# The Transgender Studies Reader 2

## Edited by
## Susan Stryker and Aren Z. Aizura

NEW YORK AND LONDON

First published 2013
by Routledge
711 Third Avenue, New York, NY 10017

Simultaneously published in the UK
by Routledge
2 Park Square, Milton Park, Abingdon, Oxon OX14 4RN

*Routledge is an imprint of the Taylor & Francis Group, an informa business*

*Library of Congress Cataloging in Publication Data*
The transgender studies reader 2 / edited by Susan Stryker and
Aren Z. Aizura. – 1 Edition.
    pages cm
  Includes bibliographical references and index.
  1. Transgenderism. 2. Transvestism. 3. Transgender people.
  4. Transvestites. I. Stryker, Susan. II. Aizura, Aren Z.
  HQ77.9.T72 2013
  306.76′8–dc23                                    2013001292

ISBN: 978-0-415-51772-0 (hbk)
ISBN: 978-0-415-51773-7 (pbk)

Typeset in Minion by
HWA Text and Data Management, London

# The Transgender Studies Reader 2

Over the past 20 years, transgender studies has emerged as a vibrant field of interdisciplinary scholarship. First collected in Routledge's own *The Transgender Studies Reader* in 2006, the field has moved on, rapidly expanding in many directions. *The Transgender Studies Reader 2* gathers these disparate strands of scholarship and collects them into a format that makes sense for teaching and research.

Complementing the first volume, rather than competing with it, *The Transgender Studies Reader 2* consists of 50 articles, with a general introduction by the editors, explanatory head notes for each essay, and bibliographical suggestions for further research. Unlike the first volume, which was historically based, tracing the lineage of the field, this volume focuses on recent work and emerging trends. To foster more interactivity, and to keep pace with this rapidly changing area, the reader will now have a companion website, with images, links to blogs, video, and other material to help supplement the book.

**Susan Stryker** is Associate Professor of Gender and Women's Studies, and Director of the Institute for LGBT Studies, University of Arizona.

**Aren Z. Aizura** is Mellon Postdoctoral Associate at the Institute for Research on Women and the Department of Women's and Gender Studies at Rutgers University.

# Contents

# Acknowledgments

At Routledge, Kimberly Guinta was an enthusiastic champion of this volume and of the importance of transgender studies as an emerging discipline. We're also grateful to Rebecca Novack, our editorial assistant at Routledge. Zuryannette Reyes Borrero, Antonia Leotsakos, Lisa Logan, and Abe Weil provided research and editorial assistance. Sophia Starmack helped with proofreading and manuscript assembly. Ben Singer developed this volume's online website for additional resources. Finally, we thank the authors featured in this volume, particularly those who contributed original work; we regret any uncorrected errors that have been introduced to your texts during the production of the *Reader*.

# Introduction

## Transgender Studies 2.0

SUSAN STRYKER AND AREN Z. AIZURA

In 2006, Routledge published the *Transgender Studies Reader*. Clocking in at a hefty 758 pages, and bearing a striking resemblance to that proverbial pre-internet-era artifact, the phone book, its fifty chapters spanned scholarly writing on gender variance from Krafft-Ebing's work on inversion circa 1886 to new essays written in 2005 that self-consciously articulated themselves as part of the new field of transgender studies. The *Transgender Studies Reader* was one part historical snapshot of how medical, legal, social, and cultural discourses have required bodies to conform to gender norms across the long twentieth century; one part account—autoethnographic and otherwise—of how a significantly large number of people have defied or evaded such regulation; and one part explanation of how we came to understand and denominate such bodies, identities, and practices as "transgender" in the first place. The *Reader* had been preceded by a number of edited collections and themed journal issues on transgender topics—reflecting the understanding of transgender as a "special issue" rather than a wide-reaching scholarly undertaking—but that volume was the first to definitively mark out a place for a *transgender studies* within the academy.

As the introduction to the 2006 *Reader* noted, to assert the emergence of transgender studies as a field only in the 1990s rests on a set of assumptions that permit a differentiation between one kind of work on "transgender phenomena" and another, for there had of course been a great deal of academic, scholarly, and scientific work on various forms of gender variance long before the 1990s. What changed in the early 1990s was the relatively sudden appearance of new possibilities for thinking about, talking about, encountering, and living transgender bodies and lives. These changes derived in part from new political alliances forged during the AIDS crisis, which brought sexual and gender identity politics into a different sort of engagement with the biomedical and pharmaceutical establishments. They emerged as well from shifting generational perspectives on gender, identity, embodiment, and social roles as the first post-baby-boomers came into adulthood; from new strategies for managing bodies and populations within the neoliberal world order that became hegemonic in the aftermath of the Soviet collapse; from the increasingly broad dissemination of poststructuralist and performative theories of subjectivity and embodiment within academe, which allowed a different kind of sense to be made of transgender phenomena; from new forms of media and communication that fostered new social and communal forms; and from *fin de mille* futurist fantasies of technologically enhanced life in the impending twenty-first century.

The convergent effect of such contingencies was that self-identified trans people found new ways to enter into conversation with others about the objective and subjective conditions of gendered

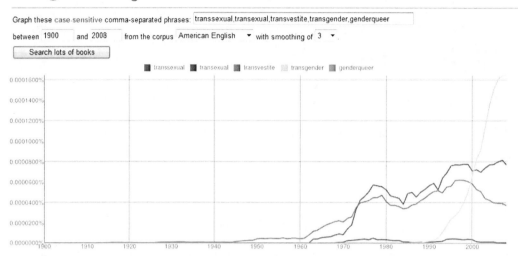

**Figure 0.1** The ascendance of "transgender" from 2000 to 2008

embodiment, rather than remaining mere objects of knowledge in the discourses of others about them, or continuing to speak in constrained autobiographical modes that, for the most part, narrated diagnostic categories from first-person perspectives. Psychopathology, in other words, was no longer the dominant mode of trans coherence and intelligibility. If pre-1990s discourse could be described as the *performance* of certain objectifying and minoritizing ways of understanding trans phenomena, then what came afterwards could be conceptualized as a kind of *performance studies* that treated this earlier work as its own archive and object of inquiry; to the extent that the earlier work understood itself as constituting a *science* of the sexed and gendered self, then the later field bracketed and historicized the truth claims of that science somewhat in the manner of *science studies*. The changes in optics and objects of knowledge were profound enough, and pervasive enough, that a newly articulated concept—"transgender" itself, rather than transvestite, transsexual, or a bevy of other existing terms—seemed necessary to mark the conceptual and perceptual transitions.

Figure 0.1 is a screen-grab of search results from the Google Books Ngram Viewer, which charts the relative frequency with which several terms have appeared in the millions of books scanned into the Google Books project—*transsexual* and its alternate spelling *transexual*, *transvestite*, *transgender*, and *genderqueer*—between 1900 and 2008 (the most recent year for which results were available). As the chart demonstrates, since about 1992, *transgender* has experienced a meteoric rise in popularity compared to other familiar terms for describing gender nonconforming practices. Considering English-language materials alone, twenty-five new dissertations have been written in the field; about a dozen special issues of peer-reviewed journals and anthologies have appeared from various academic presses, and there have been hundreds of papers presented at scores of conferences and symposia at universities and colleges.[1] A simple search of Google Scholar indicates that about 2500 books have now been published with the words "transgender" or "transsexual" in the title (excluding those that mention these words as part of some permutation of the phrase "gay, lesbian, bisexual, and transgender"); nearly 40,000 academic articles reference transgender topics, as do approximately two million newspaper and periodical stories. According to one recent poll, 91 percent of people living in the U.S.A. report that they have heard the term transgender, of which roughly three-quarters give an essentially accurate definition without prompting.[2] Transgender, in other words, is not an obscure, minor, exotic, or emergent topic. It is a common—increasingly common—feature of our world, and we need to ask ourselves why it is perpetually positioned in media and public discourse as "only now" arriving on the horizon of intelligibility, and why it is too often considered too insignificant, too novel, too ephemeral, too complicated, or too strange to matter or merit serious attention.

The field of transgender studies is, in many ways, an effort to account for the profound shifts in culture, society, and political economy that are indexed by *transgender*'s dramatic emergence and rapid dissemination more than two decades ago. It has explored a range of phenomena related to deep, pervasive, and historically significant changes in attitudes toward, and understandings of, what gender means and does in our sometimes chaotically (post)modernizing world. The work of transgender studies as a field is to comprehend the nature of these historical transformations and the new forms of sociality and cultural production that have emerged from them. It seeks as well to reevaluate prior understandings of gender, sex, sexuality, embodiment, and identity in light of more recent transgender phenomena, from critical perspectives informed by and in dialog with transgender practices and knowledge formations. From this analytical point of purchase, the field has begun to offer a wide-ranging critique of the conditions of contemporary life, as well as new understandings of the past, and novel visions of futurity. With the pop cultural cachet of transgender phenomena seeming to increase with every new episode of *RuPaul's Drag Race*, every mass-media mention of Chaz Bono dancing with the stars, every new film or television program featuring transgender characters or themes, transgender studies seems increasingly necessary, simply for mapping the quotidian features of capitalist hypermodernity in the early twenty-first century.

The 2006 *Transgender Studies Reader* can be taken as an account of field formation. It was organized in roughly chronological fashion, covering important works in the history of sexual science, feminism, and gay and lesbian studies that laid important foundations for transgender studies, before moving on to document the fruitful (and sometimes contentious) dialog with queer theory; it concluded with a series of special topics of particular importance in the first decade or so of work in the field: identity politics, community formation, trans masculinities, bio-ethics, and intersectional analyses of transgender, race, ethnicity, and location that called attention to the unmarked whiteness and Eurocentrism of the field without remedying those limitations.

If the first iteration of the transgender studies field was defined, in the words of a foundational essay by Sandy Stone, as "posttranssexual," to the extent that it exceeded then-extant categories of identity and analysis, then the second iteration of the field, which we somewhat glibly refer to in this introduction as "Transgender Studies 2.0," is "postposttranssexual."[3] It simultaneously refers back to the previous histories, problematics, and arguments that enabled the articulation of a field, but also engages with new and different sets of material circumstances and conceptual developments that have taken shape over the past twenty years.

The first iteration of the field engaged in the kind of identity politics necessary to gain speaking positions within discourse, and consequently featured a good deal of autoethnographic and self-representational work by trans subjects. It offered critiques of and resistance to the medico-juridical pathologization of gender-variance, as well as of gay and feminist discourses that positioned themselves as more sexually modern or progressive than a transgenderism it imagined as primitive, backward, unenlightened, and less advanced. It traced potential alliances between trans communities and other subordinated groups in an effort to rethink the politics of minority oppression and reframe transgender issues as not-necessarily a sexual identity modeled on gay or lesbian experience, and it engaged in recovery projects that tried to pry "subjugated knowledges" pertinent to contemporary transgender struggles from the structures of power that occluded and enclosed them.

The second iteration of the field, fueled in part by another shift in generational perspective as the so-called "millennials" replaced "Generation X" as the youngest adult demographic cohort, has taken shape under conditions of state surveillance and border securitization scarcely imaginable in the pre-9/11 cultural landscape of the U.S.A. Within this increasingly militarized state apparatus, new imperatives and opportunities for "transgender normativity" have taken shape that secure citizenship for some trans bodies at the expense of others, while replicating many forms of racism, xenophobia, and class privilege. Transgender studies 2.0 takes critical aim at such developments, and it does so in the context of deepening global economic and ecological crises that make effective critique, pragmatic counter-action, and creative alliance-building all the more urgent. As a consequence, the second iteration of the transgender studies field often directs its critical gaze at the inadequacies of the field's first iteration, in order to correct them, taking aim at its implicit whiteness, U.S.-centricity, Anglophone bias, and the sometimes suspect ways in which the category *transgender* has been circulated transnationally. It seeks to propagate *transgender* rhizomatically, in unexpected ways that trace lines of flight from the harsh realities of the present moment.

The fifty articles assembled here, in the *Transgender Studies Reader 2* (which retrospectively recasts its companion collection as volume one), are representative of these new directions in the field. They are part of the flood of new work that has appeared in print since 2005. Eleven were commissioned specifically for this anthology, and only three of the remaining thirty-nine were published prior to 2005: José Esteban Muñoz's classic essay on drag superstar Vaginal Creme Davis, "The White to Be Angry," which really should have been in the first volume but seems even more timely now, with its prescient attention to terrorism; a selection from Joan Roughgarden's *Evolution's Rainbow*, which set the stage for much of what was to follow in biologistic approaches to sex and gender diversity in the new queer/trans animal studies; and Michelle O'Brien's "Tracing This Body," a commodity-chain analysis of hormones used to alter gender-signifying aspects of embodiment, first delivered as a public talk in 2003.

The *Transgender Studies Reader 2* highlights some of the best of the most recent work in the field; it tries to orient its audience to a vast amount of new material, and it identifies some main lines of investigation in this burgeoning field of knowledge. It is intended to complement, rather than compete with, volume one. The book is organized into ten sections of five articles each. The relationship between transgender studies and feminist or women's studies continues to evolve, and one section—featuring work by Cressida Heyes on debates about transgender within feminism after the rise of queer studies, Viviane Namaste and Georgia Sitara on transfeminist pedagogy, A. Finn Enke on the concept of "cisgender," Bobby Noble on white transgender feminist masculinities, and Julia Serano on transmisogyny—documents recent interventions in this multifaceted conversation. Intersectional analyses, such as that offered by Eli Clare on what ableist trans movements can learn from disability activism, also continue to be important, but the intersection of trans studies with such other fields and issues as disability, (post)colonialism, transnationalism, and racialization are integrated throughout the volume rather than being confined to one section, as in the previous volume.

Other important lines of work, also dispersed across several sections of the volume, draw on transgender critiques of biopolitics, neoliberal economies, state formations/effects within Eurocentric modernity, and social policy; examples include Dan Irving's neo-Marxist interpretation of "normalized transgressions" and the production of legitimated transgender subject/citizens, Toby Beauchamp's critique of U.S. border securitization post-9/11 and the surveillance of gender non-conforming bodies, Ruthann Robson's thought-piece on transsexual marriage, and Nick Gorton's defense of the psycho-medical diagnosis of gender identity disorder and gender dysphoria. One section demonstrates the contribution that transgender studies is making to broad questions of historicity and temporality in the study of gender/sex/sexuality; other sections on "location" and "mobility" similarly demonstrate trans studies' contribution to thinking about those issues geospatially. Work that investigates the blurry boundary between the human, the non-human, and the post-human is increasingly common within transgender studies, and has its own section within this volume, including Myra Hird's survey of what she calls "Animal Transsex" and Eva Hayward's "Lessons from a Starfish," lessons than run the gamut from morphological regeneration to pop music criticism. One section of the *Reader* explores the interpretation and reception of recent transgender cultural production in such areas as dance, textiles, performance, and film; yet another section tackles a miscellany of perpetually contentious issues and intersections, such as psychoanalytic theory's tendency to pathologize transgender identifications, which Shanna Carlson masterfully addresses and reworks in her Lacanian account of sexual difference, or the tendency within some progressive, feminist, queer, and popular discourses to cast trans people as "evil deceivers and make-believers," as Talia Bettcher phrases it in the title of her article on the murder of transgender teen Gwen Araujo. Our goal, overall, in selecting work and organizing it thematically, has been to document the breadth of work now taking place under the rubric of transgender studies.

## NEW INSTITUTIONAL FORMS

The increasing momentum of transgender studies' disciplinary formation at conferences, in journals and other publications, and in community-based intellectual and cultural production, has compelled interdisciplines—gender and women's studies, sexuality studies, LGBT studies, American Studies, and science and technology studies—as well as traditional humanities and social science disciplines, to offer transgender-related material in curricula and mentorship, and support for graduate students researching transgender-related topics. North American intellectual publics now appear amenable to incorporating studies of non-normative gender into history, literature, anthropology, sociology, psychology, and public policy. Transgender subjects are increasingly understood to constitute populations to be researched, and from whom data can be collected and analyzed in the name of rendering them visible, promoting their health, conferring them with rights, and marketing to their needs. In June 2011, to note but one example, a team of epidemiologists, demographers, quantitative social scientists, and public policy experts known as the GENIUSS Group (Gender Identity in U.S. Surveillance) began meeting to discuss how general population surveys commissioned by the U.S. federal government can more effectively count transgender people. Elsewhere in the world, Nepal and Pakistan recently added third-gender categories to their national identification documents, and Australia is considering an "X" designation, akin to a "decline to state" status, on passports. Clearly, understandings of how "gender" as a social and administrative system structures bureaucratic practices and informs the regulation of bodies are morphing in ways that exceed the familiar binary of man/woman. However harshly religious and political conservatives might judge such developments, and however maladept states might be in adjusting their practices of government in response to these shifts, gender systems and the identities that emerge from them are changing worldwide in unprecedented ways that demand our attention—and transgender studies offers a vital perspective on this emergent aspect of contemporary society.

Consequently, the demand to teach trans subject-matter in universities is increasing globally—and the push often comes from students themselves, whose social experience of gender increasingly diverges from that of preceding generations. Teaching about transgender bodies, politics, and cultural practices has now extended far beyond the piecemeal "token transgender week" or trans special guest format in introductory gender studies, cultural studies, or queer theory courses.[4] At many universities and liberal arts colleges in the U.S.A. there are more and more opportunities to take a range of transgender studies courses at introductory and advanced levels, including graduate seminars; to encounter transgender content in general education courses; and to experience a steady stream of transgender academics, experts, and culture-makers presenting work to knowledgeable campus audiences.

Transgender phenomena are curiously prominent in such currently fashionable interdisciplinary fields and methodologies as affect theory, Foucauldian biopolitics, animal studies, haptic media, assemblage theory, critical embodiment studies, the posthumanities, and Deleuzoguattarian approaches to anything and everything. Their prevalence stems, no doubt, from the manner in which they exceed and thus call attention to the epistemic limits of Eurocentric modernity, and thereby become grist in various mills of critical inquiry into the contemporary conditions of life. And for similar reasons, transgender studies raises questions central to modern disciplinary knowledge formations. For history, it asks why we think "man" and "woman" are any more transhistorical, or less contingent, than any other category of identity, and why we persist in the presentist fallacy of ontologizing a current framework and imposing it on the strangeness of the past. For sociology, it compels attention to emergent forms of relationality involving novel types of social actors. It confronts psychology with viable subjects whose differences and atypicalities resist reduction to either the normal or the pathological, and call for new models of psychical processes. And in its increasingly global dissemination and uptake by various populations in various locations for various reasons, it challenges how anthropology has conceptualized cross-cultural analyses of the variable configuration of sex, gender, sexuality, identity, and embodiment.

These new developments are cause for optimism, but also, if not outright cynicism, then at least a measure of caution. Under neoliberalism, the humanities have tended to endorse and speedily exhaust new cultural turns and disciplines, particularly those involving interdisciplinary scholarship, or those that take shape as subaltern sources of knowledge production. A cautionary example is afforded by queer theory, which Teresa de Lauretis (often credited with coining the term) disavowed in 1994 as a "conceptually vacuous creature of the publishing industry," just as it became institutionally recognizable—and wildly popular—as "queer studies."[5] Queer theory, of course, survived this disavowal and is still the source of much of the most important thinking on non-normative sexuality and deviant modes of life; it has been transformed by two generations of scholars who both creatively pervert it and contribute to its continuity as a framework for understanding the world.

If transgender studies is not to become another such "conceptually vacuous creature," we need to attend to the ways in which many transgender and gender nonconforming people live lives that are abstracted and theorized in ways that do not materially benefit them. Contrary to what the uninformed might think, given the spectacularization of transgender phenomena in the media, most transgender lives are not fabulous. Through the operations of employment and housing discrimination, lack of access to health care and social services, and the persistence of both state-sanctioned and unchecked popular violence against many gender-variant individuals, transgender populations are disproportionately incarcerated, living in poverty, and unable to access higher education.[6] These differences in opportunity and vulnerability map starkly onto the intersections of structural racism, gender inequality, and neoliberal economics: trans women of color are far more likely to be poor, to be incarcerated, and to be the victims of street violence (not to mention the institutional violences present in the welfare, education, and prison systems). Transgender studies in the academy therefore must—whatever else it does—address itself to these injustices and be part of the process of redistributing financial, cultural, and intellectual resources from pockets of greater abundance to broader territories of greater need. Several essays in this collection pay particular attention to racism and incarceration, notably Jin Haritaworn and C. Riley Snorton's account of transsexual necropolitics, Che Gossett's essay on the memorialization and forgetting of trans political resistance, and the abolitionist manifesto jointly authored by Dean Spade, Morgan Bassichis, and Alex Lee. Such work reminds us of the need to keep transgender studies relevant to its roots in social justice work—without, we hope, defining beforehand precisely what justice might consist of, or who the proper subject of transgender politics ought to be.

As an academic field, transgender studies must also address the institutions of higher education itself, and contest the ways in which the organization and administration of the university assumes its faculty, staff, and students to be non-transgendered. Teaching transgender studies cannot succeed fully unless it is accompanied by infrastructural change: trans-friendly dorms, gender-neutral bathrooms, the ability to change one's name and gender markers in college databases, a faculty and staff who—at a minimum—are literate about the issues facing transgender and gender non-conforming students, and at best are gender-diverse enough themselves that such students can see themselves reflected back in affirming and inspiring ways. This seems an especially pressing need for trans-feminine individuals, who lag far behind trans-masculine individuals in access to education, in finding welcoming campus climates, and in moving into the ranks of the academically employed.

Another persistent thread woven through this volume is the concern that, as trans subjects become "countable," we also become vulnerable to new modes of biopolitical regulation, including the increasingly tight management of precisely what combination of surgical and hormonal bodily transformations are required to legally define a person's sex or transgender status. It is important to locate the potential complicities between such regulatory schema and an institutionalized transgender studies—particularly if the definition of "transgender" comes to signify a static identity category or specific ways of being in the world, rather than circulating as multiple modes of analysis. The danger of complicity seems particularly acute in relation to concepts of "transgender health," as psychopathological models of transgender are replaced by difference-management models. Health should not become a euphemism for the production of gender normativity through the extension of regulatory apparatuses; it must also encompass new potentials for unexpected becomings, and it must accommodate the manifestation of unforeseen, emergent potentials of bodily being. Wildness, even more than cultivation or care, should characterize the health of our gender ecologies. Transgender studies should therefore actively participate in the proliferation and articulation of new modes of embodied subjectivity, new cultural practices, and new ways of understanding the world, rather than becoming an enclosure for their containment.

The response to this danger is not, we think, to reject the formation of transgender studies wholesale. Rather, it is to be fully cognizant of the ways in which the increasingly neoliberally-structured, corporatized, for-profit university operates in the twenty-first century, and to attempt to keep open a space in which the scholarship articulated through transgender studies can continue to spill forth. This requires a bold and perhaps reckless ambition to nurture a transgender political imaginary that moves beyond a rights-and-representation based framework. It means, following Fred Moten and Stefano Harney, to approach the university as an undercommons, an "unsafe neighborhood" we seek refuge in, subvert, steal resources from, and transform from the inside and outside all at once.[7] Concretely, this means intervening into the redistribution of higher education resources, especially in light of current economic austerity measures; it also means being aware of how capital accrues to certain participants in transgender studies—not just in terms of money in the form of salaries, but also as cultural capital, racial capital, and national capital—and redirecting those flows as best we can. It's worth noting, however, that the currency of transgender studies can feel very tenuous, precisely because the field is relatively new and because of the fraught condition of higher education at the historical moment of transgender studies' consolidation. In an atmosphere where one prevailing sentiment is that the entire academic edifice might crumble tomorrow, it's tempting to reach for as much institutional legitimacy as possible right now, and to do with it what we can.

## TRANSGENDER AS GLOBAL ASSEMBLAGE

As the range of geographical locations and cultural experience covered by this collection illustrates, transgender studies is clearly no longer, if it ever really was, merely a concern of the North American Anglophone academy. Essays such as Sima Shakhsari's on transsexual asylum claims in Turkey and Iran, Marcia Ochoa's on the redefinition of citizenship by Venezuelan *transformistas*, Susan Stryker's on the appearance of U.S. transsexual celebrity Christine Jorgensen in the 1962 Filipino film *Taming Mga Talyada*, Vek Lewis's on transgender figures in Latin American cinema and literature, and Mel Chen's on (among other things) Chinese conceptual artist Xu Bing all emphasize the transnational scope of the field. As editors, we want to stress that this selection came about not because of a representational anxiety to "include international perspectives" or "highlight diversity," but rather because the field of transgender studies is moving strongly in transnational directions.

"Gender" is not merely the representation in language and culture of a biological sex; it is also an administrative or bureaucratic structure for the management of sexual difference and reproductive capacity (the ticking off of M's and F's on state-issued or state-sanctioned forms). In this sense, and to the extent that "gender identity" is understood as the psychical internalization and somaticization of historically contingent modes of embodied personhood, *transgender* is intimately bound up with questions of nation, territory, and citizenship, with categories of belonging and exclusion, of excess and incorporation, and with all the processes through which individual corporealities become aggregated as bodies politic. All current transgender phenomena are thus local and national phenomena that encounter transnationalizing forces. This insight invites research agendas within transgender studies that span nations, languages, peoples, and periods.

The current transnationalization and globalization of transgender studies may help counteract the perception of transgender studies as *only* a conceptual export of the global north and west that is being spread to the global south and east, or that begins *only* in a "highbrow" academic setting from which it trickles down to a street that finds it irrelevant. David Valentine's 2005 book *Imagining Transgender: The Ethnography of a Category* facilitates precisely such a critique. Valentine argued that *transgender* itself is a category often imagined as a form of progressive modernity that supplants outmoded "traditional" understandings of sex, sexuality, embodiment, gender, and identity. This plays out not only within the U.S.A. (along race and class lines) but also globally, between the global "north" and the global "south." Particularly within the discipline of anthropology, he argues, transgender increasingly functions as a means of organizing and interpreting cross-cultural variations in embodied personhood according to Eurocentric ontological categories and modernization narratives. One implication is that the academic institutionalization of transgender studies, which advances the goal of transgender social legitimization through the development of an expertise structured by the foundational preconditions of transgender's intelligibility (which is implicitly raced/classed and Anglocentric/Anglophone), risks a kind of theoretical imperialism that masks and marginalizes a more heterogeneous class of phenomena than can ever be encompassed adequately within transgender's conceptual framework.

In directing our attention to those ways in which transgender activism and advocacy fit hand-in-glove with the logic of a globalizing neoliberalism, Valentine offers an important corrective to naïve liberationist and progressivist discourses, and usefully points out their racial, class, and linguistic biases. When transgender is understood to include all gender variant practices and identities rather than a specific understanding of sex, gender, and identity with a recent and local past, we risk rendering other understandings of sex, gender, and sexuality unintelligible, and risk erasing as well violent colonial histories of knowledge production about sex and gender. After all, cataloguing divergences from modern Eurocentric understandings of sex, gender, sexuality, embodiment, and identity in different cultures or classes; assigning meaning to such "abnormalities," and exploiting or fetishizing that difference according to the developmental logic of colonialism and capitalism have all been central features of Euro-American societies for over five hundred years.

While much queer work in anthropology has sought to decolonize the anthropological analysis of sex/gender variance, and while the ethnographic documentation of global gender variance springs from many motivations, including support for the political struggles of non-European gender variant people, we nevertheless have steered away from including in this collection what we think of as "cross-cultural analysis" of sex/gender diversity, for two reasons. First, we seek to resist a common interpretive stance (one, admittedly, more characteristic of the past than the present) that represents non-European gender-variant cultural practices as timeless "traditions" bound to a particular location to which they are indigenous and authentic, and which are perpetually at risk of being polluted or diluted by the introduction of exogenous modern forms—rather than seeing such practices as living, evolving, responsive, and refigurable assemblages that circulate alongside and across the medicalized and juridical forms of transsexual and transgender life. Second, to resist the implicit bias in much of this "cross-cultural" work that privileges "homosexual" or "queer" optics over trans-oriented heuristics as its default mode. Our goal is not to replace "homo" with "trans" as a purportedly new-and-improved conceptual lens, but rather to insist that failing to account for the critique offered by transgender studies occludes a vital set of questions and also reproduces many gestures of colonialism.

There is a surprising degree of resistance, in work that is quick to cast transgender as a vector of a northern and western conceptual imperialism which inflicts the damages of modernity on colonized locals, to acknowledging the ways in which "homosexuality" is an equally conceptually violative way of framing varying configurations of what the modern west understands as sex, gender, identity, desire, and embodiment. Homosexuality can function in this manner precisely because the categories that undergird it—man and woman, female and male—are presumed to be ontologically given, and stable across cultures. That is, because "we" in the west recognize both bodies in a particular sexual dyad as being of the "same sex" according to an unexamined assumptions about what constitutes both sex and sameness, to call that dyad homosexual somehow seems less problematic than to recast it in terms of a "foreign" transgender framework. We insist, however, that the ontologization of sex difference through unexamined cultural beliefs about the meaning of biological materiality is itself a modern Eurocentric construct that is imposed onto other cultural phenomena. Demystifying and analyzing the ontological labor performed by *man*, *male*, *female*, and *woman*, and insisting on their historicity and cultural contingency, is part of transgender critique: those terms are no less constructed than *transgender* itself, and they circulate transnationally in discourse and analysis with no less risk of being conceptually colonizing. What new understandings of the vitality and diversity of bodily being, we ask, might emerge from putting as much pressure on the categories of *man*, *woman*, and *homosexuality*, as on *transgender*?

What kinds of questions and practices, then, can transgender studies offer that advance an anti-colonialist agenda, and that resist the subsumption of non-western configurations of personhood into western-dominant frameworks that privilege either "homo" or "trans," or assume the ontological given-ness of the concepts *man* and *woman*? What might an anti-colonial or decolonizing transgender studies look like?

At the very least, we contend, it would involve careful attention to the movement of transgender phenomena, knowledges, and practices across regions, nations, and rural–urban spaces. It concerns, and it would acknowledge, that the relationship between highly mobile medicalized categories such as "transsexual," and culturally specific terms that tend to travel shorter distances, is not a monolithic one in which the purity of an ethnic practice is polluted and diminished by the introduction of a standardized modern import; cultures make their own uses of those things that find their way to them. We also think it must concern itself with how various local phenomena imagine their own relationship to those things that "transgender" can often evoke—modernity, metropolitanism, Eurocentrism, whiteness, globalization, transnationalism. It would explore the multiple reworkings of identity that "transgender" accomplishes locally and globally—whether "transgender" is experienced as a form of colonization, as an avenue for alliance building or resource development, as a way of resisting local pressures, as an empowering new frame of reference, as an erasure of cultural specificity, as a counter-modernity, as an alternative to tradition, or as a mode of survival and translation for traditional cultural forms that are unintelligible within the conceptual double binary of man/woman and homo/hetero associated with the modern west. This kind of work is what we have sought to include in the *Transgender Studies Reader 2*

As essays in this collection attest, current trans of color critique resists imperialist forms of knowledge production precisely by calling attention to which transgender bodies—and they are almost always the non-white ones—are made to represent the traumatic violences through which claims for rights are articulated. Trans of color critique disrupts as well the racializing logic through which white gender-variant bodies become—more often than not—the only gender-variant bodies recognizable as the legitimate subjects of rights. The production of transgender whiteness as a process of value-extraction from bodies of color both within and outside of the global north and west therefore remains an important target of criticism, even as we promote transgender studies as a site where radical anti-racist and anti-imperialist work can be accomplished.

It is equally important to be cognizant of the novel and multiplying ways in which transgender assembles the world, not all of which can be reduced to operations of power applied (wittingly or unwittingly) to vulnerable, unwilling, or uncomprehending subjects. There are many transgenders—critical, queer, feminist, transnational, local, identitarian, institutional—and many of them seem politically promising. However much transgender, like other contemporary categories of identity, operates within neoliberal conditions, it has also offered powerful critiques of both homo- and hetero- nationalisms and normativities, as well as critiques of gender regulation itself as a tool of biopolitical governmentality. However much transgender has been a site of race, class, and anti-colonial struggle, it has also been generative of counter-narratives that imagine alternate, anti-, post- and a-modernities in which bodies can come to mean differently, across a range of bodily differences. This collection seeks to contribute to the proliferation of such improper transgenders and renegade versions of transgender studies, while anticipating a future in which our own visions will be eclipsed by new imaginaries that might not even call themselves transgender at all.

## A USER'S GUIDE

Even a work as massive as the *Transgender Studies Reader 2* is necessarily filled with unfortunate lacunae: a few that we see and seek to acknowledge are the relative absence of studies of transgender phenomena in relation to indigeneity, new media, popular culture, disability, HIV/AIDS, porn, sexuality, and sex-work; all are touched on to some degree, but none receive the extended attention they deserve. Transgender legal work, policy analysis, and interventions into public health and medical-psychotherapeutic service provision are all developing so rapidly, and changing so quickly, that we chose—wisely or lazily—to leave, with few exceptions, the work of anthologizing and analyzing that material to our colleagues who work more directly in those areas. Nevertheless, in spite of the many gaps in coverage (some of which we've tried to remedy in part through our suggestions for further reading, and through the supplemental online resource that accompanies this volume), we trust that readers will be as inspired as we are by the sheer breadth and depth that transgender studies has gained over the past half-decade or so.

The Table of Contents, read from beginning to end, offers one map of some broad thematic concerns and current preoccupations within transgender studies: we invite users to imagine other organizational schemas and associative threads between the selected works. Readers who peruse the book section-by-section will not find in each section an exhaustive survey of a given topic, but rather some suggestive examples of how a particular topic or theme has been addressed in transgender studies, how transgender scholarship might reimagine or reframe a particular discipline's familiar questions in new ways, or how disciplinary methodologies might themselves transform the way we do transgender studies.

Readers who skip around will find plenty of instances where the theme or approach of one section occurs in another; this is by design. In the section on trans-historicity, Mary Weismantel challenges archeology to enlarge its interpretation of the prehistoric world to include gender diversity; Deborah A. Miranda argues for an indigenous reading of archives documenting the genocide of gender-variant Native people during the conquest of the western U.S.A in order to salvage a historical anchor for contemporary Two-Spirit lives; Karma Lochrie uses medieval European texts to demonstrate the extent to which the concept of "normal" has infused all of modern sexuality and rendered it difficult to grasp the meaning of premodern female sexual variation; Robert Hill offers a genealogy of the gender-variant terminology and its relation to the concept of transgender in the subcultural literature of mid-twentieth-century North American cross-dresser communities; and Afsaneh Najmabadi's account of sexual subcultures in Iran immediately before and after the 1979 revolution investigates how categories of personhood bearing the same name came to mean very different things in new political circumstances: all these essays envision different methods for excavating pasts that certainly contained gender-variant cultural practices, without necessarily imposing the name "transgender" on those historical moments.

Todd Henry's piece on cross-dressed Tokyo sex-workers during the post-World War II U.S. occupation could certainly have been included in the section on history and temporality, but we chose instead to thematize it as a spatial study—of Tokyo as a specific place—and thereby to link it conceptually to very different kinds of work on space by Gayle Salamon, who critiques feminist philosopher Luce Irigaray's contention that sexual difference is rooted in a sense of the body's spatial contours, and to Sheila Cavanagh's analysis of the public toilet as a peculiarly powerful space for rewarding gender normativity and abjecting bodily difference. Similarly, we could have included Julian Carter's work on transitional movements in dance in the section titled "Going Somewhere," where its presence would have suggested productive linkages between bodily movement and other forms of mobility discussed in articles by Aren Aizura on medical tourist travel to Thai sex-reassignment clinics, Don Romesburg on the border-crossings of transracial transgender performer Rae (or Ray or possibly Ramon) Bourbon, and Lucas Crawford's Deleuzian take on migration and geo-affectivity; that we ultimately grouped it with other essays on cultural production—such as film theorist Eliza Steinbock's work on Hans Scheirl's phantasmagorical *Dandy Dust*, Jeanne Vaccaro's discussion of tactility in the work of mixed-media artist Emmett Ramstad, and J. Jack Halberstam's influential reworking of Laura Mulvey's notion of the cinematic gaze in "The Transgender Look"—should not obscure the theoretical connections there to be made between one kind of trans-movement and the others.

We imagine many such ways of reading or teaching this book that emphasize affinities between essays that are not "sectioned off" together. Marlon Bailey's performance ethnography of public health "intraventions" within Detroit's ballroom scene, which we have grouped with policy-related work, could just as easily have been part of the section on cultural production. Essays critiquing capital are not limited to the section on "radical political economy": such perspectives can be found elsewhere in Kale Fajardo's study of transoceanic shipping routes in which the transport of Pinoy men familiar with trans masculine life queers both Filipino masculinity and the global circulation of commodities; in Bailey Kier's account of how toxic industrial landscapes become generative of "ecological transsexes" that demonstrate the ongoing transformability of the conditions of life; and in Beatriz Preciado's garish vision of pharmaceutical capitalism and its pornographic incitements to consume. Readers interested in understanding how some experiences of transgender politics, subcultures, and communities can efface others—particularly through the cuts of racializing difference—might read Sarah Lamble's critique of Transgender Day of Remembrance, or Jessi Gan's tribute to Puerto Rican trans icon Sylvia Rivera. Students of biopolitics can compare Paisley Currah and Lisa Jean Moore's account of birth-certificate regulation in New York, included in the section on "social policy," with Laura Norton's similar work on gender-recognition in Japan, or contrast it with other work grouped together in the section explicitly devoted to biopolitics, such as Clare

Sears's work on the use of anti-cross-dressing law in nineteenth-century San Francisco to produce gender-normative public space, or Nael Bhanji's autoethnographic account of diasporic trans of color subjectivity.

The point is this: in whatever order the essays in this collection are taught or read, we anticipate that such a large volume of work can be mined again and again to locate diverse strands of thematically related material whose elucidation will enrich the conversation within transgender studies, and multiply the points of connection between transgender studies and other disciplines and fields, as well as between academic study, activism, cultural production, policy work, and service provision. Ironically, at the same time, we are very much aware of how much truly fine work has been left out by the need to limit this volume to *only* fifty articles. The field of transgender studies has grown with unexpected speed to unanticipated dimensions over the past few years: if the near future resembles the recent past, we can scarcely imagine what a *Transgender Studies Reader 3* might look like. It's our hope that by engaging with the work collected here, many of our readers will actively participate in shaping the contours of whatever such a book might come to be.

## NOTES

1. Some recent journal issues focusing on transgender include *Feminist Studies'* special issue on "Transgender and Race," 37: 2 (2010); *Hypatia: Journal of Feminist Philosophy*'s issue on Transgender and Feminism, 24: 3 (2009); *WSQ: Women's Studies Quarterly* 36: 3–4 (2008); two issues of *Sexuality Research and Social Policy* themed "The State We're In: Locations of Consent and Coercion in Trans Policy," 4: 4 (2007) and 5: 1 (2008); *Inter-Asia Cultural Studies* 8: 4 (2006); as well as work in the late 1990s including *GLQ: A Journal of Lesbian and Gay Studies* 4: 2 (1998).
2. See http://publicreligion.org/research/2011/11/american-attitudes-towards-transgender-people/
3. See Sandy Stone, "The Empire Strikes Back: A Post-Transsexual Manifesto," originally published in Kristina Straub and Julia Epstein (eds), *Body Guards: The Cultural Politics of Gender Ambiguity* (New York: Routledge, 1991), 280–304, and reprinted in the *Transgender Studies Reader Volume One*, 221–236.
4. For critiques of the token "transgender week" tendency in women's and gender studies, see Shana Agid and Erica Rand, "Teaching Trans Now: Beyond the 'Special Guest'," *Radical Teacher* 92 (2011), 5–9, and Kate Drabinski, "Identity Matters: Teaching Transgender in the Women's Studies Classroom," *Radical Teacher* 92 (2011), 10–20.
5. Teresa de Lauretis, "Habit Changes," *differences: a Journal of Feminist Cultural Studies* 6: 2–3 (1994), 297.
6. See Dean Spade and Sel Wahng, "Transecting the Academy," *GLQ: A Journal of Lesbian and Gay Studies* 10: 2 (2004), 243. For a comprehensive theorization of how the disproportionate vulnerability of trans people is also cut across by race and class, and how this can be intervened on politically, see Dean Spade, *Normal Life: Administrative Violence, Critical Trans Politics and the Limits of Law* (Boston, MA: South End Press, 2011).
7. Fred Moten and Stefano Harney, "The University and the Undercommons: Seven Theses," *Social Text* 22: 2 79 (2004), 103.

# I

## *TRANSGENDER PERSPECTIVES IN (AND ON) RADICAL POLITICAL ECONOMY*

# 1

## *Normalized Transgressions*
### Legitimizing the Transsexual Body as Productive

Dan Irving

Dan Irving, a Canadian political scientist, incorporates a critique of class and race politics into research on transsexuality, both historically and in the present day. His target in this chapter is the "transsexual working body." Analyzing 1950s-era medical studies of transsexuality by the sexologist David O. Cauldwell, early transsexual autobiographies, and contemporary trans activist discourse, Irving shows how all three discourses frame the legitimacy of transgender embodiment by whether trans people can be productive members of society. Cauldwell argued that medically assisted "sex change" would thwart bodies otherwise capable of being industrious and lead them into low lives, while the "Real Life Test" imposed on gender variant people seeking to transition medically functioned not only as a way to regulate "appropriate" candidates for transition but to test transsexual people's capacity to integrate into middle-class society: finding a respectable gender-appropriate job, marrying, and fitting in to heteronormative life. Irving points out that these dictates were not only about gender normativity but also class: they functioned to discriminate against those trans people who could not access middle-class privilege. A contemporary neoliberal analog to such discourses, he writes, can be located in how some large corporations claim to encourage transgender employees as "diversity-building," which harnesses better competitiveness. Irving's article joins a growing body of transgender studies scholarship that deploys Marxian critiques of political economy in order to understand how class and social mobility inflect ways of understanding transgender. Irving concludes that calls for transgender social legitimacy fracture transgender communities: not only are these requirements individually alienating, but they also divide middle-class trans people from those who are economically disadvantaged.

Have yourself replaced as soon as possible and come back here, after which we shall think about the way to make a new place for you in society.

—Monsignor's advice to Herculine Barbin

In 1966, Gene Compton's eatery in San Francisco's Tenderloin district was the site of the first recorded incident of transgender resistance to police harassment.[1] The Compton Cafeteria riot broke out after police assaulted a drag queen inside the establishment; she responded by throwing coffee at them. This incident sparked an immediate reaction from other gender-variant, gay and lesbian people who frequented the restaurant. Rioters smashed windows, destroyed furniture, and set fire to a car.[2] This act of resistance to the state regulation of lived expressions of sex/gender identity lasted for the entire day, and picketing followed for another week. Those subjugated by norms regulating their sex, gender, sexuality, and occupation (many were sex workers) fought back against the disciplining of their lives. The well-known Stonewall Riots in New York three years later were also led by trans people, as well as by butch lesbians and drag queens, fighting diligently against the police for the right to transgress sex/gender binaries in public spaces free from discrimination and violence.

Who were these trans activists? Their collective militancy in the face of police brutality seems a distant memory when compared to much contemporary trans theorizing and politics. Why have we not inherited this legacy? What barriers to radical theorizations of gender variance and politics must be stormed to open emancipatory queer futures for trans people? How have possibilities for debate concerning these futures and strategies to shape them been foreclosed by efforts to construct *proper trans social subjects* that can integrate successfully into mainstream North American society? This essay addresses these questions by discussing the integral links between regimes of sex/gender and exploitative economic relations of production as mutually constitutive systems of domination. While various strands of feminist commentary,[3] along with scholarship from within critical sexuality studies,[4] have demonstrated the intersectional relations of power among heteronormative gender roles, sexuality, and the demands of capitalist (re)productive regimes of accumulation, these vital correlations have not been made explicit by most trans researchers and activists.[5] Scholars within trans studies rarely contextualize trans identities, subjectivities, and activism within historical and contemporary capitalist relations. Much scholarship seeks to save trans identities from invisibility, as well as to counter the ongoing reproduction of the heteronormative binary of sex/gender through detailed analyses of the vast array of existing trans identities.[6] There is a tendency within this commentary to reify trans identities as solely matters of sex/gender and to challenge state and institutional dominance over trans people by emphasizing the necessity of self-determination of sex/gender. Such advocacy of self-determination is often coupled with arguments for human rights protections.[7] Progressive scholars must question the theoretical and political implications of putting forward individualistic strategies of sex/gender self-determination, especially within the contemporary neoliberal context, where the minimalist state and a free-market economy demand individual self-sufficiency.

While some texts address the impacts of capitalist socioeconomic relations on trans people's lives, a critical analysis of the exploitative labor relations that comprise the logic of capital remains lacking.[8] Although poverty, which often results from the marginalization of many trans people from the legal labor force, is a major theme, impoverishment is most often comprehended as a barrier to the full realization of sex/gender identities and their embodied expressions. When employment within the legal wage labor economy is addressed, the tenor of discussion is often assimilatory.[9] The necessity of integrating some trans people into the labor force, and of protecting the employment status of others, appear to foreclose critiques of capitalist productive relations and of the embeddedness of trans subjectivities within capitalist systems of power. Likewise, critical analyses of the impact of capitalist productive relations on trans subjectivities are rarely offered. Also underexamined are the ways in which hegemonic capitalism's socioeconomic and political relations are reproduced vis-à-vis the transsexual body.

This essay addresses these lacunae in trans studies literature by specifically addressing the ways in which medical experts, transsexual individuals, and contemporary trans researchers, activists, and allies seeking justice for gender variant people contribute to the construction of transsexual subjectivities in ways that reinforce dominant exploitative class relations. The mediation of transsexuality through capitalist productive relations carries implications extending beyond trans individuals ourselves. I argue that an emphasis on the transsexual as an economically productive body has important effects on the shaping of transsexual subjectivities and of political strategizing for emancipatory futures. Constructions of transsexuals as viable social subjects by medical experts, transsexual individuals, researchers, and allies were, and continue to be, shaped significantly by discourses of productivity emerging from and reinforcing regimes of capitalist accumulation. To move toward achieving social recognition, the transsexual body must constitute a productive working body, that is, it must be capable of participating in capitalist production processes. This legacy impacts the trajectories of political organizing to achieve social justice for trans communities.

To make this argument, this essay is divided into three sections. The first analyzes early medical approaches to the treatment of transsexuals including those made by influential doctors hostile to transsexuality (e.g., David O. Cauldwell), as well as by those considered compassionate (e.g., Harry Benjamin). Close attention is paid to the ways in which transsexuals are characterized in terms of their class, social status, and creative and employment potential. The second section highlights early trans theorization and activism spearheaded by trans people and their allies. I assert that these efforts were primarily directed at engaging with medical experts to depathologize transsexuality. This approach emphasized respect for transsexuals in order to enable increased access to state-based social services, human rights protections, and public spaces. An underlying goal of these initiatives to achieve sociopolitical, legal, and economic validation for transsexuals was to establish their worth as citizens. Appeals to mainstream society to accept transsexuals as legitimate subjects often emphasized their valuable contributions to society through their labor. The third section focuses on contemporary theorizations of transsexual identities and politics within a neoliberal context. I pay particular attention to subtexts emphasizing worthiness, value, and productivity in order to demonstrate the complicity of trans theorists and activists in naturalizing the exacerbated gendered labor relations characteristic of the neoliberal order that seeks to increase profits through decreasing wages.

The analysis offered in this essay is anchored in critical political economy. As defined by Gary Browning and Andrew Kilmister, this approach "rests on two main pillars; the drawing of links between the economic and other areas of social life and the recognition of the economic when these links are drawn."[10] Critical political economy centers on the productive sphere of capitalism while simultaneously working to cultivate a wider understanding of productive relations. This is achieved through analyzing the numerous components that comprise the sphere of the productive including the home, public space, and communities, as well as other vectors of power such as sex and gender. In addition, power operates discursively as meaning is created and circulated throughout society. For example, discourses of productivity naturalize the exploitative labor relations characteristic of capitalism; despite this naturalization, these discourses influence the treatment and conceptualizations of the transsexual body.

Clearly, sites of commodity production do not produce all meaning. Nor can we claim that all facets of life are determined by exploitative class relations, which maximize profit through the extraction of increasing amounts of surplus value. Social meanings are not created through direct and one-dimensional transference from the workplace to the bodies and consciousness of members of society. Embodied identities, such as transsexuality, are the result of complex amalgamating relations of domination, exploitation, and agency. Defining critical political economy as such begs the question: Why write an essay directing attention toward subtexts of value, worth, and citizenship within medical texts, transsexual narratives, and political agendas that correlate directly with participation in the legally paid labor economy? To be sure, regimes of accumulation—such as Fordism or late capitalism—do not, on their own, shape transsexual existences. That the organization of (re)production wields a significant influence on the social construction of sex and gender is a rudimentary point of feminist political economy. The construction of transsexual identities vis-à-vis capitalist productive relations serves to enrich our understanding of the ways that sex/gender are constructed as regulatory regimes.[11] In addition, considering transsexual subjectivities in light of past and contemporary regimes of accumulation opens new opportunities for theorizing trans identities and for strategizing an emancipatory politics that resists systemic oppression and enriches the lives of trans people.

## MEDICALLY CONSTRUCTING TRANSSEXUAL BODIES THAT WORK

Early discursive and physiological constructions of transsexual bodies by medical experts and their patients exemplify the reciprocal relationship between economic regimes of accumulation and sex/gender categories. Trans researchers, notably Sandy Stone and Jay Prosser, have established that medical professionals wielded enormous power over the range of possible ways that gender-variant individuals could express gendered identities.[12] This was particularly the case in North American locations, such as the Canadian province of Ontario, where the state funded hormone therapy and sex reassignment surgeries (SRS).[13] Gender Identity Clinics (GICs) required that gender-variant individuals seeking medical transition submit to numerous physical and psychological evaluations to qualify for state-funded SRS.[14] Thus qualification for paid SRS depended on a process that pathologized transsexual people as suffering from a set of mental maladies known first as "gender dysphoria" and later as "gender identity disorder."

Because they served as conduits between transsexuals and the physical expression of their sex/gender identities, doctors and psychological professionals exerted considerable authority over their patients. The reinforcement of heteronormative categories of sex, gender, and sexuality through these engagements has been well documented; however, the economic facets of these diagnoses and recommendations for treatment are less well analyzed.[15] By assessing their transsexual patients in terms of their aptitudes, earning potentials, education, and class backgrounds, medical professionals also strengthened hegemonic discourses of citizenship and productivity that buttressed the economy.

Four economic themes appear as subtexts in medical discourse on the treatment of transsexuality. The first concerns the class backgrounds of transsexual patients. Medical experts required detailed information from individuals or their families regarding their class as defined by occupation and social status. This information often appears in the writings of medical doctors as they grapple with the meaning of gender variance. For example, in documenting "Case 131" concerning Count Sandor, a female-bodied person living as male, Richard von Krafft-Ebing noted that Sandor hailed from an "ancient, noble and highly respected family of Hungary."[16]

The writings of the prolific American sexologist David O. Cauldwell (1897–1959) offer an additional example of the way class background factored into physicians' comprehension of transsexuality. Cauldwell characterized "psychopathic transsexuality" in terms of delayed development, sexual immaturity, and frivolity. For him, one's class location played a clear role in fostering this disorder; asserting a higher prevalence of transsexualism among "well to do families," he explained that impoverished people, consumed by the obligations of providing bare necessities for themselves and their families, did not have the means or time for such "deviant" pursuits. For Cauldwell, then, poverty served as a deterrent to transsexualism. The link between one's propensity toward expressing gender variance and class location is demonstrated further in his account of "Earl," a female-to-male (FTM) transsexual patient, whom he identified as having been born a "normal female" into a prominent and wealthy family. Noting that one of Earl's maternal relatives was a doctor whose son became a lawyer and that his paternal grandfather was involved in politics and civic affairs, Cauldwell interpreted Earl as one who squandered his life; in other words, he understood Earl's potential to cultivate his talents and contribute to society as thwarted due to his fixation on expressing his masculine identity. Indeed, Cauldwell asserted that such fixations would most likely result in Earl engaging in criminal activity.[17]

Class discipline also received emphasis within medical literature. The majority of gender-variant individuals who enlisted medical experts for substantive assistance were white, middle-class, able-bodied male-to-female trans people more likely to be able to finance medical transition. This class location emerged as a prominent component of the pathologization of transsexual identities. It is here that the productive body intersects with the creation of pathology as a disciplinary technique. Doctors who opposed any medical intervention enabling one to change sex did so in part because they believed that this transition would thwart the industrious potential of the middle-class, able-bodied (presumed) male and (re)productive potential of the (presumed) female. Because they understood the economic value created by individuals through their labor as a social concern, some medical professionals refused to support deliberate medical interventions that would compromise capable bodies.

Transsexuals were disciplined partially because their sex/gender variance violated social codes that contributed to the growth, development, and global expansion of the domestic economy. Like other citizens, doctors often internalized the social expectations of the upper and middle classes that undergirded hegemonic discourses of productivity. The Hippocratic oath extended beyond their professional obligation to heal individual patients to encompass a broader sense of civic duty. In other words, doctors understood their professional obligation to restore health to individuals as part of a broader imperative to act as moral, upstanding citizens. As physicians, their value lay in contributing to the vitality of the nation. In the case of physicians who adamantly refused to engage in medical transition processes, this contribution was realized through relegitimizing the normatively sexed and gendered body (i.e., one biologically genetically determined) as "the" productive body.

These sex/gendered dimensions of class discipline were clearly elucidated by Cauldwell, who highlighted the civic duty of doctors to ensure the wealth of the nation through the provision of healthy (re)productive bodies. For Cauldwell, this social responsibility trumped all other considerations, including the self-identity of transsexual patients whose understandings of sex/gender he interpreted as destructive to society. He positioned the transsexual individual who requested or demanded medical help as an adversary to the ethical, law-abiding citizen; writing in 1949, he asserted that "the psyche is already ill and sanity is seriously involved when an individual develops a compulsion to be rid of his natural organs and places his insane desires ahead of the rights of others."[18] Cauldwell proved so adamant in his understanding of sex reassignment surgery as mutilation that he claimed that "it would be criminal of a doctor to remove healthy organs."[19] The criminal nature of the surgical act is rooted in Cauldwell's belief that to operate on the transsexual body is to destroy its capacity for a (hetero)sexual life by thwarting the individual's reproductive potential.[20]

It is important to note that even experts who supported medical intervention as a treatment for transsexuality sounded the theme of class discipline. Unlike their peers who reinforced hegemonic sexed/gendered bodies as productive subjects through their refusal to assist in transition procedures, doctors who advocated for "sexual reassignment" through hormonal therapy and surgeries contributed to the economic vitality of the nation through the construction of a working body. Based on their understanding of the so-called dysphoric condition as largely unresponsive to psychotherapy, medical experts asserted the necessity of physiological interventions to construct a sexed body that reflected the self-image held by transsexuals. They grounded this hormonally and surgically assisted transformation in a social context framed in part by conceptualizing the national value ascribed to individuals in terms of their productive capacity.

While critiques by trans scholars of the gatekeeping function of medical professionals have offered compelling analyses of the investment of medical experts in heteronormative sex/gender categories, they have paid scant attention to the ways in which professionals understood these categories in relation to economic production. Prosser, for example, has directed attention to the construction of hegemonic sex/gender categories through diagnostic criteria and requirements of transsexual patients prior to their receiving hormone therapy and SRS.[21] He explains that "narrativization as a transsexual necessarily precedes one's diagnosis as a transsexual; autobiography is transsexuality's proffered symptom."[22] Prosser explains that medical experts have analyzed such narratives to ensure that supposedly proper gender norms of behavior were understood. Other scholars raise concerns regarding the reinforcement of heterosexuality by GICs: while transsexuals were required to divulge explicit details of their heterosexual fantasies, they were prohibited from acting on these fantasies prior to sex reassignment.[23] As Jason Cromwell explains, doctors governed the production of heterosexual subjects by refusing to approve surgery for transsexuals who were gay, bisexual, or lesbian.[24]

Yet the valorization of the maleness or femaleness of post-transition transsexuals hinged in part on understandings of their productive capacity. Value was ascribed to the actual contribution of one's labor power to the economy. The economic element of the "real-life test" illustrates this point. As an integral component of the Benjamin Standards of Care developed to anticipate the kinds of psychic and social challenges that the transsexual patient might encounter, the real-life test was administered by GICs to monitor the ability of the transsexual patient to live entirely as a demonstrable member of the opposite sex. If deemed successful in this endeavor by the team of doctors and psychologists managing the case, the individual was approved for hormone therapy and SRS. The real-life test functioned as an oppressive appraisal of endurance that disciplined transsexuals through the reiteration of their sex/gender variance as problematic and abnormal.[25] Transsexuals were forced to undergo the real-life test before hormone therapy modified their appearance and thereby made it easier to pass as a man or woman. Medical experts believed that the individual who succeeded in withstanding the daily harassment and discrimination that accompanied the real-life test demonstrated a genuine dedication to pursuing transition and therefore deserved to be diagnosed as transsexual.

It is important to understand that the real-life test had an economic component that cannot be conceptualized entirely as an exercise in sex/gender endurance; the test also monitored the future occupational capacities for the postoperative subject. The real-life test contained a facet of economic rehabilitation that required transsexual patients to obtain employment while living full time in their self-identified sex/gender.[26] Regardless of the personal intentions of medical experts, the employment requirements of the real-life test worked to legitimize sex/gender divisions of labor that buttressed the use of gender to maximize profits.

Within the context of heteronormativity during the post–World War II era, the ability of the male body to be economically industrious signified "authentic" manhood. Some clinical understandings of FTM transsexuals made increasingly apparent the connection between supposedly genuine maleness and productive capacity. The willingness of many FTM transsexuals to demonstrate their masculinity through an avid participation in the labor market trumped their nonnormative, nonreproductive embodiment of masculinity. According to the prominent sexologist John Money,

> There is a general consensus among professionals in transexualism that female-to-male transexualism is not an exact homologue of male-to-female transexualism. *Whereas the gender coding of the male-to-female transsexual is prevalently that of the attention-attracting vamp, not the devoted Madonna, the masculine gender coding of the female-to-male transsexual is prevalently that of the reliable provider, not the profligate playboy.* Throughout Europe, America and the English speaking world, clinicians of transexualism agree that a successfully unobtrusive sex-reassigned life is more prevalent in female-to-male reassignment than male to female reassignment even though the success of the female-to-male sex-reassignment surgery leaves something to be desired, namely an erectile penis.[27]

For Money and other medical professionals, the binary system of sex/gender naturalized the devaluation of women, as well as of nonnormative masculinities (i.e., effeminate gay men or FTM transsexuals who do not pass as men). This sex/gender-based degradation, which resulted in systemic oppression, was not practiced only by governmental and institutional bureaucracies. It was also appropriated within spheres of capitalist production, and it is within sites of commodity production where we can witness the amalgamation of exploitation with relations of domination. Oppressed sex/gender and sexual minorities such as women, trans people, gays, and lesbians have always been overrepresented within low-wage, part-time, nonunionized, and precarious sectors of the labor market.[28]

The naturalization of these gender relations is reflected in the writings of doctors who discuss how they judged the "authenticity" of their patients' claims to sex/gender identities. For instance, the influential sexologist Harry Benjamin questioned whether male-to-female patients realized fully that they would likely be unable to maintain their vocation and would experience lower job status and lower wages as women.[29] The success of their sexual reassignment was measured partly through their complacency (an ideal mark of femininity) and their willingness to assimilate into these gendered and exploitative relations.

Social parasitism represents another theme in the medical literature that demonstrates the link between processes of wealth accumulation and the construction of productive bodies. This theme, too, reveals the linkages among transsexualism as pathology, discourses of citizenship, and the economic welfare of the nation. Often medical professionals identified transsexualism as a mental disability—a preoccupation with sex/gender identities and expressions that impeded the ability of transsexuals to contribute to society. As such, they configured the transsexual as threatening and dangerous. The writings of Cauldwell exemplify this pejorative conceptualization of transsexuality. He included "parasitism" as one of the characteristics of psychopathology and marked this quality as abhorrent in his discussion of "psychopathia transsexualis."[30] Cauldwell characterized transsexuals as "sex destructionists" and characterized such destruction as a social act. Those suffering from this "self-hating psychosis . . . turn destruction on themselves [and] impose on society by *becoming burdens to it*."[31] Cauldwell understood transsexuals as socially burdensome in part because he claimed that they refused to participate in the labor economy. In relation to the case of Earl discussed above, Cauldwell wrote: "By now we were beginning to learn something of the real Earl. We knew that her [*sic*] ambitions were to live parasitically *She* [*sic*] *would not work*."[32]

Medical professionals' concern with social parasitism extended beyond employment; many believed that the propensity of gender-variant individuals toward social dependence also manifested in the leeching of public resources, especially those provided by state-funded institutions such as prisons and mental hospitals. Cauldwell advised one gender-variant individual who self-identified as a closeted homosexual and a transvestite to continue to live contrary to his identity for society's sake. Cauldwell explained that "if he continues to live his life in such a way as not to openly offend society he is *a far more valuable citizen* than hundreds (or thousands) of others who, because they are incapable of psychologically adjusting themselves, eventually land in public institutions."[33]

Doctors who reinforced the supposed knowledge that sex is immutable advocated punitive actions when transsexuals proved adamant about expressing freely their chosen sex/gender. They believed not only that disciplinary measures would promote emotional stability for gender variant individuals, but also that these measures would have a restorative effect on society. In response to a family requesting advice on dealing with a FTM transsexual relative, Cauldwell positioned gender variance as pathological with probable negative social implications. He proposed cutting this youth off from material resources as punishment. Cauldwell argued that increasing the vulnerability of transsexuals would eventually construct a productive body:

> Should the young women [*sic*] here involved be put fully on her own and refused financial assistance the results . . . although unpleasant for a number of people, might be the best in the long run for all concerned and this may be considered to include society as a whole. Just as it is said of people who are regarded as wayward, there always is a possibility that these individuals will in time settle down and become significantly well adjusted to avoid causing serious social concern.[34]

Analyzing critically the ways in which transsexualism as a category of sex/gender variance was isolated from other nonnormative gender identities such as transvestism (presently labeled "cross-dressing") reveals the concrete presence of such productive logics and the significant role they played in medical approaches to the treatment of transsexuality. For doctors like Cauldwell and Benjamin, cross-dressing was not as threatening because it was understood as an erotic fetish. Medical experts asserted that many cross-dressers were heterosexuals and professionals and often were happily married men with families and stable employment. Their desire to derive pleasure from dressing in feminine attire was interpreted as an activity that could be contained easily within private spaces (i.e., their own homes or at gatherings with other cross-dressers). Benjamin explains that "the typical or true transvestite is a completely harmless member of society. He derives his sexual pleasure and emotional satisfaction in a strictly solitary fashion."[35] For Benjamin and other sexologists, cross-dressing represented a nonnormatively gendered practice that contributed only to a facet of one's identity, rather than an all-encompassing compulsion that impinged on one's ability to perform the roles of husband, father, and/or worker.

Such was not the case with transsexuality. Doctors described transsexual individuals as consumed by the need to align their bodily sex and gender identity. Therefore, a hierarchy of gender-variant identities existed among medical experts, with transsexuals occupying the bottom echelons of this taxonomy. Regardless of their views concerning the mutability of sex and the scientific facilitation of transitioning, the majority of medical professionals classified transsexuals as the most damaged — and *damaging* — among nonnormatively gendered individuals. Frequently borrowing terminology from psychological professionals, doctors degraded transsexuals as narcissistic, destructive, and self-loathing.[36] This characterization extended beyond the frame of individual abnormality to encompass socially corrosive forms of deviance.

A reading of the medical literature reveals a dominant belief that transsexuality, framed as a mental disorder, renders the body unproductive. According to this literature, the sex/gender "preoccupations" of transsexual individuals undermined their productivity and created states of dependency. The transsexual burdened society rather than contributing to it. Thus, given their broad social commitment to healing, most doctors would not condone a decision to live as a transsexual. They maintained that if untreated, this disorder would likely have a devastating impact on the transsexual individual. Medical commentaries, including those of Cauldwell and Benjamin, interpreted problems faced by gender-variant individuals —including depression, substance abuse, and self-mutilation — not as evidence of the personal implications of unrealized desires to embody one's sex/gender identity but, rather, as evidence of the social and economic threats that such individuals posed to a broader public. Discourses of economic productivity contributed to the degradation of transsexuality and the systemic erasure of transsexual individuals. Within a heteronormative capitalist society organized around binary sex/gender and exploitative labor relations, transsexuality did not work.

## INITIATING TRANS RESISTANCE: TRANSSEXUALITY CAN WORK!

The creation of transsexual subjectivities is a multidimensional process arising through an engagement with dominant societal institutions. In this way, transsexuals are not entirely victims of external authority. They internalize power and participate actively in disciplinary techniques that lend meaning to the transsexual body as productive. The efforts through which transsexual people seek validation for their sex/gender identities and embodied expressions have economic components. The emergence of transsexual voices in and beyond academe echo hegemonic socioeconomic and political discourses grounded in conceptualizations of citizenship defined through laboring bodies. In a manner that resonates with medical practitioners' concerns regarding the practical capacity of transsexual bodies that impacts their ability to exist as responsible citizens, transsexuals also articulate understandings of their sex/gender identity grounded in the logic that buttresses wealth accumulation. Regarding (trans) citizenship, the scholar Aren Aizura asserts that "citizenship here means fading into the population . . . but also the imperative to be 'proper' in the eyes of the state: to reproduce, to find proper employment; to reorient one's 'different' body into the flow of the nationalized aspiration for possessions, property, [and] wealth."[37]

Aizura's claims are demonstrated in transsexual autobiographies, for example, which reveal a tacit commitment to a gendered logic of capitalist production. These autobiographies are often written by transsexual participants in gender-identity programs to gain a "favorable" diagnosis necessary to undergo transition. The underlying logic of economic productivity presented in these autobiographies makes Gramscian "common sense" to both expert and patient. Whether transsexuals individually subscribe to this particular notion of productive citizenship is not at issue here. It was common knowledge among patients at GICs that only a particular transsexual narrative — one that subscribes to hegemonic and heteronormative categories of sex/gender—will be accepted as a reflection of genuine transsexualism.[38] Yet even if some individuals produce these rigid narratives only for functional purposes, the rearticulation and circulation of these narratives serves to embed trans-sexuality within a discourse of productive citizenship.

It is important to read these early autobiographies with an eye toward connections drawn between the reinforcement of supposedly proper gender roles and the structures of the wage labor economy. Such connections are frequently obscured given that transsexual clients of GICs did not address employment directly.[39] Nevertheless, the understood need to make social contributions is reflected in the tenor of transsexual autobiographers' expressions of their future aspirations. The prospects of life after medicalized transition are often expressed in assimilatory terms. These writings reinforce the understanding that genuine transsexuals are those who seek integration into mainstream society as "normal"—and productive —men or women. In his book entitled *The Transsexual Phenomenon* (1966), Harry Benjamin quotes from the autobiography of a transsexual woman who explained that "we prefer the normalcy's [*sic*] of life and want to be accepted in circles of normal society, enjoying the same pursuits and pleasures without calling attention to the fact that we are 'queers' trying to invade the world of normal people."[40]

While it could be suggested that the above quote privileges heterosexuality, other transsexual authors expose more clearly the economic elements of normality. Early transsexual biographies frequently narrated a trajectory of economic difficulty (and, in some cases, failure) prior to transition, followed by integration into society post-transition.[41] For example, Christine Jorgensen, perhaps the most well-known transsexual during the 1950s, wrote of her frustration living as a shy, underweight man "who was unable to find a place in society where he could earn a living and move up in the world."[42] On returning to the United States post-transition, Jorgensen enjoyed a successful career as a public transsexual. Her self-image was embedded in an understanding of the productive potential of her transsexuality. For example, she described her invited addresses at charity events (i.e., voluntary labor) in terms of supporting her community: "It seemed to me an opportunity to prove myself a useful member of the community . . . [to make] some sort of contribution."[43] Of an appearance at Madison Square Garden, Jorgensen remembered that "the brief speech I addressed to the audience was a simple expression of the honor accorded me . . . and the opportunity to be a useful citizen of New York City."[44] Unlike the shy underweight man who could not secure an upwardly mobile position and career, Jorgensen became a financially independent and cosmopolitan woman who worked as a nightclub entertainer.[45]

In addition to transsexual autobiography, research on transsexual lives reinforces the link between gendered dimensions of power and exploitative economic relations. When analyzed through the lens of critical political economy, efforts made by academic commentators to combat characterizations of transsexuals as deviant, abnormal, criminal, and socially destructive do not achieve significant distance from the experts who articulate these characterizations. The urgency to gain social legitimacy for transsexuality often forecloses possibilities for critically theorizing the formation of transsexual subjectivities within a socioeconomic and political context. For example, prominent trans scholars and activists who have made historical arguments advocating the tolerance and social integration of transsexual people have often embedded these arguments within a socioeconomic framework that invokes a model productive citizen. Such literature seeks to challenge efforts of medical professionals to make transsexuality disappear, but it does so through the construction of productive bodies. Likewise, this literature attempts to validate transsexuality as a legitimate sex/ gender identity by demonstrating the productive capacity of this identity. In the influential book *Transgender Warriors,* for example, Leslie Feinberg yearns for a society that resembles a past when trans people were "viewed with respect as vital contributing members of our societies."[46] Scholars like Jason Cromwell invoke the historicized lives of gender-variant people to argue that if historical individuals whose embodied lives did not subscribe to binary sex/gender systems were alive today, these would most likely define themselves as transsexual.

In both of these cases, the authors focus not on the discrepancy between historical actors' sex/ gender identity and their physical embodiment, but on their contributions as workers and dutiful citizens. Such historical narratives frequently speak to the convergence of gender and nation via accounts of the trans man as soldier.[47] Other archival efforts make contributionist claims by focusing on transsexuals in professional occupations. In most of these cases, authors focus on the ways in which these historical figures passed as men or women until illness or death resulted in the discovery of their bodily incongruence. The message one can derive from such accounts is that rather than seeking to make "gender trouble," these historical actors devoted their energies to their professions and families. Trans scholars also often succumb to working within dichotomous categorizations that effectively normalize heteropatriarchal and capitalist relations. When constructing transsexual subjectivities as deserving of social recognition, researchers and activists often employ hegemonic notions of "normal," "healthy," "able-bodied," and "productive." Therefore, since transsexuals are neither unhealthy nor mentally unstable, many of them heal the sick. They are not threats to the security of the country; they fight to defend their nations in war. They are not drains on the system; they are successful workers who provide for themselves and their families (in atypical cases, they are eccentric billionaires who fund the research of doctors like Benjamin, as did the FTM transsexual millionaire Reed Erickson).[48] They are not freaks in carnival shows; they are successful entertainers.[49]

This reactionary approach to achieving trans visibility, accessibility, and inclusion is problematic. To flip dichotomies so that the abnormal becomes normal, the unproductive becomes productive, and the uncreative becomes artistic is to plant some dangerous seeds that jeopardize the state of trans theory and politics. This particular understanding of trans people privileges those within transsexual communities who have the potential to become respectable social subjects. One must acknowledge transsexual individuals who are excluded as subjects and continue to exist on the margins of society, including transsexuals of color, those who do not pass as men or women, those with illnesses or disabilities, those who are impoverished, those who are unable or unwilling to be employed within the legal wage labor economy and thus work in the sex trade, as well as those incarcerated in prisons or mental institutions. Their narratives largely remain untold.

## NEOLIBERAL ACCUMULATION STRATEGIES; OR, TRANSSEXUALITY, INC.

The new millennium has marked the concretization of trans studies wherein trans people have become the subjects of scholarly inquiry rather than its objects.[50] In many respects, trans scholars are setting the research agenda rather than responding to the commentary provided by medical professionals. Yet the need for legitimization that precipitates social recognition for trans people, particularly transsexuals who embody physically a reassigned sex, remains urgent. Transsexual people often live a marginalized existence in which they are unable to secure legal employment, housing, and meet other rudimentary needs. The urgency stemming from the dire circumstances in which many transsexual people find themselves fosters commentary that veers away from a critical analysis of the socioeconomic and political context that structures trans subjectivities and abjection. Much emphasis is placed on integrating trans people as nonnormatively sexed/gendered into heteronormative capitalist society. Such a focus reproduces problematic approaches to transsexuality, which began with medical doctors such as Cauldwell and Benjamin who pathologized transsexual individuals. Contemporary scholarship is haunted by the specter of pathologization due to the continuous reproduction of the heteronormative sex/gender binary system.

This specter emerges as especially troubling in our current neoliberal moment wherein claims to rights and equality have been easily subsumed within a discourse of economic productivity. While it is beyond the scope of this essay to provide a detailed discussion of the multiple facets of neoliberalism, two main pillars should be highlighted in relation to transsexual subjectivities. First, neoliberalism is defined according to an economic restructuring that marks the resurgence of the free-market economy.[51] To increase the accumulation of wealth, concentrated efforts have been made to push wages downward. Such efforts have contributed to the significant growth of certain sectors such as the service sector, as well as to the expansion of "home work" and contract work,[52] which are for the most part precarious, part-time, low-wage positions with few or no benefits.[53] These developments have also produced ever-expanding pools of un(der)employed workers whose vulnerability creates conditions of desperation.[54] Although capital's appropriation of other relations of power (i.e., colonization, race, sexuality, sex/gender) is not unique to neoliberalism, this current "policy project" has given new form to intersecting relations of dominance.[55] Many transsexual individuals, people of color, nonstatus immigrants, migrant workers, and gays and lesbians who do not pass as straight are overrepresented in the above-mentioned hyperexploitative sectors of the economy.

The minimalist state constitutes the second major pillar of neoliberalism. According to the logic of the free-market economy, the role of the minimal state is to provide the infrastructure and support necessary for the accumulation of capital. Within a North American context, this has meant the dismantling of the welfare state. Programs that provided citizens with social assistance, unemployment insurance, and publicly funded heath care have steadily declined, which has contributed to an environment hospitable to hyperexploitative labor relations and to an increased vulnerability of many segments of society, including many transsexual individuals. I will offer two examples most relevant to the critical political economic analysis of transsexual subjectivities. First, discourses concerning citizenship have shifted away from notions of social citizenship,[56] wherein one has clear expectations of the state to provide for one's well-being in cases of economic hardship. Neoliberal notions of citizenship do not carry these same expectations; instead, good citizens are defined as those who can contribute to their nation's advancement in the global political economy. Related closely to the dominant notion of the deserving citizen, as revived under neoliberalism, is a second discourse, which espouses the necessity of an individual to cultivate an "entrepreneurial spirit." The onus has thereby shifted from the state to individual members of society who are expected to make adjustments and sacrifices to provide for their own material needs, as well as for those of their family and communities. This may include self-care (i.e., taking care of one's physical and mental well-being), education, and training to obtain employment.[57]

Discourses of the good, deserving citizen who cultivates an entrepreneurial spirit fuel a volatile context that Angela Harris refers to as the "cultural wars."[58] The anxieties of many middle- and working-class people resulting from neoliberal restructuring are alleviated through rendering the logic of capitalist accumulation strategies invisible. Instead of focusing on these strategies, media, state, and community institutions continuously construct socioeconomic and political discourses that represent segments of middle- and working-class populations as innocent victims and upstanding citizens while simultaneously (re)constructing others as enemies, threats, and drains on the system. It is through the predominance of these discourses among the majority of middle- and working-class society that transsexuality is rendered suspect. Therefore many commentators and LGBT (lesbian, gay, bisexual, and transgender) organizations deliberately emphasize the transsexual individual as a contributing member of society when appealing for recognition of trans subjects and for access to employment. The understanding of the transsexual body as productive provides the subtexts for differing representations of transsexuality.

For example, major newspapers have recently featured transsexuals who hold corporate positions. The *Toronto Star* published an article featuring Angela Wensley, a senior manager for MacMillan Bloedel Ltd., one of Canada's leading forestry companies, who transitioned on the job. Geared toward an audience comprised mainly of businesspeople, academics, and other professionals, these articles focus primarily on values of capability and achievement. Wensley vows continued success as head of the corporation's corrosion and materials engineering group in spite of being transsexual: "A lot of women in this company have told me they're counting on me because I'm one of only a few here to make it above the glass ceiling. I'm afraid my career advancement is on hold . . . but I'm going to prove to them that not only am I as good as the man I was before, I'm better as a woman."[59] This subtext of industriousness also permeates many contemporary transsexual autobiographies. [...] Autobiographies by trans activists often follow a similar trajectory. [...]

To prove to employers just how efficiently transsexual people can function, trans activists and allies stress the capacity of transsexuals to be loyal and diligent employees. For example, the Center for Gender Sanity makes a case for the value transsexual people add to economic operations through their labor. In *Transsexual Workers: An Employer's Guide* (2003), Janis Wolworth makes the case for hiring transsexual workers, as well as for maintaining the employment status of those transitioning. It is here that (trans)sex and gender mediate economic needs to render the transsexual laboring body industrious, and in ways that are strikingly similar to how the neoliberal political economy renders all workers susceptible to decreasing wages, fewer benefits, and precarious positions (such as contract work). As Wolworth writes, "while in transition, transsexuals are strongly motivated to earn enough money to pay for the desired procedures and to maintain above-average performance in order to keep their jobs." Furthermore, corporations can influence the construction of effective transsexual bodies through investing in procedures for sexual reassignment and instituting antidiscriminatory policies that protect gender identity and expression. She states, "Once transition is completed, a transsexual employee is likely to become more productive."[64]

Transsexual individuals can be viewed as viable neoliberal subjects: they have proven to be flexible and fluid, self-sufficient, and major contributors to their families, workplaces, communities, and societies. To many, emphasizing the normative potential of transsexuality has been a successful strategy to counter the marginalizing effects of pathologization. The legitimizing of the transsexual worker, however, does not offer serious challenges to heteronormativity nor does it illuminate the conditions of hyperexploitation that structure neoliberalism. In fact, these narratives dovetail with hegemonic discourses concerning the upstanding citizen and the necessity of entrepreneurialism.[65] The interest expressed by major corporations such as IBM demonstrates the ease with which capital continues to appropriate the oppressed minorities, such as sex/gender variants, into its accumulation strategies. As part of its "managed diversity" programs, IBM actively recruits trans people, racial minorities, Native Americans, gay men and lesbians, and women.[66]

The changing tides of neoliberal restructuring amid the continuation of the heteronormative sex/gender binary has created a receptive atmosphere for transsexual incorporation into the productive spheres of capital. Unlike medical experts such as Cauldwell who chastised nonnormative sex/gender identifications as frivolities that distracted from one's potential as a laborer, corporate executives view these tenuous identifications as advantageous to present regimes of accumulation. Difference is appropriated not only as a market niche but also as a resource for capital accumulation when transsexual bodies are valorized socially because of the value their labor contributes to the economy. As explained to members of sex/gender minorities by IBM, "When you join IBM's diverse team you are *encouraged to share your unique perspectives and capabilities.* At IBM we recognize individual differences and appreciate *how these differences provide a powerful competitive advantage* and a source of great pride and opportunity in the workplace and marketplace."[67]

## TOWARD RADICAL FUTURES

Much like modern gay and lesbian movements that have veered away from liberationist approaches toward assimilatory goals, transsexuals have overwhelmingly responded to pathologization and erasure by cultivating social subjectivities that demonstrate their ability to contribute to economic progress. However, claims to self-sufficiency, morality, and a positive work ethic undermine the potential for a politics of resistance and create fractures within transsexual communities based on class, race, citizenship status, and ability (to name a few). Whose bodies are the most productive and most effortlessly absorbed into capitalist employment pools? Appealing to mainstream society through a rearticulation of dominant socioeconomic discourses comes at a cost to those within trans communities who cannot be easily assimilated into normative categories, such as those who do not pass as men or women or those who are physically or mentally ill or incarcerated.

A second division resulting from these assimilatory strategies extends beyond transsexual communities. This strategy within the context of neoliberalism distances transsexual people from other economic outsiders who are also configured as parasitic, abnormal, or deviant. Progressive trans scholars and activists ought to think through the complex ways that heteronormativity and capitalism impact the lives of many other individuals who are understood as improperly sexed/gendered such as single mothers, women and men of color, those on social assistance, and those engaged in sex work. Further, these efforts to normalize trans bodies as productive forego the possibility of establishing alliances with anticapitalist and antiglobalization activists who engage in queering all facets of political economy. While the urgent need for employment is deniable for many trans people, it is important to ask: Whose interests are ultimately served by the formation of dutiful, self-sufficient, hardworking transsexual subjectivities?

Certainly, the lasting legacy of the medicalization of trans people demands our continued resistance. We also need to acknowledge the ways in which neoliberal prescriptions for thought and behavior have influenced the lived experiences that contribute to trans theory and activism despite transsexuals' rich history of militant opposition to systemic power structures. The actions of the trans and gender-noncompliant Compton Cafeteria rioters and of those who fought police at Stonewall ought to occupy a more significant place in the queer collective memory. In the midst of a political climate in which we are told that "there is no alternative," their activism can still spark radical imaginations of a queer future.

## NOTES

1. I use the term *transsexual,* a specific category that defines gender-variant individuals who communicated their desires to have their sex reassigned, as coined by medical experts. In other words, transsexual people did not create the term; rather, it was introduced by Magnus Hirschfeld in 1923, but did not become an official diagnostic category until 1980. I use the term *trans* to denote the current terminology used. It reflects a movement away from the transsexual/transgender divide and acknowledges diversity among gender-variant identities and expressions including genderqueers, transmen, transwomen, and so on. I also use the term *gender variant* to mark the exclusion of all trans people from the hegemonic sex/gender binary.
2. Larry Buhl, "Historic 1966 Transgender Riot Remembered," Intraa, www.intraa.org/story/comptons (accessed May 8, 2007).
3. For examples, see Rosemary Hennessy, *Materialist Feminism: A Reader in Class, Difference, and Women's Lives* (New York: Routledge, 1997); Gayle Rubin, "Thinking Sex: Notes for a Radical Theory of the Politics of Sexuality," 1984,

in *Social Perspectives in Lesbian and Gay Studies: A Reader,* ed. Peter M. Nardi and Beth E. Schneider (New York: Routledge, 1998), 100–133.

4. Donald Morton, ed., *The Material Queer: A LesBiGay Cultural Studies Reader* (Boulder, CO: Westview, 1996); Amy Gluckman and Betsy Reed, *HomoEconomics: Capitalism, Community, and Lesbian and Gay Life* (New York: Routledge, 1997).

5. Leslie Feinberg and Dean Spade are notable exceptions to this scholarly act of omission.

6. For examples of the myriad of texts describing trans identities, see Ann Bolin, *In Search of Eve: Transsexual Rites of Passage* (New York: Bergin and Garvy, 1988); Holly Devor, *FTM: Female-to-Male Transsexuals in Society* (Bloomington: Indiana University Press, 1997); Kate Bornstein, *Gender Outlaws: On Men, Women, and the Rest of Us* (New York: Random House, 1995); Judith Halberstam, *Female Masculinities* (Durham, NC: Duke University Press, 1998).

7. For an example of literature concerning human rights debates, see Paisley Currah, Richard M. Juang, and Shannon Price Minter, eds., *Transgender Rights* (Minneapolis: University of Minnesota Press, 2006).

8. For texts that address trans poverty, see, for example, Dean Spade, "Compliance Is Gendered: Struggling for Gender Self-Determination in a Hostile Economy," in Currah, Juang, and Minter, *Transgender Rights,* 217–41.

9. For scholarly publications on trans employment, see Viviane Namaste, "Beyond Leisure Studies: A Labour History of Male to Female Transsexual and Transvestite Artists in Montreal, 1955–1985," *Atlantis: A Women's Studies Journal* 29 (2004): 4–11; Christine Burnham, *Gender Change: Employability Issues* (Vancouver: Perceptions, 1994). For transcommunity publications, see Marty Wilder, "First Day on the Gender," *FTMI Newsletter* 51 (2002): 8–9; Janis Wolworth, *Transsexual Workers: An Employers Guide* (Los Angeles: Center for Gender Sanity, 1998).

10. Gary Browning and Andrew Kilmister, *Critical and Post-critical Political Economy* (London: Palgrave, 2006), 4.

11. Judith Butler, "Gender Regulations," in *Undoing Gender* (New York: Routledge, 2005), 41.

12. Sandy Stone, "The Empire Strikes Back: A Posttranssexual Manifesto," in *The Transgender Studies Reader,* ed. Susan Stryker and Stephen Whittle (New York: Routledge, 2006), 232; Jay Prosser, *Second Skins: The Body Narrative of Transsexuality* (New York: Columbia University Press, 1998), 101.

13. SRS was delisted from the Ontario Health Insurance Plan in 1998.

14. The John Hopkins Gender Identity Clinic in Baltimore is one of the most notable U.S. clinics, whereas the former Clarke Institute (presently the Centre for Addictions and Mental Health) in Toronto and the Gender Dysphoria program in Vancouver are Canadian examples.

15. For example, see Vernon A. Rosario, "Trans (Homo) Sexuality? Double Inversion, Psychiatric Confusion, and Hetero-hegemony," in *Queer Studies: A Lesbian, Gay, Bisexual, Transgender Anthropology,* ed. Brett Beemyn and Mickey Eliason (New York: New York University Press, 1996), 35–51.

16. Richard von Krafft-Ebing, "Selections from Psychopathia Sexualis with Special Reference to Contrary Sexual Instinct: A Medico-Legal Study," in Stryker and Whittle, *Transgender Studies Reader,* 22.

17. David O. Cauldwell, "Psychopathia Transexualis," *International Journal of Transgenderism* 5, no. 2 (2001), www.symposion.com/ijt/cauldwell/cauldwell_02.htm.

18. Ibid.

19. David O. Cauldwell, "Questions and Answers on the Sex Life and Sexual Problems of Transsexuals," *International Journal of Transgenderism* 5, no. 2 (2001), www.symposion.com/ijt/cauldwell/cauldwell_04.htm.

20. Cauldwell, "Psychopathia Transexualis."

21. For similar commentary, see Dean Spade, "Mutilating Gender," in Stryker and Whittle, *Transgender Studies Reader,* 325–29.

22. Prosser, *Second Skins,* 104.

23. Stone, "Empire Strikes Back," 228.

24. Jason Cromwell, "Queering the Binaries: Transituated Identities, Bodies, and Sexualities," in Stryker and Whittle, *Transgender Studies Reader,* 511.

25. While the real-life test is addressed using past tense to indicate a time in the history of transsexuality when GICs were prevalent, this requirement before any access to a medicalized transition still exists for many. Transsexuals located in suburban and rural locations, where trans awareness is lacking among medical professionals, continue to be referred to GICs still in operation.

26. It was John Money who referred to the employment requirement of the real-life test as economic "rehabilitation." Money, a psychologist and a sexologist, was a professor of pediatrics and psychology at John Hopkins University from 1951 until his death in 2006. He worked within the Sexual Behaviors Unit that researches SRS. See John Money, *Gay, Straight, and In-Between* (Oxford: Oxford University Press, 1989), 88.

27. Ibid., 92; emphasis mine.

28. Jo Hirschmann, "TransAction: Organizing against Capitalism and State Violence in San Francisco," *Socialist Review* (2001): 4, www.findarticles.com/p/articles/mi_qa3952/is_2ooioi/ai_n8932894.

29. Harry Benjamin, *The Transsexual Phenomenon* (Dusseldorf: Symposion, 1997), www.symposion.com/ijt/benjamin/chapt_07.htm.

30. Cauldwell, "Psychopathia Transexualis."

31. David O. Cauldwell, "Sex Transmutation—Can Anyone's Sex Be Changed?" *International Journal of Transgenderism* 5, no. 2 (2001), www.symposion.com/ijt/cauldwell/cauldwell05.htm; emphasis mine.

32. Cauldwell, "Psychopathia Transexualis"; emphasis original.

33. Cauldwell, "Questions and Answers"; emphasis mine.

34. Ibid.

35. Benjamin, *Transsexual Phenomenon.*

36. Ibid.; Cauldwell, "Psychopathia Transexualis"; David O. Cauldwell, "Desire for Surgical Sex Transmutation," *International Journal of Transgenderism* 5, no. 2(2001), www.symposion.com/ijt/cauldwell/cauldwell_03.htm.

37. Aren Z. Aizura, "Of Borders and Homes: The Imaginary Community of (Trans)sexual Citizenship," *Inter-Asia Cultural Studies* 7(2006): 295.

38. The two failed attempts to receive the necessary access to medicalized transition procedures by the renowned FTM activist Lou Sullivan—a gay man who refused to comply with the imperative that transsexual men must desire women—demonstrate the rigidity of this narrative. For a discussion of Sullivan, see Pat Califia, *Sex Changes: The Politics of Transgenderism* (San Francisco: Cleis, 1997), 186.

39. While direct references may have been made to employment elsewhere, they were not at all prominent within sexology literature.

40. Benjamin, *Transsexual Phenomenon.*

41. Bernice Hausman, "Body, Technology, and Gender in Transsexual Autobiographies," in Stryker and Whittle, *Transgender Studies Reader,* 350.

42. Ibid., 341.

43. Christine Jorgensen, "Christine Jorgensen: A Personal Autobiography," in *Sexual Metamorphosis: An Anthology of Transsexual Memoirs,* ed. Jonathan Ames (New York: Vintage, 2005), 72.

44. Ibid., 73.

45. Joanne Meyerowitz, *How Sex Changed: A History of Transsexuality in the United States* (Cambridge, MA: Harvard University Press, 2002), 79.

46. Leslie Feinberg, *Transgender Warriors: Making History from Joan of Arc to Dennis Rodman* (Boston: Beacon, 1996), 88.

47. Jason Cromwell, *Transmen and FTMs: Identities, Bodies, Genders, and Sexualities* (Urbana: University of Illinois Press, 1999), 63–72; Nan Alamilla Boyd, "Bodies in Motion: Lesbian and Transsexual Histories," in Stryker and Whittle, *Transgender Studies Reader,* 423–24.

48. Aaron Devor and Nicholas Matte, "ONE Inc. and Reed Erickson: The Uneasy Collaboration of Gay and Trans Activism," in Stryker and Whittle, *Transgender Studies Reader,* 387–406.

49. Namaste, "Beyond Leisure Studies," 4–11.

50. Viviane Namaste, *Invisible Lives: The Erasure of Transsexual and Transgendered People* (Chicago: University of Chicago Press, 2000); C. Jacob Hale, "Suggested Rules for Non-Transsexuals Writing about Transsexuals, Transsexuality, or Trans ____," www.sandystone.com/hale.rules.html (accessed May 8, 2007).

51. Thorn Workman, *Banking on Deception: The Discourse of Fiscal Crisis* (Halifax: Fernwood, 1996), 23–24.

52. Roxana Ng, "Homeworking: Dream Realized or Freedom Restrained? The Globalized Reality of Immigrant Garment Workers," *Canadian Women's Studies* 19, no. 3 (1999): 110.

53. Jamie Swift, *Wheel of Fortune: Work and Life in the Age of Falling Expectations* (Toronto: Between the Lines, 1995), 13.

54. Thorn Workman, *Social Torment: Globalization in Atlantic Canada* (Halifax: Fernwood, 2003), 105.

55. Angela Harris, "From Stonewall to the Suburbs? Toward a Political Economy of Sexuality," *William and Mary Bill of Rights Journal* 14 (2006): 1541.

56. Stephen McBride and John Shields, *Dismantling a Nation: The Transition to Corporate Rule in Canada* (Halifax: Fernwood, 1997), 26.

57. For an example, see Thomas Dunk, Stephen McBride, and Randle W. Nelson, eds., *The Training Trap: Ideology, Training, and the Labour Market* (Winnipeg: Society for Socialist Studies, 1996).

58. Harris, "From Stonewall to the Suburbs," 1542.

59. Kathleen Kenna, "Engineer 'Just Knew' He Was Really Female," *Toronto Star,* August 4, 1990.
    […]

64. Wolworth, *Transsexual Workers,* 54.

65. Within the Western patriarchal capitalist system, one can say that gender and economic activity have always combined to produce an understanding of fully realized humanity. It is not coincidental that the titles of many recent texts written by transsexual men make use of the notion of the economic man to attempt to access hegemonic masculinity. Examples include Henry Rubin, *Self-Made Men: Identity and Embodiment among Transsexual Men* (Nashville, TN: Vanderbilt University Press, 2003); and Paul Hewitt with Jane Warren, *A Self Made Man: The Diary of a Man Born in a Woman's Body* (London: Headline, 1995).

66. For a general overview of the purpose of IBM's Executive Task Forces and a sample of the questions task forces comprised of GRLT people, Native Americans, and women were asked, please see IBM's Web site, especially Global Task Forces, www-03.ibm.com/employment/us/diverse/50/exectask.shtml (accessed May 12, 2007).

67. IBM, "Diversity at IBM," www-03.ibm.com/employment/ca/en/diversity.html; emphasis mine (accessed May 12, 2007).

# 2

## *Retelling Racialized Violence, Remaking White Innocence*

### The Politics of Interlocking Oppressions in Transgender Day of Remembrance

SARAH LAMBLE

SARAH LAMBLE IS A CANADIAN LEGAL SCHOLAR AND ACTIVIST who has critiqued the prison industrial complex and written on gender, sexuality, and the law. This article first appeared in a special issue of *Sexuality and Social Policy* on transgender law and politics. In it, Lamble looks at how race plays into the remembering of trans people killed due to anti-transgender violence or prejudice. She looks mostly at Transgender Day of Remembrance (TDOR), a day observed on November 21 each year to commemorate those who have been killed in the past year. Lamble points to the differences between the people who are remembered—overwhelmingly poor people of color, often sex-workers—and those who organize TDOR events, often comparably privileged white middle-class activists on college campuses. They argue that TDOR events often understand the murderous violence directed at trans people as specifically anti-transgender violence, to which the solution is better legal protections for transgender people. For Lamble, this reduces the complexity of events in which poverty, institutionalized racism, inadequate healthcare, sex-worker stigma and a punitive justice system contribute to particular gender variant people being far more vulnerable to violence. In short, this work questions whether framing "transgender" as the primary target of violence obscures how being brown and poor may increase one's *vulnerability* to violence. Lamble's conclusion is that transgender activists need to rethink their political strategies in ways that target those particular vulnerabilities rather than fighting for, for example, inclusion of transgender in hate crimes legislation.

In the last nine years, Transgender Day of Remembrance (TDOR) has become a significant political event among those resisting violence against gender-variant persons. Commemorated in more than 250 locations predominantly throughout North America but also in Europe, Australia, New Zealand, South America, and Southeast Asia, this day honors individuals who were killed due to anti-transgender hatred or prejudice. Although various memorial activities are organized at a grassroots level, most of these events are linked through two sister websites: the Remembering Our Dead project (http://www.rememberingourdead.org/about/core.html), which records transgender deaths, and the official TDOR site (http://www.gender.org/remember/day/), which provides educational resources and publicizes transgender vigils occurring around the world. Projects of the nonprofit organization Gender Education & Advocacy, both websites provide vital tools for local community mobilization and play an influential role in shaping transgender remembrance practices worldwide.[1] Indeed, these projects have played a crucial role in raising public awareness about the extreme violence regularly perpetrated against gender-variant persons. Despite their importance as resources for activism, the TDOR website and the Remembering Our Dead project are nonetheless limited in the scope of their analysis of the factors causing violence against gender-variant individuals and of the potential responses to such violence. By focusing on transphobia as the definitive cause of violence, the websites do not fully contextualize incidents of violence within their specific time and place, thus obscuring the ways in which hierarchies of race, class, and sexuality situate and constitute such acts. In the process, transgender bodies are universalized along a singular identity plane of victimhood and rendered visible primarily through the violence that is acted upon them.

Taking the TDOR/Remembering Our Dead project as a case study for considering the politics of memorialization, as well as tracing the narrative history of the Fred F. C. Martinez murder case in Colorado, I aim to demonstrate how deracialized accounts of violence produce seemingly innocent White witnesses who can consume these spectacles of domination without confronting their own complicity in such acts. Without addressing violence as a systemic effect of power, I argue that current manifestations of TDOR potentially limit the possibilities for resisting racialized gender violence in meaningful and effective ways.

This article is not written to denigrate the important work of activists who struggle against violence,[2] nor is it to suggest that we should abandon remembrance practices that honor those who have suffered from violence. Such practices serve multiple purposes and mark important forms of collective healing, community gathering, and public denunciations of violence. Rather, this article critically questions the politics of who and how we remember, interrogates the implications of speaking on behalf of the dead, and examines what is at stake in taking up particular kinds of remembrance practices. I argue that if we[3] are to engage in effective struggle against violence, we must resist remembrance practices that rely on reductionist identity politics; we must pay attention to the specific relations of power that give rise to acts of violence; and we must confront violence in its structural, systemic, and everyday forms.

Narratives of remembrance are not merely problems of representation. The stories we take up in remembrance are constituent practices: They tell us who we are and how we know the world. As Roger Simon (2005) noted, "Practices of remembrance are questions of and for history as a force of inhabitation, as the way we live with images and stories that intertwine with our sense of limits and possibilities, hopes and fears, identities and distinctions" (p. 3). In other words, narratives as practices of remembrance have material effects on the social ordering of relations of power and the ways in which we come to know ourselves in relation to the dead. These effects are neither politically neutral nor socially inconsequential: "In these practices of remembrance, there is a prospective orientation that seeks to legitimate and secure particular social relations, making normative claims on the conduct of human behaviour" (Simon, p. 4). Underlying this article is more than a debate about what version of a story is told, how particular persons are presented, or who is included and excluded—I wish to address a broader concern about what kinds of spaces for resistance narratives of remembrance help create and how those narratives determine the boundaries and possibilities for enacting change.

## DECONTEXTUALIZED VIOLENCE: DERACING TRANSGENDER BODIES

The Remembering Our Dead project was founded by trans activist Gwendolyn Ann Smith in response to the death of Rita Hester, an African American transwoman who was murdered in her Massachusetts apartment in November 1998. Concerned that deaths of transgender persons were poorly documented and quickly forgotten, Smith began gathering and publicizing information about transgender deaths so that trans communities would better know their own histories. In November

1999, Smith organized the first TDOR, a candlelight vigil in San Francisco. Now an annual event, TDOR has become "the largest multi-venue transgender event in the world" (Smith, 2003).

As part of the ongoing Remembering Our Dead project, a small group of volunteers compile and record the name, date, location, and cause of death for trans-related murders worldwide. As of November 2007, the list included 378 individuals.[4] The comprehensiveness of the list is no doubt limited by an unavoidable reliance on mainstream media sources, which consistently fail to provide thorough reporting on transgender deaths, as well as reports from law enforcement officers, which often reflect inadequate responses to violence against transgender persons (Moran & Sharpe, 2004). Indeed, as Smith (2000) noted, "The media's reluctance to cover our deaths lies near the heart of this project". Chronic underfunding and limited resources within transgender communities poses further challenges to the project, and the emotional burden of collecting this information can be high (Smith, 2001). Nevertheless, the project is a collaborative one, with international appeals for reports and strong links with a range of gender-related social justice organizations (Remembering Our Dead, 2006a, 2006b, 2006d). Likewise, many of the resources posted on the TDOR website are produced by other allied groups in the United States, such as the Gay, Lesbian and Straight Education Network, the Gay-Straight Alliance Network, and the Transgender Law Center.

The TDOR website acknowledges that "not every person represented during the Day of Remembrance self-identified as transgendered—that is, as a transsexual, crossdresser, or otherwise gender-variant—[but] each was a victim of violence based on bias against transgendered people" (TDOR, 2004b). Both the TDOR website and the Remembering Our Dead project are thereby explicit in privileging transphobia as the exclusive motivation for violence: "Over the last decade, more than one person per month has died due to transgender-based hate or prejudice, *regardless of any other factors in their lives* [italics added]" (Smith, 2000). Evident here is a deliberate effort to isolate transphobia from any other form of prejudice or cause of violence. From this vantage point, other factors are deemed not only to complicate our understanding of violence, but also to pose a threat to the legitimacy of the project's political goals. The authenticity of the cause is secured through the authority of a particular community: The murder list includes "only those deaths that are known to the transgender community or that have been reported in the media" (TDOR, 2004b). But who makes up this community that determines who will be remembered? Who is the subject we are asked to remember?

The answers to these questions are not simple. First, there is no clear consensus on what constitutes transgender, let alone transgender community. Emerging in the early 1990s as an umbrella term to include a multiplicity of gender experiences and practices that transgress dominant norms of gender expression (including trans-identified persons who use medical interventions to express their gender and those who do not, cross-dressers, pan-gendered people, intersex persons,[5] two-spirited individuals, etc.), the term *transgender* has been broadly used as an identity around which gender-variant individuals could gather and organize political strategies.[6] The term also emerged in resistance to pathologizing labels imposed by the medical establishment and in contestation of the trivialization of gender-variant behavior in popular culture. However, fierce debates persist on how the term should be used, whom it includes—and what proximity it has to queer, gay, lesbian, and bisexual organizing (Califia, 1997; Currah, 2006; Feinberg, 1996; Moran & Sharpe, 2004; Namaste, 2005; Phelan, 2001; Valerio, 2002). These debates go beyond simple semantics and strike at the root of political struggles revolving around citizenship rights and protection from harm. For individuals whose membership in a particular group can greatly affect their claims to medical care, protection from violence, and legal recognition of identity, the stakes are high.[7]

These divisions over who is included in the community resurface within projects such as TDOR, where belonging through victimhood is the platform for political agency. For example, the 1993 high profile murder of Brandon Teena[8] sparked fierce sectarian battles among transgender, transsexual, and lesbian and gay activists, who each wanted to claim this murder as an attack against their own kind (Halberstam, 2005; Hale, 1998). A similar example can be found in the 1996 murder of three sex workers in Toronto who were shot within hours of each other by Marcello Palma. Two of the victims, Deanna/Thomas Wilkinson and Shawn Keagan, were identified as cross-dressers and are listed on the Remembering Our Dead website as victims of transphobic violence. Yet they are also included in Douglas Janoff's (2005) recent inventory of homophobic violence in Canada. From a third camp, Mirha-Soliel Ross and Viviane Namaste (2005) maintained that these deaths arose from antiprostitute and class-based discrimination, an argument based on the fact that the perpetrator described street people and prostitutes as scum and demonstrated no clear evidence of transphobia.[9] Similarly, Ross and Namaste noted that Grace Baxter, a fully passable, postoperative transsexual sex worker who is also listed on the Transgender Remembrance website, was killed by a john who was unaware of her trans status. Ross thus denounced TDOR as "a big, bold and sickening political fraud" (quoted in Namaste, p. 92).

Within this political framework of claiming victims, activists—whose struggles are ultimately linked—can become ensnared in what Razack and Fellows (1998) described as competing marginalities. In this model, justice claims rest on proof that one group is not only most oppressed but also most innocent; that is, the group in question must convey itself as bearing no responsibility in the oppression of others (Razack & Fellows). Identities are thus marked as constituting so-called good and bad victims, and these categories tend to fall along particular class, gender, and racial lines. The supposedly perfect victim is the one who is believed to be most pure, innocent, and helpless— typically the White, middle-class girl child. It is not surprising, then, that Matthew Shepard and Brandon Teena, both marked as young, White, barely masculine (and, in Shepard's case, also middle-class), have become the poster children for protesting homophobic and transphobic violence.[10] In contrast, cases involving victims of color, prostitutes, and street people are rarely noticed, particularly by mainstream media, politicians, and service organizations (Ott & Aoki, 2002). When less ideal victims *are* taken up by the media or championed by political groups, undesirable facts or complex dimensions of identity are often omitted from the story so as to produce a good-victim narrative. By predicating political strategies on innocent victimhood, violence against individuals who deviate from the ideal becomes less visible and more tolerable. Consequently, "those who are the most severely affected victims of sexism and racism (e.g. prostitutes or teenaged black males in the juvenile justice system) qualify least as 'genuine' victims of crime" (Simon, 2000, p. 1132). Hence, the claims of the most privileged groups are advanced through the disavowal of other groups' claims.

Activists, no doubt, have strategic reasons why they continue to employ this tactic. As Razack and Fellows (1998) noted, "One reason we feel compelled to secure our own place on the margin as the most oppressed is that not to do so is to risk erasure" (p. 339). This concern is a vital one for trans people, whose invisibility—induced by dominant power relations of sex and gender norms—makes it difficult for them to secure such basic rights and services as health care and housing. Historically treated as freaks of science, sources of entertainment, or fodder for academic theorizing, trans people struggle to define visibility on their own terms (Namaste, 2000). Even among groups who claim solidarity with transgender people, tokenism and exclusionary practices persist (Namaste, 2005; Phelan, 2001). Within this context, there is "much pressure to conform to the totalizing and essentializing dimensions of identity if claims of access to resources and demands for recognition of citizenship of transgender people are to have the gloss of legitimacy" (Moran & Sharpe, 2004, p. 412). Moreover, when the urgency of addressing violence is coupled with limited resources, time pressures, and media demands for soundbite politics, the simpler, more rhetorical strategies can easily win out over complex and nuanced analysis.

Not surprising, then, is that the political narrative of TDOR has been reduced to a singular cause (transphobia) and a singular identity (victim of transphobic violence). The website achieves this narrative not only with its self-description but also through the remembrance archive itself. The list of victims in the archive includes no information on the age, race, class, ability, or particular circumstances of each individual who was murdered— nor is any such information provided about the people who committed each crime, even when the perpetrators are known. Although a handful of victim profiles include a photo of the person, most include only a generic silhouette image.[11] Each case is abstracted from its history and context: Each murder is decontextualized and reabsorbed within a unified narrative and a universalized body of the dead trans subject. The narrative encoding of gender violence dovetails with a narrative decoding of racial violence, class violence, and sexual violence. Within this framing, each individual death can stand in and be substituted for another; difference is subsumed within sameness.

Because the archive provides so few details about each case, the cause of death becomes the most powerful marker of inclusion within the community of remembrance. The gruesome details of violence, which are repeated at vigils and reiterated through the remembrance archive, have strong visceral impact; we do not remember the names of the victims so much as we remember the violence that was done to them. Just as Western feminism's historical reliance on a universal female victim has tended to define gender as what is done to women, the gender identity of trans people is signified by what is done to their bodies (Razack, 2001). Deliberately unmarked by race, class, age, ability, sexuality, and history, these individuals— otherwise unknown—are rendered visible solely through the violence that is enacted upon them. The very existence of transgender people is verified by their death. Violence thus marks the body as belonging to the trans community. In this way, violence simultaneously obliterates and produces a particular trans subject—both materially (in the act of killing) and symbolically (in the subsequent narration).

Defined by the details of brutality, violence is reduced to the snapshot of a crime scene, a momentary fragment in time between perpetrator and victim. Without history or context, the systemic roots of violence are rendered invisible; violence is comprehensible only at the microlevel whereby individual transphobia becomes the only viable explanation. Besides being incomplete, this picture undermines the scope of antiviolence efforts. Several scholars have illustrated the problem of using phobias as a primary explanation for violence (Spade & Willse, 2000). As Gary Kinsman (1996) noted of homophobia, "It individualizes and privatizes gay and lesbian oppression and obscures the social relations that organize it" (p. 33). Hence, the trans murder victim emerges as the product of an individual hatred or fear rather than the result of the accumulative effect of social institutions (such as legal, economic, and political systems) that are founded on, and perpetuate, complex hierarchies of power and violence (such as White supremacy, patriarchy, and heteronormativity).

By accumulating a collective list of murder victims, the TDOR website does make efforts to demonstrate that acts of violence against transgender people are not isolated events. One of the educational handouts, titled "Anti-Trans Murder: Over One A Month." conveys the frequency with which such violence occurs. Yet the prevalence of murders is provided as further evidence of widespread transphobia, an idea that invariably returns to individual perpetrators as the root cause of violence. This analysis is confirmed by the handout's conflation of justice with individual punishment and retribution: "Those who are caught seldom receive sentences commensurate with their crimes. In over 200 cases, only one such murderer is currently on death row, and just two others are serving life sentences" (TDOR). The wording suggests that justice would be better fulfilled if more perpetrators were given life—or death—sentences. Indeed, the Remembering Our Dead project actively supports harsher penalties for transgender-related hate crimes.

Such so-called solutions, however, fail to confront systemic causes of violence (such as the criminal justice system itself) and ignore state complicity in authorizing violence (Spade & Willse, 2000). As Wendy Brown (1995) aptly demonstrated, the call for such judicial responses "casts the law in particular and the state more generally as neutral arbiters of injury rather than as themselves invested with the power to injure" (p. 27). Moreover, because hate crime claims require the entrenchment of a fixed identity in order to prove a victim's disadvantaged status, identities are reduced to stereotypical categories that appear natural and immutable rather than as the effects of power relations (Brown). In other words, as Jonathan Simon (2000) put it, "The satisfaction that comes from avenging oppression caries the price of reinforcing the very categories of the original victimization" (p. 11). Consequently, the TDOR website's efforts to illustrate the rifeness of violence are undermined by its singular focus on transphobia.

The overarching political narrative of transphobia, however, is not absolute; it is destabilized by the highly racialized visual imagery conveyed through photos on the website. Educational handouts and other resources include photos of selected murder victims, a majority of which depict non-White faces. Of the names listed, many are non-Anglo, and several are accompanied by a parenthetical pronunciation key (e.g., "Julio Argueta [HOO-lee-o ar-GET-tah]" [TDOR, 2005a, p. 3]), which speaks to a White Anglo audience presumed to be unfamiliar with such names. Marked as racialized others, these names and faces both reinforce the website's narrative norm of Whiteness and contest its totality. Against the political narrative that denies racialized violence, these photographic images suggest that race cannot be ignored.[12]

Hence, two overlapping discourses are at work: the narrative voice of the activist cause, which refuses to formally acknowledge race, and the visual messages— captured by the names and the photos of racialized others—which explicitly call on race as a marker of victimhood. Yet these discourses do not operate with equal cognitive effect. The activist narrative (which, arguably, saturates the entire site) is overtly teleological, relying on a coherent story line of cause (transphobia) and effect (violence), with death marking the moment of truth at the end of the story. By contrast, the racialized images, which are scattered randomly throughout the site, operate at a more subconscious, yet nonetheless vivid level; they hover as a ghostly reminder of the dead, a lingering specter of race. Because these images are few in number, their visual force is particularly striking against the text-heavy website, further highlighting the significance of race even as race is formally written out of the official activist narrative. These seemingly conflicting messages work symbiotically to produce both a naturalized White subject and a brutalized body of color. The website's photos depicting activists— seen at vigil ceremonies, marches, and speech-making events—predominantly comprise White faces, whereas the victim profiles depict predominantly people of color. When these images are juxtaposed, White activists are positioned as saviors of victims of color. In this way, the brutalized body of color is called upon to advance a political agenda that reinforces racial hierarchies at the same time as it disavows the significance of race (Razack, 2001).

Although the deracialized narratives of the TDOR/Remembering Our Dead project emerge from a particular political strategy, they are also the product of a broader social context that promotes individually focused and legally oriented responses to violence. In particular, because corporate media are the primary source of reporting on violence and law enforcement is the primary mechanism for redressing violence, these institutions play a significant role in setting the stage for activism. For example, although antidiscrimination and hate crime law in the United States and Canada have been strongly critiqued for their repeated failure to address multiple, intersectional, and structural forms of oppression (see Crenshaw, 1989; Ehrenreich, 2002; Grabham, 2006; Spade & Willse, 2000), legal responses are still treated as a key remedy for violence. Because raising public consciousness is a key activist strategy, the naming power of hate crime legislation (i.e., identifying violence as perpetrated against specifically oppressed groups) remains politically appealing (Spade & Willse). In seeking such recognition, however, activists must adhere to the state's limited criteria and logic for identifying and prosecuting hate crimes. Similarly, because corporate media are often the first source of reporting about violence, such sensationalized accounts can set the tone for subsequent narratives. The Fred (F. C.) Martinez murder case, for example, shows how law enforcement agencies and mainstream media shape the terms by which activists respond to and recount incidents of violence. Tracing these narratives, one can begin to see the depth to which deracialized accounts of violence are socially embedded and collectively authorized.

## THE ERASURE OF RACE IN THE FRED (F. C.) MARTINEZ MURDER

On June 21, 2001, the brutalized and decomposing body of 16-year-old Fred (F. C.) Martinez was found in a shallow canyon on the outskirts of Cortez, Colorado. Martinez, a Navajo high school student who identified as openly gay and transgender, suffered blunt-force trauma to the head, as well as cuts to his abdomen and wrists. It was reported that on the night of June 16, 2001, Martinez had been chased by his attacker to a desolate, rocky area known as the Pits, run into a barbed wire fence, struck in the head with a rock, and left to die (Quittner, 2001). Shaun Murphy, a White 19-year-old from Farmington, New Mexico, subsequently pleaded guilty to second-degree murder, after witnesses reported him bragging that he had "bug smashed a *joto* [Spanish derogatory slang for a gay or effeminate male]" (Emmett, 2001i).

At the onset of investigation, Montezuma County Sheriff Joey Chavez stated that detectives were "looking at the boy's sexuality, as well as the fact that he was Native American, as possible motives in the crime" (Emmett, 2001b). But race quickly disappeared as a relevant factor. District attorney Joe Olt refused to prosecute the murder as a hate crime, treating the case as though the severity of the physical violence was all that mattered. As Olt explained to the local press: "We're looking at it as a murder that is heinous enough....To me, a murder is a hate crime" (GenderPAC, 2001a).

The failure to treat the crime as legally hate motivated was widely attributed to the fact that Colorado's crime-bias legislation (Ethnic Intimidation Act of 1988) did not include sexual orientation or gender identity as grounds for special prosecution (Colorado State General Assembly, 2005). The fact that the legislation included race, color, and ancestry was considered—by both news reporters and victim-advocacy groups—irrelevant (Emmett, 2001e; GenderPAC, 2001a). Some news reports even implied that Colorado had no hate crime legislation at all (Colorado Anti-Violence Program, 2001b; GenderPAC, 2002; Heidelberg, 2002).[13] The outrage over the Martinez murder was subsequently channeled into lobbying efforts to reform Colorado's bias-crime statutes to include sexual orientation—changes that were successfully adopted in 2005 (Colorado State General Assembly, 2005; Lambda Legal, 2001).[14] When the Martinez case received brief national attention, it was attributed to the antigay and anti-transgender dimensions of the crime, and not at all to factors of race (Colorado Anti-Violence Program, 2001a; Mimiaga, 2002). When the story hit national news feeders via the Associated Press, Martinez's Navajo identity was not even acknowledged (Gay and Lesbian Alliance Against Defamation [GLAAD], 2001). The farther the story traveled, the more race disappeared.

Although most regional press stories tacitly noted Martinez's Navajo identity, few articles considered it more than a supplementary detail. The controversy instead focused on whether the case constituted a hate crime and, if so, whether it was motivated by homophobia or transphobia; either way, race was deemed largely inconsequential. Although Martinez's mother, Pauline Mitchell, repeatedly described racism as a factor in her son's death and the subsequent legal proceedings, this perspective was mostly absent from the press coverage. Aside from public statements made by the Two Spirit Society of Colorado (which were mainly ignored in the mainstream press), even victim advocacy groups did not specifically discuss race.[15] In almost all accounts, sexuality and gender consistently eclipsed race as an important factor in the crime. By the time the Martinez case reached the TDOR website, the issue of race was completely absent. The website currently memorializes the case as "Fred Martinez, Jr. (aka Fredericka, F.C.). Cortez, Colorado. 16-Jun-01. Bludgeoned to the head" (TDOR, 2007, 25).[16]

A careful examination of the case, however, clearly demonstrates that racialized hierarchies of power were in operation before, during, and after the murder. Martinez's mother, Pauline Mitchell, described numerous incidents that she attributed to racism, many of which began long before her son's death. Noting that Martinez was often a target for harassment and violence at school, Mitchell felt that school officials not only failed to protect her son but also frequently blamed Martinez and subjected him to regular discipline (Quittner, 2001; TG Crossroads, 2002). As Mitchell described,

> He was sent home often. I would have to leave work to go pick him up because they sent him home so much. The principle [sic] and vice-principle [sic] made so many complaints. Too many Native American kids are sent home from school.
>
> (GenderPAC, 2001b)

Mitchell recalled several occasions in which Martinez was sent home from school for wearing what school officials called gender-inappropriate clothing—incidents she believed were also racialized:

> One time, Fred went in wearing the same shoes this other girl was wearing. They were sandals. Nike. She didn't get sent home, but Fred did. I complained to the school, but of course they aren't going to listen to me because I'm Native American.
>
> (GenderPAC, 2001b)

Racial discrimination continued in the aftermath of Martinez's death. Although Mitchell reported that her son was missing on June 18, the police did not notify her when the (unidentified) body was first discovered on June 23,[17] nor did they inform her of the arrest and arraignment of Shaun Murphy. Mitchell learned of both, after the fact, from a newspaper (GenderPAC, 2001b; Lambda Legal, 2001).[18] When she complained to the district attorney (DA) that it was her right to bear witness for her son at the court proceedings, he claimed that there had been insufficient time in which to contact her (Emmett, 2001g). Apparently, however, there had been ample time to notify Murphy's family: His mother, grandmother, girlfriend, and daughter were all present at the arraignment (Lambda Legal). Requesting that she be kept informed of any details of her son's death, Mitchell was subsequently assured by the DA that she would be notified when the autopsy was complete. However, the police released the autopsy results to the media without informing Mitchell; she learned about the gruesome details of her son's murder in a newspaper (Emmett; GenderPAC; Human Rights Campaign, 2001). Mitchell also expressed concerns that the police had not investigated the crime scene adequately. When she examined the site herself, Mitchell found evidence that police had not removed, including some of her son's hair, which was matted with blood (Human Rights Campaign). For Mitchell, the disrespectful treatment by police was symptomatic of racism (GenderPAC). Describing another indignity, she noted:

> When they had Fred's body bagged, I wanted to look at his body, to make sure. When they showed it to me, they had left a bunch of blood and rubber gloves with him. It hurt and it made me mad. They were willing to leave these gloves and blood like this with my baby. They treat me this way because I'm an Indian.
>
> (GenderPAC, 2001b)

Later, when she was at the police station, she noted that "all the Native Americans have handcuffs on them, even leg-cuffs. But white kids and Shaun, they have nothing on them. They can move around freely. It's just not right" (GenderPAC, 2001b). [...]

Contrary to the media narratives, Mitchell refused to reduce her son's death to a single cause. When asked why her son was killed, she stated repeatedly that it was because he was different (Emmett, 2001f; GenderPAC 2001b; Quittner, 2001). According to Mitchell (2002):

> F.C. [Martinez's nickname] had many difficult times in his short life. Much of this was related to the fact that he was Navajo living in a world that does not honor and respect different ways, and also that he was Nadleeh—Two-Spirit—and he could comfortably walk the path of both male and female, that he would love differently from most. F.C. also felt the pain of what comes when your family is poor, but very proud. It is not easy to grow up as Navajo, Nadleeh and poor.

Mitchell's statement describes how race, gender, sexuality, and class hierarchies collectively constituted the circumstances of her son's death. At the same time, Mitchell (2002) refused to reduce these factors to simple identity labels. For Mitchell "labels mean nothing—and they meant nothing to F.C. He used these terms to make other people comfortable, not himself". By rejecting these labels, Mitchell eschewed a logic that would reduce difference to an inherent quality about her son. As Razack (2001) argued, "When difference is thought to reside in the person rather than in the social context, we are able to ignore our role in producing it" (21). In no way did Mitchell deny the factors that marked her son as different, but she recognized that such differences are always relational; otherness can be understood only against its norm. In this way, Mitchell insisted on situating her son's death within its broader social context and thereby called on collective responsibility for such oppression. [...]

Martinez was attacked not simply because he failed to embody proper masculinity and heterosexuality; Martinez did not conform to a certain kind of heterosexual masculinity—namely, White, middle-class, able-bodied heterosexual masculinity. Masculine heterosexuality is not a universal, abstract hegemonic ideal; it is contextually bound, ordered by time and place. Black masculinity, for example, is not governed by the same standards as White masculinity. Just as gender is a cue for sexuality, so is race a cue for sexuality, gender, and class. [...] For these reasons, we cannot say that Martinez was killed primarily because he was gay and transgender but also because he was Navajo and poor; this additive approach fails to account for the ways in which the racial and class dimensions of identity are produced by and through the other. Race and class do not simply complicate violence—they enable it (Razack & Fellows, 1998). Indeed, race and class, like gender and sexuality, are also constituted *through* violence (Smith, 2005). [...]

Mitchell understood her son's death in [a colonial] context: not as a singular attack by one individual against her son, but as part of a long history of colonial oppression. The sexualized, racialized, and gendered dimensions of the violence that Martinez experienced are certainly consistent with the legacy of colonization. As Andrea Smith (2005) powerfully demonstrated, sexualized violence is deeply embedded in, as well as constitutive of, colonial relationships. Colonization required careful management of gender and sexual relations, a task achieved largely through institutionalized violence. Reflecting this legacy, the Two Spirit Society of Colorado released a formal statement acknowledging that Martinez's murder was not an isolated incident, but part of the historic violence against Native Americans. Mitchell concurred: "I will tell you [that] here in Cortez, too many Indians die. They just let it go and nothing is done about it" (GenderPAC, 2001b). [...]

## PRODUCING INNOCENT ONLOOKERS: SPECTACLE AND WITNESS AS COMPLICITY

As long as violence is attributed to the single act of an individual, the role of the witness—the one who is left to remember—is rendered innocent. At most, our duty as witnesses is to spread awareness. This orientation is reflected in the George Santayana quote that prefaces the Remembering Our Dead portal on the Gender Education & Advocacy website (http://www.gender.org/): "Those who cannot remember the past are doomed to repeat it" (n.d.). But as Simon and Rosenberg (2005: 84–85) argued, memorialization practices that function as warnings or simple object lessons are insufficient to dislodge our own complicity in deep-seated patterns of violence:

> On such terms, initiating and participating in remembrance defines one's own responsibility as one of educating others (since one already knows about the events in question), a practice that too often and too easily slides into a postponement of what one needs to do oneself.

Without critical reflexivity, the exercise of educating others serves to entrench a sense of self that is beyond reproach. Those who know and educate are positioned as morally superior to those who are ignorant; we congratulate ourselves for our political awareness without moving outside the comfort zone of moral authority and self-knowing. Such positions of moral superiority are usually classed and raced: the well-educated, supposedly enlightened White subject is juxtaposed against the ignorant redneck, the high school dropout, the presumably backwards ethnic other (Ott & Aoki, 2002).

Our innocence as witnesses is also secured through outpourings of public sympathy. Particularly when we are called to remember those whom we did not know personally, we are invited into a community of shared grief and called upon to experience a sense of collective sympathy. But, as Susan Sontag (2003) argued, "So far as we feel sympathy, we feel we are not accomplices to what caused the suffering. Our sympathy proclaims our innocence as well as our impotence" (102). In this way, sympathy is seductive. By recognizing the pain of others, we tell ourselves, we engage in a shared sense of humanity. We identify with the other through the recognition of our own pain. But in doing so, we risk appropriating another's pain for our own purposes—or, as Razack (2007) called it, stealing the pain of others.

When the deracialized narrative of Fred Martinez's murder is held up to further the transgender cause, the pain of colonial violence is erased and usurped and the racialized nature of oppression is obscured, allowing witnesses to deny the ways in which hegemonic Whiteness is enacted and sustained through violence. In other words, in such accounts, the witnesses uphold the myth of White innocence. Perpetuating this narrative of power, the witnesses are also constituted by it; in this sense, the witnesses become White. This process of White witnessing is, of course, never stable or absolute, particularly for racialized witnesses, who are already constituted as not White even as they are ushered into a White narrative. Indeed, the social and political effects of a racialized witness engaging in a White discourse (which ultimately marks the further pain of silencing, erasure, and assimilation), is different from the effects for a subject whose Whiteness is being reaffirmed and reprivileged through that discourse. Yet the overall effect is one that enables White complicity;[23] the narrative allows Whites to deny the ways in which we/they enable and benefit from the ongoing legacy of colonial and racialized violence. White witnesses do not have to consider the ways in which our/their daily practices contribute to, authorize, or uphold racialized power relations that enable violence. Such witnessing thereby uses the pain of others to reaffirm a sense of self.

This process of witnessing is evident in a remembrance ritual whereby the living speak for the dead. Among the resources provided by the TDOR website is a set of first-person narratives. For example:

> My name is China Zainal (CHI-na zy-NALL), and I was a forty-six year old Indonesian-born sex worker living in Sydney, Australia. On November thirtieth of two thousand and three, two witnesses saw me staggering down one street before collapsing in another. They called an ambulance, which took me to St Vincent's Hospital. I died at the hospital from nine stab wounds to the neck and upper torso.
>
> (TDOR, 2004a: 1)

[...]

[W]hat does it mean to speak for the dead in this way? Is this how these individuals would want to be memorialized, by the gruesome details of their death? In taking the voice of the other as our own, we colonize the bodies of the dead. These narratives speak not to the honoring of life, but to the fetishization of death. Once again, the violent act itself—and not the social conditions that facilitate violence—takes center stage. The details of these killings pander to an imagination that is enticed by images of shock and suffering. Thus, death becomes spectacle and the horror of violence eclipses the humanity of those who have died. [...]

Remembrance practices also inform the political priorities of social movements, generating further material consequences. Because remembrance narratives define problems of violence on certain terms, they directly influence the kinds of solutions proposed in response. For example, when the bulk of an advocacy group's funds are used to lobby for hate crime legislation rather than to advocate for transgender prisoners, or for increased community policing rather than decriminalization of sex work, or for corporate employee benefits rather than universal health care, it is often low-income people of color who lose. For this reason, activists have an obligation to continuously examine how their political strategies affect those who are most disenfranchised. If the most privileged within the community benefit at the expense of the most marginalized, such strategies are not worth pursuing.

## CONCLUSION: REMEMBERING OTHERWISE

The narrative erasure of racialized violence in the TDOR/Remembering Our Dead project is arguably not isolated, but symptomatic of broader racial hierarchies within transgender politics. [...] Despite these critiques, I am not suggesting that we should cease remembering those who are commemorated by the Remembering Our Dead project. As Simon (2005) noted, "The task of working for social transformation is not to forget the past, but to remember it otherwise" (p. 9). The question, then, is: how do we remember otherwise? What would it mean to remember in such a way that confronts *structural violence* (i.e., processes of domination that are socially, politically, and economically instituted over time) and requires examination of our own complicity? [...]

Our task, then, is to push these efforts further—not only with respect to TDOR but also in the many ways we recount and confront violence. None of us are innocent. We must envision practices of remembrance that situate our own positions within structures of power that authorize violence in the first place. Our task is to move from sympathy to responsibility, from complicity to reflexivity, from witnessing to action. It is not enough to simply honor the memory of the dead—we must transform the practices of the living.

## NOTES

1. Although some websites include independent information about Transgender Day of Remembrance (TDOR), most provide a direct link to either the Remembering Our Dead project or the TDOR website.
2. This article arose from my own involvement in Transgender Day of Remembrance and my participation as a nontrans person in ongoing struggles against trans-related oppression. I wrote this piece cautiously; I do not wish to replicate the history of nontrans persons who have critiqued, demonized, and pathologized trans struggles. At the same time, I take seriously the call for self-reflexivity within activism and my analysis emerges from concerns raised within my local trans and genderqueer communities about the overall effectiveness and broader implications of current manifestations of Transgender Day of Remembrance.
3. I recognize that some readers may feel excluded from, or wish to remain outside, the various significations of the word *we* as I use it in this article. Although my use of *we* does presume readers' general interest in working to end oppressive violence, I do not intend the term to denote inclusion or exclusion of any specific community. Rather, I invite readers to participate in the process of self-reflexive questioning of remembrance practices.
4. Several lists of transgender murders are available online. However, the most comprehensive and widely cited list is maintained on the Remembering Our Dead (2006c) and Transgender Day of Remembrance (2007) websites.

5. Although intersex persons are often included within the scope of transgender struggles, a consensus is emerging among gender activists that intersex issues and transgender issues, though related, should not be conflated (Currah, Juang, & Minter, 2006; Intersex Society of North America, 2006).
[...]

7. For example, when legal definitions of transgender identity require surgery or hormones as proof of transition, individuals who are unable or choose not to pursue such medical interventions may be denied gender-appropriate identification on key documents, such as passports, drivers licenses, birth certificates, and health cards. [...]

8. I use the name Brandon Teena here because it is the most commonly recognized name. [...]

9. I would argue that this case is more complicated than what was presented by any of the previously noted accounts; the evidence suggested that class, race, gender, and sexuality were all factors in the murder.

10. The racial identities of both individuals are nonetheless complex. Qwo-Li Driskill (2004) noted, for example, that Brandon Teena was of mixed White and Sioux Indian ancestry. Although the significance and meaning of this heritage warrant further discussion, Driskill rightly pointed out that the Native American dimension of Brandon Teena's identity is rarely acknowledged in queer and transgender accounts.

11. My drawing attention to the prevalence of silhouette images is not meant as a critique of the project organizers, who, as I noted previously, do not have the resources to find photographs of every victim listed on the site. Rather, my emphasis here is on the narrative effects of such images.

12. A few online lists of transgender deaths explicitly note the racial identity of victims, highlighting the significance of race. For example, of the 51 individuals included on GenderPAC's (2007) list of murder victims, 37 are identified as persons of color, the vast majority of which are African American and Latina transwomen.

13. Technically, the Ethnic Intimidation Act (1988) did not, at that time, include the term *hate crime,* but it effectively served the same purpose. Where crimes were shown to be motivated by particular forms of bias, stiffer criminal penalties could be applied (Ethnic Intimidation Act).

14. In every annual legislative session since 1994, lobbyists had introduced legislation that would enhance penalties for violence motivated by prejudice against the victim's sexual orientation, but the bills were defeated each time (TG Crossroads, 2002).

15. Gay and Lesbian Alliance Against Defamation (GLAAD), a media advocacy group that assessed press coverage of the case, did criticize news media that did not include Martinez's Navajo identity in their coverage. However, the organization nonetheless did not make race a central point of analysis.

16. Although this description is consistent with that of the other deaths listed on the website (i.e., racial identity is generally excluded for all murders noted on the list), it remains an important factor in tracing how this narrative of violence became deraced as it circulated in various media networks.

17. According to Mitchell, she reported her son missing on June 18, 2001, phoned in to follow up two days later, and then called again on June 23 when she read in the newspaper that a body had been found near her home. The sheriff's office denied Mitchell's claims, saying that she only filed a missing persons report on June 23, 2001 (Emmett, 2001g).

18. According to the sheriff's office, when the body was first found, its decomposed state made it difficult to determine how the individual had died, how long the body had been there, or "even the ethnicity of the man" (Emmett, 2001a, ¶ 4). [...]
[...]

23. By complicity, I do not mean to suggest direct involvement or intentional collaboration with acts of violence; rather, I refer to less visible and more mundane actions that nonetheless contribute to structural injustice or perpetuate social processes that enable violence. [...] Responsibility must be structurally oriented, socially connected, and collectively enacted (Veitch, 2007; Young, 2006).

## REFERENCES

Brown, W. (1995). *States of injury: Power and freedom in late modernity.* Princeton, NJ: Princeton University Press.

Califia, P. (1997). *Sex changes: The politics of transgenderism.* San Francisco: Cleis Press.

Churchill, W. (1998). *A little matter of genocide: Holocaust and denial in the Americas 1492 to the present.* Winnipeg, Manitoba, Canada: Arbeiter Ring Publishing.

Colorado Anti-Violence Program. (2001a, July 3). Colorado Anti-Violence Program responds to death of Fred Martinez, Jr. [Press release]. Retrieved May 28, 2007, from http://www.coavp.org/content/view/44/2/

Colorado Anti-Violence Program. (2001b, July 5). CAVP applauds apprehension of suspect in murder of Fred Martinez, Jr. [Press release]. Retrieved May 28, 2007, from http://www.coavp.org/content/view/40/2/

Colorado Department of Public Safety. (1993). The Victim Rights Act. Retrieved November 12, 2005, from http://dcj.state.co.us/ovp/vra_eng.htm#VRA

Colorado State General Assembly. (2005). House Bill 05-1014. Retrieved November 12, 2005, from http://www.leg.state.co.us/Clics2005a/csl.nsf/fsbillcont3/C6D3343F14EC755A87256F5D007858C1?Open& file=1014_enr.pdf

Crenshaw, K. (1989). Demarginalizing the intersection of race and sex: A Black feminist critique of antidiscrimination doctrine, feminist theory and antiracist politics. *The University of Chicago Legal Forum, 1989, 139*–166.

Crisalide Azione Trans Nazionale. (2002a). Comunicato stampa del 18 novembre 2002. Retrieved August 11, 2007, from http://www.crisalide-azionetrans.it/dor_comstampa.html.

Crisalide Azione Trans Nazionale. (2002b). Resoconti delle veglie a: Genova, Bologna. Retrieved August 11, 2007, from http://www.crisalide-azionetrans.it/dor_resoconti.html#resoconti.

Currah, P. (2006). Gender pluralisms under the transgender umbrella. In P. Currah, R. M. Juang, & S. Price Minter (Eds.), *Transgender rights* (pp. 3–31). Minneapolis: University of Minnesota Press.

Currah, P., Juang, R. M., & Minter, S. P. (2006). Introduction. In P. Currah, R. M. Juang, & S. Price Minter (Eds.), *Transgender rights* (pp. xiii–xxiv). Minneapolis: University of Minnesota Press.

Delgado, R., & Stefancic, J. (Eds.). (1997). *Critical White studies: Looking behind the mirror.* Philadelphia: Temple University Press.

Driskill, Q. (2004). Stolen from our bodies: First Nations two-spirits/queers and the journey to a sovereign erotic. *Studies in American Indian Literatures, 16*(2), 50–64.

Dyer, R. (1997). *White.* London: Routledge.

Ehrenreich, N. (2002). Subordination and symbiosis: Mechanisms of mutual support between subordinating systems. *UMKC Law Review, 71*, 252–324.

Emmett, A. (2001a, June 23). Man's body found near trailer park. *Cortez Journal.* Retrieved December 6, 2005, from http://www.cortezjournal.com/archives/1news1438.htm

Emmett, A. (2001b, June 28). Suspects questioned in boy's murder. *Cortez Journal.* Retrieved November 19, 2005, from http://www.cortezjournal.com/archives/1news1453.htm

Emmett, A. (2001c, July 7). Former Cortez resident arrested in murder. *Cortez Journal.* Retrieved August 28, 2007, from http://www.cortezjournal.com/archives/1news1479.htm

Emmett, A. (2001d, July 12). Killing raises specter of hate crime. *Cortez Journal.* Retrieved December 6, 2005, from http://www.cortezjournal.com/archives/1news1494.htm

Emmett, A. (2001e, July 14). Don't blame Cortez, says anti-bias group. *Cortez Journal.* Retrieved December 6, 2005, from http://www.cortezjournal.com/archives/1news1500.htm

Emmett, A. (2001f, July 19). Martinez's mother releases statement. *Cortez Journal.* Retrieved December 6, 2005, from http://www.cortezjournal.com/archives/1news1524.htm

Emmett, A. (2001g, August 9). Martinez's mother says Olt violating victims' rights. *Cortez Journal.* Retrieved December 6, 2005, from http://www.cortezjournal.com/archives/1news1587.htm

Emmett, A. (2001h, August 14). Murphy advised on new charge. *Cortez Journal.* Retrieved December 6, 2005, from http://www.cortezjournal.com/archives/1news1600.htm

Emmett, A. (2001i, September 8). Murphy's mother arrested on charges of intimidating witness. *Cortez Journal.* Retrieved December 6, 2005, from http://www.cortezjournal.com/archives/1news1669. htm

Emmett, A. (2002, February 2). Court hears motions in Fred Martinez murder case. *Cortez Journal.* Retrieved December 6, 2005, from http://www.cortezjournal.com/asp-bin/article_generation.asp?article_type=news&article_path=/news/news 020202_1.htm

Ethnic Intimidation Act, 18-9-121, C.R.S. (1988).

Feinberg, L. (1996). *Transgender warriors: Making history from Joan of Arc to Dennis Rodman.* Boston: Beacon Press.

Frankenberg, R. (1993). *White women, race matters: The social construction of Whiteness.* Minneapolis: University of Minnesota Press.

Gay and Lesbian Alliance Against Defamation. (2001, July 13). Coverage round-up: The murder of Fred Martinez, Jr. Retrieved November 12, 2005, from http://www.glaad.org/action/calls_detail.php?id= 2957

Gay and Lesbian Alliance Against Defamation. (2007). Transgender Day of Remembrance 2007. Retrieved November 20, 2007, from http://www.glaad.org/media/resource_kit_detail.php?id=4108

Gay, Lesbian and Straight Education Network. (2007). Transgender Day of Remembrance. Retrieved August 10, 2007, from http://www.dayofsilence.org/tdr.html

Gay-Straight Alliance Network. (2006). Transgender Day of Remembrance. Retrieved August 10, 2007, from http://www.gsanetwork.org/resources/dayofremembrance.html

Gender Education & Advocacy. (n.d.). Portal to Remembering Our Dead website. Retrieved October 19, 2007, from http://www.gender.org/remember/

Gender Education & Advocacy. (2003a). Welcome to Gender.org. Retrieved August 10, 2007, from http://www. gender.org/

Gender Education & Advocacy. (2003b, August 21). Two murders, one critically injured in D.C. trans attacks [Press release]. Retrieved August 15, 2007, from http://www.gender.org/vaults/dc_atvm.html

GenderPAC. (2001a, August 27). GenderPAC condemns Martinez killing—Urges FBI to investigate [Press release]. Retrieved November 19, 2005, from http://www.gpac.org/archive/news/notitle.html?cmd=view& archive=news&msgnum=0329

GenderPAC. (2001b, September 4). Interview with the mother of Fred Martinez. Retrieved November 19, 2005, from http://www.gpac.org/archive/news/notitle.html?cmd=view&archive=news&msgnum=0338

GenderPAC. (2002, March 1). GenderPAC expresses concern over plea bargain in Martinez killing [Press release]. Retrieved November 19, 2005, from http://www.gpac.org/archive/news/notitle.html?cmd=view& archive=news&msgnum=0368

GenderPAC. (2006). 50 under 30: Masculinity and the war on America's youth—A human rights report. Retrieved August 10, 2007, from http://www.gpac. org/50under30/50u30.pdf

GenderPAC. (2007). Spring 2007 national campaign— Victims by state. Retrieved August 10, 2007, from http:// www.gpac.org/press/victims-state.html

Grabham, E. (2006). Taxonomies of inequality: Lawyers, maps, and the challenge of hybridity. *Social & Legal Studies, 15*, 5–23.

Groupe Activiste Trans. (2006). Actu. Retrieved August 12, 2007, from http://transencolere.free.fr/actu/actu. htm

Halberstam, J. (2005). *In a queer time and place: Transgendered bodies, subcultural lives.* New York: New York University Press.

Hale, J. (1998). Consuming the living, dis(re)membering the dead in the butch/FTM borderlands. *GLQ: A Journal of Lesbian and Gay Studies, 4,* 311–348.

Heidelberg, K. (2001, August 14). Slaying prompts vigil, talk on tolerance. *Cortez Journal.* Retrieved December 6, 2005, from http://www.cortezjournal. com/archives/1news1600.htm

Heidelberg, K. (2002, June 4). Murphy sentenced to 40 years. *Cortez Journal.* Retrieved November 19, 2005, from http://www.cortezjournal.com/asp-bin/article_generation.asp?article_type=news&article_path=/ news/news020604_1.htm

Hooks, B. (1992). *Black looks: Race and representation.* Toronto, Ontario, Canada: Between the Lines Press.

Houston Transgender Unity Committee. (2006). Remembrance history. Retrieved August 10, 2007, from http:// tgdor.org/about.shtml

Human Rights Campaign. (2001, August 10). HRC urges FBI to assist in the investigation and prosecution of Colorado hate crime [Press release]. Retrieved November 12, 2005, from http://temenos.net/remember/ martinez/article_4.htm

Ignatief, N. (1996). *How the Irish became White.* New York: Routledge.

Intersex Society of North America. (2006). What's the difference between being transgender or transsexual and having an intersex condition? Retrieved August 12, 2007, from http://www.isna.org/faq/transgender

Iverson, P. (2002). *Diné: A history of the Navajos.* Albuquerque: University of New Mexico Press.

Janoff, D. V. (2005). *Pink blood: Homophobic violence in Canada.* Toronto, Ontario, Canada: University of Toronto Press.

Kinsman, G. (1996). *The regulation of desire: Homo and hetero sexualities.* Montreal, Quebec, Canada: Black Rose Books.

Lambda Legal. (2001). Partnering with GLAAD and PFLAG, Lambda assists mom of murdered 16-year-old Fred Martinez [Press release]. Retrieved November 19, 2005, from http://www.lambdalegal. org/our-work/ in-court/other/partnering-with-glaad-and.html

Leonardo, Z. (2004). The color of supremacy: Beyond the discourse of "White privilege." *Educational Philosophy and Theory, 36,* 137–152.

Martinot, S., & Sexton, J. (2003). The avant-garde of White supremacy. *Social Identities, 9,* 169–181.

Mason, G. (2002). *The spectacle of violence: Homophobia, gender and knowledge.* New York: Routledge.

Mimiaga, J. (2002, May 23). Murphy opts not to change plea. *Cortez Journal*. Retrieved December 6, 2005, from http://www.cortezjournal.com/asp-bin/article_generation.asp?article_type=news&article_path=/news/news020523_2.htm

Mitchell, P. (2002, June 3). Statement of Pauline Mitchell at the sentencing hearing on June 3, 2002 of Shawn [sic] Murphy, who pled guilty to the murdered [sic] her son Fred Martinez, Jr. in Cortez, Colorado last June. Retrieved November 19, 2005, from Families United Against Hate website: http://www.fuah.org/fuah_cortez.html

Moran, L., & Sharpe, A. (2004). Violence, identity and policing: The case of violence against transgender people. *Criminal Justice, 4,* 395–417.

Namaste, V. (2000). *Invisible lives: The erasure of transsexual and transgender people.* Chicago: University of Chicago Press.

Namaste, V. (2005). *Sex change, social change: Reflections on identity, institutions and imperialism.* Toronto, Ontario, Canada: Women's Press.

National Organization for Women. (2004). NOW commemorates Transgender Day of Remembrance on November 20. Retrieved August 10, 2007, from http://www.now.org/issues/lgbi/041119remembrance.html

Ott, B., & Aoki, E. (2002). The politics of negotiating public tragedy: Media framing of the Matthew Shepard murder. *Rhetoric & Public Affairs, 5,* 483–505.

Peirce, K. (Writer/Director), & Bienan, A. (Writer). (1999). *Boys don't cry* [Motion picture]. Canada: 20th Century Fox.

Phelan, S. (2001). Strangers among "us": Secondary marginalization and "LGBT" politics. In S. Phelan, *Sexual strangers: Gays, lesbians, and dilemmas of citizenship* (pp. 115–138). Philadelphia: Temple University Press.

Pinar, W. (2003). "I am a man": The queer politics of race. *Cultural Studies, Critical Methodologies, 3,* 271–286.

Postel, D. (1997). An interview with Noel Ignatief. *ZMagazine*. Retrieved August 28, 2007, from http://www.zmag.org/ZMag/articles/jan97postel.htm

Press for Change. (2007). News links—Trans history. Retrieved August 11, 2007, from http://www.pfc. org.uk/node/651

Quittner, J. (2001, August 28). Death of a Two Spirit— Case of Fred C. Martinez Jr., murdered for sexual preferences. *The Advocate*. Retrieved November 19, 2005, from http://www.findarticles/com/p/articles/mi_m1589/is_2001_August_28/ai_77660063

Razack, S. (2001). *Looking White people in the eye: Gender, race, and culture in courtrooms and classrooms.* Toronto, Ontario, Canada: University of Toronto Press.

Razack, S. (2007). Stealing the pain of others: Reflections on Canadian humanitarian responses. *The Review of Education, Pedagogy, & Cultural Studies, 29,* 375–394.

Razack, S., & Fellows, M. L. (1998). The race to innocence: Confronting hierarchical relations among women. *The Journal of Gender, Race & Justice, 1,* 335–352.

Simon, J. (2000). Megan's Law: Crime and democracy in late modern America. *Law & Social Inquiry, 25,* 1111–1150.

Simon, R. (2005). Remembering otherwise: Civil life and the pedagogical promise of historical memory. In R. Simon, *The touch of the past: Remembrance, learning and ethics* (pp. 1–13). New York: Palgrave Macmillan.

Simon, R., Di Paolantonio, M., & Clamen, M. (2005). Remembrance as praxis and the ethics of the inter-human. In R. Simon, *The touch of the past: Remembrance, learning and ethics* (pp. 132–155). New York: Palgrave Macmillan.

Simon, R., & Rosenberg, S. (2005). Beyond the logic of emblemization: Remembering and learning from the Montreal Massacre. In R. Simon, *The touch of the past: Remembrance, learning and ethics* (pp. 65–86). New York: Palgrave Macmillan.

Smith, A. (2005). *Conquest: Sexual violence and American Indian genocide.* Cambridge, MA: South End Press.

Smith, G. (2000). Remembering Our Dead: About this site. Retrieved August 10, 2007, from http://www.rememberingourdead.org/about/core.html

Smith, G. (2001). Transmissions 29: A moment to remember. Retrieved August 10, 2007, from http://www.gwensmith.com/writing/transmissions29.html

Smith, G. (2003). Remembering Our Dead, hate crimes contributing writers. Retrieved August 10, 2007, from    http://www.glaad.org/publications/resource_doc_detail.php?id=3496&PHPSESSID=d7dbbcbb47

4f0c11b1a1f7949f8d01e5#smith; article no longer available online—downloaded document in personal possession of the author.

Sontag, S. (2003). *Regarding the pain of others*. New York: Picador.

Spade, J., & Willse, C. (2000). Confronting the limits of gay hate crimes activism: A radical critique. *UCLAW Chicano-Latino Law Review, 21,* 38–52.

Support Transgenre Strasbourg. (2005). Événements passés (historique). Retrieved August 12, 2007, from http://www.sts67.org/

TG Crossroads. (2002, February 8). Murphy pleads guilty to murder of F.C. Martinez: Sentencing set for May 16. Retrieved December 15, 2005, from http://www.tgcrossroads.org/news/?AID=168&IID=31&type=Headlines

Trans Alliance Society. (2003). Anti-transgender violence did not end with Gwen Araujo. *tranScribes: the newsletter of the trans alliance society, 1*(2), 10. Retrieved August 12, 2007, from http://www.transalliancesociety.org/newsletters/2003/0311.pdf

Transgender Day of Remembrance. (2004a). First person biographies of murder victims, 2004. Retrieved October 4, 2005, from http://www.remem-beringourdead.org/day/how.html.

Transgender Day of Remembrance. (2004b). Trans murder statistics 1970 to 2004. Retrieved October 4, 2005, from http://www.gender.org/resources/dge/gea02002.pdf

Transgender Day of Remembrance. (2005a). First person biographies of murder victims, 2005. Retrieved October 4, 2005, from http://www.gender. org/remember/day/files/first_person_bios.doc

Transgender Day of Remembrance. (2007). Reported anti-transgender deaths, 1970–2007. Retrieved November 19, 2007, from http://www.remembering-ourdead.org/day/files/rmbrdead_full.doc

Valerio, M. W. (2002). Why I'm not "transgender." Retrieved December 5, 2005, from http://www.gay.com; article reposted on http://darkdaughta.blogspot.com/2006/03/max-wolf-valeriofiercely-transsexual.html

Vancouver Transgender Day of Remembrance. (2006). Description. Retrieved August 12, 2007, from http://groups.yahoo.com/group/VancouverTransgenderDayOfRemembrance/

Veitch, S. (2007). "Not in our name"? On responsibility and its disavowal. *Social & Legal Studies, 16,* 281–300.

Victoria. (2006, November 16). Transgender Day of Remembrance tribute—Parts 1 and 2. Retrieved August 10, 2007, from YouTube website: http://www.youtube.com/watch?v=mtADG7j7w8c

White, H. (1980). The value of narrativity in the representation of reality. *Critical Inquiry, 7,* 5–27.

White, H. (1984). The question of narrative in contemporary historical theory. *History and Theory, 23,* 1–33.

Wilchins, R. A., Lombardi, E., Priesing, D., & Malour, D. (1997). *GenderPAC First National Survey of Transgender Violence*. Washington, DC: Gender Public Advocacy Coalition.

Young, I. (2006). Responsibility and global justice: A social connection model. *Social Philosophy & Policy, 23*(1), 102–130.

Young, I. M. (1997). *Intersecting voices: Dilemmas of gender, political philosophy and policy*. Princeton, NJ: Princeton University Press.

# 3

## Artful Concealment and Strategic Visibility

### Transgender Bodies and U.S. State Surveillance After 9/11

TOBY BEAUCHAMP

IN THE AFTERMATH OF AL QAEDA'S ATTACKS ON SEPTEMBER 11, 2001, the United States government put in place many new surveillance and security measures. Most of these seemingly had little to do with transgender concerns (although one advisory from the U.S. Department of Homeland Security to security personnel worldwide noted that male terrorists might try to disguise themselves as women). And yet, as cultural studies and critical security studies scholar Toby Beauchamp makes clear, all such policies are in fact implicated in the production of normatively gendered bodies and behaviors. They disproportionately affect people who differ from dominant gender norms for whatever reason—whether or not those people claim a transgender identity. Beauchamp argues that gender variant individuals caught up in security and surveillance apparatuses are often assumed to be practicing deception because of their perceived gender presentation, and thus may be more readily suspected of criminal intent. He is critical of the gender-normativizing aspects of security surveillance, but he is equally critical of transgender political advocacy efforts that promote "transgender rights" in ways that reinforce nationalist prejudices, increase the policing of deviant bodies, ground patriotic citizenship in adherence to conventions, and serve racially and economically privileged trans-identified people better than others.

On September 4, 2003, shortly before the two-year anniversary of the attacks on the World Trade Center and Pentagon, the U.S. Department of Homeland Security released an official Advisory to security personnel. Citing ongoing concerns about potential attacks by Al-Qaeda operatives, the advisory's final paragraph emphasizes that terrorism is everywhere in disguise: "Terrorists will employ novel methods to artfully conceal suicide devices. Male bombers may dress as females in order to discourage scrutiny" (Department of Homeland Security 2003). Two years later, the Real ID Act was signed into law, proposing a major restructuring of identification documents and travel within and across U.S. borders. Central components of this process include a new national database linked through federally standardized driver's licenses, and stricter standards of proof for asylum applications. In response to both the Advisory and the Real ID Act, transgender activist and advocacy organizations in the U.S. quickly pointed to the ways trans populations would be targeted as suspicious and subjected to new levels of scrutiny.

Criticizing what they read as instances of transphobia or anti-trans discrimination, many of these organizations offer both transgender individuals and government agencies strategies for reducing or eliminating that discrimination. While attending to the very real dangers and damages experienced by many trans people in relation to government policies, in many cases the organizations' approaches leave intact the broader regulation of gender, particularly as it is mediated and enforced by the state. Moreover, they tend to address concerns about anti-trans discrimination in ways that are disconnected from questions of citizenship, racialization or nationalism. Nevertheless, by illuminating the ways that new security measures interact with and affect transgender-identified people and gender-nonconforming bodies, transgender activist practices and the field of transgender studies are poised to make a significant contribution to the ways state surveillance tactics are understood and interpreted. The monitoring of transgender and gender-nonconforming populations is inextricable from questions of national security and regulatory practices of the state, and state surveillance policies that may first appear unrelated to transgender people are in fact deeply rooted in the maintenance and enforcement of normatively gendered bodies, behaviors and identities. I argue here that transgender and gender-nonconforming bodies are bound up in surveillance practices that are intimately tied to state security, nationalism and the "us/them," "either/or" rhetoric that underpins U.S. military and government constructions of safety. At the same time, the primary strategies and responses offered by transgender advocacy organizations tend to reconsolidate U.S. nationalism and support the increased policing of deviant bodies.

## NORMALIZING GENDER: MEDICO-LEGAL SURVEILLANCE

In many ways, transgender studies provides an ideal point of entry for thinking through state surveillance of gendered bodies. The field has frequently and primarily dealt with the topic of surveillance in terms of medical and psychiatric monitoring of trans people. [...] Central to this standardized definition of trans identity, however, is the expectation that trans people will, through the process of transition, eliminate all references to their birth gender and essentially disappear into a normatively gendered world, as if they had never been transgender to begin with.

Thus two major forms of surveillance operate relative to trans people in the medical and psychiatric institutions. The first is the monitoring of individuals in terms of their ability to conform to a particular medicalized understanding of transgender identity and performance.[1] But more salient to my argument is the second component, which is the notion that the primary purpose of medical transition is to rid oneself of any vestiges of non-normative gender: to withstand and evade any surveillance (whether visual, auditory, social, or legal) that would reveal one's trans status. To blend. To pass. Medical science relies on a standardized, normative gender presentation, monitoring trans individuals' ability to pass seamlessly as non-trans. Medical surveillance focuses first on individuals' legibility *as* transgender, and then, following medical interventions, on their ability to *conceal* any trans status or gender deviance.

Yet medical science itself determines normative gender through a particular form of raced, classed and sexualized body. [...] To be classified as normatively gendered is also to adhere to norms of racial and economic privilege. Under this logic, marginalized gender identities can approximate the norm in part through clinging to ideals of whiteness and class status. Concealing gender deviance is about much more than simply erasing transgender status. It also necessitates altering one's gender presentation to conform to white, middle class, able-bodied, heterosexual understandings of normative gendering.

The notion of "concealment" via medical intervention remains tied to legal gender as well, a link made clear by the fact that most states deny changes of gender on identity documents without proof of irreversible "sex reassignment surgery." Attorney Dean Spade notes that U.S. law depends on medical evidence as proof of gender identity in almost every case involving trans people. Medical science is considered, in his words, "the cornerstone of the determination of [...] rights" (Spade 2003: 18). Moreover, Spade argues that medical science continues to rely on an ideal of "success" when diagnosing and "treating" trans people, where success is typically defined as "the ability to be perceived by non-trans people as a non-trans person" (26). Spade's work points to the ways that medicine and the law work together primarily to "correct" individuals whose bodies or gender presentations fall outside of the expected norm, promoting the concealment of trans status in order to reestablish that norm.

The discourse of concealment haunts transgender populations across a number of cultural sites. The impossibility of fully erasing one's sexed history is evident in the fact that many states still refuse to change gender markers on birth certificates, or allow only a partial change in which the original gender marker is merely crossed out and replaced. Legal gender in these cases cannot be altered, but only cloaked. Similarly, cultural representations of gender variant people depend on the popular notion that with enough scrutiny, one's "true" gender can be revealed at the level of the body. [...] Echoing this perspective, legal cases dealing with violence against gender variant individuals often revolve around the victim's responsibility to disclose their trans status or birth-assigned sex. Such cases imply or outright claim that the individual's dishonest concealment of their "true" sex was the root cause of the violent actions taken against them. [...] In [many] instances, the interplay of medical, legal and cultural representations of transgender populations works to associate the notion of transgender identity with that of secrecy, precisely because it is always understood that the secret can and will eventually be discovered.

## THE THREAT OF AMBIGUITY: NEW STATE SECURITY MEASURES

With such a pervasive cultural emphasis on concealment, it may come as no surprise that the slang used by many trans people to describe non-disclosure of trans status is "going stealth." Trans people who are living "stealth" are unknown as transgender to almost everyone in their lives—co-workers, employers, teachers, friends—and instead living only as their preferred genders. The term itself invokes a sense of going undercover, of willful secrecy and concealment, perhaps even of conscious deception. Use of this undeniably militarized language also implies a connection to the state, and going stealth does involve a great deal of complicity with state regulation of gender, for example in the changing of legal identity documents such as passports, drivers licenses and immigration paperwork. These are changes that themselves require documentation of particular medical interventions to "irreversibly" change one's physical sex characteristics. The state requires compliance with specific legal and medical procedures, and ostensibly offers in return official documentation that enables stealth status.

But such complete secrecy is never fully possible in relation to the state. The very idea of "going stealth" depends on the constancy of "going"—of continuing to conceal one's trans status, though that concealment can never be airtight. Granting medical and legal changes of gender enables the state to simultaneously keep ongoing records of these very changes: a paper trail of past identity markers. Moreover, the state's own policies and procedures for gender changes are internally inconsistent. Legal measures to document trans people's gender status frequently conflict with one another, even as they all work towards stricter regulation and surveillance of legal gender. Some states refuse to change the gender marker on birth certificates, while others do so only with documentation of surgery. Other states first require amended birth certificates in order to change the gender marker on driver's licenses, and in some cases state and city regulations contradict each other in their surgical requirements for documentation changes.[2] Such administrative conflicts now emerge in even greater relief as governmental agencies increase their policing of immigrant populations: since

1994, the Social Security Administration has sent "no-match" letters to employers in cases where their employee's hiring paperwork contradicts employee information on file with SSA. Ostensibly used to alert otherwise law-abiding employers to the possibility that they are unwittingly hiring undocumented immigrants, the no-match policy intensified after 9/11, with 2002 seeing more than eight times the typical number of letters mailed than in 2001 (Bergeron et al. 2007: 6). The letters and related data are now also accessed by the Department of Homeland Security, which sends employers guidelines about how to correct the problem and avoid legal sanctions.

The no-match policy aims to locate undocumented immigrants (and potential terrorists) employed under false identities, yet casts a much broader net. Because conflicting legal regulations often prevent trans people from obtaining consistent gender markers across all of their identity documents, gender-nonconforming individuals are disproportionately affected by the policy, whether they are undocumented immigrants or not. The National Center for Transgender Equality (NCTE) website notes that the organization "receives calls regularly from transgender people across the country who have been 'outed' to their employers by the Social Security Administration's (SSA's) unfair gender 'no-match' employment letter policy" (National Center for Transgender Equality 2007). Documents always contain traces of the past, and we might argue that this has never been as true as it is in our contemporary moment. Dean Spade's work and other activist projects have pushed for changes in particular states' approaches to gendered identity documents and moved away from the pathologizing of trans identities and bodies. But such changes emerge within a broader context of U.S. nationalism and the War on Terror that serves to justify ever-closer scrutiny of travel, identity documents and bodies.

It is in this cultural landscape of intensified medical, legal and social surveillance that the DHS Advisory appears. By warning security personnel of the gendered disguises that terrorists may appear in, the Advisory neatly fuses the threat of terrorism-in-disguise with perceived gender transgression, marking particular bodies as deceptive and treacherous. that rely on the links between gender and national identities: Algerian women pass as French to deliver bombs into French civilian settings, while Algerian men attempt to pass as women in hijabs, their disguises broken when French soldiers spy their combat boots. [...]

That the Advisory does not specifically name transgender populations in its text does not make it any less relevant to those populations. The focus on non-normative gender does raise questions about how this framing of state security affects transgender-identified people. But it also raises questions about how state institutions might view non-normative gender presentation as an act not limited to—perhaps not even primarily associated with—transgender identities. In the context of current security rhetoric related to the War on Terror, transgender individuals may not be the primary target of such advisories, particularly if those individuals are conforming to normative racial, class and national presentations. Medical science purports to normalize unruly transgender bodies through surgery and hormones. These interventions are intended to eliminate any signs of deviant gendering, creating a non-threatening body that is undetectable as trans in any way. Transgender bodies that conform to a dominant standard of dress and behavior may be legible to the state not as transgender at all, but instead as properly gendered and "safe."

But not all gendered bodies are so easily normalized. Dominant notions of what constitutes proper feminine or masculine behavior are grounded in ideals of whiteness, class privilege and compulsory heterosexuality, and individuals might be read as non-conforming depending on particular racial, cultural, economic or religious expressions of gender, without ever being classified as transgender. For example, Siobhan Somerville historicizes the ways that black people have been medically and culturally understood to have racialized physical characteristics that directly connect to their perceived abnormality in terms of gender and sexuality. She traces this history back to the public displays in the mid-1800s of Saartje Baartman, an African woman popularly known as the Hottentot Venus, whose womanhood was deemed abnormal precisely through racialized readings of her genitalia (Somerville 2000: 26). [...] Somerville argues that legal cases such as *Plessy v. Ferguson* advanced racial segregation by inciting panic about the supposed sexual danger white women experienced at the hands of black men (35). [...] Joy James draws on this history to analyze contemporary racialized state violence, arguing that state practices of surveillance and discipline read sexual and social deviance or danger through racialization processes. Moreover, she writes, "some bodies appear more docile than others because of their conformity in appearance to idealized models of class, color, and sex; their bodies are allowed greater leeway to be self-policed or policed without physical force" (James 1996: 26). These examples demonstrate that perceived gender normativity is not limited strictly to gender, but is always infused with regulatory norms of race, class, sexuality and nationality. Thus individuals need not be transgender-identified to be classified as gender-nonconforming. Bodies may be perceived as abnormal or deviant because of gender presentations read through systems of racism, classism, heterosexism, and particularly in the case of the Advisory's focus on Al-Qaeda, Islamophobia.

The impetus for state classification and surveillance of deviant bodies has increased dramatically in the context of amplified monitoring of immigration and heightened nationalist security measures justified by the rhetoric of the War on Terror. This environment spurred the passage of the Real ID Act in 2005; legislation endorsed by the 9/11 Commission, which noted that "for terrorists, travel documents are as important as weapons" (Department of Homeland Security 2008). The Real ID Act establishes minimum standards for U.S. driver's licenses and non-driver IDs, with the intention that by 2013 any ID card that is non-compliant with these standards will be invalid for activities such as air travel, access to government buildings, or access to federal funding such as Social Security. Stricter standards are to be used to verify identities, citizenship, names and birthdates. Draft regulations also specify that Real ID cards and all supporting documents used to create them (birth certificates, Social Security cards, court-ordered name changes, etc.) be linked through a federal database and stored there for 7-10 years.

It is noteworthy that the Act was passed through Congress with little debate (and with unanimous final approval from the Senate), four years after 9/11 and as the U.S. waged war in at least two countries. The ease with which the Act passed may be attributed to the fact that it was tacked onto an emergency spending bill to fund the wars in Afghanistan and Iraq. [...]

The Real ID Act and the discourses surrounding it echo much of this rhetoric. In the context of U.S. nationalism that seeks to eradicate the foreign, the Act is most overtly directed at the figures of the immigrant and the terrorist, certainly not imagined as mutually exclusive categories. To eliminate these figures, the Act increases state surveillance of identity by requiring and storing a single identity for each individual. But maintaining a singular, consistent, and legally documented identity is deeply complicated for many gender-nonconforming people: for example, common law name changes mean there is no court order to be filed with a Real ID card. Similarly, different state agencies define "change of sex" differently (with some requiring one surgical procedure, some another, and others no surgery at all), making a single gender marker on the Real ID card difficult if not impossible. Ironically, the state's own contradictory methods of determining and designating legal gender and sex render Real ID cards ineffectual. Even as these cards would work to create and enforce singular and static identities for individuals, they simultaneously work to expose the fluidity and confusion characterizing state policies on identity documents. As Jane Caplan and John Torpey argue, "[t]he very multiplicity of these documents may [...] disrupt the state's ostensibly monolithic front" (Caplan 2001: 7). Thus state regulation of gender and gendered bodies can actually function to reveal ambiguities in the state itself.

Moreover, such policies point to the ways that concealing and revealing trans identity actually depend on one another, demonstrating the impossibility of thinking these actions as binary opposites.

To conceal one's trans status under the law requires full disclosure to the medico-legal system, which keeps on public record all steps taken toward transition. That same system is later invoked when individuals seek to prove their trans status through medical and legal documents that ostensibly serve to obscure or even disappear such status. Thus concealment necessarily entails disclosure, and vice versa.

That the Real ID Act, created as part of a war funding bill and approved in a climate of fear and militarization, seeks to maintain individual identities and make them more accessible to state agencies speaks to the ways that multiple, ambiguous or shifting identities are viewed as menacing and risky on a national scale. Alongside more overt statements like the DHS Advisory, the Real ID Act and SSA no-match letters function as significant state practices and policies that link gender ambiguity with national security threats. Like other new security measures, the Real ID Act is promoted as benign—even beneficial—for those citizens with nothing to hide. Yet concealment is strongly associated with the category of transgender, a perception fueled by cultural depictions of trans deception and by the medico-legal system that aims to normalize trans bodies while simultaneously meticulously tracking and documenting gender changes. Reacting to these cultural and legislative constraints, transgender activist and advocacy organizations increasingly engage with new state security measures in efforts to maintain safety both of the nation and of individual transgender-identified people.

## NOTHING TO HIDE: ORGANIZATIONAL RESPONSES

In their responses to the DHS Advisory, the Real ID Act and the SSA no-match letters, transgender advocacy organizations have opposed these measures' effects on transgender individuals. But they have not typically considered the implications for state regulation of gender presentation more broadly, particularly as it might resonate for individuals marked as gender deviant who are not transgender-identified or linked in any obvious way to trans communities or histories. Nor have they addressed the ways in which particular groups of trans-identified people may be targeted differently by such policing. For example, in a 2006 statement to DHS regarding the no-match letter policy, NCTE recommends that gender no longer be one of the pieces of data used to verify employees, arguing that employers are not legally required to submit gender classification to SSA, and therefore any exchange of information about employees' gender is "an invasion of private and privileged medical information" (Keisling 2006: 2). In an effort to protect transgender employees, the NCTE statement aims to limit the information shared between SSA and DHS. Yet it also works to support no-match letters as a form of regulatory state surveillance, by stating clearly the importance of "avoiding fraud" through Social Security number confirmation. The statement does not oppose state surveillance measures more broadly, but instead seeks to improve them, offering recommendations on behalf of trans employees "in order for the employee verification system to be efficient and equitable" (1).

While arguing for privacy rights may benefit some gender-nonconforming employees, this strategy assumes equal access to privacy and legal recourse for all transgender people and fails to consider how privacy rights are compromised or nonexistent for undocumented immigrants, prisoners, and individuals suspected of terrorism, who may or may not be transgender-identified or perceived as gender-nonconforming. Diminished rights to privacy are particularly evident in the wake of the 2001 USA PATRIOT Act, legislation that provides much of the ideological and legal foundation for more recent state surveillance measures. [...] Passed in the flurry of anti-immigrant nationalism and increased racial profiling that followed 9/11, the Act bolsters particular understandings of the relationships between citizenship, race, privacy and danger that underpin surveillance measures like the Real ID Act and SSA no-match policy. Though absent from the NCTE statement, this context demonstrates the frailty of any claim to privacy rights, particularly for trans and gender-nonconforming immigrants and people of color. The statement seeks to protect transgender employees, but remains within—and is limited by—the constraints of the current medico-legal system.

That medico-legal system itself works to track and document gender-nonconforming bodies and transgender identities, such that at some level, trans people's medical and legal information was never private or privileged. With this in mind, it is perhaps not surprising that the primary strategy of transgender advocacy and activist groups has been to advise trans individuals to make themselves *visible* as transgender to authorities that question or screen them at places like airports and border checkpoints. In response to the DHS Advisory, The National Transgender Advocacy Coalition (NTAC) released its own security alert to transgender communities, warning that given the recent Advisory, security personnel may be "more likely to commit unwitting abuses" (National Transgender Advocacy Coalition 2003). NTAC suggests that trans travelers bring their court-ordered name and gender change paperwork with them, noting, "while terrorists may make fake identifications, they won't carry name change documents signed and notarized by a court." The organization recommends strategic visibility as a safety precaution, urging those who might otherwise be "going stealth" to openly disclose their trans status to state officials and to comply with any requested searches or questionings. Calling the potential violence and violations against travelers "unwitting abuses" suggests that authorities enacting these measures cannot be blamed for carrying out policy intended to protect the general public from the threat of hidden terrorism. Such a framework neatly sidesteps any broader criticism of the routine abuses of immigrant, Arab and Arab-appearing individuals that have been justified in the name of national security, and implicitly supports the state's increased policing of "deviant" or apparently dangerous individuals. The demand for trans people to make themselves visible as such is couched in terms of distinguishing between the good, safe transgender traveler and the dangerous, deviant terrorist in gendered disguise. This distinction rests on an implicit understanding of trans travelers as compliant and non-threatening, yet such status is only made possible through the linking of deviance to bodies outside of the white middle-class norm, as Somerville and others have demonstrated. In other words, it is only by effacing the particular scrutiny leveled at trans people of color and trans immigrants that the figure of the non-threatening trans traveler emerges. This figure is imagined to be scrutinized on the basis of gender alone, such that medical and legal documentation are assumed to be a readily available and comprehensive solution. Such a move simultaneously entails displacing the racialized elements of state surveillance onto the figure of the terrorist, implicitly marked as both racialized and non-trans in the logic of NTAC's statement. Moreover, by avoiding any larger critique of state surveillance or policing, NTAC also positions *itself* as a non-threatening, safe, even patriotic organization.

Interestingly, the call for strategic visibility does, to a certain degree, resonate with Sandy Stone's call in the late 1980s for trans people to resist the medical impetus to erase or hide their trans status. Urging trans people to remain visible *as transgender* regardless of their medical transition status, Stone writes "in the transsexual's erased history we can find a story disruptive to the accepted discourses of gender" (Stone 1991: 295). Arguing for the transformation of dominant understandings of transsexuality and gender identity, Stone asserts "it is difficult to generate a counterdiscourse if one is programmed to disappear" (295). [...]

In both Stone's work and NTAC's press release, the recourse to strategic visibility remains grounded in assumptions that *in*visibility was ever possible. Which bodies can choose visibility, and which bodies are always already visible—perhaps even hyper-visible—to state institutions? For whom is visibility an available political strategy, and at what cost? While (some) trans people gain (a particular kind of) visibility through attention from popular media and medical research, such gains must always be evaluated in relation to their dependence on regulatory norms of race, class and sexuality. Not all trans people can occupy the role of the good, safe transgender traveler that NTAC recommends. Moreover, this recommendation does not consider how increased visibility simultaneously places one under greater scrutiny and surveillance by state institutions. Bodies made visible as abnormal or unruly and in need of constraint or correction may likely experience increased vulnerability and scrutiny. For a number of gender-nonconforming individuals, then, visibility may wield more damage than protection. Which bodies would be read under the DHS Advisory's warning as gender deviant, dangerous or deceptive even if they *did* produce paperwork documenting their transgender status? Such documentation may work to decrease suspicion for some bodies, while compounding scrutiny for others.

NTAC is certainly not the only organization to advocate for the rights of legitimate transgender citizens by distinguishing those citizens from the figure of the threatening terrorist. The Transgender Law Center in San Francisco has also released security alerts and recommendations aimed at transgender-identified communities, including one statement jointly issued with NCTE, in which the two organizations criticize new security measures like the DHS Advisory and Real ID Act. They note that although these measures were originally conceived in response to "legitimate security concerns" regarding false documentation used by terrorists, they ultimately create undue burdens for transgender individuals who seek to "legitimately acquire or change identification documents" (Transgender Law Center 2005: 1). Like NTAC's concern that non-threatening transgender travelers could be mistaken for terrorists, the responses from NCTE and the Transgender Law Center refuse to critically engage the rhetoric of terrorism justifying current state regulation of gender more broadly, and in fact depend upon the figure of the (presumably non-trans, racialized) terrorist to play against the figure of the legally compliant trans person. Recalling Joy James, here again we might ask how ideals of compliance are grounded in normative understandings of race, class and sexuality. The organizations' statement not only avoids a critique of state surveillance measures, but also asks for rights and state recognition on the basis of "legitimacy." In relation to trans populations, such a label is already infused with the regulatory norms maintained by medical science and government policies. Legal legitimacy is typically based on identity documents, most of which require sex reassignment surgery for a change of gender marker. Yet in almost all cases, surgeons request a formal diagnosis of Gender Identity Disorder—a diagnosis that itself turns on the language of correction and normalization. Moreover, none of these organizations' responses to new security measures address the fact that pervasive surveillance of gender-nonconforming bodies is inextricably linked to the racialization of those bodies. Within the framework of the statement from the Transgender Law Center and NCTE, which bodies can be read as legitimate, and which bodies are always cast as suspicious?

The Sylvia Rivera Law Project, an organization in New York providing legal services to low-income gender-nonconforming people, argues that the current political climate of "us vs. them" leads to the polarization of communities that could otherwise work in coalition, as individuals attempt to divert surveillance onto other marginalized groups. The Law Project suggests that assimilation—"going stealth," or claiming status as a good transgender citizen—has become a primary tactic for escaping state surveillance, targeting or persecution. But assimilation strategies are often used in conjunction with the scapegoating of other communities. Jasbir Puar and Amit Rai convincingly address such polarization in their article "Monster, Terrorist, Fag: The War on Terror and the Production of Docile Patriots," arguing that the demand for patriotism in response to past and future terrorist attacks produces "docile patriots," who normalize themselves precisely through distinguishing themselves from other marginalized groups. [...]

This reliance on the notion of legitimacy—as good citizens, as safe travelers, as willing patriots—is similarly evident in the statements made by many transgender advocacy organizations about new security measures that target perceived gender deviance. Suggesting that trans people bring their court documents with them, cooperate with authorities and prove their legitimacy, the advocacy groups no longer rely on the strategy of concealing one's trans status, or what I named earlier as "going stealth." Instead, their primary advice is to *reveal* one's trans status, to prove that trans travelers are good citizens who have nothing to hide. Particularly in the context of the War on Terror, we might reread the notion of "going stealth" to mean not simply erasing the signs of one's trans status, but instead, maintaining legibility as a good citizen, a patriotic American—erasing any signs of similarity with the deviant, deceptive terrorist. The concept of safety thus shifts: rather than protecting trans people from state violence, the organizations now focus on protecting the nation from the threatening figure of the terrorist, a figure that transgender travelers must distinguish themselves from by demonstrating their complicity in personal disclosure. Creating the figure of the safe transgender traveler necessarily entails creating and maintaining the figure of the potential terrorist, and vice versa. Because some bodies are already marked as national threats, the ability to embody the safe trans traveler is not only limited to particular bodies, but in fact requires the scapegoating of other bodies.

While surveillance measures like the DHS Advisory may appear to primarily target transgender individuals as suspicious, the bodies being policed for gender deviance are not necessarily trans-identified, but rather demonstrate non-compliance with gender norms that may have as much to do with race, religion, class and sexuality as with transgender identity. Surveillance of these bodies centers less on their identification as transgender *per se* than it does on the perceived deception underlying transgressive gender presentation. Because normative, non-threatening gender is always read through ideals of whiteness, economic privilege and heterosexuality, "going stealth" is an option available only to those segments of the transgender population able to achieve or approximate those ideals. And in the context of national security and the U.S. War on Terror, going stealth may be less grounded in passing as non-transgender than in maintaining the appearance of a good, compliant citizen, an appearance solidified by the fact that these bodies need not conceal anything from state institutions or authorities, because they have nothing to hide. Approaching the relationship between gender-nonconformity and state surveillance in this way means resisting the urge to think about surveillance of gendered bodies as limited only to medical and legal monitoring of specifically transgender-identified individuals. In fact it points to the importance of thinking more broadly about the interactions between regulatory gender norms, racialization processes and ideals of citizenship. Moreover, it refuses a view of state surveillance as something disconnected from or unconcerned with gender, and instead foregrounds the ways that gendered and racialized bodies are central both to perceptions of safety and security and to the structuring of state surveillance practices. As these bodies attempt to evade surveillance either through careful invisibility or through strategic disclosure—each of which entails engaging the other to some degree—they do so not in isolation, but in the context of war, nationalism and militarization, and power relations that are themselves ever more starkly revealed in the act of going stealth.

## ACKNOWLEDGMENTS

An early draft of this work benefited from comments at a presentation sponsored by the Consortium for Women and Research at the University of California, Davis, in late 2007. For their careful readings and generous criticism, I am grateful to Cynthia Degnan, Benjamin D'Harlingue, Caren Kaplan and Liz Montegary, as well as two anonymous reviewers.

## NOTES

1. In "The *Empire* Strikes Back," gender and technology studies scholar Sandy Stone argues that as medical science made available more information about the standards for determining the category of transsexual, individuals were more able to deliberately perform to these standards, to convince doctors of transsexual identities and personal histories in order to gain access to medical transition. In *Sex Changes,* Patrick Califia discusses similar tactics taken up by trans-identified people in postoperative interviews and medical surveys.

2. For more in-depth analysis of gender reclassification policies and the standardization of U.S. identity documents, see Dean Spade's "Documenting Gender."

## REFERENCES

Agar, Jon. 2001. Modern horrors: British identity and identity cards. In *Documenting Individual Identity: The Development of State Practices in the Modern World,* ed. Jane Caplan and John Torpey, 101-120. New Jersey: Princeton University Press.

Bergeron, Claire, Aaron Matteo Terrazas, and Doris Meissner. 2007. Social security "no match" letters: a primer. *MPI Backgrounder* 5: 1-11, (October), http://www.migrationpolicy.org/pubs/BR5_SocialSecurityNoMatch_101007.pdf (accessed July 22, 2008).

Califia, Pat. 2003. *Sex Changes: Transgender Politics.* San Francisco: Cleis Press.

Caplan, Jane and John Torpey. 2001. Introduction. In *Documenting Individual Identity: The Development of State Practices in the Modern World,* ed. Jane Caplan and John Torpey, 1-12. New Jersey: Princeton University Press.

Department of Homeland Security. 2003. DHS advisory to security personnel; no change in threat level. Department of Homeland Security. http://www.dhs.gov/xnews/releases/press_release_0238.shtm (accessed July 28, 2007).

Department of Homeland Security. 2008. Real ID. Department of Homeland Security. http://www.dhs.gov/xprevprot/programs/gc_1200062053842.shtm (accessed July 28, 2008).

James, Joy. 1996. *Resisting State Violence: Radicalism, Gender, and Race in U.S. Culture.* Minneapolis: University of Minnesota Press.

Kaufman, Michael T. 2003. What does the pentagon see in 'Battle of Algiers'? *New York Times,* September 7, Sec. 4, p. 3.

Keisling, Mara. 2006. NCTE no-match comment. National Center for Transgender Equality. http://nctequality.org/Issues/I-9-nomatch-comment.pdf (accessed July 22, 2008).

National Center for Transgender Equality. 2007. Social security gender no-match letters and transgender employees. National Center for Transgender Equality. http://nctequality.org/issues/nomatch.html (accessed July 21, 2008).

National Transgender Advocacy Coalition. 2003. Security alert: "males dressed as females" to be scrutinized when traveling. Transgender Crossroads. http://www.tgcrossroads.org/news/archive.asp?aid=767 (accessed July 30, 2008).

Puar, Jasbir and Amit S. Rai. 2002. Monster, terrorist, fag: the war on terror and the production of docile patriots. *Social Text* 20 (3): 117-148.

Somerville, Siobhan. 2000. *Queering the Color Line: Race and the Invention of Homosexuality in American Culture.* Durham: Duke University Press.

Spade, Dean. 2003. Resisting medicine, re/modeling gender. *Berkeley Women's Law Journal* 18: 15-37.

Spade, Dean. 2008. Documenting gender. *Hastings Law Journal* 59: 731-842.

Stone, Sandy. 1991. The *empire* strikes back: a posttranssexual manifesto. In *Body guards: the cultural politics of gender ambiguity,* ed. Julia Epstein and Kristina Straub, 280-304. New York: Routledge.

Sylvia Rivera Law Project. (n.d.)The impact of the war on terror on LGBTSTQ communities. Sylvia Rivera Law Project. http://www.srlp.org/index.php?sec=03M&page=wotnotes (accessed July 15, 2008).

Transgender Law Center and National Center for Transgender Equality. 2005. The Real ID Act: bad law for our community." Transgender Law Center. http://transgenderlawcenter.org/pdf/Joint%20statement%20on%20the%20Real%20ID%20Act%20-%20final.pdf (accessed July 22, 2008).

Volpp, Leti. 2002. The citizen and the terrorist. *UCLA Law Review* 49: 1575-1599.

# 4

# *Tracing This Body*
## Transsexuality, Pharmaceuticals, and Capitalism

Michelle O'Brien

Michelle O'Brien was an independent scholar working in an HIV service agency in Philadelphia when she first wrote "Tracing This Body," which was originally given as a speech at Bryn Mawr College during Out Week in 2003; O'Brien later published it as an article on her personal website. Read online and emailed from friend to friend in the manner of a fanzine, "Tracing This Body" had achieved cult status among transgender theorists and activists by the late 2000s. In it, O'Brien traces the links of a commodity chain: from her own consumption of feminizing hormones to the pharmaceutical corporations that produce, market, and distribute synthetic estrogens; to health insurance companies that exclude coverage of transgender healthcare; to government agencies that regulate pharmaceutical distribution; and to transnational free trade agreements that structure the imbalances that make buying medicines in Mexico or Canada more "affordable" than in the U.S.A. O'Brien notes that these same pharmaceutical companies fought bitterly to prevent the production of low-cost HIV medications in countries with high rates of HIV infection. Finally, O'Brien traces the circulation and regulation of hypodermic needles: instruments of liberating bodily transformation for transgender people, but illicit and criminalized "drug paraphernalia" to governments pursuing a failing war on drugs. All of these chains of connection intimately enmesh trans people within the contradictory logics of transnational capitalism. Written just as the focus of resistance to global geopolitics was shifting from the World Trade Organization to the War on Terror, and as a major struggle was being fought to make HIV antiretrovirals accessible for the poor majority of the world's HIV positive population, "Tracing This Body" reads as a trans manifesto for the counter-globalization movement. What are our responsibilities, it asks, if we are targeted for control by the same structures that we depend on for our freedom? ← *maybe question "freedom" altogether*

## INTRODUCTION: THE STORY I'M HERE TO TELL

*personal narrative*

Every morning, when I wake up, I swallow a single pill of Proscar, a five milligram dosage of Finasteride. Every two weeks I give myself an intramuscular injection of one ml of Delestrogen, a synthetic hormone. I do these things because I like what they do to my body. I take these drugs because my body, for as long as I could remember, never fit quite right. And I believe that these drugs will help me find myself, be myself and live as myself.

Eventually I developed a story about my gender to talk about this bad fitting, this mismatch between what I felt and what people saw. This story helped me understand that I wanted to use these

56

drugs, that I wanted to grow breasts and experience their other effects. It's a story I've encountered elsewhere, that other people I've met also tell about themselves. A story about being trans.

But the story of my gender is not quite what I want to talk about today. Instead, I'd like to tell a story about these drugs. About how they locate my body, in this world. I want to trace how my body fits within structures of transnational capital, the pharmaceutical industries, and the state authority of the U.S. empire. How through these drugs I am placed and how I place myself in struggles over race and class. I want to talk about how I relate to technology, biomedicine and the play of power, domination, and resistance that crisscrosses the globe.

In doing so, I want to come a bit closer to understanding what it might mean as a body, as a gendered and racialized body, to live right now, in this world. We all, in our own ways, struggle with being a part of things we aren't so happy about. Both my complicity and resistance to the rule of capital happens in every facet of my life. In talking about these drugs and how they locate me in this world, perhaps I'll tell a story where you can find something about yourself as well.

## PAYING FOR HORMONES

Despite having one of the best medical health insurance plans my city has to offer, I pay for both of my medications out of pocket. This isn't uncommon. Most insurance plans, including my own, have an explicit exclusion of transgender healthcare. I end up spending about a third of my income on paying for my basic prescriptions. I manage to get my health insurance to cover my meetings with my hormone doctor, but only because he cites my condition as an "unspecified endocrine disorder," carefully excluding the mention of transsexuality.

For poor trans people who are uninsured or on State-funded medical assistance, the exclusion of transgender care in health plans can easily make the costs of transitioning under a doctor's care inaccessibly expensive. About two thirds of trans women in Philadelphia, according to one 1997 needs assessment, end up getting their hormones off the street. The lack of supervised medical care can have many consequences, including severe liver damage. Many women have become HIV+ through sharing street hormone needles.

Many trans people have begun talking about taking on the health insurance companies in demanding access to basic medical care. This will not be an easy task. Health insurance companies are incredibly powerful; they are massive, profitable industries. The third largest skyscraper in downtown Philadelphia is entirely dedicated to the office of the health insurance company Independence Blue Cross, making them one of the primary employers in Center City. According to their annual report, they cover about four million people in the region, having a net income of about $120 million in 2002.

One trans woman in Philly has already successfully got Keystone Mercy, her medical assistance HMO, to pay for her hormones. She argued they constituted basic medical care, and medical assistance HMOs were legally required by Pennsylvania State law to cover all basic medical care. It's an exciting and positive sign, and one we will no doubt organize around in the coming years.

These health insurance corporations are defining what medical care they consider to be appropriate, and which they do not. The basic medical needs of trans people are systematically, explicitly, and actively excluded from their plans. This reflects and reproduces the overall transphobia of the medical industry. The lack of coverage drastically reduces the number of trans people who can affordably access care. It discourages doctors and drug companies from taking seriously the needs of trans people.

Ultimately, this lack of coverage fuels a widespread institutionalized perception that the bodies and needs of trans simply do not matter. These line-item exclusions from insurance plans are

*crucial*

FDA

*market for hormones non-trans*

the bureaucratic expression of the brutal violence trans people often face out in the streets—the devaluation of our bodies as worthless.

Health insurance companies often don't even need to rationalize these exclusions. The political movements around trans healthcare are not yet big enough to successfully take on these corporations, or to even get them to notice us.

When these corporations do justify their denial of basic medical care to trans people, one rationalization comes up repeatedly: the U.S. Federal Food and Drug Administration has not given approval for the use of any medications for transgender body modification. The Federal government does not supervise, regulate, approve, or acknowledge the use of hormones to alter the gendered characteristics of one's body. The FDA has never acknowledged, I believe, that trans people even exist. *troubling*                                    *market exclusion*

When I buy my Finasteride and Delestrogen, they come to me, as most medications do, with small neatly-folded inserts outlining their proper use and potential side-effects. These texts are carefully regulated by the FDA. Nowhere in those long texts am I mentioned. They never discuss their use by transgender people, never acknowledge their potentially transformative effects when used with certain bodies, never even acknowledge that anyone under fifty would ever have a reason to take them. Similarly, I am never reflected in the advertisements for these drugs. Their extensive websites or occasional magazine ads have no trace of trans bodies. In the vast, proliferating world of consumer capitalism, trans people just don't constitute a market niche when it comes to drugs.

I am invisible to my health insurance company, invisible to the FDA, and invisible to the pharmaceutical industries. This invisibility is how these institutions express their transphobia and the hatred of trans bodies. We are not seen. For some, this lack of institutional acknowledgement has dire consequences. Already excluded from the wage economy, many poor trans women in Philadelphia turn to sex work to pay for their hormones. Poverty, police abuse, and HIV have taken a severe toll on the lives of trans women in the city. As trans people modifying our bodies, we are using these corporation's drugs towards unapproved and unacknowledged ends: the gendered rebuilding of our bodies. We pay the bill, and we live with the consequences. For me, choosing to take hormones is the best decision I've ever made.

These medications are on the market for reasons besides their use by transsexual people. If I am an improper, unauthorized user of these drugs, there are others who are thoroughly approved. Other people's bodies are taken seriously as objects of biomedical research and healthcare industries. It is for them these drugs circulate on the market. In the case of the two medications I take, both were developed to treat medical conditions for people in their fifties and sixties, a main generational age concentration in industrialized countries.

Delestrogen, like most estrogen-related hormones, was developed to ameliorate the symptoms of menopause. Many baby-boomer, non-trans women are reaching ages when their bodies' overall endocrine system goes through the drastic change of no longer producing significant levels of estrogen. The reduced hormonal levels cause a wide range of often uncomfortable and unpleasant effects, including hot flashes, loss of calcium and strength in the bones, sagging breasts, vaginal dryness and redistribution of body fat to the stomach. With a generational concentration of women in their forties, fifties, and sixties in industrialized countries, and the long life-spans of women with access to adequate medical care, addressing the symptoms of menopause has become a major industry. Estrogen-related hormonal therapies are in extremely high demand, constituting one of the major booms for pharmaceutical corporations. Women are eager to hold off the symptoms of menopause, and they and their health insurance companies are happy to pay.

Proscar, meanwhile, has a similar use among non-trans men to manage the more difficult effects of aging. While not as dramatic as non-trans women's hormonal systems, many older baby boomer men are also dealing with conditions related to changing hormonal levels. Elevated levels of testosterone in aging bodies can produce a number of effects. Proscar is on the market to help treat a condition related to enlarged prostates, known as hyperplasia. Proscar reduces the manufacture and circulation of testosterone in a body, treating such conditions. It is a five-mg form of the drug Finasteride.

In its two-mg form, Finasteride is sold under the brand name Propecia. Search on any web browser for Propecia, and hundreds of responses will come flooding back. It is a cosmetic medication to treat male-pattern balding, also an effect of testosterone. As a cosmetic medication, many health insurance companies won't cover the use of Finasteride in its two-mg form. Many non-trans older men are left, like myself, searching the web for their best buy in getting Propecia. While none of these websites ever mention trans people, they show countless men in their sixties proudly displaying full heads of hair. These men are the idealized, correct bodies that multinational pharmaceutical industries are eager to please. *crucial?*

As I pay for both medications out of pocket, I spend a lot of time looking for the best buy. By far, the best prices I've found are in Canada and Mexico. Most of us, I hope, remember a bit of the massive political battles that surrounded the approval of NAFTA and the FTAA. NAFTA established Canada and Mexico as near economic colonies of U.S. and transnational capital. It facilitated corporations relocating manufacturing operations to Mexico to pursue cheaper manufacturing costs. Meanwhile, NAFTA made easier the massive resource extraction from Canada in the forms of mining, oil drilling, and logging. A long history of coercive, neocolonial economic exploitation allows me to purchase more affordable drugs. Mexico's pharmaceutical manufacturing workers are paid far less than their U.S. counterparts, making for cheaper medications. Mexico has been chronically underdeveloped by exploitative capital, leaving a country struggling with widespread poverty. Coupled with the suppression of independent labor movements, Mexico constitutes a prime area for manufacturing interests. *free trade agreement*

Canada offers an equally appealing option for drug purchasing for Americans. The overall inequitable, exploitative organization of U.S.–Canadian economic relations contributes to an exchange rate that favors the U.S. dollar, contributing to cheaper drug costs for American consumers. Further, tight regulation of pharmaceutical costs, price caps, and a ban on drug advertising to the consumer all contribute to significantly lower drug costs. As a U.S. consumer, I'm able to directly benefit from differing corporate regulatory practices around the world. In Mexico, a less regulated economy contributes to cheaper products; in Canada, it is increased regulation that makes the drugs affordable. Either way, U.S. middle class consumers—a highly privileged if a bit tenuous minority in the neocolonial world—directly benefit.

The Proscar I take is manufactured by Merck & Co, Inc. A major transnational pharmaceutical industry, Merck maintains its main corporate office in New Jersey. They have contributed significantly to biomedical research and development throughout Canada, maintaining significant Canadian operations. As a corporation, they are traded on the New York Stock Exchange, and have a current market capitalization of about $120 million. I'm not entirely sure what this means, but I think it has something to do with how much the company is worth. According to their company website, their profits for the last five years ran over $51 million. Merck is one of the six manufacturers of HIV antiretroviral medications. *again profiting from trans suffering*

My Delestrogen is also manufactured by a major producer of HIV antiretrovirals: Bristol Meyers Squibb Company. Though a BMS subsidary originally developed and patented the drug, and continue to manufacture it, they sold its patent rights to King Pharmaceuticals in 2001. Delestrogen is marketed by Monarch Pharmaceuticals, a wholly owned subsidary of King. The names seem somehow appropriate in the world of corporate control that increasingly resembles some new revisioning of feudal states. Headquartered in Bristol, Tennessee, King is a less known, but rapidly up-and-coming and extremely profitable, drug company. In 2001 they purchased the rights to four medications, Delestrogen among them. Their corporate literature at the time heralded this purchase as a major step forward for the company. The year before BMS had netted sales of Delestrogen alone at

*against Marxist thought*

$12 million. With no promotion from BMS, sales of Delestrogen grew by 6 percent for the year. King had optimistic plans for its own intentions to aggressively and effectively market the drug. King was especially optimistic for Delestrogen's market viability, as it has no competition—the drug is without a generic alternative. At the time of its purchase, King foresaw its potential 2002 revenue at just over a billion dollars. King doesn't, however, have particularly good relations with Canadian pharmacies, and Delestrogen is particularly hard to locate online compared to many hormone therapies.

All this information is off these corporations' websites.

## IMMUNOWARS

Pharmaceutical corporations are major players in the global economy. The six major corporations that manufacture HIV medications are all Fortune 500 companies and have done well on the stock market. Together, they have organized heavily to define and regulate international trade law, the development and management of public health systems around the globe, and the political economy of medicine. HIV medications are ground zero in the battles of the politics of bodies sweeping the globe. The big six pharmaceuticals have a massive stake of profit and power in these wars. Much of the research for the section below is taken from the website of the Critical Path AIDS Project.

Estimates of global AIDS cases range around forty million. In industrialized countries, many people have access to antiretroviral treatment, powerful drugs that have drastically slowed down the degenerative advance of HIV disease within people's bodies. According to the Global Treatment Access Campaign, about 95 percent of the people living with AIDS around the globe do not have access to affordable medications. Vast populations of people across Africa, Latin America, and Asia are being denied access to basic medications.

Throughout these countries, there are major movements of people living with HIV organizing around demanding access to affordable healthcare. These movements are pushing governments to begin to manufacture low-cost, accessible, generic HIV medications. Brazil has already been implementing such programs, with tremendous success. Such programs are illegal under international trade law, violating the patent protections held by pharmaceutical corporations.

These transnational drug companies have sued under the World Trade Organization to halt the construction of low-cost medications. They are working actively to deny access to care for millions of people around the globe. These corporations, quite simply, are making a profit off people dying. They have instead launched heavily publicized, yet inept, inadequate, and pitifully small charitable contributions to global HIV care. These movements continue to demand affordable HIV care, a restructuring of international trade regulations, and the rights and urgent need of governments to address their populations' healthcare.

These battles over HIV meds are a part of massive global struggles over race and class power. In the last few decades, transnational corporations have dramatically consolidated economic and political power around the world. The long-standing colonial exploitation of people in poor countries has rapidly intensified. Transnational capital is having a dramatic impact on the social organization, governmental policy, and economic management of countries throughout the globe. Increasingly, through the pressure and control of capital interests and their representatives in the International Monetary Fund, the World Bank, and the World Trade Organization, governments are forced to adopt policies favorable to the interests of profit. Policies such as privatization of major industries, paying exorbitant patent costs for basic medications, massive expansion of the prison industrial complex, suppression of labor movements, and organizing of industries around profit-driven exports have dramatically worsened the standard of living for billions of people. An economic war against the poor people of color around the world has already cost hundreds of millions of lives, as people die from malnutrition, disease, and war.

In Philadelphia, AIDS care is a major industry. Philly has about 21,000 AIDS cases according to the CDC, and an unknown number of people living with HIV. Large Federal block grants are allocated for HIV care, covering most people living with HIV in the city. GlaxoSmithKline, a major pharmaceutical manufacturer of antiretroviral drugs, occupies a large building downtown and is one of the major corporations with headquarters in the city. Former basketball star Calvin "Magic" Johnson serves as their major advertising spokesperson. Johnson's face is plastered over billboards across the poorest neighborhoods of Philadelphia, alongside advertisements for corporate R&B radio, the videogame Grand Theft Auto, Vice City, and malt liquor contests. Glaxo's global sales for 2002 exceeded $31 million. I'm one of hundreds of HIV case workers in Philadelphia, charged with helping people access the complex system of care and services surrounding treatment.

Philadelphia is also a major city for AIDS activism and advocacy. ACT-UP Philadelphia is one of the most significant U.S. organizations participating in the international movements for access to affordable HIV treatment. ACT-UP Philly is one of the strongest, most militant, and best organized AIDS action groups in the world. They and other Philly AIDS activism groups have made a dramatic impact on metropolitan and global politics. Organizing around the healthcare of HIV+ poor people in prisons and in underdeveloped countries, Philly AIDS advocacy groups have pushed forward a sophisticated analysis of global race and class politics within HIV care.

Trans people are heavily engaged in HIV/AIDS organizing. Here in Philadelphia, many trans people are actively involved in HIV social services and advocacy. Internationally, gender variant people have played a significant role in expanding awareness of HIV and building movements to demand healthcare for all. Trans people, particularly trans women, face unusually high rates of HIV infection. As well, the issues of access to HIV medications are deeply interwoven with the rights of trans people to access hormones—a demand made of medical industries in the name of our health, our bodies, and our survival.

## NEEDLES IN THE DRUG WAR

I inject my hormones with a twenty-one-gauge, three-cc syringe manufactured by the Terumo Medical Corporation. I pick these needles up at a local needle exchange, where I periodically volunteer. Standing in line for syringes, I find myself alongside people who actively use heroin, cocaine, speed, and other intravenous drugs.

Needles are hard to find in the region. For those without a prescription, possession of an injection needle in most of Pennsylvania and New Jersey is criminal. Here in Philadelphia, only a mayoral order allows any needle exchange programs to legally operate.

The difficulty in getting clean needles has serious consequence. People using injectable drugs face extremely high rates of hepatitis C and HIV. As well as viral infections, people reusing needles face a significantly increased risk of bacterial infections. The lack of access to clean needles is a major, life-threatening health concern for injectable drug users. Needle exchanges have been demonstrated through extensive study to drastically reduce viral infection rates, mortality, and the health of drug users.

The difficulty in getting clean needles is a part, of course, of what we call the drug war. In the last twenty-five years, the U.S. has adopted a policy of massive criminalization of drug use. Through militarizing the police system to serve as occupying armies in working class urban neighborhoods, dramatically expanding the profits of the prison industry, and changing sentencing guidelines, over two million people are currently incarcerated in the U.S. This is the highest rate in the industrial world, and acts as an implement of massive suffering in poor communities of color. Prisons and police occupation destroy families and people's lives, and rob communities of political and economic self-determination.

The focus of this racist and classist state violence has been directed against drug users themselves. Legally denied access to basic social services, healthcare, housing, or employment, active drug users are among the most intensely marginalized segment of U.S. society. U.S. policies toward drug users only make sense as strategies to kill off drug users, totally devaluing people's lives and bodies as less than worthless. Humane, effective, and respectful services to active drug users, such as a decent needle exchange, are criminalized or barred from access to funding.

In the midst of this nightmarish political landscape, some people have been organizing around the rights of drug users and against the prison system. Active drug users, in coalition with the more progressive currents of social services, have been organizing against incarceration and criminalization, and in favor of adequate healthcare, housing, and other basic needs. These movements are often called "harm reduction," a phrase developed to refer to a method of social services that places respect for the person, their own self-determination, and the concrete need to reduce their suffering as paramount. The Harm Reduction Coalition of New York and San Francisco brings together many such organizations. Trans people, both as active illegal drug users and in accessing services, have participated in and benefited from this work.

While not as widely respectful to the experiences of current drug users, a broad range of antiracist, working-class, anti-capitalist, or anti-imperialist organizations have built a movement to challenge mass incarceration and the prison industrial complex. The Prison Activist Resource Center offers an excellent website that lists many such organizations.

Harm reduction has been inspiring to me as a trans activist. Learning about harm reduction has deepened and enriched my understanding of the ways meeting people's basic needs can be linked to a project of social liberation. In reading harm reduction thought, I've encountered a great deal about the right of personal self-determination in accessing healthcare and social services, a basic respect unjustly denied to many drug users and trans people. Trans people engaged in the struggle for liberation have a great deal to learn from movements against the prison complex and in defense of drug users. Trans people, whether we use drugs or not, have a tremendous stake in putting an end to the war on drugs.

## CAPITAL FLOWS, BODY FLOWS

These battles over HIV, transgender health, and drug use are real, with millions of people's lives on the line. Politics is changing fast around the world, as old resistance movements have disintegrated, and new forms of domination are deepening their entrenched authority. Capital flows more and more rapidly around the globe, while access to healthcare is strictly limited and regulated. Wars of healthcare, over the terrain of our bodies, are among the most significant political battles in the world today. Healthcare is a major site in defining, and transforming, what race and class domination mean in our day-to-day lives. This fight is so profound, so real, so important, precisely because it is the place where the three levels of flows come together: 1. those flows of T cells and hormones, of viruses and antivirals, of methadone and heroin, within our own bodies; 2. those flows of our selves, families, and lives through our communities; and 3. those flows of capital and institutional power across the globe.

All people are always living across these multiple interlocking systems of the body, social communities, and transnational capitalism. Across the bodies of trans people, people living with HIV, and active drug users, this is just a lot more obvious. But ultimately these insights, and the need to think across multiple modes of struggle and power, are relevant to everyone.

Some of the language I use here, and much of my understanding of the deep interconnection between different flows of power, I take from the remarkable writing of Felix Guattari and Gilles Deleuze. They wrote a two-volume set together subtitled *Capitalism and Schizophrenia*. Both I'd highly recommend to folks who like to read wild, incomprehensible books and are looking to discuss transnational capitalism.

When I give myself an injection of Delestrogen, I am locating myself and am located within global flows of power. I am connected to the complex political, economic, and social histories of how these drugs were manufactured and by whom) I am bound within the international trade systems that allow those corporations to function, that bring the hormones to my door in a brown envelope. I am facing the systems of violence that render my body invisible, that make it impossible for many to get drugs at all. By taking hormones, I am doing what we all do in various ways: I am participating within the system of transnational capital. These systems are racist, classist, sexist, homophobic, and transphobic to their core. They are systematically structured on a hatred of the bodies of trans people, poor people, people living with HIV, and drug users. And yet, all of us are deeply, inexorably dependent on these very structures. Quite literally, we need them to keep us alive.

## TRANS BODIES, CYBORG BODIES

While I use these corporate-produced medications, like many others, I am using them counter to their purpose. Just as a Brazilian rail worker picking up his antiretrovirals at a health clinic that violates international patent law, or an old woman in South Philly using her controlled, managed quantities of methadone to live with a brain permanently dependent on opiates, my survival depends on interfacing global capitalism, but interfacing it improperly. We are corrupting, redirecting, and redefining the products of this medical system to serve our ends. Our survival is not respected by these corporations, our needs are not taken seriously. We have to meet our needs, not through isolation, purity, or refusal, but through accessing and redefining care in ways counter to the institutions involved.

The politics of our bodies—as trans people, as drug users, as people living with HIV—require a sophisticated grasp of multiple contradictions. We are dependent on the very systems that oppress us. We make demands for change, and we appropriate the refuse of capital for our own survival. We live in the flows, suffer in the flows, envision a new world in these flows.

Many theories of power and politics offer little to grapple with such a struggle of bodily survival. I grew up working in radical environmental movements in Oregon, using direct action to defend ancient forests. The anti-capitalist analysis of many such activists relied on a fanatical commitment to purity and an attempt at a total refusal to participate or be complicit in any form of corporate rule. Veganism, do-it-yourself punk ethics, buying natural and local, lesbian-feminist separatism, back-to-the-land self-sustaining agriculture, and especially eco-primitivism and other movements common around Eugene, Oregon, all frequently rely, to various extents, on a commitment to non-participation in global capitalism and certain idealized notions of purity. Since then, I've encountered similar phenomena in many political spaces, from AIDS denialists working in animal rights organizing to the MOVE family of Philadelphia, from genderqueer denunciations of medicalized body modification to the glorification of drop-out travelers by the anarchist writing network known as CrimethInc.

There is obviously a great deal that is admirable and wonderful about these movements. I continue to seek political, spiritual, and environmental value in trying to be conscious of, limit, and redefine my forms of consumerism and capitalist participation. Much of my life, including living in a collective anarchist home, eating vegan, riding my bike as transportation, and getting my clothes from thrift stories, are rooted in values I share with many environmental movements.

At the same time, when taken in certain directions these movements can be horrifically inadequate, obnoxiously useless, or just downright oppressive to trans people, people living with HIV, and active drug users.

*certain things*
*↑ you need*

*so so so*
*important*

If your survival depends on substantially accessing global pharmaceutical industries, a politics of purity and non-participation just doesn't get you that far. I would have killed myself if it wasn't for these hormones I order from Canada. Most of my HIV+ clients would be dead, as they can't afford elaborate drug-free raw foods treatments popular among denialists in San Francisco. Similarly, any crude and dualistic politics that sets people completely against industrial systems of oppression just doesn't help me try to understand the many relationships of participation, resistance, complicity, and challenge I actually have with these structures.

These languages of purity and non-participation are frequently counterposed by the glorifying ideological cheerleaders of capitalist domination. Every major U.S. newspaper, every president and senator, every corporate trade journal is aggressively advancing the absurd notion that capitalism is the best avenue to manage and stop human suffering. Believing that state power and corporate tyranny will somehow make a decent world has a major impact on the popular discourses of science, technology, and industrial production. Such pro-capitalist perspectives are of no use to me.

*read Haraway*

Instead, I've tried through this paper to trace other ways of thinking through the relationship between my body and capitalism. At each step, I've tried to simultaneously recognize my participation and complicity, and trace the possibilities of resistance and liberation. In trying to describe the complexity of these relationships, I've found inspiration in Donna Haraway's essay "A Cyborg Manifesto: Science, Technology and Socialist-Feminism in the Late Twentieth Century." A truly remarkable text, Haraway's essay brilliantly cuts through polarized debates characterizing science as either a wonderful tool of capitalist improvement or the evil bane of patriarchy. Instead, Haraway describes the figure of the cyborg. The cyborg is the bastard child of the patriarchal realms of capitalism, nature, and technoscience. Rather than reproduce their systems of command, control, and communication, the cyborg can radically challenge, undermine, and resist domination. The cyborg is a new vision of feminist consciousness, a radical means of relating to technology and science. The cyborg is never pure, never free of the systems it subverts, never belonging to a realm before or outside of capitalist technoscience and patriarchy. But the cyborg is also a revolutionary, an effective, empowered, conscious being that reworks, redirects, and restructures the oppressive systems that birthed it.

This vision of the feminist cyborg has been very useful and inspiring to me in understanding my own body and in struggling to the liberation of trans people. Like the cyborg, we are both complicit in and a challenge to the biomedical industries. We are drastically rebuilding our bodies with the aid of technology, surgery, and drugs. And we are doing this all on our own terms, committed to our own well-being, striving to our own liberation. Far from the dupes of doctors or the crude escapists of eco-primitivism, we are living amidst the systems we are always subverting. Trans people live in that hybrid edge of technology, science, nature, and capital that Haraway correctly and brilliantly identifies as a tremendously powerful space of resistance and movement.

We are all in the midst of structures of tremendous violence, oppression, and exploitation. There is no easy escape or pure distance from them. Our ability to resist, in this world, at this time, is deeply inseparable from our ongoing connection to these very systems. But resist we do. Every day, in so many ways, we are all struggling towards a new world of liberation, healing, and respect.

## A SYRINGE AND A DREAM

It's here my story brings me. In my bag I have a pack of new, clean syringes from the exchange site up on 10th and Fairmount. In a neighborhood wracked by decades of consuming poverty, police violence, and institutionalized racism, I talked with an older black women who was picking up a bag of syringes for a dozen others—friends, she explained. In a few minutes, I'm going to go home from work and pick up a cheap order of progesterone from my pharmacy. I go there because it's across the street from a major free HIV clinic. The people there are nicer than most, and don't give anyone hassle for the drugs they are picking up. My Delestrogen refill might have arrived from Nova Scotia today, I'm not sure.

It is here we are. We are poised at the cusp of a new millennium. Here, where I am feeling the yearning so deep in my heart for a new world, for a different kind of society. In the midst of these flows of power and resistance, investment and violence, we must struggle to find ourselves. We must fight to piece together lives of profound beauty, love, respect, and dignity. Our globe is torn with centuries of racist and classist war, war where we are all fighting to survive. This story of my body, of these drugs, brings me to where my writing often leaves off—with a pain of desperation, hope, and longing. Longing I have for a revolution of the spirit and the overthrow of the empire. And with it, the welcoming of spaces of love within us all.

*[handwritten margin notes: Positively, goddamn]*

*[handwritten note: Beautiful]*

## REFERENCES

Guattari, Felix and Gilles Deleuze. 2004a. *Anti-Oedipus*, trans. Robert Hurley, Mark Seem, and Helen R. Lane. London: Continuum.

Guattari, Felix and Gilles Deleuze. 2004b. *A Thousand Plateaus*, trans. Brian Massumi. London Continuum.

Haraway, Donna. 1991. "A Cyborg Manifesto: Science, Technology and Socialist-Feminism in the Late Twentieth Century", 149–182. *Simians, Cyborgs, and Women: The Reinvention of Nature*. London: Free Association, 1991.

*[handwritten notes at bottom of page:]*
*formule*
*4 present problem*
*4 share hope*
*4 emphasize a great deal of work*
*still to be done*

# 5

# *Trans Necropolitics*
## A Transnational Reflection on Violence, Death, and the Trans of Color Afterlife

C. RILEY SNORTON AND JIN HARITAWORN

IN THIS JOINTLY AUTHORED ARTICLE, C. RILEY SNORTON AND JIN HARITAWORN bring a transnational perspective to bear on systemic forms of often deadly violence experienced by trans people of color. They suggest that postcolonial theorist Achille Mbembe's concept of "necropolitics," which describes a form of power that marks some fraction of a population for death even while it deems other fractions suitable for life-enhancing investment, accurately reflects the circumstances of trans of color existence. They assert that value extracted from the deaths of trans people of color vitalizes projects as diverse as inner-city gentrification, anti-immigrant and anti-muslim moral panics, homonationalism, and white transnormative community formation. Snorton, assistant professor of Communications Studies at Northwestern University, first offers an account of the 1995 death of Tyra Hunter, an African-American trans woman from Washington D.C., and of the many uses to which her death subsequently has been put. Sociologist Jin Haritaworn, assistant professor of Gender, Race and Environment at York University, then traces how trans of color bodies such as Hunter's have circulated in contemporary Berlin. In general, Haritaworn claims, the lives of trans people of color in the global North and West are celebrated, and their deaths memorialized, in ways that serve the white citizenry and mask necropolitical violence waged against gender variant people from the global South and East.

The concept of an afterlife has a particular resonance for transgender studies. It provides a framework for thinking about how trans death opens up political and social life-worlds across various times and places. Whether through the commemorative, community-reinforcing rituals of Transgender Day of Remembrance (TDOR) or as an *ex post facto* justification for hate crime and anti-discrimination policies, trans deaths—and most frequently the deaths of trans women or trans-feminine people of color—act as a resource for the development and dissemination of many different agendas. Through the concept of the afterlife, this essay addresses the complex interrelationships between biopower and necropolitics, to consider the discursive and representational politics of trans death and trans vitality. Our formulation of trans necropolitics draws on Achille Mbembe's (2003) necropolitics—a concept he develops for making sense of the centrality of death in contemporary social life. This enables us to understand how biopower—the carving out of subjects and populations (Foucault 1978)—can profess itself at the service of life and yet generate death, in both quotidian and spectacular forms. We also draw on current queer theorizing that attempts to make sense of the expansion of liberal LGBT politics and its complicity with racism, Empire, border fortification, gentrification, incarceration, and the "war on terror" (Puar 2007; Haritaworn, Kuntsman and Posocco forthcoming).

Working transnationally and intersectionally, we ground our analysis in trans of color critique, whose most urgent present task is explaining the simultaneous devaluation of trans of color lives and the nominal circulation in death of trans people of color; this circulation vitalizes trans theory and politics, we claim, through the value extracted from trans of color death. We bring into one frame the everyday lives of trans and gender non-conforming people of color and the symbiotic (and sometimes parasitic) relationships that develop after their deaths with globalized homonormative and transnormative political projects.

One illustration of the need to think transgender both transnationally and intersectionally is the current globalization of hate crime activism. How is this political method mobilized and assimilated in various locations; what constituencies are interpellated there? What are its seductions for a trans activism for whom traumatized citizenship is more than merely an identitarian pitfall (Brown 1993; Berlant 2000), and is rather a key condition of its own emergence (Agathangelou, Bassichis and Spira 2008)? We ask: how do the biopolitics and necropolitics of trans death and trans vitality play out on the privileged stages of North America and Europe? What are the conditions and effects of their travels? We observe that as a result of U.S. hegemony, the unequal and exploitative stakes in violence and anti-violence are replicated elsewhere, and this forces us to interrogate trans organizing transnationally.

We need to ask how subjectivities and political methodologies travel in predictable directions, from North to South, and West to East (Grewal and Kaplan 2001). Earlier critiques of global feminism and homo-neo-colonialism bear helpful lessons, yet we must be wary of analogizing categories like women, gay and trans, or even "queer of color" and "trans." Rather, the social movements organized under these umbrellas intersect, compete with, and condition each other in complex ways that demand our attention. While important work has examined the uneven ways in which "women's liberation" and "gay liberation" became respectable and assimilable through the abjection of gender non-conformity (see e.g., Namaste 1996; Rivera 2002; Spade 2003), we must question a conception of transgender as first and foremost victimized. Rather, it is necessary to interrogate how the uneven institutionalization of women's, gay, and trans politics produces a transnormative subject, whose universalized trajectory of coming out/transition, visibility, recognition, protection, and self-actualization largely remains uninterrogated in its complicities and convergences with biomedical, neoliberal, racist, and imperialist projects. Thus, while global feminist and homonormative anti-violence politics have been subject to critique, the same is not true for a comparable trans politics. Trans of color positions in particular are as yet so barely conceivable that trying to articulate them (or even marking their absence) almost automatically becomes the "p.c. that goes too far" (Haritaworn 2005).

In Europe, the subject of transgender has gained visibility and viability by joining an older archive of violence and anti-violence discourse, which after years of racist homonationalist mobilizing is already heavily raced and classed. There, the hate crime paradigm arrived in highly racialized and spatialized ways: following a decade-long moral panic over "homophobic Muslims," the figure of "the violent subject" was instantly recognizable as Muslim. The current juncture in Europe between welfare and neoliberal regimes, and the ambivalent desires for diversity and disposal that it produces, invite novel performances of transness as innocent, colorfully diverse, and entitled to survival and protection. Nevertheless, these biopolitical and necropolitical conversions do not accrue value equally to all trans people. While those whose multiple vulnerabilities lend the moral panic its spectacularly violated bodies are continually reinscribed as degenerate and killable, the same process secures a newly professionalizing class of experts in the realm of life. This forces us to examine the rise of trans movements transnationally against the globalization and intersection of various industrial complexes: the prison, non-profit, and increasingly also the academic industrial complex.[1]

How do the deaths, both social and actual, of trans people of color provide the fuel and the raw material for this process?

This essay offers two sets of observations on issues of particular relevance to the experiences of trans women of color. The first, on the afterlife of Tyra Hunter, is grounded in Riley Snorton's work; the second, on trans vitality and anti-violence activism in Berlin, is based on Jin Haritaworn's work. We offer meditations on the ways that visibility, legibility, and intelligibility structure a grid of imposed value on the lives and deaths of black and brown trans women. This value grid speaks to some of the intricacies we briefly discussed above—it demonstrates how biopolitics and necropolitics, in addition to being modes of governance, are also technologies of value extraction. We demonstrate how these technologies shape the lives and afterlives of particular persons, as well as broader social, cultural, and political projects at this particular historical juncture.

## THE AFTERLIFE OF TYRA HUNTER

On October 28, 2009 United States President Barack Obama signed into law the Matthew Shepard and James Byrd, Jr. Hate Crimes Prevention Act, which expanded on previous, similar legislation to include gender identity among other "protected categories." The Act is the first federal law to extend legal "protections" to transgender people. In addition to giving federal authorities greater ability to pursue hate crime enhancements for bias-motivated violent crime, the law also requires the Federal Bureau of Investigation (FBI) to collect data on hate crimes perpetrated against transgender people. As Dean Spade has written, support for such legislation is shored up by advocates' desires for a symbolic declaration of societal/governmental inclusion, which also increases the positive visibility of transgender people (Spade 2009: 356). Hate crimes laws thus legally articulate the value of transgender people's lives, even as this articulation of inclusion is produced by and through their deaths. Simultaneously, hate crimes legislation contributes to a broader biopolitical imperative to manage poor people and people of color by channeling them into a massive carceral project, a "prison industrial complex," through which capital gains through the privatization of prisons.

At one level, centering the experiences of transgender people of color means tuning our critical attention to the biopolitics of everyday life; on another, it requires a raising of the dead, as it were, and an understanding of what Sharon Holland describes as the knowledge of our death, that "determines not only the shape of our lives but also the culture we live in" (Holland 2000: 15). Consequently, I structure this section around the story of a twenty-four-year-old black transgender hairdresser, Tyra Hunter, to illustrate how we might pursue the vexed relationships between neoliberalism and violent forms of governmentality that are materially hostile to trans of color survival.

Drawing on Alexis Pauline Gumbs' work (2010) on the queer survival of black feminism, I suggest that transgender of color survival—and its queer persistence in life and death—provides a vantage point through which to explore the ruptural theoretical and political possibilities precipitated by centering our analysis on transgender people of color. As scholars have noted, biopower found an early and violent instantiation during the Atlantic Slave Trade (Mbembe 2003; Abdur-Rahman 2006; Mirzoeff 2009). This history framed blackness not simply in terms of racial aberrance, but of sexual and gender deviance as well. Thus the un-gendering (or perhaps trans-gendering) of blackness under slavery serves as generative ground for understanding black trans subjectifications and their relationships to contemporary biopolitics. For as Nicholas Mirzoeff explains, "any deployment of 'life' also exists in relation to the 'natural'" (Mirzoeff 2009: 290). The discursive construction of the transgender body—and particularly the transgender body of color—as unnatural creates the precise moment where we as scholars, critics, and activists might apprehend a biopolitics of everyday life, where the transgender body of color is the unruly body, which only in death can be transformed or translated into the service of state power.

Tyra Hunter was headed for work in the passenger side of a vehicle in Washington D.C. on August 7, 1995, when her car was broadsided at an intersection. When fire department personnel arrived on the scene, onlookers already had pulled Tyra and the driver from the car. As a crowd gathered, firefighter Adrian Williams and others began treating the injured—that is, until Williams cut open Tyra's pant leg and noticed she had male genitalia. At that point, according to eyewitnesses, Williams stood up and backed away from Tyra, who was semi-conscious, complaining about her pain, and gasping for breath. Williams was quoted by one witness as saying, "This bitch ain't no girl…. It's a nigger, he got a dick" (Juang 2006: 712). Another witness heard another firefighter say, "Look, it's got a cock and balls" (Levi n.d.: 1). While the firefighters stood around making derisive remarks, Tyra's treatment was interrupted.

As the "jokes" continued, bystanders began to plead with the emergency responders to resume working to save Tyra's life. One bystander was quoted as saying, "It don't make any difference, he's [sic] a person… a human being" (Anna 2011). After some time, other firefighters attended to Tyra's injuries, and she was transported to D.C. General Hospital, where she was placed under the care of Dr. Joseph A. Bastien, who failed to provide a necessary blood transfusion or insert a chest tube necessary for Tyra's medical care. She was pronounced dead later that day.

Of course, the "treatment" Tyra received is not an isolated incident. Popular transgender lore would interpret the events precipitating Tyra's death as medicalized transphobia, which of course they are. But a broader politico-theoretical framework allows us to understand Tyra's body (before and after the accident) as a site where the medical establishment enacted what Henry Giroux calls a "biopolitics of disposability," a "new kind of politics… in which entire populations are now considered disposable, an unnecessary burden on state coffers, and consigned to fend for themselves" (Giroux 2006: 174). Thus neoliberal ideologies provide biopower with new ammunition in the creation of life-enhancing and death-making worlds, and offer an insidious addendum to rationales for population control. The consequence of this logic effaces the way power and life are maintained and reproduced through the deaths of certain others.

To return to Tyra's story is to think of her life after death, and to make sense of the excess that constitute her afterlife. In death, Tyra was almost exclusively referred to as Tyrone Michael Hunter. In the series of *Washington Post* articles that chronicled her death, Tyra was described as a man in women's clothes, as a gay man, as a transgender man, and sometimes as a man who lived his life as a woman. Some of this disturbing misattribution of gender is attributable to transphobia in journalistic reporting. But it also underscores why it is necessary to think specifically about transgender of color experiences as distinct from queer subjectivities. A D.C.-based anti-violence coalition, GLOV (Gays and Lesbians Opposing Violence) responded immediately to Tyra's death by calling for the fire department to investigate the incident. Their work turned up eight witnesses willing to testify that the behavior of Williams and others was unacceptable. However, both the media and local government officials framed the death of Tyra—referred to as Tyrone— as a "gay issue." Jessica Xavier, at the time a spokesperson for GLOV and herself a transwoman, was quoted as saying that such transphobic events occur because transgender people "are walking, talking, living, breathing stereotypes of what it means to be gay. They're just trying to lead ordinary lives free from discrimination and violence."

Jin Haritaworn's (2008) analysis of the appropriation of trans of color lives by white queer theorists provides an incisive theoretical framework for understanding Tyra's after-death transformation by layering race onto trans theorist Jay Prosser's supposition about the degree to which transgender and transsexual inclusiveness might really stand in for queer inclusivity. Prosser asks, "to what extent this queer inclusiveness of transgender and transsexuality is . . . the mechanism by which queer can sustain its very queerness . . . by periodically adding subjects who appear even queerer precisely by virtue of their marginality in relation to queer" (1998: 40); we wonder to what degree queer and trans anti-discrimination and anti-violence movements are produced and sustained by the violent and frequently murderous impulses specifically directed toward trans feminine people of color.

Xavier's comments are a key example of a larger project of reincorporating transgender bodies of color under a more legible sign; in this case, the representation of Tyra as a spectacularized gay male body. Whenever the work of legibility is enacted upon transgender bodies, it is always a process of translation—with risks (of appropriation) and payoffs. One "payoff" in this instance was the $2.8 million lawsuit Tyra's mother, Margie Hunter, won against the city and hospital on December 11, 1998, when a jury found them guilty of negligence and malpractice. While $500,000 was awarded for damages attributable to the withdrawal of medical care at the accident scene, a further $1.5 million was awarded for conscious pain and suffering endured by Tyra in the emergency room as the result of medical malpractice. The sanitizing of Tyra's transgender body undoubtedly allowed her to be understood more sympathetically as a son. Indeed, Margie Hunter told *Washington Post* reporters, "Tyrone always was so sure he would be famous, that he'd be on the television," she said. "I don't think he meant this way. I know I didn't. But maybe this is God's will and something good will come of it" (Slevin 1998).

It is important to look beyond statist and mainstream media discourses to see what "good" came from Tyra's life and death. Over 2,000 people attended her funeral. A candlelight vigil/protest at the D.C. fire department headquarters drew more than 200 demonstrators. The *Washington Times* quoted Cathy Renna, then co-chairman of the Gay and Lesbian Alliance Against Defamation, as saying, "I have never seen a cause that crossed so many boundaries: gay and straight, black and white... All of our work should be this cooperative." The intersections of sexism, transphobia, and racism became the context for an insurgence of political activity, and Tyra's name lives on in the acronym, T.Y.R.A. (or Transgender Youth Resources and Advocacy), a Chicago-based program that continues to support transgender youth of color.

But Tyra Hunter's story is not unique. Her name, frequently invoked at TDOR events, is simply one appellation among many that gestures toward trans of color death. In doing so, it indexes a transnational complicity with racist, transphobic, classist, misogynist, and homophobic violence. This violence has continued even after the signing of the Matthew Shepard Act. As a recent report of the National Gay and Lesbian Task Force (NGLTF) suggests:

> It is part of social and legal convention in the United States to discriminate against, ridicule, and abuse transgender and gender non-conforming people within foundational institutions such as the family, schools, the workplace and health care settings, every day. Instead of recognizing that the moral failure lies in society's unwillingness to embrace different gender identities and expressions, society blames transgender and gender non-conforming people for bringing the discrimination and violence on themselves.[2]

Tyra's life and the lives of other transgender people of color gesture in less moral terms toward an understanding of various forms of transgender repudiation. They require a rigorous reconsideration of lives structured alternately by illegibility and spectacle. Those lives also carry a productive force—particularly in death—that sheds light on the borders where biopower and necropower brush against each another in everyday life. These lives stand at the limit of what is livable, and transgender of color survival—in its ghastly presence, which occurs before and after life subsides—becomes a unique vantage point for understanding how one might persist in the space of hetero/homonormative unincorporability. As Haritaworn recounts in the subsequent section, Tyra Hunter's story is not confined to a North American context. In fact, her death sutures together a number of transnational political projects that hinge on anti-violence legal protections and transgender-inclusive legislation. In recounting details of her life and death, the aim is not simply to rehearse transmisogynistic violence, but rather to provide an example of how trans women of color act as resources—both literally and metaphorically—for the articulation and visibility of a more privileged transgender subject. The extraction of value from trans of color lives through biopolitical and necropolitics technologies not only serves the sovereign, but also indexes much more subtle and complex shifts in power. Trans rights activists' participation in and complicity with this process is what compels us to make this intervention.

## TRANSGRESSIVE CITIZENSHIP IN GERMANY

Hate crime discourse made its entry onto the German scene in 2008. It found its first bodies on the genderqueer scene: in the summer of that year, a group of visitors and performers at Berlin's Drag Festival were involved in a violent incident that was quickly attributed to men of Turkish origin, and which gave rise to media and policy responses that first introduced the term *Hasskriminalität* (hate crime) to a wider German public. The privileged place assumed by the gender non-conforming body in the institutionalization of the hate crime framework may at first surprise. Racialized violence discourses were certainly not alien to white-dominated queer and trans scenes, yet the actors who had invested in them most systematically followed a homonormative politics. The figure of the victim of transphobia nevertheless became instantly legible as the offspring of an already-existing migrant *homo*phobia script. Unlike in the U.S.A., where the death of a homonormative subject—the white, middle-class, college student Matthew Shepard—was instrumental in forging consent for the inclusion of homophobia and transphobia, German hate crime discourse found its first victims in radical queer and gender non-conforming people, some of whom were migrants. The key "event" that launched the odd neologism *Hasskriminalität* into the German vocabulary was the Drag Festival, an internationally publicized gender/queer performance event, which culminated in an altercation during which several festival visitors and performers were beaten up. Dovetailing with a decade-long moral panic over "homophobic Muslims," and set in the gentrifying "Turkish" area of Kreuzberg—a crime scene par excellence—the incident instantly became an "event" that circulated rapidly through a ready-made queer and trans audience.[3] The representations that followed in its wake, partly as a result of the white festival organizers' own press releases, were highly ambivalent about transgender. In fact, there was an abundance of transphobic images of ridiculous, repulsive, and excessive bodies, and it was the homonormative, homoracist trope of "Turks beating up lesbians" that ultimately came to define the incident (Haritaworn 2011). Nevertheless, and maybe for the first time, the gender non-conforming subject emerged as a body worthy of both protection and celebration. It became an important symbol of the diverse neighborhood that can be colorful even while its older poor and racialized inhabitants are ghosted from it through gentrification and policing. The very excess of the gender non-conforming subject here served to demonstrate how far the tolerant society will go—both in the kind of bodies it is willing to protect, and in the punishments it is willing to mete out to Others who, in a post-Fordist and neoliberal context, had been reduced to diversity's constitutive outside.

Spectacularized through the injured bodies of gender non-conforming subjects, the perpetrator of hate crime is nevertheless instantly recognized as the *homo*phobic migrant. This figure emerges in public discourse in the late 1990s, when the big gay organizations turn to "migrants," hitherto marginal to mainstream gay politics, in search of new constituencies, new *raisons d'être*, and an expanded public audience for the recognition of sexual politics as part of a broader, national agenda. Rather than incidental to or a natural result of migrant particularity, the racialization of gender and sexuality that constitutes the ground on which hate crimes discourse arrives is the result of a performative labor which, as Sarah Ahmed puts it, conceals itself through repetition and affective proximities (see Ahmed 2004: 91–92). The homophobic migrant fits this family well—he is instantly adopted as a newcomer whose resemblance makes him seem to have been here forever. The ease with which the homophobic migrant becomes common sense in 2000s Germany belies the decade-long efforts that go into crafting this figure. Its landmarks include, first, the simultaneous integration debates and the Europe-wide "crisis in multiculturalism," blown up into a panic big enough to include even gay expertise (an assimilation which occurs by performing an Other as unassimilable). Second, a domestic violence paradigm increasingly Orientalized as a function of "Muslim" cultures and gender relations, which thus creates space for new metonymies between Muslim sexism and Muslim homophobia, and between women of color and white gay men, who are imagined to suffer from identical forces. Third, the so-called "Muslim Test" of German nationality, which attempts to shore up a belatedly reformed law of blood, or *ius sanguinis*, by inventing new traditions, or "core values," of women-and-gay friendliness. Fourth, the Simon study, a quantitative psychosocial study of homophobic attitudes in "migrant" versus "German" pupils in Berlin, commissioned by the biggest gay organization, funded by the state, and disseminated by the mainstream media, which renders scientific and respectable what by then everybody knows: that "migrants" are *more homophobic* than "Germans," and that the twain, as the unhyphenable categoric opposition under comparison already suggests, shall never meet (see Haritaworn and Petzen forthcoming for an in-depth historiography).

The Drag Festival is thus but the latest episode of a well-rehearsed drama, which nevertheless launches a new victim-subject onto the stage (see Kapur 2005). As so often with moral panics, one incident leads to another, cramming the archive of violence and anti-violence as far as it will stretch (Gilmore 1999; Sudbury 2006). In addition to producing more victim-subjects, the moral panic about "homophobic Muslims" has served to proliferate hate crime scenes and cases, perpetrator profiles, experts, numbers, actions, action plans, projects, media, policy, and academic texts, along with government funds for more of the same.[4] While homonormative activists have been the main beneficiaries, trans (and radical queer) activists too have joined the stage, with little complication or mutual protest, to co-star in a drama that is characterized by symbiosis and mimesis as much as competition. In summer 2009 the Berlin district of Schöneberg became known as a similarly dangerously "homophobic" and "transphobic" place as neighboring Kreuzberg. Significantly, Schöneberg is home to both the gayborhood and to Frobenstrasse, one of the poorest streets in Berlin, which that summer proved to become a highly productive hate crime scene. Recent migrants from Bulgaria and Romania, many of whom are Roma and/or from the Turkish-speaking minority, live, work, and socialize in the street amidst other people of color with longer histories in the area. The area has long been a site of trans street sex work, and many of the new migrants, both trans women, trans-feminine people, non-trans women, and queer- and straight-identified men, use it to sell sex. Of course migrant sex workers of all gender and sexual identities have experienced all kinds of violence for a long time: from residents who blame them for littered condoms and other signs of chronic disinvestment, from police and other authorities who variously target and exclude them as under-documented migrants and sex workers, and from the utterly unremarkable and uneventful neglect and exploitation to which poor, racialized people and sex workers are regularly subjected. Nevertheless, their lives were long completely uninteresting to queer and trans activists in Berlin. It is arguable that beyond their capacitation as injured victims of hate crime they have largely remained so. Archived as trans sex workers being beaten up by migrant youth gangs, this "event" of violence both fed the moral panic over criminal and violent Muslim youth and accrued value and visibility to more powerful queer and trans positions. In September 2009, a coalition of mainly white trans, mainly non-trans queer of color, and mainly white and non-trans sex work organizations organized a "Smash Transphobia" demo at Frobenstrasse (Siegessäule TV 2009). The demo was visited by mainly white queer and trans activists, most of whom had probably never been to the street before, and would never return thereafter. The speeches, slogans, and posters interpellated a transnormative, protectionist victim-subject of "violence against trans people" or "trans women" and called for policy attention to this hitherto neglected group. While sex work occasionally made it into the speeches, the local context was barely mentioned, and where it was, this again occurred in highly racialized and classed ways:

> "You may be unemployed but this is no excuse" (call through the loudspeaker into the open windows of random residents) .

> "Transphobic people go to hell" (poster held by a white and presumably secular/Christian organizer).

> "This is our street, too!" (slogan at the demo).

Although the event was ostensibly organized for the benefit of migrant trans sex workers, as happens so often, those injured in the event of violence benefited the least from the remedies offered by a traumatized citizenship model. The two biggest gay organizations were not directly involved in either the Drag Festival or the Frobenstrasse organizing, and indeed continue to show no interest in trans people, let alone migrant trans sex workers. However, their long-standing investment in the adjacent gayborhood and ample expertise in racializing homophobia enabled them to swiftly capitalize on the panic. In many ways, the policy attention that resulted from these two spectacles of transphobia fulfilled a long-standing attempt by these organizations, who had authored the first press releases about "homophobic migrants" in the area years earlier, to describe Schöneberg as a dangerous area where (white) gay men live in constant fear of Muslim youth (Haritaworn and Petzen forthcoming). While the bodies that were injured, first in Kreuzberg and then in Frobenstrasse, less than a kilometer away from the office of the Lesbian and Gay Association Germany (LSVD), radically exceeded this binary, the events nevertheless served to consolidate a homonormative constituency and to insert it firmly within urban policies of gentrification, touristification, and securitization. Projects that became possible in their wake include the "Rainbow Protection Circle," an association of local businesses and non-governmental organizations (NGOs) led by the Berlin branch of the LSVD. It was inaugurated in the town hall of Schöneberg in 2010 by the district mayor, who announced that additional police were now allocated in the area specifically for the protection of LGBT people. In November 2011, the LSVD's smaller sister organization Maneo (originally an anti-violence hotline) organized a big international conference entitled *Building a Queer and Tolerant Neighborhood* that explored the "potential benefits and development possibilities" that rainbow neighborhoods like Schöneberg, whose "importance lies in the signal that they can give to city managers that the city is socially open and tolerant" (Maneo 2011). The conference program featured representatives from "metropolitan cities from across the world," and included presentations on gayborhoods such as Chicago's Boystown, San Francisco's Castro, Sydney's Oxford Street, Montreal's Gay Village, and Cape Town's Green Point. According to one report by a visitor from Chicago, it was attended by international diversity officials, law enforcement officers, entrepreneurs, and NGO representatives (*Windy City Times* 2011). It is also said to have included scholars from more radical generations of queer space activism.

The anti-transphobia organizing around violence in Berlin thus points to multiple genealogies and complicities in gay, queer, and trans organizing around space, violence, and visibility that deserve careful unpacking. We would like to resist the easy ascription of these complicities to neoliberalism. Rather, the homonormative narrative of the creative-class member, who ventures into hitherto ungentrifiable territory and performs himself as a productive citizen and consumer *in contrast to those whose unproductiveness and excessive reproductiveness mark their intimacies as disposable in the current diversity regime*, is sprouting transgressive offshoots that equally need addressing.[5] Thus, as argued by Haritaworn (2011), the degenerate, regenerating ghetto enables a trans subject to emerge whose colorful difference, in a context which increasingly lets go of its people of color, for the first time becomes a pleasant sight. This is also brought home by the fact that white trans activists in Berlin did manage to institutionalize the new space won in the anti/violence archive. In November 2009, a few months after the demo at Frobenstrasse, TDOR—a fairly new and until then more DIY event in Berlin—likewise took place in the town hall of Schöneberg.[6] Co-organized by the same predominantly non-trans queer of color group that had collaborated with white trans activists on the Smash Transphobia demo, it nevertheless remained an overwhelmingly white event, and it closely followed the U.S. formula of remembrance (Lamble 2008; Bhanji forthcoming). Most of these dead people were trans people of color from both the Global North and the Global South, whose exotic presence in this overwhelmingly white German trans and ally space was brought home by the chuckles that some of their badly pronounced names evoked. "Their" deaths were not in vain, one of the speakers is said to have stated: "they" made it possible for "us" to come together today. Among "them" was Tyra Hunter.[7] Like so many of its globalizing predecessors, the Berlin TDOR thus incited a trans community into life whose vitality depends upon the ghosting of poor trans people, trans people of color, and trans people in the Global South.

Who benefits from these dominant methodologies of violence and anti-violence? Instead of those most in need of survival, the circulation of trans people of color in their afterlife accrues value to a newly professionalizing and institutionalizing class of experts whose lives could not be further removed from those they are professing to help. Immobilized in life, and barred from spaces designated as white (the good life, the Global North, the gentrifying inner city, the university, the trans community), it is in their death that poor and sex working trans people of color are invited back in; it is in death that they suddenly come to matter.

## CONCLUSION

How do Tyra Hunter and other dead trans women of color circulate, and what are the corporeal excesses that constitute their afterlives as raw material for the generation of respectable trans subjects? We have examined this circulation, which adds value through nominal and numeric repetition, as paradoxically giving birth to both the conditions that allow more recognizable trans subjects to mobilize and ascend into life, and to the forces that immobilize subaltern trans lives. The resulting trans vitalities and socialities must be examined transnationally, as bringing trans people into community (both with each other and with a newly sympathetic public) through intensified violence. Thus, we have examined how the ascendant politics are symbiotic with the death-making capacities of the market and the state, and cannibalistic upon the lives of other sexually and gender non-conforming people. What would a trans politics and theory look like that refuses such "murderous inclusion" (see Haritaworn, Kuntsman and Posocco forthcoming)? While radical formulations of violence and anti-violence have tended to focus on colonial feminist and homonormative subjects, dominant trans subjects are rarely held accountable and remain awkwardly frozen in positions of analogy and equivalency with other "diversely diverse" locations. Maybe it is time to push our accounts of violence and anti-violence beyond limited formulas such as "race, gender, and class," in both their intersectional and post-identitarian formulations. We certainly have examples of such politics to build on (Gossett, this volume).

## NOTES

1. These activations are, of course, terrains of struggle and open to contestation and reappropriation. Particularly in contexts where decolonial struggles have been won, events like TDOR can reflect broader critical agendas, as was the case with the memorial for Sanesha Stewart by Queers for Economic Justice, Audre Lorde Project, and others in 2008, and for Nizah Morris in Philadelphia in 2002 (Che Gossett, personal communication with Jin November 17, 2011.)
2. Grant, Jaime M., Lisa A. Mottet, Justin Tanis, Jack Harrison, Jody L. Herman, and Mara Keisling (2011). *Injustice at Every Turn: A Report of the National Transgender Discrimination Survey, Executive Summary*. Washington, D.C.: National Center for Transgender Equality and National Gay and Lesbian Task Force.

3. The "event" was heavily contested. Thus, one of the "beaten up" trans people described it as a mutually escalating drunken traffic altercation whose adversaries were conspicuously blond.
4. For example, see the racialized homophobia study by psychologist Simon (2008); the special issue on the Drag Festival aftermath in the left-wing weekly *Jungle World* (2008); and the homophobia and sexual diversity action plans by the red-red government (SPD/Die Linke 2009) and the Green opposition (Bündnis 90/Die Grünen 2009). See Haritaworn and Petzen (forthcoming) for a careful mapping of this proliferation.
5. For critiques of queer gentrification, see Manalansan (2005); Fierce (2008); Hanhardt (2008); and Decolonize Queer (2011).
6. Jin would like to credit another trans of color activist in Berlin, who would prefer not to be named, for sharing his brilliant analyses of homo- and trans-whiteness in Berlin.
7. For example, Tyra Hunter appears twice on the list and images of "remembered" trans people on Berlin TDOR's myspace page: http://www.myspace.com/TDoR#{%22ImageId%22%3A18354015}, http://www.myspace.com/TDoR#!/tdor/photos/4495414 accessed January 12, 2012.

## WORKS CITED

Agathangelou, Anna, Morgan Bassichis, and Tamara Spira (2008). "Intimate Investments: Homonormativity, Global Lockdown and the Seductions of Empire." *Radical History Review* 100, 120–143.

Ahmed, Sara (2004). *The Cultural Politics of Emotion*. Edinburgh: Edinburgh University Press.

Aliyyah I. Abdur-Rahman (2006). "'The Strangest Freaks of Despotism': Queer Sexuality in Antebellum African American Slave Narratives," *African American Review* 40(2): 223–237.

Anna (2011) "Black and Transgendered: Double the Suffering?" *DCentric*, 9 February 2011. http://dcentric.wamu.org/2011/02/black-and-transgendered-double-the-suffering/index.html. Accessed September 25, 2012.

Berlant, Lauren (2000). "The Subject of True Feeling: Pain, Privacy and Politics." In S. Ahmed, J. Kilby, C. Lury, M. McNeil, and B. Skeggs (eds), *Transformations: Thinking Through Feminism*, 33–47. London: Routledge.

Bhanji, Nael (forthcoming). *Trans Necropolitics* (working title). PhD thesis, Women's, Gender and Sexuality Studies Department, York University.

Brown, Wendy (1993). "Wounded Attachments." *Political Theory* 21: 3, 390–410.

Decolonize Queer (2011). "From Gay Pride to White Pride? Why Marching on East London is Racist." *Decolonize Queer*, http://www.decolonizequeer.org/?p=1 (accessed January 1, 2012).

Fierce (2008). "LGBTQ Youth Fight for a S.P.O.T. on Pier 40." *Fierce*, September 15, http://fiercenyc.org/media/docs/3202_PublicHearingPressRelease.pdf (accessed February 19, 2009).

Foucault, Michel [1978] (2004). *The Birth of Biopolitics: Lectures at the Collège de France 1978–1979*. London: Palgrave.

Gilmore, Ruth Wilson (1999). "Globalisation and US Prison Growth: From Military Keynesianism to Post-Keynesian Militarism." *Race and Class* 40: 2–3, 171–188.

Giroux, Henry (2006). "Reading Hurricane Katrina: Race, Class, and the Biopolitics of Disposability." *College Literature* 33: 3, 171–196.

Grewal, Inderpal and Caren Kaplan (2001). "Global Identities: Theorizing Transnational Studies of Sexuality." *GLQ: A Journal of Lesbian and Gay Studies* 7: 4, 663–679.

Gumbs, Alexis Pauline (2010). *We Can Learn to Mother Ourselves: The Queer Survival of Black Feminism*. Dissertation, dukespace.lib.duke.edu (accessed June 1, 2011).

Hanhardt, Christina B. (2008). "Butterflies, Whistles, and Fists: Gay Safe Streets Patrols and the New Gay Ghetto, 1976–1981." *Radical History Review* 100, 61–85.

Haritaworn, Jin (2011). "Colorful Bodies in the *Multiklti* Metropolis: Trans Vitality, Victimology and the Berlin Hate Crime Debate." In Trystan Cotto (ed.), *Transgender Migrations: Bodies, Borders, and the (Geo)politics of Gender Trans-ing*, 11–31. New York: Routledge.

Haritaworn, Jin (2005). "Queerer als wir? Rassismus, Transphobie, Queer-Theory" (Queerer than us? Racism, Transphobia, Queer Theory). In E. Yekani Haschemi and B. Michaelis (eds.), *Queering The Humanities*, 216–238. Berlin: Querverlag.

Haritaworn, Jin (2008). "Loyal Repetitions of the Nation: Gay Assimilation and the 'War on Terror,'" *DarkMatter*, No. 3: Special Issue on Postcolonial Sexuality. http://www.darkmatter101.org/site/2008/05/02/loyal-repetitions-of-the-nation-gay-assimilation-and-the-war-on-terror/

Haritaworn, Jin and Jennifer Petzen (forthcoming). "Invented Traditions" (working title), in C. Flood and S. Hutchings et al. (eds.), *Islam in its International Context: Comparative Perspectives*. Cambridge: Cambridge Scholars Press.

Haritaworn, Jin, Adi Kuntsman, and Silvia Posocco (eds.) (forthcoming). *Queer Necropolitics*, book project (in review).

Holland, Sharon (2000). *Raising the Dead: Readings of Death and (Black) Subjectivity*. Durham, NC: Duke University Press.

Juang, Richard (2006). "Transgendering the Politics of Recognition", in Susan Stryker and Stephen Whittle, *The Transgender Studies Reader*. New York: Routledge, 2006.

*Jungle World* (2008). "Bissu schwül oder was?" (You gay or wha'?). Special issue, 26 June 2008.

Kapur, Ratna (2005). "The Tragedy of Victimisation Rhetoric: Resurrecting the 'Native' Subject in International/ Postcolonial Feminist Legal Rhetorics." In *Erotic Justice: Postcolonialism, Subjects and Rights*, 95–136. London: Glass House Press.

Lamble, Sarah (2008). "Retelling Racialized Violence, Remaking White Innocence: The Politics of Interlocking Oppressions in Transgender Day of Remembrance." *Sexuality Research and Social Policy: Journal of NSRC* 5: 1, 24–42.

Levi, Jennifer (n.d.) Statement before the Joint Committee on Judiciary in Support of Raised Bill No. 5723, An Act Concerning Discrimination. Gay and Lesbian Alliance Against Defamation (GLAAD). http://www.glad. org/uploads/docs/advocacy/Testimony_CT_Transgender_2008_03_18.pdf.

Manalansan, Martin F. IV (2005). "Race, Violence, and Neoliberal Spatial Politics in the Global City." *Social Text* 23: 3–4, 141–155.

Maneo (2011). "The International Maneo Conference 2011." http://www.maneo.de/en/maneo-konferenz.html (accessed January 6, 2012).

Mbembe, Achille (2003). "Necropolitics." *Public Culture* 15: 1, 11–40.

Mirzeoff, Nicholas (2009). "The Sea and the Land: Biopower and Visuality from Slavery to Katrina." *Culture, Theory and Critique* 50: 2, 289–305.

Namaste, Ki (1996). "Tragic Misreadings: Queer Theory's Erasure of Transgender Subjectivity." In B. Beemyn and M. Eliason (eds.), *Queer Studies: A Lesbian, Gay, Bisexual, and Transgender Anthology*, 183–203. New York: New York University Press.

Prosser, Jay (1998). *Second Skins: The Body Narratives of Transsexuality*, New York: Columbia University Press. 1998, Second Skins: The Body Narratives of Transsexuality, (New York: Columbia University Press).

Puar, Jasbir (2007). *Terrorist Assemblages: Homonationalism in Queer Times*. Durham, NC: Duke University Press.

Rivera, Sylvia (2002). "Queens in Exile: The Forgotten Ones." In J. Nestle, C. Howell and R. Wilchins (eds.), *Genderqueer*, 67–85. Los Angeles, CA: Allyson Books.

Siegessäule TV (2009). "Transphobe Gewalt im Berliner Frobenkiez–Solidarität mit den Sexarbeiterinnen." http://www.youtube.com/watch?v=YT_krTlkBzQ&feature=related (accessed December 23, 2011).

Simon, Bernd (2008). "Einstellungen zur Homosexualität: Ausprägungen und psychologische Korrelate bei Jugendlichen mit und ohne Migrationshintergrund (ehemalige UdSSR und Türkei)." *Zeitschrift für Entwicklungspsychologie und Pädagogische Psychologie* 40, 87–99.

Slevin, Peter (1998)."Suit Over Bias in Rescue Goes to Trial; Attorney for Dead Transvestite's Mother Says D.C. Workers Mocked, Mistreated Son", *Washington Post Metro*, November 11, B04.

Spade, Dean (2003). "Remarks at Transecting the Academy Conference, Race and Ethnic Studies Panel," *Make Zine*. http://www.makezine.org/transecting.html (accessed 13 September 2012).

Spade, Dean (2009). "Keynote Address: Trans Law and Politics on a Neoliberal Landscape." *Temple Political and Civil Rights Law Review* 18: 2, 353–373.

SPD/Die Linke (2009). *Initiative Berlin tritt ein für Selbstbestimmung und Akzeptanz sexueller Vielfalt*. http://www. spdfraktion-berlin.de/var/files/pdfzumthema/antrag_sexuelle_vielfalt.pdf (accessed February 15, 2009).

Sudbury, Julia (2006). "Rethinking Antiviolence Strategies: Lessons from the Black Women's Movement in Britain." In Incite! (eds.), *Color of Violence: The Incite! Anthology*, 13–24. Cambridge, MA: South End Press.

*Windy City Times* (2011). "International MANEO-Conference Looked at LGBT Neighborhoods Worldwide, Chicago Viewed as Model for Developing, Sustaining LGBT Neighborhoods." http://www. windycitymediagroup.com/gay/lesbian/news/ARTICLE.php?AID=35180 (accessed January 6, 2012).

# II

## *MAKING TRANS-CULTURE(S): TEXTS, PERFORMANCES, ARTIFACTS*

# 6

# *"The White to Be Angry"*
## Vaginal Davis's Terrorist Drag

José Esteban Muñoz

THIS CLASSIC TEXT BY PERFORMANCE STUDIES SCHOLAR JOSÉ ESTEBAN MUÑOZ, about drag superstar Vaginal Creme Davis, is perhaps even more relevant now, with its prescient attention to the trope of terrorism, than when it was originally published in *Social Text* in 1997, as part of the first collection of essays within queer theory to grapple with the new problematics introduced by transgender issues. Muñoz uses Davis's productively off-kilter satirization of white supremacist terrorism, brilliant aesthetic reworkings of Black Power militancy, postmodern glosses on gay male drag performance, and unironic embrace of the aggressive urgency of urban punk subcultures to exemplify his influential concept of disidentification. Muñoz defines disidentification as "a performative mode of tactical recognition that various minoritarian subjects employ in an effort to resist the oppressive and normalizing discourse of dominant ideology;" it is a practice that refuses the interpellating call of ideology to become a fixed subject within a state apparatus. Disidentificatory practices such as Davis's function instead, for Muñoz, as third terms by means of which queer selves create the option of just "saying no" to the dead-end dichotomy of, on the one hand, a melancholy surrender to normativity, or, on the other hand, a simplistic anti-normative stance. They allow us to begin imagining and enacting new relations to the social, and to envision alternative futures. The article is noteworthy as well for the early gesture it makes toward the work of Felix Guattari, which has yet to command the full attention within Anglophone queer and transgender studies that it richly deserves.

Nineteen eighty saw the debut of one of the L.A. punk scene's most critically acclaimed albums, the band X's *Los Angeles*. X was fronted by John Doe and Exene Cervenka, who were described by one writer as "poetry workshop types"[1] and who had recently migrated to Los Angeles from the East Coast. They used the occasion of their first album to describe the effect that the West Coast city had on its white denizens. The album's title track, "Los Angeles," narrates the story of a white female protagonist who had to leave Los Angeles because she started to hate "every nigger and Jew, every Mexican who gave her a lot of shit, every homosexual and the idle rich." Today, the song reads for me like a fairly standard tale of white flight from the multiethnic metropolis. Yet I can't pretend to have had access to this reading back then, since I had no contexts or reading skills for any such interpretation.

Contemplating these lyrics today leaves me with a disturbed feeling. When I was a teenager growing up in South Florida, X occupied the hallowed position of favorite band. As I attempt to situate my relation to this song and my own developmental history, I remember what X meant to me back then. Within the hermetic Cuban American community I came of age in, punk rock was not yet the almost-routine route of individuation and resistance that it is today. Back then it was the only

*avant-garde to a site of resistance*

avant-garde that I knew, the only cultural critique of normative aesthetics available to me. Yet there was a way in which I was able to escape the song's interpellating call. Though queerness was already a powerful polarity in my life, and the hissing pronunciation of "Mexican" that the song produced felt very much like the epithet "spic," with which I had a great deal of experience, I somehow found a way to resist these identifications. The luxury of hindsight lets me understand that I needed X and the possibility of subculture it promised at that moment to withstand the identity-eroding effects of normativity. I was able to enact a certain misrecognition that let me imagine myself as something other than queer or racialized. But such a misrecognition demands a certain toll. The toll is one that subjects who attempt to identify with and assimilate to dominant ideologies pay every day of their lives. The price of the ticket is this: to find self within the dominant public sphere, we need to deny self. The contradictory subjectivity one is left with is not just the fragmentary subjectivity of some unspecified postmodern condition; instead, it is the story of the minoritarian subject within the majoritarian public sphere. Fortunately, this story does not end at this difficult point, this juncture of painful contradiction. Sometimes misrecognition can be *tactical.* Identification itself can also be manipulated and worked in ways that promise narratives of self that surpass the limits prescribed by dominant culture. → *redefining self.*

*CRUCIAL*

*denial of self to find self*

In this paper I will discuss the cultural work of an artist who came of age within the very same L.A. punk scene that produced X. The L.A. punk scene worked very hard to whitewash and straighten its image. While many people of color and queers were part of this cultural movement, they often remained closeted in the scene's early days. The artist whose work I will be discussing in this paper came of age in that scene and managed to resist its whitewashing and heteronormative protocols.

The work of drag superstar Vaginal Creme Davis, or, as she sometimes prefers to be called, Dr. Davis, spans several cultural production genres. It also appropriates, terroristically, both dominant culture and different subcultural movements. Davis first rose to prominence in the L.A. punk scene through her infamous zine *Fertile Latoya Jackson* and through her performances at punk shows with her Supremes-like backup singers, the Afro Sisters. *Fertile Latoya Jackson's* first incarnation was as a print zine that presented scandalous celebrity gossip. The zine was reminiscent of *Hollywood Babylon,* Kenneth Anger's two-volume tell-all history of the movie industry and the star system's degeneracy. The hand-stapled zine eventually evolved into a video magazine. At the same time as the zine became a global subcultural happening, Davis's performances in and around the L.A. punk scene, both with the Afro Sisters and solo, became semilegendary. She went on to translate her performance madness to video, starring in various productions that include *Dot* (1994), her tribute to Dorothy Parker's acerbic wit and alcoholism; *VooDoo Williamson: The Dona of Dance* (1995), her celebration of modern dance and its doyennes; and *Designy Living* (1995), a tribute to Noel Coward's *Design for Living* and Godard's *Masculin et Feminine.*

According to Davis's own self-generated legend, her existence is the result of an illicit encounter between her then forty-five-year-old African American mother and her then twenty-one-year-old Mexican American father. Davis has often reported that her parents only met once, when she was conceived under a table during a Ray Charles concert at the Hollywood Palladium in the early 1960s.

While her work with the Afro Sisters and much of her zine work deal with issues of blackness, Davis explores her Chicana heritage with another one of her musical groups, ¡Cholita!, a band that is billed as the female Menudo. This band consists of both men and women in teenage Chicana drag who sing Latin American bubblegum pop songs with titles like *"Chicas de hoy"* ["Girls of today"]. ¡Cholita! and Davis's other bands all produce socially interrogative performances that complicate any easy understanding of race or ethnicity within the social matrix. Performance is used by these theatrical musical groups to, borrowing a phrase from George Lipsitz, "rehearse identities"[2] that

*rehearse toxic identities*

have been rendered toxic within the dominant public sphere but are, through Davis's fantastic and farcical performance, restructured (yet not cleansed) so they present newly imagined notions of the self and the social. This paper focuses on the performance work done through *The White to Be Angry*, a live show and a compact disc produced by one of Davis's other subculturally acclaimed musical groups, Pedro, Muriel, and Esther. (Often referred to as PME, the band is named after a cross section of people that Davis met when waiting for a bus. Pedro was a young Latino who worked at a fast-food chain, and Muriel and Esther were two senior citizens.) This essay's first section will consider both the live performance and the CD. The issue of "passing" and its specific relation to what I am calling the cultural politics of *disidentification* will also be interrogated. I will pursue this question of "passing" in relation to both mainstream drag and a queerer modality of performance, which I will be calling Davis's *terrorist drag*. In the paper's final section I will consider Davis's relation to the discourse of "antigay."

*TERRORIST DRAG, ANTIGAY*

## WHO'S THAT GIRL?

Disidentification is a performative mode of tactical recognition that various minoritarian subjects employ in an effort to resist the oppressive and normalizing discourse of dominant ideology. Disidentification resists the interpellating call of ideology that fixes a subject within the state power apparatus. It is a reformatting of self within the social, a third term that resists the binary of identification and counteridentification. Counteridentification often, through the very routinized workings of its denouncement of dominant discourse, reinstates that same discourse. In an interview in the magazine *aRude*, Davis offers one of the most lucid explications of a modality of performance that I call *disidentificatory*. Davis responds to the question "How did you acquire the name Vaginal Davis?" with a particularly elucidating rant:

*Not just counterid.*

> It came from Angela Davis—I named myself as a salute to her because I was really into the whole late '60's and early '70's militant Black era. When you come home from the inner city and you're Black you go through a stage when you try to fit the dominant culture, you kinda want to be white at first—it would be easier if you were White. Everything that's negrified or Black—you don't want to be associated with that. That's what I call the snow period—I just felt like if I had some cheap white boyfriend, my life could be perfect and I could be some treasured thing. I could feel myself projected through some White person, and have all the privileges that white people get—validation through association.[3]

The "snow period" Davis describes corresponds to the assimilationist option that minoritarian subjects often choose. Though sanctioned and encouraged by the dominant culture, the snow period is not a viable option for people of color. More often than not, snow melts in the hands of the subject who attempts to acquire privilege through associations (be they erotic, emotional, or both) with whites. Davis goes on to describe her next phase:

> Then there was a conscious shift, being that I was the first one in my family to go to college—I got militant. That's when I started reading about Angela and the Panthers, and that's when Vaginal emerged as a filtering of Angela through humor. That led to my early 1980's acapella performance entity, Vaginal Davis and the Afro Sisters (who were two white girls with afro wigs). We did a show called "we're taking over" where we portrayed the Sexualese Liberation Front which decides to kidnap all the heads of white corporate America so we could put big black dildos up their lily white buttholes and hold them for ransom. It really freaked out a lot of the middle class post-punk crowd—they didn't get the campy element of it but I didn't really care.[4]

Thus the punk rock drag diva elucidates a stage or temporal space where the person of color's consciousness turns to her or his community after an immersion in white culture and education. The ultramilitant phase that Davis describes is a powerful counteridentification with the dominant culture. At the same time, though, Davis's queer sexuality, her queerness *and* effeminacy, kept her from fully accessing Black Power militancy. Unable to pass as heterosexual black militant through simple counteridentification, Vaginal Davis instead disidentified with Black Power by selecting Angela and *not* the Panthers as a site of self-fashioning and political formation. Davis's deployment of disidentification demonstrates that it is, to employ Kimberlé Crenshaw's term, an *intersectional strategy*.[5] *Intersectionality* insists on a critical hermeneutics that registers the copresence of sexuality, race, class, gender, and other identity differentials as particular components that exist simultaneously with each other. Vintage Black Power discourse contained many homophobic and masculinist elements that were toxic to queer and feminist subjects. Davis used parody and pastiche to remake Black Power, opening it up via disidentification to a self that is simultaneously black and queer. (Elsewhere, with her group ¡Cholita!, she performs a similar disidentification with Latina/o popular culture. As Graciela Grejalva, she is not an oversexed songstress, but instead a teenage Latina singing sappy bubblegum pop.)

Davis productively extends her disidentificatory strategy to her engagement with the performative practice of drag. With the advent of the mass commercialization of drag—evident in suburban multiplexes, which program such films as *To Wong Foo, Thanks for Everything, Julie Newmar* and *The Bird Cage,* or in VH1's broadcasts of RuPaul's talk show—it seems especially important at this point to distinguish different modalities of drag. Commercial drag presents a sanitized and desexualized queer subject for mass consumption, representing a certain strand of integrationist liberal pluralism. The sanitized queen is meant to be enjoyed as an entertainer who will hopefully lead to social understanding and tolerance. Unfortunately, this boom in filmic and televisual drag has had no impact on hate legislation put forth by the New Right or on homophobic violence on the nation's streets. Indeed, I want to suggest that this "boom" in drag helps one understand that a liberal-pluralist mode of political strategizing only eventuates a certain absorption, but nothing like a productive engagement, with difference. So while RuPaul, for example, hosts a talk show on VH1, one only need click the remote control to hear about the new defense-of-marriage legislation that "protects" *the* family by outlawing gay marriage. Indeed, the erosion of gay civil rights is simultaneous with the advent of higher degrees of queer visibility in the mainstream media.

But while corporate-sponsored drag has to some degree become incorporated within the dominant culture, there is also a queerer modality of drag that is performed by queer-identified drag artists in spaces of queer consumption. Felix Guattari, in a discussion of the theatrical group the Mirabelles, explains the potential political power of drag:

> The Mirabelles are experimenting with a new type of militant theater, a theater separate from an explanatory language and long tirades of good intentions, for example, on gay liberation. They resort to drag, song, mime, dance, etc., not as different ways of illustrating a theme, to "change the ideas" of spectators, but in order to trouble them, to stir up uncertain desire-zones that they always more or less refuse to explore. The question is no longer to know whether one will play feminine against masculine or the reverse, but to make bodies, all bodies, break away from the representations and restraints on the "social body."[6]

Guattari's take on the Mirabelles, specifically his appraisal of the political performance of drag, assists in the project of further evaluating the effects of queer drag. I don't simply want to assign one set of drag strategies and practices the title of "bad" drag and the other "good." But I do wish to emphasize the ways in which Davis's *terroristic drag* "stir[s] up uncertain desire[s]" and enables subjects to imagine a way of "break[ing] away from the . . . restraints on the 'social body,'" while sanitized corporate drag and even traditional gay drag is unable to achieve such effects. Davis's political drag is about creating an uneasiness in desire, which works to confound and subvert the social fabric. The "social body" that Guattari discusses is amazingly elastic and able to accommodate scripts on gay liberation. Drag like Davis's, however, is not easily enfolded in that social fabric because of the complexity of its intersectional nature.

There is a great diversity within drag. Julian Fleisher's *Drag Queens of New York: An Illustrated Field Guide* surveys underground drag and differentiates two dominant styles, "glamour" and "clown."[7] New York drag queens like Candis Cayne or Girlina, whose drag is relatively "real,"[8] rate high on the glamour meter. Other queens like Varla Jean Merman (who bills herself as the love child of Ethel Merman and Ernest Borgnine) and Miss Understood are representative of the over-the-top parody style of clown drag. Many famous queens, like Wigstock impresario and mad genius The "Lady" Bunny, appear squarely in the middle of Fleisher's scale.[9] On first glance Vaginal, who is in no way invoking glamour or "realness" and most certainly doesn't *pass* (in a direct sense of the word), seems to be on the side of clown drag. I want to complicate this system of evaluation and attempt a more nuanced appraisal of Vaginal Davis's style.

*passing in drag*

Vaginal Davis's drag, while comic and even hilarious, should not be dismissed as just clowning around. Her uses of humor and parody function as disidentificatory strategies whose effect on the dominant public sphere is that of a counterpublic terrorism. At the center of all of Davis's cultural productions is a radical impulse toward cultural critique. It is a critique that, according to the artist, has often escaped two groups who comprise some of drag's most avid supporters: academics and other drag queens.

> I was parodying a lot of different things. But it wasn't an intellectual-type of thing—it was innate. A lot of academics and intellectuals dismissed it because it wasn't smart enough—it was too homey, a little too country. And gay drag queens hated me. They didn't understand it. I wasn't really trying to alter myself to look like a real woman. I didn't wear false eyelashes or fake breasts. It wasn't about the realness of traditional drag—the perfect flawless make-up. I just put on a little lipstick, a little eye shadow and a wig and went out there.[10]

*"smart enough"*

It is the innateness, the homeyness, and the countryness of Davis's style that draw this particular academic to the artist's work. I understand these characteristics as components of the artist's guerrilla style, a style that functions as a ground-level cultural terrorism that fiercely skewers both straight culture and reactionary components of gay culture. I would also like to link these key words—*innateness, homeyness,* and *countryness*—that Davis calls upon with a key word from the work of Antonio Gramsci that seems to be a partial cognate of these other terms: *organic.* Gramsci attempted to both demystify the role of the intellectual and, at the same time, reassert the significance of the intellectual's role to a social movement. He explained that "Every social group, coming into existence on the original terrain of an essential function, creates together with itself, organically, one or more strata of intellectuals which give it homogeneity and an awareness of its own function not only in the economic but also in the social and political fields."[11] Davis certainly worked to bolster and cohere the L.A. punk scene, giving it a more significant "homogeneity"[12] and "awareness." At the same time, her work constituted a critique of that community's whiteness. In this way, it participated in Gramsci's project of extending the scope of Marxist analysis to look beyond class as the ultimate social division and consider blocs. Blocs are, in the words of John Fiske, "alliance[s] of social forces formed to promote common social interests as they can be brought together in particular historical conditions."[13] The Gramscian notion of bloc formation emphasizes the centrality of class relations in any critical analysis, while not diminishing the importance of other

*cultural terrorism*

*hegemony theory*

*bloc?*

*[handwritten top margin: It doesn't accomplish everything she needs.    hardcore w/ gay reach]*

*[handwritten left margin: Organic Intellectual]*

cultural struggles. In the lifeworld of mostly straight white punks, Davis had, as a black gay man, a strongly disidentificatory role within that community. I will suggest that her disidentifications with social blocs are productive interventions in which politics are destabilized, permitting her to come into the role of "organic intellectual." While Davis did and did not belong to the scene, she nonetheless forged a place for herself that is not *a place*, but instead the still important *position* of intellectual.

A reading of one of Davis's spin-off projects, *The White to Be Angry,* a live show and CD by her hard-core/speed metal band, Pedro, Muriel, and Esther, will ground this consideration of Vaginal Davis as organic intellectual. While I focus on this one aspect of her oeuvre, it should nonetheless be noted that my claim for her as organic intellectual has a great deal to do with the wide variety of public performances and discourses she employs. Davis disseminates her cultural critique through multiple channels of publicity: independent video, zines, public access programming, performance art, anthologized short fiction, bar drag, the L.A. punk-rock club Sucker (for which she is a weekly hostess and impresario), and three different bands (PME and ¡Cholita! as well as the semi-mythical Black Fag, a group that parodies famous North American punk band Black Flag). In the PME project she employs a modality of drag that is neither glamorous nor strictly comedic. Her drag is a terroristic send-up of masculinity and white supremacy. Its focus and pitch are political parody and critique, anchored in her very particular homey-organic style and humor.

*[handwritten left margin: this is amazing]*

*[handwritten right margin: → this is empirical to my argument point M (Oscar)]*

## "THE WHITE TO BE ANGRY" AND PASSING

It is about 1:30 in the morning at Squeezebox, a modish queercore night at a bar in lower Manhattan. It is a warm June evening, and PME's show was supposed to start at midnight. I noticed the band's easily identifiable lead singer rush in at about 12:30, so I had no expectation of the show beginning before 1:00. I while away the time by watching thin and pale go-go boys and girls dancing on the bars. The boys are not the beefy, pumped-up white and Latino muscle boys of Chelsea. This, after all, is way downtown where queer style is decidedly different from the ultramasculine muscle drag of Chelsea. Still, the crowd here is extremely white, and Vaginal Davis's black six-foot-six-inch frame towers over the sea of white post-punk club goers.

*[handwritten: holy shit]*

Before I know it Miss Guy, a drag performer who exudes the visual style of the "white trash" Southern California punk waif,[14] stops spinning her classic eighties retro-rock, punk, and new wave discs. Then the Mistress Formika, the striking leather-clad Latina drag queen and hostess of the club, announces the band. I am positioned in the front row, to the left of the stage. I watch a figure whom I identify as Davis rush by me and mount the stage.

*[handwritten left margin: plurality of deauthorized identities]*

At this point, a clarification is necessary. Vaginal is something like the central performance persona that the artist I am discussing uses, but it is certainly not the only one. She is also the Most High Rev'rend Saint Salida Tate, an evangelical church woman who preaches "Fornication, no! Theocracy, yes!"; Buster Butone, one of her boy drag numbers who is a bit of a gangsta and womanizer; and Kayle Hilliard, a professional pseudonym that the artist employed when she worked as an administrator at UCLA.[15] These are just a few of the artist's identities; I have yet to catalog them all.

The identity I will see tonight is a new one for me. Davis is once again in boy drag, standing on stage in military fatigues, including camouflage pants, jacket, T-shirt, and hat. The look is capped off by a long gray beard, reminiscent of the beards worn by the 1980s Texas rocker band Z Z Top. Clarence introduces himself. During the monologue we hear Vaginal's high-pitched voice explain how she finds white supremacist militiamen to be *really hot,* so hot that she herself has had a race and gender reassignment and is now Clarence. Clarence is the artist's own object of affection. Her voice drops as she inhabits the site of her object of desire and identifications. She imitates and becomes the object of her desire. The ambivalent circuits of cross-racial desire are thematized and contained in one body. This particular star-crossed coupling, black queen and white supremacist, might suggest masochism on the part of the person of color, yet such a reading would be too facile. Instead, the work done by this performance of illicit desire for the "bad" object, the toxic force, should be considered an active disidentification with strictures against cross-racial desire in communities of color and the specters of miscegenation that haunt white sexuality. The parodic performance works on Freudian distinctions between desire and identification; the "to be or to have" binary is queered and disrupted.

When the performer's voice drops and thickens, it is clear that Clarence now has the mike. He congratulates himself on his own woodsy militiaman masculinity, boasting about how great it feels to be white, male, and straight. He launches into his first number, a cut off the CD *Sawed Off Shotgun*. The song is Clarence's theme:

> I don't need a 'zooka
> Or a Ms. 38
> I feel safer in New York
> Than I do in L.A.
>
> You keep your flame thrower
> My shotgun is prettier
>
> Sawed off shot gun
> Sawed off
> Shotgun
>
> My shot gun is so warm it
> Keeps me safe in the city
> I need it at the ATM
> Or when I'm looking purdy
> In its convenient carrying case
> Graven, initialed on the face
> Sawed off shot gun
> Sawed off
> Shotgun
> Yeah . . . wow!

*[handwritten margin note: militancy, terrorism]*

*[handwritten margin note: Abnormal performativity]*

The singer adopts what is a typical butch, hard-core stance while performing the song. The microphone is pulled close to his face, and he bellows into it. This performance of butch masculinity complements the performance of militiaman identity. The song functions as an illustration of a particular mode of white male anxiety that feeds ultra-right-wing movements like militias and that is endemic to embattled straight white masculinity in urban multiethnic spaces like Los Angeles. The fear of an urban landscape populated by undesirable minorities is especially pronounced at privileged sites of consumerist interaction like the ATM, a public site where elites in the cityscape access capital as the lower classes stand witnesses to these mechanical transactions that punctuate class hierarchies. Through her performance of Clarence, Vaginal inhabits the image of the paranoid and embattled white male in the multiethnic city. The performer begins to subtly undermine the gender cohesion of this cultural type (a gender archetype that is always figured as heteronormative), the embattled white man in the multiethnic metropolis, by alluding to the love of "purdy" and "prettier" weapons. The eroticizing of the weapon in so overt a fashion reveals the queer specter that haunts such "impenetrable" heterosexualities. Clarence needs his gun because it "is so warm" that it keeps him "safe in the city" that he no longer feels safe in, a city where growing populations of Asians, African Americans, and Latinos pose a threat to the white majority.

Clarence is a disidentification with militiaman masculinity—not merely a counteridentification that rejects the militiaman, but a *tactical misrecognition* that consciously views the self as a militiaman. This performance is also obviously not about passing inasmuch as the whiteface makeup that the artist uses looks nothing like real white skin. Clarence has as much of a chance passing as white as Vaginal has passing as female. Rather, this disidentification works as an *interiorized passing*. The interior pass is a disidentification and tactical misrecognition of self. Aspects of the self that are toxic to the militiaman—blackness, gayness, and transvestism—are grafted on this particularly militaristic script of masculinity. The performer, through the role of Clarence, inhabits and undermines the militiaman with a fierce sense of parody.

But Davis's disidentifications are not limited to engagements with figures of white supremacy. In a similar style Clarence, during one of his other live numbers, disidentifies with the popular press image of the pathological homosexual killer. The song "Homosexual Is Criminal" tells this story:

> A homosexual
> Is a criminal
> I'm a sociopath, a pathological liar
> Bring your children near me
> I'll make them walk through the fire
>
> I have killed before and I will kill again
> You can tell my friend by my Satanic grin
> A homosexual is a criminal
>
> A homosexual is a criminal
>
> I'll eat you limb from limb
> I'll tear your heart apart
>
> Open the Frigidaire
> There'll be your body parts
> I'm gonna slit your click
> Though you don't want me to
> Bite it off real quick
> Salt'n peppa it too.

At this point in the live performance, about halfway through the number, Davis has removed the long gray beard, the jacket, and the cap. A striptease has begun. At this point Clarence starts to be undone and Davis begins to reappear. She has begun to interact lasciviously with the other members of her band. She gropes her guitarist and bass players as she cruises the audience. She is becoming queer, and as she does so she begins to perform homophobia. This public performance of homophobia indexes the specters of Jeffrey Dahmer, John Wayne Gacy, and an entire pantheon of homosexual killers. The performance magnifies images from the homophobic popular imaginary. Davis is once again inhabiting phobic images with a parodic and cutting difference. In fact, while many sectors of gay communities eschew negative images, Davis instead explodes them by inhabiting them with a difference. By becoming the serial killer, whose psychological profile is almost always white, Vaginal Davis disarticulates not only the onus of performing the positive image, which is generally borne by minoritarian subjects, but also the Dahmer paradigm where the white cannibal slaughters gay men of color. The performance of "*becoming* Dahmer" is another mode of hijacking and lampooning whiteness. Drag and minstrelsy are dramatically reconfigured; performance genres that seemed somewhat exhausted and limited are powerfully reinvigorated through Davis's "homey"-style politics.        *"hysterical body" — John Maw*

By the last number Vaginal Davis has fully reemerged, and she is wearing a military fatigue baby-doll nightie. She is still screaming and writhing on the stage, and she is soaked in rock'n'roll sweat. The Clarence persona has disintegrated. *Long live the queen.* During an interview Davis explained to me that her actual birth name is Clarence.[16] What does it mean that the artist who negotiates various performance personas and uses Vaginal Creme Davis as a sort of base identity reserves her "birth name" for a character who represents the nation's current state of siege? Davis's drag, this reconfigured cross-sex, cross-race minstrelsy, can best be understood as terrorist drag—terrorist    *CRUCIAL* insofar as she is performing the nation's internal terrors around race, gender, and sexuality. It is also an aesthetic terrorism: Davis uses ground-level guerrilla representational strategies to portray some of the nation's most salient popular fantasies. The fantasies she acts out involve cultural anxieties around miscegenation, communities of color, and the queer body. Her dress does not attempt to index outmoded ideals of female glamour. She instead dresses like white supremacist militiamen and black welfare queen hookers. In other words, her drag mimesis is not concerned with the masquerade of womanliness, but instead with conjuring the nation's most dangerous citizens. She is quite literally in "terrorist drag." → *Drag as terrorist*

While Davis's terrorist drag performance does not engage the project of passing as traditional drag at least partially does, it is useful to recognize how passing and what I am describing as disidentification resemble one another—or, to put it more accurately, how the passing entailed in traditional drag implicates elements of the disidentificatory process. Passing is often not about bald-faced opposition to a dominant paradigm or a wholesale selling out to that form. Like disidentification itself, passing can be a third modality, where a dominant structure is co-opted, worked on and against. The subject who passes can be simultaneously identifying with and rejecting a dominant form. In traditional male-to-female drag "woman" is performed, but one would be naive and deeply ensconced in heteronormative culture to consider such a performance, no matter how "real," as an actual performance of "woman." Drag performance strives to perform femininity, and femininity is not exclusively the domain of biological women. Furthermore, the drag queen is disidentifying— sometimes critically and sometimes *not*—not only with the ideal of woman but also with the a priori relationship of woman and femininity that is a tenet of gender-normative thinking. The "woman" produced in drag is not a woman but instead a public disidentification with woman. Some of the best drag that I have encountered in my research challenges the universalizing rhetorics of femininity.     *need to pay attention to humiliated Self*

Both modalities of performing the self, disidentification and passing, are often strategies of survival. (As the case of Davis and others suggests, often these modes of performance allow much more than mere survival, and subjects fully come into subjectivity in ways that are both ennobling and fierce.) Davis's work is a survival strategy on a more symbolic register than that of everyday practice. She is not passing to escape social injustice and structural racism in the way that some people of color might. Nor is she passing in the way in which "straight-acting queers" do. Her disidentification with drag plays with its prescriptive mandate to enact femininity through (often white) standards of glamour. Consider her militiaman drag. Her dark brown skin does not permit her to pass as white, the beard is obviously fake, and the fatigues look inauthentic. Realness is neither achieved nor is it the actual goal of such a project. Instead, her performance as Clarence functions as an intervention in the history of cross-race desire that saturates the phenomenon of passing. Passing is parodied, and this parody becomes a site where interracial desire is interrogated.     *Not an attempt to define realness*

Davis's biting social critique phantasmatically projects the age-old threat of miscegenation, something that white supremacist groups fear the most, onto the image of a white supremacist. Cross-race desire spoils the militiaman's image.[17] It challenges the coherence of his identity, his

*militant language*

essentialized whiteness, by invading its sense of essentialized white purity. The militiaman becomes a caricature of himself, sullied and degraded within his own logic.

Furthermore, blackface minstrelsy, the performance genre of whites performing blackness, is powerfully recycled through disidentification. The image of the fat-lipped Sambo is replaced by the image of the ludicrous white militiaman. The photographer Lyle Ashton Harris has produced a series of elegant portraits of himself in whiteface. Considered alongside Davis's work, Harris's version of whiteface is an almost *too literal* photonegative reversal. By figuring the militiaman through the vehicle of the black queen's body, Davis's whiteface interrogates white hysteria, miscegenation anxiety, and supremacy at their very core. Eric Lott, in his influential study of minstrelsy in the dominant white imagination, suggests that

> The black mask offered a way to play with collective fears of a degraded and threatening—and male—Other while at the same time maintaining some symbolic control over them.[18]

Harris's photography replicates traditional whiteface so as to challenge its tenets in a different fashion than Davis does. Harris's technique addresses the issue of "symbolic control," but does so in the form of a straightforward counteridentification. And while counteridentification is certainly not a strategy without merits, Davis's disidentification with minstrelsy offers a more polyvalent response to this history. Davis's disidentificatory take on "whiteface" both reveals the degraded character of the white supremacist and wrests "symbolic controls" from white people. The white supremacist is forced to cohabit in one body with a black queen in such a way that the image loses its symbolic force. A figure that is potentially threatening to people of color is revealed as a joke.

The dual residency in Davis's persona of both the drag queen and the white supremacist is displayed in the CD's cover art. The illustration features Clarence cleaning his gun. Occupying the background is a television set broadcasting a ranting white man reminiscent of right-wing media pundit Rush Limbaugh, a monster-truck poster titled "Pigfoot," a confederate flag, a crucifix, assorted pornography, beer bottles, and a knife stuck in the wall. Standing out in this scene is the framed photo of a black drag queen: Vaginal Davis. The flip side of the image is part of the CD's interior artwork. Vaginal sits in front of a dressing mirror wearing a showgirl outfit. She is crying on the telephone as she cooks heroin on a spoon and prepares to shoot up. A picture of Vaginal in boy drag is taped to the mirror. Among the scattered vibrators, perfume bottles, and razors is a picture of Clarence in a Marine uniform. These images represent a version of cross-racial desire (in this instance the reciprocated desire between a black hooker/showgirl and a white supremacist gun nut-militiaman) that echoes what Vaginal, in her 1995 interview, called "the snow period" when "some cheap white boyfriend" could make one's life perfect, permitting the queen of color to feel like "some treasured thing," who hopes for "the privileges that white people get—validation through association." The image of the snow queen, a gay man of color who desires white men, is exaggerated and exploded within these performances. It is important to note that this humor is not calibrated to police or moralize against cross-racial desire. Instead, it renders a picture of this desire in its most fantastic and extreme form. By doing so it disturbs the coherence of the white militiaman's sexual and racial identity, an identity that locates itself as racially "pure." Concomitantly, sanitized understandings of a gay identity, which is often universalized as white, are called into question.

Davis has remarked that academics and intellectuals have dismissed her work as "homey" or "country." I have attempted in this section to point to the ways in which these low-budget performances intervene in different circuits of publicity: predominantly white post-punk queercore spaces like Squeezebox and, further, the spaces of predominantly white masculinity that are associated with hard-core and speed metal music. I want to suggest that Davis's signature "homeyness," which I have already linked to an *organic* and terroristic politics, also permits us to further understand her as

an "organic intellectual," that is, an intellectual who possesses a "fundamental connection to social groups."[19] These social groups include but are certainly not limited to various subcultural sectors: punks, queers, certain communities of color. In the wake of deconstruction the word *organic* has become suspect, implying a slew of essentialist and holistic presuppositions. By linking *organic* to Davis's notion of "homey" and "country" I wish to take some of the edge off the word. My invocation of *organic intellectual* is meant to foreground the importance of cultural workers to ground-level politics of the self while avoiding the fetishizing of the minoritarian intellectual.

Gramsci's work offers a view of Davis not only as organic intellectual but also as philosopher. Gramsci contended that philosophy was

> a conception of the world and that philosophical activity is not to be conceived solely as the "individual" elaboration of systematically coherent concepts, but also and above all as a cultural battle to transform the popular "mentality" and to diffuse the philosophical innovations which will demonstrate themselves to be "historically true" to the extent that they become concretely—i.e. . . . . historically and socially—universal.[20]

Davis's work fits in with this Gramscian model of philosophy insofar as her cultural production attempts to dismantle universals within both the dominant public sphere and various subcultures, both of which are predominantly white. The Gramscian notion of "a philosophy of praxis" helps transcend a more traditional Marxian binary between praxis and philosophy.[21] Vaginal Davis's performance attempts to unsettle the hegemonic order through *performance* of praxis (a performance that imagines itself as praxis). The performances that are produced are rooted within a deep critique of universalism and the dominant power bloc.

The cultural battle that Davis wages is fought with the darkest sense of humor and the sharpest sense of parody imaginable. Her performances represent multiple counterpublics and subjects who are liminal within those very counterpublics. She shrewdly employs performance as a modality of counterpublicity. Performance engenders, sponsors, and even *makes* worlds. The scene of speed metal and post-punk music is one which Davis ambivalently inhabits. Her blackness and queerness render her a freak among freaks. Rather than be alienated by her freakiness, she exploits its energies and its potential to enact cultural critique.

[...]

Disidentification, as a mode of analysis, registers subjects as constructed and contradictory. Davis's body, her performances, and all her myriad texts labor to create critical uneasiness and, furthermore, to create desire within uneasiness. This desire unsettles the strictures of class, race, and gender prescribed by what Guattari calls the "social body." A disidentificatory hermeneutic permits a reading and narration of the way in which Davis clears out a space, deterritorializing it and then reoccupying it with queer and black bodies. The lens of disidentification allows us to discern seams and contradictions and ultimately to understand the need for a war of positions.

## NOTES

1. Barney Hoskyns, *Waiting for the Sun: Strange Days, Weird Scenes, and the Sound of Los Angeles* (New York: St. Martin's, 1996), 307.
2. George Lipsitz, *Dangerous Crossings: Popular Music, Postmodernism, and the Poetics of Space* (New York and London: Verso, 1994), 17.
3. Tommy Gear and Mike Glass, "Supremely Vaginal," *aRude* 1 (fall 1995): 42.
4. Ibid.
5. Kimberlé Williams Crenshaw, "Beyond Racism and Misogyny: Black Feminism and 2 Live Crew," in *Words That Wound: Critical Race Theory, Assaultive Speech, and the First Amendment,* ed. Mari J. Matsuda et al. (Boulder, Colo.: Westview, 1993), 111–32.

6. Felix Guattari, *Soft Subversions,* ed. Sylvere Lotringer, trans. David L. Sweet and Chet Wiener (New York: Semiotext(e), 1996), 37.

7. Julian Fleisher, *The Drag Queens of New York: An Illustrated Field Guide* (New York: Riverhead, 1996).

8. "Realness" is mimetic of a certain high-feminine style in standard realist terms.

9. Many of the performers I have just mentioned appear in the film documentation of New York's annual drag festival, *Wigstock: The Movie.*

10. Gear and Glass, "Supremely Vaginal," 77.

11. Antonio Gramsci, "The Formation of Intellectuals," in *The Modern Prince and Other Writings,* trans. Louis Marks (New York: International, 1959), 181.

12. Here I do not mean *homogeneity* in its more quotidian usage, the opposite of *heterogeneous,* but, instead, in a Gramscian sense that is meant to connote social cohesion.

13. John Fiske, "Opening the Hallway: Some Remarks on the Fertility of Stuart Hall's Contribution to Critical Theory," in *Stuart Hall: Critical Dialogues in Cultural Studies,* ed. David Morley and Kuan-Hsing Chen (New York: Routledge, 1996), 213–14. Also see Dick Hebdige's classic analysis of subcultures for an analysis that uses what is in part a Gramscian lens to consider group formations, *Subculture: The Meaning of Style* (London: Routledge, 1979).

14. Miss Guy's image was featured in designer Calvin Klein's CK One ad campaign. Her androgynous, nontraditional drag was seen all over the nation in print and television advertisements. This ad campaign represented a version of gender diversity that was not previously available in print advertising. Yet, once again, the campaign only led to a voyeuristic absorption with gender diversity and no real engagement with this node of difference.

15. Queercore writer Dennis Cooper, in an attempt to out the "real" Davis in *Spin* magazine, implied Hilliard was the artist's true identity. The joke was on Cooper, since Davis's professional identity as Hilliard was another "imagined identity." Davis has explained to me that her actual birth name is Clarence, which will be an important fact as my reading unfolds.

16. An alternate yet complementary reading of the name Clarence that I am offering here would link this white militiaman and the act of cross-race minstrelsy to the Bush-appointed Supreme Court Justice Clarence Thomas, an African American who has contributed to the erosion of civil rights within the nation.

17. Here I risk collapsing all antigovernment militias with more traditional domestic terrorist groups like the Ku Klux Klan or neo-Nazis. Not all militiamen are white supremacists, and the vast majority of white supremacists are not in a militia. But Davis's Clarence is definitely concerned with racist militias whose antigovernment philosophies are also overtly xenophobic and white supremacist.

18. Eric Lott, *Love and Theft: Blackface Minstrelsy and the American Working Class* (New York: Oxford, 1993), 25.

19. Antonio Gramsci, *Selections from the Prison Notebooks* (New York: International, 1971), 14.

20. Ibid., 348.

21. For an example of this divide in classical Marxism, see Karl Marx, *Theses on Feuerbach,* in *The Marx-Engels Reader,* ed. Robert C. Tucker (New York: Norton, 1972), 145.

# 7

# *Felt Matters*

JEANNE VACCARO

JEANNE VACCARO REDIRECTS EXISTING TRANSGENDER VOCABULARIES to talk about art and embodiment along an unexpected, novel, and radical trajectory: felt, the fabric. For Vaccaro, felt matters. Felt matters in multiple ways, primarily as a metaphor to talk about the "textured" and affective labors performed in making transgender subjectivities and embodiments. Drawing on Deleuze and Guattari, Vaccaro theorizes a poetics of literal felt: as a fabric, it resists the gridlike rigidity, reproducibility, and homogeneity of other fabrics. Using felt's mattedness and three-dimensionality as a metaphor for embodiment enables her to refuse the assumption that a "social body" (clothing, gesture, cosmetics) overlays a "biological body." Addressing these insights to the specificities of transgender embodiment, felt, for Vaccaro, also confounds the unidirectional narrative of medical transition as a logical endpoint of trans-ing. Transgender embodiment as felt, therefore, is more a matter of something handmade, textured, crafted—with all the implications of that term as women's work or amateurism, and also as a collaborative and communal process. Vaccaro considers a number of textile artworks by the artist Emmett Ramstad that incorporate handmade paper, felt, lace, and articles of clothing: art that engages with a politics of transgender embodiment by privileging "becoming" as an interdependent embodied process.

"Felt," write Deleuze and Guattari in 'The Smooth and the Striated,' is a

> supple solid product that proceeds altogether differently, as an anti fabric… An aggregate of intrication of this kind is in no way *homogenous*: it is nevertheless smooth, and contrasts point by point with the space of the fabric (it is in principle infinite, open, and unlimited in every direction; it has neither top nor bottom nor center.
>
> (1987, 475)

Felt, the "anti-fabric," cannot be known mathematically, calculated, quantified or mapped on a horizontal-vertical grid like textiles. It is the result of the destruction of a grid. There is no pattern to follow; felt is freestyle. Deleuze and Guattari privilege felt's infinite zigzags and aimless directionality, and I am seduced by felt because it is a nonformula for an organic, mashed up mode of becoming. My interest here is the relation between matter and feeling within experience, specifically the sensation (bodily, cognitive and otherwise) of gender in transition. The many valences of felt account for the dimensionality of such an experience, and importantly, do not privilege a single mode of transition (hormonal, surgical or legal) or reinforce narratives of gender "realness".

This exploration of the intersection of transgender embodiment and what I call the politics of the handmade generates a turn away from ideological accounts of identity reproduction and toward the singularity of subject formations. I am proposing a non-predictive theory of gender in which predetermination of gender identity or expression is neither possible nor desirable. The non-predictive references craft's anti-machinic quality, its insistence on individuality and embrace of amateur aesthetics. Connecting transgender corporealities to the politics and labor of the handmade is a way to explore alternate modes of identity production, and to resist institutional and institutionally sanctioned gender formation. It offers a productive counter to medicalized and psychiatric discourses that pathologize non-normative transgender transitions and the body's dependence on external technologies. With craft—too often dismissed as low art, amateurism, or merely "women's work"— we may take a step toward generating a landscape of feminist labor, collective process and quotidian aesthetics. As "women's work," craft provides a rich lens through which to observe gender and its relationship to labor. By embracing that energy and history, this essay is in direct conversation with feminist and queer discourses on the body and engages art as an alternate form of theory to create new modes of language. This is an exploratory gesture that cultivates, rather than dismisses, the potential of "women's work," configured as feminist labor and collectivity.

In assembling points of contact between transgender embodiment and fiber arts—including ideas of process, duration, comportment, materiality, among others—I explore non-representational efforts to create space and room to circulate in and through regulatory and oppressive forces. Craft is a practice, object, method and theoretical strategy, and is principally a way for me to theorize the handmade and politicized models for self-determined and directed labor. The proximity of craft to themes of labor, process, materiality, amateurism, and gender make it an ideal site to access and foreground embodied, affective and dimensional forms of transgender embodiment. It might seem strange to theorize identity and identity politics with craft, even as art and aesthetic worlds are regularly called upon to illuminate the social. One aim of this essay is to interrogate such logic and contest the maligned status of craft within art criticism. My intention is not to elevate craft or equalize its relation to art, but to think through its "outsider" position and negative reputation. This will require privileging some voices that have been silenced.

How might craft contribute to feminist and queer configurations of the body? To understand the potential of craft to speak to identity, and generate new ways of thinking about the body, it is important to recall the over determined and shifting identities craft has accumulated since the initial division of liberal and mechanical arts. Craft has variously been characterized as skilled labor, a pre-modern or "primitive" form of art making, feminine handicraft, and an elite activity of the leisure class. Art, meanwhile, is untethered from identity categories, a supposedly neutral, pure and transcendental practice. Why do some materials (paint, for example) accumulate value within art, while others are degraded as craft? Craft is defined by its *lesser* materiality, like wood, fiber, clay and other objects associated with everyday use. It is the unexceptional character of these materials that make craft a rich site through which to consider quotidian performances of gender. Craft is also characterized by its close and sustained relationship to materiality, a connection that remains after a work is complete. An artwork, however, is only defined by its medium while in process (once a painting is painted, for example, it becomes conceptual and visual). Art transcends the material and is abstracted from its surface or canvas, however the sensory encounter inherent to craft—with materiality, process, labor and object-ness—remains. Again, my intention is not to defend craft or restore balance between art and craft, but to capitalize on its already excessive relationship to identity, with particular attention to categories of gender, race and ethnicity, labor and class.

Fiber is an especially rich site to explore embodiment. Soft, flexible and textured materials like wool, rubber and fiberglass are reminiscent of skin, hair and veins. The everyday and unexceptional character of transgender experience receives little attention in studies of transgender subjectivity.

Utilitarian transitions are somehow not "queer" enough for theorizing, nor are bodies that have not yet or will never undergo hormonal or surgical intervention. How does the everyday threaten queerness, and become a burden to theorizing? Why theorize transgender identities as transgressive, exceptional, non-normative, as opposed to ordinary, boring and practical? [...]

In fiber arts and textiles we may initially think of metaphors that dress the body in a protective mask or identity, something that can be changed into and out of at will. By now we are familiar with metaphors that fabricate the body, fashion its presentation, sew its clothes and construct its identity. However, my theoretical turn to fiber is not a method to imagine an outside for a supposed inside. I think with the tactility and metaphor of fiber to disavow the belief that transgender identity is a condition of either interiority or exteriority. Rather, it is the connective tissue between these dimensions. I am interested in the movement between these places and spaces and exploring what it feels like to embody gender in transformation. As a response to popular metaphors and pathological renderings of transgender subjectivity, like feeling trapped in the "wrong" body, I consider aesthetic and identificatory practices that are not defined by binaries of surface/depth or before/after.

Turning to fiber as a metaphor, not clothing or other cultural marks of signification, places necessary pressure on flat, one dimensional gender and disrupts the notion that the social body is layered on top of the biological body. Here, it is useful to recall Eve Sedgwick's work on affect and texture in *Touching Feeling* and her invocation of the term besides as a remedy to that which is beneath or beyond. Sedgwick seeks "to explore some ways around the topos of depth or hiddenness, typically followed by a drama of exposure"—themes of particular resonance to transgender identities and politics (2003, 8). For Sedgwick, "*Beside* permits a spacious agnosticism about several of the linear logics that enforce dualist thinking...*Beside* comprises a wide range of desiring, identifying, representing, repelling, paralleling, differentiating, rivaling, leaning, twisting, mimicking, withdrawing, attracting, aggressing, warping, and other relations" (2003, 8). Thinking with the theoretical frame of "beside" and the textured imprints of fiber generates a dimensional account of transgender subjectivity that integrates bodily experience with material, social and political modes of being and becoming.

The affective labor I want to mark is that of bodies (literal and figurative, human and beyond) making contact, or being moved emotionally and/or physically. This movement is critical insofar as economies of "wrong" embodiment privatize transgender identities and practices inside medical and psychiatric clinics, effectively denying the movement of bodies in space, as well as political organization and coalition. It is important to distinguish emotion from affect, and from the questions of texture, sensation and trace that I argue are illustrative of trans-corporeality, although I do want to put pressure on so-called negative emotions or bad feelings like "feeling trapped in the 'wrong' body" as foreclosing of certain affective possibilities. My work participates in a genealogy of scholarship that maintains a crucial distinction between emotion and affect. "Affect," notes Jasbir Puar, "is something of a residual phenomenon that escapes emotion" (2009, 161). To generate another landscape, one in which transgender is legible beyond the limitations of identity and the discrete boundaries of the body, I foreground the language of "elsewhere" in place of "in between." Gesturing toward the potential of elsewhere is not meant to discount what Jay Prosser describes as "the feeling and experience of being transexed" or privilege the production of theory over bodies (1998, 67). Sara Ahmed's invocation, in *Queer Phenomenology*, of the term "orientation" is useful here, as it emphasizes the body's continual and dynamic orientation at or towards something and further reminds us that metaphors of sexuality are normatively directional. [...]

The affective, textured and dimensional labor of transgender embodiment also finds theoretical resonance with Deleuze's concept of the fold. Folding is a process of subjectivity, of body, memory and time folding into each other to produce the subject. The gesture of the fold—a doubling back of outsides in—disrupts the directional logic of "wrong" embodiment and generates an account of

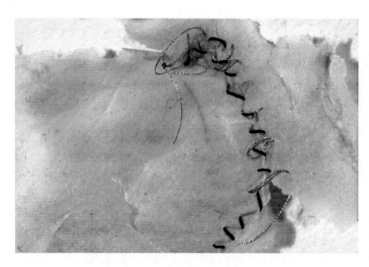

**Figure 7.1** Emmett Ramstad, *Becoming* (2006). Handmade flax paper and cotton thread.

transgender subjectivity not reducible to its location on or inside the body. As Deleuze writes, "I am forever folding between two folds, and if to perceive means to unfold, then I am forever perceiving within the folds" (1993, 93). The fold produces an opening between sight and speech. In these folded elements, which include past and present, creased skin and scar tissue, we observe affect as a site of meaning and value. The body *becomes*. It becomes with and over time. It becomes with and through other bodies that are human, possibly "transgender" or "queer" or "sexed" in manners similar to one another, as well as objects, species, events, infrastructures and institutions. The body *becomes* with and through its movement and proximity to these other bodies. In this way, *the* body is *a* body is *my* body is *your* body, a choreographed set of spatial relations and discursive practices.

We might ask, then, how the body enacts transition, before and without external prompts and approval—when a doctor says so, drugs are prescribed or surgery is performed. This question is not dismissive of hormonal or surgical transitions, but is more nearly an effort to recognize myriad forms of bodily capacity. Again, the theory of gender I am proposing is "non-predictive", a process in which predetermination of gender identity or expression is neither possible nor desirable. It is a theory of embodiment that does not seek totality or coherence of self, precisely because legible subjectivity is an unwanted and often impossible achievement for many gender variant people. The lived experience of trans people will always exceed the biomedical and juridical models that pathologize gender variance as Gender Identity Disorder. My aim is to resist the logical endpoints of gender transition, and to think outside of and beyond gender binarism by deterritorializing transgender subjectivity from the medical and representational models unavailable and undesirable to many transgender people for financial, political, and personal reasons. Deterritorialization, though, is always a reterritorialization—not an abandonment or abstraction of the body, but a rearrangement. [...]

Transgender subjectivity—its origins, essence, bodily difference and psychic structures—is too often reduced to its *location* on or inside the body. Such of formation maintains that transition is defined by the totalizing, yet superficial language of exchange, a movement between two discrete genders and sexes, while the liminal space and time between registers as merely a temporary stop en route to a fixed destination. The normative directionality of this movement can only be thought through horizontality and verticality, with coordinates of male and female and hetero/homo sexuality. The body is thus demoted to an act of expression, its primary function to communicate internalized feelings, private depth and symptomized pathology, as in "Help! I'm trapped in the wrong body!" Partial and contingent embodiment is subsequently eclipsed by wholesale evacuation

**Figure 7.2** From Emmett Ramstad, *Little Boy Pussy* (2008). Handmade paper and lace.

and re-habitation. To strategically deploy feelings of "wrong" embodiment—for the benefit of a therapist, surgeon, case worker, welfare administrator, and so on—has the effect of depoliticizing and privatizing gender identity, and also contributes to Ann Pellegrini's idea of a confessional culture. The force of this performative utterance constructs a barrier that splits the subject pre- and post-transition, effectively erasing the past, and nullifying the existence of—and any possible continued relationship with—the so-called "wrong" body.

Oakland based textile artist Emmett Ramstad works with paper, lace, felt, animal skins and other handmade fibers to create soft sculpture, body casts and embroidered drawings. His artwork directly engages his experiences as a transgender person; however, it is decidedly uninterested in a cohesive and complete narrative of gendered and sexual subjectivity. In *Embodiment* (2006) Ramstad made paper with a gauze infrastructure and stained it deep brown to simulate post-surgical skin and blood. The stitched scars pucker, creating movement, dimension and texture. The body, in Ramstad's configuration, is unfinished and in process, regardless of its status pre- or post- sex reassignment

**Figure 7.3** From Emmett Ramstad, *Embodiment* (2006). Hand stitching on cotton.

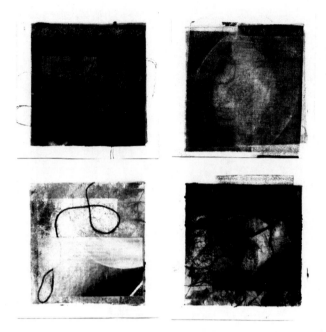

**Figure 7.4** Emmett Ramstad, *String Series* (2005). Monoprints with gauze.

surgery, hormone therapy or legal name change. His artwork counters the normatively directional force of "wrong" embodiment, and generates a new mode of masculinity defined by its critique of patriarchy, of particular significance for representational politics of trans-masculinities.

In *String Series* (2005), Ramstad created a set of mono-prints inspired by post-surgical drains, visualizing the landscape of embodied transition. The string process evokes blood fibers, threads and veins, creating an x-ray-like, textured image. Though his work frequently references surgical interventions on the body, Ramstad is critical of representations that reify transgender subjectivity as complete and embodied *post* transition. The transition his artwork imagines is neither complete nor perfect, but a stillness that we can understand as *enough*. Stillness is not oppositional to the movement I have repeatedly and insistently invoked; indeed, we can observe stillness in movement and movement in stillness, particularly by recognizing multiple forms of embodied labor—cellular, felt and otherwise. The labor of cisgender (or "non-transgender") embodiment must also be acknowledged here; unmarking the neutrality of cisgender embodiment is critical to dismantling the privileges of race and ethnicity, class, sexuality and ability.

Ramstad's embodied aesthetic challenges the performative force of diagnosis in transgender discourse and disorients corollary of affect and action, affirming Lucas Cassidy Crawford's observation that "no bodily sensation carries its own self-evident meaning or orders for action prior to our reformulating these affects into narratives" (2008, 132). Ramstad's artwork abandons the logical endpoints of transition, refusing legible subjectivity's demand for totality and coherence. Disrupting the causal relationship of affect and signification—such that how something feels necessarily predicts meaning and therefore action—marks and confronts the force by which trans bodies become trans identities. Further, it situates action within the hetero-patriarchal logics of state incentives to live full time in the "opposite" sex.

Recent contributions within queer scholarship to the theory of time couple with Ramstad's aesthetic practice to critically reassess transgender subjectivity and the medicalized temporal demands placed on transgender subjects—years spent in therapy and living "full-time" in the "opposite" sex, being merely a few examples. [...] The material objects Ramstad deploys—flexible fibers, disintegrating papers, and textured encasements—signal a convergence of tactility, materiality and affect. These disintegrating materials cooperate with time, forming a relationship in which time is not an enemy, something to resist or outpace. Ramstad's material objects will fade *with* time. His artwork collaborates with time, participating in a temporal economy that is to the side of the art market. [...]

In *Cruising Utopia: The Then and There of Queer Futurity*, José Muñoz states, "Queerness is not yet here. Queerness is an ideality. Put another way, we are not yet queer" (2009a, 1). Queerness in his figuration is not "here" or "now," but it is nonetheless imaginable and desirable. Utopia signals another temporal-spatial moment, marking a conceptual shift from "then to now" to "then to here." It is also a critical methodological practice, gesturing to what Elizabeth Povinelli calls "diagonal genealogies" (2006, 46). Though utopian thought is desirous and oriented to another time and place, that time is not necessarily the future. Muñoz cautions us not to define utopia this way, because such a move takes us out of the present—and the present cannot be abandoned. The present, or the everyday, is the site of local politics, of current struggles, and embodied (rather than alienated) liberation. Utopianism is also a reparative strategy, engaging what has come before not merely to imagine and project a future tense but to critique the present. An embodied narrative of transgender or gender non-conforming subjectivity retains a multiplicity of times and places—of names, body parts, senses of self, familial and community affiliations in transition. The theory of transgender temporality I am foregrounding in dialogue with Muñoz and Halberstam is expansive and able to contain these varied and at times conflicting genealogies of self. These queer philosophies of time, taken together with Ramstad's aesthetic project, displace the medical and biopolitical frames that coercively structure so much of transgender experience and the other modes of political affiliation and relation that remain possible there.

Scars, scarred bodies, and scar tissue emerge in Ramstad's aesthetic as "a model of humanity that is becoming." He engages the layered and evolving meanings of skin in transformation as a metaphor for transgender politics. Scars immediately speak a history of transmasculine identities, but also of breast cancer, a C-Section, or any number of other vulnerable cuts into the body. In Ramstad's aesthetic, a long line stretching across the torso—evidence of a bilateral mastectomy's double incision—doesn't simply represent surgical intervention. Scars perform an archive of corporeal labor and become an optic lens marking the ways "scars come to define communities" and "create landscape" for transmasculine communities (2007, 26). The visual landscape Ramstad creates doesn't fix a singular or prescribed trans identity, or authorize Joan Scott's idea of an "evidentiary experience" (1991). Rather, he privileges individual desires to confront bodily limitations and constraint that are too often reprocessed into medical narratives of trans identity, citing Dean Spade on the notion of "norm-resistant, politicized, and feminist desire for gender-related body alteration," and contextualizing choice and access within the normalizing schema of medical and psychiatric discourse (2006, 319).

Scars evidence a certain bodily or psychic trauma, but also call attention to the body's capacity for dimension and texture. The collagen fibers that are randomly aligned and disorganized at the initial wounding become an organized matrix in scar development and healing; if tension is not relieved at the scar site, cells over-proliferate into repeated remodeling and tissue formation. The various orientations of collagen in the body make evident this labor of transformation at the temporal and spatial scale of the cellular. In *Transcape* (2006), a series of mono-prints with cotton stitching, Ramstad took inspiration from the mass of bodies gathered and marching for the Trans Day of Remembrance in San Francisco. The leans and puckers of the cotton stitching are reminiscent of the double incision, emphasizing the affective labor of transitioning or transgressing normative gender practices.

**Figure 7.5** From Emmett Ramstad, *Transcape* (2006). Monoprint with cotton stitching.

In this scene community action is a diverse and expansive collective body, a form of embodied coalition that is necessarily singular and excessive, balancing the tensions between *the* body and *a* body. The neutrality of *the* body, its assumed physical ability and whiteness, is a set of privileges Ramstad marks with discomfort in his artwork and writing. In his aesthetic of transition the body is not containable in a single unit, or by the disciplines—scientific, medical and legal—which monitor, control and theorize its practices. This is to say that the body is in excess of meaning. As Elizabeth Grosz observes: "the body is not simply a sign to be read, a symptom to be deciphered, but also a force to be reckoned with" (1994, 120).

In his *Becoming* (2006) series Ramstad used handmade flax paper and cotton thread to create sculptural body forms. The translucent shedding is stitched together with dark thread, seams exposed, and suspended in air; it is reminiscent of and references Eva Hesse's *Contingent* (1969).

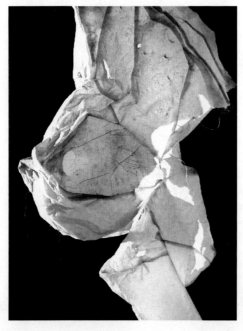

**Figure 7.6** From Emmett Ramstad, *Becoming* (2007). Handmade flax paper and cotton thread.

**Figure 7.7** From Emmett Ramstad, *Becoming* (2007). Handmade flax paper and cotton thread.

Ramstad suspended the three-dimensional bodies at varying heights and angles in order to create multiple points of visual access and meaning. Walking through and among the suspended, hollow forms, visitors in the gallery meet the fibrous, paper skins as another surface, another body coming into contact. In this encounter the viewer is transformed into a participant, another body in the installation of unknowable forms and formations, and the handmade assemblage invites a bodily reorganization and non-predictive engagement with processes of labor and becoming. The aesthetic experience that Ramstad cultivates in his work puts to practice the Deleuzian notions of surface and fold, making of them not merely conceptual or topological points, but material processes.

In his artwork Ramstad aims to develop a language of queer desire and foreground "the transgender voice in visualization" (2007, 7). He theorizes this voice in his M.F.A. thesis, stating that it articulates "not just the performativity and fantasy of gender and sex, but a lived experience that stands at odds with any binaries" (2007, 8). Ramstad's artistic and conceptual practice is directly in dialogue with the transgender look Judith Halberstam theorizes in *In A Queer Time and Place*. [...] For Halberstam, the transgender look "inscribes abrupt shifts in time and space directly onto the gender ambiguous body, and then offers that body to the gaze as a site of critical reinvention." It is, she continues, "a mode of seeing and being seen that is not simply at odds with binary gender but that is part of a reorientation of the body in space and time (2005, 7).

Ramstad's art demonstrates both the exceptional and quotidian nature of transgender embodiment and foregrounds a new mode of trans-masculinity defined by its critique of patriarchy. It belies the emphasis on "wrong" embodiment in transgender discourse, and challenges the privatization and closeting of transgender experience. His aesthetic process is a response to Sandy Stone's observation, "the highest purpose of the transsexual is to erase him/herself and fade into the 'normal' population" (2006, 230). Foregrounding performance, craft, and visual culture de-centers the psychiatrist, surgeon, social worker, and lawyer in trans discourses, and privileges the individually collective labor of transgressing normative gender. Further, by deterritorializing transgender subjectivity we can recognize the body's capacity to labor and transition among genders before and without external prompts and approval. Turning to the politics of the handmade generates evidence, previously unrecognizable or intangible, or what a body and its different might be.

The conditions in which transgender identities emerge—and are subsequently defined and managed by social service and government agencies, policy makers, scholars and activists—can be thought through the body's relationship to a specific event: the linguistic event that is the performative utterance "I am transgender." With this statement, flesh becomes a social body, bound in both particular and evolving ways. From this body, information is extracted, knowledge produced and transmitted. This body, though, has its own power to produce and its own response to articulate. Performativity theory thus opens a space to observe gender through its *doing*, not *being*. It is not merely a semantic endeavor to displace *being* with *doing* or *becoming* or *activation*, though we can surely debate the quality and effectiveness of such a move; with this theoretical shift I aim to produce an *attentiveness*. Alone this might seem slim or unimportant, but realigning our resources—visual, perceptive and cognitive—enables recognition, makes room for things to happen, or not, challenges the way identities are defined and measured and made to "measure up."

## WORKS CITED

Ahmed, Sara. 2006. *Queer Phenomenology: Orientations, Objects, Others*. Durham: Duke University Press.

Crawford, Lucas Cassidy. 2008. "Transgender Without Organs? Mobilizing a Geo-affective Theory of Gender Modification." *WSQ: Women's Studies Quarterly* 36: 3 & 4, 127-143.

Deleuze, Gilles. 1993. *The Fold: Leibniz and the Baroque*. Minneapolis: University of Minnesota Press.

Deleuze, Gilles and Felix Guattari. 1987. "1400: The Smooth and the Striated." *A Thousand Plateaus: Capitalism and Schizophrenia*. Minneapolis: University of Minnesota Press, 474-500.

Grosz, E. A. 1994. *Volatile Bodies: Toward a Corporeal Feminism*. St. Leonards, NSW: Allen & Unwin.

Halberstam, Judith. 2005. *In A Queer Time and Place: Transgender Bodies, Subcultural Lives*. New York: New York University Press.

Kirby, Vicky. 1997. *Telling Flesh: The Substance of the Corporeal*. New York: Routledge.

Muñoz, José Esteban. 2009a. *Cruising Utopia: The Then and There of Queer Futurity*. New York: New York University Press.

Muñoz, José Esteban. 2009b. "From surface to depth, between psychoanalysis and affect." *Women & Performance: a journal of feminist theory*, Vol. 19, No. 2, 123-129.

Povinelli, Elizabeth A. 2006. *The Empire of Love: Toward a Theory of Intimacy, Genealogy and Carnality*. Durham: Duke University Press.

Prosser, Jay. 1998. *Second Skins: The Body Narratives of Transsexuality*. NY: Columbia University Press.

Puar, Jasbir K. 2009. "Prognosis time: Towards a geopolitics of affect, debility and capacity." *Women & Performance: a journal of feminist theory*, Vol. 19, No. 2, 161-172.

Ramstad, Emmett. 2007. "Scars as Metaphor for the Body in Process." MFA Thesis, Minneapolis College of Art and Design.

Salamon, Gayle. 2010. *Assuming a Body: Transgender and the Rhetorics of Materiality*. New York: Columbia University Press.

Scott, Joan. 1991. "The Evidence of Experience." *Critical Inquiry*. Vol. 17, No. 4, 773-797.

Sedgwick, Eve Kosofsky. 2003. *Touching Feeling: Affect, Pedagogy, Performativity*. Durham: Duke University Press.

Stone, Sandy. 2006. "The Empire Strikes Back: A Posttranssexual Manifesto." *The Transgender Studies Reader*. Susan Stryker and Stephen Whittle (Eds.) New York: Routledge, 221-235.

# 8

# *Groping Theory*
## Haptic Cinema and Trans-Curiosity in Hans Scheirl's *Dandy Dust*

ELIZA STEINBOCK

IN "GROPING THEORY," Netherlands-based cinema studies scholar Eliza Steinbock considers affective engagement with media through a discussion of *Dandy Dust*, a film directed by the Austrian filmmaker and artist Hans Scheirl. *Dandy Dust* is the anti-story of Dandy, a character whose gender remains permanently in question. As Steinbock points out, *Dandy Dust* doesn't have a linear narrative—it meshes sci-fi, splatter, porn, art film, and other genres, and resists any effort by the viewer to impose a narrative on the chaotic proceedings. Drawing on a diverse materialist tradition of theorizing affect and cinema (including Brian Massumi, Steven Shaviro, and Linda Williams), Steinbock reads *Dandy Dust* through a concept of haptic spectatorship that critically revises Freudian notions of scopophilic pleasure. By refusing to privilege sight as the key to proper knowledge and sense-making, watching the film must take place though straining to grasp or grope the bodies on-screen. The non-linearity of the film's structure invites a spectator to uncover meaning on an affective plane: groping, floundering in confusion, thrown back on one's own somatic sensations, pleasures, and discomforts. Refusal of closure through numerous false endings implies a body that is always in the process of composition. Finally, Steinbock invites transgender studies to "use affective operations to mobilize curiosity" in ways that destabilize the normalized, identity-based understanding of transgender as a medical transition, a one-way trip, arriving at a logical conclusion.

Each time I watch Hans Scheirl's experimental feature film *Dandy Dust*,[1] I feel nauseous, disoriented, and, by its end, excited. Its viewing requires cruising through multiple worlds, swiftly changing scale and points of view from that of an insect to god's eye, from the cosmos to the interior of a bodily cavity. Scheirl, a filmmaker and professor of contextual painting at the Vienna Academy of Art who made his international reputation as Angela Hans Scheirl with the lesbian cult classic *Flaming Ears*,[2] both directed the film *Dandy Dust* and played the eponymous title character, Dandy Dust. Scheirl, along with many of his ensemble cast, was beginning to experiment with testosterone injections during filming, which resulted in female-bodied persons who often (yet not consistently) present as masculine, both on-screen and off.[3] In the film's companion text, "Manifesto for the Dada of the Cyborg-Embrio," Scheirl explains that the proper pronoun for Dandy Dust is neither *she* nor *he*, but rather *cy*, short for cyborg.[4] Scheirl's hormonal "experiments," as he called them, as well as *Dandy Dust*'s experimental style, together articulate a form of "ethologic" research in the vein of Baruch Spinoza, who stated that "we do not yet know what a body can do."[5] In experimenting with encounters that redefine the body's experiences of motion and rest, its capacity to affect and be affected by other bodies, the film poses the question, "What can a body do, or be made to do?" within the mediated and ideological contexts of contemporary cinema.

Like its shape-shifting protagonist, the film jumps genres—from science fiction, to mystery, to horror, to splatter, to porn. It refuses to maintain a singular gender identity or, for that matter, embodiment for its lead character, who appears on-screen as a young boy of color, an older Caucasian tomboy, a talking flame, and a dusty mummy. The stable characteristic of Dandy Dust the character, as well as *Dandy Dust* the film, is neither gender nor genre, but rather, in the words of Scheirl's collaborator Johnny de Philo, a "vastly overgrown appetite for curiosity."[6] All of the film's genre referents are in fact closely tied to a viewer's curiosity about bodies. Laura Kipnis points out that science fiction is closely related to the genre of porn, as both take a "what if?" approach to bodies and societies, replacing commonalities with alternative corporeal universes.[7] Further, Linda Williams argues that pornography and horror cinema belong to the category of "body genres," in that each transforms the body's affective dimensions, whether to induce arousal or fear.[8] *Dandy Dust's* narrative, to the extent that there is one, is full of false plot turns and stylized omissions that subvert the quests for knowledge that it seems to launch.

Dandy Dust's curiosity pushes and pulls cy through various worlds, to collect or disperse fluid and fragmented bits of self, but the curiosity that drives this decidedly posthumanist *bildungsroman* is more than a mere plot device; curiosity is the central affect of the film. It is expressed formally in the film's narrative style as well as its visual aesthetics, and it is thematized primarily as a curiosity about gender-transition.

As Laura Mulvey notes, a film image's sensuous address of a viewer's curiosity drives the viewer's appetite for deciphering meaning. *Dandy Dust's* aesthetic certainly aims to generate just such a curiosity on the part of the spectator; its flickering images enchant, but do not readily give up their meaning.[9] *Dandy Dust's* "Fun-Punk" sensibility exploits the sensuous quality of film through images peppered with cheap special effects and such mixed formats as animation, Super8, 16mm, and video. Scheirl intended that his extremely low-budget effects produce an abstract sense of shape and saturated color that is metonymic of the notion of a rich field of aesthetic experience more generally.[10] He was especially enamored of a "particular 'glow'" produced by shooting on video, filming off the monitor, and then transferring the film image back to video, that made the film grain seem to come alive. He claimed, in fact, that the real protagonist of *Dandy Dust* "IS the film grain and the TV-noise [*Fernsehrauschen*, or static]," which visually and aurally represents the interstitial space between technology and corporeality.[11]

The film-goer who encounters *Dandy Dust* becomes an experiential hub of curiosity: witnessing flagrant representations of transgenderism, encountering the film's tactility and its body genres, and participating in the investigation. Hence, unlike activist cinemas concerned with delivering a cogent message, or entertainment cinema with a goal-oriented plot, *Dandy Dust* forgoes accumulating new knowledges or reproducing old ones. Instead, the film's curious style and form engage in what I call "cinematic research."

In what follows, I explicate *Dandy Dust* in relation to Freudian notions of curiosity about sex difference, but I underscore the difference between a haptic (and anal) curiosity and Freud's own optical (and penile) approach. I draw on film theorist David Bordwell to discuss the film-goer's cognitive responses to the narrative, as well as Jonathan Crary's concept of "the carnal density of vision," and the works of such feminist film scholars as Linda Williams and Vivian Sobchack, who argue for an understanding of cinema's touching and moving affectivity. Finally, extrapolating from *Dandy Dust's* cinematic research to "curious" encounters with cultural objects, I draw out an anti-Oedipal carnality potentially at work in transgender studies' production of knowledge.

## OPTICAL AND HAPTIC CURIOSITY

For Freud, the "thirst for knowledge seems to be inseparable from sexual curiosity," but the infantile libido focusing on problems of the distinction between the sexes and the mystery of reproductive sexuality (the Oedipal and castration complexes) must become sublimated into adult intellectual interest.[12] Freud regards psychoanalysis as a mode of recovering the sexual impulse that fuels curiosity, which he applies to his case of Little Hans. When Hans watches the bathing of his seven-day old sister, he comments, "But her widdler's quite small.... When she grows up it'll get bigger all right."[13] Freud muses on why Hans did not report what he "really saw," namely, the absence of a penis. He accounts for Hans' "faulty perception" as a mistake that conceals a truth he cannot yet understand.[14] Although Freud writes that Hans' interest in widdlers "also impelled him to *touch* his member," any consideration of touching as a mode of meaning-making equal to or complementary to vision remains unanalyzed.[15] Freudian curiosity, with its focus on investigating the genitals as a visual problem, plays directly into the Enlightenment desire to see and thereby know the world—a framework that raises sight to the "noblest of the senses."[16]

Hans, however, acknowledges that he pleasurably "gropes" towards knowledge through the kinesthetic exploration of his own embodiment. When Hans' mother finds him touching himself, she threatens to send for a doctor to "cut off your widdler"; she asks, "then what'll you widdle with?" to which Hans responds, "With my bottom."[17] Freud diagnoses this moment as Hans' acquisition of the castration complex, when the child perceives that his genitals, the most important pleasure center, are threatened. Hans, however, effectively dodges the importance that Freud and his parents place on the presence of *the* widdler (the penis) as a reproductive or gender-specifying problem by shifting pleasurable curiosity to his bottom. A curiosity that begins not from the penis, but from the bottom, points to a haptic or groping curiosity not partial to the difference a widdler makes.

That Freud insists Little Hans' parents distinguish the form of widdlers once and for all as a penis suggests Freud's privileging of visuality. Art historian Aloïs Riegl asserts that whereas optical images of distinct forms must be perceived from a distance, haptic images (from *haptein*, to fasten) draw in the viewer.[18] Building on Riegl's insight, film scholar Laura Marks claims that film can orientate spectators towards a haptic visuality, in which "the eyes themselves function like organs of touch."[19] Similarly, Anne Rutherford suggests that haptic visuality locates the perceiver *in* an environment, perceiving the significance of surfaces in relation to one's body. Thus, perception is "more akin to a millipede than to a camera or camera obscura—a thousand tentacles feeling their way through a space rather than a single lens taking it in view."[20] This corporeally-involved spectator is poised to exploit the bodily pleasures of being touched by the folds of filmic space.

*Dandy Dust* opens with what I experience as haptic images that "invite a look that moves on the surface plane of the screen for some time before the viewer realizes what she or he is beholding," and conversely, "create an image of such detail ... that it evades a distanced view."[21] In challenging the viewer to fasten onto images she cannot pretend to fully know or view, the viewer must approach those images through other sensory modes. This approach has far-reaching implications for the understanding of the film's bodily environ and the spectator's sensuous engagement with its gendered space.

After the title sequence, *Dandy Dust* begins with a black screen accompanied by the sound of air whirling around space. The setting places the viewer in a groundless position, akin to an astronaut or God. It then displays a flimsy white ball made from plaster and wraps, which moves vertically to the center of the frame. A shaky zoom at the slowly turning ball reveals the flickering light to be a projection of black and white images (Figure 8.1). A masculine voice-over narrates, "Wars are raging through the centuries on the Planet of White Dust." The zoom continues until the planet fills the screen and the sound of shrill cries and whirring machines become louder, as if the spectator were about to crash onto its surface.

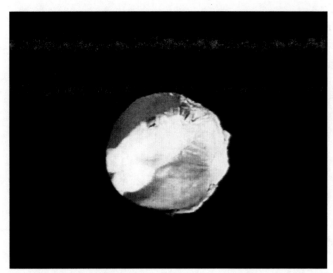

**Figure 8.1** Close-up, the Planet of White Dust

A hard cut dangles the viewer above a white dusty surface populated with animated insects, bones, and toy airplanes. Shifting the point of view, the viewer is positioned amidst a scene in which, as the narrator describes, "scavengers from the surrounding galaxies ravage [the planet's] cadaverous surface." *Dandy Dust* then moves the spectator to a deep crease in the flat surface, and then to the center of the planet, where naked and greased bodies stand on each others' shoulders. Their grim physical struggle in an enclosed space suggests they are working in a shaft of the planet. The voice-over tells the viewer that the workers "pump the mechanism for death and destruction" that runs on the white dust of crushed bones. A tightly framed close-up of a screw spinning and flashing, with an intercut black shot, continues longer than necessary to establish the object, which has the effect of unnerving the viewer, who cannot get away from almost seeming to fall into the grinder. A twenty-five-second-long follow-up shot of white dust falling against a black background fascinates the eye. Less menacing than the screw, the dust shines, reflecting light as it falls directly from above—a movement in which rushing cinematic images seem to stream down like a waterfall.

The spectator's body becomes implicated in each shot: not close enough, then too close for comfort, and finally unable to grasp. The opening sequence suggests that *Dandy Dust* likely will not appeal to the spectator's desire for a goal-oriented narrative, or offer an identification with the as-yet unannounced protagonist. Rather, it addresses the spectator bodily, to locate him or her in a physical, haptic relation to the imagery of the film. As Bordwell claims, a film's beginning is crucial for how a spectator's "hypothesis" about the film finds an anchor point. *Dandy Dust's* anchor point is not with a character, however, but with an environment. As the exposition continues for the film's first ten minutes, the spectator is introduced to another three environments, all of which recall various parts of the body and place the action in their midst. The spectator travels to a parental dwelling-place on the "Planet of Blood and Swelling," to Dandy's mother's flying "Mother-Ship" (shaped like a uterus and fallopian tubes), and to the bladder of "Planet 3075," in which naked hermaphroditic beings live connected by tubes diffusing nectar.

The cinematic construction of such worlds maps *Dandy Dust's* "filmscape" as a "bodyscape." To borrow Marks' phrase, the spectator, touched by "the skin of the film," first contacts outer cutaneous surfaces, then slips inside the bodily cavity, only to be pushed out again. At no point can a spectator physically or cognitively grasp the unity of the film's given "body." Through a haptic visuality, however, the viewer might travel along its organs, capillaries, and pock-marked surfaces. Though a viewer's perceptual location is in the immediacy of the image, she sits in her chair, perhaps sweating, frowning, or leaning forward. Since the film consists of a sort of body not accessible to optical vision alone, it seems that the sexualized elements must belong to a loosely defined, gender-flexible bodyscape.

Scheirl's "Manifesto for the Dada of the Cyborg-Embrio" provides clues as to how the spectator might navigate the film. He writes that rather than moving in and out of spaces, the film's figures travel in the dimension of "scale."[22] Instead of judging inside or outside, Dandy Dust, along with the spectator as fellow traveler, moves through a "big" universe, and then approaches a "small" one.[23] For instance, from the depths of space, the spectator lands on the open surface of the Planet Dust, then enters the constricted anal canal. Whereas Freud relates "big" and "small" to the size of the male member, for the protagonist, the experience of space changes according to cy's movement within and across the bodyscape. Similarly, the spectator cannot rely solely on the optical, distanced, and phallocentric point of view. The body's movement, sensations, and responsive affects determine the scale and shape of this kind of space, suggesting that it is organized through touch, or for the viewer, through a haptic visuality keyed to an environment.

Scheirl likens these constant fluctuations of spatial scale to a tight-ringed doughnut, infinitely folding "in/out/side insideout" to create "a transgendered arsehole!"[24] Scheirl describes anal space as "transgendered," or non-gender specific, or gender-irrelevant, rather than associating it with gay men or homosexuality. Rejecting the phallic rendering of folds that privileges the form of the penis, Scheirl declares *Dandy Dust*'s corporeal scale to follow "the politics of bulge and cavity."[25] The transgendered bulge and cavity, and not the "present" penis or the "absent" vagina, form *Dandy Dust*'s undulating bodyscape. Scheirl's depiction of *Dandy Dust*'s bodyscape thus renders the haptic experience of the film as an ever-shifting scale, sensitive to minute changes.

Relating to the film as an "arsehole" does not cancel out the other sexualized forms in the bodyscape; I understand it as a strong reference to touch, which blurs the distinction between inside and outside, internal cavities and external projections. Hence, "transgender," in association with "arsehole," refuses the imperative to maintain the self as singular. In the manifesto, and manifestly in *Dandy Dust*, Scheirl reframes identity as a "complex system of inwards & outwards bulging hyrarchical [sic] identities with the potential to blow up to pieces."[26] He goes on to profess that "only where there are multiple identities, fear of identity termination fades."[27] The effect of bulging in three dimensions reflects an understanding of transgender as embracing forms of bodily uncertainty.

The potential of losing or growing an identity "part" provides the trans subject of *Dandy Dust* with more options and directions to experience the folds of space. The film offers the viewer a chance to sidestep the horrors of the castration complex, in effect to touch and widdle "elsewhere" on the body. The multiple identities available in experiencing the body as having ever-changing inward cavities and outward bulges translates into a *lack of fear* over losing (or not having to begin with) a widdler, putting to rest the psychological or social need to *fear a lack*. Freud would have done well to heed Little Hans' advice: there are always other bulges and cavities with which to widdle, should one be lost (or not found).

## THE STAIN OF CARNALITY

Several interconnected theoretical texts inform my approach to *Dandy Dust*. Jonathan Crary's term the "carnal density of vision" describes how the relocation of vision through film's coordination of the viewer's sensual corporeality confers a "palpable opacity" to the experience of movies.[28] Exploiting the double meaning of "carnal" as referring both to flesh and sexual intercourse, porn theorist Linda Williams develops Crary's turn of phrase in relation to mass-produced "dirty pictures" to explain the pleasurable, even sexual, sensations experienced while viewing images due to "haptic

**Figure 8.2** Naked future Dandy

immediacies."[29] Wagering that the sex in (audio-)visual pornography is mere pretext for triggering haptic, masturbatory actions, Magnus Ullén claims that porn's interactive format is its essential "pornographicity."[30] Vivian Sobchack's phenomenological conception of embodied viewing specifies that the cinematic spectator comes back to her or his own body through an intentional arc that originates and ends with the spectator, not with the image-world; the inability to literally touch, smell, or taste whatever it is that solicits her desire means that her body's intentional trajectory "will *reverse its direction* to locate its partially frustrated sensual grasp on something more literally accessible," namely her own "subjectively felt lived body."[31] The compensation of herself as the sensible object might be roughly understood as a masturbatory action. The lived body "turning back" to itself has the effect of both growing sensual awareness and diffusing its specific content. In this sense, cinematic pleasures and masturbatory pleasures can be seen as relying on the same increase of general carnal density. Although Sobchack's carnally intense and substantialized viewer does not explicitly refer to a viewer enjoying pornography, it provides a model for understanding the "rebound" effect of haptic cinematic images.

*Dandy Dust*'s carnality is concerned not only with density— it also ramps up in intensity. Film scholars have sought to account for cinema's ability to mobilize the spectator: to charge her or his affective disposition. Summarizing this concern, Rutherford writes, against competing cognitive theories of narration, "[c]inema is not only about telling a story; it's about creating an affect, an event, a moment which lodges itself under the skin of the spectator."[32] An exemplary sequence of intense and dense pornographicity in *Dandy Dust* revolves around Dandy's auto-erotic relation to other selves in the film.

The setting is in a European mansion circa 1780, in which the character "Spider-Cuntboy" visits Dandy in cy's bedroom late at night. Waking Dandy by stimulating cy's genitals, Spider-Cuntboy takes cy time-travelling to see a future self, "speeding up" cy's sexual development. The masculine Dandy of the eighteenth century observes the Dandy of 3075: a breasted figure amongst other short-haired and breasted beings naked on all fours, being filled by fluorescent tubes of fluid (Figure 8.2). Spider-Cuntboy remarks that "Dandy was so shaken by seeing his sexually-fluid self that he went nuts!" (Figure 8.3). What is implied is that *he* becomes turned on by seeing *herself* sucking and being penetrated. Dandy's response, thrown back into cy's body, indicates an experience of carnal vision.

While the content of the sequence includes sexual acts, the *mise en scène* of cy's sexual awakening, including setting, the behavior of the figures, and the use of costume as well as props,

**Figure 8.3**  Response shot of past Dandy

reflect on the viewer's position as masturbator. The sequence demonstrates the autoeroticism of a separated self, one hand grasping outward and one compensatory hand towards the self. The scene emphasizes that masturbatory cinematic pleasures require the exclusion from the image in order to feel a tactile thrust in compensation. However, the depiction of sex is hardly a mere pretext for this pornographicity. *Dandy Dust*'s exhibition of sexual fluids, tumescence, and physical action indicates a sexuality that potentially spreads and stains the viewer as much as it does Dandy. In other words, the viewer's body absorbs the affect of arousal precisely because it is excluded from direct participation in what is seen.

The self-pleasuring scene, starring the future Dandy, initiates the uneducated Dandy's acting out of lasciviousness, including rubbing trees, biting legs, eating beasts, etc. Heavy, distorted techno music carries over from the future to the past, connecting worlds through a sound bridge. The following sequence, situated in a late eighteenth-century setting, shows the increasingly dramatic activities that sexually "going nuts" entails. The viewer can see from a low angle that Dandy stands alone in a tree. Seeming to recall cy's other self, cy closes cy's eyes. Cy rubs cy's now pronounced crotch, which centers the shot. Depicted in slow motion and moving in closer, the viewer now sees cy humping the trunk, apparently building up steam. The self-love imagery of Dandy's goes deeper: a biological slide of flesh, perhaps of cy's organ, is seen as if from under a microscope. The sound of blood pumping accompanies a flash from blue to red. The animated family house shown next receives the same treatment: it shows lust by a hot red color, which surrounds the blue-lit figurine of a house perched on a globe; red then flows into it, making it throb.

Though the editing depicts the characters as separate, the pleasurable feelings seem to spread from the future fluid Dandy to the eighteenth-century teenager. Although the colorful liquids do not literally spray on cy, the scene revolves on the idea of transfer. The fluid self relates at once to the sexual fluids the hermaphroditic beings enjoy, and signals the mobility that is possible as one "grows up." The sexual development of Dandy Dust progresses on a scale of acceleration and deceleration, or from being centralized and dispersed and back, rather than cycling through Freud's stages to adulthood. Like Little Hans' widdling, masturbation figures here as the igniting of sexuality and as a key action towards carnal knowledge. That the spread of throbbing blood from Dandy's body flows into the family house indicates that arousal might also be directed towards the family, establishing an incestuous connection that shortly becomes apparent. For the moment, however, the seepage into the family house suggests that sexuality in *Dandy Dust* functions through the contagion of affect.

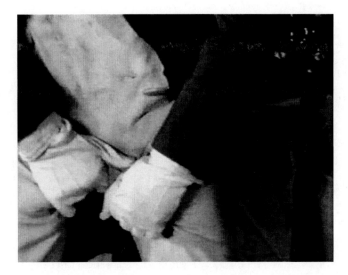

**Figure 8.4** Stained crotch

The following cut begins the "dinner party" portion of the sequence, which shows Dandy behaving badly during a formal gathering in his father's household. The first part of the sequence focuses on tight, tilted shots that capture Dandy's barbaric stuffing of food into his mouth and trousers. The effect is a disorienting, almost subjective camera, spinning out of control as it follows Dandy's wild gyrations and waving of a knife. In Figure 8.4, Dandy has just grasped onto some reddish fruit that he squeezed through his fingers at crotch level to create a mushy penis shape. The remains have been inserted quickly into his pants and further mashed into the white fabric. The color contrast has a metaphorical function: the material transformed into blotches of color brings to light the intangible affect of arousal. On the surface of the body, textile and stain mark a mounting tension. At this point, the color red becomes a motif, indicating the spreading of arousal, marked like a virus that is stained to be traceable.

Besides grabbing cy-self, Dandy also moves around the table quickly, following cy's eyeing and poking at the goodies available. The intense affect thus spreads from the future self, to Dandy's body, to surround the house, inside it, and now across the whole of the banquet spread. Distracted by a guest's stare and overt popping of cleavage, even of a nipple (Figure 8.5), Dandy (and the music)

**Figure 8.5** Come hither

**Figure 8.6** Group shot, flipped

briefly stops to check out this new fascination. Dandy even wonders out loud, "Who the hell is that?" The red filter over the woman's white-caked skin highlights that the contagion has spread. The disheveled look she casts at Dandy shows she has become undone by the intensity of her interest.

Once Dandy crosses to the side of the guests, the table is left for another kind of spread. The camera work notes the new interest through a change in style. Though Dandy is situated amongst the guests, the camera aligns not with Dandy but with the guests' perspective: it becomes more static, staying at a distance of long to medium shots. The distance frames the guests, who sit and stand facing the camera. The change of overall style from volatile gestures to shots that emphasize a particular arrangement creates the impression of an especially stilted scene.

Visually, the camerawork now seems to obey the characteristics of the *tableau vivant*: a theatrical device that renders a live performance still, players freeze into an expressive formation. Hence, it indicates a Victorian obsession with the control of movement: the staging of animation or aliveness (*vivant*) in a still picture (*tableau*). Lynda Nead's study of moving bodies in the 1890s claims that *tableau vivant* predates the perceived problems of pornographic arousal, which arises from nudity in combination with movement, such as the strip film.[33] While this staging is typical for painting or still photography, its inclusion in the motion picture opens the possibility of disrupting the contained eroticism of the genre.

Dandy's arousal ripples through the arrangement, gradually animating the bodies. The guests are caught rubbing their breasts and coyly smiling to flirt with him. The slightest motion indicates raging desire. Standing behind the characters done up in petticoats and bodices, Dandy's entrance coincides, as if cy's presence causes it, with the image flipping upside down (Figure 8.6). Once righted again, cy tugs at feathers stuck in hats, then whips up a skirt to crawl under it, and then through it on the way to cy's interest: grasping her, cy bites the tender leg of this "lady." Cy's motions cause a stir from which the guests try to recover, struggling to regain composure as they smooth down dresses, readjust gloves and headgear.

Distracted, Dandy follows a rat-like creature that scurries under the table. On cy's way, cy grabs a ladle from the punch bowl and sprays the drink around the room. The red liquid echoes the sexual fluids of cy's future self: cy has caught up with the accelerated development instigated by Spider-Cuntboy. The fluids inscribe the spread of affect through color and form. In the commotion, the tablecloth is pulled off the table, comically scattering the dishes piled high around the room. Larger bits of stuff spread the arousal. The lust built through stuffing, biting, and rushing about seems about to explode in a visual orgasm. The reaction shot of the guests depicts them undone, giggling amidst the food raining down on them.

From the guests, the sequence cuts back to a close-up of Dandy greedily eating the rat-thing. As lumpy blood oozes out of his mouth, cy moans in pleasure. The abjectness of the image perhaps lies in the blood evoking regurgitated semen, or suggesting a death scene. The flirtatious woman moves back across the room, drawn to Dandy. In one quick motion, cy grabs her and lunges in for a kiss, smearing her face with the blood. Disgusted, then grabbing cy by the crotch, she pushes cy down to the ground, and smacking cy repeatedly across the face. Lust then gets the best of her: the music plays in reverse, signaling a change in direction. She kisses cy back hard. The camera's point of view, following the flow of affect, then jumps to Sir Sidore, who watches over the scene. The narrator says, "Sir Sidore's desire is aroused. And his hate is a volcano ready to erupt," while an image of a red pulsating light under his white pants illustrates his throbbing penis. Desire has now spread throughout the scene, dangerously from son to father.

Rutherford argues that the elements of *mise en scène* are vehicles, through which sensory intensification can be translated from the screen to the audience.[34] This proposition specifies the carnal recourse of which Sobchack writes. The banquet table and the *tableau vivant* lay out for the viewer delights on which to grab and feast. Both sorts of tables, banquet and "living," arrange and focus the desire of Dandy and likely also the viewer. Yet, the viewers cannot get at the delicacies; they are excluded from sitting down to join the fun. The inability of the viewer to touch the objects redirects the grasp from the party setting, back to the fleshy delights of his or her own sensuality. The dinner party scene exemplifies a "pornographic" aesthetic not so much because of its perversity, but rather because of taunting the spectator with an over-the-top haptic field, one in which he or she cannot fully participate.

In *The Cinematic Body*, Steven Shaviro describes cinema as a site of visual fascination, in which the spectator's sensorium is "powerless not to see" or to be touched, and yet strains towards the image.[35] Drawing from Blanchot's theory of the subject's "passion for the image," Shaviro's cinema always involves a haptic curiosity that wishes to touch back in order to connect and produce sensate meaning.[36] One quality of the image that Shaviro singles out as responsible for fascination is the image's appeal to tactility in combination with its simultaneous exclusion from touch. Shaviro describes it as follows, "I cannot take hold of it in return, but always find it *shimmering* just beyond my grasp."[37]

This shimmering quality triggers a haptic response in the spectator: called to action, she lifts a hand, seeking to become caught up in the flux of images. The image's impact instigates a blurring between the subject's senses of the visual and the tactile. The shimmering of the image, though achieved by visual effects, also creates a texture, a rhythmic beating on the spectator's body. While the allure of shimmering is most easily taken as a visual effect, its appeal may also refer to affective, haptic contact. The social aspect of affect means that it extends beyond individuals, while registering its effect in the body. The dinner table and the *tableau vivant* organize the viewer's interest in the goodies on display, but it is the tablecloth that hangs over them, extending the pro-filmic surface of the table towards the characters. This textile meets with the movie screen, further extending the skin prickled by affect towards the viewer. The pro-filmic tablecloth acts as a skin the viewer can brush up against to catch the scene's affect.

Psychologist Silvan Tomkins describes affects as the essential "amplifiers" of drives and the directors of cognitive systems, "because without its amplification nothing else matters and with its amplification anything else can matter."[38] The amplification of interest to the level of arousal, for instance, offers an account of curiosity's erotic dimension during film viewing. Yet, only when the physiological sensation of affect, here the nervous excitation of interest, is "owned" does it transform into a subjective feeling of curiosity. Brian Massumi explains this action of owning or possessing affect is the "socio-linguistic fixing of the quality of an experience."[39] Hence, curiosity moves from affect's carnal intensification into a signifier of arousal precisely when the subject grasps for meaning. The spreading of sensation between bodies and material objects on screen might not mark the viewer with red fluid, but the comportment of the viewer's body registers the transmission of the stain, or here rather the *strain*, of arousal. The spectator's curiosity pitches him or her forward, straining towards the image and meaning-making, which prove elusive.

The groping motion of embodied thinking that Shaviro describes, and that *Dandy Dust* invites, consists in the subject seeking a foothold in the image, a handgrip to guide towards knowability. Knowledge becomes the most elusive outcome of the process initiated by the spectator's evaluated response to shimmering images. The spectator's dalliance with *Dandy Dust* performs what Shannon Bell terms "pornosophy," a philosophy that emerges from the carnal.[40] The practice of pornosophy, Susan Stryker elaborates, consists in a "refusal to discredit what our own carnality can teach us."[41] Inspired by *Dandy Dust*'s pornographicity, I wish to address the haptic knowledge generated by a grasping, groping subject.

## GROPING THEORY

"The film begins, again. Always again. Sometimes the film begins to begin again in the middle of the film, sometimes at the end. Sometimes it doesn't begin at all. Sometimes it just gestures to the beginning, as if to say, 'you lazy bastards out there in t.v. land, get off your butts and go start the film,'" Johnny de Philo writes in the catalogue for *Dandy Dust*.[42] Dandy Dust appears for the first time only in minute twelve. Cy begins cy's journey the same way as the film instructs the viewer to "get off your butt." Rotating in a void, Dandy Dust seems to ponder cy's existence, while the narrator offers the advice: "Sometimes, when we know too much, we forget everything; Dust was bored from watching telly-vision" (Figure 8.7). "Knowing too much" here means not knowing how to know new things. Suddenly, the protagonist notices a new planet flickering on the horizon and asks, "When did that grow? Let's go check it out!" Cy cures cy's boredom in the instant of seeing a new planet and taking action, de Philo continues, "flying into the projection screen of life, arms outstretched, whimsical and full of the kind of wonder only untamed horses and fashion models know is theirs for certain" (Figure 8.7).[43] This is not a self-conscious wonderment, but a dispossessing curiosity.

Dandy Dust's trajectory in the film is to allow cy-self to be thrown off track, to redo actions, and change dwelling places. The fact that Dandy thrice returns to a monitor to watch flashbacks as well

**Figure 8.7** Dandy Dust, bored in a void

as to escape into a "trippy story" (read, disorientating and freeing) indicates that curiosity "starts the film," over and again. The openness or wonder that Dandy Dust displays brings cy into contact with a host of inadvertent incidences. In wondering, cy seems to ask, or is forced to ask, "What if?" This cinematic gesture has much in common with academic research, which, according to Christopher Bollas, feels something like this: "I often find that although I am working on an idea without knowing exactly what it is I think, I am engaged in thinking an idea struggling to have me think it."[44] The practice of beginning again, struggling to think, "What if?," I propose, suggests a theory of curiosity, as well it offers a demonstration of how one may produce "groping theory" in the interdiscipline of transgender studies.

Jonathan Culler emphasizes that theory be defined in terms of "practical effects," and hence, he continues, "it is less a particular content, it seems, than something one can do or not do, something one can study, teach, or ignore, be interested in or hate."[45] Culler's broad strokes suggest that theory is a *practice*, a successful one if it succeeds in making one *feel* by "challenging and reorienting thinking" in their own field and new fields.[46] Whereas Culler focuses on the "scariness" and "intimidation" one might feel when confronted with a lack of delineation, *Dandy Dust* also articulates the *appeal* of theory in terms of the erotic amplification of curiosity.[47] The possibility of new understanding that comes from the openness of a theorist at the interstices of disciplines, or of a plot juncture, might summon pleasure, not just fear. The desire to become reoriented, perhaps through the disorienting process of juxtaposing disciplines, may account for why some become interested in "doing" theory.

Mieke Bal's theoretical practice of cultural analysis insists on the trajectory of learning the difference between an unreflective use of a word and a historicized concept. Concepts only become useful when lending understanding to the object, "*on its*—the object's—*own terms*."[48] The dynamism that Bal describes in turn encourages and conditions what she calls "a groping" towards understanding.[49] The groping involved in the process of defining a *meaning* of a particular concept, provisionally and partly, produces an experience, a learning moment. Situated in relation to the object and confronted with a concept, she comes to learn something about what the concept can *do*: the ways in which it can inflect, deflect, and reflect the object.[50] Bal maintains that "it is in the groping that the valuable work lies," emphasizing not the so-called determination of meaning, but the performative dimension of what it can do and what affects it may prompt.[51]

The learning moment in *Dandy Dust* comes from the film's non-linear structure, which implores the viewer to open up the film, to try to assert meaning and infer connections. In Bal's paradigm, the cognitive action of groping for a provisional concept in relation to the object offers an alternative to both mastery ("without claiming to know it all") as well as "floundering" in confusion.[52] A method of groping suggests that one starts from where one is, and necessarily goes from there. The practice of groping challenges the theorist to become reoriented towards the object and to become unstuck from his or her epistemological trajectory. A daughter who is also a son, for instance, confronts the viewer to retrace the film, try again, and reconnect her concept of gender to bodily formations. Opening out to the object forces a dispossession: entering the world requires one to leave "home," wherever that might be at a given point for the researcher, or Dandy Dust. The posture of arms out, embracing what may come, means that one's interest eclipses "knowledge" itself, since this knowing "is always knowing about, knowing of, knowing towards."[53] Like grasping for a cinematic image, a theoretician's groping towards the object and for a reasonable concept proves elusive. Dandy's face-forward movement suggests that the push and pull that directs cy's route towards knowledge also prohibits the arrival of mastery (Figure 8.8). The shimmering lights of the "screen of life" that Dandy sails through are the affective backdrop to the groping theory produced as the practitioner moves towards, and is moved towards, "knowing." At best, Bal suggests, one might find a provisional resting place, from which to write.[54]

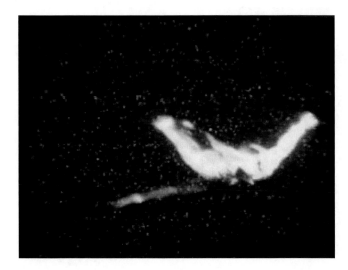

**Figure 8.8**  Dandy Dust, flying

In the logic of *Dandy Dust* that requires regular kick-starts, one finds few rest stops in between starting again. The multiple endings, however, demonstrate a commitment to open-ended knowledge. The final part of the film begins with fusing the separated state of Dandy and Dust, suggesting closure at first. After facing rape and eventual death by Sir Sidore's penis, Dandy's electronic remains return to a holding in the Mother-Ship. Through a cinematic operation of a green-screen special effect, in which the image of a flame, the essence of "Dust," merges with Dandy's head, the entities unify (Figures 8.9 and 8.10). The technological nature of this operation is specified in the top right corner, which depicts the running time, a video's plea for the viewer to "look at me, see what tricks I can do." An animation of a shriveled clay heart pulsing confirms Dandy Dust's reanimation. The theme song sounds to signal the end of the film. But the events continue: a voice-manipulator multiplies the protagonist's voice into different tones, shouting, "You've got the best, you got them all. Now dance." Interrupting the dance, Aunt Theodora asks, "Who's that now?" To which the protagonist proudly claims, "I am Dandy Dust." Theodora says, "Oh that makes sense. Do me a favor and stay that way for a while," before going back to her tinkering with a wrench. The "for a while" extends the film for a bit longer, or at least casts doubt on attempts at closure.

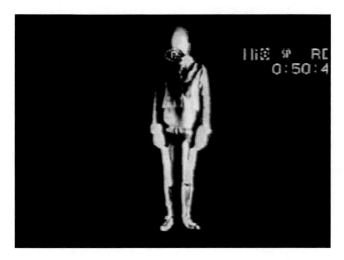

**Figure 8.9**  Unification with flame

**Figure 8.10** "You've got the best, you've got them all!"

The resolution of the protagonist's main problem, his split-self, makes for a proper ending to the goal-oriented narrative. However, as one might by now expect, the flame-headed protagonist then sits down to watch the film, beginning it again, launching a new investigation and another reading (Figure 8.11).

The narrator takes up the plot when Dandy was killed off and brought into the Mother-Ship. The sequence of gruesome surgeries, including the stitching of over-sized genitals with thick yarn, closed mouths, and baby fingers onto adult hands, ends with the theme song coming on, once again. The voice-over now instructs the protagonist and viewer to "stay tuned," as the film begins to end again, framed by the red flame encasing the monitor (as shown in Figure 8.11). Yet, the next sequence offers a recap of events, followed by the camera pulling out to reveal who is still watching: the flame-headed Dandy Dust reclining on the couch. After getting a copy of the "trippy story," cy attempts to face "no more detours" to take cyself in cy's own hands, to go cy's own path. Now the film should surely end. Instead, Dandy Dust announces cy's trip back to the Mother-Ship to confront history. Entering the scene, cy is immediately grabbed by all family members. They force cy into a gynecological chair, strapping cy down and forcing cy's legs open to reveal an open wound. The surgery commences

**Figure 8.11** Dandy Dust, at monitor

**Figure 8.12** Dandy Dust, mad child

with cy's mother, Cyniborg, shouting, "We shall end sloppy patchwork. We shall breed clean and intelligent. Replant our future," as everyone pummels Dandy Dust with squirting oversized bats, far too large to penetrate. Rising up and impervious to the violence, cy cries, "I am Dandy Dust. I am without fear! Come you feeble fleas, come feed from my rivers, come and see that I'm burning," ending with a cackle.

The narrator announces, "Bravo, Dandy Dust, you've said it, but too late. Shock, horror. Remember the extra selves—waste products of unification?" Grinning madly while looking into the camera, a reverse-shot then shows Dandy Dust (and the viewer), that each character reveals that cy is in their costume by the removal of a mask representing the mother, father, and twins. The ripping off of the masks provokes the viewer to reconsider the events of the last ninety-odd minutes. If Dandy Dust was always all the other characters as well, then…? The confounding "thinking" of *Dandy Dust* delivered in each affective operation, each reorientation, gestures away from a beginning or an ending, but outwards to the edges of possibility.

The last image before the credit sequence is of Dandy Dust back in the shimmering void, the projection screen of life that makes possible the contradictions of multiple identities (Figure 8.12).

Pants down around ankles, squatting with bottom in the air, a flower dart thrust into cy's anus, Dandy Dust blathers nonsense in between bursts of laughter. This widdling child playing with cy's bottom has less interest in explanation than in provocation and pleasure. Cy coaxes to the viewer to join, "Come to me baby," only then to grab at the figurines of father and mother, of Sir Sidore and Cyniborg. Dandy Dust performs a transgressive "regression"; his swinging of the parent dolls recalls Little Hans wresting control of his parents and their threat of castration. Like cy's groping of sexual difference, cinematic curiosity consists in, to borrow a phrase from Brian Massumi, "a thousand tiny performative struggles," that differ the body in unpredictable ways.[55] The starting, stopping, and starting again signal the machinic assemblage of body and cinema. The mutual "deterritorialization" of body and cinema struggling together involves multiple, perhaps infinite, operations; thousands of tiny shifts in the body that "differ" the (boundary of) the "body" territory in relation to the territory of "affect." The final image of Dandy Dust rotating in the shimmering void manifests a body that cannot be said to be composed with any sense of finality, but always remains in a state of composing. *Dandy Dust*'s refusal to provide closure to meaning as well as to the subject's ontology indicates that its groping research for new subjectivities underpins its transgender politics.

Lucas Cassidy Crawford's "Transgender without Organs? Mobilizing a Geo-Affective Theory of Gender Modification" introduces affect into the debate on transgender embodiment in terms of what it "feels like" to be transgender. Examining the narratives of transsexual transitions, which often involve moving from one place to another, Crawford argues that transitions involve an orientation to place as much as to the body.[56] Countering the "proper" trans affect of coming home to the self, he suggests considering a different style of affect that involves the deterritorialization of the self: "the process of leaving home, of altering your habits, of learning new tricks."[57] The impetus might then become directed towards composing forces that undermine "our best attempts at deciding, conclusively, on identities and selves."[58]

According to Crawford, and in accordance with the affective style of transgender in *Dandy Dust*, where one dwells and moves are technologies of the subject who is done and undone in affective operations, "equally as much as those surgical and hormonal technologies we recognize more easily as body/gender modification."[59] Placing affect on a par with the hard technologies of surgery does not question the necessity of the kind of surgery that generates "transgender" bodies, but highlights other possible arenas of operation.[60] The mobile character of transgender bodies, in Crawford's view, may "deterritorialize gender rather than settle it ... to help us experiment rather than solve a problem, and to take us wayward rather than directly from one point to the next."[61] While of course not all cinema operates with a transgender commitment towards open-endedness, the potential for cinema to practice trans-curiosity lies in enabling the force of affect to disorient and excite.

Transgender studies might use affective operations to mobilize curiosity, to commit to knowing new things, to refuse to settle, to accept the constraints of an unlivable narrative. Sue Golding (a.k.a. Johnny de Philo) suggests that affect and the force of curious thinking may offer a livability that is not available by other means: "It is amazing how people have survived some horrible things, and one of the things that have actually made them survive is curiosity, that is thinking the most famous radical question of all: Supposing that it could be otherwise?"[62]

With this notion of survival, my discussion of curiosity approaches the gravity of the ways in which aesthetic experience might invigorate and amplify thinking. The value in thinking "anew" might be appreciated in relation to the distance it gains from the "horrible things" that threaten one's existence. Though it is scary not to be able to commit to meaning, the appeal of transgender studies may well register in the commitment to curiosity, to asking questions that lead one astray and far from home.

## NOTES

1. *Dandy Dust*, dir. Hans Scheirl, 1998, 95 min, Austria/United Kingdom.
2. *Flaming Ears*, dir. A. Hans Scheirl and Ursula Puerrer, 1992, 84 min, Austria.
3. Hans Scheirl, "Manifesto for the Dada of the Cyborg-Embrio," in *The Eight Technologies of Otherness*, ed. Sue Golding (London: Routledge, 1997), 50. In his artist statement for a solo show of paintings, "Hans in Transition," he writes "[t]he term 'transition' is used in the transsexual and transgender community for the stretch of time it takes a person to change into the other gender. Now, i'm [sic] not going from A to B, but rather zigzagging my way through a large, open space of possibilities." Hans Scheirl, "Hans in Transition: Paintings by Hans Scheirl," last modified September 2004, http://www.transitiongallery.co.uk/htmlpages/hans/hans_pr.html.
4. Scheirl, "Manifesto," 46. A cyborg embodiment is closely associated with a transgender kind of identity; each explicitly trouble the notion of (singular) identity. As the chapter will discuss, the technologies afforded by film and video form an interface with flesh and blood bodies in a mutual re-making of Scheirl's character's techno-body, following Donna Haraway's "A Cyborg Manifesto: Science, Technology, and Socialist-Feminism in the Late Twentieth Century" description.
5. In *Spinoza: Practical Philosophy*, (1988, San Francisco, CA, City Lights Books)Gilles Deleuze provides a definition for Spinoza's general study of the body: "Ethology is first of all the study of the relations of speed and slowness, of the capacities for affecting and being affected that characterize each thing" (125). The significance for ethics of Spinoza's seemingly simple acknowledgement (stated above) is that beforehand, prior to a specific arrangement or encounter one does not know what a body is capable of, what good or bad. Hence, the body, for Spinoza, is not essentially any quality, but a potentate for them all.

6.  Sue Golding [as Johnny de Philo], "To Tremble the Ejaculate," in *[Cyborg. Nets/z] Catalogue on Dandy Dust* (Hans Scheirl, 1998), ed. Andrea B. Braidt. (Vienna: BKA Filmbeirat, 1999), 69.
7.  Laura Kipnis, "Ladies First: The Utopian Fantasy of Deep Throat," posted online 11 February 2005, at http://www.slate.com/id/2113399/.
8.  Linda Williams, "Film Bodies: Gender, Genre and Excess" in *Feminist Film Theory: A Reader*, ed. Sue Thornham (Edinburgh: Edinburgh University Press, 1999), 267–281.
9.  Laura Mulvey, *Fetishism and Curiosity Fetishism and Curiosity* (London: BFI, 1996), xi.
10. Andrea Braidt, "I am opposed to the practice of not showing the horrible things," interview with Hans Scheirl, in *[Cyborg.Nets/z] Catalogue on Dandy Dust* (Hans Scheirl, 1998), ed. Andrea B. Braidt (Vienna: BKA Filmbeirat, 1999), 19.
11. Ibid.
12. Sigmund Freud, "A Phobia in a Five-Year-Old Boy" [1909], in *Case Histories I. 'Dora' and 'Little Hans'*, trans. Alix and James Strachey (New York: Penguin, 1977), 173.
13. Freud, "A Phobia," 175.
14. Freud, "A Phobia," 175, note 2.
15. Freud, "A Phobia," 171.
16. René Descartes quoted in Martin Jay, *Downcast Eyes: The Denigration of Vision in Twentieth-Century French Thought* (Berkeley, CA: California University Press, 1993), 21. Jay argues that from the Greeks to the present day, Western visuality has formed what he calls an "ocularcentric discourse" that informs the tightly bound relationship between intellectual inquiry and the experience of vision.
17. Freud, "A Phobia," 171.
18. Aloïs Riegl quoted in Laura U. Marks, *The Skin of the Film: Intercultural Cinema, Embodiment, and the Senses* (Durham, NC: Duke University Press, 2000), 162.
19. Marks, *Skin of the Film*, 162.
20. Anne Rutherford, "Cinema and Embodied Affect," *Senses of Cinema* 25 (2003): n/p, http://www.sensesofcinema.com/2003/feature-articles/embodied_affect/.
21. Marks, *Skin of the Film*, 162–163.
22. Scheirl, "Manifesto," 55.
23. Ibid.
24. Ibid.
25. Ibid.
26. Schierl, "Manifesto," 51.
27. Ibid.
28. Jonathan Crary, *Techniques of the Observer: On Vision and Modernity in the Nineteenth Century* (Cambridge, MA: MIT Press, 1990), 150.
29. Linda Williams, "Corporealized Observers: Visual Pornographies and the 'Carnal Density of Vision,'" in *Fugitive Images: From Photography to Video*, ed. Patrice Petro (Bloomington, IN: Indiana University Press, 1995), 3–4, 11. Williams' article focuses on the mechanical "cranking" of the body that early cinema machines such as the mutoscope required that paralleled the male cranking himself, i.e. masturbating. Cinema, in extension, provides mechanical tactile pleasure; itself a possible substitute, though by no means an equal or equitable, sexual partner.
30. Magnus Ullén, "Pornography and its critical reception: Toward a Theory of Masturbation," *Jump Cut: A Review of Contemporary Media* 51 (2009), 9. http://www.ejumpcut.org/currentissue/UllenPorn/index.html.
31. Vivian Sobchack, *Carnal Thoughts: Embodiment and Moving Image Culture* (Berkeley, CA: California University Press, 2004), 76.
32. Rutherford, "Cinema and Embodied Affect," 10.
33. Lynda Nead, "Strip: Moving Bodies in the 1890s," *Early Popular Visual Culture* 3: 2 (2005), 141.
34. Anne Rutherford, "Precarious Boundaries: Affect, *Mise en scène* and the Senses in Angelopoulos' Balkan Epic," *Senses of Cinema* 31 (2004). http://www.sensesofcinema.com/2004/featurearticles/angelopoulos_balkan_epic
35. Steven Shaviro, *The Cinematic Body* (Minneapolis, MN: Minnesota University Press, 1993), 47.
36. Shaviro asserts Blanchot's question is central to any theory of embodied spectatorship: "What happens when what you see, even though from a distance, seems to touch you with a grasping contact, when the matter of seeing is a sort of touch, when seeing is a contact at a distance?"
37. Shaviro, *The Cinematic Body*, emphasis mine, 47.
38. Silvan Tomkins quoted in Ernst van Alphen, "Affective Operations of Art and Literature," *RES* 53/54 (2008), 23.
39. Brian Massumi, "The Autonomy of Affect," *Cultural Critique* 31 (1995), 88.
40. Shannon Bell, "Fast Feminism," *Journal of Contemporary Thought* 14 (2001), 93–112.
41. Susan Stryker, "Dungeon Intimacies: The Poetics of Transsexual Sadomasochism," *Parallax* 46 (2008): 39.
42. Golding [as de Philo], "To Tremble," 69–70.
43. Golding [as de Philo], "To Tremble," 69.
44. Christopher Bollas, quoted in Mieke Bal, *Travelling Concepts in the Humanities: A Rough Guide* (Toronto: Toronto University Press, 2002), 96.

45. Jonathan Culler, introduction to *The Point of Theory: Practices of Cultural Analysis*, (Amsterdam: Amsterdam University Press, 1994), 13.
46. Ibid.
47. Culler, "Introduction", 16–17.
48. Bal, *Travelling Concepts*, 8.
49. Bal, *Travelling Concepts*, 11.
50. Ibid.
51. Ibid.
52. Bal, *Travelling Concepts*, 55.
53. Steven Connor, "A Short Stirring to Meekness," in *Inside Knowledge: (Un) Doing Ways of Knowing in the Humanities*, eds. Carolyn Birdsall, Maria Boletsi, Itay Sapir, Pieter Verstraete (Newcastle: Cambridge Scholars, 2009), 202.
54. Bal, *Travelling Concepts*, 55.
55. Brian Massumi, "Introduction," *A Shock to Thought: Expression after Deleuze and Guattari,* ed. Brian Massumi, (New York: Routledge, 2002), xix.
56. Lucas Cassidy Crawford, "Transgender without Organs? Mobilizing a Geo-Affective Theory of Gender Modification," *WSQ: Women's Studies Quarterly* 36: 3–4 (2008), 129.
57. Gilles Deleuze quoted in Crawford, "Transgender without Organs?," 133.
58. Crawford, "Transgender without Organs?," 133.
59. Crawford, "Transgender without Organs?," 137.
60. In footnote 2, Crawford does question the efficacy of genitalia-focused surgeries to the transition or leaving home that changing gender involves. However, rather than dismiss such surgeries his emphasis is to think twice about the centrality of sexual organs to gender.
61. Crawford, "Transgender without Organs?," 139.
62. Sue Golding, "A Bit(e) of the Other: An Interview with Sue Golding," by Joanna Zylinska *Parallax* 13 (1999), 154.

# 9

# *The Transgender Look*

## J. Jack Halberstam

Queer theorist J. Jack Halberstam has been one of the most prolific, provocative, and influential voices in transgender studies for nearly two decades. "The Transgender Look" is a chapter from Halberstam's book, *In a Queer Time and Place: Transgender Bodies, Subcultural Lives*. In the book, this chapter links a lengthy, preceding discussion of the print and visual media archives that have accumulated around the figure of Brandon Teena, the murdered transgender teen whose story was famously fictionalized in the Academy Award-winning film *Boys Don't Cry*, and a subsequent analysis of a much broader archive of visual representations of gender ambiguity. The crucial conceptual pivot on which the chapter turns is the "transgender gaze," through which Halberstam reworks the key term in Laura's Mulvey's canonical essay, "Visual Pleasure and Narrative Cinema." Mulvey's essay depends on a rigid, binary economy of masculine and feminine subject positions from which a film is seen, its characters identified with, and in accordance with which the film-viewer finds his or her opportunities for "visual pleasure." Given that narrative cinema, in Mulvey's formulation, is structured by the "male gaze," women's cinematic pleasures are construed as either masochistic (identifying with the fetishized object of the male gaze) or voyeuristic (appropriating the active desire of the masculine subject presumed to be gazing). Halberstam complicates Mulvey's schema by introducing transgender and genderqueer perspectives that proliferate the possibilities for identificatory pleasure and embodied spectatorship, before explicating the operation of the "transgender gaze" in several important films with trans content, including *The Crying Game* and *By Hook or By Crook*.

Certain social groups may be seen as having rigid or unresponsive selves and bodies, making them relatively unfit for the kind of society we now seem to desire.

—Emily Martin, *Flexible Bodies*

In the last two chapters, we have seen how an archive of print and visual materials have accumulated around the figure of Brandon Teena, a young transgender man who defied the social mandate to be and to have a singular gender identity. Here, I continue to build on that archive with a consideration of the feature film *Boys Don't Cry*, but I also try to expand the archive of visual representations of gender ambiguity, placing this expanded archive within what Nick Mirzoeff calls "the postmodern globalization of the visual as everyday life" (Mirzoeff 1999, 3). I begin with a study of the transgender gaze or look as it has developed in recent queer cinema (film and video), and then in the next chapter, turn to photography and painting to examine the clash between embodiment and the visual that queer art making has documented in vivid detail. Gender ambiguity, in some sense, results from and contests the dominance of the visual within postmodernism.

The potentiality of the body to morph, shift, change, and become fluid is a powerful fantasy in transmodern cinema. [... T]he body in transition indelibly marks late-twentieth- and early-twenty-first-century visual fantasy. The fantasy of the shape-shifting and identity-morphing body has been nowhere more powerfully realized recently than in transgender film. In films like Neil Jordan's *The Crying Game* (1992) and *Boys Don't Cry*, the transgender character surprises audiences with his/her ability to remain attractive, appealing, and gendered while simultaneously presenting a gender at odds with sex, a sense of self not derived from the body, and an identity that operates within the heterosexual matrix without confirming the inevitability of that system of difference. But even as the transgender body becomes a symbol par excellence for flexibility, transgenderism also represents a form of rigidity, an insistence on particular forms of recognition, that reminds us of the limits of what Martin has called "flexible bodies." Those bodies, indeed, that fail to conform to the postmodern fantasy of flexibility that has been projected onto the transgender body may well be punished in popular representations even as they seem to be lauded. And so, Brandon in *Boys Don't Cry* and Dil in *The Crying Game* are represented as both heroic and fatally flawed.

Both *The Crying Game* and *Boys Don't Cry* rely on the successful solicitation of affect—whether it be revulsion, sympathy, or empathy—in order to give mainstream viewers access to a transgender gaze. And in both films, a relatively unknown actor pulls off the feat of credibly performing a gender at odds with the sexed body even after the body has been brutally exposed. Gender metamorphosis in these films is also used as a metaphor for other kinds of mobility or immobility. In *The Crying Game*, Dil's womanhood stands in opposition to a revolutionary subjectivity associated with the Irish Republican Army (IRA), and in *Boys Don't Cry*, Brandon's manhood represents a class-based desire to transcend small-town conflicts and a predictable life narrative of marriage, babies, domestic abuse, and alcoholism. While Brandon continues to romanticize small-town life, his girlfriend, Lana, sees him as a symbol of a much-desired elsewhere. In both films, the transgender character also seems to stand for a different form of temporality. Dil seems deliberately removed in *The Crying Game* from the time of the nation and other nationalisms, and her performance of womanhood opens up a ludic temporality. Brandon in *Boys Don't Cry* represents an alternative future for Lana by trying to be a man with no past. The dilemma for the transgender character, as we have seen in earlier chapters, is to create an alternate future while rewriting history. In *Boys Don't Cry*, director Peirce seems aware of the imperative of queer time and constructs (but fails to sustain) a transgender gaze capable of seeing through the present to a future elsewhere. In experimental moments in this otherwise brutally realistic film, Peirce creates slow-motion or double-speed time warps that hint at an elsewhere for the star-crossed lovers that is located in both time and space.

The transgender film confronts powerfully the way that transgenderism is constituted as a paradox made up in equal parts of visibility and temporality: whenever the transgender character is seen to be transgendered, then he/she is both failing to pass and threatening to expose a rupture between the distinct temporal registers of past, present, and future. The exposure of a trans character whom the audience has already accepted as male or female, causes the audience to reorient themselves in relation to the film's past in order to read the film's present and prepare themselves for the film's future. When we "see" the transgender character, then, we are actually seeing cinematic time's sleight of hand. Visibility, under these circumstances, may be equated with jeopardy, danger, and exposure, and it often becomes necessary for the transgender character to disappear in order to remain viable. The transgender gaze becomes difficult to track because it depends on complex relations in time and space between seeing and not seeing, appearing and disappearing, knowing and not knowing. I will be identifying here different treatments of the transgenderism that resolve these complex problems of temporality and visibility.

In one mode that we might call the "rewind," the transgender character is presented at first as "properly" gendered, as passing in other words, and as properly located within a linear narrative; her exposure as transgender constitutes the film's narrative climax, and spells out both her own decline and the unraveling of cinematic time. The viewer literally has to rewind the film after the character's exposure in order to reorganize the narrative logic in terms of the pass. In a second mode that involves embedding several ways of looking into one, the film deploys certain formal techniques to give the viewer access to the transgender gaze in order to allow us to look *with* the transgender character instead of *at* him. Other techniques include ghosting the transgender character or allowing him to haunt the narrative after death; and doubling the transgender character or playing him/her off another trans character in order to remove the nodal point of normativity. *The Brandon Teena Story,* discussed in chapter 2, provides an example of the ghosting technique, and in this film, Brandon occupies the space of the ghost; he literally haunts the film and returns to life only as an eerie voice recorded during a brutal police interrogation. Two other transgender films, Kate Davis's documentary *Southern Comfort* (2001) along with Harry Dodge and Silas Howard's feature film *By Hook or by Crook* (2001), work through the strategy of doubling. In *Southern Comfort,* the transgender man, Robert Eads, is in the process of disappearing as the film charts his decline and death from uterine and ovarian cancers. Robert is doubled by other male transgender friends, but also by his transgender girlfriend, Lola. By showing Robert to be part of a transgender community rather than a freakish individual, the film refuses the medical gaze that classifies Robert as abnormal and the heteronormative gaze that renders Robert invisible. Instead, *Southern Comfort* portrays Robert as a transgender man among other transgender people.

In *By Hook or by Crook,* transgenderism is a complex dynamic between the two butch heroes, Shy and Valentine. The two collude and collaborate in their gendering, and create a closed world of queerness that is locked in place by the circuit of a gaze that never references the male or the female gaze as such. The plot of *By Hook or by Crook* involves the random meeting of two trans butches and the development of a fast friendship. Shy tries to help Valentine, who has been adopted, find his mother, while Valentine introduces the lonely Shy, whose father has just died, to an alternative form of community. The dead or missing parents imply an absence of conventional family, and afford our heroes with the opportunity to remake home, family, community, and most important, friendship. As the story evolves into a shaggy-dog tale of hide-and-seek, we leave family time far behind, entering into the shadow world of queers, loners, street people, and crazies. Transgenderism takes its place in this world as a quiet location outside the storm of law and order, mental health, and financial stability. Unlike other transgender films that remain committed to seducing the straight gaze, this one remains thoroughly committed to the transgender look, and it opens up, formally and thematically, a new mode of envisioning gender mobility. In this chapter, I pay close attention to three versions of the "transgender film"—*The Crying Game, Boy's Don't Cry,* and *By Hook or by Crook*—to track the evolution of a set of strategies (each with different consequences) for representing transgender bodies, capturing transgender looks, and theorizing transgender legibility.

## CRYING GAMES

> *crying—verb:* announce in public, utter in a loud distinct voice so as to be heard over a long distance; *noun:* the process of shedding tears (usually accompanied by sobs or other inarticulate sounds); *adj.:* conspicuously bad, offensive or reprehensible.
>
> —*Oxford English Dictionary*

When *The Crying Game* was released, the media was instructed not to give away the "secret" at the heart of the film—but what exactly was the film's secret? Homosexuality? Transsexuality? Gender construction? Nationalist brutalities? Colonial encounters? By making the unmasking of a transvestite character into the preeminent signifier of difference and disclosure in the film, director

Jordan participates, as many critics have noted, in a long tradition of transforming political conflict into erotic tension in order to offer a romantic resolution.[1] I want to discuss *The Crying Game* briefly here to illustrate the misuse or simply the avoidance of the transgender gaze in mainstream films that purport to be about gender ambiguity. By asking media and audiences to keep the film's secret, then, *The Crying Game's* producers created and deepened the illusion that the film would and could offer something new and unexpected. In fact, the secrecy constructs a mainstream viewer for the film and ignores more knowing audiences.

*The Crying Game* concerns a number of different erotic triangles situated within the tense political landscape of the English occupation of Northern Ireland. The film opens by animating one triangle that links two IRA operatives Fergus and Jude, to the black British soldier, Jody, whom they must kidnap. Jude lures Jody away from a fairground with a promise of sexual interaction, and then Fergus ambushes Jody and whisks him away to an IRA hideout. The whole of the opening scene plays out to the accompaniment of "When a Man Loves a Woman." The song equates femininity with trickery falsehood, and deceit, and it sets up the misogynist strands of a narrative that envision the white male as unknowing victim of feminine wiles. The first third of the film concerns the relationship between captors and captive and particularly between the warmhearted Fergus and the winning Jody. Fergus and Jody bond and connect over the picture of Jody's absent lover, Dil. After Jody dies in a foiled escape effort, Fergus leaves Ireland to escape the IRA and heads to England, where he becomes a construction worker. Fergus goes looking for Dil, and when he finds her, he romances her while seemingly unaware of her transgender identity. The last third of the film charts the course of Fergus's discovery of Dil's secret and his reentanglement with the IRA.

There are three major narrative strands in *The Crying Game,* all of which seem bound to alternative political identities, but none of which actually live up to their own potential. In the first strand, which involves the IRA we expect to hear a critique of English colonialism, English racism, and the occupation of Northern Ireland by England. Instead, the film uses Jody to critique Irish racism and Fergus to delegitimize the IRA. The second narrative strand, which concerns the romance between Fergus and Dil, seems committed to a narrative about the "naturalness" of all types of gender expression, and here we expect to see the structures of heteronormativity exposed and the male gaze de-authorized. Instead, *The Crying Game* uses Dil's transvestism only to re-center the white male gaze, and to make the white male into the highly flexible, supremely human subject who must counter and cover for the gender rigidity of the transvestite Dil (rigidity meaning that she cannot flow back and forth between male and female; she insists on being recognized as female) and the political rigidity of the IRA "fanatic" Jude. [...] The third narrative strand has to do with cinematic time, and it projects an alternative ordering of time by positioning Dil as a character who seems to be able to cross back and forth between past, present, and future. When we first see Dil, she appears in a photograph representing Jody's past. When Fergus finally meets Dil, she represents his new present-tense life away from the IRA, and as the film winds down, Dil represents for Fergus a conventional future of marriage and family that awaits him when he obtains his release from jail, where he is "doing time." The seeming temporal fluidity of Dil is undercut, however, by the normative logic of the narrative's temporal drive, which seeks, through Fergus, to pin Dil down within the logic of heteronormative time.

Ultimately, the transgender character Dil never controls the gaze, and serves as a racialized fetish figure who diverts the viewer's attention from the highly charged political conflict between England and Ireland. The film characterizes Irish nationalism as a heartless and futile endeavor while depicting England ironically as a multicultural refuge, a place where formerly colonized peoples find a home. To dramatize the difference between Irish and English nationalism, the kidnapped black soldier, Jody, describes Ireland as "the only place in the world where they'll call you a nigger to your face." England, on the other hand, is marked for him by class conflicts (played out in his cricket tales), but not so much by racial disharmony. By the time Dil enters the film, about a third of the way in, England has become for Fergus a refuge and a place where he can disappear.

Disappearing is, in many ways, the name of the crying game, and the film plays with and through the fetishistic structure of cinema itself, with, in other words, the spectator's willingness to see what is not there and desire what is. In a series of scenes set in the gay bar, the Metro, where Dil performs, the viewer's gaze is sutured to Fergus's. In the first few scenes, the bar seems to be populated by so-called normal people, men and women, dancing together. But in the scene at the Metro that follows Fergus's discovery of Dil's penis, the camera again scans the bar and finds the garish and striking faces of the drag queens who populate it. Like Fergus, we formerly saw bio men and women, and like Fergus, we suddenly see the bar for what it is: a queer site. And our vision, no matter how much we recognized Dil as transgender earlier, makes this abrupt detour around the transgender gaze along with Fergus. Indeed, *The Crying Game* cannot imagine the transgender gaze any more than it can cede the gaze to an IRA perspective. Here the revelation of a queer bar community sets up new triangulations within which the relationship between Fergus/Jimmy and Dil is now coded as homosexual. The homo context erases Dil's transsexual subjectivity, and throws the male protagonist into a panic that is only resolved by the symbolic castration of Dil when Fergus cuts Dil's hair. He does this supposedly to disguise Dil and protect her from the IRA, but actually the haircut unmasks her and serves to protect Fergus from his own desires. [...]

## BOYS DON'T CRY: BEYOND TEARS

Given the predominance of films that use transgender characters, but avoid the transgender gaze, Peirce's transformation of the Brandon story into the Oscar-winning *Boys Don't Cry* signaled something much more than the successful interpretation of a transgender narrative for a mainstream audience. The success of Peirce's depiction depended not simply on the impressive acting skills of Hilary Swank and her surrounding cast, nor did it rest solely on the topicality of the Brandon narrative in gay, lesbian, and transgender communities; rather, the seduction of mainstream viewers by this decidedly queer and unconventional narrative must be ascribed to the film's ability to construct and sustain a transgender gaze. [...] The success of *Boys Don't Cry* in cultivating an audience beyond the queer cinema circuit depends absolutely on its ability to hijack the male and female gazes, and replace them surreptitiously with transgender modes of looking and queer forms of visual pleasure.

In a gesture that has left feminist film theorists fuming for years, Laura Mulvey's classic essay "Visual Pleasure and Narrative Cinema" argued, somewhat sensibly, that the pleasure in looking was always gendered within classic cinema. Mulvey went on to claim that within those classic cinematic narrative trajectories that begin with a mystery, a murder, a checkered past, or class disadvantage, or that advance through a series of obstacles toward the desired resolution in heterosexual marriage, there exist a series of male and female points of identification (Mulvey 1990). [...] These gendered characters play their parts within a field of extremely limited and finite variation, and yet, because gendered spectators have already consented to limited and finite gender roles before entering the cinema, they will consent to the narrow range of narrative options within narrative cinema. Entertainment, in many ways, is the name we give to the fantasies of difference that erupt on the screen only to give way to the reproduction of sameness. [...]

How does conventional narrative cinema allow for variation while maintaining a high degree of conformity? [...S]ometimes, as we saw in *The Crying Game*, the transgender character will be evoked as a metaphor for flexible subjecthood, but will not be given a narrative in his/her own right. But every now and then, and these are the instances that I want to examine here, the gendered binary on which the stability, the pleasure, and the purchase of mainstream cinema depend will be thoroughly rescripted, allowing for another kind of gaze or look. Here, I track the potentiality of the transgender gaze or the "transverse look," as Nick Mirzoeff describes it. Mirzoeff suggests that in an age of "multiple viewpoints," we have to think beyond the gaze. He writes about a "transient, transnational, transgendered way of seeing that visual culture seeks to define, describe and deconstruct with the transverse look or glance—not a gaze, there have been enough gazes already" (Mirzoeff 2002, 18).

While Mulvey's essay created much vigorous debate in cinema studies on account of its seemingly fatalistic perspective on gender roles and relations, the messenger in many ways was being confused with the message. [...] Within conventional cinema, Mulvey proposed that the only way for a female viewer to access voyeuristic pleasure was to cross-identify with the male gaze; through this complicated procedure, the female spectator of a conventional visual narrative could find a position on the screen that offered a little more than the pleasure of being fetishized. Mulvey suggests that the female viewer has to suture her look to the male look. Others have talked about this as a form of transvestism—a cross-dressed look that allows the female spectator to imagine momentarily that she has the same access to power as the male viewer. The problem with the cinematic theory of masquerade, of course, is that it requires no real understanding of transvestism and of the meaning of male transvestism in particular. [...] But what happens [...] when gender constructions are overthrown and sexual difference is shaken to its very foundations?

In the classic Hollywood film text, the camera looks from one position/character and then returns the gaze from another position/character, thereby suturing the viewer to a usually male gaze and simultaneously covering over what the viewer cannot see. This dynamic of looking is called shot/reverse shot and it occupies a central position within cinematic grammar. The shot/reverse shot mode allows for the stability of narrative progression, ensures a developmental logic, and allows the viewers to insert themselves into the filmic world by imagining that their access to the characters is unmediated. The dismantling of the shot/reverse shot can be identified as the central cinematic tactic in *Boys Don't Cry*. In her stylish adaptation of the true-to-life story of Brandon, director Peirce self-consciously constructs what can only be called a transgender look. *Boys Don't Cry* establishes the legitimacy and the durability of Brandon's gender not simply by telling the tragic tale of his death by murder but by forcing spectators to adopt, if only provisionally, Brandon's gaze, a transgender look.[4] The transgender look in this film reveals the ideological content of the male and female gazes, and it disarms, temporarily, the compulsory heterosexuality of the romance genre. Brandon's gaze, obviously, dies with him in the film's brutal conclusion, but Peirce, perhaps prematurely, abandons the transgender look in the final intimate encounter between Lana and Brandon. Peirce's inability to sustain a transgender look opens up a set of questions about the inevitability and dominance of both the male/female and hetero/homo binary in narrative cinema.

One remarkable scene, about halfway through the film, clearly foregrounds the power of the transgender look, making it most visible precisely where and when it is most threatened. In a scary and nerve-racking sequence of events, Brandon finds himself cornered at Lana's house. John and Tom have forced Candace to tell them that Brandon has been charged by the police with writing bad checks and that he has been imprisoned as a woman. John and Tom now hunt Brandon, like hounds after a fox, and then they begin a long and excruciating interrogation of Brandon's gender identity. Lana protects Brandon at first by saying that she will examine him and determine whether he is a man or a woman. Lana and Brandon enter Lana's bedroom, where Lana refuses to look as Brandon unbuckles his pants, telling him, "Don't. . . . I know you're a guy." As they sit on the bed together, the camera now follows Lana's gaze out into the night sky, a utopian vision of an elsewhere into which she and Brandon long to escape. This is one of several fantasy shots in an otherwise wholly realistic film; Peirce threads these shots in which time speeds up or slows down through the film, creating an imagistic counternarrative to the story of Brandon's decline.

As Brandon and Lana sit in Lana's bedroom imagining an elsewhere that would save them from the impoverished reality they inhabit, the camera cuts back abruptly to "reality" and a still two-shot of Brandon in profile and Lana behind him. As they discuss their next move, the camera draws back slowly and makes a seamless transition to place them in the living room in front of the posse of bullies. This quiet interlude in Lana's bedroom establishes the female gaze, Lana's gaze, as a willingness to see what is not there (a condition of all fantasy), but also as a refusal to privilege the literal over the figurative (Brandon's genitalia over Brandon's gender presentation). The female gaze, in this scene, makes possible an alternative vision of time, space, and embodiment. Time slows down while the couple linger in the sanctuary of Lana's private world, her bedroom; the bedroom itself becomes an otherworldly space framed by the big night sky, and containing the perverse vision of a girl and her queer boy lover; and the body of Brandon is preserved as male, for now, by Lana's refusal to dismantle its fragile power with the scrutinizing gaze of science and "truth." That Lana's room morphs seamlessly into the living room at the end of this scene, alerts the viewer to the possibility that an alternative vision will subtend and undermine the chilling enforcement of normativity that follows.

Back in the living room—the primary domestic space of the family—events take an abrupt turn toward the tragic. Brandon is shoved now into the bathroom, a hyperreal space of sexual difference, and is violently de-pantsed by John and Tom, and then restrained by John while Tom roughly examines Brandon's crotch. The brutality of John and Tom's action here is clearly identified as a violent mode of looking, and the film identifies the male gaze with the factual, the visible, and the literal. The brutality of the male gaze, however, is more complicated than simply a castrating force; John and Tom not only want to see the site of Brandon's castration but more important, they need Lana to see it. Lana kneels in front of Brandon, confirming the scene's resemblance to a crucifixion tableau, and refuses to raise her eyes, declining, again, to look at Brandon's unveiling.

At the point when Lana's "family" and "friends" assert their heteronormative will most forcefully on Brandon's resistant body, however, Brandon rescues himself for a moment by regaining the alternative vision of time and space that he and Lana shared moments earlier in her bedroom. A slow-motion sequence interrupts the fast and furious quasi-medical scrutiny of Brandon's body, and shots from Brandon's point of view reveal him to be in the grips of an "out-of-body" and out-of-time experience. Light shines on Brandon from above, and his anguished face peers out into the crowd of onlookers who have gathered at the bathroom door. The crowd now includes a fully clothed Brandon, a double, who returns the gaze of the tortured Brandon impassively. In this shot/reverse shot sequence between the castrated Brandon and the transgender one, the transgender gaze is constituted as a look divided within itself, a point of view that comes from two places (at least) at the same time, one clothed and one naked. The clothed Brandon is the one who was rescued by Lana's refusal to look; he is the Brandon who survives his own rape and murder; he is the Brandon to whom the audience is now sutured, a figure who combines momentarily the activity of looking with the passivity of the spectacle. And the naked Brandon is the one who will suffer, endure, and finally expire. [...]

Not only does *Boys Don't Cry* create a position for the transgender subject that is fortified from the traditional operations of the gaze and conventional modes of gendering but it also makes the transgender subject dependent on the recognition of a woman. In other words, Brandon can be Brandon because Lana is willing to see him as he sees himself (clothed, male, vulnerable, lacking, strong, and passionate), and she is willing to avert her gaze when his manhood is in question. With Brandon occupying the place of the male hero and the male gaze in the romance, the dynamics of looking and gendered being are permanently altered. If usually it is the female body that registers lack, insufficiency, and powerlessness, in *Boys Don't Cry*, it is Brandon who represents the general condition of incompleteness, crisis, and lack, and it is Lana who represents the fantasy of wholeness, knowledge, and pleasure. Lana can be naked without trauma while Brandon cannot; she can access physical pleasure in a way that he cannot, but he is depicted as mobile and self-confident in a way that she is not. Exclusion and privilege cannot be assigned neatly to the couple on the basis of gender or class hierarchies; power, rather, is shared between the two subjects, and she agrees to misrecognize him as male while he sees through her social alienation and unhappiness, recognizing her as beautiful, desirable, and special.

By deploying the transgender gaze and binding it to an empowered female gaze in *Boys Don't Cry*, director Peirce, for most of the film, keeps the viewer trained on the seriousness of Brandon's masculinity and the authenticity of his presentation as opposed to its elements of masquerade. But toward the end of the film, Peirce suddenly and catastrophically divests her character of his transgender look and converts it to a lesbian and therefore female gaze. In a strange scene following the brutal rape of Brandon by John and Tom, Lana comes to Brandon as he lies sleeping in a shed outside of Candace's house. In many ways, the encounter between the two that follows seems to extend the violence enacted on Brandon's body by John and Tom since Brandon now interacts with Lana *as if he were a woman*. Lana, contrary to her previous commitment to his masculinity, seems to see him as female, and she calls him "pretty" and asks him what he was like as a girl. Brandon confesses to Lana that he has been untruthful about many things in his past, and his confession sets up the expectation that he will now appear before Lana as his "true" self. Truth here becomes sutured to nakedness as Lana disrobes Brandon, tentatively saying that she may not know "how to do this." "This" seems to refer to having sex with Brandon as a woman. They both agree that his whole journey to manhood has been pretty weird and then they move to make love. While earlier Peirce created quite graphic depictions of sex between Brandon and Lana, now the action is hidden by a Hollywood dissolve as if to suggest that the couple are now making love as opposed to having sex. The scene is disjunctive and completely breaks the flow of the cinematic text by having Lana, the one person who could see Brandon's gender separate from his sex, now see him as woman. Moreover, the scene implies that the rape has made Brandon a woman in a way that his brutal exposure earlier in the bathroom and his intimate sex scenes with Lana could not. And if the scene seems totally out of place to the viewer, it apparently felt wrong as well to Hilary Swank. There are rumors that Swank and Peirce fought over this scene, and that Peirce shot the scene without Swank by using a body double. A close reading of the end of the scene indeed shows that the Brandon figure takes off his T-shirt while the camera watches from behind. The musculature and look of Brandon's back is quite different here from the toned look of Swank's body in earlier exposure scenes.

The "love" scene raises a number of logical and practical questions about the representation of the relationship between Brandon and Lana. First, why would Brandon want to have sex within hours of a rape? Second, how does the film pull back from its previous commitment to his masculinity here by allowing his femaleness to become legible and significant to Lana's desire? Third, in what ways does this scene play against the earlier, more "plastic" sex scenes in which Brandon used a dildo and would not allow Lana to touch him? And fourth, how does this scene unravel the complexities of the transgender gaze as they have been assembled in earlier scenes between Brandon and Lana? When asked in an interview about this scene, Peirce reverts to a tired humanist narrative to explain it and says that after the rape, Brandon could not be either Brandon Teena or Teena Brandon and so he becomes truly "himself," and in that interaction with Lana, Brandon "receives love" for the first time as a human being.[5] Peirce claims that Lana herself told her about this encounter and therefore it was true to life. In the context of the film, however, which has made no such commitment to authenticity, the scene ties Brandon's humanity to a particular form of naked embodiment that in the end requires him to be a woman.

Ultimately in *Boys Don't Cry*, the double vision of the transgender subject gives way to the universal vision of humanism; the transgender man and his lover become lesbians, and the murder seems to be simply the outcome of a vicious homophobic rage. Given the failure of nerve that leads Peirce to conclude her film with a humanist scene of love conquers all, it is no surprise that she also sacrificed the racial complexity of the narrative by erasing the story of the other victim who died alongside Brandon and Lisa Lambert. As discussed earlier, Philip DeVine, a disabled African American man, has in general received only scant treatment in media accounts of the case, despite the connections of at least one of the murderers to a white supremacist group (Jones 1996, 154). Now in the feature film, Philip's death has been rendered completely irrelevant to the narrative that has been privileged. Peirce claimed that this subplot would have complicated her film and made the plot too cumbersome, but race is a narrative trajectory that is absolutely central to the meaning of the Brandon murder. Philip was dating Lana's sister, Leslie, and had a fight with her the night he showed up at Lisa's house in Humboldt County. His death was neither accidental nor an afterthought; his connection to Leslie could be read as a similarly outrageous threat to the supremacy and privilege of white manhood that the murderers Lotter and Nissen rose to defend. By taking Philip out of the narrative and by not even mentioning him in the original dedication of the film ("To Brandon Teena and Lisa Lambert"), the filmmaker sacrifices the hard facts of racial hatred and transphobia to a streamlined romance.[6] Peirce, in other words, reduces the complexity of the murderous act even as she sacrifices the complexity of Brandon's identity.

In the end, the murders are shown to be the result of a kind of homosexual panic, and Brandon is offered up as an "everyman" hero who makes a claim on the audience's sympathies first by pulling off a credible masculinity, but then by seeming to step out of his carefully maintained manhood to appear before judge and jury in the naked flesh as female. [...] *Boys Don't Cry* falls far short of the alternative vision that was articulated so powerfully and shared so beautifully by Brandon and Lana in Lana's bedroom. But even so, by articulating momentarily the specific formal dimensions of the transgender gaze, *Boys Don't Cry* takes a quantum leap away from the crying games, which continued in the past to locate transgenderism in between the male and female gazes and alongside unrelenting tragedy. Peirce's film, in fact, opens the door to a nonfetishistic mode of seeing the transgender body—a mode that looks with, rather than at, the transgender body and cultivates the multidimensionality of an indisputably transgender gaze.

What would a transgender film look like that did not punish the transgender subject for his or her inflexibilities and for failing to deliver the fantasy of fluidity that cinematic audiences so desire? *By Hook or by Crook* offers the spectator not one but two transgender characters, and the two together represent transgender identity as less of a function of bodily flexibility and more a result of intimate bonds and queer, interactive modes of recognition.

## LOVELY AND CONFUSING: *BY HOOK OR BY CROOK* AND THE TRANSGENDER LOOK

We feel like we were thrown almost every curve in the game. And we managed to make this thing by hook or by crook.

—Harry Dodge and Silas Howard, *By Hook or by Crook* directors

*By Hook or by Crook* marks a real turning point for queer and transgender cinema. This no-budget, low-tech, high-concept feature, shot entirely in mini digital video, tells the story of two gender bandits, Shy and Valentine. Described by its creators as "utterly post-post-modern, a little bit of country and a little bit of rock and roll," the film conjures up the twilight world of two loners living on the edge without trying to explain or rationalize their reality. [7] The refusal to explain either the gender peculiarities of the heroes or the many other contradictions they embody allows directors Howard and Dodge instead to focus on developing eccentric and compelling characters. While most of the action turns on the bond between Shy and Valentine, their world is populated with a stunning array of memorable characters like Valentine's girlfriend, Billie (Stanya Kahn), and Shy's love interest, Isabelle (Carina Gia). [... These appearances] establish the world of *By Hook or by Crook* as a specifically queer universe. [...]

Both *The Crying Game* and *Boys Don't Cry* relied heavily on the successful solicitation of affect—whether revulsion, sympathy, or empathy—in order to give mainstream viewers access to a transgender gaze. And in both films, a relatively unknown actor (Jay Davidson and Hilary Swank, respectively) performs alongside a more well-known actor (Stephen Rea and Chloe Sevigny, respectively); the relative obscurity of the transgender actors allow them to pull off the feat of credibly performing a gender at odds with the sexed body even after the body has been brutally exposed. *By Hook or by Crook* resists the seduction of crying games and the lure of sentiment, and works instead to associate butchness and gender innovation with wit, humor, and style. The melancholia that tinges *The Crying Game* and saturates *Boys Don't Cry* is transformed in *By Hook or by Crook* into the wise delirium of Dodge's character, Valentine. Dodge and Howard (Shy) knowingly avoid engaging their viewers at the level of sympathy, pity, or even empathy, and instead they "hook" them with the basic tools of the cinematic apparatus: desire and identification.

Dodge and Howard pioneer some brilliant techniques of queer plotting in order to map the world of the willfully perverse. As they say in interviews, neither director was interested in telling a story about "being gay." Nor did Dodge and Howard want to spend valuable screen time explaining the characters' sexualities and genders to unknowing audiences. In the press kit, Dodge and Howard discuss their strategy in terms of representing sexuality and gender as follows: "This is a movie about a budding friendship between two people. The fact that they happen to be queer is purposefully off the point. If you call them something, other than sad, rambling, spirited, gentle, sharp or funny . . . you might call them '*butches*.'" [...]

In the film, Shy and Valentine visit cafes, clubs, shops, and hotels where no one reacts specifically to their butchness. This narrative strategy effectively *universalizes queerness* within this specific cinematic space. Many gay and lesbian films represent their characters and their struggles as "universal" as a way of suggesting that their film speaks to audiences beyond specific gay and lesbian audiences. But few do more than submit to the regulation of narrative that transforms the specific into the universal: they tell stories of love, redemption, family, and struggle that look exactly like every other Hollywood feature angling for a big audience. *By Hook or by Crook* actually manages to tell a queer story that is more than a queer story by refusing to acknowledge the existence of a straight world. Where the straight world is represented only through its institutions such as the law, the mental institution, or commerce, the queer cinematic world comes to represent a truly localized place of opposition—an opposition, moreover, that is to be found in committed performances of perversity, madness, and friendship. [...] *By Hook or by Crook* universalizes queerness without allowing its characters to be absorbed back into the baggy and ultimately heterosexist concept of the "human."

Different key scenes from the film build, capture, and sustain this method of universalizing queerness. In one scene soon after they meet, Shy and Valentine go to a club together. The club scene, filmed in San Francisco's notorious Lexington Bar, is a riotous montage of queer excess. The camera lovingly pans a scene of punky, pierced, tattooed, perverted young queers. [...] In *The Crying Game*, the bar scenes were used first to establish the credibility of Dil's womanhood and then, after she has "come out" to Fergus as male bodied, the bar scenes are used to cast her womanhood as incredible. [...] Dodge and Howard situate the queer bar as central to an alternative vision of community, space, time, and identity. In the bar, Valentine dances wildly and ecstatically while Shy sits apart from the crowd watching. The camera playfully scans the bar and then lines up its patrons for quick cameos. Here, Dodge and Howard are concerned to represent the bar as both a space of queer community and a place of singularity. The singularity of the patrons [...] reveals a difference to be a shared and a collaborative relation to normativity rather than an individualist mode of refusal.

After watching Valentine dance, Shy gets up and steals Valentine's wallet before leaving. The theft of Valentine's wallet should create a gulf of distrust and suspicion between the two strangers, but in this looking-glass world, it actually bonds them more securely within their underground existence. Shy uses Valentine's wallet to find out where she lives, and when Shy returns Valentine's wallet the next day, she is greeted like a long-lost brother—this has the effect of inverting the morality of the world represented in this film by the police. Other scenes deepen this refusal of conventional law and order. The two butches as wannabe thieves try to hold up a drugstore only to be chased off by an aggressive salesclerk; they try to scam a hardware store and, in a citation of Robert De Niro's famous scene from *Taxi Driver,* they pose with guns in front of the mirror in Shy's run-down motel room. All of these scenes show Shy and Valentine as eccentric, but gentle outlaws who function as part of an alternative universe with its own ethics, sex/gender system, and public space.

[... While] De Niro's character accidentally hits a vein of humor with his mohawked "fuck you," Shy and Valentine deliberately ride butch humor rather than macho vengeance into the sunset. If the vigilante wants to remake the world in his image, the queer outlaws of *By Hook or by Crook* are content to imagine a world of their own making. When asked about the title of the film, Silas Howard responded: "The title refers to what is involved in inventing your own world—when you don't see anything that represents you out there, how can you seize upon that absence as an opportunity to make something out of nothing, by hook or by crook. We take gender ambiguity, for example, and we don't explain it, dilute it or apologize for it—we represent it for what it is—something confusing and lovely!"

The recent explosion of transgender films forces us to consider what the spectacle of the transgender body represents to multiple audiences. For some audiences, the transgender body confirms a fantasy of fluidity so common to notions of transformation within the postmodern. To others, the transgender body confirms the enduring power of the binary gender system. But to still other viewers, the transgender body represents a Utopian vision of a world of subcultural possibilities. Representations of transgenderism in recent queer cinema have moved from a tricky narrative device designed to catch an unsuspecting audience off guard to truly independent productions within which gender ambiguity is not a trap or a device but part of the production of new forms of heroism, vulnerability, visibility, and embodiment. The centrality of the figure of Brandon in this drama of postmodern embodiment suggests [...] that we have a hard time thinking of seismic shifts in the history of representations separate from individual stories of transformation. The hopes and fears that have been projected onto the slim and violated body of one transgender loner in small-town Nebraska make clear the flaws of "representative history," and call for the kind of shared vision that we see in *By Hook or by Crook*—a vision of community, possibility and redemption through collaboration.

## NOTES

1. For an excellent discussion of the political contradictions of *The Crying Game,* see Shantanu Dutta Ahmed, " 'Thought You Knew!' Performing the Penis, the Phallus, and Otherness in Neil Jordan's *The Crying Game*" (1998). [...]
4. Patricia White has argued in "Girls Still Cry" (2001) that the gaze in *Boys Don't Cry* is Lana's all along. [...]
5. Interview by Terry Gross on *Fresh Air,* PBS Radio, March 15, 2001.
6. In the review copy of the film I saw, *Boys Don't Cry* was dedicated "To Brandon Teena and Lisa Lambert." This dedication seems to have been removed later on, possibly because it so overtly referenced Philip's erasure.
7. Unless otherwise attributed, all quotes from directors Howard and Dodge are taken from the press kit for *By Hook or by Crook,* http://www.steakhaus.com/bhobc/.

# 10

# *Embracing Transition, or Dancing in the Folds of Time*

Julian Carter

In this meditation on transgender time and movement, Julian Carter performs a close reading of contemporary choreographer Sean Dorsey's dance work *Lou* (2009), about Lou Sullivan, a transsexual activist who, among other things, kept a diary from age eleven, started FTM International, and promoted the visibility of trans men like himself who identified as gay. Carter begins his essay with a consideration of that paradigmatic expression of transness as physical immobility, "the soul of a woman trapped in a man's body." He points out that the word typically translated from the original Latin phrase as "trapped"—*inclusa*—can also be interpreted as meaning embraced or enfolded. What happens to the "wrong body" transsexuals are often thought to be trapped in, Carter asks, if we begin to rearticulate *inclusa* as a condition of possibility for being enfolded or moved toward something else? Carter notes that "transition," in addition to being transgender argot for changing genders, is a choreographic term for how movements are linked; he then offers dance criticism of the transitional gestures and movements that Dorsey uses to stage Lou's transition from social womanhood into a gay male community. Carter reads Dorsey's staging of transition as "inherently relational"; it is communal, interconnected, and generative not only of individual trans subjects but of sexual communities. In a final section, Carter offers a way to understand differently the time and space of gender transition (what he names "transitional time"). Rather than conceiving transition as a linear progression, what would happen, he asks, if we imagined transitions between genders, like choreographic transitions, as places in time in which numerous movements—forward, backward, sideways, tangential—are equally possible and can coexist?

*Anima mulieris in corpore virilis inclusa*: the soul of a woman imprisoned in a man's body. Karl Ulrichs' 1862 account of trans- experience echoes into our own time in variants of the phrase "trapped in the wrong body." Culturally powerful and politically controversial, claimed and resisted in many ways, such descriptions can feel like a potent form of truth-telling about gender even while they mobilize a troubling vision of embodiment as a form of constraint. To imagine the body as a prison for the soul is to participate, however reluctantly, in a conceptual universe where our flesh is inconvenient matter which limits the free expression of our inner and nobler being. Such a vision seems to cement us into a position of permanent helpless struggle. In this depressive figuration, simply to be embodied is already to be trapped by a wrongness inseparable from the condition of materiality. The historico-cultural slippage from ascription to evaluation—from Ulrich's sexed body to the more contemporary wrong body—deepens the sense of hopeless entrapment: physical sex easily becomes a condition of existential inadequacy. No way out.

But this impasse is not inevitable. *Inclusa* is the feminine perfect passive participle of the Latin verb *includere*, which means to enclose or include. You can use the same word to describe arms extending in embrace, pulling you in. Fem(me)inist explorations of sexual receptivity demonstrate that such gestures of welcome and desire are neither static nor passive but involve active bodily participation in social relationships.[1] It follows that to be *in corpore inclusa*, enfleshed, is not necessarily a trap, but rather the condition of possibility for movement toward one another. Do away with the (assumption of the) trap, and questions arise about what kinds of gestures toward sociality our "wrong" embodiment enables. Do away with the trap, and we can begin to explore the range of motion inherent in the dynamic prefix *trans-*.[2]

I wonder how the wrong body trope can be addressed differently if I put the emphasis on how trans- embodiment mobilizes us. I'm not the first to draw attention to the spatial dynamism of sex/gender change: a powerful tradition in trans- studies theorizes transition as movement, especially movement into the territory of the transformed, the unnatural and monstrous, the cyborg and the transspecies.[3] My focus here is more quotidian. I want to consider transition in terms of physical gestures, movements from place to place (*trans/situ*) that simultaneously shift our relations with our own bodies and the bodies of others. But gesture is not only physical.[4] The English word derives from the Latin *gesturus*, a future active participle of the verb *gerere*, to carry or bear; *gesturus* means "I am about to carry." Gesture is an anticipatory performance of our physical bearing. If we listen to the futural temporality embedded in the word's root, we can hear not only intentionality in relation to actions as we undertake them, but also a triple meaning of the word "to bear," which means to comport one's body in a particular way, to carry something, and to endure. To gesture, then, is to embody one's intention, and may entail assuming a certain open-ended responsibility for what one carries. Taking gender transition literally, as a matter of gesture, can facilitate thinking about its impact on relationality in ways that attend to the physicality of embodiment without bracketing the body's social, psychic, and affective dimensions.

Considering gender transition as embodied gesture also raises questions about related issues of continuity, retroflexion, and anticipation.[5] In trans- contexts the term "transition" is most often used to refer to the period of time during which one shifts the sex/gender of one's anatomical body and/or presentation of self in the world. As I'll show, such shifting in space can open time so that developmental sequences, backward turns, and futural impulses coexist and intertwine. Dance has a highly developed technical vocabulary for talking about just such movements in spacetime. In dance worlds, transitions are shifts from one kind of movement to another. They are physical strategies—which may include gestures, motion pathways, adjustments of weight or tension or tempo—that redirect embodied energies so that (for instance) a forward movement becomes a sideways step, or a slowly moving body accelerates. Transitional gestures are the small, often unobtrusive movements that connect and contextualize poses, positions, sequences, or ways of moving that might otherwise seem disjunctive; or conversely they can be ways of interrupting a predictable flow, heightening contrast or calling attention to the moment where one sequence of movements changes into another. Or transitional awareness can index the energetic exchange between bodies, their capacity to sense the presence and proximity of other beings. Transition, as it's realized in dance, joins references to time and references to space in ways that allow us to consider the dimension of embodied relationality that involves movement. As such, dance provides an appropriate analytic framework for trans- work: it is the technical language par excellence of bodies in motion. This essay, then, brings dance's precision about physical movement to bear on embodied trans- subjects.

## *LOU*

All dance proceeds via transitions, but very little dance represents transition in terms of gender. Trans- choreographer Sean Dorsey's critically acclaimed work *Lou* (2009) is therefore an especially useful source for this discussion. *Lou* is Dorsey's homage to FTM (female-to-male) activist Lou Sullivan (1951–1991). In 1976 Sullivan began seeking sex reassignment but was routinely rejected from gender clinics because then-current medical protocols defined eligibility for sex change according to medico-psychiatric gatekeepers' assessment of whether the person seeking to transition would be able to function socially as a "normal" man or woman.[6] As a woman whose erotic gestures were directed toward men, Sullivan's social movements already appeared to conform to normative expectations for his embodiment; therefore his desire for transition seemed simply perverse to his doctors. His insistence on the legitimacy of his intention to move in the world as a gay man, and his persistent post-transition engagement with psychiatrists positioned to parlay their convictions into recommendations for practice, were instrumental in changing standards of care to accommodate queer outcomes: Sullivan's trailblazing activities expanded opportunities for medically-assisted transition toward embodiments legible as gay for later generations of trans men.[7] He also helped to found an international FTM community, initially through a support group in San Francisco and later through editing a newsletter that circulated nationally and internationally, linking its readers through community announcements, political and medical news, and historical anecdotes. And almost every day for thirty years, Lou Sullivan kept a diary in which he detailed his relationship to himself as well as his many and varied encounters with thousands of people.[8]

This is the figure at the center of Dorsey's *Lou*. The dance is performed by four men moving to an original score featuring spoken excerpts from Sullivan's diaries, supplemented with Dorsey's reflections on those texts and on his own affective and creative responses to the issues they raise. At the core of this piece is a certain productive refusal to maintain clear subjective and temporal boundaries between the choreographer and the object of his homage. Not only does Dorsey mix his words with Sullivan's, he physically embodies his sense of Sullivan's experience by dancing the title character's role.[9] But while Dorsey's physical re-creation and inhabitation of Sullivan's social gestures work to extend Sullivan's presence into the moment of performance, Dorsey's written text insists that the past is gone and can't be regained. The first and last movements of *Lou* are meditations on the permanence of loss, the transience of memory, and the unreliability of history. "History," Dorsey declares, "is a trick the living play on the dead," not least because it so often forgets or conceals the poverty of its representation of their lives.

*Lou* thus stages the tension between the material reality of historical loss—the past as dead and gone—and the equally material reality of physical rememory—the past as embodied in the living present.[10] The four dancers' gestures are not literal enactments of the voice-over text. Instead they develop a bodily representation of loss that can't be separated from their simultaneous fleshly recreation of and relationship to the lost subject. For instance, one of the dance's core motifs is a sequence in which one dancer embraces another's chest and shoulders, then stands while the one being held dips his knees to slide out of the embrace and step away. The result is an empty circle of arms with the palms turned inward toward the face (Figure 10.1).

Dorsey's voice-over tells us that people die and we are left with the space they once filled, until over time we come to imagine that space as an adequate reflection of who they were in life. Yet while the words are about absence and grief, the changing experience of loss is made tangible on stage through the continued living presence of the "dead" subject, theatrically embodied by the very survivor who mourns its loss.

When we experience the dead as present in living flesh that nonetheless invokes, remembers, and mourns their absence, we are sensing time's ability to fold in on itself. This isn't another way of indicting our untrustworthy memories or faulty accounts of the past. The *when* of the dance in

**Figure 10.1** The embrace, emptied

performance and the *when* it depicts in its movements lie over one another like transparencies in an anatomical textbook, in which the layers of the body are necessarily perceived simultaneously and as a whole, while they are also palpably, if not always exactly visibly, distinct and separable. Watching, we see that the body's past both is and is not present in the present. Further, the present is not the past's future so much as its re-embodiment. The present does not merely cite the past (acknowledging, tacitly or overtly, that it is pointing to something outside of and other than itself in order to claim a particular relation of identity or alterity in relation to it), but is instead a rematerialization of it.

This approach to the past is a sensuous operation as well as an analytic one. The body is always in its present, which does not prevent it from both rubbing up against and remaking its past in a way that utterly defies historical logic. Embodiment provides a compelling model for developmental, sequential history in its progressive physical maturation through years of growth and aging, and yet at the same time the body's capacity not only to index but also to embody a past it never experienced presents a major challenge to any such notion of linearity. This complexly invaginated, profoundly relational experience of temporality is especially significant in the sections of Dorsey's dance that stage Sullivan's transition from female to male. The first of these sections, titled "I Want to Look Like What I Am," presents gender transition as entry into relationship, an entry that sends time swirling around itself and around people who are set in motion by the decision to change sex. The second section, "Desire," stages the physicality and consequentiality of trans- interventions into the social.

## JOY

"I Want to Look Like What I Am" opens with the cast reading excerpts from Sullivan's diaries that highlight both Sullivan's pre-transition identification with gay men and his uncertainty about making that identification real through transitioning. As the other dancers file off the stage and leave Dorsey alone, the soundtrack continues with Dorsey's voice reading the words *"I want to look like what I am, but I don't know what someone like me looks like."* Wandering passages of movement, frequently executed with Dorsey's back to the audience or with his focus curled into his torso, provide visual counterpoint to the soundtrack's evocation of solitary self-questioning. We hear how Sullivan's library research yields no evidence that anyone like him has ever existed, and learn the consequences for him of this lack of human recognition: *"Hidden from view I'm losing touch."* Sullivan's choice of words is telling: the split subjectivity of the unrealized transsexual produces both the sensation and the performance of a physical disconnection indistinguishable from lack of social engagement.

Dorsey interrupts his performance of isolation by staging the classic transgender experience of wrong embodiment. Walking downstage center, face to face with the audience, Dorsey introduces gender transition as a move toward relationality via folds in time, recognition, and embodiment. As he faces us, his recorded voice says: *"I look in the mirror and say to myself, that's you? That girl over there is you."* The proscenium stands in for the frame of the mirror such that the audience is positioned as looking through it at him while he looks at himself. What we see there is importantly different from what he tells us he sees in that the person on the stage does not occupy a social space marked "girl." The resulting stumble of perception marks Dorsey's queer inscription of his viewing audience into the wrong-body narrative. We are called to occupy the position of the outsider whose visual perception of sexed embodiment doesn't align with the transsexual sense of self. Yet at the same moment and through the same summons to relationship we are positioned as transsexuals, at risk of seeming deluded because we perceive Dorsey's masculinity even though the "objective reality" that pertains within the dramatic situation—what we are told the mirror reflects—says "girl." And we in the audience are summoned as affirmative witnesses to the temporal transitivity of the transgender embodiment on the stage in front of us. Through the looking glass we see the trans man's body standing in for its own potential before it was brought into being.

On one level, "I Want to Look Like What I Am" follows a conventional narrative arc that maps neatly onto a triumphalist model of time as progress: in this section, we see Lou Sullivan moving from isolation and confusion toward self-realization and, eventually, sociosexual affirmation. But the arc of that story is the narrative equivalent of the proscenium arch in that, while it lends authority to a particular view of the action on the stage, it does not fully contain the potential of the movement that unfolds there. Dorsey's depiction of transition as progress toward sociality provides a stabilizing frame for his depiction of transition as an elaborately transtemporal relational formation. Such an arrangement may appear like an aesthetic compromise, a pulling-back from his own exploration of transitional time in the interests of accessibility; audiences are comfortable with that narrative arc, and telling tales of becoming-transsexual transpiring within its frame may serve a normalizing, universalizing function. One could come away from this piece with dreams of social progress confirmed, the hope for a more perfect body renewed. But it's also true that Dorsey shows triumphalist and invaginated time as co-existing, a convergence which challenges the assumption that they are opposed and mutually exclusive modes of temporality. In doing so he pushes us to consider through what gestures, and through what physical relationships, the time of transition unfolds.

Transition pleats time, and in so doing transforms our relational capacities. Dorsey enacts that folding as inseparable from Sullivan's frustrated need for embodied social contact: *"My voice and my body betray me. I mean, no-one looks deeper than the flesh, do they. So practice being invisible. Learn to look in the mirror and see only the mirror."* At this point dancer Brian Fisher walks up behind Dorsey and stands at his back, mirroring his moves (Figure 10.2) while Dorsey's recorded voice, speaking Sullivan's words, announces an intention to *"See only the person there that I imagine myself to be. And make this change."*

With this utterance Dorsey shifts from Sullivan's remembrance of the "years of this wondering, not validated by anybody" to his own enactment of Sullivan's transition. This is simultaneously a narrative transition from female to male and a choreographic transition in which Dorsey turns away from his imaginary mirror and toward a physical relationship with another dancing body on the stage.

**Figure 10.2** The shadow in the mirror

These transitions are explicitly romantic in gesture and in utterance. The core movement motif of this section is an embrace, and Sullivan's words record his experience of transition as a romance that is none the less social because it is with the self: *"I think of myself as two people, finally coming together in peace with each other, but of my other half I sing, 'Nobody loves me, but me adores you.' I am positive I want to do this, this change. My own body. This limitless joy. Imagine. I am finally going to be able to look in the mirror and see the person there I imagine myself to be."* Holding hands, the dancers twine (Figure 10.3).

They step around one another's legs and through one another's arms, resting their heads against one another, lifting one another off the floor and circling one another with their weight until Dorsey pulls Fisher face to face and suddenly Fisher is leading this same-sex couple in a few measures that quote a tango. We are being shown that they are passionate partners in a movement pattern that is formally structured by gender, but which does not duplicate the conventional heterogendered relations of social dance. Then, just as suddenly, Dorsey turns out of Fisher's arms, pulls him against his back, closes Fisher's arms around his chest and dips his knees to slide out of the embrace he has made.

With this movement Dorsey repeats the core motif of the opening section of *Lou*, the sequence that enacts the transition from loss to grief to memory to history. This slipping-through is a repetition of the previous gesture but it is enacted now to the words *"I am positive I want to do this."* This is a repetition with a difference, a gesture that fills the space of loss with the realization of connection.[11] Dorsey, who has slipped out of Fisher's grasp, turns his back to his partner and faces us with the words *"My own body,"* just as Fisher's hands land softly on Dorsey's hips and Dorsey opens his arms soft and wide as his weight wavers in Fisher's hands. In its earlier iteration this gesture signified memory, the last personal trace of the dead before they are abstracted into history. Repeated now, it combines the lightness and uncertainty of flight toward the future, and it is grounded in the present by his partner's touch. Dorsey is staging "this change" as the transtemporal enactment of self-love, a relation of mutual trust and reliance between the gay man who is coming into being and the person

**Figure 10.3** Partnering the shadow self

who has been a girl and a woman before this point in his life. As the narrator anticipates *"I am finally going to be able to look in the mirror,"* the dancers, facing one another, take turns creating openings with their arms for the other to slip through. The gestural sequence that once performed loss and memory's fading into historical misrepresentation now communicates not only transformation but also the delights of looking forward to a scene of secure recognition.

Yet the transformations and recognitions the dancers anticipate have in fact already taken place. Dorsey offers a vision of transsexual self-fashioning in which the gay man who will be the end product of transition guides and supports the trans man-in-the-making as he begins to realize himself. The trans man dancing the role of a female-bodied person just embarking on transition could be seen as a turn toward the past that Dorsey and Sullivan, as trans men, can be said to share insofar as both were once girls: but it is also a kind of folding forward of her life into his, a suggestion that her body held its breastless future just as his holds its breasted past. The supple cisgendered gay man dancing the role of the trans fag who has not yet come into being is also folding time forward, toward the erotic masculinity that transition enabled Sullivan to access, and back toward a past in which the trans man was a man all along. Time's pleating here is inseparable from affective and intercorporeal connection.

This magical temporality, where many layers of anticipation, experience, loss, and memory fold into one another, takes physical shape as an extraordinarily delicate intimacy between the dancers. Fisher, in black, melts visually into the dark stage so that his movement can be perceived primarily as his body shadows the cream-clad Dorsey. Like a shadow, his body is not quite the same as Dorsey's, but instead of rendering Dorsey's embodiment uncanny or inauthentic in its similitude without sameness, Fisher's shadow-role serves to provide Dorsey's embodiment with a visual depth of field that is emotionally analogous to intersubjective context. One embodied aspect of the self dances with another. We witness transsexual self-fashioning as inherently, physically relational, and as deeply tender.

The narration underscores this relational quality by introducing an interlocutor; the voice-over tells us *"He asked if I was scared and I said 'Just the opposite.' Afraid for so long, I now know I can do anything, be anything, exactly who I am."* On this phrase, Dorsey walks forward with Fisher at his back, holding Fisher's hands gently on his hips and stopping downstage center in a spotlight. We are looking through the mirror again. Head turned to the side, remaining in touch with his partner, Dorsey's hands follow Fisher's briefly as Fisher circles Dorsey's chest, but this time Dorsey doesn't slip through. Instead Fisher lifts Dorsey's shirt from the bottom hem. For a moment Dorsey's hands hover, suspended, and then together they slide the shirt off over his head. As Dorsey stands and looks at himself in his imaginary mirror, his mouth slightly open and his hand on his solar plexus, the narration folds time in on itself again with the whisper "*I always knew it would turn out to be like this.*"

The movement of taking off a shirt is simple both as gesture and as concept, but in this context it has disproportionate performative force. It is not a moment of coming out; we already know that Lou Sullivan and Sean Dorsey are transsexual men. When Dorsey bares his chest, he occupies Sullivan's bodily re-making for us to witness and celebrate. The gesture's evident communicative content, in this performance context, is something like "look at Sullivan's success by looking at my success! We are no longer wrongly embodied." But the physical presence in the spotlight exceeds its overt reference to the prior achievement of gendered rightness. Both dancers are sweating and breathing hard, and in their, and our, larger stillness, it's impossible not to feel the labor of their ribcages' pulsing, their collarbones rising with the air they suck. The gestures of respiration Dorsey presents at this moment reveal and solicit the sheer physical work of making connection. Knowledge here precedes both the existence of its object—the realized trans- body—and the existence of the subject who will know that body in and through its movement of disrobing. It's the attempt to make connection that sets these bodies in motion, that makes time fold and pleat. Watching these men breathe together while their larger travels from place to place are temporarily suspended, we see transition as a physical practice that exceeds alterations in individual embodiment. It's not only about the contours of Dorsey's chest, but also about the way his rematerialization of Sullivan's relation to himself performs and transforms the spatial and temporal transitivity of bodies. The fold in time produces a fold toward relationship: Dorsey turns his head as though to ask his shadow "*Did you know? I always knew it.*" Still holding his hip with one hand, the other caressing an arm, Fisher rests his head on the back of Dorsey's shoulder and the two of them sway with their shared breath as the narrator whispers "*Limitless joy. Just, joy.*"

## DESIRE

To push at what thinking transition as embodied movement can accomplish, I want to consider transitional gestures. Recall that transitions, in dancer-talk, are movements that accomplish change; they redirect moving bodies' relation to tempo, energetic focus, spatial orientation or intercorporeal connection. The transitional sequence of *Lou* to which I now turn is about forty seconds long and connects the duet that ends "I Want to Look Like What I Am" to the next movement of *Lou*, a full-company segment titled "Desire." I want to linger on a very brief—three-second—passage within this transitional sequence. Such lingering is not only for the pleasure it yields, though pleasure turns out to be a lot of what's at stake here. It also allows me to demonstrate transition's effectiveness as a conceptual tool for unpacking movement that is not explicitly or intentionally "about" changing sex.

After Dorsey takes off his shirt the stage goes dark and in that darkness Dorsey's recorded voice reads passages from Sullivan's diary about his emergence as a gay man. Three dancers enter wearing white boxer briefs and tank-tops. Spread out in a line near the back of the stage, they pose while we hear Sullivan exulting in his discovery that he is "a social being." "*I am desired, and I desire other men. I've got lost time to make up for,*" he tells us. "*I've got to make up for lost time.*" Again a temporal fold enables Sullivan's turn toward embodied relationship; the fantasy of re-occupying the past, using it better, animates his determination to occupy his masculinity through sexual contact. As the narrator invokes time, the dancers reach toward one another. Wrists crossed and holding hands (Figure 10.4),

**Figure 10.4** Three gay cygnets

**Figure 10.5** Unraveling the cygnets' chain

they sketch the first steps of *Swan Lake*'s Dance of the Cygnets before unraveling their tidy full-frontal pattern into a loose chain (Figure 10.5).

While the three men—still holding hands—turn and twist through one another's arms, the narrator reads from Sullivan's diary about the sexual acceptance and pleasure he experienced among gay men.

The three seconds Dorsey borrows from *Swan Lake* serve as a transition from a sequence in which the men preen as individuals, connected only by the precise timing of their movements, to a sequence in which their gestures become socially intertwined so that they respond to and flow out of one another's bodies. In between—during the cygnets' steps—they hold hands and step in unison, physically and temporally connected but not yet motivating or responding to one another's gestures. It's a moment of proximity that has not yet become sociality. On the level of narrative, it connects the longing to embody masculinity depicted in "I Want to Look Like What I Am" to the longing to touch other men. It takes us from the desire for gender to sexual desire, from the desire to be a man to the desire to have men.[12] And it accomplishes that transition into the social through a gestural image that returns us to the "wrong body" trope, this time heavily laden with normative expectations for the gendered temporality through which we enter into relationships.

*Swan Lake*'s Dance of the Cygnets is a famous *pas de quatre* for four young women who demonstrate the purity and precision of their ballet technique by executing increasingly bravura steps side by side while holding hands across one another's waists. It stages mutual support among adolescent girls as a charming phase to be superseded by heterosexual pairing: in the ballet world, a cygnet transitions into a swan when she is offered a romantic *pas de deux* with a male lead, a framing expectation that sentimentalizes the ephemerality of same-sex companionship. The cygnets' shoulder-to-shoulder configuration embodies the cultural demand that girls identify with other girls. Simultaneously, it displays them for an implied masculine viewer, anticipating the dissolution of their identificatory intimacy through sexual competition.

When Dorsey gives these girlish steps to three adult men, the choreography's references to conventional gender and sexual development fracture into a representation of a particularly gay temporality. Three men are not four girls, and as such they are clearly the wrong bodies for the Dance of the Cygnets. Or one could say that the Dance of the Cygnets is a culturally wrong movement for adult male bodies: whether you place the emphasis on the form or the gesture, morphologies and movements don't line up in conventional ways. Much of that queer disjunction has to do with time. Because these men dance steps that "belong" to adolescents, they can be imagined as performing their own developmental failure.[13] For a grown man to embody a cygnet suggests a perverse refusal to grow out of same-sex intimacies: men acting like teenagers materialize their homosexuality as an arrest of development. Further, because the men's gestures invoke a past in which they were girls, these gestures suggest that the putative effeminacy of proto-gay boys overlaps the youthful femininity of the trans man-to-be.[14] The temporal disjunctions launched by the cygnets' steps serve to connect the three dancing men to one another along an axis of shared physical and dynamic wrongness, which, in turn, launches their creation of a mutually supportive intimacy. When adult men's arms and ankles cross to compose the cygnets' network of intersecting lines, *Swan Lake*'s sentimental homophobia is replaced with a web of connection. These cygnets transition us into gay community. And by staging this transition with three dancers instead of *Swan Lake*'s four, Dorsey opens a space on the stage where the fourth dancer belongs even before he appears.

His entry will matter all the more because his absence carries such a powerful charge. Dorsey is offstage during this transitional sequence, which means that the figure of the gay trans man literally stands to one side of the Dance of the Cygnets. His spatial marginalization during this sequence suggests that the intersection of gay tropes of arrested development with trans- tropes of wrong embodiment works differently for trans- subjects than for gay ones. The narrator has already hinted that Sullivan's transition will enable his entry into gay men's public sexual culture, where he'll "make up for lost time," but he can't do that by turning toward the adolescent femininity the cygnets' steps evoke. Retroflexion and delay would seem particularly complex for trans- subjects. Because Sullivan once embodied the category "teenage girl," arresting his development at that stage would foreclose his access to gay masculinity, not confirm it.[15] For Dorsey to dance toward girlhood, however gay the irony, does not constitute a queer arrest of development as much as a return to a non-consensually feminized past. In its movement away from trans- self-realization, such a return rejects futurity and in doing so forecloses Sullivan's desire to make up for the sexual time he lost by being embodied as a girl on his first tour through adolescence. When the future is refused, the past loses its dynamic potential and the subject finds itself stuck on the margins of time and social relationship. Making up for lost time requires a return with a difference, rather than an arrest.

Hence Dorsey/Sullivan does not—in some senses, cannot—do the cygnets' dance. This matters because that dance provides the choreographic transition that brings spatially separate, though visually connected, individuals into physical contact and communication. If the trans man cannot physically take the place of the fourth cygnet, how can he enter into gay sexual community? Dorsey answers with a return to the embrace. Still holding hands, the trio melts out of the little swans' lateral formation to collaborate on a low traveling lift, two of the men containing the third with their linked hands circling his waist, one pair of hands clasping in front and the other behind. The

**Figure 10.6** Three cygnets meet the fourth dancer

gesture sustains and intensifies the cygnets' interwoven arms. Held between his partners' hands and propelled by their forward motion, the third dancer arches back and extends his neck. The gesture feels intensely sexual in its exaggerated openness and sense of being carried along, as though the boundaries of the self were dissolving in sensation—but if the self dissolves, it's safely contained by the intimate touch of surrounding bodies.

We've just seen another form of intimate, containing touch in the embrace at the end of "I Want to Look Like What I Am," in which Fisher's hands provide physical and symbolic stabilization for Dorsey/ Sullivan as he commits himself to realizing his masculinity in his flesh. What's different about this embrace is the affect generated by its traveling execution with four arms, two dancers' hands clasped around a third body. Intimacy looks and feels different when it involves three people. *Pas de deux*— movement passages for two dancers who sustain physical contact with one another—are conventionally used to develop and express romance. Dorsey staged Sullivan's gender transition as a *pas de deux* in a way that emphasizes his vision of transition as expressing love for and reconciliation between halves of the self (one masculine, one feminine). In the transitional movement borrowed from the Dance of the Cygnets, Dorsey expands the embrace in a way that expands the relational connections among the bodies on stage. Through this visual reference to a *ménage à trois* we're offered a vision of eroticism as social contact, an expansion beyond privatized dyadic romantic love toward the sex clubs Sullivan frequented. Then the embrace expands again: the three cygnets land the traveling embrace face to face with Dorsey/Sullivan, who has entered quietly and stands watching their approach (Figure 10.6).

They look at one another for a heartbeat, then two, before the cygnets extend their hands and Dorsey joins their chain, weaving through their arms. His passage through their hands concludes with his chest arched back and neck extended, ecstasy running through his spine.

## FOLDING

Dorsey offers us a vision of the embrace as a gesture that transitions bodies to new sociotemporal contexts. At the beginning of *Lou*, circling arms indicate the progressive stages of response to death— from loss, to grief, to memory, to history. In "I Want to Look Like What I Am," variations on the same motif move the Sullivan character along a developmental path from isolation and confusion to self-recognition and, eventually, love. But other uses of this gesture interrupt conventional expectations of linear temporal and affective development. For instance, when Dorsey draws on the embrace used in partnered social dancing to depict the psychic and physical process of gender transition, he stages that transition as inherently relational in a way that makes time fold around the subject. In

"Desire," increasing expansions of the cygnets' embrace generate a sexual community wide enough to include Sullivan despite his temporal difference from other gay men. The expanded embrace produces a ripple effect out from the individual body of the transsexual man into the social body: the *ménage à trois* becomes a quartet, suggesting the possibility that we could keep adding more and more partners in an almost infinite expansion of possible intimacies. Further, the trans man's disruptive effect on the cygnets' signifying chain stages the historical expansion of the category "gay" to include transsexuals, and the category "transsexual" to include "gay," at the end of the 1980s. Such transformations demonstrate that bodies can change the social contexts in which they move. Dorsey shows us that Sullivan's transition did more than make him a gay man: it helped widen the social worlds in which bodies natally assigned to femininity could embrace, and be included in, erotic manhood. Because we watch Dorsey's work in a moment subsequent to the historical change he depicts, our current engagement with Sullivan's past must involve our own willingness to allow time to fold around our bodies as well. Thus the remaking of the body that is becoming-transsexual changes both the content and the form of social relationships, with profound temporal implications.

This essay can't finish with a conventional conclusion because the medium it engages works against tidy endings. Movement doesn't conclude when the dancers bow. There's always another transition ahead, another step, another opportunity to change direction and approach other bodies; not to attend to that embodied and relational reality would be to betray this project's deepest investments. Besides, there's something compelling about the circular, recursive temporality that emerges from the gesture of the embrace. And so we circle back to the question with which I began: how the wrong-body trope works differently when being *in corpore inclusa* is considered not as a flesh trap but as the condition of possibility for our movement toward other bodies. The wrong-body trope most often drives an understanding of gender transition as a reparative process through which one alters a bad form so that its structure aligns with and reflects a particular content more precisely. That understanding presumes that content exists prior to and separate from its expression; further, it tends to impose a linear temporality on transition so that it serves as a hinge between two distinct conditions linked and separated by a point of redirection in an otherwise intact timeline (e.g., not this future, in a woman's body, but that future, in a man's body).[16] The problem with such accounts of transition is that they can consider time only as an inert substance linking physical moments or embodied states that are static in themselves. In contrast, Dorsey offers us a vision of transitional time, and transitioning bodies, as dynamic and relational negotiations of wrongness. He shows us how transition enfolds the body in its own material substance, yet allows for that substance's alteration. Anticipation, retroflexion, and continuity co-exist in the same body, at the same moving moment of space and time. Transitioning subjects anticipate a gender content they generate recursively out of their physical medium's formal potential in relation to the context of its emergence. One might say transition wraps the body in the folds of social time.

Transitional time's folds may drag on the body in a way that produces the sense of arrest, deferral, and delay so richly explored by queer theorists of temporality.[17] Queer time is widely theorized in opposition to temporal straightness, the normative and limiting "logic of development" that subtends and legitimizes many objectionable discursive constructions and sociopolitical formations, from individual maturation through reproduction to eugenic imperialism.[18] From this analytic perspective, when Dorsey opens a representation of gay sexual community by having adult men execute steps choreographed for adolescent girls, he is staging the social and libidinal joys of arrested development—joys worth celebrating not only for their physical pleasure but also for their interruption of normative expectations for how, and through which forms of relationality, individual lives should progress. This works fine as a description of the way that Dorsey's choreography communicates the gay sexuality of the three men dancing together, but, as I suggested above, queer valorizations of temporal lag are not quite adequate to theorizing the fourth dancer's absence, or the way his entry shifts the social field. As the temporal lag of arrested development opens the space for same-sex bonding and polymorphous perversity, it simultaneously shuts down the space for becoming-trans. For a trans- subject like Lou Sullivan, developmental arrest can lead to imprisonment in a wrong body: remaining a teenage girl forecloses rather than instantiates his adult male homosexuality.

Fortunately, transitional time's folding can have other effects beyond drag. It may heighten the body's sensitivity, invaginating it so that it touches itself in several different moments at once; thus, after transition materializes Sullivan's adult gay masculinity, he might return to his girlhood as a site of youthful effeminacy. He might embody the boy, the girl, and the adult man all at the same time. Or transitional time's pleats may propel the body forward: Sullivan left girlhood behind to become a man. Sex change does involve purposive movement toward an embodied future, even as that future is summoned into being in and through a body that does not yet exist, and while the body that does exist in the present is the medium for the future body's becoming-form. Transitional time's incorporation of both straight and queer temporalities exemplifies a certain heuristic spaciousness in the concept of trans-, a spaciousness wide enough to enclose the notion of queer time in a trans-embrace.

## NOTES

1. In addition to Joan Nestle's classic works, especially *A Restricted Country* (San Francisco, CA: Firebrand Books 1987), see descriptions of femme sexual agency in Heidi Levitt and Katherine Heistand, "Gender Within Lesbian Sexuality: Butch and Femme Perspectives," *Journal of Constructivist Psychology* 18 (2005): 39–51; Juana María Rodríguez, "Gesture and Utterance: Fragments from a Butch/Femme Archive," in *A Companion to LGBT Studies*, ed. George Haggerty and Molly McGarry (Malden, MA: Blackwell Publishing, 2007), 282–291.
2. On the trans- prefix see Susan Stryker, Paisley Currah, and Lisa Jean Moore, "Trans-, Trans, or Transgender?" *WSQ* 36: 3–4 (2008), 11–22.
3. Several essays in *The Transgender Studies Reader*, ed. Susan Stryker and Stephen Whittle (New York: Routledge, 2006) provide an introduction to these themes. See especially Susan Stryker, "My Words to Victor Frankenstein above the Village of Chamounix: Performing Transgender Rage" (244–256); Donna Haraway, "A Cyborg Manifesto: Science, Technology, and Socialist-Feminism in the Late Twentieth Century" (103–120). For a critical exploration of the social and legal consequences of phobic figuration of transsexuality as monstrous, see Abigail Lloyd, "Defining the Human: Are Transgender People Strangers to the Law?" *Berkeley Journal of Gender, Law and Justice* 20 (2005), 150–195. See also Myra Hird, "Animal Transsex" in *Queering the Non/Human*, ed. Noreen Giffney and Myra Hird (London: Ashgate, 2008), 227–248; Eva Hayward, "More Lessons from a Starfish: Prefixial Flesh and Transspeciated Selves," *WSQ* 36: 3–4 (2008), 64–85.
4. Adam Kendon, *Gesture: Visible Action as Utterance* (Cambridge: Cambridge University Press, 2004); David McNeill, *Gesture and Thought* (Chicago, IL: University of Chicago Press, 2007); Carrie Noland, *Agency and Embodiment: Performing Gestures/Producing Culture* (Boston, MA: Harvard University Press, 2009).
5. Current queer theoretical examinations of temporality emphasize the extent to which non-normativity can scramble time, undoing the linear sequentiality characteristic of straight temporality; but despite Halberstam's work on trans-subjects in *In a Queer Time and Place: Transgender Bodies, Subcultural Lives* (New York: New York University Press, 2005), this critical literature rarely treats gender in terms sensitive to or informed about trans- scholarship and experience. See, for instance, Carolyn Dinshaw *et al.* "Theorizing Queer Temporalities: A Roundtable Discussion," *GLQ: A Journal of Lesbian and Gay Studies* 13: 2–3 (2007), 177–195; Elizabeth Freeman, *Time Binds: Queer Temporalities, Queer Histories* (Durham, NC: Duke University Press, 2010).
6. "Medical Correspondence Regarding Sex-Reassignment, 1976–1990," especially correspondence with the Stanford Gender Dysphoria Clinic, Louis G. Sullivan Papers, 97-1, San Francisco GLBT Historical Society.
7. Susan Stryker, "Portrait of a Transfag Drag Hag as a Young Man: The Activist Career of Louis G. Sullivan," in *Reclaiming Gender: Transsexual Grammars at the Fin de Siecle*, ed. Kate More and Stephen Whittle (London: Cassells, 1999), 62–82.
8. "Guide to the Louis Graydon Sullivan Papers," 97-1, San Francisco GLBT Historical Society.
9. This subjective overlapping extends offstage, where Dorsey is a trailblazing transgender presence in dance and the founder of an important arts organization, Fresh Meat, which stages a festival of trans- arts each June. As a writer of texts and of dances, and as a trans- community organizer, Dorsey extends Sullivan's social roles into a historical and cultural moment Sullivan didn't live to see.
10. "Rememory" is the term Toni Morrison uses in her novel *Beloved* (New York: Alfred A Knopf, 1987) to capture the complexity of memories that exceed individual experience and consciousness. See Caroline Rody, "Toni Morrison's Beloved: History, 'Rememory' and a 'Clamor for a Kiss,'" *American Literary History* 7:1 (1995), 92–119.

11. See Judith Butler, *Undoing Gender* (New York: Routledge, 2004), especially Chapter One, "Beside Oneself: On the Limits of Sexual Autonomy."

12. The phrase "the desire for gender" has been floated by at least two previous theorists, Sheila Jeffreys and Robyn Weigman. For Jeffreys, the desire for gender is a symptom of collusion with the existing sexist binary system; she assumes that "gender" is a reflection of heteronormativity, such that without its asymmetrical polarizations "gender" would have no meaning. See "Heterosexuality and the Desire for Gender," *Theorizing Heterosexuality*, ed. Diane Richardson (Buckingham, UK: Open University Press, 1996), 75–90. For Weigman, the desire for gender describes a feminist analytic: it "serves as a way to name how, as gender has been pursued as an object of study, it has proliferated, instead of settled, meaning, becoming one thing and then another as it has traveled across different domains where it has been wielded, differently, as both explanation and solution to the problems it has named." "The Desire for Gender," in *A Companion to LGBT Studies*, 231.

    My usage is (oddly enough) more aligned with Jeffreys' political argument than with Weigman's analytic, in that Jeffreys does think of the desire for gender in terms of the longing to take up a particular embodied place in the social order and thus making oneself available for particular kinds of relationships; further, she recognizes that gender has an erotic dimension and that much eroticism mobilizes gender. Susan Stryker would seem to concur, describing "gender categories (like man and woman)" as enabling "desire to take shape and find its aim." "Transgender Studies: Queer Theory's Evil Twin," *GLQ: A Journal of Lesbian and Gay Studies* 10:2 (2004), 212.

    In my usage, the desire for gender is not an alternative to sexual desire—so much of eroticism is bound up with gender, and vice versa, that any firm theoretical distinction (let alone opposition) between them will inevitably falter on the evidence of experience. But the desire for gender does not always overlap sexual desire in the sense that desire may prioritize gender itself as its aim. For instance, when Dorsey stages Sullivan's romance with his own futural dream of gay manhood, the relationship unfolding on stage is a materialization of Sullivan's longing to occupy masculinity, a longing that contains a fantasy of the social but that is nonetheless distinct from the social act of moving toward another person.

13. Juana María Rodríguez, writing about erotic gesture, has argued that no movement can be said to "belong" to a particular group ("Gesture and Utterance," 284). The point holds for ballet. Yet gestures also embody cultural traditions of which bodies will perform them and how—traditions that necessarily inflect their performance by other bodies.

14. Boyish effeminacy can also lead to a transfeminine future, of course. My formulation here is not meant to occlude this point but instead reflects the fact that in the context of Dorsey's dance, what's at stake is the way that femininity in youth can be a precursor to adult gay masculinity.

15. I am arguing here against Judith Halberstam's stance that "For queers, the separation between youth and adulthood quite simply does not hold... I want to return here to the notion of queer time, a different mode of temporality that might arise out of an immersion in ... queer sex cultures." Judith Halberstam, "What's That Smell," *In a Queer Time and Place*, 174. Such a valorization of delay and arrest works to marginalize a trans subject like Sullivan, for whom access to queer sex cultures depended on leaving adolescence.

16. The linear temporality of this construction has a spatial counterpart that appears in the travel narrative of trans-becoming, which figures sex change as a journey. Aren Aizura offers an able and elegant critique in "The Persistence of Transgender Travel Narratives," *Transgender Migrations: The Bodies, Borders, and Politics of Transition*, ed. Trystan T. Cotten (New York: Routledge, 2011), 139–156.

17. See especially J. Jack Halberstam, *In a Queer Time and Place*; Heather Love, *Feeling Backward: Loss and the Politics of Queer History* (Cambridge, MA: Harvard University Press, 2005); Kathryn Bond Stockton, *The Queer Child: Growing Sideways in the Twentieth Century* (Durham, NC: Duke University Press, 2009).

18. Elizabeth Freeman, "Time Binds, or Erotohistoriography," *Social Text* 23 (2005), 57–58; 59. Also see Julian Carter, *The Heart of Whiteness: Normal Sexuality and Race in America* (Durham, NC: Duke University Press, 2007) for a discussion of evolution's developmental narrative. Against developmental timelines and their political consequences, queer theorists have argued for the critical importance of putting on the brakes, turning backward or stepping sideways: evasive movements undertaken in part out of the conviction that resisting neoliberalism's claims for privatization as progress necessarily involves rejecting all developmental accounts or, for some, rejecting futurity as inherently complicit with reproductive investments that work to recreate a corrupt social order in its own image. See Lee Edelman, *No Future: Queer Theory and the Death Drive* (Durham, NC: Duke University Press, 2004); against Edelman, see José Esteban Muñoz, *Cruising Utopia: The Then and There of Queer Futurity* (New York: New York University Press, 2009); Juana María Rodríguez, "Queer Sociality and Other Sexual Fantasies," *GLQ: A Journal of Lesbian and Gay Studies* 17: 2–3 (2011), 331–348.

# III

## *TRANSSEXING HUMANIMALITY*

# 11

# Sex and Diversity, Sex Versus Gender, and Sexed Bodies

## Excerpts from *Evolution's Rainbow: Diversity, Gender, and Sexuality in Nature and People*

### Joan Roughgarden

Joan Roughgarden is an evolutionary biologist at Stanford University. In her general-audience text *Evolution's Rainbow*, she elaborates on the simple idea that population diversity—including diversity of gender—is beneficial for species and for the biosphere. Often considered a concept peculiarly applicable to humans, Roughgarden argues that gender, as well as sex, is also part of non-human life. She first defines "sex" as a reproductive strategy that requires bringing together complementary gametes (egg and sperm)—cells that contain only part of the genetic material necessary to produce a new organism; this is in contrast to asexual reproduction, which takes place when cells containing all the necessary genetic material for a new individual divide and multiply in a clonal fashion. She then defines "gender" not as the "cultural construction" or representation of sex-difference within language and society, as it is commonly considered to mean for humans, but rather as "the appearance, behavior, and life history of a sexed body." In the selection that follows, Roughgarden describes many diverse sexual reproductive strategies as well as a variety of genders across many different species. If an individual creature bearing one type of gamete looks like, acts like, and shares portions of particular life-paths with individuals of the same species who bear different gametes, can such creatures be considered "transgendered"?

## SEX AND DIVERSITY

All species have genetic diversity—their biological rainbow. No exceptions. Biological rainbows are universal and eternal. Yet biological rainbows have posed difficulties for biologists since the beginnings of evolutionary theory. [...]

### Diversity—Good or Bad?

Rainbows subvert the human goal of classifying nature. Even worse, variability in a species might signify something wrong, a screwup. In chemistry a variation means impurity, a flaw in the diamond. Doesn't variability within a species also indicate impurity and imperfection? The most basic question faced by evolutionary biology is whether variation within a species is good in its own right or whether it is simply a collection of impurities every species is stuck with. Evolutionary biologists are divided on this issue. [...]

## SEX VERSUS GENDER

To most people, "sex" automatically implies "male" or "female." Not to a biologist. [To a biologist], sex means mixing genes when reproducing. Sexual reproduction is producing offspring by mixing genes from two parents, whereas asexual reproduction is producing offspring by one parent only, as in cloning. The definition of sexual reproduction makes no mention of "male" and "female." So what do "male" and "female" have to do with sex? The answer, one might suppose, is that when sexual reproduction does occur, one parent is male and the other female. But how do we know which one is the male? What makes a male, male, and a female, female? Indeed, are there only two sexes? Could there be a third sex? How do we define male and female anyway?

"Gender" also automatically implies "male" and "female" to most people. Therefore, if we define male and female biologically, do we wind up defining gender as well? Similarly, for adjectives like "masculine" and "feminine," can we define these biologically? Moreover, among humans, is a "man" automatically male and a "woman" necessarily female? One might think, yes, of course, but on reflection these key words admit lots of wiggle room. This chapter develops some definitions for all these words, definitions that will come in handy later on.

When speaking about humans, I find it's helpful to distinguish between social categories and biological categories. "Men" and "women" are social categories. We have the freedom to decide who counts as a man and who counts as a woman. The criteria change from time to time. In some circles, a "real man" can't eat quiche. In other circles, people seize on physical traits to define manhood: height, voice, Y chromosome, or penis. Yet these traits don't always go together: some men are short, others are tenors, some don't have a Y chromosome, and others don't have a penis. Still, we may choose to consider all such people as men anyway for purposes like deciding which jobs they can apply for, which clubs they can join, which sports they may play, and whom they may marry.

For biological categories we don't have the same freedom. "Male" and "female" are biological categories, and the criteria for classifying an organism as male or female have to work with worms to whales, with red seaweed to redwood trees. When it comes to humans, the biological criteria for male and female don't coincide 100 percent with present-day social criteria for man and woman. Indeed, using biological categories as though they were social categories is a mistake called "essentialism." Essentialism amounts to passing the buck. Instead of taking responsibility for who counts socially as a man or woman, people turn to science, trying to use the biological criteria for male to define a man and the biological criteria for female to define a woman. However, the definition of social categories rests with society, not science, and social categories can't be made to coincide with biological categories except by fiat.

### Male and Female Defined

To a biologist, *"male" means making small gametes, and "female" means making large gametes.* Period! By definition, the smaller of the two gametes is called a sperm, and the larger an egg.˙ Beyond gamete size, biologists don't recognize any other universal difference between male and female. Of course, indirect markers of gamete size may exist in some species. In mammals, males usually have a Y chromosome. But whether an individual is male or not comes down to making sperm, and the males in some mammalian species don't have a Y chromosome. Moreover, in birds, reptiles, and amphibians, the Y chromosome doesn't occur. However, the gamete-size definition is general and works throughout the plant and animal kingdoms.

Talk of gamete size may seem anticlimactic. Among humans, for example, centuries of poetry and art speak of strength and valor among men, matched by beauty and motherhood among women. Saying that the only essential difference between male and female is gamete size seems so trivial. The key point here is that "male" and "female" are biological categories, whereas "man" and "woman" are social categories. Poetry and art are about men and women, not males and females. Men and women differ in many social dimensions in addition to the biological dimension of gamete size.

Yet, biologically, the gamete-size definition of "male" and "female" is far from anticlimactic. In fact, this definition is downright exciting. One could imagine species whose members all make gametes of the same size, or several gamete sizes—small, medium, and large—or a continuum of gamete sizes ranging from small to large. Are there any such species? Almost none. Some species of algae, fungi, and protozoans have gametes all the same size. Mating typically occurs only between individuals in genetic categories called "mating types." Often there are more than two mating types.[1] In these cases, sex takes place between the mating types, but the distinctions of male and female don't apply because there is only one gamete size.[2] By contrast, when gametes do come in more than one size, then there are generally only two sizes, one very small and the other very large. Multicellular organisms with three or more distinct gamete sizes are exceedingly rare, and none is known to have a continuum of gamete sizes.

More than two gamete sizes occur in some colonial single-celled organisms, the protozoans. In the green ciliate *Clamydomonas euchlora,* the cells producing gametes may divide from four to sixty-four times. Four divisions result in relatively big gametes, whereas sixty-four divisions produce lots of small gametes. The cells that divide more than four times but less than sixty-four make various intermediate-sized gametes. Another ciliate, *Pandorina,* lives in colonies of sixteen cells. At reproduction, some cells divide into eight big gametes and others into sixteen small gametes. However, any two of these can fuse: two big ones, one big and one small, or two small ones.[3] These species are at the borderline between single-celled and multicellular organisms.

In the fruit fly *Drosophila bifurca* of the southwestern United States, the sperm is twenty (yes, twenty) times longer than the size of the male who made it! These sperm don't come cheap. The testes that make these sperm comprise 11 percent of the adult male's weight. The sperm take a long time to produce, and males take twice as long to mature as females. The sperm are so expensive that males conserve them, "offering" them to females in small amounts, leading to a one-to-one gamete ratio.[4] So much for the vision of one huge egg surrounded by zillions of tiny sperm. Although giant sperm are a marvelous curiosity, the important finding is that some species of *Drosophila* have three sperm sizes—one giant type and two smaller varieties that overlap somewhat, totaling four gamete sizes (three sperm sizes plus one egg size). In *Drosophila pseudoobscura* from Tempe, Arizona, the tail of the big sperm is 1/3 millimeter long, and the tail lengths of the two small types are 1/10 and 1/20 millimeter.

Female *Drosophila* in some species can store sperm for several days or even up to a month after mating. About one-third of the sperm are the giant type; the remaining two-thirds are small. Females preferentially store the large sperm, although some small sperm are stored too. Females also control which sperm are used for fertilization and preferentially select the large sperm. Whether the small sperm are ever used for fertilization has been hard to demonstrate. The amount of material in a large sperm is about one hundred times that of a small sperm. Therefore, to break even, the fertilization rate for small sperm needs to be only 1/100 of the fertilization rate of large sperm, and this low rate would be hard to detect.[5]

If different individuals made the different-size gametes, we could have as many as four sexes in *Drosophila,* one for each gamete size. In this species, however, every male apparently makes all three of the sperm sizes in the same ratio, so all the males are apparently the same. If further research reveals that the sperm makers differ in the ratio of sperm sizes they produce, we will have discovered a species with more than two sexes. Such a discovery would not violate any law of nature, but it would be very rare and would certainly make headlines. So, for practical purposes, male and female are universal biological categories defined by a binary distinction between small and large gametes, sperm and egg.

Why are two gamete sizes practically universal in sexually reproducing species? The current theory imagines a hypothetical species starting with two mating types that produce gametes of the same size. These gametes fuse with each other to produce a zygote, and each gamete contributes half the genes and half the cytoplasm needed by the zygote. Then the gamete in one of the mating types is hypothesized to evolve a smaller size to increase quantity while sacrificing quality. The gamete in the other mating type responds by evolving a larger gamete size to compensate for the lowered quality of the small gametes now being made by its counterpart. Overall, this back-and-forth evolutionary negotiation between the mating types with respect to gamete size culminates in one mating type making the tiniest gametes possible—gametes that provide genes and nothing else, whereas the other mating type makes gametes large enough to provide genes as well as all the cytoplasm the zygote needs to start life.[6]

This little story of how the gamete binary originates is completely conjectural and untested, and points to the need for much further thought on such an important issue. This story also leaves unexplained why some groups, such as fungi, persist with only one gamete size, and why rare groups such as *Drosophila* occur with multiple sperm sizes.

### Gender Defined

Up to now, we've come up with two generalizations: (1) Most species reproduce sexually. (2) Among the species that do reproduce sexually, gamete size obeys a near-universal binary between very small (sperm) and large (egg), so that male and female can be defined biologically as the production of small and large gametes, respectively. Beyond these two generalizations, the generalizing stops and diversity begins!

The binary in gamete size doesn't extend outward. The biggest error of biology today is uncritically assuming that the gamete size binary implies a corresponding binary in body type, behavior, and life history. No binary governs the whole individuals who make gametes, who bring them to one another for fertilization, and who interact with one another to survive in a native social context. In fact, the very sexual process that maintains the rainbow of a species and facilitates long-term survival automatically brings a cornucopia of colorful sexual behaviors. Gender, unlike gamete size, is not limited to two.[7]

"Gender" usually refers to the way a person expresses sexual identity in a cultural context. Gender reflects both the individual reaching out to cultural norms and society imposing its expectations on the individual. Gender is usually thought to be uniquely human—any species has sexes, but only people have genders. With your permission, though, I'd like to widen the meaning of gender to refer to nonhuman species as well. As a definition, I suggest: *Gender is the appearance, behavior, and life history of a sexed body.* A body becomes "sexed" when classified with respect to the size of the gametes produced. Thus, gender is appearance plus action, how an organism uses morphology, including color and shape, plus behavior to carry out a sexual role.

Now we're free to explore the zoological (and botanical!) counterpart of human gender studies. So, we may ask: How much variety occurs in gender expression among other species? Let's take some favorite stereotypes and see. We'll look mostly at vertebrates; even more variety occurs with invertebrates and plants.

- *An organism is solely male or female for life.* No, the most common body form among plants and in perhaps half of the animal kingdom is for an individual to be both male and female at the same, or at different times during its life. These individuals make both small and large gametes during their lives.
- *Males are bigger than females, on the average.* No, in lots of species, especially fish, the female is bigger than the male.

- *Females, not males, give birth.* No, in many species the female deposits the eggs in the pouch of the male, who incubates them until birth. In many species, males, not females, tend the nest.
- *Males have XY chromosomes and females XX chromosomes.* No, in birds, including domesticated poultry like chickens, the reverse is true. In many other species, males and females show no difference in chromosomes. In all alligators and crocodiles, some turtles and lizards, and the occasional fish, sex is determined by the temperature at which the eggs are raised. A female can control the sex ratio among her offspring by laying eggs in a shady or a sunny spot.
- *Only two genders occur, corresponding to the two sexes.* No, many species have three or more genders, with individuals of each sex occurring in two or more forms.
- *Males and females look different from one another.* No, in some species, males and females are almost indistinguishable. In other species, males occur in two or more forms, one of which resembles a female, while the others are different from the female.
- *The male has the penis and the female lactates.* No, in the spotted hyena, females have a penislike structure externally identical to that of males, and in the fruit bat of Malaysia and Borneo, the males have milk-producing mammary glands.[8]
- *Males control females.* No, in some species females control males, and in many, mating is a dynamic interaction between female and male choice. Females may or may not prefer a dominant male.
- *Females prefer monogamy and males want to play around.* No, depending on the species, either or both sexes may play around. Lifelong monogamy is rare, and even within monogamous species, females may initiate divorce to acquire a higher-ranking male.

One could tick off even more examples of gender stereotypes that are often thought to be "nature's way" but that have no generality within biology. Instead, let's look closer at the lives of these organisms to see whether what they do makes sense to us. Be prepared, though, to shrug your shoulders and wonder about the mystery of life.

Note that by defining gender as how an organism presents and carries out a sexual role, we can also define masculine and feminine in ways unique to each species. "Masculine" and "feminine" refer to the distinguishing traits possessed by most males and females respectively. Cross gender appearance and behavior are also possible. For example, if most females have vertical stripes on their bodies and males do not, then a male with vertical stripes is a "feminine male." If most males have antlers and females do not, then a doe with antlers is a "masculine female."

Politically, locating the definition of male and female with gamete size keeps society's gender categories at arm's length from biology's sex binary. We don't have to deny the universality of the biological male/female distinction in order to challenge whether the gender of whole organisms also sorts into a male/female binary. In humans specifically, a gender binary for whole people is not clear-cut even though the difference between human sperm and egg is obvious—a size ratio of about one million to one.

## SEXED BODIES

### *What Fish Can Tell Us*

[...]

### *Females Changing to Male*

Sex change is only one of several interesting aspects of coral reef fish society. The bluehead wrasse is named for the blue head of the largest males. When small and just entering sexual maturity, fish of both sexes look similar. Later three genders develop. One gender consists of individuals who begin life as a male and remain so for life. Another gender consists of individuals who begin as females and later change into males. These sex changed males are larger than those who have been male from the beginning. The third gender consists of females who remain female. We'll call the two male genders the "small unchanged males" and the "large sex-changed males," respectively. The large sex-changed males are the biggest individuals of the three genders, and they attempt to control the females. In some species, the large sex-changed males maintain and defend the females, and in others they defend locations that females appear to prefer.

Fertilization is external—a female releases eggs into the water and a male then releases a cloud of sperm around the eggs to fertilize them. The unfertilized eggs are out in the open and can potentially be fertilized by any male in the vicinity.

The small unchanged and large sex-changed males are hostile to each other. The large sex-changed males chase the small unchanged males away from the territory or from females they control. The small unchanged males are more numerous than the large sex-changed males and may form coalitions to mate with females that a large sex-changed male is trying to control. The small unchanged males mate by darting in and fertilizing the eggs that a large sex-changed male was intending to fertilize. Some small unchanged males keep the large sex-changed male busy while others are mating.

Different ecological circumstances favor unchanged and sex-changed males. The wrasses live both on coral reefs and in the seagrass beds nearby. In seagrass, females nestled among grass blades can't be guarded very well, and the balance of hostilities tips in favor of the small unchanged males. This situation leads to only two genders, unchanged males and females. On the coral reef, clear water and an open habitat structure permit the large sex-changed males to control the females, and the balance tips in their favor.[3] This situation encourages the presence of all three genders. Simple population density also shifts the gender ratios. At high densities females are difficult to guard and small unchanged males predominate, whereas at low densities a large sex-changed male can control a "harem."[4] Whether females prefer either type of male isn't known.

The sex changes are triggered by changes in social organization. Another type of wrasse is the cleaner wrasse, named for its occupation of gleaning ectoparasites from other fish. When a large sex-changed male is removed from his harem, the largest female changes sex and takes over. Within a few hours, she adopts male behavior, including courtship and spawning with the remaining females. Within ten days, this new male is producing active sperm. Meanwhile the other females in the harem remain unchanged.[5] I haven't been able to find out whether any female can turn into a male if she is the biggest female when the existing male dies, or whether females divide into two groups—those who remain female no matter what and those who change sex when circumstances are right.

Does this animal society seem oh-so-bizarre? It isn't. Aspects of this system appear again and again among vertebrates, especially the themes of male control of females or their eggs, multiple male genders, hostility among some of the male genders, flexible sexual identity, and social organization that changes with ecological context. Still, if you think the coral reef fish scene is bizarre, you're not alone—so did the biologists who first witnessed it. We're only just realizing that the concepts of gender and sexuality we grew up with are seriously flawed.

*Male Changing to Female*

Sex changes from male to female also occur. A group of damselfish are called clown fish because their bold white strips remind one of the white makeup used by clowns. These fish live among the tentacles of sea anemones, which have cells in their tentacles that sting any animal who touches them. To survive in this lethal home, a clown fish secretes a mucus that inhibits the anemone from discharging its stinging cells. Although living within the anemone's tentacles provides safety for the clown fish, the size of its house is limited by how big its sea anemone grows. An anemone has space for only one pair of adult clown fish and a few juveniles.

The female is larger than the male. If she is removed, the remaining male turns into a female, and one of the juveniles matures into a male.[6] The pair is monogamous. Female egg production increases with body size. A monogamous male finds no advantage in being large because he's not controlling a harem of females. The advantage for males of remaining small and for females of becoming large may account for the developmental progression from male to female.[7]

### Male and Female Simultaneously

Hamlets, which are small coral reef basses, don't have to worry about choosing their sex: they are both sexes at the same time. However, they cross-fertilize and must mate with a partner to reproduce. These simultaneous hermaphrodites change between male and female roles several times as they mate. One individual releases a few eggs and the other fertilizes them with sperm. Then the other releases some eggs, which the first fertilizes with sperm, and so on, back and forth.[8]

No one has offered any suggestions about why hamlets are simultaneous hermaphrodites. Deep-sea fish also tend toward simultaneous hermaphrodism, which for these species is viewed as an adaptation to extremely low population density.[9] Hamlets don't have a strange appearance, nor do any other hermaphroditic fish. Hermaphroditic fish look like, well, just fish. Hamlets are not particularly rare, nor are they derived from ancestors who were rare or lived in the deep sea. So just why hamlets are simultaneously hermaphroditic remains mysterious.

### Male and Female Crisscrossing

Changing sex once may seem a big deal, but some fish do it several times during their life span. An individual may change from an unsexed juvenile to a female, then to a male, and then back to a female. Or it may change from a juvenile to a male, then to a female, and then back to a male. In certain species, sexual identity can be changed as easily as a new coat.

Sex crisscrossing was first discovered in a species of goby, which is the largest family of fish. Gobies are tiny and often live on coral reefs—in this case, on the Pacific island of Okinawa.[10] These gobies live as monogamous pairs on branching coral, and the males care for the eggs. About 80 percent of the juveniles mature female, and the rest mature male. Some of the females later switch to male, and some of the males later switch to female. Of those that have switched once, a small fraction later switch back again—the crisscrossers.

Why go to the expense of changing one's sexual wardrobe? One theory envisages pair formation in gobies as resulting when two larvae drop out of the plankton together onto a piece of coral.[11] They awake after metamorphosis to discover that they are both the same sex. What to do? Well, one of them changes sex. Changing sex has been suggested as a better way of obtaining a heterosexual pairing than moving somewhere else to find a partner of the opposite sex when traveling around is risky. Thus this theory comes down to a choice: switch or move. This theory is rather heterosexist, though. As the hamlets show, a heterosexual pair is not necessary for reproduction, because both could be simultaneously hermaphroditic and not have to bother with crisscrossing.

A species of goby from Lizard Island on Australia's Great Barrier Reef has recently been discovered to crisscross, but in a way that is interestingly different from the Okinawan goby.[12] In the Australian goby, all the juveniles mature into females, with some later becoming males. The males, however, can change back into females. In fact, the meaning of male is ambiguous here. The investigators defined a male to be any fish with at least some sperm production. All males, however, contain early-stage oocytes—cells that develop into eggs—in their gonads. So all the males remain part female. The species therefore consists of two genders at any one time: all-female fish and part-male-part-female fish.

Among flowering plants, populations with hermaphrodites and females are common,[13] more so than populations with males and females. These mixed hermaphrodite/single-sex species contrast with most plant species, which are entirely hermaphroditic. (Perhaps as more gobies are investigated, a species will be found consisting of females and hermaphrodites, just as in plants.)

Plants also offer the most amusing examples of crisscrossing sex changes. In a tropical ginger from China, some individuals are male in the morning, making pollen, while others are female in the morning, receiving pollen. Then they switch sexes in the afternoon. This phenomenon, called flexistyly, is known in eleven families of flowering plants.[14] The ginger's diurnal sex change is not too different from how hamlets mate, where members of a mating pair switch back and forth between male and female once a minute.

These examples of sequential, simultaneous, and crisscrossing hermaphrodism show that male and female functions don't need to be packaged into lifelong distinct bodies. Hermaphroditic vertebrate species are successful and common.

## NOTES FOR "SEX VERSUS GENDER"

\* A gamete is a cell containing half of its parent's genes. Fusing two gametes, each with half the needed number of genes, produces a new individual. A gamete is made through a special kind of cell division called meiosis, whereas other cells are made through the regular kind of cell division, called mitosis. When two gametes fuse, the resulting cell is called a zygote. A fertilized egg is a zygote.

1. See: Y. Iwasa and A. Sasaki, 1987, Evolution of the number of sexes, *Evolution* 41: 49–65.

2. Having one gamete size is called isogamy. Having more than one gamete size is called anisogamy. See: G. Bell, 1982, *The Masterpiece of Nature,* University of California Press; R. Hoekstra, 1987, The evolution of sexes, pp. 59–91 in S. Sterns, ed., *The Evolution of Sex and Its Consequences,* Birkhäuser.

3. V. A. Dogiel, 1965, *General Protozoology,* Clarendon Press.

4. C. Bressac, A. Fleury, and D. Lachaise, 1994, Another way of being anisogamous in *Drosophila* subgenus species: Giant sperm, one-to-one gamete ratio, and high zygote provisioning, *Proc. Nat. Acad. Sci. (USA)* 91:10399–402; S. Pitnick and T A. Markow, 1994, Male gametic strategies: Sperm size, testes size, and the allocation of ejaculate among successive mates by the sperm-limited fly *Drosophila pachea* and its relatives, *Amer. Natur.* 143:785–819; S. Pitnick, G. S. Spicer, and T. A. Markow, 1995, How long is a giant sperm? *Nature* 375 109.

5. R. R. Snook, T. A. Markow, and T. L. Karr, 1994, Functional nonequivalence of sperm in *Drosophila pseudoobscura,* *Proc. Nat. Acad. Sci. (USA)* 91:11222–26; C. Bressac and E. Hauschteck-Jungen, 1996, *Drosophila subobscura* females preferentially select long sperm for storage and use, *J. Insect Physiol.* 42:323–28; R. R. Snook, 1997, Is the production of multiple sperm types adaptive? *Evolution* 51:797–808. See also: P. Lee and A. Wilkes, 1965, Polymorphic spermatozoa in the hymenopterous wasp, *Dahlbominus, Science* 147:1445–46; R. Silberglied, J. Shepherd, and J. Dickinson, 1984, Eunuchs: The role of apyrene sperm in lepidoptera? *Amer. Natur.* 123:255–65; P. Cook, I. Harvey, and G. Parker, 1997, Predicting variation in sperm precedence, *Phil. Trans. R. Soc. hond.,* ser. B, 352:771–80; M. Watanabe, M. Bon'no, and A. Hachisuka, 2000, Eupyrene sperm migrates to spermatheca after apyrene sperm in the swallowtail butterfly, *Papilio xuthus L.* (Lepidoptera: Papilionidae), *J. Ethol.* 18:91–99.

6. The state where both mating types, A and B, have the same gamete size has the interesting property of being an ESS (evolutionary stable strategy) that is dynamically unstable. If the optimal size for a zygote is say 2 mg, then the optimal size for each gamete is 1 mg, so they sum to 2 mg upon fusing. Therefore, conditional on type A having a gamete size of 1 mg, then the optimal gamete size for type B is also 1 mg, and a mutation within A that deviates from this optimal size of 1 mg will not increase when rare. Conversely, conditional on type A having a gamete size of 1 mg, the optimal gamete size for type A is also 1 mg, and any mutation within A that deviates from this size will not increase when rare. Thus the state where both type A and type B have a gamete size of 1 mg is an ESS. But this state is not dynamically stable to perturbation. If the gamete size of type A decreases somewhat, then selection favors increasing the gamete size within type B to compensate, in an escalating progression leading to increasingly divergent gamete sizes, culminating in one being as small as possible and the other as big as needed to fully provision the zygote. See: G. Parker, R. Baker, and V. Smith, 1972, The origin and evolution of gamete dimorphism and the male-female phenomenon, *J. Theor. Biol,* 36:529–53; N. Knowlton, 1974, A note on the evolution of gamete dimorphism, *J. Theor. Biol.* 46:283–85; G. Bell, 1978, The evolution of anisogamy, *J. Theor. Biol,* 73:247–70; J. Maynard Smith, 1978, *The Evolution of Sex,* Cambridge University Press; R. Hoekstra, 1980, Why do organisms produce gametes of only two different sizes? Some theoretical aspects of the evolution of anisogamy, *J. Theor. Biol,* 87:785–93; G. Parker, 1982, Why so many tiny sperm? The maintenance of two sexes with internal fertilization, *J. Theor. Biol.* 96:281–94; H. Matsuda and P, Abrams, 1999, Why are equally sized gametes so rare? The instability of isogamy and the cost of anisogamy, *Evol. Ecol. Research* 1:769–84; I. Eshel and E. Akin,

1983, Coevolutionary instability of mixed Nash solutions, *J. Math. Biol,* 18:123–34; J. Madsen and D. M. Waller, 1983, A note on the evolution of gamete dimorphism in algae, *Amer. Natur.* 121:443–47.

7.  J. Butler, 1990, *Gender Trouble,* Routledge, rpt. on pp. 80–88 in C. Gould, ed., 1997, *Key Concepts in Critical Theory: Gender,* Humanities Press; S. Kessler, and W. McKenna, 1978, *Gender: An Ethnomethodological Approach,* University of Chicago Press.

8.  C. Francis, E. L. P. Anthony, J. Brunton, and T. H. Kunz, 1994, Lactation in male fruit bats, *Nature* 567:69 1–92.

## NOTES FOR "SEXED BODIES"

[…]

3.  D. Robertson and R. Warner, 1978, Sexual patterns in the labroid fishes of the western Caribbean: II. The parrotfishes (Scaridae), *Smithsonian Contributions to Zoology* 255:1–26.

4.  R. Warner and S. Hoffman, 1980, Local population size as a determinant of a mating system and sexual composition in two tropical reef fishes (*Thalassoma* spp.), *Evolution* 34:508–18.

5.  D. Robertson, 1972, Social control of sex reversal in a coral reef fish, *Science* 1977:1007–9; J. Godwin, D. Crews, and R. Warner, 1996, Behavioral sex change in the absence of gonads in a coral reef fish, *Proc. R. Soc. Lond.,* ser. B, 263:1683–88; J. Godwin, R. Sawby, R. Warner, D. Crews, and M. Grober, 1999, Hypothalamic arginine vasotocin mRNA abundance variation across the sexes and with sex change in a coral reef fish (unpublished manuscript).

6.  H. Fricke and S. Fricke, 1977, Monogamy and sex change by aggressive dominance in coral reef fish, *Nature* 266:830–32; J. Moyer and A. Nakazono, 1978, Protandrous hermaphrodism in six species of the anemonefish genus *Amphiprion* in Japan, *Japan. J. Ichthyology* 25:101–6. See also: J. Moyer and A. Nakazono, 1978, Population structure, reproductive behavior and protogynous hermaphrodism in the angelfish *Centropyge interruptus* at Miyake-jima, Japan, *J. Ichthyology* 25:25–39.

7.  A test of this idea may be possible by comparing with clown fish, such as those from Batavia Bay in Indonesia, who do live in anemones large enough to support more than one pair of adults and in whom polygamy may occur instead of monogamy. A table reviewing these species appears in J. Roughgarden, 1975, Evolution of marine symbiosis—a simple cost-benefit model, *Ecology* 56:1201–8.

8.  E. Fischer, 1980, The relationship between mating system and simultaneous hermaphrodism in the coral reef *Hypoplectrus nigricans* (Seranidae), *Anim. Behav.* 28:620–33; P. Pressley, 1981, Pair formation and joint territoriality in a simultaneous hermaphrodite: The coral reef fish *Serranus tigrius, Z. Tierpsychol.* 56:33–46.

9.  G. Mead, E. Bertelson, and D. M. Cohen, 1964, Reproduction among deep-sea fishes, *Deep Sea Research* 11:569–96.

10. Discussion based on T. Kuamura, Y. Nakashima, and Y. Yogo, 1994, Sex change in either direction by growth-rate advantage in the monogamous coral goby, *Paragobiodon echinocephalus, Behav. Ecol.* 5:434–38.

11. Ibid.

12. Discussion based on P. Munday, M. Caley, and G. Jones, 1998, Bi-directional sex change in a coral-dwelling goby, *Behav. Ecol. Sociobiol.* 43:371–77.

13. A population with both females and hermaphrodites is called gynodioecious, and a population with both males and hermaphrodites is called androdioecious. See: M. Geber, T. Dawson, and L. Delph, eds., 1998, *Gender and Sexual Dimorphism in Flowering Plants,* Springer Verlag; D. Charlesworth and M. Morgan, 1991, Allocation of resources to sex functions in flowering plants, *Phil. Trans. R. Soc. Lond,* ser. B, 332:91–102; J. Pannell, 1997, The maintenance of gynodioecy and androdioccy in a metapopulation, *Evolution* 51: 10–20; A. Liston, L.H. Rieseberg, and T. Elias, 1990, *Datisca glomerata* is functionally androdioecious, *Nature* 343:641–42.

14. Qing-Jun Li, and Zai-Fu Xu, W. John Kress, Yong-Mei Xia, Ling Zhang, Xiao-Bao Deng, Jiang-Yun Gao, and Zhi-Lin Bai, 2001, Flexible style that encourages outcrossing, *Nature* 410:432; S. Barrett, 2002, The evolution of plant sexual diversity, *Nature Reviews: Genetics* 3:274–84.

# 12

---

## *Animal Trans*

### Myra J. Hird

---

Transdisciplinary scholar Myra Hird is a Professor at Queen's University (Canada), where she teaches science and technology studies, sociology of knowledge, and feminist, queer, and trans theory. In this article, Hird reviews materialist feminist critiques of trans embodiment that, in their presumption of an irrefutable and incommensurable biological sex difference, position transsexual embodiment as, at best, a cosmetic alteration of bodily surface that does not truly "change sex," and that represent transgender identification as some species of error. Hird finds such views to be limited by their anthropocentrism, and she argues for a wider, more comprehensive perspective on the world of biological sex diversity of which human gender, sex, and sexuality are but small parts. She seeks to expand materialist feminist accounts of sex difference by putting them in conversation with biological studies of non-human reproduction and embodiment. In doing so, Hird opens new lines of interdisciplinary research into bodily difference and biological processes, and she argues for a reconsideration of the customary divisions not only between male and female, but between human and non-human animals, and between nature and technoculture. Throughout, she resists the temptation to conceptualize some species as "queer" or "trans" simply because they confound anthropocentric notions of sex difference and reproduction, and asks instead that we try to grapple with the world in a rigorously non-anthropocentric manner: what might human practices of embodiment such as transgendering mean—if anything—for the many other kinds life with which humans share the biosphere, and which (like microbial life) make human bodies their homes?

The universe is not only queerer than we suppose, it is queerer than we can suppose.

(Haldane 1928, 298)

When animals do something that we like we call it natural. When they do something that we don't like, we call it animalistic.

(Weinrich 1982, 203)

## INTRODUCTION

Punky and Elvira, two female red-faced Japanese macaques, have lived together for fifteen years and raised three adopted juvenile monkeys together. Whether or not they want to marry (or have any recognition of this distinctly human concept) remains beside the point for the moment, as the state of Ohio, and indeed the whole of America it seems, is embroiled in a heated debate about gay marriage. On one side of the debate, Angela Murray, executive director of the Human Rights for

Animals organisation argues that it is Punky and Elvira's right to have a full wedding that carries the same legal entitlements as human marriages. At the opposite end, Roberta Crombs, president of the Christian United Movement disagrees: "Animals marrying? That's beyond being 'under attack'. These zealots have scaled the walls and society has begun to crumble!" (Busse 2004, 2)

Nonhuman animals have for some time been overburdened with the task of making sense of human social relations. In most cultures, and for most people, nonhuman animals are symbolic. It matters less how nonhuman animals behave, and more how we think they behave. Nonhuman animals supposedly exemplify human animal qualities like the family, fidelity, selfless care for young and, perhaps above all, sex complementarity (that femininity and masculinity are categorically different and complementary). As the quotes at the beginning of this chapter allude, nonhuman animal morphology and behaviour are most often cited to confirm our assumptions about the nature of things and human beings' relationship to this nature, even though these meanings may indeed have very little to do with the biological and social realities of nonhuman animals (Bagemihl 1999). Moreover, and as in the case of Punky and Elvira, discussions of animal behaviour often move quickly to moral debates about topics such as gay marriage, the nuclear family and gender relations. As I will argue, morality and nature enjoy an interesting relationship: nature is often invoked in discussions of morality in so far as natural behaviours are considered to be morally superior. Punky and Elvira incite debate because they are nonhuman animals (natural) who are engaged in homosexual behaviour (unnatural and therefore morally inferior), thus disrupting the historic Judaeo-Christian association between nature and moral superiority.[2]

It is certainly of value, then, to exercise caution when the behaviour of nonhuman living organisms is cited in the service of discussions of human socio-cultural relations. And yet, in recent years there has been a rejuvenation of feminist interest in ethology and biology, with a number of scholars making the specific argument that the study of nonhuman living matter might usefully inform debates about social structures and relations. [...]

A number of feminist studies have also begun to think through the implications of analysing human understandings of embodiment, sexual difference and sexuality with nonhuman studies. Arguing more generally for the recognition of sex and sexual diversity amongst nonhuman animals, Sharon Kinsman states:

> Because most of us are not familiar with the species, and with the diverse patterns of DNA mixing and reproduction they embody, our struggles to understand humans (and especially human dilemmas about "sex", "gender" and "sexual orientation") are impoverished ... Shouldn't a fish whose gonads can be first male, then female, help us to determine what constitutes "male" and "female"? [...] Shouldn't the long-term female homosexual pair bonding in certain species of gulls help define our views of successful parenting, and help [us] reflect on the intersection of social norms and biology?
>
> [2001, 197]

Elizabeth Wilson (2002) furthers this invitation to consider nonhuman species through her analysis of Charles Darwin's work on barnacles. Whilst first assuming that the classification of this organism would occupy little time, it would eventually take years to accomplish, involve correspondence with scientists and collectors around the world, and require the dissection of hundreds of specimens. Through dissection, Darwin discovered that most species of barnacles are intersex: each barnacle has female and male organs. Other barnacles first appeared to be sex dimorphic, but closer inspection led to an interesting discovery. What Darwin initially discarded as tiny barnacle-infesting parasites turned out to be male barnacles. Completely different in bodily shape and microscopically small, the male barnacles lived, embedded, inside the body of the female. This was not "simply" the case of one sex living inside the other; *multiple* (sometimes thousands of) males live inside single females.

So barnacles can be intersex but they can also be something else—something we have yet to have a common term for. Wilson points out that "these females and hermaphrodites with many husbands are not simply the intermediary stages in the evolution of barnacle form; they are also evidence of the somatic diversity that nature produces." (284)

To some extent, then, feminist interest in nonhuman animal morphology and behaviour has extended beyond feminist evolutionary biologists and ethologists. I see this interest as part of a wider concern with "new materialism" (See Hird 2006). Briefly, new materialism attends to a number of significant shifts in the natural sciences within the past few decades to suggest agency and contingency (Grosz refers to this as "emergence, which is neither free nor determined but both constrained and undecidable" (1999, 19)) within the living and nonliving world.[3] New materialist developments within the natural sciences have made a significant impression on feminist scholars who increasingly find themselves grappling with issues involving life and matter (for instance, in debates about the body, the sex/gender binary and sexual difference).[4] These analyses acknowledge the reluctance of feminist theory to engage with the natural sciences in so far as matter has been traditionally understood as inert, stable, concrete, unchangeable and resistant to socio-historical change; and that the principal means of studying matter, science, has been used to shore up the subordination of women within patriarchy. The reluctance on the part of feminist theory has meant that, while feminism has cast light on social and cultural meanings of concepts such as sex, gender and sexual difference, there seems to be a hesitation to delve into the actual physical processes through which stasis, differentiation and change take place. Only a minority of feminist studies analyse how physical processes, and particularly nonhuman processes, might contribute to feminist concerns.[5]

This chapter aims to contribute to the growing interest in new materialist approaches to understanding sex, gender and sexual difference. More specifically, I want to bring together two hitherto largely mutually exclusive literatures—new materialism and transsex/transgender/trans—in order to suggest that the study of nonhuman trans might make a useful contribution to a number of debates engendered within the trans literature. These debates include questions about the authenticity of sex and gender and the extent to which trans is transgressive. The analysis of trans is important for feminist theory in as much as it keys into wider debates about the ontology of sexual difference, the vicissitudes of sexuality and the limits of subjectivity. I will argue these debates tend to occur within cultural analyses, as though assuming that trans is a distinctly and exclusively cultural phenomenon. This has serious consequences for some of these debates, such as the authenticity of trans in so far as the debate is anchored by a sense of what is natural about sex. [...]

I want to explore evidence that trans exists in nonhuman species and what this evidence might suggest about cultural explanations that implicitly rely upon a nature/culture distinction. In this effort, I want to extend feminist interest in trans as a specifically sexed enterprise (as in transitioning from one sex to another), but also in a broader sense of movement across, through and perhaps beyond traditional classifications. [...] What appeals to me about the concept of trans is that it works equally well both between and within matter, confounding the notion of the well-defined, inviolable self which precedes Western culture's "stories of the human place in nature, that is, genesis and its endless repetitions" (Haraway 1997, 60). [...] With this in mind, I turn now to a short review of feminist approaches to trans with a view to then exploring how animal trans might usefully inform these approaches. [...]

## LIVING ORGANISM TRANS

Feminist analyses of trans, like those by social scientists generally, have tended to argue from socio-cultural perspectives, as though trans is a distinctly human enterprise. I now want to consider how the concerns about authenticity and transgression outlined above might be affected by a consideration of trans in other species. The diversity of sex and sexual behaviour amongst (known) species is much greater than human cultural notions typically allow. This diversity confronts cultural ideas about the family, monogamy, fidelity, parental care, heterosexuality, and perhaps most fundamentally, sexual difference. [...]

Nor do many animals have sex solely or primarily in order to reproduce. There is a general lack of acknowledgement of pleasure as an organising force in relations between nonhuman animals, and neo-Darwinism generally. [...] Many female animals engage in sex when they are already pregnant. Birth control is not restricted to humans; many animals practice forms of birth control through vaginal plugs, defecation, abortion through the ingestion of certain plants, ejection of sperm and, in the case of chimpanzees, nipple stimulation. Embryos are also known to kill each other before birth.

Perhaps the single most popular debate about sexual diversity, however, is whether or not homosexual behaviour is natural or unnatural. Homosexual behaviour is part of our evolutionary heritage: it can be traced back at least 24–37 million years (Vasey 1995). Homosexual behaviour occurs in over 450 different species of animals, is found in every geographic region of the world, in every major animal group, in all age groups, and with equal frequency amongst females and males (Bagemihl 1999). [...]

Whether homosexual behaviour is still considered a deviation from the heterosexual norm, there is a list of other sexual behaviours classified as abnormal that few people question. Sex between different species is one of them.[10] Yet findings are beginning to emerge to suggest that sexual behaviour amongst nonhuman animals is again much more plastic and diverse than human culture allows. Sexual behaviour between flowers and various insects is so commonplace that it is rarely recognised as transspecies sexual activity. But other examples have been found. [...]

In sum, nonhuman living organisms display a wide diversity of sexual behaviour. But nonhuman living organisms also display a wide diversity of sex. Nonhumans eschew the assumption that sex involves two (and only two) distinct (and opposite) entities (female and male) and further, that these two sexes behaviourally complement each other. Virtually all plant, and many animal species are intersex. That is, living organisms are often both sexes simultaneously—which means that there are not really two sexes at all. Most fungi have thousands of sexes—Schizophyllum, for example, has more than 28,000 sexes. And sex amongst these promiscuous mushrooms is literally a "touch-and-go" event, leading Jenni Laidman to conclude that for fungi there are "so many genders, so little time..." (2000). Nor are living organisms genetically sex dimorphic. Studies of people with intersex conditions reveal that there are many variations of sex in humans: XXY XXXY, XXXXY, XXYY and XXXYY to name only a few. There is also great diversity in nonhuman animal chromosome structures: male birds are homogametic with two Z chromosomes and females are heterogametic with one Z and one W chromosome—thus female birds determine the sex of their offspring (Snowdon 1997). Some reptile and amphibian species have no sex chromosomes, and the sex of offspring is determined by the temperature of egg incubation. The platypus has five X chromosomes and five Y chromosomes (Australian Broadcasting Corporation 2004).

Many species also transsex. For ethologists and biologists, sex change typically refers to an organism that functions as one sex during one breeding season and the "other" sex during another breeding season. This definition excludes those organisms that can change sex within one breeding season. David Policansky (1982) documents some of the widely distributed geographically and taxonomically sex-changing species. Given the selective and reproductive advantages of changing sex, Policansky questions why more species do not change sex, rather than attempting to explain why some species do have this ability. In other words, in some families of fish, transsex is so much the norm that biologists have created a term for those "unusual" fish that do not change sex—gonochoristic. The coral goby, for instance, changes sex both ways, between female and male, depending on environmental circumstances. As further examples, earthworms and marine snails are male when young and female when they grow older. Chaetopod annelids show a similar development, but in certain environmental circumstances will change back into males. For instance, when two females are confined together, one female may kill the other female by biting her in half or eating all the available food. When this female has had sex with a male, the male might then turn into a female and bite her in two (Denniston 1980).

Researchers have also found transvestism to be widespread amongst nonhuman animals. Sometimes transvestism takes a physical form, when animals physically resemble the opposite sex.[11] Transvestism might also be behavioural, when a nonhuman animal behaves in ways associated with the opposite sex of their species. Some entomologists, for instance, describe transvestism in various insect species. Denis Owen (1988) describes female *Papilio phorcas* (a type of butterfly) who take on "male pattern" wings of other male butterflies that fly faster and are better able to avoid prey (see also Roughgarden 2004).

Thus, in so far as most plants are intersex, most fungi have multiple sexes, many species transsex, and bacteria completely defy notions of sexual difference, this means that the majority of living organisms on this planet would make little sense of the human classification of two sexes, and certainly less sense of a critique of transsex based upon a conceptual separation of nature and culture.

## THE CURIOSITY OF SEX DIMORPHISM

In this concluding section, I want to reconsider the concerns of feminist scholars in light of new materialist evidence of sex and sexual diversity in nonhuman organisms. As outlined, the concerns include the authenticity of trans, the ontology of sexual difference, the material artificiality of human trans and the limits of trans as a transgressive identity or being.

### Authenticity

Some feminist critiques reject the ability of a trans person (usually a trans woman) to authentically experience a gender other than the one assigned at birth.[12] Wilton, for instance, rejects the ability of a trans woman to authentically experience life as a woman. Whether or not nonhuman animals "feel" themselves to be feminine or masculine is a difficult, if not impossible, question to answer, not least because it requires judgements about what constitutes femininity or masculinity in any given species as well as how this experience might feel, and how we might assess how this experience feels. However, we may assert that nonhuman animals do experience femininity and masculinity to the extent that any given species' behaviour is gender segregated. To the ethologist, the coral goby fish experiences life as a female coral goby when she reproduces. To suggest that the coral goby is *only* female if and when she reproduces would be the equivalent of reducing human experiences of womanhood to sexual reproduction, something feminist scholars and activists have argued against for over a century.

### The Ontology of Sexual Difference

The second, related, feminist critique argues for an ontology of sexual difference which makes impossible any transition from one sex to another.[13] In the case of all nonhuman living organisms who do trans sex or who completely defy the categorisation of sex dimorphism, this argument cannot be sustained. It might be counter-argued that sex dimorphism is a characteristic of higher life forms and that sex diversity is reserved for lower organisms. To my mind, this hierarchical taxonomy invokes the worst kind of anthropomorphism. As Eileen Crist highlights in her book *Images of Animals* (1999), naturalists like Darwin have been heavily criticised for attributing supposedly unique human qualities (such as affection, fear, anger and joy) to nonhuman animals.

Since then, the almost complete hegemony of ethology and sociobiology within neo Darwinism has asserted a rigid separation between human and nonhuman organisms, not only of degree but of kind.[14] At one time, to challenge this hierarchy (and its Judaeo-Christian origins) was to risk being labelled "unscientific." However, such challenges have now begun to filter into mainstream biology. For instance, while George Herbert Mead distinguished humans from all other animals through our supposedly unique ability to recognise ourselves as objects, recent studies conclude that chimpanzees and orangutans recognise themselves, and subordinate simians hide copulations from other males (Mead 1997; Margulis and Sagan 1997). Language is another trait that human animals favour in distinguishing themselves as entirely unique and superior. However, all nonhuman animals communicate—indeed, the recent discovery of symbolic communication by honeybees "upsets the very foundation of behaviour, and biology in general" (Griffin, quoted in Margulis and Sagan 1995, 150).

From Darwin's perspective, all surviving species are equally successful, and any other classification of superiority or inferiority is based upon human-made criteria. Further, the homogenisation of nonhuman animals shifts attention away from contemplating the possible similarities of organisms (humans share 98 per cent of the same genes with chimpanzees), and more disturbingly, the possible "superiority" of nonhuman organisms in certain respects. We might, for instance, consider that particularly with regard to sex, humans and other primates should be considered inferior to some other organisms. Evolution is commonly assumed to favour sexual reproduction over non-sexual reproduction and sex differences over sex diversity. These assumptions, however, are based more on competing evolutionary theories than on Darwin's original thesis. New materialism, on the other hand, has generated a renewed interest in what I argue have become more silent, yet nevertheless intrinsic, elements of Darwinian theory: contingency, diversity, nonlinearity and self-organisation (all of which are distinctly non-functional). As Wilson argues, "there is no pre-given identity of form or function to be found anywhere in nature, [Darwin] argues; rather there is mutation, inconstancy and radical interconnectivity that produces the identities and differences we recognize as individuals and species" (2002, 284).

Take bacteria for instance: "Bacteria are biochemically and metabolically far more diverse than all plants and animals put together" (Sagan 1992, 377). On their curriculum vitae, bacteria cross species barriers (indeed, bacteria cannot be referred to as a species), perform hypersex, pass on pure genes through meiosis, shuffle genes and successfully resist death. Although the subject of a paper in its own right, it is worth noting that much of the brave new world of reproductive technologies is human mimicry of well-worn, millions-year-old bacterial practices. Our remote ancestors continue to promiscuously exchange genes without getting hung up on sexual reproduction. Bacteria are not picky, and will avidly exchange genes with just about any living organism anywhere in the world, including the human body. Thus bacteria are beyond the female/male dichotomy of human discourse (Margulis and Sagan 1997, 89). Since bacteria recognise and avidly embrace diversity, they do not discriminate on the basis of sex differences at all. The bacteria that move freely into and within our bodies are already infinitely sex diverse.[15]

But until recently, the bacterial world has been under-researched, precisely because of assumptions made about the unimportance of bacteria in sustaining the living and nonliving environment. But as Lucien Mathieu and Sorin Sonea note:

> The every day contribution of bacteria to life on Earth is momentous in terms of the maintenance of global homeostasis, the dependence of living organisms (including humans) on bacteria for processes such as digestion, and, indeed, the origin of species themselves—perhaps it is telling that we feel the need to distance ourselves through a taxonomic hierarchy from our earliest ancestors.
>
> [1996, 3]

Sociobiologists and social scientists alike have tended to overlook the sex lives of bacteria in order to adhere to a paradigm that *a priori* defines the kind of sexual reproduction humans engage in as superior. But as Lynn Margulis and Dorion Sagan argue:

> Our own biologically parochial existence as sexually reproducing beings does not mean ... that there is only copulatory, genital-based sex or that sex has anything necessarily to do with reproduction ... Sex is not equivalent to reproduction. On the one hand, any organism can receive new genes—can indulge in sex—without reproducing itself. On the other hand, plants bud, bacteria divide and cells with nuclei reproduce all without any requirement for sex.
>
> [1997, 17]

Evolutionarily speaking, sexual reproduction is a recent phenomenon. Margulis and Sagan argue that sexual reproduction evolved by accident as a necessary by-product of the evolution of multicellularity and cellular differentiation (Margulis and Sagan 1986). In multicellular organisms, cells begin to specialise and carry out different functions: "mixis ... becomes a consequence of the need to preserve differentiation ... mixis itself is dispensable and ... was never selected for directly" (180).[16] Put another way, "multicellularity provided evolutionary advantages and sex came along for the ride" (Fausto-Sterling 1997, 53). Thus, rather than deliberate on how most living organisms are able to reproduce without sex, scientists are more puzzled by those species that *do* engage in sexual reproduction. Sexual reproduction consumes twice the energy and genes of parthenogenic reproduction (Bagemihl 1999). After an extensive search of the biological literature on sex, Mackay concluded:

> The most intriguing aspect of my research was why we have sex at all. After all, sexual reproduction in animals started only 300 million years ago. Life on earth got on pretty well for 3000 million years before that with asexual reproduction ... [Sexual reproduction] takes more time, it uses more energy, and mates may be scarce or uncooperative.
>
> [2001, 623]

### The Material Artificiality of Human Trans

To argue that human transsex relies entirely upon technology is to significantly circumscribe the definition of technology to the human sphere. As Arthur Clarke points out, "we never invent anything that nature hasn't tried out millions of years earlier" (2000, 333). At a basic level, life itself is, and has always been, technological in the very real sense that bacteria, protoctists and animals incorporate external structural materials into their bodies (Margulis and Sagan 1997). Bacteria also invented all major forms of metabolism, multicellularity, nanotechnology (controlling molecules in ways that continue to elude scientists) and metallurgy. Given that Western societies routinely deploy technology in a plethora of varying circumstances, the specific regulation of technology in the case of transsex becomes a more transparently moral exercise, raising again the association between morality and the nature/culture distinction. For instance, Wilton describes the from-birth vagina as "a complex organ, muscular, self-maintaining and dynamic," compared with the surgical construction of a vagina in which "you flay the penis, turn it inside out, and insert it into the pelvic cavity between the bowel and abdominal wall" (Wilton 2000, 245). Most surgery, I am thinking here particularly of eye and heart, makes for pretty grim reading, and yet may be attributed entirely positive meanings, as in skin "flaying" for burn victim skin-grafting. This use of technology to distinguish between nature and culture obscures the very real and energetic invention and use of technology by nonhuman living organisms (termite high-rise cities include "birth chambers, hatcheries, the insect equivalent of schools, hospitals, honeymoon quarters, workshops and morgues" all under sensitive climate control) as well as the extent to which so-called human technologies actually mimic technology already invented by other species (Margulis and Sagan 2002). The continued focus on technology also further limits the discussion to transsex rather than considering the lived experiences of transpeople more generally.

### Trans as Non-transgressive

In terms of the debate within feminist theory about the transgressive potential of trans, it seems to me that if trans and queer studies concern the ways in which we might work within current structures to transform sex, gender and sexuality then the study of trans amongst nonhuman living organisms is a vital part of this project. Wilson notes that feminists have positively reclaimed the notion of perversity for its supposed defiance of nature, in so far as heterosexuality is venerated as normal because it is natural. By taking on board Darwin's finding that "nature is already generatively and happily perverse," feminist theory might reconsider the ways in which this "natural perversity [might] reorganize our culture-centric theories of difference, embodiment and identity" (Wilson 2002, 284). Indeed, as Phil Macnaghten (2004) writes, "from this perspective, trans isn't 'transgressive' at all—it's natural."

Elsewhere I critiqued queer theory for what I saw as an implicit assumption that queer is constituted through the domain of culture (Hird 2006). I argued that the morphologies and behaviours of many living organisms are queer in that they challenge heteronormativity. The problem with my argument, it seems to me now, is that I read nonhuman living organisms through the lens of queer, rather than critically reflecting upon how we socio-culturally constitute queer and how we might read queer through a nonhuman lens. Referring to Darwin's barnacles, Elizabeth Wilson distils this alternate term of reference:

> ... to characterize Darwin's barnacles as queer is too glib—if by this characterization we mean that the barnacle simply mimics those human, cultural and social forms now routinely marked queer (the transgender barnacle! The polyandrous barnacle!). This characterization has more punch if it is used, contrariwise, to render those familiar human, cultural and social forms more curious as a result of their affiliation with barnacle organization. The queerness of Darwin's barnacles is salutary not because it renders the barnacle knowable through its association with familiar human forms, but because it renders the human, cultural and social guises of queer less familiar and more captivated by natural and biological forces.
>
> [2002, 284]

We need to consider the viability of continued discussions of human trans as though it were an entirely socio-cultural phenomenon. To take Wilson's point, we need to resist the temptation to name certain species as queer—queer barnacles, queer Schizophyllum, queer fish, queer lichen. It is much more interesting to consider how we might understand trans in humans from, say, a bacterial perspective. From such a perspective, given the diversity of sex amongst living matter generally, and the prevalence of transsex more specifically, it does not make sense to continue to debate the authenticity of trans when this debate necessarily relies upon a notion of nature that implicitly excludes trans as a nonhuman phenomenon.

Perhaps given its prevalence amongst living matter, we should be concerned with how infrequently humans transsex. As Birke, Bryld and Lykke point out:

> ... there are sets of practices and performativities, both human and non-human, *which reproduce "the animal" as something apart, as different* ... we need to understand more about "animality"—and hence "humanness"—and how that cuts across gender. But that must be done in ways that allow for animal agency, participation, and performativity—whether they are stag beetles, laboratory rodents, or companions by the feminist fireside.
>
> [2004, 178, emphasis added]

## NOTES

1. The chapter previously appeared as "Animal Transsex" (2006), *Australian Feminist Studies,* 21(49): 35–48. Permission kindly granted by Taylor and Francis. See <http://www.informaworld.com>.
2. Punky and Elvira's case evinces one side of the ambivalent relationship between nature and morality. Animals also represent all that is base or inferior in humans. See Daston and Park (1998).
3. For examples of these shifts see De Landa (1997a; 1997b); Deleuze and Guattari (1987); Jonson (1999); Kirby (1997; 1999, 2001); Margulis and Sagan (1997); Rabinow (1992); Sagan (1992).
4. Indeed, elsewhere I suggest that some of the most thought-provoking and promising explorations of new materialism have recently been produced by Australian feminists (Hird, 2003b).
5. For example, much has been written within feminism on eating disorders and the body, including the social construction of dieting, fitness, beauty and the patriarchal system that regulates women's relationships with their own bodies (see Orbach 1986; Bordo 1993). Despite the enormous number of feminist analyses on the gendered construction of eating disorders, "these analyses consider the cellular processes of digestion, the biochemistry of muscle action, and the secretion of digestive glands to be the domain of factual and empirical verification... only a certain understanding of the body has currency for these feminist analyses, an understanding that seems to exclude 'the biological body'" (Wilson 1998, 52).
   [...]
10. People recognise that sexual intercourse between a horse and donkey might produce an ass, but, on the whole, transspecies sex is considered impossible.
11. Bruce Bagemihl notes that transvestism does not mean caking on activities or behaviours that are considered to be either typically 'female' or 'male'. For instance, the sexual reproduction of offspring is typically considered a female prerogative. But for seahorses and pipefish, the male bears and gives birth to offspring. So male seahorses and male pipefish are not practising transvestism when they produce offspring. Bagemihl notes this is also the case for behaviours involved in what biologists term 'courtship'. In many species, females are more aggressive than males in these behaviours. Should a female in these species behave passively, she would be practicing transvestism (see Bagemihl 1999). It is worth noting here that nonhuman animals who engage in transvestite behaviour, like their human counterparts, specifically avoid homosexual behaviour. The misconception that transvestites (usually male) attempt to be 'feminine' in order to attract sexual relationships with males is as erroneous for the nonhuman, as the human animal world.
12. This scepticism is not limited to academia. Witness the outcry that ensued in 1995 when Kimberley Nixon, a trans woman, attempted to train as a volunteer counsellor for women sexual assault survivors at Vancouver Rape Relief organisation. When Nixon revealed herself to be trans, the Rape Relief organisation refused to allow her to engage in counsellor training. This decision culminated in a British Columbia Supreme Court ruling, and a case that remains ongoing. See Prasad (2005); Namaste (2000). The case pivots on arguments about the authentic embodiment of femaleness.
13. Ontology tends to (as in Wilton's case) be morphologically defined.
14. I refer to ethology as a postmodern synthesis of Darwinian theory here.
15. I am not the only social scientist interested in bacteria. For example, Donna Haraway provides a superb example of how knowledge of biological diversity can inform key feminist debates about embodiment and subjectivity. Haraway describes *Mixotricha paradoxa,* a minute single-celled organism that lives in the gut of the South Australian termite. For Haraway, this tiny organism engenders key questions about the autonomy of identity (we tend to assume that single organisms are defined by the possession of nucleated cells), or as Haraway puts it "the one and many." *Mixotricha paradoxa* lives in a necessary symbiotic relationship with five other organisms, none with cell nuclei but all with DNA. Some live in the folds of the cell membrane, whilst others live inside the cell, whilst simultaneously not being completely part of the cell. Haraway asks: "is it one entity or is it six? But six isn't right either because there are about a million of the five non-nucleated entities for every one nucleated cell. There are multiple copies. So when does one decide to become two? And what counts as *Mixotricha*? Is it just the nucleated cell or is it the whole assemblage?" Advancing a similar argument, Joost Van Loon uses symbiosis theory within nonlinear biology to argue the parasite with the body as the ultimate "Other", and invites a reconsideration of a politics of difference from inside the body. See Haraway (2001); Van Loon (2000).
16. Mixis refers to the "production of a single individual from two parents by way of fertilization occurring at level of fused cells or individuals." See Margulis and Sagan (1986, 232).

## REFERENCES

Adams C. (1995), *Neither Man Nor Beast: Feminism and the Defense of Animals* (New York: Continuum).
Australian Broadcasting Corporation (2004), "It's Official—The Platypus is Weird." *ABC Online,* 25 October: 1.
Bagemihl, B. (1999), *Biological Exuberance: Animal Homosexuality and Natural Diversity* (New York: St. Martin's Press).
Birke, L. (1994), *Feminism, Animals and Science: The Naming of the Shrew* (Toronto: McGraw Hill).

Birke, L., Bryld, M. and Lykke, N. (2004), "Animal Performances: An Exploration of Intersections Between Feminist Science Studies and Studies of Human/Animal Relationships." *Feminist Theory* 5(2): 167–83.

Bordo, S. (1993), *Unbearable Weight: Feminism, Western Culture, and the Body* (Berkeley and Los Angeles: University of California Press).

Brown, N. (1999a), "Debates in Xenotransplantation: On the Consequences of Contradiction." *New Genetics and Society* 18(2/3): 181–96.

Brown, N. (1999b), "Xenotransplantation: Normalizing Disgust." *Science as Culture* 8(3): 327–55.

Brown, N. and Michael, M. (2001), 'Transgenics, Uncertainty and Public Credibility', *Transgenic Research* 10: 279–83.

Busse, P. (2004), "The Far-Right's Fight Against Gay Monkey Marriage." *The Portland Mercury,* July: 1–3.

Butler, J. (1993), *Bodies that Matter: On the Discursive Limits of 'Sex'* (New York: Routledge).

Clarke, A. (2000), *Greetings, Carbon-based Bipeds!* (London: HarperCollins).

Crist, E. (1999), *Images of Animals: Anthropomorphism and Animal Mind* (Philadelphia: Temple University Press).

Daston, L. and Park, K. (1998), *Wonders and the Order of Nature* (New York: Zone Books).

De Landa, M. (1997a), "Immanence and Transcendence in the Genesis of Form." *The South Atlantic Quarterly* 96(3): 499–514.

De Landa, M. (1997b), *A Thousand Years of Nonlinear History* (New York: Swerve Editions).

Deleuze, G. and Guattari, F. (1987), *A Thousand Plateaus* (London: Athlone Press).

Denniston, R.H. (1980), "Ambisexuality in Animals." In J. Marmor (ed.), *Homosexual Behaviour: A Modern Reappraisal* (New York: Basic Books).

Donovan J. and Adams, C. (eds) (2000), *Beyond Animal Rights: A Feminist Caring Ethic for the Treatment of Animals* (New York: Continuum).

Fausto-Sterling, A. (1997), "Feminism and Behavioural Evolution: A Taxonomy." In P. Gowaty (ed.), *Feminism and Evolutionary Biology: Boundaries, Intersections, and Frontiers* (New York: Chapman and Hall).

Feinberg, L. (1996), *Transgender Warriors: Making History from Joan of Arc to Dennis Rodman* (Boston, MA: Beacon Press).

Gaard, G. (ed.) (1992) *Ecofeminism: Women, Animals, Nature* (Philadelphia, PA: Temple University Press).

Grosz, E. (1999), "Thinking the New: Of Futures Yet Unthought." In E. Grosz (ed.), *Becomings: Explorations in Time, Memory, and Futures* (Ithaca, NY and London: Cornell University Press).

Haidane, J. (1928), *Possible Worlds and Other Papers* (New York: Harper and Brothers).

Haraway, D. (1989), *Primate Visions: Gender, Race, and Nature in the World of Modern Science* (London and New York: Routledge).

Haraway, D. (1991), *Simians, Cyborgs, and Women: The Reinvention of Nature* (London and New York: Routledge).

Haraway, D. (1997), *Modest_Witness@Second_Millennium.FemaleMan©_Meets_On-coMouse™* (New York and London: Routledge).

Haraway, D. (2001), "More than Metaphor." In M. Mayberry, B. Subramaniam and L. Weasel (eds), *Feminist Science Studies* (New York: Routledge).

Haraway, D. (2003), *The Companion Species Manifesto: Dogs, People, and Significant Otherness* (Chicago, IL: Prickly Paradigm Press).

Hird, M. (2002a), "For a Sociology of Transsexualism." *Sociology* 36(3): 577–95.

Hird, M. (2002b), "Re(pro)ducing Sexual Difference." *Parallax* 8(4): 94–107.

Hird, M. (2003a), "From the Culture of Matter to the Matter of Culture: Feminist Explorations of Nature and Science." *Sociological Research Online* 8(1) <http://www.socresonline.org.uk/8/1 /hird.html>.

Hird, M. (2003b), "New Feminist Sociological Directions." *Canadian Journal of Sociology* 28(4): 447–62.

Hird, M. (2003c), "A Typical Gender Identity Conference? Some Disturbing Reports from the Therapeutic Front Lines." *Feminism and Psychology* 13(2): 181–99.

Hird, M. (2004a), "Chimerism, Mosaicism and the Cultural Construction of Kinship." *Sexualities* 7(2): 225–40.

Hird, M. (2004b), "Feminist Matters: New Materialist Considerations of Sexual Difference." *Feminist Theory* 5(2): 223—32.

Hird, M. (2004c), "Naturally Queer." *Feminist Theory* 5(1): 85–9.

Hird, M. (2004d), *Sex, Gender and Science* (Basingstoke: Palgrave Press).

Hird, M. (2006), "The Evolution of Sex Diversity: Trying to Get Beyond the Study of the Evolution of Homosexuality." *The Psychologist* 19(1): 30–32.

Jonson, A. (1999), "Still Platonic After All These Years: Artificial Life and Form/Matter Dualism." *Australian Feminist Studies* 14(2):, 47–61.

Kinsman, S. (2001), "Life, Sex and Cells." In M. Mayberry, B. Subramaniam and L. Weasel (eds), *Feminist Science Studies* (New York: Routledge).

Kirby, V. (1997), *Telling flesh: The Substance of the Corporeal* (New York: Routledge).

Kirby, V.(1999), "Human Nature." *Australian Feminist Studies* 14(2): 19–29.

Kirby, V. (2001), "Quantum Anthropologies." In F. Simmons and H. Worth (eds), *Derrida Downunder* (Palmerston North: Dunmore Press).

Krizek, G. (1992), "Unusual Interaction Between a Butterfly and a Beetle: 'Sexual Paraphilia' in Insects?" *Tropical Lepidoptera* 3(2): 118.

Laidman, J. (2000), "Reproduction a Touch-and-Go Thing for Fungus." *Nature,* 24 July: 1–3.

Mackay, J.L. (2001), "Why Have Sex?" *British Medical Journal* 332(7285): 623.

Macnaghten, P. (2004), "Animals in their Nature: A Case Study on Public Attitudes to Animals, Genetic Modification and 'Nature'." *Sociology* 38(3):533–52.

Margulis, L. and Sagan, D. (1986), *Origins of Sex. Three Billion Years of Genetic Recombination* (New Haven, CT: Yale University Press).

Margulis, L. and Sagan, D. (1995), *What is Life?* (Berkeley: University of California Press).

Margulis, L. and Sagan, D. (1997), *What is Sex?* (New York: Simon and Schuster).

Margulis, L. and Sagan, D. (2002) *Acquiring Genomes. A Theory of the Origins of Species* (New York: Basic Books).

Mathieu L. and Sonea, S. (1996), "Time to Drastically Change the Century-Old Concept about Bacteria," *Science Tribune,* August: 3.

Mead, G.H. (1934), *Mind, Self and Society* (Chicago, IL: University of Chicago Press).

Namaste, V. (2000), *Invisible Lives: The Erasure of Transsexual and Transgendered People* (Chicago, TL: University of Chicago Press).

Orbach, S. (1986), *Hunger Strike: The Anorectic's Struggle as a Metaphor for Our Age* (London: Faber).

Oring, L., Fleischer, R., Reed, J., and Marsden, K. (1992), "Cuckoldry Through Stored Sperm in the Sequentially Polyandrous Spotted Sandpiper." *Nature* 359: 631–3.

Owen, D. (1988), "Mimicry and Transvestism in Papilio phorcas." *Journal of Entomological Society of Southern Africa* 51: 294–6.

Pavelka, M. (1995), "Sexual Nature: What Can We Learn from a Cross-Species Perspective?" In P. Abramson and S. Pinkerton (eds), *Sexual Nature, Sexual Culture* (Chicago, IL: University of Chicago Press).

Policansky, D. (1982), "Sex Change in Plants and Animals." *Annual Review of Ecology and Systematic;* 13: 471–95.

Prasad, A. (2005), "Reconsidering the Socio-Scientific Construction of Sexual Difference: The Case of Kimberly Nixon." *Canadian Woman Studies* 24(2/3): 80–84.

Rabinow, P. (1992), "Artificiality and Enlightenment: From Sociobiology to Biosociality." in J. Crary and S. Kwinter (eds), *Incorporations* (New York: Urzone Books).

Raymond, J. (1979), *The Transsexual Empire* (New York: Teachers College Press).

Reite, M. and Caine, N. (eds) (1983), *Child Abuse: 'The Nonhuman Primate Data* (New York: Alan R. Liss Inc.).

Roughgarden, J. (2004), *Evolution's Rainbow: Diversity, Gender, and Sexuality in Nature and People* (Berkeley, Los Angeles, London: University of California Press).

Sagan, D. (1992), "Metametazoa: Biology and Multiplicity." in J. Crary and S. Kwinter (eds), *Incorporations* (New York: Zone Books).

Snowdon, C. (1997), "The 'Nature' of Sex Differences: Myths of Male and Female." In P. Gowaty (ed.), *Feminism and Evolutionary Biology. Boundaries, Intersections, and Frontiers* (New York: Chapman and Hall).

Taylor, J. (1995), "The Third Sex." *Esquire* 123(4): 102–12.

Van Loon, J. (2000), "Parasite Politics: On the Significance of Symbiosis and Assemblage in Theorizing Community Formations." In C. Pierson and S. Tormey (eds), *Politics at the Edge* (New York: St. Martin's Press).

Vasey, P. (1995), "Homosexual Behaviour in Primates." *International Journal of Primatology* 16: 173–204.

Weinrich, J. (1982), "Is Homosexuality Biologically Natural?" In W. Paul, J.D. Weinrich, J.C. Gonsiorek, and M.E. Hotveldt (eds), *Homosexuality: Social, Psychological, and Biological Issues* (Beverly Hills, CA: Sage Publications).

Whittle, S. (2003), "The Becoming Man: The Law's Ass Brays." In K. More and S. Whittle (eds), *Reclaiming Genders* (London: Cassette College Audio).

Wilson, E. (1998), *Neural Geographies: Feminism and the Microstructure of Cognition* (New York and London: Routledge).

Wilson, E. (2002), "Biologically Inspired Feminism: Response to Helen Keane and Marsha Rosengarten, 'On the Biology of Sexed Subjects'," *Australian Feminist Studies* 17(39): 283–5.

Wilson, E.O. (2000), *Sociobiology: The New Synthesis: 25th Anniversary Edition* (Cambridge, MA: Harvard University Press).

Wilton, T. (2000), "Out/performing Our Selves: Sex, Gender and Cartesian Dualism," *Sexualities* 3(2): 237–54.

Zita, J. (1998), *Body Talk: Philosophical Reflections on Sex and Gender* (New York: Columbia University Press).

# 13

# *Animals Without Genitals*
## Race and Transsubstantiation

MEL Y. CHEN

IF THE CONCEPT OF "THE HUMAN" as it has been developed in the modern Western tradition is predicated on marking a salient distinction from "the animal" as well between the genders, then it stands to reason that concepts of transgenderedness and animality, in conversation with one another, might have something interesting to say. Not only to each other and about themselves, but about the domain of the human itself from their respective positions of exteriority to it. In this article, Mel Chen, a theorist of gender, race, and science at the University of California-Berkeley, analyzes three eclectic cultural texts, all of which stage encounters between humans and non-human animals in which genitals are present and/or absent in various permutations: filmmaker Nagisa Oshima's interspecies love story involving a chimpanzee, *Max, mon amour*; philosopher of language J. L. Austin's curious use of a monkey to illustrate a variety of linguistic performativity in his famous series of essays, *How to Do Things With Words*; and artist Xu Bing's conceptual work, *Cultural Animal*, in which a live male pig mounts and penetrates an androform mannequin. Chen teases out the associative links between genitals, castration, gender transposition, animality, blackness, racialization, and (post)colonialism that operate in and across these texts, which are seemingly far removed from any direct consideration of the lives of transgender and transsexual people. And yet, Chen's interpretation of these works is animated by insights drawn from transgender theory; what emerges is a conceptual map of the porous and refigurable boundaries that join and separate sexes and species along racialized lines.

How might one think about modes of trans-ness in conjunction with animality? Invoking the theoretical lens of a Deleuzian "body without organs," I bring into suggestive conversation several disparate instances of cultural production from the last few decades of the twentieth century, each of which ostensibly opposes nonhuman animals to humans in ways that crucially implicate gender. This is a transgeneric thought piece, intentionally speculative in tone as well as consciously promiscuous as it crosses various borders of cultural analysis to examine performatively and rhetorically independent examples that are drawn from film, contemporary art, and language philosophy. I argue that each plumbs animals' symbolic force as a third term, and hence bears its own particular imprint of racialization, sexualization, and globalization in a shared era of geopolitical contestation and postcoloniality. In doing so, I consider the epistemological lessons made possible by thinking about trans-animality in terms of sex.

If mattering turns irrevocably on gender—if, as Judith Butler writes, questions of gender are irretrievably interwoven with questions of materiality, and if human substantiation enduringly depends on the expulsion of animals—then it is imperative that we ask questions about how animals matter sexually.[1] To examine the transness of animal figures in cultural productions or philosophical discourses (beyond their biology, queerness or pure animality, for instance) is to also interrogate how humans' analogic mapping to and from animals (within imagined, lived or taxonomic intimacies) paradoxically survives the cancellation wrought by the operations of abjection, casting a trans light back on the human. By considering the simultaneous relevance of race, gender, sexuality, and geopolitics in the examples below, each chosen for their potent ambivalences, as well as for their diverse consideration of how trans-animality looks and functions, this piece builds on recent work that treats animal spaces intersectionally.[2] It makes use of the simultaneous mobility, stasis, and border-violation shared among transgender spaces and other forms of trans-being: transnationality, transraciality, translation, transspecies. This is not to conflate these various, importantly distinct terms, but to instead try to think them together in new constellations.

Making the science studies observation that "biology has always meant the thing itself and knowledge of what it is, and equally notoriously, these two biologies have not always been identical," Sarah Franklin (thinking through Haraway) dubs "transbiology" an intensified making of "new biologicals" via "the redesign of the biological in the context of contemporary bioscience, biomedicine and biotechnology,"[3] identifying what might be thought of as a significant shift in the specific depth of imaginative technologies in crafting matter—a shift in the participants in what Charis Thompson has called "ontological choreography."[4] [...] Here, thinking less in terms of biotechnologies than attending to the role of visual representation and morphology in mattering, I turn directly to the "trans" in "transbiology." With "trans," I focus on how animal-human boundaries are articulated *in terms of* sex and gender by examining perhaps the most consistent missing morphology in cultural representations of animals: the genitalia.[6]

## ANIMAL SPACES: *MAX, MON AMOUR*

In the 1988 bilingual French film *Max, mon amour*, directed by Nagisa Oshima, Margaret (played by Charlotte Rampling), the wife of a British diplomat named Peter (played by Anthony Higgins), recounts to her husband that she has fallen in love with a chimpanzee named Max, purchased Max and taken Max home. The film, saturated in bourgeois settings with the blatant exception of Max, proceeds with the ambivalent games of the husband to cope with Max's entrance into the family, Max's moving into the family home, Max's resistances to Peter's mistreatments and violences, Margaret's insistence upon keeping her relationship with Max during a climactic scene during which a rifle changes hands from Peter to Max, and the ultimate, happy reconstitution of the family, Max included.

Max's *linguistic* gender is, throughout, consistently male. Yet the embodied creature is not terribly convincing as a chimpanzee. The non-integrity of the creature is made evident by the fact that the eyes shift around inside the sockets of the chimpanzee hood as Max moves. To a queer (and perhaps forgiving?) skeptic, the middling chimp costume begs further questions, such 1980s special effects notwithstanding: it lacks any form of visible genitalia or easily legible "secondary sex characteristics." While such a visual absence, all else equal, might provoke a tentative reading of "female," it is also true that the default movie sex for costumed monkeys and apes can remain unspecified, genderless, in almost a literalization of the genericity of the animal type. In addition, individual animal specificities like sex cannot survive in a costume unless it is intended as "anatomically accurate," bucking the neutering costume traditions for genitalia. Such a confounding and ultimate undeterminability of possible linguistic and visual sexes and genders points, no less so in the relatively ludicrous case of Max, to the porosity underlying gender/sex systems that structure Western cultural spaces.

How might these cultural spaces intersect with, or differentiate themselves from, animal spaces? The terms "animal spaces" and "animal places" are used by Chris Philo and Chris Wilbert in an articulation of critical animal geographies, where "animal space" signifies the kinds of domains in which non-human animals appear and inside which they come into particular being (such as experimental animal labs) and "animal places" signifies the "proper location" of animals in a human typology.[7] Myra Hird writes that "non-human animals have for some time been overburdened with the task of making sense of human social relations."[8] This is as true for race as for any social construct. Given that humans, as indefatigable denizens of the symbolic, inherit and project such responsibilities onto non-human animals, the trick seems to be how to objectify this symbolic responsibility given to non-human animals, as well as our dependence upon their symbolic labor, and to contextualize it such that our ideas about animality are not be automatically affectively or structurally reliant upon this dependence.

Watching the film, my colleagues and I took pleasure in the "failure" of the costume and the awkward monkey-moves of the actor inside. There were gender-queering possibilities: on top of the expected bestial kinkiness offered by a human-animal coupling, why not add a Rampling/chimpanzee lesbian coupling, rather than—as the film seems only to intend—a neatly contained heterosexual narrative?[9] And perhaps, given that the chimp actor was self-evidently a person in a costume, was Margaret's sexual preference in fact for Furries [...]?

For all the amusement of such questions, what cannot be ignored in *Max, mon amour* is the virtual stampede of Africanized racial invocations, overdetermined by Margaret's British husband's diplomatic status and the Parisian locus of the film as both a colonial metropolis, and a host to unwelcome racialized colonial subjects. Such racialized staging was evident from moment to moment in the chimp's expressive limitations, marked "impoliteness" and unfamiliarity with its "civilized" surroundings, its surfeit of embodiment, aggression, and emotional lability in the face of white upper-class cultural sophistication, formal "goodwill," and expressive minimalism. All of these are conditioned by seasoned colonial narrative and visual tropes.[10] The recognizable "fakeness" of the costume's face further invites comparisons to blackface minstrelsy, in which there lingers the possibility that a mask conceals a differently racialized human, undermining the film's pointedly surrealist overtones with a historical legacy of European racism and colonialism.[11]

## AUSTIN'S MARRIAGE

In 1955, the British language philosopher J.L. Austin put forward a theory of language and action called *How to do things with words*, consisting of a series of transcribed and edited lectures. As the lectures progressed, Austin developed the concept of the performative from a simple class of utterances characterized by special main verbs in finite form, to a more complex tripartite typology of *acts* that not merely the special verbs, but all utterances, would involve: locutionary (speech) content, illocutionary (conventional) content, and perlocutionary (effective) content. In an early lecture, Austin was working off the simple definition of the performative, such as in the example "I thee wed" in a marriage ceremony.

Stating that a performative could not succeed without supporting conditions, Austin wrote: "Suppose we try first to state schematically . . . some at least of the things which are necessary for the *smooth or 'happy' functioning* of a performative (or at least of a *highly developed* explicit performative …)" (my emphasis). [...] Austin's model was also premised on the assumption that communication is "normally" good-willed, and relies on the proper positioning of that person delivering the performative. He wrote: "One might … say that, where there is not even a pretence of *capacity* or a *colourable* claim to it, then there is no accepted conventional procedure; it is a *mockery, like a marriage with a monkey*" (my emphasis).[12]

Proper capacity and goodwill were critical to the success of Austin's performative, and these conditions remained through complex developments of the theory. In the moment of defining a critical aspect of the successful performative, Austin turned to marriage [...]

What does Austin's marriage with a monkey suggest, and on what does it rely to make this kind of sense? While Austin's articulation "mockery, like a marriage with a monkey" seems mundane in the sense that monkey-invocations often function as normative dismissals, we can look more closely at the significance of its collocations. More specifically, we can consider what a queer reading might offer. "A mockery, like a marriage with a monkey" equates a particular kind of animal with the performative's excess (and, perhaps, an affective excess inappropriate to the encounter)— that which must be sloughed off for the performative to work efficiently and effectively.[13] Austin's backhanded dismissal of the animal monkey, and his matter-of-fact exclusion of the monkey from the institution of marriage, together consign the marrying monkey to queer life. In citing a particular kind of marriage just as he asserts its invalidity, Austin is responding to a sensed threat. Someone's heteronormative and righteous marriage must be protected against the mockeries of marriage; and we might imagine that someone's righteous and heteronormative speech must be protected against the mockery of performative improprieties, which for all practical purposes are open to convenient definition.

But it is worth asking what might have most registered as a threat. Austin delivered these lectures informed by the social and political context of mid-1950s Britain. The 1950s was a period of intensive societal and legal flux, in which immigrants from formally decolonized sites were arriving in greater numbers as Britain went through the intensified strains of post-colonial revision. 1948 saw the first group of West Indian immigrants enter Britain from sites in the Commonwealth, having been granted citizenship through the *British Nationality Act*. Violence and discrimination against the immigrants grew in the 50s, resulting in 1962's restrictive *Commonwealth Immigrants Act* (also the year of publication of *How to Do Things with Words*). Of course, Austin's monkey was not necessarily innocent of a more generalized history. There was already a long history of British and European associations of apes and monkeys with African subjects, fed and conditioned by the imperialist culture of colonial relations; these were underlain by an abiding pseudo-Darwinian mapping which temporally projected non-European peoples and non-white racialized groups onto earlier stages of human evolution.

The powerfully racialized undertones of "mockery" have been theorized by thinkers such as Homi Bhabha, who opens his essay "Of mimicry and man: On the ambivalence of colonial discourse" with a citation from Sir Edward Cust (1839) that reads: "To give the colony the forms of independence is a mockery."[14] Thus we might say that a racial—*and* freakishly gendered—body haunts Austin's monkey, just as British whiteness may haunt Austin's authorized speaker. Once again, a colonial past might lurk inside a presumably "innocent" cultural form which seems to deploy a presentist animal figure. Austin was working in a specific social and political context, and to tease out the undertones of his language is also to explore contemporary hauntings or habits of epistemological projection with regard to animality, sex, and race. We might also use this example to understand some linguistic animal figures as before-the-fact racialized and sexualized, especially if used in contexts where race has a history of social or cultural presence.

## CASTRATED ANIMAL

A queer analysis of either Max or Austin's monkey, however, does not suffice; for both of these figures are simultaneously engaged with transgender meaning. This dance between *queer* and *trans* evokes debates that have been taken up in recent scholarship, particularly about what degree one might excavate the *trans-* in what has been taken and subsumed under the rubric of *queer*. Ultimately, the opposition of *trans* and *queer* suggests a false dichotomy: just as gender and sex are unavoidably linked, so too are trans and queer. They can be considered as independent factors which participate in intersectional spaces.[15] A *trans critique* is thus invited in the instance of what David Eng calls racialized castration, a kind of transing which is not always considered under a trans rubric, except in the case of male to female transsexuality.[16]

Myra Hird invokes feminist biologist Sharon Kinsman to argue for the idea that human understandings of sex respond not merely to humanity's own intraspecies evidences, but also to those of non-human animals as well, such as fish whose gonads shift from male to female. Concomitantly Hird thinks in terms of "trans" not as an exclusively human construct, challenging readers to fairly consider the implications of evidence of trans in non-human animals. Such analysis perhaps suggests a sense of trans that extends beyond sex alone; as Hird writes, "I want to extend feminist interest in trans as a specifically sexed enterprise (as in transitioning from one sex to another), but also in a broader sense of movement across, through and perhaps beyond traditional classifications." [17]

Of what might be labeled an "organ," the genitals bear tremendous weight, particularly, arguably, in the West/Global North. They are a tremendously loaded "organ," for they simultaneously impute both gender and sexuality and, as so many race and sexuality theorists have demonstrated, race and class.[18] Therefore the "genitals" are directly tied to geopolitical and social orders which are vastly more complex and intersectional than to systems of gender alone. Genitality can be prosthetized through other accoutrements in a society which is still wrapped up in styles of modesty. While much has been written of histories in which non-white racialized men are often, due to racism, subject to symbolic castration and representation as non-human animals, less has been suggested of the possibility that the castrated animal is not only a substitute for, but coextensive with, and forming meanings equally with, castrated racialized men.[19]

Frantz Fanon in *Black Skin, White Masks*, in analyzing the postcolonial psychic state of a racialized subject, theorizes relations among animality, castration, and black sexual threat, and in so doing offers us a condensed image of the social possibility of simultaneous *castration* and phallic *presence*.[20] [...] Given the sacrosanct importance of the penis or phallus, we might extend the concurrence of castration and phallic presence to the possibility that non-genitality could impute genitality, or the threat thereof—the threat of genitality's eventual presence.

The introduction of species difference yields a yawning gap around the unresolved question of gender and sexuality, precisely around questions of genericity and gender. If Max, for instance, is a blend between actual (if materialized through costume only) and figural chimpanzee, should there not be another layer of gender confusion between human/animal and actual/figure? [...]

Conveniently perhaps for the design of the film *Max, mon amour*, no linguistic contradictions need be enacted: the French grammatical gender for chimpanzee (*le chimpanzee, lui, il*) is the same as the purported gender/sex of the chimpanzee Max, who is supposed to be a masculine, male chimp. Yet for all the profusion of linguistic gender, in *Max, mon amour*, the incursion of species difference also introduces the presumably threatening possibility of a *genderless* relation, produced by the genericity of the type but literalized in the costume itself. Rampling and the chimp's affections thus yielded something that was *trans* in the sense of the undecidability, elusiveness, or reluctance toward fixity of the chimp's sex, which in spite of its linguistic reinforcements surpasses its otherwise presumptive maleness; that is, to what extent can one trust that a male chimp is sexed *or* gendered "like" a human male?

Returning to the example of Austin's "marriage with a monkey," the genericity of "a monkey" implicates that the monkey threatens being genderless: first, in a general sense, a creature without a gender identity somehow threatens the smooth running of heteronormative society which itself relies on a robust organization of its gender systems; second, a creature without a gender identity must also lack a sex, and thus threaten the possibility of bringing an abject, queer sexuality into (the institution of) marriage. By including "the institution of marriage," I suggest that though Austin insisted in some sense that the performative verbs themselves (like *wed* in "I thee wed") were fixed in purpose and meaning and thus robust, his use of mockery here and the invocation of a kind of animality linked to discourses of colonial and species threat reveals, perhaps, a fear that the institution of marriage (or conventions of language, or rigidities of gender and sex, or divisions of race and nation) itself might be maligned and indeed transformed by a performative's misuse.[23]

Thus, while considering Max's "bad" costume may seem an indulgence, it nevertheless points to the fact that any decision about including or excluding genitals on an imagined non-human animal cannot help but be loaded, since species difference itself cannot help but be fraught with anxieties about reproduction (e.g. miscegenation and animality in discourses of eugenics). Once again the queer/trans relationship is made explicit in the case of Max.

Thus, "trans-animality" can simultaneously refer to gender and species, while sexuality, geopolitics and race remain in full scope. In other words, an analysis of trans-animality must simultaneously identify the quiet imputations of race that are shuttled in along with the animal. Definitions of both "trans-" and "animal" vary both disciplinarily and politically. I consider *animality* not a matter of non-humanity or of creatures considered non-human (for instance the accepted logics of pets or agricultural livestock and our stewardship of them), so much as a quality of animalness, one equally attributable to humans as well as non-human animals. Likewise, *trans* is not as a linear space of mediation between two monolithic, autonomous poles, as for example "female" and "male," not least because the norms by which these poles are often defined too easily conceal, or forget, their interests and contingencies. Rather, *trans* is conceived of as more emergent than determinate, intervening with other categories in a richly intersectional space. Much in the way that the idealized meaning of *queer* signifies an adjectival modification or modulation, rather than a substantive core such as a noun, I wish to highlight a *prefixal* "trans-" not preliminarily limited to gender.

By mobilizing a different form of trans-, I do not mean by any means to evacuate trans entirely of its gendered possibilities. To the contrary, I reassert the complex, multi-factored cultural contingency of transgendered actualizations and affirm that gender is omnipresent, though I am suggesting that it is rarely monolithically masculine or feminine. As Susan Stryker, Paisley Currah, and Lisa Jean Moore write, "The hyphen... marks the difference between the implied nominalism of 'trans' and the explicit relationality of 'trans-,' which remains open-ended and resists premature foreclosure by attachment to any single suffix [including gender]." [24] Such a prefixal "trans-" is a way to explore that complexity of gender definition that lies between human gender systems and the gendering of animals.

## ANIMALS WITHOUT GENITALS/BODY WITHOUT ORGANS

In two successive coauthored works, *Anti-Oedipus: Capitalism and Schizophrenia*, and *A Thousand Plateaus*, Gilles Deleuze and Félix Guattari describe what they call a "body without organs."[25] The body without organs is that body which actively refuses its own subjectivity, by engaging the dis-ordering of its "organs." In the body without organs, no given organ has merely one functionality, and the organism itself cannot be represented as an ordered system. Instead, the body without organs makes impossible such a systematicity by affirming an infinite functionality and interrelation of the "parts" within, "parts" which can only be individuated by one of an infinite number of permutations of the body into "parts." We might say that in biological research, it does seem that the actual human body is being found to approach the body without organs and to move away from a regularized, systemic representation, both in terms of the multifunctionality of a given organ (the appendix's function has just been discovered, for example), and the increasing numbers of communicative relationships among "organs" that converge to produce behavioral or emotional appearances or effects (e.g. neurophysiological constructs are understood to interact with bodily hormone systems in new ways that influence the measurable emotionality of a body).

Quite unlike Deleuze's "body without organs," the "animal without genitals" would seem to be a body-with-organs-without-genitals, that is, a body with organs from which the genitals have been extracted or pointedly neglected. Nevertheless, the "animal without genitals'" *affective* valence bears closer attention, for I suggest that the animal-without-genitals, just as the directionality of biological research on organism systematicity towards more multiplicity, marks or symbolizes a kind of affective impulse towards a human hope OR repulsion from a marginless being, even as it reiterates the porosity of the very human-animal border. Thus, the animal-without-genitals AFFIRMS the body without organs, while carrying dramatically variant affective valences. The ghostly logic of the racialized, castrated human male/present phallus explored by Fanon and Fuchs is perhaps why, alternatively, the racialized figurative animal that is deployed for purposes of human signification is a body *with* organs *without* genitals, since the body with organs *needs* genitals. Furthermore, affectivities, while they may help leverage narratives to a satisfying conclusion, also yield a result which is ambivalent about the abjection of animality vis-à-vis the weakly solidified human, because the analogies are so vibrant—indeed vital.

## CULTURAL ANIMAL

In Chinese conceptual artist Xu Bing's 1994 installation/performance work *Cultural Animal*, a live male pig, with nonsense words made up of letters from the Roman alphabet painted all over its body, was introduced to a male mannequin posing on all fours, which it eventually mounted, in front of a live audience in Beijing. The mannequin had nonsense Chinese characters inscribed on its body. In personal accounts of this piece, Xu Bing explained that he had applied the scent of a female pig onto the mannequin.[26] In this queer, transspecies encounter, certain common scenarios of relative clarity and obfuscation are reversed: the live pig's genitals are made central and clearly visible, while the mannequin is a "dead/fake figure" whose genitalia are never made explicit in the photographic documentation.

What does this suggest, or generate? Certain easy conflations do not succeed here: in this representation/performance, "the animal" is not so easily filled in by the "dead/fake figure," despite that figure's quadripedal stance. If traditions of human-animal encounter in representation and performance privilege or enhance the liveness or subjectivity of the human against the counterexample of the animal, then *Cultural Animal* scrambles given codes of reading.

"Reading," in fact, is an equal participant in the spectatorship of this performance. Xu Bing's work frequently deploys nonsense words in both Englishlike and Chinese-like forms, and it is commonly interpreted as "scrambling" received semiotic relations between East and West. While such a lexically dependent strategy might in itself seem an obvious rendering of the impossibility of cultural translation, when juxtaposed with the actors of the performance and the emergent actions this scrambling generates a possible critique of the ready recourse of human-animal renderings into symbolic certainties (or the ready assignation of passive mannequin to "East" and penetrating pig to "West"). What the pointed and productive restaging of otherwise common priorities makes possible here is a Deleuzian "becoming-animal": without the fixity of animal-human difference in place, the audience is provoked into the multiplicity of possible encounters of self and other—perhaps even of dissolution of borders between animal and human and self and other.

In the case of Max, the fictive chimpanzee in an actual animal suit in a fictional film, Max's transspecies identity is incontestable. Narratively, Max is a chimpanzee with unruly passions and who is deeply attached to Margaret; visually, "Max" is a chimpanzee costume with no known sex and a somewhat disembodied voice, barely concealing the actor inside, who is of unknown sex, gender, or age. The standards of opacity applied to this actor are much lower than those applied to Rampling in character. The consequences of reading the not-so-chimp chimp are manifold. Another layer is opened up; the chimp figure, which is already itself a complex blend of species, race, gender and sexuality, animates a body without organs, releasing our determinative hold on the events in the film as the sincere construction of truth, and allowing surrealist ironies to unfold. What is trans-animality here is not that we sometimes see the chimp as alternatively chimp and unskilled human actor, so much as the fact that the presence of this "flimsy chimp" can serve as a "key" that enables us to move outside and away from the overdetermined racialized and other spaces Max occupies, and to critically read the confluences by which he has been constructed.

In the conceptions offered by this paper, several senses of "trans-" have been mobilized and put into conversation: transgender (living outside normative gender definition, or undergoing shift in gender identity), transmogrification (changing of shape or form to something fantastical), translation (across languages), and of course, transspecies (across species). Each of these terms suggests a movement or dynamism, from one site to another, as in the sense of "across." I attempted to make the case for a trans-theorizing that recognizes the distinctness of queer, but at the same time embraces the collaborative possibilities of thinking trans alongside and across queerness. In analyzing a number of theoretical and cultural productions and their (often hostile) articulations or imputations of transness, this paper worked very far away from lived transgender and transsexual lives and identities and does not intend to be in direct conversation with them. Rather, it attended to the coercive conceptual workings of these productions and their way of crafting forms of cultural exile premised on already marginal loci in gender, race, species, and sexuality matrices. Simultaneously, it located zones of possibility that work around and against such coercions, such as the analogic survival of transness that can always be purported back to the human.

Deleuze and Guattari's "body without organs" is both honored and merely suggested in the three examples elaborated in this essay. Their simultaneous limitation and promise is precisely that the genitals (or non-genitals) within them *matter*, but are not necessarily constrained by normative gender and sexuality, and these "animals with/out genitals" possess a trans-materiality which is characterized by a radical uncertainty and a generative affectivity. And so this essay might be thought of as an invitation to consider queer-trans animality, even in its politically most closed of circumstances, not as a tired and fatal venue for human self-making but as a site of unpredictable investment for untraceable animal futurities.

## NOTES

1. Butler 1993.
2. Animal studies is still being formed, and its borders are still in contention. It is a multidisciplinary field, reaching across environmental studies, science and technology studies, psychoanalysis, ecocriticism, and literary and cultural studies. In addition to Donna Haraway's corpus, some representative texts include work by Thompson 2002; Anderson 2000; Lutz and Collins 1993; Shukin 2009; Franklin 2007.
3. Franklin 2006.
4. Thompson 2005.
5. Halberstam 2008. Additionally, Akira Lippit (2000) considers the discourse of the animal as a "third term."
6. For two other studies on the intersection of transness and animality, see Hansen 2008; Hayward 2008.
7. Philo and Wilbert 2000.
8. Hird 2006.
9. Of course, this is a playful reading well outside of standard film criticism, bringing contemporary economies of animal and sexual representation to bear on earlier film practices that did not employ them. For a critically positive psychoanalytic reading of *Max, mon amour*, see Barbara Creed (2006). Creed frames *Max, mon amour* as one example of new "zoocentric" cinema that reflects its interest in resolving questions that remain of a Darwinian blurring of the boundary between human and non-human animal. Creed notes that Margaret's desire for Max foregrounds an even more mysterious female "jouissance" that lies threateningly outside of the male symbolic order (and thus beyond Peter's ken).
10. Shohat and Stam 1994.
11. For work on blackface minstrelsy in the US context, see Lott 1993.
12. Austin 1962, 24.
13. Does this animal expulsive strain still exist in performativity theory itself? To the degree that performative authority is conferred onto to those in strict categories of human role membership (such as a minister), that expulsive strain must live. If performativity theory (thinking here of Judith Butler's *Excitable speech*) delinks performance from the notion of the individual and casts it into realms of iterable citation, I suggest that unless it is extinguished that strain—the

human-animal divide and the expulsion inherent inside it—replicates along with scenes of iteration, in ways that might be similar to the ways that traumas might be ushered forth in the reiterations of injurious speech. See Butler 1997.
14. Bhabha 1994, 85.
15. For work that considers the queer-trans relationship, see for example work by Susan Stryker, Jay Prosser, J. Halberstam, and Judith Butler.
16. See Eng 2001.
17. Hird 2006, 37.
18. See, for example, work by Siobhan Somerville, Sander Gilman, Gail Dines, and Patricia Hill Collins.
19. Eng's *Racial castration* offers a brilliant cogent psychoanalytic study of the vexed sexualization of the Asian American male.
20. Fanon [1952] 1994.
    […]
23. The insecurity I attribute to Austin here is equivalent to a recognition of the importance of iterative renewal for the performative itself to retain its normativity.
24. Stryker, Currah, and Jean Moore 2008.
25. Deleuze and Guattari 1977, 9.
26. Skype interview with Xu Bing in Beijing, December 2009.

## REFERENCES

Anderson, Kay. 2000. "The beast within": Race, humanity, and animality. *Environment and Planning D: Society and Space* 18, no. 3: 301–20.
Austin, J.L. 1962. *How to do things with words*. William James Lectures, Harvard University, 1955. Oxford: Clarendon.
Bhabha, Homi. 1994. *The location of culture*. London: Routledge.
Butler, Judith. 1993. *Bodies that matter: On the discursive limits of sex*. London and New York: Routledge.
Butler, Judith. 1997. *Excitable speech: A politics of the performative*. New York and London: Routledge.
Creed, Barbara. 2006. A Darwinian love story: *Max Mon Amour* and the zoocentric perspective in film. *Continuum* 20, no. 1: 45–60.
Cust, Edward. 1839. *Reflections on West African affairs . . . addressed to the Colonial Office*. London: Hatchard.
Deleuze, Gilles, and Félix Guattari. 1977. *Anti-Oedipus: Capitalism and schizophrenia*. New York: Penguin Classics.
Eng, David. 2001. *Racial castration: Managing masculinity in Asian America*. Durham, NC: Duke University Press.
Fanon, Franz. [1952] 1994. *Black skin, White masks*. Trans. Constance Farrington. New York: Grove Press.
Franklin, Sarah. 2006. The cyborg embryo: Our path to transbiology. *Theory, Culture and Society* 23, nos. 7–8: 167–87.
Franklin, Sarah. 2007. *Dolly mixtures: The remaking of genealogy*. Durham, NC: Duke University Press.
Freccero, Carla. Forthcoming. "Les chats de Derrida." In *Derrida and Queer Theory*, ed. Michael O'Rourke. Basingstoke: Palgrave.
Fuchs, Cynthia. 1995. Michael Jackson's penis. In *Cruising the performative*, ed. Sue-Ellen Case, Philip Brett, and Susan Leigh Foster, 13–33. Bloomington: Indiana University Press.
Halberstam, Judith. 2008. Animating revolt/revolting animation: Penguin love, doll sex and the spectacle of the queer nonhuman. In *Queering the Non-Human*, ed. Noreen Giffney and Myra Hird, 265–81. Hampshire: Ashgate.
Hansen, Natalie Corinne. 2008. Humans, horses, and hormones: (Trans) gendering cross-species relationships. *WSQ: Women's Studies Quarterly* 36, nos. 3–4: 87–105.
Hayward, Eva. 2008. Lessons from a starfish. In *Queering the non-human,* ed. Noreen Giffney and Myra Hird, 249–63. Hampshire: Ashgate.
Hird, Myra. 2006. Animal transex. *Australian Feminist Studies* 21, no. 49: 35–50.
Lippit, Akira. 2000. *Electric animal: Toward a rhetoric of wildlife*. Minneapolis: University of Minnesota Press.
Lott, Eric. 1993. *Love and theft: Blackface minstrelsy and the American working class*. New York, Oxford University Press.
Lutz, Catherine A., and Jane L. Collins. 1993. *Reading National Geographic*. Chicago and London: University of Chicago Press.
Philo, Chris, and Chris Wilbert. 2000. Introduction to *Animal spaces, beastly places,* ed. Chris Philo and Chris Wilbert. London: Routledge.

Shohat, Ella, and Robert Stam. 1994. *Unthinking Eurocentrism: Multiculturalism and the media.* New York and London: Routledge.

Shukin, Nicole. 2009. *Animal capital: Rendering life in biopolitical times.* Minneapolis and London: University of Minnesota Press.

Stryker, Susan, Paisley Currah, and Lisa Jean Moore. 2008. Introduction, "Trans-." *Women's Studies Quarterly* 36, nos. 3–4: 11–22.

Thompson, Charis. 2005. *Making parents: The ontological choreography of reproductive technologies.* Cambridge, MA: MIT Press.

Thompson, Charis. 2002. When elephants stand in for competing philosophies of nature. In *Complexities: Social Studies of Knowledge Practices*, ed. Jon Law and Annemarie Mol. Durham, NC: Duke University Press.

Xu Bing. 2009. Interview, by Residential Research Group members, "Species Spectacles: Transnational Coordinations of Animality, Race, and Sexuality" at the University of California Humanities Research Institute, Irvine, CA. Beijing, December 2009, with Tonglin Lu translating.

# 14

## Lessons From a Starfish

EVA HAYWARD

ONE OF SEVERAL ESSAYS IN THIS VOLUME that refuse an identity-based theory of transgender embodiment, Eva Hayward's "Lessons From A Starfish" weaves together music criticism, zoology, philosophy and deeply personal poetics. The article begins by quoting the lyrics from "Cripple and the Starfish," a song recorded by Antony and the Johnsons. If lead singer Antony Hegarty is, as Hayward suggests, intelligible as trans in some way, what might the phrase "I'll grow back like a starfish" teach us about transsexual embodiment? From here, the essay explodes into a poetic meditation on the metaphor of cutting as it intersects with gender reassignment surgeries. If we resist the idea of cutting as mutilation (as some interpretations of transsexuality would have it), how does it change the game to understand cutting as regenerative? The "growing back" capacities of the starfish in the song become a metaphor for thinking through the difference between "transformative" and "regenerative" in transsexual discourse. For Hayward, regeneration feels like a more capacious category than transformation: while transformation implies something that changes the body itself, regeneration suggests "re-shaping and re-working bodily boundaries" contained within and initiated by the same body. Moving to a zoological account of real sea stars, Hayward pushes the starfish to be more than a metaphor. Some starfish, Hayward writes, can break off limbs and regenerate them; sometimes the limb itself can grow into a new starfish capable of reproduction. But the starfish will not be digested as a mere metaphor for human concerns. Invoking Akira Lippit's concept of "animetaphor," Hayward suggests that nonhuman organisms devour and exceed their representations, to touch us materially. The starfish in the song thus intensifies a moment in which human and non-human, transsexual and non-transsexual beings mingle in a "voluptuary of trans-speciation."

### Cripple and the Starfish

Mr Muscle forcing bursting
Stingy thingy into little me, me, me
But just "ripple" said the cripple
As my jaw dropped to the ground
Smile smile

It's true I always wanted love to be
Hurtful
And it's true I always wanted love to be
Filled with pain
And bruises

Yes, so Cripple-Pig was happy
Screamed "I just completely love you!"
And there's no rhyme or reason
I'm changing like the seasons
Watch! I'll even cut off my finger
It will grow back like a Starfish!
It will grow back like a Starfish!
It will grow back like a Starfish!
Mr Muscle, gazing boredly
And he checking time did punch me
And I sighed and bleeded like a windfall
Happy bleedy, happy bruisy

I am very happy
So please hit me
I am very happy
So please hurt me

I am very happy
So please hit me
I am very very happy
So come on hurt me

I'll grow back like a Starfish
I'll grow back like a Starfish
I'll grow back like a Starfish
I'll grow back like a Starfish

I'll grow back like a Starfish
I'll grow back like a Starfish
I'll grow back like a Starfish
I'll grow back like a Starfish
Like a Starfish...
(Antony and the Johnsons 2000)

*I call this piece a critical poetics rather than a cultural account, so as to foreground the process of writing in it. For I want this to be a doing and a knowing that I get woven into—a kind of phenomenological telling. I am not only describing and articulating, not merely charting the geography, but am pulled into the gerunds of what I write out. That is to say, I am not creating a new narrative; rather I'm simply pulling at the stitches of ongoing processes. I am here not to confess, but to confect; I bear witness through relating.*

## OF SPECIES AND SEXES

I have been in an email exchange with Susan Stryker.[1] During this correspondence, Stryker brought to my attention a particular song, "Cripple and the Starfish" by Antony and the Johnsons.[2] Stryker thinks that Antony is probably "trans or at least gender-queer," and that the song seems to point toward "a yearning for transformation." Although it is difficult to say anything definitive about someone else's "transition" or gender identity, I agree with Stryker.[3]

I listen to the song; I find the layered tones in Antony's voice haunting, and the lyrics startling: "I'll even cut off my finger"; "I'll grow back like a Starfish"; "Happy bleedy, happy bruisy." My iTunes player calls the song "alternative", that ambiguous over-populated term. The music "ripples" through styles and textures. Antony's voice vibrates (vibrato), fluctuating and undulating with emotional expressiveness: sometimes soft and tender and ripe with satiety and fulfillment ("I am very happy/ So please hit me") then shifting in cadence to declarative and triumphant ("I'll grow back like a Starfish"). Following the rise and fall of the song, Antony's voice shifts between low and high, deep and bright. Antony's voice creates a waving space, a singing sea—the pace and rhythm of his/her phrasing expresses frenetic and calm movements, the periodicity or the punctuated changes of things and events. Could it be that Antony sings the tones of whales calling, the syncopation of herds, the transfiguring surf? This is to ask: how do the tone and the wording of "Cripple and the Starfish" put us in touch with things that it mentions or hints at?

I wonder, thinking about the transsexual *trans*-formations and the starfish re-generations that are suggested in the song, "What is the transformative and relational power of prefixes like *trans*- or *re*-?" I mentioned this wonderment to Stryker. She wrote in response, "What this calls my attention to is the need to become more specific in how we think about the *re*-/*trans*-distinction in trans discourse." My question grew insistent; I wanted to understand how *re*-(as is re-turn or re-new) and *trans*- (as in elsewhere) were differently embodied. Beyond my own identity as a transsexual woman, or the political formation of transgender/transsexual,[4] I wasn't certain about the ontological processes of bodily transformation (my own or others'). How does *re*-assignment define transitioning for some trans-subjects? Moreover, I wondered if starfish—"I'll grow back like a Starfish"—or more properly "sea stars," might provide some prefixial lessons or guides through language, metaphor and other tropological terrains. Do some starfish not re-generate themselves from injury? Is the "cripple" not re-pairing him/herself through the act of cutting? Is transsexual transformation also re-generative? Am I not in part a transsexual through the re-working and re-folding of my own body, my tissue and my skin? In being transsexual, am I also becoming "like a starfish" as the song suggests? When does metaphor transform into metonymy? Is the metaphorical device of "likeness" ("like a starfish" or like a woman) too clumsy a rhetorical device for the kind of poetic and material enactments of trans-sexing/speciating?

In addition to stirring my interest, Stryker also provided me with several interviews with Antony and other promotional materials. I have excerpted two key quotations from Antony that evocatively link the group (and Antony him/her-self) both to trans histories and human-animal relationships. During an interview with *Velle Magazine*, Antony, the founder of Antony and the Johnsons, discusses the emergence of the band:

> The Johnsons's name is a reference to a hero of mine named Marsha P. Johnson, who was a street activist from the mid sixties all the way through to her death in the early nineties. Marsha P. Johnson was a street prostitute and a very visible figure on Christopher Street through the seventies and eighties, very renowned for her kindness. You know, her nickname was Saint Marsha. She was a very gregarious sort of outsider street presence and she was rumored to have thrown the first bottle in the Stonewall Riot—I mean whether that was true or not was a bone of contention among several different queens.[5]

Marsha Johnson,[6] or Saint Marsha, and Sylvia Rivera,[7] an important figure in the nascent "transgender" civil rights movement, started a group in 1970 called STAR, Street Transvestite Action

Revolutionaries.[8] In Antony's own words, a transgender legacy is written into the music group; "she", an "outsider", a queen of color, who threw "the first bottle", who was murdered in 1992, structures the creative and political intent of the band. Johnson is Antony's "hero", perhaps, and I say this only speculatively, an ego ideal.

Antony is clear to emphasize the "collage" quality of her/his music and sound in relation to her/his creative process:

> I think my creative process has always been what I've described as accumulative. I collect a lot of different shards and pieces, and I create something that feels meaningful to me by finding relationships between them and putting them into a kind of a collage ... You know, for me, I'm really drawn to singers that are full of feeling and are seeking transformation. I like transformative singing, you know, singing that starts one place and ends in another place.[9]

Classification is evaded for something more "transformative", something "that starts one place and ends in another place." *Trans-*, a prefix weighted with across, beyond, through (into another state or place), does the now-familiar work of suggesting the unclassifiable. To be trans is to be transcending or surpassing particular impositions whether empirical, rhetorical, or aesthetic. Antony speaks of the affective force of his/her transformation in songs and in singing. Transformations—not unlike transgenders—are produced through emotive forces. "Shards" and "pieces" (again, of something broken) are reworked into meaningful integrities, but not wholes.

In another interview with *The Guardian*,[10] Antony discusses her/his album, *I Am a Bird Now*, which was included in the 2004 Whitney Biennial.[11] The record has been described by Antony as "A record of transformations and survival. Its characters move between states—life and death, male and female, human and animal—searching for sanctuary and fulfillment." Antony proposes transformation as a trope for reworking the relationality of male and female, human and animal. Perhaps I am the only one hearing it, but in the texture of Antony's voice, the instrumental variations and in the lyrics themselves, boundaries of sexual and species differences, artificial and authentic orderings, and nature and culture are affectively and literally *trans*-ed in their music.

"Trans" is meant to disturb purification practices; the well defined is confounded at multiple material and semiotic levels. Psychical and corporeal experiences are blended. For example, gender and the embodiment of gender are contingencies that may hold for a moment then fall away into another set of relationships. Species exist in taxonomic differences (*Homo sapiens sapiens* are not the same as *Octopus vulgaris*), but species are also *always already* constitutive of each other through the spaces and places we cohabit—this of course includes language and other semiotic registers. Indeed, species are relationships between species—relationality is world-hood. Matter is not immutable, Antony and the Johnsons suggest, it is discursive, allowing sexes and species to practice trans-materialization. The meat and meaning for humans and starfish have no structuring lack, no primordial division, but are sensuously intertwined.

## TRANS-FORM

In "The Cripple and the Starfish," transformation is indeed a fusing of organisms, energies and sexes. I am intrigued by the phrase "cut off my finger, it'll grow back like a starfish." Let us start with the cut—the "cripple" wants "Mr Muscle" to "please hurt me" and "cripple" will "even cut off my finger." From what has been suggested by the song and Antony him/herself, I presume that "cripple" wants to transform through cutting (amputation or castration); the "cripple" can be heard as a transsexual/transgender M2F seeking transformation.[12] At first, the cut finger leads me, and perhaps other listeners/readers, to think that the cut is an act of castration—the finger works as a substitute for the penis. "Cripple" wants to become a "woman" through the cutting-off of her penis. Certainly, some transsexual women "cut off" their penises in order to have solidarity with females[13] or to become female themselves.

I am not interested in how the cut is an absence (as in castration) but how it is a generative enactment of "grow[ing] back" or healing. The cut enacts trans-embodiment—to cut is not necessarily about castration, but an attempt to re-cast the self through the cut body. The whole (body) and the part (cut) are metonymically bound in an attempt to trans-form *in toto*. However successful or not, however uncomfortable for listeners/readers, however seemingly masochistic, "cut off my finger" and "please hit me" can be understood as wished-for metamorphosis by the "cripple". To cut off the penis/finger is not to be an amputee, but to produce the conditions of physical and psychical re-growth. *The cut is possibility.* For some transsexual women, the cut is not so much an opening of the body, but a generative effort to *pull the body back through itself* in order to feel mending, to feel the growth of new margins. The cut is not just an action; the cut is part of the ongoing materialization by which a transsexual tentatively and mutably becomes. The cut cuts the meat (not primarily a visual operation for the embodied subject, but rather a proprioceptive one), and a space of psychical possibility is thereby created. From the first, a transsexual embodiment does not foreground a wish to "look like" or "look more like a woman" (that is, passing). The point of view of the looker (those who might "read" her) is not the most important feature of trans-subjectivity—the trans-woman wishes to be *of* her body, to "speak" from her body.

When I pay my surgeon to cut my penis into a neo-vagina, I am moving *toward myself through myself.* As the surgeon inserts the scalpel and cuts through the thickness of my tissue, my flesh immediately empurples. For weeks afterward, my groin remains discolored and swollen. Between the surgeon's efforts and my body's biomechanics, my cut spills blood and affect. My cut enacts a regeneration of my bodily boundaries—boundaries redrawn. Through my cut, I brush up against invocations and revelations; my cut is not passive—its very substance (materially and affectively) is generative and plays a significant role in my ongoing materialization. My cut is *of my* body, not the absence of parts of my body. The regenerative effort of my cut is discursive; my transfiguring cut is a material-discursive practice through which I am *of my* body and *of my* transself. My cut penis entails being and doing, materiality and affect, substance and form. My cut is generative within material limits but not with affective fixity, my tissues are mutable in so far as they are made of me and propel me to imagine an embodied elsewhere.

Not surprisingly, scholars, activists, students and artists have questioned the meaning and significance of transsexual/transgender embodiment. Some have suggested that the experience of transsexuals is determined, both negatively and positively, by the forms of our bodies. Rather simplistically, it has been suggested that the pre-operative transsexual feels constrained by the "wrong body" and longs to acquire the whole or healed body, which is represented by the male or female form. According to this account, transsexual selfhood is entangled with images of bodily wholeness—what's more, there is an idea of "inside" and "outside" of the body that are at odds. The body is a container—a body-bag of nouns to keep the proper ones in order. The transsexual aspires to make the so-called "defective body" intact, entire, complete, in order that it may be owned as mine, as me. It is undeniable that such agonizing experiences of bodily disownment are true and important for some transsexuals, nor is it difficult to believe that transsexual alterations are not simply chosen or kinds of mutilation, but the transformation of an unliveable, fragmented body into a "liveable whole."

What I find disconcerting about this description of the transsexual is not the trouble of containment; it is the limiting of the body to containment alone. To be comfortable in one's own body is not *only* to be restricted, limited, contained, or constrained, or not this alone. It is to be able to live out the body's vicissitudes—its (our) ongoing process of materialization. The body (trans or not) is not a clear, coherent and positive integrity. The important distinction is not the hierarchical, binary one between wrong body and right body, or between fragmentation and wholeness. It is rather a question of discerning multiple and continually varying interactions among what can be defined indifferently as coherent transformation, de-centered certainty, or limited possibility. Transsexuals do not transcend gender and sex. We create embodiment by not jumping *out* of our bodies, but by taking up a fold in our bodies, by folding (or cutting) ourselves, and creating a transformative scar of ourselves. For example, neo-vaginas are made from originary penises or skin grafts, and the beards of F2Ms emerge from their own testosterone-invigorated hair follicles. There is no absolute division, but continuity between the physiological and affective responses of my different historical bodies. Again, I am of my body in order that I might experience a subjective, energetic transformation.

A transsexual (myself, for example) is never discontinuous from different states of embodiment, or at least I am only generally distinguished from different historical states of my own beingness. By nature, the body has something tautological about it: skin here is always intractably skin. It is as if a M2F transsexual always carries her various embodiments with herself. Let me be clear here, I am not suggesting anything as banal as that "male privilege" is carried into female embodiment—I am not making a sociocultural argument about authenticity (such arguments should be put to rest by now!). If my subjective embodiment has always been "transgender", then my material transformation is meant to congeal my differently trans-embodied experiences of body and mind. What I am suggesting when I say that embodiment is coherence, is that I am always *of* my tissue even in its ongoing transformation. Whatever the transsexual grants to vision, the subjective embodiment is always only partially visible. We see the physical efforts, but the psychical energies only express themselves within the limits of the both.

Changeability is intrinsic to the transsexual body, at once its subject, its substance and its limit. Our bodies are scarred, marked and reworked into a liveable "gender trouble", sex trouble, or uneven epidermis. Transsexuals survive not because we become whole, but because we embody the reach and possibility of our layered experience—we have no choice. This is all to say, the transsexual body, my body, is a body created out of necessity, ingenuity and survival—to carry the heft of social identity. I, like many transsexuals, may desire some mythic wholeness, but what is truly intact for me, what I live, what I must be part of, is a body pliant to a point, flexible within limits, constrained by language, articulation, flesh, history and bone.

## RE-FORM

"I'll grow back like a starfish." From the start, I notice two things: first, my finger has been substituted for "I"; secondly, we have moved from the metonymy of the cut to the metaphor of trans-speciation. The starfish seemingly appears as a stand-in for transsexual transformation—the animal appears only as a tool for thinking about beingness. Let us not forget, the metaphor is a displacement: a nominative term is displaced from its everyday context and placed elsewhere so as to illuminate some other context through its reconfiguration. Thus, the relationship is based on the relationship of ideas rather than objects—metaphor does not owe any allegiance to the literal object. The "cut", in contrast, is structured by a metonymy of embodied correspondences and correlations. Metonymy is a tropological operation quite different from metaphor. Metonymy brings together two objects, each of which constitutes a separate whole. Metonymy refers to conditions of correspondence: cause to effect, instrument to purpose, container to content, "cut" to trans-body.

I wonder if the starfish is more than metaphor (not that metaphor isn't enough). Playing on the side of zoomorphism, I wonder if being starfish shares in the ontological imaginary of becoming trans-sexed. I don't want to propose that transsexualism is the *same as* trans-speciation, but rather that both share in the materialization of the trans-figure described in "The Cripple and the Starfish." Both the starfish and the transsexual "grow back", differently but with similar phenomenological goals of bodily integrity and healing. Is it possible, and here I take a leap, that while the "cut" has a metonymic force in trans-embodiment, could not "like a starfish" also suggest a metonymy of trans-speciation. For example, literal animals are always part of figural animals; animals cannot be displaced by words, rather words carry the nervous circuitries, the rhythms, the tempos of the literal. Animals are always constitutively formed in language—human and not, animal and not. Animals (though not necessarily animals alone—but that is for another collection of essays) are bound in language such that language cuts into flesh but does not completely devour the body. The literal "cut" bleeds around the word "cut", which is where the conditions of subjective transformation emerge. Likewise, the starfish, an echinoderm, a regenerating body, an invertebrate that can in some species reproduce new individuals through bodily divisions, exceeds the metaphoricity of "likeness" because the starfish is only ever partially digested, defined, explained, used by language.

Some species of starfish also reproduce asexually by fission, often with part of an arm becoming detached and eventually developing into an independent individual sea star. Some sea stars have the ability to regenerate lost arms. Most species must have the central part of the body intact to be able to regenerate, but a few can grow an entire starfish from a single ray. This bit of morphological knowledge leads me to wonder about *transformative* versus *regenerative*. *Trans-* the prefix has more to do with the sense of across, through, over, to or on the other side of, beyond, outside of, from one place, person, thing or state to another. If we think about *re*-prefix however, the original sense of *re-* in Latin is that of "back" or "backwards", but in the numerous words formed by its usage, the prefix acquires various shades of meaning. For example, *re*-generate: to form, construct, or create anew, especially in an improved state; to give new life or energy to; revitalize; and in biology, to replace (a lost or damaged organ or part) by the formation of new tissue.

How might the "Cripple" yearn for *regeneration* in order to transform? "I'll even cut off my finger. It will grow back like a Starfish." To me, this is a literal instantiation of sea star biodynamics—s/he will *re*-grow her/his finger, but not necessarily *trans*-form her/his finger. In broader terms, s/he is also *re*-sexed body just as she/he also becomes subjectively transsexed. Although subtle, the work might be in how prefixes shape and re-shape the prepositions of the discourse; *re-* is *of* the body, not *in* the body (as trans embodiment is often articulated—for example, "trapped in the wrong body"). *Re-* makes all enactments constitutive of the "form-er" (even if that "form-er" is an ongoing process of materialization). *Re-* might offer a more "crippling" approach to the limit and containment of the flesh. Re-generativity is a process that is enacted through and by containment (the body). In this way, regeneration is a re/iterative enactment of not only growing *new* boundaries (re-bodying), but of imperiling static boundaries (subjective transformation). Re-generation can attend to desire, pathos, trauma, but also to modes of corporeal intimacy, fleshy possibility and, most importantly, re-embodiment.

Re-generation is something that both transsexuals and starfish do. Transsexuals and starfish do other kinds of prefixial relationships between inside/outside, subject/object, or predator/prey, but in re- they share a phenomenological experience of re-shaping and re-working bodily boundaries. How might prefixes help us to understand the ways that we (starfish, transsexuals and others) autonomize and generate embodiment? Re-grow, re-differentiate, re-pattern, re-member, re-nucleate: our bodily structures, our biodynamics, are materiality enacted through ongoing relationships with the world, as part of that world. Transsexuals and starfish challenge disembodied metaphors (such as "like," resemblance, or simile), and propose ways in which we are metonymically stitched to carnal substrates. In other words, I'm not like a starfish; I am of a starfish. I am not trapped in my body; I am of my body.

## MEAT OF MEANING

As for language, I turn to Akira Mizuta Lippit's important discussion of "animetaphor" (a play on anti-metaphor and animal-metaphor; that is, animals exceed metaphoricity). Lippit writes, "The animetaphor is ... never absorbed, sublimated, or introjected into the world but rather incorporated as a limit ... The animetaphoric figure is consumed literally rather than figuratively" (Lippit 1998, 1115). The "animetaphor" (that which tries to speak for/about specific animals) is metonymic, foregrounding the ways that the lived being always already inhabits language, grammar, syntax and metaphor. The "animetaphor" is about how animals *exist within* practices of signification— nonhuman animals are not merely subjected to primate language; nonhuman animals are always already reworking language. The real animal is constantly present in Adam's Genesis. Animals, in their own ways, inhabit language. Language emerges from an ontology that is ecological, *anima,* the animal den, the wave and the invertebrate.

Lippit suggests that the "animetaphor" foregrounds the complex ways that animal representations are always haunted, vexed, reworked and enfolded by real animals. Animals expose the limits of representation. Lippit shows how animality, animal spirits and organisms themselves reside as "real" within representations. He writes:

> On the verge of words, the animal emits instead a stream of cries, affects, spirits, and magnetic fluids. What flows from the animal touches language without entering it, dissolving memory, like the unconscious, into a timeless present. The animal is magnetic because it draws the world-building subject toward an impossible convergence with the limits of world, toward a metaphysics of metaphor. The magnetic animal erases the limits of the metaphor, affecting an economy of the figure that is metamorphic rather than metaphoric. It forces a transformation of the figure.
>
> [1998, 1120]

Lippit posits that metaphors and representations create spaces where nonhuman animals can be pointed to "without naming," subsumed "without securing." That is to say, the animetaphor, the living metaphor, is always pointing to a space (even if it is always already in language) outside of language, exposing the limits of language.[14]

Working with the "animetaphor" figure of Nicholas Abraham and Maria Torok (1994), Lippit is suggesting here that, animals in language are always transforming figure into flesh, always *dis-figuring* representation. Animals are always troubling the language that attempts to name them. In this way, nonhuman animals seem to put an oral void into language. Animals cannot be named without invoking the limits of the process of naming. This is not a tautology. Animals are *in and of* language and representation, but their lived bodies are always restoring words to beings. Lippit writes, "When the metaphoricity of the metaphor collapses, the concept becomes a metonymic thing that can be eaten" (1998, 1122). Animals in language rest at the edges of the mouth, my mouth; I taste the failure of language to describe animals, and savor the presence of real animals flanking my sentences, my words. My language cannot digest the tissue and meat of nonhuman animals—a meal that cannot be digested.

Taking Lippit's "animetaphor" and applying it to "The Cripple and the Starfish," "starfish" point to the limits of representation, where "like a starfish" has corporeal meaning. The starfish referent is constantly touching me and devouring its representation. Antony's starfish is fiercely present as a regenerating body in the song about it. Eating and hearing are collapsed as phenomenological modes of encounter within this starfish song. Antony's starfish consumes me through the excess of its referentiality. The listening subject (myself, for example) is wholly or partially touched by the soma of the named starfish. The referent itself establishes itself as *that-which-is-re-embodying-this.* As I listen to Antony's song, rather than anthropomorphizing the starfish through identification, I am simultaneously chewing on and being chewed on an economy of excess, carnality, materiality and indexicality.

The word "starfish" puts me in contact with starfish themselves. As Antony sings "starfish", the literal starfish resounds in his/her voice. The word maps out the dense tissue of starfish lifeways. For me, Antony intensifies the encounter, the meeting between the bodies of species. "Like a starfish" enacts an artistry on the starfish and the subject of the "animetaphor". "I will grow back like a starfish" solicits both "I" and the starfish to inhabit those words; with those words we move into life. "I" is a word that finds roots in oneself; "starfish" transplants a figural element into a literal one. Out of the murmuring sensations of "The Cripple and the Starfish" come words and the babble of others that are uttered into oneself, into one's bone marrow, one's anatomy and one's circadian rhythms. This inter-somaticity of starfish (material) and "starfish" (semiotic), of "I" and me is a kind of loving, a kind of nearness that invokes a voluptuary of trans-speciation, and imagines a co/passionate kind of presence. Language and music enacts a caressing, a sensuous immersing in the ardent materiality of world-hood.

## RIPPLE

"Ripple" (Oxford English Dictionary):
1. A slight cut, scratch, or mark. Verb: to scratch slightly; to graze or ruffle.
2. A piece of shallow water in a river where rocks or sand-bars cause an obstruction; a shoal.
3. A light ruffling of the surface of water, such as is caused by a slight breeze; a wavelet.
4. A wave on the surface of a fluid the restoring force for which is provided by surface tension rather than by gravity, and which consequently has a wavelength shorter than that corresponding to the minimum speed of propagation.
5. A sound as of rippling water.
6. To mark with or as with ripples; to cause to undulate slightly.

"Ripple" creates the ruffling within the subject that allows "Happy bleedy, happy bruisy" to become the conditions for bodily regeneration, psychical transformation and trans-speciation. "Ripple" tears and fiddles with the idea that language/representation is a cut between the phenomenal world and the knowing subject. "Ripple" with "The Cripple and the Starfish" creates the carnal foundations for prefixial enactments that take meat and meaning seriously. The "cripple" and "like a starfish" provide an extreme collapse between the figural and the real. In other words, prefixes (trans- and re-) are kinds of relationships that ripple and rupture the field of representation. The starfish and the transsexual point beyond the limits of language, allowing both figures to exceed any kind of palliative function ("like a woman" or "like a starfish").

The transsexual—again I speak of this experience not to the side of my body, but because of my body—energetically ripples the body, marks the meat, with re-form, re-grow, re-shape so that subjective transformation may occur: transition, transsex, trans-be; this is prefixial rippling. The prefix re- must take up the body order that trans- might become. The starfish, depending on species, can re-grow a damaged ray. The lost ray, again in some species, may become another individual, rippling into another state of being. This is to say, the starfish changes its bio-geometry in relationship to its environment—it is entangled and reshaped and transfigured through encounters. Moreover, the metonymic qualities of embodiment always links semiotics to matter. "Starfish" is a representation with tube feet; transsexual is an identity that bleeds and is cut.

"Ripple" reminds me of starfish locomotion. Starfish have hydraulic water vascular systems that facilitate movement. Ocean water comes into the system via the madreporite (a small opening in the aboral surfaces of starfish). Saltwater is then circulated from the stone canal to the ring canal and into the radial canals. The radial canals carry water to the ampullae and provide suction to the tube feet. The tube feet latch on to surfaces and move in a wave, with one body section attaching to the surfaces as another releases. "Ripple" defines the biomechanics of tube feet.

"Ripple", on a somatic level, reminds me of my own physical vulnerability—my animate transsex flesh. Might I share this same somatic sensitivity with the starfish in the most basic sense of redressing harm: regeneration as an act of healing. Transsexing is an act of healing. This is some kind of mutuality—some kinds of shared ontology. Trans-morphic as zoomorphic—if we can understand the cut as an act of love, then can we not imagine that "like a starfish" is an enactment of trans-speciating? We, transsexuals and starfish, are animate bodies; our bodies are experienced and come to be known through encounters with other animate bodies. These epistemological moves describe a shared phenomenological ontology. This is sensate intertwining—inter-corporeal zones between these bodies in language and in experience. Starfish and transsexuals share world-hood both semiotic (as metonymic kinds) and phenomenological enactments—is this not some form of inter-somaticity?

"It's true I always wanted love to be hurtful," sings Antony in "The Cripple and the Starfish." If, as I hope I've illustrated here, the literal and the figural—the *matter that means* and the *meaning that means*—emerge as interlocking and dynamic. "Hurt" is not a masochistic enactment (or, at least, not this alone), but signals a breach in language and a tear in the traditional subject/object formation. The material, the literal matter of being, surfaces and resurfaces as a constitutive force that cannot be digested in the acid fluids of anthropic concerns. "Animetaphor" and metonymy applies a figurative sense as a literal one, while yet retaining the look or feel of figurality. A phenomenology of the rippling subject having and making sense of the song reveals to us the inter-corporeal function of lived bodies—as both carnal and conscious, sensible and sentient—and how it is we can apprehend the sense of the song both figurally and literally.

Correlatively, a phenomenology of the experience of this lived inter-somaticity and differentiation in the song reveals to us—in the metonymic articulations of language—the reversible and oscillating structure of the lived body's experience of language. To put it simply (if densely): in the act of "making sense" of the song, metonymy is to language as rippling is to lived bodies. Ambivalently subtending fusion and difference, ambivalent in its structure and seemingly ambiguous in meaning, metonymy not only points to the "gap" between the figures of language and literal lived-bodies experiences but also inter-corporeally, rippling, "bridges" and intertwines a sensate ontology. Thus, "The Cripple and the Starfish" mobilizes, differentiates and yet entangles lived bodies and language, and foregrounds the inter-somaticity of sensible matter and sensual meaning. As zoomorphic, *re*-morphic and *trans*-morphic subjects, then, we possess an embodied knowledge that both opens us beyond our discrete capacity for listening to a song, opens the song far beyond its containment in iTunes's "alternative" and opens language to a metonymic and biodynamic knowledge of specific carnal origins and limits. This is what my being transsexual knows about being a starfish.

## NOTES

1. Susan Stryker has enormously influenced this essay. She was the first to suggest to me that the song was about transgender transformation, and that the song demonstrated how transformation is a means of "addressing a hurt, and of moving through that hurt." Thank you, Susan.

2. Claire Carré has made a "spec" video of Antony and the Johnsons' "The Cripple and the Starfish." To watch the video, visit <http://www.elairesquare.com/starfish.html>. To read Carre's comments about the video and its reception by Rebis Music, visit <http://www.Justonestar.com/forum/viewtopic.php?p=8613&sid=7b35b23c5702726c6b283b69dd468106>.

3. In a Björk Podcast (#6), Antony explicitly defines as "transgender". However, I think the content of the song illustrates a kind of transgender/transsexual embodiment regardless of Antony's own identity—after all, musicians do not need to be faithful to their identities.

4. I use transgender and transsexual interchangeably in this essay. I do so not to elide the significant differences between these identities, but to foreground the shared concerns and desires for embodiment. This is to say, being transgender does not exclude bodily change, nor does being transsexual mean one will have sex-reassignment surgery.

5. Antony interviewed by Rebecca K. Uchill <http://www.vellemagazine.com/contenta/music/antony/antony.shtml>, 18 January 2007.

6.  Several links that offer biographical material on the late Marsha P. Johnson: <http://en.wikipedia.org/wiki/Marsha_P_ Johnson>; an obituary <http://gender.org/remember/people/marshajohnson.html>; a poem by Qwo-Li Driskill, <http://www.lodestarquarterly.com/work/248/>.

7.  For a bio on Sylvia Rivera, which sadly is also an obituary, see <http://www.workers.org/ww/2002/sylvia()3()7.php>.

8.  My suggestion that STAR was a "transgender" political organization is a bit ahistorical, considering that "transgender" as a social identity was still only emerging during these years. All too often, gender variant communities and their contributions to social change, however, get lost in more traditional gay/lesbian historiographies. So, I risk playing the part of a "bad historian" in the hopes of encouraging more inclusive historical projects.

9.  Antony interviewed by Rebecca K. Uchill <http:/www.vellemagazine.com/contenta/music/Antony/antony.shtml>, 18 January 2007.

10. Antony interviewed by David Peschek <http://arts.guardian.co.uk/features/story/0,,1438695,00.html>, 18 January 2007.

11. Antony and the Johnsons collaborated with filmmaker Charles Atlas and thirteen trans women from New York City on a concert/live video installation staged in London, Rome and Paris in autumn 2007. During "TURNING", Antony and the Johnsons present a concert while Atlas creates live video portraits of each model. "TURNING" was first presented as a part of the 2004 Whitney Biennial in New York City.

12. Again, I risk reading the "Cripple" as a trans-subject not to iterate the pathologization of trans-folks, but to explore the imaginings of the song. For the transsexual/transgender subject, gender assignments can feel "disabling", even wounding. I'm speaking about this traumatic experience, not about transgressive exceptionalism in which gender/sex changes prompt "revolutionary potential." I am simply returning to my own bodily knowledge—carnal logics—of pain and possibility.

13. I use solidarity to suggest something other than identification. I'm not suggesting that transsexual women do not become female (some certainly do), but I want to hold out the possibility that the transsexual woman can also become a kind of woman *made of* her various ontologies. I want to value the experience of becoming transsexual as something particular to transsexuals, even as that experience is constitutive of other sexes and their constitutiveness—together all the way down. This line of reasoning is explored in Stone (1993).

14. Lippit is working here from Jacques Derrida's work on the limits of subjectivity (Derrida and Dufourmantelle 2000; Derrida and Kamuf 1991).

## REFERENCES

Abraham, N. and Torok, M. (1994), "Mourning or Melancholia: Introjection Versus Incorporation," in N. Rand (ed. and trans.), *The Shell and the Kernal* (Chicago, IL: University of Chicago Press).

Antony and the Johnsons (2000), "Cripple and the Starfish," on *Antony and the Johnsons* (song title on music album).

Derrida, J. and Dufourmantelle, A. (2000), *Of Hospitality, Cultural Memory in the Present* (Stanford, CA: Stanford University Press).

Derrida, J. and Kamuf, P. (eds) (1991), *A Derrida Reader: Between the Blinds* (New York: Columbia University Press).

Lippit, A.M. (1998), "Magnetic Animal: Derrida, Wildlife, and Animetaphor," *MLN* 113(5): 1111–25.

Stone, S. (1993), "The Empire Strikes Back: A Posttranssexual Manifesto" <http://www.actlab.utexas.edu/~sandv/empire-strikes-back>, accessed 21 August 2007.

# 15

# *Interdependent Ecological Transsex*

## Notes on Re/production, "Transgender" Fish, and the Management of Populations, Species, and Resources

BAILEY KIER

BAILEY KIER CONDUCTS RESEARCH ON GENDER, RACE AND CLASS from the interdisciplinary perspective of American Studies. When he asserts that everyone on the planet is now encompassed within the category of transgender, he is asking us to acknowledge the basic instability of static, binary conceptualizations of gender within the biological and ecological world. Our world, he contends, is objectively changing—and, along with it, our capacity to separate cleanly nature, environments, culture, technology, animals, and humanity. With sweeping ambition, Kier suggests that we refuse rights-based identity politics and move past culture-based feminist and queer scholarship. Instead, he argues, we must acknowledge the interdependence of human cultural formations and the non-human dynamics and processes that underpin human interactions and infrastructures along with the rest of the material world. This is most important in circumstances in which the environment is being managed according to the logic of sustainability—an implicitly xenophobic logic, he contends, that privileges certain (white middle-class) populations as the inheritors of an earth immunized from its "undesirable" human surplus. Kier shows how ecologies themselves are replete with processes and substances that disrupt "normal" biological development: specifically, endocrine-disrupter chemicals (EDCs), byproducts of petrochemical production that have been linked with the increased emergence of "transgender fish" in post-industrial river ecologies. While it is possible to understand the transsexing fish as the signifier of ecological catastrophe, Kier refuses to frame the natural world as innocent, victimized, and lacking agency. Instead, he suggests we understand transsexing fish as a "technology beyond our grasp"—as one resilient, adaptive precursor among many of a new re/productive regime in the making.

## INTRODUCTION

I contend that everybody on the planet is now encompassed within the category of transgender. I illustrate this proposition by tracing some of the not-so-visible links of how this shared rearrangement of sex and re/production is unfolding. I also contend that we might be better off responding to this rearrangement, not through fear of the eco-catastrophic assumptions transsex invokes, but by embracing our shared interdependent transsex, a term that is about queering ideas of re/production, and refers to dynamic ecosystemic relations of multiple "bodies," energies, and things—animals, humans, lakes, plants, uranium, etc—which compose broader economic re/productive relations and energies of the bioscape.[1] Shared interdependent transsex refers to "bodies" as constant processes, relations, adaptations, and metabolisms, engaged in varying degrees of re/productive and economic relations with multiple other "bodies," substances, and things, in which no normal concept of re/production, as based on our common categories of sex, gender, and sexuality, exists. It is a phrase that questions human-centered understandings of re/production, family, species and kind, which align with developments of agriculture, capitalism and the rise of the corporate (trans)national state as a governing apparatus that increasingly manages the basic elements necessary for human and animal life; e.g., water, food, shelter, meaningful work, pleasure, and a re/productive landscape and/or waterscape. The perpetual transformations and adaptations that transsex constantly engages in order to re/produce are what "bodies" have in common. Commonality does not mean sameness, and crosses populations, species, and things of incalculable differences.

Embracing our shared transsex is one component of many that will be needed to address the vast social and ecological problems we face in the unfolding century. As some of the basic necessities for human and animal life—water, forests, agriculture, seeds, migration, knowledge, and shelter—become increasingly privatized, owned, and controlled by world corporations, evolutionary re/productive arrangements and relations, which are composed of thousands—perhaps millions—of years, are being rearranged in a very short period of time. This rearrangement in the speed of re/production is made possible largely through the concentrated energy of oil, the backbone of the corporate economy and possibly the most politically charged substance of the twentieth and twenty-first centuries, which continues to be centered in the political and economic decisions of the world's elite. Non-elite human and non-human bodies also make "decisions" in re/productive and economic relations that need greater consideration in the politics of globalization. Political ecology should not just refer to the decisions humans make to manage their ecological land and waterscapes, but should include the decisions non-humans make as well. Interdependent transsex as a mode of conceptualizing systemic relations queers ideas about politics and identity, in order to create the possibility for humans to observe and interpret the "decisions" non-human bodies, relations and systems make. This perspective situates humans as merely one component among many in re/productive relations—and one which has a great deal to learn from the politics of interdependent transsex, or the various interrelated decisions systems and things make.

I illustrate our interdependent transsex through two seemingly separate but interrelated re/productive rearrangements. Specifically, I consider the re/production of particular sectors of the human population through "progressive" contraceptive and sterilization interventions in humans alongside the recent emergence of "transgender" fish in the Potomac River—two seemingly separate phenomena, connected by hormones and hormone-mimicking substances such as EDCs (endocrine-disruptor chemicals). EDCs refers to a multitude of petrochemical, agricultural, and industrial products, processes and wastes, which interfere, mimic, and/or disrupt human and animal hormonal endocrine systems.

These rearrangements in re/production emerge at the cusp of what Donna Haraway has called naturecultures, or "the co-histories and co-evolutions of humans and other organisms."[2] These co-histories and co-evolutions are where "flesh and signifier, bodies and words, stories and worlds" are joined, various parts "don't add up to wholes," and only "partial connections" are possible.[3] Connections, if valued as partial, can illustrate "counter-intuitive geometries and incongruent translations necessary to getting on together, where the god-tricks of self certainty and deathless communion are not an option."[4] This essay engages partial connections and negates fantasies for quests of an (inter)disciplinary whole; it attempts to think more systemically about the interdependence of living and non-living systems, while realizing at the same time that a complete holistic view of the world is never possible. It attempts to engage Evelynn Hammond's notion of a queer geometry for knowledge worlds, capable of illustrating what gets produced as invisible silence in relation to what is knowable, discernable, and readily apparent. Hammond, concerned with the invisible silence of black women's sexuality, wrote that mere visibility "does not erase a history of silence nor does it challenge the structure of power and domination," but that our goal "should be to develop a 'politics of articulation'" capable of interrogating "what makes it possible" for people "to speak and act."[5] Additionally, considering co-histories and co-evolutions of "transgender" fish and re/productively managed human populations and resources requires situating them within the major organizing classificatory knowledge infrastructures of Western thought: sex/gender/sexuality, human/animal, and nature/culture.

Our shared transsex, emerging through natural/cultural assemblages of fish, hormones, EDCs and neoeugenics, becomes more visible when situated within the politics of knowledge infrastructures and critical engagement to expose the work normative categories do to make certain ideas knowable and others impossible. I attempt to make some of the unfathomable imaginable by providing a working and flexible re/productive orientation for feminist and queer critique, thereby partially interrogating the classificatory infrastructures of Western thought in order to expand notions of re/production in directions we're not so used to. I then consider a few ideas emerging from recent developments in queer ecological studies to illustrate ways in which the reorganization of sex and re/production are being thought about and to suggest additional ways we might begin to think through these rearrangements. Lastly, I turn to partial connections and co-constitutions that "transgender" fish and reproductively managed human populations share through the prism of hormones and EDCs, in order to promote a systems approach.

## TOWARD RE/PRODUCTIVE ORIENTATIONS FOR FEMINIST AND QUEER CRITIQUE

My claim that everybody—in this case, literally every body—is interdependently transsex is not intended as the next inclusionary progressive step in the explosion since the 1990s of signifiers, aesthetics, bodies, commodities and identities that have increasingly become encapsulated within the category trans. In fact, I am rather apprehensive of (although interdependent and indebted to) the use of trans as solely associated with individual human identities and the economies of desires and consumption surrounding identity as we mostly know it. I am not against identity, but I think identity needs to be radically re-conceived in ways that de-center the human, so that various, perhaps endless, interrelated components of global ecology can be regarded as giving life (and dare I say death) to the human.

It is for the de-centering of the human I seek to reimagine the concepts of both trans and identity. Transgender is a category associated mostly with post-industrialized nations of the West, but which is also meaningful in other parts of the world. It is mostly used to describe individuals who do not fit neatly into normative notions of human re/production in which the category of sex has an imagined clear, distinctive, and essential male and female. Transgender relies upon an understanding of gender that is dependent and distinguished, yet closely associated with the category of imagined essential sex. Gender is largely thought of as a constructed human category, a cultural universal displaying diversity across cultures, while sex is considered an essential universal of "Nature," although much scholarship in the humanities and social sciences now situates sex as a socially constructed category. The prefix trans—meaning to cross, go beyond, and to change—when combined with gender, means to go beyond, to change and to cross the anthropocentric category of socially constructed gender. Transgender as a category is also closely associated with ideas about human individual identities and imagined and real human collective communities, even as David Valentine has shown that the category conveys different meanings to many of those who use it and to those it is used to describe in the same local contexts.[6] So why does the term transgender continue to commonly be held in close association with the human, when the term literally means to change and disrupt the human-centeredness of the category of gender itself? Transgender as a category is just as much about queering the human as it is about queering sex and gender. Because of the human-centered paradox of the category of transgender, I prefer the term transsex in this essay, in an attempt to use another (just as problematic) signifier to expand the trajectory of transgender studies and to describe the eco-systemic relations and negations of re/production of multiple species and things. To change, go beyond and across normal meanings of sex is to expose the queer relations of re/production of multiple species and things.

[...]

My use of the term transsex seeks to point to the interdependent earthly needs of multiple species and things, and attempts to queer human-centered notions of economy. Perhaps the emerging bioeconomy, information economy, and service economies are heavily saturated and centered upon the human, but these economies would not be possible without the raw materials, resources, tools, energy, and labor of multiple species and things. Transsex intentionally queers economy, in order to illustrate that economies extend far and wide beyond capital and the human. The classificatory infrastructure of nature/culture is perhaps the broadest, most universal knowledge infrastructure, engrossing several other major classificatory infrastructures such as sex(nature)/gender(culture), and human(culture)/animal(nature).[23]

We must complicate the limits of solely socio-cultural paradigms by considering many other dynamics and processes, both human and non-human, that enable and uphold culture as a classificatory infrastructure guiding most scholarship in the humanities and much of the social sciences.[24] Works by scholars such as Lisa Duggan and Aihwa Ong insist that cultural analyses are not enough, and a more accurate theoretical framework in the neoliberal era requires considering the intersections of culture, politics, and economics.[25] But how can we continue talking about culture, politics and economy without considering interdependent relational re/productive ecological economies as the backbone of all three? Even the advent of the bioeconomy, which speculates value, requires ecological symbioses and divisions to make raw materials and energy, and labors to make the machines, computers, and various infrastructures of the bioeconomy possible.

My thinking of re/productive orientations initially stemmed from Henri Lefebvre's *The Production of Space*, for his attempt to unearth and connect "naturalized" discourses about re/production, the family, re/producing the labor force for capitalism, and re/producing the social relations necessary for re/production—the family, capitalism, and culture. Lefebvre explained "three interrelated levels" in which social space is produced: "(1) *biological reproduction* (the family); (2) *the reproduction of labour power* (the working class per se); and (3) the *reproduction of the social relations of production*—that is, of those relations which are constitutive of capitalism and which are increasingly (and increasingly effectively) sought and imposed as such."[26] When these three components are made visible, it becomes clear that a system of symbolic representation works "to maintain these social relations in a state of coexistence and cohesion," displaying "them while displacing them . . . concealing them in symbolic fashion—with the help of, and onto the backdrop of nature."[27] In other words, the production of space (or how capitalism produces space) becomes "naturalized," though for Lefebvre, the process is entirely social.

Lefebvre's work allows for linking normative ideas of sexuality, human re/production and the management of labor and populations to the various components of economic production involving the production and management of resources, populations, species and the landscape. Through Lefebvre's model, we can decipher that capitalism is a human social process and structure, and the "fitness" and "success" of white European and American exploitation, while hanging upon the backdrop of "nature," is in fact a social process made invisible through normative discourses and the symbolic realm. There is nothing distinctively "natural," or beyond the grasp of humans, about the exploitations of capitalism; these exploitations are political decisions made by groups of people about other groups of people, resources, and species. Additionally, Lefebvre's work allows us to shift thinking about the category of "sexuality" to the realm of "re/production," which expands the category of normative sex, gender, and sexuality to account not just for humans having babies, but also maintaining and managing labor pools, resources, species and the social and economic relations necessary for those labor pools and resources to re/produce for capitalism. However, Lefebvre's work barely addresses the material world and species beyond humans, except to briefly explain "nature" as a "source and resource," that is "part of the forces of production and part of the products of those forces."[28] Lefebvre's model can be expanded by adding a fourth interrelated level—ecological re/production—to the production of space, which consists of the non-human ecological relations, materials, and species that make human reproduction possible in the first place. The literal re/production and exponential growth of the human species would not be possible without the multiple other species we rely on for food, food pollination, tools, labor, and the mitigation of disease and predation. The list of what Donna Haraway calls "companion species" is vast, and includes species of bees, cedar, dogs, rats, grass, fish, etc. This fourth level of ecological re/production can produce space independently of humans, outside of capitalism and the symbolic realm, but can also be manipulated, although not completely controlled, by humans to produce space for capitalism. It is noticing the discrepancies that arise between "Nature's" ability to independently produce space and human production of space through capitalism that has the potential to illustrate useful tools and ideas for devising more equitable and ethical economic orders. By paying attention to nature outside the human urge to control it, one can see that "Nature" has a different system of valuation and profit than that of capitalism. There is not one "natural" economy called capitalism but multiple interactive and adaptive economies at work, in sync and in contestation with capitalism. Paying attention, observing, and documenting "Nature's" systems of valuation and profit has further capacity to demystify capitalism as part of the natural order, illustrating our interrelated co-constituted situatedness in global ecological economies of people, resources, things, desires, and processes. Interdependent transsex, as illustrated through "transgender" fish and the fear EDCs invoke about human re/production, is just one example. Re/productively altered factory cattle are another example, pumped with synthetic hormones and antibiotics that humans consume directly as meat and milk and then indirectly through waterscapes of agricultural runoff (EDCs) and also through the fish we consume.

This re/productive model seeks to push the politics of thinking about thinking into the realm of conceiving our being, our knowing, and our practice as located simultaneously within the histories and knowledge infrastructures of capitalism, but also within multiple other "economic" processes of life, death, and matters that involve other species and resources. What would it mean for feminist and queer thought to radically rethink ideas of sex, gender, and sexuality in this re/productive light? I'm not suggesting doing away with categories like sex or gender altogether; too much history is caught up in these concepts merely to forget them. But I do think queer and feminist critique could be greatly enhanced by an interrelated, interdependent worldview of re/production that understands that multiple processes, species and things—what we call resources, energy, and labor—all make the human and its various knowledge infrastructures possible. Feminism and queer thought will have to find some way to begin to address the reorganizations of re/production that are unfolding in the age of transgenic engineering and "artificial" intelligence. The current classificatory infrastructure of sex/gender/sexuality will not be adequate, nor will any other category, if it is dependent upon the idea of individual identity. Partial re/productive models will also not be enough, but they are a step in addressing multiple levels of re/production in order to consider the transformations of re/production that are now unfolding.

Biotechnology and the bioeconomy emerging since about the 1970s now saturate everyday life: from the food chain of transgenic organisms we grow, buy and eat, to the experimental medical therapies improving (or diminishing) quality of life for those who can afford them, to the cross pollination between GMO crops and "conventional" crops. There is no way to escape biotechnology's impact. We cannot simply reject the advent of human-produced biotechnology and/or ignore its implications—implications that can be potentially horrifying, but also contain possibilities for transformations of knowledge infrastructures, with the potential to lead to more ethical earthly interrelations and social worlds.

Biotechnology, and its focus on life and matter at the molecular level, represents a reorganization in material re/productions, and also a crisis in human symbolic and taxonomic classificatory infrastructures which are central to Western thought. For instance, as Sarah Franklin points out in her brilliant examination of the reorganization of re/production illustrated by Dolly, the world's first "cloned" sheep; the language describing this reorganization of re/production is imprecise and in crisis around questions of sameness and difference. Franklin writes that Dolly represents "both sameness and difference as a clone," but this reorganization of sex and re/production is hard to grasp through Dolly "because she slips out of familiar kinds: her existence does not parse within familiar categories" and "is syntactically noncompliant within the normative arboreal grammars of reproduction and descent; her queer genealogy haunts the very basis of the formal biological categories that once affirmed the stability of a known sexual and reproductive order."[29] If Dolly and other reorganizations of re/production do represent a queer genealogy that challenges normative categories, then we really need to begin asking questions about what exactly a queer critique of the normative entails in terms of re/production. If the biotechnology industry emerged in tandem with the neoliberal restructuring of the US economy, as Melinda Cooper suggests, and transformations in both neoliberal global economics and technoscience no longer serve or emulate what is popularly conceived as the heteronormative family, then what exactly does queer critique entail?[30] Is genetic engineering and biotechnology the queer culprit, or is biotechnology merely inventing new norms that are not yet decipherable because we do not have the language to precisely describe these transformations?

One major assumption that drives a lot of scholarship considering biopolitical and bioeconomical reorganizations of re/production is that humans make biotechnology a possibility through our inventions, tools, computers, and a molecular view of the world. However, biotechnologies such as the manipulation of metabolism and possible capabilities of horizontal gene transfer exist in other life forms in ways that we may never be able to completely comprehend or mimic. For instance, Myra Hird suggests that by looking at the reproduction of bacteria, we can see that interspecies gene transfer is a technology much older than ourselves, which humans have just begun to engage through recent reproductive technologies. For Hird, bacteria have "invented all major forms of metabolism, multicellularity, nanotechnology (controlling molecules in ways that continue to elude scientists) and metallurgy," that we might "consider that particularly with regard to sex, humans and other primates should be considered inferior to some other organisms."[31] Might we follow Hird's lead and possibly consider that "transgender" fish's ability to change "sex" due to the toxic presence of EDCs represents a technology beyond our grasp? We are most certainly "endangering" wild native fish, but we also need to begin asking what technologies, processes, and relations fish are using to change sex. Is this changing of sex a response, an adaptation, or both? Is this change a sign of resilience or a degenerative "defect"?

## SCOPES AND SCALES OF INTERDEPENDENT TRANSSEX: SOME REORGANIZATIONS OF RE/PRODUCTION THROUGH THE PRISM OF HORMONES AND HORMONE-MIMICKING SUBSTANCES

The recent emergence of "transgender" fish in the Potomac River and more recent developments in birth/population control are two examples I use for tracing more specific examples of re/productive relations of our interdependent, shared transsex. I use the term "transsex" to refer to the transformations in the re/production of the larger earthly, interdependent ecologies that have been radically altered through world wars, industrialization and expansive exploitation of resources, species, and populations. I use transsex as a term broadly defined through a hormonal, metabolistic, and adaptive prism to constitute not just human transsexuals, but multiple and possibly endless other bodies, including but not limited to welfare recipients and Native women in the US, livestock, fish, bodies of water and even the so-called normative bodies of white, middle class Americans who may or may not eat meat and dairy but who consume water, food and products that contain EDCs. Even self-defined transgender or genderqueer-identified people who don't intentionally take hormones share transsex through their relationships with meat, dairy, plastics, cosmetics, drinking water, occupation, etc. The scope of transsex defined through this hormonal prism is far reaching and global, and potentially encompasses every *body* on the planet.

[...]

Perhaps we need to look for resilience in species, populations, and things, instead of or in addition to a fixed idea of sustainability. "Transgender" fish are an excellent example with which to begin considering not just resilience but the hormonal links across bodies and species of interdependent transsex, and the ways in which our interdependent transsex transpires through the byproducts of (post)industrialization and mono factory agriculture.

"Transgender" fish were first noticed in the Potomac River in 2003 when scientists with the West Virginia Division of Natural Resources and the United States Geological Survey examined widespread and pervasive fish kills and discovered that smallmouth bass exhibited widespread reproductive anomalies. They found that nearly 80 percent of male smallmouth bass exhibited an intersex condition in which eggs were found inside the testes.[43] Since then, there has been extensive coverage in both mainstream and scientific media on what are referred to as "transgendered," "intersex," or "sexually confused" fish, linking the rise of this new phenomenon to alarming amounts of EDCs found in synthetic chemical waste, sewer and agricultural runoff and "treated" grey water. The correlation between toxic conditions in waterways and reproductive anomalies is not a recent phenomenon. Since the late 1970s, reports by English anglers of "sexually confused fish" caught the attention of both media and researchers and it now appears that correlations between EDCs and reproductive anomalies are widespread and pervasive not only geographically, but across multiple species as well, including alligators, birds, panthers, turtles, mink, otters, and even large mammals such as polar bears and humans.[44] In fact, the issue has become enough of a concern that legislation was submitted to Congress in December 2009 to push for the *Endocrine Disruption Prevention Act* H.R. 4190, which if passed would legislate government-funded research investigating the sources of the problem.

It is interesting to consider why the idea of transgenderedness is being used to represent toxicity and eco-catastrophe, instead of the various economic and political aspects of "development" that create toxic endocrine disrupting conditions in the Potomac River. Stated simply, why is "transgender" the signifier and not "Merck & Co, Inc.," or "Perdue, Inc."? But even more interesting is that people and fish share this re/productive reorganization of endocrinology. Some of the visible pollutions of the Potomac River include plastics and anything imaginable that can float—things containing EDCs that people use and that then make their way into the river. Additionally, the Potomac River and other equally polluted bodies of water are the sources of drinking water for much of urban and suburban Washington, DC. The Potomac River and many of its tributaries obtain agricultural, industrial, suburban, and urban runoff and then empty into the Chesapeake Bay. The Chesapeake Bay contains "dead zones" (low dissolved oxygen levels that kill most species of an ecosystem) in which contributing factors include "polluted runoff from farms and feedlots, deforestation and wetland loss, discharges by wastewater treatment plants, air pollution from cars, as well as the loss of oysters that would filter algae and other organic matter from the water column."[45]

Humans as much as fish are caught up in the transformations of re/production that are unfolding as a result of human-made EDCs circulating in the environment, water, and food chains. Although fish may hold EDCs in their bodies at higher concentrations than humans, humans share a habitat with plastics, pesticides, and factory farming, just at different scopes and varying degrees of intimacy depending on where one works, what one eats and drinks, and where one lives. But if we are to de-center the human in this unfolding problem, what does it really matter that humans absorb lower concentrations of EDCs than fish, if EDCs are possibly creating marine "dead zones" in rivers, water tables, bays and estuaries that are used to hydrate and feed glocal populations? Instead of eating locally and coastally, the majority of humans in the United States now eat from the agricultural and factory farms which are themselves their own tributaries for EDCs, draining to create "dead zones" of the world's major bays and estuaries. EDCs are part of the food, productive and re/productive chain of non-human and human life and we will need to devise ways, just like fish, to adapt to their influence.

EDCs clearly do not cause everyone to transition gender in the same ways and capacities as transsexual humans using medically prescribed hormones. But certainly most humans on the planet have most likely come into contact with EDCs; especially the pesticide DDT, the resin BPA (bisphenol A) and PCBs (polychlorinated biphenyl); all of which are highly estrogenic and at different points in time have saturated most parts of the globe. DDT and PCBs saturated industrial, urban, suburban and agricultural land and waterscapes through the mid-twentieth century, and even though DDT is now banned in many places and levels have dropped, PCBs in the production of coolants, pesticides, sealants, PVC coatings, and many other home and industrial construction products still saturate our living environments. BPA in the epoxy resins of hard plastics also surround us in our homes, offices, cars, and bottled drinking water.

So why do mainstream media representations of EDCs and this larger global ecological reorganization of re/production focus on the spectacle of the transgender fish? The use of "transgenderedness" as a sensationalized cultural signifier of re/productive eco-catastrophe illustrates that certain assumptions about re/production are at play and entangled with specific human socio-cultural categories in these mainstream media discourses. The fearful assumption that human-made environmental problems led to "transgender" fish, and possibly other "transgender" organisms that cannot re/produce, seems to be a motivating fear in governmental and scientific intervention into the problem. But I presume EDCs are not going anywhere anytime soon. Many EDCs come from oil and the thousands of products made from oil, and a transition from an economy of oil, plastics, pesticides, and factory agriculture will take time. How might we begin to grapple with this time? Embracing our shared transsex is a first step, not out of fear that we might not be able to re/produce or be clearly distinguished as male or female, but out of the knowledge that life in many ways is simultaneously fragile, resilient, adaptive, and that transsex exhibits the ability to find ways to transform the possibilities of re/production. Perhaps our "emerging" interdependent transsex is only one step in the larger adaptation to adjusting to the damages that humans have caused to the larger Earthly ecology. That isn't to say that we shouldn't clean up our act, but what would it mean to imagine that transgender fish might just in fact be the "fittest" in the dance of life and death that is survival?

## NOTES

1. I use the term bioscape instead of biosphere for a few different reasons. The term biosphere conjures assumptions of life contained within a round objectified planet earth. Bioscape here refers to both life and energies in relation to an imperfect spherical earth, but also its relations to multiple other possible planes, elements, assemblages, and processes. These various scapes may or may not be considered "alive" by conventional human standards, but all contain energy in some form and/or relation and from or for some time. Commercial and military jetscapes, oilscapes, foodscapes, microwavescapes, surveillancescapes, mountainscapes, sunscapes, and waterscapes, are a few examples of various systemic energy infrastructures. Bioscapes is a terminology tactic to unpack various processes, components, and "bodies" within, among and beyond the biosphere.
2. Haraway 2003, 12.
3. Ibid., 20, 25.
4. Ibid., 25.
5. Hammonds 1994, 141.
6. Valentine 2007.

   [...]

23. The sex(nature)/gender(culture) combination is a bit tricky because the word sex has many meanings. In my work I assume sex to refer to the two main categories male and female which signify their division based on reproductive functions. And even trickier is popular culturally speaking sex defined in regards to reproductive capacity, assumed to belong to the classificatory infrastructure of "Nature," while in the historical "progression" of queer and feminist thought, the concept of sex has transformed from being the natural category from which the social or cultural category of gender could develop. However, since at least the 1990s, the category of sex has been increasingly framed as socially constructed and thus been associated with the cultural realm. For an introduction to the social construction of sex see: Fausto-Sterling 2000; Meyerowitz 2002; Schiebinger 1989.
24. I am especially indebted to Mary Sies for her sustained critique and insistence that I not limit and inhibit my thinking by merely trying to do away with a cultural paradigm and simply replace it with a spatial in hope that it would somehow miraculously incorporate the interrelated dynamics of "Nature," and the ecologies which are the backbone of much of human political economies and organizations of space. John Caughey also provided useful critique and suggestions.
25. Duggan 2003; Ong 2006.
26. Lefebvre 1991, 32.
27. Ibid.
28. Ibid., 343, 347.
29. Franklin 2007, 28.
30. Cooper 2008.
31. Hird 2008, 239, 241.

    [...]

43. Chambers and Leiker 2006, 7.
44. Langston 2003, 129–32.
45. Faber 2001, 8.

## REFERENCES

Bagemihl, Bruce. 1999. *Biological exuberance: Animal homosexuality and natural diversity.* New York: St Martin's Press.

Bowker, Geoffrey C., and Susan Leigh Star. 1999. *Sorting things out: Classification and its consequences.* Cambridge, MA: MIT Press.

Chambers, Douglas B., and Thomas J. Leiker. 2006. *A reconnaissance for emerging contaminants in the South Branch Potomac River, Cacapon River, and Williams River Basins, West Virginia, April–October 2004.* Reston, VA: US Geological Survey.

Colborn, Theo, Frederick S. von Sall, and Ana M. Sota. 1993. Developmental effects of endocrine-disrupting chemicals in wildlife and humans. *Environmental Health Perspectives* 101, no. 5: 378–84.

Cooper, Melinda. 2008. *Life as surplus: Biotechnology and capitalism in the neoliberal era.* Seattle, WA: University of Washington Press.

Duggan, Lisa. 2003. *The twilight of equality: Neoliberalism, cultural politics, and the attack on democracy.* Boston: Beacon Press.

Edwards, Clive A., and David Pimentel. 2002. The future of human populations: Energy, food, and water availability in the twenty-first century. In *Just Ecological Integrity: The Ethics of Maintaining Planetary Life,* ed. Peter Miller and Laura Westra, 119–39. Lanham, MD: Rowman & Littlefield.

Faber, Scott. 2001. *Bringing dead zones back to life: How Congress, farmers and feedlot operators can save America's most polluted bays.* Environmental Defense website. http://www.edf.org/documents/817_DeadZone.PDF

Fausto-Sterling, Anne. 2000. *Sexing the body: Gender politics and the construction of sexuality.* New York: Basic Books.

Franklin, Sarah. 2007. *Dolly mixtures: The remaking of genealogy.* Durham, NC: Duke University Press.

Fuss, Diana. 1996. Introduction: Human, all too human. In *Human, all too human*, ed. Diana Fuss, 1–7. New York: Routledge.

Halberstam, Judith. 2005. *In a queer time and place: Transgender bodies, subcultural lives.* New York: New York University Press, 2005.

Hammonds, Evelynn. 1994. Black (w)holes and the geometry of Black female sexuality. *differences: A Journal of Feminist Cultural Studies* 6, nos. 2–3: 126–45.

Haraway, Donna. 2003. *The companion species manifesto: Dogs, people, and significant otherness.* Chicago: Prickly Paradigm Press.

Hird, Myra J. 2008. Animal trans. In *Queering the non/human*, ed. Noreen Giffney and Myra J. Hird, 227–47. Burlington, VT; Ashgate.

King, Katie. 2005. Feminist theory through and beyond critique: Rupturing epistemologies and transforming relationships to global realities. (Course syllabus.) University of Maryland website. http://www.womensstudies.umd.edu/wmstfac/kking/teaching/602/602syll.html

Langston, Nancy. 2003. Gender transformed: Endocrine disruptors in the environment. In *Seeing nature through gender*, ed. Virginia J. Scharff, 129–66. Lawrence, KS: University of Kansas Press.

Lefebvre, Henri. 1991. *The production of space.* Malden, MA: Blackwell.

Meyerowitz, Joanne J. 2002. *How sex changed: A history of transsexuality in the United States.* Cambridge, MA: Harvard University Press.

Naz, Rajesh K., Satish K. Gupta, Jagdish C. Gupta, Hemant K. Vyas, and G.P. Talwar. 2005. Recent advances in contraceptive vaccine development: A mini-review. *Human Reproduction* 20, no. 12: 3271–83.

Oliver, Kelly. 2009. *Animal lessons: How they teach us to be human.* New York: Columbia University Press.

Ong, Aihwa. 2006. *Neoliberalism as exception: Mutations in citizenship and sovereignty.* Durham, NC: Duke University Press.

Puar, Jasbir. 2007. *Terrorist assemblages: Homonationalism in queer times.* Durham, NC: Duke University Press.

Roberts, Dorothy. 1997. *Killing the Black body: Race, reproduction, and the meaning of liberty.* New York: Vintage Books.

Roughgarden, Joan. 2004. *Evolution's rainbow: Diversity, gender, and sexuality in nature and people.* Berkeley: University of California Press.

Roughgarden, Joan. 2009. *The genial gene: Deconstructing Darwinian selfishness.* Berkeley: University of California Press.

Schiebinger, Londa L. 1989. *The mind has no sex?: Women in the origins of modern science.* Cambridge, MA: Harvard University Press.

Sturgeon, Noël. 2009. *Environmentalism in popular culture: Gender, race, sexuality and the politics of the natural.* Tucson, AZ: University of Arizona Press.

Sze, Julie. 2006. Boundaries and border wars: DES, technology, and environmental justice. *American Quarterly* 58, no. 3: 791–814.

Valentine, David. 2007. *Imagining transgender: An ethnography of a category.* Durham, NC: Duke University Press.

Weil, Simone. 2002. *The need for roots: Prelude to a declaration of the duties towards mankind.* New York: Routledge.

Wohlforth, Charles. 2010. Conservation and eugenics: The environmental movement's dirty secret. In *Orion Magazine: Nature/Culture/Place*, July/August, pp. 22–8.

# IV

## *TRANSFEMINISMS*

# 16

# *Feminist Solidarity after Queer Theory*

## The Case of Transgender

### CRESSIDA HEYES

FEMINIST PHILOSOPHER CRESSIDA HEYES is Canada Research Chair at the University of Alberta. In this article, she makes the case for solidarity across differences within an expansive notion of feminism. Heyes notes that transgender, transsexual, intersex, and queer activist scholarship has issued fundamental challenges to the ways in which feminism was framed in the previous generation; she notes as well that feminists whose backgrounds in the women's movement of the 1970s and 80s have rendered them skeptical, hostile, or otherwise ill-equipped to engage with the theoretical and political challenges raised by these previously-mentioned forms of identity are nevertheless engaged in meaningful and necessary social justice work. How might such irreconciled factions be brought together in a more encompassing vision of a just and livable society that resists oppression based on gender and sexuality? For Heyes, the crucial task for all concerned is to engage in ethical self-transformation. She calls upon all of us to keep in mind the limits placed on individual agency by supra-individual structures of state and society (which she sees as a traditional concern of feminist critique), as well as the mutability of embodied selfhood that lies, for Heyes, at the heart of transgender and queer modes of life.

"Transphobia" (literally, the fear of the subject in transition), the stigmatization of transsexuals as not "real men" and "real women," turns on this conception of transsexuals as constructed in some more literal way than nontranssexuals—the Frankensteins of modern technology's experiments with sexual difference.

—Jay Prosser

Perhaps I've insisted too much on the technology of domination and power. I am more and more interested in the interaction between oneself and others and in the technologies of individual domination, the history of how an individual acts upon himself, in the technology of the self.

—Michel Foucault

It is by now clear that feminist politics needs to speak to (and be spoken by) many more subjects than women and men, heterosexual women and lesbians. How—in theory and in practice—should feminism engage bisexuality, intersexuality, transsexuality, transgender, and other emergent identities (or anti-identities) that reconfigure both conventional and conventionally feminist understandings of sex, gender, and sexuality?[1] For me this question takes its most pressing forms when I am thinking about how effective alliances can be forged in feminist spaces. How should feminists imagine and create communities that take the institutions and practices of sex, gender, and sexuality to be politically relevant to freedom? How might such communities incorporate our manifest and intransigent diversity, *and* build solidarity? In this chapter I work through these questions with reference to the leitmotif of transgender. Following Susan Stryker, I use "trans" as a broad umbrella adjective intended to capture the multiple forms of sex and gender crossing and mixing that are taken by their practitioners to be significant life projects. I use "transgendered" to describe all those who live a gender they were not perinatally assigned or that is not publicly recognizable within Western cultures' binary gender systems, and I use "transsexed" to describe all those who undergo (or hope to undergo) any of a number of physical interventions to bring their sexed body more closely into line with their gender identity.[2]

Feminists of all stripes share the political goal of weakening the grip of oppressive sex and gender dimorphisms in Western cultures, with their concomitant devaluing of the lesser terms "female" and "feminine." This move has opened up new possibilities for individuals, but it is also, over time, generating a whole new field of meaning within which some identities may eventually cease to exist while others are being created. At this very general level, a wide range of gendered subjects stands to gain from challenges to enforced binaries within the nexus of sex, gender, and sexuality. At a more specific level, however, the complexities of oppression and privilege, and conflicting ideological and strategic approaches to politics, have conspired to fracture feminist and queer communities along identity fault lines. Despite the fact that most transgendered people are daily the victims of the most intense and public attempts to discipline gender in ways feminists have long criticized, "trans liberation" and "feminism" have often been cast as opposing movements. This chapter seeks to explain and argue against this division, without entirely conceding the normative concerns that motivate it.

However political resistance through transforming gender has been articulated, the struggle has been on the disputed terrain where the life of the individual meets its institutional and historical conditions of possibility. Part of feminism is changing those institutions and creating new history, but in the interim feminists must make sense of the scope and limits of our agency *within* structures of oppression and privilege. In this space, ethics meets politics: feminism entails not only organizing for change, but also changing oneself. Another backdrop to all the work in this book, then, is my larger interest in the ethics of self-transformation, taken up through specific cases of decision making that involve reworking one's identity by working on one's body. Although gender is often experienced as a deeply authentic aspect of the individual self, many theorists have persuasively argued that gender identities must be understood as *relationally* formed. With theorists such as Jessica Benjamin (1995), I start from the claim that gender is not best understood simply as an attribute of individuals, but rather as a set of often hierarchical relations among differently gendered subjects. Thus any project that takes up the ethics of self-transformation will be necessarily linked to the questions about our responsibilities to others I want to raise.

Initially, I offer a critical analysis of two very different feminist texts: the 1994 reissue of Janice Raymond's notorious *The Transsexual Empire: The Making of the She-Male* (originally published in 1979) and Bernice Hausman's 1995 book *Changing Sex: Transsexualism, Technology, and the Idea of Gender*. Rather than understanding transgendered people as working within an ethics of self-transformation with which all feminists must grapple, Raymond's and Hausman's otherwise theoretically contrasting texts represent the transsexual (qua monolithic representative of all transgender subjectivities) as uniquely mired in pathology. Both commentators draw on the classification of transsexuality as a mental "disorder" to make their case; by persistently foreclosing all possibilities for political resistance to a disease model, they construct trans people as lacking both agency and critical perspective. By showing in some detail how these strategies of foreclosure work, I hope, first, to develop the negative case presented by Sandy Stone (1991) that influential non-trans feminists have orientalized the trans subject and concomitantly failed to investigate their authorial locations as stably gendered subjects.[3] This reductive characterization of the transsexual as the dupe of gender then permits the conclusion that transgender politics writ large has no feminist potential.

Charges of political quietism against transsexuals present one set of challenges to meaningful political alliances between trans and non-trans feminists. A second set of difficulties is raised by the genre of popular trans feminist polemic, epitomized by authors such as Kate Bornstein, Leslie Feinberg, and Riki Anne Wilchins. This literature voices the views of trans people with radical gender politics, moving beyond the traditional forums of sensationalized autobiography or objectifying psychological studies. These authors properly advocate the right to express and develop a gender identity not determinately linked to birth sex; however, I'll argue that too often this literature falls back onto an implausibly atomistic self that is given normative free rein to assert its gender. Taking Feinberg's remarks in hir book *Trans Liberation: Beyond Pink and Blue* (1998) as exemplary, I contest hir implication that a feminist politics should tolerate any "gender expression." (Feinberg prefers to be described with the gender-neutral pronouns *ze,* in place of he/she, and *hir,* in place of her/his, and I shall follow this usage.) A failure to understand gender as relational (and hierarchical) leads Feinberg to elide certain normative implications of hir account. Specifically, ze does not examine the fact that the expression of one gender may limit the possible meanings or opportunities available to others. Adopting the language of individual freedom of expression with regard to gender, then, will sidestep important questions that arise from gender relations and the demands of politics.

Thus feminist writing about transgender needs to define and articulate a middle ground in which an ethics of self-fashioning can be developed. Such an ethics should recognize the discursive limits on individual self-transformation without denying agency to gendered subjects. It must also engage the politics of self-transformation in a broader field, where one's choices affect others' identities and possibilities. Throughout this book, I hope to show some of the constraints and possibilities for this project writ large, although in this chapter my goals are more parochial. I argue that certain phenomenological and ethical conflicts concerning transformation of the body are related in important ways, and raise similar dilemmas for all feminists—transgendered or not—trying to live a good life. This conclusion has important implications for feminist solidarity after queer theory.

## WHERE IS THE AUTHOR?

I am acutely aware of the pitfalls of writing about trans people from the vantage point of a non-trans woman, and as someone who is not actively involved with extra-academic trans communities.[4] Questions about the location of a non-trans author in writing primarily concerned with trans issues are important, and while I don't want to engage in autobiography for its own sake, my personal motivations are, as always, deeply intertwined with the structure of my arguments. This is particularly important to acknowledge when much of what has been written about trans people by non-trans feminists has not only been hostile, but has also taken an explicit *dis*identification with transsexuals' experiences as its critical standpoint.[5] This move runs counter to familiar feminist political commitments to respecting what the marginalized say about themselves, and seems to ignore the risks of orientalism. It also inhibits alliances between trans and non-trans feminists; theorists' inclination to stress deep differences between these groups attenuates the political motivation to investigate shared experiences. In fact, for a long time I sustained a marked feminist suspicion of transsexuality, based largely on popular (feminist) portrayals.[6] However, the first two transsexual people I came to know socially (one male-to-female [MTF], one female-to-male [FTM])[7] disrupted this suspicion: both were feminists, and involved (in very different ways) in queer communities.

I have since read, listened to, and corresponded with many more trans people in the context of my feminist theoretical work. I am not claiming any definitive epistemic authority here, and this is certainly not a representative sample—any more than my genetic women colleagues in feminist studies are. However, I have also known a lot of other people who have struggled with gender—as butches, femmes, women working in male-dominated occupations, female and male survivors of sexual violence, male feminists, gay men, bisexual feminists, and so on. Over several years, I have come to see connections among these different people that make me less inclined to separate out transsexuals, or trans people in general, as traitors to a cause certain others share.

[...]

## TRANS LIBERATION?

I now want to take up the second horn of the dilemma I identified at the beginning of the chapter and turn to trans feminist writing—specifically, Feinberg's *Trans Liberation*. In this text I identify an understanding of gender as a property of individuals rather than relations that hampers the development of feminist coalitions in which agents are held morally accountable for the consequences of their gender expression for others.

In the emerging genre of popular trans feminist polemic (as in much of popular feminist writing) the rhetorical emphasis is squarely on the right of individuals to express their gender as they choose or to engage in free gender play. Hausman's brief critique of Bornstein finds fault with the "liberal humanist" model of the self such claims imply, and, philosophically speaking, I concur that Bornstein risks eliding a number of concerns about the embeddedness of gendered subjects (although Hausman also underestimates Bornstein's sophistication in this regard). However, I also see gender voluntarism as playing an important rhetorical role for transgendered intellectuals. For most of the modern history of transsexuality, the public trans person has typically been manipulated as a talk-show gimmick, sexual fetish, or tell-all sensationalist. These images are still there, but there is also now a genre of writing by feminist activists such as Kate Bornstein (1995; 1998), Leslie Feinberg (1998), Sandy Stone (1991), Susan Stryker (1994), the *Taste This* collective (1998), and Riki Anne Wilchins (1997), who use both first-personal narratives and polemical commentary on gender to motivate more critical understandings of what trans liberation might mean—for, as the subtitle of Bornstein's book suggests, "men, women, and the rest of us." One challenge for these activists, as for other feminists, is to bridge the gap between dominant popular understandings of gender (ultraconservative through liberal) and academic trans studies (radical feminist through Foucauldian through poststructuralist). The struggle to write a popular book on transgender without playing only to the liberal crowd in part defines a genre particularly vulnerable to scholarly critique. Interpreting *Gender Outlaw* or *Read My Lips* as the final word in trans politics is rather like seeing *The Female Eunuch* or *The Beauty Myth* as the epitome of feminism—each text captures particular moments in political movement, defends particular theses perhaps, but need not define the scope of critique or remedy.

Feinberg's work on trans liberation as a political movement "capable of fighting for justice" must be read against this background.[18] This movement, on Feinberg's account, includes "masculine females and feminine males, cross-dressers, transsexual men and women, intersexuals born on the anatomical sweep between female and male, gender-blenders, many other sex and gender-variant people, and our significant others" (1998, 5). Indeed, in the short "portraits" by other contributors, an impressively wide range of queer identities and stories inflected by class, race, and age are represented: from a male transvestite who became a full-time transgendered woman talking with her wife about their relationship, to a drag queen recalling New York street life and Stonewall, to a gay trans man on the significance of his Native heritage, to an intersexed activist discussing the emergence of the intersex movement. Feinberg never hesitates to draw parallels with the oppression of women, and hir extensive connections to feminist activism are made explicit throughout hir writing. Hir stated primary goal is to "refocus on defending the [gender] diversity in the world that already exists, and creating room for even more possibilities" (28), with a particular emphasis on rupturing the connection between sexed bodies and gender identities.

Despite the book's many virtues, there are interesting dissonances between Feinberg's analysis of trans oppression, and hir emphasis on freedom of individual self-expression: "Each person's expression of their gender or genders is their own and equally beautiful. To refer to anyone's gender expression as exaggerated is insulting and restricts gender freedom" (24). And "since I don't accept negative judgments about my own gender articulation, I avoid judgments about others. People of all sexes have the right to explore femininity, masculinity—and the infinite variations between—without criticism or ridicule" (25). This freedom is characterized very much as a property of individuals, and the language of choice appears throughout the book in such slogans as "Every person should have the right to choose between pink or blue tinted gender categories, as well as all the other hues of the palette"; "These ideas of what a 'real' woman or man should be straightjacket the freedom of individual self-expression" (4). In certain contexts I think Feinberg's appeal for blanket tolerance of all and any gender expressions is appropriate. The notion of gender freedom ze espouses is important in speaking against both the crashing weight of the dominant culture's gender discipline, and some of feminism's more doctrinaire moments: "There are no rights or wrongs in the ways people express their own gender style. No one's lipstick or flattop is hurting us.... Each person has the right to express their gender in any way that feels most comfortable" (53).

This approach, however, avoids important normative questions. In particular, in defending toleration Feinberg moves from an otherwise materially inflected and feminist account of gender to a curiously aesthetic and depoliticized version. As ze seems to recognize elsewhere, the privilege of white bourgeois male masculinity is implicated in the cultural visibility of minority male masculinities, cultural disdain for femininity, and cultural intolerance and disgust directed against any gender "deviance." These social structures inform and support normative heterosexuality and white bourgeois patriarchy. Gender expression is thus not only an aesthetic choice about cosmetics or hairstyle, skirts and suits. It is also implicated in politically fraught behaviors, economic marginalization and exploitation, and political consciousness. So even if the aesthetic choices of individuals are not up for moral grabs (as I agree they shouldn't be), "gender expression" must surely (on Feinberg's own account) occupy an ethical terrain.

For example, many feminists have argued that misogynist violence is constitutive of certain kinds of masculinity, but it is hardly a form of gender expression that Feinberg can condone. When ze discusses hir experience of police brutality against gay drag kings and drag queens, ze concludes: "I believe that we need to sharpen our view of how repression by the police, courts, and prisons, as well as all forms of racism and bigotry, operates as gears in the machinery of the economic and social system that governs our lives" (11). Such analysis should also include critique of the gender work accomplished by, for example, male police officers who assault gender-queers. Their self-expression may be equally deeply felt or essential to maintaining a gendered identity, but it clearly needs to be fought against. To express masculinity (no matter what one's birth sex) is often to despise femininity, just as to express femininity is often to implicate oneself in one's own oppression. Once when I heard Feinberg speak, I asked hir, with this problem in mind, "What's good about masculinity?" Ze seemed to miss the political import of the question, referring in hir answer instead to the diversity of masculinities across and within time and place, and again alluding to the freedom of individuals to express their gender without fear of reprisal. This is an important goal, but in posing the question I was thinking more of the ethical dilemmas faced by men who want to avoid participating in sexism. This is a complex straggle—including for pro-feminist "genetic" men. As David Kahane puts it: "Men have to face the extent to which fighting patriarchy means fighting themselves.... But even if men become part of the solution and find rewards in this role, we shouldn't deceive ourselves that we can cease being part of the problem" (1998, 213). It is probably even more difficult to combine the demands of maintaining a viable public identity as a trans man with a commitment to feminism (see Hale 1998). How does one consolidate a livable masculinity without participating in sexism? Answering this question is a project that feminists of any gender have barely begun, but it raises a set of ethical questions that are no less applicable to trans men than to any other men committed to feminist politics.

Feinberg thus tries to sidestep the ethical field into which one invariably stumbles when talking about the merits of various "gender expressions." This elision comes from hir willingness to treat gender as an *individual* matter, rather than as a web of relations in ongoing tension and negotiation. It is not so clear that, as Feinberg likes to think, ending gender oppression will benefit everyone. Implicitly addressing hir non-trans readers, ze says: "all your life you've heard such dogma about what it means to be a 'real' woman or a 'real' man. And chances are you've choked on some of it" (1998, 3). The chances of this are far greater, however, if one is either a woman or a trans person; Feinberg doesn't acknowledge that far from "choking," there are many people who lap up gender ideology precisely because it supports their privilege. This refusal to pass judgment on others' choices contributes to the appeal of Feinberg's rhetoric throughout hir work, in the same way that Raymond's dogmatism detracts from hers. But it also sometimes evades hard political questions about who is damaged and privileged by configurations of gender that themselves need to be transformed, sometimes from within the subject's own political consciousness. In other words, Feinberg's approach here elides a crucial aspect of progressive gender politics: the demand that we change ourselves. No doubt ze would resist such a demand on the reasonable grounds that trans people have too often been forced to conform to damaging gender norms, or been oppressively criticized—as I have already shown—for having the "wrong" sort of consciousness. But this response does not allow for important political distinctions between progressive transformations of consciousness initiated from within marginalized communities and disciplining moves that attempt only to reinforce established divisions. Missing from this rhetoric is any rich account of the ethics of self-transformation, which would be informed by consideration of how specific gendered ways of being fit into a web of possibilities and repressions. This omission is politically frustrating—including, I suspect, to feminist commentators like Raymond and Hausman. Filling in this gap might mitigate some of the legitimate anxieties of non-trans feminists that transgender politics will be inattentive to the relations that hold stigmatized concepts of "woman" in place.

## "US AND THEM": FEMINIST SOLIDARITY AND TRANSGENDER

Either feminists elide, with Feinberg, the ethical questions that are raised by self-fashioning in the context of gender relations, or, with Hausman and Raymond, we condemn any trans move as merely another iteration of oppressive norms. One important characteristic of the middle ground excluded by these positions is a relational, historicized model of the self that remains sensitive to context, while broadening the scope of Foucauldian analysis to encompass "technologies of the self"—"matrices of practical reason" that "permit individuals to effect by their own means, or with the help of others, a certain number of operations on their own bodies and souls, thoughts, conduct, and way of being, so as to transform themselves" (TS 225). In the case of trans identities, I have pointed out that these technologies are unusually literal, and the stakes are particularly high for subjects often denied any gender home unless they undertake them. Rather than treating transgender as a special case, however, we might see SRS as one technology of the self among many others implicated in histories of normalization. In beginning to articulate some connections among SRS, dieting, and cosmetic surgeries, I am not suggesting that they are directly equivalent—experientially, ethically, or politically.

Rather, I am suggesting that the dilemmas these practices raise for feminists are worth comparing with an eye to finding the family resemblances among them. Starting from lived experience is particularly important here. Dismissing women (and transsexuals) who change their bodies in allegedly gender-conforming ways as simply the victims of false consciousness erases the very place from which an ethics of self-transformation might begin. Ultimately, the purpose of bringing "to our attention historical transformations in practices of self-formation," whether explicitly indebted to Foucault or not, is "to reveal their contingency and to free us for new possibilities of self-understanding, new modes of experience, new forms of subjectivity, authority, and political identity" (Sawicki 1994, 288).

How might non-trans feminists temper critique of trans identities without adopting a laissez-faire account of gender, and while recognizing our own parallel straggles with identity? In the context of her critique of transgender politics, Hausman asks—supposedly rhetorically—"Are subjects who change their sex in order to make their bodies 'match' some kind of internal experience of the self defined as gender really able to question the 'system' that so clearly demarcates their choices?" (1995, 199). Consider the following two variations on this theme: "Are subjects who identify unquestioningly as 'heterosexual' in order to accommodate the demands of heteropatriarchy really able to question the 'system' that so clearly demarcates their choices?" "Are subjects who define themselves as 'lesbian' in order to make sense of their sexual desire for other women really able to question the 'system' that so clearly demarcates their choices?" Adopting a framework in which choice must be understood through the deep construction of subjects cannot apply only to the construction of transsexuals. The categories "women," "men," "lesbian," "gay," "heterosexual" have their own histories that congeal in contemporary individuals, structuring consciousness and determining possibilities. An agnosticism with regard to the causal histories of these various identities (which are quite clearly interconnected) might better serve the critical project of working from within them to change the world.[19]

To make this point more forcefully, imagine Q, a lesbian feminist who subscribes enthusiastically to the notion that her life constitutes a resistance to institutionalized heterosexuality, yet who in autobiographical moments resorts to the language of "I've always known I was a lesbian" and who sees no other social-sexual choice available to her. Q recalls a childhood fraught with ambivalence and trauma: she had unrequited crushes on other girls, she experimented briefly and unsuccessfully with dating boys, and agonized over imagining herself the married mother that her culture expected her to become. After years in the closet, trying to pass as heterosexual, she finally decided that she would "come out" and create a life as a lesbian. This caused her family a great deal of anguish, and many people tried to persuade her that sexuality was quite malleable and in fact she could continue simply to pass as heterosexual. Q was well aware that she lived in a culture where "sexuality" is treated ahistorically and quasi-scientifically as a core ontological fact about individuals. As a devotee of Foucauldian feminism, she was convinced, by contrast, that "lesbian" is in fact a relatively recent category of being, created by economic change, urbanization, shifting kinship relations, and feminist social movement. This intellectual attitude, while it shaped her way of being in the world, nonetheless coexisted uneasily with her sense that things could not have been otherwise except at the cost of great anguish and self-deception.

Q's story bears a striking resemblance to the autobiographies of many trans people. Of course, just as there is a standard "coming out" story for gays and lesbians, so, as I have discussed, there is a set of tropes that define the genre of autobiography, and particularly the autobiographies of transsexuals (Martin 1988, Phelan 1993, Mason-Shrock 1996, Prosser 1998). These tropes in both cases may well inspire post hoc interpretations of a life that fit a recognizable template. But just as non-trans feminists take seriously the experience of "growing up as a lesbian," so there is no less of a moral commitment to respect the testimony of those who describe early lives marked by gender confusion and distress:

> As our (modern Western) world is now, failure to conform to the norms of gender is socially stigmatizing to an unbearable extent: To be human just is to be male or female, a girl or a boy or a man or a woman. Those who cannot readily be classified by everyone they encounter are not only subject to physically violent assaults, but, perhaps even more wounding, are taken to be impossible to relate to humanly.... In such a world, boundary blurring carries psychic costs no one can be asked to pay, and the apparently conservative gender-boundary-preserving choices (surgical, hormonal, and behavioral) of many transsexuals have to be read in full appreciation of what the real options are.
> (Scheman 1997, 132–33)

It may well be the case that a larger institutional history creates those subjects, but that does not make their experience any less real or deeply felt on an individual level. Thus one cannot say of any feminist subject that she is simply the hapless product of social shifting, nor that she simply upped and chose to be a lesbian—or a transsexual. Rather it suggests a complex intermediate space, where individuals are thrown into particular subject-positions that are the contingent product of larger historical dynamics, within which they work to resist or exceed norms that are simultaneously the conditions of their own possibility.

Raymond recognizes the important fact that denial is very deeply built into the structure of privilege, and, hence, that people read as men are likely to underestimate the psychic impact of their male privilege. I have certainly seen transsexuals act in ways that I thought showed poor political judgment on matters of oppression and privilege. But I've seen lesbians misstep, too, and increasingly I have been impressed by the political commitment and sophistication of many trans activists. The politically resistant choices that trans people are making, especially in the context of the emerging trans liberation movement, often do challenge the terms of medical practice, as well as the depoliticized queer aestheticism that some feminists find objectionable (Bolin 1994; Califia 1997, 221–44; Feinberg 1998). The trans person who most obviously epitomizes Raymond's and Hausman's claims is the politically conservative, heterosexual MTF transsexual with both the desire and the economic resources to seek out SRS. Yet many FTMs in particular refuse surgeries, especially lower body surgeries. The cosmetic and functional inadequacy of phalloplastic techniques is undoubtedly a major element of this resistance (and a valid one: who wants a lousy surgical outcome?), but resistance is also motivated by the feminist recognition that the penis does not make the man (Devor 1997, 405–13; Cromwell 1999, 112-17, 138–40). Many MTF transsexuals are developing their own forms of feminist consciousness, and expressing their politics by both refusing certain medical interventions and asserting their rights to transform medical requirements. For example, many MTFs who do not want to engage in penile-vaginal intercourse after SRS (including those who resist medical demands further by defining as lesbians) resist the heterosexist demand to excessively dilate or surgically extend their newly constructed vaginas, or even to have one constructed in the first place (Bornstein 1995, 15–19, 118–21). In general, it seems as though increased access to critical information about medical procedures, a growing political consciousness, and expanded community has caused those trans people who do seek medical services to be increasingly concerned with the *limits* of SRS as a route to an authentic identity.

I have shown that Hausman's and Raymond's claims that transsexual identity is overdetermined by its medicalization are, conceptually speaking, tautological, and, empirically speaking, false. Rather, transgendered people face a complex set of choices about which, if any, medically managed changes to the body they want to make. At the very end of her book, Hausman claims that "the transgenderist['s]... ingestion of hormones, or participation in other procedures such as plastic surgery, merit medical attention because of the inherent dangers of reconfiguring the body's tissues" (1995, 200). In a similar vein, Raymond states that "medicalized intervention produces harmful effects in the transsexual's body that negate bodily integrity, wholeness, and being" (1994, 18). Both critics are right that such interventions carry medical risks not yet fully understood, and one of the frustrations of much philosophy of the body is precisely that it treats flesh as infinitely malleable, bloodless, and acquiescent. Yet it is precisely those people who must grapple with the pros and cons—physically as well as politically—of hormone treatments and surgeries who are most aware of the trauma and risks of changing one's body. These pros and cons include consideration of the quality of one's future life, in turn dependent on how desperately uncomfortable, unsafe, or unhappy one would be without altering one's body. In making decisions about hormones, surgery, passing, and gender conformity, trans people—especially if they are feminists—face ethical and political dilemmas. These dilemmas, again, might be best understood as lying at one end of a spectrum that includes others faced by non-trans feminists.

In the remainder of this chapter, let me just make a few suggestions about how this spectrum might be defined, to set the stage for the later case studies of dieting and cosmetic surgery. First, when I think about what it means to diet and exercise to keep one's body as close to slim as possible (something over which few people have very much real control), I see a number of parallels. I know many intelligent feminists who actively resist gaining weight, even though they would agree with the proposition that fat people should not be discriminated against, whose ideal world would not include any particular normatively upheld body type, and who even actively write and work against the "tyranny of slenderness." This lived contradiction is a well documented part of feminist consciousness for some women, and one deeply imbricated with gender identity. Being slim means being heterosexually attractive, which is the aspect of slenderness most available for feminist critique. However, more profound connotations of thinness include being in control of one's body (and hence one's life), and, as I suggested earlier, being fashionably slender is also associated with upward mobility and intellectual acumen. The deep unhappiness and discomfort experienced by many women with what are euphemistically called "body image problems" tells us a great deal about how femininity is disciplined in this culture. But unfortunately many feminists also know that reading *Fat is a Feminist Issue,* attending consciousness-raising groups, and stripping at music festivals are only partial solutions. For many women, regrettable though this is, nothing solves the problem quite as well as working on the body (including, of course, by losing weight). So is every woman who diets a dupe of the patriarchy, acceding to a disciplinary regime that has overdetermined her choices, and reinforcing objectifying images that degrade fat people? Although there certainly are radical feminist models that reiterate this reduction in the case of dieting (implicitly drawing a negative parallel with transsexuality), it is far more obvious in this context that there are other philosophical perspectives that give greater emphasis to the lived experience of embodied conflicts. And, crucially, many non-trans women can identify with this particular psychic struggle.

[...]

To ground a theory of resistance simply in the claim that such changes to the body are naïve capitulations to patriarchy is not only to ignore the complexities of women's experiences, but also to ignore that identity is always already written on the body. The objection that we should leave the body alone in its natural state erases the ubiquity of our embodied construction. Even if one has a theoretical commitment to maintaining one's "natural" body this proves a stubborn and elusive goal. (Is the fit body "natural" in today's sedentary cultures? A body fortified with vitamin supplements? A body that has been operated on to restore "normal" functioning?) To be sure, bodily inscriptions range vastly in their physical consequences—getting a tattoo is not the same deal as SRS. But in a deeply technological world, analysis must begin from the fact that the "natural body" is an unknowable, fictive entity.

In this vein, instead of simply rejecting body modification *tout court,* Kathryn Morgan argues that a possible "response of appropriation" in resisting the demands of beauty is to reclaim the "domain of the ugly," including through the technology of cosmetic surgery (1998, 340–42). There are fascinating intersections here with the work of performance artist Orlan, who has in fact had her face remodeled in a number of disturbing surgical performances, which have left her looking far from conventionally beautiful. Davis remarks on the interconnection of her work with Orlan's, pointing out:

> There are, indeed, similarities between Orlan's statements about her art and how the women I interviewed described their reasons for having cosmetic surgery. For example, both Orlan and these women insisted that they did not have cosmetic surgery to become more beautiful. They had cosmetic surgery because they did not feel "at home" in their bodies; their bodies did not "fit" their sense of who they were. Cosmetic surgery was an intervention in identity. It enabled them to reduce the distance between the internal and external so that others could see them as they saw themselves.
>
> (2003, 110)

Again, this could easily be a description of the phenomenology of transsexuality. As Davis goes on to describe, there are also dissimilarities between Orlan and her interviewees: the former is making "a public and highly abstract statement about beauty, identity, and agency," while the latter want to "eliminate suffering" and "do not care at all about changing the world; they simply want to change themselves" (2003, 110, 111). Within the trans community, we might compare Davis's "ordinary women" with the "average" transsexual who abhors publicity, while Orlan's project jibes with the work of such highly visible trans critics as Sandy Stone and Susan Stryker. In Stryker's words:

> I who have dwelt in a form unmatched with my desire, I whose flesh has become an assemblage of incongruous anatomical parts, I who achieve the similitude of a natural body only through an unnatural process, I offer you this warning: the Nature you bedevil me with is a lie. Do not trust it to protect you from what I represent, for it is a fabrication that cloaks the groundlessness of the privilege you seek to maintain for yourself at my expense. You are as constructed as me.
>
> (1994, 240–41)

We in Western, wealthy countries are all faced with decisions about when and how to request or permit intervention on our bodies, and they are rarely without political significance. Thus all political theoretical discussion of the fraught relationship between transgender, modern medicine, and feminism needs to see hormone treatments and SRS as practices on a continuum with other interventions in which we are all implicated. I don't want to minimize the possible consequences for physical health of any form of intervention with the body's functions. But it seems obvious that side-effects, complications, risks, and even a shortened life are considered well worth it by rational individuals contemplating a variety of embodied goals. The transsexual body fascinates our culture precisely as an orientalized example of the discourse of corporeal self-improvement to which we are all—in one way or another—attached.

## FEMINIST SOLIDARITY AFTER QUEER THEORY

My feminist utopia definitely does not include rigid disciplining of dimorphic sex and gender categories, an enforced normative ideal body type, objectification, or abjection. In this I am joined by all of the authors I have discussed in this chapter, and sharing these goals for me defines a potential for feminist solidarity. Whether gender should eventually cease to exist remains, I think, an open (and unanswerable) question. A space outside normalization is conceptually and institutionally unavailable to us, and thus feminist subjects have to live in the uncomfortable psychic space that our legacy as normalized bodies and our critical consciousness defines. The one thing we can definitely do to change the contours of that space is to resist struggling alone. To be able to live in a body that has one's resistance to patriarchy written on it requires a space within which one can be protected from the worst excesses of body disciplining (or within which one can simply be *intelligible*). The different positioning of many different subjects with regard to patriarchal discipline, however, creates numerous opportunities for strategies of divide and conquer, and nowhere has this been more apparent than in the debates about transgender within feminist theory.

The arguments I have made in this chapter are intended to open up an ethical field that I explore later, but one within which trans and non-trans feminists will continue to argue. Whether one *should* diet, have cosmetic surgery, have SRS, or in any other way self-consciously mold one's body are questions that will no doubt continue to preoccupy many feminists, even as we continue to engage in such practices. Although my argument is intended to motivate solidarity, the connections I have made will likely be resisted by some trans people who see their struggles as unique, far from the triviality of cosmetic surgeries or dieting. I am not arguing for a one-size-fits-all theory of embodied identities, or minimizing the grave emotional and pragmatic implications of moving in the world with a sexed body at odds with one's gender.[20] Often the psychic battles of those considering diets and cosmetic surgeries are not accessible to others as embodied dissonances; they have the dubious luxury of seeming "normal," and the steps they take to transform themselves are usually less dramatic and can be part of a less disjointed life story. Nonetheless, we all feel the weight of a culture where identities and bodies are supposed to line up, and despite our deep differences we share the goal of making our existence as gendered critics of gender livable, while opening possibilities for new kinds of lives (Butler 2004, 17–39).

In this chapter I have tried to show that the differences between the ethical and political dilemmas faced by feminists who are transgendered and those who are not are not as great as some theorists have suggested. I have highlighted some rhetorical moments in the ways non-trans feminists tend to theorize transgender: hostility, the construction of the Other, objectification, homogenization, and denial of agency. These approaches may say more about non-trans feminists' failure to interrogate our own identities, and our comfort with our own gender, than they do about the realities of trans communities or political movement. Acknowledging this, I have argued, leads us toward the recognition of some political common ground, and thus to the question of how feminist alliances can be formed. Very different experiences and identities can motivate very similar feminist goals, and the political Zeitgeist is such that solidarity must, of necessity, start from the deep diversity of agents. As Scheman puts it, "the issue... is not who is or is not really whatever, but who can be counted on when they come for any one of us: The solid ground is not identity but loyalty and solidarity" (1997, 152–53). Solidarity will founder, however, if we detach ourselves from each other and our mutual implication in favor of a demand for individual freedom.

## NOTES

1. The very separability and meaningfulness of the terms "sex," "gender," and "sexuality" are called into question by many of these identities. In particular, this chapter raises questions that implicitly challenge the distinction between "sex" (the body as male or female), and "gender" (the social role of the individual as a man or a woman). Thus I'll use the phrase "sex/gender identity" to avoid the impression that this distinction is being upheld.
2. This usage follows Stryker 1994, 251–52, n. 2. Of course, these terms are contested within trans communities: see Prosser 1998, esp. 200–205, for an alternative reading, and Cromwell 1999, esp. 19–30, for yet another.
3. I am thinking here of "Orientalism" in all of the senses invoked by Said, but the most striking analogy with feminist treatments of transgender is with his claim that "Orientalism can be discussed and analyzed as the corporate institution for dealing with the Orient—dealing with it by making statements about it, authorizing views of it, describing it, by teaching it, settling it, ruling over it: in short, Orientalism as a Western style for dominating, restructuring, and having authority over the Orient" (Said 1978, 3).
4. I have tried to write this chapter in the spirit of Jacob Hale's (1997) "Suggested Rules for Non-Transsexuals Writing About Transsexuals, Transsexuality, Transsexualism, or Trans——."

5. In his critique of Bernice Hausman, Jay Prosser argues that Hausman blocks out her own gender identity and embodiment in order tacitly to justify her authorial location "outside of" transsexuality as "the authoritative site from which to speak" (1998, 132). Janice Raymond's text is similarly at pains to show that transsexuals' attitudes are fundamentally inimical to a particular kind of identity politics, while being devoid of any critical examination of the author's location and investments in the identity being defended.

6. See Gamson 1998 for analysis of the intense manipulation of representations of trans people in U.S. talk shows. There's a remarkable continuity between some of the stereotypes Gamson discusses and those upheld within feminist contexts.

7. The terms "male-to-female" and "female-to-male" are disputed in trans communities. Some prefer the terms "female-to-female" or "male-to-male" to capture the subjective experience of transition rather than its perception by others.
   [...]

18. An earlier version of this critique of Feinberg was first published in Heyes 2000b.

19. When Foucault was asked, "Do you have any conviction one way or another on this issue [of the distinction between innate predisposition to homosexual behavior and social conditioning]?" he replied, "On this question I have absolutely nothing to say. 'No comment.'" (SCSA 142). He goes on to say that this is "not my problem" and "not really the object of my work." I read Foucault not simply as demurring due to lack of expertise (as if the question had a correct answer that he did not know), but also again shifting the focus of political conversation, as I would like to, away from the allure of causal pictures.

20. In her commentary on the city of San Francisco's decision to extend health-care coverage for its employees to SRS, for example, columnist Norah Vincent argues aggressively that this move is inconsistent with a refusal to pay for "nonessential cosmetic surgeries" for non-transsexuals (which she assumes to be a non-starter). In a way Vincent is right to point out that "these are the kinds of plastic surgeries your average Jane and Joe undergo at their own expense, though, ostensibly, for the same reason that transsexuals do—because they are unhappy with the way they look." But Vincent raises only to dismiss one of the most plausible justifications for this policy, namely, that "plastic surgeries... are a means of self-realization to transsexuals. Without them, transsexuals literally cannot be themselves" (Vincent 2001).

# 17

# *Inclusive Pedagogy in the Women's Studies Classroom*
## Teaching the Kimberly Nixon Case

VIVIANE K. NAMASTE, WRITTEN IN COLLABORATION WITH
GEORGIA SITARA

"IS A TRANSSEXUAL WOMAN A WOMAN?" This banal question, Namaste and Sitara contend, has initiated many discussions of transsexuality within feminism and in gender studies classrooms. Taking the case of Kimberly Nixon, a transsexual woman who was barred from the Vancouver Rape Relief volunteer training program in 1995, this chapter pushes the question of trans women's inclusion in feminist spaces beyond the question of identity. The authors explore both Vancouver Rape Relief's defense of their actions, and writing by Nixon's supporters to show how the case can be used as a pedagogical tool for diverse topics in gender studies. Nixon's case can be used to illustrate the limits of the assumptions that all non-transsexual women share all the same experiences of being a woman. It similarly highlights problems with depending on the state as the arbiter of feminist social justice. It further demonstrates why making an analogy between gender and race (i.e. the claim, "A man wanting to be a woman is like a white person wanting to be black") doesn't work. Finally, it underscores the imperialist history of feminism in Canada and elsewhere. Framed as a pedagogical discussion, this chapter does, in fact, dissect feminist arguments that trans women are not women. Its cleverness lies in showing how the holes in such an argument are so large as to engulf the question in a host of problematics within feminist thought more generally. Canadian gender scholar Viviane Namaste is the author of *Invisible Lives* and *Sex Change, Social Change*, from which this chapter is excerpted. Historian Georgia Sitara has taught gender and women's studies at the University of Victoria.

This article explores questions of teaching and pedagogy in women's studies classrooms, with a particular case study on addressing transsexual and transgendered issues in that setting. Through a study of the Kimberly Nixon case—in which a male-to-female transsexual was denied the right to train as a volunteer counselor at Vancouver Rape Relief—we want to provide some reflection, offer some pointers, and raise some critical questions about how to begin to address these issues raised by the Nixon case.

We feel the need to intervene in this debate because, in many ways, the Nixon case is coming to stand in as a litmus test for the relations between (non-transsexual) feminists and transsexuals in Canada. There is more and more discussion of this case in the context of English-Canadian women's studies classrooms, and the case has been taken up in recent academic work.[1] The case is also examined in the English- and French- language popular media, from the *National Post* to the feminist magazines *La Gazette des Femmes* and *Herizons*.[2] In this regard, one of the objectives of this article is to provide an overview of the case and the debates as a useful resource for teachers and students.

We are equally concerned with how this debate is framed within the teaching context, a discussion that focuses on whether or not transsexual women are women. We find this focus limited insofar as it understands the issue exclusively as a question of identity. Our observations of discussion of the Nixon case indicate that the case is used to raise the question, "Who is a woman?" It offers an opportunity for teachers to introduce the different ways in which sex and gender can be defined, broaching questions of genitals, chromosomes, social role, psychological identity, and biological determinism. We do think these questions are important and need to be addressed in the context of women's studies. Yet we think this focus on identity can obscure other critical issues raised by the Nixon case. A second objective of this article, then, is to encourage ways of teaching about transsexuality that move the debate beyond that of identity.

Third, we believe that the Nixon case raises central questions about an inclusive vision of feminism, particularly with respect to race. The Nixon case provides an occasion to think through how an appeal to "woman's experience" made by some feminists is an appeal to the experiences of certain white women. We hope to offer some reflection on how teachers can help students understand the limitations of such a universalist position. Our third objective of this article is to explore the issues in light of the history of imperialism in feminism, as well as to take seriously a commitment to diversity and inclusivity in feminist scholarship and politics.

Fourth, we are interested in thinking about these issues in relation to questions of the state. We are particularly invested in these questions because the discussion of the Nixon case to date has not, in our opinion, adequately incorporated this matter into its analysis. We will draw on different historical examples to raise questions about the complicated relations between feminist politics and state formation, and to suggest how a critical teacher can use the Nixon case as a way to bring these questions out in the classroom. Our fourth objective of this article is to encourage teachers to reflect on the definitions of the state deployed by feminist groups such as Vancouver Rape Relief.

Finally, we want to reflect on a feminist appeal to "protecting" the autonomy of (non-transsexual) women's groups. Historically, the notion of "protection" has been invoked under the banner of "women's rights" in a deeply conservative manner, supporting the work of imperialism and calling on the state to enforce a particular practice of morality. In this regard, we want to interrogate the argument made by some feminists that the Nixon case is important with respect to protecting women's interests.

This article seeks to offer reflection and to stimulate further thought and dialogue on these issues. We do not offer a detailed exposition or analysis of the Nixon case in its entirety. Nor do we simply take a position with respect to the Nixon debate. Rather, we raise questions for teachers to take up in their work of critical pedagogy.

## BACKGROUND AND AN OVERVIEW OF SOME OF THE MAIN ARGUMENTS

Kimberly Nixon is a male-to-female transsexual woman who volunteered for a training program of the Vancouver Rape Relief (VRR) and Women's Shelter in 1995. Upon discovery of her transsexuality, Nixon was excluded from the program. She filed a complaint with the British Columbia Human Rights Commission, arguing that she was a victim of discrimination because of her transsexual status. The BC Human Rights Tribunal on the case commenced in December 2000 and concluded in February 2001. In January 2002, the Tribunal found in favor of Nixon, awarding her $7,500 in damages, the highest damage award in the tribunal's history. In June 2002, VRR filed an appeal with the BC Supreme Court. The BC Supreme Court overturned the decision of the

BC Human Rights Commission and argued that Vancouver Rape Relief did not discriminate against Nixon.[3]

A variety of arguments are made in this case.[4] In the first instance, Nixon maintains that she was subject to discriminatory treatment as a transsexual woman, and that VRR was in violation of human rights legislation with respect to sex. VRR, in its defense, contends that the particular circumstances of the VRR volunteer training program are not covered by the existing Human Rights Code. Since the training program is volunteer and unpaid, it cannot be considered under the rubric of employment.[5] Moreover, the unique program of VRR cannot be considered as a service, insofar as Nixon was not denied access to *receiving* a service, but rather was denied access to training to provide a service.[6] VRR maintains that existing human rights legislation protects individuals who receive services, but not those who provide them. As such, there is no legal precedent for a finding of discrimination.

Even if the volunteer training program is to be considered as a protected ground under the rubric of employment or services with respect to human rights legislation, VRR argues that exclusion of Nixon from the program does not constitute discrimination since she does not have the life experience of living as a woman. VRR maintains that this is a *bona fide* requirement for participation in the volunteer training program. Indeed, this position is central to VRR's defense. They contend that only women who have the life experience of being raised and living as women are in a position to counsel women victims of rape and domestic violence. This appeal to "life experience" is at the core of their argument.

VRR argues that the Nixon case raises fundamental questions about minority groups in society defining their membership. They appeal to legislation that allows for members of minority groups to organize amongst themselves—freedom of association (Section 41 of the BC Human Rights Code). Freedom of association contends that disadvantaged groups have the legal right to exclude members who do not share their characteristics without it constituting discrimination, with an aim towards collective mobilization and social change. In other words, Mennonites can organize together and exclude non-Mennonites, if the aim of their organizing is to improve their social condition. This position outlines the difference between *distinction* and *discrimination*. VRR uses this framework to argue that the Code's use of the term "sex" ought also to be applied in this regard: (non-transsexual) women have the right to organize amongst themselves to promote (non-transsexual) women's interests without such a distinction constituting discrimination.[7] For VRR, non-transsexual women have the right to define who is a woman, and therefore who can participate in their training program.

VRR's position raises a variety of questions, and some feminists have seen in this case an important one concerning the autonomy of women's organizing. Judy Rebick, former president of the National Action Committee on the Status of Women, for instance, testified at the Tribunal and declared,

> The issue at stake is whether or not a women's group has the right to decide who its members are.... there's no question that transgendered people suffer from discrimination, they suffer a great deal. So of course, in your heart as a feminist you want to be on their side in every fight but you can't because there's a conflict of rights. It goes to the heart of what the women's movement is and what feminism is. It's a very important discussion and a difficult one![8]

Rebick's comments help situate the importance of the Nixon case for the women's studies classroom. This situation is perceived by many non-transsexual feminists, such as Rebick, as fundamental to the autonomy of the women's liberation movement. VRR also takes this position, and links it to the notion of protection. They argue that human rights legislation needs to protect (non-transsexual) women's rights to define who is a woman. In a response to Mary-Woo Sims, former chief commissioner of the BC Human Rights Commission, they write, "Human rights advance with each advance in the equality and liberation of women. We believe that it is critical to protect women's right to assess the significance of life experience and determine with whom and how we will be organized in order to protect and nurture the potential of the women's liberation movement."[9]

Having provided some background information and an overview of some of the main arguments, we turn our attention now to the pedagogical opportunities opened up by the Nixon case. Our comments address several questions that a critical teacher can take up with students: different definitions of "experience" in feminist theory and politics; diversity and inclusivity within feminist thinking and politics; faulty analogies between race and gender made by both anti-transsexual and pro-transsexual feminists; definitions of the state implicit in the appeal to the law made by VRR's defense; and an invocation of the notion of "protection" as linked to "women's rights." We conclude with some general comments on pedagogical approaches to these matters.

## DIFFERENT DEFINITIONS OF "EXPERIENCE"

VRR's defense is premised on the assumption that transsexual women cannot counsel victims of sexual assault and/or domestic violence because they do not share a common experience of being raised as girls. This appeal to "life experience" thus functions as the mitigating difference between women who are transsexual and those who are not.

Such an invocation of "experience" allows the critical teacher to present a variety of different ways in which feminist theorists and thinkers have defined the notion of "experience." This type of pedagogy would be especially pertinent at the introductory level, as a way of offering students an overview of different feminist positions on the same issue. It would also lend itself quite well to teaching feminist theory, since it provides an occasion for students to think through different paradigms in feminist thought. In this regard, teachers can use the Nixon case as a way to introduce, or to revisit, some fundamental traditions within feminist thought.

How do feminists influenced by standpoint theory rely on the notion of "experience"? How is "experience" defined and used by radical feminists? What do post-structuralist feminists say about the notion of "experience"? What are the different underlying assumptions about knowledge and being of each of these positions? What are their epistemological and ontological foundations? Having provided such an overview, teachers can encourage students to situate VRR's response in relation to particular traditions of feminist thought. The objective of such an exercise is not so much to have them debate the merits of VRR's position, but rather to encourage them to think theoretically: to understand the claims about knowledge and being that underlie their position and to be able to situate these claims within a history of feminist scholarship.

Having introduced some basic theoretical traditions in feminist thought, a critical pedagogue can also encourage students to reflect on the relations between theory and practice, knowledge and action. What forms of political action become possible, or impossible, based on a particular way of understanding the world? If women are understood to be non-rational, as they were by many Enlightenment thinkers, how could they even make a claim to desire access to education? If transsexual women are understood, *a priori,* to be other than women, how can they make a claim to equal access to the public sphere as women?

The Nixon case allows students to understand that the work of doing "theory" is deeply political, since it determines what forms of political action are possible in various traditions of (feminist) thought. Furthermore, the case illustrates quite well that political work is always informed by a particular theoretical perspective. Politics contain specific assumptions about knowledge, being, and the social world. Pedagogically, then, the Nixon case helps the women's studies instructor to demonstrate that thinking theoretically can help illuminate a specific political issue. These relations between theory and politics, knowledge and action, are central to the work of teaching in the women's studies classroom.

## DIVERSITY

VRR argues that Nixon cannot counsel women victims of sexual assault and/or domestic violence because she does not share the experience of living as a woman since birth. Such an experience is necessary, according to VRR, in order to establish rapport and to build trust between volunteer counselors and clients. Indeed, one of the witnesses called in their defense contended that she would not want her daughter to be counseled by Nixon.[10] Within this discourse, the shared "lifelong" experience of women is understood as a necessary precondition to successful counseling.

Yet interestingly, such a criterion of "experience" is only invoked with regard to transsexual women as volunteers. There is no similar appeal to the common "experience" of volunteers with other kinds of differences. VRR does not require, for instance, that its volunteers have lived for their entire lives as prostitutes in order to effectively counsel clients who are prostitutes. Nor does VRR demand that volunteers have been physically disabled since birth as a precondition to counseling women who are physically disabled and who have been sexually assaulted. Presumably, it is only the difference of transsexuality that seems to matter to VRR.

Fortunately, the decision of the BC Human Rights Tribunal recognized the discriminatory nature of treating transsexual women differently. Commenting on VRR's argument that volunteers need to have the lifelong experience of living as a woman, Heather MacNaughton writes,

> I accept that there may be some basis for that argument. However, it assumes that all the women who access Rape Relief for services, and who provide services, have a homogeneous common life experience. Rape Relief is prepared to make that assumption about all other women who apply to them without making any inquiry about it, and without having in place a policy that makes it necessary. The only criteria they have in place for their volunteer trainees is that they accept the four basic principles on which Rape Relief operates, and that they are not men. Ms. Nixon accepted the four basic principles and is not a man.[11]

VRR's exception with respect to transsexuals is significant, and it speaks to the implicit assumptions about violence advocated by VRR. Indeed, VRR is quite explicit in its conception of violence as one perpetrated by men against women.

> Rape Relief deals with all forms of male violence against women. Rape Relief was especially interested in overriding Social Services' delivery categories around incest, wife assault, and rape. Rape Relief thought the political similarity was more important. The political similarity is that it's men who are attacking women and women as a group need to resist.[12]

This position establishes an immediate connection amongst women as victims of male violence. It is based on this perceived connection of womanhood—defined as the common experience of living under sexism—that allows VRR to make its claim as to rapport and trust that only a non-transsexual woman as service provider or as volunteer can establish with another non-transsexual woman as client.

This argument places priority on sex above other differences such as race and class. Yet such a position actively ignores a rich history of debates within feminist scholarship and activism with respect to race and class differences. Women of color have criticized the ways in which this type of discourse appeals to a universal experience of "womanhood" that effaces differences within and across cultures, which forces women of color to locate their political commitments primarily in terms of sex (not race), and which quietly bypasses the history of imperialism and oppression enacted by white women.[13]

Yet when we examine the complexities of violence against women, it becomes increasingly problematic to make such claims to universalism. Consider a variety of different experiences of violence against women in the Canadian context: that of a South Asian immigrant woman, living in Canada, having been sponsored by her legal husband who abuses her; the Native woman in Vancouver who works as a street prostitute and is beaten by a client; or the young white woman who injects heroin daily and who is beaten by a drug dealer for nonpayment of debts. All of these situations reflect complicated dynamics and social relations that cannot be subsumed into a universal "experience" of "violence against women." Furthermore, the skills required to intervene in these situations demand much more than a simplistic appeal to "a life-long experience of living as a woman" as the VRR position implicitly maintains. These scenarios demand knowledge of different cultures, familiarity with street prostitution, and/or an awareness of harm-reduction strategies when working with intravenous drug users. [...] Clearly, an appeal to the lifelong experience of living as a woman is an insufficient ground for solidarity.

VRR maintains that as an organization, it adopts an anti-racist position. Yet its conception of violence is one that cannot account for the different ways in which violence is organized. The organization's implicit appeal to a "sisterhood" established through the lifelong experience of living as a woman effectively requires that violence be understood primarily in terms of gender—which is to say, the violence of men against women: "[I]t's men who are attacking women and women as a group need to resist."[14] We would question this understanding of anti-racism, to the extent that VRR's position in the Nixon case requires a virtual erasure of the specificity of violence in different racial and ethnic contexts.

One of the limitations of this argument is that it highlights questions of sex and gender while downplaying those of race. Significantly, however, it also supports an underlying assumption about the nature of women. By understanding violence as something perpetrated by men against women, this position effectively precludes the possibility of women who enact violence against other women. [...]

VRR's appeal to the trust and rapport established between women as victims of violence and non-transsexual volunteers emerges from this simplistic conception of violence. It necessarily ignores the violence that women enact against other women. Indeed, if some women can abuse other women, this means that women as victims of violence and as service providers or as volunteer counselors do not, *a priori*, share any essential connection, regardless of the fact that they may have been raised since birth as girls and women. Furthermore, when we position women as victims of violence it becomes difficult to analyze the violence that women perpetrate on their own children.

We think that a critical pedagogue can help students to think through these issues. Teachers can ask their students how the position of VRR addresses the diversity amongst women, including the varied articulations of violence in different class and race contexts. Students can be encouraged to think about the function of universalism—the appeal to a common bond between (non-transsexual) women that is at the core of VRR's argument. How does this universalist appeal work to exclude transsexuals? What are its assumptions about the essentially good, moral nature of women? How does this appeal to morality relate to the work of early feminists in Canada, who appealed to the moral nature of Anglo-Saxon women and whose politics was marked by overt racism and imperialism?[16] In what ways does this position force feminists to place a priority on matters of sex, downplaying questions of race and class? How have feminist theories and politics made use of universalism in the past? Has this use of universalism been critiqued by some feminists, and if so, how?

## ANALOGIES OF RACE AND GENDER

In the previous section, we have outlined how the position of VRR works with a universalist conception of women and violence that effaces the complexity of violence as it is organized and manifested in different cultural, ethnic, and class contexts. We also suggested some particular strategies for teachers to help students better understand these issues. One of our central arguments was that VRR's position demands an understanding of violence primarily in terms of gender, downplaying questions of race and class.

Yet VRR is not the only party to engage in such a tactic—which is to say, one that situates the Nixon debate primarily with respect to violence against white women. Indeed, some supporters of Nixon make an analogy between race and gender that also effaces the realities of non-white people. In a community forum on the Nixon case published in *Herizons,* Dodie Goldney, a non-transsexual woman who self-identifies as a "radical lesbian feminist woman," writes,

> I can do nothing but wholeheartedly embrace transgendered women as my sisters. I am also a white woman and I embrace women of color as my sisters. To me, the issues are similar. To say that a woman might not feel comfortable receiving counseling or support from a transgendered woman is similar, to me, to saying that a white woman might not feel comfortable receiving counseling from a woman of color, or that a heterosexual woman might not feel comfortable receiving counseling from a lesbian.[17]

This position is also articulated by the lawyer for Nixon. In a press release issued after the Tribunal rendered its verdict in favor of Nixon, barbara findlay writes,

> The decision will make it clear that it is no more acceptable to say that they [members of a women's organization] cannot imagine working in a rape crisis center with a transsexual woman, than it would be to say that they cannot imagine working in a rape crisis center with a woman of color, a lesbian, or a woman with a disability.[18]

The statements of both Goldney and findlay establish a similarity between gender and race. While they are clearly in support of Nixon's struggle, and of equal access for transsexual women in women's organizations, they mobilize this support by invoking the similarity of transsexual women providing services with women of color providing services. In this discourse, *gender is like race.*

We suggested earlier that critical teachers can use the Nixon case to raise important questions of diversity and inclusion in feminist politics. While it is necessary to think through the ways in which the position of VRR privileges gender over race, it is equally important to unpack the false analogies of race and gender established by supporters of Nixon.

Not all transsexuals are white. This statement shows the limitations of the argument put forward by Goldney and findlay. Through their analogy, they implicitly suggest that all transsexuals are white. Of course, this type of reasoning and comparison needs to be interrogated, and the critical teacher can help students in such an exercise. We believe it is particularly important to do so given the general context of the discussion of the Nixon case—which is to say, the case is about violence against women, about the work done in a woman's service organization, and about the city of Vancouver. Non-white transsexuals make up a significant proportion of the transsexual population in Vancouver, particularly when one considers street prostitutes. To make an analogy between race and gender, as Goldney and findlay do, effectively erases the realities of the Native, Filipina and other non-white transsexuals who live and work in Vancouver. Analogies between race and gender are sometimes deployed by white feminists in an attempt to undermine the viability of transsexuality. Marisa Swangha addresses this issue in taking up the white feminist statement "A man wanting to be a woman is like a white person wanting to be Black." As Swangha elegantly argues, this statement evacuates the realities of non-white transsexuals. In her words,

I have many problems with this ignorant racist statement. First, it implies that all transsexuals are white, that all transsexuals are MTF (male-to-female) and that being a woman is like being Black. But most of all it negates the millions of lives of transsexual/transgendered peoples of *First Nations, Afrikan,* and *Asian* descent, who are the world *majority* of transsexuals.

An Afrikan/Asian/Native "man wanting to be" an Afrikan/Asian/Native woman is not "like a white person wanting to be Black," it is like a "man" of a certain color wanting to be a woman of the same color as "he" already is. *Gender is not like race.*[19]

Swangha's intervention addresses the consequences of establishing a false analogy between gender and race. While her critical inquiry helps us to undo the racism of an anti-transsexual discourse advocated by some white feminists, it can also assist us in thinking through the limitations of a pro-transsexual discourse advocated by some white allies and white supporters of transsexuals.[20]

In this regard, the Nixon case offers an excellent pedagogical opportunity to help students think through the dangers of analogies between race and gender too often made by liberal thinkers. We suggest that teachers have students list some of the arguments put forward in support of Nixon, drawing on the discussion published in *Herizons* and the press release issued by findlay. Having outlined some of these arguments, teachers can help students think about the invocation of "race" in certain positions. What is the connection put forward between gender and race? How is this invocation of race connected to the lives of non-white transsexuals in Vancouver? Having asked these questions, teachers can use the reflections offered by Swangha to assist students in understanding the limitations of these supposedly "progressive" positions.

We believe that this type of teaching—helping students to understand the limitations of making analogies between race and gender—is a fundamental aspect of anti-racist pedagogy in the women's studies classroom.

## APPEAL TO THE LAW

The Nixon case is further useful from a pedagogical perspective given the appeal of feminists—both Nixon and VRR—to the terms of the law.

Nixon makes her case by arguing that she suffered discrimination as a transsexual woman. Interestingly, the response of VRR to this allegation also invokes the law. In their early defense—before the case arrived before the BC Human Rights Tribunal—they made an argument before the BC Supreme Court that the Human Rights Code did not explicitly protect transsexual and/or transgendered people.[21] Since the Code did not set out such formal protection, VRR argued, they could not be found to be in violation of the existing legislation. The BC Supreme Court rejected this argument, and found that the use of the term "sex" did include transsexuals in British Columbia.

In their defense at the Tribunal, VRR also made several arguments that maintained that the organization did not discriminate. In the first instance, they contended that the situation involved an individual who was to work as a volunteer counselor. This particular circumstance was not covered under existing human rights legislation, they argued, which limited its scope to either the category "employment" or "services." VRR maintained that since Nixon was neither an employee of the organization, nor a recipient of services, the group could not be found in breach of human rights legislation in BC. They maintained that Nixon was denied access to training to provide a service, but that this cannot be confused with receiving a service or with employment. The Tribunal disagreed with this position, basing its decision on some previous human rights cases in British Columbia with respect to volunteer labour.[22]

We wish to highlight here the strategy adopted by VRR with respect to the law and the state. In the first instance, they maintained that since the existing law does not include transsexuals, groups like VRR that exclude (male-to-female) transsexuals are not engaging in a discriminatory practice. This position thus understands that "discrimination" can only be what is set forth in the law. Importantly, such a strategy places the burden on marginalized peoples to ensure that their specific differences are incorporated into human rights law. It shifts the responsibility away from institutions and organizations that then do not need to prove that they did not discriminate in treating an individual differently based on a particular characteristic. Moreover, such a strategy opposes the practice of human rights law, which is always to be interpreted in an open manner in the interests of ensuring equal access to all citizens. The Tribunal judgment included a statement on precisely this purpose and function of human rights law: it "must be interpreted broadly and purposively."[23] In this regard, we find that the strategy chosen by VRR is a deeply conservative move that is detrimental not only to transsexuals, but to all marginalized peoples whose difference is not explicitly named in existing human rights legislation.[24] [...]

Moreover, this recourse to the law is further ironic given a strong feminist critique of the ways in which the law has not historically represented the interests of women. [...] More radically, some feminists contend that the law actively organizes oppressions of race and of gender.[27]

Given this historical background, in which feminists have been deeply critical of the law, what does it mean now that VRR appeals to the terms of the law in its defense? Is it possible that the law has been clearly discriminatory in an historical sense, but that the possibility of such discrimination no longer exists?

We see in VRR's appeal to the law a position that is entirely uncritical of the state and how it works, a position here mobilized under the name of "feminism." And we find it problematic that VRR adopts such a statist position with respect to this human rights case when their mission is clearly critical of the state. In their summary of the key evidence, VRR argues that the organization was established to move beyond the limitations of the state's services with respect to violence.[28]

This contradiction offers a wonderful pedagogical opportunity for teachers. Instructors can raise the obvious question with respect to VRR's defense: how is it that the organization can critique the functioning of the state with respect to its conception of violence against women, and use this critique as a foundation for the need of VRR's services, yet at the same time appeal to the terms of the state and its laws in order to argue that the organization has not discriminated against Kimberly Nixon? Can these two elements of their position be reconciled? What is the theory of the state that underlies them? Are there different feminist understandings of and appeals to the state? If so, which (feminist) tradition does VRR invoke in its defense? These questions lend themselves particularly well to discussions about women and politics, women and the law, and women and the state. In this regard, the Nixon case is useful not for discussion about who is or who is not a woman. Rather, the Nixon case allows teachers to introduce different theories of the state—including feminist theories—and to discuss how these theories inform political action.[29]

## PROTECTION

The final issue we would like to address is an appeal made by VRR to "protecting" the interests of women. Indeed, certain feminists (such as Judy Rebick) see in the Nixon case a fundamental struggle over the autonomy of women's groups. VRR's press release announcing an appeal of the Tribunal decision makes this perfectly clear. Suzanne Jay of VRR states, "[W]e are fighting this case as a test case on the protection of women's rights to women-only organizing."[30] And as we cited earlier, the organization's response to Mary-Woo Sims, former chief commissioner of the BC Human Rights Commission, also appealed to this notion of "protection":

> Human rights advance with each advance in the equality and liberation of women. We believe that it is critical to protect women's right to assess the significance of life experience and determine with whom and how we will protect and nurture the potential of the women's liberation movement.[31]

The position of VRR establishes a crucial link between the autonomy of women's groups, women's rights, and this notion of "protection." Their argument opens up a pedagogical opportunity for teachers to better understand the function, and consequences, of such an appeal to "protection." Here, we believe it is important to understand these issues historically, learning from some of the ways in which feminists have mobilized support through an appeal to "protection," and thinking critically about some of the ways in which the concrete organizing efforts of such feminists have failed, in point of fact, to improve the social conditions of women. [...]

Once we consider the deeply conservative political work that occurs in the name of protection, it is necessary to rethink the equation made between "women's rights" and "human rights" as proposed by VRR. We do not accept the claim that "human rights advance with each advance in the equality and liberation of women."

Indeed, critical scholars have shown us that the history of a struggle for "women's rights" in Canada is also a history of imperialism.[34] Feminists such as Nellie McClung and Emily Murphy held deeply racist beliefs, and their projects of social reform were intimately linked to colonialism and a settler society. Emily Murphy, for instance, is often hailed as one of the feminist leaders instrumental in getting women the vote in Canada. She was also active in matters of social reform such as drug policies and drug laws. In her book *The Black Candle,* Murphy argues that it is important to combat the trafficking in drugs because it weakens the nation. Together with a declining birth rate, this factor will be the downfall of the British Empire, Murphy contends.[35] Elsewhere in the book she writes of how white female addicts are enslaved to the "negro" and Chinese men who corrupt them through drugs.[36] In this regard, the political work of feminists like Murphy and McClung with respect to "women's rights" was carried out in service to the British Empire. These limitations of their political organizing challenge the assertion made by VRR that "human rights advance with each advance in the equality and liberation of women." In point of fact, the historical evidence in Canada shows that efforts to advance the legal equality of women had detrimental consequences for human rights more broadly.

We believe it is important for students and teachers to learn from this history. Careful reflection in this regard cautions us against making faulty equations between the advancement of "women's rights" and those of "human rights." Indeed, the task of the critical scholar includes understanding how an appeal to "women's rights" has been instrumental in the work of imperialism as well as in the functioning of a moralist state.

Teachers in the women's studies classroom can help students learn from the history of a feminist appeal to "protection." Given this history, what does it mean when VRR invokes the notion with respect to the Nixon case? Can we trust this appeal to "protecting" women's interests to be other than a conservative move, and if so, on what basis? How have feminists in the past linked the autonomy of women to the notion of protection? Does the position advocated by VRR differ from this history?

The Nixon case allows teachers to present the history of imperialism in feminism, a discussion particularly suited to courses on the history of women in Canada, as well as courses in feminist thought and anti-racism. Furthermore, it creates an opportunity for teachers to help students think about fundamental concepts used to advance a political agenda—in this instance, the notion of "protection." Such pedagogy is particularly useful in courses on feminist theory, although of course it can be usefully applied in any women's studies classroom.

## CONCLUSION

In recent years, the Kimberly Nixon case is discussed more and more within university-based feminist circles. Frequently, analysis of the case limits itself to questions of identity. Is Nixon a woman? How do we define who is a woman? Can transsexual women be active members of (non-transsexual) women's groups?

Our reflections on the Nixon case seek to move teachers and students beyond this narrow framework. We have argued that the Nixon case is pedagogically useful and important not with respect to identity ("who is a woman?"), but rather in relation to some fundamental questions of feminist history, theory, and politics. The case allows teachers to introduce different theoretical traditions of feminist thought and how they define the concept of "experience." It creates an opportunity for teachers in the women's studies classroom to help their students think about an appeal to a universal women's experience, as well as the attending race and class biases of such an argument. The Nixon case can also help students to reflect on analogies made between race and gender within a liberal framework and the limitations therein. Furthermore, the case lends itself well to discussion on women and politics, since different positions with respect to the Nixon case embody different definitions of the state. Finally the Nixon case provides an occasion for the critical teacher to facilitate learning with respect to an invocation of "protecting" women's rights, understanding how this notion of protection has been deployed in a conservative manner historically.

These reflections offer different ways to refocus the debate. We believe that it is necessary and productive to reorient how feminists think about the Nixon case in order to offer a broader conception of justice. In this regard, we take issue with Judy Rebick's statement at the Tribunal that:

> The issue at stake is whether or not a women's group has the right to decide who its members are.... there's no question that transgendered people suffer from discrimination, they suffer a great deal. So of course, in your heart as a feminist you want to be on their side in every fight but you can't because there's a conflict of rights. It goes to the heart of what the women's movement is and what feminism is.[37]

Rebick's comments illustrate the implications of understanding the Nixon case exclusively with respect to identity. When the debate is framed as a matter of whether or not transsexual women are women, it becomes possible to advance the somewhat incredulous argument that there exists a "conflict of rights" between transsexual women and non-transsexual women.

Yet before we accept the terms set out by Rebick, we think it useful to reflect on how she can establish a "conflict of rights" between marginalized peoples. How is it that she can understand the oppression of people within a framework of conflict and competing interests? How does she reconcile this position with feminism's commitment to understanding the links among oppression? What are the social, political, and institutional conditions that produce divisive thinking like that of Rebick? Can feminists advocate a program of justice that appeals to competing rights? How have feminists resisted this type of analysis, and how have they adopted it?

We hope that this article helps both teachers and students to think critically about the Nixon case, in ways that move beyond the identity-based frame of reference advocated by Rebick. Analysis of the Nixon case that moves beyond identity can assist feminists in the development of truly inclusive conceptions and practices of justice.

## NOTES

1. Patricia Elliot, "Who Gets to Be a Woman? Feminism, Sexual Politics and Transsexual Trouble," presentation at the Transgender/Transsexual: Theory, Organizing, Cultural Production Symposium, Graduate Programme in Women's Studies, York University, Toronto, November 29 2002; Patricia Elliot, "Who Gets to Be a Woman? Feminist Politics and the Question of Trans-Inclusion." *Atlantis: A Women's Studies Journal* 29.1 (Fall 2004): 13–20; barbara findlay, "Real Women. *Kimberly Nixon* v. *Vancouver Rape Relief.*" *UBC Law Review* 36.1 (Winter 2003).
2. Ian Bailey, "Rebick Defends Rape Centre's Right to Reject Transsexual." *National Post* December 19, 2000; Mary-Woo Sims, "Why Transgendered People Need Human Rights Protection." *Horizons* Fall 2001: 19–21, 28; Vancouver Rape Relief, "Vancouver Rape Relief Responds to Mary-Woo Sims Remarks." *Horizons* Fall 2001: 29; "Can a Transgendered

Person Be 'One of Us'?" *Herizons* Fall 2001: 22–3, 27; "Faut-il intégrer les transsexuelles?" *La Gazette des femmes* 25.5 (janvier-février 2004): 9–10.

3. The decision, *Vancouver Rape Relief v. Nixon et al.,* can be consulted online at www.courts.gov.bc.ca/Jdb-txt/SC/03/19/2003BCSC1936.htm.

4. We outline some of the main arguments here that are particularly relevant for the women' studies classroom. A detailed reading of the Tribunal transcripts, submissions to the Tribunal, and the decision would, of course, offer additional arguments and evidence.

5. Christine Boyle, "Vancouver Rape Relief and Women's Shelter Legal Argument Part 1." Presented January 24-26, 2001. Available online at www.rapereliefshelter.bc.ca/issues/knixon_cboyle_argurn.htrnl.

6. *Ibid.*

7. Vancouver Rape Relief, *"Nixon v. Vancouver Rape Relief Society:* Pending before the B.C. Human Rights Tribunal." January 2002. (Available online at www.rapereliefshelter.bc.ca/issues/knixon_outline.html)

8. Cited in Ian Bailey, "Rebick Defends Rape Centre's Right to Reject Transsexual." *National Post* December 19, 2000.

9. VRR, "Vancouver Rape Relief Responds to Mary-Woo Sims Remarks." *Herizons* Fall 2001: 21.

10. Rape Relief's Summary of Key Evidence by Issue, Sections 63, 64. Presented January 24-26 2001. Available online at www.rapereliefshelter.bc.ca/issues/knixon_summary.html.

11. Heather MacNaughton, *Nixon* v. *Vancouver Rape Relief Society,* 2002 BCHRTi, S 202. Available online at www.bchrt.gov.bc.ca/decisions/2002/index.htm.

12. Rape Relief's Summary of Key Evidence by Issue, Section 8. Presented January 24–26, 2001. Available online at www.rapereliefshelter.bc.ca/issues/knixon_summary.html.

13. See, for instance, Audre Lorde, *A Burst of Light* (Ithaca, NY: Firebrand Books, 1988).

14. Rape Relief's Summary of Key Evidence by Issue, Section 8. Presented January 24–26, 2001. Available online at www.rapereliefshelter.bc.ca/issues/knixon_summary.html.

[...]

16. Carol Bacchi, *Liberation Deferred? The Ideas of the English Canadian Suffragists, 1877–1918* (Toronto: University of Toronto Press, 1983).

17. Goldney in "Can a Trans-gendered Person Be 'One of Us'?" *Herizons* Fall 2001:23.

18. findlay, "Nixon Wins against Rape Relief," press release circulated via e-mail January 17, 2002.

19. Swangha, "A man wanting to be a woman is like a white person wanting to be Black." *Gendertrash* 3 (Winter 1995): 23–4.

20. These reflections can also be applied to the ruling of the BC Supreme Court in the Nixon case. The decision refers to case law with respect to Métis communities in Canada, and then extends this analysis of race to the matter of gender. See *Vancouver Rape Relief v. Nixon et al.,* www.courts.gov.bc.ca/Jdb-txt/SC/o3/19/2003BCSC1936.htm.

21. *Vancouver Rape Relief Society v. BC Human Rights Commission,* 2000 BCSC 889. Cited in Heather MacNaughton, *"Nixon v. Vancouver Rape Relief Society* 2002 BCHRT I, S 3." Available online at www.bchrt.gov.bc.ca/decisions/2002/index.htm.

22. Heather MacNaughton, *"Nixon v. Vancouver Rape Relief Society,* 2002 BCHRT I, Sections 47–73." Available online at www.bchrt.gov.bc.ca/decisions/2002/index.htm.

23. Heather MacNaughton, *"Nixon v. Vancouver Rape Relief Society,* 2002 BCHRT I, S 52." Available online at www.bchrt.gov.bc.ca/decisions/2002/index.htm.

24. Cf. findlay, "Nixon Wins against Rape Relief," press release circulated via e-mail January 17, 2002. [...]

27. See, for instance, Sherene Razack, ed. *Race, Space, and the Law. Unmapping a White Settler Society* (Toronto: Between the Lines, 2002).

28. Rape Relief's Summary of Key Evidence by Issue. Presented January 24–26, 2001. Available online at www.rapereliefshelter.bc.ca/issues/knixon_summary.html.

29. On this subject, it is worth pointing out that the decision of the BC Supreme Court argues that:

> Rape Relief did not discriminate against Nixon because her exclusion from the agency did not take place in public, and because the organization is a private one. In the words of the ruling, "exclusion by a small relatively obscure self-defining private organization cannot have the same impact on human dignity as legislated exclusion from a statutory benefit program.... Rape Relief's exclusion of Ms. Nixon was private. That does not mean it was subjectively less hurtful to her, but it was not a public indignity." Cited from Vancouver Rape Relief v. Nixon et al., available at www.courts.gov.bc.ca/Jdb-txt/SC/03/19/2003BCSC1936.htm.

> This argument is deeply conservative in that it maintains that discrimination in the private sphere is not the same as discrimination in the public sphere. Feminists, of course, have been critical of the ways in which such a public/private division has been used to oppress women. So the ruling of the BC Supreme Court violates one of the fundamental tenets of feminist theory and politics, that the "private" realm is also political. In this regard, regardless of the position taken by feminists with respect to the inclusion of male-to-female transsexuals, it remains quite problematic to celebrate this decision as any kind of victory for feminism.

30. "Vancouver Rape Relief Seeks BC Supreme Court of Appeal of Human Rights Decision in Women-Only Case," press release, June 24, 2002.

    [...]

34. Bacchi, *Liberation Deferred? The Ideas of the English-Canadian Suffragists, 1877–1918* (Toronto: University of Toronto Press, 1983).

35. Emily Murphy, *The Black Candle* (Toronto: Thomas Allen, 1922), 46–7.

36. *Ibid.,* 302–3.

37. Cited in Ian Bailey, "Rebick Defends Rape Centre's Right to Reject Transsexual." *National Post* December 19, 2000.

# 18

## *Skirt Chasers*
## Why the Media Depicts the Trans Revolution in Lipstick and Heels

JULIA SERANO

JULIA SERANO, A RESEARCH BIOLOGIST, PERFORMANCE ARTIST, musician, and transfeminist activist, has argued that much of the antipathy directed towards trans women can be understood as a virulent form of misogyny—and that, furthermore, the cultural prejudices against femininity and woman-identification can actually be seen with extraordinary clarity when they are projected against a purportedly male body (a practice she describes as "transmisogyny"). In this article, Serano suggests that transmisogyny actually harms and holds back the broader transgender activist agenda in an antifeminist manner, by belittling the whole transgender movement through the disparagement of femininity. She analyzes the mainstream media portrayal of male-to-female transsexuals, and identifies two predominant representations: the "deceptive" and the "pathetic" transsexual. As Serano explains, these portrayals highlight instances of hyperfemininity in order to assert the inauthenticity of transsexual women's femininity: beneath the makeup and the dresses, transsexual women are "really" men who embrace stereotypical views of womanhood. Serano's goal, as a feminist, is to show how such representations are fueled by a pervasive sexism and the hypersexualization of all women's bodies, whether or not they are transsexual.

As a transsexual woman, I am often confronted by people who insist that I am not, nor can I ever be, a "real woman." One of the more common lines of reasoning goes something like this: *There's more to being a woman than simply putting on a dress.* I couldn't agree more. That's why it's so frustrating that people often seem confused because, although I have transitioned to female and live as a woman, I rarely wear makeup or dress in an overly feminine manner.

Despite the reality that there are as many types of trans women as there are women in general, most people believe that all trans women are on a quest to make ourselves as pretty, pink, and passive as possible. While there are certainly some trans women who buy into mainstream dogma about beauty and femininity, others are outspoken feminists and activists fighting against all gender stereotypes. But you'd never know it by looking at the popular media, which tends to assume that all transsexuals are male-to-female, and that all trans women want to achieve stereotypical femininity.

The existence of transsexuals—who transition from one sex to the other and often live completely unnoticed as the sex "opposite" to the one we were assigned at birth—has the potential to challenge the conventional assumption that gender differences arise from our chromosomes and genitals in a simple, straightforward manner. We can wreak havoc on such taken-for-granted concepts as *woman* and *man*, *homosexual* and *heterosexual*. These terms lose their cut-and-dried meaning when a person's assigned sex and lived sex are not the same. But because we are a threat to the categories that enable traditional and oppositional sexism, the images and experiences of trans people are presented in the media in a way that reaffirms, rather than challenges, gender stereotypes.

## TRANS WOMAN ARCHETYPES IN THE MEDIA

Media depictions of trans women, whether they take the form of fictional characters or actual people, usually fall under one of two main archetypes: the "deceptive transsexual" or the "pathetic transsexual." While characters based on both models are presented as having a vested interest in achieving an ultrafeminine appearance, they differ in their abilities to pull it off. Because the "deceivers" successfully pass as women, they generally act as unexpected plot twists, or play the role of sexual predators who fool innocent straight guys into falling for other "men."

Perhaps the most famous example of a "deceiver" is the character Dil in the 1992 movie *The Crying Game*. The film became a pop culture phenomenon primarily because most moviegoers were unaware that Dil was trans until about halfway through the movie. The revelation comes during a love scene between her and Fergus, the male protagonist who has been courting her. When Dil disrobes, the audience, along with Fergus, learns for the first time that Dil is physically male. When I saw the film, most of the men in the theater groaned at this revelation. Onscreen, Fergus has a similarly intense reaction: He slaps Dil and runs off to the bathroom to vomit.

The 1994 Jim Carrey vehicle *Ace Ventura: Pet Detective* features a "deceptive transsexual" as a villain. Police lieutenant Lois Einhorn (played by Sean Young) is secretly Ray Finkle, an ex-Miami Dolphins kicker who has stolen the team's mascot as part of a scheme to get back at Dolphins quarterback Dan Marino. The bizarre plot ends when Ventura strips Einhorn down to her underwear in front of about twenty police officers and announces, "She is suffering from the worst case of hemorrhoids I have ever seen." He then turns her around so that we can see her penis and testicles tucked between her legs. All of the police officers proceed to vomit as *The Crying Game*'s theme song plays in the background.

Even though "deceivers" successfully "pass" as women, and are often played by female actors (with the notable exception of Jaye Davidson as Dil), these characters are never intended to challenge our assumptions about gender itself. On the contrary, they are positioned as "fake" women, and their "secret" trans status is revealed in a dramatic moment of "truth." At this moment, the "deceiver"'s appearance (her femaleness) is reduced to mere illusion, and her secret (her maleness) becomes the real identity.

In a tactic that emphasizes their "true" maleness, "deceivers" are most often used as pawns to provoke male homophobia in other characters, as well as in the audience itself. This phenomenon is especially evident in TV talk shows like *Jerry Springer*, which regularly runs episodes with titles like "My Girlfriend's a Guy" and "I'm Really a Man!" that feature trans women coming out to their straight boyfriends. On a recent British TV reality show called *There's Something About Miriam*, six heterosexual men court an attractive woman who, unbeknownst to them, is transsexual. The broadcast of the show was delayed for several months because the men threatened to sue the show's producers, alleging that they had been the victims of defamation, personal injury, and conspiracy to commit sexual assault. The affair was eventually settled out of court, with each man coming away with a reported 125,000 British pounds (over 200,000 U.S. dollars at the time).[1]

In the 1970 film adaptation of Gore Vidal's novel *Myra Breckinridge*, the protagonist is a trans woman who heads out to Hollywood in order to take revenge on traditional manhood and to "realign the sexes." This "realignment" apparently involves raping an ex-football player with a strap-on dildo, which she does at one point during the movie. The recurring theme of "deceptive" trans women retaliating against men, often by seducing them, seems to be an unconscious acknowledgment that both male and heterosexual privilege is threatened by transsexuals.

In contrast to the "deceivers," who wield their feminine wiles with success, the "pathetic transsexual" characters aren't deluding anyone. Despite her masculine mannerisms and five o'clock shadow, the "pathetic transsexual" will inevitably insist that she is a woman trapped inside a man's body. The intense contradiction between the "pathetic" character's gender identity and her physical appearance is often played for laughs—as in the transition of musician Mark Shubb (played as a bearded baritone by Harry Shearer) at the conclusion of 2003's *A Mighty Wind*.

Unlike the "deceivers," whose ability to "pass" is a serious threat to our culture's ideas about gender and sexuality, "pathetic transsexuals"—who barely resemble women at all—are generally considered harmless. Perhaps for this reason, some of the most endearing pop culture portrayals of trans women fall into the "pathetic" category: John Lithgow's Oscar-nominated portrayal of ex-football player Roberta Muldoon in 1982's *The World According to Garp*, and Terence Stamp's role as the aging showgirl Bernadette in 1994's *The Adventures of Priscilla, Queen of the Desert*. More recently, the 1998 indie film *The Adventures of Sebastian Cole* begins with its teenage protagonist learning that his stepdad Hank, who looks and acts like a roadie for a '70s rock band, is about to become Henrietta. A sympathetic character and the only stable person in Sebastian's life, Henrietta spends most of the movie wearing floral-print nightgowns and bare-shouldered tops with tons of jewelry and makeup. Yet despite her extremely femme manner of dress, she continues to exhibit only stereotypical male behaviors, overtly ogling a waitress and punching out a guy who calls her a "faggot" (after which she laments, "I broke a nail").

In the case of Henrietta, this extreme combination of masculinity and femininity does not seem designed to challenge audiences' assumptions about maleness and femaleness. On the contrary, Henrietta's masculine voice and mannerisms are meant to demonstrate that, despite her desire to be female, she cannot change the fact that she is really and truly a man. As with *Garp's* Roberta and *Priscilla's* Bernadette, the audience is encouraged to respect Henrietta as a person, but not as a woman. While we are supposed to admire their courage—which presumably comes from the difficulty of living as women who do not appear very female—we are not meant to identify with them or to be sexually attracted to them, as we are to "deceivers" like Dil.

Interestingly, while the obvious outward masculinity of "pathetic transsexual" characters is always played up, so too is their lack of male genitalia (or their desire to part with them). In fact, some of the most memorable lines in these movies are uttered when the "pathetic transsexual" character makes light of her own castration. At one point during *Priscilla*, Bernadette remarks that her parents never spoke to her again, "after [she] had the chop." In *Garp*, when a man is injured while receiving a blow job during a car accident, Roberta delivers the one-liner, "I had mine removed surgically under general anesthesia, but to have it bitten off in a Buick . . ." In the 1994 fictionalized biography *Ed Wood*, Bill Murray plays another "pathetic transsexual," Bunny Breckinridge. After seeing Wood's film *Glen or Glenda*, Bunny is inspired to go to Mexico to have a "sex change," announcing to Wood, "Your movie made me realize I've got to take action. Goodbye, penis!"

The "pathetic" transsexual's lighthearted comments about having her penis lopped off come in stark contrast to the revelation of the "deceiver," who is generally found out by someone else in an embarrassing, often violent way. A Freudian might suggest that the "deceptive" transsexual's dangerous nature is symbolized by the presence of a hidden penis, while the "pathetic" transsexual's harmlessness is due to a lack thereof. A less phallic interpretation is that the very act of "passing" makes any trans woman who can do so into a "deceiver." Ultimately, both "deceptive" and "pathetic" transsexual characters are designed to validate the popular assumption that trans women are truly men. "Pathetic" transsexuals may want to be female, but their masculine appearances and mannerisms always give them away. And while the "deceiver" is initially perceived to be a "real" female, she is eventually revealed as a wolf in sheep's clothing—an illusion that is the product of lies and modern medical technology—and she is usually punished accordingly.

## THE FASCINATION WITH "FEMINIZATION"

In virtually all depictions of trans women, whether real or fictional, "deceptive" or "pathetic," the underlying assumption is that the trans woman wants to achieve a stereotypically feminine appearance and gender role. The possibility that trans women are even capable of making a distinction between identifying as female and wanting to cultivate a hyperfeminine image is never raised. In fact, the media often dwells on the specifics of the feminization process, showing trans women putting on their feminine exteriors. It's telling that TV, film, and news producers tend not to be satisfied with merely showing trans women wearing feminine clothes and makeup. Rather, it is their intent to capture trans women *in the act* of putting on lipstick, dresses, and high heels, thereby giving the audience the impression that the trans woman's femaleness is an artificial mask or costume.

An excellent example of this phenomenon is *Transamerica* (2005), a "buddy" road-trip movie pairing up trans woman Bree Osbourne (played by Felicity Huffman) with a son that she was previously unaware she had. In the opening five minutes of the film, we see Bree practicing along with the instructional video *Finding Your Female Voice,* putting on stockings, padding her bra, donning a pink dress suit, painting her nails (also pink), and putting on lipstick, eye shadow, powder, and other cosmetics. This scene (not coincidentally) is immediately followed by the first dialogue in the movie, where Bree tells a psychiatrist that she's been on hormone replacement therapy for three years, has undergone electrolysis, feminine facial surgery, a brow-lift, forehead reduction, jaw recontouring, and a tracheal shave. This opening flurry of cosmetic and medical feminization is clearly designed to establish that Bree's female identity is artificial and imitative, and to reduce her transition to the mere pursuit of feminine finery.

Throughout the rest of the film, feminine apparel and cosmetics are repeatedly used as a device to highlight Bree's fakeness. There are excessive scenes in which Bree is shown in the act of dressing and undressing, as though her clothing represented some kind of costume. We also see her applying and fixing her makeup nearly every chance she gets, and it is difficult not to view the thick layers of foundation she constantly wears as a mask that is hiding the "real" (undoubtedly more masculine) Bree underneath. While many MTF crossdressers often wear heavy makeup to cover up their beard shadow, a trans woman like Bree—who has already undergone electrolysis and been on hormones for three years—would not need to do this. Indeed, the fact that her foundation begins to develop a sheen from perspiration at several points in the movie, and that she stumbles in her high heels on more than one occasion—faux pas that never seem to afflict cissexual women in Hollywood—makes it clear that the filmmakers purposely used these female accessories as props to portray Bree as "doing female" rather badly. And they certainly succeeded, as Felicity Huffman comes off seeming infinitely more contrived than the several real-life trans women (such as Andrea James and Calpernia Addams) who appear briefly in the film.

The media's willingness to indulge the audience's fascination with the surface trappings that accompany the feminization of "men" also tarnishes nonfiction and serious attempts to tell the stories of trans women. For example, the 2004 *New York Times* article "As Repression Eases, More Iranians Change Their Sex" is not sensationalistic, describing the rise of transsexual rights in Iran.[2] Yet, one of the two photos that accompany the piece depicts an Iranian trans woman putting on lipstick. In 2003, *The Oprah Winfrey Show* aired a two-part special on transsexual women and their wives. The entire first episode featured a one-on-one interview with Jennifer Finney Boylan, author of the autobiography *She's Not There: A Life in Two Genders.* While Oprah Winfrey's conversation with Boylan was respectful and serious, the show nonetheless opened with predictable scenes of women putting on eye makeup, lipstick, and shoes, and the interview itself was interspersed with "before" pictures of Boylan, as if to constantly remind us that she's really a man underneath it all.

Mass media images of "biological males" dressing and acting in a feminine manner could potentially challenge mainstream notions of gender, but the way they are generally presented in these feminization scenes ensures that this never happens. The media neutralizes the potential threat that trans femininities pose to the category of "woman" by playing to the audience's subconscious belief that femininity itself is artificial. After all, while most people assume that women are naturally feminine, they also (rather hypocritically) require them to spend an hour or two each day putting on their faces and getting all dressed up in order to meet societal standards for femininity (unlike men, whose masculinity is presumed to come directly from who he *is* and what he *does*). In fact, it's the assumption that femininity is inherently "contrived," "frivolous," and "manipulative" that allows masculinity to always come off as "natural," "practical," and "sincere" by comparison.

Thus, the media is able to depict trans women donning feminine attire and accessories without ever giving the impression that they achieve "true" femaleness in the process. Further, by focusing on the most feminine of artifices, the media evokes the idea that trans women are living out some sort of sexual fetish. This sexualization of trans women's motives for transitioning not only belittles trans women's female identities, but encourages the objectification of women as a whole.

Of course, what always goes unseen are the great lengths to which producers will go to depict lurid and superficial scenes in which trans women get all dolled up in pretty clothes and cosmetics. Shawna Virago, a San Francisco trans activist, musician, and director of the Tranny Fest film festival, has experienced several such incidents with local news producers. For instance, when Virago was organizing a forum to facilitate communication between police and the trans community, a newspaper reporter approached her and other transgender activists to write an article about them. However, the paper was interested not in their politics but in their transitions. "They wanted each of us to include 'before' and 'after' pictures," Shawna said. "This pissed me off, and I tried to explain to the writer that the before-and-after stuff had nothing to do with police abuse and other issues, like trans women and HIV, but he didn't get it. So I was cut from the piece."

A few years later, someone from another paper contacted Virago and asked to photograph her "getting ready" to go out: "I told him I didn't think having a picture of me rolling out of bed and hustling to catch [the bus] would make for a compelling photo. He said, 'You know, getting pretty, putting on makeup.' I refused, but they did get a trans woman who complied, and there she was, putting on mascara and lipstick and a pretty dress, none of which had anything to do with the article, which was purportedly about political and social challenges the trans community faced."[3]

Trans woman Nancy Nangeroni and her partner Gordene O. MacKenzie, who together host the radio program *GenderTalk,* described two similar incidents on one of their programs. In both cases, while they were being filmed, the media producers wanted to get footage of the two of them putting on makeup together (requests that Nangeroni and MacKenzie denied).[4] I myself had a similar experience back in 2001, just before I began taking hormones. A friend arranged for me to meet with someone who was doing a film about the transgender movement. The filmmaker was noticeably disappointed when I showed up looking like a somewhat normal guy, wearing a T-shirt, jeans, and sneakers. She eventually asked me if I would mind putting on lipstick while she filmed me. I told her that wearing lipstick had nothing to do with the fact that I was transgender or that I identified as female. She shot a small amount of footage anyway (sans lipstick) and said she would get in touch with me if she decided to use any of it. I never heard back from her.

When audiences watch scenes of trans women putting on skirts and makeup, they are not necessarily seeing a reflection of the values of those trans women; they are witnessing TV, film, and news producers' obsessions with all objects commonly associated with female sexuality. In other words, the media's and audience's fascination with the feminization of trans women is a by-product of their sexualization of all women.

## THE MEDIA'S TRANSGENDER GAP

There is most certainly a connection between the differing values given to women and men in our culture and the media's fascination with depicting trans women rather than trans men, who were born female but identify as male. Although the number of people transitioning in each direction is relatively equal these days, media coverage would have us believe there is a huge disparity in the populations of trans men and women.[5]

Jamison Green, a trans man who authored a 1994 report that led to the city of San Francisco's decision to extend its civil rights protections to include gender identity, once said this about the media coverage of that event: "Several times at the courthouse, when the press was doing interviews, I stood by and listened as reporters inquired who wrote the report, and when I was pointed out to them as the author I could see them looking right through me, looking past me to find the man in a dress who must have written the report and whom they would want to interview. More than once a reporter asked me incredulously, 'You wrote the report?' They assumed that because of my 'normal' appearance that I wouldn't be newsworthy."[6]

Indeed, the media tends to not notice—or to outright ignore—trans men because they are unable to sensationalize them the way they do trans women without bringing masculinity itself into question. And in a world where modern psychology was founded upon the teaching that all young girls suffer from penis envy, most people think striving for masculinity seems like a perfectly reasonable goal. Author and sex activist Patrick Califia, who is a trans man, addresses this in his 1997 book *Sex Changes: The Politics of Transgenderism*: "It seems the world is still more titillated by 'a man who wants to become a woman' than it is by 'a woman who wants to become a man.' The first is scandalous, the latter is taken for granted. This reflects the very different levels of privilege men and women have in our society. Of course women want to be men, the general attitude seems to be, and of course they can't. And that's that."[7]

Once we recognize how media coverage of transsexuals is informed by the different values our society assigns to femaleness and maleness, it becomes obvious that virtually all attempts to sensationalize and deride trans women are built on a foundation of unspoken misogyny. Since most people cannot fathom why someone would give up male privilege and power in order to become a relatively disempowered female, they assume that trans women transition primarily as a way of obtaining the one type of power that women are perceived to have in our society: the ability to express femininity and to attract men.

This is why trans women like myself, who rarely dress in an overly feminine manner and/or who are not attracted to men, are such an enigma to many people. By assuming that my desire to be female is merely some sort of femininity fetish or sexual perversion, they are essentially making the case that women have no worth beyond the extent to which they can be sexualized.

## FEMINIST DEPICTIONS OF TRANS WOMEN

There are numerous parallels between the way trans women are depicted in the media and the way that they have been portrayed by some feminist theorists. While many feminists—especially younger ones who came of age in the 1980s and 1990s—recognize that trans women can be allies in the fight to eliminate gender stereotypes, other feminists—particularly those who embrace gender essentialism—believe that trans women foster sexism by mimicking patriarchal attitudes about femininity, or that we objectify women by trying to possess female bodies of our own. Many of these latter ideas stem from Janice G. Raymond's 1979 book *The Transsexual Empire: The Making of the She-Male*, which is perhaps the most influential feminist writing on transsexuals. Like the media, Raymond virtually ignores trans men, dismissing them as "tokens," and instead focuses almost exclusively on trans women, insisting that they transition in order to achieve stereotypical femininity. She even argues that "most transsexuals conform more to the feminine role than even the most feminine of natural-born women."[8] This fact does not surprise Raymond, since she believes that femininity itself is an artificial by-product of a patriarchal society. So despite the fact that trans women may attain femininity, Raymond does not believe that they become "real" women. (To emphasize this, she refers to trans women as "male-to-constructed-females" and addresses them with masculine pronouns throughout the book.) Thus, Raymond builds her case by relying on the same tactics as the media: She depicts trans women as hyperfeminine (in order to make their female identities appear highly artificial) and she hyper-sexualizes them (by playing down the existence of trans people who transition to male).

Unlike the media, Raymond does acknowledge the existence of trans women who are not stereotypically feminine, albeit reluctantly. She writes, "I have been very hesitant about devoting a chapter of this book to what I call the 'transsexually constructed lesbian-feminist.'"[9] Because she believes that lesbian-feminists represent "a small percentage of transsexuals" (a claim that she never verifies), she does not seem inclined to discuss their existence at all except for the "recent debate and divisiveness [the subject] produced within feminist circles."[10] Being that Raymond believes that femininity undermines women's true worth, you might think that she would be open to trans women who denounce femininity and patriarchal gender stereotypes. However, this is not the case. Instead, she argues, "As the male-to-constructed-female transsexual exhibits the attempt to possess women in a bodily sense while acting out the images into which men have molded women, the male-to-constructed-female who claims to be a lesbian-feminist attempts to possess women at a deeper level."[11] Throughout the rest of the chapter, she discusses how lesbian-feminist trans women use "deception" in order to "penetrate" women's spaces and minds. She says, "although the transsexually constructed lesbian-feminist does not exhibit a feminine identity and role, he does exhibit stereotypical masculine behavior."[12] This essentially puts trans women in a double bind: If they act feminine they are perceived as being a parody, but if they act masculine it is seen as a sign of their true male identity. This damned-if-they-do, damned-if-they-don't tactic is reminiscent of the pop cultural "deceptive"/"pathetic" transsexual archetypes. Both Raymond and the media ensure that trans women—whether they are feminine or masculine, whether they "pass" or not—will invariably come off as "fake" women no matter how they look or act.

While much of *The Transsexual Empire* is clearly over the top (the premise of the book is that "biological woman is in the process of being made obsolete by bio-medicine"), many of Raymond's arguments are echoed in contemporary attempts to justify the exclusion of trans women from women's organizations and spaces. In fact, the world's largest annual women-only event, the Michigan Womyn's Music Festival (often referred to simply as "Michigan"), still enforces a "womyn-born-womyn"-only policy that is specifically designed to prevent trans women from attending.[13] Many of the excuses used to rationalize trans women's exclusion are not designed to protect the values of women-only space, but rather to reinforce the idea that trans women are "real" men and "fake" women. For example, one of the most cited reasons that trans women are not allowed in the festival is that we are born with, and many of us still have, penises (many trans women either cannot afford to or choose not to have sex reassignment surgery). It is argued that our penises are dangerous because they are a symbol of male oppression and have the potential to trigger women who have been sexually assaulted or abused by men. So penises are banned from the festival, right? Well, not quite: The festival does allow women to purchase and use dildos, strap-ons, and packing devices, many of which closely resemble penises. So phalluses in and of themselves are not so bad, just so long as they are not attached to a trans woman.

Another reason frequently given for the exclusion of trans women from Michigan is that we supposedly would bring "male energy" into the festival. While this seems to imply that expressions of masculinity are not allowed, nothing could be further from the truth. Michigan allows drag king performers who dress and act male, and the festival stage has featured several female-bodied performers who identify as transgender and sometimes describe themselves with male pronouns.[14] Presumably, Lisa Vogel (who is sole proprietor of the festival) allows this because she believes that no person who is born female is capable of exhibiting authentic masculinity or "male energy." Not only is this an insult to trans men (as it suggests that they can never be fully masculine or male), but it implies that "male energy" can be measured in some way independent of whether the person expressing it appears female or male. This is clearly not the case. Even though I am a trans woman, I have never been accused of expressing "male energy," because people *perceive* me as a woman. When I do act in a "masculine" way, people describe me as a "tomboy" or "butch," and if I get aggressive or argumentative, people call me a "bitch." My behaviors are still the same; it is only the context of my body (whether people see me as female or male) that has changed.

This is the inevitable problem with all attempts to portray trans women as "fake" females (whether media or feminist in origin): They require one to give different names, meanings, and values to the same behaviors depending on whether the person in question was born with a female or male body (or whether they are perceived to be a woman or a man). In other words, they require one to be sexist. When people insist that there are essential differences between women and men, they further a line of reasoning that ultimately refutes feminist ideals rather than supporting them.

From my own experience in having transitioned from one sex to the other, I have found that women and men are not separated by an insurmountable chasm, as many people seem to believe. Actually, most of us are only a hormone prescription away from being perceived as the "opposite" sex. Personally, I welcome this idea as a testament to just how little difference there really is between women and men. To believe that a woman is a woman because of her sex chromosomes, reproductive organs, or socialization denies the reality that every single day, we classify each person we see as either female or male based on a small number of visual cues and a ton of assumption. The one thing that women share is that we are all *perceived* as women and treated accordingly. As a feminist, I look forward to a time when we finally move beyond the idea that biology is destiny, and recognize that the most important differences that exist between women and men in our society are the different meanings that we place onto one another's bodies.

## NOTES

1. Steve Rogers, "Lawsuit Settled, 'Crying Game'–Like 'There's Something About Miriam' Premieres in UK," RealityTVWorld.com, February 23, 2004; Debi Enker, "Reality Reaches New Low," *The Age,* May 20, 2004; Emily Smith, "Miriam's Secret," *The Sun Online* (www.thesun.co.uk).
2. Nazila Fathi, "As Repression Eases, More Iranians Change Their Sex," *New York Times,* August 2, 2004.
3. Shawna Virago, in correspondence with author, April 12, 2004.
4. Nancy Nangeroni and Gordene O. MacKenzie, in conversation on *GenderTalk,* program 538, November 26, 2005 (www.gendertalk.com/real/500/gt538.shtml).
5. Meyerowitz, *How Sex Changed,* 9, 148, 276–277; Califia, *Sex Changes,* 61.
6. As quoted in Califia, *Sex Changes,* 239.
7. Ibid., 178. It should be noted that Pat Califia and Patrick Califia are the same person; he is a trans man, and I refer to him as Patrick Califia, the name he currently uses, throughout the text. In the notes section, I use whichever name appears on the book that I am citing.
8. Raymond, *The Transsexual Empire,* 79.
9. Ibid., 99.
10. Ibid., 100.
11. Ibid., 99.
12. Ibid., xix.
13. Lisa Vogel, "Michigan Womyn's Music Festival Sets the Record 'Straight,'" press release issued by Lisa Vogel, August 22, 2006.
14. Anderson-Minshall, "Michigan Or Bust"; Sarah Liss, "Politics of Pussy: Bitch and Animal on a Revolutionary Gender-Bender," *Now* (Toronto), July 25, 2002.

# 19

## *The Education of Little Cis*
### Cisgender and the Discipline of Opposing Bodies

A. FINN ENKE

IN THIS ARTICLE, TRANSFEMINIST HISTORIAN A. FINN ENKE reflects on the history of attempts in North American activist communities and higher-education contexts to name the difference between trans people and others. S/he does so by giving an account of the prefix "cis-" which was first proposed in 1994 as a handy term for marking the trans/not-trans distinction. Although Enke has found cis- to be pedagogically useful in conversations about social privilege based on gender normativity, after nearly two decades of teaching trans issues in the classroom s/he has concluded that insisting on a clear cis-/trans- dichotomy creates more problems than it solves. Enke draws on disability studies, critical whiteness studies, and queer feminism to show how the privileges associated with legible, coherent, and persistent gender markers (as well as the vulnerabilities associated with their absence) are the effects of multiple intersecting systems of body-regulation; they cannot be located in, or limited to, two qualities defined by "cis-" and "trans-". One particularly instructive section of the article is an auto-ethnographic account in which Enke writes of hir own positioning athwart cis-/trans- divides, and enacting a principled refusal to say what s/he "really" is.

I am trying to assess campus climates for the transgender community.... Issues of interest are transphobia, hostility, general knowledge and understanding, attitudes of the queer community and cisgendered people, etc.

(Dana Leland Defosse, 1994)

I just kept running into the problem of what to call non-trans people in various discussions, and one day it just hit me: non-trans equals cis. Therefore, cisgendered.

(Carl Buijs, 1996)

In other words, it's the opposite of transgender.... So why are y'all tripping, cisgender people? Cisgender isn't an insult.

(Monica Roberts, *TransGriot*, 2009)

Biologist Dana Leland Defosse is generally credited as the first person to put the neologism "cisgender" (based on the Latin root "cis-", which prefixes things that stay put or do not change property) into public circulation in 1994, using it in a Web-based call for research on campus climate and transgender subjectivities (quoted in the epigraph above). Defosse explained at the time why cis- might serve as a linguistic complement to trans-. Within molecular biology, cis- is used as a prefix (as in cis-acting) to describe something that acts from the same molecule (intramolecular), in contrast to trans-acting things that act from different molecules (intermolecular); in organic chemistry, cis- refers to substituents or groups that are oriented in the same direction, in contrast to trans-, wherein the substituents are oriented in opposing directions. Defosse—followed by others—saw the potential of cisgender to describe the condition of staying with birth-assigned sex, or congruence between birth-assigned sex and gender identity. Nowadays, cisgender commonly implies staying within certain gender parameters (however they may be defined) rather than crossing (or trans-ing) those parameters.

But cisgender does not stay put. It is even now traversing contexts, and—like genders and many other substituents—it is changing in the crossing. Cisgender is still only sparsely used in trans* communities across the country;[1] nevertheless, the word is seeing new life on college campuses, particularly within student organizations and classrooms that critically interrogate the categories of gender. Cisgender's migrations can tell us about the power of language to transform gender politics and queer alliances, for better or worse. Specifically, the term appears to encourage investments in a gender stability that undermines feminist, trans*, queer, and related movements.

Although I had offered the terms cisgender and cissexual as conceptual tools in my undergraduate gender and sexuality courses as early as the mid-1990s, they had too much of a subcultural "insider" feel at that time to be democratically adopted in the classroom. I was surprised, then, around 2008, when an increasing number of queer-savvy students began to casually toss "cis" into their classroom comments. They used such phrases as "she's cis," or, "the cis man in the film said...," or, "as a cis woman, I...." Required to explain for the benefit of the class, they typically defined "cis" along these lines: "cis is short for cisgender, which is non-trans." A more elaborate explanation often included, "You are cisgender if your gender identity matches your sex, the sex you were assigned at birth."[2] Subsequent conversations occasionally problematized such definitions but rarely led to doubt about the *use* of the word. On the contrary, even critical conversations about cisgender had the effect of educating students who had not known the word in how to become disciplined users.

What role is cis playing here, and how can we understand its market value in this context? This deserves some explanation, not least because the term does have its share of detractors. In 2009, *TransGriot* blogger Monica Roberts suggested that it is people who are not transgender who object to the word; in her analysis, "cisgender people" feel insulted by the word "cisgender" because transgender (i.e. stigmatized minority) people dare to name and to *other* them.[3] It is also clear that many people object to being interpellated as cis because cis is generally conflated with normativity, and they do not think of themselves that way. More recently, trans* people have become the most vocal critics of cisgender.[4] Although trans activism initiated discourses of cis, the word's broader uptake may be an effect not of trans activism in itself, but rather a particular expression of ally desire. In the classroom, people bring cisgender into being as a performative ally-identity, explicitly reserving the term "trans" for others. It is all the more pressing, then, to analyze the campus and classroom context, because it reveals troubling contradictions behind the adoption of cis.

In this article, I first elucidate the discursive uptake of cis, emphasizing its use within social-movement contexts and the Queer-Studies classroom.[5] I offer a critique through the lens of trans, queer, disability, and feminist—what I call transfeminist—theory and politics. The performative uptake of cis should invite questions about its cultural value not just to classrooms but to the multidiscipline of gender and women's studies as a whole.[6] Cisgender may hold appeal for maintaining gender and women's studies as an arena that produces and disciplines "women" and "men" as self-evident categories, contrary to gender and women's studies' more radical potentials. How troubling: just when queer and trans theory remind us that gender and sex are made and have no a priori stability ("one is not born a woman"), cisgender arrives to affirm not only that it is possible for one to *stay* "a woman" but also that one *is* "born a woman" after all.

*[handwritten: crucial → works against the theoretical project by definition]*

## THE GENEALOGY OF CIS

The history of cisgender begins with transgender activism. Transgender and transsexual activism has a long history in North America, but in the early 1990s, a transgender liberation movement by that name came into its own with a groundswell of concerted action that had momentum and staying power. At that time, "transgender" was most broadly conceived to encompass "the whole spectrum" of gender non-normative practices, communities, and identities.[7] The transgender liberation movement was to recognize and to address the connections among many different forms of gender-based oppressions and the economic, nationalist, and racist structures that buttress those oppressions; simultaneously, it would forge alliance among *all* the diverse gender-variant communities and identities that arise out of such oppressions.[8] Transgender signaled dissident politics and a positive embrace of new possibilities. As Currah, Green, and Stryker put it, transgender

> was meant to convey the sense that one could live non-pathologically in a social gender not typically associated with one's biological sex, as well as the sense that a single individual should be free to combine elements of different gender styles and presentations, or different sex/gender combinations... [I]t represented a resistance to medicalization, to pathologization, and to the many mechanisms whereby the administrative state and its associated medico-juridical-psychiatric institutions sought to contain and delimit the socially disruptive potentials of sex/gender non-normativity.[9]

Transgender also emerged as a politicized identity category, as activists sought to collectively instantiate social viability for gender variant persons. Transgender furthermore described individuals by what they *do*, as in Susan Stryker's articulation of transgender as "people who move away from the gender they were assigned at birth, people who cross over (trans-) the boundaries constructed by their culture to define and contain that gender."[10]

The term "cisgender" arose in the context of this groundswell, articulated most often by people who visibly crossed normative gender signifiers and/or experienced significant cross-gender identification. This naming made visceral sense, as the world indeed seems divided between trans and non-trans epistemologies. Within trans activist circles, non-normative gender variability is normalized: the array of things we do with our bodies, pronouns, names, and histories is a necessary (in measures both joyful and coerced) aspect of being human in a gendered society. In the 1990s, collectively attempting to clear a wider path, while faced with the inflexibilities of most social institutions, confirmed that "the public" was (and still is) an explicitly and often violently trans-exclusive and disenfranchising space. People who reject medico-juridical determinations of sex at birth or who in any other way occupy a less legibly male or female sex/gender comportment can attempt to buy access to social arenas: we can supply specific narratives to garner specific diagnoses to attempt to win a legal status that will allow the most privileged among us access to sex-segregated spaces, jobs, housing, and health care.[11] We need the exact right combination of *visible* "difference," passability *and* nonvisibility (a combination assisted by whiteness, abledness, legal citizenship, employment, and noncriminal status) to hope to be granted authenticity, transparency, and belonging within a chosen gender.[12]

The distinction between living a life in congruence with static medico-juridical determinations of one's sex/gender and living a life in defiance of that congruence is a highly consequential one, because our social institutions are structured to uphold and privilege the former. It is hard to overstate how dramatically sex/gender congruence, legibility, and consistency within a binary gender system buy a

*Privilege of congruency*

*pairing*

*cis*

privileged pass to social existence, particularly when accompanied by the appearance of normative race, class, ability, and nationality. The term "cisgender" was to name that privileged pass.

As the name of normative privilege, cisgender characterized the transphobic institutions and the everyday practices of a stunningly trans-ignorant and willfully normative public. Simultaneously, the word purported to challenge the naturalization of "woman" and "man" by making visible their rootedness in the interested achievement of social hierarchies, thereby also exposing the non-natural privileges and exclusions gained by successfully performing them. The word "cisgender" spread as a strategy of social critique that resonated with similar strategies from feminism, critical race theory, whiteness studies, and dis/ability rights, among other arenas of radical politics. Utilizing this familiar style of theoretical and political intervention, cisgender was able to move outside as well as within trans communities. As Emi Koyama, an activist author who works for intersex, trans, disability, race, and class justice, put it in 2002:

> I learned the words "cissexual," "cissexist," and "cisgender," from trans activists who wanted to turn the table and define the words that describe non-transsexuals and non-transgenders rather than always being defined and described by them. By using the term "cissexual" and "cisgender," they de-centralize the dominant group, exposing it as merely one possible alternative rather than the "norm" against which trans people are defined. I don't expect the word to come into common usage anytime soon, but I felt it was an interesting concept—a feminist one, in fact—which is why I am using it.[13]

In 2002, Koyama did not expect the "common" adoption of cisgender "any time soon," but by signing the statement, "In Cisterhood," Koyama invited broader, allied use of the terms "cisgender" and "cissexual."

Related to all the previous factors, cisgender additionally emerged as a critique of the way that queer and LGBT organizations often define "queer" and "LGBT" by dissident sexual desires and *not also* by gender variance. The pointed use of the acronym "LGB *not* T" critically makes explicit the actual exclusions of purportedly "LGBT" arenas: although LG(B) and queer groups may fetishize gender fluidity and non-normativity while tokenizing transgender people, very few embrace trans politics as an integral and essential priority.[14] In this context, cisgender became a way of distinguishing queers who do not have trans histories, identities, and perspectives from trans people who do. Koyama thus spoke to a small but growing movement of people who would make cisgender a political act that could be hailed by queer sympaticos of all kinds.

*crucial*

Cisgender (or cis) became a more common enculturated word and identity category, particularly among some activist communities that interface with academics.[15] Neoliberal rights discourses that feed on identity politics further promoted the sense that people are *either* transgender *or* cisgender; cisgender, that is, did not simply name privilege, but also could be used to describe individuals.

*crucial Neoliberal discourse*

Widely accessible texts, such as Julia Serano's *Whipping Girl* (2007), also helped authorize cis identifications. Foremost a treatise on transsexual politics and the misogyny that undergirds transphobia, *Whipping Girl* is the first book to elaborate cisgender and cissexual privilege. Serano defines cissexual as "people who are not transsexual and who have only ever experienced their physical and subconscious sexes as being aligned"; cisgender more simply refers to "people who are not transgender."[16] If not lost, the distinction Serano implicitly draws between cisgender and cissexual allows nuance: people can be cissexual but not necessarily cisgender. One could feel congruence with one's assigned body sex and thus consider one's self cissexual but not identify with the gender that is typically associated with that sex and thus not be cisgender. Reading between the lines, gender-queer and transgender people who do not strongly identify with either part of the gender binary (maleness *or* femaleness) might not experience trans*sex*-ness or cis*gender*-ness, as *both* cisgender and transsexual suggest primary identification with one sex/gender in a binary

*cis variability* (margin note)

system (male or female). In theory, this suggests variability within cis-ness, just as there is variation within transness.[17]

Serano's critique of cissexual privilege, much like critiques of race privilege, ableism, and heteronormativity, successfully brings attention to the ways that people construct normative hierarchies through everyday behaviors. Her initial definition of cissexual privilege as "the double standard that promotes the idea that transsexual genders are distinct from, and less legitimate than, cissexual genders" names one fundamental root of the transphobia that undergirds most social institutions. Cissexual privilege is instantiated in part through the activity of "reading" and assigning male or female sex/gender to others. All people make assumptions about other's sex/gender, "whether we are cissexual or transsexual, straight as an arrow, or queer as a three-dollar bill."[18] But one privilege of cissexuality is that it performs as the arbiter of real, true, or natural gender. Cissexuality by definition is rarely required to, but can always legally and socially prove itself; as such, it serves to judge the realness or legitimacy of all people's sex/gender. Cissexual privilege is authorized in part through connected practices: a) assuming everyone is cissexual (erasure of trans existence), b) demanding that trans men and women come out as trans rather than simply as men and women, and, simultaneously, c) requiring that transsexual men and women "pass" or "be believable to others as" the sex/gender they "claim to be" to make their trans-sex more palatable to people who feel that birth-assigned sex/gender is the only legitimate (true) sex/gender.[19] Serano's discussion effectively invites readers to see how the presumption that sex/gender is transparent naturalizes binary gender construction and pathologizes transgender existences; moreover, sexism and misogyny particularly pathologize all people on a feminine spectrum.

*reading bodies* (margin note)

*feminine in particular* (margin note)

*common reception of the text* (margin note)

This is the kind of "eye-opening" that many students in a gender or sexuality course find satisfying: to see and to name systemic oppressions. In my experience, however, non-trans students assume the book is about someone else (transsexuals) who face an entirely foreign set of oppressions, and therefore it cannot also be about the very same sexism, misogyny, and binary gender system that they learn to analyze in Women's Studies 101. Neither do readers tend to see themselves in the generalizations about how cissexuals think and feel. But some—in effort to *not be* the kind of transphobic or trans-ignorant "cissexual people" critiqued in the book—may take up the ally mantle and "own" their privilege as "cis" people.

The uptake of cis among students in university contexts is also inspired by its use in community educational spaces, such as Camp Trans, in part because such spaces confirm the word's subcultural authenticity. Camp Trans is a week-long protest staged annually down the road from the Michigan Womyn's Music Festival (MWMF).[20] As a physical site comprising workshops, speeches, reports, performances, community-building activities, and direct actions, and as a generator of its own and related Web sites, blogs, and YouTube posts, its influence extends far beyond its temporal and geographic location.

Among the many productive outcomes of Camp Trans is that it began with insistence on self-identification, which was and is a fundamental tenet of trans activism: people's gender identity must be respected, regardless of how they may appear.[21] Camp Trans also generated some of the earliest articulations of the classism and racism embedded in the use of surgical status as a criterion for passable gender status. Emphasis on people's surgical status has frequently accompanied considerations of exclusion/inclusion policies in "women-only" community spaces; as one of the most well-known women-only spaces, MWMF occasioned some of the first critiques of the relationship among racism, classism, and transphobic definitions of women.[22]

Over the last decade, the term "cis" has gained platform at Camp Trans. The use of cisgender in this context, acting as it does in binary opposition to trans*, seems to cause an unfortunate amnesia of prior lessons about the relationship between binary gender and race and class hierarchies. As is

*amnesiatic* (margin note)

true elsewhere, use of the term "cis" has not generally been subject to race, ability, and class analysis; instead, its use reinforces gender as a self-evident, autonomous category. *which is not entirely accurate*

As do many trans* spaces, Camp Trans makes explicit its intended constituency. Before elaborating its "Inclusion" and "Exclusion" policies, the Camp Trans Web site offers a "note on wording":

> Used on this page, please consider "trans" to be the broadest possible usage of the word, commonly written as "trans*" to include people who self-identify as trans, transgender, transsexual, transcending the gender binary, transvestite, and gender queer…. Similarly, as used here, "cis" is to be taken with the broadest possible definition, to include anyone not identifying under the umbrella usage of "trans."[23]

The suggestive list following trans* is meant to be elaborated into "the broadest possible" range of trans identities. Cis is identically broad, perhaps ironically, as seemingly none of the above. *Dominant as a category, of N/A*

The Inclusion/Exclusion policy disciplines by positing cis people as the sole agents of cisgender privilege. According to the Inclusion policy ("who is camp for?"), "Camp is secondarily a place where trans and genderqueer people are centralized. This does not mean that cis people are not allowed at Camp at all, but it does mean that Camp is not set up to play to the privilege cis people experience."[24] The Exclusion policy (under the heading, "who shouldn't come to camp?") states, "A cis person who wants to learn about trans and genderqueer people. A cis person who does not understand concepts of gender privilege and oppression. Please note that this applies to cis partners of trans people coming to Camp as well."[25] These statements have been important to the preservation of Camp Trans as a space for trans organizing. Furthermore, such guidelines instruct insiders and outsiders in basic respect for Camp Trans as a trans-centric space that gains its vulnerable efficacy from its education and outreach mission, its proximity to MWMF, and its high profile to people seeking "real-life" queer classrooms. *pedagogical concerns*

Such statements contribute to cis's appeal as an ally-identity in college classrooms: the term offers a certain cultural capital to those who are close enough to trans contexts not only to imbibe vocabularies but also to be able and willing to address gender privilege and oppression outside trans-literate contexts. *ally*

But we must see that the compulsion to name cis (as that which is not trans) demonstrates that the difference between trans and non-trans mobilities is far more concrete in our everyday lives than the rather elastic distance between male and female. *elasticity of "cis"*

In an effort to restore some nuance, Defosse generously reentered the fray on the Web in 2006: "As a biologist, I simply used the prefix cis as the complement to that of trans. In the simplest interpretation, cis means on the same side and trans means across. *Cis and trans are not just where something is, however; they extend to the realms of their respective effects.*"[26] Here, rather than being fixed in identities, cis and trans describe locations and effects. This is a critical point. Trans studies scholars have noted the extent to which trans invokes a person's (or body's) orientation in space and time.[27] Cis theoretically must also be *effected through* time and space, despite the presumption of stasis. Furthermore, cisgender's value from a social-movement perspective comes from the recognition and denaturalization of its powerful *effects*. *effects* *temporality and positionality*

Notwithstanding claims that cis is simply "the opposite of transgender" in some neutral way, its effects are inextricably associated with transphobia. *Transgriot* Monica Roberts's claim that calling people cisgender "is not an insult" thus rings rather untrue; it seems that the best cis can hope for is ally status. Cautionary reminders about the costs of identity politics have held little sway, as cis becomes a subject position in the performance of allyship. In the process, cis and trans both shrink, in exactly the way living things do when they desiccate and ossify.

## ENTER THE UNMARKED CIS-ALLY

From its social-movement origins, cisgender and simply cis wound their way into gender and women's studies' hallways, where they found audiences eager to understand and to confess their places in a world of hierarchies, violences, and privileges. Here, further organizing comes in the concept of ally and the practice of allyship education that is increasingly popular on college campuses and elsewhere. Related to antiracist education, allyship education speaks to the desire of some members of "majority communities" (e.g., white, heterosexual) to solve rather than to participate in the oppression, stigmatization, and marginalization of "minority communities" (e.g., people of color, gays, lesbians). Inherent to the concept of allyship is acknowledgment of the relative privilege of being seen as part of majority communities and also of the relationship between that privilege and the perpetuation or redress of injustice. Ally is a paradoxical identity, however, claiming simultaneous proximity to and distance from those of whom one becomes an ally.[28]

Increasingly popular trans ally trainings depart from antiracist and anti-oppression education in several respects.[29] As Vik DeMarco, Christoph Hanssmann, and others have rightly observed, white antiracist and anti-oppressive education emphasizes learning about and taking responsibility for one's racism and racial privilege; in contrast, trans ally trainings tend to take the form of "Trans 101," in which participants learn (usually in an hour or two) about the plight of the mysterious others we call transgendered. They are virtually never asked to consider their own transphobia or passing privilege.[30] Defining, tokenizing, and fetishizing transgender individuals according to their greater oppression, such education suggests absolute and *discernable* difference between trans and "everyone else," the presumptive majority. Trans allyship confirms not-trans identity by investing in a definition of trans as *someone else*, a more oppressed other. In just the way that "LGBT ally" effectively marks one as straight, "trans ally" is a discursive practice that resecures some portion of normativity.

The concept of cisgender *privilege* provides a necessary critique of structural hierarchies built around binary sex/gender, and it has the potential to intervene in the "Trans 101" model of allyship. However, such phrases as "as a gender-queer cis woman I...," or "the cis man in the film said..." don't simply acknowledge but in fact reinforce this privilege by enacting a distinction between cis and trans. Such speech invokes trans by its absence; and this absence is predicated on a definition of trans as a rare but visible embodiment of "cross-sex" identification. When cis is taken up as an admission of privileged identity, it is cis- privilege itself that reifies trans as most oppressed—so oppressed, in fact, that it cannot speak out of character.

And finally, one of the most repercussive limitations of the discursive production of cisgender is the lack of attention to the *multiple* hierarchies on which cis status depends. Although trans studies increasingly acknowledge the extent to which sex/gender is constituted through class hierarchies, racializations, nationalisms, ableisms, and so forth, cisgender has thus far remained impervious to theorizations of the multiple dimensions of dominance inherent to its privilege.[31] Cisgender privileges are surely most commonly conferred and achieved when the appearances of normative race, class, and ability are also achieved, along with a host of other normative mobilities. Scholars have shown that gender normativity is all but dependent on and reserved for whiteness, legal citizenship, and normative ability. David Valentine, Dean Spade, and others have also shown that the institutionalization of the term "transgender" inheres a history of race and class hierarchies and violences.[32] Cisgender then necessarily plays out as a normatively racialized ally status confirming its privilege through association with whiteness, legality, and ability. Can this be part of its appeal, even as people use the term in an attempt to critique systemic hierarchy?

## WILL THE REAL CIS PLEASE STAND UP?

How do we determine the distance between cis and trans, and at what point in time should this distance be measured? As someone who peed standing up as a child, who spent more than twenty years terrified that someone would discover that I was "really" male, and who passes almost consistently as a woman, I would hate to rely on the American Psychiatric Association's *Diagnostic and Statistical Manual of Mental Disorders* (DSM) to answer that question. For most of my lifetime, the DSM has used "rejection of urination in a sitting position" or "desire to urinate from a standing position" as one criterion toward the diagnosis of Childhood Gender Identity Disorder, but only when it occurs in children with vulvas; neither the desire nor the behavior are diagnostic when they occur in children with penises, because such children presumably *naturally* urinate standing up.[33]

In the summer of 2010, out of curiosity, I let my light beard grow in, and I was not sorry to find that it has thinned over the years. Writing now, I pause, because I know that all parts of that statement can signify a lot of different things depending on one's political persuasions, what one thinks of the relationship between beards and genders, and, more specifically, what is assumed about my body and my history. But as a historian, I want to say that history-making is a highly suspect business. Particularly when it comes to identity confirmation, narratives do their work by selectively collapsing time and place into the present through the use of undisrupted signifiers.[34] What must stay the same and what must change to determine the distance between cis and trans? Or, is it not the fact of changing but rather the *method* by which one changes that distinguishes cis from trans?

As an adolescent, I secretly began to interfere with my body's endogenous hormonal balance to inhibit certain (gender-laden) body changes and to encourage others—and I did so at some cost to my health. After five years, others ferreted this out, and I submitted (under duress but not force) to medical authority's technique of using exogenous hormones to "restore" a more stereotypical sex/gender endogenous hormonal balance (this, too, at some cost to my health). In my late twenties, I dispensed with the conventional medical program. I became a lesbian, and, for the first time in my life, I lost most of the fear that someone would discover that I was "really" male and thereby forever deny me whatever moments of self-determination I had won. Alongside the joys of those liberations, I wince whenever I am called "ma'am" or "sir" (which is nearly constant, because in most places, gendering others is considered polite rather than violent).

Or perhaps the cis/trans distinction depends most on place and privilege.

During my grade school years in Michigan, I imagined myself becoming a monk to live and work in a monastery that I loved to visit. In addition to the sublime silence, I felt my gender "matched" that of the community, and it was one of few places I could imagine being a viable adult self. Forty years later in Wisconsin, I work as a tenured professor. Here, I wear a braid and men's clothes, and I pass as locally legible: the combination of locale, the deference accorded to my race and class status, my job security, and a workplace culture formed by a prior generation of feminists all contribute to the common interpretation of my appearance as a white, middle-class, lesbian-woman academic, which, after all, is a category of person that earlier won a place in this institution. Such interpretation projects onto me a history that erases uncertainty and secures my legitimacy as "woman" rather than as trans woman, trans man, cross-dressed trans woman, or "unknown." My birth certificate and passport match this interpretation; I pass security checks and cross borders—uneasily and often under scrutiny, but the law is on my side. Crossing the threshold to the women's room still gives me the willies; I don every item of privilege, entitlement, and history available to me every time I enter.

I offer these selective disclosures with skepticism, not about the veracity of the points but about the ends they might serve. I could be coming out as something or other. I could be asserting my right to belong in some space built around politicized identity categories. I could be anticipating interrogation—who am I, after all, to be writing on this topic? I do not seem to be claiming my own transparency (relying on the privileges available to me, I can afford to obscure signifiers), but might

I want self-representation?[35] It would be easy to narrate a true history of gender consistency across my lifetime, and it would be equally easy to narrate a true history in which my expressed and/or perceived gender has changed dramatically across time and place. Critically, I could show how being read as male or female at various times and places was not about gender alone; in fact, it was at least as much my race and class privilege, my perceived age, and my perceived mobility and ability that have served as the functional cues leading to people's interpretations of my sex/gender.

In the summer of 2010, my department of Gender and Women's Studies moved from one building where we had an almost wheelchair-accessible, single-occupancy restroom to a renovated building with wheelchair-accessible, multistalled restrooms that have mutually exclusive signs on the doors. I go there, braided and bearded, and am furious to discover the options. Workplace bathrooms acknowledge that workers are biological beings; the signs, on the other hand, suggest that some bodies—most pressingly in this moment, mine—somehow need not be biological. The signs provide social messages, too, telling other people that they should defend this territory that is clearly marked as *theirs*. But I also know that here, due to my relatively high status in the university's hierarchies, I can walk through *either* door, and I will not be physically or verbally assaulted. I enter the one that says "women" and, at a sink that is too high and set too far back to use from a wheelchair, I splash my face with cold water. I am not using a wheelchair. And I am white, and I am a professor, and, actually, no one is looking. I kick the door as hard as I can on my way out. Do I make the signs impossible, or do they make me impossible?

Despite the fact that the majority of transsexuals will have no transition-related surgeries in their lifetimes (due to lack of access or desire), medico-juridical transition continues to be a defining feature in the constitution of trans as a category, and never more so than when trans is elicited by cis. By announcing its own sex/gender consistency, cis makes the *across* (n.) that trans *crosses over* refer to the "line" between "male" and "female," as though we agree upon what and where that line may be as well as on what constitutes male and female.[36] Doing so effectively asserts the naturalness of medico-juridical determinations of and control over trans existence. At the same time, cis further distances from trans by establishing its own relative normativity.

As trans studies scholars emphasize, trans theoretically inheres movement and change, or space and time. But when we posit cis in binary opposition to trans, cis and trans *both* must erase their temporality and location. At precisely what point in time do trans-ness and cis-ness depart from each other? I think a lot about Dr. Marci Bowers, a surgeon and gynecologist who offers sex reassignment surgery (SRS—also known as gender confirmation surgery) and one of the more famous women with a transsexual history. Practicing in Trinidad, Colorado, she is willing to use her status to create publicized platforms for education around transgender issues. Dr. Bowers seems to enjoy her notoriety as SRS's "transsexual rockstar."[37] But she tells me to "get the *nomenclature* right": She does not think of herself as a transsexual or a transsexual woman; "that's all in the past; I am a woman."[38] While not rejecting transsexuality, Bowers marshals several entitlements to successfully reject the *abjection* that neoliberal discourses of oppression cast upon transsexuals. This strategy is available to few people, and it may leave most others (poor and unemployed people, people for whom surgeries are not available, people of color, and so forth) disenfranchised.[39] But if we take Bowers at her word—and I think we must—her perspective suggests that at an *earlier* time, perhaps but not necessarily including when she was living as a boy and later as a man, Bowers was a transsexual woman. Then—also "in the past"—she transitioned: she became a woman and *now* is a woman. One might say she is a cisgender, cissexual woman. This suggestion flies in the face of most assumptions that attend the cis/trans binary, not least of which is that a transsexual history makes one forever trans and precludes cissexuality at *all* points in time.[40] Cis's peculiar ontology erases location and effects through time and space. To preserve the stasis of cis as non-trans, trans must never have been or become cis but instead be consistently trans across all time and in all spaces.

## BUMPING INTO WALLS

Trans studies and disability studies together provide compelling insight about movement and change. Movement is integral to trans studies, but disability studies may do a better job of recognizing that bodies, abilities, and core identities change. For example, disability studies will not reify ability as a static *condition*: cis-abled?! Impossible. Although people with disabilities constitute 20 percent of the population, only 15 percent of people with disabilities (roughly 3 percent of the whole population) were born with disabilities; the other 97 percent of the population is likely to enter the status of disabled at various times and places even though they may presently feel securely abled. Moreover, built environments reflect social normativities and biases, and thus, by design, they also constitute dis/ability. Moving from one context to another, an individual may be abled then disabled then abled again. Disability and ability, along with identity and subjectivity, are situational, temporal, spatial, and culturally constructed; barriers are in the same measure social, physical, and psychological— which is to say, always political.[41] Bringing transgender studies and disability studies together, we can see that physical movement and habits elicit ableist judgments and social gendering simultaneously.[42]

Trans, queer, and disability movements suggest that we should not assume anything about a person's gender identity, sex, desires, abilities, personal history, *or* future. Trans-ness, for example, more often than not is nonvisible to outside observers regardless of how queer-savvy those observers may be. But positing the existence of the cis-normative subject seems to encourage the assumption that the people around us—our peers, coworkers, and students, as well as "the man in the film"—are cis unless they provide visible and narrative proof of trans-ness.[43] Alternatively, knowing that trans-ness is among us regardless of whether it shows itself as such makes it impossible to assume that anyone here is non-trans.

Social spaces that depend on identity categories—as most do—are constituted through the constant surveillance and policing of those within. The presence of "difference" from the operative identity category is simultaneously invoked and erased: social spaces suggest that all people within them *pass* as *really being* members of the social category that the space thereby helps produce.[44] Thus, normative social spaces are structured around the presumed absence of disabled, queer, trans, and other marginalized subjects, which is to say that such spaces inscribe exclusion.[45] Disability and trans theories insist that we challenge this cultural logic, a logic that believes that "the physical body is the site of identic intelligibility."[46] How can we interrupt the erasures enacted by normativity? The strategy of identity politics believes that if we first *get in* (accept the pass granted by the presumed absence of queer, trans, and/or disabled subjects), then we can interrupt this presumption by performing or making visible our own non-normativity by *coming out* as disabled, and/or queer, and/or trans. However, such solutions underwrite visibility politics and attendant discriminatory practices, as well as hierarchies between those who can pass and those who never will.[47]

The effects of cis make clear that we cannot simply add trans to the list of "differences" covered in our classrooms without launching a simultaneous critique of the impulse to name cis as trans's absence. Wittingly or not, gender and women's studies derives a disciplining security from the embrace of cis. This occurs in the presumption that "women" is not "trans" and in the presumption that "trans" is limited to a relatively small fraction of human existence that does not intersect with habituated definitions of "gender" in the title "Gender and Women's Studies."[48] As cis circulates, it renders "woman" and "man" more stable, normative, and ubiquitous than they ever were. In the very same gesture, the cis ally reduces "trans" to the most oppressed and institutionally defined object fighting for recognition within a framework of identity politics and additive "rights." Whatever else it may accomplish, cisgender forces transgender to "come out" over and over through an ever-narrower set of narrative and visual signifiers. This erases gender variance and diversity among everyone while dangerously extending the practical reach and power of normativity. That is to say, little cis and its step-cister ally can only rediscipline gender.

As so much feminist, queer, and trans theory has suggested, the compulsion to identify or even to posit a cis/trans binary is an effect of neoliberal politics in which identity categories are crafted to maximize a share of normative privilege. Feminist and queer theory and gender and women's studies as a whole have therefore been challenged to develop perspectives on lives, power, and oppression that do not require speaking as or speaking for the next identity category to be "included." This challenge has helped produce our best resources. Recalling Sandy Stone's charge that "passing means the denial of mixture," we might take greater pause at the constrictions wrought by cis.[49]

As a teacher and activist, I am humbled by the extent to which we exceed the English language. Words fail utterly, as do all conventions of naming the variety of ways we live with gender. We make up pronouns and prefixes—languages change, after all—and then we wrestle with how to use them, because they do not escape systemic gender policing. We inevitably cloak ourselves in paper suits of biocertification, all the while tearing at the seams.[50] But perhaps it is in this very wrestling that we can find hope and be changed. Otherwise, to paraphrase Ryka Aoki, our classrooms may only encourage us to make our mistakes more eloquently.[51] As a transfeminist teacher and activist, I have a vested interest in keeping the categories woman, man, and trans* wide open, their flexible morphologies blending into one another and becoming accessible in more ways than we can even imagine.

## EPIGRAPHS

Dana Leland Defosse, original call posted on http://groups.google.com/group/alt.transgendered/browse_thread/thread/69c04e35666a9a1b/69ebde0bf2af8dc6?lnk=st&q=cisgendered+dana+defosse&rnum=1&hl=en#69ebde0bf2af8dc6.

Carl Buijs, "A new perspective on an old topic" (April 16, 1996), posted on http://groups.google.com/group/soc.support.transgendered/msg/184850df15e48963?hl=en.

Monica Roberts, "Cisgender Isn't an Insult," posted July 10, 2009, http://transriot.blogspot.com/2009/07/cisgender-isn't-insult.html.

## NOTES

1. Across the U.S.A. and Canada, use of the terms "cisgender" and "cis" varies by location and the political orientation of any given community.
2. Recorded quotes from students in the courses "Lesbian(?) Contexts," "Trans/Gender in Historical Perspective," and "Advanced Seminar in LGBT Studies," 2008, 2009, 2010.
3. Monica Roberts is one of very few people to bring up issues of race in connection to the term "cisgender," and she does so as an African-American trans woman to make an analogy rather than to question whether cisgender itself may carry racist hierarchies: "I believe the people having a problem with the word are wailing in unacknowledged cisgender privilege. They are taken aback that there is a trans community term coined by trans people to describe them. [It's like] how many [white] peeps get upset and call me 'racist' over the 'vanilla flavored privileged' term I used to describe white privilege.... [T]hey call me 'racist' anytime I criticize the underlying structural assumptions that buttress whiteness" (from "Cisgender Isn't an Insult") posted July 10, 2009, http://transgriot.blogspot.com/2009/07/cisgender-isn't-insult.html.
4. Trans and genderqueer critique of cis has grown in the last two years, all in informal and unpublished venues. The term became the subject of Kate Bornstein's Twitter account for several days during and following my talk on cisgender at the Postposttranssexual Conference, in Bloomington, Indiana, in April 2011. A member of the Trans-Academics listserv brought up the term and elicited more than sixty elaborate submissions in what became a conversation among twenty-eight different people between May 16 and 19, 2011.
5. By "Queer Studies classroom," I mean environments in which gender, sex, and/or sexuality are explicitly engaged, regardless of discipline and not limited to university settings.
6. We often ask what is being brought into or excluded from purview in (or despite) such titles as Gender and Women's Studies, LGBT Studies, Sexuality Studies, Gender Studies, and Queer Studies. The burgeoning field of Transgender Studies does not find a "natural" home in either Women's Studies or LGBT Studies. [...]
7. Holly Boswell, "The Transgender Alternative," *Chrysalis Quarterly* 1:2 (1991–1992): 29–31.
8. Leslie Feinberg's extraordinarily influential 1992 pamphlet "Transgender Liberation: A Movement Whose Time Has Come" (New York: World View Forum) offers a Marxist and feminist analysis of (trans)gender oppression as the basis

for forging a movement that linked, rather than separated, all manifestations of gender oppression and all marginalized communities and identities that are born of such oppression.

9. Paisley Currah, Jamison Green, and Susan Stryker, "The State of Transgender Rights in the United States of America" (paper prepared for the National Sexuality Resource Center, San Francisco, CA, 2008).

10. Susan Stryker, *Transgender History* (Berkeley, CA: Seal Press, 2008), 1.

11. The list of institutions that typically require sex/gender legibility and consistency is infinite. To mention a few here: social services such as rape crisis centers, homeless shelters, and medical clinics; educational and job-training services; housing; employment; public accommodations, including restrooms; marriage; rights to custody of children; inheritance; health insurance; incarceration in gender-appropriate facilities; and identity records (passport, driver's license, and so forth), all of which use legal gender for purposes of identification.

12. Wilchins, *Read My Lips*, 33–40; Joanne Meyerowitz, *How Sex Changed: A History of Transsexuality in the U.S.* (London: Harvard University Press, 2002); Nikki Sullivan, "The Role of Medicine in the (Trans)Formation of 'Wrong' Bodies," *Body and Society* 14 (2008), 105–116; Dean Spade, "Mutilating Gender," in *The Transgender Studies Reader*, ed. Susan Stryker and Stephen Whittle (New York: Routledge, 2006), 315–332.

13. Emi Koyama (06/07/ 2002), posted on Koyama's blog site, http://eminism.org/interchange/2002/20020607-wmstl.html.

14. This is true in academic contexts as well, as programs integrate gay and lesbian and queer studies but fail to integrate trans and bi studies. Robert McRuer has observed, "Queer theory and LGBT studies have arguably come together with disability studies more than many other 'identity'-based fields." And yet his version of "queer/disabled" history excises trans when he suggests that "gay liberation distanced from disability" by winning the removal of homosexuality from the DSM III. Where does trans fit into this? From a trans-conscious queer/disability perspective, there is no institution more consequential (not liberating) to transsexuality and trans lives than the DSM and the weight of Gender Identity Disorder. Robert McRuer, "Shameful Sites: Locating Queerness and Disability," in *Gay Shame*, ed. David Halperin and Valerie Traub (Chicago, IL: University of Chicago Press, 2009), 181–187.

15. S. Bear Bergman and J. Wallace, "Open Log: IM on Identity," *Women and Environments* (2009), 5–8; Julia Serano, *Whipping Girl: A Transsexual Woman on Sexism and the Scapegoating of Femininity* (Emeryville, CA: Seal Press, 2007).

16. Serano, *Whipping Girl,* 12 and 33, respectively. Serano's definition of cisgender depends on the definition of transgender, but Serano does not offer a definition of transgender.

17. Serano does not elaborate on the cisgender/cissexual distinction in her book as much as she has in personal conversation. *Whipping Girl* is not concerned with transgender, but, uniquely, its purpose is to see transsexuals "develop our own language and concepts that accurately articulate our unique experiences and perspectives and to fill in the many gaps that exist in both gatekeeper and transgender activist language" (162). Serano and others rightly critique the academic and social movements' prioritizing and privileging of transgender, genderqueer, and gender fluidity at the expense of transsexual politics and existence.

18. Serano, *Whipping Girl*, 162.

19. One of Serano's interventions is to challenge naturalizing vocabularies, such as the very common tendency to refer to non-trans people as "biological" or "genetic" males and females. As Serano explains, "I usually interject that, despite the fact that I am a transsexual, I am not inorganic or nonbiological in any way.... When you break it down ... it becomes obvious that the words 'biological' and 'genetic' are merely stand-ins for the word that people want to use: 'natural'" (174–175, and 161–193 passim). Serano and others critique the concept of "passing" for the way it implies that the trans person is doing the action while masking the fact that passing is about what other people—observers and interpreters—do.

20. People began protesting MWMF's anti-trans policies in 1992. Since then, Camp Trans has experienced major transformations in mission, demographics, and strategy.

21. Leslie Feinberg most forcefully articulated this in a speech delivered at Camp Trans in 1993 ("Building Bridges") and in an interview with Davina Anne Gabriel, "The Life and Times of a Gender Outlaw: Leslie Feinberg," *TransSisters: The Journal of Transsexual Feminism* (September–October 1993), 4–13.

22. Cf. Emi Koyama, "Whose Feminism Is It Anyway? The Unspoken Racism of the Trans Inclusion Debate" (first on http://eminism.org, now available in a collection of Koyama's transfeminist essays under the same title); reprinted in *The Transgender Studies Reader*, 698–704.

23. Camp Trans Web site, www.camp-trans.org.

24. "Camp is first and foremost a place for people who wish to actively oppose policies which exclude trans women from 'women's-only' spaces, most specifically, Michigan Women's [sic] Music Festival."

25. First and last in the Exclusion list, respectively: "ANY person, no matter their gender, orientation, identity, or partnership status, who does not oppose (who either supports or does not have an opinion on) policies which exclude trans women from women's spaces, specifically Michigan Women's [sic] Music Festival;" and "Any person not dedicated to building a week-long community space where trans people are as free as possible from the repression and constraints placed upon them by the larger society."

26. Defo0008 04:40, 6 July 2006 (UTC), posted on http://en.wikipedia.org/wiki/Talk:Cisgender; emphasis added.

27. "Transgenderism is constituted as a paradox made up of equal parts of visibility and temporality." Judith Halberstam, *In a Queer Time and Place: Transgender Bodies, Subcultural Lives* (New York: New York University Press, 2005), 77. "We invite our readers to recognize that 'trans-' likewise names the body's orientation in space and time; we ask them to...

begin imagining these phenomena according to *different* spatio-temporal metaphors." Susan Stryker, Paisley Currah, and Lisa Jean Moore, "Introduction: Trans-, Trans, or Transgender," *WSQ: Women's Studies Quarterly* 36: 3–4 (2008), 11–22, 13; emphasis added.

28. The emergence of the term "trans ally" as distinct from "LGBT ally" reflects the failure of "LGBT" organizations as well as most academic institutions to function as trans-inclusive entities; trans allyship specifically recognizes trans issues.

29. In response to growing social-movement visibility, trans ally trainings are now offered in a host of educational contexts, including to social- and medical-service providers as well as student organizations and outreach groups on college campuses.

30. Vik DeMarco, "Ally Exceptionalism: Problems in Approaches to Allyship Trainings" (B.A. Honors Thesis, Gender and Women's Studies, University of Wisconsin Madison, 2010); Christoph Hanssmann, "Training Disservice: The Productive Potential and Structural Limitations of Health as a Terrain for Trans Activism," in Anne Enke, ed, *Transfeminist Perspectives: In and Beyond Gender Studies* (Philadelphia, PA: Temple University Press, forthcoming 2012). On anti-oppressive education see Kevin Kumashiro, "Toward a Theory of Anti-oppressive Education," *Review of Educational Research* 70: 1 (2000), 25–53.

31. See, e.g., Eli Clare, *Exile and Pride: Disability, Queerness, and Liberation* (Boston, MA: South End Press, 1999); Susan Stryker, "We Who Are Sexy: Christine Jorgensen's Transsexual Whiteness in the Postcolonial Philippines," *Social Semiotics* 19 (2009), 79–91; Kenji Tokawa, "Why You Don't Have to Choose a White Boy Name to Be a Man in This World," in *Gender Outlaws: The Next Generation*, ed. Kate Bornstein and S. Bear Bergman (Berkeley, CA: Seal Press, 2010), 207–212; Zev Al-Walid, "Pilgrimage," in *Gender Outlaws*, 261–267; Dean Spade, "Compliance is Gendered: Struggling for Gender Self-Determination in a Hostile Economy" in *Transgender Rights*, 217–240; Richard M. Juang, "Transgendering the Politics of Recognition," in *Transgender Rights*, 242–261; Koyama, "Whose Feminism Is It Anyway?"

32. David Valentine, *Imagining Transgender* (Durham, NC: Duke University Press, 2007); Dean Spade, "Trans Law and Politics on a Neoliberal Landscape," *Temple Political and Civil Rights Law Review* 18:2 (2009), 353–373; Spade, "Documenting Gender." *Hasting Law Journal* 59:4 (2008) Also cf. Cathy Cohen, "Punks, Bulldaggers, and Welfare Queens: The Radical Potential of Queer Politics?" in *Black Queer Studies*, ed. E. Patrick Johnson and Mae Henderson (Durham, NC: Duke University Press, 2005), 21–51.

33. The exact language is "in girls, rejection of urination in a sitting position," with no discussion of "boys'" urination preferences. In the late 1950s, physicians used "urinating in the standing position" as diagnostic proof that the sex of a gender-ambiguous subject under scrutiny was male. Harold Garfinkel, "Passing and the Managed Achievement of Sex Status in an 'Intersexed' Person," in Harold Garfinkel, *Studies in Ethnomethodology* (Oxford: Polity, 1967).

34. See, for example, Halberstam, *In a Queer Time and Place*; Jay Prosser, *Second Skins* (New York: Columbia University Press, 1998); Jean Bobby Noble, *Sons of the Movement* (Toronto, Ontario: Women's Press, 2006); Kath Weston, *Render Me, Gender Me: Lesbians Talk Sex, Class, Color, Nation, Studmuffins* (New York: Columbia University Press, 1996).

35. On compulsory narrative and resistance to such, see Rachel Pollack, "Archetypal Transsexuality," *TransSisters: The Journal of Transsexual Feminism* 9 (1995), 39–41; Lucas Cassidy Crawford, "Transgender without Organs? Mobilizing a Geo-affective Theory of Gender Modification," this volume; Nikki Sullivan, "Transmogrification: (Un)Becoming Other(s)," in *The Transgender Studies Reader*, 552–563.

36. Defosse's entry goes on, "I think the use of cisgender also captures a subtle and nondualistic aspect of the issue at hand; cisgender reinforces and reflects itself, while transgender originates where cisgender begins but extends into a greater dimension by 'crossing over.'" Defosse 04:40, 6 July 2006 (UTC), posted on http://en.wikipedia.org/wiki/Talk:Cisgender. Other subtle renderings of cisgender failed to take hold as well. For example, unsigned added to Defosse's comments, "I also coined cisgendered as a term around 1994 in publicity for the GLQSOC-L, the Gay, Lesbian, Queer Social Science listserv, to describe those who move from one mode of masculinity or femininity to another. This usage never caught on." Unsigned 68.162.116.127 (talk) 00:12, 15 October 2007 (UTC), posted on http://en.wikipedia.org/wiki/Talk:Cisgender.

37. Countless mainstream and trans* community news articles have conferred this title on Bowers.

38. Author interview with Dr. Marci Bowers, July 25, 2009, Trinidad, Colorado. Bowers has insisted on this point in numerous public interviews and documentaries as well.

39. Since the 1960s, trans* communities have debated umbrella categories, such as transgender. Inherent to the debate are strong feelings about activism and whether one should be "out" about one's trans* history. Sandy Stone, "The Empire Strikes Back" (in *Body Guards: The Cultural Politics of Gender Ambiguity*, New York and London: Routledge, 1991); Jamison Green, "Look! No, Don't! The Visibility Dilemma for Transsexual Men," in *The Transgender Studies Reader*, 499–508. Other aspects of the debate include boundary policing and the challenge of forming alliances among people with disparate proximities to the privileges accorded to normativity.

40. Serano rightly notes that many people whose gender identity is in congruence with the sex they were assigned at birth object to the suggestion that SRS, transition, and male-to-female (MTF) identity can turn a male-bodied person into a woman. I am also aware that many trans-identified people object to the erasure of transsexuality implied by the claim that Bowers is now a cisgender/cissexual women, because it buys into cis privilege. Both objections invest in a cis/trans binary that ultimately supports cis privilege. I prefer a trans* politics that does not reject trans identity but that also does not depend on possession and retention of ur-trans identity.

41. One of the best articulations of this, including a critique of the imperialism embedded in concepts of disability, is Michael Davidson, *Concerto for the Left Hand: Disability and the Defamiliar Body* (Ann Arbor, MI: University of Michigan Press, 2008).

42. Cf. Tobin Siebers, *Disability Theory* (Ann Arbor, MI: University of Michigan Press, 2008); Terry Galloway, "Tough," in *Gay Shame*, 196–200; Dominique Bednarska, "Passing Last Summer," in *Nobody Passes: Rejecting the Rules of Gender and Conformity*, ed. Mattilda Bernstein Sycamore (New York: Avalon, 2006), 71–82; Clare, *Exile and Pride*; Rosemary Garland-Thomson, *Extraordinary Bodies: Figuring Physical Disability* (New York: Routledge, 1996).

43. If, as Serano points out, all people engage in assumptions about others' sex/gender, it is also the case that most people, regardless of identity, assume that most other people are cis.

44. Anne Enke, *Finding the Movement: Sexuality, Contested Space, and Feminist Activism* (Durham, NC: Duke University Press, 2007).

45. Ellen Samuels, "My Body, My Closet: Invisible Disability and the Limits of Coming-Out Discourse," *GLQ: A Journal of Lesbian and Gay Studies* 9: 1–2 (2003), 233–255.

46. This phrase comes from Elaine Ginsburg, ed., *Passing and the Fictions of Identity* (Durham, NC: Duke University Press, 1996), 4.

47. Trans and disability studies engage "masquerade" and the many meanings of "passing." Cf. Siebers, *Disability Theory*.

48. LGBT Studies is not exempt from this tendency, although it is perhaps more frequently in conventional disciplines whose methodological, theoretical, and pedagogical practices depend on binary gender stability and normativity.

49. Stone, "The Empire Strikes Back," 231.

50. Thanks to Ellen Samuels for this image of paper suits. Carrie Sandahl makes paper suits of biocertification graphic in her performance piece "The Reciprocal Gaze," which she discusses in "Ahh, Freak Out! Metaphors of Disability and Femaleness in Performance," *Theatre Topics* 9:1 (1999), 11–30. Samuels discusses biocertification at length in *Fantasies of Identification: Disability, Gender, Race* (book manuscript in process).

51. Ryka Aoki, "When Something Is Not Right," in Enke, ed, *Transfeminist Perspectives*.

# 20

# *Our Bodies Are Not Ourselves*

## Tranny Guys and the Racialized Class Politics of Incoherence

BOBBY JEAN NOBLE

EXCERPTED FROM CANADIAN SCHOLAR BOBBY NOBLE'S BOOK *SONS OF THE MOVEMENT*, "Tranny Guys and the Racialized Class Politics of Incoherence" explores the racial and class privilege of white masculinity as it inflects transgender experience. Drawing on Richard Dyer's influential book, *White*, Noble's strategy is to turn toward whiteness the gaze more often directed toward the racialized Other, which produces racial knowledge as its effect. Noble is interested specifically in how white transgender masculinity is constructed and reproduced. He uses his own experience as a "formerly off-white and now White" person as a tool to explain the shift from being read as a working-class butch woman (located in a gendered "No Man's Land") to being read as a man who bears the representational burden of hegemonic masculinity and white supremacy. By claiming space as a "race traitor," Noble shows how to refuse the ideology of naturalized white masculinity that white trans men may unwittingly (or consciously) subscribe to. Instead, he argues for a transgender masculinity that holds itself accountable for the privileges it accrues; as Noble neatly puts it, he seeks a way to be a man without becoming "The Man." This chapter is noteworthy for its interrogation of race and transgender masculinity at a time when such critiques weren't yet circulating widely. Written at a time when transgender masculinities were becoming increasingly culturally visible in North America, "Tranny Guys" complicates the optimism with which trans masculine subcultures theorized the work of self-making.

That was when I realized a shocking thing. I couldn't become a man without becoming The Man. Even if I didn't want to.

—Jeffrey Eugenides (2002: 518)

In my first department meeting as a professor at York University, one held during the CUPE strike on our campus in 2000, the department was attempting to address the gender imbalance among its rank of full professors. Given that many of the full professors are male, the department was taking the very important step of finding a remedy to this situation. One senior professor (but not full professor), a woman who teaches, among other things, feminist literature, made the very curious claim that given how easy it is these days to change one's gender—and this even after the Ontario government de-listed sex-reassignment surgeries—that she would volunteer to do so if it would allow her to access the pay increase that accompanied a full professorship. A round of laughter ensued in which all seemingly agreed that this was indeed an easy process and the meeting continued. I sat a little dumbfounded that—in the midst of the CUPE 3903 union labor action on the campus, a local that has been remarkably progressive in its inclusion of trans issues in its mandate, and in the face of the aggressive de-listing of sex-reassignment procedures *and* the sad reality that male full professors still outranked the females—any of these matters would be so easily the source of laughter among faculty. This work is addressed to, in part, not only the female professor in question but to those folks inside of feminism who might claim that trans is not a feminist issue.

As I have been suggesting so far, issues around the prefix *trans-* present not only theoretical but lived opportunities to refine our intersectional reading practices. The perspective I want to explore here is one that will allow us to see trans issues as not only those of gender but also those of race and class as well. The titles of two significant feminist books on class—Dorothy Allison's *Skin* and bell hooks's *Where We Stand*—signal the precise articulation I want to explore here: that between (trans-)[1] embodiment, class, and labor. Each text argues, among other things, that materializing class within feminist theoretical paradigms is often accomplished through corporeal metaphors. Moreover, each also suggests to us that class, the one term within our intersectional frameworks that is often neglected, is itself perceived to be about a kind of hyper-embodiment and hyper-visibility, especially for those of us who are working class and racialized White. If the anti-racist field of whiteness studies is correct, as I will argue later it is, then being classed as White is whiteness racialized as visible, especially since whiteness operates through ironic codes of invisibility and, hence, epistemological and discursive power. That is, whiteness comes into visibility as whiteness when it is articulated through class. If that is true, then under what conditions can transed bodies, bodies that similarly matter when invisible and/or fetishized, emerge within the feminist analytical intersections of capitalism, class, and race? I want to play in those fields by offering my own trans body—which is White but formerly off-White,[2] formerly lesbian but now female-to-male trans-sexual—as a case study in resistance. A practice of strategically unmaking the self—that is, working the labor of self-making against the categorical imperative—is a class, trans, anti-racist, and union politic I want to cultivate in this era where "self" is the hottest and most insidious capitalist commodity.[3]

The union motto that I want to borrow—an injury to one is an injury to all—has been in my life since I was very young.[4] My maternal grandmother was a member of CUPE for her entire working life; she was a hospital worker when services, like laundry and food, were still provided in-house. She worked in a hospital laundry for almost 40 years. I spent one summer as a young teenager working in that same laundry with her and just barely lasted the first month. Conditions were horrific. Unpacking the laundry from the hospital hampers was one of the nastiest jobs I have ever witnessed. Thankfully, I suppose, the staff wouldn't let me near the job of separating soiled sheets, bloodied towels from the operating rooms, and so on. Temperatures were extremely high and dangerous. Between massive pressing machines that ironed linens and sheets, the huge dryers, and washers that laundered sheets at very high temperatures, workers were dehydrated on a regular basis. After working for 40 years in daily conditions like these, my grandmother was given a CUPE ring that I still have and wear on a chain around my neck. I remember visiting her on her lunch break when I was much younger; I would wait for her in the hospital cafeteria and when the laundry women came into the room, they certainly were quite a sight. Into that otherwise unremarkably populated cafeteria walked a group of White, working-class, big, tough-looking, often hard-drinking women dressed in white dress-uniforms that looked out of place on them. They lumbered into the cafeteria, lit cigarettes, opened their homemade lunches, and stared down all who dared to look. Those women, a formidable bunch of working-class women who were literally at the bottom of the health-services industry but upon whom it depended, made a mark on me. Much later when I walked the CUPE 3903 picket line at York University with my teaching assistants as a new faculty member, something of those early workers infused my determination to see that strike through to its conclusion. I doubt that much of CUPE 3903's current work on trans-sexual issues would have made much sense to those women with whom my grandmother worked, although I suspect a couple of them might have understood the stakes. Because of the political commitment to social justice issues, CUPE 3903 has passed a number of resolutions that include the struggles of trans-sexual peoples into their primary mandate. They also support their trans-sexual members with funding; when I had surgery, CUPE 3903's Ways and Means fund helped me pay for a procedure that has been de-listed in the Conservatives' butchery of Ontario health care.[5]

The men in my family were less union-affiliated but just as affected by the class-based issues of labor activism. My grandfather was one of the "Little Immigrants," groups of White, working-class, orphaned British children shipped to Canada from the homes of Thomas John Barnardo, a philanthropist in 19th-century London, England. Thomas Barnardo, along with others, established a series of reformatory and industrial schools known as "ragged schools" (because of the ragged clothing of the attendees) for homeless and abandoned children. In the 19th century, they struck a deal with the Canadian government whereby they would export large numbers of these children to Canada to work as "farm" help and "mother's helpers" in Canadian homes and farms (Bagnell 1990: 91). At its peak, this emigration was responsible for shipping between 80,000 and 100,000 (orphaned or abandoned) children to Canada, a ready-made, exploitable "servant" class (Bagnell 1990: 9). Most of these children, now known as the Barnardo kids, would end up working as indentured domestic servants. My grandfather was one of those who came to Canada via Montreal in 1916 as a young boy to be adopted into a farm family, or so he thought. Instead, he lived in the barn, was ill fed, beaten, and overworked until he was old enough to run away. He did, and set up a life for himself in Canada as a laborer, eventually marrying my grandmother in northern Ontario. As one of the students of a ragged school, my grandfather was still unable to read and write when he died in 1992.

About one thing I felt certain: these were the primary influences on my gender. My grandfather had an entirely ambivalent relationship with England: I suspect he had always felt abandoned and banished from it, although as a young boy from a very poor family, he had already lived the life of an exile on the streets of London. He remained vehemently class-identified and anti-British for his entire life, continuously evoking cultural traces of England and, unknowingly, its particular form of class whiteness while constantly disparaging both at the same time. I find traces of both grandparents in the words I use to describe myself ("a guy who is half lesbian") and, in finding these traces, have built a sense of self quite different from their own. The rough and yet somehow vulnerable masculinity of the butches and FtMs brings my grandmother back to me, while, in some kind of temporal and geographical displacement, I find traces of my grandfather's off-whiteness in the class-based traces of manhood I now wear as corporeal signifiers.

To be sure, my family and I are all White. When I say "off-White," I do not mean to suggest at all that somehow being poor and/or working class means that one is no longer White. What I mean is that whiteness, like gender and class, has a history of invention, construction, and utility. Embedded in those histories are the processes that manufacture whiteness in the service of modern nation building. I was reminded of this when I watched the film, *Gangs of New York* (2002). For all of its problems, the least of which is its final ideological return to pre-September 11 United States *vis-à-vis* images of the World Trade Center's twin towers, *GONY* depicts the simultaneous whitening of Irish immigrants and the utilitarian invention of the nation-state. The thing that renders the "tribal" or "gang" conflict inconsequential, in the final scenes of the film, is the intervention of the American government through its military.[6] Through its need to govern a people, the United States government first had to invent them. This, of course, occurs long before the timeline represented in the film, but the film is an allegory of the process whereby certain groups of light-skinned immigrants into the "Americas" purchased their way into White citizenry. Amsterdam (Leonardo di Caprio) and Bill the Butcher (Daniel Day-Lewis) are equally made subject to the American government and can become just plain American men (code for American White men) because they have what James Baldwin referred to as the price of the ticket.

If racialized bodies are the product of both our own labor and the work of a racial social manufacturing machine, then developing not just a tolerance for, but an acquired taste, for destabilizing paradoxes within our feminist vocabularies might be one way to trouble that machinery. Female-to-male trans-sexuals embody but are also articulated by paradox: Loren Cameron's (1996) photographs in *Body Alchemy,* to which I will return in my afterword, visually represent this paradox. The guys whom Cameron photographs, especially those without clothes, really are half guy, half something else. My own body does this too: from the waist up, with or without clothes, I display a White male chest. Naked, from the waist down, my body reads closest conventionally female body even though that is not how it reads to me. Clothed, from the waist down, my body is overdetermined by signifiers of whiteness and masculinity and I am just a guy. Given that the surgical production of a penis leaves much to be desired—and the penis they can build costs so much that it is out of reach for most guys—trans men cannot leave the "trans" behind and be "men." Self-naming and, by implication, self-definition, then, these crucial axioms that feminist movements fought long and hard for become tricky: I find myself at an even greater loss when it comes to finding a language to describe myself. Just recently, I have settled upon the following paradox: "I am a guy who is half lesbian." I have a long lesbian history, which I do not deny despite tremendous pressure, but have just recently come out as a straight (albeit trans-sexual) man or "I am a lesbian man:" Identifying myself through paradox as a "guy who is half lesbian" really comes closest to bringing a number of historical moments together to form *something like an identity.*

Refracting identity through simile ("something like" or "closest to") is crucial to my sense of self. While I am suggesting *something like*—that is, something comparable or similar to—I am also suggesting but *something that fails to*—that is, something that fails to cohere as a thing unto itself, hence the need for the comparison to begin with. In the case of my own sense of self, for instance, the tension between "guy" and "lesbian" does the work of articulating in language what my body is currently doing through gender signifiers. The result, of course, is that many FtMs cannot always be read as "men" (without the quotation marks) in every circumstance, presuming, of course, that any man can. Take gym locker rooms as an example. These are sites of poignant contradiction within our current capitalist discourses about bodies. Gyms and health clubs are strange sites of Marxist alienation and disembodiment even in the face of an apparent hyper-embodiedness. Fragmenting bodies into "legs," "abs," "chest," "shoulders," and "arms" (and then systems like "cardio"), the class culture of working out before or after work (not employment/work as physically demanding) requires one to become, quite literally, subject to or to step into a machine that has been designed to isolate a muscle or set of muscles and work them with the goal of having them look like they do more than get worked on at the gym. The gym body is developed not necessarily from use but from an extreme form of docility, repetition, and discipline. Capitalism requires each of these when manufacturing laboring bodies. Don't get me wrong: working out is not necessarily a terrible thing to do. After years of disembodiment, I decided to take the plunge and sign up with a fitness program. Like most gyms, it relies heavily on a gendered division of space determined by conventional understandings of the supposed self-evidence of the body. Given that I read completely as male, showering in public would compromise that reading. Being undressed in a locker room—and given the degree to which straight men furtively but quite decidedly look at each other—would, quite literally, be my undoing.

Then again, signifying as a guy, which I do more consistently now that I no longer have breasts, I do so with a success that makes me politically suspect to some lesbians while at other times interesting to gay men. Toronto's Pride 2003 was an interesting experience; two things happened that marked a shift in my identity from very masculine lesbian to guy. First, I seemed to be much more interesting to gay men as an object of desire. This is evident by the way in which I am now just more noticeable;

gay men flirt with me now in a way they've not done so before. At dinner, in a queer-esque restaurant, a number of men stopped by our table to say hello, pass on a pride greeting or, in one case, to invite me upstairs to an event that was happening later that night. But let me describe myself to you: in my life as a "woman," I failed miserably. I signified as extremely butch, stone butch, macho even. I am heavy-set, continue to wear a kind of crew cut, dress in black pants and crisp shirts, and do not communicate signals that could be easily construed as gay (read: gay man) in any way at all. And yet precisely because of my gender performance (if categories are necessary, I could be considered a smallish bear), I am cruised on a regular basis by gay men.

But masculinity is not the only subject of unmaking found in No Man's Land. The other thing I felt quite compelled to do during the weekend's activities was to insist that my very out lesbian-femme girlfriend of African descent hold my hand as much as possible.[7] This irony resonates even more strongly for several reasons. In a historical moment where femmes are accused of not being lesbian enough, or where queer femininity is cast in a suspicious light, it was a bit of an oddity to realize that I passed as *less than bio-guy* when outed as *something else* through my lesbian partner. Queer femininity or, as Anna Camilleri calls it, femininity gone wrong, is equally bound by contradiction, paradox, and, in the best sense of the term, perversion. The curious difference, though, where trans-folks often need to be recognized for their gender resignifications, queer femmes often rearticulate sexual scripts and do not receive enough credit for that very political work. That is, to be very specific, as a trans guy it is extremely important to me to be seen as male whereas for my femme partner, it's far more important for her to be seen as lesbian. My partner is a woman of African descent, which means that, because of our impoverished and anti-intersectional economies, a battle of dualities plays out on her body to claim her—through identification or dis-identification—either as "Black" or "queer" (but rarely both) in No Man's Land. This is not her battle but a battle over how her body is being read. The signifiers most easily read as femme and/or lesbian in our culture are those of White femininity. Lesbians of color, including many femmes and butches, have written extensively about the whiteness of gay, lesbian, bisexual, and trans language, signifiers, histories, and so on. The semiotic deficiencies of subjectivity within White supremacy disallow signifying as Black and femme simultaneously. For my partner, visibility is frequently conditional: either she is read as her sexuality or she is read as her race. Being a racialized, gendered, and sexualized subject all at the same time is seen as unthinkable within our current paradigms of identity, which privilege—indeed, demand—singularity of identification. Models of intersectionality, which allow me, for instance, to read myself as raced (White, British), gendered (masculine), and sexualized (hetero-gendered and queerly straight) all at the same time are still sadly missing in our political lexicons. If FtMs wear masculinity as what Jay Prosser calls a second skin in order to feel visible and, strangely, invisible at the same time, femmes, on the other hand, wear a queer gendered-ness as a second skin that renders them invisible as lesbians. Femmes of color, to risk an awkward phrase, are hailed as racialized subjects, which can render them invisible as queers *inside* queer communities. Each of these are accomplished through a triangulation, each through the other, and tell us that despite the work we have done, we have still so much more to do.

One of the most significant things I have done to unmake this supposedly femininely signified body is to have top surgery to remove my breasts. On June 9, 2003, I underwent top surgery, a euphemism for a surgical procedure properly known as bilateral mastectomy with male chest reconstruction. As I sat at my desk several days after the procedure, I wore a wide binder around my now scrawny-looking white chest. Underneath that binder, strangely similar to one I had worn when I wanted to bind my breasts, are two lateral scars where those breasts used to sit. Just above those scars are my nipples, grafted onto my newly configured chest but still healing under dressings to ensure that the grafts take. To be clear, in this procedure, the graft (the nipples) are removed completely from the skin. Once the breast tissue is removed, the nipples are then reattached as grafts.

After about two weeks, the "new" nipples have attached again to the skin, only this time in a new position on the newly configured chest. But the *metaphor* of grafting is an interesting one and all too relevant to what I have just come through in this "transition."

I prefer the trope of "grafting" to "transition" because it allows me to reconfigure what I mean by trans-gender or trans-sexual. All too often, the relation between the "trans" and either "gender" or "sexual" is misread to mean that one transcends the other or that trans people, in essence, are surgically and hormonally given "new" bodies. That is, the terms "trans-gender" or "trans-sexual" are often misread to suggest a radical departure from birth bodies into squeaky clean new ones. But the terms are often misread as transcending the gender of those birth bodies into an entirely new gender. I counter that belief in my earlier book *Masculinities without Men?* but also now on and through my body; indeed, even more so now since my nipples were literally grafted back onto my chest: neither of these misreadings are as helpful as they could be.[8] My *gender* now looks different from the one I grew up with but my body is, paradoxically, almost still the same. I have the same scars, the same stretch marks, the same bumps, bruises, and birthmarks that I have always had, only it is all different now. Grafting allows me to think that relation. Not only does this trope allow me to look at the way my "new" body is grafted out of, onto, through my "old," but it is also a way of rethinking trans-gendered (read: differently gendered) bodies as effects of the sex/gender system in crisis and transition. It means my newish-looking gender is the effect of a productive failure of that manufacturing system, not its success. In those failings, trans men can become "men" in some contexts; some, but not all. But neither do trans-sexual and trans-gender folks transcend the sex/gender system; instead, trans-folks are an important site where its inabilities, as Judith Butler argues, to live up to its own imperatives (that gender be the artifact of sex) are rendered obvious.

The process of grafting, as self-remaking and queer reproduction outside of a heteronormative model, spawns (certainly for FtMs) something else outside of our sexual vocabularies and grammars. But this is not androgyny, a mix, or blending of both (read: natural) genders. As Doan (1994:153) puts it, "the notion of hybridity resonates with doing violence to nature, which results [...] in the scientific equivalent of freaks, mongrels, half-breeds and crossbreeds." This is a strategy of naturally denaturalizing biological essentialisms with a "sexual politics of heterogeneity and a vision of hybridized gender constructions outside an either/or proposition" in order to naturalize "cultural oddities, monstrosities, abnormalities, and [what appear to be] conformities" (Doan 1994: 154). The trope of grafting thus allows me to articulate the paradox signaled by "I am a lesbian man" or "I am a guy who is half lesbian." This picture of transed bodies as grafted, where one materialization is haunted by the other, as opposed to crossing or exiting, also allows me to articulate the radical dependencies that these identities (lesbian and trans guy or, to update the lexicon, female masculinity and trans-sexual masculinity) have for me but also with each other historically (the invert + the lesbian + the transsexual). To say "I am a lesbian man" or "I am a guy who is half lesbian" both materializes or externalizes a body that is not always immediately visible yet is still absolutely necessary for the performative paradox to work. It means to answer "yes" to "Am I that name?"[9] and to amend the question so that it reads multiply instead of singularly: "Am I this and that at the same time?" Thus, intelligibility for the female-to-male trans-sexual man means contesting the alignment of bodies, genders, and sexualities to force a crisis by grafting articulations onto each other in the same way that my nipple grafts work. I remember the day I heard a trans man say about his former breasts: "It's such a paradox to have to cut some part of myself off in order to feel whole." Those words are inscribed painfully across my chest today more than ever, but make no mistake: this is the body not as foundation but as archive; this is the same chest, the same body, the same flesh I have always known, only now its text is totally different.[10]

For all my bravado around top surgery, one of the things I have learned through the process is that these are costly choices. Certainly they are costly financially and now that many provincial governments have de-listed these services, trans-folks are left to their own devices to pay for vital procedures. In addition, there's something about going to my extremely trans-friendly doctor that I find profoundly disturbing. My anxiety traces a particular distress around the medically overdetermined conditions of embodiment. This is still the medicalization of bodies, genders, and lives, and as much as the diagnosis "gender identity disorder" is a formal alibi, it still reflects the reality that trans-folks are forced to make the best choices for ourselves in a field of overdetermined possibilities. Even though Toronto's Clark Institute is no longer the sole gatekeeper of sex-reassignment procedures, the job of dispensing hormone therapies and giving referrals to surgeons, etc., still rests with usually non-transed physicians. And the means of rendering oneself intelligible, which is especially true for FtMs who do not achieve full embodiment of their chosen gender, is still the clinical alibi of "gender identity disorder."

That said, politically, the pressure to complete paperwork to change my former F to an M is tremendous. While I signify a version of White masculinity, I have chosen to keep the F. The existence of that F, though, has led me to draw some rather interesting conclusions about its limits. When I have handed that document over to various individuals, most people seem to pay little attention, if any, to the F. I am often, because of my gender presentation, dis-identified with that F Similarly, my image of myself as masculine is becoming reoriented in the process as well. Such incommensurability between self and body is the No Man's Land in which transed lives are lived. While medicalized interventions render this gap less dangerous, they do not, at least for FtMs, render the gap non-existent. Since my surgery, I am aware that I signify quite differently and that I need to transform my own consciousness to keep up. I now find myself asking what kind of *guy* am I presenting because masculinity on the perception of a male body is quite different than masculinity on the perception of a female body. But I am still a guy with an F designation. This discursive contradiction, paradox even, allows me, as Duggan and McHugh suggest (1996: 110) in the "Fem(me)inist Manifesto," to "inhabit normal abnormally." It means, as the best feminist interventions have always told us, that I need to be painfully aware of how I signify, of what kinds of power accrue to my whiteness and masculinity, and then work against both of those to challenge those power grids. It means, as a White man, outing myself whenever and wherever possible as a race traitor, not because I am partnered with a woman of color but because of my commitment to an anti-racist critical practice that includes doing the pedagogical work of challenging racism among other straight White men. Who better to occupy the space of *guy* but former lesbians who have walked the streets as women, loved as fierce and sometimes stone butches, and who have come of political age in the context of lesbian-feminism? For me, that's a proud history that does not get left behind in the operating room.

But it is precisely *because* of that same gender performance that some lesbians, on the other hand, have expressed frustration when I, a straight White man, appear in lesbian (although not lesbian/woman only) spaces. The most pernicious of these chills occurred at United Kingdom 2: International Drag King Show, a trans-friendly and literate event produced in Toronto that showcases drag king performances from across North America and, this year, Amsterdam. The irony resonates strongly: at an event that offers female and trans masculinity for consumption, I passed so well as a non-transed person—indeed, as just a straight White guy—that my presence was troubling to one young woman in particular who felt little discomfort about communicating her disapproval. That chill was repeated a number of other times during Toronto's Dyke March day (I did not go on the dyke march) so that I quite aggressively hunted down a t-shirt that would, at the very least, dis-identify my seemingly heterosexual masculinity with heteronormativity.

That said, then, if it is possible to render my masculinity anti-hetero-normative, then might it also be possible to remake whiteness, not necessarily just self-conscious but similarly incoherent? That is, if I've been suggesting that trans men risk incoherence, can White masculinity also risk incoherence as a political strategy, one that refuses the hegemonic bargains offered to White trans manhood?

White masculinity is, of course, an intersection of parts where a fantasy of singularity is privileged instead. As I have indicated earlier in conversation with James Baldwin, whiteness, in other words, is secured by its violent imperative of universal, categorical singularity (that is, non-intersectionality). Trans manhood has the ability to exist on a similar frequency as biological masculinity without the coherence or clarity of meaning. Trans White masculinity is key for its failure to cohere, as I indicated at the end of Chapter 1, into hegemonic or visible *matter*. (Again, simile is key here.) Dionne Brand presents a similar argument about this in her work, *A Map to the Door of No Return,* when she writes of bodies as matter being socially constructed with extremely potent stakes:

> There are ways of constructing the world—that is, of putting it together each morning, what it should look like piece by piece—and I don't feel that I share that with the people of this small town. Each morning I think we wake up and open our eyes and set the particles of forms together—we make solidity with our eyes and with the matter in our brains. [...] We collect each molecule, summing them up into "flesh" or "leaf" or "water" or "air." Before that everything is liquid, ubiquitous and mute. We accumulate information over our lives which brings various things into solidity, into view. What I am afraid of is that waking up in another room, minutes away by car, the mechanic wakes up and takes my face for a target [...] He cannot see me when I come into the gas station; he sees something else [...] as if I do not exist [...] or as if something he cannot understand has arrived—as if something he despises has arrived. A thing he does not recognize. Some days when I go to the gas station [...] I drive through the possibility of losing solidity at any moment.
>
> (Brand 2002: 141–142)

Brand argues for race what Fausto-Sterling and Butler argue about sex and gender and what I want to advocate as a trans practice of masculinity:

> To be material is to speak about the process of materialization. And if viewpoints about [identity] are already embedded in our philosophical concepts of how matter forms into bodies, the matter of bodies cannot form a neutral, pre-existing ground from which to understand the origin of [...] different. Since matter already contains notions of [identity], it cannot be a neutral recourse on which to build "scientific" or "objective" theories of [the trans subject] ... the idea of the material comes to us already tainted, containing within it pre-existing ideas about [identity] ... the body as a system [...] simultaneously produces and is produced by social meanings.
>
> (Fausto-Sterling 2000: 22–23)

Entrance into these fictionalities of matter, of coherent White skin, is purchased through an ideological belief in a naturalized whiteness and naturalized masculinity. The reading of a body as gendered male and racialized White involves presenting signifiers within an economy where the signifiers accumulate toward the appearance of a coherently gendered and racialized body.

Baldwin's work on the price of the White ticket is crucial here. "White people are not white," writes James Baldwin (1985: xiv), "part of the price of the white ticket is to delude themselves into believing that they are." Baldwin echoes sentiments of thinker WE.B. Du Bois, who argued that there is no such thing as pure categorical whiteness. The existence of the White race produces the unconscious (at best) willingness of those assigned to it to place their racial interests above class or any other interests they hold. Whiteness, in other words, is bound by and is, in effect, secured by its imperative of universal singularity. Entrance into the fictionality of whiteness is purchased through an ideological class belief in naturalized whiteness. What White is, then, is a class-based race: the higher up you go, the whiter you get. One is not born White, one buys his or her way into whiteness and *becomes* White. That price, Baldwin writes, includes, necessitates even, believing in the fiction of whiteness as signifier of the universal subject, the just plain, simple, and singular Man and Woman. But the price is afforded by what later theorists of whiteness will call its psychological and social wages: skin color and class (upward) mobility. This is what the men and women of my ancestry purchased for me off the labor of their class-based whiteness (what I previously called off-White, White, but not middle-class White): entrance, as an educated adult, into a whitened middle class. While I grew up on welfare, we became *whiter* through the generations.

While I am no longer working class (the transition into that whitened middle class was a far harder transition for me than "changing" genders), I continue to be very aware of a rising discourse of whiteness, which, as some writers detail, is racializing class-based whiteness in what seem to me to be all the wrong ways. Five years ago I would have argued that self-consciousness for White people could be anything but wrong. But as many race theorists have taught us, White supremacy, like other colonial systems, is historical and amenable to new circumstances and critique. In the last few decades, there has been a huge proliferation of thinking and writing about whiteness. The emerging field of critical whiteness scholarship has an interdisciplinary past, influenced by work being done in two fields simultaneously: on the one hand, the work of American historiographers have produced very interesting articulated histories of class and race. Historian David Roediger's books: *Towards the Abolition of Whiteness* and *The Wages of Whiteness* both explore the emergence of whiteness as a labor force in the post-slavery U.S. Theodore Allen's book, *The Invention of the White Race* similarly traces the way that Irish immigrants, like those portrayed in *Gangs of New York,* settled in the U.S. and *became* White. While the work of historians has provided critical accounts of the moments when White identities first began to do particular types of work in North America, the work of novelists and literary critics or cultural theorists began to theorize the impact of representational and canon-formation practices that construct their canons and readers as White.

[...]

What's at stake in this particular set of arguments is a denaturalization of whiteness. That is, denaturalizing whiteness means to universalize whiteness, not as the norm but as just another race among a spectrum of racial identities that could do the work of articulating both whiteness and anti-racism work differently, albeit another race with systemic power.

[...]

I have been suggesting all along that the labor of making oneself—indeed, of becoming a man—is fraught with responsibilities that go with the territory whether we know it or not. This labor is not unlike the labor of capitalized waged work, especially when, as the whiteness theorists have told us, whiteness accrues with it an additional social and psychological wage. The question then is less how much of ourselves do we sell with intention and more how much we are willing to articulate our bodies against the hegemonic bargain offered to us. For me, that is the measure of the privilege of masculinity without also being The Man.

I like to think that my grandmother and her co-workers understood something of these stakes as working-class and union women. If class and race are the subject of invention and ideological production, then theorizing trans-sexual issues as *labor* also does not seem that strange to me. In many ways, that's precisely the argument of this book. Gender identities—that is, gendered selves— are the product of, but also condition, particular kinds of labor. If the sex/gender system works, like any other ideological system, through misrecognition where we misperceive ourselves as natural human beings rather than as ideologically produced subjects, then it requires, as many theorists have pointed out, our complicit co-operation in order to accomplish that misrecognition. One of the rewards of that activity is the belief in a natural gender that is not man-made. Feminism has been arguing now for over a century that active insubordination with the imperatives of that system is one of the ways to make change happen and to refuse to allow that system to accomplish itself. A new century demands that feminism also begin to acknowledge its own complicity with the biological essentialisms at the core of the sex/gender systems. If it is true that gender identities are acts of co-production, then the process of becoming a self, of making a self, which is so much a part of what trans-identities tell us, is also labor that can be used against the sex/gender system. A North Carolina drag king named Pat Triarch calls gender queers and trans-folks "deconstruction workers," who, by quite literally putting misfitting bodies on the (dis-assembly) line, begin to resist and rebuild the *man-made* gender imperatives that pass as those of nature. These bodies are not bodies as foundation but trans-bodies as archive, witness, risking political incoherence.

## NOTES

1. The pedantic distinction between "transgender" and "transsexual" cannot hold, especially for female-to-male transsexual men for whom surgeries are always incomplete. To avoid being repetitive here, I used the prefix *trans-* to signify subjectivities where bodies are at odds with gender presentation, regardless of whether that misalignment is self-evident in conventional ways or not. The entire question of what's visible, when, how, and by whom is precisely what is at stake in this chapter, so policing or prescribing or hierarchizing kinds of political embodiment is a topical identity politic and moral panic that I eschew.

2. I am not claiming to be outside of White supremacy, nor am I claiming that somehow working-class whiteness is not White. What I am trying to explore here is the possibility within intersectionality of different kinds of whiteness, positioned at different angles to power in White supremacy, where the type of power is mitigated by overlapping and intersecting vectors of power by class, able-bodied-ness, sexuality, gender, and so forth. But the relation to racialized power is constant and I am not at all suggesting otherwise.

3. There is a curious and undertheorized history of what has come to be known as the "self-help discourse"; there was a time in early second wave feminism, due to the work of rape crisis and battered women's/shelter activists/workers, when recovering from the trauma and violence of the sex/gender system was an inherently political act of resistance. Hegemonic appropriations of these ideas rearticulated this notion of a reconfigured self in extremely conservative ways: self is what cosmetic procedures provide ("The Swan"); it's the product of an upper-class leisure-time activity (in most recent years, "Oprah"); self is what's taken up by the beauty myths and also what's used as an advertising strategy (see Subway's new campaign for lighter food consumption, which shows several people stating why they prefer Subway's new light menu, including a young, blonde, White woman from the anorexia demographic saying "I choose to actually eat"); a newly configured self is what Dr. Phil's diet campaign berates and shames folks into becoming. One of the few feminist texts to begin examining this history is Ann Cvetkovich's (2003) *An Archive of Feelings: Trauma, Sexuality and Lesbian Public Cultures.*

4. This is, of course, the primary trope and political rallying cry of Leslie Feinberg's (1991) novel, *Stone Butch Blues,* one of the most important working-class and trans narratives to call for a practice of strategic unmaking.

5. The CUPE 3903 Women's Caucus has not only counted trans-sexual women amongst its members, but in a truly unprecedented intervention in this border war, recently changed its name (it is now the "Trans Identified and Women Identified" Caucus) to create space for trans-sexual men as well. It is clear that this local is able to fold the concerns of its trans-sexual and trans-gendered members into its mandate as issues of labor, not "lifestyle" as the Ontario Conservative government has so deemed.

6. By "tribal" I refer to the tribal organization of premodern Ireland as it was depicted in the film, not the current obnoxious fashion among White folks (read: "Survivor") to imagine themselves as members of urban tribes.

7. The work of this section owes a debt to OmiSoore H. Dryden, my partner, with whom I have spent many pleasurable hours in delightful conversation.

8. *Masculinities without Men?* (2004).

9. This is an allusion to Denise Riley's (1988) extremely important work, *"Am I That Name?": Feminism and the Category of "Women" in History.*

10. See Ann Cvetkovich, *An Archive of Feelings.* On the relation between trauma and counter-cultural resistance movements as an archive or record of trauma but also of resistance, Cvetkovich (2003: 20) writes: "I am interested [...] in the way trauma digs itself in at the level of the everyday, and in the incommensurability of large-scale events and the ongoing material details of experience .... I hope to seize authority over trauma discourses from medical and scientific discourse in order to place it back in the hands of those who make culture, as well as to forge new models for how affective life can serve as the foundation for public but counter-cultural archive as well."

# V

## *CROSS TALK: CONTENTION AND COMPLEXITY IN TRANS-DISCOURSES*

# 21

# *Body Shame, Body Pride*
## Lessons From the Disability Rights Movement

ELI CLARE

ELI CLARE IS A WRITER AND ACTIVIST who lives at the intersection of trans, genderqueer, disability, peace, and anti-racist movements for social justice. In this short text, adapted from a keynote address Clare delivered at a 2007 conference in Milwaukee, Wisconsin (USA) for trans men and their broader communities, Clare examines the differing manifestations of pride and shame related to different-bodiedness that characterize his experiences in the disability rights movement and in ableist trans communities. As his title suggests, most of Clare's remarks have to do with what he feels the trans movement can learn from crip and disability perspectives. Clare notes, among other things, that trans people who seek to medicalize their gender transitions should not expect medicalization to confer normalcy, or to offer a cure for the social stigma of being different. That, for him, is a longing rooted in shame—a lesson learned long ago by disability activist communities. He urges caution, too, when trans activists seek to resist pathologization by advocating for the removal of Gender Identity Disorder from the *Diagnostic and Statistical Manual of Mental Disorders* (DSM). He sees shame at work here, too, in the fear of being diagnosed with a psychopathology and subjected to the disabling consequences that such a diagnosis can trigger.

## INTRODUCTION

I wrote the following first as a keynote speech for a FTM conference in Milwaukee, Wisconsin, in 2007. Imagine a hotel ballroom full of trans people—mostly on the FTM spectrum, but not exclusively—and our friends, family, lovers, spouses, and allies. We've spent the last two days attending workshops and talking politics, dancing and flirting, sitting in community, and listening to stories. From the podium as I look over the jam of people, I see more genders than I can count. I feel a tremendous responsibility to all the overlapping communities gathered in this corporate hotel. What follows is a revised version of what I read that night.

\*\*\*

All my life as a genderqueer crip, I have puzzled my way through bodily difference, struggling with my own shame and love, other people's pity and hatred. Tonight as I stand here in this ballroom overflowing with people, I'm reminded of the incredible importance of community, how bodily difference means one thing in isolation and quite another when we come together, finding ourselves reflected in each other's stories.

My first experience of queerness—of bodily difference—centered, not upon sexuality or gender, but upon disability. Early on I understood that my body was irrevocably different from my neighbors, classmates, playmates, siblings: shaky, off balance, speech hard to understand, a body that moved slow, wrists cocked at odd angles, muscles knotted with tremors. But really, I am telling a kind of lie, a half-truth. Irrevocably different would have meant one thing. Bad, wrong, broken, in need of repair meant quite another. I heard these every day as my classmates called *retard*, *monkey*, *defect*; as nearly everyone I met gawked at me, as my parents grew impatient with my clumsiness. Irrevocably different would have been easy compared to this. I stored the taunting, gawking, isolation in my bones; they became the marrow, my first experience of bodily difference.

Because of that, I always come to community hungry, seeking reflection, wanting dialogue, hoping for a bridge. I know I'm not the only one. Tonight I want to continue my puzzling through bodily difference, spanning the distance between disability politics and trans experience. Of course I could start with the substantial presence of disabled folks in trans communities, and by disability I mean chronic illness and intellectual, cognitive, learning, sensory, and psych disability, as well as physical disability. Or I could start with the truisms about bringing experiences of multiple oppressions and identities to our work. Or start with the long overdue need for accessible spaces, the importance of integrating ableism—that is disability-based oppression—into our understanding of oppression.

But really I want to delve beyond the rhetoric we often don't pay attention to, delve into the myriad of lived bodily differences here in this room tonight and think hard about three lessons I've learned from the disability rights movement. The first is about naming; the second, about coming out and disclosure; the third, about living in our familiar, ordinary bodies.

First, naming: I often hear trans people—most frequently folks who are using, or want to use, medical technology to reshape their bodies—name their transness a disability, a birth defect. They say, "I should have easy access to good, respectful health care, just as other disabled people do. I simply need a cure." The word *defect* always takes my breath away; it's a punch in the stomach. But before I get to that, I need to say the whole equation makes me incredulous, even as I work to respect the people who frame their transness this way. Do they *really* believe disability ensures decent—much less good and respectful—health care? I could tell you a litany of stories, cite you pages of statistics, confirming that exactly the opposite is true. Disabled people routinely deal with doctors who trivialize and patronize us, who believe some of the worst ableist stereotypes, and who sometimes even think we'd be better off dead. I could rant for hours about ableism in medical contexts. But my frustration doesn't stop here.

To couple disability with the need for cure accepts wholesale some of the exact bigotry that I and other disabled people struggle against every day. It takes for granted that disability is an individual medical problem curable, or at least treatable, by doctors. It runs counter to the work of disability activists who frame disability as an issue of social justice, not of medical condition: disability lodged not in paralysis, but rather in stairs without an accompanying ramp; not in depression or anxiety, but rather in a whole host of stereotypes; not in dyslexia, but in teaching methods unwilling to flex. It ignores the reality that many of us aren't looking for cures, but for civil rights.

I've been asked more than once whether I'd take the hypothetical cure pill, always asked in ways that make it clear there's only one real answer: "Why, of course, in a heartbeat." But that's not my answer. For me, having cerebral palsy is like having blue eyes and red hair. I simply don't know my body any other way. Thank you very much, but no: no to the New Age folks who have offered crystals and vitamins, no to the preachers who have prayed over me, no to the doctors who have suggested an array of drugs and possible surgery, all with uncertain outcomes.

All of this gets complicated when I turn back to trans community, to those of us who seek to reshape our gendered and sexed bodies. But really it's not our desire or need for bodily change that I'm challenging here. Rather, it's how we name those desires and needs, because to claim our bodies as defective, and to pair defect with cure, not only disregards the experiences of many disabled people, it also leaves us as trans people wide open to shame.

Of course there's another important strand of naming at work in our communities—a strand that declares transness not a disease, gender non-conformity not a pathology, and bodily uniqueness not an illness—a strand that turns the word *dysphoria* inside out, claiming that we are not the ones dysphoric about our genders, but rather dysphoria lives in the world's response to us. This naming acts as a necessary counterbalance. But I have to ask: what about those of us who do in truth deal with deep, persistent body dissonance, discomfort, dysphoria? A social justice politics by itself will never be enough to resist shame. *SO IMPORTANT* ✳

And now let me move close to the word *defect* because it keeps ringing in my ears. It's an intense word, loaded in this culture with pity and hatred, a word that has tracked me all my life and brought nothing but shame. The bullies have circled round, calling, *defect, monkey, retard, hey defect*, leaving me no escape. Complete strangers on the street have asked, *What's your defect?*, curiosity and rudeness splaying my skin. Doctors have filled my chart with the phrase "birth defect," observed my gait, checked my reflexes, measured my muscle tone. That word is certainly a punch in the stomach.

And so when folks name their transness a birth defect, invoking some horrible bodily wrongness and appealing to cure as a means to end that wrongness, I find myself asking a disbelieving why. Why would anyone freely choose that word for themselves? But the question really needs to be: what leads us to the belief that our bodies are defective in the first place? The answer has to include shame, which medical technology alone will never cure. *AGAIN, CRUCIAL*

Don't get me wrong: I'm not dismissing medical transition as caving into the gender binary or into shame itself. In truth, hormones and surgery can be powerful tools along the way for those of us who have the money or health insurance necessary to access health care in the U.S.A. And just as powerful are the choices to live in all kinds of gendered and sexed bodies—as a man with breasts, as a woman with a penis, as some third, fourth, fifth gender, the possibilities way too many to name. All I mean is that medical technology will never be the whole answer for any of us. → *NOT A RHETORICAL Q,*

Rather than resorting to some naïve and stereotyped notion of disability, we need to grapple with the complex twine of gender dysphoria and body shame. What are the specifics of our shame? How do we move through hatred, disgust, numbness, toward comfort and love, all the while acknowledging body dissonance as a real, sometimes overwhelming, force? Let's lean towards places where we name our bodily differences, even through our ambivalence, grief, and longing, in ways that don't invite and encourage shame. *part of naming, disclosure*

*(might not be positive, but it can't be through shame, it's unproductive.)*

***

That's naming, and now let me move on to a second lesson I've learned from the disability rights movement, a lesson about disclosure and coming out. In trans communities we talk a lot about disclosure, but so often that talk is full of misunderstanding and accusation. Folks who choose to be "stealth" are accused of shame, and folks who choose to be "out" are told they'll regret it later. In these community controversies, we lose all the nuance—the layers of history, fear, protection, exhaustion, resistance, pride, and pure practicality—that come with being out or not. I want us to nurture the most complex conversations possible about how we disclose our bodies and identities to strangers, friends, co-workers, lovers, tricks, doctors, family. I want to honor all the losses and gains contained in each decision about outness. At the same time, I want to challenge the argument I hear sometimes that being trans is simply a private bodily and medical matter, no one's business beyond our closest intimates.

The ability to keep bodily matters private is a privilege that some of us don't have. Just ask a poor person on welfare, a fat person, a visibly disabled person, a pregnant woman. Ask a person of color whose ethnic heritage isn't seemingly apparent. Ask an African-American man who's been pulled over by the cops for "driving while black." Just ask a seriously ill person, a gender ambiguous person, a non-passing trans man or trans woman. All these people experience public scrutiny, in one way or

*VISIBILITY*

*It is inherently not afforded to us.*

another, of their bodies. In this culture bodily difference attracts public attention. For many of us, privacy is simply not an option.

*choosing privacy*

Certainly as a disabled person, I never get a choice about privacy. Sometimes I can choose how to deal with gawking, how to correct the stereotypes and lies, how to live with my particular bodily history. But I don't get to choose privacy, much less *medical* privacy. The first thing people want to know is what's wrong with me. Sometimes they ask carefully about my *disability*, other times demand loudly about my *defect*. But either way they're asking for a medical diagnosis. And if I choose not to tell, they'll just pick one for me anyway and in the picking probably make a heap of offensive assumptions. The lack of privacy faced by poor people, fat people, disabled people, people of color, and visibly queer and gender nonconforming people has many consequences connected to a variety of systems of oppression. I'm not saying that bodies should be public, just that many people don't have access to bodily privacy. *Some people have to disclose*

*Difference in medical privacy*

And so when I hear the argument that being trans is a private matter, I want to ask: do you know that bodily privacy is a privilege regulated by systems of power and control? And if you have that privilege, how are you using it, even when it's laced with ambivalence and stress? In asking these questions, I'm not suggesting that all trans people need to come out all the time, nor that those of us who choose to be "stealth" are suspect. As a genderqueer who lives in the world as a white guy, I certainly understand the challenges and risks of disclosure on a daily basis. In a transphobic world all the available options are fraught. And it goes without saying that non-consensual disclosure is just plain wrong, and in some cases, deadly. Yet if we are to make a sustaining community that profoundly challenges shame and nurtures pride, we need to acknowledge the political implications that trail our personal, individual decisions and question the value some trans people place on privacy.

*NEED TO DISCLOSE? WHY.*

In contrast, the disability rights movement values self-determination. Who gets to make which choices about our bodies—where we sleep, what we eat, who we socialize with? A popular disability slogan declares, "Nothing about us without us." For peoples who have long histories of institutionalization in nursing homes, group homes, psych wards, state-run hospitals, and rehab centers, self-determination is a radical and liberating politics. We get to determine how and when to explain ourselves, bodies not reduced to medical histories and issues but rather belonging fully to us, doctors playing only small, bit roles. A politics of self-determination declares that only we—not doctors, psychiatrists, physical therapists, case workers, social workers, the folks ruling on our SSI and food stamp applications—have authority over our bodies, know what works for us and what doesn't, can say who we are and what we want. It discards the notion that our bodies are medical curiosities, scientific theories, social burdens and perversities. It is a simple, matter-of-fact, and entirely profound politics. By valuing self-determination, we invite many different kinds of bodies to the table. We reach toward liberation rather than privilege.

*we define our narrative*

*pwr*

Turning back to trans disclosure, I remember what intimate and risky work it is, so full of conflicting urges and emotions—exhaustion, frustration, necessity, fear, desire. What would disclosure look like if trans communities shaped a politics around self-determination, rather than privacy?

\*\*\*

Naming, disclosure, and now I'll turn to a third lesson I've learned from the disability rights movement, a lesson about living in our familiar, ordinary bodies. I watch marginalized people in a variety of communities yearn towards—or make declarations of—normality. So many FTMs aspire to be normal men, MTFs to be normal women. There are trans folks who don't want to be queer in any way, and others who embrace their queerness loudly and with pride. Personally I'd like to completely discard the idea of normality. I don't mean that everyone ought to be queer; it's just that the very idea of normal means comparing ourselves to some external, and largely mythical, standard. But being normal or being queer aren't the only choices.

*Foucault and a sort of ordinary*

*mythology / Barthes*

All too often in trans communities we buy into the wholesale medicalization of our bodies and lose what is simply ordinary and familiar about them. I think of the long-standing argument that trans activists are embroiled in about the DSM and Gender Identity Disorder. Does the diagnosis that trans people use to access medical technology belong in the DSM; is transness a *psychiatric* disorder; where does it belong if not in the DSM? This conversation has been, and continues to be, long and fraught. The details are important, and I find myself agreeing with parts of both arguments. But in the end, I think we're asking the wrong questions.

These debates have highlighted the need for a diagnosis for transsexuality, underscored the differences between a psychiatric and a medical framework, and articulated the trouble with the word *disorder*. Still we haven't questioned the fundamental relationship between trans people and the very idea of diagnosis. Many of us are still invested in the ways we're medicalized. How often have you heard trans people come out by saying, "I have Gender Identity Disorder," explain and defend their choices by referencing that diagnosis? We praise our doctors, rail against their quirks, measure our transitions in medical terms. Even trans folks who have no interest in medical transition are assumed to be in relationship to it. How many female-assigned genderqueer people are sick of the question, "When are you going to start testosterone?"

In counterpoint, the disability rights movement fiercely resists the medicalization of bodies. Certainly disabled people sometimes need medical technology to sustain our very life's breath, but that doesn't transform our bodies into mere medical conditions. We have become practiced at defining ourselves from the inside out, stepping away from the shadow called normal, understanding what doctors can offer and what they can't, knowing our disabled bodies as familiar and ordinary. If trans people took up this disability rights lesson and defined ourselves on our own terms rather than through the lens of medicine, we'd still care about finding good doctors and getting good medical treatment, but our bodily truths wouldn't ultimately be medical truths. From this place of power, the question of psychiatric versus medical diagnosis would become less pressing.

At the same time, issues surrounding psychiatric diagnosis are often about life and death for many folks trapped inside the mental health system. As we talk about the DSM, let's not act as if trans people don't belong in the DSM because we aren't *really* "crazy," unlike the "crazies" over there—folks labeled with depression, bipolar disorder, dissociative behavior, schizophrenia, and so on. Let's work from the knowledge that the DSM wields incredible power and causes tremendous trouble for so many different people. Let's remember the gender nonconforming youth who endure psychiatric abuse, the transsexuals who need drug treatment programs but can't find placements because their transness is seen as psychiatric illness.

With a disability politics, we could learn to use diagnosis without being defined by it, all the while resisting the institutions that hold power over us. Simply changing where Gender Identity Disorder lives without changing our relationship to the idea of diagnosis isn't nearly enough. Rather than being attached to diagnosis, we could understand our lives and histories as *ordinary* from the inside, even as we're treated as curious, exotic, unbelievable, deceptive, sick, threatening from the outside. We could frame bodily difference as neither good nor bad, but as profoundly *familiar*.

***

In the end I'm reaching toward a disability politics of transness, not one of simple analogy, but one that delves into the lived experiences of our bodies, that questions the idea of normal and the notion of cure, that values self-determination, that resists shame and the medicalization of identity—a politics that will help all of us come home to our bodies.

# 22

# The Pharmaco-Pornographic Regime

## Sex, Gender, and Subjectivity in the Age of Punk Capitalism

BEATRIZ PRECIADO

"WE ARE FACING A NEW KIND OF CAPITALISM THAT IS HOT, PSYCHOTROPIC AND PUNK," according to Spanish architectural theorist and transdisciplinary sexuality scholar Beatriz Preciado, who coins a new term—*farmacopornográfico* (pharmaco-pornographic)—to describe the post-World War II confluence of drugs, surgery, biotechnology, mass media, new media, cybernetics, and hypersexuality that s/he claims now governs our lives. Preciado draws on the work of Michel Foucault to argue that sex, sexuality, sexual identity, and erotic pleasure have become crucial vectors for the governance of life. But whereas, in the era of capitalism that is now passing, the body was a target of external "ortho-architectural" disciplinary practices aimed at controlling workers and work processes, in the new pharmaco-pornographic regime, technologies of control physically enter the body to merge with it and incite desire at the molecular level: they dissolve in the body and become part of the body, thereby blurring the boundaries between *soma* and *techné*. Everything from moods and affects, to sexual function and reproduction, to attention and relaxation and sleep increasingly falls under psycho-pharmacological regulation, through which existence becomes subjugated to a neoliberal logic of efficiency, productivity, and the optimization of costs and benefits. Within such a biotechnological society, bodies and machines grow increasingly interpenetrated, and the technical means of bodily control becomes literally incorporated. For more than half a century, the figure of the transsexual—hormonally altered and surgically modified, rendered hypersexual and deemed obscene—has functioned as an emblem of the pharmaco-pornographic era. For Preciado, the figure of the transsexual represents the style of technocultural embodiment through which we all increasingly live; but also, and perhaps more importantly, transsexual/transgender political activism and critical theory offer powerful critiques of the conditions of contemporary life, that in turn suggest new ways of ethical living that may be of much more general relevance.

During an era, recent and already irretrievable, Fordism and the automobile industry synthesized and defined a specific mode of production and of consumption. It instituted a Taylorist protraction of life: a smooth and polychrome aesthetic of the unanimated object, a way of thinking about interior space and of living in the city, a conflicting promise of the body and of the machine, a discontinued manner of desiring and of resisting. In the years following the energy crisis and the collapse of the assembly line, new sectors were said to explain the transformations of the global economy. Thus economic "experts" begin to speak of the biochemical industry, electronics, informatics or communication as the new industrial supports of capitalism.[1] But these discourses are not sufficient to explain the production of value and of life in contemporary society.

It seems possible and politically crucial to draw a new cartography of the transformations occurring in industrial production over the last century. With certain radical changes in view, the political management of body technologies that produce sex and sexuality can be seen to progressively become *the* business of the new millennium. It is today philosophically pertinent, following Foucault, to carry out a somatic-political analysis of the "world economy."[2] Economists usually situate the transition to a third type of capitalism around the seventies, after industrial and slavery regimes. These have traditionally been said to set in motion a new type of "governmentality of the living," emerging from the corporal, physical and ecological urban ruins of the Second World War.[3] The mutation of capitalism that we witness in our time can be characterized by the conversion of "sex", "sexuality", "sexual identity" and "pleasure" into objects used for the political management of life, and also by the fact that this "management" itself takes place through the innovative dynamics of advanced techno-capitalism, global media, and biotechnologies. But first let us review some of the somatic-political events in recent history.

During the period of the Cold War, the United States invested more dollars in scientific research related to sex and sexuality than any other country had done before throughout history. Let us remember that the period between the beginning of the Second World War and the first years of the Cold War constitutes a moment without precedence for women's visibility in public space as well as the emergence of visible and politicized forms of homosexuality in such unexpected places as, for example, the American army.[4] Alongside this social development, American McCarthyism— rampant throughout the 1950s—added to the patriotic fight against communism the persecution of homosexuality as a form of anti-nationalism while exalting at the same time the family values of masculine labour and domestic maternity.[5] Meanwhile, architects Ray and Charles Eames collaborated with the American army to manufacture small boards of molded plywood to use as splints for mutilated appendages. A few years later, the same material was used to build furniture that came to exemplify the light design of modern disposable American architecture.[6] In 1941, George Henry carried out the first demographic study of "sexual deviation," a quantitative study of masses known as *Sex Variants*.[7] The Kinsey Reports on human sexual behaviour (1948 and 1953) and Robert Stoller's protocols for "femininity" and "masculinity" (1968) followed in sexological suit. During the early fifties and into the sixties, Harry Benjamin systemized the clinical use of hormonal molecules in the treatment of "transsexualism", a term first introduced in 1954. In 1941 the first natural molecules of progesterone and estrogens were obtained from the urine of pregnant mares (Premarin) and soon after synthetic hormones (Norethindrone) were commercialized. In 1957, Enovid, the first contraceptive pill was invented using synthetic estrogens, a hormone that would soon become the most used pharmaceutical molecule in the whole of human history.[8] In 1947, the laboratories Eli Lilly commercialized the molecule called Methadone (the most simple opiate) as an analgesic, which became in the seventies the basic substitution treatment for heroin addiction.[9]

Between 1946 and 1949 Harold Gillies was performing the first phalloplastic surgeries in the UK, including work on Michael Dillon, the first female-to-male transsexual to have taken testosterone as part of the masculinization protocol.[10] In 1952, U.S. soldier George W. Jorgensen was transformed into Christine, the first transsexual person discussed widely in the popular press. In 1953, Hugh Hefner founded *Playboy*, the first North American "porno" magazine to be sold in newsstands, with a photograph of Marilyn Monroe naked on the front page of the first publication. In 1957, the North American pedo-psychiatrist John Money coined the term "gender", differentiating it from the traditional term "sex", to define an individual's inclusion in a culturally recognized group of "masculine" or "feminine" behaviour and physical expression. Money famously affirmed that it is possible to "change the gender of any baby up to 18 months."[11] In 1960, the laboratories Eli Lilly commercialized Secobarbital, a barbiturate with anaesthetic, sedative and hypnotic properties conceived for the treatment of epilepsy, insomnia and as an anaesthetic for short surgery. Secobarbital, better known as "the red pill" or "doll", becomes one of the drugs of the rock underground culture of the '60s. At the start of the '60s, Manfred E. Clynes and Nathan S. Kline used the term "cyborg" for the first time to refer to an organism technologically supplemented to live in an extraterrestrial environment where it could operate as an "integrated homeostatic system."[12] They experimented with a laboratory rat, which received an osmotic prosthesis implant that it dragged along—a cyber tail. The first antidepressant that intervenes directly in the synthesis of a neurotransmitter called serotonin was invented in 1966. This would lead to the conception in 1987 of the molecule called Fluoxetine that would be commercialized under various names, the most renowned being Prozac©. In 1969, as part of a military investigation programme, Arpanet was created; it was the predecessor of the global Internet, the first "net of nets" of interconnected computers capable of transmitting information. [...] In 1972, Gerard Damiano produced the film *Deep Throat*. The film, starring Linda Lovelace, screened widely in the United States and became the most watched movie of all times, grossing more than $600 million. From this time on, porn film production boomed: from thirty clandestine films in 1950 to 2500 films in 1970. Homosexuality was withdrawn from the *Diagnostic and Statistical Manual of Mental Disorders* (DSM) in 1973. The soviet Victor Konstantinovich Kalnberz patented, in 1974, the first penis implant using polyethylene plastic rods as a treatment for impotency, resulting in a permanently erect penis. These implants were abandoned for chemical variants because they were found to be "physically uncomfortable and emotionally disconcerting." In 1977, the state of Oklahoma introduced the first lethal injection composed of barbiturates similar to the "red pill" to be used for the death penalty. The same method had already been applied in a Nazi German program called Action T4 for "racial hygiene" that euthanatized between 75,000 and 100,000 people with physical or psychic disabilities. The program was abandoned because of the high pharmacological cost; instead they substituted it for the methods of gas chambers or simply death caused by inanition. In 1983, Gender Identity Disorder (clinical form of transsexuality) was included in the DSM with diagnostic criteria for this new pathology. In 1984 Tom F. Lue, Emil A. Tanaghoy and Richard A. Schmidt implanted a "sexual pacemaker" in the penis of a patient. The contraption was a system of electrodes inserted close to the prostate that permitted an erection by remote control.

During the '80s, new hormones were discovered and commercialized such as DHEA or the growth hormone, as well as numerous anabolic steroids that would be used legally and illegally in sports. In 1988, the pharmacological use of Sildenafil (commercialized as Viagra© by Pfizer laboratories) was approved of for the treatment of penile "erectile dysfunction." It is a vasodilator without aphrodisiac effects that induces muscular relaxation and the production of nitric oxide in the cavernous body of the penis. From 1996 on, American laboratories produced synthetic oxyntomodulin, a hormone found to suppress human appetite by affecting the psycho-physiological mechanisms that regulate addiction; it was quickly commercialized to induce weight loss. At the beginning of the new millennium, four million children are being treated with Ritalin for hyperactivity and for the so-called "Attention Deficit Disorder" and more than two million children consume psycho-tropics destined to control depression.

During the Second World War, we see the exponential multiplication of the production of transuranic elements (the chemical elements with atomic numbers greater than 92—the atomic number of uranium) for use in the civil sector. This included plutonium, which had previously been used as nuclear fuel in military operations. The level of toxicity of transuranic elements exceeds that of all other elements on Earth, creating a new form of vulnerability for life. At the same time, a viscous, semi-rigid material that is waterproof, thermally and electrically resistant, produced by artificial propagation of carbon atoms in long chains of molecules of organic compounds derived from petroleum, and whose burning is highly polluting, became generalized in manufacturing the objects of daily life. The mass consumption of plastic defined the material conditions of a large-scale ecological transformation resulting in the destruction of other (mostly lower) energy resources in the world, rapid consumption, and high pollution. The *Trash Vortex*, a floating mass of the size of Texas in the north Pacific Ocean made of plastic garbage, was to become the most significant architecture of the twenty-first century.[13]

We are facing a new kind of capitalism that is hot, psychotropic and punk. These recent transformations indicate new micro-prosthetic mechanisms of control emergent from advanced bio-molecular techniques and media networks. The new world economy does not function without the simultaneous and interconnected production and deployment of hundreds of tons of synthetic steroids, without global dissemination of pornographic images, without the manufacturing of new varieties of legal and illegal synthetic psycho-tropics (e.g. enaltestovis, Special K, Viagra©, speed, crystal, Prozac©, ecstasy, poppers, heroin, omeoprazole) without the global dispersal of mega-cities of misery knotted into high concentrations of capital,[14] or without an informatic treatment of signs and numeric transmission of communication.

These are just some snapshots of a post-industrial, global and mediatic regime that I will call from here onwards *pharmaco-pornographic*. This term refers to the processes of a bio-molecular (pharmaco) and semiotic-technical (pornographic) government of sexual subjectivity—of which "the Pill" and *Playboy* are two paradigmatic offspring. During the second half of the twentieth century, the mechanisms of the pharmaco-pornographic regime are materialized in the fields of psychology, sexology and endocrinology. If science has reached the hegemonic place that it occupies as a discourse and as a practice in our culture it is precisely thanks to what Ian Hacking, Steve Woolgar and Bruno Latour call science's "material authority," that is to say, its capacity to invent and produce techno-living artifacts.[15] Techno-science has established its "material authority" by transforming the concepts of the psyche, libido, consciousness, femininity and masculinity, heterosexuality and homosexuality, intersexuality and transsexuality into tangible realities. They are manifest in commercial chemical substances and molecules, biotype bodies, and fungible technological goods managed by multinationals. The success of contemporary techno-science consists in transforming our depression into Prozac©, our masculinity into testosterone, our erection into Viagra©, our fertility/sterility into the Pill, our AIDS into Tritherapy without knowing which comes first: if depression or Prozac©; if Viagra© or an erection; if testosterone or masculinity; if the Pill or maternity; if Tritherapy or AIDS. This performative feedback is one of the mechanisms of the pharmaco-pornographic regime.

Contemporary society is inhabited by toxic-pornographic subjectivities: subjectivities defined by the substance (or substances) that supply their metabolism, by the cybernetic prostheses and various types of pharmaco-pornographic desires that feed the subject's actions and through which they turn into agents. So we will speak of Prozac© subjects, cannabis subjects, cocaine subjects, alcohol subjects, Ritalin subjects, cortisone subjects, silicone subjects, hetero-vaginal subjects, double-penetration subjects, Viagra© subjects, $ subjects…

There is nothing to discover in nature, there is no hidden secret. We live in a punk hyper-modernity: it is no longer about discovering the hidden truth in nature; it is about the necessity of specifying the cultural, political and technological processes through which the body as artifact acquires natural status. The Oncomouse, the laboratory mouse biotechnologically designed to carry a carcinogenic gene, eats Heidegger.[16] Buffy, the mutant vampire on television, eats Simone de Beauvoir. The dildo, a synthetic extension of sex to produce pleasure and identity, eats Rocco Siffredi's cock. There is nothing to discover in sex nor in sexual identity, there is no *inside*. The truth about sex is not a disclosure; it is *sexdesign*. Pharmaco-pornographic bio-capitalism does not produce *things*. It produces mobile ideas, living organs, symbols, desires, chemical reactions and conditions of the soul. In biotechnology and in porno-communication there is no object to be produced. The pharmaco-pornographic business is the *invention of a subject* and then its global reproduction.

In this period of the body's techno-management, the pharmaco-pornographic industry synthesizes and defines a specific mode of production and of consumption, a masturbatory temporization of life, a virtual and hallucinogenic aesthetic of the body, a particular way of transforming the inner in outer space and the city in a private junkspace[17] by means of self-surveillance devices and ultra fast information distribution, resulting in continuous and uninterrupted loops of desire and resistance, of consumption and destruction, of evolution and self-extinction.

## THE HISTORY OF TECHNO-SEXUALITY

In thinking about the transformations of European society at the end of the eighteenth century, Foucault describes the transition from what he calls a sovereign society towards a disciplinary society. A new form of power that calculates life technologically in terms of population, health and national interest, he notes, displaces a prior form of power that decided and ritualized death. Foucault calls this new diffuse set of *dispositifs* to regulate life *biopower*. This power overflows the legal and punitive spheres, to become a force that penetrates and constitutes the body of the modern individual. This power no longer behaves as a coercive law or as a negative mandate, but becomes versatile and responsive. Biopower is a *friendly-power* that takes the form of an art for governing life. As a general political technology, biopower morphs into disciplinary architectures (prison, barracks, schools, hospitals, etc.), scientific texts, tables of statistics, demographic calculus, employment options and public hygiene. Foucault underlined the centrality of sex and of sexuality in the modern art of governing life. The biopower processes of the feminine body's hysterization, children's sexual pedagogy, regulation of procreative conduct and the psychiatrization of the pervert's pleasures will be to Foucault the axes of this project that he distinguishes, not without irony, as a process of sexuality's modernization.[18]

The sex-political devices that develop with these new aesthetics of sexual difference and sexual identities are mechanical, semiotic and architectonical techniques to naturalize sex. These devices include *The Atlas of Human Sex Anatomy*, treatises on maximizing the natural recourses available from population growth, judiciary texts about the penalization of transvestism or of sodomy, handcuffs that restrain the hands of masturbating girls to their beds, iron ankle spreaders that separate the legs of hysterics, silver films that engrave photographic images of the dilated anuses of passive homosexuals, straitjackets that hold the indomitable bodies of masculine women....[19] These devices for the production of sexual subjectivity take the form of a political architecture *external* to the body. These systems have a firm command of orthopedic politics and disciplinary exoskeletons. The model for these techniques of subjectivization, according to Foucault, could be Bentham's architecture for the prison-factory (and in particular, panopticism), the asylum or military barracks. If we think about devices of sex-political subjectivization then we must also speak about the net-like expansion of "domestic architecture." These extensive, intensive and, moreover, intimate architectural forms include a redefinition of private and public spaces, the management of sexual commerce, but also gynecological devices and sexual orthopedic inventions (the corset, the speculum, the medical vibrator), as well as new media techniques of control and representation (photography, film, incipient pornography) and the massive development of psychological techniques for introspection and confession.

It is true that up till here Foucault's analytical overview, though not always historically and chronologically exact, is critically sharp. However, it is also true that the valuable insights he offers begin to blur the closer the analysis comes to contemporary societies. It seems that Foucault does not consider the profound changes, beginning during the Second World War, that occur with a new set of technologies for producing sexual subjectivity. As I see it, these somatic-political technologies require us to conceptualize a third regime of power-knowledge, neither sovereign nor disciplinary, neither pre-modern or modern, in order to take into consideration the deep and lasting impact of these new body technologies on contemporary constructions of subjectivity. In the Postscript of *A Thousand Plateaus*, Deleuze and Guattari are inspired by Williams S. Burroughs to name this "new monster" of social organization derived from biopolitical control a "society of control."[20] I prefer to call it, reading Burroughs along with Bukowski, *pharmaco-porn-power*: a politically programmed ejaculation is the currency of this new sexual-micro-informatic control.

The somatic-political context after the Second World War seems to be dominated by a set of new technologies of the body (e.g. biotechnologies, surgery, endocrinology) and of representation (e.g. photography, film, television and cybernetics) that infiltrates and penetrates everyday life as never before. We live in an era of proliferating bio-molecular, digital and high-speed technologies; of the soft, light, slimy and jelly technologies; of the injectable, inhalable, and incorporable technologies. Testosterone gel, the Pill and psychotropics all belong to this set of *soft technologies*. We are heavily involved in something that can be called—recalling the work of Zygmunt Bauman—a sophisticated form of "liquid" control.[21]

Whereas in the disciplinary society, technologies of subjectivation control the body from the outside as an ortho-architectonic exterior device, in the pharmaco-pornographic society of control, technologies enter the body to form part of it: they dissolve in the body; they become the body. Here somatic-politics become tautological: techno-politics take the form of the body; techno-politics becomes (in)corporate. In the middle of the twentieth century, the first signs of the new somatic-political regime's transmutation were the electrification, digitalization and molecularization of devices of control that specifically produce sexual difference and sexual identities. Little by little, the orthopedic sexual mechanisms and disciplinary architectonics are being absorbed by pharmacological micro-informatics and instant audiovisual transmission techniques. If in the disciplinary society, architecture and orthopedics served as models to understand the relation of body-power, in the pharmaco-pornographic society, the models for body control are micro-prosthetics: pharmaco-porn-power acts through molecules that become part of our immune system; from the silicon that takes the form of breasts, to a neurotransmitter that modifies our way of perceiving and acting, to a hormone and its systematic affect on hunger, sleep, sexual excitation, aggression and the social codification of our femininity and masculinity. The devices of surveillance and control that are common to a disciplinary sex-political regime will thus progressively assist the pharmaco-pornographic subject's miniaturization, internalization and reflexive introversion (a twist towards the inside, towards the space that is considered to be intimate, private). A common trait of the new soft technologies of micro-control is that they take the form of the body; they control by transforming into "body", until they become inseparable and indistinguishable from it. Soft technologies become the stuff of subjectivity. Here the body no longer inhabits disciplinary spaces, but is inhabited by them. The bio-molecular and organic structure of the body is a last resort for these control systems. This moment contains all the horror and exaltation of the body's political potential.

Unlike the disciplinary society, pharmaco-pornographic society no longer works over a modern *corpus*. The new pharmaco-pornographic body does not have its limits at the skeletal wrapping that the skin delineates. This new body cannot be understood as a biological substratum outside the framework of production and cultivation, typical features of techno-science. As Donna Haraway teaches us, the contemporary body is a techno-living being, "a networking techno-organic-textual-mythic system."[22] Organism and machine, nature and culture are obsolete disciplinary fictions. This new condition of the body blurs the traditional modern distinction between art, performance, media, design, and architecture. The new pharmacological and surgical techniques set in motion tectonic construction processes that combine figurative representations derived from cinema and from architecture (editing, 3D modelling or personality design, etc.), according to which the organs, the vessels, the fluids (techno-blood, techno-sperm, etc.) and the molecules are converted into the prime material from which our pharmaco-pornographic corporality is manufactured. Techno-bodies are either not-yet-alive or already-dead: we are half fetuses, half zombies. Thus, every politics of resistance is a monster politics.

## TECHNO-GENDER

The invention of the category *gender* announces the arrival of the new pharmaco-pornographic regime of sexuality. Far from being the creation of 60s feminism, the category of gender belongs to the bio-technological discourse from the 1950s. "Gender," "masculinity," and "femininity" are inventions of the Second World War that would see their full commercial expansion during the Cold War, along with objects such as canned food, the computer, plastic chairs, nuclear energy, television, the credit card, the disposable pen, the bar code, the air bed and the artificial satellite.

Arguing against the rigidity of the nineteenth century concept of "sex", John Money, who conducted the first methodological treatment of intersex babies, advanced the technological plasticity of "gender." In 1957, Money used the notion of "gender" for the first time in speaking about the possibility of technologically modifying, through the use of hormones and surgery, the bodily presentation of babies born with "unclassifiable" (according to medicine's visual and discursive criteria) feminine or masculine genital organs and/or chromosomes. With Anke Ehrhardt and Joan and John Hampson, Money would later develop his claim into a strict clinical procedure for tinkering with young intersexual bodies.[23] When Money uses the term "gender" to refer to "psychological sex," he basically thinks about the exciting possibility of using technology to modify the deviant body, in order to bring it into accordance with pre-existing prescriptive ideals for feminine and masculine human bodies. If in the nineteenth century disciplinary system sex was natural, definitive, untransferable and transcendental, then *gender* now appears to be synthetic, malleable, variable, and susceptible of being transferred, imitated, produced and technically reproduced.

Far from the rigidity of exterior techniques to normalize the body practiced by the disciplinary system at the end of the nineteenth and beginning of the twentieth century, the new gender techniques of the bio-capitalist pharmaco-pornographic regime are flexible, internal and assimilable. Twenty-first century gender functions as an abstract device of technical subjectivation: it is glued, it is cut, it is displaceable, it is named, it is imitated, it is swallowed, it is injected, it is grafted, it is digitalized, it is copied, it is designed, it is bought, it is sold, it is modified, it is mortgaged, it is transferred, it is downloaded, it is applied, it is transcribed, it is falsified, it is executed, it is certified, it is exchanged, it is dosed, it is provided, it is extracted, it shrinks, it is subtracted, it is denied, it is renounced, it is betrayed, it mutates.

Gender (femininity/masculinity) is not a concept, it is not an ideology, and it is not simply a performance: *it is a techno-political ecology*. The certainty of being a man or a woman is a somatic-political fiction that functions as an operational program of subjectivity through which sensorial perceptions are produced that take the form of affections, desires, actions, beliefs, identities. One of the defining results of this technology of gender is the production of an interior knowledge about oneself, of a sense of the sexual "I" that appears to one's consciousness as emotional evidence of reality. "I am man," "I am woman," "I am heterosexual," "I am homosexual" are some of the formulations that condense specific knowledges about oneself, acting as hard biopolitical and symbolic nuclei around which it is possible to attach a set of practices and discourses.

The pharmaco-pornographic regime of sexuality cannot function without the circulation of an enormous quantity of semiotic-technical flows: hormonal flows, silicon flows, digital flows, textual and of representation. *Definitively, this third regime cannot function without the constant trafficking of gender bio-codes.* In this political economy of sex, the normalization of difference depends on the control, re-appropriation and use of these flows of gender.

Nowadays, the synthetic molecules of testosterone, oxytocin, serotonin, codeine, cortisone, estrogens, etc. are edible somatic-political programs for the manufacturing of subjectivity and its affects. We are equipped techno-biopolitically to fuck, to reproduce or to control the possibility of reproduction. We live under the control of molecular technologies, of hormonal straitjackets, forever destined to invest in the power of gender. The objective of these pharmaco-pornographic technologies is the production of a living political prosthesis: namely, the production of a body docile enough as to put its total and abstract capacity to the task of creating pleasure in the service of capital's production. Outside of these somatic-political ecologies that regulate gender and sexuality there is no man or woman, just as there is no heterosexuality or homosexuality.

What I call *gender programming* is a pharmaco-pornographic technology for modelling a subjectivity that permits its productive (or successful) subjects to think and to act as individual bodies. Hence, such gender-producing subjects understand themselves as delimited spaces and as private property, with a gender identity and a fixed sexuality. The programming of a dominant gender starts from the following premise: an individual=a body=a sex=a gender=a sexuality. There are a wide variety of models for genderization, for so-called gender programs, depending on the historical moment and on the political and cultural context. Some gender programs have lost their potential for achieving subjectivization (i.e. the systems of matriarchal genderization or of Greek paedophilia) because the *political ecologies* that activated them have become extinct. Still others are in complete transformation, as is the case for our current genderization model.

In the pharmaco-pornographic regime, gender is constituted in the "nets" of biopolitical materialization. Gender, as Judith Butler has brought sharply into focus, is produced and socially consolidated in the act of performance, in an image in movement, in digital worlds, in cyber code, constantly recreated as "a practice of improvisation in a scene of constraint."[24] There is no longer a masculine or feminine gender unless it is facing a public, that is to say, gender is a somatic-discursive construction of a collective kind, apparent only when facing the scientific community or the net. Gender is public, it is the scientific community; it is the net itself.

Our contemporary societies are enormous sex-political laboratories where gender is being produced. The body, the body of each and every one of us, is the precious enclave where complex transactions of power are taking place. My body=the body of the multitude. That what we call sex, but also gender, masculinity/femininity and sexuality are *techniques of the body*, bio-technological extensions that belong to the sex-political system whose objective is production, reproduction and colonial expansion of heterosexual human life on the planet.[25]

Since the Second World War, the new biopolitical ideals of masculinity and femininity are created in laboratories. These ideals of gender cannot exist in a pure state; they only exist in our *confined sexual techno-ecosystems*. As sexual subjects we inhabit a bio-capitalist theme park (providing entertainment, education, excitement, leisure...) surrounded by a gigantic junk backstage. We are laboratory man and woman. We are the effects of a kind of political and scientific bio-Platonism. But we are alive: at the same time we materialize the power of the pharmaco-pornographic system and its possibility of failure.[26]

We are molecularly equipped to remain complicit with dominant repressive formations. But the contemporary pharmaco-pornographic body, just like the sex-disciplined body from the end of the nineteenth century, (different from what Foucault affirms) is *not* docile.[27] This body is not simply an effect of the pharmaco-pornographic systems of control; it is first and above all the materialization of "*puissance de vie*," "power of life" that aspires to transfer to all and to every body. This is the paradoxical condition of contemporary resistance and revolt: pharmaco-pornographic subjectivity is at the same time the effect of biopolitical technologies of control and the ultimate site of resistance to them.[28]

The body in the pharmaco-pornographic era is not a passive substrate but a techno-organic interface, a biopolitical standard-of-living-package segmented and territorialized by different political models (textual, computing, bio-chemical).[29] As legal theorist Dean Spade has shown, there are no successions of models that will be historically superseded by others, no ruptures, no radical discontinuities, but unconnected simultaneity, transversal action of several somatic-political models that operate at diverse intensities, diverse rates of penetration, and diverse grades of effectiveness in the production of subjectivity.[30]

How to explain otherwise that at the beginning of the twenty-first century, nasal surgery is considered to be a cosmetic surgery while vaginoplasty (surgical construction of the vagina) and phalloplasty (surgical construction of the penis) are considered as sex reassignment surgeries that require psychiatric assessment and legal authorization? We could say that nowadays, and inside the same body, the nose and the sexual organs are understood, produced, and explained by two completely different regimes of power. The nose is regulated by a pharmaco-pornographic power in which an organ is considered as an individual property and a market object, while the genitals are still enclosed in a pre-modern and almost sovereign regime of power that considers them to be state property (and in extension of this theocratic model, God's property) by virtue of a transcendental and immutable law. But the statute of the organs in the pharmaco-pornographic regime is undergoing a rapid change, so that a shifting multiplicity of production systems operates simultaneously on any given body. Those who survive the current mutation will see their body change from a semiotic-technical system; in other words, they will no longer be the bodies they were.

Forty years after the invention of the endocrine gender control techniques (like the Pill) all sexual bodies are subject to a *common* pharmaco-pornographical platform. Today a bio-man will take a hormonal testosterone supplement to increase his performance in sports; a subcutaneous compound of estrogens and progesterone, active over three years, will be implanted in an adolescent as a contraconceptive; a bio-woman who defines herself as a man could sign a protocol of sex change and access an endocrinology therapy based on testosterone that will make him grow a beard and moustache, increase musculature and pass socially as a man in less than eight months; a sixty-year-old bio-woman who ingested a high dose of estrogens and progesterone in her contraceptive pills for over twenty years will have kidney failure or breast cancer and receive chemotherapy similar to the kind administered to the victims of Chernobyl; a heterosexual couple will turn to in vitro insemination after discovering that the male of the couple cannot produce sufficient mobile spermatozoids to fertilize the ovule of his partner, due to a high intake of tobacco and alcohol...

All this indicates that the diverse sexual identities, the various models of having sex and producing pleasure, the plural ways of expressing gender coexist with a *"becoming-common"*[31] of the technologies that produce gender, sex and sexuality.[32]

## RESISTANCES, MUTATIONS...

But a process of deconstructing and constructing gender that Judith Butler has called "undoing gender" is always already taking place.[33] Dismantling these gender programmes requires a set of denaturalizing and disidentification operations. These take place, for example, in drag king and criss-cross practices, hormonal self-experiments, crip and post-porn practices which in political terms function as techniques for de-installing gender.

In the year 2000, establishing in a certain way our corporal future in the new millennium, the Scottish surgeon Robert Smith became the subject of an international bioethics controversy for accepting the petition of Gregg Furth, a patient who applied for the amputation of his healthy legs. He was suffering from what is known today under the nomenclature of Body Integrity Identity Disorder (BIID), an illness of misidentifying one's real and imagined corporal integration. Furth perceived his own biped body to be contrary to what he thought was *his* ideal body image. Even though the bioethics committee prevented the operation from taking place, Smith confirmed that he had amputated several patients with similar pathologies of "corporal dysmorphism" between 1993 and 1997. To some, nostalgic for the modern body, these operations are considered to be appallingly aberrant. But who would dare to cast the first stone at Furth: candidates for lifting and liposuction, people fitted with pacemakers, consumers of "the Pill," addicts to Prozac, to Tranquimazin or to cocaine, slaves of the hypo calorie regime, consumers of Viagra, or those who spend an average of eight hours per day connected to an informatic-mediatic prosthesis, i.e. computers, television, games on the net?

Furth is not an isolated madman who wants to submit himself, under medically controlled conditions, to a chirurgical bacchanal worthy of *Texas Chainsaw Massacre*. On the contrary, he is one of the known creators of a set of micro-political movements that demand the right to redefine the living body outside of a hegemonic society's normative restrictions for legitimate able bodies. The political defenders of elective mutilation adopt the slogan of Mies Van der Rohe "less is more" as the new economy for their project's ideal corporal architecture. The BIID project resists corporal normalization imperatives and brutally brings to light the cultural and political law constructed out of the binary disability/normality.

In parallel, activists of the self-styled "crip" movement are putting the medical industry on the rack by refusing to receive cochlear electronic prostheses implants that would enable them to hear. Crip activists, inspired by the political tradition of the feminist, black and queer movements, defend their right to stay in the "culture of deafness." They argue that access to sound through prosthesis is a normative imposition that forces them to be part of the dominant auditory culture. Similarly, at the end of the 80s, the transgender movement commenced by criticizing the enforced use of technologies for sex changes, which sought to normalize the transsexual's body. Bio-men and the bio-women (indistinctly heterosexuals and homosexuals), but also those transsexuals who have access to chirurgical, endocrinological or legal techniques to produce their identity, are not simple economical classes in the Marxist sense of the term, but authentic *pharmaco-pornopolitical factories*. These subjects are at the same time prime pharmaco-pornopolitical *material* and the *producers* (rarely the proprietors), as well as consumers of gender's bio codes. Activists like Kate Bornstein, Pat Califia, Del LaGrace Volcano, Dean Spade, Jacob Hale, Sandy Stone and Moisés Martínez reject the psychiatrization of transsexuality (until now defined, in a similar way as BIID, as gender dysphoria) and defend their right to define their own sex, reappropriating hormonal and chirurgical techniques to construct themselves, in loud disagreement with normative codes of masculinity and femininity. They produce self-designed sexes.

Hackers use the Internet and 'copyleft' programs for the free and horizontal distribution of information tools. They affirm that the social movement that they lead is within everyone's reach, via the Internet. The copyleft pharmaco-pornographic movement has a techno-living platform far more accessible than the Internet: the body. But not the naked body, or the body as immutable nature, but the techno-life body as biopolitical archive and cultural prosthesis. Your memory, your desire, your sensibility, your skin, your dick, your dildo, your blood, your sperm, your vulva, your gonads, etc. are the tools of a possible *gender-copyleft* revolution. Gender-copyleft tactics should be subtle but determinant: the future of sex and the open gender of the species is at stake. There should not be one single name that can be patented. It will be our responsibility to remove the code, to open political practices, to multiply possibilities. This movement—that has already begun—could be called Postporno, Free Fuckware, Bodypunk, Opengender, Fuckyourfather, PenetratedState, TotalDrugs, PornTerror, Analinflaction, TechnoPriapismoUniversalUnited…

By voluntarily declining politically marginal identities or by electing their own sex-political status, these corporal self-determination movements show that the desired "normal body" is the effect of violent devices of representation, control and cultural production. What the BIID, crip or transgender movements teach us is that it is no longer a question of making a choice between a *natural body* and a *techno body*. No, now the question is whether we want to be docile consumers of biopolitical techniques and complicit producers of our own bodies, or, alternatively, if we want to become conscious of the technological processes of which we are made. Either way, we must collectively risk inventing new ways of installing and reinstalling subjectivity.

## NOTES

Thank you to Yvette Vinke and Eliza Steinbock for helping me with the translation and to Susan Stryker for her sharp reading and editing of the text.

1.  Some of the most influential analyses of the current transformations of industrial society and capitalism relevant to my own work are: Mauricio Lazzarato, "*Le concept de travail immaterial: la grande enterprise*," in *Futur Antérieur*, n.10 (1992); Antonella Corsani, "*Vers un renouvau de l'économie politique, anciens concepts et innovation théorique*," in *Multitudes*, n.2 (2000); Antonio Negri and Michael Hardt, *Multitudes* (Paris: Editions La Decouverte, 2004); Yann Moulier Boutang, *Le capitalismo cognitif. La grande transformation* (paris: Ámsterdam, 2007).
2.  I refer here to Foucault's notion "*somato-pouvoir*" and "*technologie politique du corps*." See Michel Foucault, *Surveiller et punir* (Paris: Gallimard, 1975), pp.33–36, and Michel Foucault, "*Les rapports de pouvoir passent à l'intérieur du corps*," *La Quinzaine Littéraire*, 247 (January 1977), pp.4–6. Also, here I draw on the well-known expression used by Immanuel Wallerstein in *World-Systems Analysis: An Introduction* (Durham, North Carolina: Duke University Press, 2004).
3.  Michel Foucault, *Du gouvernement des vivants* (Collège de France, 1980) (unpublished).
4.  Alan Berube, *Coming Out Under Fire: The History of Gay Men and Women in World War Two* (New York: The Free Press, 1990).
5.  John D'Emilio, *Sexual Politics, Sexual Communities: The Making of a Homosexual Minority in the United States, 1940–1970* (Chicago: Chicago University Press, 1983).
6.  See Beatriz Colomina, *Domesticity at War* (Cambridge, MA: MIT Press, 2007), p. 29.
7.  Jennifer Terry, *An American Obsession: Science, Medicine, and Homosexuality in Modern Society* (Chicago: The University of Chicago Press, 1999),178–218.
8.  Andrea Tone, *Devices and Desires. A History of Contraceptives in America* (New York: Hill and Wang, 2001), 203–231; Lara V. Marks, *Sexual Chemistry: A History of the Contraceptive Pill*, (New Haven: Yale University Press, 2001).
9.  Tom Carnwath and Ian Smith, *Heroin Century* (New York: Routledge, 2002), 40–2.
10. Harold Gillies and Ralph Millard Jr., *The Principles and Art of Plastic Surgery Volume II* (Boston: Little, Brown, 1957), 385-88; Michael Dillon, *Self: A Study in Ethics and Endocrinology* (London: Heinemann, 1946). See also Bernice L. Hausman, *Changing Sex, Transsexualism, Technology, and the Idea of Gender*, (Durham, London: Duke University Press, 1995), 67.
11. John Money, Joan Hampson, and John Hampson, "Imprinting and the Establishment of Gender Role", *Archives of Neurology and Psychiatry* 77 (1957), 333-36.
12. M. E. Clynes and N. S. Kline, "Cyborgs and Space," in *Astronautics* (September, 1960).
13. See Mike Davis, "Planet of Slums," *New Left Review* 26 (April–March 2004).
14. Ian Hacking, *Representing and Intervening: Introductory Topics in the Philosophy of Natural Science* (Cambridge: Cambridge University Press, 1986), and Bruno Latour and Steve Woolgar, *La vie de laboratoire. La construction des faits scientifiques* (Paris: La Découverte, 1979).
15. See: Donna Haraway, *Modest_Witness@Second_Millennium. FemaleMan©Meets_OncoMouse™: Feminism and Technoscience* (New York: Routledge, 1997), 54; Susan Freinkel, *Plastic: A Toxic Love Story* (Boston: Houghton Mifflin Harcourt, 2011).
16. See Donna Haraway, "When Man™ is on the Menu," *Incorporations*, ed. Jonathan Crary and Sanford K. Winter (New York: Zone Books, 1992).
17. See Rem Koolhaas's notion of "junkspace" in "Junkspace," *October* 100 (June 2002), 175–190.
18. Michel Foucault, *Histoire de la sexualité* (Paris: Gallimard, 1976), 136–39; Michel Foucault, *Naissance de la biopolitique: Cours au Collège de France, 1978-1979* (Paris: Gallimard/Seuil, 2004).
19. For a visual history of hysteria see Georges Didi-Huberman, *Invention of Hysteria: Charcot and the Photographic Iconography of the Salpetriere* (Cambridge, MA: MIT Press, 2004)
20. Gilles Deleuze, "Post-scriptum sur les sociétés de contrôle," *Pourparlers* (Paris: Minuit, 1990), 241.
21. Zygmunt Bauman, *Liquid Modernity* (Cambridge: Polity Press, 2000).
22. Donna Haraway, *Simians, Cyborgs, and Women. The Reinvention of Nature*, (New York: Routledge, 1991), 219.
23. John Money, Joan Hampson, and John Hampson, "Imprinting and the Establishiment of Gender Role", *Archives of Neurology and Psychiatry* 77 (1957), 333-36.
24. Judith Butler, *Undoing Gender* (New York: Routledge, 2004), 1.
25. See Marcel Mauss, "Techniques du corps" [1934], *Sociologie et anthropologie* (Paris: PUF, 2001).

26. About this relationship between power, failure and resistance see Judith Butler, *Undoing Gender* (New York: Routledge, 2004), 15–16.

27. I am referring here to Michel Foucault's notion of "*corps docile*" in *Surveiller et punir*, first chapter of the third section.

28. For the elaboration of this Spinozan concept of "*puissance*" see Maurizio Lazzarato, *Puissance de l'invention* (Paris: Les empêcheurs de penser en rond, 2002).

29. Donna Haraway, *Simians, Cyborgs, and Women: The Reinvention of Nature* (New York: Routledge, 2000), 162.

30. Dean Spade, "Mutilating Gender," in *The Transgender Studies Reader*, ed. Susan Stryker and Stephen Whittle (New York: Routledge, 2006), 315–32.

31. I am using here the notion of "becoming-common," "*devenir-commun*" invoked by Michael Hardt and Toni Negri to explain the new common condition of biopolitical work. See: Michael Hardt and Toni Negri, *Multitude: War and Democracy in the Age of Empire* (New York: Penguin Press, 2005), 142.

32. See Antonio Negri and Michael Hardt, *Multitudes*.

33. Judith Butler, *Undoing Gender* (New York: Routledge, 2004).

# 23

# *Evil Deceivers and Make-Believers*

## On Transphobic Violence and the Politics of Illusion

TALIA MAE BETTCHER

PHILOSOPHER AND GENDER STUDIES SCHOLAR TALIA BETTCHER analyzes the tragic case of Gwen Araujo, one of many murdered transgender youth who have come to symbolize the prevalence of anti-transgender violence, in order to address larger questions about the systems of representation that sustain and inform transphobic actions and feelings. In Araujo's case, as in many other similar instances, attempts were made to justify assault and murder by claiming that the victim had practiced a deception upon the perpetrator—that is, the victim was presenting as one gender, but was really the other. If the victim's supposedly "real" gender (that is, biological sex) should first come to light in a moment of sexual attraction or intimacy, the perpetrator typically claims that a panic over unwittingly participating in an act perceived as homosexual excuses and legitimates the act of anti-transgender violence. As Bettcher argues, this scenario depends on philosophies of representation and of the body. The biological materiality of the sex-differentiated body is typically thought to determine the reality of subjective gender identity; furthermore, a gendered sense of self is typically represented as an interior reality that should be aligned with the appearance and apparent meaning of the body. The confluence of these two assumptions, along with their disruption by transgender phenomena, enables the "rhetoric of deception" that so often produces harm for transgender individuals. Bettcher concludes by noting that medical and legal techniques for changing gender in ways that make the embodied self more congruent with these underlying assumptions (surgery, hormones, state-issued identity documents) are more available to white people, due to racialized economic discrimination, than they are to people of color, which thereby unjustly distributes the effects of transphobic violence.

In Newark, California, on October 3, 2002, Gwen Araujo was beaten, killed, and then buried 150 miles away in the Sierra wilderness.[1] Afterward, the four men who buried her apparently stopped to enjoy a drink at a McDonald's restaurant. The slaying occurred at a party held at a private home and the violence apparently occurred in front of many of the partygoers. The events, however, remained undiscovered until two weeks after the fact. Although the reports about what happened that evening have been to some degree conflicting, it appears that at some point Araujo was subjected to forced genital exposure in the bathroom, after which it was announced that "he was really a man" (Reiterman, Garrison, and Hanley 2002). Indeed, this seems to have been the crucial event that precipitated the subsequent acts of torture and murder.

Araujo had three years earlier come out to her mother (Sylvia Guerrero), asked her to refer to her as Gwen (a name which she had chosen after Gwen Stefani of the band No Doubt), and expressed the intention to have "sex-change surgery." According to Sylvia Guerrero, who reportedly had originally struggled accepting her child's identity, "He felt like a girl trapped in a man's body." Araujo had also experienced persistent harassment at school, as well as difficulty finding employment because her appearance as a girl did not match her legal name on job applications (Reiterman, Garrison, and Hanley 2002). Her brutal murder at age seventeen followed closely on the heels of consistent discrimination.

The murder itself was subsequently surrounded by suggestions that Araujo had herself engaged in wrongdoing (namely "sexual deception"). For example, Jose Merel (charged in the murder, but pleading innocent) was quoted as saying, "Sure we were angry. Obviously she led us on. No one knew she was a man, but that's no excuse for anyone to hurt someone. I don't believe two wrongs make a right" (Fernandez and Kuruvila 2002). Accusations of wrongdoing were also embedded within murder-excusing and blame-shifting rhetoric. For example, Jose Merel's mother Wanda Merel was quoted as saying, "If you find out the beautiful woman you're with is really a man, it would make any man go crazy" (Reiterman, Garrison, and Hanley 2002). And Zach Calef (writer for the *Iowa State Daily*), despite the fact that the only sexual assault that we know to have occurred is the forced genital exposure to which Araujo herself was subjected, argued that Araujo's murder was not a hate crime because Araujo had raped some of her killers, ones she allegedly had sex with. According to Calef, "The men did what they did because Araujo violated them. He used lies and deception to trick them into having sex. He was not honest with them and had he been, none of this would have happened. A hate crime should not even be considered. No one killed him because he was a cross-dresser. These men were truly violated. They were raped" (2002).

Such allegations of deception were subsequently taken up during the trial of the three men charged with the first-degree murder of Gwen Araujo: Jason Cazares, Michael Magidson, and Jose Merel.[2] Both Jack Noonan, Merel's attorney, and Mark Thorman, Magidson's attorney, argued that their clients were only guilty of manslaughter on the basis of what came to be known as the "trans panic defense" (a variant of the gay panic defense).[3] The slaying, they argued, was committed in the "heat of passion" upon discovery of Araujo's "biological sex" (Locke 2004b).

Apparently, both Merel and Magidson had earlier entered into sexual relations with Araujo and had also already been discussing Araujo's identity several days prior to the slaying. Yet Thorman nonetheless spoke of the "extreme shock, amazement and bewilderment" at the public disclosure of Araujo's identity, subsequently using allegations of "sexual deception" as a main tactic in his defense (Kuruvila 2003). In particular, he argued that the discovery of "Eddie's true sex" had provoked the violent response to what Thorman represented as a sexual violation "so deep it's almost primal" (Locke 2004a). "Sexuality, our sexual choices, are very important to us," claimed Thorman in his closing argument, "That's why the deception in this case . . . was such a substantial provocation—sexual fraud, a deception, a betrayal" (St. John 2004). By contrast, the prosecution argued that, far from constituting manslaughter, the slaying involved premeditation constituting murder in the first degree. And Gloria Allred, Sylvia Guerrero's attorney, represented the slaying as a "Tony Soprano-style murder" (Lagos 2004).

The jury itself failed to reach a verdict for any of the men charged with the first-degree murder of Gwen Araujo. They reportedly deadlocked 10-2 against a first-degree conviction for both Merel and Cazares, while deadlocking 7-5 for conviction in the case of Magidson. Judge Harry Sheppard was forced to declare a mistrial. According to informal polling of prosecutor Chris Lamiero, none of the jurors had accepted the trans panic defense, but remained divided on the question of whether the three were guilty of first-degree murder or second-degree murder, a killing promoted by an "unconsidered rash impulse" (Wronge 2004). In seeming contradiction to this, however, Thorman countered that some of jurors had in fact agreed that sexual provocation led to the killing (Locke 2004b). And he claimed, "The prosecution's case is likely to hang no matter how many times you try it" (Wronge 2004). After a second trial, both Magidson and Merel received second-degree murder convictions, while the jury again could not reach a verdict for Cazares, who subsequently pleaded no-contest to voluntary manslaughter. The jury, however, did not find in favor of hate-crime enhancement for either Magidson or Merel.

## PRELIMINARIES

I write this essay as a white, Anglo, transsexual woman. The work reflects inspiration from my personal involvement in Los Angeles–based grass roots responses to transphobic violence and my experience moving through the intersections of race, class, and gender within transgender communities, as well as a sexist, racist, and transphobic society more generally. My perspective is culturally located in ways that allow for insight as well as obliviousness. This essay is a personal attempt to think through the meaning of transphobic violence and its embeddedness within other systems of oppression.

My central goal is to provide a reply to the charges of deception, betrayal, and rape made against Gwen Araujo and many other people like her. In doing so, I hope to provide a deeper understanding of the nature of what I call "transphobia." A second, related goal is to argue that this notion of sexual deception is fundamentally grounded in sexual violence against women and in race-based oppression. My aim is to request help in ending transphobic violence by those who are currently indifferent to it, as well as motivating those particular transpeople who are currently not so motivated to take seriously broader issues of gender- and race-based oppression.[4]

[...]

## TRANSPHOBIA

I use the term *transphobia* not necessarily to imply the fear of transpeople, but simply any negative attitudes (hatred, loathing, rage, or moral indignation) harbored toward transpeople on the basis of our enactments of gender.[6] Such attitudes no doubt lie at the root of much violence against transpeople. In 2003, fourteen murders of transpeople were reported in the United States, and thirty-eight were reported worldwide. Most were MTFs, and most were people of color.[7] Recent studies also indicate a consistently high degree of reported transphobic verbal abuse against transpeople—80 percent or higher—and reported transphobic physical assault—30 percent to almost half (Lombardi et al., 2001; Clements 1999; Reback et al. 2001; and Lombardi unpublished). Once again, it also appears that transpeople of color may have a higher rate of abuse.[8]

In this essay, I am specifically concerned with the ways in which victims of transphobic violence can be subject to blame shifting through accusations of deception and the way in which transphobic violence may be understood in terms of the related notions of 'exposure,' 'discovery,' 'appearance,' and 'reality.' To be sure, the transphobia that motivated the murder of Gwen Araujo appears, at first blush, to be a straightforward case of homophobia. This is because the violence clearly involved the implication of her killers' own sexual desire toward her.

Yet it also seems to me that the relationship between transphobia and homophobia is far more complicated than it might initially appear. The view that the murder was grounded in homophobia only makes sense on the condition that we view Araujo as "really a boy"—specifically contrary to her own way of identifying—or at least on the condition that we privilege the attitudes of her killers in providing such an account. Beyond these obvious problems, it is clear that this type of account, while successfully explaining the attitudes of Araujo's killers, would fail to explain the transphobic charge of wrongful "sexual deception" and constitute yet another transphobic denial of Araujo's own identity. It cannot, therefore, be accepted as an account.[9]

To repeat, then, I am concerned with the rhetoric of deception. Rage at having "been deceived" may play a role in some transphobic hostility, interwoven, of course, with homophobic and possibly sexist attitudes. More generally, the persistent stereotype of transpeople as deceivers and the equation of deception with rape need explanation. In addition to contributing to transphobic hostility, the stereotype plays a significant role in blame-shifting discourse that can be deployed to justify or excuse violence against transpeople. ✳

Blame-shifting

The rhetoric of deception appears deeply connected to deployments of gender attributions that run contrary to a transperson's own self-identifications (I'll use the phrase *identity enforcement*). For example, while Araujo was represented as a "boy who dressed like a woman," she understood herself to be a girl and presented herself in that manner. Such gender attribution, of course, is frequently intertwined with notions of appearance, reality, and discovery. For example, some of the rhetoric that surrounded the slaying of Araujo involved the idea of "discovering" that she was "really a boy," appearances notwithstanding.

Genital exposure as sex verification may also be implicated in some forms of transphobic violence. For example, both of the highly publicized murders of Gwen Araujo and Brandon Teena involved forced genital exposure (sex verification) that occurred in a bathroom amid accusations of deception and betrayal, followed by extreme violence and finally murder.[10] Identity enforcement may itself involve a kind of violence, such as the raping of Brandon Teena one week prior to his murder. And it seems fair to say the deceiver representation (with its related identity enforcement) in and of itself constitutes considerable emotional violence against transpeople through its impeachment of moral integrity and denials of authenticity. ✳ *crucial*

formulaic nate

emotional violence

The rhetoric of deception appears to apply most appropriately to people who present gender that may be construed (at least at the specific moment of transphobia) as "unambiguously" masculine or feminine as opposed to transpeople who present in ways that may be construed as "inconsistent," "androgynous," or "incomprehensible." By "unambiguously" I mean that the gender presentation can be read as "misaligned" with the sexed body (either successfully or not). My account should be understood to apply in such cases rather than those involving more ambiguity. [11]

## DECEIVERS AND PRETENDERS

Fundamental to transphobic representations of transpeople as deceivers is an appearance-reality contrast between gender presentation and sexed body. For example, an MTF who is taken to misalign gender presentation with the sexed body can be regarded as "really a boy," appearances notwithstanding. Here, we see identity enforcement embedded within a context of possible deception, revelation, and disclosure. In this framework, gender presentation (attire, in particular) constitutes a gendered appearance, whereas the sexed body constitutes the hidden, sexual reality. Expressions such as "a man who dresses like a woman," "a man who lives as a woman," and even "a woman who is biologically male" all effectively inscribe this distinction.

complicating and conflating sex and gender

Frequently connected to this appearance-reality contrast is the view that genitalia are the essential determinants of sex. This identification is of a piece with what Harold Garfinkel called "the natural attitude about gender" (1957, 122–33; see also Kessler and McKenna, 1978, 113–14; Bornstein 1994, 45–51).[12] According to Garfinkel, individuals (whom he called "normals") maintain fundamental beliefs that constitute a kind of pretheoretical common sense about gender and sex ("the natural attitude"). While this view is obviously naïve,[13] the essentiality of genitalia in determining sex status also remains a deeply entrenched view pervading dominant cultural mainstream conceptions of gender in the United States (Kessler and McKenna 2000). To my mind, it seems clear that such a position is connected to this distinction between gender appearance and sex reality, where genitalia play the role of "concealed truth" about a person's sex. We may gain an intuitive understanding of this through recognizing how often expressions such as "really a man," "discovered to be male," and so forth, are linked with genital status.

genitalia as determinant concealed

*when their histories are discovered*

To be sure, even transpeople who have undergone genital reconstruction surgery have been represented as deceivers.[14] Nonetheless, I do not believe this fact seriously undermines the significance of genitalia as "concealed truth or reality" about a person's sex. Transpeople who have undergone genital reconstruction surgery challenge some of the basic tenets of the natural attitude, whereas it is less clear that those who have not undergone such surgery do so in the same way. In addition to regarding genitals as essential to sex, for example, the natural attitude also maintains that sex is invariant. It would seem, then, that genital reconstruction surgery forces rejection of either genital essentiality or the invariance of sex. How "normals" are to treat such cases, however, is a complicated and unpredictable affair; certainly, the status of a postsurgical transperson is both controvertible and fragile. Notably, however, those "normals" who come to believe that such surgery legitimately constitutes a sex change (and thereby reject their view that sex is invariant) or else view gender self-identity as the essential determinant of sex (and thereby reject genital essentiality) will generally not regard such a surgically transformed transperson as a deceiver.[15]

Basic to the natural attitude is the tendency to dismiss counterexamples as "exceptional" and "abnormal." In fact, both the invariance of sex and the essentiality of genitals can be maintained by dismissing surgically constructed genitals as "artificial" in conjunction with the ad hoc stipulation that birth genital status determines sex. To the extent that such a view underlies the belief that even transpeople who have undergone genital reconstruction are deceivers, the role of genitals in determining sex remains in full force. (Only now there has been a new ad hoc clarification that surgically constructed genitals are invalid.)

Of course, it is also true that there are many other ways of determining sex. For example, one might cite chromosomes as a way of claiming that a transperson is "really a so and so." And the actual complexities of sex and sex determination are certainly treated with greater sophistication in more specialized medical, legal, and psychotherapeutic discourses. However, those who embrace the natural attitude tend to be suspicious of more theoretical notions of sex (see Hale 1996). For insofar as the natural attitude constitutes a kind of pretheoretical common sense about sex, it tends to maintain itself even in the face of clear-cut evidence that the attitude is false.

Notably, there are ways in which the natural attitude affects even these more specialized discourses. A professional working in a specialized discourse nonetheless must leave her job and move through a world in which the natural attitude tends to prevail. Moreover, such an individual may not herself be immune to the force of the natural attitude—maintaining it at some visceral level, while rejecting it in a professional capacity. Indeed, it often seems that specialized discourses themselves aim, in part, to preserve as much of the natural attitude or common sense about sex as possible (Hale 1996). It therefore seems to me that even an appeal to chromosomes to disallow genital reconstruction surgery as sex-change surgery may be underwritten by, or at least deployed in defending, the deeper ("natural") view that sex is invariant and that surgically reconstructed genitalia are artificial or invalid. For these reasons, I think, the application of "deceiver" to transpeople who have undergone genital reconstruction surgery must nonetheless also be understood fundamentally in terms of a contrast between gender presentation (appearance) and genital status (reality).[16]

## A DOUBLE BIND

The contrast between gender presentation (appearance) and sexed body (reality), when intersected with possibilities of either being or not being visibly trans, yields a dangerous double bind. In speaking of a double bind, I am explicitly drawing on the work of Marilyn Frye, who has characterized oppression as a complex network of immobilizing social barriers and forces (1983, 2–4).[17] To understand this bind, we need only examine the rhetoric of deception and disclosure that informed the murder of Gwen Araujo. While she was considered a deceiver for failing to disclose her "true status," one can only imagine the reaction that she would have received had she simply

*appearance-reality*

announced herself as trans. For in coming out, she would have no doubt been interpreted as "really a boy, who dressed up like a girl." Hence the option: disclose "who one is" and come out as a pretender or masquerader, or refuse to disclose (be a deceiver) and run the risk of forced disclosure, the effect of which is exposure as a liar.

I want to be clear that far from mere "stereotype" or "ignorant misconception" this double bind between deception and pretense actually reflects the way in which transpeople can find ourselves literally "constructed" whether we like it or not. That is, if these are somehow "stereotypes," then they are "stereotypes" that we can find ourselves involuntarily animating. Views, particularly when they are held by many and have consequences in terms of how people behave, speak, and interact, can be far more than mere negative attitudes existing only in the minds of some people. Rather, they can help constitute "who one is" in a situation that is utterly beyond one's control.

Recognizing this allows us to characterize more fully the two sides of the bind. On the one hand, visibility yields a position in which what one is doing is represented as make-believe, pretending, or playing dress up. Some of the general difficulties with this side of the bind run as follows: (1) having one's life constructed as fictitious; and so (2) failing to have one's own identifications taken seriously; (3) being viewed in a highly condescending way; and (4) being the subject of violence and even murder. On the other hand, to opt for invisibility is to remove one's life from the domain of masquerade into actual reality. Yet this is complicated by the way in which the visible/invisible contrast tracks the deception side of the bind. For the movement from invisible to visible generates the effect of revelation, disclosure, or exposure of hidden truth. Hence, some of the possible consequences are: (1) living in constant fear of exposure, extreme violence, and death; (2) disclosure as a deceiver or liar (possibly through forced genital exposure); (3) being the subject of violence and even murder; and (4) being held responsible for this violence.

Overall, we can characterize some of the consequences of this bind as follows. Insofar as transpeople are open to constructions as "really an x," (appearances notwithstanding) we will immediately find ourselves represented in ways that are contrary to our own identifications. This construction literally *reinscribes* the position that genitalia are the essential determinants of sex by identifying that essential status as the "hidden reality or truth of sex." Through such a construction, we will invariably be represented as deceivers or pretenders. This has the effect of doubly delegitimating our own voices by constructing us as both fictitious and morally suspect. Hence, after identity enforcement, nothing we might say could possibly matter. A framework has been deployed whereby transphobic violence may be excused or justified on the grounds that deception had been involved. The only latitude appears to involve the degree to which our pretense is viewed as harmless make-believe or evil deception.

## SOME COMPLEXITIES

While the two options of the bind are to some degree distinct, they also blur into each other in important ways. First, "exposure as deceiver" does not lead to the consequence that one's life is *not* viewed as a kind of pretense or masquerade. Clearly, descriptions such as "boy who lived as a girl" indicate that precisely the opposite is the case. For while one's "acts of deception" may be taken very seriously, it hardly follows that one's own life will be regarded in that way. Second, even in cases in which one is out as trans, one may not necessarily be exempt from accusations of at least the potential for deception. Indeed, accusations of "heterosexual male" infiltration of women's space (such as restrooms) and the possibility of the intention to rape have been made against uncloseted MTFs.

Moreover, it is important to be clear that the possibilities of visibility and invisibility are not always within our control, and can shift from one to the other in complicated ways. For example, passability as non-trans may not always be an all or nothing affair, and can be a function of physical proximity as well as the degree, nature, and context of social interaction. An MTF may pass as a woman (from a distance), only to be exposed as "really a man" upon closer proximity and greater scrutiny. Consequently, some transpeople may find themselves shifting from the invisible to visible on a regular basis (and in a way that affects an "exposure" or "revelation"). Indeed, in order to avoid this "exposure" effect and the attendant representation as "revealed deceiver" it appears that a transperson must either consistently pass, fail to pass, or explicitly (and repeatedly) come out as trans in order to prevent such shifts from occurring.

There are complicated intersections of visibility/invisibility with both race and class privilege. For example, it seems that the price of visibility is a function of class (which is itself intersected with race). The thesis that degree of transphobia will be higher in geographical areas that already involve a higher degree of violence and that the likelihood of transphobic discrimination (and severity thereof) will be greater in lower-paying jobs is a plausible one. That being said, opportunities for invisibility itself are also a function of class privilege. For while it is generally acknowledged that the privilege of passing is a function of overall appearance and body type, the effects of class privilege are insufficiently acknowledged. At least in my own experience, some MTFs whose general physical characteristics may be more likely to be read as male can successfully pass given access to techniques and technologies of passing (nice wig, clothes, hormones, pedicure, and so on), whereas poor and possibly homeless MTFs who do not have similar access to these aids may sometimes be quite easily "read" and face considerable harassment and violence irrespective of physical considerations. If this is right, then as class status decreases, so will the option of invisibility while the negative consequences of visibility will increase.

Related to this, it is important to recognize that many MTFs are vulnerable to sexualization on the pretender side of the bind, where "pretense" is transformed into "sexual fantasy." This is to say that many MTFs who are uncloseted find that they are represented as whores—sexually available and disposable. This dovetails importantly with the ways in which many MTFs find themselves economically subject to forced visibility in dangerous contexts, helping to constitute the conditions that make the reality of MTF sex work. This "whorification" of MTFs constructed as make-believe contrasts sharply with the relative dearth of sexualized images of FTMs (at least in non-trans, heterosexual mainstream, and gay male subcultures). This is important, because it helps identify one of the many reasons why invisibility and erasure may be particularly relevant to FTMs while enforced, sexualized visibility may be particularly relevant to MTFs. While this sketch is crude, it may also be correct to say that MTFs and FTMs are to some extent divided across the visible/invisible border, and as a result, the deceiver/pretender bind is manifested for MTFs and FTMs in different ways.

## SEXUAL DECEPTION AS RAPE

### Gender Presentation as Genital Representation

Foundational to this appearance/reality contrast and the related deceiver/pretender bind is a representational relation that obtains between gender presentation and sexed body (that is, genitalia). Gender presentation is generally taken as a *sign* of sexed body, taken to *mean* sexed body, taken to *communicate* sexed body. And it is precisely for this reason that transpeople who "misalign" gender presentation and sexed body are construed as either deceivers or pretenders. Indeed, the very fact that transpeople are viewed as deceivers demonstrates that a representational or communicative relation is taken to hold between presentation and body. For if "misaligning" gender presentation and sexed body is tantamount to lying and misrepresentation, then "correctly aligned" cases must surely involve truth telling and accurate representation.

If this is right, then people in general disclose their genital status on a regular basis through gender presentation. This is ironic, of course, since one of the main functions of attire is to conceal the sexed regions of the body. Yet insofar as gendered attire and gender presentation more generally indicate genital status, systematic symbolic genital disclosures are secured through the very items designed to conceal sexed body. It is therefore little wonder that people who misalign gender presentation and sexed body are frequently subject to forced genital exposure as sex verification, and then subsequently represented as deceivers.

This account is important, because it shows why the common responses to accusations of sexual deception made by transgender advocates often fail to go deep enough. For example, one common response involves simply denying that there is any deception involved at all. On the contrary, according to this view, people like Gwen Araujo are merely "being themselves." A second, related response involves posing the question why somebody like Araujo should have been *expected* to announce that she was "transgender" (or declare her genital status) in the first place. After all, Araujo's killers did not have to disclose their own genital status. So, why should Araujo have had to? Both thoughts are nicely expressed by Dylan Vade (2004), cofounder of the San Francisco Transgender Law Center, who writes:

> Why do some folks feel that transgender people need to disclose their history and their genitalia and nontransgender people do not? When you first meet someone and they are clothed, you never know exactly what that person looks like. And when you first meet someone, you never know that person's full history. Why do only some people have to describe themselves in detail—and others do not? Why are some nondisclosures seen as actions and others utterly invisible? Actions. Gwen Araujo was being herself, openly and honestly. No, she did not wear a sign on her forehead that said "I am transgender, this is what my genitalia look like." But her killers didn't wear a sign on their foreheads saying, "We might look like nice high school boys, but really, we are transphobic and are planning to kill you." That would have been a helpful disclosure. Transgender people do not deceive. We are who we are.

Yet, while I do believe that it is quite right to ask the question why it should have been important for Araujo to declare her status in the first place, there are several difficulties with this response. The major difficulty is that it does not appreciate that a disclosure of genital status (or disclosure as trans) may only reinscribe a transsubject as a deceiver/pretender. In effect, this response fails to discuss the way in which it was effectively impossible for Araujo to "come out as herself" at all. Clearly, if she had publicly declared her trans status, she would have simply been constructed as a "boy living as a girl" or as a "boy pretending to be a girl." She still would have been vulnerable to the deceiver/pretender construction.

For just as we do not always have authority over how our bodies are understood, so too we do not always have authority over what our words mean. The point is worth stressing, since it is not sufficiently appreciated in current criticisms of the "trans panic defense." After all, there is an important difference between coming out as a "transgender woman" and as "really a man disguised as a woman." Yet it is often the latter that does much of the work in transphobic violence, accounts which justify or defend such violence, and accounts which blame the victim. Indeed, it is precisely the fact that transpeople often do not have their self-identifications taken seriously that is so deeply bound up with the transphobic hostility and violence. How can we ignore the fact that often "transgender woman" simply *means* "man disguised as a woman" to many people—whether that is our own understanding or not? And this surely stands in marked contrast to the hypothetical disclosures of Araujo's killers. Had they confessed their own intentions, they would not necessarily have found their claims invalidated or disregarded. They would not have been represented in ways contrary to their own self-identifications, and the very meaning of their own words would not have been interpreted in ways hostile to their very existence.

Moreover, the response does not appreciate the fact that most people do in fact regularly declare their genital status. They do so through the very gendered attire which is designed to conceal body because such attire represents genital status. Transpeople, by contrast, according to this particular system of meaning at any rate, "misalign" such genital representation and thereby opt out of the mundane, daily disclosures made by most people. This is why we are taken for deceivers in the first place. And this is why our sex, and therefore our genital status, is the subject of such (generally abusive) scrutiny. In other words, the point that it is unfair to demand that transpeople disclose our genital status when other people do not have to do so is actually dead wrong insofar as gender presentation is a ubiquitous system of genital representation that transpeople opt out of.

Finally, I believe that this response fails to acknowledge the depth of the deceiver representation. For if what I have claimed is correct then deceiver/pretender is not merely one of the many unfortunate stereotypes that plague transpeople. Rather, it flows primarily from a fundamental communicative relation that obtains between presentation and body—a relation within which even non-transpeople are implicated. For insofar as gender presentation means sexed body, we *do* engage in "false representation." In other words, it is precisely because of this communicative relation that transpeople are fundamentally constructed as deceivers/pretenders—and to that extent are liars and frauds—whether we like it or not. And given that the only "option" is between invisible deception and visible pretense, it would appear that this representational system actually prevents transpeople from existing at all (except, of course, as fakes and frauds).

To be sure, trans claims to "authenticity" may be understood as directly opposing constructions as deceiver/pretender. Thus, for example, the metaphor "really a woman trapped in the body of a man" turns the accusation of deception or betrayal on its head by representing the body itself as somehow deceptive. Similarly, claims that transpeople are "simply being true to themselves" in presenting a particular gender take up the theme of authenticity and, in their own way, contest allegations of fraudulence. Yet such contestations should also not be understood as literally claiming "authenticity" in the sense that is instituted by a gender-genital system of representation. For in saying that one is being one's true self through gender presentation or that one is a woman concealed within a betraying body, one is not identifying genitals with the deep, concealed, reality of sex.

Overall, I wish to stress that by making labels such as "deceiver" seem like inexplicable and bizarre stereotypes that are used against transpeople, or by simply claiming that transpeople are simply being ourselves, one overlooks some of the most important issues that confront transpeople. For because of the systematic representational alignment between gender presentation and sexed body, transpeople are never allowed to be ourselves in the first place insofar as we are fundamentally constructed as deceivers/pretenders. Nothing short of the elimination of this communicative relation will alter the deep social mechanism that prohibits transpeople from existing within dominant mainstream with any authenticity at all.

## Rape, Sexual Seduction, and Rate

It is not uncommon for transpeople who are "exposed as deceivers" to be sexually assaulted as a kind of punishment. And forced genital verification itself obviously constitutes sexual assault and abuse. Yet it is also a perverse fact that "sexual deception" is itself identified as a kind of rape. After all, Calef's and Thorman's remarks about Araujo are not unique. For example, in *The Transsexual Empire: The Making of the She-Male*, Janice Raymond not only accuses all male-to-female transsexuals of raping women's bodies by "appropriating them to themselves" but also accuses some of deception, equating conflations with rape.

> All transsexuals rape women's bodies by reducing the real female form to an artifact, appropriating this body for themselves. However, the transsexually constructed lesbian-feminist violates women's

sexuality and spirit, as well. Rape, although it is usually done by force, can also be accomplished by deception. It is significant that in the case of the transsexually constructed lesbian-feminist, often he is able to gain entrance and a dominant position in women's spaces because the women involved do know he is a transsexual and he just does not happen to mention it.

(1979, 104)

While a thorough account of the connections between the deceiver/pretender construction and sexual assault constitutes an enormous task, it seems to me that part of the explanation for this association is the fact that the representational relation between gender presentation and sexed body is actually a piece of the communication system that facilitates and justifies sexual violence against women as well as helping promote and justify racial oppression. If this is correct, then the deceiver/pretender bind is part of a larger system of oppression.

Begin by noticing the close analogy between the role of gender presentation in "communicating" genital status, and the role of female gender presentation in "communicating" sexual interest. All too frequently a woman's attire may be construed as a "provocative" invitation; and even such decisions as accepting the drink a man offers may be taken as an unspoken commitment to have sex. Obviously this "communicative" function of gender presentation and behavior plays a role in facilitating the tactics of seduction in date rape as well as providing the basis for the "she wanted it" defense and tactics of blaming the victim. The analogies seem especially strong once we recognize that in both cases the actual subjectivity of the "communicator" is erased through the imposition of intentions vis-à-vis the fact that the presentation is construed as communicative.

Looking more deeply, however, we see that all of this has less to do with analogy and more to do with the fact that both types of "communication" are a part of the system of sexual violence. A heterosexual framework that centers upon the model of penis-vagina penetration undoubtedly informs the genital division of male and female; and one major reason for (nonverbally) communicating genital status is to secure heterosexual engagement. Crudely put, within a dominantly heterosexual context, a man needs to know a person has a vagina for the same reason that a man needs to know about sexual willingness without actually having to ask.[18] To put it differently, insofar as genitals (as sex determining) fall within a sexualized heterosexual framework, and insofar as this framework relies upon a pursuer/pursued model—complete with refusals that supposedly mean acceptance—to this degree, the communicative function of attire with respect to genital status is simply part of a sexually manipulative heterosexuality.

Once we take the preceding considerations seriously, however, it starts to become clear why accusations of sexual deception should be *equated* with rape and that transpeople themselves should be vulnerable to rape (as identity enforcement). For example, the charge that MTFs infiltrate women-only spaces, and are thus predators in prey's attire, is predicated upon the identification of penis with rapist and the assumption that female attire communicates absence of penis.[19] And the raping of FTMs emerges as an obvious strategy for putting "women back in their rightful place." Calef's specific allegation of deception emerges as a complaint that the day-to-day operations of (hetero) sexual sexuality and the nonverbal system of communication that underwrites it were "misused." Surely, the conflation of "deception" with "rape" is hardly accidental.

Yet once we square with the fact that transphobia is fundamentally a part of (hetero)sexual systems of violence and rape mythology, we must immediately accept the view that it is also fundamentally imbricated in systems of racial oppressions, sexual violence, and racist rape mythology. For example, to the degree that gender presentation is itself racially specific the (communicative) relationship between gender appearance and sexed reality must be understood in term of racialized bodies, genitalia, sexualities, and sexual intentions. We must also recognize that white female gender presentations have a special place in dominant standards of female attractiveness (hooks 1992; Collins 2000).

Beyond this, however, we must recognize the deep historical connections between rape, rape rhetoric, and racial oppressions. Angela Davis (1981) argued, for example, that the myth of the black rapist has been used as a tool to justify lynching and imprisonment of black men—a powerful example of racial oppression. Davis has also claimed that the myth serves to obscure the historical systematic raping of black women by white men of power (itself a tool of racist domination). Correspondingly, black women, subjected to racialized sexual violence, have been animalized and sexualized as black "prostitutes" or "Jezebels."[20] Consequently, one may not simply argue that transphobic violence is embedded within a system of sexual violence without appreciating the obvious racial aspect of sexual violence and accusations of sexual violence within this country. Indeed, to demonstrate the connection between transphobia and sexual violence is ipso facto to demonstrate the connection between transphobia and racial oppression in a country with its particular history of lynching and where rape and accusations of rape continue to be used as instruments of racial subordination.

The central conclusion, then, is that gendered representation of genitals is fundamentally intertwined with a much larger, violent system of communication. And this means that there are significant grounds for coalition among trans, feminist, and antiracist politics. Yet even talk of "coalition" is deeply misleading, if we recognize that many transpeople are not merely oppressed as trans, but also as women and as people of color. In such cases, the doubling and tripling of violence as well as the deployment of hybrid forms of violence is inevitable.

[...]

We might wonder why transpeople should feel apologetic about "gender deception" in the first place. In a world that constructs us as either deceivers or pretenders to begin with—invariably denying our authenticity and preventing our very existence, surely "gender deception" must be seen as one laudable tactic of attempted survival in what appears to be an exceptionally violent, no-win situation. After all, isn't the adoption of "honesty is the best policy" only to acquiesce to the morality of oppression? Perhaps, in this respect, it may also prove useful to understand anew the contrast between appearance and concealed reality in terms of the split between dominant mainstream and trans-centered constructions of transpeople. There is a sense in which, in dominant constructions, we are always "in disguise" while the "concealed realities" are the multiply resistant community contexts that sustain us.

It may also behoove us to turn within to examine the degree to which we have been fragmented by pervasive invalidation and danger. What might it take to heal ourselves? And what should it take to begin fully to see the tremendous beauty, defiance, strength, and courage of somebody such as Gwen Araujo? Can we look past the doubling, tripling, quadrupling of identity-based oppression that foregrounded her murder? Can we peer past the discourse of deception, victim, and blame to see an agent, a living human being? Dare we forget the sheer value of one human life that is lost? And can we bring about the changes that are needed within so that we may undo the distortions that blind us to this? What might it take to be real?

## NOTES

`1. "Gwen" was not Araujo's legal name and during the party she was also using the name "Lida." I use the name "Gwen" since this was this was the name that she had asked her mother to use upon coming out to her. I refer to Araujo as "she" since she saw herself "as a girl trapped in a man's body." Araujo's mother, Sylvia Guerrero, buried Araujo dressed as a girl, and the name "Gwen" was engraved on her headstone. On June 23, 2004, Sylvia Guerrero's request for a posthumous name change was granted.

2. Jaron Nabors, also originally charged in the slaying, pleaded guilty to manslaughter in exchange for his testimony against the other three men.

3. Tony Serra argued that his client, Cazares, had only helped bury the body and was not involved in the slaying.

4. The concerns I articulate in this essay as well as the specific politics I outline are to be understood as more or less indexed to the United States. This is not to say that the concerns are limited to only what occurs within the U.S. border. On the contrary, the impact of U.S. ideology is undoubtedly felt worldwide.

[...]

6. By "gender presentation" I mean not only gendered attire but also bodily gesture, posture, manner of speech (pitch, tone, pattern, and expressive range), and socially interactive style. By "sexed body" I mean physical characteristics such as genitals, presence or absence of breast tissue, facial and body hair, fat distribution, height, bone size, and so forth. I intend for this distinction to admit of some blurriness.

7. See Gwendolyn Ann Smith, "Remembering Our Dead," www.rememberingour-dead.org. Smith is founder of the Transgender Day of Remembrance.

8. While both the GenderPAC study (2001) and the Los Angeles Transgender Health Study (2001) fail to discuss correlations between race and ethnicity, on the one hand, and reported incidence of transphobic abuse and violence, on the other, Lombardi finds in her unpublished study that African American transpeople reported the highest levels of discrimination over the past year, while white transpeople reported the lowest.

9. For a good preliminary discussion of transphobic violence and its relation to "gay bashing" see Namaste 2000 (135–56). [...] For the argument that current transgender theory and politics are not equipped to address this sort of transphobia, see Bettcher 2006.

10. John Lotter and Marvin Thomas Nissen murdered Brandon Teena on 31 December 1993 in Humbolt, Nebraska. A week earlier, Lotter and Nissen kidnapped and raped Teena after forcibly exposing his vagina. In the emerging transgender movement of the 1990s, the name Brandon Teena was solidified. There is not substantial evidence that Brandon (the name this individual used most commonly before the murder) actually used Teena as a last name. Ultimately, any name choice is problematic. For a thorough and thoughtful discussion of these issues, see Hale 1998a (311–48). [...]

11. Lombardi's (unpublished) distinction in measuring transphobic life events between trans people who present "consistent" masculine or feminine gender presentations (FTM, MTF) and those who present "inconsistent" or androgynous gender presentations (FTO, MTO; where 'O' stands for "other") indicates how these differences might matter. Her study finds that MTF and FTO individuals report more discrimination over a lifetime and over the past year than do MTO and FTM individuals. Although the differences were not statistically significant, they may indicate a trend that could not be conclusively measured due to limitations in sample size. At any rate, the account of transphobia that I discuss in this essay does not include FTO transphobic discrimination and is therefore limited.

12. The propositions that constitute this attitude include (in addition to the fundamentality of genitals): (1) there are two mutually exclusive and exhaustive categories (male and female); (2) this distinction is natural; (3) membership in a particular sex is natural and invariant; and (4) exceptions to the preceding claims may be dismissed as abnormal.

13. For a good discussion of the complexity of concepts such as 'woman' see Hale 1996 (94–121). [...]

14. Michael Lavin (1987) defends post-operative transsexuals against the charge of deception. He argues that while there is a fact of the matter what sex a person is and that this true sex is determined by genotypic considerations, this is not significant in everyday life since we do not ordinarily know what the real sex of a person is. [...]

15. Even in this situation, it seems to me that the best transpersons could hope for would be to be assigned to their sex of preference "with qualification." As such, they might still be held accountable for failing to disclose "the truth." Such a fragile achievement could be secured only to the extent the some socially recognized authority (such as medical and psychiatric authorities) were taken seriously enough to force a modification in the natural attitude.

16. There may be a way in which gendered surgical body modifications begin to threaten the distinction between gender presentation and sexed body. To the extent that bodies are culturally stylized, bodies themselves become gender presentations. Consequently, surgically enlarged breasts, reconstructed genitals, and the like can be seen as "artificial" and "mere appearance" in much the way clothes are, while undermining the very line between appearance and reality in a kind of postmodern moment.

17. I am following through on Hale's suggestion that "ignoring Frye's insight and its applicability to transsexuals also enables the more recent questions of whether transsexuals are duped or duplicitous or both" (1998b, 106).

18. I have not discussed the communicative role of attire in nonheterosexual contexts, as it is beyond the scope of this essay [...]

19. Obviously, the issues here are deep. For example, one of the tactics in feminist criticism of MTFs involves an appeal to "identity" and the effects of personal history and social upbringing. I do not wish to suggest that such concerns are irrelevant. The problem, however, is that even if this difference is granted, it does not follow that MTFs are "rapists in disguise." It only follows that there may be a difference between MTFs and non-transwomen. [...]

20. For example, see Davis 1981 and Collins 2000

## REFERENCES

Bettcher, Talia Mae. 2006. Appearance, reality, and gender deception: Reflections on transphobic violence and the politics of pretence. In *Violence, victims, justifications: Philosophical approaches,* ed. Felix Ó. Murchadha. Oxford: Peter Lang.

Bornstein, Kate. 1994. *Gender outlaw: On men and women and the rest of us.* New York: Routledge.

Calef, Zack. 2002. Double standard in reactions to rape. *Iowa State Daily,* October 24.

Clements, Kristen. 1999. *The transgender community health project: Descriptive results.* San Francisco: San Francisco Dept. of Public Health.

Collins, Patricia Hill. 2000. *Black feminist thought: Knowledge, consciousness, and the politics of empowerment.* 2nd ed. Routledge: New York.

Davis, Angela. 1981. Rape, racism, and the myth of the black rapist. In *Women, race, and class.* New York: Random House.

Fernandez, Lisa, and Matthai Chakko Kuruvila. 2002. Man says he didn't kill teen after learning of gender. *Mercury News,* October 24.

Frye, Marilyn. 1983. Oppression. In *The politics of reality: Essays in feminist theory.* New York: Crossing Press.

Garfinkel, Harold. 1957. *Studies in ethnomethodology.* Oxford: Polity Press.

Hale, C. Jacob. 1996. Are lesbians women? *Hypatia* 11 (2): 94–121.

Hale, C. Jacob. 1998a. Consuming the living, Dis(re)membering the dead in the butch/FTM borderlands. *GLQ: A Journal of Lesbian and Gay Studies* 4 (2): 311–48.

Hale, C. Jacob. 1998b. Tracing a ghostly memory in my throat. In *Men doing feminism,* ed. Tom Digby. New York: Routledge.

hooks, bell. 1992. Is Paris burning? In *Black looks: Race and representation.* Boston: South End Press.

Hutchison, Sue. 2004. Deadlocked jury sent a message of hope. *Mercury News,* June 29.

Kessler, Suzanne J., and Wendy McKenna. 1978. *Gender: An ethnomethodological approach.* New York: John Wiley and Sons.

Kessler, Suzanne J., and Wendy McKenna.. 2000. Who put the "trans" in transgender? Gender theory and everyday life. *International Journal of Transgenderism* 4 (3). http://www.symposion.com/ijt/index.htm.

Kuruvila, Matthai Chakko. 2003. Testimony in "Gwen" case. *Mercury News,* February 11.

Lagos, Marisa. 2004. Mistrial declared in transgender murder. *Los Angeles Times,* June 22.

Lavin, Michael. 1987. Mutilation, deception, and sex changes. *Journal of Medical Ethics* 13: 86–91.

Locke, Michelle. 2004a. Defense lawyers claim heat of passion in transgender killing case. *Associated Press,* June 3.

Locke, Michelle. 2004b. Prosecutors to retry transgender slay case. *Associated Press,* June 23.

Lombardi, Emilia. Unpublished. Understanding genderism and transphobia.

Lombardi, Emilia, R. Wilchins, D. Preising, and D. Malouf. 2001. Gender violence: Transgender experiences with violence and discrimination. *Journal of Homosexuality* 42: 89–101

Namaste, Viviane. 2000. *Invisible lives: The erasure of transsexual and transgender people.* Chicago: University of Chicago Press.

Reback, Cathy J., P. Simon, Paul A. Simon, Cathleen C. Bemis, and Bobby Gatson. 2001. The Los Angeles Health Study: Community Report. Los Angeles.

Raymond, Janice. 1979. *The transsexual empire: The making of the she-male.* Boston: Beacon Press.

Reiterman, Tim, J. Garrison, and C. Hanley. 2002. Trying to understand Eddie's life—and death. *Los Angeles Times,* October 20.

Roen, Katrina. Transgender theory and embodiment: The risk of racial marginalisation. *Journal of Gender Studies* 10 (3): 253–63.

St. John, Kelly. 2004. Defense in Araujo trial gives final argument. *San Francisco Chronicle,* June 3.

Vade, Dylan. 2004. No issue of sexual deception, Gwen Araujo was just who she was. *San Francisco Chronicle,* May 30.

Wronge, Yomi S. 2004. Reaction to mistrial in teenager's killing. *Mercury News,* June 23.

# 24

# *"Still at the Back of the Bus"*
## Sylvia Rivera's Struggle

Jessi Gan

"After all these years, the trans community is still as the back of the bus," says Sylvia Rivera, whose observation on the place of trans people in the LGBT community informs the title of this essay by Jessi Gan, a graduate student in American Studies at the University of Michigan when this essay was published in the Puerto Rican studies journal *Centro*. Rivera, who died in 2002, has become a legendary figure in the historical consciousness of contemporary trans people, particularly for those engaged in radical trans politics. Rivera is often reputed to have thrown the first projectile at police during the Stonewall Riots in New York in 1969 (or, as Gan claims, the *second* Molotov cocktail). Some researchers have disputed the veracity of Rivera's claim to have actually been present during the first night of rioting, though all agree on Rivera's prominent role in early gay and trans militancy, and on the continuing influence of her legacy. This essay explores the queen behind the myth, and situates Rivera's activism within broader struggles against poverty, racism, incarceration, and U.S. colonialism—all of which Rivera experienced. Rivera's role in the Stonewall Riots, the Gay Liberation Front, and Street Transvestite Action Revolutionaries (STAR) took on new significance in the early 1990s when a new generation of transgender activists struggled with non-transgender gays and lesbians over inclusion in what became known, as a result, as the LGBT community. Gan's account of the swirl of events around Rivera show how racial and class divides, as well as those centered on gender expression, created tensions within early gay liberation—notably in the exclusion of Rivera and other drag queens from the Christopher Street Liberation Day parades. Gan futher argues that Rivera's incorporation into the Stonewall mythos implies ongoing exclusions within trans communities over race, class, and politics. In asserting that Rivera's life and political involvements exceeded appropriation by any one political cause, Gan's essay contributes to the ongoing rediscovery of Rivera by a new generation of trans and queer activists eager to move transgender people out of the bus's back seats.

## I.

In New York City, the Sylvia Rivera Law Project is named in her honor, as is Sylvia Rivera Way in the West Village.[1] The history of Rivera, the Puerto Rican and Venezuelan drag queen and transgender activist who lived between 1951 and 2002, is rarely mentioned in Latin@ Studies. But since the mid-1990s, she has become increasingly invoked in transgender politics. In part, this is because Rivera was a combatant at the 1969 Stonewall Inn riots in New York, which in dominant accounts of U.S. history are said to have ignited the contemporary lesbian and gay rights movement. Because the post-1969 movement allegedly used more visible and militant tactics than its assimilationist predecessor, the homophile movement, Stonewall bridges the two periods in progressive narratives of gay history in which lesbians and gays, previously forced to occupy the private "closet," move toward a trajectory of "coming out" into the public sphere.[2] In the same way that Rosa Parks and the bus boycott in Montgomery, Alabama, became a symbol of black struggle against segregation, gays claimed Stonewall as a symbol of progress, pride, and resistance. "Today," wrote gay historian Martin Duberman, "the word resonates with images of insurgency and self-realization and occupies a central place in the iconography of modern gay awareness."[3] From the Stonewall Democrats and the Stonewall Chorale to June pride marches, the mythology of Stonewall has become integral to how many gay communities see themselves.[4]

Yet, though the iconography of Stonewall enabled middle-class white gays and lesbians to view themselves as resistant and transgressive, Stonewall narratives, in depicting the agents of the riots as "gay," elided the central role of poor gender-variant people of color in that night's acts of resistance against New York City police.[5] It was not until historian Duberman interviewed Rivera for a 1993 book called *Stonewall* that her role in the riots became widely known. She had left gay activism in 1973 and then been forgotten, sidelined in dominant accounts of queer politics.[6] Duberman's telling of Rivera's story, however, enabled transgender activists to write themselves into the heart of U.S. gay history and queer resistance as, during the 1990s, transgender activism itself took a more militant turn and transgender people fought more visibly to be included in gay institutions.[7] They could argue that since they had paid their dues at Stonewall, the names of "gay" organizations should be "lesbian, gay, bisexual, and transgender."[8] With historical authority, they could contend that the largest U.S. gay rights group, the Human Rights Campaign, should include transgender people in its mission statement, an argument to which it finally acquiesced in 2001 after years of lobbying.[9]

But just as "gay" had excluded "transgender" in the Stonewall imaginary, the claim that "transgender people were at Stonewall too" enacted its own omissions of difference and hierarchy within the term "transgender." Rivera was poor and Latina, while some transgender activists making political claims on the basis of her history were white and middle-class. She was praised for becoming visible as transgender while her racial and class visibility were simultaneously concealed. Juana María Rodríguez has pointed out that making oneself politically legible in the face of hegemonic culture will necessarily gloss over complexity and difference. "It is the experience of having to define one's sense of self in opposition to dominant culture that forces the creation of an ethnic/national identity that is then readable by the larger society," she wrote. "The imposed necessity for 'strategic essentialism,' reducing identity categories to the most readily decipherable marker around which to mobilize, serves as a double-edged sword [...]"[10] The myth that all gay people were equally oppressed and equally resistant at Stonewall was replaced by a new myth after Rivera's historical "coming out," that all transgender people were *most* oppressed and *most* resistant at Stonewall (and still are today). This myth could be circulated and consumed when, in the service of a liberal multicultural logic of recognition,[11] Rivera's complexly situated subjectivity as a working-class Puerto Rican/Venezuelan drag queen became reduced to that of "transgender Stonewall combatant."[12]

Some recovery projects lubricated by Rivera's memory—in their simultaneous forgetting of the white supremacist and capitalist logics that had constructed her raced and classed otherness—served to unify transgender politics along a gendered axis.[13] The elisions enabled transgender activist Leslie Feinberg, in hir[14] book *Trans Liberation,* to invoke a broad coalition of people united solely by a political desire to take gender "beyond pink or blue."[15] This pluralistic approach celebrated Rivera's struggle as one "face" in a sea of "trans movement" faces.[16] The anthology *GenderQueer: Voices from Beyond the Sexual Binary*, similarly, called for a "gender movement" that would ensure "full equality for all Americans regardless of gender."[17] The inclusion of Rivera's life story in the largely white *GenderQueer* lent a multicultural "diversity" and historical authenticity to the young, racially unmarked coalitional identity "genderqueer", that had emerged out of middle-class college settings.[18]

But the elision of intersectionality in the name of coalitional myth-making served to reinscribe other myths. The myth of equal transgender oppression left capitalism and white supremacy unchallenged, often foreclosing coalitional alignments unmoored from gender analysis, while enabling transgender people to avoid considering their complicity in the maintenance of simultaneous and interlocking systems of oppression.[19]

It is clear that Rivera's history and memory have been put to a variety of political uses, and not just by others. In the years before her death Rivera consciously used her symbolic power as a Stonewall veteran to raise public awareness of anti-transgender oppression, according to observers.[20] But the contours of her life and her personal statements, I will argue, reveal a figure at once complexly situated and fluid, whose inclusive political affinities resist attempts to reduce her to appropriated symbol. Her life illustrates the limits of dominant theories of queer visibility, while her political commitments challenge us to continually bypass statically reductive visions of identity and community. Rivera is, moreover, profoundly important in a Latin@, transgender, and queer historiography where histories of transgender people of color are few and far between. In the following pages, I reconstruct her life and the context of the Stonewall riot by drawing upon interviews, speeches, essays, and newspapers. With competing claims over Rivera's historical significance having intensified since her death, I have chosen to emphasize her own statements, believing that Rivera's praxis is inextricably linked to her life experience.[21] I foreground the motivations behind her political stakes through an extended narrative.

## II.

Born male, Sylvia Rivera showed early signs of femininity, as well as sexual precociousness. She started wearing makeup to school in the fourth grade, and would try on her grandmother's clothes when she wasn't home. By age seven, Rivera had already had sex with her 14-year-old male cousin; by age ten she was having sex with her fifth-grade teacher, a married man.[22] That year, she began turning tricks on the streets with her uncle because "[w]e didn't have much money and I wanted things my grandmother couldn't buy."[23] In addition to being poor, Rivera's home life was emotionally precarious. Her birth father José Rivera had disappeared, then neglected to send child support. Her mother's second husband, a drug dealer, showed disinterest in the children. When Sylvia was three years old, her mother committed suicide by ingesting rat poison, and attempted to kill Sylvia along with her, but did not succeed. Rivera's Venezuelan grandmother, Viejita,[24] who was a pieceworker in a factory, was left to raise the children by herself. She called Rivera a "troublemaker," beat her frequently, and told her she did not really want her.[25] According to Rivera, one reason for her grandmother's pique was that she had wanted a "white child." Prejudiced against darker-skinned people, she carried a grudge against Sylvia because Sylvia's father was a dark-skinned Puerto Rican. "I guess in her own strict way my grandmother loved me," Rivera related, but "I basically grew up without love."[26]

Viejita fretted about Rivera's femininity and blooming sexuality. As a preteen, Sylvia shaved her eyebrows, wore mascara, eyeliner, and tight pants, and had sex with boys and men. "My grandmother used to come home and it smelled like a French whorehouse, but that didn't stop me," Rivera said. "I got many ass-whippings from her."[27] The neighbors, evincing heterosexist beliefs, had teased Viejita about Rivera's expressed femininity, warning that she would become a despicable street-hustling *maricón*. Viejita took those criticisms, combined with her own homophobia, to heart. When Rivera came home one night with hickeys on her neck, Viejita beat her, screaming, "Next thing I know you'll be hanging out with the rest of the *maricones* on 42nd Street!"[28] Later, when a neighbor reported sighting Rivera on 42nd Street, Viejita threatened her more vehemently. Rivera attempted suicide and spent two months in a hospital. Viejita, believing Rivera was going to die, tried to remove a cross hanging from around her neck, but Rivera would not let go of it.[29] Recalling her childhood,

Rivera expressed frustration with a community that labeled her a gay maricón while foreclosing other sexual and social options. "As I've grown up, I've realized that I do have a certain attraction to men. But I believe that growing up the way I did, I was basically pushed into this role. In Spanish cultures, if you're effeminate, you're automatically a fag; you're a gay boy. I mean, you start off as a young child and you don't have an option—especially back then. You were either a fag or a dyke. There was no in-between."[30]

Unhappy with her grandmother and the neighborhood, Rivera left home at age 10 to seek a new one on 42nd Street in Times Square.[31] That was where the drag queens and the boy hustlers performed sex work. Although literally homeless and estranged from her birth family, she was able to find a new site of community and kinship. She was excited to find so many drag queens, some of whom adopted her and helped her out,[32] and elated that on her very first night on the street, a man offered her ten dollars for sex. "Ten dollars?! Wow! Ten dollars of my own! Great! Let's go!" she recalled.[33] It was expected that all of the street queens would give themselves new names, and so Ray Rivera became Sylvia Lee Rivera in a ceremony. Fifty street queens, most of them Latin@ and black, attended the celebration, which, Rivera said, felt "just like being reborn."[34]

But such life-affirming joys were rare; street life was hard. Some of the queens Rivera met at the drag balls downtown and in Harlem were affluent, but the street queens turned tricks because they had to. Prostitution was an economic necessity because many of them had left home or been kicked out as children, and because of transphobic, homophobic, and racist employment discrimination. "[I]t just wasn't feasible to be working if you wanted to wear your makeup and do your thing," as Rivera put it.[35] Most abused drugs and alcohol. "You must remember, everyone was doing drugs back then," she said. "Everybody was selling drugs, and everybody was buying drugs to take to other bars, like myself. I was no angel."[36] Near the bottom of the social hierarchy, the street queens risked violence at the hands of each other, their customers, and the police—and the threat of arrest and prison time always loomed.[37] "Back then we were beat up by the police, by everybody," recalled Rivera. "When drag queens were arrested, what degradation there was. [...] We always felt that the police were the real enemy. We expected nothing better than to be treated like we were animals—and we were. We were stuck in a bullpen like a bunch of freaks. We were disrespected. A lot of us were beaten up and raped. When I ended up going to jail, to do 90 days, they tried to rape me. I very nicely beat the shit out of a man."[38] In an environment full of dangers induced by poverty, drugs, and state violence, the presence of true friends could be lifesaving. Early in her life on the streets, Rivera met a black street queen named Marsha P. Johnson, who became her best friend for the next decade. Like a big sister, Johnson looked out for her, taught her how to apply makeup, and gave her good advice, like "show a happy face all the time, not to give a fuck about nothing, not to let nothing stop you [...] Don't mess with anyone's lover; don't rip off anyone's dope or money."[39] When, because of a police crackdown on "vice", Sylvia ended up in prison at Rikers Island in the cellblock reserved for "gay crimes," she met a black queen friend named Bambi Lamour. In jail, the two developed a reputation for being "crazy, abnormal bitches"; according to Rivera, "Nobody ever fucked with us."[40]

On the night of June 27, 1969, Sylvia was only 17 years old. It was a hot and muggy evening, and she headed to the Stonewall Inn to go dancing. Stonewall was not a drag queen bar. In fact, it allowed few drag queens inside because the owners felt gender-nonconforming people would attract trouble from the police. Racism was central to the story of Stonewall; Rivera characterized the Stonewall Inn as "a white male bar for middle-class males to pick up young boys of different races."[41] But she had connections inside the bar, so she could get in. Then, all of a sudden, police were walking through, ordering the patrons to line up and present identification. There was a New York law requiring people to wear at least three pieces of clothing "appropriate" to their birth-assigned gender, and usually in these raids, only people dressed in clothes of a different gender, people without IDs, and employees of the bar would be arrested. Everyone else would be released.[42] Transgender and gender-variant people were separated from lesbians and gays, according to Rivera: "Routine was, 'Faggots over here, dykes over here, and freaks over there,' referring to my side of the community."[43] She elaborated, "The queens and the real butch dykes were the freaks."[44] But on this night, a confrontation occurred. Who initiated the confrontation has become politically important to transgender people who wish to establish historical authenticity within queer movements. One of historian Martin Duberman's interviewees said it was "a dyke dressed in men's clothing" who resisted as the police put hir into the paddy wagon.[45] Rivera told transgender activist Leslie Feinberg that "it was street gay people from the Village out front—homeless people who lived in the park in Sheridan Square outside the bar—and then drag queens behind them and everybody behind us."[46] She said to Latino Gay Men of New York that "street queens of that era" initiated the Stonewall riots by throwing pocket change at the police.[47] She seemed aware of her role in the historical narratives of Stonewall as she joked with the Latino Gay Men audience: "I have been given the credit for throwing the first Molotov cocktail by many historians but I always like to correct it; I threw the second one, I did not throw the first one!"[48]

Though the riot took place at a bar with a largely white, normatively gendered clientele, it was the street youth and gender-variant people nearby—many of them working-class and of color—who were on the front lines of the confrontation. Those who had most been targets of police harassment, those who were most socially and economically marginalized, fought most fiercely. Seymour Pine, the deputy inspector in charge of public morals at the New York Police Department, was the lead police officer on the scene. He recalled on a 1989 National Public Radio program: "One drag queen, as we put her in the car, opened the door on the other side and jumped out. At which time we had to chase that person and he was caught, put back into the car, he made another attempt to get out the same door, the other door, and at that point we had to handcuff the person."[49] A bystander said: "I remember looking back from 10th Street, and there on Waverly Street there was [...] a cop and he is on his stomach in his tactical uniform and his helmet and everything else, with a drag queen straddling him. She was beating the hell out of him with her shoe."[50] Rivera described seeing one drag queen who got beat by the police "into a bloody pulp," and "a couple of dykes they took out and threw in a car."[51] In his historical re-examination of Stonewall, David Carter wrote that "it seems irrefutable that a highly disproportionate amount of the physical courage displayed during the riots came from the more effeminate men in the crowd" and from the street youth.[52] According to Rivera, "Many radical straight men and women" living in Greenwich Village also joined the riot.[53]

Few sources specifically denote race or ethnicity in describing the front line Stonewall combatants. However, Duberman believes it was mostly street people and drag queens who started the fighting.[54] Because many of the street queens Rivera described working with were black and Latin@, I assume that people of color played pivotal roles.[55] This view is supported by sources' occasionally racialized depictions of the riot's early moments. One recalled a "big, hunky, nice-looking Puerto Rican guy" throwing a milk carton at police near the beginning of the confrontation. According to another account, "a young Puerto Rican taunted the gays, asking why they put up with being shoved around by cops."[56] One of David Carter's interviewees said that Gino, a working-class Puerto Rican gay man, was so enraged at the sight of police mistreating a butch female that he yelled at officers to "let her go!" Others in the crowd chimed in; then Gino threw a heavy cobblestone onto the trunk of a police car, "scaring the shit" out of them.[57] It is also important to note that the Stonewall combatants' resistant acts drew inspiration from contemporaneous movements for racial justice. Uprisings against racist police brutality had accelerated during the late 1960s, and as the confrontation with police intensified that night at Stonewall, the crowd's chants of "Gay power!" and "We're the pink panthers!" referred to Black Power and the Black Panther Party.[58] Rivera confirmed, "I don't know how many other patrons in the bar were activists, but many of the people were involved in some struggle. I had been doing work in the civil rights movement, against the war in Vietnam, and for the women's movement."[59]

Published news accounts, for mainstream as well as gay publications, generally elided the roles of gender-variant people and people of color at Stonewall, while subsuming them under the term "gay." For instance, the headline of a September 1969 article in the *Advocate* magazine, originally written for the *New York Mattachine Newsletter,* was "Police Raid on N.Y. Club Sets Off First Gay Riot."[60] This formulation—that the Stonewall uprising was a "gay riot"—consolidated gender-nonconforming people, poor people, and people of color under the identity category of "gay." But it could not explain why police targeted some "gay" people for harsher treatment. It also couldn't explain why some older, wealthier, white gays turned their noses up at news of the uprising, even if later they were to claim they had supported it. According to Martin Duberman, "Many wealthier gays, sunning at Fire Island or in the Hamptons for the weekend, either heard about the rioting and ignored it […] or caught up with the news belatedly." They spoke of Stonewall as "'regrettable,' as the demented carryings-on of 'stoned, tacky queens'—precisely those elements in the gay world from whom they had long since dissociated themselves." Some of these gay people even praised the police for showing "restraint" with the combatants.[61] The body of the *Advocate* article followed the lead of its headline, describing the rioters as "homosexuals," "gay," and as "boys," while generally leaving their ethnicities unmarked.[62] But the racialized and gendered dynamics of the confrontation, and the classed and raced semiotics of the queens' otherness, occasionally break through nonetheless. At one point the article reads: "[A] cop grabbed a wild Puerto Rican queen and lifted his arm to bring a club down on 'her.' In his best Maria Montez voice, the queen challenged, 'How'd you like a big Spanish dick up your little Irish ass?'"

Though the more conservative gays may not have wished it, the national political climate did shift in the uprising's wake. Drawing from the energies of the Third World liberation, civil rights, and feminist movements, two gay political groups, Gay Liberation Front and Gay Activists Alliance, formed in the New York area.[63] Fresh from the empowering actions at Stonewall, Rivera started attending the groups' meetings with high hopes. "I thought that night in 1969 was going to be our unity for the rest of our lives," she told Martin Duberman.[64] But the appearance of political unity soon fractured as Rivera found herself shunned on the basis of her race, class, and gender expression. A founder of GAA, Arthur Bell, reported that "the general membership is frightened of Sylvia and thinks she's a troublemaker. They're frightened by street people." At GAA, wrote Duberman, "[i]f someone was not shunning her darker skin or sniggering at her passionate, fractured English, they were deploring her rude anarchism as inimical to order or denouncing her sashaying ways as offensive to womanhood." Despite feeling marginalized in the groups, Rivera had found purpose in the activism. She kept coming to meetings, where she would loudly speak her mind, and fervently engaged in all of their political actions. But some women in the groups had mixed feelings about her femininity. Events came to a head during the 1973 gay pride rally in Washington Square Park, when Jean O'Leary of GAA publicly denounced Rivera for "parodying" womanhood. Lesbian Feminist Liberation passed out flyers opposing the "female impersonators," seeking to keep queens off the stage.[65] "[B]eing that the women felt that we were offensive, the drag queens Tiffany and Billy were not allowed to perform," Rivera recalled. "I had to fight my way up on that stage and literally, people that I called my comrades in the movement, literally beat the shit out of me."[66] Rivera took the 1973 incident hard. She responded by attempting suicide and dropping out of the movement.[67] According to friend Bob Kohler, "Sylvia left the movement because after the first three or four years, she was denied a right to speak."[68]

Rivera was not only involved in GLF and GAA. Sometimes she marched with the Young Lords and the Black Panthers, and recalled a meeting with Huey Newton as transformative. She dreamed of enacting a very grounded kind of social change: creating a home for "the youngsters," the underage street queens who, like her, had begun working on the streets at age ten, and who not long afterward ended up dead. Rivera and her friend Marsha P. Johnson called their group "Street Transvestites

Action Revolutionaries." They found their refuge for the young street queens first in the back of an abandoned trailer truck, then in a building at 213 East Second Street they called STAR House and quickly proceeded to fix up. Though Sylvia tried to enlist the help of GLF and GAA members with her endeavor, they showed little interest. But she and her "STAR House kids" threw a benefit dance to raise money. Rivera set up an altar with incense and candles where the residents of STAR House would pray to the saints, particularly to Saint Barbara (reputed to be the patron saint of queer Latinos), before they went out hustling. And she began to cook elaborate dinners each night for "the children." But this situation was not to last. They were eventually evicted for nonpayment of rent. Before they left, they removed the refrigerator and destroyed the work they had done on the building. Rivera explained, "That's the type of people we are: You fuck us over, we fuck you over right back."[69]

## III.

Some formulations of queer and transgender politics assert the signal importance of visibility. They celebrate the Stonewall riots as a turning point in which queer and trans people spoke up to straight society, then found freedom, kinship, and community in their ensuing political vocality. They advocate a similar personal trajectory for gay and trans people: at some point, one must opt to break silence, come out of the sexual/gender closet, or refuse to pass as normative, in order to challenge the hegemony of hetero and gender normativity.

The disjunction between this narrative and Rivera's experience illustrates its hidden assumptions of power and privilege. As a child, Rivera involuntarily became visible to neighbors and to her grandmother as a feminine Puerto Rican boy. Poverty and discrimination, rather than pure choice, pushed her into the sex trade. Her queer visibility resulted in estrangement and sexual/gendered surveillance from her birth family and from a homophobic community. Her classed, gendered, and raced visibility as a Puerto Rican street queen resulted in incarceration and unrelenting harassment by police. Though Rivera agitated politically at the Stonewall riots and in GAA and GLF meetings, the gay communities that had "come out" together were not supportive spaces, but stifling and unwelcoming. It was only in communities of poor street queens of color, it seemed, that she felt more at home. Rivera's life shows that queer/trans visibility is not a simple binary; multiple kinds of visibilities, differentially situated in relation to power, intersect and overlap in people's lives. The consequences and voluntariness of visibility are determined in part by social location, and by the systems of power that write gendered and racialized meanings onto bodies. The space "outside" the closet that one comes out to may fail to correspond to romanticized or reductive visions of identity and community.

Political scientist Cathy Cohen has suggested that queer politics has failed to live up to its early promise of radically transforming society. Rather than upend systems of oppression, Cohen says, the queer agenda has sought assimilation and integration into the dominant institutions that perpetuate those systems. In clinging to a single-oppression model that divides the world into "straight" and "queer," and insists that straights oppress while queers are oppressed, queer politics has neglected to examine how "power informs and constitutes privileged and marginalized subjects on both sides of this dichotomy." For instance, it has looked the other way while the state continues to regulate the reproductive capacities of people of color through incarceration. Cohen suggests this is because the theoretical framework of queer politics is tethered to rigid, reductive identity categories that don't allow for the possibility of exclusions and marginalizations *within* the categories. Also dismissed is the possibility that the categories themselves might be tools of domination in need of destabilization and reconceptualization.[70]

Rivera's tense relations with mainstream gay and lesbian politics affirm Cohen's analysis.[71] In 1970 she worked hard on a campaign to pass a New York City gay rights bill that included protections for gender-variant people. A few years later, gay activists and politicians agreed in a backroom deal to raise its chances of passage by removing gender protections from the bill. "The deal was, 'You take them out, we'll pass the bill,'" Rivera bitterly recalled.[72] After dropping out of a movement that had begun "to really silence us,"[73] she spent some years homeless on Manhattan's West Side before being asked in 1994 to lead the 25th anniversary Stonewall march. Yet, the New York City Lesbian and Gay Community Center formally banned her from its premises after she vehemently demanded that they take care of homeless trans and queer youth.[74]

Mainstream gay politics' narrow, single-identity agenda situated Rivera on its margins, and viewed her and her memory as both manipulable and dispensable. By contrast, Rivera's own political affinities, while fiercely resisting cooptation, remained inclusive, mobile, and contextual. Her political practice, informed by a complexly situated life, built bridges between movements, prioritizing the project of justice above arbitrary political boundaries. Her personal identifications, similarly, eschewed categorization and resisted reductive definition. Press narratives pegged her as "gay," neighbors had called her a maricón, transgender and genderqueer activists narrated her as transgender and genderqueer, and Jean O'Leary asserted that she "parodied" womanhood. But she told Martin Duberman: "I came to the conclusion [...] that I don't want to be a woman. I just want to be me. I want to be Sylvia Rivera. I like pretending. I like to have the role. I like to dress up and pretend, and let the world think about what I am. Is he, or isn't he? That's what I enjoy."[75] Rivera elaborated: "People now want to call me a lesbian because I'm with [life partner] Julia [Murray], and I say, 'No, I'm just me. I'm not a lesbian.' I'm tired of being labeled. I don't even like the label transgender. [...] I just want to be who I am. [...] I'm living the way Sylvia wants to live. I'm not living in the straight world; I'm not living in the gay world; I'm just living in my own world with Julia and my friends."[76]

Juana María Rodríguez has written that political affinities based on identity categories have "become highly contested sites [...] based on more precise, yet still problematic, categories of identification and concomitant modes of definition. Identity politics' seeming desire to cling to explicative postures, unified subjecthood, or facile social identifications has often resulted in repression, self-censorship, and exclusionary practices that continue to trouble organizing efforts and work against the interests of full human rights, creative individual expression, and meaningful social transformation."[77] To some extent Rivera's history confirms this view. Her distance from a valued Puerto Rican/Venezuelan male subjectivity characterized by whiteness and hegemonic masculinity, resulted in much pain. Her distance from middle-class white gay maleness resulted in the condemnation of O'Leary, other feminists, and GAA and GLF members. Narratives of gay history that viewed Stonewall as a "gay" event prevented recognition of raced, classed, and gendered hierarchies at Stonewall. And viewing Rivera as a "gay man" makes her relationship to her life partner Julia Murray incomprehensible.[78]

However, Rivera's statements also support a strategic, contingent mobilization of identity categories. Speaking to gay Latinos, she said of the legacy of Stonewall: "*You* have acquired your liberation, your freedom, from that night. Myself, I've got shit, just like I had back then. But I still struggle, I still continue the struggle. I will struggle til the day I die and my main struggle right now is that my community will seek the rights that are justly ours."[79] "My community." Rivera clarified, the "our" that she was referring to, was the "transgender community"; she was sick of seeing transgender political needs continually sold "down the river" in favor of gays.[80] ("[A]fter all these years, the trans community is still at the back of the bus," she wrote.[81]) In this moment, identity labels usefully help Rivera describe her disgust with gay dominance and transgender marginality. She can verbally scold the segment of the lesbian and gay community that wants "[m]ainstreaming, normality, being normal" — to adopt children, to get married, to wear properly gendered clothes—and she can express her political distance from those assimilationist dreams.[82]

Yet, when Rivera says to Latino Gay Men of New York, "I am tired of seeing my children—I call everybody including yous [sic] in the room, you are all my children— I am tired of seeing homeless transgender children; young, gay, youth children," it becomes apparent that her visions of community are suffused with far more complexity and fluidity than a mere denunciation of certain people and a celebrating of others.[83] In that moment, Rivera's articulations of kinship, family, and community exceed models of kinship built upon heterosexual reproduction, and models of community that rely upon an identity politics that Rodríguez called "exclusionary" and "repressive." We begin to see in that sentence that her visions of kinship, family, and community are both inclusive and dynamic. Like her lifelong attempts at building "home," they are unpredictable, impatient but generous, provisional yet welcoming. They parallel the ways in which STAR House enacted a limber physical mobility, but a steadfast commitment to justice, as circumstance buffeted it. In encompassing her life partner Julia, young trans sex workers, Bambi Lamour, Marsha P. Johnson, and all those in Latino Gay Men of New York, they engage in what José Esteban Muñoz has called queer world-making.[84] Even though Rivera "grew up without love," attempts to circumscribe her personal and political positionings are challenged by her abiding ethic of love for all her children: young and old; gay, bisexual, and transgender; normatively gendered and gender variant; in the room and outside it.

## ACKNOWLEDGMENTS

Many thanks to Emma Garrett, Larry La Fountain-Stokes, Nadine Naber, and reviewers for *CENTRO Journal* for their comments on this essay. Thanks also to Matthew M. Andrews, Maria Cotera, Joelle Ruby Ryan, Amy Sueyoshi, and Xavier Totti.

## NOTES

1. Sylvia Rivera Law Project, http://www.srlp.org; James Withers, "Remembering Sylvia Rivera: Though a Divisive Figure, Trans Activist and Stonewall Rioter Gets Honored with Street Sign," *New York Blade* (25 November 2005), http://www.newyorkblade.com/2005/11-25/news/localnews/rivera.cfm.
2. The contention that Stonewall singlehandedly turned the national gay and lesbian tide is refuted by Victor Silverman and Susan Stryker's film, *Screaming Queens: The Riot at Compton's Cafeteria. Screaming Queens* uses interviews and archival research to show that San Francisco transgender prostitutes fought police in 1966, three years before Stonewall. The homophile-to-Stonewall narrative of gay history as "coming out" into liberation also ignores the lives of queer street sex workers such as Rivera. Less able to pass as "normal" than white middle-class gender-normative gays, they were more vulnerable to state violence because of their public gendered, racial, and class visibility.
3. Martin Duberman, *Stonewall* (New York: Dutton, 1993), xv.
4. See, for example, John D'Emilio, "Stonewall: Myth and Meaning," in *The World Turned: Essays on Gay History, Politics, and Culture* (Durham: Duke University Press, 2002), 147.
5. I use "gender-variant" provisionally. Because "transgender" is a relatively recent term, there is no seamless transhistorical connection between people in the late 1960s who I am describing as "gender-variant," and those today who we might call "transgender." But this essay contends that in 1969, people whose expressed genders were distant from hegemonic norms were subject to greater discrimination than those closer to norms.
6. Duberman, 282; Benjamin Shepard, "Sylvia and Sylvia's Children: A Battle for a Queer Public Space," in *That's Revolting!: Queer Strategies for Resisting Assimilation,* ed. Mattilda, aka Matt Bernstein Sycamore (Brooklyn, NY: Soft Skull Press, 2004), 101.
7. See Patrick Califia, *Sex Changes: Transgender Politics,* 2nd ed. (San Francisco: Cleis Press, 1997; 2003), 227.
8. See, for example, Andy Humm, "Transgender Rights," *Gotham Gazette* (July 2001), http://www.gothamgazette.com/article//20010701/3/183 and Michael Bronski, "Sylvia Rivera: 1951–2002," *Z Magazine* (April 2002), http://www.zmag.org/Zmag/articles/april02bronski.htm.
9. Southern Voice, "'T' Time at the Human Rights Campaign," *National Transgender Advocacy Coalition,* 29 March 2001, http://www.ntac.org/news/01/04/08southern.html.
10. Juana María Rodríguez, *Queer Latinidad: Identity Practices, Discursive Spaces* (New York: New York University Press, 2003), 10–1.
11. Elizabeth A. Povinelli, *The Cunning of Recognition: Indigenous Alterities and the Making of Australian Multiculturalism* (Durham: Duke University Press, 2002).
12. As I point out later, Rivera herself often strategically made use of this mobilization.

13. Not all recovery projects have done so. The Sylvia Rivera Law Project's mission statement importantly prioritizes those affected by "multiple vectors of state and institutional violence," and emphasizes participation in "a multi-issue movement for justice and self-determination of all people" in order to address root causes of violence. Also significant are the connections made by TransJustice, "Trans Day of Action for Social and Economic Justice" (2005), in *Color of Violence: The INCITE! Anthology,* ed. Incite! Women of Color Against Violence (Cambridge, MA: South End Press, 2006), 228–9. I do not mean to suggest that the projects I scrutinize intentionally sought to elide vectors of power. Rather, I foreground my interpretations of their unintended effects in the hopes of helping to "reenvision a politics of solidarity that goes beyond multiculturalism." Andrea Smith, "Heteropatriarchy and the Three Pillars of White Supremacy: Rethinking Women of Color Organizing," in *Color of Violence,* 73.

14. A gender-neutral pronoun.

15. Leslie Feinberg noted, "We are a movement of masculine females and feminine males, cross-dressers, transsexual men and women, intersexuals born on the anatomical sweep between female and male, gender-blenders, many other sex and gender-variant people, and our significant others." Feinberg, *Trans Liberation: Beyond Pink or Blue* (Boston: Beacon Press, 1998), 5.

16. Ibid, 106.

17. Riki Wilchins, "Gender Rights are Human Rights," in *GenderQueer: Voices From Beyond the Sexual Binary,* ed. Joan Nestle, Clare Howell, and Riki Wilchins (Los Angeles: Alyson Books, 2002), 297.

18. See Wilchins, "Queerer Bodies," in *GenderQueer,* 37. For the academic origins of "queer," see Cathy J. Cohen, "Punks, Bulldaggers, and Welfare Queens: The Radical Potential of Queer Politics?," in *Sexual Identities, Queer Politics,* ed. Mark Blasius (Princeton: Princeton University Press, 2001), 201.

19. Smith, 67.

20. Benjamin Shepard, "History or Myth? Writing Stonewall," *Lambda Book Report* (August/September 2004), 14.

21. Patricia Hill Collins, "Defining Black Feminist Thought," in *The Second Wave: A Reader in Feminist Theory,* ed. Linda Nicholson (New York: Routledge, 1997), 246.

22. Duberman, 23; Sylvia Rivera, "Queens in Exile, the Forgotten Ones," in *GenderQueer,* 68–9.

23. Rivera, 69.

24. In my sources, Rivera only refers to her grandmother as "my grandmother." However, Martin Duberman in *Stonewall* refers to Rivera's grandmother as Viejita. I assume this is Rivera's usage because Duberman interviewed her extensively for the book. Therefore I have used Viejita as an alternate way to refer to Rivera's grandmother.

25. Duberman, 21–2; Rivera, 68.

26. Rivera, 68.

27. Ibid., 69.

28. Duberman, 23.

29. Ibid., 66.

30. Rivera, 69.

31. Duberman, 24; Rivera, 70.

32. Rivera, 70.

33. Duberman, 66.

34. Ibid., 67.

35. Rivera, 70–1. Gender presentation and class were intertwined. The street queens had to hustle, and the affluent queens did not, partly because the street queens were more gender-nonconforming. See Rivera, 71, and David Carter, *Stonewall: The Riots that Sparked the Gay Revolution* (New York: St. Martin's Press, 2004), 61.

36. "Sylvia Rivera Talk at LGMNY" (manuscript, June 2001), transcribed by Lauren Galarza and Lawrence La Fountain-Stokes, 2. See also Rivera, 71; Duberman, 66, 70.

37. Rivera, 70–1; Duberman, 68–71; Eric Marcus, *Making History: The Struggle for Gay and Lesbian Equal Rights,* 1945–1990: An Oral History (New York: HarperPerennial, 1992), 189–90.

38. Feinberg, 106.

39. Duberman, 68.

40. Ibid., 123–4.

41. Rivera, 78. She also notes, "Even back then we had our racist little clubs. There were the white gay bars and then there were the very few third world bars and drag queen bars." "Sylvia Rivera Talk," 2. Rivera's depiction of the Stonewall Inn's clientele as being mostly white, middle-class, male, and gender normative is partly corroborated and partly contested by David Carter's sources. Carter, 73–7.

42. Duberman, 192; Rivera, 77–8.

43. "Sylvia Rivera Talk," 3.

44. Rivera, 78. New York Police Department Deputy Inspector Seymour Pine has confirmed that in these raids, police singled out gender-variant people for extra harassment and physical "examination" in the bathroom. It's unclear what happened during this examination. David Carter, 140–1.

45. Duberman, 196. For more on this butch person, see Carter, 150–1.

46. Feinberg, 107.

47. "Sylvia Rivera Talk," 3.

48. Ibid., 4. Rivera's role in the Stonewall riots has been questioned by David Carter. See Shepard, "History or Myth?," 12–4.

49. David Isay with Michael Schirker, producers, "Remembering Stonewall," *Weekend All Things Considered,* National Public Radio, 1 July 1989; http://www.soundportraits.org/on-air/remembering_stonewall/.

50. Ibid.

51. Marcus, 192.

52. Carter, 192, 162–3. Carter concludes that combatants were most often young, poor or working-class, and gender-variant, and also notes the participation of middle-class college graduates. Carter, 163, 262.

53. "Sylvia Rivera Talk," 5.

54. Duberman, "Stonewall Place" (1989) in *About Time: Exploring the Gay Past,* ed. Duberman (1986; rev. and expanded ed., New York: Meridian, 1991), 425.

55. In a speech, Rivera named Marsha P. Johnson, an African-American, and fellow street queens as front-line combatants. "[The confrontation] was started by the street queens of that era, which I was part of, Marsha P. Johnson, and many others that are not here." "Sylvia Rivera Talk," 3–4. However, David Carter has asserted that "of those on the rebellion's front lines, most were Caucasian; few were Latino." Carter, 262.

56. Carter, 161.

57. Ibid., 152.

58. Ibid., 164–5; Duberman, *Stonewall,* 197, 203.

59. Rivera, 77. See also Feinberg, 107.

60. Dick Leitsch, "Police Raid on N.Y. Club Sets Off First Gay Riot" (September 1969), in *Witness to Revolution: The Advocate Reports on Gay and Lesbian Politics, 1967–1999* (Los Angeles: Alyson Books, 1999), 11.

61. Duberman, *Stonewall,* 206.

62. Leitsch, 11–3.

63. Though inspired by racial justice movements, the groups generally excluded people of color. Duberman, *Stonewall,* 233–4.

64. Ibid., 246.

65. Ibid., 235–6, 238; Shepard, "Sylvia and Sylvia's Children," 99–100.

66. "Sylvia Rivera Talk," 8–9.

67. Duberman, *Stonewall,* 236; "Sylvia Rivera Talk," 9; Shepard, 100.

68. Shepard, "Sylvia and Sylvia's Children," 100.

69. Duberman, *Stonewall,* 251–5.

70. Cohen, "Punks, Bulldaggers, and Welfare Queens," 200–201, 203, 219–221, 223.

71. In her essay, Cohen is specifically addressing queer, rather than gay and lesbian, politics. However, both politics share similar logics.

72. "Sylvia Rivera Talk," 7; Shepard, "Sylvia and Sylvia's Children," 99.

73. "Sylvia Rivera Talk," 9.

74. Shepard, "Sylvia and Sylvia's Children," 101; "Sylvia Rivera Talk," 6; Bronski.

75. Duberman, *Stonewall,* 125.

76. Rivera, 77.

77. Rodríguez, 41.

78. Soundportraits.org, "Sylvia Rivera," http://www.soundportraits.org/in.-print/magazine_articles/sylvia_rivera/, from 27 June 1999 *New York Times Magazine.*

79. "Sylvia Rivera Talk," 6.

80. Ibid., 7.

81. Rivera, 80.

82. "Sylvia Rivera Talk," 7, 10.

83. Ibid., 6.

84. José Esteban Muñoz, *Disidentification: Queers of Color and the Performance of Politics* (Minneapolis: University of Minnesota Press, 1999).

# 25

# Transgender Subjectivity and the Logic of Sexual Difference

Shanna T. Carlson

Psychoanalytic theory, particularly as Freud's ideas have been interpreted by Lacan, has played an important role in many feminist projects to critique dominant sex/gender ideologies that constrain the lives of women—largely by demonstrating that gendered psyches are formed through a socio-cultural process rather than being pre-existing natural or biological facts. Feminist critiques of gender drawing on psychoanalysis (notably but by no means exclusively those of Judith Butler) have helped clear intellectual space for discussions of gender's complexities in ways that have benefited transgender discourses, identities, and practices. And yet, psychoanalytic theory has been notoriously maladept at understanding transgender subjectivity as anything other than psychopathological. In this technically difficult article, which requires some familiarity with Lacan's elaborate terminology, Romance Studies scholar Shanna Carlson argues that it is possible to bring psychoanalysis and feminist gender analysis together in ways that give better, less prejudicial, accounts of transgender psychical phenomena. In fact, Carlson suggests, taking transgender subjectivity seriously calls for a profound re-envisioning of key psychoanalytic concepts, including sexual difference, masculinity, femininity, desire, castration, and lack. In charting what this transgendering of psychoanalytic theory might entail, Carlson imagines that the psychical imperative to take up a position of sexual difference and be a sex could come to be understood as something other than a scene of compulsory heterosexuality; it could point instead toward the emerging contours of (post)human bodies and subjects yet to come.

Gender studies and Lacanian psychoanalysis share a set of common questions [...] In spite of these shared concerns, sexual difference, what it is and what it means, often becomes a point of contention. This antagonism is perhaps most stringently encapsulated in Kate Bornstein's response to Lacanian psychoanalyst Catherine Millot's text on transsexuality, when the former writes, "Gender terrorists are not the leather daddies or back-seat Betties. Gender terrorists are not the married men, shivering in the dark as they slip on their wives' panties. Gender terrorists are those who, like Ms. Millot, bang their heads against a gender system which is *real* and *natural*; and who then use gender to terrorize the rest of us. These are the real terrorists: the Gender Defenders" (236). The discourses of gender studies and Lacanian psychoanalysis collide to particularly spectacular effect around the questions of transsexuality and transgenderism. What remains to be seen is whether or not these spectacular effects might be channeled into some sort of understanding for a logic of sexual difference for present bodies as well as "the holographic and moving contours of *bodies to come, of bodies as they might come*" (Berger 64).

In *Three Essays on the Theory of Sexuality*, Freud writes that we as human animals are all bisexual (141) and that we are all perverts (160). The radical promise of Freud's words on perversion has not gone unnoticed by gender theorists, who have rightly pointed to certain strident passages in Freud's writings in order to object to a facile vilification of Freud as anti homosexuality.[4] Less attention seems to have been paid, however, to Freud's words on bisexuality and the provocative connections between perversion and bisexuality (bisexuality as related to psychical hermaphroditism and/or physical hermaphroditism, as well as bisexuality as homo- plus heterosexuality).[5] If the condition of human subjectivity as such is bisexuality, and if, as Lacan writes, Freud "posit[s] sexuality as essentially polymorphous, aberrant" (*Four* 176), then why in Lacan's reading of Freud are there only two sexual positions, masculine and feminine? Where Butler might advocate gender play, where Derrida has been said to "dream... of a sexual relationship, albeit sexed otherwise: not one that is divided into two parts, played by two recognizable partners, but one that is inscribed in multiple ways" (Berger 60), Lacan replies implacably that "there's no such thing as a sexual relationship" (*Encore* 57) and that there is a feminine way to respond to that failure and a masculine way to respond to it. How do these qualifications, that there is no sexual relationship and that there are only two sexual positions, follow from the conditions of bisexuality and polymorphous perversion? And don't these qualifications make psychoanalysis seem rather sexually impoverished with respect to other perspectives?

For Lacan, polymorphous perversion is the effect of castration, and, in the spirit of a perverse temporality, castration is equally the effect of polymorphous perversion. How is this so? In speaking of infantile sexuality, Freud provides the example of thumb sucking, explaining that in thumb sucking a child seeks a previously experienced pleasure that "is now remembered" (181). Later Freud qualifies, "The finding of an object is in fact a refinding of it" (222). For Lacan, finding and refinding objects is not only the infantile, polymorphous precursor to an eventual castration by way of shame, disgust, morality (Freud 191), and the Oedipal drama but also, or rather, the sign that the subject has already been castrated.[6]

For Lacan, as soon as there is an object, evidenced in the example of the infant's turn to the thumb, there is castration. Something, in other words, has been lost. Lacan writes,

> [W]hat makes us distinguish this satisfaction from the mere auto-eroticism of the erogenous zone is the object that we confuse all too often with that upon which the drive closes—this object, which is in fact simply the presence of a hollow, a void, which can be occupied, Freud tells us, by any object, and whose agency we know only in the form of the lost object, the *petit a*. The *objet petit a* is not the origin of the oral drive. It is not introduced as the original food, it is introduced from the fact that no food will ever satisfy the oral drive, except by circumventing the eternally lacking object.
>
> (*Four* 179–80)

Lacan points to Freud's specification that the object can be "any object" (180), commenting elsewhere, "Let us look at what he says—*As far as the object in the drive is concerned, let it be clear that it is, strictly speaking, of no importance. It is a matter of total indifference*" (168). In other words, any object may be one toward which the drive might tend; what seems new here is the reason for such *pulsion*, as well as what is signified by that object around which the drive closes. Here the regression is not precisely, for example, from thumb to breast to milk, but rather from any object to object *a* as "the eternally lacking object." Lacan tells us that object *a* is introduced from the fact that nothing, no thing—no food, no breast, no person—will ever satisfy the drive. Object *a* as "cause of desire" (*Encore* 92) is not the object that the subject seizes, nor is it the aim of desire, but rather, "It is either pre-subjective, or the foundation of an identification of the subject, or the foundation of an identification disavowed by the subject" (*Four* 186). It is, indeed, the foundation of a subject, but a contingent foundation: as Dean explains, "[T]his object counterintuitively (ungrammatically?) appears to precede the subject, to found the subject.... Yet the apparent foundationalism of object *a* betokens a radically contingent foundation, since as Ellie Ragland points out, '[w]e humans are grounded in objects that are not themselves grounded'" (*Beyond* 194). In insisting that "any object" can stand in as a representative for object *a* and that object *a* is only a further representative of "the eternally lacking object," Lacan distances himself from a reading of Freud that would see a sexual developmental progression or "maturation" from the oral to the anal to the genital drives. Instead, Lacan emphasizes the essential groundlessness of object *a* and its voidlike role in the circuitous motion of the drive (*Four* 181).

Lacan offers a variety of accounts of the "birth" or "origin" of these ungrounded objects *a*. The story of the lamella, as one such example, is Lacan's playful revision of Plato's myth in the *Symposium* as told by the narrative voice of Aristophanes. Replacing the missing parts as explained by Plato with the figure of the lamella, Lacan writes:

> This lamella, this organ, whose characteristic is not to exist, but which is nevertheless an organ—I can give you more details as to its zoological place—is the libido.
>
> It is the libido, qua pure life instinct, that is to say, immortal life, or irrepressible life, life that has need of no organ, simplified, indestructible life. It is precisely what is subtracted from the living being by virtue of the fact that it is subject to the cycle of sexual reproduction. And it is of this that all the forms of the *objet a* that can be enumerated are the representatives, the equivalents. The objets a are merely its representatives, its figures.
>
> (*Four* 197–98)

This is yet another narration of castration, this time a rather surreal mythologization [...] In fact the lamella-as-libido provides the thin, hymenium contiguity for Lacan between what the subject loses via sexed reproduction and the order of the real, for "[i]t is precisely what is subtracted from the living being by virtue of the fact that it is subject to the cycle of sexed reproduction" (*Four* 198). Lacan describes the libido as "essential" to "understanding the nature of the drive" (205), and his usage of a mythical organ to figure a real loss is strategic, for, as he writes, "This organ is unreal. Unreal is not imaginary. The unreal is defined by articulating itself on the real in a way that eludes us, and it is precisely this that requires that its representation should be mythical, as I have made it" (205). In *Encore,* meiosis will serve as the framework to tell the same story, again constituting "a thoroughly obvious subtraction" (66), whose "'waste' returns to haunt the libidinal subject in the form of object *a*" (Barnard, "Tongues" 174). [...]

Lacan's account of object *a* seems to pose no threat to any range of queer theories of sexuality insofar as it does not presuppose, for example, that a particular type of object *should* or in fact ever *could* satisfy the drive. Indeed, Lacan repeatedly mocks the institution of so-called genital primacy (*Ethics* 88). [...] Left only with a story of *a*-sexual asexuality, we might be halfway to a Lacanian narration of transgender ontology—not such a radical thought when we recall that Freud was the one who pointed out the constitutive bisexual perversion of the human unconscious. From whence, then, the feminine and masculine subject positions?

No matter where we locate the instantiation of loss in the subject (meiosis, birth, thumb sucking), it is clear that for psychoanalysis we are dealing with a desiring subject, a subject who lacks not simply some locatable object (e.g., a penis) but who lacks being as such. But, according to Lacan, there is not only one way to desire. This is another way of saying that there is not only one way to apprehend the lack in the Other. There are two sexual positions available to human subjects because, as Lacan asserts in *Encore* using the language of logic and mathematical formalization, subjects are positioned differently with respect to one term: the phallic function. There are two sexual positions insofar as every subject is either "all" or "not-all" under the phallic function. [...]

Veering into yet another scene of castration, the formulas of sexuation provide the "logical matrix" (Salecl 2) of the deadlock of sexual difference. As Lacan recounts, the formulas consist of the following: the right side of the formula, which reads $\exists x \overline{\Phi} x$ and $\overline{\forall} x \Phi x$, figures the "feminine" side and can be translated to state that there is not one x that is not subject to the phallic function and that not every x is subject to the phallic function. The feminine subject finds "herself" "not-all" by way of negation insofar as "she" forms part of an open set, open and thereby infinite because it is not constituted by an exceptional figure. No shared trait—aside from the absence of any such shared trait—serves to define the set; no constitutive outside functions close her set. Exceptionally lacking exception, though, and being only loosely linked by virtue of an absence offers/burdens the feminine subject (with) a particular perspective on the phallic function and thus on what grounds the masculine subject, which Barnard describes as "a view to the contingency of the signifier of the Other in its anchoring function... [S]he 'knows' that the signifier of phallic power merely lends a certain mysterious presence to the Law that veils its real impotence" ("Tongues" 178). One of the logical consequences of such a position, of "being in the symbolic 'without exception'" (178), is that she has a different relation than the masculine subject, not only to the symbolic but also to the lack in the Other.

The "anchoring function" lacking to the feminine subject is located on the "masculine" side of Lacan's formula: "On the left, the lower line— $\forall_x \overline{\Phi}x$ —indicates that it is through the phallic function that man as whole acquires his inscription... with the proviso that this function is limited due to the existence of an x by which the function $\overline{\Phi}x$ is negated...: $\exists x \overline{\Phi}x$ " (*Encore* 79). This exception also immediately takes on a truly exceptional status, from the standpoint of the masculine subject who is established by it, for the exception proffers the outside that closes "his" set and the limit that grounds "his" being; it thereby proffers a sort of support not afforded the feminine subject. One figure of this exception would be that of the mythical primal father, he who evades castration and thereby enjoys unlimited jouissance. In other words, the masculine subject is only "whole" or "all" as a result of the fact that he is permitted (permits himself?) the fantasy of one who escapes the very same set that grounds his being: "That is what is known as the father function—whereby we find, via negation, the proposition..., which grounds the operativity (*exercice*) of what makes up for the sexual relationship with castration, insofar as that relationship is in no way inscribable. The whole here is thus based on the exception posited as the end-point *(terme)*, that is, on that which altogether negates $\overline{\Phi}x$ " (Lacan, *Encore* 79–80). As Lacan makes explicit here, castration/sexual difference is something that fundamentally, if incompletely, makes up for the absence of the sexual relationship. By this logic, the sexual positions borne of sexual difference figure as solutions, no doubt principally unsatisfying ones, for the loss of a sort of relation that was in fact never possible, a relation of One-ness or complementarity, or for the loss of that missing half that Plato tells us, somewhat cruelly, we once had. [...]

At least in this *Encore* explanation of the formulas of sexuation, Lacan's introduction to the feminine side reads quite differently from his introduction to the masculine side. Perhaps in the spirit of approximating form and content, the masculine description is considerably more formulaic. Immediately following his definition of the masculine side, his words concerning the feminine side posit a proviso that will prove fruitful for the turn to questions of transsexuality and transgenderism:

> On the other side, you have the inscription of the woman portion of speaking beings. Any speaking being whatsoever, as is expressly formulated in Freudian theory, whether provided with the attributes of masculinity—attributes that remain to be determined—or not, is allowed to inscribe itself in this part. If it inscribes itself there, it will not allow for any universality—it will be a not-whole, insofar as it has the choice of positing itself in $\overline{\Phi}x$ or of not being there. (80)

Of course part of what is at stake in this particular citation is the status of the word *choice*. Is it significant that the matter of choice comes up in his description of the feminine side of the formula? And when Lacan states that any speaking subject has the choice to position itself or not in $\overline{\Phi}x$, what is the relationship between the "choice" signaled here and any possibility of "choice" occasioned by Butlerian notions of gender play? Meanwhile, how do Butler's and Lacan's regimes of choice articulate with Susan Stryker's observation that "performativity" and its promises do not always speak to "the self-understanding of many transgender people, who consider their sense of gendered self *not* to be subject to their instrumental will, not divestible, not a form of play" (10)? And what are the differences between the experiences of transsexualism and those of transgenderism when it comes to thinking about "choice?"

Already we can see further sets of challenges, knotting around questions of disciplinary allegiance, contestation, dissidence, identity politics, and ontology. These issues, too, will necessitate delicate unraveling as we continue to explore what Lacanian psychoanalysis and gender studies have to offer one another. Still, it is statements like Lacan's, above, that offer hope, beyond the fears and objections of theorists like Butler and Copjec, that there *is* room for meeting ground between Lacanian psychoanalysis and gender studies, over and above—in fact, sometimes revolving precisely around— the divisions concerning (and that are perhaps inherent in) sexual difference.

Dean further supports such optimism when he declares that "psychoanalysis *is* a queer theory" (*Beyond* 215), meaning, in part, that Lacanian psychoanalysis has "antinormative potential" (217). One of the principal stakes of Dean's project is "to think sexuality outside the terms of gender" (185). In accordance with many thinkers, he considers the debate between essentialism and constructivism, or what he calls foundationalism and rhetoricalism, a false alternative, and he takes a view on sexuality that he describes as "both immoderately antifoundationalist *and* antirhetoricalist" (178). In this way, he takes exception to Butler's account of sexuality as outlined in *Bodies That Matter*, for, as he argues, Butler's is a rhetoricalist approach. According to Dean, "rhetoricalist theories of sexuality effectively evacuate the category of desire from their accounts" by failing to take account of "what in rhetoric or discourse exceeds language" (178). Desire will prove essential to Dean's own account of sexuality; in his project to deheterosexualize desire, Dean develops the notion of object *a* in order to theorize sexuality "outside the terms of gender *and* identity" (222).

Dean demonstrates that a Lacanian theory of desire is "determined not by the gender of object-choice, but by the object *a* (*l'objet petit a*), which remains largely independent of gender" (216). By this move, Dean, via Lacan, goes further than Freud did in his account of humans' constitutive bisexuality. Dean reminds readers of Freud's claim that "we've all made a homosexual object-choice" (219). However, as Dean makes clear, such a pronouncement presupposes that an object be gendered in the first place; by relying on humans' "bisexuality," Freud leaves intact the possibility that objects may be "somehow identifiable as masculine or feminine" (219). Object *a*, on the other hand, is not so easily assimilated to either hetero- or homosexual frames. Dean reminds readers of Lacan's "unthinkable list" of possible objects a—"lips..., the rim of the anus, the tip of the penis, the vagina, the slit formed by the eyelids, even the horn-shaped aperture of the ear..., the mamilla, faeces, the phallus (imaginary object), the urinary flow..., the phoneme, the gaze, the voice—the nothing" (Lacan quoted in *Beyond* 251–52).

Part of what is at stake in Dean's insistence on object *a* as the queerly "ordering" term for sexuality is his wish to relocate the scene of desire from one revolving around the phallus, which, according to Lacan, is the name for a certain lack borne of the desire of the Other ("Meaning" 83). Dean is sensitive to various feminist and queer critiques of Lacanian terminology, noting that suspicions about such terms as *lack* and *the phallus* are warranted, given, in part, the theological origins of lack and the psychoanalytic legacy of associating homosexuality with deficiency (*Beyond* 248). Master terms such as *lack, loss, castration, death,* and *sexual difference* are not ideologically neutral, and Dean advises caution about how different terms may "imply invidious distinctions or otherwise embed normative ideologies of gender and sexuality" (248).

According to Dean, the limitation of situating the phallus at the center of a theoretical account of desire is not only that the phallus has such a problematic history but that it is a single term; object *a*, on the other hand, "implies multiple, heterogeneous possibilities for desire" (250). Dean wishes to figure desire within "terms of multiplicity" (249) rather than principally according to an "ideology of lack" (247). He cites Lacan's assertion that "[d]esire is a relation of being to lack" (quoted in *Beyond* 247) but emphasizes, too, that "the question of conceptualizing desire in terms of lack remains a stubborn problem" for a variety of queer- and feminist-minded projects (248). Dean identifies the latter resistance as having precisely to do with the way that the ideology of lack intersects with castration in psychoanalytic theory (248). In favor of such a scene, Dean turns instead to polymorphous perversion as a site of multiplicity, contending that theorizing desire from the point of excess instead of from the point of lack "makes desire essentially pluralistic, with all the inclusive implications of pluralism" (249).

For Dean, one of the advantages of theorizing desire from the starting point of polymorphous perversion arises from Freud's understanding of polymorphous perversion as preceding normative— that is, genital—sexuality; in this way, perversion comes to represent a sort of "paradise lost" that "normal sexuality" will try, but never completely manage, to supplant (235). In rehearsing Freud's decision to classify perversion in terms not of content but rather of "exclusiveness and fixation" (236), Dean will go so far as to suggest that "*the process of normalization itself is what's pathological,* since normalization 'fixes' desire and generates the exclusiveness of sexual orientation [heterosexual or homosexual] as its symptom" (237).

Thus for Dean, polymorphous perversion figures as a model for desire to which he would have subjects return, both foundational and desirable insofar as it predates normalization. This move serves to shift focus from a scene of desire dependent on castration, "one that threatens to return us to the binary categories of complementarity and homogeneity so inhospitable to non-normative sexualities" (*Beyond* 249), to one dependent on a multiplicity of objects. While he knits polymorphous perversion and object *a* together with multiplicity, heterogeneity, and possibility, it seems important to acknowledge once again that primary perversion remains deeply imbricated with loss: it names the "stage" that inculcates desire via the production of objects, and, as we have seen, these objects are always already irremediably lost objects. Primary perversion also figures loss insofar as it is a lost stage, replaced as it is, to whatever extent that may be, by processes of normalization such as the formation of a sexual (orientation) identity. Perversion thus takes on a curious status in Dean's thought, for from one perspective it constitutes a state of desire that is less lacking—the sheer multiplicity of objects available gestures in this direction. But insofar as these objects all remain lost objects, the opposite could be argued as well: via polymorphous perversion, the subject is more lacking by entertaining more (lost) objects. However, this change in the scenery of desire, from lacking phalluses to abundant objects, represents a provocative and productive development [...]

I am interested in going in a slightly different direction than that outlined in *Beyond Sexuality*. While Dean is abundantly clear that he is not interested in gender, he also specifies that sexual difference (which, as we know by now, should not be collapsed into the category of gender) cannot be so summarily discounted: "Let me make clear that I'm not claiming that sexual difference is inconsequential to this account of sexuality, just that it is secondary. Desire emerges before sexual difference" (267). No doubt. Insofar as desire is the other side of lack/loss/castration, desire has been with the subject since the days of the lost lamella. However, what is not of interest to Dean, at least in this text, is Lacan's assertion that masculine and feminine subjects *relate differently* to object *a*. According to Lacan, it is the masculine subject that is principally occupied with object *a*. Queer as it is, could Dean's account of desire be lacking the feminine?

Lacan writes that "the object—from at least one pole of sexual identification, the male pole—the object... puts itself in the place of what cannot be glimpsed of the Other" (*Encore* 63). By contrast, for the feminine subject, "something other than object *a* is at stake in what comes to make up for the sexual relationship that does not exist" (63). Here again, we see Lacan specifying that via sexual difference, something tries to make up for the absence of the sexual relation. However, there is a fundamental asymmetry at play in the making up for lost/fantasized complementarity, for feminine and masculine subjects make up for the loss, in part, with recourse to different types of others. [...]

Perhaps the position of object *a* in Lacan's depiction is a little deceiving. The sexuation graph seems to imply that feminine subjects lose all connection to object *a*, but we could read this instead to suggest that the feminine subject simply is not *as* invested in object *a* insofar as she might be overwhelmed with interrogating the phallic signifier and with a certain queer, inscrutable relation with the barred, lacking Other. To my knowledge, Lacan does not anywhere specify that feminine subjects lose all connection with object *a*; rather, he writes simply that "something other than object *a* is at stake in what comes to make up for (*suppléer*) the sexual relationship that does not exist" (*Encore* 63). Of importance here is that one consequence of sexual difference is that while the masculine subject becomes principally invested in object a—wherever he may locate it/them—as one compensation for the lack of the sexual relation, the feminine subject "is 'twice' related to the Other" (Barnard, "Tongues" 172). I take this to mean that the feminine subject is related both to object *a* (*autre*, or other) as that "scrap of the real" lost through sexed reproduction and to the Other conceived of as the lacking Other.

Dean's reading of Lacan's representation of sexual difference suggests there may be something to Butler's critique that the Lacanian notion of sexual difference enjoins compulsory heterosexuality, if not in the formulas themselves, then at least in one way of reading the sexuation graph representation. In both *Bodies That Matter* and *Antigone's Claim*, Butler performs readings of the subject's entry into the symbolic via sexual differentiation, and two of her principal charges are that Lacan's symbolic is normative and that the assumption of a sexed position enjoins compulsory heterosexuality. In *Antigone's Claim*, Butler turns from matters of discourse and materiality to the scene of kinship in order to explore how psychoanalysis might both/either compel and/or inhibit the forging of new kinds of community ties, ties that Butler subsumes under the promising header "radical kinship." [...]

Butler's investment in the possibility of imagining new forms of kinship ties has a strong affective and political attraction, which she wields to good end, for example, in her listing of the ways that "kinship has become fragile, porous, and expansive" (*Antigone's* 22). Butler cites the mobility of children who, because of migration, exile, refugee status, or situations of divorce or remarriage, "move from one family to another, move from a family to no family, move from no family to a family, or live, psychically, at the crossroads of the family, or in multiply layered family situations" (22). She points to the blending of straight and gay families, to gay nuclear families, and to straight or gay families where a child may have no mother or no father, or two mothers or two fathers, or half-brothers as friends (22–23), asking: "What has Oedipus engendered?... What will the legacy of Oedipus be for those who are formed in these situations, where positions are hardly clear, where the place of the father is dispersed, where the place of the mother is multiply occupied or displaced, where the symbolic in its stasis no longer holds?" (22–23). No doubt this is a time of potentially unprecedented familial mobility. Some would evaluate these realities as the sign of a crisis in "family values"; others would celebrate the more positive effects of the new types of ties and encounters. In this text, though, Butler is also taking aim at a particular strain of psychoanalysis that would seem unexpectedly to ally itself on some levels with defenders of the heterosexual nuclear family. Butler references such positions as she has encountered them, including psychoanalysts opposed to or at least worried about gay adoption as a possible source of psychosis for the adopted children, Jacques-Alain Miller's alleged opposition to male homosexual marriage on account of its likely infidelity, and others' suggestion that autism can be traceable to lesbian parenting (70). Butler concludes, "These views commonly maintain that alternative kinship arrangements attempt to revise psychic structures in ways that lead to tragedy again, figured incessantly as the tragedy of and for the child."

I, too, would object to the efficacy or relevance of such concerns, for many reasons. As one objection, these views appear to share the assumption that something like "gender" needs to accord to (or succeed in according to) a sexual position. In other words, these views, where they exist (meaning both in some Lacanians' readings of sexual difference and in Butler's reading of Lacan's understanding of sexual difference), suggest once again that gender accords with unconscious sexuation. What, for example, is a "lesbian" according to those concerned about autism in children? What if an apparently "woman"-loving "heterosexual" "man" could be said to be unconsciously "feminine?" If "he" is in a relationship with a subject also describable as unconsciously "feminine," is "he" a "lesbian?" Perhaps this divorcing of gender from unconscious sexuation sounds like another queer utopia and is for this reason, for some, unviable, but I think it is the logical consequence of Lacan's claim that "[a]ny speaking being whatsoever, as is expressly formulated in Freudian theory, whether provided with the attributes of masculinity—attributes that remain to be determined—or not, is allowed to inscribe itself in [the woman portion of speaking beings]" (*Encore* 80). I would like to join Butler in imagining sexuation otherwise than as a scene of compulsory heterosexuality. However, I do not think that doing so requires locating a loophole in the Oedipal narrative, as Butler does in her interpretation of the Antigone story. For while Butler is quite right to lament and fear the compulsory heterosexuality that provides a potent backdrop to many societal norms and ideals, no one knew better than Lacan that, as he put it, "[i]deals are society's slaves" (Dean, *Beyond* 229).

In her argument, Butler seems to cast the Oedipal scene as the only available solution within psychoanalysis to the failure of the sexual relation, as in her observation that, for Lacan, the symbolic is "the realm of the Law that regulates desire in the Oedipus complex" (*Antigone's* 18). True, all subjects enter the symbolic, but the Oedipal drama is a principally "masculine" (and indeed a principally "obsessional," if not a principally heterosexual) solution to the failure of the sexual relation, one that hallucinates an object as prohibited. But as we have seen, there is not only one solution to the failure of the sexual relation: there are two! In this way, Butler is quite right to turn to Antigone as an alternative to the Oedipal solution. In Butler's reading, Antigone helps us envisage new forms of kinship and, correspondingly, the "possibility of social transformation" (24). [...] Through the figure of Antigone, Butler explores a non-Oedipal solution to the failure of the sexual relation, one that in Lacan's reading entails a specifically feminine encounter with the signifier. However, she does so without avowing that this solution was available to subjects from the start, that it was not the Oedipal drama that engendered it.

At some points, one might be led to wonder if Butler's configurations of the allegedly sedimentary symbolic might owe a bit more to Claude Lévi-Strauss than to Lacan's own reformulation, as for example when she writes,

> *The Elementary Structures of Kinship* was published in 1947, and within six years Lacan began to develop his more systematic account of the symbolic.... On the one hand, we are told that the rule of prohibiting incest is universal, but Lévi-Strauss also acknowledges that it does not always "work." What he does not pursue, however, is the question, what forms does its nonworking take? Moreover, when the prohibition appears to work, does it have to sustain and manage a specter of its nonworking in order to proceed?
>
> (*Antigone's* 16–17)

Perhaps, in contrast to Lévi-Strauss, Lacan is more explicit: the form the nonworking of the incest prohibition takes is femininity. Feminine figures testify precisely to the failure of the prohibition, for, as Copjec eloquently plots out, "Lacan answers that the woman is not-all because she lacks a limit, by which he means she is not susceptible to the threat of castration; the 'no' embodied by this threat does not function for her" (226).

While the "universal" incest prohibition does not "work" for the feminine subject, this does not necessarily mean that she has incestuous relations with or desires toward someone in her family (which may be composed as radically or as porously as permitted by the limits of our imaginations)— though she very well may, and I see no reason to shy away from Butler's suggestion that Antigone's desire for her brother Polynices is incestuous: "Is it perhaps the unlivable desire with which she lives, incest itself, that makes of her life a living death, that has no place within the terms that confer intelligibility on life?" (*Antigone's* 25). Nonetheless, I would emphasize that incest as one possible disruptive form of radical kinship is not the only stake here. Rather, according to Lacan, *no* object—mother, father, brother, sister—is marked as prohibited for the feminine subject. Not only is incest not prohibited; *no one thing* is prohibited. Thus, for the masculine subject, the point is not that he need necessarily be a heterosexual, ostensibly "biological" boy barred access to his heterosexual, "biologically" female mother, but that he be a subject who has fallen under the blow of some prohibition and by consequence takes up a position as unconsciously masculine. And as McNulty has noted, "To believe that [the prohibited object is] the mother is a specific symptom, a particular way of resolving castration... by attributing it to the father and thereby making it 'avoidable' through obedience or submission to norms. [In other words,] it also reveals the ideology of norms as a way of avoiding castration" (pers. comm.). On the other hand, for the feminine subject, the point is perhaps even more radical: regardless of her "gender," the feminine subject is she to whom no prohibition is addressed. No universal can be made of or for her. The relief given the masculine subject, composing prohibitions as limits, does not transpire for the feminine subject. Instead, the nonworking of the prohibition is what ushers the feminine subject toward... maybe (who knows?) her brother/half-sister/stepmother/adoptive cousin/grandfather, and definitely toward a contingent encounter with the symbolic. With this in mind, I would suggest that Antigone's claim on a future for kinship, or a future for relationality, as well as a future for psychoanalysis, has just as much, if not more, to offer by way of what she does as a feminine figure confronting a symbolic that she is "totally, that is, limitlessly inscribed within" (Copjec 227) as with what she does as a would-be incestuous figure that "represents not kinship in its ideal form but its deformation and displacement" (Butler, *Antigone's* 24).

Curiously, then, if we attempt a still more fragile point of contact between Lacanian psychoanalysis and gender studies, a contact on the question of femininity, we open onto the sort of radical clearing wished for and envisaged by gender theorists' calls for a safer, more just world for queer and transgender subjectivities and relations. What has been overlooked in Dean's narration of desire and disavowed in Butler's reading of kinship is the possibility and exploration of a feminine perspective. The feminine perspective brings with it a relation both to the radically contingent *and* to intractability, or the real, precisely by virtue of the fact that the feminine subject is not afforded the same sort of support and limits by the phallic function spared the masculine subject. And as Dean rightly cautions, "[A]ny queer or feminist political theory that refuses to acknowledge intractability will remain less effective than it otherwise might be, because it will ceaselessly encounter the real as an unfathomable blockage of its political aims" (*Beyond* 92). In other words, to respond at last to the question I raised above, as to whether or not psychoanalysis may seem rather sexually impoverished with respect to (some) other perspectives, I would like to argue that no, it does not. On the contrary.

Where psychoanalysis may appear limited resides in part in what I interpret as the too easy capitulation of the *terms feminine* and *masculine* to "gendered" readings. This happens both for gender theorists reading and sometimes writing psychoanalytic texts and for psychoanalytic theorists reading and writing psychoanalytic texts. As we saw earlier, some Lacanians participate in a logic of sexual difference whereby it magically turns out again and again that subjects with apparently female genitalia "are" "women," and so on. Butler damningly maps out the consequences of such readings with respect to family relations:

> And when there are two men or two women who parent, are we to assume that some primary division of gendered roles organizes their psychic places within the scene, so that the empirical contingency of two same-gendered parents is nevertheless straightened out by the presocial psychic place of the Mother and the Father into which they enter? Does it make sense on these occasions to insist that there are symbolic positions of Mother and Father that every psyche must accept regardless of the social form that kinship takes?
>
> (*Antigone's* 69)

It seems important to imagine a queerer future for Lacanian psychoanalysis wherein terms like "the desire of the mother" and "the law of the father," still very much in currency, might be replaced (not, of course, without haunting remainders) by some new terminology that would better reference the psychical functions these terms index. But terminology shifts alone will not a queer theory make of contemporary deployments of psychoanalysis; we must also bear in mind Dean's rigorous reminder that objects *a* emerge outside of and in excess to the frame of gender. And with respect to sexual difference, we must insist on the ways in which, for Lacan, the terms *masculine* and *feminine* signal two different logics, two different modes of ex-sistence in the symbolic, two different approaches to the Other, two different stances with respect to desire, and (at least) two different types of jouissance. Nothing here indicates "gender" as we might more conventionally conceive of it.

What would it look like to consider transgender identity as an expression of the logic of sexual difference? What are the implications of such a move? This depends in part on what, generally speaking, we mean by the word *transgender,* and how it relates to the term *transsexual.* In the foreword to the *Transgender Studies Reader,* Stephen Whittle uses simply the word *trans* instead of either *transgender* or *transsexual,* reflecting the popular shift to the usage of a new, apparently more all-encompassing term. As he writes,

> A trans person might be a butch or a camp, a transgender or a transsexual, an mtf or ftm or a cross-dresser; they might, in some parts of the world, consider themselves a lady boy, katoey, or even the reclaimed Maori identities whakawahine or whakatane. Some communities and their terms are ancient, such as the Hijra from Northern India, but many are more modern. The word "trans," referring to a "trans woman" or "trans man" (of whatever subtype of trans identity) is a very recent take on the umbrella term "transgender." (xi)

While I am moved by the suggestiveness of a term like *trans* for forging politically motivated identificatory alliances, I would like to narrow down my own definitions of *transgenderism* and *transsexualism* in the interest of a provisional amount of coherence, but with the expectation that no one definition of either of these words could satisfy or suffice. I would like to define the transsexual subject as a person who identifies with a gender that is not consonant with the gender assigned at birth. In some cases, but certainly not all, the transsexual subject will go to whatever efforts possible (hormone therapy, sex or genital reassignment surgery, etc.) to "pass" as that gender. Inasmuch as the transsexual subject strives to pass *and/or* (for not all transsexuals strive to pass) identifies with one gender or another with an apparent degree of certainty, he or she is psychically no different than any other subject who lines up under one banner or the other.[8] *Ostensibly* "nontranssexual" subjects also strive to pass; they also identify with an apparent degree of certainty with one gender or another. In other words, "transsexuality" is not in and of itself anymore extreme a type of symptom than is "man" or "woman." Where transsexual subjects' experiences may be different from those of ostensibly nontranssexual subjects, of course, arises in part from the fact that the latter have not, so far, proven particularly welcoming: from under the meager protection of their banners, they have not yet realized that they have no monopoly on the psychic experience of the semblance of "gender certainty." Oftentimes, the upshot of this false monopoly on a piecemeal "certainty" is that transsexual subjects—particularly those who do not rigorously fit the demands of the public's "incessant need to gender every person they see as female or male" (Serano 117)—are excluded, objectified, exploited, scapegoated, and silenced.

Transgenderism presents a slightly different situation, and this is the one with which this article has been occupied. For it could be argued that the transgender subject—as someone who is not necessarily or only very strategically invested in "passing" as one gender or another (e.g., someone who could be described as "bigendered" or "gender-fluid" [Serano 27]), as someone who may be invested in embodying a gender that would attest to what he or she may define as the constructedness of gender (e.g., "genderqueer" [Serano 27])—would be the human subject as such, the unconsciously bisexual subject for whom sexual difference is only ever an incomplete, unsatisfactory solution to the failure of the sexual relation. In this way, transgenderism would figure as a solutionless solution to the impasses of sexual difference, a sort of unconscious scene of undecideability, but an undecideability fundamentally shared by all human subjects, no matter their seeming "gender."

But there is another way of reading transgenderism, or another transgenderism available to subjects, wherein transgenderism figures not as a solutionless solution to the impasses of sexual difference, but rather as an expression of the logic of sexual difference: a feminine solution. Hysteria as it is defined by Lacan is a profoundly feminine phenomenon and is characterized by the question, "Am I a man, or am I woman, and what does that mean?" The hysteric tends to interrogate societal norms at large, oftentimes embodying a subversive attitude that arises in part from a profound suspicion that her own sexed and sexual body is incommensurate to cultural injunctions regarding gender identities. As Ellie Ragland-Sullivan writes, "Lacan saw the hysteric as embodying the quintessence of the human subject because she speaks, as agent, from the lack and gaps in knowledge, language and being" (164). The hysteric is, in some senses, interested in nothing *but* the lack that, for example, Dean may be read to circumvent by focusing on the apparent multiplicity of object *a*. The failure, deadlock, and trauma of sexual difference returns for the hysterical/feminine transgender subject, irreducibly, in her insistent interrogation of the phallic function and in her very queer relation to the lacking Other. Our question, then, might read as follows: what will the feminine/transgender subject do confronting a symbolic that she is "totally, that is, limitlessly inscribed within" (Copjec 227)? For this, we do not have to look far—we might consider Antigone, or, if we wish to be more timely, we might pay attention to art, writings, memoirs, and scholarship by various present-day transgender or, sometimes, transsexual-identified subjects. If part of the point this essay is trying to make, though, is that there is something transgendered about the human subject, and that this transgenderism transcends notions of gender, it follows that we need not be restricted by rigid definitions of gender identities to encounter the question, "Am I a man, or am I woman, and what does that mean?" Feminine subjects identify in multiple directions. More importantly, they demonstrate another sort of agility as well: "[Lacan] implied that for all the difficulties woman had with speech and the signifier, mistrusting its promises because they de facto fail her, a certain freedom to play was available to woman… [A]ccording to Lacan, 'Women are less enclosed by discourse than their partners in the cycle of discourse'" (MacCannell 198–99). When we recall that discourses are "forms of the social tie" (Lacan quoted in MacCannell 235) and that discourses as social ties move to cover over the lack of the sexual relation, we could argue by extension that the hysteric feminine subject in particular is structurally well situated to cycle through and fall between the cracks of discourses. Preoccupied as the hysteric is with the very question that discourse wishes to mask, she may be particularly well situated to "do something" to the social tie itself. And yet, despite (but also because of) her "freedom to play," the feminine/transgender subject's speech does not stop insisting that discursive flexibility, lest it be mistaken for a merry-go-round of liberating multiplicity, is a flexibility borne of and about at least two overlapping lacks: castration and a certain exclusion. Feminine/transgender speech materializes (sometimes, painfully silently) hollowed out by the deafening significance of what it "is" to "be" a (divided) (feminine) subject, a truth that echoes across gender divides *and* blurs.

Ragland cautions as well: "Given that the hysteric's fundamental question in the signifier is 'Am I a woman or a man?' she is at risk of being overtaken by the real in both the symbolic and the imaginary" (69). She later adds more pointedly:

> How, then, does the hysteric reveal a truth worth noting? Subversion for its own sake or acting out is not admirable.... It is, rather, this, that the subject, any subject except a psychotic, is divided. In varying ways, all individuals who are divided suffer from this. The master represses it in the place of truth. The academic puts it in the place of repressed knowledge. The analyst interrogates it. But the hysteric lives it; it is her badge of honor that she lives castration at the surface of her life and discourse.... The hysteric does not say, as poststructuralists would claim, I am man and woman, the difference makes no difference.... For her it is an either/or question.

This is the heart of Lacanianism: either/or. Either one is masculine or one is feminine. One is not both, except in the suffering of hysteria. Both is the position of suffering, not liberation. It is this truth of the hysteric to which Lacan pays heed. (85)

Ragland's explicit cautions notwithstanding, something seems to slip through the cracks here, and it again references the hysteric's contortionist cycles, overlappings, and subversions: "One is not both, except in the suffering of hysteria," Ragland writes, carefully. Consistently excepted, the feminine/transgender subject is perhaps in a unique position to enact social transformation. Being wholly within the symbolic but at an exclusive remove, she may have special affinities with what it means to change that which is "external" by a motion that cuts in immeasurable, infinitesimal directions, inside and out, for "the symbolic is not a set of conditions external to the subject, and..., as a result, the subject who labors to change the world is already its product. The notion of a 'change in the symbolic,' understood as 'outside' the subject, must therefore be supplemented by a 'change in the subject' as well" (Shepherdson 39). This recalls Lacan's explanation:

> There can be no act outside a field which is already so completely articulated that the law is located within it. There are no other acts than those that refer to the effects of this signifying articulation and include its entire problematic—with on the one hand whatever loss [chute] the very existence of anything at all that can be articulated as subject entails, or rather is, and with on the other what preexists it as a legislative function.
>
> (*Other* 125)

As she who *lives* the loss, "the very existence of anything at all that can be articulated as subject entails," and as she who is limitlessly inscribed in that symbolic that preexists her, the act of the feminine/transgender subject may indeed "refer to the effects of this signifying articulation and include its entire problematic."

Might we not also hear in Ragland's words on the suffering of hysteria queer resonances of the precise sentiment of Whittle, who, while "(self-consciously) no more able to stand in as 'spokesperson' for a collective transgender community than The Woman is able to exist," nonetheless states, "[I]t has been through this articulation of the imposition of gendering on us by others that the position of suffering of those with trans identities has been heard"? Whittle speaks here to an order to which trans identities might be exceptional and to the suffering that implies, and, of course, he speaks of speaking. Just after, he identifies one of the new possibilities opened up for trans people thanks to the increased opportunity for "public articulation of a trans voice and trans consciousness": "[T]o turn away, ultimately, from the relative safety of queerness and go beyond that to claim a unique position of suffering" (xv). If we are to dream of some liberatory remainder to this suffering subversion, it may—as Butler suggests from a different perspective—be locatable precisely there where Antigone speaks her "aberrant" words (*Psychic* 58)—yes, where, sometimes, "gender is displaced" (82), but sexual difference is not. As Slavoj Žižek writes in response to Butler's *Psychic Life of Power*:

> The Lacanian answer to this is clear—"to desire something other than its continued 'social existence'" and thus to fall "into some kind of death," that is, to risk a gesture by means of which death is "courted or pursued," points precisely towards the way Lacan reconceptualized the Freudian death-drive as the elementary form of the ethical act. Note that the act, insofar as it is irreducible to a "speech act," relies for its performative power on the pre-established set of symbolic rules and/or norms. Is this not the whole point of Lacan's reading of Antigone?

At the beginning of this essay, I asked what gender studies and Lacanian psychoanalysis have to offer one another and whether it might be possible to integrate the two domains. To answer quite simply, Lacanian psychoanalysis offers gender studies what I read as a richly malleable framework for thinking through matters of sex, subjectivity, desire, and sexuality. Likewise, gender studies offers Lacanian psychoanalysis readers who are deeply, productively mistrustful and whose compelling perspectives on diverse social issues are driven by passionate commitment. Integration of the two domains can only ever be a scene of fruitful contestation, but it could also go further if contemporary psychoanalytic thinkers were willing to listen to their compatriots' desires and to redefine some of their more exclusionary "shibboleths" (Dean, *Beyond* 226), and if gender theorists were willing to reread psychoanalysis, again.

## NOTES

[…]

4. See, for example, Teresa de Lauretis's discussion of "Freud's negative theory of sexuality" (xi), where "'normal' is conceived only by approximation, is more a projection than an actual state of being, while perversion and neurosis (the repressed form of perversion) are the actual forms and contents of sexuality" (xii). [...]
5. The excellent work of Gayle Salamon is a notable exception. See, in particular, "The Bodily Ego and the Contested Domain of the Material."
6. On the roles of shame, disgust, morality, and the Oedipal drama as forces of castration, Freud writes, "On this view, the forces destined to retain the sexual instinct upon certain lines are built up in childhood chiefly at the cost of perverse sexual impulses and with the assistance of education" (232).

[...]

8. See Serano.

## WORKS CITED

Barnard, Suzanne (2002) "Introduction." In Suzanne Barnard and Bruce Fink, eds, *Reading Seminar XX: Lacan's Major Work on Love, Knowledge, and Feminine Sexuality.* Albany: SUNY Press, 1–19.

Barnard, Suzanne (2002) "Tongues of Angels." In Suzanne Barnard and Bruce Fink, eds, *Reading Seminar XX: Lacan's Major Work on Love, Knowledge, and Feminine Sexuality.* Albany: SUNY Press, 171–85.

Barnard, Suzanne, and Bruce Fink, eds (2002). *Reading Seminar XX: Lacan's Major Work on Love, Knowledge, and Feminine Sexuality.* Albany: SUNY Press.

Berger, Anne (2005). "Sexing Differences." *differences: A Journal of Feminist Cultural Studies* 16: 3, 52–67.

Bornstein, Kate. "Gender Terror, Gender Rage." In Susan Stryker and Stephen Whittle, eds, *Transgender Studies Reader.* New York: Routledge, 236–43.

Butler, Judith (1993). *Bodies That Matter: On the Discursive Limits of Sex.* New York: Routledge.

Butler, Judith (1997). *The Psychic Life of Power: Theories in Subjection.* Stanford: Stanford University Press.

Butler, Judith (2000). *Antigone's Claim*. New York: Columbia University Press.

Copjec, Joan (1995). "Sex and the Euthanasia of Reason." *Read My Desire: Lacan against the Historicists*. Cambridge, MA: MIT Press, 201–36.

de Lauretis, Teresa (1994). Introduction. *The Practice of Love: Lesbian Sexuality and Perverse Desire*. Bloomington: Indiana University Press, xi–xx.

Dean, Tim (2000) *Beyond Sexuality*. Chicago: University of Chicago Press.

Dean, Tim (2001) "Homosexuality and the Problem of Otherness." In Tim Dean and Christopher Lane, eds, *Homosexuality and Psychoanalysis*. Chicago: University of Chicago Press, 120–46.

Dean, Tim, and Christopher Lane, eds (2001). *Homosexuality and Psychoanalysis*. Chicago: University of Chicago Press.

Dean, Tim, and Christopher Lane. (2001) "Introduction." In Tim Dean and Christopher Lane, eds, *Homosexuality and Psychoanalysis*. Chicago: University of Chicago Press, 3–42.

Freud, Sigmund (1953). *Three Essays on the Theory of Sexuality*. 1905. *The Standard Edition of the Complete Psychological Works of Sigmund Freud*. Trans. and ed. James Strachey. Vol. 7. London: Hogarth, 130–242. 24 vols. 1953–74.

Lacan, Jacques (1999). *Encore: The Seminar of Jacques Lacan, Book XX. On Feminine Sexuality, The Limits of Love and Knowledge, 1972–1973*. Ed. Jacques-Alain Miller. Trans. Bruce Fink. New York: Norton.

Lacan, Jacque (1992). *The Ethics of Psychoanalysis, 1939–1960. The Seminar of Jacques Lacan, Book VII*. Ed. Jacques-Alain Miller. Trans. Dennis Porter. New York: Norton.

Lacan, Jacque (1998). *The Four Fundamental Concepts of Psychoanalysis: The Seminar of Jacques Lacan, Book XI* Ed. Jacques-Alain Miller. Trans. Alan Sheridan. New York: Norton.

Lacan, Jacque (1985). "The Meaning of the Phallus." *Feminine Sexuality: Jacques Lacan and the* école freudienne. Juliet Mitchell and Jacqueline Rose (eds.) Trans. Jacqueline Rose. New York: Norton, 74–85.

Lacan, Jacque (2007). *The Other Side of Psychoanalysis: Seminar XVII*. Jacques-Alain Miller (ed). Trans. Russell Grigg. New York: Norton.

MacCannell, Juliet Flower (2000). *The Hysteric's Guide to the Future Female Subject*. Minneapolis: University of Minnesota Press.

Ragland, Ellie (2006). "The Hysteric's Truth." *Reflections on Seminar XVII: Jacques Lacan and the Other Side of Psychoanalysis*. Ed. Justin Clemens and Russell Griggs. Durham: Duke University Press, 69–87.

Ragland-Sullivan, Ellie (1992). "Hysteria." *Feminism and Psychoanalysis: A Critical Dictionary*. Ed. Elizabeth Wright. Cambridge: Blackwell, 163–65.

Robinson, Paul. "Freud and Homosexuality." In Tim Dean and Christopher Lane, eds, *Homosexuality and Psychoanalysis*. Chicago: University of Chicago Press, 91–97.

Salamon, Gayle (2004). "The Bodily Ego and the Contested Domain of the Material." *differences: A Journal of Feminist Cultural Studies* 15: 3, 95–122.

Salecl, Renata (2000). Introduction. *Sexuation*. Ed. Renata Salecl and Slavoj Žižek. Durham: Duke University Press, 1–9.

Serano, Julia (2007). *Whipping Girl: A Transsexual Woman on Sexism and the Scapegoating of Femininity*. Emeryville: Seal.

Shepherdson, Charles (2000). *Vital Signs: Nature, Culture, Psychoanalysis*. New York: Routledge.

Stryker, Susan (2006). "(De)Subjugated Knowledges: An Introduction to Transgender Studies." In Susan Stryker and Stephen Whittle, eds, *Transgender Studies Reader*. New York: Routledge, pp. 1–17.

Stryker, Susan, and Stephen Whittle, eds (2006). *Transgender Studies Reader*. New York: Routledge.

Whittle, Stephen (2006). "Foreword." In Susan Stryker and Stephen Whittle, eds, *Transgender Studies Reader*. New York: Routledge, xi–xvi.

Žižek, Slavoj (1998). "From 'Passionate Attachments' to Dis-identification." *umbr(a)* 1 (1998). http://www.gsa.buffalo.edu/lacan/zizekidentity.htm.

# VI

## TIMELY MATTERS
### Temporality and Trans-historicity

# 26

## *Towards a Transgender Archaeology*
### A Queer Rampage Through Prehistory

MARY WEISMANTEL

ANTHROPOLOGIST MARY WEISMANTEL, AN EXPERT ON CERAMICS from the pre-Columbian Moche culture of Peru, has written widely on issues of sexuality, race, and gender in prehistory, and on the interpretative challenges of recovering social information from nonliterary material artifacts. In this article, she provides an overview of several tantalizing archeological finds in the past few decades that may offer evidence for questions raised within transgender studies. In discussing cultural patterns from long ago, Weismantel makes an argument similar to those of transgender studies scholars who examine the biological diversity of sex difference: that is, she highlights the wide range of variation observable in the material world with regard to what we now call sexuality and gender, and she points as well to the historically contingent and limited nature of modern thinking about such things. Weismantel writes not only about what archeology can offer transgender studies, but what transgender studies can offer archaeology. Taking as her point of departure the figure of the "monster," which has been fruitfully elaborated within trans studies as well as in studies of premodern history, Weismantel turns a critical "transgender rage" against the heteronormativizing assumptions of the contemporary archeological profession that fail to recognize the material trace of styles of embodiment, desire, and social gender in past human cultures that do not comply with the modernist ontology.

The Vix burial has attracted considerable attention because of ... the much-debated sex assessment of the principal burial.... Since its excavation in the 1950s, this individual has been described variously as a ... "nomad princess" ... a "lady" ... a "man who did not mind wearing women's clothing" ... a "transvestite priest" ... a "rich woman and possibly a chief or tribal ruler" ... [or] an "honorary male"...

(Knüdson 2002: 278)

The "Princess of Vix," an Iron Age tomb in France containing an apparently female skeleton surrounded by gold and bronze artifacts usually associated with males, is only one of many archaeological discoveries that hint at a diversity of sexual histories hidden in the ancient past.[1] Very few people outside of professional archaeology know about this intriguing find, and it is not easy for non-specialists to get accurate information about it. The Wikipedia entry about "the Vix grave," for example, describes the fabulous objects found in the tomb, but does not mention the maelstrom of controversy that has raged over the small body buried with so much pomp and circumstance.[2]

The silence that surrounds this grave suggests that archaeology needs to be brought under transgender studies' broad interdisciplinary umbrella. The time is right: professional archaeology is finally starting to shake off its long history of "sex negativity" and self-censorship (Voss 2008: 318), and, as it does so, a profusion of incredibly rich evidence of diverse forms of gender identity and gender expression is spilling out from ancient sites around the globe.[3] This newly available data raises provocative questions. Was the body buried at Vix, for example, a woman who attained a lordly political status usually reserved for men? Or an intersex individual who attained the status of a religious leader or shaman,[4] partly because of her unusual body,[5] which was small, asymmetrical, and mostly but not entirely female?[6]

If transgender scholars ignore these archaeological puzzles, we risk impoverishing our sense of the past, and our understanding of who we are and where we came from—not to mention missing out on a whole lot of (somewhat wonkish) fun. It's fascinating to read about the bronze-studded chariot that rolled the bier into the grave at Vix, and the accompanying *krater* (a bronze vessel imported from Greece), the largest and fanciest ever found in the Celtic world—four feet in diameter and five feet tall, and entirely filled with mead (an alcoholic drink made of honey). Or to pore over photographs of the Princess's jewelry, lavish adornments of a kind worn by both men and women, such as the enormous gold *torc* (a large flat necklace or breastplate) adorned with winged horses, lion's paws, and poppies (Knüdson 2002).

However, in inviting you to enjoy these things, I am also inviting you to share my rage. Why is it that the burial at Vix was originally discovered in 1952, but information about the corpse's anomalous sex was not made public until feminist archaeologist Bettina Arnold published a re-study in 1991? Why do so many twenty-first century archaeologists continue to suppress information about discoveries like these? To enter the archaeological record from a transgender perspective is not just a romp through a queer fairyland. In fact, it can turn into a queer *rampage* driven by an angry determination to overturn this systematic repression of knowledge, which constitutes a form of structural violence perpetrated against people, past *and* present, who do not conform to contemporary norms of gender.

Rage can be a defining aspect of transgender identity, as Susan Stryker reminds us in her powerful essay "My Words to Victor Frankenstein above the Village of Chamounix: Performing Transgender Rage" (1994). That rage has its origins in the many forms of violence—physical and psychological, material and symbolic—inflicted on transgender bodies. Transgender scholars transform that rage into a mandate: to write the history of violence so as to bring it back into public memory—and, when we can, to undo it.

Some violence is ancient. For instance, although we remember Classical Greece as a place where sculptors carved sensuous images of the god Hermaphrodite, whose body is both female and male, documents from the period tell a more complicated story. The same society that produced those statues also put women to death by public drowning or burning alive if their bodies were determined by the authorities to be partly male (Ajootian 1995: 102–103). But my focus here is on a modern form of violence: the systematic erasure of lives and histories that are inconveniently queer. Viewed through transgender eyes, the modern history of archaeology looks a little like the history of medicine: where the body of evidence does not fall neatly into a gender binary, the academic doctors just lopped off what doesn't fit.

The first step in creating a transgender archaeology, then, is a destructive one: tearing off the layers of unsupported assumptions about sex and gender that encrust the archaeological record, and freeing the queerly formed bodies trapped underneath. The first section of this article, "Towards a Transgender Archaeology," summarizes the challenges currently facing archaeologists who study sex and gender. The second part surveys some of the work of archaeologists who have moved beyond the gender binary, and shows what an "ungendering" of the archaeological record can do. Ungendering the past has the potential to release us from even the most harmful beliefs about what it means to be human, such as those that denigrate the bodies of transgender persons as "monstrous," "unnatural," or "abnormal." In studying precapitalist, non-Western societies, archaeologists and art historians encounter ontologies of the body in which the damaging modernist fiction of the "natural," with its abhorrence of bodies assembled rather than birthed, never existed. The third and final section of this essay, "Here Be Monsters," enters the arena of the monstrous body. This is the difficult terrain on which Susan Stryker compared her own body to that of Frankenstein, and on which Gloria Anzaldúa called herself "Coatlicue" after the terrifying Aztec goddess (1987). It is here, where the deepest trauma lies, that transgender studies stakes out its most profound battles; and it is here that archaeology offers its most radical promise.

## TOWARDS A TRANS ARCHAEOLOGY

The "Princess," who died some time around 450 BC, is a little too old to be called "transgender"—a newly minted term that came into its own in the 1990s.[7] Nevertheless, this find, and others around the globe, demonstrate that many of the behaviors associated with transgender today—"occasional or more frequent cross-dressing, permanent cross-dressing and cross-gender living" (Whittle 2006: xi); "transsexuality ... some aspects of intersexuality and homosexuality, ... [and] myriad specific subcultural expressions of 'gender atypicality'"(Stryker 2006)—were also part of ancient life.

Vix is far from an isolated case. The evidence defying binary models of gender and sex is truly global, and stretches across the entirety of human history. Let's start with rock art, that earliest and most ubiquitous form of human self-expression. Carved and painted images on caves and cliffs from Australia to Colorado, some of them tens of thousands of years old, provide a rare glimpse of how early humans (and more recent foraging societies) perceived the human body. Surveying these images, Kelley Hays-Gilpin finds little evidence of two sexes. Instead, "With surprising frequency, one encounters figures with something fancy between the legs that can't readily be assigned to one of two categories, neither penis nor vagina" (2004: 15–16).

Interpreting evidence like this from a transgender perspective doesn't mean artificially forcing ancient phenomena into a new and ill-fitting category. If anything, the opposite seems true. It is as if the premodern past had to wait for transgender scholarship to arrive, and with it, an understanding that "'gender'... is more complex and varied than can be accounted for by the currently dominant binary sex/gender ideology of Eurocentric modernity" (Stryker 2006: 3).

The gender diversity of the past matters for transgender activism. The dominant vision of human history is an oppressive one: an unbroken legacy of manly men and womanly women compelled by biology to create nuclear families devoted to reproduction. Transgender people need to know that the accumulated weight of archaeological data does not support this vision of human history (Joyce 2008). The study of history and prehistory is an inherently political activity, because it reveals this normativizing narrative as the distorting, selective, constructed artifice that it is.

The goal of a transgender archaeology is not to re-populate the ancient past with modern trans men and trans women—that would be a blatant distortion of the archaeological record and of the goals of transgender studies.[8] What we can do is to replace the narrow, reductive gaze of previous researchers with a more supple, subtler appreciation of cultural variation. According to what feminist philosophers of science call "standpoint theory" (Wylie 2003), this is simply good science: turning to the perspective of people from outside the mainstream in order to arrive at hypotheses that a normative person might never generate. Modern researchers' vision of human possibility is inevitably limited by their own cultural biases and personal experience; incorporating a plurality of perspectives is one way to circumvent this limitation.

However, introducing a transgender eye among the archaeology guys will be no easy task. The dominant archaeological model still assumes that every human group, always and everywhere, has been composed of two distinct sexes, male and female:

> ...the way gender is experienced today is homogenized, made to seem a natural given, and projected back into a timeless past of men and women living life as demanded by genetic capacities and reproductive imperatives deemed to be universal.
>
> (Joyce 2008: 18; see also Voss 2008: 318)

A small but growing number of archaeologists are arguing for a very different picture of human history—one that does not assume a two-sex model, the universality of the nuclear family or the timelessness of heteronormativity. But the work of changing the dominant paradigm is an uneven, ragged, and conflictual process that is far from complete.

The status of research on gender and sexuality in archaeology these days is contradictory. On the one hand, research on women is a well-established subfield. There has been an outpouring of excellent feminist work since the 1980s,[9] and studies of masculinity followed in the 1990s.[10] Anthropology departments at major universities like U.C. Berkeley and Stanford University now boast senior faculty in archaeology who are outspoken feminists. Nevertheless, these researchers and their students are isolated enclaves in a field still largely dominated by heteronormative men, and by research agendas focused on masculinist topics such as warfare and state-level politics.

The picture for the study of sexuality is far more dismal. Although professional archaeologists laugh at their public image as "Indiana Jones," the dominant culture of the discipline is unapologetically testosterone-driven and heteronormative, creating an atmosphere at large mainstream professional meetings that keeps queers barely visible and non-normative voices silent. A small minority of rebels—many of them students of the feminist professors mentioned above—have produced a few really excellent publications and conferences on the archaeology of sexuality, but to many established archaeologists, the very notion of such a subfield is simply ludicrous. With feminist work on gender and queer work on sexuality still struggling to establish a foothold, a transgender archaeology is hard to imagine—and more necessary than ever.

## UNGENDERED

In *Ancient Bodies, Ancient Lives: Sex, Gender and Archaeology*, Rosemary Joyce advocates an archaeology free from "the normative two-sex/two-gender model" (2008: 18). At the moment, though, that binary sex/gender model remains so thoroughly integrated into most archaeological research paradigms that it is invisible—even to the investigators themselves. Gender binaries appear to originate in the data, not in our heads. Occasionally, though, we can glimpse the gap between the actual evidence, which is usually inconclusive, contradictory, and open to multiple interpretations, and the rigid gender straightjacket imposed by the researchers, who may not even be aware that they have foreclosed on the possibility of seeing gender variation in their data.

In the summer of 2011, for example, I saw a colleague make a presentation, which he intended to illustrate some new insights into social structure and site planning at an ancient Middle Eastern city. Inadvertently, however, he showed us something else instead: an unusually graphic illustration of the way restrictive assumptions about gender get superimposed on the open-ended ambiguities of the past. The ancient city in question is a famous one: Çatalhöyük, a Neolithic site in the Anatolian region of Turkey that was occupied between 7500 and 5700 B.C.; this colleague and I were both part of a small international group of researchers who had gathered for a small conference at the site.

The last slide in my colleague's presentation showed an artist's re-creation of the ancient city. I liked the drawing, which showed a multi-storied compound of rooms, rooftops, and activity areas, with a few people and dogs for scale. What I didn't like was what the speaker had done to it. In thick red lines, he had superimposed a circle over part of one building, to indicate that it was an individual household, and annotated the circle with the words "FAMILY = M + F + others." In assigning these gender markers, and tucking them into a nuclear family, he had recreated a modern middle-class ideal that was not very common in ancient agricultural societies.

In a way, we should be grateful for egregious examples like this, because they make it easy to peel off the offending words and take a look at what lies underneath. At Çatalhöyük, what shows up once we strip away our modern assumptions is fascinating and unexpected. Years of intensive excavation and analysis have resulted in a wealth of information about life in an urban settlement nine thousand years ago, when most human beings still lived in nomadic bands. The gender picture that is emerging at this early city bears little resemblance to the simplistic model suggested by the words "M + F."

There are two reasons that a different kind of picture is developing at Çatalhöyük. The most important source is the data itself; but we would not necessarily know about that data were it not for another important factor, which is that some of the archaeologists working at the site share Joyce's innovative perspective. After the talk, one of those archaeologists came up to thank me for objecting to the slide: Lynn Meskell, a researcher known for her boldly original work on gender and sexuality. Meskell had particularly good reason to be irritated by the red scrawl projected on the screen, and must have wondered whether the speaker had been listening earlier, when she had presented her research, or whether he had read any of her publications about the site. He seemed oddly unaware that her conclusions differ quite radically from his own. According to Meskell, "[W]hat seems to have been most salient at Çatalhöyük was... not a specifically gendered person with discrete sexual markers, but an [unsexed]... human form."

When asked, the speaker freely admitted that the idea that Çatalhöyük was inhabited by "M + F"s, rather than by individuals who may not have been "specifically gendered" was based purely on assumption, unsupported by any data. Meskell's conclusions, in contrast, are the result of a long and intensive investigation based on a carefully constructed research paradigm. That work has focused on the hundreds of small clay and stone figurines that litter the site: archaeologists interested in gender often study anthropomorphic figures as evidence of how people in the past conceptualized their own bodies, or the human body in general.

What sets Meskell's work apart from most figurine studies, including earlier work on figurines at Çatalhöyük, is that she did not begin with a binary model, which assumes that all humans are either males or females, and separate the artifacts accordingly into two piles. According to archaeologist Naomi Hamilton, most "interpretation[s] of prehistoric anthropomorphic figurines from eastern Europe and the Near East" rely upon "a methodology which classifies figures primarily by sex and then translates sex into stereotyped Western gender roles which may have no relevance to prehistory" (2000: 17).

Meskell's project is a welcome exception to this gloomy assessment of the status quo. In her research design, the categories used to analyze the figures are developed from differences observed within the corpus of figurines itself, not based on how people are categorized today. As a result, she and her team were able to see one of the hardest things of all for us to perceive: the *absence* of the gender binary that is so deeply inscribed in modern life. In her re-study of the Çatalhöyük figurines, Meskell provided a positive identification for a number of figurines that previous investigators, looking for whole bodies of women and men, had labeled "indeterminate" (Nakamura and Meskell 2009). For Meskell, indeterminacy is not illegibility. Where others speculated that clumsy workmanship had prevented the artist from creating a recognizably sexed body, she sees a deliberate effort to create blurred boundaries.

Of course, figurines are only images, and it is difficult to know how representations relate to lived reality. But another set of researchers at Čatalhöyük—the bioarchaeologists, who study skeletal remains—found a similarly ungendered pattern in the actual bodies of the people who lived there.

At many other archaeological sites around the world, bioarchaeologists find gender deeply inscribed onto the bones of the dead. This is a dramatic instantiation of the effects of gender: physical evidence that the patterns of health, life, work, and diet imposed on biological males and females during their lives were so different from one another that they resulted in two different sets of permanent physical alterations. In many parts of ancient North America, for example, women's skeletons show the effects of long hours spent grinding corn on a metate (work that might also have changed the skeletons of biological males who adopted a feminine or two-spirit role during life).[11] In Central Asia, archaeologists were surprised when they looked at the skeletons of the first humans to ride horses, and discovered that these riders were all female.[12] At Čatalhöyük, however, the meticulously analyzed biological data does not reveal this kind of binary pattern. Regardless of their apparent genital or skeletal sex, every individual had similar (relatively healthy) patterns of morbidity and mortality, performed equally demanding physical work, and ate the same abundant and varied diet.[13]

In addition to this biomorphological data and Meskell's analysis of the figurines, there is a third strand of evidence about gender at Čatalhöyük: the treatment of corpses at burial shows very little evidence of socially assigned gender (Nakamura and Meskell 2009: 208). Many societies differentiate between social males and females at death—for example, by burying a woman in her bridal gown and a man in a suit, or (as in the ancient Americas) by placing weaving tools in a woman's grave and weapons or agricultural tools in a man's. Not so at Čatalhöyük. Burials are simple: every adult of any sex was placed in a shallow grave with, at most, one or two grave goods such as a necklace or a clay pot. Not only were men and women buried in similar ways; their bodies were often placed in the same tomb, and over time, the bones were mixed together haphazardly or deliberately re-combined without regard to gender—a point I return to below.

Finally, one very recent study looks at yet another line of evidence, and casts a new kind of doubt on the implications built into the phrase "FAMILY=M + F + others." The custom at Čatalhöyük was to bury the dead under the floors of their houses; it seems logical to assume that the people buried together within one building had lived there together, like families do. But when researchers analyzed the genetic make-up of people from the same grave, the results were a shock—at least, to those who assume that households are "naturally" constituted through heterosexual reproduction. Instead of one biological male, one biological female, and their biological offspring, the people buried together at Čatalhöyük are genetically unrelated individuals of various ages and sexes, grouped together in numbers ranging from one to several dozen (Pilloud and Larsen 2010). If these clusters of people represent families, their families were big, variable, and chosen: not small, heteronormative, and biological.

Overall, then, the available data supports a simple hypothesis: the absence of gender was a structural feature of Čatalhöyük society. Later societies of the Middle East would enlarge and elaborate the difference between male and female into a major feature of every aspect of social and spiritual life—a process that may already have begun at other communities in the region while Čatalhöyük was flourishing. But in this particular place, over a period of more than a thousand years, it seems that gender difference was typically, and deliberately, left unmarked.

"Ungendering" our interpretations doesn't mean claiming that gender didn't exist in the ancient past. Ungendering means conceptual uncoupling: pulling apart biology and culture, and de-linking aspects of gender and society that seem inseparable today. One of the most striking things about Čatalhöyük, for example, is that gender is not linked to inequality. The striking lack of emphasis on gender differentiation (and male dominance) is part of a general pattern at the site, where there seem to have been no forms of structural inequality at all.

For most of human history, people lived in small, egalitarian groups, where gender may well have been as insignificant as it apparently was at Čatalhöyük. But as societies became larger, they became more unequal—and gender mattered more. Large, unequal societies typically denigrate women and punish gender deviance. And once gender inequality has been established as fundamental and "natural," it provides a basis for other structures of inequality, such as race and class.

The egalitarian world of Čatalhöyük is more alien to us than the complex and oppressive systems that followed; but even when they are unequal and rule-bound, non-Western and precapitalist societies are not gendered like us. In studying them, we need to be more careful than ever to ungender our preconceptions. For example, in many ancient societies, ritualized cross-dressing was mandated for political and religious leaders. Cross-dressing is an important form of transgender performance today, but to understand it in past societies, we have to be careful to make no assumptions; otherwise, we can only see what we expect to see and learn what we already know, missing the more complicated and interesting stories that the past might be able to teach us instead.

For example, a recent archaeological find in South America, the "Lady of Cao," is fun to read about but treacherous to interpret. This individual lived and died far more recently than the people of Čatalhöyük: the tomb dates to the first millennium A.D., and was found on the North Coast of Peru. Whoever this individual was, s/he was fierce. The "Lady" died young—in his/her early twenties—and was buried in an elaborate tomb in a temple overlooking the sea. Like other "royal" burials of the Moche period, the corpse was laid to rest surrounded by finery: adornments of copper, silver and gold; shimmering cloaks and banners made of feathers and metal bangles; and even the sacrificed bodies of male and female retainers. The dry North Coast winds have preserved the body perfectly. We can still see the long hair, braided into dozens of tiny braids, and the arms, the skin richly tattooed with spiders, serpents, and seahorses.

The person in the tomb surprised the archaeologists who excavated it. More than a dozen equally fabulous Moche tombs have been discovered over the last few decades, each of them quite different from the others.[14] But what the researchers did not expect to find was a morphologically female corpse—that was buried grasping two enormous gold-headed war clubs, one in each hand.[15] In their publications about previously discovered tombs, Moche experts had described a pattern of strict segregation by gender. On the one hand, there were the men, like the famous "Lords of Sipán": male corpses surrounded by tremendous wealth, and by the bodies of lesser individuals, possibly including wives.[16] Archaeologists called these masculine individuals "Lords" because they were buried with weapons of war and insignia of power.

And then (according to the Moche experts) there were the "Priestesses": women who were also buried with great pomp and circumstance, but without weapons. Instead, the clothing and accessories that accompanied these bodies, including a special goblet, were said to have purely ritual and religious significance. Instead of rulers and warriors, these were said to be priestesses and healers—and perhaps the cup-bearers who accompanied male priests in bloody rites of human sacrifice.[17]

The weapon-bearing "Lady of Cao" is clearly an anomaly within this gendered system—and so, too, is another recent discovery. According to unpublished reports, one of the "Priestesses" is actually a biological male; could this be a man who lived and dressed as a woman, or perhaps a cross-dressing priest?

These fascinating finds upend existing pictures of Moche society. But before we assume that these are non-normative individuals who violated gender expectations, we have to ask where those gender norms actually originate. Can we see them in the archaeological record, or are they modern impositions that would not be recognized by the ancient Moche? (We might note Hamilton's (2000) comment that archaeologists are too quick to label males as "warriors" and women as "healers".)

Rather than rushing to anoint the warlike Lady of Cao and the male Priestess as our gender-bending ancestors, we would do better to look again at all of the Moche burial data. If we did as Meskell did with the Čatalhöyük figurines, and began without assuming that "M" and "F" are inevitably meaningful categories, what might we see?

If the most significant difference between the body buried at Cao and the one at Sipán is *not* that one is morphologically female and the other is morphologically male, other possibilities suddenly become apparent. For the elites who ruled these valleys, maybe it wasn't especially transgressive for a biological female to carry weapons, or a male to take the "feminine" role in a ritual—as long as they respected other traditions that marked their membership in a particular lineage. We might be too focused on the apparent mismatch between the woman and her large, phallic-looking maces, and the man with the feminine outfit and the delicate cup. Their own people—the ones who carefully placed their dead daughter or brother in the tomb with these particular artifacts—may have cared more about a different kind of symbolism. The really meaningful thing, for example, might have been those sea horses tattooed on the body at Cao, or the astounding necklace of gold and silver beads hammered into the shape of peanuts, that had been placed around the neck of the body at Sipán. These may have marked forms of identity that, for the Moche elites, trumped sex.

It matters that these were elites: in complex, stratified societies, the rules of gender vary by social class. Gender variance without fear of stigma or punishment can be a freedom allotted to the privileged few, who are free to indulge in sexual and gender experimentation forbidden to others. But not necessarily; in other societies, the public lives of elites—especially elite women—were even more constrained than those of ordinary people. In still other cases, as for the kings of the ancient Maya, cross-dressing was an important component of royal performance. At this point, we don't know how to read the fierce performance of the "Lady of Cao," with "her" gold-headed maces, braided hair and sea horse tattoos; a carefully ungendered re-analysis of all the "Lords," "Ladies," and "Priestesses" of Moche would be one step towards finding out.

Some of the most sophisticated archaeological research on gender to date comes from Mesoamerica (a region that comprises Mexico and parts of Central America). While standard textbooks about Mesoamerican archaeology still describe an unbroken tradition of "men and women engaged in familiarly gendered tasks," several decades of intensive research have overturned that conventional picture. New data has peopled the Aztec cities and Mayan temples with "men wearing women's clothing... gods with male and female aspects... androgynous figures... [and] women rulers..." (Stockett 2005: 568).

This is not an ungendered world: instead, it is multiply gendered—and elaborately hierarchized. In the delicate, aristocratic art produced for royalty, cross-dressing kings and gender-morphing gods abound. Androgyny is also a theme that runs throughout Mesoamerican art, much to the confusion of modern viewers. Even experts have been slow to abandon the binary altogether, and to recognize that, sometimes, a ferocious argument about whether a figure is male or female should be answered with a simple "yes."

Consider, for example, the history of the Las Limas statue, a beautiful stone figure found in a cornfield by two Mexican children in 1965. This enigmatic seated figure with a flat chest and a rounded, feminine face holds an inert smaller figure lying in the larger figure's lap. The children and their parents initially worshiped this image as the miraculous "Virgin of Las Limas": a Mother holding her Child. But archaeologists quickly recognized the sculpture as pre-Christian. To an informed eye, the graceful, intricate tattoos incised on the larger figure, and the "were-jaguar" facial features of the smaller figure, immediately identify it as Olmec. The experts re-named the statue the "Lord" of Las Limas: a young man holding a sacrificial victim (or possibly an ancestor).

Efforts to affix stable gender identities to this Olmec figure seems somewhat misguided, given that a few centuries later, during the Classic Maya period and after, Mesoamerican deities appeared in both male and female manifestations—and sometimes as both/neither. At the Maya site of Palenque (a jewel-like complex of palaces, temples, and plazas in southern Mexico famed for its exquisite bas-relief depictions of rulers and deities), walls and doorways were adorned with the lovely face of the Young Maize God, usually described by modern viewers as a very feminine young man.[18] The god was the epitome of perfect beauty—and a perfect androgyne.

This androgynous god lets us question one of the most unquestioned and most damaging assertions of modern gender/sex ideology, namely, that the idea of two sexes originates in nature itself, and expresses the will of God. Ancient Mesoamericans learned a quite different lesson from the natural and supernatural worlds. The Maize God is the human incarnation of the young maize or corn plant—a plant notorious for its sexual ambiguities. Corn and squash, the staples of Native American societies in Mexico and in the U.S. Southwest, reproduce sexually, producing visibly "male" and "female" parts—each with shapes that unmistakably resemble human genitalia. Glyphic depictions of the Maize God as a young lord often feature the glossy, pollen-laden strands of silk that erupt from the plant's male sex organs (Taube 1985: 173). But like human parents, corn and squash plants do not always produce fully "male" or fully "female" blooms: ambiguous organs with characteristics of both are extremely common, and healthy plants may produce an exuberance of sexual variations on a single stalk.

The domestication of corn was a great achievement—and one that made generations of Native peoples intimately familiar with the natural phenomenon of intersex individuals. The gently smiling, enigmatic face of the Young Maize God, which hovers so delicately between masculinity and femininity, incarnates the changeable sexuality of this life-giving plant. For the corn farmers who created the great civilizations and religions of Mexico, nature itself offered proof that male and female are mutable categories. Olmec and Maya artists made this connection implicit when they depicted human bodies as ears of corn (Taube 1985, 1996). For ancient Mesoamericans, this—not the inevitability of a fixed biological "nature"—is the message that the biological world offers to the cultural one.

(It is worth noting, though, that this liberating message did not necessarily translate into gender freedom for everyone. Great lords and powerful priests arrayed themselves in elaborate costumes that incorporated aspects of male and female clothing, as well as maize, flowers, the plumage of birds, and the skins of jaguars. For ordinary people, however, opportunities for mobility and flexibility may have been tightly constrained.)

Ungendering our analyses, then, does not produce only one way of seeing ancient societies. Looking at Çatalhöyük, we are struck by how insistently its egalitarian residents refused to differentiate by gender, in life or in death. In contrast, the rulers and gods of the Maya world appropriated every form of gendering—masculine, feminine, androgynous, even vegetative—as signs of their own multiplicitous power. These glimpses of the past affect our vision of the present: archaeology does its best ungendering when it undermines the claim that modern gender/sex systems are both universal and natural.

## HERE BE MONSTERS[19]

Archaeology can certainly contribute to transgender studies' mission of "cross-cultural and historical investigations of human gender diversity" (Stryker 2006: 3). At first glance, though, it seems limited in the insights it might provide into contemporary transgender experience. The ritual cross-dressing of ancient kings is an interesting historical footnote, but modern medical practices like hormone replacement and gender reassignment surgery are phenomena of an entirely different order, about which the ancient past presumably has little to say.

Wrong. A deeper look—not at practices but at ontologies—shows that it is precisely here, in thinking about the twenty-first century transsexual body, that a transgender archaeology may have the most profound contribution to make. By juxtaposing premodern, modernist, and posthuman understandings of the body, archaeology can perform transgender studies' most critical task: to "disrupt... denaturalize... rearticulate... and make... visible the normative linkages we generally assume to exist between [gender and] the biological specificity of the sexually differentiated human body" (Stryker 2006: 3).

As it turns out, the idea of constructing one's body through appropriating and suturing together disparate body parts from diverse origins is not modern at all; many ancient societies would find this way of thinking about oneself completely familiar. It is a peculiarly *modern* state of affairs to have become so estranged from the idea of the body as a hybrid creation, assembled after birth and multiple in its identities and origins. Modernity may have produced the medical system that invented techniques we use today in transitioning, but it also gave rise to an ontology that abhors the constructed body that results, rejecting it as antithetical to the "truth" of the "natural" body (Stryker 1994).

The modern conception of the sexed body claims to be based in immutable, natural truth. One benefit of a cross-cultural and transhistorical perspective is that it helps us see that this "nature" is not natural at all: it is a carefully constructed intellectual artifice, the product of contingent histories. Like the androgynous Maize God, the two-sex model rests upon a highly selective engagement with nature, one that ignores as much biology as it recognizes, and that was developed to meet specific cultural and ideological needs.

In the canonical modernist novel *Frankenstein,* the unhappy being who inhabits a surgically created body is a monster. This abject role is taken up by Susan Stryker, who claims—and reinvents—monstrosity for her own transsexual body, "torn apart and sewn together again in a shape other than that in which it was born" (1994). Mary Shelley, *Frankenstein*'s author, portrayed the unnatural creature as inherently tragic, a being with no future and no past. Stryker absorbs this message and then, like the monster in the novel, rises up in rage to reject it and claim a different history for herself. The transgender body, she suggests, might not belong to the modernist present or the immediate past at all. It might instead be part of a future only now coming into being, in which the constructed body is not terrifyingly inhuman, but "exhilaratingly posthuman"—perhaps one of Haraway's feminist cyborgs (1994) or Rosi Braidotti's "cyberbodies" (2002).

Stryker claims her surgically assembled body as something powerful and new; we might also call it powerful and old. Throughout ancient Europe, the ubiquitous figurines that archaeologists worked so hard to divide into two little piles, male and female, have constantly confounded them with anomalies: a woman/centaur, a man seated on a birthing stool, bodies with a penis and breasts (Hamilton 2000).

In the ancient Americas, a basic premise of Pre-Columbian art is that living beings gain power and beauty through appropriating the body parts of others. At the great Peruvian oracle of Chavín, for instance, stone carvings depict pilgrims processing into the temple accompanied by jaguars and supernatural beings. Humans and superhumans alike are composites: a man wears metal breastplates that are literally shaped like a pair of breasts; the "angel" on a stone cup has the wings of a bird, the face of a jaguar, and a human hand that grasps a baton. Two utterly fantastic composite beings who stand guard at the entrance of the temple may be a male and female pair—but their fearsome, tooth-lined genitalia far exceed anything found on actual bodies of any sex (Burger 1992).

In the Western tradition, too, artists use the contrast between women and men, humans and animals to portray power—but never by contaminating the male body with the taint of the female. Instead, tableaux of conquest show the masculine man dominating lesser beings. In the Pre-Columbian tradition, humans demonstrate superiority quite differently: by rising above the limitations of the birthed body through incorporating the bodily aspects of others. To show femininity in this context makes a man more powerful, not less. Underlying this hybrid imagery is a basic theory of the body as permeable and protean, growing throughout life through physical and metaphysical intercourse with others. Because Westerners fear losing control over the boundaries of the body and the self, the art produced in the ancient Americas sometimes creates discomfort and dislike. But for those who do not occupy a privileged body that is masculine and white—or at least respectably feminine and willing to submit—the great corpus of Pre-Columbian art stands as a repository of revolutionary ideas.

In claiming the territory of the monstrous, Stryker walks in the footsteps of Chicana lesbian writer Gloria Anzaldúa, who revolutionized Latino Studies when she embraced the monstrous image of an Aztec goddess, the fearsome Coatlicue, as her own (1987). It was here, in the art of ancient Latin America, that this rebellious writer found a context within which to understand her own nature, which she experienced as both masculine and feminine—and a place where she could embrace her own uncontrollable rage. Coatlicue and her fellow goddesses, Coyalxauqui and Tlaltecuhtli, are ferocious amalgams of human and non-human, masculine and feminine, mother and killer. Standing, like Anzaldúa, in their protective shadows, it becomes easier to follow Styker in claiming "monstrosity" as a state of redemptive power for gender non-normative people—and for all of us who are stigmatized as deviant in modern Western thought.

The image that Anzaldúa chose is one of the most unforgettable in Pre-Columbian art. At the heart of the Aztec empire, in the center of one of the largest cities in the world, Tenochtitlan (today Mexico City), three enormous female statues were placed in the precincts of the great central temple (Carrasco et al. 1988). For modern Latin Americans, Coyalxauqui is the easiest to understand, and she is the most beloved of Mexicans today. She is a beautiful young woman dressed as a warrior— and killed in combat by her own brother. In the carving, her graceful limbs have been severed from her naked torso, and her eyes are closed in death on her decapitated head. In keeping with modern sensibilities, she is the tragic feminine heroine, young, lovely, and safely dead.

Anzaldúa chose a more difficult figure: not the dead sister, but the vengeful mother. This is Coatlicue, an enormous and terrifying body, human in form but incorporating a fearsome array of non-human creatures. Her head is formed of intertwined serpents; her feet are the curved talons of birds of prey; and, most terrifying of all, her hands are live obsidian blades. The blades are sacrificial knives, and she wears a gruesome necklace of the hearts and hands of her victims. But she herself seems to have been decapitated: the snakes pouring out from her neck and forming her face can also be read as streams of life blood pumping out from a headless corpse. This is no passive victim: erect and powerful, the goddess rises from the dead, her blood forming new and more fearsome dual snakeheads to replace the human head that was taken from her.

Since Anzaldúa wrote her paean to Coatlicue, archaeologists have discovered a third figure, as large and elaborate as the others. This ten-ton stone carving portrays Tlaltecuhtli, a god often portrayed in masculine form, but here a goddess who squats in the birth position, even as sacrificial blood pours from her mouth like tongues.[20] This iconography makes explicit the symbolism of birth and death implicit in the other two; unlike them, she was created as the cover for a coffin, which held the body of a male emperor, Ahuitzotl.

These three goddesses are huge and deadly, and their bodies incorporate more than just elements of masculinity. They are both alive and dead, life-giving and life-taking, and their bodies are composed of bone, blood, flesh, and stone; bird, snake, and woman. They are powerful images, but after all, they are just that: representations of bodies, not real ones.

There is ample evidence, however, that ancient people also saw their actual bodies as things that were assembled over life rather than given at birth—and that this process of accumulating bits and pieces of others was a beneficial process, even though it necessarily involves giving away parts of oneself too. We see this perhaps most strikingly in burial practices: whereas archaeologists originally assumed that the bodies in tombs were intact individuals, new evidence from around the globe shows that premodern people preferred to mix it up. In addition to mass graves, even graves that apparently contain only one person often turn out to contain one whole skeleton—composed of body parts from multiple individuals. In Mexico, Peru, and Turkey, there is evidence that graves were repeatedly re-entered, so that the living could interact with their dead in commemorative rites (see for example Millaire 2004). In the process, they often exchanged, added, or subtracted bones, as for example in the grave of a woman at Çatalhöyük who cradles a man's head in her lap, or another young female whose own head has been replaced with that of a man who died long after her.

Theoretically inclined archaeologists are starting to absorb the implications of this data. It suggests that ancient people did not think of themselves and their own bodies in the modern Western sense, as individual bodies with individual identities—a belief that makes interfering with the bodily integrity of a corpse reprehensible. Instead, they conceived of life as a process of constant exchange between bodies, and wished only that such exchange might continue after life. Feminist theorist Marilyn Strathern says that in non-Western societies such as tribal Papua New Guinea, people are not "individuals" but "dividuals" whose bodies and selves—including their gendered sense of themselves as female and male—are multiple and composite in their very essence (1988).

In addition to the bones, there is another body part that provides evidence of this ontology: the detachable penis. A few years ago, I gave a lecture at a Peruvian university on my research into the "Moche sex pots"—sexually explicit works of art found in ancient tombs like the one that held the "Lady of Cao" (Weismantel 2004, 2011). The prominent archaeologist who had invited me expressed skepticism about the validity of studying sex during my talk; but afterwards, as we toured his labs, he confided that he had himself found some artifacts that he was at a loss to interpret. One of these was a clay penis discovered in a woman's tomb. He became extremely uncomfortable when I asked him where, exactly, it was found. "It was... sort of by her waist," he replied, and then said fiercely, "but it wasn't... *inside* her or anything." The only relationship between a penis and a biological female that he could imagine was penetration: the possibility of a woman claiming the penis as her own possession, to be attached to her own body, apparently never even crossed his mind.

Like many archaeologists, this intelligent, highly educated man was ill-prepared to think through this particular find: there was little in his own life experience or his many years of training that he could bring to the task. In the end, the confusing artifact remained in a laboratory drawer, while he and his team returned to the more familiar task of publishing evidence they found less threatening, such as gruesome scenes of men inflicting torture on war captives.

However, there are other archaeologists working elsewhere in the world, and some of them have no fear of a detachable penis or two. One of them is Meskell, who identified a number of the ceramic and stone figurines at Çatalhöyük as "phallic." However, these small penises were, like everything else at the site, surprisingly ambiguous. Some could be read as either a torso or genitals, while others were just amorphous. The most interesting were simultaneously male and female: a penis and testicles when looked at from one angle, they became breasts or buttocks when rotated (Nakamura and Meskell 2009). This visual punning suggests a fundamentally different attitude towards gender, one that emphasizes the mutability, not the fixity, of bodily sex. Recent work on figurines elsewhere in Europe has noticed similar effects: some of the female bodies can be turned upside down to become life-sized—if somewhat abstract—sets of male genitalia (Joyce 2008).

For our purposes, the most important thing about these ancient penises is that they were usually pierced for wearing, probably hung from a cord around the neck. As Meskell points out, these detachable body parts could be attached to any kind of body, including that of a child. (Similarly, in my own research on Moche, I found that ceramic effigies of male genitalia appeared in all kinds of tombs, not just those of men.)

This detachability indicates a body that is partible rather than unitary. It warns against the assumption that is too often made, that a penis is inevitably a metonym for a whole gendered person, for masculinity as an abstraction, or for "phallic" power. Instead, as Strathern found in her ethnographic research in twentieth century New Guinea, elements of maleness and femaleness may be partible elements that inhere in the products of men's and women's labor, as well as within their bodies, and so can be exchanged, divided, ingested, or temporarily held within individual persons (1990). Within this ontology, bodies and persons are not conceptualized as discrete bounded individuals, but as constellations of qualities and potencies that come alive through constant interaction with others. Gender, like sexuality, becomes a matter of object choice and the play of difference, rather than the search for an elusive unitary identity that torments the modern imagination.

To ungender Čatalhöyük, then, or any society, is not to imagine (or create) a blandly uniform social landscape without appetites or organs. It is to conceptualize bodies and persons as vital assemblages interacting in a field of dynamic material entanglements, where the physical properties of the flesh are not inescapable markers of absolute difference and limitation, but desirable and detachable gifts that can be exchanged in real and imagined interactions between mutable social agents.

## TO CONCLUDE: AN INVITATION

I have taken you, my readers, on a romp and a rampage through the archaeological record, sharing my pleasures and my rages in a rather wanton fashion. I would like to express my gratitude for the opportunity to do so; the invitation to write this essay let me reinvent my own thinking about the archaeological study of the ancient past by looking at it through a transgender lens. I want to respond with an invitation in return: it is my hope that this article might inspire some smart, angry transgender intellectuals to invade archaeology—and transform it forever.

I have told stories about the transphobic and heteronormative attitudes of some practicing archaeologists; my purpose in doing so was not just to vent (although that felt good, too). These are tales of double impoverishment: archaeologists like the man who hid the penis in the drawer have been impoverished by the limited education about gender and sexuality that most students receive. In return, he can only offer the impoverished and distorted record of gender diversity in the ancient past—the only account typically made available to the public. This cycle is endlessly self-perpetuating—unless and until activist scholars insist on changing the political and intellectual landscape. That kind of transformation is what transgender studies is all about.

## NOTES

1. I am very grateful to Susan Stryker for the invitation to contribute this article to the second *Transgender Studies Reader*; to my partner, Simon Z. Aronoff, for his careful reading and astute commentaries on various drafts; and to my research assistant, Pilar Escontrias, for her help in assembling the bibliography.
2. The Wikipedia entry is an interesting artifact of the current gender/sex wars in archaeology. On the one hand, it is a triumph for archaeologist Bettina Arnold that the skeleton is described in the entry as female; she fought hard to get Celtic archaeologists to recognize that not all elaborate burials were male. However, neither that debate, nor the further controversy over whether the skeleton might be intersex or occupy an intermediate gender between male and female, is mentioned directly. The fight over gender and sex in archaeology does emerge obliquely in an angry note in the discussion section, which erroneously insists that there is never any doubt about the sex of a skeleton. (On this point, see the recent discussion over osteological identification at the 2011 meetings of the Society for American Archaeology, where a symposium entitled "Exploring Sex and Gender in Bioarchaeology" coined the phrase "the sexism of sexing" to refer to this kind of insistence that identifying biological sex is a simple and unambiguous matter.)
3. Throughout this essay, I use "ancient" as a broad umbrella term to refer to a wide variety of precapitalist and non-Western societies that have been studied by archaeologists. I am regretfully excluding an entire gamut of excellent archaeological work on sex and gender in historical and Western settings; see for example the essays by historical archaeologists in Schmidt and Voss 2000 and Casella and Voss 2010.
4. The word "shaman" has taken on so many meanings in both popular and academic writing that it should be used with caution (Klein et al. 2002).
5. I use the female pronoun in accordance with other authors. All researchers agree that this was the individual's primary biological sex, and I do not wish to countervene Bettina Arnold's argument that Celtic individuals buried in this way are not inevitably male.
6. On the Vix debate, see Arnold 1991; Knüdson 2002; and the discussion in Joyce 2008: 75–76 and Voss 2008.

7. Stryker (2006) and Whittle (2006) describe the "transgender phenomenon" as a development of the 1990s, the crystallization of cultural effects as diffuse as the rise of the internet, the availability of medical technologies, and the maturation of the feminist and LGBT movements.
8. We no longer naively imagine that other peoples' histories can be treated as a sort of giant thrift shop where we are free to rummage around among discarded and outmoded identities, picking and choosing what pleases us without regard for how our selections were meant to be used, or what might have happened to the original owners. While acknowledging the cultural importance of books like Leslie Feinberg's *Transgender Warriors* for trans people today, or Walter Williams' *The Spirit and the Flesh* for gay men a generation ago, we have seen the ugly racial politics that can ensue. A notable example is the Native American two-spirit tradition, a complex and constantly evolving cultural and religious phenomenon that was reduced by enthusiastic gay outsiders to the simplistic notion of the *berdache* (a term that was itself a homophobic insult, imposed by French colonialists on a cultural phenomenon they neither understood nor respected). For indictments of the cultural whiteness of LGBTQ culture and queer studies, see for example Smith 1977; Harris 1996; Ferguson 2004; Johnson 2005; McBride 2005; Manalansan 2003.
9. Feminist archaeology has a substantial scholarly history today, beginning with the seminal article by Conkey and Spector (1984). A flurry of gender volumes and articles followed (see, for example, Gero and Conkey 1991; Brumfiel 1992; Jacobs et al. 1997; Nelson and Rosen-Ayalon 2002).
10. See for example Joyce 2000; Buechli 2000; Yates 1993.
11. See, for example, Medrano Enriquez 2006.
12. Kanne, pers. comm., Evanston IL 2010; see also Linduff and Rubinson 2008.
13. Richards and Pearson 2005, cited in Nakamura and Meskell 2009: 208.
14. Moche society was very stratified: while the elite were buried with piles of gold, silver, fine art, and precious materials, ordinary fisherfolk and farmers were placed in shallow graves with, at most, a simple basket or crude ceramic pot.
15. Quilter 2010: 71; http://www.fundacionwiese.com/in/arqueologia/lasradecao/html, accessed January 22, 2012.
16. Alva and Donnan 1993.
17. Castillo-Butters 2005, 2006; Donnan and Castillo-Butters 1994.
18. Looper 2003; see also Klein 2001, Bassie-Sweet 2002. Taube 1985: 171 and passim; although note the discussion of the female-bodied aspects of the Maize God on 1985: 178.
19. Early European cartographers wrote "here be monsters" on the edges of their maps when they reached the limits of the known world.
20. See www.mexicolore.co.uk/index.php?one=azt&two=aaa&id=286&typ=reg, accessed February 7, 2012.

## BIBLIOGRAPHY

Ajootian, Aileen (1995). "Monstrum or Daimon: Hermaphrodites in Ancient Art and culture." *Greece and Gender*: 93–108. Papers of the Norwegian Institute at Athens. http://digital-ub.uib.no/1956.2/2994, accessed May 21, 2012.

Alva, Walter and Christopher Donnan (1993). *Royal Tombs of Sipán.* Los Angeles: Fowler Museum of Cultural History at the University of California.

Anzaldúa, Gloria (1987). *Borderlands/La Frontera: The New Mestiza.* San Fancisco, CA: Aunt Lute Books.

Arnold, Bettina (1991). "The Deposed Princess of Vix: The Need for an Engendered European Prehistory." In Dale Walde and Noreen Willows (eds), *The Archaeology of Gender: Proceedings of the 22nd Annual Chacmool Conference*, 366–374. Calgary: Department of Archaeology, University of Calgary.

Bassie-Sweet, Karen (2002). "Corn Deities and the Male/Female Principle." In Lowell Gustafson and Amy Trevelyan (eds), *Ancient Maya Gender Identity and Relations*, 169–190. Westport, CT: Greenwood Press.

Blackwood, Evelyn (1984). "Sexuality and Gender in Certain Native American Tribes: The Case of Cross-Gender Females." *Signs* 10: 1, 27–42.

Braidotti, Rosi (2002). *Metamorphoses: Towards a Materialist Theory of Becoming.* Cambridge: Polity Press.

Brumfiel, Elizabeth (1992). "Distinguished Lecture in Archaeology: Breaking and Entering the Ecosystem: Gender, Class, and Faction steal the show." *American Anthropologist* 94: 3, 551–567.

Buechli, Victor. (2000). "Constructing Utopian Sexualities: The Archaeology and Architecture of the Early Soviet State." In Robert Schmidt and Barb Voss, eds. *The Archaeologies of Sexuality*, 67-88. London: Routledge Press.

Burger, Richard L. (1992). *Chavín and the Origins of Andean Civilization.* New York: Thames and Hudson.

Carrasco, David, Eduardo Matos Moctezuma, and Joanna Broda (1988). *The Great Temple of Tenochtitlan: Center and Periphery in the Aztec World.* Berkeley, CA: University of California Press.

Casella, Eleanor and Barbara Voss, eds. (2010). *The Archaeology of Colonialism, Gender, and Sexuality.* Cambridge: Cambridge University Press.

Castillo-Butters, Luis Jaime (2005). "Las Señoras de San José de Moro: Rituales funerarios de mujeres de élite en la costa norte del Perú." In *Divina y humana, la mujer en los antiguos Peru y Mexico*, 18–29. Lima: Ministerio de Educación.

Castillo-Butters, Luis Jaime (2006). "Five Sacred Priestesses from San José de Moro: Elite Women Funerary Rituals on Peru's Northern Coast," *Revista Electronica de Arqueologia PUCP* 1(3): 1–10.

Conkey, Margaret and Janet D. Spector (1984). "Archaeology and the Study of Gender." *Advances in Archaeological Method and Theory* 7: 1–38.

Donnan, Christopher B. and Luis Jaime Castillo-Butters (1994). "Excavaciones de Tumas de Sacerdotisas Moche en San Jose de Moro, Jequetepeque." In Santiago Uceda and Elias Mujica, eds. *Moche: Propuestas y Perspectivas*, 415–424. Travaux de l'Institut François d'Etudes Andines 79. Lima: Institut François d'Etudes Andines

Feinberg, Leslie (1996). *Transgender Warriors: Making History from Joan of Arc to Dennis Rodman*. Boston, MA: Beacon Press.

Ferguson, Roderick A. (2004). *Toward a Queer of Color Critique: Aberrations in Black*. Minneapolis, MN: University of Minnesota Press.

Gero, Joan M. and Margaret W. Conkey, eds. (1991). *Engendering Archaeology: Women and Prehistory*. Chichester: Wiley.

Hamilton, Naomi (2000). "Concepts of Sex and Gender in Figurine Studies in Prehistory." In Moira Donald and Linda Hurcombe, eds. *Representations of Gender From Prehistory to the Present*, 17-30. Basingstoke: Palgrave Macmillan.

Haraway, Donna (1994). "A Manifesto for Cyborgs: Science, Technology, and Socialist Feminism in the 1980s." In Steven Seidman (ed ) *The Postmodern Turn: New Perspectives on Social Theory*, 82-118. Cambridge University Press.

Haraway Donna (2006). "A Cyborg Manifesto: Science, Technology and Socialist-Feminism in the Late Twentieth Century." In Susan Stryker and Stephen Whittle (eds), *The Transgender Studies Reader*, 103–118. New York: Routledge.

Harris, Laura Alexandra (1996). "Queer Black Feminism: The Pleasure Principle." *Feminist Review* 54: 3–30.

Hays-Gilpin, Kelly A. (2004). *Images: Gender and Rock Art*. New York: Rowman Altamira.

Jacobs, Sue-Ellen, Wesley Thomas, and Samantha Lang, ed. (1997). *Two-Spirit People: Native American Gender Identity, Sexuality, and Spirituality*. Urbana, IL: University of Illinois Press.

Johnson, E. Patrick (2005). "Introduction: Queer Black Stadius/'Quaring' Queer Studies." In E. Patrick Johnson and Mae G. Henderson (eds), *Black Queer Studies*, 1–20. Chapel Hill, NC: Duke University Press.

Joyce, Rosemary A. (2000). "A Precolumbian Gaze: Male Sexuality among the Ancient Maya." In Robert Schmidt and Barbara Voss (eds), *Archaeologies of Sexuality*, 263–283. New York: Routledge.

Joyce, Rosemary A. (2004). "Embodied Subjectivity: Gender, Femininity, Masculinity, Sexuality." In L. Meskell and R.W. Preucel (eds), *A Companion to Social Archaeology*, 82–93. Oxford: Blackwell.

Joyce, Rosemary A. (2008). *Ancient Bodies, Ancient Lives: Sex, Gender and Archaeology*. New York: Thames and Hudson.

Klein, Cecelia, ed (2001). *Gender in Pre-Hispanic America*. Washington, DC: Dumbarton Oaks.

Klein, Cecelia, Eulogio Guzmn, Elisa Mandell, and Maya Stanfield-Mazzi (2002). "The Role of Shamanism in Mesoamerican Art." *Current Anthropology* 43: 3, 383–419.

Knüdson, Christopher (2002). "More Circe than Cassandra: The Princess of Vix in Ritualized Social Context." *European Journal of Archaeology* 5: 275–308.

Linduff, Katheryn and Karen S. Rubinson, eds. (2008). *Are All Warriors Male? : Gender Roles on the Ancient Eurasian Steppe*. Lanham, MD: Altamira Press.

Looper, Matthew George (2003). *Lightning Warrior: Maya Art and Kingship at Quirigua*. Austin, TX: University of Texas Press.

McBride, Dwight A. (2005). *Why I Hate Abercrombie & Fitch: Essays on Race and Sexuality*. New York: New York University Press.

Manalansan, Martin F. (2003). *Global Divas: Filipino Gay Men in the Diaspora*. Durham, NC: Duke University Press, 2003.

Medrano Enríquez, Angélica María (2006). "Jardines flotantes y actividad ocupacional: Los chinamperos prehispánicos de San Gregorio Atlapulco." In Lourdes Márquez Morfín and Patricia Hernández Espinoza, eds. *Salud y sociedad en el México prehispánico y colonial*, 367–394. Mexico City: Conaculta and Inah.

Millaire, Jean-François (2004). "The Manipulation of Human Remains in Moche Society: Delayed Burials, Grave Reopening, and Secondary Offerings of Human Bones on the Peruvian North Coast." *Latin American Antiquity* 15: 4, 371–388.

Nakamura, Karen and Lynn Meskell. 2009. "Articulate Bodies: Forms and Figures at Çatalhoyük." *Journal of Archaeological Method and Theory* 16: 205–230.

Nelson, Sarah Milledge and Myriam Rosen-Ayalon (2002). *In Pursuit of Gender: Worldwide Archaeological Approaches.* Walnut Creek, CA: AltaMira Press.

Pilloud, Marin A and Clark Spencer Larsen. 2011. "Official and 'practical' kin: Inferring social and community structure from dental phenotype at Neolithic Çatalhoyük." *American Journal of Physical Anthropology* 4:519–530.

Quilter, Jeffrey (2010). *The Moche of Ancient Peru: Media and Messages.* Boston, MA: Peabody Museum Collection Series.

Schmidt, Robert A. (2002). "The Iceman Cometh: Queering the Archaeological Past." In Ellen Lewin and William L. Leap (eds), *Out in Theory: The Emergence of Lesbian and Gay Anthropology*, 155–185. Urbana, IL: University of Illinois Press.

Schmidt, Robert A. and Barbara J. Voss (2000). *Archaeologies of Sexuality.* New York: Routledge.

Smith, Barbara (1977). "Toward a black feminist criticism." In Gloria T. Hull, Patricia Bell Scott, and Barbara Smith (eds), *All the Women are White, All the Blacks are Men, but Some of us are Brave*, 157–175. New York: Feminist Press.

Stockett, Miranda (2005). "On the Importance of Difference: Re-Envisioning Sex and Gender in Ancient Mesoamerica." *World Archaeology* 37: 4, 566–578.

Strathern, Marilyn (1988). *The Gender of the Gift*, Berkeley, CA: University of California Press.

Strathern, Marilyn (1990). *The Gender of the Gift: Problems with Women and Problems with Society in Melanesia.* Berkeley, CA: University of California Press.

Stryker, Susan (1994). "My Words to Victor Frankenstein above the Village of Chamounix: Performing Transgender Rage." *A Journal of Lesbian and Gay Studies* 1: 3, 237–254.

Stryker, Susan (2006) "(De)subjugated Knowledges: An Introduction to Transgender Studies." In Susan Stryker and Stephen Whittle (eds), *The Transgender Studies Reader*, 1–18. New York: Routledge.

Taube, Karl (1985). "The Classic Maya Maize God: A Reappraisal." In Virginia M. Fields (ed), *Fifth Palenque Round Table, 1983.* Proceedings of the Fifth Palenque Round Table Conference, June 12–18, 1983, Palenque, Chiapas, Mexico. Washington DC: Dumbarton Oaks.

Taube, Karl (1996). "The Olmec Maize God: The Face of Corn in Formative Mesoamerica." *RES: Anthropology and Aesthetics* 29/30, 39–81.

Voss, Barbara L. (2000). "Feminisms, Queer Theories, and the Archaeological Study of Past Sexualities." *World Archaeology* 32(2): 180–192.

Voss, Barbara L. (2008)."Sexuality Studies in Archaeology." *Annual Reviews in Anthropology* 37: 317–336.

Weismantel, Mary (2004). "Moche Sex Pots: Reproduction and Temporality in Ancient South America." *American Anthropologist* 106: 3, 495–505.

Weismantel, Mary (2011). "Obstinate Things." In Barbara Voss and Eleanor Casella (eds), *The Archaeology of Colonialism, Gender, and Sexuality*, 203–222. Cambridge: Cambridge University Press.

Whittle, Stephen (2006). "Foreword," in Susan Stryker and Stephen Whittle (eds), *The Transgender Studies Reader*, xi–xvi. New York: Routledge.

Williams, Walter L. (1986). *The Spirit and the Flesh: Sexual Diversity in American Indian Culture.* Boston, MA: Beacon Press.

Wylie, Alison (2003). "Why Standpoint Matters." In Robert Figueroa and Sandra Harding (eds), *Science and Other Cultures: Issues in Philosophies of Science and Technology*, 26–48. New York: Routledge.

Yates, T. (1993). "Frameworks for an Archaeology of the Body." In Christopher Tilley (ed), *Interpretive Archaeology*, 31–72. Oxford: Berg.

# 27

## *Before the Tribade*

## Medieval Anatomies of Female Masculinity and Pleasure

### Karma Lochrie

EXPLICITLY OR IMPLICITLY, MUCH OF CONTEMPORARY TRANSGENDER SCHOLARSHIP addresses the question of what it means to live in a modern capitalist society that organizes itself according to norms of embodied subjectivity. Differences from norms become the targets of regulatory and disciplinary power, sites of struggle for control, and opportunities for excess or noncompliance to function as vectors of subversion, liberation, creativity, political mobilization, and futurity. But what if society were not organized in this manner? What if power operated in some other fashion than through the promulgation of norms by scientific and social-scientific means? This is a question that motivates the research of medievalist Karma Lochrie, who seeks to understand "female sexuality when normal wasn't." The turn Lochrie takes is a significant one for transgender studies, if the field is to continue developing its analytical and theoretical reach. Although she raises the question of "a-normativity" in its historical dimension, seeking to understand the organization of embodiment, desire, and subjectivity prior to the advent of Eurocentric modernity, the same question could be asked of contemporary non-Eurocentric (post-colonial) socio-cultural formations, as well as of any form of social organization we might hope to actualize in the future. In this excerpt from Chapter 4 of her book *Heterosyncracies*, Lochrie contests early modern anatomists' so-called "discovery" of the clitoris, which comes to function as a privileged site for the installation of modern schemas of sexuality and gender, by recounting what earlier medieval texts made of this particular bit of throbbing gristle. In doing so, she traces figurations of female masculinity and pathways of female homoeroticism that lie outside of modernity.

Fallopius arrogates unto himself the Invention or first Observation of this Part. And Columbus gloriously, as in other things, he is wont, attributes it to himself. Whereas nevertheless *Avicenna, Albucasis, Ruffus, Pollux,* and others, have made mention hereof in their Writings.
—Caspar Bartholin, Bartholinus' Anatomy, 1668

The Renaissance discovered the clitoris, according to Katharine Park and Valerie Traub. Or rather, European anatomists rediscovered from Arab sources the *capacity* of the clitoris for pleasure, and with this rediscovery female erotic pleasure achieved nothing less than "a new articulation and heightened cultural capital."[1] The importance of this rediscovery is, as both scholars have argued, that it produced a significant shift both in the understanding of female sexual pleasure and in the discourse about sex between women. The Middle Ages, as Park notes, knew of the clitoris but was woefully misinformed on the subject:

> Although the clitoris as an anatomical organ (rather than a general locus of female sexual pleasure) had been well known to late Greek writers on medicine and surgery, that knowledge had been lost to medieval medical authors. Misled by the linguistic imprecision of their Arabic sources, exacerbated by the uncertain terminology of Latin translators, they tended either to identify it with the labia minora, or following the eleventh-century Persian medical authority Avicenna, to think of it as a pathological growth found in only a few women.[2]

Avicenna's pathological clitoris is usually cited as evidence of the medieval tendency to acknowledge the clitoris only in its monstrous incarnations and to ignore its role in normal female pleasure.

In turn this representation of medieval medical ignorance of the clitoris provides the necessary scaffolding for the discovery of the clitoris in the Renaissance, thanks to the new practice of dissection, and with that discovery, nothing less than the breakdown of the one-sex model of sexual difference and the emergence of the lesbian for the first time in the Western cultural imagination.[3] Park identifies a two-stage development in the discovery of the clitoris and the association of female homosexuality with that discovery: the first stage was Jacques Daléchamps's "preliminary version of the tribade" in the *Chiurgie françoise* of 1570. According to Park, Daléchamps was the first to have "fabricated the connection between clitoral hypertrophy and female homoeroticism by consolidating what were in fact two separate topics in his ancient texts and then to have authorized his construction by projecting it back onto those texts." The critical passage in the *Chiurgie françoise* observes that all Egyptian women and "some of ours" are endowed unusually large clitorises, so that "when they find themselves in the company of other women, or their clothes rub them while they walk, or their husbands wish to approach them, it erects like a male penis, and indeed they use it to play with other women, as their husbands would do." Though Daléchamps attributes this information to the Greek authors Paul of Aegina, Aetius, and pseudo-Galen, none of these authors or his Arabic sources "in fact connected an enlarged clitoris (or labia) with female homoerotic desire or behavior," Park contends.[4]

The second step in the formation of a clitorally-endowed female homoeroticism was achieved by the "explosion of anatomical knowledge· based on systematic human dissection... and the anatomical debates surrounding the newly discovered clitoris." The "definitive *tribade*, in all her Phallic glory," was born.[5] Credit for this scientific discovery through human dissection is attributed to Gabriele Falloppia (a name to which another part of the female reproductive system is indebted), not only by Renaissance scholars but by Falloppia himself. We can thus date the discovery of the clitoris to 1561, when Falloppia published his *Observationes anatomica*. In fact, Falloppia insists that, the claims of other anatomists to the contrary, he discovered it first in 1550 and everyone else stole it from him. Among alleged plagiarists of his discovery is one Realto Columbo, who in his 1559 study, *De re anatomica*, takes the liberty of naming "these projections" that "no one has discerned... the love or sweetness of Venus."[6]

The narrative of the Renaissance discovery of the clitoris and concomitant initiation of a "profusion and variety of representations" of the tribade and female homoeroticism "unique to the early modem era" thus depends on three intersecting developments: the medical discovery of the clitoris, the recognition of that part of the sexual anatomy as the source of female pleasure independent of heterosexual intercourse and the aims of reproduction, and the explicit association of a hypertrophied clitoris with female homosexual desire and sexual predation. Before the

Renaissance, the clitoris languished in medieval confusion inherited from Arabic sources, and therefore, the "definitive *tribade*," to borrow Park's words, was powerless to be borne in the medieval cultural imagination. This would explain the comparative absence of discourse generally concerned with female homoerotic desire in medieval culture and the "explosion" of that same discourse in Renaissance texts so extensively documented by Traub.

It would, that is, if this narrative were accurate. It seems to be true that the practice of dissection in the early modern period contributed to an increased awareness of the role of the clitoris in female pleasure. It also seems to be the case, at least so far, that female homoeroticism figures much more pervasively as a site of cultural anxiety and erotic possibility in Renaissance texts from the medical to the dramatic than it does in medieval texts, where it is much less in evidence. The case remains to be made, however, for the absence of a medical knowledge of the clitoris in the Middle Ages. It also remains to be seen what it would mean if the Middle Ages did in fact know more than Renaissance scholars believe it did. Since a clitoris does not necessarily a lesbian make, the question of what it means that the Middle Ages might not only have known about the clitoris, but also have associated it with female homosexual tendencies, needs to be raised. Finally, if the clitoris did indeed have a history before the Renaissance, the current narrative of its renaissance in the early modern period needs some modification, if not some acknowledgment of the medieval "prediscovery" of the Renaissance clitoris.

Even if the medieval prehistory of the clitoris is more continuous with its Renaissance self-fashioned discovery than it is radically discontinuous, early modernists would maintain that a crucial difference lies in the normalization of the clitoris as an effect of Renaissance anatomical science. Medieval medicine discussed the clitoris only as "an illness or anatomical peculiarity," while Renaissance anatomists conferred normalcy on the clitoris by rendering it a regular part of the female sexual anatomy. All women, not just hermaphrodites or imprudent ones, were endowed with a clitoris that afforded them an independent source of sexual pleasure and the biological wherewithal to desire and have sex with other women. As a result, female pleasure becomes normal and homoeroticism possible. My problem with this argument is that the evidence of Renaissance discourse actually continues to pathologize both the clitoris, particularly where it is the instigator of female homoeroticism and female sexuality. If there was a normal clitoris during the Renaissance (which I seriously doubt, since as I have argued, norms were not installed in the scientific method), it existed in the shadows of its pathological counterpart, just as it did in the Middle Ages.

Finally, there is the problematic claim itself to rediscovery of the clitoris. As early as the seventeenth century, anatomists themselves recognized the speciousness of the claims of Falloppia and Columbo in particular to have discovered this part of the female anatomy. Caspar Bartholin, the famous seventeenth-century Danish anatomist, is responsible for the quotation that opens this chapter, attributing the claims of Falloppia and Columbo to sheer professional self-promotion rather than scientific discovery. Bartholin notes that Avicenna, Albucasis, and others had long known about the clitoris, and he implies that nothing new is to be gained from the scientific verification of their writings. By repeating the claims of Falloppia and others, Renaissance scholars have revived and replicated the competition over who discovered the clitoris without acknowledging the sheer professional rivalry that marks the claims of Falloppia and Columbo. In the meantime, one of the most interesting questions to be raised in the original debate goes unasked: why did Renaissance anatomists choose this organ as the site on which to stake their reputations, and what, exactly, were they claiming? Thomas Lacqueur's answer to the second question is "not much":

> The somewhat silly but complicated debate around who discovered the clitoris is much less interesting than the fact that all of the protagonists, shared the assumption that, whoever he might be, someone

could claim to have done so on the basis of looking at and dissecting the human body. A militant empiricism pervades the rhetoric of the Renaissance anatomists.[7]

In the end, what differentiates Falloppia's or Colombo's clitoris from Avicenna's is not a new pleasure principle or normalizing effect, but the argument for militant empiricism itself and the case for a new anatomical science. The clitoris was not newly discovered, only newly legitimized by anatomists who were interested in establishing names for themselves and for a "self-consciously revisionist" science.[8] The clitoris became, in effect, a trophy of the new militant empiricism of anatomists such as Falloppia, and like all trophies, it did more to confer visibility on its discoverers and legitimacy on the practice of dissection than it did to inform medicine about female sexual pleasure or homoeroticism.

The argument of this chapter, as the reader might have guessed, is that the evidence from medieval medical texts suggests that the Middle Ages was not as confused about the role of the clitoris in female pleasure as has been maintained, and beyond this, that it linked the hypertrophied clitoris with deranged female homoerotic desire long before Daléchamps discussed the anatomy of Egyptian women, and before Gabriele Falloppia claimed to have recuperated its role in female sexual pleasure from the neglect of anatomy.[9] Although there was some medieval confusion regarding the clitoris, as Park and Traub have claimed, there was likewise some of the same confusion in the Renaissance, as indeed, there has been ever since. To accept as true the claims of the Renaissance anatomists to have discovered the clitoris is, in a sense, to make the same empirical fallacy that they made. To see and identify a clitoris does not necessarily amount to a new understanding of female pleasure or to less confusion about it. After all, as Park notes, even after its alleged discovery, the clitoris was often mistaken for the labia, and vice versa.[10] Prior to the sixteenth century, anatomists had already begun dissecting human corpses at the end of the thirteenth and beginning of the fourteenth century, but this did not necessarily eliminate their confusion about the clitoris.[11] Confusion is, in fact, a crucial part of the history of the clitoris, since it is the association of clitorises "in all their phallic glory" that gives rise to premodern theories of female same-sex desire in the first place. Falloppia and Columbo's rival claims are as dubious as those of Sigmund Freud in 1905, the next man who claims to have discovered the clitoris. Few today would credit Freud with much real knowledge of female sexuality; rather, his discovery led to a new cultural denial of the clitoris in favor of the mythical vaginal orgasm.[12]

The history of the clitoris is therefore less a trajectory from more to less confusion, from inaccurate to accurate appraisals of its function, or from absence to presence, than it is an overlapping discourse. The Renaissance bears the residue of medieval accounts of the clitoris without ever entirely displacing those accounts. Early modern medical discourse might have waxed more voluminous on the subject than medieval medicine did, but it did not change fundamentally the medieval understanding of the clitoris with all its confusion.

## DESPERATELY SEEKING THE MEDIEVAL CLITORIS

What did the Middle Ages know of the clitoris and when did it know it? The evidence does not, unfortunately, fit neatly into a linear model from ignorance to knowledge. It reveals, instead, a messy and sometimes incoherent flux of ideas derived from ancient authorities and modern dissection simultaneously. Of the authorities on anatomy available to the Middle Ages, the primary ones who discussed the clitoris were Galen, Soranus, Caelius Aurelianus, Albucasis, and Avicenna. Galen's clitoris seems to be very much in evidence, but its function is confused, and this confusion will be carried wholesale into the medical texts of medieval surgeons, such as Henri de Mondeville, in the fourteenth century. Galen's description of the external female genitals includes the part he calls the "nymph," a term that would become standard for some anatomists and surgeons into the Renaissance:

As for the outgrowths of skin at the ends of the two pudenda, in woman they [the labia majora and minora] were formed for the sake of ornament and are set in front as a covering to keep the uteri from being chilled;... The part called *nympha* [the clitoris] gives the same sort of protection to the uteri that the uvula gives to the pharynx; for it covers the orifice of their neck by coming down into the female pudendum and keeps it from being chilled.[13]

Since Galen was analogizing the female sexual anatomy to the male, he privileged the vagina and womb over the external organs, rendering the labia ornament to those more functional components. The clitoris, too, becomes secondary to the vagina, forcing Galen to search for its function in the lore of gender myth. The idea that women were especially susceptible to external influences was so common that Avicenna, the Arabic physician, claimed that mares could be impregnated by the wind, and Albert the Great much later could recount the pleasure one woman received from the "caress of a breath of wind."[14] Galen rescues the nymph from its seemingly anomalous place in the female sexual anatomy and, at the same time, perpetuates one of the medical ideas of women that would persist beyond the Middle Ages.

Elsewhere, however, Galen attributes the vulva to being the seat of female sexual pleasure. He recounts the story of a widow who suffered from "nervous tension." The midwife who examined her diagnosed her as having a retracted uterus. She cured her by applying heat and manual "contact with [the woman's] sexual organs," causing "contractions associated with the pain and pleasure similar to that experienced during intercourse."[15] Galen is vague about what the midwife did with her hand to arouse the woman to orgasm, but he nevertheless endorses such methods for relieving women of retained sperm. Pleasure and sexual health are Galen's concern in this passage even if the clitoris is not specifically recognized.

Before Galen, Soranus of Ephesus offered a different vision of the clitoris's function. His *Gynaecia*, written in the first century AD, was available to the Latin West since its translation in the sixth century by Moschion. In two sections of this work, Soranus uses two different names for the clitoris, the *landica*, an indecent term in Classical Latin, and *tentigo*, a more technical term that meant "tension" and conceived of the clitoris in terms of its capacity for erection.[16] First, Soranus's description of the "normal" clitoris:

> Quid ipse sinus muliebris?
> membranum nervosum maioris intestini simile. intus autem est spatiosissimus, foris vero angustus, in quo coitus virorum et usus venerius efficitur. quem vulgo cunnum appellant. cuius foris labra graece pterigomata dicuntur, latine pinnacula dicta sunt, et a superiore parte descendens in medio dicta est landica.

> What is the woman's *sinus* [cavity]?
> A nervous membrane like the large intestine: very spacious on the inside, the opening, in which coitus with men and venereal acts take place, is truly narrow; it is vulgarly called *cunnus;* outside of which are the labia called *pterigomata* in Greek, in Latin, *pinnacula,* and from the upper part descending in the middle is what is called the *landica.* (My italics.)[17]

The location and description of the clitoris in Moschion's translation of Soranus appear to be more accurate than Galen's, but he does not describe its function in conjunction with those venereal acts of coitus he identifies with the vagina. Whatever its function, the *landica* is no more pathological in this text than are the other parts, the labia or the vagina. It is only when the *landica* becomes morbidly enlarged that Soranus treats it as a pathology that can only be remedied by surgery. Here, too, emerges evidence of that tribade and anxieties about female pleasure that Traub and Park attribute to Renaissance anatomists. In his chapter "on the immoderate *landica*," Soranus waxes alarmist: "Turpitudinis symptoma est grandis yos nymfe. quidam vero adserverant pulpam ipsam erigi similiter ut viris et quasi usum coitus quaerere" (The "nymph" of great size is a shameful symptom, which flesh is said to become aroused in a way that is similar to men and as if seeking the act of coitus).[18] Although Soranus does not explicitly attribute tribadism to the enlarged clitoris, he does suggest that women possessing this shameful condition are in a state of heightened desire. Comparison to the aroused penis in search of coitus assigns the possessors of the enlarged clitoris the appetites of men, as another version of Soranus makes more explicit: "ipse adfecte tentigine virorum similem appetentiam sumunt et in venerem coacte veniunt" (those possessed of the *tentigo* [clitoris] assume an appetite resembling that of men and they engage in the venereal act).[19] The type of venereal acts that women possessed of the enlarged *tentigo* seek out is nowhere specified, but the hyperbolic desire and masculine impersonation described does imply tribadism in other medical texts of the Greek and Arabic traditions.

The last Greek text that was available to the Middle Ages was the fifth-century work of Caelius Aurelianus, *On Chronic Diseases*. In this work, the tribade assumes a kind of phallic glory long before she sprang full-fledged from the minds and dissections of Renaissance anatomists. In the course of describing effeminate men, Caelius compares them to the female victims of the same affliction, the tribades:

> Indeed, the victims of this malady may be compared to the women who are called *tribades* because they pursue both kinds of love [heterosexual and homosexual?]. These women are more eager to lie with women than with men; in fact, they pursue women with almost masculine jealousy, and when they are freed or temporarily relieved of their passion ... they rush, as if victims of continual intoxication, to new forms of lust, and sustained by this disgraceful mode of life, they rejoice in the abuse of their sexual powers.[20]

Caelius's work may not have been very influential during the Middle Ages, according to some scholars of the history of medicine, but it does provide evidence of a kind of lore of the tribade that might have circulated around the remarks about this condition of hypertrophied clitorises.[21] Caelius was, after all, a translator of Soranus. Even if Soranus never labeled his shamefully endowed woman a tribade, his description provided Caelius with a template for his tribade, and for her companion in sexual pathology, the effeminate man.

It is in the Arabic medical tradition that the hypertrophied clitoris takes a backseat to another disorder that looks very similar, at least to Avicenna and Albucasis, *ragadia* of the womb. In other words, the enlarged clitoris–wielding women who assumed masculine desires were now the possessors of another penis-like genital, but one that developed from either a prolapsed uterus or an abscess of the womb. The confusion of this new disorder with the enlarged clitoris does not mean that it was ignored by medieval medicine, or that the clitoris was somehow unknown to the Middle Ages. I would rather propose that medieval medicine had two clitorises instead of one and that both of them were dangerous.

Albucasis, whom Caspar Bartholin cites in the quote at the beginning of this chapter, was one of three Arab physicians who were known and quoted throughout the Middle Ages and Renaissance, the other two being Avicenna, the most famous, and Rhazes. Albucasis's *Chirurgia* (tenth–eleventh centuries) was translated by Gerard of Cremona in the twelfth century, along with the works of the other two Arab authors. It is in Gerard's translations of the Arabic into Latin that a new term for clitoris is coined, *batharum*, a fairly literal transliteration of the Arabic. This word becomes synonymous with the two words already quoted in the Latin translations of Greek medical texts, *tentigo* and *landica*.[22] In his discussion of the clitoris and "fleshy growths in the female genitalia," Albucasis treats the two deformities together:

> The clitoris may grow in size above the order of nature so that it gets a horrible deformed appearance; in some women it becomes erect like the male organ and attains to coitus.... As to the fleshy growth, that is, flesh growing in the cervix and filling it, and also often protruding like a tail (on which account some of the Ancients "caudate disease"); this too you should cut away as you do for the clitoris and dress until healed.[23]

Albucasis makes no mention of the deranging effects of the enlarged clitoris or the rather alarming cervical polyps, but he does imply the one is used for coitus.

In Avicenna the two disorders become separated, and while he says little about the enlarged clitoris except on the subject of its removal, he does have quite a bit to say on the fleshy growth called *ragadia* that emerges from the wombs of some women. Traub and Park themselves confuse Avicenna's discussion of the "pathological clitoris" for her cousin, the pathological fleshy growth (this time, *baccarum* in the Latin) that causes women to pursue other women and engage in coitus with them, just like the Renaissance tribade.[24] Avicenna discusses the surgical procedure for removing the enlarged clitoris without reference to any adverse sexual behaviors affecting women who have it. However, he also discusses separately another affliction, *ragadia* of the womb, which inflames some women with inordinate sexual desire and impels them to seek out other women for sex. Avicenna writes (by way of Gerard of Cremona's translation):

> Quandoque oritur in ore matricis caro addita et quandoque apparet super mulierem res que est sicut virga commouens sub coitu. Et quandoque aduenit ei vt faciat cum mulieribus simile quod fit eis cum quibus coitus. Et quandoque est illud baccarum magnum. Et furfus quidem est caro addita orta in ore matricis que quandoque prolongatur, et quandoque abbreuiatur et non pro-longatur nisi in estate et abbreuiatur in hyeme. Et summa quidem medicorum testificatur illud sicut Archigenes et Galen et negat illud Hyppocrates medicus.

> Sometimes there arises additional flesh in the mouth of the womb, and sometimes there appears on a woman a thing that is just like the penis aroused in coitus. And sometimes it occurs to her to perform with women a coitus similar to what is done to them with men. And sometimes it is one large clitoris. And this disease of the skin is indeed the additional flesh arising in the mouth of the womb that is sometimes extended and sometimes shortened and not extended, except in summer; it is shortened in winter. And indeed the majority of physicians testify to this, such as Archigenes and Galen, though Hyppocrates the physician denies it.[25]

Avicenna via his Latin translation invokes the Arabic word for clitoris, *baccarum,* here to describe what is clearly not a clitoris at all but either a prolapsed uterus or a nasty abscess. As "one large clitoris," it seems to suffer from its own form of seasonal affective disorder in which it is extended during the summer and withdrawn or contracted during the winter. Avicenna might indeed confuse a "true" clitoris with something that merely quacks like one, and this confusion no doubt matters in the history of anatomy, but it matters less to the history of the clitoris and women's pleasure. Avicenna is clearly aware that the clitoris is the center of female pleasure. Furthermore, he conceives of the enlarged clitoris as a penis in drag and the woman who possesses it, a masculine woman with lesbian-like desires. A large clitoris, wherever it may pop up (or down), is the sign of a woman with an inordinate sex drive directed at other women. The clitoris itself is the cause of that drive, as its appearance coincides with the desire to engage in coitus with other women. To paraphrase Avicenna, "that is one large clitoris," with Galen and Archigenes to vouch for it.

Even if Avicenna's text exhibits some of that uncertainty about the true clitoris that has been used to characterize medieval medicine generally, Avicenna was in fact quite clear about what the clitoris's function was, which is why he mistook the engorged flesh extending from the vulva for one. In another passage of his *Canon of Medicine* Avicenna explicitly advises men on the art of foreplay, including instructions about the importance of rubbing the "seat of pleasure" in a woman before intercourse:

> Amplius prolongent ludum, et proprie cum mulieribus quorum complexiones non sunt male. Langat ergo vir eius mammillas cum facilitate, et tangat pectinem eius et obuiet ei non permiscendo se ex permixtione vera. Quandoque desiderat et affectat permisceatur ei fricando de ea quod est inter anum eius desuper et vuluam. Alle enim locus est delectationis eius. Consideret ergo in ea horam in qua fortis fit in ipsa adherentia et incipiunt oculi eius mutari in rubedinem, et eius anhelitus eleuari, et verba eius balbutire.

> Men should take their time over playing with women who do not have a poor complexion. They should caress their breasts and pubis, and enfold their partners in their arms without really performing the act. And when their desire is fully roused, they should unite with the woman, rubbing the area between the anus and the vulva. For this is the seat of pleasure. They should watch out for the moment when the woman clings more tightly, when her eyes start to go red, her breathing becomes more rapid and she starts to stammer.[26]

Kinsey would have been pleased with Avicenna's description of the signs of female arousal (although he added the curling of women's toes to the picture). Avicenna does not mention the clitoris here, and that silence permits another sort of confusion, but he is clear on the importance of female pleasure, which importance is picked up by many Renaissance anatomists directly from him. Thus Ambroise Paré, the famous French surgeon who wrote on female hermaphrodites with enlarged clitorises who desired other women, writes about foreplay with less detail than Avicenna but with a clear echo of the Arab surgeon's instructions:

> When the husband commeth into his wives chamber hee must entertaine her with all kinde of dalliance, wanton behaviour, and allurements to venery: but if he perceive her to be slow, and more cold, he must cherish, embrace, and tickle her, [without penetration] ... intermixing more wanton kisses with wanton words and speeches, handling her secret parts and dugs, that she may take fire and bee enflamed to venery, for so at length the wombe will strive and waxe fervent with a desire of casting forth its owne seed.[27]

Paré is indebted to Avicenna's principle of play, or "entertainment," in this passage, his prescription for the woman of slower temperaments or complexions, and his more explicit directions to caress and "handle" the "secret parts." It is interesting that Avicenna's is the more explicit text, identifying the area wherein woman's pleasure is found and the signs of her arousal, while Paré leaves both to the husband's imagination. There is no more accuracy, anatomical correctness, or scientific knowledge in Paré's description than there is in Avicenna's, and Paré is clearly working more from Avicenna than he is from observation. A comparison of the two passages suggests that Avicenna was at least, if not more, attuned to the function of the clitoris and physiological signs of female pleasure than was Paré, with all his scientific knowledge.

Latin translations of the Arab and Greek medical texts produced a number of words for the clitoris in the Middle Ages, some of which continued to be used in the Renaissance: *batharum, baccarum,* and *badedera* (Arab words rendered in Latin), *nymphe, tentigo, landica, virga* (a word also used for penis), and *ragadia* (as in Avicenna's Canon).[28] Considering the variety of words used for clitoris, it would be naive to assume that medieval medicine did not know about the clitoris in its normal or pathological states, or that it did not recognize its function as the site of female sexual pleasure. It is true, as we have seen, that there were at least two clitorises in medieval medicine: one that we recognize today as the true one, and the other, a disease of the womb that produced something that looked like an enlarged clitoris. This confusion, however, far from obscuring the phallically-endowed sexual lover of women, in fact contributes to it as much as the Renaissance hermaphrodite does. Avicenna's *ragadia*-wielding woman is not too far removed from the hermaphrodite, which was also known and discussed in Arab medical literature.[29] In any case, confusions about real versus pathological clitorises reflect cultural anxieties about female sexual pleasure and same-sex desire as much as early modern tribadic mythologies do. The fact that, from the thirteenth century through the Renaissance, Avicenna's *Canon* "was one of the most widely used university medical textbooks," and that even Renaissance anatomists continued, like their medieval predecessors, to rely heavily on Avicenna, means that, despite dissection and the new science, the old science dating back to Arab medicine continued to exert a strong influence on ideas about female anatomy and pleasure.[30]

In fact, some of the confusion that persisted from the Middle Ages into the Renaissance was due to the unresolved use of inconsistent sources. What Joan Cadden remarks about the Middle Ages holds for the Renaissance as well: "In part, the lack of clarity and agreement about the geography of pleasure is the result of the different contexts in which the comments are made.... In part, too, the differences can be traced to different sources, which the scholastic authors did not attempt to resolve or harmonize." Renaissance anatomists who continued to rely on sources that contradicted their empirical evidence were following the "cultural politics of representation and illusion," not "the evidence of organs, ducts, or blood vessels," according to Laqueur: "No image, verbal or visual, of 'the facts of sexual difference' exists independently of prior claims about the meaning of such distinctions."[31] Renaissance illustrations of the female anatomy, therefore, depended for their meaning on some prior claims established from Avicenna through medieval medicine, as Bartholin was keen to point out.

Once Avicenna had been translated in Latin, both his clitoris with all its lesbionic effects and his theory of female sexual pleasure contained in the procedural foreplay segment of the *Canon* set two paths in medical discourse about the clitoris. The one trajectory leads to that pathological clitoris to which Park and Traub allude, while the other recognizes the importance of clitoral stimulation to female pleasure in coitus. The normal and the pathological clitorises and female sexual pleasures, however, are not as distinct as early modernists argue they are for the Renaissance. They are different modalities of the same sexology that analogized the clitoris to the penis, recognized the independence of female sexual pleasure from coitus, and posited female desire as inexhaustible.

One of the most important interpolators of Avicenna's *ragadia*-wielding women in the thirteenth century was William of Saliceto, a professor and surgeon at the medical school at Bologna. William's *Summa conservationis et curationis* (1285) addresses both the regular functioning of female sexual pleasure and the errant condition of *ragadia* described by Avicenna. Following the Arabic tradition, William emphasizes pleasure in the sexual act, devoting an entire chapter of his *Summa* to the subject. Like Avicenna, he stresses the importance of touching the breasts, genitals, and hair of the vulva, and the signs of female arousal, eye motion, breath rate, and babbling.[32] In the chapter on *ragadia* of the womb, the phallic female who preys on other women for sex makes a stunning appearance. First William explains where the *ragadia* comes from and then describes the forms it takes and its effects.

The telltale linkage of this condition to a seasonal affective disorder smacks of his source, the *Canon of Medicine*:

> Ragadie sunt scisure cum quibusdam eminentii carnosis a quibus per fricationem cum virga et etiam per se emanat sanguis: fiunt aliquando propter siccitatem loci eminentem vt contingit in partu difficili aut propter aposthema quod rumpitur et advenit quandoque quod consolidatur et acquirunt formam verucarum et porrorum et apparent ragadie matricis quandoque in collo matricis intra aut extra itaquod videri possunt: quandoque preter ragadías oritur in ore matricis caro addita: et quandoque apparet res super muliere que est sicut virga commouens sub coitu: et quandoque advenit ei vt faciat cum mulieribus similiter quod fit eis cum quibus coitus: et quandoque est bothor magnum vel eminentia.

> Ragadiae are tears in the womb accompanied by certain prominent fleshy growths from which blood also oozes caused by friction with a penis. They are caused sometimes by the particular dryness of the area as occurs in a difficult childbirth or on account of an abscess because it has ruptured, and sometimes it hardens and acquires the form of small growths or warts. Sometimes the fissures of the womb appear in the neck of the womb within or without so that they can be seen. And sometimes in addition to the fissures extra flesh arises in the mouth of the womb; and sometimes a thing appears on a woman that is just like a penis aroused during coitus; and sometimes it occurs to her to do what men do with women, that is, have coitus with women; and sometimes there is a great clitoris [Arabic, *bothor*] or protuberance.[33]

As in Avicenna, William's *ragadia* is one version of the clitoris. Caused by dryness from friction with a penis or an abscess, the *ragadia* grows into a penis-like appendage, causing its bearer to desire coitus with other women. Like Avicenna, William recommends the surgical removal of the *ragadia* to remedy the condition, which presumably is neither painful nor debilitating so much as it is undesirable to the physicians writing about it. Neither physician expresses any moral outrage at the condition, however; it is treated with the same equanimity that hemorrhoids are treated.

William of Saliceto's very concept of the *ragadia*-afflicted woman, like that of Avicenna, would not be possible without an understanding of the clitoris as the center of female sexual pleasure. At the same time, there is no question that the pendant *ragadia*-as-clitoris is anatomically incorrect. This confusion, however, does not mean that William and Avicenna were ignorant about the function of the clitoris in female pleasure or the alarming independence of female pleasure from intercourse. The *ragadia*-wielding woman who desires other women represents a hypertrophied version of the "normal" woman, a version inflected by masculine anxiety. The analogy of the clitoris to the penis as locus of sexual pleasure contributes to the easy slippage from woman to masculinized, pathologically sexed, *ragadia*-wielding woman. The one-sex model, according to which woman's genitals were merely the inverted version of man, may explain the *ragadia*-deranged woman whose clitoris is, in fact, her vagina in reverse. Whatever the case, the pathology described by William of Saliceto is not at all inconsistent with an understanding of the clitoris as the center of female sexual pleasure.

William devotes, in fact, an entire chapter to the subject of "those things that add desire in sexual intercourse." Drawing mostly on Avicenna and other Arabic works, he advises rubbing the area around the vulva and making certain facial and eye motions to increase female delight. The telltale signs are the woman's eye motions, breathing rate, babbling, and incomplete sentences.[34] This kind of advice is found throughout the medical literature, from William of Saliceto to Arnold of Villanova, who translated Avicenna's Canon and wrote the De *regimen santitatis* (ca. 1311). The clitoris is not explicitly named in these sex manuals, but the "seat of female pleasure" is located outside the vagina in the vulva in each case. Clearly, it is independent of sexual intercourse.

The first major medical writer in England, Gilbert the Englishman, a priest and royal physician to King John, wrote the *Compendium medicinae,* "one of the first works to take advantage of new Latin translations of Arabic medical and philosophical texts."[35] Although Gilbert's discussion of sexual desire and coitus is concerned almost solely with men's experience, in his chapter on sexual impotence, he picks up Avicenna's advice on foreplay as a way of increasing women's desire: "Maior iterum videtur esse in delectatione mulieris concupiscentia ex molli fricatione nervorum et villorum matricis et irroratione puri et summe delectabilis vt dixi" (a greater desire is seen in the pleasure of a woman from the gentle rubbing of the nerves [clitoris] and the tuft of hair of the uterus and by the emission of moisture, and this is intensely pleasurable as I have said).[36] The word *nervus* usually refers to the penis, but here it is used for the clitoris. Gilbert locates Avicenna's vague "seat of desire" in the clitoris and, at the same time, emphasizes the friction of this organ that will come to be associated with tribades. In both William of Saliceto and Gilbert the Englishman, we can see a persistent understanding of female pleasure in its ordinary and extraordinary forms and a mythologizing of the phallic woman who desires other women.

In the early fourteenth century the great natural philosopher and physician Peter of Abano compiled scientific and medical authorities in his *Conciliator.* His language is less vague than Gilbert's or Avicenna's in the discussion of provoking female desire: "Likewise [women are driven to desire] especially by having the upper orifice near their pubis rubbed; in this way the indiscreet (? *curiosi*) bring them to orgasm. For the pleasure that can be obtained from this part of the body is comparable to that obtained from the tip of the penis."[37]

While Peter of Abano may have been an early champion of the "true" clitoris, other writers continued either to parrot Avicenna on the subject or to perpetuate Galen's confusion about its function in protecting the womb from wind. In his *Lilly of Medicine* (1303), for example, Bernard of Gordon, a professor at Montpellier, adopts Avicenna's language on the subject of exciting women, writing that "the man should excite the woman to coitus" by "speaking, kissing, embracing, and touching her breasts, abdomen, and pubic region."[38] Using much the same language, John of Gaddesden, who entitled his treatise Rosa *Anglica* (ca. 1314) in honor of Bernard's work, also instructs men on the solicitation of women to coitus beyond the customary speaking, kissing, embracing, and touching the breasts and perineum, with the unusual counsel to "take the entire vulva in your hands and strike the buttocks" to cause the woman to eagerly desire intercourse.[39] Although the clitoris is nowhere singled out for special attention in the erotic art of arousing women, there is clearly knowledge of the vulva as an erogenous zone that is aroused independently of intercourse.

Medieval misunderstandings regarding the clitoris existed side by side with more accurate descriptions of its location and function. In the fourteenth century, two important French surgeons, Henri de Mondeville and Guy of Chauliac, represented two very different clitorises, one according to the Galenic model and the other a compilation of Arabic and later authors. First Henri, who wrote his *Chiurgia* in 1306. It was translated into French in 1314 and afterwards used as a vernacular textbook for surgeons and barbers. He compiles the many words for clitoris, but gets its function wrong:

> In the middle it has a brawny membrane which hangs out somewhat and which is called by Rhazes in the second [book] of the *al-Mansuri* and chapter seven of Albucasis, *tentigo.* The uses of this membrane are twofold: first, that urine could issue through it so that it does not spill into the uterus through the vulva; and second, it is able to alter the air that enters the womb through the vulva.[40]

Even though the Latin word for the clitoris, *tentigo,* would have suggested lust, erection, and sexual tension to Henri de Mondeville, his analysis of its functions here desexualizes it and, in the process, occludes female sexual pleasure entirely. This is, indeed, a confusion, but it is not a confusion that is limited to the Middle Ages, for in the sixteenth century, Thomas Vicary is still insisting on the clitoris's dual function as a channel for urine and a prophylactic against wombal windiness.[41]

In contrast to Henri's desexualization of the clitoris's functions, Guy of Chauliac writing in 1373 compares the clitoris to the penis, lending it a sexual function by analogy. The Middle English translator's vernacular rendering of the terminology strongly indicates the sexual nature of the clitoris. The early fifteenth-century English translation of Guy of Chauliac's *Inventarium seu collectorium in parte cyrgicali medicine* begins by describing the penis-like vagina, womb, and testicular ovaries. The clitoris follows: "It haþ also þe priue schappe or chose as a hellynge and mytre. It haþ also a þriue poynte as þe hole in þe ȝerde" (It also has a sexual organ or vulva like a glans penis and urethra. It also has a sexual point [in another Middle English version, *tentigo*], like the hole in the penis).[42] Guy of Chauliac's one-sex model of sexual anatomy, according to which the woman's internal organs are inverted versions of the male sexual organs, is here rendered incoherent by the clitoris, which he also compares to the penis. Clearly, he and other medieval surgeons could live with the contradiction, even as Renaissance anatomists did later.

In the same vernacular translation of Guy of Chauliac's surgical treatise, the hypertrophied clitoris makes an appearance not as a *ragadia* of the womb, which is treated sepatately, but as an enlarged *tentigo,* or to use the translator's coinage for Middle English, a *kikir*:

> When þat echyng of flesche þat cleped þe kikir groweþ somtyme to suche a quantite in þe priue chose þat it maketh displesynge and noye, þe cure þerof forsothe (after albucasis) is þat it be kytte with a byndinge or wiþa rasoure and noght vnto þe botume for drede of bledynge.

> When that protuberance of flesh that is called the *kikir* grows sometimes to such a quantity in the private part [vulva] that it causes discomfort and disgust, the cure is truly (after Albucasis) that it be cut with a binding or with a razor and not to the bottom to avoid bleeding.[43]

Guy of Chauliac says nothing about the sexual proclivities of the woman suffering from an enlarged *kikir,* and this is odd. He is more than familiar with the writings of Avicenna and William of Saliceto, both of whom he extols in his history of surgery, yet he is silent on the sexual side effects of the hypertrophied *kikir*.[44] Why he omitted this detail is impossible to say, whether because it was common medical knowledge or because it was no longer accepted. The first possibility is very likely, as Guy follows Avicenna in everything else, including his surgical solution to the female hermaphrodite who has "a ȝerde and priue stones" above her vulva. Whatever the reason for Guy of Chauliac's omission of the side effects of large clitorises, he clearly assigns a sexual function to the clitoris that conflicts with his one-sex model of sexual anatomy. Even dissection, which Guy of Chauliac and other medieval surgeons practiced to develop their skills and to fund their knowledge, did not remedy this anomaly.[45]

Obviously, there is more in medieval medical discourse about the clitoris than is currently apprehended in the early modernists' claims for the Renaissance discovery of the clitoris. In spite of the coexistence of incommensurable accounts of the clitoris in medieval texts, certain consistencies also emerge from the discourse. First, the clitoris was sometimes understood by homology with the penis as both a natural organ of sexual pleasure and the seat of female pleasure. Second, this understanding of the clitoris's function produced theories of foreplay in medical texts from Avicenna to Peter of Abano to William of Saliceto that assumed the independence of female pleasure from reproduction. Moreover, the pathologizing of the clitoris, comparatively sparse as the medieval evidence is, extends the gender ideology of female hypersexuality to its natural conclusion, unnatural lust, perversion, and gender transgression. Whether in the form of the uteral lesion known as the *ragadia* or the enlarged *kikir,* the hypertrophied clitoris sometimes predisposed her to inordinate lust directed at other women. Obviously, any woman was susceptible to this erotic proclivity insofar as any woman was susceptible to diseases of the womb and deformations of her sexual organs. Female homoeroticism was the morphological limit case for all women.

What is missing from medieval medical discourse by comparison with early modern texts is the conflation of the tribade with the hypertrophied clitoris. That peculiar "psychomorphology" of the clitoris described by Traub does seem to be peculiar to the Renaissance.[46] The fact that the Middle Ages seems not to have imagined the tribade, however, does not mean that it did not have other models of gender instability and transgression through anatomical anomalies. "Virago" was the term applied to another kind of gender disorder in which a woman's body underwent a physiological sex change through the retention of menses. Avicenna's description of this condition is curiously free of any pathologizing perspective. He presents it simply as a variation, and not an unnatural or morbid one, of the female menstrual function:

> And indeed the natures of these women become similar to the natures of men, for they have power over digestion and necessary distribution and expulsion of superfluities the way that men expel them. And these women are fat, nervous, and muscular, and among them are strong viragos whose hips are narrower than their chests, and whose extremities are heavier. They experience many evacuations through medicines, exercise, nosebleeds, hemorrhoids, wounds, and other ways.[47]

Not only do these "viragos" develop masculine bodies, but their menstrual retention becomes compensated for in masculine forms of disposing of bodily superfluities. While women typically give off their residues less efficiently than men due to their temperamental coldness through menstruation, men shed their superfluities more efficiently, and this leads to such markers of sexual difference as an increased libido and beards. When women are afflicted with amenorrhea, or obstruction of the menstrual function, then they become more like men, assuming masculine sexual desires and even beards. From Avicenna through the English physicians contemporary with Chaucer, the virago who retains menses is described as having, in the words of Bernard of Gordon repeating Avicenna, "greater desire because of the tickling and itching [retained] menstrual blood induces," while John of Gaddesden describes the little beards that appear on these women. Their beards, in fact, reflect their greater sexual drives, according to medieval physiology, because both are produced by the greater heat of men's bodies as well as their greater ability to process superfluities. When women retain menses, therefore, they assimilate to male physiology, and this in turn, besides producing beards, produces a psychomorphic change that the physicians sought to remedy, but did not condemn.[48]

Two separate models of anomalous female sexualities and genders thus emerge from medical texts in the Middle Ages. The first is the hypertrophied clitoris–wielding woman, whose inflated sexual desire was directed to other women, the other, the virago, whose physiological assimilation to masculinity through the retention of menses led to exorbitant sexual desire and masculine strength. In both cases, morphology, physiology, and anatomy precede excessive lust and sexual proclivities. In the case of the virago, it precedes a kind of female masculinity that did not necessarily imply female homoeroticism. Could the two figures of female gender and sexual transitivity have been imagined together?

[...]

The trajectory from Avicenna's conception of the *ragadia* of the womb to late medieval diagnoses of the symptomatic virago [...] is freighted with anxieties about female masculinity and desire, but these anxieties are not heteronormative reflexes. Heterosexuality, we might say, is "notwithstanding," that is, it is irrelevant to the medical and literary representations of the virago and *ragadia*-afflicted woman. Female sexuality is partly constructed through an "anatomical essentialism" that Traub attributes to early modern anatomists, with a difference.[49] The medieval virago did not give rise to the tribade, or "rubster," but instead to an otherwise "heterosexual" woman whose sexual anatomy predicts her masculinity. Her sexuality is anything but heteronormative.

## NOTES

1. Traub, *Renaissance of Lesbiansim*, 89. See also Park "Rediscovery of the Clitoris."
2. Park, "Rediscovery of the Clitoris," 173. [...]
3. Thomas Laqueur explains that, prior to the eighteenth century, a one-sex model of sexual difference dominated medical thinking. According to this one-sex model, the female sexual anatomy is but an imperfect, inverted version of the male: her vagina an internal penis, her womb a scrotum, and her ovaries testicles. This premodern model is differentiated from the modern, which construes women and men as opposites based on the incommensurability of their sexual anatomies. See Laqueur, *Making Sex*. Park argues that the rediscovery of the clitoris in the early modern period undermined the one-sex model much earlier than Laqueur suggests in his book.
4. Park, "Rediscovery of the Clitoris," 175 and 176.
5. Park, "Rediscovery of the Clitoris," 176. Traub's account relies upon Park's narrative of the clitorally endowed early modern lesbian: *Renaissance of Lesbianism*, 205.
6. Quoted in Laqueur, *Making Sex*, 65 and 64. Traub discusses their competing claims in *Renaissance of Lesbianism*, 205.
7. Laqueur, *Making Sex*, 65.
8. Laqueur's words in *Making Sex*, 64.
9. For an account of this discovery, see Park, "Rediscovery of the Clitoris," 177. Falloppia makes this claim in his *Observationes anatomicae*, vol. 1, fol. 193r-v.
10. Park, "Rediscovery of the Clitoris," 178. See also Laqueur, *Making Sex*, 98.
11. For the new anatomy of the late thirteenth and early fourteenth centuries and persistent confusion, see Jacquart and Thomasset, *Sexuality and Medicine*, 35–36.
12. See Freud, *Three Essays on the Theory of Sexuality*, 86–87. Laqueur also argues that Freud's theory of the vaginal orgasm initiated "a great wave of amnesia" in science: *Making Sex*, 234.
13. Galen, *On the Usefulness of the Parts of the Body,* vol. 2, 15.3.660–61.
14. Jacquart and Thomasset, *Sexuality and Medicine,* 47.
15. *Galen on the Affected Parts,* trans. Siegel, bk. VI, chap. 5, p. 185. I have discussed this passage in the context of the *Secret of Women* in Covert *Operations*, 126–27. Helen Rodnite Lemay also discusses Galen's cure and later suppressions of it in "William of Saliceto on Human Sexuality," 177.
16. For the history of the term *landica,* see Adams, *Latin Sexual Vocabulary,* 97–98. Adams does not include *tentigo,* but Jacquart and Thomasset do: *Sexuality and Medicine,* 206 n. 103.
17. Muscio, *Sorani "Gynaeciorum,"* 8–9. All translations from Latin are my own unless otherwise cited.
18. Muscio, *Sorani "Gynaeciorum,"* 106.
19. Aurelianus, *Gynaecia,* 113.
20. Aurelianus, *On Acute Diseases and* On *Chronic Diseases,* 900–903: "Nam sicut feminae tribades appellatae, quod utramque venerem exerceant, mulieribus magis quam viris misceri festinant et easdem invidentia paene virili sectantur, et cum passione fuerint desertae seu temporaliter relevatae, ea quaerunt aliis oblicere quae pati noscuntur iuvamini humilitate duplici sexu confectam, velut frequenter ebrietate corruptae in novas libidinis formas erumpentes, consuetudine turpi nutritae, sui sexus iniuriis gaudent."
21. See De Moulin, "Influence of Caelius Aurelianus." Cited in Lemay, "William of Saliceto on Human Sexuality," 179 n. 74.
22. As Jacquart and Thomasset point out, *batharum* appears also as *badedera* in other Latin translations, and Simon of Genoa links the word to Moscio's *landica* in his fourteenth-century *Synonyms: Sexuality and Medicine,* 45–46.
23. Albucasis, *On Surgery and Instruments,* 456. The "caudate disease," say the editors, is "possibly a cervical fibroid or polyp with a long pedicle."
24. Traub quotes Park, who summarizes without quoting Avicenna and his followers, saying they "think of it as a pathological growth found only in a few women," in "Rediscovery of the Clitoris," 173, and Traub, *Renaissance of Lesbianism,* 87–88.
25. Avicenna, *Liber canonis,* Lib. III, fen. xxi, tr. 1, chap. 22, p. 377v.
26. Avicenna, *Liber canonis,* Lib. III, fen. xxi, tr. 1, chap. 10, p. 363v. The translation is from Jacquart and Thomasset, *Sexuality and Medicine,* 131.
27. Quoted in Traub, *Renaissance of Lesbianism,* 85.
28. See Adams, Latin *Sexual Vocabulary,* 97-98, and Jacquart and Thomasset, *Sexuality and Medicine,* 45–46. Compare with the words in Renaissance anatomical treatises in Traub, *Renaissance of Lesbianism,* 89–96.
29. See Albucasis, On *Surgery and Instruments,* 454, and Avicenna, *Liber canonis,* Lib. III, fen. xx, tr. 2, chap. 43, p. 358r.
30. The quote is from Siraisi, *Medieval and Early Renaissance* Medicine, 59. Not only Avicenna but Albucasis continued to inform surgical knowledge and practice in the Renaissance, according to Siraisi (p. 161). Both Traub and Park cite the indebtedness of some Renaissance authors, such as Jacques Duval, to Avicenna's and Albucasis's clitoridectomy procedure for hermaphrodites. See Park, "Rediscovery of the Clitoris," 183. Traub notes Avicenna's contribution to the Renaissance discourse on foreplay: *Renaissance of Lesbianism,* 86. It is puzzling, then, how they can conclude that the Renaissance discovered the clitoris, the tribade, or female pleasure.
31. Cadden, *Meanings of Sex Difference,* 139. Laqueur, *Making Sex,* 66.
32. I am indebted to Helen Rodnite Lemay's summary of William's treatise, "William of Saliceto on Human Sexuality."
33. Guilielmus de Saliceto, *Summa conservationis et curationis,* chap. 168, p. 65rb, fol. i2rb.

34. I am relying on Lemay's summary of William's treatise in "William of Saliceto on Human Sexuality," 166–70.

35. Getz, *Medicine in the* English *Middle Ages,* 3.

36. Gilbertus Anglicanus, *Compendium medicinae,* bk. VII, fol. 284r.

37. Quoted in Jacquart and Thomasset, *Sexuality and Medicine,* 46.

38. Bernard de Gordon, Opus *lilium medicinae inscriptum,* 633: "Masculus debet excitare foeminam ad coitum ... osculando, amplexando, mammillas tangendo, pectinem et peritonaeum."

39. John of Gaddesden, Rosa *Angelica,* 555: "totamque vulvam accipiendo in manus et nates percutiendo."

40. Henri de Mondeville, *La Chiurgie,* 1:112. The Latin version concludes by comparing the function of the clitoris to that of the uvula in the throat. See Jacquart and Thomasset, *Sexuality and Medicine,* 45.

41. See Laqueur, *Making Sex,* 98. The OED and Laqueur limit the *tentigo's* associations with lust and the clitoris to the seventeenth century, but the word's Latin meaning would have had the same associations for the Middle Ages, as Adams proves, Latin *Sexual Vocabulary,* 97–98.

42. Guy of Chauliac, *The Cyrurgie,* 67. This text is made from the only full translation of the *Cyrurgie* found in Paris, Bibliothèque Nationale, MS Anglais 25. For another Middle English rendering of the same passage in which *tentigo* is used where *point* is used in the partial translation of the *Cyrurgie,* London, British Museum, MS Sloane 965, see Guy of Chauliac, *The Middle English Translation,* 136.

43. Guy of Chauliac, *The Cyrurgie,* 529–30.

44. See Guy of Chauliac, *The Cyryrgie,* 8–9.

45. For more on dissection as part of surgical education, see Rawcliffe, *Sources for the History of Medicine,* 46 and 49–50, and Gottfried, *Doctors and Medicine in Medieval England,* 173–74 and 241. Apparently, dissection was more a practice in continental medicine than it was in English medicine, although even the barbers were allowed one cadaver a year to study.

46. See Traub's chap. 5, *Renaissance of Lesbianism,* 188–228.

47. Avicenna, *Liber canonis,* Lib. III, fen. xxi, tr. iii, chap. 25, p. 373r–v: "Et huiusmodi quidem mulierum nature virorum similes existunt naturis et sunt potentes super digestionem vitimam et distributionem necessariam et expulsionem superfluitatum secundum modum quo expellunt eas viri, et iste sunt pingues nervose lacertose, de quibus sunt fortes viragines quarum anche ipsarum pectoribus sunt strictiores et ipsarum extremitates sunt pingues plus, et sunt multarum evacuationum cum medicinis et exercitiis et proprie sanguis fluentes per nares aut emorroydas aut plagas aut alia."

48. See Avicenna's discussion of amenorrhea, cited above; also Bernard of Gordon, *Opus lilium medicinae inscriptum,* 619: "Octavo intelligendum, quod in retentione menstruorum, mulleres magis appetunt propter titillicium et pruritum quem inducunt." John of Gaddesden follows these two sources in his description of the virago sporting "barbi sicut si esset vir" (whiskers as if she were a man): Rosa *Anglica,* 100r. See Cadden's discussion of the medical links between body hair, libido, masculine physiology, and sexual difference: *Meanings of Sex Difference,* 181–83.

49. Traub, *Renaissance of Lesbianism,* 208.

# 28

# *Extermination of the* Joyas
## Gendercide in Spanish California

### Deborah A. Miranda

Deborah A. Miranda, a Native American scholar and poet, offers in "Extermination of the *Joyas*" both a historical and political treatise. Miranda's historical project is to offer a broad account of how gender variant Native people were treated by Spanish colonizers in what became California. Through this excavation, Miranda reconstructs a history of Two-Spirit existence in Native societies, connecting with and informing contemporary Two-Spirit traditions. The stakes are high: Miranda's goal is nothing less than resistance to cultural genocide—the loss of Native tradition and knowledge—through writing history. Rejecting the anthropological term *berdache* once used to describe Two-Spirit traditions, Miranda offers instead the term *joya*, the Spanish word for "jewel," which was used from the sixteenth century onward to denote third-gender people in written records of the Spanish conquest. Since most of the *joyas* were exterminated, Miranda explains, the Spanish archives are often the only traces left of their existence. Accounts of gender-variant Indians are thus mostly brutal tales of conquest: for instance, when the first Spaniard to cross the Isthmus of Panama, Vasco Nuñez de Balboa, came across forty indigenous males dressed as women, he had them torn apart by dogs trained to kill humans. Later, mission priests forcibly regendered *joyas*, according to European conventions, under threat of severe corporal punishment. While most historical accounts understand sodomy (or homosexuality) as the primary target in that instance, Miranda defines the violence instead as gendercide, "an act of violence committed against a victim's primary gender identity."

Attempting to address the many communities from which she spoke, Paula Gunn Allen once asserted: "I cannot do one identity. I'm simply not capable of it. And it took me years to understand that that's one of the features of my upbringing. I was raised in a mixed cultural group—mixed linguistic, mixed religion, mixed race—Laguna *itself* is that way. So I get really uncomfortable in any kind of mono-cultural group."[1] Although Allen does not speak specifically of another community—her lesbian family—in this quotation, her legacy of activism and writing document the unspoken inclusion of sexual orientation within her list of identities. Like Allen, my own identity is not monocultural: by blood, I am Esselen and Chumash (California Native) as well as Jewish, French, and English. I was born at UCLA Medical Center, raised in trailer parks and rural landscapes, possess a PhD, and teach at a small, private southern liberal arts university. I am fluent in English, can read Spanish, and was called to an *aliyah* at the bat mitzvah of my partner's niece. Who am I? Where is home?

In my poetry and my scholarship, I have worked through issues of complex identities for much of my life, primarily those relating to my position as a mixed-blood woman with an Indian father and European American mother. But one of the most urgent questions in my life—the intersection of being Indian and being a lesbian—has always been more complicated, less easily articulated, than anything else. Here again, Allen's body of work has been most helpful. In a poem titled "Some Like Indians Endure," Allen plays with concepts of just what makes an Indian an Indian—and asks if those qualities, whatever they are, are necessarily exclusive to Indians. At the heart of this poem is this thought:

> I have it in my mind that
> dykes are indians
> they're a lot like Indians …
> they were massacred
> lots of times
> they always came back
> like the gas
> like the clouds
> they got massacred again. …[2]

This poem illustrates the multiple directions of Allen's thought: while defending the concept of Indian as something different and distinguishable from colonizing cultures around it, Allen simultaneously compares the qualities of being Indian with those of being lesbian. She comes up with lists of similarities for both identities, the lengthiness of which overwhelms her ability to keep the two apart. While Allen recognizes balance and wholeness in both her Laguna and lesbian identities, this is not necessarily something that completely expresses my own situation.

While researching material for my book "Bad Indians: A Tribal Memoir," however, I came across a page of the ethnologist J. P. Harrington's field notes that provided a doorway for me to enter into a conversation about complex identities with my ancestors.[3] Tracing my California Native ancestors from first contact with Spanish missionaries through contemporary times, my research required that I immerse myself in a rich variety of archival resources: correspondence between missionaries and their supervisors in Spain; mission records of baptism, birth, and death as well as finances and legal cases; the as-told-to testimonies of missionized Indians both before, during, and after the mission era; as well as newspapers, family oral history, photographs, and ethnological and anthropological data from earliest contact through the "salvage ethnology" era and into the present.[4] None of these archival materials came from unfiltered Indian voices; such records were impossible both because of their colonizing context and the prevalence of an oral tradition among California Indians that did not leave textual traces. The difficulties of using non-Indian archives to tell an Indian story are epic: biases, agendas, cultural pride, notions of Manifest Destiny, and the desire to "own" history mean that one can never simply read and accept even the most basic non-Native detail without multiple investigations into who collected the information, what their motivations were, who preserved the information and their motivations, the use of rhetorical devices (like the passive voice so prevalent in missionization histories: "The Missions were built using adobe bricks" rather than "Indians, often held captive and/or punished by flogging, built the Missions without compensation"). Learning how to "re-read" the archive through the eyes of a mixed-blood California Indian lesbian poet and scholar was an education in and of itself, so the fact that this essay emerges from one short, handwritten piece of information gleaned by Harrington from one of my ancestors about older ancestors should not be surprising.

To tell the story of this field note, for which I use the shorthand title "Jotos" (Spanish slang for "queer" or "faggot"), I must pull threads of several stories together. The field note is like a petroglyph; when I touch it, so much else must be known, communicated, and understood to see the power within what looks like a simple inscription, a random bit of Carmel Mission Indian trivia. Once read, this note opens out into deeper and deeper stories. Some of those stories are full of grief—like the one that follows—yet they are all essential to possessing this archival evidence and giving it a truly indigenous reading. When I say "indigenous reading," I mean a reading that enriches Native lives with meaning, survival, and love, which points to the important role of archival reconstruction in developing a robust Two-Spirit tradition today.[5] In the last two decades, the archaeology of sexuality and gender has also helped create new ways to use these biased primary sources, and I hope to pull together the many shards of information available in order to glimpse what contemporary California Indians might use in our efforts to reclaim and reinvent ourselves.[6] This essay, then, examines methods employed by the Spaniards to exterminate the *joya* (the Spanish name for third-gender people); asks what that extermination meant to California Indian cultures; explores the survival of this third gender as first *joyas*, then *jotos* (Spanish for homosexual, or faggot); and evaluates the emergence of spiritual and physical renewal of the ancestral third gender in California Indian Two-Spirit individuals.[7] It is both a personal story and a historical struggle about identity played out in many indigenous communities all over the world.

## WAGING GENDERCIDE 101

Spanish colonizers—from royalty to soldier to padre—believed that American Indians were intellectually, physiologically, and spiritually immature, if not actual animals.[8] In the area eventually known as California, the genocidal policies of the Spanish Crown would lead to a severe population crash: numbering one million at first contact, California Indians plummeted to about ten thousand survivors in just over one hundred years.[9] Part of this massive loss were third-gender people, who were lost not by "passive" colonizing collateral damage such as disease or starvation, but through active, conscious, violent extermination. Speaking of the Chumash people living along the southern coast (my grandmother's tribal roots), Pedro Fages, a Spanish soldier, makes clear that the soldiers and priests colonizing Mexico and what would become California arrived with a deep abhorrence of what they viewed as homosexual relationships. In his soldier's memoir, written in 1775, Fages reports:

> I have substantial evidence that those Indian men who, both here and farther inland, are observed in the dress, clothing, and character of women—there being two or three such in each village— pass as sodomites by profession (it being confirmed that all these Indians are much addicted to this abominable vice) and permit the heathen to practice the execrable, unnatural abuse of their bodies. They are called *joyas,* and are held in great esteem. Let this mention suffice for a matter which could not be omitted,—on account of the bearing it may have on the discussion of the reduction of these natives,—with a promise to revert in another place to an excess so criminal that it seems even forbidden to speak its name … But we place our trust in God and expect that these accursed people will disappear with the growth of the missions. The abominable vice will be eliminated to the extent that the Catholic faith and all the other virtues are firmly implanted there, for the glory of God and the benefit of those poor ignorants.[10]

Much of what little we know about *joyas* (Spanish for "jewels," as I discuss below) is limited to observations like that of Fages, choked by Eurocentric values and mores. The majority of Spanish soldiers and priests were not interested in learning about California Indian culture and recorded only as much as was needed to dictate spiritual and corporeal discipline and/or punishment; there are no known recorded interviews with a *joya* by either priest or Spaniard, let alone the salvage ethnologists who arrived one hundred years later. In this section, I provide an overview of what first contact between *joya* and Spaniard looked like, and how that encounter leaves scars to this day in California Indian culture. The key word here is not, in fact, encounter, but *destruction*.

### Weapons of Mass Destruction: The Mastiffs

As I show, while the Spanish priests' disciplinary methods might be strict and intolerant, they were at least attempting to deal with *joyas* and *joya* relationships in ways that allowed these Indians to live, albeit marginalized and shamed.

Spanish soldiers had a different, less patient method. They threw the *joyas* to their dogs. Shouting the command "Tómalos!" (take them, or sic 'em), the Spanish soldiers ordered execution of *joyas* by specially bred mastiffs and greyhounds.[11] The dogs of the conquest, who had already acquired a taste for human flesh (and were frequently fed live Indians when other food was unavailable), were the colonizer's weapon of mass destruction.[12] In his history of the relationship between dogs and men, Stanley Coren explains just how efficient these weapons were: "The mastiffs of that era … could weigh 250 pounds and stand nearly three feet at the shoulder. Their massive jaws could crush bones even through leather armor. The greyhounds of that period, meanwhile, could be over one hundred pounds and thirty inches at the shoulder. These lighter dogs could outrun any man, and their slashing attack could easily disembowel a person in a matter of seconds."[13] Columbus brought dogs along with him on his second journey and claimed that one dog was worth fifty soldiers in subduing the Natives.[14] On September 23, 1513, the explorer Vasco Nuñez de Balboa came on about forty indigenous men, all dressed as women, engaged in what he called "preposterous Venus." He commanded his men to give the men as "a prey to his dogges," and the men were torn apart alive.[15] Coren states matter-of-factly that "these dogs were considered to be mere weapons and sometimes instruments of torture."[16] By the time the Spaniards had expanded their territory to California, the use of dogs as weapons to kill or eat Indians, particularly *joyas*, was well established.

Was this violence against *joyas* classic homophobia (fear of people with same-sex orientation) or gendercide? I argue that gendercide is the correct term. As Maureen S. Heibert comments:

> Gendercide would then be … an attack on a group of victims based on the victims' gender/sex. Such an attack would only really occur if men or women are victimized because of their *primary* identity as men or women. In the case of male gendercide, male victims must be victims first and foremost because they are men, not male Bosnians, Jews, or Tutsis. Moreover, it must be the perpetrators themselves, not outside observers making ex-poste analyses, who identify a specific gender/sex as a threat and therefore a target for extermination.
>
> *As such, we must be able to explicitly show that the perpetrators target a gender victim group based on the victims' primary identity as either men or women.*[17]

Or, I must add, as a third gender? Interestingly, although Heibert doesn't consider that possibility, her argument supports my own definition of gendercide as an act of violence committed against a victim's primary gender identity.

Consider the immediate effect of Balboa's punishment of the "sodomites": when local Indians found out about the executions "upon that filthy kind of men," the Indians turned to the Spaniards "as if it had been to Hercules for refuge" and quickly rounded up all the other third-gender people in the area, "spitting in their faces and crying out to our men to take revenge of them and rid them out of the world from among men as contagious beasts."[18] This is not homophobia (widely defined as irrational fear of or aversion to homosexuals, with subsequent discrimination against homosexuals); obviously, the Indians were not suddenly surprised to find *joyas* in their midst, and dragging people to certain death went far beyond discrimination or culturally condoned chastisement. This was fear of death; more specifically, of being murdered. What the local indigenous peoples had been taught was gendercide, the killing of a particular gender *because of their gender*. As Heibert says in her description of gendercide above, "It must be the perpetrators themselves, not outside observers making ex-post analyses, who identify a specific gender/sex as a threat and therefore a target for extermination." Now that the Spaniards had made it clear that to tolerate, harbor, or associate with the third gender meant death, and that nothing could stand against their dogs of war, the indigenous community knew that demonstrations of acquiescence to this force were essential for the survival of the remaining community—and both the community and the Spaniards knew exactly which people were marked for execution. This tragic pattern in which one segment of indigenous population was sacrificed in hopes that others would survive continues to fester in many contemporary Native communities where people with same-sex orientation are no longer part of cultural legacy but feared, discriminated against, and locked out of tribal and familial homes. We have mistakenly called this behavior "homophobia" in Indian Country; to call it gendercide would certainly require rethinking the assimilation of Euro-American cultural values and the meaning of indigenous community.

Thus the killing of the *joyas* by Spaniards was, indeed, "part of a coordinated plan of destruction"— but it was only one strategy of gendercide.

### (Re-)Naming

Father Juan Crespi, part of the 1769 "Sacred Expedition" from Mexico to Alta California, traveled with an exploration party through numerous Chumash coastal villages. "We have seen heathen men wearing the dress of women," he wrote. "We have not been able to understand what it means, nor what its purpose is; time and an understanding of the language, when it is learned, will make it clear."[19] Crespi's willingness to wait for "an understanding of the language" was not, unfortunately, a common sentiment among his countrymen, and although he describes but does not attempt to name these "men wearing the dress of women," it wasn't long before someone else did.

Erasure of tribal terms, tribal group names, and personal tribal names during colonization was a strategy used by European colonizers throughout the Americas. The act of naming was, and still is, a deeply respected and important aspect of indigenous culture. Although naming ceremonies among North American Indians followed many traditions, varying according to tribe and often even by band or time period, what has never changed is an acknowledgment of the sense of power inherent in a name or in the person performing the act of naming, and the consequent right to produce self-names as utterances of empowerment. Renaming both human beings and their own names for people or objects in their world is a political act of dominance. As Stephen Greenblatt writes of Christopher Columbus's initial acts of renaming lands whose indigenous names the inhabitants had already shared with him, "The founding action of Christian imperialism is a christening. Such a christening entails the cancellation of the native name—the erasure of the alien, an exorcism, an appropriation, and a gift ... [it is] the taking of possession, the conferral of identity."[20] To replace various tribal words for a Spanish word is indeed an appropriation of sovereignty, a "gift" that cannot be refused, and perhaps more properly called an "imposition."

Therefore, when Spaniards arrived in Alta California and encountered a class of Indians we would now identify as being "third gender," it makes sense that in exercising power over the land and inhabitants, one of the first things the Spaniards did was invent a name for the third-gender phenomenon, a name applied only to California Indians identified by Spaniards as men who dressed as women and had sex with other men. Interestingly, although Spanish morality disapproved of "sodomy" within their own culture and had a collection of words and euphemisms available to describe "el acto pecado nefando" ("the silent/unspoken sin") and its participants (*hermafrodita, sodomía, bujarrón, nefandario, maricón, amujerado*), they did not choose to apply these existing Spanish labels to California Indians.[21] Instead, overwhelmingly, primary sources use the word *joya*. As early as 1775, only six years after Crespi made his observation, the term *joya* was already in widespread use. In describing the customs of Indian women in 1775, Fages writes, "The Indian woman takes the little girls with her, that they may learn to gather seeds, and may accustom themselves to carrying the basket. In this retinue are generally included some of the worthless creatures which they call *joyas*."[22] Although Fages states that "they" (Indians) use the word *joyas*, the slippage is obvious when we note that in 1776 or 1777, the missionaries at Mission San Antonio also reported that

> the priests were advised that two pagans had gone into one of the houses of the neophytes, one in his natural raiment, the other dressed as a woman. Such a person the Indians in their native language called a *joya*. Immediately the missionary, with the corporal and a soldier, went to the house to see what they were looking for, and there they found the two in an unspeakably sinful act. They punished them, although not so much as deserved. The priest tried to present to them the enormity of their deed. The pagan replied that that *joya* was his wife ... along the Channel of Santa Barbara ... many *joyas* are found.[23]

In precontact California, the linguist Leanne Hinton writes, "Over a hundred languages were spoken here, representing five or more major language families and various smaller families and linguistic isolates."[24] Adding in estimates of hundreds of different dialects, it seems clear that every California tribe would have had its own word for third-gendered people, not the generic *joya* that Spanish records give us. For example, at Mission San Diego, Father Boscana describes the biological men who dressed and lived as women or, as he put it, those who were accustomed to "marrying males with males." He writes, "Whilst yet in infancy they were selected, and instructed as they increased in years, in all the duties of the women—in their mode of dress—of walking, and dancing; so that in almost every particular, they resembled females. ... To distinguish this detested race at this mission, they were called '*Cuit*,' in the mountains, '*Uluqui*,' and in other parts, they were known by the name of '*Coias*.' "[25] *Joya*, then, is a completely new term and must have been fashioned one way or another by the Spaniards, perhaps from an indigenous word that sounded like "joyas" or as commentary on the *joyas*' fondness for women's clothing, jewelry, and hairstyles (Spanish explorers in Mexico called hummingbirds *joyas voladores*, or "flying jewels").[26] It seems doubtful that the Spaniards would retain a beautiful name like "jewel" to describe what they saw as the lowest, most bestial segment of the Indian community unless it was meant as a kind of sarcasm to enact a sense of power and superiority over the third-gendered people. James Sandos has some sense of this as well, writing that "the Spanish called them (jewels), a term that may have been derisive in Spanish culture but inadvertently conveyed the regard with which such men were held in Chumash culture."[27] By "derisive," Sandos perhaps means that the Spaniards were making fun of what they perceived to be a ridiculous and shameful status.

Another possibility for the origins of *joya* lies in a linguistic feat, the pun. For years, people have assumed that the California town La Jolla (the double *l* in Spanish is pronounced as a *y*) is simply a misspelling of *joya*. However, Nellie Van de Grift Sanchez writes: "*La Jolla*, a word of doubtful origin, said by some persons to mean a 'pool,' by others to be from *hoya*, a hollow surrounded by hills, and by still others to be a possible corruption of *joya*, a 'jewel.' The suggestion has been made that La Jolla was named from caves situated there which contain pools."[28] Yet another similar sounding Spanish word is *olla*, which means jar or vessel. What all these things have in common—a pool, a hollow, a vessel—is that each is a kind of container, a receptacle. Ethnologists and Spaniards alike agree that the *joya*'s role as a biological male living as a female meant, among many other things, *joyas* were sexually active with "normative" men as the recipients of anal sex. In fact, a *joya* would never consider having sex with another *joya*—this was not forbidden, simply unthinkable—so this may truly have been a case of "I'm not *joya* but my boyfriend is!"

All in all, the renaming of the *joyas* was not likely meant to be a compliment, but strangely enough, it does reflect the respect with which precontact California Natives regarded this gender. Perhaps, as with the word *Indian*, *joya* has strong potential for reappropriation and a new signification of value. By choosing this word and not one of their established homolexemes, this act of renaming reinforces the notion that Spanish priests and soldiers sensed something else—an indefinable gender role, a "new" class of people?—going on here, something more or different than the deviant "sodomites" of their own culture.

On an individual basis, the changing of California Indian personal names is recorded in the mission baptism records.[29] An Indian from Cajats was baptized at Mission Santa Barbara in 1819, stripped of the name Liuixucat and renamed Vitor Maria.[30] Yautaya from Chucumne, near Mission San Jose, became Robustiano in 1823.[31] In 1832 an Indian from Liuayto, near the San Francisco Mission, came in with the name Coutesi but was baptized Viador.[32] These same three people, brought into missions for baptism at ages thirty-two, thirty-three, and forty-five, respectively, had notations on their baptism records of another kind of naming: "*armafrodita o joya*," "*joya*," or "*joya o amugereado*." The padres applied Spanish words meaning "hermaphrodite" or "effeminate," as well as (in all three cases) *joya*. Vitor Maria died in 1821, just two years after baptism. Robustiano died in 1832, nine years after baptism. There is no death record for Viador, who may have been one of the many mission runaways. Interestingly, *joya* or other gender identifiers do not appear on the death records available, unlike the baptisms. Had Vitor and Robustiano learned to hide their gender, or was it simply accepted and no longer noted? It seems most likely that in the interest of survival (coming into the missions as grown adults, in this late era, usually meant starvation and/ or capture), a *joya* would at least attempt a form of assimilation such as assuming male dress and work roles. However, as Sandos comments, "If contemporary study is any guide, these berdache, especially when they entered the missions, were important links between the new, European-imposed culture and traditional Chumash ways."[33] The entrance of older *joyas*, raised to revere and preserve cultural and spiritual continuity, into California missions where Native culture was disparaged and forbidden, must have provided a powerful infusion of Native language, religion, and values that contributed to or delayed assimilation. (Indeed, on a larger scale, tremendously high death rates combined with perilously low birth rates meant a constant "restocking" of the missions with "wild" Indians captured from farther and farther away as time went on, creating a situation where the Spanish language and European farming/herding skills were not passed from one generation to the next but had to be retaught to each incoming wave. This breakdown in transference of culture actually allowed California Natives a chance to retain more indigenous culture, albeit at great personal loss.)

### Punishment, Regendering, and Shame

The Spanish priests, viewing themselves *in loco parentis*, approached the *joya*'s behaviors through the twin disciplinary actions of physical and spiritual punishment and regendering. Both of these terms are euphemisms for violence. The consequences for being a *joya*—whether dressing as a woman, doing women's work, partnering with a normative male, or actually being caught in a sexual liaison with a man—included flogging with a leather whip (braided leather typically as thick as a fist), time in the stocks, and *corma* (a kind of hobbling device that restricted movement but allowed the Indian to work). Enforced, extended rote repetition of unfamiliar prayers on knees, verbal harassment and berating, ridicule, and shaming in front of the *joya*'s community were other forms of discipline. The Ten Commandments were beaten into Indians who spoke fragmented Spanish by priests who spoke little if any Indian language, so misunderstandings were frequent and devastating. In a culture where corporal punishment was unknown, even for children, the Spaniards quickly learned that "the punishing of Indians with lashes … in the case of the old and married produces shame and sarza of mind, so that at times the victims die of chagrin and melancholy, or desert to the mountains, or, *if women, are rejected by their husbands*."[34] As *joyas* were treated like women by their tribal communities, married or partnered to "normative" men, they too would be subject to rejection by their partners or community. Father Boscana wrote that *joyas*, "being more robust than the women, were better able to perform the arduous duties required of the wife, and for this reason, they were often selected by the chiefs and others, and on the day of the wedding a grand feast was given."[35] Often, *joyas* were driven from their communities by tribal members at the instigation of the priests and made homeless; this, after a lifetime of esteem and high status, must have been a substantial blow to both physical well-being and emotional health.

In one case, Father Palóu described a group of natives visiting at Mission Santa Clara; soldiers and priests noticed that one native among the women was actually a man. Father Palóu wrote:

> Among the gentile [Indian] women (who always worked separately and without mixing with the men) there was one who, by the dress, which was decorously worn, and by the heathen headdress and ornaments displayed, as well as the manner of working, sitting, etc., had all the appearances of a woman, but judging by the face and the absence of breasts, though old enough for that, they concluded that he must be a man, but that he passed himself off always for a woman and always went with them and not the men. Taking off his aprons they found that he was more ashamed than if he really had been a woman. They kept him there three days, making him sweep the plaza, but giving him plenty to eat. But he remained very cast down and ashamed. After he had been warned that it was not right for him to go about dressed as a woman and much less thrust himself in with them, as it was presumed that he was sinning with them, they let him go. He immediately left the Mission and never came back to it, but from the converts it was learned that he was still in the villages of the gentiles and going about as before, dressed as a woman.[36]

Close reading ("thrust himself in") suggests that the priest and soldiers completely misunderstood the situation, and assumed that this man was "sinning"—that is, sneaking into the women's work area dressed as a woman to flirt or have sex with them. The idea that a man would *choose* to dress and work as a woman with other women—and that the community accepted and in fact benefited from that choice—was inconceivable to the Spaniards. Probably because of this misunderstanding, this *joya* was able to escape and find another community (at least temporarily). After a taste of regendering by the Spaniards, no doubt even unfamiliar villages looked better than remaining with one's own family and friends. At this point in the missionization process, leaving for life with the "gentiles" was still a possibility.

As time went on and escapes like the one above became less viable, *joyas* trapped in the missions or brought in as adults by raiding parties suffered from a kind of social dislocation that must have been deeply troubling for individuals accustomed to a rich but specialized community network. Precontact native Californian societies operated under a gender separation that generally kept men and women working at separate tasks, away from the opposite sex, most of the day. Women had their work areas and were accustomed to withdrawing to them to weave, harvest, process and prepare food, care for children, and so on. *Joyas* were always a part of this women's world and did not cross over into the men's territory. The mission priests, however, demanded that *joyas* spend all their time in "masculine" company, doing "masculine" work, rather than in the company of women and benefiting from the camaraderie, friendships, and sense of worth found there. Aside from the emotional shock of being cut off from friends and community, *joyas* were also faced with what, to them, was an inappropriate mixing of genders. In a culture where work and play were gendered activities (although not necessarily gendered as the Spanish would think of them), being forcibly placed in the "wrong" group would have been both extremely uncomfortable and unfamiliar for *joyas*. Remember that Father Palóu remarked of the *joya* found in his mission, "Taking off his aprons they found that he was more ashamed than if he really had been a woman." In a kind of involuntary gender-reassignment, *joyas* were made to dress as men, act as men, and consort with men in contexts for which they had little if any experience. For the "normative" men, having a *joya* among them all day and night—let alone someone stripped of appropriate clothing, status, and respect—must have also been disturbing and a further disruption of cultural signification. Women, too, would have noticed and missed the presence of *joyas* within that smaller, interdependent feminine community.

As a consequence of this regendering, renaming, and murder, one of the *joya*'s most important responsibilities, on which the well-being of the tribe depended, was completely disrupted; prohibited by the priests, the complex and deeply spiritual position of undertaker became a masterful example of colonization by appropriation.

### Replacement

Most research on the indigenous third gender agrees that a person living this role had particular responsibilities to the community, especially ceremonial and religious events and tasks.[37] In California, death, burial, and mourning rituals were the exclusive province of the *joyas*; they were the undertakers of their communities. As the only members of California Indian communities who possessed the necessary training to touch the dead or handle burials without endangering themselves or the community, the absence of *joyas* in California Indian communities must have constituted a tremendously disturbing crisis.[38] As Sandra E. Hollimon states, "Perhaps most profoundly, the institution of Catholic burial programs and designated mission cemeteries would have usurped the traditional responsibilities of the *ʾaqi* [Ventureno Chumash word for *joya*]. The imposition of Catholic practices in combination with a tremendously high death rate among mission populations would undoubtedly have contributed to the disintegration for the guild."[39] It is hard to overstate the chaos and panic the loss of their undertakers must have produced for indigenous Californians. The journey to the afterlife was known to be a prescribed series of experiences with both male and female supernatural entities, and the *ʾaqi*, with their male-female liminality, were the only people who could mediate these experiences. Since the female (earth, abundance, fertility) energies were so powerful, and since the male (Sun, death-associated) energies were equally strong, the person who dealt with that moment of spiritual and bodily crossing over between life and death must have specially endowed spiritual qualities and powers, not to mention long-term training and their own quarantined tools. Baskets used to scoop up the earth of a grave, for example, were given to the *ʾaqi* by the deceased person's relatives as partial payment for burial services, but also because they could never again be used for the life-giving acts of cooking or gathering.[40]

The threshold of death was the realm of the *ʾaqi*, and no California Indian community was safe or complete without that mediator. Asserting that undertakers were exclusively *ʾaqi* or postmenopausal women (also called *ʾaqi*), Hollimon speculates that perhaps "the mediation between death and the afterlife, and between human and supernatural realms, was entrusted by the Chumash to individuals who could not be harmed by symbolic pollution of the corpse, and who were no longer (or never had been) capable of giving birth."[41] Hollimon's archaeological work allows us to understand that the "third gender" status of *joyas* may have been extended, in some fashion, to postmenopausal women as well, should they desire to pursue a career as undertaker. Another strong possibility is that elderly women stepped into the role of undertaker when persecution reduced the availability of *joyas*.

With the loss of the *ʾaqi*, then, came an instant and urgent need for some kind of spiritual protection and ritualization of death. This would have suited the Roman Catholic Church, which had more than enough ritual available—and priests were anxious to institute new rituals to replace what they regarded as pagan practices. While founding the San Francisco Mission, Fray Palóu wrote, "Those who die as pagans, they cremate; nor have we been able to stop this," indicating that burial—as tribes farther south practiced—was the only mortuary practice considered civilized.[42] At these same cremations, in reference to funeral rituals, Palóu noted that "there are some old women who repeatedly strike their breast with a stone ... they grieve much and yell quite a bit."[43] It would have been difficult to tell an elderly *joya* dressed as a woman from an elderly woman, if one did not know of the connection between *joyas* and the death ceremony; in fact, years later, when Harrington interviewed Maria Solares, a Chumash survivor of

Mission Santa Ynez (and one of his major consultants), she told him that all undertakers ("aqi") were women, strong enough to carry bodies and dig deep graves, and that the role was passed from mother to daughter.[44] Harrington pointed out that the Ineseño word for *joto* was also *'aqi*, that it was strange that "women should be so strong to lift bodies," and Solares agreed, though still puzzled.[45] It seems that by the mid-1930s, the memory of *'aqi* as beloved members of the community no longer matched Solares's cultural understanding of *joto*—the long-term damage of homophobia was substantial even in linguistic terms, let alone human terms. It is not hard for me to imagine my ancestors, fearing for their spiritual well-being, their loved ones, and what remained of their communities, turning to Catholicism out of desperation. As the diseases and violence of colonization took their toll, communities were under intense pressure about the many burials or cremations to be carried out. The turn to, and dependence on, Catholic burial rituals was a form of coerced conversion that had nothing to do with Christianity, and everything to do with fear.

Through these methods, then—murder, renaming, regendering, and replacement—the *joya* gendercide was carried out. The destruction seems to cover every aspect of *joya* identity and survival. Yet, I argue, *joya* identity did not disappear entirely.

## SURVIVING GENDERCIDE

How could *joyas* survive such devastation? Where are they? What is their role in contemporary California Indian life?

First, it is important to note that mission records show baptisms of adult *joyas* as late as 1832, almost sixty years after Fages expressed his outrage in 1775. "Late arrivals" to the mission—adult Indians who, having lived most of their lives as "wild" Indians, were rounded up and brought in for forced baptism—actually slowed the missionization process considerably. In combination with the low life expectancy of mission-born children (two to seven years), a strong influx of adult indigenous cultural practices probably also kept the role of *joya* from fading away as quickly as might otherwise be expected (allowing younger Indians to witness or know *joyas*, as well as pass on that information orally to future generations).[46]

Second, just as the extermination of California Indians, while extensive, has been exaggerated as complete, so too is the idea that *joyas* could be gendercided out of existence. A *joya*'s conception does not depend on having a *joya* parent, unlike normative male and female sexes, who depend on both male and female for conception; as long as enough of the normative population remains alive and able to bear children, the potential for *joya* gender to emerge in some of those children also remains. To exterminate *joyas* entirely, *all* California Indian people would have had to be killed, down to the very last; thus it makes sense that during missionization and postsecularization, as in the past, *joyas* rose out of the general population spontaneously and regularly. However, those *joya* had virtually no choice but to hide their gender. Like Pueblo tribes who took their outlawed religious ceremonies underground until it was safe to practice more openly (although outsiders are understandably rarely allowed to partake or witness the ceremonies), *joyas* in California may have taken a similar tactic, removing themselves from ceremonial roles with religious connotations and hiding out in the general population. Sadly, the traditional blend of spiritual and sexual energy that was a source of *joya* empowerment suffered an abrupt division; as time passed and the few surviving elder *joyas* passed on, younger *joyas* would have been forced to function without role models, teachers, spiritual advisers, or even—eventually—oral stories of their predecessors. Walter Williams reports that he "could not find any traces of a *joya* gender in oral traditions among contemporary California Indians from missionized tribes," but adds, "that does not mean that a recognized and respected status for berdache no longer existed, or that same-sex behavior vanished. To find evidence of such continuity is extremely difficult."[47]

[...]

## RECONSTRUCTING A SPIRITUAL, COMMUNITY-ORIENTED ROLE FOR TWO-SPIRIT PEOPLE

In conclusion, I suggest that contemporary California Two-Spirits are the rightful descendents of *joyas*.[72] Two-Spirit people did not cease to exist, they did not cease to be born, simply because the Spaniards killed our *joya* ancestors. This, in fact, is a crucial point: the words *gay* or *lesbian* do not fully define a Two-Spirited person, because those labels are based on an almost exclusively sexual paradigm inherited from a nonindigenous colonizing culture. The Chumash *'aqi*, or *joyas*, fulfilled important roles as spiritual community leaders, so although genocide and gendercide worked to erase their bodies, neither their spirits nor the indigenous community's spiritual needs could be murdered. This is what comes down to us as Two-Spirit people: the necessity of our roles as keepers of a dual or blended gender that holds male and female energy in various mixtures and keeps the world balanced. Although Two-Spirit people often had children in the past, and continue to do so in the present, and will into the future, we do not expect or train our children to follow in our footsteps. A Two-Spirit person is born regardless of biological genealogy. Thus we will always be with you. We *are* you. We are not outsiders, some other community that can be wiped out. We come from you, and we return to you.

Simply identifying as both Indian and gay does not make a person Two-Spirit, although it can be a courageous and important step; the danger of that assumption elides Two-Spirit responsibilities as well as the social and cultural needs of contemporary indigenous communities in relation to such issues as suicide rates, alcoholism, homelessness, and AIDS. What steps can we take to reconstruct our role in the larger indigenous community? I look back at this research on my family and find guidance, examples, strategies, and lessons that converge around six key actions:

1   reclaim a name for ourselves;
2   reclaim a place for ourselves within our tribal communities (which means serious education and presence to counteract centuries of homophobia—a literary presence, a practical presence, and a working presence);
3   resist violence against ourselves as individuals and as a community within Native America;
4   work to determine what our roles as liminal beings might be in contemporary Native and national contexts;
5   work to reclaim our histories from the colonizer's records even as we continue to know and adapt our lives to contemporary circumstances and needs; and
6   create loving, supportive, celebratory community that can work to heal the wounds inflicted by shame, internalized hatred, and fear, dealing with the legacy that, as the Chickasaw poet Linda Hogan says, "history is our illness."[73]

With the adoption of the name "Two Spirit," we have already begun the work of our lifetimes. As Sue-Ellen Jacobs, Wesley Thomas, and Sabine Lang write, "Using the word 'Two-Spirit' emphasizes the spiritual aspect of one's life and downplays the homosexual persona."[74] Significantly, this move announces and enhances the Two-Spirit need for traditionally centered lives with the community's well-being at the center. Still, we face a great problem: the lack of knowledge or spiritual training for GLBTQ Native people, particularly the mystery of blending spiritual and sexual energies to manage death/rebirth. In traditional times, there would have been older *joyas* to guide inexperienced ones; there would have been ceremony, role modeling, community support, and, most importantly, there would have been a clear role waiting to be filled.

The name Two-Spirit, then, is a way to alert others, and remind ourselves, that we have a cultural and historical responsibility to the larger community: our work is to attend to a balance of energies. We are still learning what this means; there has been no one to teach us but ourselves, our research, our stories, and our hearts. Maybe this will be the generation to figure it out. Maybe this will be the generation to reclaim our inheritance within our communities. And if it is not, I take heart from the history of the *joyas*, the impossibility of their true gendercide, and the deep, passionate, mutual need for relationship between Two Spirits and our communities.

## NOTES

1. Paula Gunn Allen, "I Don't Speak the Language That Has the Sentences: An Interview with Paula Gunn Allen," *Sojourner: The Women's Forum* 24, no. 2 (1999): 26–27.
2. Paula Gunn Allen, "Some Like Indians Endure," in *Living the Spirit* (New York: St. Martin's, 1988), 9–13.
3. Elaine Mills, ed., *The Papers of John Peabody Harrington in the Smithsonian Institution, 1907–1957*, microfilm (White Plains, NY: Kraus International, 1981).
4. *Salvage ethnology* is a term coined by Jacob Gruber to refer to the paradoxical obsession of Westerners to collect artifacts, linguistic traces, and cultural knowledge of cultures that they had previously spent much effort to colonize or exterminate. Rather than basic ethnological research, the study of a culture, "salvage ethnology" was concerned with an almost fanatic search (and often the hoarding of) any remains of a colonized culture. See Jacob Gruber, "Ethnographic Salvage and the Shaping of Anthropology," *American Anthropologist*, n.s., 72 (1970): 1289–99.
5. I use this name as it was coined during the Third International Two Spirit Gathering, to provide a positive alternative to the unacceptable term *berdache*: Two-Spirit people are "Aboriginal people who possess the sacred gifts of the female-male spirit, which exists in harmony with those of the female and the male. They have traditional respected roles within most Aboriginal cultures and societies and are contributing members of the community. Today, some Aboriginal people who are Two-Spirit also identify as being gay, lesbian, bisexual or transgender" ("Background and Recent Developments in Two-Spirit Organizing," International Two Spirit Gathering, http://www.intltwospiritgathering.org/content/view/27/42/ [accessed July 28, 2009]).
6. The archaeology of sexuality refers to a fairly recent movement within archaeology that brings together theoretical work from gender and women's studies, science studies, philosophy, and the social sciences on sex and gender to study material remains and to approach questions often considered accessible only through texts or direct observation of behavior, such as gender or multiple genders. An excellent collection of articles on this topic is Robert Schmidt and Barbara Voss, eds., *Archaeologies of Sexuality* (London: Routledge, 2000).
7. My use of the term *third gender* relies on and refers back to work done by Will Roscoe, Sabine Lang, Wesley Thomas, Bea Medicine, and others as a way to identify a gender that is neither fully male nor fully female, nor (more importantly) simply "half and half," but a unique blend of characteristics resulting in a third or other gender. See Sue Ellen Jacobs, Wesley Thomas, and Sabine Lang, eds., *Two-Spirit People: Native American Gender Identity, Sexuality, and Spirituality* (Urbana: University of Illinois Press, 1997). As Brian Gilley summarizes, "The institution of the third gender [in Native American precontact societies] was less about an individual's sexuality and more about the ways their special qualities were incorporated into the social and religious life of their community" (*Becoming Two-Spirit: Gay Identity and Social Acceptance in Indian Country* [Lincoln: University of Nebraska Press, 2006], 11).
8. Father Gerónimo Boscana, a Franciscan priest who kept extensive notes about Native culture and customs during his stay at Mission San Juan Capistrano from 1812 until 1826, wrote that the "Indians of California may be compared to a species of monkey" ("Chinigchinich," in Alfred Robinson, *Life in California: During a Residence of Several Years in That Territory, Comprising a Description of the Country and the Missionary Establishments*, ed. Doyce B. Nunis Jr. [New York: Wiley and Putnam, 1846], 335). Postsecularization, perceptions had not changed much; in 1849 Samuel Upham commented on California Indian genealogy and eating habits: "Like his brother, the gorilla, he is a vegetarian and subsists principally on wild berries and acorns, occasionally luxuriating on snails and grasshoppers" (*Notes of a Voyage to California Via Cape Horn, Together with Scenes in El Dorado, in the Years 1849–50* [New York: Arno, 1973], 240). This attitude persisted when John Audubon wrote in his journal of a Miwok child "eating [acorns] with the judgment of a monkey, and looking very much like one." Although the journal covers the years 1840–1850, it was published in 1906, perpetuating the distorted view of California Indians into the twentieth century (John Audubon, *Audubon's Western Journal: 1840–1850*, ed. Frank Heywood Hodder [Cleveland: Clark, 1906], 213).
9. Although most scholars still use the population estimates by Martin Baumhoff (*Ecological Determinants of Aboriginal California Populations* [Berkeley: University of California Press, 1963]) and Sherburne Cook (*The Population of the California Indians, 1796–1970* [Berkeley: University of California Press, 1976]), many contemporary scholars view their numbers (150,000–350,000) as greatly outdated. In *American Indian Holocaust and Survival: A Population History since 1492* (Norman: University of Oklahoma Press, 1987), Russell Thornton, for example, writes that California Indian precontact population was "approaching 705,000" (200). In private correspondence with the author about more current population data, William Preston writes that "at this point I think Thornton's high number is totally reasonable. In fact, keeping in mind that populations no doubt fluctuated over time, I'm thinking that at times one million or more Native Californians were resident in that state." William Preston, e-mail message to author, July 8, 2009.
10. Pedro Fages, *A Historical, Political, and Natural Description of California by Pedro Fages, Soldier of Spain*, trans. Herbert Priestley (Berkeley: University of California Press, 1937), 33.

11. Stanley Coren, *The Pawprints of History: Dogs and the Course of Human Events* (New York: Free Press, 2003), 67–80.

12. Coren, *Pawprints of History*, 76.

13. Coren, *Pawprints of History*, 72–73.

14. Coren, *Pawprints of History*, 74.

15. Peter Martyr d'Anghera, "The Third English Book on America" [*De Orbe Novo*], trans. Richard Eden, in *The First Three English Books on America: [?1511]–1555 A.D.*, ed. Edward Arber (Birmingham, 1885), 138.

16. Coren, *Pawprints of History*, 76.

17. Maureen Heibert, " 'Too Many Cides' to Genocide Studies? Review of Jones, Adam, ed. Gendercide and Genocide," H-Genocide, H-Net Reviews, www.h-net.org/reviews/showrev.php?id=10878 (accessed December 17, 2008); emphasis added.

18. D'Anghera, "Third English Book on America," 138.

19. Herbert E. Bolton, trans. and ed., *Fray Juan Crespi: Missionary Explorer on the Pacific Coast* (Berkeley: University of California Press, 1927), 171.

20. Stephen Greenblatt, *Marvelous Possessions: The Wonder of the New World* (Chicago: University of Chicago Press, 1991), 83.

21. Wayne Dynes, "Gay Spanish," Homolexis, December 25, 2006, homolexis.blogspot.com/2006_12_01_archive.html.

22. Fages, *Historical, Political, and Natural Description of California*, 59.

23. Francisco Palóu, *Palóu's Life of Fray Junipero Serra*, ed. and trans. Maynard J. Geiger (Washington, DC: American Academy of Franciscan History, 1955), 33.

24. Leanne Hinton, *Flutes of Fire: Essays on California Indian Languages* (Berkeley: Heyday, 1994), 13.

25. Boscana, "Chinigchinich," 284.

26. Connie M. Toops, *Hummingbirds: Jewels in Flight* (Stillwater, MN: Voyageur, 1992), 15.

27. James Sandos, "Christianization among the Chumash: An Ethnohistoric Perspective," *American Indian Quarterly* 15 (1991): 71.

28. Nellie Van de Grift Sanchez, *Spanish and Indian Place Names of California: Their Meaning and Their Romance* (San Francisco: Robertson, 1914), 44.

29. Huntington Library, "Early California Population Project Database, 2006" (ECPPD), www.huntington.org/Information/ECPPmain.htm (accessed September 30, 2007).

30. ECPPD, Santa Barbara, Baptismal #04128.

31. ECPPD, San Jose, Baptism #04733.

32. ECPPD, San Francisco Solano, Baptism #00977.

33. Sandos, "Christianization among the Chumash," 71.

34. Irving Berdine Richman, *California under Spain and Mexico, 1535–1847* (Whitefish, MT: Kessinger, 2007), 442; emphasis added.

35. Boscana, "Chinigchinich," 245.

36. Palóu, *Palóu's Life of Fray Junipero Serra*, 214–15.

37. For a general survey, see Jacobs, Thomas, and Lang, *Two-Spirit People*; and Will Roscoe, *Changing Ones: Third and Fourth Genders in Native North America* (New York: St. Martin's, 1998).

38. J. Alden Mason writes, "That the mention of the dead was as serious an offence among the Salinans as with other Californian Indians is well illustrated by the incident that when asked jocularly for a Salinan word of profanity, Pedro Encinales gave ca MteL and translated it 'go to the devil' (ve al diablo). [Father] Sitjar writes chavmtel 'cadaver.' " Sitjar, who compiled a useful list of Salinan words and phrases, knew enough of the Indian language to make his own translation, which apparently Pedro Encinales, the indigenous speaker, wasn't comfortable speaking (J. Alden Mason, *The Ethnology of the Salinan Indians* [Whitefish, MT: Kessinger, 2006], 167).

39. Sandra E. Hollimon, "Archaeology of the 'Aqi: Gender and Sexuality in Prehistoric Chumash Society," in *Archaeologies of Sexuality*, ed. Robert Schmidt and Barbara Voss (New York: Routledge, 2000), 193.

40. Holliman, "Archaeology of the 'Aqi," 192.

41. Holliman, "Archaeology of the 'Aqi," 182.

42. Palóu, *Palóu's Life of Fray Junipero Serra*, 193.

43. Palóu, *Palóu's Life of Fray Junipero Serra*, 445.

44. Linda B. King, *The Medea Creek Cemetery (CA-LAN-243): An Investigation of Social Organization from Mortuary Practices*, UCLA Archaeological Survey Annual Report, no. 11 (Los Angeles: University of California Press, 1969), 47. I call Solares a "consultant" here rather than use the traditional ethnological term *informant* out of respect for all Native peoples who have retained and chosen to share their cultural knowledge and expertise; my purpose is to acknowledge that Indigenous knowledge puts Native consultants on an equal intellectual level with scientists and academics.

45. Hollimon suggests that "daughters" of male-bodied 'aqi were probably fictive kinships (such as adoption) formed with other members of the same guild or role or premenopausal children of women who took up the 'aqi role late in life, and when colonization had created a shortage in the usual mortuary profession (Holliman, "Archaeology of the 'Aqi," 185).

46. For information about the life expectancy of mission-born children, see Robert H. Jackson and Edward Castillo, *Indians, Franciscans, and Spanish Colonization: The Impact of the Mission System on California Indians* (Albuquerque: University of New Mexico Press, 1995), 53–56.

47. Walter L. Williams, "The Abominable Sin: The Spanish Campaign against 'Sodomy,' and the Results in Modern Latin America," in *The Spirit and the Flesh* (Boston: Beacon, 1992), 129.

[…]

72. Other indigenous peoples around the world attributed special powers and rights to Two-Spirits within their tribes; although they were not always the mediators between life and death, similar patterns may be found. Because of the limitations of this essay, I leave that to future scholars and seekers.

73. Linda Hogan, *The Woman Who Watches Over the World: A Native Memoir* (New York: Norton, 2001), 59.

74. Jacobs, Thomas, and Lang, *Two-Spirit People*, 3.

# 29

# *Before Transgender*

## *Transvestia's* Spectrum of Gender Variance, 1960–1980

### Robert Hill

Robert Hill is an American Studies scholar who earned his Ph.D. from the University of Michigan. His dissertation offered the first full-length history of the heterosexual male cross-dressing community in the U.S.A. In this article, Hill lays out the complex taxonomy of identity terms that developed over the course of twenty years, 1960–1980, in the pages of *Transvestia* magazine, the most significant and widely-read publication in this community. Hill's recovery of this terminological evolution is important not only for the window it offers us on U.S. gender ideology during the Cold War era, but for the ways in which the hair-splitting debates about gender presentation and identification within this community during these years shaped the connotations and contours of the term *transgender*—prototypical forms of which first emerged in this context. As Hill explains, *transgender* was first used to distinguish heterosexual male cross-dressers who lived as women full-time from transsexuals who surgically and hormonally altered their male bodies. Although he claims that this earlier meaning was "lost" by the 1980s, thereby making the term available for creative adaptation and reuse by a new generation of gender-variant persons in the 1990s, important continuities between earlier and later usages of transgender remained. Most important, the term continued to be a self-applied label that promoted a socially affirming identity, designed to counter public and professional discourses that depicted a wide range of gender-variant phenomena as pathological, perverse, or criminal.

*Transvestia* is here for those whose development has taken them to the point of FemmePersonation, which differs from simple transvestism in much the same way as being a champion Olympic swimmer differs from the person who simply puts on a bathing suit and gets in the pool.[1]

In 2001, I came across a near complete run of the underground magazine *Transvestia* in a vast collection of transgender-related periodicals and ephemera that Dallas Denny had recently bestowed on the University of Michigan's Special Collections Library.[2] *Transvestia* was edited and published from 1960 to 1980 by Virginia Prince, a white, heterosexual, male-to-female (MTF) cross-dresser from Los Angeles.[3] Published bi-monthly and averaging around eighty pages per issue, the magazine sought to entertain, educate, and instruct MTF cross-dressers, or heterosexual transvestites, to use the lingo of the time.[4] More broadly, it promoted a socially affirming identity script designed to counter public discourses that depicted transvestism as sinful, pathological, and criminal. The magazine went from twenty-five initial subscribers to several hundred across the U.S.A. and dozens in Canada, England,

and Australia over the twenty years of Prince's editorship.[5] In addition to her editorial column, "Virgin Views," Prince published around 120 life histories and 300 letters to the editor from readers of the magazine. In these letters and histories, writers profoundly engaged questions of identity, desire, and embodiment, all within the context of Cold War gender roles, sexual norms, and domestic ideals.

With most of the content comprising testimonials, editorials, and also self-portraits, the pages of *Transvestia* document an era when "trans" identities, practices, and modes of personhood were created and contested by a variety of gender variant individuals and groups, many of whom would help shape and fill the category of "transgender" in the 1990s. Most of the narratives in *Transvestia* came from persons who called themselves "TVs," short for transvestites. But not all fit comfortably within this category. For example, one interesting narrative came from Prince's part-time assistant, Mary, an MTF transvestite with a strong sense of cross-gender identification. Mary handled secretarial tasks at Prince's Chevalier Publications, and sometimes answered letters and counseled *Transvestia*'s readers during Prince's extended public relations trips. Mary had been working for Prince for two years when she wrote her life history for *Transvestia* in 1969. What we learn from her history is that after her mother died in 1966, Mary began to think seriously about sex reassignment surgery (SRS). In preparation, she underwent electrolysis and began taking hormones to induce feminine characteristics. During this time, Prince and Mary frequently argued about the benefits of SRS. Mary desired surgery because she felt that the results of the operation would make her a "real" woman subjectively and also in the eyes of society. However, she eventually arrived at Prince's belief that gender identity, behavior, and presentation need not conform to sexual anatomy. What she really wanted, then, was a "change of gender" rather than a sex change. Consequently, in late 1967, Mary decided to begin living her life both privately and socially in the feminine gender role, without surgical alteration.

In her history, Mary underscored the fact that this decision was not made on a whim. She emphasized that transitioning from a life of periodically and privately cross-dressing to living as a woman on a "full-time" basis involved several sacrifices:

> You don't just decide to take this step. I had a good job with a secure future. This would have to be given up. I knew I would have to live on savings for at least a year while going to school and getting established. You think awhile before you give up a job that you like, with people who like and respect you. You know that you will have to move from a house you have lived in for a number of years. Then there are many of the friends you had whom you will never hear from again, because you know that they would not accept your new ways of life.

Mary stressed that many aspects of feminine living—the "femme-life" idealized by most of the magazine's readership—take on less glamorous meanings when conducted out of necessity and when taken from the framework of fantasy to the reality of actually living the everyday life of a woman. Cultivating a passable feminine appearance becomes more of a chore and less of an act of pleasure and leisure. Mary further reflected on her transition, saying that she was happy that she did not follow through with the surgery.

> Eventually I realized that I was not a transsexual and that surgery was not for me. Life today is better than I had ever dreamed it could be. I have achieved my original goal to be a woman, but I have done it by my own efforts and not just from the necessity following an irreversible act of surgery.

Mary's statement reflected the belief that she could become a "legitimate" woman without extensive bodily alterations, especially surgical castration. The validity of her self-definition rested on a crucial distinction she made between anatomical sex and subjective gender identity.[6]

Mary's narrative illustrates the identity work characteristic of a person in the "male-woman" or "transgenderist" category, one of several gendered designations represented in Prince's magazine. In this essay, I explore the range of identities that *Transvestia*'s history and letter writers fashioned along the magazine's spectrum of gender variance in the years between 1960 and 1980. I observe how they variously embraced, negotiated, complicated, and destabilized the category of heterosexual transvestism and the narrow identity script promoted by the magazine. I then discuss the hierarchy of designations that resulted, as *Transvestia*'s writers engaged in a relentless and oftentimes vicious politics of respectability when classifying and differentiating types of (trans) gender embodiments, practices, and identities.

The identity formation and contestation that took place within *Transvestia* can be situated within a taxonomic revolution that occurred in the decades following the Second World War. During this formative era of transgender history, doctors, sexologists, and psychologists, along with persons who identified as transsexuals, transvestites, and homosexuals began to map and sort out the overlapping subcultures of gender and sexual variance and make ontological distinctions among the categories of "sex," "gender," and "sexuality."[7] Other historians of the LGBT experience have described aspects of this taxonomic revolution, as well as the "border skirmishes" fought among gender and sexual minorities.[8] My work draws upon this important scholarship and deepens it with an account of how heterosexual transvestites, specifically those who belonged to *Transvestia*'s gender community, contributed to this taxonomic enterprise.

In the 1960s and 1970s, heterosexual transvestites like Prince and most of her readers were part of a broader social formation of gender and sexual minorities that included, among other identifications, MTF and female-to-male (FTM) transsexuals, drag queens, street queens, hair fairies, female impersonators, effeminate gays, butch lesbians, and transvestite clothing fetishists. All of these diverse groups transgressed gender norms, that is, displayed non-normative variations of the sex/gender relationship. Yet most all of them were lumped together in the public's mind under the broad category of "sexual deviancy." After the Second World War, these groups, along with gender normative gays and lesbians, sorted themselves out from the mix of gender and sexual variance. As they courted public favor, homosexuals, transvestites, and transsexuals began to develop a mutual aversion to one another, each believing that the other groups hurt their cause for public acceptance. In turn, they played a politics of respectability, intensified greatly amidst the heightened public anxiety over individuals who deviate from conventional gender roles and sexual norms. Consequently, homophobia ran rampant within transvestite and transsexual networks; transphobia characterized many gay and lesbian organizations. All sorts of infighting erupted within each group, often having to do with proper gender and sexual behavior. My analysis of the "trans" taxonomies featured in *Transvestia* and contested within the framework of respectability concludes around 1980, but cross-dressers and the constituents of other gender and sexual communities would continue to use print and media and a politics of respectability to mark and contest their identities, desires, and practices long after *Transvestia* ceased publication.

Although it is difficult to know the exact statistics of who comprised the magazine's readership of several hundred, it is difficult to believe that a magazine like *Transvestia* did not, at least initially, attract a motley group of gender-variant folk with varying styles, practices, and modes of identity. The representations of male-bodied gender diversity featured in the letters and histories that Prince published probably represented only a portion, albeit a large one, of the magazine's potentially diverse readership. Without question, thousands of individuals who cross-dressed moved in social circles and networks outside of *Transvestia*'s gender community. In fact, *Transvestia*'s readership represented only a small slice of a much broader social formation of gender and sexual minorities in the U.S.A.

Two letters that Prince published acknowledged the assortment of gender and sexual non-conformity that existed in postwar American society. The first of these letters came from Rita from New York. Rita "loved lingerie, high heels, panty hose, and pretty dresses," but had never gone out in public dressed as a woman. She represented a rare example of a self-identified "true transvestite" who acknowledged familiarity with a range of desires, interests, and practices engaged in by cross-dressers but encouraged the readership to stop disparaging those who deviate from the norms established in the magazine. Her letter read:

> It has been my pleasure in life to meet quite a few TVs [transvestites] like myself, except that most of them differ from one another in many ways such as some are gay, some like bondage and paddling, others love to be dressed in leather or rubber…. Some TVs frown on others if they stray from the straight and narrow path of just dressing like a woman. I think we should all stop and think of our strong desire to dress up in pretty finery and stop censoring others who have desires just as strong for other things while enjoying the art of being a TV at the same time.[9]

Given the many admonishments directed toward non-respectable forms of cross-dressing and the ridicule and scorn exhibited by other writers towards homosexuals and fetishists, Rita's tolerance for and defense of these identities and practices is striking. Rita's letter was published in 1960, along with the following one from Dorothea:

> There are degrees and variations among TVs just like in any other group. This applies to intelligence, knowledge, intensity of TV drives, frequency of desires to dress and the extent of dressing. By this I mean some of us are content in dressing periodically, some want to do it more frequently and some want to do it all the time. Some are content with only hosiery and lingerie; others must be complete as to dress, makeup, figure, voice, mannerisms, etc.[10]

As Dorothea astutely recognized, transvestism was not a monolithic social category in the 1950s and early 1960s. She upheld that many variations existed among male-bodied individuals who enjoy cross-dressing. Most notably, Dorothea did not assign value or rank to the variations she listed. Rita and Dorothea's acceptance of the diversity of styles and practices associated with cross-dressing were rare articulations in the pages of *Transvestia*, and it is not surprising that both letters were written and published in 1960, when the push towards respectability and promotion of a narrow identity script had not yet gained force. The following years would typically see Prince and most of *Transvestia*'s writers struggle to tame the multiplicity and censure the more ostensibly erotic strands of cross-dressing that Rita and Dorothea delighted in.

Prince conceptualized *Transvestia* as a tool that would help advance the cause of a particular breed of transvestite—heterosexual men who cultivate and periodically express de-eroticized and respectable renditions of femininity. She wanted to disassociate heterosexual transvestism from forms of deviant sexuality that doctors and the public associated with cross-dressing, particularly homosexuality. Tiring of the widespread usage of "transvestite" as a reference for a variety of gender and erotic minorities, Prince began to invent new terms to describe heterosexual males who enjoy expressing femininity through the act of cross-dressing. In early 1961, she coined the term "feminiphilia," which she defined as "a condition in which an anatomically and physiologically normal male who is heterosexually oriented feels driven to partake of all things feminine as an expression of his inner personality needs."[11] Prince contended that every feminiphile (one who had the condition of feminiphilia) harbored a feminine personality needing and deserving outward expression. She also invented a more frequently used term, "femmepersonation," to better capture what true transvestites do when they don the clothing of women and behave effeminately. Femmepersonators were not *impersonating*—a word with a prefix that denoted fraud and falsity. Rather, they were *personating*—giving life to the feminine side of their personalities.[12]

Susanna Valenti, the fashion and gossip columnist for *Transvestia*, popularized a term to describe this buried feminine personality: the "girl-within." A transvestite who adhered to the tenets of femmepersonation cultivated a second personality—a feminine persona—to express his desire to look and act the part of a woman. In a manner that preserved the gender dichotomies of the postwar era, femmepersonators separated the feminine persona from the masculine self. In many of their minds, mixing the two would "make an unholy mess out of things." Because the girl-within was less formed than the masculine self, it needed to be developed through practice in behaving like a "true lady," with all of the class and racial markers Prince, Valenti, and other femmepersonators associated with the term. Within this new lexicon of meaning, transvestism was reformulated from a sexual fetish into an affirmative mode of identity.

Even though many did not adopt Prince's terminologies, *Transvestia*'s letter and history writers made a home within the ideological parameters of femmepersonation. In their narratives, they described how they strove to achieve their ideal of feminine authenticity by self-regulating their behaviors, honing their skills, and assiduously monitoring the progress of their "femme-selves." These narratives documented improvement, evolution, and transformation. "I admire the qualities that women possess," remarked Nancy, "and hope that I'm expressing some of them now and will express more as I acquire more insight. I've taken a certain pride in Nancy and have done my best to perfect her makeup, dress, and mannerisms and to make her as authentic as possible."[13] As Nancy indicates with her use of the third person, femmepersonators wrote as if the feminine personas they cultivated represented completely different beings with unique personalities of their own. Jean, who practiced cross-dressing with "great care and utmost discretion," maintained that she felt great happiness in living two lives but much preferred her femme-self. Like many other writers, she described the differences between her masculine and feminine personas. "My male nature is quiet and reserved, mild-natured and of even temperament. The Girl is cheerful and fun-loving, though not overly demonstrative. She is a Lady at all times." As for managing her two personalities:

> My open public disclosures are decidedly male and incur no indication of the existence of another [feminine] "self". My private life centers about the female personality within me that is the more natural existence. To experience the transference into the feminine world is exhilarating and inspiring beyond words. I become a whole being and live life to its fullest, which contrasts to my otherwise average existence.[14]

Jean captured the duality that lies at the core of *Transvestia*'s gender community—a much stated desire to live the best of both gendered worlds, but also a strong feeling that life as a woman far surpasses the mundane existence of life as a man. Bobbie also touched on this sentiment:

> I feel strongly that a TV needs to give expression to the woman inside the male body. ... As a man I was typical—acceptable—reasonable—personable—an average conservative scientist and business man. But as a woman I seemed to catch fire and really come alive with a sparkle in my eyes and a vivacity that truly expressed the being within. A woman has so much more opportunity than a man to express her feelings and personality in clothes, make-up, mannerisms, and all the little nuances that mean so much. I can sum it up by saying: As a man I exist; as a woman I live.[15]

Jean, Bobbie, and other writers, many of whom were husbands and fathers, reveled in the freedom, frivolity, and feelings of self-actualization that cross-dressing engendered. In many ways, the practice of femmepersonation helped transvestites with wives and families to navigate the treacherous paths produced by the confluence of transvestism and domesticity in "John Wayne's America." Early on, Prince saw a danger lurking and counseled her readers accordingly:

> Try to employ perspective in seeing FemmePersonation as an adjunct to your masculine personality, not a substitute for it. We were all born male, trained in masculinity, and have acquired most of our experience in that role. Thus we are expected by society and by our loved ones to function adequately in that role. *Transvestia* does not exist for the purpose of impairing or destroying the masculine but rather to allow those who are aware of their feminine side to extract the full benefits from it. We can experience some of the feminine side of life, express part of our personality that way, and be better persons and citizens for it IF we utilize and express our desires with WISDOM; in MODERATION; and apply PERSPECTIVE to keep the whole matter in balance and under control.[16]

What Prince's advice indicates is that the constituents of *Transvestia*'s gender community, particularly the husbands and fathers, wanted to normalize transvestism—contain its most abnormal elements and make it fit comfortably within the cultural narratives of gender, home, and national belonging that circulated with ferocity in the postwar era. The fear of becoming stigmatized as sexually deviant greatly structured the ideology, practices, and aesthetics of this gender community. In response to Cold War gender strictures, Prince and the *Transvestia* readership developed a social script to justify their practices and dignify their identities. To further manage the stigma, they created dress codes and conduct guidelines and downplayed the erotic aspects of transvestism. They purported that their respectable looks outwardly reflected inner virtue. Engaging in a politics of respectability, they contended that the desire to dress as "ladies" and express such traits as grace, beauty, and gentleness safely distinguished them from the true sexual deviants that loomed large in the Cold War cultural imaginary.[17]

Nevertheless, as some of the testimonials above indicate, a fair number of *Transvestia*'s writers experienced a sense of cross-gender identification, a profound sense of being or wanting to become the other gender than the one assigned at birth, which only complicated attempts to balance dual personalities. Cross-gender identification could yield a life of periodic cross-dressing, a life of permanent living as the gender of one's choice, or a quest for bodily change to match one's perceived gender identity. While cross-gender identification and transvestism are technically separate phenomena, self-identified transvestites did, in fact, experience these intense longings associated with wanting to be the gender opposite the one assigned at birth. Several of *Transvestia*'s writers pushed their self-definitions beyond the established tenets of femmepersonation in terms of the frequency and intensity of their desires to cross-dress. With respect to intensity, consider this excerpt from Georgette's history:

> In addition to the love of the clothes, there is a deep, deep desire to be a girl, and a deep, deep feeling that I should be a girl. … I think feminine thoughts, can act like a woman with the greatest of ease, and use feminine expressions in preference to typically male ones. … I would love to be a girl in every minute physical detail. As I am one in mind and—who knows? In spirit.[18]

Georgette titled her life history "I Am a Transvestite," but her articulation of identity suggested a mode of being more along the lines of transsexuality than the form of transvestism advocated by Prince in the early 1960s. Georgette probably held a broader definition of transvestism, but that is beside the point. Georgette's "deep, deep desire" to be a woman "in every minute physical detail" destabilized the category of heterosexual transvestism.

The same could be said for Eleanor from Connecticut, who wrote that "all my life I have wanted to be a woman, to live and dress as a woman, to take my place in life and take the secondary role of a woman which I honestly feel I can fulfill. I am inadequate as a male."[19] Eleanor's articulation of identity, particularly her declaration: "I am inadequate as a male," indicated a mode of cross-gender expression more befitting of what was becoming the prevailing narrative of transsexuality. Wanting permanently to take the "secondary role" of a woman distinguished her from femmepersonators, who typically desired periodic feminine expression and wanted the best of both gendered worlds. Although Eleanor expressed no stated desire or plan for a sex change operation, she seemed to want to *be* a woman. Interestingly, despite the availability of the term, Georgette and Eleanor did not identify as transsexual. In fact, only a few of *Transvestia*'s letter and history writers self-identified using the classification "transsexual."[20]

Several other writers did, however, describe how, at various points in their lives, they had flirted with the idea of requesting sex-reassignment surgery. Myrtle Ann from Oklahoma described how she had longed to be transformed into a woman, even before Christine Jorgenson became a media sensation in 1953. In more recent years, Myrtle Ann sought out a surgeon but was turned down as a candidate for SRS, she claims, because she was married with children and too old. A psychiatrist advised Myrtle Ann to partially satisfy her yearnings by beginning a life of periodic feminine expression. For three years, she shopped, dined, and traveled *en femme*, and she took charm and sewing classes. Myrtle Ann's new life as a "part-time woman" seemed to alleviate the stress that had plagued her former years as a closeted transsexual. When the opportunity for surgery became available to her, she decided against it. At the time of her writing, Myrtle Ann enjoyed being a woman almost all the time except when working.[21]

Myrtle Ann probably represented scores of other readers of *Transvestia* who, if life circumstances had permitted, would have requested SRS. Instead, depending on their individual situations, they settled for a life of periodic feminine expression and, for a few, full-time living as a woman without surgical alteration. In later years, and as I will detail later in this essay, the categories of "transgenderist" and "male-woman" would emerge as options for Eleanor and Myrtle Ann and others, some desirous of SRS, others not, but all expressing a belief that socially and psychologically they *were* women despite what biology, anatomy, or culture might say.[22]

As I have briefly illustrated here, *Transvestia*'s spectrum of gender variance featured fairly diverse identifications, some of which destabilized the parameters of heterosexual transvestism. But as Prince's push for respectability and social distinction intensified, a hierarchy of trans- taxonomies began to take shape. To be sure, the rankings of this hierarchy were not explicitly spelled out. Rather, the hierarchy of designations that I will map out is based on my interpretation of Prince and Susanna Valenti's columns and the letters and histories of the magazine's readership. It is to this retrospective hierarchy that I now turn.

*Transvestia*'s writers relegated individuals who cross-dressed primarily for sexual gratification to the bottom, including homosexual fairies and street queens who were presumed to cross-dress only for sexual favors, and any "kinky" group, such as some bondage enthusiasts, whose cross-dressing was incidental to some other (presumably sexual) purpose.[23] It was the transvestite clothing fetishist, also placed at the bottom of the hierarchy, which warranted the most concern from Prince and those who subscribed to her philosophy. Prince prescribed "wisdom, moderation, and perspective" in cross-dressing primarily in order to distinguish heterosexual cross-dressers with a sense of aesthetics and respectability from the unsavory character of the fetishistic transvestite. "There are two general kinds of males interested in crossdressing," she contended, "those who have a feeling for the feminine gender role, and those who are fixated on the fetishistic, erotic level where the clothes simply serve to stimulate and satisfy the masculine personality and do nothing to unlock, release or aid in the development of a feminine personality."[24] While early on she tended to obscure and downplay the erotic components of transvestism, in the late 1960s and 1970s, Prince seldom shied away from acknowledging the relationship between eroticism and cross-dressing. "I think it is safe to say that 95% of all femmepersonators start out cross-dressing with sexual involvement."[25] Prince described the typical pattern. At an early age, transvestite boys developed an erotic association with certain items of feminine clothing, such as high heels, nylon stockings, satin nightgowns, taffeta dresses, or silk panties. During adolescence, most derived sexual rewards from the touching or wearing of these articles of clothing, as well as entire outfits. While Prince never denied that cross-dressing originated as an erotic activity or might continue to serve as a sexual outlet throughout adolescence and adulthood, she did challenge the assumption that the erotic impulses that shaped early compulsive behavior patterns remained the same throughout the life cycle. Other factors and motivations, she contended, come into play as the sexual novelty wanes over time. Susanna Valenti also argued that while a sexual component existed, transvestism entailed a way of life, an avenue for relaxation, and a way to alleviate the pressures of social manhood more than it represented a form of erotic expression. "You are in the midst of a fascinating adventure," she wrote, "and breathing life into a totally new individual, teaching her (or allowing her) to do new things. All the facets that make human beings are now at play—social, intellectual, physical, aesthetic. They are all finding new channels for expression."[26]

According to Prince, after the fetishistic stage, three levels of behavior would gradually sort themselves out. Some individuals would continue to fetishize their special article or articles of clothing and thus remain clothing fetishists. Other cross-dressers would gradually incorporate additional articles of clothing until they discovered satisfaction in wearing an entire outfit. Individuals in this second level simply cross-dressed and did not attempt to cultivate a feminine persona. They were "simple transvestites." Prince believed that the third behavior pattern represented the largest group within the magazine's readership, the femmepersonator faction. These were cross-dressers who possessed "feelings of femininity above and beyond the merely visual and tactile satisfactions of wearing clothes," although their experiences varied widely in intensity and development.[27] The third group, however, developed an awareness of a feminine "gender-personality" that clothing fetishists and simple transvestites purportedly lacked. They developed their "femme-selves" according to whatever cultural models of femininity they had become accustomed to emulating. The result was the blossoming of a second personality.

The narrative of Phyllis from Michigan illustrates this gradual progression from fetishism to aesthetic transvestism. Phyllis reported that she had "lost, or better, replaced, an all compulsive urgency, ringing like a fire alarm, that made dressing a clandestine type of thing…":

> A thing, not of beauty, but needed and always ridden with guilt. Now, with your help, I find I can savor the anticipation, much as one looks forward to a good play or meeting an old friend; no more like an animal stalking its prey on which to glut itself. Consequently the end result finds me a gentle and respectable Phyllis, unlike the secretive, often garish girl of the dark of yore.[28]

Phyllis interpreted her former self as a guilt-ridden transvestite in what was commonly referred to as the "locked-room stage" among the magazine's readership, meaning one's expressions of femininity or cross-dressing practices were confined to a private room and kept secret from everyone else. A hint of illicit eroticism haunted both her analogies. She employed the phrase "ringing like a fire alarm" to describe her "compulsive urgency" to cross-dress. A more overt note of erotic compulsion resided in the second analogy that compared her former insatiable desires to that of a gluttonous animal stalking its prey. Phyllis credited Prince and the magazine for helping her to adopt more respectable dressing habits and to develop a disciplined mindset. Phyllis achieved respectability only with the removal of the secrecy and illicit nature of the practice. Phyllis recorded a transformation to what she considered a higher expression of transvestism. Her former feminine persona was a "garish" girl. By implication, she had now learned the proper codes of dress and behavior advocated by Prince and Susanna Valenti.

Not surprisingly, at the top of the hierarchy stood the "true transvestites"—the femmepersonators or feminiphiles—who successfully divided and balanced their masculine and feminine personalities. Those who identified as femmepersonators believed that their renditions represented a more authentic and truer image of femininity (based on their own definitions and criteria, of course). To rise above "simple transvestism" and reach the level of femmepersonation, though, entailed rigorous self-improvement. Because they were socialized to be men, transvestites who aspired to reach that level believed that they needed to develop the "girl-within." This group issued a multitude of directives, advice, and guidelines in their letters and histories. *Transvestia*'s fashion and gossip columnist Susanna Valenti led the way.

Valenti became the most prominent voice and critic amidst the contestation that erupted among *Transvestia*'s readership over proper and improper ways to dress and behave. In her fashion column, "Susanna Says," Valenti offered an incisive examination of the "femme-personality" that she believed was created as one practiced the art of cross-dressing and improved in the skill of behaving femininely. Along with Prince, she strongly advocated keeping each personality separate and distinct from the other. "If we allow 'him' to express himself through 'her,'" Susanna contended, "then we are going to create a horrible caricature which is neither fish nor fowl…":

> Or should "she" sneak in some of her traits when "he" is around, I'm afraid his reputation won't be worth a plug nickel around the office. That is why, whether it is scientifically correct or not, for purely practical purposes, I find it most helpful to think and talk as if two different entities were occupying one single body. … It is very useful as a practical tool, as a guide, to prevent Susanna from being nothing but a "man in skirts."[29]

Authentic expression was the central component of Valenti's ideology. She considered posture, gestures, walk, and voice inflection the four biggest challenges for cross-dressers who attempted to emulate women. Through practice and professional lessons, Valenti tried to improve in these areas, and she implored her readership to strive for "realness" and authenticity, as well. "The real fun about being a TV," she proclaimed, "is in the CONSTANT IMPROVING."[30] In her column, Valenti would offer her readers advice and many tips on how to look and behave authentically feminine. For example:

> I only see swishing as a tool with which we can learn to break long entrenched masculine movements, poses, and habits. Before you embark in social life as a TV, learn to swish—exaggerate feminine mannerisms to break the masculine patterns. Later, you'll be surprised how easily you'll drop back to that happy medium that tells a lady from a tramp or a drag queen."[31]

Initially, Valenti resisted Prince's attempts to draw semantic lines around the desired readership. At the beginning of her tenure as fashion and gossip columnist, she recognized the variety, fluidity, and complexity of styles that comprised the transvestite category. Transvestism "is not a static state of mind," she argued in her November 1960 column.

> Like everything human, it moves, sometimes forward, sometimes backward, but it does not stay the same. This applies to the intensity of the desire to dress, its frequency, and the forms it takes regarding preferences as to styles, make-up, lingerie, hairdo and even as to activities we like to engage in.

Not only did Valenti acknowledge transvestism's multiplicity, she also evoked a non-judgmental attitude of its assortment when she followed these statements with the assertion that transvestism "grows in any of many directions and there are constant subtle changes in the inclinations of every TV I've met including myself." Yet, the carefree tone of her fashion advice would take a more critical and harsh turn two years later. Although she would never adopt Prince's terms (e.g. femmepersonator) into her vocabulary, an event that occurred in 1962 pushed Valenti into becoming an enthusiastic watchdog who guarded the parameters of "heterosexual transvestism" with respect to dressing practices, aesthetics, style, and behavior.

The event that compelled Valenti to jump on Prince's taxonomic bandwagon was the famed October 1962 convention of around seventy transvestites, several wives, and a few sexologists at Valenti's resort property in Hunter, a town in the Catskills of upstate New York. Valenti operated the 150 acre resort during the summer season for a marginal profit. Throughout the 1950s and 1960s, she and her wife hosted small numbers of transvestite friends on weekends during the off-season. "Casa Susanna" was a self-described "TV haven"—a place where transvestites could visit and be completely free to cross-dress around the resort grounds. In her columns, Valenti extended an invitation to her readers to visit the resort. She suggested that if enough transvestites could get together at the same time, then they could hold classes on make-up, sewing, dancing, and poise. Many adventures were had by those who managed to find their way to Casa Susanna. The stories recounted by Valenti and her guests in *Transvestia* indicate that the resort was a sanctum for self-expression, creating a sense of normalcy and community for those who visited:

> Scene: The porch in the main house at … our resort in the Catskill Mountains. The time: 4 o'clock in the morning as Labor Day is ready to awaken in the distant darkness. The cast: four girls just making small talk and getting to know each other. It's been a strenuous day for everybody but we are greedy; we don't want to say goodnight yet, and we squeeze a few more hours from a day that's already gone. It's dark in the porch; just a row of lights illuminate part of the property at intervals … perhaps a bit chilly at 2,400 feet of altitude, but we don't seem to care … bare shoulders, bare arms … the feel of that long hair that strangely has become part of our own selves. An occasional flame lighting a cigarette throws a glow on feminine faces … smiling, serene, relaxed, happy faces…. Just a weekend at the resort, hours in which we know ourselves a little better by seeing our image reflected in new colors and a new perspective through the lives of new friends.[32]

The idea for a transvestite convention came to fruition. The convention met at Valenti's resort during a cold weekend in October of 1962. In their respective columns, Valenti and Prince wrote about the momentous affair and commented on the guests, several of whom did not fit the respectable mold promoted by the magazine. One cross-dresser, in particular, evoked the ire of both Valenti and Prince. According to Valenti, this guest did not bother shaving and wore a simple knee-length nightgown. But what really shocked and infuriated her was when this lazy cross-dresser lit up a cigar. The sight of so many motley renditions of femininity focused Valenti and Prince's attention on the fact that variety was more the norm of transvestism than previously realized. The convention weekend, then, was not only a defining moment in the history of heterosexual transvestism, it helps explain Valenti's move towards policing the lines of respectability drawn around the magazine's model of femmepersonation. The weekend's assortment of participants compelled Valenti, along with Prince, to close ranks to an even greater degree. Following the retreat weekend, she unleashed a series of hard-hitting columns centered on themes of self-improvement, including dressing tips and guidelines on appropriate conduct. She would become increasingly annoyed by cross-dressers who did not try to look and act the part of a proper woman. For Valenti, it was not enough just to wear women's clothes, make-up, and a wig. It was the cultivation of "inner femininity" that distinguished and elevated a true transvestite above drag queens, transsexuals, and clothing fetishists.

Through a discourse of social uplift, Valenti, Prince, and many of the letter and history writers elevated cross-dressing from a practice that was commonly and clinically perceived as a sexual peculiarity and mental disorder to what they considered to be an artful, beautiful mode of gender expression. Viewed within the lens of femmepersonation, true transvestites were not the compulsive, masturbating weirdoes popularly depicted in the tabloid, medical, and pornographic press. Rather, they were rendered as respectable males who just happened to enjoy expressing the femininity that was suppressed by a society invested in the "pink and blue division." "[T]he outer-girl we create," remarked Valenti, "is the indispensable container from which our heart emits all the feelings that—as men—we have not been able, nor been permitted to express."[33] This respectable framing, however, necessitated making other distinctions from groups precariously close to femmepersonators—various identifications that fell along the middle of the hierarchy.

With femmepersonators at the top and clothing fetishists and other "kinky" groups at the bottom, the middle of the hierarchy comprised a motley group of female impersonators, transsexuals, and "simple transvestites" with various clothing styles, aesthetic tastes, and modes of gender presentation—all judged to be woefully deficient.

A sizeable number of *Transvestia*'s cross-dressers enjoyed female impersonator shows, and a few envied the glamorous looks and embodiments that professional female impersonators and drag queens perfected on stage. A transvestite named Ana Bertha remembered when she and her male buddies jokingly went to "see the gay queens" at a local club. But for Ana Bertha the experience was no joke. "I wanted to look just like that queen I had seen, dressed as she was and with face made up as hers was!"[34] Another writer, Marilyn, remembered a summer visit to Finnochio's, a popular tourist nightclub in San Francisco that featured female impersonation shows. "To see these female impersonators truly 'set me off.' I was thrilled that there were those who could dress as girls and in public too! I too wanted to dress up. ..."[35]

A few self-identified transvestites even dabbled in amateur female impersonation. Valenti sometimes performed in the impersonator show at her vacation resort. In a letter to Prince, Eloise from Massachusetts related her initial foray into impersonation when she played a female part on stage. After describing this "chance to live his dream," she offered a few admonitions that showed her disrespect for the lewd performances done by many female impersonators. "We don't need to be afraid of female impersonation on stage in the proper atmosphere," she wrote, but we should "avoid any of the standard ploys of the nightclub type shows, especially the lewd routine of the typical emcee and the strip-teasing."[36] As Eloise's admonition suggests, the envy and admiration many of *Transvestia*'s cross-dressers felt towards professional female impersonators and drag queens could quickly turn if they judged either's performance of femininity as a lewd enactment or crude appropriation. Many heterosexual transvestites considered the typical drag queen's style as flashy, outlandish, and unladylike, definitely not the kind of appearance any self-respecting femmepersonator would want to emulate unless she were to make a mockery of femininity.

As Esther Newton documents, drag queens and female impersonators also held unfavorable opinions of heterosexual transvestites. The Midwestern professional stage impersonators and drag queens that Newton interviewed in the 1960s utilized the derogatory term, "transy drag," to condemn fellow impersonators who violated the "glamour standard" with an everyday, ordinary presentation of femininity. An appearance designated "transy drag" directly linked the violator to the kinds of hideous, non-stage enactments of femininity that professional female impersonators and drag queens perceived to be the province of the "lone wolf" transvestites. Indeed, many of *Transvestia*'s cross-dressers sought to emulate traditional or everyday models of femininity, such as the suburban housewife.[37] As Valenti contended, "one of the nicest compliments a TV can get from a non-TV is not that she looks beautiful or pretty (the friend is probably lying) but that she looks real."[38] As is evident here, the mutual distaste felt between transvestites and drag queens partly stemmed from each group's contrasting ideals of femininity and notions of authenticity.

Also situated in the middle of the hierarchy were "simple transvestites" who enjoyed dressing completely in women's clothing but did not strive to improve their appearance and mannerisms. Many femmepersonators considered simple transvestites as just "men in drag." However, they also knew that any man in complete feminine attire, no matter how crudely made up, was uncomfortably akin to themselves in the eyes of the public. In 1968, Sheila Niles, a columnist of the magazine, popularized the derogatory term "whole girl fetishist" to classify these unruly, lazy, and stubborn types of cross-dressers who for whatever reason would not adopt the behavioral codes and dressing guidelines associated with femmepersonation. "The pipe smoking, swearing, and bread devouring whole girl fetishist can create the same type of shock with his incongruous behavior as the shock we get when someone draws a moustache on a portrait of Sophia Loren," remarked Valenti. "And if he cannot or simply does not feel like modifying his behavior to match his appearance, then … stay behind your locked doors and enjoy your appearance to your heart's content."[39] The pejorative deployment of the whole girl fetishist category was a further attempt on the part of Prince, Valenti, and other femmepersonators to define authenticity as having a convincing feminine appearance and respectable deportment. Attaining this level of authenticity entailed creating a feminine persona from head to toe and from within and without. Doing anything less was deemed substandard. The stigma assigned to the category of whole girl fetishism derived from the assumption that one's unwillingness to fashion oneself in the mode of "true femininity" automatically signaled fetishistic impulses.

To be sure, whole girl fetishism was not applicable to transvestites who were thought to be on the path to femmepersonation. Some cross-dressers may have been judged deficient in their attempts but not for lack of trying. The main problem with those perceived to be whole girl fetishists, then, was that they did not strive for any standard of perfection. They purportedly achieved just enough of a feminine look to stimulate sexual excitement. With the achievement of orgasm, the masquerade ended. Cross-dressing, then, was the means to a sexual end, rather than a means to a higher plane of virtue, morality, and respectability. Respectable and aesthetically skilled transvestites now had a classification for these dissidents. The category of whole girl fetishism served as a linguistic tool to elevate femmepersonators and distinguish them from a deviant group presumed to be undermining the image of heterosexual transvestism.

The last type within the hierarchy's middling ranks that I will discuss is the transsexual, a pervasive symbol within the pages of *Transvestia*. *Transvestia*'s writers' attitudes regarding transsexuality were mixed. Celebrity transsexuals, such as Christine Jorgenson, Charlotte McLeod, Roberta Cowell, and Tamara Rees, whose sex-change surgeries garnered unprecedented media publicity in the mid-1950s, were heroines to many of *Transvestia*'s cross-dressers. However, some correspondents also displayed disdain, prejudice, and resentment towards ordinary individuals who had SRS. Reading between the lines, I detect a great deal of envy, as well. Quite a few of *Transvestia*'s writers described early childhood feelings of desperately wanting miraculously to be changed into girls. As young adults, these same individuals often read with intense interest the sensationalized stories about sex change published in the popular press.[40] Many transvestites, including Prince, even made scrapbooks of collected news clippings pertaining to transsexuality and cross-dressing.

Despite their envy and admiration for celebrity transsexuals, most of *Transvestia*'s writers held everyday transsexuals in low regard and considered them tragic, pathetic, or delusional individuals. They were quick to point out that post-operative transsexuals often had to settle for lower paying jobs and that many, out of desperation, entered prostitution to make ends meet. The perceived social costs of surgical castration—the fear of what life would be like without having the status in society that having a penis conferred to a male—undermined many of their desires for surgery. Like Prince's assistant Mary, discussed at the beginning of this essay, many transvestites who had at one time or another flirted with the idea of SRS decided otherwise after contemplating the social and economic costs of the procedure.

As I have previously discussed, even as the desire for bodily change and obtainment of SRS became the lines of demarcation separating transsexuals from transvestites, the two categories often overlapped, as many self-identified transvestites, including Prince, took hormones and underwent electrolysis and other cosmetic procedures to enhance their feminine appearance.[41] Some of these individuals decided to live full-time as women without having SRS. They called themselves "full-time transvestites," or sometimes "male-women," and later, in the 1970s, some began referring to themselves as "transgenderists." For the readers of *Transvestia*, male-women and transgenderists joined femmepersonators atop the hierarchy. Prince, in fact, made this transition. Her movement from periodic cross-dressing towards full-time living as a woman in the late 1960s deserves further discussion, as scholars have credited her for having coined the term "transgenderist," the linguistic ancestor of "transgender."[42]

In the autumn of 1968, Prince greatly complicated her place on *Transvestia*'s spectrum of gender variance when she decided to live full-time as a woman rather than dress as one periodically. This momentous decision undercut many components of her philosophy of "wisdom, moderation, and perspective" from the early 1960s. As she recounted in the August 1968 issue, in an essay entitled "My Goal Achieved," a profound experience at a nudist therapy retreat that she attended enabled her to reconcile a contradiction that had bothered her for years:

> For about twenty hours I was as naked as the day I was born, but for those same twenty hours I was still Virginia to myself and to all the rest. Although there could be no doubt as to my maleness (sex), nobody seemed inclined to doubt my femininity (gender), and I was treated in all respects as one of the girls by men and women alike. So from that time on I knew and know that I AM Virginia and Virginia is for real. This is the end of the road in the self-acceptance battle—to be able to know and maintain one's gender orientation in spite of the visible evidence of maleness.[43]

Having fully accepted herself "genderally," Prince informed her readers of her plans to live full-time as "Virginia." In subsequent columns, she would have to explain and rationalize her decision to readers who pointed out what they considered a contradiction in relation to her previous stances, if not an outright hypocrisy. Prince would later tell them that she regretted publishing "My Goal Achieved," admitting that it was not very wise in light of the many wives who read the magazine and who would surely fear that their husbands might take a similar path. She admitted that her enthusiasm for her self-discovery clouded her judgment, and she assured her readers that while she had gone further on the "gender train" than any other heterosexual cross-dresser, she had not "jumped the rails."[44] "I merely came to a point where I have extended the feminine phase into a long term condition of life, but Charles [her masculine self] is always with me, anatomically, physiologically and mentally…. My change has not been one of sex but one of gender."[45] In 1971, she testified that

> Me, myself, and I reside and originate in my head, not my genitals."[46] And almost ten years after her transition, she continued to maintain that "I have managed to get my self-image, my self-identity out from between my legs and into between my ears. In short my identity as a woman does not either depend upon nor is it hampered by the state of my genitals. I am perfectly comfortable with the designation of 'male woman' even though to most people that seems a contradiction in terms because they can't separate sex from gender.[47]

It is out of these rationalizations following "My Goal Achieved" that Prince invented language to describe the gender position she envisioned herself inhabiting between transvestism and transsexuality. In 1969 she designated herself "trangenderal" in order to deflect claims that she was on a path to transsexuality. However, she never used this term again, at least not in print. Ariadne Kane, co-founder of Fantasia Fair, also deserves credit for working out the meaning of this new identity category and maybe even coining it. In an interview with the *Gay Community News*, published January 31, 1976, Kane identified as a "transgenderist" and explained:

> A transgenderist goes beyond crossdressing to convey an image and express feelings we usually associate with femininity. Some of these characteristics are behavioral—the way one walks, sits,

crosses one's legs, carries himself. Some are physical—such as hair removal or hormone injections to develop secondary sexual characteristics. Some transgenderists live most of their lives in their preferred gender role, functioning as women or men socially but not biologically. For others this is not enough. When a person decides that he or she can no longer live in a physical body that does not match his or her preferred gender, he or she may opt for reassignment surgery. Then we use the classification "transsexual."[48]

Although Prince has been credited for originating the term, it was not until 1978 that she used the term "transgenderist" in print. At a conference that year, Prince read "The Transcendents or Trans People." In this paper, which was later reprinted in *Transvestia*, she distinguished sex from gender, discussed how individuals have historically been gendered in a binary system, and then described three classes of people who transcend the gender binary: transvestites, transgenderists, and transsexuals. She defined "transgenderists" as "people who have adopted the exterior manifestations of the opposite sex on a full-time basis but without surgical intervention."[49]

It is somewhat irrelevant who first coined "transgenderist." The meaning both Prince and Kane attached to it—a third way between transvestism and transsexuality—would be lost at some point during the 1980s. Then, in the early 1990s, a variation of it, "transgender," appeared with a politicized meaning, entirely different from Prince and Kane's connotation. Activists employed "transgender" as an umbrella term to mobilize and ally "all individuals who [are] marginalized or oppressed due their difference from social norms of gendered embodiments."[50]

This essay rewound to a formative era, before transgender, when a non-patient, textual community of transvestites marked their turf in the 1960s and 1970s. "Street queens," "transvestite fetishists," "simple transvestites," "drag queens," "whole girl fetishists," "transsexuals," "female impersonators," "true transvestites," "femmepersonators," "male-women," and "transgenderists": these were several of the designations known to *Transvestia*'s readership. Some of them, such as "femmepersonation," "whole girl fetishism," and "transgenderism," were produced within *Transvestia*'s gender community in order to further delineate differences between their kind and a repudiated Other—differences that would likely go undetected by mainstream observers but were viewed by the readership as important markers separating respectability from deviance. Those who encountered the magazine evaluated and measured their identities, experiences, and desires in relation to the designations and scripts they encountered in *Transvestia*'s columns, letters, and life histories. In this process of negotiation and contestation, each defined for him or herself an identity in accordance with or in opposition to (or somewhere in between) the magazine's prescriptive models.

Although the nomenclature would fade away, *Transvestia*'s spectrum of gender variance was an important battlefront of the taxonomic war fought among a host of gender outlaws in the decades after the Second World War—warriors who would later drop their shields of respectability and answer the call of a transgender nation.

## NOTES

1. Virginia Prince, "Virgin Views," *Transvestia* 14 (April 1962).
2. In addition to the National Transgender Library and Archive at the University of Michigan, I conducted research at the Kinsey Institute at Indiana University, the One Institute in Los Angeles, and the University of California at Northridge, which holds the Vern and Bonnie Bullough Collection on Sex and Gender. Although my oral research is not reflected in this essay, I interviewed Virginia Prince by phone several times and met with her once in person. I also corresponded with three former members of Prince's national transvestite sorority Phi Pi Epsilon, including Katherine Cummings, who shared many important stories and photographs of her friendship with Prince and of her experiences socializing in transvestite social circles in the 1960s and 1970s. She recounts these experiences and her developing transsexual identity in her autobiography, *Katherine's Diary: The Story of a Transsexual* (Woy Woy, NSW: Beaujon Press, 2007).
3. Prince's birth name was Arnold Lowman. In the 1950s, Lowman adopted "Virginia Prince" as a pseudonymous feminine name and "Charles" as a pseudonymous masculine name. For most of her adult life, Prince was a chemist and part owner

of a pharmaceutical plant. She died on May 2, 2009, at the age of 96. Scholarship on Prince is sparse. My work represents the first substantial historical examination of Prince, *Transvestia*, and the transvestite sorority Phi Pi Epsilon. See, Robert Hill, "'As a Man I Exist; As a Woman I Live': Heterosexual Transvestism and the Contours of Gender and Sexuality in Postwar America" (Ph.D. diss., The University of Michigan, 2007) and "'We Share a Sacred Secret': Gender, Domesticity, and Containment in *Transvestia*'s Histories and Letters from Crossdressers and Their Wives," *Journal of Social History* 44: 3 (2011): 729–750. An informal biography of Prince was written and self-published by psychologist Richard Docter, a personal friend of Prince. See *From Man to Woman: The Transgender Journey of Virginia Prince* (Northridge, CA: Docter Press, 2004). More biographical information on Prince can be found in Vern Bullough, *Before Stonewall: Activists for Lesbian and Gay Rights in Historical Context* (New York: Routledge, 2002) and *Cross Dressing, Sex, and Gender* (Philadelphia, PA: University of Pennsylvania Press, 1993). Richard Ekins and David King have edited a special issue of the *International Journal of Transgenderism*, 8 (2005), which brings together five of Prince's most significant essays.

4. I use the terms "cross-dresser" and "transvestite" interchangeably to refer to genetic males who identify as heterosexual and who enjoy periodically dressing in clothing that their society views as socially and culturally belonging to women. Within the print culture and social world they created, transvestites identified and addressed one another with their feminine names and used feminine pronouns. In spite of their anatomical sex, I utilize third person feminine pronouns in this essay to respect their self-definition.

5. Richard Docter writes that Prince informed him that *Transvestia* never surpassed 1000 subscribers. Docter, *From Man to Woman*, 83.

6. Mary, "Mary Makes It," *Transvestia* 62 (February 1970).

7. For important taxonomic work done by doctors, sexologists, and mental health professionals during this formative era, see David Cauldwell, *Transvestism: Men in Female Dress* (New York: Sexology Corporation, 1956); Harry Benjamin, *The Transsexual Phenomenon* (New York: Julian Press, 1966); Robert J. Stoller, *Sex and Gender: On the Development of Masculinity and Femininity* (New York: Science House, 1968); and John Money, *Man and Woman; Boy and Girl: Gender Identity from Conception to Maturity* (Baltimore, MD: Johns Hopkins University Press, 1972). For a short history of Alfred Kinsey's collaborations and correspondence with transvestites and transsexuals, see Joanne Meyerowitz, "Sex Research at the Borders of Gender: Transvestites, Transsexuals, and Alfred C. Kinsey," *Bulletin of the History of Medicine* 75: 1 (2001), 72–90. As one might expect, historical evidence in published form of the taxonomic production and contestation "on the ground" from this period is less abundant. I will highlight some obscure sources that relate to this essay. Louise Lawrence, an MTF transvestite from San Francisco, was an early trans pioneer who informally collaborated with doctors on the subject of cross-dressing and gender variance. Lawrence's correspondence, including letters to and from Alfred Kinsey and Harry Benjamin, comprises folders 5 through 15 of box 1 in the Louise Lawrence Collection at the Kinsey Institute. Lawrence also published "Transvestism: An Empirical Study" under the name "Janet Thompson" in *The Journal of Sexology* (May 1951). Prince published her ideas and findings in professional journals. For example, see C.V. Prince, "Homosexuality, Transvestism, and Transsexualism: Reflections on Their Etiology and Differentiation," *American Journal of Psychotherapy* 11: 1 (1957), 80–85; and Virginia Prince and P.M. Bentler, "A Survey of 504 Cases of Transvestism," *Psychological Reports* 31 (1972), 903–917. Prince published three books on cross-dressing with her press Chevalier Publications: *The Transvestite and His Wife* (1967); *How to be a Woman, Though Male* (1972); and *Understanding Cross Dressing* (1981). In *A Year Among the Girls* (New York: Lyle Stuart, Inc. 1966), Darrell G. Raynor recounts his experiences socializing in a transvestite network in the early 1960s and candidly writes about Prince and other personalities associated with *Transvestia*.

8. Jennifer Terry, *An American Obsession: Science, Medicine, and Homosexuality in Modern Society* (Chicago, IL: University of Chicago Press, 1999); Joanne Meyerowitz, "Sexual Revolutions," in *How Sex Changed: A History of Transsexuality in the United States* (Cambridge: Harvard, 2002), Chapter 5; Martin Meeker, *Contacts Desired: Gay and Lesbian Communications and Community, 1940s through 1970s* (Chicago, IL: University of Chicago, 2006); David Valentine, *Imagining Transgender: An Ethnography of a Category* (Durham, NC: Duke, 2007); and Susan Stryker, *Transgender History* (Berkeley, CA: Seal Press, 2008).

9. Letter from Rita, *Transvestia* 5 (September 1960).

10. Letter from Dorothea, *Transvestia* 5 (September 1960).

11. Prince coined the terms "feminiphilia" and "feminiphile" in *Transvestia* 7 (January 1961). The spelling of these terms would change over the years to "femmiphilia" and "femmiphile," sometimes capitalized, other times, not.

12. Virginia Prince, "Targets, Titles, and Terminology," *Transvestia* 12 (December 1961). Prince did not use these terms consistently throughout the 1960s and 1970s, and neither did the readership. She made a strong push for their use among her readers in the early 1970s, including advocating the use of "FP" instead of the popular "TV," but eventually the terms would fade away, probably due to their awkwardness. However, the letters and histories indicate that many readers adopted the philosophy and practice of "dual personality expression" that characterized feminiphilia/femmepersonation even if they preferred to use more popular designations like "TV."

13. Nancy, "My Year," *Transvestia* 14 (April 1962).

14. Jean, "I Could Not Win Till I Lost," *Transvestia* 18 (December 1962).

15. Bobbie, "Bobbie Goes Private," *Transvestia* 22 (August 1963).

16. Virginia Prince, "Virgin Views," *Transvestia* 16 (August 1962).

17. Hill, "We Share a Sacred Secret."

18. Georgette W., "I Am a Transvestite," *Transvestia* 30 (December 1964).

19. Letter from Eleanor, *Transvestia* 5 (October 1960).

20. For example, see Winfie, "The Wish to Be a Girl and Wear Girl's Clothing," *Transvestia* 18 (December 1962).

21. Letter from Myrtle Ann, *Transvestia* 61 (1970).

22. Prince and other writers mentioned more than a handful of *Transvestia* subscribers who had "done the deed" or were planning to do so. As Meyerowitz has argued, transvestite social circles were sometimes the "training grounds" for participants who would later develop transsexual identities. Meyerowitz, *How Sex Changed*, 170.

23. Evidence of these fetishistic expressions abound in the underground magazines *Bizarre* and *Exotique* and the erotic correspondence mediums La Plume, Contact, and Clique. The Kinsey Institute for Research in Sex, Gender, and Reproduction at Indiana University, Bloomington, holds these publications.

24. Virginia Prince, "Virgin Views," *Transvestia* 28 (August 1964).

25. Virginia Prince, "Virgin Views: Eroticism and Femmiphilia," *Transvestia* 65 (1970). Prince wrote her most candid essay about the relationship between eroticism and heterosexual cross-dressing in this column.

26. Susanna Valenti, "Susanna Says," *Transvestia* 8 (March 1961).

27. Prince, "Virgin Views: Eroticism and Femmiphilia."

28. Letter from Phyllis, *Transvestia* 26 (April 1964).

29. Susanna Valenti, "Susanna Says," *Transvestia* 19 (February 1963).

30. Ibid.

31. Susanna Valenti, "Susanna Says," *Transvestia* 55 (February 1969).

32. Susanna Valenti, "Susanna Says," *Transvestia* 17 (October 1962). Robert Swope and Michel Hurst found a collection of about 400 photographs belonging to Valenti at a flea market in Manhattan in the early 2000s. The snapshots depicted scenes from the resort, including pictures of Prince and others who belonged to *Transvestia*'s gender community. Swope and Hurst edited and published part of the collection. See, Robert Swope and Michel Hurst, eds. *Casa Susanna* (New York: Powerhouse Books, 2005). As publicity for this book, a journalist wrote a story on Casa Susanna. See Penelope Green, "A Safe House for the Girl Within," *New York Times*, September 7, 2006.

33. Susanna Valenti, "Susanna Says," *Transvestia* 61(February 1970).

34. Anna Bertha, "The Life of a Mexican Sister," *Transvestia* 51 (June 1968).

35. Letter from Marilyn, *Transvestia* 13 (February 1962).

36. Letter from Eloise, *Transvestia* 60 (December 1969).

37. Esther Newton, *Mother Camp: Female Impersonation in America* (Chicago, IL: University of Chicago Press, 1972), 51 and 52. "Female impersonators do not refer to themselves as transvestites…. To female impersonators, the real transvestites are the lone wolf isolates whose individual and private experiments with female attire are described as 'freakish.' To them, the transvestite is one who dresses as a woman for some 'perverted' sexual purpose outside the context of performance (either informal, as in the gay bar, or formal, i.e. professional)."

38. Susanna Valenti, "Susanna Says," *Transvestia* 36 (December 1965).

39. Susanna Valenti, "Susanna Says," *Transvestia* 55 (February 1969).

40. Joanne Meyerowitz, "Sex Change and the Popular Press: Historical Notes on Transsexuality in the United States, 1930–1955," *GLQ: Journal of Lesbian and Gay Studies*, 4 (1998), 159–187.

41. For an account of how the request for surgery became the distinguishing feature or line separating transvestism and transsexuality, see Meyerowitz, *How Sex Changed*, 176.

42. For example, see Richard Docter, *Transvestites and Transsexuals: Toward a Theory of Cross-Gender Behavior* (New York: Plenum, 1988); Gordene Olga MacKenzie, *Transgender Nation* (Bowling Green, OH: Bowling Green State University Popular Press, 1994); and Phyllis Randolph Frye, "Facing Discrimination, Organizing for Freedom: The Transgender Community," in John D'Emilio, William B. Turner, and Urvashi Vaid (eds). *Creating Change: Sexuality, Public Policy, and Civil Rights* (New York: St. Martin's Press, 2000), 451–468.

43. Virginia Prince, "Virgin Views," *Transvestia* 52 (August 1968).

44. Virginia Prince, "Virgin Views," *Transvestia* 53 (October 1968).

45. Virginia Prince, "Virgin Views," *Transvestia* 56 (April 1969).

46. Virginia Prince, "Virgin Views," *Transvestia* 66 (1971).

47. Virginia Prince, "Virgin Views," *Transvestia* 89 (1977).

48. My source for this interview came from its reprint in *Hose and Heel* 5 (1976), the newsletter of a cross-gender organization named the National Alliance for Heterosexual Male Feminism. The name of the newsletter was later changed to "The Journal of Male Feminism." The vertical file on this organization in the Kinsey Institute has around twelve issues of the newsletter, dated from 1976 to 1979.

49. Virginia Prince, "The Transcendents or Trans People," *Transvestia* 95 (1978). Prince first read this paper at the Western Regional Meeting of the Society for the Scientific Study of Sex, held in Santa Barbara in June of 1978.

50. Susan Stryker, "(De)Subjugated Knowledges: An Introduction to Transgender Studies," in Susan Stryker and Stephen Whittle (eds). *The Transgender Studies Reader* (New York: Routledge, 2006).

# 30

# *Reading* Transsexuality *in "Gay" Tehran (Around 1979)*

Afsaneh Najmabadi

Prior to the Iranian Revolution in 1979, historian Afsaneh Najmabadi points out, Tehran had a reputation in the West as being a "gay paradise." In the present day, Iran attracts Western attention for the apparent contradiction that sodomy (often conflated with modern gay identity) is punishable by death while transsexuality is a state-sanctioned practice through which individuals may change gender markers and obtain reassignment surgeries. Both narratives obscure a complex history of transsexuality within Iran. Najmabadi, an Iranian feminist historian and professor at Harvard, offers a detailed account of how gender reassignment was treated by the Iranian state from about 1970, in the waning days of the Pahlavi regime, until just after the revolution of 1979. She tells a story of friction between older and newer gender and sexual categories, of changing medical discourses about gender reassignment and sex-change, and of individuals who were creative and resourceful in living their lives in an atmosphere of anxiety about shifting gender norms. Drawing on mass media and medical documents as well as interviews, this chapter shows how gender non-conforming people carved out spaces of relative acceptance in the entertainment and media professions, and demonstrates the ways in which lines between what was then designated as *gay* and trans were far blurrier than they subsequently became in post-revolutionary Iran. With this historical background to Maryam Mulk-ara's successful petition for a fatwa permitting transsexuals to transition legally, Najmabadi tracks the emergence of a transsexuality that operated alongside, but independently of, different transsexualities in Europe, North America, and elsewhere.

Tehran in the early 1970s offered a spectrum of overlapping conceptions of maleness and masculinities. This spectrum structured everyday practices of life with regard to non-heteronormative male gender/sexual desires, and it construed non-heteronormative maleness as being at once criminal, immoral, and theatrical. This article offers a preliminary mapping of that scene. It is not, and cannot be, a social history of "gay Tehran." Although the available scholarly writing on this topic agrees on the existence of an "active gay subculture"[1] in 1970s Tehran, this literature is anecdotal, and the critical archival research necessary to produce a proper history remains yet to be done. But I also want to argue that to name the 1970s as the decade of a *gay* Tehran obscures important (in)distinctions between what is now named gay (always considered male in this context by all writers on the topic) and what is now considered male-to-female (MtF) trans. My purpose is thus to offer an initial survey of the complex overlaps and connections between these sorts of non-heteronormative lives. I want to trace continuities across the "before" and "after" of the 1979 revolution, as well as note the ruptures introduced by regime change into the scene of male non-heteronormativities. Simply casting the advent of the Islamic Republic as the brutal end of Gay Tehran does not do justice to the complexity of the tale.

The story of "Gay Tehran" in the 1970s has been articulated in at least two domains. At the time, there were a number of articles about Tehran's "gay scene" in the American gay press, which reported its extermination by the policies of the Islamic Republic in the 1980s.[2] There is an implicit progressivist dynamic to these stories: the emerging gay subculture of Tehran would have evolved naturally into a livelier, more open, gay Tehran, except that its life was cut short through the 1979 revolution and subsequent Islamization of society. As Jerry Zarit's end-of-the-decade article put it succinctly, "Iran was for me, and for others like me, a sexual paradise. In terms of both quantity and quality it was the most exciting experience of my life."[3] The quests of Western gays for a sexual paradise in Iran specifically, while unselfconsciously reenacting broader cultural tendencies to sexualize an exotic "Orient," were most likely influenced by the publication and enormous popularity of Mary Renault's *The Persian Boy* in 1972, which was widely reviewed and reported on in the American gay press in the 1970s.[4]

A second domain for the formation of the "Gay Tehran" story has been within Iranian diasporic gay communities—some members of which personally experienced the 1970s there.[5] But their recollections are narrated through later *gay* identification developed in their new homes, which, in the 1980s and 1990s when much of this immigration took place, were dominated by a particular style of sexual identity politics. The Iranian gay diasporic progressivist narrative was informed by this sensibility—and through the lens of later identities, earlier sexual and gender subjectivities and practices came to be seen as problematic and backward.

From its earliest manifestation in the diasporic press, Iranian gay identity marked its emergence through a disidentification with that past. This included a very clear demarcation between *hamjinsgara'i* (same-sex inclination/orientation) and *hamjinsbazi* (same-sex playing).[6] The former has been embraced as a modern form of identification that outwardly expresses a true inner self; *hamjinsbazi*, on the other hand, has been disavowed, perhaps because of its pejorative use by government officials, in condemnatory religious texts, in pathologizing contexts by medical professionals, or in hostile general usage within Iranian society and culture at large. The disavowal of *hamjinsbazi* by diasporic gays has been articulated through turning societal and cultural abjection back onto the concept itself: they disavow same-sex playing due to its presumed abusive character, and its being marked by disparities of age and economics. This is in contrast to same-sex-oriented relations (characterized as *hamjinsgara'i*) that allow for genuinely egalitarian romantic relationships among same-sex partners.[7] The differentiating move between *hamjinsgara'i* and *hamjinsbazi* thus articulates a homonormative response to an anti-heteronormative project.[8]

The imaginary of "Gay Tehran" works differently in these two domains. For the growing gay liberation movement of the 1970s in the U.S.A., traveling to "Gay Tehran," in fiction or in person, was a search for one's "own kind" beyond national borders. In that sense, it fit well with liberationist dreams of the internationalization of activism, and with solidarity work based on "finding the same everywhere" (as in, "Sisterhood is Global").[9] Within diasporic Iranian gay activist politics, imagining the "Gay Tehran" of the 1970s offered a critical intervention into the Iranian cultural politics of denial that insisted on the foreignness of non-normative gender/sexual desires and practices. My point here is not to question the sociological existence of such non-normative desires and practices, but to suggest, rather, that imagining them and the period of 1970s as *gay* may prevent other, equally pertinent ways of thinking about the scene of male non-normative gender/sexuality during that decade. Actively un-familiarizing ourselves with what already has been read through the prism of "Gay Tehran" would, I hope, open up the possibility of seeing differently, and asking different questions about, non-heteronormative practices of life at that time.

## THE SPECTACLE OF UNMANLY MALES

The "Gay Tehran" I wish to reread was part of a complex, rapidly growing urban society, in certain domains of which particular styles of non-heteronormative male lives were becoming somewhat visible. This was particularly the case in the growing entertainment industry, which ran the gamut from high-quality modern film and television shows to nightclubs that catered to a range of class-inflected tastes. "Lower-class" clubs were performance venues that sustained older and more traditional forms of male dance and entertainment, while the performance of such dances in newer, more cosmopolitan nightclubs, and in film, made them more visible to a layer of the urban middle-class population that may not have been exposed to them in earlier decades; indeed, the urban middle class may well have developed its sense of modern-ness in part from the disavowal of such cultural enactments.

Stories of females living unusual masculine lives fascinated the public during this period; such stories were common features in history books, neighborhood gossip, newspapers, and magazines from the 1950s through the 1970s.[10] In many of these cases, especially in the women's press of the 1960s, the stories of females living masculine lives would be rescued from the suspicion of "improper sexuality" through the affirmation of a modern marriage ideal, the failure of which had pushed women into these unusual paths, through cruel arranged marriages or good-for-nothing husbands. Alternatively, economic hardship and the social inhospitality of many professions to women were said to have forced the choice of masculine living. This acceptable configuration of public female non-normative gender self-styling did not have an equivalent for males: males who did not or could not marry and perform their "marital duties" could not get away from their social obligations through a surfeit of feminine performance.

In earlier eras, a male dressing as a woman and opting for a womanly career constituted "housewifery," that is, becoming a male kept by a man.[11] By the mid-twentieth century, such a practice of life was no longer possible; it would have added scandalous shame to the insult and injury of refusing adult manhood. Males who wanted to *live* womanly lives tended to keep it a secret, fearing censure and punishment. Such was the fate of a male person who had worked for 19 years as a masseuse in a women's public bath.[12] In another case, a male person who had lived and worked for the previous 50 years as a woman was forced into men's clothes, with her hair shaved off her head.[13] In yet another case, a male person refused to leave the hospital in men's clothes, after being forced to undergo "disambiguating sex-surgery," and declared her intention to continue living a womanly life.[14] Reports of such incidents in the press never had an admiring or approving edge to them; rather, they were cause for apprehension and incomprehension.

A less scandalized report on a "young man who dresses and behaves in a completely contrary fashion," who wore his hair long and was a dancer, constituted an exception: he was considered to stand out as "a red bean on the surface of rice pudding" (i.e., he was a spectacle). The magazine *Khvandaniha*'s lengthy account of the case was made possible in part through displacing his contrarian self-presentation onto his "unusual background," the product of an Azerbaijani father and a mother from Istanbul.[15] The report vacillated in tone, sometimes sympathetically presenting the "young man" as a philosophically-oriented intellectual, at other times as a weird recluse, and sometimes as someone whose unconventional self-presentation produced unwanted social reaction: he was followed by curious street kids who made fun of him; he had been arrested twice for appearing inappropriately in public. A line drawing of his face (compared to a full stature photograph) made his face look more female by emphasizing his plucked eyebrows and giving him fuller hair. He was said to have eventually opted for a more routine life, by opening a sandwich shop on Maulavi Street in a popular southern Tehran neighborhood. This "young man's" style of public self-presentation, and his former profession as a performer in an Azerbaijani dance troupe, positioned him at the very limit of social tolerance: there was an accepted, if marginal, vocation for males to dance or otherwise perform female roles in theater and the cinema.

The figure of the male performer or dancer has a long history in Iran. Anthony Shay's numerous essays offer us a rich conceptual vocabulary for understand the cultural work of this figure and its history, not only for the Tehran of the 1970s, but also into the present. Several of Shay's propositions are pertinent here. He challenges "the romantic views that many gay men hold that the presence of male dancers and the sexual interest expressed toward them by Middle Eastern men somehow constitutes evidence for an environment accepting of homosexuality and a utopian gay paradise," and "the oft-expressed viewpoint that male dancers were imitating or parodying women.... The presence of male dancers, professional and nonprofessional, in public and private space requires a (re)evaluation of the meaning of these male bodies."[16] Shay argues that in the 1970s in Iran, modern choreographers attempted to eradicate traces of the earlier male choreographic tradition by creating what he calls hypermasculine styles of movement for male dancers, often within "folk dance" choreographies, "suitable to the urban Westernized male and their sensitive elite audiences."[17] As he notes, the older style of male dancers continued their performances in the "gritty underworld" of nightclubs and cafés. Indeed, "In the late 1960s and early 1970s a wave of nostalgia for Qajar-era [pre-1925] performing and decorative styles swept through Tehran, where a number of cafés sprang up in which former boy dancers, now elderly but still capable performers, appeared."[18] The sharp contrasts between the two modes of male dance performance, Shay concludes, point to "the underlying changes in attitudes toward sexuality and gender."[19]

Because male dancers and *zan-push* (woman-attired) actors continued to work in the café entertainment scene as well as in some of the "grittier" nightclubs, these more traditional male dancers and entertainers increasingly may have been marked, for the emerging urban middle classes, as a lower-class taste tainted by the immorality of a suspected sexual availability. But the figure of the female-attired male actor/dancer attained a new, somewhat more respectable, life in the cinema and in "legitimate" theatrical productions.[20] The dominant style of male-actors-performing-female-roles was what William Beeman has called "pretend mimic," that is, looking like a woman but achieving a "distance" from the female through the exaggeration of clothing, make-up, voice, and body movements. It was a style of performance already prevalent in the 1940s and 1950s, and there was a significant traffic, even then, between the worlds of stage and screen and the ongoing public conversations about sex-change, which circulated around such figures.

In 1955, for example, *Khvandaniha* published in its regular "Album of Artists" page a picture of the actor 'Ali Tabish, dressed as woman, along with a commentary entitled "Is this a man or a woman?" (Figure 30.1):

> You have frequently read in the press that in such and such corner of the world, for example in Europe or America, a woman or a man was fed up with her/his own (sex!) and with a surgery her/his constitution was changed.
>
> This (twentieth century whim) has not yet found adherents in Iran, so the man you see in this picture in women's clothes, standing with special coquettishness, is our very own famous actor 'Ali Tabish. Since he hasn't had any luck with manhood, he decided to don for a few hours the attire of (devil's apprentices), not in street and public but in the play (Charley's Aunt) in which he plays the role of a capricious woman.[21]

*Zan push* performances were included in many pre-Revolutionary films of the so-called "Film Farsi" period, including *Madmuvazil Khaleh* (*Ms. Auntie*, 1957, dir. Amin Amini) with 'Ali Tabish playing the aunt figure; *Zalim-bala* (translated on the film posters as *The Naughty Girl*, 1957, dir. Siamak Yasami); and *Shabaji Khanum* (1958, dir. Sadiq Bahrami). The anxious fantasy of waking up as

**Figure 30.1** 'Ali Tabish as Charley's Aunt', *Khvandaniha*, October 1, 1955, page 37.

the other sex was reflected in the satirical 1959 film, *'Arus Kudumeh? (Which One is the Bride*, dir. Farrukh Ghaffari).[22]

As Beeman notes, "Sexuality is also an important undertone for the 'mimetic' female portrayers.... Since these actors, with few exceptions, claim to be fully heterosexual males, this situation can be an uncomfortable social position for them."[23] This "uncomfortable social position" was much murkier for male dancers who performed in the "gritty world" of lower-class nightclubs. In the 1950s, *Khvandaniha* and other magazines would publish alarming reports, with lurid photographs, about the nightclub life of Tehran (as well as major European cities), emphasizing that these spaces were populated by men dressing up as women to exploit male clients.[24] They depicted a steamy and seamy nightlife in which hard-working citizens, lured by the temptations of alcohol, music, and dance, would be taken advantage of and robbed by "available" male and female performers. According to one 1954 report, of a total of 332 cafés and restaurants in Tehran, only a dozen actually offered musical and dance performances. These were said to be clustered largely in two areas of Tehran—Laleh-zar and the district around Shahr-i nau (Tehran's red-light district). The report further implied an overlap between sex-work and the entertainment offered in these nightclubs by describing several of them as run by women named Khanum, a designation often used, in this context, for women who bossed their own group of sex-workers. The report included several photographs of performers and clients, including one of a male dancer, Baqir Namazi (Figure 30.2).[25]

At other times, a male dancer would come to public attention accidentally—often in the context of charges of "taking advantage" (ighfal, a word with a high sexual charge) of men, or of scuffles leading to injuries and pressing of charges, all of which worked to consolidate the association of criminality and public disturbance with non-normative gender/sexual presentations. Such was the case of Akbar Burzabadi, who was arrested after knifing one of a group of young men who had been harassing him on a Tehran street. Akbar was "a woman-presenting man [mard-i zan-numa] who makes himself up as a woman and works at one of Tehran's popular musical [saz-u-zarbi] café-restaurants. Yesterday evening, Akbar, with wig and heavy make-up, left home to go to work." He was

باقر نمازی در چندکشور خ دلمالی کرده وباعث تفریح
وشگفتی عموم شده است وی‌گویا اخیرا بنابدعوتیکی
ازکاباره‌ها خیال دارد بابانو پروانه بهیروت برود

**Figure 30.2** Male dancer Baqir Namazi, said to have performed well in several countries. *Khvandaniha*, September 25, 1954, page 37.

followed and harassed by a group of young men, and eventually attacked them with a knife, injuring one of them, who filed a complaint. The paper added, "The officers [at the police station] indicated that he had been booked several times in the past on the charge of taking advantage of men; he sits at café customers' tables, looking like a woman, and taking advantage of them."[26]

In the context of Tehran's nightlife, a "distancing" style of feminine mimesis could signal particular kinds of gender/sexual desire: it could be enacted by males who wanted to present themselves as female-acting non-females (thus the need for "distancing exaggerations") who wanted to be desirable to men who desired female-presenting non-females. At the same time, some males opted for "complete" mimesis—working as female dancers and intending to be taken totally for women. This style of mimesis allowed some males to live as women.[27] Such, for instance, was the case of one café dancer known as Nargis Salihi who was believed to be a woman and had worked for five years before it was found out that s/he was born male, as Nasir Salihi (Figure 30.3). The "outing" resulted from a café scuffle that led to Salihi and a number of clients being detained at the local police station. When interrogated at the police station, Salihi explained that she had moved to Tehran from the small provincial town of Arak five years ago. Because she "was very fond of wearing women's clothes," she explained,

> I made myself look like a young woman. I then went to the town registry in Ray [at the time, a small suburb of Tehran] and declared my birth certificate lost and requested a new one in the name of Nargis Salihi. With the new birth certificate, I began a career of singing and dancing and have developed a circle of admirers."[28]

Both styles of self-fashioning continue to inform MtF public presentations in Iran today, and are often cause for tension between those who want to completely live as women, and thus argue against the exaggerated femaleness of those other MtFs, who, in their opinion, "are giving a bad name to the community."[29] In the 1970s, these two analytically distinct styles of male non-heteronormativity existed more as a continuum, which also included a range of other strategies for males-living-as-

**Figure 30.3** Nargis Salihi at the police station. *Kayhan*, May 13, 1969, page 18.

women. Some were individuals such as Nargis, who lived as women without undergoing any form of medicalized body modification, but a growing number of people opted for various degrees of hormonal and surgical intervention.

The world of non-heteronormative males was visible in the 1970s not only in the world of "gritty" entertainment. The upper echelons of an expansive art world—painters, photographers, television producers and performers—were also rumored to harbor non-masculine males. Indeed, the two poles of the culture industry were not sealed off from each other. At elite parties catering to males who dressed as women, members of high society mingled with *khanums* who worked in menial day jobs.[30] One difference was that the very rich could dress at home and be safely driven to such parties by their chauffeurs, whereas the less affluent had to change clothes on arrival. These get-togethers were the non-heteronormative male equivalent of *daureh* parties (women's-night-out parties that rotated on a circuit between different women's homes). The more well-to-do males would throw lavish parties and invite the rest of their circles—sometimes numbering in the hundreds.

Not all men-loving men in Iran during this period opted for feminine styles, of course.[31] Many lived lives scarcely distinguishable from other men, but they often socialized with the more "flamboyant" non-masculine-attired males.[32] These spaces of socialization gained the name of "gay parties" or "gay bars" in international gay media coverage, as well as in collective memories of 1970s Tehran for Iranians in later decades. But males-living-as-women who socialized through these networks did not consider themselves homosexual, and they defined their relationship with men in heterosexual terms. Within these intimate (*khaudi*) circles, they addressed each other by their female names. Many lived double lives. By day they dressed as men and went to work as such; some were even married and had children. At night, they lived as women.[33] The parties they attended were not a space for finding potential lovers or partners, but rather a place to dance and have fun, to exchange gossip about one's adventures, and to meet people like oneself (which by definition excluded people who were one's target of desire).

Some of these trends continue into the present. Today's "gay parties" similarly are seen to be for people of the same kind. Behzad, a gay-identified man in his early fifties when I interviewed him in

Tehran in 2007, seemed resigned to a single life. When I asked him why he didn't go to gay parties to try to meet someone, he was puzzled:

> why would I go to a party to spend time with people like myself? Years ago, in my twenties and thirties, when I was still trying to figure things out for myself, I used to go to some of these parties— they are good for the younger folk so they don't feel they are the only ones who are not like others.[34]

Cyrus, a gay-identified man in his early thirties, similarly did not consider the parties a place to find a partner, describing them rather as places "for hanging out with like-minded men." He met his last two partners at the gym, and noted: "the men who pick me up, they are all either married—and I move away from them as soon as I find out—or else I lose them to marriage sooner or later. It is very depressing."[35] The distinction within the party scene that Behzad and Cyrus both described is between those who (like them) do not look very different from straight men, and those who have what Behzad called "girlie-like" styles of self-presentation. But all the attendees would be looking "out there," not within the gay parties, for potential lovers and partners. This structure of desire and identification reflects the dominance of a larger discourse in twentieth-century Iran that has transformed males and females into "opposite sexes," and which depends on the notion that "opposites attract"—a discourse that sets the parameters of sexual/gender subjectivity, whether normative or not.[36]

We have no ethnographies, nor published memoirs, that would help map this non-heteronormative culture in the 1970s. We have instead a vast circulation of rumors from the time that have since acquired the status of fact. It was, and still often is, said that by the 1970s Iranian television had become a safe haven for *gay* men, who enjoyed the protection of not only Reza Qotbi, the director of National Iranian Radio and Television and a cousin of Queen Farah Pahlavi, but, somewhat equivocally, of the Queen herself. When the Tehran daily *Kayhan* published a report about the purported wedding celebration of two gay men in a club, the Queen is said to have reacted negatively and asked the men involved and their friends to behave more responsibly and avoid such excesses in the future. In their defense, the men are said to have clarified that the celebration was a birthday party that had been misreported in the press.[37] Kavus, a self-identified gay in his late fifties in 2007, similarly recalled the public view of such marriages as a misrecognition: "How could two khanums get married?" He laughed. He described such occasions as carnivalesque "dressing-up parties," in which two *khanums* would present themselves as a bride and groom.[38] In real life, he added, "both of them would be interested in *straight* [pronounced as in English] married men. Targeting married men was like a conquest, a proof of womanliness. In these parties, they would brag about who had succeeded in breaking up which marriage." If a *khanum* developed a special relationship with a lover, sometimes, s/he would "marry" this guy. But the occasion was not a public ritual, nor was it celebrated by a "wedding party." At most, for a keepsake, they would go to a commercial photographer for a "wedding portrait," for the occasion of which the *khanum* might change into a wedding gown.

## THE SHAME OF UNMANLY MALES AND THE HOPE OF GENDER AMBIGUITY

The emergence in the 1970s of more visible scenes of non-heteronormative maleness, along with increased knowledge of such scenes circulating in speech and print, was widely perceived as a moral corruption of Iranian culture through Westernization. The perception had class connotations: only elite society in Tehran was assumed capable of fostering such calamities. The extensive circulation of extravagant rumors about high-society circles of non-heteronormative males became part of the criticism of Pahlavi Court culture, which was seen as corrupt and as encouraging further corruption. While subsequent to the establishment of the Islamic Republic and the world-wide growth of Islamist movements, one tends to associate such criticism with an "Islamist backlash," in the 1970s, attacks against an "excess of cultural liberties" were a much more broadly voiced concern.[39] What sustained the power of non-heteronormative maleness as a sign of excessive liberty (or, as it was by then commonly called "Westoxication"),[40] was the overwhelming feeling of shame and disgust associated with any public spectacle of non-masculine maleness and non-heteronormative sexuality.

What made "it"—this preferably un-named horror—a cultural assault and moral insult was above all *not* its putative Western origin, but the shame of being *kuni*. The most derogatory word in the realm of sexuality, *kuni* literally means anal, but in Persian it exclusively means to be receptive of anal penetration. Young male adolescents often first become familiar with the word as that which signals the edge of abjection; for instance, when parents warn their young son to stay away from certain activities (such as dance) and from certain (ill-reputed) persons, lest they become *kuni*. The equivalent word for women, *baruni*, does similar disciplinary work, but its moral load is much lighter.[41]

The gut-shame associated with *kuni* seems to have made it resistant to any measure of self-appropriation and re-signification. When the word *gay* began to arrive in Tehran from the West, some did not take to it. Behzad said he initially "disliked *gay* because in my mind I would translate it into *kuni* and I stayed away from it."[42] Ironically, the more recent acceptance and circulation of *gay* in Persian signifies the same thing: the need for a word that is not-*kuni*.[43] What does that "gut" feeling of revulsion speak to? Why does the spectral threat of be(com)ing *kuni* seem to be so shattering to a modern (male) Iranian's sense of self? It is impossible—or, at any rate, it is not my project—to give a convincing etiology of disgust. But it is critical to ask what cultural work disgust performs. What does it do to "the disgusting"? What does it achieve for "the disgusted"? Miller asks, "Why is it that disgust figures so prominently in routine moral discourses, even more so perhaps than the idioms of other moral emotions such as guilt and indignation?"[44] And how does this sense of profound aversion to *kuni* relate to the rise in visibility and the increasing prevalence of MtF trans inflections of woman-presenting maleness?

Another source of anxiety directed at males in the 1970s was that of "gender confusion," or ambiguity. Numerous social commentators wrote essays about the current state of youth lamenting the disappearance of manly valor, and of young men with long hair whose demeanor was that of a flirtatious girl, especially when they danced to rock music—all in "blind imitations of the West."[45] For a modern Iranian masculinity that had crafted itself through hetero-gendering previously androgynous concepts of beauty, and by the adoption of more disciplined and uniform sartorial practices during the first half of the twentieth century, the new fashions and tastes of the young seemed nothing short of a threat to national honor.

Part of this gender anxiety resided in fear of the failure of sex/gender recognition and of what that misrecognition would cause. One woman wrote:

> Once upon a time when we looked at men, we had no doubt that they were men. But now with these Beatle-style hair-dos and [tight] pants that show the body and high-heel shoes and manicured nails, we are forced to look again and again to remove our doubt. In the old days, if you called a man woman, that was an insult, but now they try to make themselves look like women. Several days ago, in Nasir Khusrau Street in Tehran, I ran into a man who had braided hair, was displaying a lot of jewelry and exactly like women had plucked his eyebrows and wore heavy make-up. It is astonishing that these men who always considered women beneath them and thought of themselves as the superior sex are putting themselves in women's place when it comes to dressing and make-up.[46]

Connecting such gender/sex ambiguity to sexual deviation was an easy imaginative leap. Under the bold headline, "The Danger of Women and Men Looking Alike," another newspaper article cautioned against the clothing, lifestyles, and work of women and men becoming too similar. This kind of confusion threatens today's civilization, in the same manner that two thousand years ago civilized nations such as Greece and Rome … were overthrown. In ancient Athens, before they were defeated by the Spartans, men had begun to make themselves up like women…. In ancient Rome too, similar things happened…. Moreover sexual deviancy, as it is today, became so prevalent that it caused their overthrow and destruction.[47]

The spaces opened up by a more visible non-heteronormative maleness and by gender/sex ambiguity nevertheless offered some hopeful possibilities for women-presenting males. As I have already argued, "Gay Tehran" was inclusive of a broad spectrum of male non-heteronormativity. Press reports of genital surgeries beginning to be performed in Iran at this time were particularly important in informing woman-presenting males of more affordable possibilities for changing their bodies, which until then had seemed to be available only at great cost in Europe. On February 17, 1973, the daily *Kayhan* (p. 19), under the headline "In Shiraz, a Man Voluntarily Became a Woman!" reported:

> A thirty-one-year-old man was operated in Namazi Hospital in Shiraz and became a woman. This man, who does not wish to reveal his/her [non-gender marked pronoun *u* in original] identity, was a perfectly healthy man, but had an intense desire to become a woman and for a long time s/he was wearing women's clothes and injected female hormones. The patient is a resident of Tehran, had consulted several psychologists before surgery, and the Legal Medical Board in Tehran and Shiraz considered the surgery permissible. The former man has said that soon s/he will be marrying a man who knows her/his condition completely. Doctors say s/he is capable of marriage.

Unlike previous reports of "sex-change" in Iran, which typically involved disambiguation surgery performed on intersex persons, this report specifically emphasized that the person had been "a perfectly healthy man." Inadvertently, it also advertised to any interested reader what the process of sex-change would entail: psychological consultation and acquiring permission from the Legal Medical Board. Most hopefully, it ended in a "happy marriage."

The next year, the women's weekly *Ittila'at-i banuvan* ran the life story of Rashil (formerly Sa'id) Sa'idzadeh over eight weeks.[48] The coverage in a popular women's weekly transformed the coverage of sex-change from short medical news items into a full-length, melodramatic human-interest story. In the first issue, a huge headline, running the entire width of the page, declared "The 28-Year-Old Newborn to the World of Women." A supra-title exclaimed "wondrous, extraordinary, unbelievable … but true!" while a subtitle explained that "'Sa'id' whom everyone thought of as a man has now become a coquettish woman!" Every week, the story was accompanied by her post-change photographs and, as if "seeing was not believing," Rashil's various medical and legal documents were reproduced as well. Most importantly, Rashil's story was narrated as her own story and in the first person. After a long, patronizing, introductory editorial note in the first installment (as well as shorter editorials in every issue), the story unfolds in Rashil's narrative voice. The sustained narrative, serialized in the tradition of short novellas, accompanied with her photographs and legal and medical documents, fully fleshed out the story of a livable sex/gender-transitioned life. This was not a story of misery, misfit, and disorder, though all these elements were part of her story. This was instead a "sweet and interesting" story with a happy ending. The eight-week run of Rashil's story in a popular women's weekly, which built upon previous decades of news of intersex surgeries reported as sex-change as well as reports of prominent international sex-change surgeries, transformed the idea of sex-change into a tangible possibility within public imagination. Rashil's detailed life story contributed to a pattern of life-narratives that would structure much of the scientific and popular writings, including autobiographical writings, about transgender/sexuality to the present day.

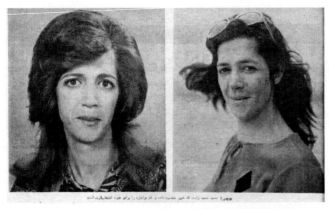

**Figure 30.4** Two photos of Rashil Saʻidzadeh, *Ittilaʻat-i banuvan*, January 9, 1974, page 13

**Figure 30.5** Rashil again. *Ittilaʻat-i banuvan,* January 30, 1974, page 13

As the story of Rashil Saʻidzadeh indicates, it was still possible to write, even at great length, about trans persons (especially if their gender/sexual non-normativity could be vaguely associated with a physical intersex condition) in a way that was unthinkable to write about non-surgically-modified, cross-dressed males living as women. Rashil's story was framed with sympathy, and at times as a form of heroism that triumphed against all odds. The woman-presenting males, on the other hand, could be laughed at, mocked, sniggered about, or tolerated in hostile silence. They could be subject to moral outrage and criminal suspicion. By the mid-1970s, however, the medical establishment, possibly alarmed at the growing rate of sex-change surgeries performed outside any norms of institutional medical supervision, transferred the moral judgment against homosexuality onto trans persons. It took the professional and disciplinary power of the Medical Council of Iran (MCI) to bring the full weight of opprobrium associated with homosexuality to bear on the life-options of woman-presenting males, and thereby to delineate and enforce a kinship relationship between male homosexuality and MtF trans.

## SCIENCE RULES ON UNMANLY MALES

Formed only in 1969, the MCI established a whole series of regulations for medical practice during the first years of its operation. It also acted as the authority where complaints about medical practice could be filed and reviewed.[49] In the early 1970s, it began to produce guidelines on new medical

«مونیکا» یکی از دؤجنسی هائی بود که بعد از
۲۳ سال «نه مرد و نه زن بودن» پس از یك عمـل
جراحی به سلك زنها پیوست، دوستانش رویا، فیروزه
و سحر (که هر سه پسرند و تمایلات زنانه دارند) با
حسرت به او نگاه می کنند . معلوم نیست دیگر آرزوی
عمل جراحی و تغییر جنسیت در این سه تن، هرگز
بتواند تحقق یابد.

**Figure 30.6** Three woman-presenting males visiting a friend, Monica, after her surgery. The caption reads in part: "Roya, Firuzeh, and Sahar (who are all boys who have womanly inclinations) look at her enviously. It is not clear if their wish to have surgery and change sex could be fulfilled any longer." *Kayhan*, October 11, 1976, page 5.

practices, such as acupuncture. Indeed, its rulings on sex-change surgery and acupuncture were decided in the same session of the Board of Directors on September 28, 1976. Alarmed by the apparent increase in genital surgeries among woman-presenting males, and by the growing public knowledge of these practices, the MCI decided to ban sex-change surgeries, except in the case of the intersex. A huge front-page headline in the daily *Kayhan* informed the public of this decision on October 10, 1976. The newspaper explained that the decision "meant that sex-change through surgical operations and the like which are aimed to solely change someone's apparent condition is no longer permitted." It quoted "an informed source" as saying that "this operation can cause psychological and physical harm and that is why MCI has banned it.... From now on any doctor who performs such operations will be legally prosecuted." The paper added that, "up to now some 30 sex-change operations have been performed in Iran."

The full text of the decision was first published some three years later in the *Newsletter of the Medical Council of Iran*. It read:

> In general, changing the apparent sex through surgical operations and the like is not possible, "neither from a psychological nor from a physiological respect." Since this type of young men—who now insistently ask that their apparent condition be changed—cannot become a future perfect woman and become married to a man as a woman, and since the hole that is created for them will most likely become a source of chronic infections, and since there is a high probability that they will then express enmity toward the persons who have changed their condition and their sex, or at least they will express regret under conditions that a reversal to their prior condition is not possible, therefore such persons must be considered mental patients, they must be treated psychologically, and one cannot permit that they would be moved out of their current condition and appearance.[50]

The delay in publication perhaps indicated a level of disagreement among medical practitioners on this issue, and may have reflected debates within the medical community that dated back to the

1940s, when Iran's preeminent gynecologist, Dr. Jahanshah Salih, in his seminal textbook, had argued strongly against the possibility, advisability, and morality of sex-change. Indeed, this difference of opinion continues to inform conceptions and practices of sex-change in Iran today. The statement is a remarkable document on many levels. It implies that to be a "perfect woman" is to be a perfect "hole," and that surgically modified MtF trans individuals are deficient in womanhood to the extent that the surgeries they receive produce unsatisfactory holes. The concern expressed is evidently driven in part by the expressed dissatisfaction with the quality of surgery woman-presenting males were receiving. But it was also a move to put medicine's house in order, in keeping with other efforts to promote professionalization.

Officially, no sex-change surgeries took place in reputable hospitals after 1976. Dr. Yahya Behjatnia was a prominent gynecologist who for many years headed the Family and Infertility Clinic of Jahanshah Salih Hospital in Tehran, the primary teaching hospital for gynecological training, and the hospital known for having a team of surgeons who operated on the intersex; he recalled that many woman-presenting males would visit him and beg him to change their sex. Often, he explained, by the time such persons would come to him for removal of male sexual organs and vaginal construction, they were already dressing as women and looking like women, and had already obtained hormonal treatment and already had breasts. But he would tell them that genital sex-change was not a permitted practice. If they insisted, he would advise them to go abroad for the surgery.[51] Some surgeons in the late 1970s, however, still carried out sex-change operations. They either did it surreptitiously in smaller private clinics, or they manipulated the medical system simply by listing their clients as intersex on hospital records.

Another prominent gynecologist, Dr. Mehdi Amir-Movahedi, was a highly regarded specialist in uterine surgeries, intersex surgeries, and vaginal construction for women who were born without vaginas, or with vaginas with very restricted openings.[52] He served on the Board of Directors of MCI for several years, and he echoed the observations of his colleague Dr. Behjatnia. He compared the situation to that of women seeking abortion. At the time, this was illegal except under strict exemptions, such as a pregnancy that threatened the mother's life. Yet with the right connections and money, many doctors would perform abortions.[53] At Jahanshah Salih Hospital, Dr. Movahedi explained,

> We were very strict, we would not do anything that was against regulations, nor would we train medical students for illegal surgeries. I worked there for some 20–30 years and I do not recall a single case of sex-change surgery. If any of our trainees performed this in their own clinic, the MCI would prosecute them.

Why, then, did the MCI issue an official statement on sex-change, I asked? "If there were any related complaints, it was not when I served there. But many in the old days would do things for money and perhaps that is what happened."[54]

Peculiarities in the timing of the publication of the MCI decision on surgical sex-change, coupled with later interviews with prominent gynecologists who worked at the time in Jahanshah Salih Hospital but insist that no sex-change surgeries were performed by reputable surgeons in this period, lead one to speculate that despite persistent disavowals, reputable surgeons were indeed carrying out a whole range of surgeries that began to endanger the reputability of other surgeons. The division was not a matter of differing professional opinions about the advisability of genital surgery for woman-presenting males; rather, it involved matters of moral reputation. By this time, in the dominant scientific discourse, intersex and trans persons had come to belong to distinctly different categories. The latter had become affiliated with sexual deviancy, rather than birth defect. It was the morality of sex-change—or rather, the moral status of the persons requesting or performing sex-change—that was at issue. This was indeed at the heart of public conversations at the moment of the MCI decision against surgical sex-change in 1976.

The 1976 MCI decision had paradoxical effects. It must have made some surgeons more cautious about sex-change operations; but the practice of surgical sex-change continued, along with media interest in it. The medical community as well, even in the publications of the MCI itself, continued to produce articles that covered the subject of sex-change in supportive terms.[55] Indeed, the MCI's insistence on the impossibility of sex-change, along with the simultaneous banning of surgeries deemed impossible, combined with the prominent coverage of the decision in the national dailies, created a productive public conversation that circulated knowledge of surgical sex-change on an unprecedented scale. Against the MCI's intentions, perhaps, the very possibility of such operations came to broader attention.

Noushin, for example, now in her fifties, said she had no idea such operations were possible in Iran before she read these newspaper reports. In the 1970s, she socialized as part of circle of singers and entertainers. Her/his parents had noticed her/his "incredible voice" when s/he was a teenager, and encouraged her/him to take voice lessons. She became a singer, and continues to be much in demand even today, although she now performs only at private parties.[56] Noushin counted among her friends many of the famous male and female vocal artists of the 1970s. She and another close friend, the son/daughter of a high-ranking army officer, had been planning in the mid-1970s to go to Europe for their sex-change surgeries. Her friend's father was making arrangements for them to be seen at a famous London clinic. The MCI decision and the subsequent newspaper coverage made them realize they might possibly get what they wanted in Iran. Noushin and her friend visited Dr. Taqavi in Asia Hospital (the same hospital and surgeon who had operated on Rashil Saʿidzadeh), as well as Dr. Behjatnia. Both advised them to go abroad under the current circumstances. Eventually, in 1977, after a period of hormone therapy in Iran, they both went abroad for their operations.[57]

Aside from going abroad or using "back-street" surgeons, the other option remained living as a woman-presenting male without surgical transformation (obtaining hormones seems to have continued to be as possible as before). Many took this latter route. One such woman-presenting male, now internationally known, was Maryam Khatun Mulk-ara.[58] Born male in 1950, Mulk-ara, according to her many accounts of her earlier life, was already going out to parties dressed as a woman by her late teens.[59] At age eighteen, walking home from such a party, a car stopped and she noticed the occupants were "three *transsexual* males just like me." The moment she joined them in the car marked for Mulk-ara the beginning of a new life; she referred to this accidental meeting "as the true moment of my entry into a collectivity, a group of people like myself.… In those days, there was no distinction between *gay*, two-sexed people, or *transsexuals*. Everyone knew these individuals existed, but no one knew exactly what the problem was. People referred to all these individuals as 'iva-khvahar' [o'sister]" (p. 7). Mulk-ara described the gatherings and parties she attended with her friends as "a place where everyone was a woman, that is, even though they were known as males in social norms of recognition, but they were women. The ambience was just like the ambience of womanly gatherings. We talked about fashion and other women's issues."[60] In the early 1970s, Mulk-ara started working at the Iranian National Radio and Television, and she went to work dressed as a woman. It was there that she was first encouraged to go abroad for a sex-change operation. She spent some time in London in 1975 to learn more about herself and to look into various possibilities, and it was there, she claimed, that she "learned about *transsexuality* and realized I was not a passive *homosexual*."[61] Upon returning from London, Mulk-ara began to lobby various authorities to see what could be done in Iran, but everyone told her that because of the prevailing social atmosphere, the government could not do anything. By this time, of course, the MCI had closed the emerging medical possibilities for sex-reassignment surgery in Iran.

During this same period, Mulk-ara became concerned about the implications of her practices from a religious point of view. "I was in a religious conundrum [*az lihaz-i sharʿi sardargan*]." She visited Ayatollah Bihbihani, who consulted the Qurʾan; it opened on the Maryam chapter. Mulk-ara consided this a very auspicious sign, for Maryam is the only chapter bearing a woman's name; this occasion provided her with her eventual post-op name, Maryam). Ayatollah Bihbihani suggested that

Mulk-ara should contact Ayatollah Khomeini on this issue, who at the time was in Najaf. Ayatollah Khomeini confirmed that "sex-change was permitted and that after surgery, she must live her life as a woman."[62] At this point, she began to plan to go to Thailand, but by then the years of revolutionary upheavals had erupted.

Mulk-ara eventually did go to Thailand for her surgery, in 2002. But in the early months of 1979, once the general strikes came to an end, she, like most people, simply went back to work—and here her troubles began.

> They asked me who are you? Why do you look like this? When I insisted that I had a condition, they set up a meeting for me with a doctor at Day Clinic [a top private clinic]. But the doctors' treatment of me was unbelievable; it was gross. This was just the beginning of a series of arrests, questioning me over and over again.... Dr. Bahr al-'Ulum and the director of Sida va Sima's [the Islamic Republic of Iran Broadcasting (IRIB), which was previously National Iranian Radio and Television (NIRT)] health clinic threatened me, saying they would set me on fire. Eventually they forced me to take male hormones and go into male clothes.... This kind of treatment continued till early 1980s; these were bad years for *gays* and *dau-jinsi* [double-sex] people. I heard several were arrested and spent time at Evin prison.

Mulk-ara was not the only woman-presenting male forced out of NIRT/IRIB. Haideh, now in her late forties, used to teach animation classes there before she was expelled. Eventually, she opted for sex-change in the late 1990s and now has her own graphic design business. Natasha was a young make-up artist, similarly forced out of NIRT/IRIB. For a while, she tried to find jobs in private film studios, but these studios were also under increasing scrutiny for perceived immoral conduct. Eventually, she opened her own hair-dressing salon and has become quite well-known in Tehran. Today, two other MtFs are also employed in her salon.

In the early 1980s, as the Islamic Republic was taking shape, Maryam Mulk-ara began her persistent lobbying of various authorities to change the situation for woman-presenting males who did not wish to dress and live as men. Under the new regime, the moral purification of society became a systemic priority. Moral purification measures included closing down sites that were considered spaces of corruption, such as the red-light district businesses, bars, night-clubs, and many cafés and cinemas. It meant a series of horrifying public executions of women and men on charges of prostitution and sodomy. It meant intense scrutiny of all institutions, especially those such as the mass media and the universities, which were considered critical for the production of a new revolutionary Islamic culture and society, but were thought to be populated by corrupt persons who had to be purged. As Mulk-ara puts it in her interview, these were indeed "bad years for *gays* and *dau-jinsi* people."

The spectrum of non-heteronormative male-bodied persons in the 1970s had included woman-presenting males as well as males who did not dress as or look like women. The latter's non-heteronormativity was focused on their desire for men, while they continued to live lives largely indistinguishable—to the uninitiated—from normative males. These males, some of whom now name themselves as *gay* or are so named by others, had shared in the increased visibility of non-heteronormative males of the 1970s. That visibility became dangerous in the years following the 1979 change of regime. These men had to adopt a more circumspect style of life, something that indeed had been a way of life for many of them already. But while the sexual politics of the new government could be warded off by some non-heteronormative males simply by living more circumspect lives, woman-presenting males faced a peculiar challenge in the new republic, when public gender-separation emerged as an important ethical project. A totally homosocial gendering of public spaces was seen as the ideal, although it was considered largely unachievable in practice. Nevertheless, strict codes of dress and gender presentation in public were put in place by a series of measures over the period 1979–1981.[63] The self-perceptions and preferred styles of living for some non-heteronormative males included, and at times critically depended on, their ability to present themselves as women and to be visibly feminine in public—but the gender norms set in place in the early days of the IRI made that nearly impossible. As Mulk-ara and others explained, many people like her felt forced to grow mustaches and beards and live, at least in daytime, as men. Living a double life by presenting as a woman at night, which was practiced by many woman-presenting males even in the 1970s, suddenly became much more hazardous, to the extent that it remained possible at all.

As we have seen, in the 1970s, woman-presenting males had carved for themselves spaces of relative acceptance in particular places and professions. The more public spaces of such "acceptability," for instance in the entertainment industry, were at once spaces of "disrepute" but also spaces in which non-normative living could be safely cordoned off and marginalized. They provided not only a measure of safety for woman-presenting males, but also for their containment and confinement from the larger society. Woman-presenting males performed the vulgar and the deviant, and the deployment of these semi-licit styles in the popular entertainment of the 1970s provided for partial tolerance of those deemed deviant.[64] The 1979 revolution, particularly the cultural purification campaigns of the first few years of the new republic, ruptured this dynamic. The vulgar, taken in the Islamist discourse (and indeed on the political Left as well) to represent the extreme embodiment of late-Pahlavi corruption, became yet another ground for massive repression of social deviance.

The enforcement of public gender codes in the post-1979 years disrupted the old continuum of male non-heteronormativity. While it was possible to be a closeted *gay* man, living openly as a woman-presenting male became increasingly impossible. Woman-presenting males not only carried the stigma of male same-sex practices, they also transgressed the newly imposed regulations of gendered dressing and presentation in public. They were always assumed to be "passive homosexuals," facing the same severe interrogations, sometimes anal rape, imprisonment, or death. Transdressed males walking in the streets would be arrested on charges of prostitution. Some, like Mulk-ara, were forced to take male hormones and change into male clothing, and could no longer go to work looking "like that." One key effect of the policies of the early 1980s was thus the categorical bifurcation of *gay* and *transsexual*. The practices of everyday life within both categories depended on the public disavowal of homosexuality, and both were likewise predicated on the public expression of gender normativity. Given the religious sanction to sex-change offered by Ayatollah Khomeini, the categorical bifurcation of non-heteronormative maleness played out quite differently in the IRI, in the years ahead, than it did in Europe and the United States. Being *transsexual*, rather than gay, emerged as the more socially acceptable way of being a non-heteronormative male.

## ACKNOWLEDGMENTS

This paper is based on Chapter Five of my manuscript, *Sex-in-Change: Configurations of Gender and Sexuality in Contemporary Iran* (forthcoming, Duke University Press) and was made possible by the superb editorial work of Susan Stryker. I am deeply grateful.

## NOTES

1. See, for instance, Janet Afary, *Sexual Politics in Modern Iran* (Cambridge: Cambridge University Press, 2009). Afary states, "By the 1970s, a small gay male subculture was gradually taking root in elite circles of Tehran, mostly as a result of interaction with American and European advisors who lived in the country" (243). Similarly, Firoozeh Papan-Matin has suggested, "By the 1970s, Iran had a small and active gay subculture." "The Case of Mohammad Khordadian, an Iranian Male Dancer," *Iranian Studies*, 42: 1 (February 2009): 127–138; quote from 128.

2. For reports of persecutions and executions in the early months and years of the establishment of the Islamic Republic, see *The Advocate*, 266, May 3, 1979, 7; 267, May 17, 1979, 7, and 12–13; 276, September 20, 1979, 17; 281, November 29, 1979, 12; 283, December 27, 1979, 8; 293, May 29, 1980, 12. See also *Homan*, No, 16 (Spring 2000), 16–17, for Iranian newspaper clips of executions from this period on the charge of *lavat* (sodomy). See also Afary, *Sexual Politics*, 265. In

much of such coverage, it is routinely said that Islamic law prohibits homosexuality—even though there is no notion of homosexuality in Islamic law—or that the Islamic Republic made homosexuality a capital offense and that gay men are executed in Iran for expressions of open homosexuality or on charges of homosexuality. On this issue as far as recent executions and the international campaigns are concerned, see Scott Long, "Unbearable Witness: How Western Activists (Mis)recognize Sexuality in Iran," *Contemporary Politics* 15: 1 (March 2009), 119–136. The slippage is important for contemporary politics of sexuality in Iran.

3. Jerry Zarit, "The Iranian Male—an Intimate Look," *GPU* [Gay Peoples Union] *News*, October 1979, 19.

4. See Mary Renault, *The Persian Boy* (New York: Pantheon, 1972), and, for instance, Jim Kepner's review in *The Advocate*, January 31, 1973, 26.

5. The two domains are highly interactive: Jerry Zarit's article in *GPU News* was translated and published in one of the earliest diasporic Iranian gay journals, *Homan*, published first in Sweden (first issue dated May–June 1991) and later in the U.S.A. See *Homan* 5, April–May 1992, 2–5.

6. In these distinctions, what often is lost is the very modernity of *hamjinsbazi* itself. The nineteenth-century vocabulary of what is at times conceived as the pre-history of modern same-sex relations—such as *amradbazi* (playing with a male adolescent), "*ubnah-'I*" ("afflicted" with a desire for anal penetration), *bachchah'bazi* (playing with a young person)—did not place the two sides in one category (*jins*) of person whether in a pejorative sense (same-sex player) or in its more recent recuperation as same-sex orientation. Even today, some in "same-sex" relationships do not recognize themselves of the same kind.

7. See for instance, Avaz, "Tafavut-i 'hamjins-gara' ba hamjins-baz va bachcheh-baz dar chist?" ["What is the difference between 'the same-sex-inclined' with the same-sex-player and child-player?"] *Homan* 9 (October–November 1994), 27–33.

8. See Sima Shakhsari, "From *Hamjensbaaz* to *Hamjensgaraa*: Diasporic Queer Reterritorializations and Limits of Transgression." Unpublished paper.

9. For a feminist critique, see Janet Jakobsen, *Working Alliances and the Politics of Difference: Diversity and Feminist Ethics* (Bloomington, IN: Indiana University Press, 1998).

10. *Khvandaniha*, June 30, 1956, 29, reprinted from *Payam*. For other reports of women opting to live and work as men, see *Ittila'at-i banuvan*, June 17, 1963, 12 and 75; *Zan-i ruz*, special New Year issue, March 1965, 12–14.

11. See Chapter Two in Afsaneh Najmabadi, *Women with Mustaches and Men without Beards: Gender and Sexual Anxieties of Iranian Modernity* (Berkeley, CA: University of California Press, 2005) for some examples of "keeping a young man" (*amrad-dari, adam-dari*), as it was then called.

12. *Khvandaniha* May 4, 1947, 13–14.

13. *Kayhan*, January 5, 1977, 2, and again January 6, 1977, 1.

14. See Chapter Two of my manuscript, *Sex-in-Change: Configurations of Gender and Sexuality in Contemporary Iran* (Duke University Press, forthcoming) for further discussion of these cases.

15. *Khvandaniha*, January 29, 1955, 20–22.

16. Anthony Shay, "The Male Dancer in the Middle East and Central Asia," *Dance Research Journal* 38: 1–2 (2006), 137–162. Quotes from 137 and 138, respectively.

17. Shay, "The Male Dancer," 139.

18. Anthony Shay, "Choreographic Hypermasculinity in Egypt, Iran, and Uzbekistan," *Dance Chronicle: Studies in Dance and the Related Arts*, 31, 2 (2008), 211–238. Quote from 234.

19. Shay, "The Male Dancer," 139.

20. *Zan-push*, literally meaning dressed in women's clothes, refers to male actors who played women's roles in traditional theatrical performances, whether in passion plays (*ta'zieh*) or in *ruhauzi* plays (literally over the pond, because the stage was a garden pond covered with planks of wood) at celebratory occasions. For an important analysis of different styles of enacting female personas in these plays, see William O. Beeman, "Mimesis and Travesty in Iranian Traditional Theatre," in Laurence Senelick, ed., *Gender in Performance: The Presentation of Difference in the Performing Arts*, (Medford, MA: Tufts University Press, 2002), 14–25. The expression *zan-push* has now become part of trans-vocabulary for MtFs who change to female clothes.

21. *Khvandaniha* October 1, 1955, 37. Parenthetical punctuations in original. Other issues of this journal similarly carried news and photographs of male actors in female roles. See October 13, 1955, 37, for a picture of Majid Muhsini (an actor) in women's clothes, replacing a female actress who was sick on that performance day; December 22, 1955, 39, picture of another male actor, Mr. Hushmand, in another production of the play *Charley's Aunt* in Rasht; January 12, 1956, 39, again Tabish as "Charley's Aunt"; March 21, 1961, 98, pictures of four male actors, Tabish, Vahdat, Qanbari, and Bahmanyar, all in female roles. The journal had similar brief reports on non-Iranian performances of male actors in female roles. See September 1, 1959, 16 (Jack Lemon and Tony Curtis trans-dressed as female musicians in *Some Like it Hot*); June 11, 1960, 19 (picture of an Italian male actor in a female role); December 19, 1961, 39 (another picture of female-dressed Tony Curtis) among many other similar ones.

22. For an informative history of Iranian cinema and its different genres, see Hamid Naficy, "Iranian Cinema," in Oliver Leaman, ed., *Companion Encyclopedia of Middle Eastern and North African Film* (London: Routledge, 2001), 130–222.

23. Beeman, "Mimesis and Travesty," 22.

24. See "Khatirat-i jalib-i yik ruznameh nigar-i Irani: dar in shahr mardan ba libas-i zananeh az hamjinsan-i khaud pazira'i mikunanad" ["Fascinating Memoirs of an Iranian Journalist: In this City Men in Women's Clothes Entertain People of

Their Own Sex"], for a report on West Berlin's night life, in *Khvandaniha*, August 18, 1959, 16–19; also "Mauvazib bashid khanumi kih kinar-i shuma nishasteh mard nabashad!" ["Watch out, lest the woman sitting next to you is a man!"], *Khvandaniha*, April 25, 1959, 52–54 (reprinted from *Umid-i Iran*).

25. 'Ali Sha'bani, "Gardishi dar kafeh-ha va risturanha-yi Tehran" ["A Tour of Tehran's Cafés and Restaurants"]," *Khvandaniha*, September 25, 1954, 22–25 and 36–37. Such reports continued to appear in the 1960s and 1970s. The emphasis, however, shifted to highlighting the growth of dance clubs as part of the "cultural turn" to dance among the youth. For one example, see Gregory Lamya, "Raqqas-khaneh-ha-yi zirzamini-i Tehran bazar-i garmi yafteh-and" ["Tehran's Underground Dance Dins Have a Heated Market"], *Kayhan*, January 25, 1969, 16. See also *Ittila'at*, October 6, 1976, 7, reporting on a Turkish singer appearing in women's clothes and make-up.

26. *Kayhan*, 19 April 1973, 22. For another similar report, see *Kayhan*, October 11, 1973, 22. This was the case of two young males, 18 and 19 years of age, "in women's clothes and make-up," arrested on Tehran-Saveh road, and charged with fooling men and stealing their money. The men denied the charges and stated that they were music performers (*mutrib*), working in the area villages. "We make up ourselves as women and in weddings make the guests laugh and be amused by imitating women's movements." Both reports carry photographs of arrested women-presenting males.

27. I have specifically opted not to name this category of males living-as-women "transwoman" because of the specific meaning of that word in today's English-speaking context.

28. *Kayhan*, May 13, 1969, 18.

29. The latter's style is seen as a signal to men who desire non-masculine males—whether for hire or not. The stigma of that kind of MtF-ness is elaborated in terms of its collapse onto sex-work; it is assumed that exaggerated female appearance is always a sign of commercial availability. It demarcates one style of MtF-ness as virtuous, pressing the other to the outside of domain of acceptability to community membership—this other is not seen as truly trans. It is marked by the weight of social shame associated with "passive" homosexuality. Among self-identified gay men, on the other hand, the distancing is seen as a defense against the bodily changes that would turn a gay man into a deformed woman.

30. *Khanum* is a generic form of address for an adult female. I, for instance, am often addressed as Khanum Najmabadi in Iran. In this period, it was also used as an "insider" designation for males-living-as-women. Information presented here about this subculture of Tehran life in the 1970s is based on conversations with several men in their fifties who now identify as gay, and several male-born adults who now identify as MtF.

31. It is more common today, especially in middle-class urban circles, for men-loving men to self-reference themselves as gay (the English word pronounced exactly the same in Persian). This was rare in the 1970s.

32. One self-identified gay man reported noticing a growing presence of what he referred to as *trans* women in these gatherings. Behzad, interviewed summer 2006—evidently this observation was from the vantage point of 2006 and within a conversation about transsexuality today.

33. For a sensitive depiction of one such life, see Farhad Rastakhiz, "Mardi dar hashieh" ["A Man on the Margin"], in a volume of two short stories, *Mardi dar hashieh* (Hamburg: Nashr-i Kalagh, nd), in which the main character/narrator, Mr. Qurayshi, is an assistant principle in a high school by day and lives a lone womanly life at home. I am grateful to Elham Gheytanchi for bringing this story to my attention.

34. Behzad, interviewed summer 2007. Johnson, in the context of southern Philippines, has noted, "most find repulsive the idea that one would have sex with their 'own kind.'" See Mark Johnson, *Beauty and Power: Transgendering and Cultural Transformation in the Southern Philippines* (Oxford: Berg, 1997), 90.

35. Cyrus, interview, fall 2007.

36. In the 1970s, when the word gay was not a dominant self-reference, few would use homosexual (in its French pronunciation in Persian—*humausiksual*) either. It was largely used in psycho-medical discourse. In recent decades, gay has become a more acceptable word, though its meaning, as the above articulations indicate, is not identical with its usage in English. Often, Persian words are used as in-words, which if used to refer to someone, would be recognized by another knowing person, but would be safely assumed to mean differently by the unknowing audience. As these words continue to be used in Iran today, I have refrained from recording them here. Some of these patterns recall somewhat similar configurations in the pre-1940s New York world of male-male intimacy as documented and analyzed in George Chauncey, *Gay New York: Gender, Urban Culture, and the Making of the Gay Male World 1890–1940* (New York: Basic Books, 1994), especially Chapter 10, "The Double Life, Camp Culture, and the Making of a Collective Identity."

37. Behzad, interviewed summer 2007. Whatever the meaning of these rumored "gay weddings" may have been at the time, today both in Iran and in the Iranian diasporic gay and lesbian communities, they are considered "gay weddings" in a more recent sense and as an indication of the lively "gay culture" of the 1970s. These weddings between men constituted a most scandalous public event toward the end of 1970s that continues to be remembered today, in conversations and in print. The event narrated by Behzad is now included in a proto-official publication, Ruhallah Husaynian, *Fisad-i darbar-i Pahlavi* [Corruption of Pahlavi Court], Markaz-i Asnad-i Inqilab-i Islami [Islamic Revolution Documentation Center]. Online edition, last visited: July 19, 2009. Part 3: http://www.irdc.ir/fa/content/4915/default.aspx.

38. Martha Vicinus has suggested that these marriages are reminiscent of "what went on in the early 18th-century London molly houses" (email communication, September 28, 2009). One difference, however, seems to be that the marriages in molly houses seem to have been about ceremonials of two men who would possibly be sexual partners even if for a brief time. See Alan Bray, *Homosexuality in Renaissance England* (New York: Columbia University Press, 1982), Chapter Four. Marriages between two *khanums* seem to have excluded that possibility.

39. See, for instance, anonymous report, "Yadi az jashn-i hunar-i Shiraz va barrisi-i iftizahat-i 'an. ..." ["Notes on the Shiraz Art Festival and its Scandalous Embarrassments"] in which one of the criticisms is explicit talk of homosexuality in one of the plays. *Khvandaniha*, November 21, 1972, 13 and 54–55.

40. *Gharbzadigi*, a concept that gained popularity through Jalal Al Ahmad's essay. For an English translation, see *Gharbzadegi—Weststruckness*, trans. John Green and Ahmad Alizadeh (Lexington, KY: Mazda Publishers, 1982). For a critical discussion, see Mehrzad Boroujerdi, *Iranian Intellectuals and the West: the Tormented Triumph of Nativism* (Syracuse, NY: Syracuse University Press, 1996).

41. *Baruni* literally means raincoat—I have not been able to trace where this word comes from. Another difference between the two words is that *kuni* is used to designate an individual man; *baruni* is used within the context of a relationship between at least two women—as in so-and-so is so-and-so's *baruni*.

42. Behzad, interviewed summer 2007.

43. The need for a word that is not derogatory but also not an in-word signifies the emergence of a broader semi-open circulation of these conversations. For that reason, the circulation of *gay* also marks the space of this semi-openness. For a similar dynamic between *gay* and *bantut* in the Philippines, see Johnson, *Beauty and Power*, 89; and for Thailand, between *gay* and *kathoey*, see Megan Sinnott, *Toms and Dees: Transgender Identity and Female Same-Sex Relationships in Thailand* (Honolulu, HI: University of Hawai'i Press, 2004), 6.

44. William Ian Miller, *The Anatomy of Disgust* (Cambridge: Harvard University Press, 1997), xi.

45. No author, "Javanan-i ma chizi mian dukhtar va pisar hastand!" ["Our Youth are Something Between Girls and Boys!"], *Khvandaniha*, March 6, 1971, 18, reprinted from *Khurasan*.

46. Nadereh Shahram, "Men of the Twentieth Century?" *Zan-i ruz*, August 3, 1974, 7 and 86. For another similar essay, see Mahmud 'Inayat, "Jaff al-qalam, jall al-khaliq," *Kayhan*, December 6, 1972, 5.

47. *Khvandaniha*, "Khatar-i hamrikhti-i zanan va mardan" ["The Danger of Women and Men Looking Alike"], translated by Dr. Kuhsar (no author or source of translation is specified), April 6, 1973, 36–38. Reprinted from *Danishmand*, a general science journal.

48. *Ittila'at-i banuvan*, January 9, 1974, 12–13 and 81; January 16, 1974, 12–13, and 80; January 23, 1974, 11 and 83; January 30, 1974, 13 and 79; February 6, 1974, 21; February 13, 1974, 12, 81, and 83; February 20, 1974, 13 and 82; and February 27, 1974, 19 and 83.

49. Attempts to form an association of health professionals had a much longer history. See Cyrus Schayegh, "*Who Is Knowledgeable Is Strong*": *Science, Class, and the Formation of Modern Iranian Society, 1900–1950* (Berkeley, CA: University of California Press, 2009), 54–60.

50. *Newsletter of the Medical Council of Iran* 12, July 23, 1979, 29 (quotation marks in original).

51. Interview, December 2007. When I asked about the operation reported in the press in February 1973 that took place in Namazi Hospital of Shiraz, he thought that was a possibility since that hospital had American and American-trained doctors. Doctors trained by Dr. Salih were trained to refuse sex-surgeries except for the intersex. Information about Dr. Behjatnia in the following section is based on interview and on his biographical entry in Muhammad Mahdi Muvahhidi, *Zindigi-nameh-i pizishkan-i nam-avar-i mu'asir-i Iran* [*Biographies of Famous Contemporary Iranian Physicians*] 2 (Tehran: Abrun, 2000) 61–64.

52. Information about Dr. Amir-Movahedi is based on interview and on his biographical entry in Muvahhidi, *Zindigi-nameh-i pizishkan* 2, 53–59.

53. Interview, December 2007. On abortion regulations, see the text of revision of Article 42, Point 3 of the Penal Code, May/June 1973, in Gholam Reza Afkhami (ed.), *Women, State, and Society in Iran 1963–78: An Interview with Mahnaz Afkhami* (Bethesda, MD: Foundation for Iranian Studies, 2003), 268–269.

54. Interview, December 2007.

55. See, for example, "Akhlaq-i pizishki dar barabar-i pizishki-i nauvin: masa'il-i ikhtisasi-i akhlaq-i pizishki" ["Medical Ethics Confronting New Medicine: Special Problems of Medical Ethics"], *Journal of Medical Council of Iran*, 6: 5 (1978): 445–447.

56. Interview, August 2007.

57. Interview, August 2007. The experience was a harrowing one: bad surgeries in several countries over many years, interrupted by the revolution and the closing of borders in the early years of Iran–Iraq war (1980–1988).

58. Mulk-ara has been the subject of numerous interviews and reports, in Iran and internationally, both in print and film, about Iranian transsexuals. In the book project from which this article is drawn, I will discuss more fully her critical role in creating (and controlling) spaces for trans-activism in Iran over the past decade.

59. I have depended on the following sources for this sketch of Mulk-ara's life. By far, the most extensive interview with her (and the only one in which she talked at length about her life in the 1970s) appeared as part of a four-page social reportage in the daily *I'timad* (May 8, 2005, 7–10). Mulk-ara, including a picture of her at the center of page 7, was featured on 7 and 10 (interviewed by Hamid Riza Khalidi, the total page coverage was over one fourth of the full dossier. Unless noted otherwise, the quotes in this section are all from this interview). This dossier remains the most substantive and serious press coverage of transsexuality in Iranian press, though many other newspapers and magazines have covered various aspects of the issues. Other sources on Mulk-ara are a short interview with her as part of a dossier on transsexuals in a popular weekly, *Chilchiraq* (May 26, 2007, 7–13, interview on 11) and several phone conversations with her during summer and fall 2006.

60. In my conversations with her, Mulk-ara spoke about two circles in which she socialized in this period; one she called *darbariha*, the Court circle, which according to her included the Shah's cousin, his chief of staff, and several others she named. The other circle, she referred to as lower middle class *zir-i mutivassit*. The two circles overlapped in that many of the women most desired in the courtly circles were from the lower middle-class circles and would be brought to parties.

61. Interview, summer 2006. The account of how and when she first identified herself, or was identified by a doctor, as a *transsexual* differed in this conversation from those reported in the *I'timad* and *Chilchiraq* interviews in which she said she was sent to a specialist by the National Iranian Radio and Television who diagnosed her as *transsexual* and suggested she should go for surgery. Nowadays, this moment of "learning about *transsexuality*" has become a central narrative feature in the self-presentation of woman-presenting males. In particular, learning to distinguish oneself from "a passive homosexual" has become a key moment for feminine male-bodied persons. My interviews with Mulk-ara were carried out in 2005–2007 and to some extent reflect the retroactive naming of the consolidation of this distinction in contemporary discourses and practices of transsexuality.

62. "Taghyir-i jinsiyat bilamani' ast va ba'd az 'amal taklif-i yik zan bar shuma vajib ast." Noushin and two other MtFs I interviewed each claimed that it was them who had obtained the first fatwa from Ayatollah Khomeini on permissibility of changing sex. Interviews, summer 2006 and 2007. I discuss the significance of these multiple "firsts" in the book from which this article is drawn.

63. There is a huge literature on this period's state policies and resistance by large sections of women against it. Though successfully implemented by the early 1980s, women's dress public code has remained a perennial site of contestation between sections of the government, dissenting women, and, at times, young male youth. See Parvin Paidar, *Women and the Political Process in Twentieth-century Iran* (Cambridge: Cambridge University Press, 1995); Minoo Moallem, *Between Warrior Brother and Veiled Sister: Islamic Fundamentalism and the Politics of Patriarchy in Iran* (Berkeley, CA: University of California Press, 2005); and Hamideh Sedghi, *Women and Politics in Iran: Veiling, Unveiling, and Reveiling* (Cambridge: Cambridge University Press, 2007).

64. Johnson also discusses, in a different context, the paradox of the *gay/bantut* being "both celebrated as masters of beauty and style and circumscribed as deviant and vulgar," and notes "the historical significance of the beauty parlors as both the site and means for gays' successful occupational reinvention of themselves." One could argue that in the 1970s Iran, the entertainment industry had become such a site for performers such as Farrukhzad and others, who found a place such as NIRT a site of relative acceptance and flourishing of their performative skills. See *Beauty and Power*, 146–147.

# VII

## *BEING THERE*

### *The (Im)material Locations of Trans-Phenomena*

# 31

## *Between Surveillance and Liberation*

### The Lives of Cross-Dressed Male Sex Workers in Early Postwar Japan

Todd A. Henry

Todd A. Henry, a historian of twentieth-century Japan and Korea, makes splendid use of the ephemeral, tabloid *kasutori* press of U.S.-occupied Japan to offer a detailed account of individuals described as *danshō*, which he translates as "cross-dressed male sex workers." Henry uses this racy, popular literature to map the underground sexual economy of Tokyo in the late 1940s and early 1950s, and he situates *danshō* in the broader social landscape he describes—the ways in which utter defeat in war shattered the masculinist military culture of Japan, as well as the widespread unemployment and homelessness that fed into public commercial sex subcultures. Henry's work takes its place amid a growing body of literature that details the profound, worldwide shifts in sex/gender taxonomies in the mid-twentieth century. During this period, new categorical distinctions between what are now separately understood as "homosexual" and "transgender" identities began to emerge, and older continuities between sexuality and gender played out in new ways due to Cold War geopolitical pressures and the spread of a social-scientific framework for understanding the self.

…the body-for-itself can never be known as an object of knowledge like other objects. This body is lived, not known.[1]

## INTRODUCTION

On the morning of November 23, 1948, the Japanese public awoke to startling newspaper headlines of a captivating incident that had occurred the night before. According to one report, the Tokyo police chief was patrolling Ueno Park just after 7 pm as part of a crackdown on crime when he came across a group of cross-dressed male sex workers (*danshō*). A group of newspaper photographers accompanying the police chief indiscriminately flashed pictures of these sex workers, who responded by trying to wrest the intrusive cameras from the paparazzi. Fearful of what might happen to him, the police chief retreated behind a statue of Saigō Takamori, only to find ten more sex workers emerge from this epicenter of male prostitution. Together, they ganged up on the cameramen, forcing the police chief to retreat once again in search of back-up. When he returned to the scene with an additional ten officers, the angry sex workers continued their protest by taking shots at the police force and the cameramen, leaving a number of them injured. It took another ten men to finally detain the sex workers, five of whom were arrested in what this sensational report described as an incident of "group violence."[2]

Although perhaps distanced in time and place, this spectacular struggle—waged among the managerial concerns of the state, the profit-oriented interests of the media, and the determined agency of *danshō* themselves—encapsulates many of the issues that have come to animate transgender studies since the 1990s.[3] One purpose of this short essay is to capture some of these unexpected convergences, making postwar Japan relevant to questions of embodied personhood, epistemologies of the self, and meaning making around the sexed body. Although this particular "case" clearly resonates with many themes in transgender studies, I also want to leave open the possibility that local experiences of what we call gender and sexuality, analytical categories that are neither universal to all times nor all places, have different implications for the lives of people who did not necessarily embrace (at least at this time) the model of identity-based politics and rights so often associated with Euro-American modernities.[4] A critical understanding of post-war *danshō* as part of an increasingly globalized transgender studies, therefore, requires a careful grounding in local specificities, the second aim of this essay. One wants to know, for example, why this particular category, with a genealogy dating back to the so-called "erotic-grotesque-nonsense" of Japan's own twentieth-century modernity, became a salient way of forging a sense of self that was ontologically satisfying and/or strategically useful to survival during an era of intense material privation.[5] In placing emphasis on the specificity of "Japanese traditions," however, I also want to avoid the "area studies" pitfalls of either essentializing non-Western cultures as hermetically sealed from the outside world, or romanticizing them as more tolerant and accommodating of what scholars tend to lump together as "transgender" (or "queer") phenomenon.[6] As the otherwise titillating story that opened this essay suggests, cross-dressed sex workers in early postwar Japan were also engaged in a significant form of struggle—in this case, to protect and promote some combination of their material interests, sexual desires, and gendered sense of selves.

With these problematics in mind, the following pages analyze this struggle in terms of a contested process of bodily meaning making between the objectifying lenses of the postwar media and the lived experiences of *danshō* subjects. To date, most histories of sex work in the aftermath of Japan's defeat in the Asia-Pacific War (1937–1945) and its subsequent occupation by the U.S.A. (1945–1952) have focused on heterosexual relations between the so-called *panpan* girl and her male customers, especially American GIs.[7] However, as the aforementioned "incident" suggests, the figure of the cross-dressed male sex worker also received considerable attention in the postwar media, whose racy magazines, to quote John Dower, "celebrated self-indulgence and introduced such enduring attractions as pulp literature and commercialized sex."[8] Even as their cross-dressed bodies allowed them to superficially blend in with the female *panpan*, the *danshō* emerged as a related but separate category of sex worker who, through intense police surveillance and media scrutiny, was mapped onto the sexual landscape of a ravaged Tokyo.[9] They received particularly close attention from the pulp press, which featured them in pathologizing medical reports, titillating ethnographic exposés, graphic short stories, and saucy comic strips. The first part of this essay surveys these representational genres in order to show how a profit-seeking media spotlighted the "strange" bodies and practices of *danshō*, thereby rendering these elusive figures visible, if not intelligible. On the one hand, their hyper-visibility in the pulp press allowed the police to more effectively monitor these transgressive sex workers—as my opening anecdote suggests. On the other hand, the frequent appearance of *danshō* in the pulp press encouraged fascinated readers to participate, if vicariously, in the queer world of Tokyo's pubic sites—a tradition of "curiosity hunting" which had also consumed prewar readers of popular sexology.[10] In this way, the pathological and scopophilic lenses of the media rendered *danshō* as objects of scientific knowledge and popular fantasy, or what Jean-Paul Sartre once called the "body-for-others."[11]

To counter these objectifying tendencies of the pulp press, the second part of this essay adopts a phenomenologically-inspired approach to the bodies and practices of *danshō* which "considers the embodied experience of the speaking subject, who claims constative knowledge of the referent topic, to be a proper—indeed essential—component of the analysis of transgender phenomenon."[12] To this end, I pursue a close textual reading of roundtable discussions in order to reveal the embodied experiences of working class *danshō* and their relationships to the discourses and institutions that acted upon and through them. Defeat in a hyper-masculine war allowed these individuals, many former soldiers, to reposition themselves as male-bodied "women" within a society whose sex/gender system remained overwhelmingly hetero-normative. To be sure, the socioeconomic vagaries of early postwar society presented these cross-dressed male sex workers with great difficulties in realizing their dreams to leave the profession and become middle-class "housewives" of a stable male patron. However, their efforts to assert an ontologically satisfying sense of self which could also promote their material well-being demonstrate the resilience with which *danshō* transformed themselves into new beings during an era of great uncertainty.

## SETTING THE STAGE: TOKYO'S UENO PARK

According to an article published in 1952, there were seven major areas in Tokyo where cross-dressed male sex workers congregated alongside *panpan* girls.[13] While most of these areas could boast no more than twelve or thirteen male sex workers, Ueno Park was home to the largest population of *danshō*, twenty to thirty of whom had gathered there from early 1946.[14] Before World War II, Ueno Park, presented to the residents of Tokyo in 1924 as a gift from the Emperor, had been one of the city's most important cultural spaces, boasting national museums, Buddhist temples, and a zoological garden. At the same time, however, its back alleys were still known as home to a number of tea houses specializing in male prostitution.[15] Like Asakusa, Ueno Park was also in close proximity to another long-standing area of sexualized entertainment, the Yoshiwara, which catered to heterosexual liaisons. One of several licensed pleasure quarters dating back to the Tokugawa period (1600–1868), the Yoshiwara continued to flourish under administrative oversight by the modern Japanese state until MacArthur's 1946 decree formally abolished state-sanctioned prostitution.[16]

In spite of these legal measures, earlier traditions of sex work quickly re-emerged in the early postwar period around historic sites like Ueno Park—a major railroad hub that, between September 1945 and December 1946, unloaded five million demobilized soldiers and Japanese expatriates returning from its former empire.[17] With sex work deregulated by the early postwar state, the chaotic park and its environs quickly became a down-and-out site for drug trafficking, gangster activities, a flourishing black market, and a population of nearly 2,000 homeless people.[18] A 1949 magazine article entitled "A Cageless Zoo," a pejorative reference to the animalistic tendencies of the park's sex workers, suggests that *danshō*, although far outnumbered by their female counterparts, occupied a relatively high position in the spatialized class hierarchy of Ueno Park.[19] For example, the so-called "night hawks," dressed in baggy work trousers and inexpensive wooden clogs worn by women during the war, worked in the heights of the park's hills, where they covered their faces and serviced customers on a portable straw mat. By contrast, *panpan* girls, who tended to wear more expensive Western clothes and high heels, worked at ground level in the park by the south exit of the train station. The *danshō*, many of whom preferred less expensive and looser fitting Japanese dress to disguise themselves as women, also worked within the confines of the park.[20] References to these male-bodied, cross-dressed sex workers frequently placed them near the statue of Saigō Takamori, a symbolic reference to the late nineteenth-century samurai leader from Satsuma, a southwestern district of Japan known as a hotbed for homosexuality until the early twentieth century.[21] According to one former soldier who eventually entered the prostitution business after the war, the scene of fashionable *danshō* milling around the statue of Saigō, himself apparently fond of "beautiful boys," convinced this reluctant man to join the growing number of cross-dressed male sex workers in Ueno Park.[22]

Following their attack on the police, officials issued an ordinance in December 1948 that closed the park grounds after dark, one of nearly sixty such decrees aimed at controlling commercial sex in Tokyo.[23] However, none of these hetero-normative regulations specifically pertained to male-bodied sex workers, who could only be tried on the more shaky charge of swindling, requiring "proof" from a concerned witness.[24] Although never fully enforced, the night-time regulation also threatened the business practices of *danshō*, who often relied on darkness to disguise themselves as women for their primarily male clients. During the daytime, the ordinance did not prevent them from using the southern fringes of the park to continue their trade. Meanwhile, these innovative sex workers played up their immunity from the law as one of many "benefits" distinguishing them from the even greater surveillance of the *panpan*. Other "benefits" actively advertised by *danshō* included the relatively low incidence of sexually-transmitted diseases and their ability to serve customers more caringly than their female counterparts.[25] Even after various police interventions, reports suggest that the number of cross-dressed sex workers actually increased, reaching approximately sixty by 1952. And whereas many *panpan* girls moved to other locations after 1949, Ueno Park remained the stomping grounds for most of Tokyo's *danshō*. Although accounting for less than ten percent of the park's sex workers in 1946, by 1952 they comprised nearly fifty percent of Ueno prostitutes. So entrenched had cross-dressed sex workers become in this part of Tokyo that some veterans even opened a nearby *danshō* school where their aspiring disciples could learn the arts of makeup application, dressing, sewing, and female speech patterns.[26]

## THE BODY-FOR-OTHERS: PATHOLOGIZING AND SCOPOPHILIC GAZES

As their presence in Tokyo's sexual landscape became increasingly common, *danshō* quickly became the object of intense media scrutiny, spotlighted in a variety of representational forms. As mentioned above, popular knowledge of cross-dressed male sex workers was produced, in part, through police surveillance of the city's prostitution business, which officials associated with the black market, drug use, vagrancy, gangster activities, and petty crime. As members of this down-and-out society, *danshō* and other transgressive figures like the *panpan* girl thus figured prominently in discussions about re-establishing "healthy" sexual mores from the chaos of Japan's ravaged social landscape. [27] In one discursive guise, Japanese experts, drawing on prewar traditions of medical pathology, cast a distinctly sexological gaze on the cross-dressed male sex workers of Ueno Park.[28] Minami Takao, a professor of medicine at Keio University, was one such individual.[29] Also on staff at the Sakuragaoka Sanatorium, Minami collaborated with the welfare bureau of the Tokyo metropolitan government in forcefully expelling vagrants from Ueno Park and other locations throughout the city. On one 1947 roundup of individuals "deemed psychologically abnormal," Minami discovered a cross-dressed male sex worker with a Meiji (1868–1912) hairdo and a red skirt. Later detained and hospitalized, this *danshō*, along with another Ueno Park male sex worker already confined at the sanatorium, became the basis for a more thorough investigation of twenty such individuals.

Published in a journal entitled *Clinical Medical Digest* in July of 1948, Minami's report includes graphic photographs of his first two *danshō* patients, one of which features them completely naked against the sterile backdrop of the sanatorium examination room. To further expose their sexual souls, Minami subjected his patients to a litany of diagnostic tests, including questions regarding their family and occupational histories, bodily and psychological symptoms as well as their life experiences. From these case studies, Minami paints a picture of an economically downtrodden group of individuals whose own predilections for cross-dressing and same-sex sexuality drew them into prostitution. Although he failed to find the physiological signs of their feminization, a common pathology used to diagnose homosexuality (rather than what many today would call transgenderism),

Minami also took great pains to establish the empirical basis for their femininity. As evidence, he cited the "woman-like" ways in which they walked and spoke, previous employment they held in the cross-dressed *kabuki* theater or as eroticized café and restaurant waiters, and their own semi-coerced confessions of hoping to become nurturing housewives for future husbands. In spite of these findings, Minami struggled to square their feminized gender with the sexual practices of the twenty *danshō* he interrogated, sixty percent of whom had apparently engaged in sexual relations with women.[30] Dismissing "hermaphrodite" as a suitable diagnosis, he concluded his analysis by categorizing their condition as *dōsei sōshinshō*. Although the literal meaning of this term resonates with what scholars now call "homo-sociality," Minami, citing Western sexologists' understandings of this condition, diagnosed it as an abnormal disease and a sexual perversion.[31]

It was this incongruence and instability between what Minami considered the distinct categories of "gender" and "sexuality" that the popular media also addressed. However, rather than simply objectifying *danshō* as a problem to comprehend in rational, sexological terms, the pulp press sensationalized them as a matter of fascination, curiosity, and profit-making. Such a scopophilic gaze characterizes the writing of Sumi Tatsuya. In early 1949, Sumi penned *The Grove of Cross-Dressed Male Sex Workers*, a semi-fictional novel about the *danshō* of Ueno Park which later became a popular theatrical performance. The author himself was a postwar product of Ueno Park, having lived there for three years as a homeless vagrant who sold underground newspapers and begged for a living. In his production notes of the novel, Sumi described being startled by the "bizarre" lifestyles of the park's *danshō*. However, after working in the local welfare consultation office, he apparently came to understand how their sexual desires (rather than gendered personhood) had become a motivating force closely linked to their vagrancy and their struggle for survival. Through an inside story of their lives, Sumi thus aimed to question preconceived notions of *danshō* as pathological "perverts."[32] In spite of his stated intentions, the publication of *The Grove of Cross-Dressed Male Sex Workers* infuriated the *danshō* of Ueno Park—who accused the protagonist, a male sex worker named Tomio, of collaborating with Sumi to make a profit by exposing their lives. They became particularly irate when Sumi attempted to stage Tomio, a former actor of female roles in the *kabuki* theater, in a

**Figure 31.1** Photo exposé of *Danshō* lifestyles

**Figure 31.2** *Danshō* and their "perverted" customers

theatrical performance of his highly popular novel. Although he convinced Tomio to appear on stage by promising to give her all the proceeds from his novel, Sumi apparently reneged on his agreement, claiming that he had never made such a statement, and accused his star performer of extortion.[33]

As Sumi capitalized on sensationalizing the life of Tomio and her *danshō* friends, other writers in the pulp press followed in his footsteps, spotlighting the "bizarre" lifestyles of cross-dressed male sex workers in lurid photographic exposés.[34] Just four months after the release of Sumi's novel, a magazine called *All Novels* featured an eye-catching *danshō* applying makeup on the cover of a special issue devoted to crime—once again establishing the imagined (if not real) connection between this subversive practice and that of sex work. The caption accompanying Figure 31.1 makes direct reference to Sumi's work, crediting him for establishing *The Grove of Cross-Dressed Male Sex Workers* as a popular expression of the times.

The following pages featured semi-nude images of *danshō* in the men's side of the public bath, a practice that perhaps enticed potential customers. The caption accompanying the left image of Figure 31.2 explained the talents of some cross-dressed male sex workers who could fool other male bathers into thinking that they were of the opposite sex by disguising their private parts with a towel. The pathologizing caption also suggests that this practice, commonly undertaken by women and often mentioned in discussions of male sex workers, had become instinctual for the latter, thus proving their "feminization."

The caption accompanying the right image of Figure 31.2 introduced their customers, some of whom apparently knew *danshō* were not anatomical females and still willingly engaged in sexual relations with them.[35] It concludes by describing these male customers and their cross-dressed prostitutes as suffering from "sexual perversion," an expression that medical professionals like Minami had also used to diagnose *danshō*. In this way, the disparate terms of the media spotlight converged in unclothing these figures, revealing individuals who had allegedly strayed from the gender/sex system.

Even as many media reports bemoaned their alleged abnormality, others reveled in the perversity of *danshō*. Some even encouraged their readers to experiment with non-normative forms of gender and sexuality. In one short story entitled "Residence of Male Prostitutes," for example, the male protagonist encounters a cross-dressed male sex worker in the entertainment district of Asakusa, not far from Ueno Park.[36] Rather than turning around and going home, however, the protagonist is suddenly overtaken by a strong feeling of curiosity. He remarks on her smooth, white skin and her slim figure, and thinks she might be a woman. Soon, however, he notices a ball of cloth stuffed in her bosom and a bulge in her crotch. Although unwilling to answer the protagonist's question about her anatomical sex, she invites him back to her residence, where she lives with twelve other *danshō* in a secret organization. After a few days at their residence, they give him the female name of the cross-dressed male sex worker he had recently met on the street, Eriko. Before long, Eriko begins to train as a *danshō* himself, learning how to speak and act like a woman—albeit with only gradual success. Finally, after two months of gender training, the protagonist engages in his first "strange experience" of being penetrated and penetrating another man, an encounter which transforms him into a regular sex worker at Ueno Park.[37] Even as the pulp press drew on the pathological language of medical professionals and subjected cross-dressed sex workers to its own scopophilic gaze, the profit-oriented media also enticed readers to engage in their own practices of "curiosity hunting," thereby subverting the state's efforts to control public sexuality during a chaotic time of deregulation.[38]

## THE BODY-IN-ITSELF: *DANSHŌ* AS SPEAKING AND ACTING SUBJECTS

Although the media thus tended to objectify the bodies of *danshō*, one particular genre of the pulp press, the roundtable discussion (Figure 31.3), allows us to approach the embodied experiences and circumscribed agency of cross-dressed male sex workers as speaking and acting subjects. Not unlike George Chauncey's discussion of the effeminate male "fairy" in early twentieth-century New York, the hyper-feminized model of the early postwar *danshō* "offered many men a means of constructing public personas that they considered more congruent with their 'inner natures' than conventional masculine ones, but that were also consistent with the terms of the dominant gender culture in which they had been socialized and that had, therefore, helped constitute those 'inner natures.'"[39] Many roundtable discussions reveal that Japanese men who eventually became *danshō* also struggled during their childhood and adolescence to relate the materiality of their anatomical sex with a prescribed gender role and a normative gender identity. Their testimonies also expose how early postwar sex workers used feminized practices to explain the heterosexist culture they had recently encountered during their military service. Not unlike medical pathology, the pulp press often framed currying favor with one's superior and other "feminine" practices as the background for a case study of their sexual being. However, *danshō* participants in roundtable discussions used this interactive forum to express the many slippages among the categories of sex, sexuality, and gender then circulating among doctors, journalists, and other professionals. Meanwhile, news reporters also refused to retreat from these language games, pressing sex workers to accept these categories so that their bodily sex mirrored a fixed gender role and identity.

In one 1949 roundtable discussion with the title "Confessions of a Problem," three *danshō* explain from their present position as feminized male sex workers how, as boys and adolescents, they developed the rudiments of a gendered personhood that prewar and early postwar Japanese culture ascribed primarily, if not exclusively, to women.[40] Born in 1916, Ranko, for example, recounts how she only played games with girls as a youngster, while Masako reveals that she was often called a girl while growing up. When asked by the leader of this roundtable discussion when she became a woman, Otoki expresses her "inner feelings" by categorically stating, "Mentally, I was born a woman." Adopting feminine mannerisms resonating with their gendered selves thus allowed

**Figure 31.3** A *Danshō* Roundtable (1949)

these male-bodied individuals to make ontological sense of their personhood. They also used these epistemological frames to negotiate relationships with other men, some of which became carnal in nature. Indeed, both Ranko and Masako admit to having engaged in "sexual perversion" with gender-normative men as teenagers. Although perhaps modified to fit the pathological framework of the pulp press, their words suggest that they had, at least to some degree, adopted popular terms circulating in medical and media discourses. However, the use of these terms does not imply that they simply followed an innate desire for members of the same sex, whom they seem to have pursued tentatively and with some trepidation. Rather, re-fashioning themselves as *danshō* was the particular medium that allowed these men to square their inner sense of self with their self-feminized appearance. For example, Ranko, who worked in the entertainment district of Asakusa Park during the prewar period, recalled an experience from 1933 when a man followed her along the streets of Tokyo:

> In the end I gave him my naked body that night. As a result I felt that the things I had been troubled by had been resolved and I became so absorbed with it that I couldn't bring my hands to work. From such experiences I became obsessed with this world. And seventeen years later…

(70)

Even as Ranko and others sold sex to men as cross-dressed sex workers, early postwar *danshō* continued to position their gendered subjectivities as "real women" into a framework of dichotomous gender roles. Oftentimes, *danshō* professed the desire to become a customer's "wife." Becoming a "wife" in this way could enable working-class individuals to extricate themselves from the vagaries of the sexual market and enter into a more stable, domestic partnership common to the middle classes. Having lost family members and their homes in the World War II bombing of Japan, many *danshō* explained how they chose the profession both out of economic necessity and a desire for new forms of human intimacy. Struggling to earn enough money to buy food by working as a backstage dresser

**Figure 31.4** Unfulfilled dreams of becoming "housewives"

in the *kabuki* theater, Otoki—shown in the left image of Figure 31.4, crying about not being born as a woman and dreaming about marrying a beloved husband—finally succumbed to pressures to enter the sex trade. However, when the police roundup of 1948 threatened her financial well-being, she was forced to leave Ueno Park, taking up temporary work at a nearby cabaret to make ends meet.

Such financial uncertainties formed the material backdrop against which Otoki professed her penchant for a "domestic lifestyle" or, as she explained with a distinctly feminine tone, the desire "to take hold of a man, become his wife, and prepare his food." Masako, shown in the right image of Figure 31.4, also expressed a similarly bourgeois ideal, albeit one that was marked by the economic vagaries which accompanied the sex trade. As she explained, "Last year I was so fortunate to get a man who supported me, but his bankruptcy forced me to start working again." Although Ranko admitted a stronger inclination toward dispelling her loneliness by sleeping with men, she also described her relationship with the office chief of a small company in gendered terms as a middle-class housewife—that is, by cooking for him and washing his clothes in exchange for economic dependence. However, when his company went bankrupt and he descended into poverty, she too faced the harsh realities of the postwar economy. Ranko thus had no choice but to return to the sex trade, at least temporarily, in order to provide for herself, lest she too fall into the despised socioeconomic category of "vagrant."

In the end, Ranko's dream of becoming a housewife in a stable partnership with a successful husband remained an unrealized fantasy. As a result, she struggled to measure up to the idealized image of the middle-class "woman" they actively embraced. Having rejected the masculinity prescribed for them by the dominant gender order, Ranko and other like-minded *danshō* also realized that they could not "become men," neither in terms defined by their society nor by those they had come to identify. This situation left them suspended in an unstable, precarious, and often unhealthy existence, struggling to articulate a viable future. No longer able to return to the Buddhist temple where her family used to live, Masako found her situation so dire that she felt she could only depend on potassium cyanide, a compound she considered taking to commit suicide. More of an optimist, Otoki expressed her desire to leave the sex trade and make a living by running an *oden* (stewed vegetable soup) shop. While reminding Otoki that that such an endeavor required a financial patron, Ranko, always the realist, pointed to another *danshō*, Otomi, the protagonist in Sumi Tatsuya's *The Grove of Cross-Dressed Male Sex Workers*. Although swindled out of a profit, Ranko considered Otomi a model who both honored her "inner nature" and could forge an independent livelihood. In conclusion, Ranko and the other participants of this roundtable discussion urged the public to better understand and sympathize with their plight, one not simply defined by pathological "perversion." Rather, this plight involved finding a stable socioeconomic and emotional existence as male-bodied sex workers whose gender they struggled to transform into that of "real housewives."

Although they continued to express their femininity in these class-specific ways, their male bodies forced *danshō* to engage in a number of highly creative sartorial and corporeal practices in order to bridge the dissonance of what Susan Stryker, drawing on Frederic Jameson, calls "mirror-style representation[s]."[41] Part of an epistemological construction project aimed at expressing a personal truth about their bodies, these tactics allowed them to rearticulate their gendered personhood, usually without relying on morphological sex. Central to this project of self-fashioning was the concealment of the phallus, especially from customers who might respond negatively or even violently to the discovery of their genitalia.[42] This involved a practice known as the "lotus root," a vegetable characterized by its many orifices. Cupping their hand in the form of a lotus root, *danshō* created an ersatz vagina to simulate the experience of coital sex, while taking other precautions to keep their penises away from the probing hands of aroused men. To further conceal their genitalia from potential customers, most cross-dressed sex workers, particularly older ones, wore loose-fitting kimonos rather than tighter Western-style dresses, which might have revealed the contours of their pubic area.

Other roundtable discussions reveal a litany of creative practices of self-fashioning adopted by *danshō* of different ages and physical appearances in order to re-sex their bodies as female. This project involved modifying, if temporarily, the face, neck, breasts, buttocks, crotch, and other symbolically charged parts that provided others with the somatic data customarily used to determine one's sex as either male or female. The thirty-year-old Otsune explained how her old age required that she engage in time-consuming rituals of female beautification, such as using depilatory cream, applying makeup, and enhancing her buttocks. Such cosmetic practices allowed Otsune to pass during seven years as a kimono-wearing sex worker.[43] By contrast, her roundtable counterpart Miyo (twenty-two) seems to have passed as a Western-dressed *panpan* girl due to her young age and feminine body. As Otsune enviously explained, "This child has not one facial hair, her behind is large, and her breasts protrude. Thus, if she covers her crotch, Miyo can go into the women's side of the public bath and not a single person seems to know." While Miyo claimed that entering the men's side of the bath would be embarrassing to her, Otsune expressed similar feelings about baring certain parts of her male body to women on the other side of the public bath. On other hand, she encountered difficulties passing as a man, as male bathers often stared at her slender figure (Figure 31.5) and the extended time she spent applying makeup.

In order to further re-sex themselves as women, Otsune explained how *danshō* usually carried two towels: one to dry themselves off and another to cover their groin. Many semi-nude sex workers felt uncomfortable revealing these telling areas of their male bodies, especially when they targeted heterosexual men at the public bath as potential customers.[44]

Even when fully-clothed, *danshō* had to maneuver through a complicated set of bodily codes in order to successfully present themselves as anatomical females to their male clients.[45] For example, Isoko, a thiry-nine-year-old *danshō* working out of Ueno Park, explained that questioning customers tended to recoil if a cross-dressed sex worker found it necessary to declare that she was a biological male. On the other hand, Isoko worried that it would be fraudulent to tell a suspecting customer that he was a woman. Disagreeing with such a view, Ranko, her thirty-five-year-old colleague, explained

**Figure 31.5** *Danshō* re-sexing body with bath towel

her own strategy. She invited dubious clients to experience the superior affection provided by *danshō* as compared to their *panpan* counterparts. If a potential customer still refused, Ranko returned his money and searched for a more amenable client. Kokatsu, a forty-year-old *danshō*, also explained how many customers appreciated their elaborate attempts to re-sex themselves as women, herself having yet to encounter a dissatisfied client. Relieving herself from accusations of fraud, a charge the police did use to prosecute cross-dressed sex workers, Kokatsu could only wonder how many men she had slept with without them discovering her anatomical sex. Judging from Isoko's praise of a *danshō* who spent the night with the same man six times in one month without him knowing her bodily secret, Kokatsu seems to have perfected the skill of presenting her feminized body as a woman. However, the account of the twenty-eight-year-old Tokio demonstrates the anxieties that even the most feminine cross-dressed sex workers must have felt in attempting to pass as women. It also reveals that some of their customers embraced *danshō* and even preferred them over equally feminine women. According to Tokio's account, two men from a famous cosmetics company, both in search of a cross-dressed male sex worker, once mistook her for a *panpan* girl. It was not until she was forced to disclose her male anatomy that she finally convinced customers to spend the evening together.

## CONCLUSION

In sum, these sartorial and corporeal practices worked to bridge the gap between undertaking a common form of male-oriented sex work and expressing a gendered subjectivity and/or erotic desire that was not determined in "mirror-style" fashion by one's anatomy.[46] In this way, the category of *danshō* provided a convenient, if precarious, way for individuals to negotiate and suspend the sex/gender system, but not necessarily to transgress or dismantle it in the radical ways described by some queer theorists, such as Judith Butler. Much like their transgender counterparts elsewhere during this period, "they were," to quote Joanne Meyerowitz's study of American transsexuals, "neither symbols, emblems detached from social milieu, nor heroes or villains engaged in mythic battles to further or stifle progress. They were ordinary and extraordinary human beings who searched for workable solutions to pressing personal problems."[47]

As mentioned above, the subjectivities of early postwar *danshō* took shape amidst a perceived sense of liberation from the wartime exigencies of duty and patriotism. At the same time, these subjectivities developed alongside invasive forms of surveillance from both scopophilic media entrepreneurs and a criminalizing police force. The pulp press exposed these power dynamics, as the lives of cross-dressed sex workers become increasingly visible, although not fully legible. Even in objectifying accounts catering to a reading public with an insatiable appetite for both the pathological and the bizarre, individual *danshō* as speaking subjects parried this intrusive gaze into a personal world beyond the will to know and thus the power to control. Their words, when used for the "insurrection of subjugated knowledges," remind us of the creative ways in which these individuals redefined relationships to their bodies and struggled to find meaningful forms of intimacy during a time of unprecedented privations. The police "incident" of 1948 with which this essay begins is but one spectacular manifestation of the struggles that *danshō* endured on an everyday basis. Although most readers probably did not identify with their quotidian work of gendered embodiment, some of them likely discovered in their personal stories a universalized commentary about the material re-building of their own lives in the wake of Japan's leveling defeat.

Even as the country's economic situation gradually improved, many cross-dressed male sex workers remained in Tokyo's parks, mostly out of economic necessity. Although far fewer in number, some successful *danshō* used their popularity as sex workers to engage in less precarious forms of sexualized entertainment at indoor establishments. Still others, like Kobayashi Yuri, drew on her experience as a *danshō* to open Yushima, a same-sex tea house located near Ueno Park.[48] Kobayashi's tea house joined a growing number of so-called "gay bars" which sprouted up in Tokyo during the early 1950s. The emergence of these bars coincided with a growing aversion toward working-class *danshō* among many, but not all, gender-normative men who preferred less feminized partners.[49] This development, in turn, led to greater numbers of male-dressed sex workers as well as middle-class men who dressed in Western suits and cruised for other men in public places like Hibiya Park as well as at indoor sites, such as theaters, tea houses, and even train stations.[50] Through these processes, the fluid situation characterizing the early postwar period began to solidify into more rigid categories of queer desires and sites for their expression.[51] To be sure, the re-emergent gender/sex configuration came to privilege gender-normative men (many of the growing middle-class) whose sexual object choice tended to be similarly fashioned homosexual men or androgynous-looking "gay boys" working in the bar scene.[52] However, the words and actions of non-normative men (to say nothing of their lesser-known female-bodied counterparts) continued to have an effect on what individuals considered their "gender," if only because many (but not all) of them began to separate their public presentation as anatomical men from what they understood and embraced as their disguisable "(homo)sexuality."

## ACKNOWLEDGMENTS

Research for this paper was made possible by a Professional Development Grant from Colorado State University. I thank Amy Wasserstrom, Setsuko Means, and Eiko Sakaguchi at the Gordon W. Prange Collection for facilitating my trip to the University of Maryland in spring 2007. I also wish to express my gratitude to Dr. Ishida Hitoshi who, with great care and a wonderful sense of humor, guided me through the queer archives of Tokyo during the hot summer months of 2007.

# NOTES

1. Henry S. Rubin, "Phenomenology as Method in Trans Studies," *GLQ: A Journal of Lesbian and Gay Studies* 4: 2 (1998), 268.

2. "'Yoru no otoko' no shūdan bōkō: Keishi sōkan nagurareru" ["Group violence by 'men of the night': Police chief is punched"], *Mainichi shimbun*, November 23, 1948. Another newspaper report, "Nagurareta keishi sōkan" ["Police chief is punched"], can be found in *Mainichi shimbun*, November 23, 1948. For more on the thirty-two-year-old heroine of this incident, see "Tekken no Okiyo-san" ["Okiyo-san's knockout"] in Hirooka Keiichi, *Sengo seifūzoku taikei: Waga megamitachi* [*Compendium of Sexual Customs in Postwar Japan: Our Goddesses*] (Tokyo: Asahi shuppansha, 2000), 23–33.

3. For one account chronicling the development of this field, see Susan Stryker, "(De)Subjugated Knowledges: An Introduction to Transgender Studies" in Susan Stryker and Stephen Whittle (eds.), *The Transgender Studies Reader* (London: Routledge, 2006), 1–17.

4. Afsaneh Najmabadi presents queries along these lines in "Beyond the Americas: Are Gender and Sexuality Useful Categories of Historical Analysis?," *Journal of Women's History* 18: 1 (Spring 2006): 11–21. For a related analysis of the contemporary US through the lenses of race and class, see David Valentine, *Imagining Transgender: An Ethnography of a Category* (Durham, NC and London: Duke University Press, 2007). This is *not* to say that some trans-identified people in Japan did not come to adopt this model as a basis for subsequent political struggles. For more on the diversity of "transgender" practices in postwar Japan, see Mitsuhashi Junko, "Sengo nihon toransujendā shakai no rekishiteki henyō no sobyō" ["A sketch of historical changes in the transgender society of postwar Japan"] in Yajima Masami (ed.), *Sengo nihon "toransujendā" shakaishi I* [*A Social History of Transgenderism In Postwar Japan, Vol. 1*] (Tokyo: Sengo nihon "toransujendā" shakaishi kenkyūkai, 2000); Wim Lunsing, "What Masculinity? Transgender Practices among Japanese 'Men'" in James Roberson and Nobue Suzuki (eds.), *Men and Masculinities in Contemporary Japan* (London: Routledge, 2003); and Mark McLelland, *Queer Japan from the Pacific War to the Internet Age* (Oxford: Roman and Littlefield, 2005), 111–122 and 193–220.

5. Studies on the prewar history of non-normative genders and sexualities include Gregory M. Pflugfelder, *Cartographies of Desire: Male-Male Sexuality in Japanese Discourse, 1600-1950* (Berkeley, CA and Los Angeles, CA: University of California Press, 1999); McLelland 2005; and Jeffrey Angles, "Seeking the Strange: Ryōki and the Navigation of Normality in Interwar Japan," *Monumenta Nipponica* 6: 1 (2008): 101–141.

6. For a cautionary tale in this regard, see Evan B. Towle and Lynn M. Morgan, "Romancing the Transgender Native Rethinking the Use of the 'Third Gender' Concept," *GLQ: A Journal of Lesbian and Gay Studies* 8: 4 (2002): 469–497. One promising research agenda in this regard is outlined in Ara Wilson, "Queering Asia," *Intersections: Gender, History and Culture in the Asian Context* 14 (November 2006). http://intersections.anu.edu.au/issue14/wilson.html#n45, accessed January 12, 2012.

7. See, for example, Sarah Kovner, "Base Cultures: Sex Workers and Servicemen in Occupied Japan," *Journal of Asian Studies* 68: 3 (2009): 777–804; and Michiko Takeuchi, "'Pan-Pan Girls' Performing and Resisting Neocolonialism(s) in the Pacific Theater: U.S. Military Prostitution in Occupied Japan, 1945–52" in Maria Höhn and Seungsook Moon (eds.), *Over There: Living with the U.S. Military Empire from World War Two to the Present* (Durham, NC and London: Duke University Press, 2010), 78–108.

8. John Dower, *Embracing Defeat: Japan in the Wake of World War II* (New York: WW Norton and Company, 1999), 122. In this landmark study of the early postwar period, Dower mentions the incident of November 1948 in a footnote, only to say that the topic of male prostitution, as well as the broader topic of homosexual relations among Japanese and members of the occupation force, remains unexamined (580). For extended discussions of postwar *danshō*, see Mitsuhashi Junko, "Sengo Tōkyō ni okeru 'danshoku bunka' no rekishiteki hensen: Moriba no katasumi de" ["Historical and geographical changes in 'male-male sexual cultures' in postwar Tokyo: In a corner of gathering spots"], *Gendai fūzokugaku kenkyū* 12 (March 2006): 1–15; and Mark McLelland, *Love, Sex, and Democracy in Japan during the American Occupation* (New York: Palgrave Macmillan, 2012), 156–169.

9. *Danshō* also emerged in other large cities, especially Osaka, although my discussion here will focus on the capital, Tokyo. For a similar phenomenon in postwar Germany, see Jennifer V. Evans, "Bahnhof Boys: Policing Male Prostitution in Post-Nazi Berlin," *Journal of the History of Sexuality* 12: 4 (2003): 605–636.

10. On these traditions, see Pflugfelder 1999, 286–335, and Angles 2008.

11. Jean-Paul Sartre, *Being and Nothingness: A Phenomenological Essay on Ontology* (London and New York: Routledge, 2003), 315–326.

12. Stryker 2006, 12. For more on this approach as it pertains to female-to-male (FTM) transsexuality, see Rubin 1998. Also representative is Sara Ahmed, *Queer Phenomenology: Orientations, Objects, Others* (Durham, NC and London: Duke University Press, 2006).

13. The following discussion is based on "Tōkyō gaishō bunpuzu" ["Distribution map of Tokyo's street prostitutes"], *Ningen tankyū* 27 (July 1952), 36–48.

14. Women who catered to Western men charged higher rates than those who served Japanese men. In the Yūrakuchō district, for example, the former took in between 1,000 and 1,500 yen for a "short time" encounter and 2,000 to 5,000 yen for an "all night" hotel stay, while the latter were only paid 500 to 800 yen and 1,500 to 2,000 yen, respectively, for the

same services (Ibid., 38). According to one account from 1954, *danshō* reportedly charged 3,000 to 10,000 yen for an "all night" hotel stay with foreigners versus only 3,000 to 8,000 yen for their Japanese customers. "Danshō gakkō no seitai" ["Lifestyles in the *danshō* school"], *Fūzoku kagaku* (September 1954), 111.

15. Pflugfelder 1999. On prewar Tokyo, also see Angles 2008.
16. For more on the prewar state's policy toward prostitution, see Sheldon Garon, "The World's Oldest Debate?: Prostitution and the State in Imperial Japan, 1900–1945," *American Historical Review* 98: 3 (1993): 710–732.
17. Lori Watt, *When Empire Comes Home: Repatriation and Reintegration in Postwar Japan* (Cambridge, MA and London: Harvard University Press, 2009), 1. In addition to the 6.7 million Japanese who eventually returned to Japan, the postwar state also deported over one million former colonial subjects, including Koreans. On this post-colonial history, see Tessa Morris Suzuki, *Exodus to North Korea: Shadows from Japan's Cold War* (Lanham, MD: Roman and Littlefield Publishers, 2007).
18. Sumi Tatsuya, "Ueno e iku" ["Going to Ueno"], *Junkan nyūsu* 32 (January 1, 1947), 8–12. For a detailed account of life in postwar Ueno, see Ōtani Susumu, *Ikite iru: Ueno chikadō no jittai* [*Alive: Actual Circumstances of Ueno's Underground Passageways*] (Tokyo: Yūjinsha, 1948).
19. The following description is based on Kanzaki Kyoshi, "Ori no nai dōbutsuen: Yoru no Ueno no genjō hōkoku" ["Cageless Zoo: A contemporary report on Ueno by night"], *Josei kaizō* 4: 4 (April 1, 1949), 64–72.
20. According to the responses of twenty-five *danshō* surveyed in 1955, more than half (fifteen) preferred Japanese clothing, apparently because it fit their bodies better than Western clothing and because they could easily borrow kimonos from their families and friends. By contrast, younger *danshō*, or those for whom more tight-fitting Western clothes suited their slender bodies, tended to wear dresses. Shiga Yūji, "Josō aikōsha" ["Cross-dressing enthusiasts"] in Ōta Tenrei (ed.) *Daisan no sei: Sei wa hōkai suru no ka* [*The Third Sex: Will Sexuality Collapse?*] (Tokyo: Ningen no kagakusha, 1957), 353–354.
21. On the place of Satsuma in the Meiji period (1868–1912) discourses on homosexuality, see Pflugfelder 1999, 203–212.
22. Hirano Tofumi, "Gunpuku no danshōtachi" ["Cross-dressed male sex workers who used to wear military uniforms"], *Jissō jitsuwa* 1 (May 1, 1949), 138.
23. For more on these measures, see Fujino Yutaka, *Sei no kokka kanri: Baibaishun no kingendaishi* [*The State Management of Sex: A Modern and Contemporary History of Prostitution*] (Tokyo: Fuji shuppan, 2001), 195–197.
24. "Juken yoka" ["Leisure from exam preparation"], *Keisatsu shinpō* 2: 2 (November 15, 1948), 57.
25. "Ryōki zadankai: Danshō (okama) no seitai (onoroke)" ["A roundtable discussion of the bizarre: Lifestyles of cross-dressed male sex workers"], *Kaiki zasshi* 2 (November 1, 1948), 9.
26. "Danshō gakkō no seitai" ["Lifestyles in the danshō school"], *Fūzoku kagaku* (September 1954), 111.
27. For more on these efforts, see Mire Koikare, *Pedagogy of Democracy: Feminism and the Cold War in the U.S. Occupation of Japan* (Philadelphia, PA: Temple University Press, 2009).
28. For more on the history of medical discourse on (same-sex) sexuality in prewar Japan, see Pflugfelder 1999, 193–285, and Sabine Frühstück, *Colonizing Sex: Sexology and Social Control in Modern Japan* (Berkeley, CA and Los Angeles, CA: University of California Press, 2003), 83–115.
29. The following discussion is based on Minami Takao, "Danshō ni kansuru 2, 3 no seishin igakuteki kōsatsu" ["Two or three medico-psychological observations of *danshō*"], *Shinsatsu daigesto* 3: 4 (July 10, 1948), 19–20. For Minami's other writings, see "Dōseiai ni ichiruikei (danshō) ni tsuite: Sengo no ichijiki Ueno kōen ni tamuroshita danshōgun no kansatsu o tōshite" ["On one variety of homosexuality (*danshō*) through observations of the group of cross-dressed male sex workers stationed in Ueno Park for a short period after the war"] in Minami Takao and Komine Shigeyuki, *Dōseiai to dōsei shinjū no kenkyū* [*Studies on Homosexuality and Same-Sex Suicide*] (Tokyo: Komine kenkyūjo, 1985), 268–304.
30. *Donten* was the popular argot for *danshō* who sleep with both men and women. "Danshoku shakōba" ["Homosexual gathering spots"], *Ningen tankyū* 28 (August 1952), 55.
31. In a more popular discussion on his investigation of these twenty *danshō*, he transliterated the two Chinese characters for cross-dressed male prostitute into the phonetic syllabary as "man-women" in order to capture the incongruence of their gender and sexuality. Minami states that feminized men and masculinized women do not necessarily have *dōsei sōshinshō*, but that this condition often leads to homosexuality or sexual relations with both men and women. "Danshō gidan (otoko onna no hanashi)" ["Discussions of *danshō* (stories about men-women)"], *Danwa* 1: 12 (November 15, 1948), 19–23. For another more popular discussion, see Minami Takao, "Danshō no seishin igaku: Dansei josei no seikaku ni kanshite" ["Psychological pathology of cross-dressed male sex workers: On the character of men and women"], *Fujin no seki* 6: 6 (June 25, 1948), 28–35.
32. Sumi Tatsuya, "Danshō no sekai: Danshō no mori sakusei nōto" ["The world of *danshō*: Production notes on *The Grove of Cross-Dressed Male Sex Workers*"], *Sekai hyōron* 4: 2 (February 1, 1949), 59–60.
33. "Geikai no naimaku: Danshō gekijiken no shinsō" ["The inside story on the entertainment world: The truth about the *danshō* play"], *Ekkusu* 3: 7 (June 1, 1949), 7. As a result of this confrontation, Sumi decided to extricate himself from the world of cross-dressed male sex workers and concentrate, instead, on poetry and literature. "Nogami kara enko e: *Danshō no mori* no Otomi butai ni kōsei" ["From Ueno to sitting: Otomi from *The Grove of Cross-Dressed Male Sex Workers* returns to the stage"], *Sanjunichi* 1: 2 (June 10, 1949), 30.
34. The first of such photographic exposés appears in the same issue as the first installment of Sumi's novel. See "Otoko henjō" ["Overturned men"], *Bungei yomimono*, 8: 2 (February 1, 1949), 2–8.

35. Although media reports frequently offered estimates of customers who claimed to know the anatomical sex of their *danshō* partners (approximately one-third to one-half), they failed to offer a conclusive picture of this elusive question.

36. Unless otherwise noted, the following discussion is based on Horii Shōgo, "Kagema yashiki" ["Residence of male prostitutes"], *Bēze* 2: 7 (July 1, 1949), 40–44. For another account of a man who became a *danshō* (in this case, for just one day), see Tanuma Kiyoshi, "Rinji danshōki" ["The account of a temporary *danshō*"], *Amatoria* (March 1954), 110–115.

37. Many reports claimed that *danshō* enjoyed performing the insertee role, thus equating their feminized gender with their "woman-like" sexual preferences. Others, however, mentioned that such practices reflected the demands of their customers and even suggested that many cross-dressed male sex workers preferred the inserter role. On the latter phenomenon, see Minami Satohiro, "Danshō no seiseikatsu" ["The sexual life of *danshō*"], *Ribe* 4: 4–5 (May 1, 1948), 20.

38. For other examples of both male and female curiosity hunters, see McLelland 2012, 165–177.

39. George Chauncey, *Gay New York: Gender, Urban Culture, and the Making of the Gay Male World, 1890–1940* (New York: Basic Books, 1994), 49. Unlike the American "fairy" who did not cross-dress, the Japanese *danshō*'s public persona was based on transvestitism and depended, in large part, on her ability to pass as a woman.

40. The following discussion is based on Wim Lunsing (tr.), "Confessions of a Problem: A Round-table discussion with Male Prostitutes" in Mark McLelland, Katsuhiko Suganuma, and James Welker (eds.), *Queer Voices from Japan: First-Person Narratives from Japan's Sexual Minorities* (Lanham, MD: Lexington Books, 2007), 69–79. The original, "Mondai no kokuhaku: Danshō zadankai," was published in *OK: Ero and Thrill* 2: 5 (August 1949), 12–16.

41. "In this seemingly commonsensical view," Stryker writes, "the materiality of anatomical sex is represented socially by a gender role, and subjectively as a gender identity: a (biological) male is a (social) man who (subjectively) identifies himself as such; a woman is similarly, and circularly, a female who considers herself to be one." (9)

42. Some customers consciously sought out this erotic pleasure in cross-dressed men, while others simply learned to accept it after coming to appreciate the nurturing character of *danshō*. For examples of violence committed against cross-dressed male sex workers, see Enuma Saburō and Katō Yoshirō , "Josō no kaishitai" ["A mysterious, cross-dressed corpse"], *Ryōki jitsuwa* 1 (November 10, 1947), 13–18; and "Okama satsujin jiken" ["Murder incident of faggot"], *Shōsetsu shimbun* 2 (August 1, 1949), 6.

43. "Zadankai: Danshō no sekai" ["A roundtable discussion: The world of *danshō*"], *Bungei shunjū* 3: 1 (January 1, 1949), 36–45.

44. "Ryōki zadankai: Danshō (okama) no seitai (oiroke)" ["A roundtable discussion on curiosity hunting: Lifestyles of *danshō*, or the sexual passions of faggots"], *Kaiki zasshi* 2 (November 1, 1948), 6–9.

45. Unless otherwise mentioned, the following discussion is based on "Zadankai: Danshō no sekai" ["A roundtable discussion: The world of *danshō*"], *Bungei shunjū* 3: 1 (January 1, 1949), 36–45.

46. In addition to cross-dressed male sex workers, approximately ten "*panpan* boys" (Western-dressed adolescents) reportedly trolled Hibiya Park as early as 1947 in search of male customers, which likely included Americans and other Western members of the nearby Supreme Commander for the Allied Powers headquarters. Murata Ichirō, "Yami o oyogu: Panpan bōi" ["Panpan boys who swim in the dark"], *Surirā* 3 (January 1, 1948), 27–28. Young, male-dressed sex workers were also referred to as "kakusaku (cock suck) boys." "Okame no kan: Josō no otoko" ["The homosexual segment: Cross-dressed men"] and "Kakusaku bōi no kan: Satsu no miryoku" ["The cock suck boy segment: The lure of money"], *Hanzai yomimono* 1: 3 (October 1, 1947), 12–13 and 20–21. For more on this phenomenon, see McLelland 2012, 163–164.

47. Joanne Meyerowitz, *How Sex Changed: A History of Transsexuality in the United States* (Cambridge, MA: Harvard University Press, 2002), 12–13.

48. Kabiya Kazuhiko, an amateur ethnographer of Tokyo's postwar gay scene, explains this phenomenon in market terms based on the "principle of supply and demand." "Homo no hanataba III: Dōseiai no hyakka jiten" ["A homo bouquet III: Encyclopedia of homosexuality"], *Fūzoku kagaku* (August 1953), 143. Kabiya dates the emergence of these new male-dressed sex workers to mid-1951. "Danshoku shakōba" ["Homosexual gathering spots"], *Ningen tankyū* 28 (August 1952), 47–48. For homosexual men's animosity towards cross-dressed male sex workers, see Itō Seiu and Takahashi Tetsu, "Tengoku ka, jigoku ka: Danshi dōseiai no tsudoi" ["Heaven or hell?: Gatherings of homosexual men"], *Ningen tankyū* (January 1951), 75–76, and Kabiya Kazuhiko, "Dōseiai ni okeru seishinha to nikutaiha" ["The spiritual and corporal factions of homosexuality"] *Amatoria* (August 1954), 155.

49. Based on a survey of 500 gay men interviewed between the spring of 1951 and the summer of 1953, 30 percent responded that they met other gay men in parks, 45 percent met in theaters, and only 15 percent in teahouses and bars. An additional 10 percent claimed to prefer cruising in trains and other public places. Takabatake Masurō, "Sodomia no jittai chōsa" ["An actual survey of sodomy"], *Fūzoku kagaku*, (January 1954), 173. For a description of Tokyo's gay bars in the mid-1950s, see "Lifestyles of the Gay Bars," in Mark McLelland, Katsuhiko Suganuma, and James Welker (eds.) *Queer Voices from Japan: First Person Narratives from Japan's Sexual Minorities*. (Lanham: Lexington Press, 2007). 105–138.

50. For more on this process, see Ishida Hitoshi and Murakami Takanori, "The Process of Divergence between 'Men who Love Men' and 'Feminized Men' in Postwar Japanese Media," *Intersections: Gender, History and Culture in the Asian Context* 12 (January 2006). http://intersections.anu.edu.au/issue12/ishida.html#t4, accessed January 12, 2012.

51. On the figure of the "gay boy," see McLelland 2005, 101–111.

# 32

## *An Ethics of Transsexual Difference*

### Luce Irigaray and the Place of Sexual Undecidability

GAYLE SALAMON

LUCE IRIGARAY IS A CELEBRATED FRANCOPHONE PSYCHOANALYTIC FEMINIST who, over the course of her career, has developed a thorough critique of what she, following Derrida, terms the "phallogocentric" bias of the Western philosophical tradition—that is, the tendency of Eurocentric thought to privilege determinative, positivist constructions of knowledge and to gender such forms of knowledge as masculine, phallic, and patriarchal, at the expense of "aporetic", incomplete, and indeterminate forms of knowledge gendered feminine. In this article, Gayle Salamon, a student of feminist philosopher Judith Butler and a professor of English at Princeton University, turns Derrida's deconstructive method on Irigaray herself to critique elements of Irigaray's thought that Salamon deems biological-determinist and gender-essentialist. Salamon asks how transsexual, transgender, and genderqueer embodied subjects offer new possibilities for ethical relations between self, place, and others that exceed the binaristic (and implicitly heteronormative) assumptions of penis and womb, man and woman, and masculine/feminine that animate and structure Irigaray's oeuvre. She reads against itself Irigaray's reading of Aristotle's *Physics*, in which Irigaray claims that woman finds herself by becoming a place in which man can find himself. She argues that the subject's "corporeal surveillance" of the outermost contours of its material body, which Irigaray posits as basis for feminine relationality to self and others, can be equally generative for bodies and subjects that do not cohere within sex/gender binaries, and which can generate other forms of ethical interpersonal and environmental interaction. Salamon decouples the magical chains of association that, for Irigaray, indissociably link genital morphology, masculine and feminine psychical dispositions and identifications, and social genders; she thereby opens new potentials within Irigaray's own thought for "giving difference its due as a vital force" in ways that do not foreclose possibilities for transgender, transsexual, and genderqueer personhood.

### AGAINST SEXUAL HYLOMORPHISM

Luce Irigaray raises a number of questions in "Place, Interval" about place, sexual difference, and the body as it is given through relation.[1] I want to ask whether a nonheteronormative reading of body and relation is possible within the logic of Irigaray's work in *An Ethics of Sexual Difference* and, if so, what room might be made for sexual relationships that fall outside the scope of the strictly heterosexual or bodily and identificatory configurations that cannot be understood as strictly male or female. I want to follow Irigaray in insisting on the importance of a theory of place and relation to such questions and to depart from her by moving toward a number of points at which such an intervention might begin, a queer reading of Irigaray in which bodies, boundaries, and relations of sexual difference need not exclude the sexually different or the differently sexed.

Irigaray's reading of Aristotle in "Place, Interval," like her readings of other philosophers, is primarily concerned with relation, with self and other, where *self* is figured as the masculine subject of philosophy and *other* as its elided feminine. Central to her reading of Aristotle is an inquiry into the place of that relation between self and other. Woman, Irigaray will argue, is allied with place in the same way that she is allied with matter against the masculinity of form, and, in several crucial ways, place resembles form but is not reducible to it. This is at first a surprising strategy, a reversal of the ways in which matter has been historically allied with the feminine and form with the masculine. Irigaray proceeds quite differently here, and her reading of form and boundedness, rather than matter, as feminine nevertheless places its anchor in the sexual specificity of the body. Irigaray's reading hinges on the fact that matter in Aristotle's account is both density *and indeterminacy,* and the view of matter that we are given in *Physics* IV understands it to be fundamentally without form or shape. In "Place, Interval," Irigaray reads form in Aristotle as a description of the feminine, as a description of place.

As we shall see, there is an impossibility of place for the feminine: place is what the feminine is for the masculine, but what the masculine can never be for the feminine or, indeed, what the feminine can never quite be for herself. Irigaray ingeniously reverses this and reads the feminine as the container, that which houses the masculine and functions as the fixed external boundary for his moving center. The problematic, as Irigaray poses it, is for the feminine to find or to become a place for herself and thus find herself in place, and this is accomplished so that she may become place for the masculine. The means by which she accomplishes this, a reclaiming of the skin, reads at first as a strategy that might be deployed as successfully by the masculine as by the feminine, a means of finding body and place, but there are important ways in which a "corporeal surveying" of the outermost layer of the body, the skin—or indeed, of the body *as* that which is bounded by its skin—might even confound the familiar divisions between masculine and feminine as they are articulated here.

In my reading of Irigaray's reading of Aristotle, I want to make two claims about place, the first, following Irigaray, having to do with the place of self and the second, departing from her, having to do with the place of relation. Thinking seriously about the external contours of the bodily boundary, as Irigaray suggests that we do with "skin," can help us understand how a body—especially a female body—might find its own place and thus be able to move from its own place toward relation with others.[2] The second claim I want to make is about that relation to others. Irigaray has offered sexual difference as "the major philosophical issue of our age,"[3] and she turns to Aristotle to theorize relations across sexual difference, asking how bodily and sexual relations might bridge the interval of sexual difference. I want to suggest that even with Irigaray's often dazzling conceptual reversals, interventions by which her own text comes to be folded around Aristotle's like a skin, in "Place, Interval" the question of sexual difference ends at an impasse. This impasse stems from a fundamentally *hylomorphic* understanding of sexual difference: a conviction that male and female, like matter and form, must always be ontologically conjoined.

Is it possible that Irigaray's notion of sexual difference and her insights into the ways in which sexual difference is crucially generative might be of use in an account of sexual difference that aims to challenge gender and sexual heteronormativity? What would it look like if the divide of sexual difference were not fixed in the place it now occupies, marked as the boundary between "male" and "female"? Were that boundary not mapped onto the body in strictly determinative ways, we might be able to theorize sexual difference between women, between men, or between bodies and psyches who do not find easy home or place in either of these categories. A queer reading of the place of sexual difference, then, might be able to answer my second question by way of the first.

## WHERE IS PLACE?

Midway through the *Physics,* Aristotle turns to the question of place, explaining that we must have a thorough understanding of place if we are to understand both existence and motion, "both because all suppose that things which exist are *somewhere* (the non-existent is nowhere—where is the goat-stag or the sphinx?), and because 'motion' in its most general and primary sense is a change of place."[4] Contrary to the hope that place will be sufficient to give things a solid anchor in existence, we find that place is reckoned only through relation. The place of things, and thus the "thing" of place, is only found through other things. According to Aristotle, "the existence of place is held to be obvious from the fact of mutual replacement. Where water now is, there, in turn, when the water has gone out as from a vessel, air is present. When therefore another body occupies this same place, the place is thought to be different from all the bodies which come to be in it and replace one another" (208b, l.i).

When Aristotle first introduces us to place in the beginning of *Physics* IV, he does so indirectly. We are led to infer place not from any direct experience with or of it, but because of the loss of a body or object, its displacement (or destruction) by another object. "The existence of place is held to be obvious from the fact of mutual replacement." Place is the nonmaterial residue of two different, separate bodies. The question of place is from the outset already a question of relation, of mobility, of replacement, of bodies, place reveals itself through a succession of different bodies, one supplanting the other in the same space—water then air—and the relation of these different bodies is mutual only to the extent that it is mutually exclusive: place stands as a testament to the fact that the two bodies cannot share the same space. Place is the marker of the bounded and separate identity of the two bodies, and only by virtue of this does space become transmogrified into place. Place is the space where two bodies can never coexist, the space that they cannot ever share.

Place then is testament to a lack of relation, of the progression from water to air, where neither leaves the trace of itself, leaves no mark that it was housed or held there. Place is place to the extent that it is different from either of these, water or air, and neither leaves any trace. Place persists emptily and is established through a network of relations of mutual exclusivity. Place exists to the extent that it is demarcated and separate from the things that inhabit it, and it persists to the extent that the things that inhabit it, in this first instance, at least, are different from one another and pass through it leaving no part of themselves in it.

Aristotle, then, seems to be offering place as a relation, or non-relation, of mutual exclusivity, at least at first. Place develops as the text continues, however, becoming the location where relation happens and eventually becoming that very relation. Place is eventually established as *only* relation, only established by the proximity of the two bodies who share it, neither of which is quite place. "Place," writes Aristotle, "is the boundary of the containing body at which it is in contact with the contained body." We are still presented with two separate substances, neither partaking of the other, but are now offered a place that is entirely comprised of the touch between them. Aristotle eventually concludes that "the innermost motionless boundary of what contains is place" (212a, I.20). That is, an object, a body, moves within the context of a fixed and bounded something that does not move. And that fixed and bounded something is not merely a space of contact, but is itself another body, a body that is necessary for the establishment of place but is not reducible to it, is not the same as place itself: "If then a body has another body outside it and containing it, it is in place, and if not, not" (212a, I.32). Place would then be the plane of contact between the body that encapsulates and the body that is held.

Here we may note the problematic that Aristotle touches upon briefly and Irigaray dwells upon at some length: if place is the *innermost* boundary of the body containing, this leaves the external layer of that body without its own place, outside of place. In order to see if the outermost surface of the containing body, the feminine body, might become housed in itself, or cast a place around itself, Irigaray suggests that we read this external boundary as skin: "But each of us (male or female) has a place—this place that envelops only his or her body, the first envelope of our bodies, the corporeal identity, the boundary, that which delineates us from other bodies. Form and configuration also determine one's size and all that makes one body unsubstitutable by another. Could this be called a corporeal *surveying*?"[5]

## THE GOAT-STAG OR THE SPHINX

We will return to this question of corporeal surveying: what exactly is it? Is it a scopic activity? A tactile one? What are the proper, and improper, objects for such a survey?[6] Here we will note Irigaray's claim that to become place for the man, woman must be place for herself. Like Aristotle, she introduces us to place by showing us the existence of place prior to relation, a radical boundedness into which the other does not—cannot—move. We have the place of the self established as the place of the body and the place of the body understood as its outermost boundary, its envelope, its skin. In the Aristotelian model, however, place does not yet encompass the outermost boundary of this body. The task as Irigaray describes it is to transform the skin into something that also contains, to feel the skin as its own bounding envelope so that the body might house itself. The body must perform that bounding function for itself before it can properly house the masculine. The first step toward relation between feminine and masculine, Irigaray suggests, is for woman to find and claim her body as a discrete and separate entity.

I will return in a moment to the collapse of feminine and woman here and see if it might not be possible to coax those two categories apart, in order to give them a relation to one another other than simply sameness. It is important to understand this relational bind that Irigaray describes, that woman's own emergence as a discrete entity cannot come before her encounter with the other but rather only emerges in relation to this other who is proximate to her, installed inside of her, away from whom she needs to retract to the outermost extensions of her body and being in order that she might return with something like place to offer him. In order to find the place that each of us, female and male alike, *is,* the feminine retracts into the particularity of herself, but finds the same problematic enacted at the level of her own individual body. If our skin is what "delineates us from other bodies," the other body is already installed at the exact moment and precise place at which I find myself; this other who is not me delineates my own boundary. The body belongs to the self to the extent that it "delineates us from other bodies," and thus the feminine finds her place as inescapably bordered by and bound to the place of the masculine, with the result that she cannot even extend into her own skin without feeling the press of the masculine on the other side of it.

But even though male and female are perfectly and inescapably joined, or perhaps *because* they are inescapably joined, Irigaray makes clear that we must not then understand them to be collapsible or substitutable. The shared border between male and female becomes the occasion of the shoring up of the boundary between them. And this boundary, this determinant of categorization, turns out to be bodily form, since "form and configuration also determine one's size and all that makes one body unsubstitutable by another." Irigaray, like Aristotle, reckons the body here as something more precise and distinct than merely the mass of matter of which it is comprised. Mapping my own body means feeling not only its weight, but its form and shape, and these latter are only perceptible as I feel the press of myself out toward the world where another body, another self, is located. We see again in Irigaray's text another surprising reversal: whereas what secures place in Aristotle is the substitutability of one kind of body for another, Irigaray points here toward the limits of that substitutability and suggests that the form and shape of the body secure for it an identity, though not a sameness, that allows and enables proximity. If one kind of thing is unsubstitutable for another, then two bodies might share the same space, inhabit the same place, with no fear of engulfing or annihilating each other. Though they are determined and constituted in relation to one another, their differences of form and configuration, their distinct morphologies secure and solidify their distinct identities. This last is crucial, for if one thing, in the act of replacing in space, takes over or overcomes another kind of thing, it is not only the thing that is vanquished, but place itself.

What does it mean to suggest that one body is unsubstitutable for another? And how can this help us make sense of sexual difference? I am most interested here in the ways that the singularity or unsubstitutability said to characterize bodies across sexual difference is secured by ascribing an interchangeability to bodies *within* sexual difference. The logic by which the male body is unsubstitutable for the female body is the same logic that would posit every male body as able to stand in for any other or viewing women, in some sense, as interchangeable parts of Woman. What is unsubstitutable about these bodies is not just any singular quality, not even the vicissitudes of size and shape, but their designation as "masculine" or "feminine." Irigaray writes: "For the masculine has to constitute itself as *a vessel* to receive and welcome. And the masculine's morphology, existence, and essence do not really fit it for such an architecture of place" (39). Understood in this way, it is not a difficulty of relation or a failure of imagination that makes the masculine unable to receive and welcome, it is rather the poor "fit" of the morphology of the masculine that Irigaray deems determinative. But what if we were to understand masculinity as something different from the male body, femininity as not reducible to the vessel of the, womb? What if sexual difference were not parsed between the registers of morphology so neatly, so that masculinity might be less simply a matter of morphology but also a mode of relation?

Must sexual difference be legible at the surface of the body? And is sexual difference the same thing as "natural" sex? There are, of course, a number of ways to pose the question of sexual difference that would not reduce it to the category male or female, determined by bodily or genital morphology. One could, for example, formulate sexual difference in a way that would not require the identificatory possibilities it extended to relate mimetically to the dimorphic tendencies of genital morphology assumed to be the material markers of that difference. That is, if one thinks sexual difference in other than binary terms, the category can become unyoked from determinative bodily materiality in a way that makes it easier to resist the temptation to posit genital morphology as essentially determinative not only of sexual difference but also of the self. If sexual difference is categorically and functionally indistinguishable from *genital* difference, which is itself understood to manifest (as) a binary, than sexual difference is genital difference is genital dimorphism.

Like the goat-stag or the sphinx, Aristotle and Irigaray would seem to agree that the sexually undecidable does not exist and is located nowhere ("The non-existent is nowhere—where is the goat-stag or the sphinx?"). The goat-stag and the sphinx, who are themselves ambivalently located and fundamentally undecidable in terms of sexual difference, appear in the first sentence of book 4 in order to proclaim that they are located nowhere. Aristotle seems at first to be offering this monstrous couple to demonstrate that everything that exists must have its proper place. The passage as it stands, however, appears to be making this claim from the other direction: what secures the ontological primacy of place is precisely the fact that anything that is categorically undecidable cannot be located in any proper place. What renders a thing or being impossible is literally that it *has no place*. It is not quite that an understanding of place might be discerned by a thorough examination of existence, but rather that a proper orientation toward place can help us determine what things exist. We look around, in no place do we find a goat-stag or a sphinx, and this absence is evidence for our conclusion that such things do not exist.

We look around, we notice that the beings we encounter are male or female, and we make a swift and sure conclusion about the place of gender and of sexual difference. The feminine is the female is the one with a womb is woman, the masculine is male, and this of "morphology, existence, and essence." It remains to be determined, however, by what measure, what method of corporeal surveying the masculine or the feminine might be decided.

## CORPOREAL SURVEILLANCE AND SEXUAL UNDECIDEABILITY; OR, MINDING THE GAP

What if the bodies that we survey resist conforming to that most familiar of binaries, male and female? What if the objects of surveillance were transgendered bodies or other bodies that challenge the familiar divides by which we are accustomed to parsing sexual difference? Irigaray suggests that coexistence in place, the establishment of a place where masculine and feminine could reside together, is the ultimate goal of relation and can only be established once the distance between masculine and feminine is closed, "if the split between them (in the division of both work and nature) were bridged" (37), and she suggests a "corporeal surveying" as the method by which the establishment of this new place might become possible. The corporeal surveying Irigaray suggests would then close up the interval between the two bodies, span the gap between them, and allow masculine and feminine to coincide in sameness, in place.

And yet, even granting this interval exists (although Aristotle is quite deliberate in demonstrating that this interval is an illusion, a trick of form, in 2iib, I.15–20), it is unclear that the most productive response to this split, this gap, this embodied difference is to close it up. Indeed, we might think "corporeal surveying" as a method of apprehending not only the difference of the other, as Irigaray suggests, but also as a way of taking measure of the difference that inheres in my own flesh. Irigaray insists that we attend the difference that is always already installed at the level of not merely the blunt materiality of my body but also the labile boundary with the other that finally comprises my form. In this way, place becomes not the shared and self-identical space of sameness, but, more generatively and more radically, the place where I confront the otherness of the other without annihilating or canceling that difference or replicating the other in my own image.

What, then, are the effects of this corporeal surveying? It is attempted in order to close up the gap between the male and female, but I will suggest that this is only an incidental effect of the survey. Its aim is to find the outermost boundary of woman, which must be located and inhabited for woman to be able to establish place for herself. Locating this boundary is crucial for woman in particular because she is, for Irigaray, perpetually open, never closed off or sealed up. But the unbounded body can never be whole, whether that body is a mundane material object or the human form. Woman relies for her coherence on the boundary of difference that demarcates her singularity, the external edge of the masculine. What this corporeal surveying seems to show us is a condition of bodily being in which the masculine acts as place to house the feminine—an exact reversal of Irigaray's most familiar figuration of sexual difference—to define her borders and guarantee her existence. As place is coincident with the thing and boundaries are coincident with the bounded, so too is masculine necessarily always coincident with feminine, male always coincident with female. Whereas we are accustomed in Irigaray's work to understanding the feminine and the female as the condition of possibility for the masculine and the male, within this scene the masculine becomes the constitutive outside of the feminine, her condition of being.

Although Irigaray would seem to offer us the concept of the interval as a way of circumventing the logic of masculine form giving shape to the otherwise formless unboundedness of the feminine, we must stray far from the Aristotelian model to consider this possibility, as it requires an impossible extension between bodies. As these bodies are shown to be always in necessary continuity with another, we then have man and woman inescapably conjoined *as a direct result* of Irigaray's insistence that these bodies are male and female.

## TO BE MORE THAN TWO

Thus is magically guaranteed an indissoluble nearness between two categories that are at first posited as entirely separate. The insistence on the radical boundedness of each kind of being across the divide of sexual difference secures for each not only a coherent and concrete identity but also an eternally proximate point of contact and place of meeting. This suggestion that the relation between members of different categories will be nearer and more vital than the relation between members of the same category is a particularly Aristotelian formulation, encapsulated in his observation that "bodies which are united do not affect each other, while those which are in contact interact on each other" (212b, 130). It is the same logic that underlies Irigaray's proclamation that "man and woman is a most mysterious and creative couple" (199).

Striking as the consequences of this position are for theorizing relations across sexual difference, they turn out to be still more stark when we consider relations among people who are nominally "of" the same sexual category. That is: relation within sexual difference turns out to be no relation at all. Woman's position relative to another woman can only be one of sexual indifference. There has been much contention on this point, and her work on ethical relations and sexual difference has been located at various points on the spectrum between heteronormative and homophobic. Irigaray has responded to charges of this kind by affirming the primacy of sexual difference, suggesting homosexuality is a question of sexual *choice* rather than sexual *difference* and that the problem of sexual difference is as primary for homosexuals as it is for heterosexuals. Their homosexuality, in Irigaray's eyes, is merely a flight from this problem, not a renegotiation of its terms.

This is absurd for a number of reasons: its insistence that sexual choice and sexual difference are strictly separate and separable realms, its figuration of "choice" as the proper rubric for understanding homosexuality, further emphasizing her view of both heterosexuality and proper gendering as compulsory. Perhaps most alarming is the assertion that homosexuality is a flight from difference, merely love of the same that has no relationship of difference at work within it. In order to achieve an ethical relationship, Irigaray has said that it is necessary for a couple *to be two*; as she understands things, this is not something that a gay or lesbian couple—or some other, queerer pairing—can ever quite manage.

And yet, even as she appears to be dismissing homosexuality as a flat and frictionless nonrelation, her own theory of relation offers the tools for describing its possibilities otherwise. What is presented as an insurmountable dilemma becomes immediately more potent and promising if we reconfigure the location of the sexuate border that Irigaray proposes, if we shift its *place*. For if we do not restrict our scope to the categories of male and female as they are most strictly conceived, and extend our consideration to the myriad ways in which gender is performed even within the category of, for example, femaleness, we can begin to discern differences, perhaps even difference itself. These are differences that are emphatically bodily, and undeniably material, even as they are also psychic, emotional, and relational differences.

What seems useful—crucial, even—within Irigaray's schema is its insistence on locating difference at the heart of relation, in insisting on the importance and generative power of the border between self and other. This boundary between male and female is characterized by Irigaray at times as a vaporous gulf, an immaterial divide or chasm that cannot be spanned, and at other times as a tactile boundary, as palpable and dense as flesh. But in insisting on the importance of the divide of sexual difference, what or who is served in drawing that divide only and always between male and female?

If we take the example of a butch/femme couple and note that they may exemplify different and contrasting modes of comportment, styles of embodiment, methods of bodily inhabitation, and affective tendencies, what investments demand the withholding of the term *sexual difference* as a descriptor of these oppositions? In a relationship between a transman and a straight woman, is it not clear that the difference between them is decidedly bodily and resolutely "sexuate"? Acknowledging the sexual difference between a couple consisting of a transman and a gay man in relation allows us to resist the easy collapse of all masculinities into one undifferentiated category of male, while, at the same time, recognizing that each member of this couple is indeed a man. These pairings can help us conceive of sexual difference without requiring that one sex be quarantined away from another. The trans body can also help us understand the traversal of sexual boundaries not as an unrepresentable breach but as a negotiation of difference. Recognizing that movement is possible across the borders of male and female means that the bodily envelope cannot only be understood as the symbolic marker of the absolute otherness of sexual difference. Indeed, transition itself can be understood as a means of "reclaiming the skin," the project that Irigaray enjoins women to undertake.

Irigaray's corporeal survey of sexual difference concerns itself with the primacy and place of difference and can show us that that even inhabiting one's own body necessitates an encounter with sexual difference. But it misunderstands the place of sexual difference, locating it always *over there*, in that other who is a perpetual mystery to me and never reachable or knowable. This impossibility of any true encounter with sexual difference, the assertion that it may be proximate to me but can never be known or understood, renders my sexual being closed and isolated away from difference, even as I endeavor to engage with it. When each sex is given its own proper domain, which the other can never traverse, the place of sexual difference is always beyond the scope of understanding, just out of grasp. The effect is finally an inoculation against sexual difference in the guise of an engagement with it.

It may in fact be true that there is a certain ineffable power, some enthralling and catalyzing force, in sexual difference. But it seems important to remember, as Penelope Deutscher reminds us, that the concept of sexual difference—particularly as the ground for an ethics or politics—is always animated by the tension between its possibility and its impossibility.[7] It is imperative to consider the ways in which this difference does not reside only in the contrast between male and female, where these are both understood as immutable designations. If we are to give difference its due as a vital force, as Irigaray invites us to, we must also acknowledge that femininity is compossible with the category of male, that the masculinity expressed within some iterations of femaleness is as ontologically robust as any other kind of masculinity. To exclude these pairings from the realm of ethical, productive, generative relation is to understand both sex and difference in the most reductive and biologistic of terms. Genders that find no easy home within the binary system are still animated by difference. Sexual undecidability does not condemn the subject to placelessness, but rather locates difference at the heart of both subjectivity and relation.

## NOTES

1. Irigaray, "Place, Interval."
2. Ibid., p. 35.
3. Chanter opens her book *Ethics of Eros* by reformulating this statement to point to feminist contestations of the concept of sexual difference: "One of the most powerful categories of analysis that has served the needs of feminism in recent years is that of gender" (1).
4. Aristotle, *Physics IV*, 208a, I.30.
5. Irigaray, "Place, Interval," pp. 36–37.
6. On bodily boundedness, unboundedness, and corporeal surveying in Irigaray, see Grosz, *Volatile Bodies*.
7. Deutscher, *A Politics of Impossible Difference*. This is particularly apparent in her emphasis on the uncertain temporality of sexual difference: "Sexual difference could only be that which is to come. Difference does not lie between two identities, the male and the female. That should not be sexual difference" (121).

# 33

# *Touching Gender*
## Abjection and the Hygienic Imagination

Sheila Cavanagh

WHY ARE PUBLIC TOILETS GENDER-SEGREGATED? Canadian gender studies scholar Sheila Cavanagh writes on the history of public toilets in Europe and North America, and on the ways in which these built environments participate in the production and policing of normatively gendered bodies. Public toilets are particularly emotionally loaded and symbolically freighted sites where the tenuous boundaries between the clean and the dirty, the inside and outside, the private and the communal, the intimate and the impersonal—and, she argues, the male and the female—collapse and consequently must be shored up to sustain the current social order. Cavanagh draws connections between public hygiene campaigns in the 19th and 20th centuries and the construction, through exclusion, of particular kinds of bodies subjected to surveillance within public toilets—racialized bodies, disabled bodies, poor bodies, immigrant bodies, street-walking bodies, bodies seeking sexual contacts. She situates contemporary trans and genderqueer bodies in this long lineage of the abjected. Cavanagh conjoins her historical narrative and theoretical framing with extensive interviews with a wide range of trans and genderqueer individuals in Toronto, who speak in compelling detail about their highly varied experiences of using (or avoiding) public toilets, and of the ways in which their bodies are read and misread by others in these spaces.

Society scares easily at those aspects of sensuality that it qualifies as obscene ... *Inter faeces et urinam nascimus* (we are born between excrement and urine).

(Bernard Tschumi, quoted in Lahiji and Friedman 1997, 36)

The panoptic designs of the modern toilet owe much to the plague. Cholera, diarrhea, smallpox, and typhus were [...] big worries to sanitation reformers and city planners concerned about mortality rates in Britain and Europe. When it was known through scientific testing that sewage-contaminated drinking water led to disease, efforts were made to improve city sewers and to eradicate cesspools and faecal and urinary deposits in urban streets. The ultimate fears of the early-modern era were those of disease, contagion, and death – all of which were managed by order, quarantine, and partition.

Gendered toilet designs of today are rooted in the ways Victorians and Parisians managed disease, what Foucault calls the 'great confinement' (1979, 198). But the plague was not just a physical ailment. It was a rationale upon which people could be internally divided and subject to surveillance. 'Underlying disciplinary projects the image of the plague stands for all forms of confusion and disorder; just as the image of the leper, cut off from all human contact, underlies projects of exclusion' (ibid., 199). Worries about contamination were projected onto the body of the leper, the criminal (often thought to hide out in the underground), the prostitute (culturally aligned with raw sewage, disease, and contaminating fluids), the destitute (who searches for sellable items buried in septic sludge), the vagrant (who slept in the city sewers), the scourer (who cleans city drains and sewers), and those racialized as degenerate. The trouble with disease, however, is that it does not discriminate. During the nineteenth century, epidemics of cholera and typhoid affected the bourgeois classes, the royals, and the well-to-do: 'Death seemed unwilling to bless the squire and his relations, and keep us in our proper stations' (Wright 1960, 210).

While there is no basis for gender-exclusionary designs in epidemiology, segmentation by sex in bathrooms today is often rationalized by recourse to ideas about public health and safety. Gender-segregated designs are sacrosanct because many people are preoccupied by the careful delineation of sex. This is not because one gender can infect the other but because gender disorder is sometimes *felt* to be a matter of life and death. Gender incoherence, or, rather, what is taken to be an incongruence between gender identity, the sex of the body, and the insignia on the bathroom door, is metonymically associated with disease. Sodomy is also associated with disease, HIV and AIDS in particular. There is never enough soap and disinfectant to kill whatever it is people are afraid of catching. We are subject to quarantine and compelled to purify our bodies (literally and symbolically). We cleanse the boundaries between the masculine and feminine (or separate the two) in public lavatories so as to police the borderland or indeterminate space between these two discursive and material positions. Gender purity is disciplined by hygienic imaginations and rendered sacred, while gender impurity – signified by a discord between gender identity and the way the sex of the body is intercepted by others – is profane. 'Modern cleanliness departs from ancient ablution in its extension of hygiene to the psychological interior' (Lahiji and Friedman 1997, 42). Hygiene is no longer a ritual or set of practices exclusively focused upon the material body but a pedagogy or art of government targeting gender in ways that are psychically significant.

In their discussion of modern architecture, the sink, and abjection, Lahiji and Friedman (1997) coin the term 'hygienic superego' (11) to illustrate how cleanliness is tied to the law, and to prohibitions on sensorial pleasures (other than vision). The hygienic superego polices the gap between purity and abject dirt (defilement) (ibid.). What is pure and abject is no longer (or, rather, not exclusively) determined by hygiene; it is about gender coherence. 'Prohibition against dust and dirt marks the structure of the hygienic superego. This prohibition is aggressive; it propels modernism and identifies with it. The clean body is also a plumbed body' (ibid., 42). But the plumbed body is also a carefully sculpted and coherent gendered body; one that cannot be confused with the 'other' sex. Because gender is about how we seal and delimit the body, how we navigate identifications and desires in relation to others, it should not be surprising that hygienic superegos are focused upon governing orifices and genital zones are points of interconnectivity. Panic about gender and panic about sexuality intersect. Injunctions placed on homo, queer, or perverse sex demand that olfactory[1] and tactile sensations be stifled – noses plugged and fluids kept at bay. When abject body fluids commingle, gender is sometimes felt to be at risk. Those who are seen to be impure – specifically those who are recognizably GLBT and/or intersex – are sometimes perceived by heteronormative and cissexual folk as contaminating the public body by igniting otherwise dormant sensory registers. Abject desires, those regarded as repulsive in the bathroom – such as hygrophilia (pleasure sought by physical contact with body fluids) and mysophilia (arousal by the inhalation of body secretions) – are so constituted because of the now widespread degradation of sensorial pleasure (touch and smell in particular). Erotic pleasures that involve body parts, orifices, scents, and fluids that do not abide by heteronormative and cissexist prohibitions on desire are disowned or, literally, driven underground.

Tactile and olfactory sensory systems are subordinated (rendered impure) by modern optical and acoustic designs. Modern optics and acoustics are accentuated in toilet designs because, unlike other sensory systems, they enable distance and objectification. As Laura Marks (2000) suggests in her study of film and embodiment, modern optics is a less intimate or sensuous kinaesthetic than touch or taste or smell. Hearing also preserves objectivity and is mediated by air, as vision is mediated by light. For the auditory canal, the 'exteriority of its object is preserved even as sound enters the ears' labyrinths, because the sound in itself conveys nothing but the meaning given it' (Vasseleu 1998, 100). Those at odds with the cissexist and heteronormative body politics that mandate gender purity and coherence are held up to a bright, investigatory air or light in the lavatory (much like an amoeba under an open-air microscope).

## THE GENDER OF ABJECT FLUIDS

> The abject, like the uncanny, offers a valuable means to demonstrate the connections between psyche, body and society, and the way in which these are sustained spatially, both at the level of the individual and within the surrounding social system. Boundaries, borders, and the very design of the social environment symbolize the fragile division which sustains identity.
>
> (Wilton 1998, 179-80)

> Woman, toilet: these are the apparatus by which we are undone and which we abjure, in order to be who we are.
>
> (Morgan 2002, 175)

Gender purity is established by abjection. Julia Kristeva (1982) defines the abject as that which 'does not respect borders, positions, rules. The in-between, the ambiguous, the composite' (4). The abject opposes the 'I' and exists in a 'place where meaning collapses' (2). It threatens the modern subject at its constitutive boundaries. By abjection, we rid ourselves of dirt and substances that are coded as impure or unclean. The abject (or that which is defiled) is also that which is 'jettisoned from the "symbolic system." It is what escapes that social rationality, that logical order on which a social aggregate is based, which then becomes differentiated from a temporary agglomeration of individuals and, in short, constitutes a classification system or structure' (ibid., 65). Building upon Kristeva's analytic of abjection, Butler (1990 and 1993), McClintock (1995), and Thomas (2008) further elaborate upon what they call social abjection to understand how people devalued in modern, Western industrial and capitalist nations are metonymically associated with abject body fluids, or, to be precise, treated 'like shit.' People are excrementalized. Late-modern societies expel and excommunicate people deemed to be unclean. The social body, like the individual body, polices its borders.

While there is no one-to-one correspondence between what we abject (and find grotesque) and desire in the realm of object relations, and gender identity (trans or cissexual), there is, as interviewees note, a way that gender is secured by abjection. Gender is partially ratified by what (and whom) we abject and see to be other or different from the self. By aggressive disidentifications (you are nothing like me, bear no trace of or relation to me) or projective identification (whereby a subject projects unwanted parts of the self onto others), people police gender identity. There are gender-specific choreographies modelled upon what Inglis (2002) refers to as 'toiletry habitus.' These choreographies are evident in bathroom designs and in one's orientation to base body matter. It is frequently the case that one gender is thought to be more 'dirty' or 'unclean' than another, and the cleanliness of the bathroom mirrors these assumptions. Tara, who is a genderqueer butch, notes that 'women's' toilets are always cleaner than 'men's' toilets, and asks, 'How do men's bathrooms get so dirty and filthy?' A bisexual interviewee hypothesizes that 'women are more likely to complain about dirty bathrooms, and … men that complain about dirty bathrooms are going to be seen as "effet" [effeminate] … or feminine.' Sarah, who is transgenderist, speculates that we have gender-segregated toilets because 'guys are so dirty, guys need their own bathroom … let them be dirty, we don't want

*cultivate it gendered hygienic illusion)*

to be affected by that [dirt].' As one trans man notes, bathroom designs cultivate illusions about the 'dirt' and 'stink' of gender:

> Just from the condition of bathrooms [it appears that] women's bodies are considered hygienic or made hygienic and men are considered dirty or stinky and that's okay … you know, never a paper towel to be had and no soap [in the 'men's' toilet] because you don't need it you can just stay smelly … it's fine. But in the women's room there is everything you need to [keep clean].

Some trans and non-trans queer femmes intimate that hand washing (whether or not one does it in the 'men's' room) is largely determined by the design of the porcelain receptacles (and the presence of toilet paper). In other words, the pedagogy or art of hygiene built into the lavatory is gender specific. As Emily, who is intersex, says,

> There's a very good reason for … why men tend not to wash their hands nearly as much as women do. There's no toilet paper at the urinals, for starters. You don't really need it … and so men don't tend to think of … [their hands] in contact with anything they would think of as dirty … whereas going to the bathroom as a woman, you are definitely going to get your hands wet … it's a much messier experience. And … there is much more of a visceral … drive for women to get their hands washed … so … women are much more sensitive and aware … of less clean bathrooms. *Genitalia → is the same?*

As interviewees note, personal hygiene is gendered and mediated by toilet designs. The difference between male and female, masculine and feminine is authenticated by recourse to cleanliness; the 'ladies' room is imagined to be clean whereas the 'gentlemen's' room is thought to be unclean.[2] Because women are more likely to be read as 'dirty,' and 'polluting' in Western cultural folklore (Grosz 1994, Kristeva 1982, Longhurst 2001, Shildrick 1997) than men (unless, of course, those men are racialized or classed as 'dirty'),[3] it is likely that women are held to more exacting cleaning rituals than men.

Interviewees also have much to say about colour and its relation to hygiene. They note that toilets *while* are either painted or lacquered white to denote cleanliness, or are in muted pastel shades, normally pink or blue, to signify gender. Images of gender purity (cleanliness) tend to be denoted by white or pastel colouring. Butch Coriander, who is a non-trans genderqueer butch woman, explains that public toilets are 'white broken up by a colour of some sort, some sort of pastel … like blue, maybe a light pink … It's supposed to be pure and clean. White is supposed to be pure and clean.' Tara notes that 'White has a psychological … association with cleanliness … And … it looks dirty faster … When it's white, you can see dirt. When it's black, you can't.' Toilets kept white by elaborate bleaching and disinfecting rituals are said to be racialized. Sugar, who is a non-trans queer femme, surmises that

*Racial aspect*

> Cream and beige … I think part of it's racial. Part of it goes back to that sort of 1940s, 50s, 60s, white is clean and good and we will do all in our power to bleach and whiten everything … whether that's people or our houses and washrooms and … I think that has informed paint colours in washrooms … I think it's largely informed by … needing to be white and clean and sterile and … normal.

This normality is colonial and puritan in its emphasis on virginal and pristine toilet space. As an interviewee who is bisexual notes, 'Everything [in the lavatory] is always white … which is really impossible to keep clean, and that's the whole point, it has to be pristine … I think the ideal [sought] … is that every time you go in [to the bathroom] it should look like no one has ever used it before.'

Whiteness signifies absence, or perhaps a vanishing point or horizon beyond which nothing can be seen. It is, as Richard Dyer (1997) writes, associated with 'purity, cleanliness, virginity, in short, absence' (70). Whiteness may also signify a dead end[4] or sensory limit. Colourful designs and ornamentation were characteristic of early Victorian pedestal closets and public urinals (such as the 'Gents' at Sough End Green in Hampstead, built in 1897, near the London and North Western Railway (and used to stage public sex scenes in the film *Prick Up Your Ears* based on the life of the late, gay playwright Joe Orton). However, these features disappeared as a capitalist ethic of utility, time management, and efficiency took hold. Loitering at the urinal and taking one's time on the potty were discouraged. Homosexual sex was subject to censure. The public lavatory was not to be a place of erotic contemplation, sensuality, or relaxation. Colour and lavish design came to signify unsavoury pleasures and were, over time, seen to be incompatible with public hygiene and prohibitions on public sex (sodomy in particular). Straight lines, metallic walls, and plainly tiled white surfaces replaced lavish Victorian water-closet designs, their circular patterning, ornamentation, and 'decadent' colour schemes.[5]

The visual contrast between the clean bathroom and the defecating body was amplified. 'Whiteness as an ideal can never be attained, not only because white skin can never be hue white, but because ideally white is absence: to be really, absolutely white is to be nothing' (Richard Dyer 1997, 78). This is as true of human skin as it is of the lavatory designs and fixtures inspired by the present-day hygienic imagination. Spectacles of death and transcendence (encapsulated by the story of Jesus Christ), flesh and spirit, darkness and light, impurity and purity, all haunt Western Christian nations and turn up in the way city planners, capitalists, corporate executives, architects, and engineers employed by large corporations build, design, and dictate how the populace will use public washrooms. As Joel Kovel notes,

> the central symbol of dirt throughout the world is faeces, known by that profane word with which the emotion of disgust is expressed: shit ... when contrasted with the light colour of the body of the Caucasian person, the dark colour of faeces reinforces, from the infancy of the individual in the culture of the West, the connotation of blackness with badness.
>
> (Quoted in Richard Dyer 1997, 76)

That the ethic of gender purity is colonial is evident in the historical example of Pears' Soap, which Anne McClintock (1995) uses to illustrate 'commodity racism' in Britain, in present-day hygienic rituals that remove not only bacterial build-up in public restrooms but people culturally coded as 'dirty' and 'unclean' (often the under-housed and street active – it is no coincidence that the economically dispossessed are called 'bums'),[6] and in the criminalization of sodomy (homosexuality was imagined to be a eugenic defect, and consequently a danger to what Lee Edelman (2004) calls 'reproductive futurity,' impinging upon the general health and well-being of the population).[7] Gender purity is set up against the trans and/or queer subject as whiteness (instrumental to gender purity) is set up against those racialized as non-white and impoverished (under-housed and unemployed). Those without employment and access to affordable housing, and thus dependent upon public facilities to clean themselves and to get drinking water, are sometimes branded unproductive, 'faecal' parasites.[8]

Public facilities separate the body from its faecal remains; but they also separate the so-called upstanding citizen from those culturally coded as abject. In her reworking of the Kristevian notion of abjection, Anne McClintock (1995) argues that modernity produces abject 'objects' (like the anus), abject 'states' (like coprophilia), abject 'zones' (like the toilet), and socially designated 'agents' of abjection (GLBT and/or intersex people, those with disabilities, those who are underemployed, those who are racialized as non-white, etc.) (72). 'Under imperialism ... certain groups are expelled and obliged to inhabit the impossible edges of modernity: the slum, the ghetto, the garret, the brothel, the convent, the colonial bantustan ... [and I would add the sewer, the urinal, the common

*A place of refuge in some abject way?*

latrine or cesspool]. Abject peoples are those whom industrial imperialism rejects but cannot do without' (ibid.). The crucial point to be made is that people are symbolically coded as abject (not just substances)[9] and abjected (sometimes literally from public space). In the case of the toilet, non-trans folk sometimes impose upon those who are perceived to be trans and/or queer to internalize, or to forge an identification with, that which is abject or culturally de-idealizing. In this way, cissexuals who are not gay-positive or trans-positive transfer their own gender identificatory troubles (and refused desires) onto trans and/or queer people. GLBT and/or intersex folk become the 'untouchables' of the toilet.

Prohibitions placed on touch and smell are about the management of ego boundaries. In her seminal notes on projective identifications, Melanie Klein notes that the one who projects unwanted elements of the self onto others may experience a 'weakened sense of self and identity' (Hinshelwood 1989, 179), and that aggressive disidentifications with the other are spurred on by envy. Distance taken between people may indicate not only objectification and distancing but subject-object confusion. Worries about whiteness and sanitation are, as I suggest in what follows, driven by anxiety about gender coherence (its purity and legibility). The degradation of touch and smell (the more intimate senses) is accomplished in part by the valorization of vision (and, to a lesser extent, hearing). The optical design of the toilet is meant to patrol the distance between self and other. The bathroom places occupants in a fluorescent spotlight 'so that they are clearly separated from their surroundings' (Richard Dyer 1997, 86), from abject body fluids and people coded as abject in the normative landscape.

In his discussion of the modern bathtub, William Braham (1997) notices that rules of hygiene are not just about health and safety but about visual integrity: one must be able to see the body unencumbered by dirt. 'The appearance of the modern [bathroom] surface – smooth, white, shiny, sanitized – offers sufficient guarantee of protection from disease' (217). But the glow and appeal of the oval toilet bowl receptacle, urinal, or sink basin are illusory, offering only an imaginary defence against subjective entanglement (or exposure to others). Smooth, white, porcelain tubs, toilet bowls, and urinals are desirable because they symbolize, mirror, and refract a neutral tertiary space where the body will, presumably, not be exposed to the mess and spillage of others. We pretend that the underlying worry about touching the toilet bowl, for example, is about personal hygiene, all the while forgetting that urine is a sterile substance. The rim of the toilet bowl must *appear* to be clean. This is not because people worry about disease and infection (although we do), but because people are anxious about whiteness (denoting purity) and gender integrity. When abject body fluids are left behind by others, one's own gender integrity is sometimes felt to be compromised. In other instances, one may come to question the sanitary practices of others when the rules of hygiene are violated. This questioning is gender specific. Phoebe, who is a trans woman, explains that in the 'women's' room,

*visual leaking*

It seems to me that this is a fairly constant behaviour of leaving toilet paper on the floor, tampons, like not throwing them in the disposal properly … I'm just totally surprised because this … is not the public demonstration of femininity. Femininity in its public form is considerably different. And so, I was surprised once I entered that ['women's' room] space, surprised, hell, I was shocked!

Phoebe underscores how feminine gender performances are dependent upon elaborate hygienic rituals and how these performances are interrupted by leaving abject fluids behind (or backstage, in the stall).[10]

Hygiene practices are moored by our openness to what I call cultural infection: that is, the fact that our bodies can be seen to be carriers, signifiers, or agents of abjection. While there is no one universal substance that offends in all moments (faeces notwithstanding), heterosexual matrices prescribe and set parameters upon the grotesque and the sublime. These parameters are governed by prohibitions and taboos relating to excretion and excreta.[11] Anthropological data confirm that there are widespread beliefs about how 'each sex is a danger to the other through contact with sexual fluids' (Douglas 1966, 37). The management of elimination tells us much about the hygienic superego, its gender and psychic structures.

Normative performances of disgust are gender, class, and racially specific. They reveal the inner workings of white hygienic imaginations. Disgust about urine is often about a perceived encroachment upon the border between inside and outside, private and public, self and other, masculine and feminine, white and non-white. This encroachment is evident in interviewee comments about urinary and faecal remains in the toilet. As Tulip, who is a non-trans genderqueer femme, says, 'I feel like women's bathrooms are dirtier and my theory is that women squat … I would never sit on a … public toilet ever … there is more urine on the seat in women's bathrooms than men's.' KJ, who is trans man, complains that '[Men] … miss the friggin' toilet bowl … So it's on the walls … It's horrific! It's, like, jeez … how did you do that? … the men's washroom is going to be gross, and the women's is going to be not gross.' As one trans guy laments, '[In] some of the [men's] bathrooms it looks like they're [crap testing] when they're peeing … it's all over … the stall … why can't [they] all just pee in a bowl?' Tara agrees: 'They just whip it out and whiz anywhere they damn well please … it's pretty gross.'

One of the reasons urinary spill and splatter are a point of contention in restrooms is because they are not obviously gendered. The body's interiors are curiously ungendered (with the exception of the reproductive organs, differing chromosome counts, and estrogen and testosterone levels). Despite beliefs that urine's smell, colour, and consistency vary by gender, it is not a fluid that can easily be traced back to a given subject. (It is, for example, not uncommon for a woman to say to another user, upon leaving a stall, that she was not the one who made a mess left behind on or in the toilet bowl or seat). Everyone shits and, like shit,[12] urine is a great equalizer.

Unease about urine is often played out upon the toilet seat, and obsessive attention is paid to the vertical (upright) or horizontal (downward) position of the lid. The way a toilet seat is left in a private bathroom signals the urinary position assumed by the previous user. Obsessive worries (usually in-home) about the lid of the toilet are commonplace and sometimes comical.[13] Consider the following memory of Tulip after immigrating to the United States:

> At home there were no rules or anything [about 'urinary positions'] … when we got to the States from Israel … my mom would always comment that the TV shows always had the wife and the husband fighting about leaving the toilet seat up, which was really funny because we were a family of three women and one man and my dad always sat and the one time that he would stand up he would always leave the toilet seat up and nobody cared, you just put the toilet seat down. And then we came to the States, and it was this constant joke on sitcoms and, like, 'Oh, I am going to divorce you if you don't put the seat down.'

The state of the porcelain receptacle after use may be seen as comical, or as a grave concern. 'The appearance of the modern surface – smooth, white, shiny, sanitized – offers sufficient guarantee of protection from disease. An architectural soothsayer, or even a concerned homeowner, can point to a clean tub as evidence of a healthy future' (Braham 1997, 217). A safe family home[14] is no longer *just* about the eradication of germs and disease; it is also about subject demarcation by gender. We must see our own image in the receptacle – it should be that clean and mirrorical. 'The subject who looks at this sink [receptacle or urinal] is the phenomenological, self-conscious subject: the sink itself becomes a mirror in which "I see myself seeing myself" ' (Lahiji and Friedman 1997, 37). The mirage should cultivate an illusion of absolute subject integrity in the domain of gender, and the subject should be unencumbered by abject body fluid.

> Bathroom finishes must resist the accelerated tendency of matter to change state under the influence of water ... the glazed surface of the tub and of the tiled walls in the standardized room of fixtures is unchanging, or nearly so, requiring little of the regenerative maintenance demanded by other materials.
>
> (Braham 1997, 219)

The object constancy of bathroom fixtures is designed to quell anxieties about bodily ego boundaries and their instability. By appealing to an obsessive fantasy of extermination and removal – no part objects (floaters) in the toilet bowl – the lavatory caters to a modern individualist and puritanical wish to be unencumbered by the other, his/her shit and residue.[15]

It must be remembered that, because the 'rules of cleanliness were previously the province of religious doctrine' (Braham 1997, 217), and because such inscriptions relied upon whiteness as a trope and emblem of purity, there is, in the present-day manifestation of the hygienic superego, a compulsion to exterminate (by oversanitization) that which is not white (coded unclean or abject), a compulsion reminiscent of the older, Christian practice of ablution.

[...]

Bodies, like pipes and genitals, leak. Orifices obscure imaginary boundaries and psychically invested fantasies about impermeability. Fluids are unfaithful and promiscuous. We question and get upset about their whereabouts because they give us away and reveal others to have been where we ourselves wish to be or, conversely, where we do not want to be. Fluids escape the body and thus resist mapping.[16] Abject and unruly fluids upset gender. Fluids, like odours, threaten to overtake the primacy of sight in the modern optical arena, thereby obscuring body coordinates that are consolidated by the eye's exacting dissections. The 'flows' confuse body boundaries, and the disorientations are met with disgust (and sometimes desire).

Urine, menstrual blood, faeces, saliva, semen, and female ejaculate all threaten to alter the territory of the body, what Kaja Silverman (1996) calls the proprioceptive ego or sensational body (discussed in chapter 4). When the limits and contours of the body are uncertain, our relation to the signifying chain (symbolic law) is unstable. Kristeva argues that excrement and menstrual blood are the two main polluting objects in phallocentric cultures. 'Excrement and its equivalents (decay, infection, disease, corpse, etc.) stand for the danger to identity that comes from without: the ego threatened by the non-ego, society threatened by its outside, life by death. Menstrual blood, on the contrary, stands for the danger issuing from within identity (social or sexual); it threatens the relationship between the sexes within a social aggregate and, through internalization, the identity of each sex in the face of sexual difference' (1982, 71). Both trajectories (from without and within) threaten identities in public toilets. Body fluids left in and around the white, oval, porcelain toilet bowl or urinal are met with disgust because they interfere with our internalized body maps.

Gendered anatomies are hard to decipher when they leak and smell out of place, time, and libidinally invested body coordinates. In her discussion of the 'mechanics of fluids,' Luce Irigaray (1985) notes that 'Fluid – like that other, inside/outside of philosophical discourse – is, by nature, unstable. Unless it is subordinated to geometrism, or (?) idealized' (112). The body's fluids symbolize disorder unless they are funnelled or plumbed (down the drain), subject to organizing spatial units (medical or scientific grids or geometrical maps that order and isolate fluids), or revered (as when menstrual blood was designated sacred because of its relationship to fertility in goddess worship). Irigaray also notes that fluids transgress and confuse boundaries that are integral to what science takes to be 'real.' In other words (her words), fluids defy the 'proper order' of the Symbolic and 'in large measure, *a psychical reality* that continues to resist adequate symbolization and/or that signifies the powerlessness of logic to incorporate in its writing all the characteristic features of nature. And it has often been found necessary to minimize certain of these features of nature, to envisage them, and it, only in light of an ideal status, so as to keep it/them from jamming the works of the theoretical machine' (ibid., 106–7).

We may understand what Irigaray refers to as the insistent inattention to fluids as an example of a phallocentric intolerance for the feminine coded as maternal and abject. As she says, 'Since historically the properties of fluids have been abandoned to the feminine, *how is the instinctual dualism articulated with the difference between the sexes?* How has it been possible even to "imagine" that this economy had the same explanatory value for both sexes? Except by falling back on the requirement that "the two" be interlocked in "the same" ' (116). If the feminine (or, for Irigaray, a 'sex that is not one') is absorbed into, or seen to be an inferior version of, the masculine; then it stands to reason that fluids marked as 'not coming from man' (the one and only sex) are most susceptible to abject horror. In other words, if menstrual blood in the phallocentric or cissexist economy is 'not male,' then it is the excess or remainder. Not only is menstrual blood abject, but it poses a noxious threat to non-trans heteromasculinities and to dominant ideas about an absolute and unchanging sexual difference between male and female. This is particularly the case when blood flows from bodies identifying as male or as masculine. Menstrual blood is, perhaps, along with faeces, the most culturally shameful bodily substance in those Canadian and American public cultures that have been influenced by Christianity and phallocentric reasoning. It is certainly subject to intense corporate-driven sanitary rituals.

A significant number of non-trans women and trans men interviewed are upset by the taboos surrounding menstruation and the shame those taboos provoke. Menstrual blood is subject to discipline by way of sanitation – for example, through corporate-driven advertising campaigns aligning menstruation with contaminate and pollution. Menstruation denotes a stain (blood red) upon life and codes the subject as impure (or as a harbinger of death). It should also be noted that undergarments are usually white because they are worn close to the body and meant to reveal abject body fluids. White panties, for example, show up menstrual fluids meant to be plugged up in a vaginal opening and absorbed by 'feminine hygiene' products (usually tampons). White light and clothing make menstrual blood ultra-visible, or, by contrast, demonstrate its absence (invisibility) or vanishing point.

[...]

Menstrual blood evokes shame (a revelation of the body and its insides) in public. Interviewees who bleed often say they are embarrassed by menstrual blood and by sanitary products (including how to change or dispose of them). The disgust compels a will to absorb. In her definition of the words 'absorb' and 'absorption,' Molesworth (1997) writes, '*Absorb*: to take in without echo, recoil, or reflection: to absorb shock. *Absorption*: assimilation: incorporation' (76). The early French word for 'absorb' (*assorbir*) (or *absorbere* in Latin) meant to 'swallow up' or to 'suck in.' Menses are not funnelled back inside the body (although this may be a fanatical wish in our body-fluid-phobic culture), but into a negative (absorptive or non-space) without a visual trace or echo. The plumb line is blocked and shall be seen and heard to go nowhere. Molesworth notes, as well, that the capitalist logic and management of part objects (such as body fluids) is consumption oriented. The feminine incorporates by 'taking in' or 'absorbing' menstrual flows that are otherwise contrary to (or at odds with) a heteromasculine and typically phallocentric capitalist enterprise invested in the continual production of menstrual taboos.

Having to purchase and to change tampons, pads, sponges, 'diva-cups' (made of silicone), 'keepers' (made of rubber), and so on, in public space is described as disturbing or shocking (an antonym to the word 'absorb') to onlookers in the washroom, who are also embarrassed by the sight of menses. As Rohan notes, 'Women need to be changing sanitary, menstrual devices or whatever and of course [the assumption is that we should not] ... do [it] in front of other women ... it is coded as being very dirty and very shameful and ... something you ought to keep private.' Carol, who is a non-trans woman, emphasizes the cultural focus on concealment and how people are shocked by menstrual blood in the sink:

> I started using menstrual sponges instead of Tampax, for a while. And of course, when you're using a menstrual sponge, the big challenge becomes what you do when it's time to squeeze it out … And so I got to the space where I would squeeze out my menstrual sponge in public restrooms … in the sink [area] … And … I remember at least one time, having an old lady get very big-eyed next to me and seeming a little terrified.

Chloe, who is a non-trans queer femme, makes the same point about onlookers:

> [We are supposed to] dispose of … sanitary products in a decent, unobtrusive way that almost pretends we don't menstruate … [with respect to the 'keeper'] you *do not rinse your keeper in full view of other women!* … Do not let other people know that your menstrual blood has just gone down the sink!

A third interviewee summarizes: 'I have a keeper and … the whole process … [of cleaning it creates] anxiety in, like, bathrooms, especially … if I want to, like, dump it out in the sink, forget it! Like, that's a lot of stress, [it personifies] … a leaky [feminine] body writ large.'

Trans-masculine interviewees who bleed are uniquely anxious about how to dispose of menstrual products. Menstrual blood is, as discussed above, coded as feminine and aligned with abject interiority. As C. Jacob Hale (2009) notes in his discussion of transsexuality, voice, and agency, one's insertion into language, as a social subject, demands 'gendered stability both over time and at any given time that some of us lack' (53). For those who undergo gender transitions, there are no gender pronouns or linguistic devices to denote male or female histories that may be at odds with one's present gender identity. If gender pronouns are the toilets of language, as Bobby Noble (2006) notes in his discussion of gender incoherence and trans masculinities, then it should not be surprising that a cissexist grammar is built into the architecture and designs of toilets. The grammatical coding is especially obvious in the lack of menstrual disposal facilities in the 'men's' room. Lana, who identifies as a non-trans, genderqueer, femme gimp, and who often uses the toilet with trans-masculine personal assistants, says, 'I've noticed that when I've been bleeding in the men's room, they don't have anywhere to put your pad, so it's like "Okay, what do I do with this?" There's no trash cans in their stalls. So, I had a moment where I was like "God, I'm sharing a moment with trans guys." ' The problem is confirmed by KJ, who says,

> I worked with a trans guy with a full beard and everything and he's not on hormones anymore – he was on T [testosterone] – and so he has his period. But then when you go into a male washroom and you need to get rid of whatever, sanitary napkin, wrapper, tampon, whatever – you know … How do you do that when the receptacle is obviously out[side the stall]?

Callum, who is a trans man, confirms that it would be 'traumatizing to have to come out of the stall and access it [the tampon machine] and go back in. So I was always very prepared [and brought my own product into the 'women's' bathroom].'

As indicated by the interviewees, the gendering of lavatories is painfully obvious in the presence or absence of what are called 'feminine hygiene disposal facilities.' The trouble with blood and the visibility of menses, in the 'men's' public toilet in particular, is not only that it confuses cissexist body maps attributing menstruation to female and feminine bodies exclusively but that it is at odds with a late-modern cultural imperative to absorb, or perhaps to contain, the liquidity of blood. As Foucault notes in his discussion of the symbolic of blood in the eighteenth century, blood was worrisome because it was 'easily spilled, subject to drying up, too readily mixed, capable of being quickly corrupted' (1978, 147). In other words, the bio-political regulation of the gendered and sexual body once secured by recourse to laws driven by anxieties about the unauthorized crossing of blood lines, those laws governing marriage, reproduction, kinship, and citizenship in particular, is now secured by attention to gender and sexual purity. Feminine 'hygiene' is not just about health and safety but about purifying and consolidating sexual difference, 'controlling our unruly pluralities [in the case of trans people],' as Hale (2009) notes. Gender incoherence is supposed to be eradicated by the internal grammar of the toilet. Economies of power once focused upon the symbolic of blood are now, in the Foucauldian story of sexuality, more often consolidated by the deployment of sexual purity through discourse. The precariousness of blood – its troubling menstrual flows and dark red stains – reveals insides out. The spectacle is interlinked with a worry about death as represented by the archetype of the devouring maternal-feminine (discussed above), and also signified by the king and his capacity to have one beheaded. But this threat is no longer about human mortality, death, and dying, as governed by the older regimes of power heralded by the king, or even about a threat of disease and contagion. The worry is now about gender incoherence. Gendered ways of being at odds with a coordinated system of normative signs and significations governing the border between male and female, masculine and feminine, are related to larger worries about white heterosexual reproductive futurity (Edelman 2004) and the health of the nation.

[…]

## SHIT AND ANAL IMAGINATIONS

This culture has lots of taboo stuff about shit.

(A trans male interviewee)

As everybody can tell by walking through a newly completed building, contemporary architecture has a harmful smell.

(Frascari 1997, 163)

Aversions to dung (abject par excellence) are gendered and gendering. Female gender identifications are often shaped by aversions to scatological remains, while male gender identifications are more likely to enact an imperviousness to scat (or use it to expand the symbolic territory of the body). The faecal-mass ejected may *feel* like a little penis (as hypothesized by Freud),[17] or an 'unfeminine' penetration or cut into the otherwise rigidly gendered geography of the toilet. It is certainly the case that interviewees who use the 'women's' room tend to be disgusted by shit,[18] and many abstain altogether from having bowel movements in public rooms. As Haley recalls, 'I remember being in a public bathroom in our school, and having a couple of my friends talk about how they would *never* poo in the bathroom. And they thought it was so disgusting … when people did [eject faeces].' Frieda, who is of British heritage and living in Toronto, non-trans, and queer, agrees: 'There's this unspoken code of conduct in [the] women's [room] that you don't do number two.' To leave behind, to be seen to have made, or to be surrounded by the aroma of, stool is to trouble feminine gender identifications. Stool is to be invisible (flushed away) or, as Jacob says, 'for home.'

Some interviewees talk about angst-ridden moments when they needed to defecate, but could not, or did not want to. Others said that worries about transphobia and homophobia inhibit one's capacity to discharge faeces. In Chloe's words, 'I think hassles around homophobia … Or … for some [other] reason [queer and/or trans folk] can't be relaxed enough in a public washroom to move their bowels.'

If gender protocols in the 'women's' room demand that one avoid defecation as unacceptably messy, the rules governing defecation in the 'men's' room are almost entirely reversed. For those invested in dominant, cissexually defined masculine subject positions, there appears to be pride in, or space taken up by, faecal droppings. This pride is in direct opposition to the shame sometimes felt by interviewees who use the 'women's' room. Rohan elaborates upon the gender difference as follows:

> It's funny … guys will take a dump and leave it [in the toilet bowl] and not flush; it's, like, 'Look what I left behind! Look what I did!' Like a little kid, 'Look what I made,' whereas women would never do that.

Callum also observes the gendered responses to dung:

> I think … [there is pride around not flushing for men] … like a 'Look what I made,' so everyone can see … But … then it's the same reason that you would be flushing [in the 'women's' room] because you are ashamed about it. And a woman would never not flush. Only if it's plugged, and even then it's traumatizing … [and] horrible, like, you'll close the door as you leave.

Hegemonic masculinity seems to be authenticated by a willingness to perform imperviousness to cultural infection by faeces. One's own excrement is to be made visible. In his discussion of sport and the territorial anus, Brian Pronger (1999) contends that white heteronormative masculinities are established through territorialization. He writes that there is, in dominant displays of masculinity, a 'colonizing will to conquer the space of an "other" while simultaneously protectively enclosing the space of the self, in an attempt to establish ever greater sovereignty of self and consequent otherness of the other' (376). The visual presence of the phallus is exaggerated while the anus is closed to curtail the threat of penetration and subsequent feminization. Faecal remains do not represent an open or gaping anus, however. They represent the markings of a phallic heteromasculinity that is committed to the usurpation of the other's body space. To shit in public space is to claim or mark the place as one's own. There is a none-too-subtle correlation between heteronormative masculinities and their territorialization through the spread of dung. Evidence is left behind, so to speak. As Rohan comments,

> I used to have to clean men's washrooms and women's washrooms … [and] the stuff that men do, like shitting next to the toilet on the floor. Smearing it on the wall … I've never cleaned a women's change room where women were like sitting there playing with their poop, or doing performance art with it or something.

Gay and/or trans men in this study tend to take issue with public displays of excrement and ejaculate in the 'men's' room. Interviewees' complaints about the stench in the 'men's' room may be a reaction to the aggressiveness symbolized by indiscreet and territorial droppings. Dung spilled onto floors and toilet seats or smeared on stall walls and doors projects the masculine (phallic) body into public space. This is in direct contrast to the way menstrual blood symbolizes feminine interiority and is absorbed or plugged up to relinquish a territorial and expansive claim to public space. Space is acquired symbolically by the way those who are masculine sometimes intentionally spread the dark mass. The presence of shit 'out of place' may also signal trans and homophobic hate. If the anus and the homosexual are equated in the homophobic imagination, the performed repudiation or display of shit – wiping it on walls, for example – is very likely an aggressive repudiation of anal eroticism. 'That abjectifying – and therefore effeminizing – anality is a condition that homophobic masculinity repudiates by constructing it as the distinguishing hallmark of a recognizable category of homosexual person' (Edelman 1994, 169). Insofar as the anus signifies a gap or negative space – an invagination, so to speak – it cannot solidify non-trans heteromasculinities invested in phallic, penetrative capacities and a simultaneous refusal of vaginal tissue, when, as Freud tells us, the act of defecation *feels* like penetration. Edelman suggests that the 'anatomical "cavity" denoted by the "cloaca" … [conjures up] anxiety of an internal space of difference within the body, an overdetermined opening or invagination within the male, of which the activity of defecation may serve as an uncanny reminder' (1994, 162). People less beholden to homophobic prohibitions may be more willing to avow an 'internal space of difference – an opening or invagination.' They may also be more able to deal with death and disorder signified by body matter 'out of place.' Heteronormative and cissexist displays of masculinity may be disproportionately dependent upon grandiose fantasies of invincibility and immortality.

Dominant, white heteromasculinities tend to present themselves as if they are invulnerable to the anus and to the messes it makes (coded as feminine and aligned with interiority). As Pronger notes,

> Masculine desire protects its own phallic production by closing openings, preeminently the anus and mouth … in short, any vulnerability to the phallic expansion of others. Rendered impenetrable, masculine desire attempts to differentiate itself, to produce itself as distinct and unconnected … The point of this conquering and enclosure of space is to make bodies differentiate themselves from the vortex of unbounded free-flowing desire … and thereby establish territorial, sovereign, masculine selfhood.
>
> (1999, 381)

In his discussion of the anus and the toilet, Lee Edelman (1994) makes a similar observation. He suggests that 'urinary segregation' is about the establishment of sexual difference. The phallus must be in plain view (before the urinal) to differentiate the masculine body from a feminine body – both of which, in the stall, experience a 'loosening of sphincter control, evoking, therefore, an older eroticism, undifferentiated by gender, because anterior to the genital tyranny that raises the phallus to its privileged position' (161). To shit in place is, for heteromasculine subjects, risky. 'For the satisfaction that such [intestinal] relief affords abuts dangerously on homophobically abjectified desires, and because that satisfaction marks an opening onto difference that would challenge the phallic supremacy and coherence of the signifier on the men's room door, it must be isolated and kept in view at once lest its erotic potential come out' (ibid.). Heteromasculinity demands not only that the anus be refused as a site of pleasure but that his excrement be imposed upon the space of the Other (in and around the stall).

Gay and/or trans men in my study seem to be less likely to use faeces as a means to claim public space and to seal the territory of the body. They are also more willing to acknowledge how shit can humble the body. Non-trans gay men sometimes regard faecal matter as part and parcel of what it means to be human and thus mortal. Faeces are also by-products of anal sex. As Ivan reflects, 'I'm a little bit embarrassed about crapping in public, just a little bit … Audible stuff … mainly it's the noise … it's about the body being seen as low, abject and dirty.' He also suggests that the relationship between disgust, abjection, and faeces is very much about sex and how one is able to come to terms with the liquidity of the human body:

> as a gay man who has anal sex, you come across shit, right? And heterosexuals have anal sex too, so … I'm not the kind of person who gets disgusted by these very normal, natural processes around sex … Sometimes [sex] gets dirty … So, there's shit on the condom. There's blood on the condom. There's vaginal fluid … we're messy, liquid creatures.

[…]

If the homosexual (or sodomitical scene) signifies 'no future', or rather a kind of social and reproductive death, as Edelman (2004) argues in his discussion of American culture, it is not much of a conceptual leap to surmise that homophobic preoccupations with faeces are about not only human mortality but a discomfort with ways of being together that are felt to be 'anti-family' or abject. 'The Freudian pleasure or comfort stationed in that movement of the bowel overlaps too extensively with the Kristevian abjection that recoils from such evidence of the body's inescapable implication in its death; and the disquieting conjunction of these contexts informs, with predictably volatile and destructive results, the ways in which dominant American culture could interpret the ' "meaning" of male-male sexual activities' (Edelman 1994, 161). Kristeva (1982) tells us that the abject (faeces in particular) upsets fantasies about individual integrity and is, ultimately, associated with death. Interviewees also notice how the toilet is haunted not only by the ghost of homosexuality but by the spectre of death and dying. Rohan focuses on human frailty:

> it's that [human] frailty … that idea that yes I am going to get old, my body is going to fall apart, and it's going to get progressively leakier, smellier, less controllable. I'm going to have less control over my bladder and my bowels as I age because that's just part of aging … I think that bothers people. To be confronted with that bothers people.

Velvet Steel compares the bathroom to the hospital: 'I think most people see it [the bathroom as] … a bad place to go. It's almost like going into a hospital … people [worry that] you're never going to come out!' Another trans interviewee comments on faeces and organic decay:

> Faeces doesn't smell so good. It's like the smell of rotten chicken … I think that they're waste products for a reason and decay is … we find it abhorrent because we don't want to think about decay. We are all [supposedly] perfectly healthy and we are all going to live forever there is no decay there is no rot, there's no waste product. We are all just *clean as a whistle*.

Worries about hygiene, rot, and decay are intimately tied to gender. Whiteness is about abstinence and absence (no longer here), as mentioned above, and gender purity is about obsessive attempts to police the borderlands between male and female, masculine and feminine; each is preoccupied by a negative or tertiary space, a gap or disconnect between life (coded as masculine virility) and death (symbolized by the sodomite and the maternal or devouring feminine).

Curiously, the difference between the masculine and the feminine is managed by a puritanical, white, body politic that inhibits touch. The condemnation of touch and unlawful (usually public) sex is enforced to preserve a strangely virginal and pristine whiteness in a space that is oversaturated by heteronormativity. The toilet is a site of death and disease (not life), and it is supposed to be a site of orificial (anal) disavowal (not homosexual activity or sodomy). Bathroom technologies police touch and keep bodies apart.[19] The designs and cleaning technologies channel worries about death and dying into an obsessive concern about and sexual abstinence. Olfactory and tactile emissions are disowned, or perhaps deadened, while visual and acoustic registers are employed to enact a vanishing of excrement at the still-water mark or in the pipeline.

Karl Marx wrote that modern alienation under capitalism is, in part, about an estrangement from the body's sensory apparatuses, with the possible exception of vision (and I would add acoustics). The degradation of touch and smell, what Marks (2000) refers to as the 'close' senses, fundamentally alters the social landscape. Marks argues that modern optics are predicated upon 'symbolic representation', whereas tactile epistemologies (and the relationships they engender) give rise to mimesis. She defines mimesis as a 'form of representation based on a particular, material contact at a particular moment' (138). Touch conjures up a memory encoded in the senses. Mimesis also 'presumes a continuum 'een the actuality of the world and the production of signs about that world' (ibid., 139). So, for example, the automated sink that can be turned on without touch, without the turning and release of a valve, is an alienating optical design as opposed to a mimesis. The automated technology secures distance and prohibits touch. Summarizing the foundational work of Horkheimer and Adorno (1972) and Benjamin (1978) of the Frankfurt School, Marks writes, 'Mimesis, they argued, is a form of yielding to one's environment, rather than dominating it, and thus offers a radical alternative to the controlling distance from the environment so well served by vision' (2000, 140).

There is also an uncanny aspect to mimesis because it conjures up relations now past but encoded in touch. In mimeses, one not only remembers (or senses what has been forgotten) but also yields to (does not objectify) the organic. Horkheimer and Adorno, for example, describe tactile epistemology as a 'yielding form of knowledge … [not unlike] the death instinct, the willingness to merge back with nature' (quoted in Marks 2000, 143). This epistemology is distinct from what Horkheimer and Adorno refer to as a 'mimesis unto death' (1972, 57) in which factory workers, or bathroom patrons for that matter, line up and choreograph and sequence their movements in keeping with modern capitalist ethics governing productivity, utility, and efficiency (not to mention sanitation). What might be called an insatiable capitalist mimesis shelters and segregates the self from nature, from the immediate environment, and blunts the senses in doing so.

Modern bathroom designs, which are increasingly reliant on automated technologies, cultivate a mimesis that dulls and rounds out the senses. With the deadening of the intimate (less objectifying) senses we see a refusal to validate trans-identifications and queer sexualities that do not lay claim to clean and private heterosexual body politics. There is, as suggested above, a generic and anaesthetized spatial politics of the bathroom that aligns sensory experience with a white, Westernized, privatizing, and reproduction-oriented heterosexuality. 'It seems reasonable to worry that as culture becomes globalized, sensuous experience is becoming both universal and placeless. "Non-places," or generic places (malls, airports [and I would add toilets]) are proliferating around the world … and would seem to bring with them certain sensory organizations' (Marks 2000, 244). A mimesis responsive to touch or smell is now subordinated to modern, generic optics and acoustics. Toilets are increasingly sanitized, automatic, and reliant upon globally marketed apparatus. 'When it is separated from its source and packaged, smell becomes a simulacrum, the scent of nonplace' (ibid., 245).

Although there is a modern disdain for touch and smell in the design of the toilet, space is made – however provisionally – for the organic, the sensual, and the feminine by those who use it in unauthorized ways. 'Against the tide of the commodification and genericization of sense experience, pools of local sensuous experience are continually created anew' (Marks 2000, 245). Sex in bathrooms, erotic uses of and fixations upon fluids and smells, and excitations about who may be in a neighbouring stall based upon curiosity and sensual intrigue, as opposed to phobic and exterminatory impulses, make room for new (while recalling older) modalities of mimetic engagement at present defamed in modern, Western, capitalist, cissexist, and heteronormative organizations of culture. Eroticizing partition walls (and puncturing them to make glory holes); finding pleasure in the contravention of prohibitions placed upon public mixing; making or fantasizing about an unauthorized touch while seated upon the throne or standing before the urinal – these are all ways to create new modalities of desire and identification. To queer, or to sensate, modern restrooms we must support multiple ways of being gendered and their associated structures of desire in the domain of the social. In the following chapter, I consider how gender is disciplined by prohibitions placed on sex in public.

## NOTES

1. Olfactory intolerance intersects with what Corbin (1986) refers to as 'the rise of narcissism, the retreat into private space, the destruction of primitive comfort, the intolerance of promiscuity' (232).
2. The interview data show that those who struggle with housing and employment, and those who do custodial work, are culturally aligned with faeces and 'dirt'. As Zoe notes, 'If somebody came into the washroom that was really dirty…

or … [who] was a homeless person that lived on the street … I'm guessing that people would think of those people as dirty.' For a detailed discussion of how the under-housed are refused access to public toilets, see Sandra Wachholz, 'Hate Crimes against the Homeless' (2005).

3. In her discussion of cleanliness, gender, race, and social difference, Adeline Masquelier writes that 'Unwashed hands, greasy clothes, offensive smells, grime on the skin all entered into complex judgments about not only the social position of the "dirty" person but also his or her moral worth' (2005, 6).

4. Richard Dyer (1997) argues that the 'theme of whiteness and death takes many forms. Whites often seem to have a special relation with death, to yearn for it but also to bring it to others. Death may be conceived of as something devoutly to be wished but also as terrifying' (208).

5. For a discussion of Victorian designs and ornamentation on early lavatories, see Lucinda Lambton, *Temples of Convenience and Chambers of Delight* (2007); and Kit Wedd, *The Victorian Bathroom Catalogue* (1996).

6. See Guy Hocquenghem (1978) for a good discussion of how the learning of personal hygiene is metonymically associated with private property, class, and capitalist accumulation.

7. See Andil Gosine (2009) for a discussion of the racism endemic to the criminalization of sodomy.

8. The white, sanitized bathroom aesthetic is colonial and imperialist by design. 'Ideas about cleanliness condensed a range of bourgeois values, among them monogamy (clean sex), capitalism (clean profit), Christianity (being cleansed of sin), class distinction, rationality, racial purity' (Boddy 2005, 169).

9. See Iris Young (1990) for a discussion of how 'socially abjected groups' (145) are constructed as ugly.

10. In an interesting sociological discussion of faecal habitus, Weinberg and Williams (2005) found that 'vigilance concerning breaches of body boundaries [farting, flatulence, and faecal discharge in toilets] was of greater concern for heterosexual women whose body image was mediated by cultural notions of "feminine" demeanor' (332). It is also worth noting that by keeping the anus clean, gay men mark the anus as a sexual zone. By completely removing faecal matter from the anal cavity through relatively stringent cleaning rituals, men who have sex with men preserve the anus as a sexual orifice.

11. It may seem odd to regard urine and excrement as anything but disgusting. But the unprecedented loathing of so-called body wastes is relatively modern. John G. Bourke (1891) writes, in the now classic *Scatalogic Rites of All Nations*, that modern European sewer systems and latrines were not the result of innovations in human hygiene and the control of germs and disease. Nor were they built to keep urine and faecal matter from fouling the streets of cities like London and Paris. Instead, he suggests, latrines were a means to contain the otherwise potent and sensorial powers of body fluids: 'Enough testimony has been accumulated to convince the most skeptical that the belief was once widely diffused of the power possessed by sorcerers, *et id omne genus*, over the unfortunate wretches whose excreta, solid or liquid, fell into their hands; terror may, therefore, have been the impelling motive for scattering, secreting, or preserving in suitable receptacles the alvine dejections of a community' (Bourke 1891, 134).

12. There is interesting research on the history, cultural politics, and symbolism of shit in modern cultures. See, for example, Begona Aretxaga, 'Dirty Protest' (1995), for a fascinating discussion of the excremental protest by the Irish National Liberation Army against the British government in a Northern Ireland prison. In her discussion of the 'powers of ordure', literature, satire, and the metaphor of human excrement, Kelly Anspaugh argues that the anus and the mess it makes have been subject to repression in ways even the genitals and sexual fluids (vaginal fluid and semen, for example) have not. 'Whereas sex has for centuries, at least in the Western world, been sublimated into romantic love, excrement, despite the efforts of a handful of alchemists and the Marquis de Sade, has remained irredeemably base matter' (Anspaugh 1994, 4). In his study of excrement in literature, John R. Clark (1974) writes 'For what society normally considers "low" and "sordid," rhypological and rhyparographical, is more frequently excretory than sexual. Many a man is willing to boast of his sexual prowess and caprice, but is distinctly unwilling to tender public pronouncements about the size of his faeces, the shape of his intestinal disorders, or the stature of his last bout with diarrhea. And a man might be willing to look into another man's sex life, but not into his stool' (43).

13. For a discussion of toilet humour, see Sigmund Freud, *Jokes and Their Relation to the Unconscious* (1975[1905]) and read Alfred Jarry's play *Ubu Roi* (1896), which scandalized late-nineteenth-century Parisian audiences at the Théâtre de l'Oeuvre by its satiric use and flaunting of the scatalogical.

14. Lynn Sacco (2002) convincingly argues that, in America at the turn of the twentieth century, fears about contracting sexually transmitted infections (such as gonorrhoea and syphilis) from toilet seats were less about evidence-based information about disease transmission than about denying incest in middle- and upper-class family homes. White girls from well-to-do families were said to have contracted such diseases from toilet seats. By contrast, girls with sexually transmitted infections from working-class, immigrant, African-American, and poor families were 'victims' of incest.

15. Kristeva notes that human excrement is the 'most striking example of the interference of the organic within the social' (1982, 75). Organic waste interferes with subject demarcations enabled by language in the symbolic circuit. Binary gender regimes are dependent upon clear subject positions. As literary and art critics argue (Anspaugh 1994 and 1995; Canning 1993; Clark 1974; Esty 1999), faecal matter denotes radical ambiguity, disorder, horror, alienation, mortality, and 'matter out of place' (Douglas 1966). Ordure is also used to link 'modern' sanitary engineering with the aesthetics of colonial whiteness. While metaphorics of shit figure prominently in postcolonial writing (Beckett 1970; Joyce 1961 [1922], 1976 [1939], 1976 [1916]; Soyinka 1978 [1965]; Armah 1968), less work has been done on the use of faecal imagery in literature to conjure up images of gender disorder.

16. For a discussion of the fluid-bounded body in art and literature, see Claudia Benthien, *Skin* (2002); and Steven Connor, *The Book of Skin* (2004).
17. In Freudian psychoanalysis the penis is symbolized by faeces. Sigmund Freud (1960 [1917]) gives voice to what he observes to be a repressed element of anal eroticism in the child's early, instinctual development: 'The faecal mass, or as one patient called it, the faecal "stick," represents as it were the first penis, and the stimulated mucous membrane of the rectum represents that of the vagina … during the pregenital phase they had already developed in phantasy and in perverse play an organization analogous to the genital one, in which penis and vagina were represented by the faecal stick and the rectum' (300).
18. While it may be difficult to think about human excrement as anything but unsexy in the present day, it figures prominently in histories of heterosexual love and was, in fact, regarded as an aphrodisiac. In his discussion of courtship and marriage, Bourke (1891) shares folklore of European history: 'Love-sick maidens in France stand accused of making as a philter a cake into whose composition entered "nameless ingredients," which confection, being eaten by the refractory lover, soon caused a revival of his waning affections' (216). Although use of such philtres was punishable by death, it demonstrates that human excrement was seen to have aphrodisiac qualities. In her fascinating history of chocolate, Alison Moore (2005) argues that European appetites for cocoa are related to taboos on coprophagia – a taste for human excrement. Chocolate, a gift exchanged by lovers on Valentine's Day, has, 'throughout the late modern era … been repeatedly associated, both explicitly and symbolically, with excrement' (52). Moulded into the shape of eggs, logs, and other '*lumpf*-like forms' (ibid., 59), chocolate evokes thinly disguised coprophilic fantasies. Noticing that the advent of the modern toilet coincides with the colonial appropriation of cocoa from Latin American countries, Moore argues that chocolate 'functioned as a symbol of the erotic, the infantile, and the feminine aspects attributed to primitivity and which were cast out as waste matter in the masculine, adult work of civilized society and capitalist economic order' (ibid., 52–3).
19. Allen Chun (2002) writes about what he calls the development of the 'supermodern Japanese bidet-toilet,' and the Western automated technologies and sensibilities it relies upon. The focus upon cleanliness, sanitation, and the masking of bodily sounds (primarily in the 'women's' toilet) is, he suggests, about the 'filth associated with the traditional Japanese squat toilet' (153). The racialization and concurrent degradation of the squatting toilet can also be seen in the globalization of the Western-style flush toilet.

# 34

# *Perverse Citizenship*

## Divas, Marginality, and Participation in "*Loca*-lization"

### Marcia Ochoa

California-based Colombian-diasporic anthropologist Marcia Ochoa writes in this article about her work with Venezuelan trans women, or *transformistas*. In doing so, she works through a familiar dilemma in transgender studies, and in the lives of transgender people: whether or when it is more important to conform to society's understanding of what constitutes a legitimate citizen, and whether or when it is more important to disengage from practices of "good citizenship" entirely. Ochoa's deeper philosophical problematic is to examine how "modernity extinguishes humanity yet creates other possibilities for existence." This, she contends, creates a logic of "perverse citizenship." For marginalized people, Ochoa writes, the question is not simply how to access rights, but rather how to access the "right to have rights." For example, Ochoa writes, *transformistas* are routinely detained by national guardsmen and police along Avenida Libertador in Caracas. Complaints against such arrests might make such violence more visible to a wider public, but at the same time might expose *transformistas* to extrajudicial police and military violence. Ochoa documents various strategies of political intervention used by *transformistas* in Venezuela. Through sketching these ongoing debates within transgender and *transformista* communities in Venezuela about accessing "the right to have rights," Ochoa makes an important contribution to a vast, ongoing transnational conversation about transgender political imaginaries.

Although sex work is not a crime in the Venezuelan penal code, on the streets of Caracas, the Ordenanza de Convivencia Ciudadana is the law of the land.[1] These few words, which happily proclaim the terms under which citizens might harmoniously live together, also condemn many women, *transformistas,* and men to live in a daily negotiation, expensive and at times violent, with the agents of the state, in this case, the Policía Metropolitana de Caracas (PM). *Convivencia ciudadana* (citizenly coexistence) implies a social harmony that respects all citizens as long as they respect the law.[2] But some citizens "live together" better than others, and the law always values some existences while marginalizing others.

I had to get to know the Ordenanza de Convivencia Ciudadana (or simply ordenanza), and its accompanying definition of "citizenship," to understand the context of Avenida Libertador in Caracas, where dozens of *transformistas* undertake sex work nightly. I had to get to know the ordinance this way because it helped me understand the structural factors that overdetermine the violence and marginalization that are produced on a daily basis on these streets and upon these bodies. But the truth is that the *ordenanza* is just a tool for the PM. Before the *ordenanza,* there was the Ley de

Vagos y Maleantes, before that another law, and always Morality, Order, and Good Citizenship. If the *ordenanza* is struck down tomorrow, the PM will find another way to police these *transformistas*.

When I began my work in Venezuela, I didn't expect to engage with questions of citizenship and civil society. However, as I spent more time in an increasingly polarized political environment where mechanisms of participation and collective action became more and more contested, I began to turn to these words as ways to talk about my concerns.[3] There are some sectors of the so-called civil society *(sociedad civil)* within which I function, specifically, the work of nongovernmental organizations (NGOs) and activists to HIV/AIDS and movements to articulate identity, community, and culture for people of color in the United States. However, the limitations of "civil society," and in particular of NGOs, to respond to the concerns of queer and transgender people of color have informed the skepticism with which I approach such concepts as citizenship and civil society. Rather than approaching the survival of *transformistas* through political theory, HIV prevention, or the traditions in anthropology that attend to non-Western sexualities and gender systems, I focused my work on bodily and imaginative responses to marginalization through mass media. My fieldwork, in fact, is about these mechanisms and not about what I refer to in this essay as "GLBT civil society." But the distinction between those who see themselves as political actors of *el ambiente* and those who are automatically excluded (or who exclude themselves) from "political" possibility recurred both in my interviews with members of GLBT civil society in Caracas, and in my work on Avenida Libertador.[4] I came to see citizenship as a tool that can be used perversely, one that actors within "civil society" (among whom I count myself) must be careful not to normalize.

In Venezuela, I collaborated on the production of a report about the problem of impunity and its impact on the "GLBT community" (Carrasco and Ochoa 2003). This study identifies a problematic relationship between the PM and the GLBT people in Caracas who responded to a short survey. When I ask a *transformista* what should be done about the PM, and if she is interested in participating in negotiations with them, she responds, "The PM?! *Ay no.* Because then when they see you on the street, just imagine." I began to understand, as I worked on Libertador, that these relations function in a climate of silence, in which the complaint filed serves not to change police behavior but rather to name the complainant and mark her for other possible aggressions. An intervention in this situation would have to be much more profound to avoid such aggressions.

This essay is based on my fieldwork with *transformistas* on the Avenida Libertador of Caracas.[5] It also draws on my experiences with a queer Latina/o HIV-prevention organization in the United States called Proyec-to ContraSIDA Por Vida (PCPV) and on interviews with activists working in three GLBT NGO projects in Caracas: Alianza Lambda de Venezuela, Unión Afirmativa de Venezuela, and the nascent Divas de Venezuela. From these observations, I consider how the case of *transformistas* in Venezuela might transform our concepts of politics, citizenship, and participation.

I will begin by attending to some issues of taxonomy and translation, in which I clarify the terms and usage employed in this essay. I base my taxonomic approach on the work of anthropologist David Valentine (2007), who articulates the importance of attending to and parsing out local gender categories in ethnographic fieldwork. Then I discuss the concept of *loca*-lization, a play on words that attempts to locate the *loca* within processes of modernity, nation, and globalization.[6] I follow this discussion with sections on the concepts of citizenship and civil society as they have affected my work in Venezuela and conclude with some suggestions for a politics that honors and includes *transformista* survival strategies.[7]

## TAXONOMY AND TRANSLATION

Language and naming have became central concerns to this question of citizenship and perversion, in part because citizenship in its traditional Enlightenment sense is about codifying mechanisms of recognition and participation. As Lisa Lowe (1996) has argued, the mechanisms through which noncitizens, foreigners, are made legible and thus excluded produce the conditions of possibility for a nation to define itself through the technology of citizenship. Definition, naming, confers a certain kind of visibility while obscuring that-which-will-not-be-named.

I found in Venezuela that silence, too, can be a space of possibility for *transformistas,* who often narrated their silent passage into womanhood through practices such as eyebrow plucking, hormone self-medication, and subtle shifts in wardrobe. Without asking permission, without declaring herself, a *transformista* emerges into being. By the time someone notices, by the time someone else names her difference, she has already transformed.

Throughout this work, I have encountered these problems of naming and meaning, where the stakes of specific words, even of the act of speaking, get to be very high. This is why I seek out nimble words, slippery and agile in their meanings. Terms such as "queer," *loca, de ambiente, entendido, transformista.* Those that name and define with power while refusing to be pinned down. I seek a language that honors my own slippery bilingualism, which asks you to work if you do not fully feel my form, which does not always stop to explain.

Valentine's recent "critical ethnography of the *category* 'transgender' itself (2007, 14) attends carefully both to the politics of naming and to honoring the categories and names that people use when talking about themselves. I think about this approach as a kind of taxonomy—a faithful listing, a parsing out of particularities in the genealogies and usage of the names and categories that emerge in a given social context. Here, I work to clarify these terms very carefully because they get conflated often, despite the fact that they imply very different social realities. But I also work to register the polymorphous forms of meaning and usage I've encountered. In the following section, I will define a few key terms and clarify my usage in the languages of transgender studies and queer *Latini-dad* (Rodríguez 2003).

## TRANS TAXONOMIES

*Transformista* is a word used in Venezuela to refer to people who are assigned male sex at birth and who present themselves in their everyday lives as women. The word has associations with the sex work performed by many *transformistas,* and is considered an insult by some, although it is also used for self-definition.

I am defining "transgender" as a general category that refers to people who make identitarian, physical, and social efforts to live as members of the gender that society says does not belong to the sex assigned to them at birth. *Transformistas,* fit within this definition, but not all transgender people are *transformistas.* [...] *Transformistas* are not transsexual women because (1) they are not recognized as transsexual under the diagnostic criteria, (2) may or may not desire sex reassignment surgery, and (3) may or may not have access to the medical or psychiatric care necessary to produce this category in Venezuela.

And, in case you're wondering, "travesti" and "drag queen" are words used to describe female impersonators—the *transformistas* I met on the whole did not do these kinds of performances.

## QUEER *LATINIDAD*

I want to briefly clarify my use of the concept "GLBT," and how I encountered the term in Venezuela: GLBT (pronounced *"jeleheté"* in Venezuelan Spanish) is an acronym for "gay, lesbian, bisexual, and transgender or transsexual"—something I was asked to clarify for the original Spanish-language audience of this essay. Although the exercise seems unnecessary here, it is important to note that the concept has been appropriated for the purposes of activism and human rights projects in Venezuela.[8] It has come to be used as a unified concept, in the sense that it is almost invoked as a word (*jelebeté*) rather than as an acronym. Although the words *gay, lesbiana, bisexual* and *transgénero* are now used for self-identification among the people I met in Venezuela, the language is rich with other words to talk about these existences, most particularly *homosexual, marico* (gay or fag), *camionera* or *cachapera* (lesbian), and *transformista*. Of course, these are not words to be used in polite, or should I say civil, conversation. GLBT, as a concept, names specific members of what is understood to be a "community" and is different from ideas such as *el ambiente* or "in the life," which name places or environments rather than specific actors. *El ambiente* is a Latin American concept of queer sociability, sort of like the queer "scene," although it is figured more as a place and a matrix than a staging. The difference here is between being specific (gay, lesbian, bisexual, or transgender people) or ambiguous (queer, *de ambiente*). In the end, I choose to go with ambiguity over naming, preferring slippery signifies over reified categories.

## *LOCAS*, FABULOUSNESS, PERVERSION, AND MODERNITY

> "Holly, what's it like to be a woman trapped in a man's body?" "I'm not trapped in a man's body, I'm trapped in New York City!"
>     I quipped.
>     "But what are you? Are you a man, are you a woman—"
>     "Honey" I shot back. "What difference does it make, just so long as you're fabulous!"
>                 —Holly Woodlawn, narrating an experience on the *Geraldo Rivera Show,*
>                     in *A Low Life in High Heels: The Holly Woodlawn Story*

First, "*loca*-lization." The diverse and imaginative strategies of survival that we invent continue to impress me. Among them is the talent of being "fabulous." How do people manage to make themselves "fabulous" despite great social resistance and material constraints? In talking about melodrama, Ian Ang calls this "the expression of a refusal, or inability, to accept insignificant everyday life as banal and meaningless" (1989, 79). Those who are "fabulous" sometimes appear as divas or *locas*. Of course, I use *loca* in its most generous and honorific sense, as a category used in many places *de ambiente* to refer to its boldest and most scandalous actors. The word is used to refer to effeminate gay men and also to *transformistes* and transgender women.

I would like to do several things with the idea of "*loca*-lization." First, I want to "*loca*-lize" myself, or rather I want to explain to you how and from where I arrive at this inquiry. Second, I want to signal the intersecting and transnational pathways that underscore the political and social environment where *las locas* are found. Third, I want to invoke the process called "globalization" as a very local and contingent one, to highlight that there is negotiation between transnational and local realities. Finally, I want to privilege in my analysis those citizens—good, bad or undocumented—whom I have called *locas,* who are excluded from the political imaginary, to suggest a few ways to make *polítka* a bit more *loca* and learn from the micropolitics *of locas.*

I "*loca*-lize" myself as a butch dyke baby of the Colombian brain drain, coming to consciousness as a gender-nonconforming "foreigner" in the United States of America. In this negotiation of difference, I found my base in the confluence of *jotería* in the San Francisco Bay Area—primarily (but not exclusively) Latinas and Latinos *de ambiente* surrounding the cultural project of Proyecto ContraSIDA Por Vida. At PCPV, *jotería,* an idea based in Chicana/o movement and culture and its queer participants, articulated with the idea of queerness and the people of color who found ourselves in the Mission District of San Francisco in the mid-1990s.

I am drawn to *locas* because although I fit quite easily into a "good" citizenship, I too have experienced the process of marginalization, and I want to understand how power and marginalization work so that we can begin to imagine the possibilities of our collective survival. I am drawn to *peluqueras* (hairdressers), *divas, locas,* and *putas* both because in my experience I have always been legible to them and because they often scandalize me. In my community, they have been those willing to take risks, *las atrevidas*. These trans women are important to me precisely because they complicate the political project; they are the ones who bring shame upon themselves, their families, the nation. And they are not afraid of this shame; rather, they embrace it, turn it around, use it as a weapon. If we want to elaborate a truly inclusive social project, we have to imagine that not all its citizens will be good or conform to the expectations for social participation (be educated, interested, rational, not frivolous). A project that strives for social transformation must embrace and negotiate both complexity and frustrating political subjects.

What draws my attention is a question of power; over the bodies of these divas, society violently demarcates the territory of gender. This demarcation results in their social, economic, judicial, political, and interpersonal exclusion. "Citizenship" has been a mechanism used to exclude them. They are denied social participation, their rights are violated (both as citizens and as humans), and many times they themselves refuse to participate in what could be considered a "good" citizenship. So although "citizenship" and "civil society" have not been central to the formation of my work, they are mechanisms for exercising social power.

In my research, I encountered two areas that have come to frame my understanding of the complexities of *transformista* citizenship: the relationship between perversion, modernity, and nature, and the situation of policing *transformistas* performing sex work on Avenida Libertador in Caracas.

## PERVERSION, MODERNITY, POLICING

The idea of perversion came up many times during my stay in Venezuela, but not the sort of celebratory perversion that I live and embrace in San Francisco. The idea of perversion that pervaded was more like an unintended or undesired effect. A perversion of democracy. Corruption and police abuse as perverse. Perversion—like diversion, subversion, inversion—as a directional metaphor, the place reached by a trajectory intended for somewhere else. During my time in Venezuela, I began to see the country as a profoundly and perversely modern place. I came to understand the project of being modern as inherently productive of perversions of all sorts, including my own fabulous and charming perversions. What I am trying to find is a point of reconciliation within the idea that the lives we make are embedded in a cultural logic that seeks to destroy us. That sometimes riding that razor edge between our perverse existences and the perversions of modern institutions—such as the police state, democracy, or science—is part of the fun.

There is a fundamental contradiction at work here—the process of modernity extinguishes humanity yet creates other possibilities for existence. It is the same mechanism that allows us to understand nature as a legitimizing force while at the same time it becomes the thing upon which order and civilization must be imposed, and violently. I felt this contradiction most during a conference I organized in Caracas—TRANS-foro—which brought together physicians, psychiatrists, legal scholars, and transgender people to open a dialogue and exchange information. One of the presentations was of two transgender women (who do not identify as *transformistas),* Rummie Quintero and Estrella Cerezo, and their mothers. Rummie's mother, Gisela, talked about her experience of her now-daughter in the womb, how she always "knew" that she "was different." Someone asked her what it was like, watching her son transition into a daughter, and she said: "Bueno, si se opone la naturaleza lucharemos contra ella y haremos que nos obedezca" (If nature opposes us, we will fight against her and we will make her obey us).

These words were delivered by Simón Bolívar, called "the Liberator," on March 26, 1812, in Caracas (Avemda Libertador is named after Bolívar). A massive earthquake had decimated an already struggling and war-torn Caracas. Bolívar's followers began to fear that this earthquake was God's retribution for rising up against their king. Bolívar reassured his compatriots that their struggle to impose a new order, in the land that would become the nation of La Gran Colombia and later Venezuela, was righteous, and not in a godly way. That righteousness could come from imposing order, from shaping nature and making her obey. The project of citizenship then, in nineteenth-century Venezuela, became, for people like Bolivar, the shaping of the nature of *el pueblo* to conform to the functioning of a modern nation-state. That Rummie's mother could employ this foundational bit of national ideology to describe her daughter's need to discipline a "male" body with unruly hair and testosterone into a "female" body through whatever means she had available to her seemed to me profoundly perverse. It is an appropriation of the discourses of modernity and nature employed in Venezuela precisely to *exclude transformistas,* and yet which make their existence possible, feasible, even legible.

The modern project of disciplining nature and bodies produces an aesthetic to include or exclude subjects from its realm of comprehension. As the Venezuelan political crisis unfurled before me during my fieldwork, I became particularly interested in the process of inclusion or exclusion of subjects in the project of citizenship. As undesirable citizens are culled out of civil society projects to legitimize claims within a liberal political aesthetic—as was the case with the *transformistas* and the GLBT organizing going on in Venezuela at the time—I am concerned with building the basis for interventions that privilege *transformista* strategies within their own contexts. An incident that I describe in what follows sparked my concern with the project of what I now call "perverse citizenship."

One evening on Avenida Libertador in Caracas, my outreach companion and I saw five Venezuelan national guardsmen with machine guns escort two *transformistas* under a bridge and disappear. The escort walked in silence: neither we civilians, nor the *guardias,* nor the *transformistas* in their custody spoke while they walked by. When they passed by me, I exchanged glances with one of the girls, who seemed to be saying, *"Ahora sí que estamos jodidas,"*—"Now we're really screwed"—with a faint, cynical smile and an eyebrow arched as if it were a challenge. The *guardias* took them under the bridge, we stood frozen as silent firepower paraded past us. After they passed, we slowly edged toward the bridge to see if we could see where they had gone. Not wanting to leave, I began scribbling notes about the incident on my memo pad. We couldn't see what was going on under the bridge. Five minutes passed. Everything was quiet except the passing cars. One of the soldiers had remained above as a lookout. He spotted us, and we began to edge back, not sure if our presence would help or hurt the fate of the *transformistas.* I never found out what happened to the girls—no bodies turned up, no shots were heard, the best case scenario I could imagine is that they had to perform some sexual favor for the *guardias* and then were let go. We don't know because we hailed the next cab that came by after the *guardia* saw us.

These kinds of things happen all the time on Libertador, not just with the Guardia (in fact, this was the first time I had seen them take *transformistas* in custody), but also with the Policía Metropolitana. These things happen because there are silences in which they can happen—people who are not subjects of rights are regularly subject to violations of their integrity as human beings and citizens. No complaints are filed because the complaint is not a useful tool for them. At that moment they are really, irreverently, screwed. So at any moment, some men with guns can do what they please, and if there is silence, they can continue to do so. In Venezuela I learned that this problem has a name: impunity. There are few negative consequences for these actions (which are presumably worth the risk for a free blow job).

If one were to try to produce an utterance that brought consequences—a sound in the night or a complaint filed and prosecuted the morning after—one would be attempting to intervene in the situation. But the problem is that the situation works within its spaces of silence and that the same people who are subject to its abuses have learned to take advantage of these silences. If they wanted to fight for their "rights" they would be doing so already—because they already know how to fight. While there is no such discourse that makes explicit the terms of interaction within what is now a space of silence, the parties coexist in a daily negotiation, lubricated by that very silence. The problem is that sometimes they don't coexist, and one of them ends up dead under a bridge. For those of us who, coming from another place, happen upon these realities and want to intervene, the task is not to bring "light" or "voice" somehow, presuming there was none before; it is to use the social mobility of our bodies and our language to transform relations—to treat people as legitimate subjects of rights, to mobilize the resources necessary for an intervention that makes sense to the people directly involved.

## CITIZENSHIP AND PARTICIPATION

This brings me back to the problem of citizenship. There are several ways to consider the idea. Citizenship can be a disciplinary structure (González Stephan 1996) that crystallizes identities through the control of state and ideological mechanisms, or a political structure within which the subjects of rights and political actors capable of intervening in governance are recognized (as it is defined by the Real Academia Espanola). "Citizenship," as an idea that refers to the subject position of individuals with respect to governance, contains both structural components (the law and other practices of citizenship, such as carrying a national ID card, getting a birth certificate, being recognized by the state, and voting) and affective components (feelings of belonging, participation, one's stance with respect to state recognition or lack thereof). [...] Both dimensions necessarily marginalize *transformistas*. The important thing about citizenship for my work is that it facilitates logics, aesthetics, practices, and structures of *participation*. For citizenship to be useful to *transformistas*, the very notions of politics and citizen must be transformed. To put it another way, for a person to imagine herself the "subject of rights" and to participate in the exercise of those rights there has to exist a process that *produces* this subjectivity, at the same time as there is a struggle for structural recognition in other spheres.

So, if we define a citizen as a subject of rights who exercises them, and if rights and recognition actually have any impact on the situation of social marginality, I have then proposed the idea that it would be a useful intervention for *transformistas* to cultivate a kind of citizenship. I am interested in some strategies to materialize this proposed social transformation, something that seems to me to be a very long term project with little ability to intervene in immediate problems. For example, to intervene in the moment that the Policía Metropolitana is trying to put you in the *perolón* it is much more useful to take off your acrylic heels and start running, not think about fostering your sense of citizenship. [...]

The problem of *transformista* citizenship must be seen from two vantage points: from the integration of *transformistas* into the concept of citizenship and from the transformation of the concept of citizenship. This is how Rummie Quintero puts it. Through her dance and sport activities in her barrio, an expansive 1950s-Soviet-style concrete housing project in Caracas called 23 de Enero, Quintero brings visibility to transgender women in Venezuela. To be clear, Quintero is a transgender woman who is proposing to work with *transformistas*. She does not identify herself or work as a *transformista*. She formed an NGO project called Divas de Venezuela, an organization for transgenders, transsexuals, and *transformistas* in Venezuela. She remarks:

> From the time I began my projection as a person and dancer, I began, at the same time, that social piece. Always working with communities because I always saw the respect that you win by adapting yourself, and many times, you have to adapt to the society so that you can then adapt society to yourself. That is what I'm doing now. Now I'm adapting society. First I adapted myself to the society, now I'm adapting the society to me. (2003)

For however much one can try to "polish" *transformistas* to become exemplary citizens (the normative project), so they can coexist with, for example, the residents of Avenida Libertador who always call the Policía Metropolitana to run them off, or so they begin to file complaints when their rights are violated, one would be naïve to assume that opening the door to dialogue or taking complaints would actually receive any sort of response. The years of active state and social repression have to be countered by some other sort of intervention. Quintero comes from a position that recognizes the legitimacy of society and of her community, a position that is not common among many of the *transformistas* I talked to, but that I have found among people who identify as transgender or transsexual, and not as *transformista*.

Quintero recognizes that one strategy for transforming society's views of transgender people is to respect the norms of the society, and in her experience, to stand out on your artistic merits wins you respect. This strategy works well for her, and I have been quite impressed with her ability to project a positive image of transgender people to a very wide audience of people who one might assume at first to be hostile to transgender people. But the strategy doesn't work in the criminalized and stigmatized environment of publicly visible sex work. Here I have found an aesthetic that privileges shock, scandal, and at times abjection.[9] The aesthetic involves "scandalous" activities such as sex work, aggression, public nudity, stealing, and alcohol and drug use, to name a few. But in the words of one male sex worker on Avenida Solano, a block from Libertador, "I know this is illegal and all, but the fact that I'm a human being— they shouldn't mistreat you."[10] Being a subject of rights is conditioned by the accomplishment of the aesthetics and behavior of a "good citizen." The sex worker refers to a subject of rights who has these rights based on the condition of being a human being, not a citizen. He is, of course, employing the language of international human rights advocacy and, at the same time, indicating another way of understanding the question of citizenship.

The Brazilian political scientist Evelina Dagnino identifies a difference in struggles for rights in Brazil; the sex worker's statement indicates not a struggle *for rights,* but rather a struggle for *the right to have rights.* [...] Dagnino identifies two types of rights: the right to equality and the right to difference. The right to equality corresponds to the liberal definition of citizenship, while the right to difference corresponds to what she calls the "new citizenship" (1998: 50). The new citizenship is defined outside the relationship between the state and the individual. This implies not only "access, inclusion, membership and belonging in a political system," but also "the right to participate in the definition of that system" (51). In the redefinition of citizenship, it is seen as both a political strategy and a cultural politics. [...] Dagnino also includes the GLBT movement in these struggles. But to what extent are the liberal concepts of citizenship, in fact, reproduced within new social movement struggles? Based on my experience with the "GLBT movement" in the United States, and now in Venezuela, it seems that the categorization of these actors as participants in the creation of "new citizenship" occludes the exclusionary practices and limitations in the political imaginaries that we use within the same movement.

I would like to suggest two ways to see the possibility of equality: one in which I am equal to you and another in which you are equal to me. From a position of abjection, or from absolute societal rejection, this difference implies different strategies—if I am equal to you, I conform to your aesthetic to make myself a subject of rights. If you are equal to me, and I am a person rejected in society, then you, too, in the moment of equivalence, are polluted.

In an article called "Scandalous Acts," Don Kulick and Charles Klein (2001) analyze Brazilian *travesti* scandal to understand its political possibilities. For Kulick and Klein, *travesti* scandal as a transformative distribution strategy "reterritorializes shame," that is to say, the *travesti* uses her power to contaminate, implicating the object of her scandal (a client accused of being a *maricón* and taking pleasure in being penetrated by the *travesti),* thus transforming the "battlefield" and getting what she wants. This strategy works to produce the desired effect, which in the case illustrated in the article is getting the client to pay more money. *Travesti* scandal is a resignifymg strategy: *"travestis* transgress public decorum and civil society not by rejecting shame (and championing something like *'Travesti* Pride'), but by inhabiting shame as a place from which to interpellate others and thereby incriminate those others" (2). Upon being incriminated, the object of the scandal feels shame enough to quiet the scandal by acquiescing to its demands. Kulick and Klein suggest that this strategy at times extends beyond the micropolitical sphere of *travesti-client* relations into "battlefields" of an organized, collective arena.

## *SOCIEDAD CIVIL*

If it can be said that the "economic and political direction of society" can be constructed through a consensus (Robles Gil 1998, 117), then civil society can be seen as the field of that construction, negotiation, and reelaboration. [...] What is certain is that to design interventions, it is important to understand and respect the symbolic, economic, political, and interpersonal environments that are pertinent to the transformation one wants to effect.

At various moments in the elaboration of this essay, I have asked myself: is civil society useful at all? And increasingly, I have found myself very frustrated with the whole question and landing on the idea that it is more important to know how to imagine and manifest interventions than to relate them to some idea called "civil society." But Roitter points out one way to think of the operability of the concept of civil society: "We consider that the reintroduction of this theme in the social sciences also signifies another opportunity to pay attention to how people organize themselves in autonomous ways to influence the State and the market, and confront the growing levels of exclusion and fragmentation in society" (2003).

The idea of looking at ways of organizing to make one's presence felt seems important, but I wonder how we deal with those social elements one would want to resist that are neither of the state nor of the market: for example, domestic violence, religious prohibitions on sexuality, or the cultural mechanisms for imposing racism and xenophobia. These things are beyond the state; they bear upon the market. Are the state and the market the only sites for transformation? Where can we locate internal transformations, conceptual transformations that change the way we see a problem, the place of faith, creativity, pride, shame? How do we approach the affective and imaginative dimensions of social transformation? To put it succinctly, how do we go from the intimate (and sometimes public) space of pleasure and feeling *(la rumba)* to the often very public and alienating space of political determination *(el rumbo)*?[12] In my interviews with LGBT NGO representatives in Caracas, there was a separation between "social" space and legal or juridical space.[13] For Jesús Medina, executive director of Asociación Lambda de Venezuela, the two kinds of space form part of and "an 'integral' approach" to defending LGBT rights: "You can attack a violation of rights from the juridical point of view, but also from the educational. Maybe there is also something worth looking at in health, and the social part. You can do a sports event to get a group of people together, have them meet each other, interact. And this will allow you to bring a strong group together so that when you try to attack a problem like discrimination you'll have that strong group that you created through sports" (Medina 2003).

Jesús Raveloof Unión Afirmativa (UnAf) characterizes his experiences at the Lambda meetings as having the quality of a "social encounter," or of "community."[14] Speaking about the difference between Lambda and UnAf, he remarks: "We saw in practice that ... Lambda, the couple of times that I visited them, they had their cinema group every Tuesday, and chévere, because the times I went I felt like ... there's community, or at least a part of the community is forming there. But then in these kinds of activities, I feel like it's important ... to educate" (Ravelo 2003).

This distinction is reaffirmed in the work that Lambda does to put on Orgullo GLBT (GLBT Pride) in Caracas. Orgullo is an event that convenes the "community" to promote visibility, pride, and rights for GLBT people. Lambda became the main organizer of Orgullo after a split with an HIV-services organization and the Red GLBT (GLBT Network) in 2002. The primary reason I point out this distinction is that the two spaces, social and political, are seen as spaces *apart*. In this division, Lambda becomes the organization that puts together more "social" activities (although they clearly see the political dimensions of these kinds of activities), and UnAf becomes the organization that does more "legal" or political activities. The division is also created in a context in which UnAf comes to be known not only for its activities but also for its members, as the organization for professionals and intellectuals (university professors, lawyers, political scientists, and so on). The separation created between social and political space, between doing and thinking, is an aesthetic distinction, in which the social is fun and the political is *pesado* (heavy or serious). [...]

Ravelo relates an experience that the UnAf people had, on Republicagay.com, a Venezuelan GLBT website:

> In fact in *Republica Gay,* over about a year we had a column … every two months. But the column apparently was the least visited in the entire Web site [Author: The what? The least visited? (laughter)] The least visited, yes, yes. Because there was all the rumba (party) and all the interesting news … and the Galena [the site's photo and video area, which provides free soft porn] and the Cuarto Oscuro [Dark Room, the sexually explicit photo and video area of the site]. No one wanted to hear us talk politics [laughs] no way!
>
> (Ravelo 2003)

One of the most often repeated complaints of my friends in the "GLBT civil society" of Caracas pertained to the lack of *participation* of members of the "community." Jesús Ravelo's experience indicates that the readers of Republicagay.com have many more things that interest them besides "politics," and it is in these activities that they choose to participate.

Now I would like to return to Rummie Qumtero, founder of Divas de Venezuela, who you may recall also works what she calls the "social," and who shares Jesús Medina's vision of the social as something integral to a larger project of exercising rights for GLBT people. The reasons that Quintero gives for not participating in the other GLBT organizations illustrate as much the aesthetic problem as the problem of participation for transgender and *transformista* subjects, particularly in the frustration she felt from how she was received by other NGOs:

> I have been in many sports organizations, I've been in others, and yet … there's been that … like that not hearing, no? Because all of the sudden you might see that lack of respect toward transgender people, or that lack of valuing [our contributions]. I have also found that … there are choques [clashes] with people who are not as prepared as you are, or as one is, to take on a role, and sometimes that gets to people. In other words, that is why I decided to start this NGO [Divas]. As far as organizations where there are heterosexual people, I have experienced a lot of openness. My areas they leave to me, and I handle them. And well, whenever I was the one handling them, thank God, it's gone well for me.
>
> (Quintero 2003)

Quintero feels as though she gets more respect for her organizing abilities in a non-GLBT environment. Although it can be said that Lambda and UnAf accept the participation of transgender people, there are frustrations and self-exclusions:

> You would get, "Well, we won't reject you outright because you're also with the GLB … you're the 'T'" Or rather, the gay community. But no … I actually got a *cargo* [position], in Lambda de Venezuela as cultural and sports coordinator, a position that I never really occupied, as they say, it was something

very fictitious, and that was a disappointment to me, really, because, well, if they give you a *cargo,* they should give you the importance of that *cargo.*

(Quintero 2003)

But Quintero and I have also encountered the problem of participation in trying to convene groups of transgender women and *transformistas,* and it seems to me that the act of "convening" is precisely where we encounter the problem. If Quintero herself can function within a more or less normative political model ("conform herself to society"), then there are many more transgender women and *transformistas* in particular who can't or won't.

*La rumba, locas,* and scandal are not always productive sites from which to build interventions. When I say we have to imagine a politics from the *rumba* I am not saying that it should only be imagined in that way, but rather that it is necessary to transcend the aesthetic distinctions that marginalize or cause specific actors to exclude themselves. If the idea is to bear upon those grave moments and silences in which rights are violated, we have to transform politics so that it exists in those spaces and is employed by the subjects that transit them.

## CONCLUSION

Since I wrote the first version of this essay, the landscape of organizing for transgender and GLBT people in Caracas has changed quite a bit. While the "GLBT civil society" of Caracas (that is, those who imagine themselves as the "political" actors of *el ambiente,* who attempt to intervene in situations of abuse and inequality for GLBT people) has suffered some setbacks and divisions, particularly around Venezuela's political situation and the tensions between programs that are funded to provide HIV prevention and treatment services and those that are not, there has also been a significant expansion in the landscape of activism and advocacy by and for LGBT people in Caracas, as well as the rest of Venezuela. Two trans-gender organizations were registered in 2004 with the goal of advocating for transsexuals, transgender women, and *transformistas.*

While initially Rummie Qumtero and Estrella Cerezo proposed to start one organization, *Divas de Venezuela,* the differences in their approaches made it clear that their efforts would best be served by establishing two organizations. For Quintero, cultural activities such as sporting events, aerobics, and beauty pageants are of more interest. Informed by her (very successful) efforts in barrio organizing in Caracas's 23 de Enero housing projects, Quintero privileged "self-esteem," "cultural expression," and "alternatives to delinquency" programming based on her experience with youth movements in Caracas. Quintero's work as a neighborhood and youth activist marked her approach to transgender organizing. She actively tried to counter the stereotype *of transformistas* as hairdressers or prostitutes, and this stance meant that some of the *transformistas* 1 worked with on Avenida Libertador disliked her and refused to participate in Divas because she did not accept their sex work as a legitimate vocation.

Cerezo's approach to organizing was based in her experiences with political parties, including a huge effort during the 1998 presidential elections (when current president Hugo Chávez Frías was elected) and the subsequent Constitutional Convention in 1999. Cerezo was also a founding member of Movimiento Ambiente de Venezuela (MAV), a GLBT organization founded by Oswaldo Reyes, who registered MAV with the National Electoral Commission and ran as an openly gay candidate to the 1999 Constitutional Assembly. Cerezo worked closely with Reyes on this campaign, but complained bitterly about her exclusion from MAV's charter at the time of its registration, claiming she had been excluded from the leadership of the organization for being transgender. When MAV was dissolved, she decided not to continue working with the primarily gay-male-led organizations that emerged—Unión Afirmativa and Alianza Lambda de Venezuela, suspicious that she would suffer the same treatment with them. Both Quintero and Cerezo complained about gay men's misogyny and transphobia in the Venezuelan GLBT movement. Although Cerezo had not been a sex worker (she was trained as a nurse but was turned away from every place she applied for a job after graduating), several of her friends and acquaintances were sex workers, and she was concerned about their health. She and artist Argelia Bravo began accompanying me to Avenida Libertador in the summer of 2003, having expressed curiosity about my work on the street. After investigating the possibility of joining Divas, Estrella decided to found her own organization, which she called TransVenus de Venezuela. Bravo and Cerezo decided to work together on the organization, and TransVenus was registered in April 2004. With great dedication, they have developed and maintained close relationships with many of the *transformistas* who work on Avenida Libertador, providing condoms, medical visits (in collaboration with volunteer physicians), and vigilance toward human rights violations. After collaborating with the HIV/AIDS service organization ASES de Venezuela, TransVenus applied for and received funding from the Ministry of Health and Development (MSDS) to continue its condom distribution and medical attention to *transformistas* on Avenida Libertador. Cerezo also began giving hairdressing classes to *transformistas* doing sex work. This work was supported by Fundación Artistas Emergentes.

On June 25, 2004, in conjunction with a month of Orgullo GLBT programming put on by various organizations, TransVenus organized a vigil for the human rights of *transformistas* on Avenida Libertador. Forty people attended and stood with *transformistas* where they do sex work every day, everyone holding up placards bearing the points of the United Nation's Universal Declaration of Human Rights and waving them at passing cars. The event resulted in two full pages of coverage on trans-gender issues in *El Nacional,* one of Venezuela's newspapers of record. As transgender people and *transformistas* begin to articulate individual and collective responses to the problems they face in Venezuelan society, I am inspired to see them analyzing *transformistas'* existing survival strategies and resisting the pressure to conform their demands and political imagi-naries to a liberal model that fundamentally excludes many *transformistas.*

## NOTES

1. The preceding epigraph is chapter and verse from the Ordenanza de Convivencia Ciudadana of the city of Caracas. In the tradition of the Spanish Requerim-lento, which was read in Spanish to populations of indigenous people in what was then called Yndias on the eve of conquest, I leave it untranslated. I dedicate this essay to Estrella Cerezo, Argelia Bravo, and TransVenus de Venezuela, with whom I have worked to establish condom distribution and HIV-prevention education on Avenida Libertador.
2. *Transformista* is a term used in Venezuela to refer to someone who is assigned male sex at birth and who presents herself in her life as a woman, using technologies related to hair, cosmetics, clothing, diet, hormones and implants to accomplish her femininity. The term is at times considered an insult, but is also used for in-group identification. It also implies, more often than not, the practice of publicly visible sex work as part of one's identity. Not all transgender women in Venezuela do sex work or identify as *transformistas.*
3. Note that in the polarization between the Chávez government and the opposition, the words *ciuiaiano* and *sociedad civil* have been taken up by the different sides to signify participation. *Ciudadano* has become the parlance of the Chávez administration, and of the Movimiento Quinta Republica (MVR) as it struggles to include marginalized Venezuelans in the political process. *Sociedad civil* has been appropriated by the opposition to signify dissent from an authoritarian regime, as it came to be used in Brazil, Argentina, and Chile in the late twentieth century.
4. "GLBT" refers to a kind of queer "scene" and is a term used for LGBT communities and spaces throughout Latin America. I will further define this and other terms below.
5. [...] The original Spanish version of this article was developed through my participation in the Programa de Cultura, Globalización y Transformaciones Sociales at the Universidad Central de Venezuela, Centro de Estudios Post-Doctorales (CIPOST), Facultad de Ciencias Económicas y Sociales (FACES). For the original version of this essay, see Ochoa 2004. [...]
6. Although my usage of the term *loca* emerged from my experience with gay, queer, and trans (Latino) communities in the United States, Colombia, and Venezuela, it is very much resonant with Lawrence La Fountain-Stokes's (2008) beautiful riff on *locas* and *locura.* I use the term to refer to a variety of people and will discuss this in the section on taxonomy and translation.
7. In an expanded version of this essay as well as in the original Spanish-language version, I discuss in more detail the relationship of this work to my experience with the San Francisco-based Proyecto ContraSIDA Por Vida. See Ochoa 2004, 2006.

8.  For a critique of the "Gay International," see Masad 2002. Extensive debates on the globalization of LGBT political categories have emerged in the past decade, and I will not summarize them here. For important contributions to and documentation of these debates, see Cruz-Malavé and Manalansan 2002; Boelstorff 2005, 2007.
9.  Márquez (1999, 46–47) describes the cultivation and use of an abject aesthetic among the "chupapegas" (glue-sniffers, generally boys eight to twelve years old) in Sabana Grande, the area of Caracas where the *transformistas* and other sex workers do their work.
10. "Yo sé que esto es ilegal y todo pero el hecho de ser un ser humano—no te deben maltratar" (Carrasco and Ochoa 2003; translation mine).
    [...]
12. *La rumba* translates as "the party"; *el rumbo* is "the direction," or "the sense" in which something or someone is going.
13. For one take on Movimiento Ambiente de Venezuela (MAV), see Muñoz 2003. Muñoz's article includes a content analysis of MAV's publication *Igual Género,* national press coverage, Web pages, and interviews with Jesús Medina (identified as "Jesus Rovelo") of Lambda de Venezuela and José Ramon Merentes of Unión Afir-mativa. [...]
14. Muñoz may have transposed and misspelled names. I know of no Jesús Rovelo associated with Lambda. Jesús Ravelo has not, to my knowledge, ever been part of the leadership of Lambda de Venezuela, though he has participated in Lambda events and workshops.

## WORKS CITED

Ang, Ien. 1989. *Watching* Dallas: *Soap Opera and the Melodramatic Imagination.* New York: Routledge.

Boellstorff, Tom. 2005. *The Gay Archipelago: Sexuality and Nation in Indonesia.* Princeton: Princeton U Press.

Boellstorff, Tom . 2007. *A Coincidence of Desires: Anthropology, Queer Studies, Indonesia.* Durham: Duke University Press.

Carrasco, Edgar, and Marcia Ochoa. 2003. "Informe sobre impunidad: Venezuela." Proyecto ILGALAC-OASIS-Unión Europea. Caracas: Acción Ciudadana Contra el SIDA.

Dagnino, Evelina. 1998. "Culture, Citizenship, and Democracy: Changing Discourses and Practices of the Latin American Left." In *Culture of Politics/Politics oj Culture: Revisioning Latin American social movements,* ed. Sonia E. Alvarez, Evelina Dagnino, and Arturo Escobar. Boulder, CO: Westview Press.

González Stephan, Beatriz. 1996. "Economías fundacionales: Diseño del cuerpo ciudadano." In *Cultura y Tercer Mundo 2: Nuevas identidades y ciudadanías,* comp. Beatriz González Stephan. Serie Nubes y Tierra. Caracas: Editorial Nueva Sociedad.

Kulick, Don, and Charles Klein. 2001. "Scandalous Acts: The Politics of Shame Among Brazilian Travesti Prostitutes." http://www.sociology.su.se/cgs/Con-ference/Klein%20and%20Kulick20()l.pdf(accessed    16 April, 2003).

Laclau, Ernesto, and Chantal Mouffe. 1989. *Hegemonía y estrategia socialista. Hacia una radicalizacián de la democracia.* Madrid: Siglo XXI.

La Fountain-Stokes, Lawrence. 2008. "Trans/Bolero/Drag/Migration: Diasporic Puerto Rican Theatricalities." *WSQ: Trans*-Special Issue.

Lowe, Lisa. 1996. *Immigrant Acts: On Asian American Cultural Politics.* Durham: Duke University Press.

Márquez, Patricia. 1999. *The Street Is My Home: Youth and Violence in Caracas.* Stanford: Stanford University Press.

Massad, Joseph. 2002 . "Re-Orienting Desire: The Gay International and the Arab World." *Public Culture* 14(2): 361-385.

Medina, Jesús, executive director, Lambda de Venezuela. 2003. Interview by the author, May 6, Caracas, Venezuela. Minidisc recording.

Muhoz, Carlos. 2003. "Identidades translocales y orientación sexual en Caracas: (arqueología, geneología y tecnologías de la orientación sexual." In *Políticas de identidades y diferencias sociales en tiempos de globalización,* coord. Daniel Mato. Caracas: FACES, Universidad Central de Venezuela.

Ochoa, Marcia. 2004. "Ciudadanía perversa: Divas, margmación y participación en la 'loca-lización.'" In *Políticas de ciudadanía y socíedad civil en tiempos de globalización,* coord. Daniel Mato. Caracas: FACES, Universidad Outrai de Venezuela.

Ochoa, Marcia. 2006. "Queen for a Day: *Transformistas,* Misses, and Mass Media m Venezuela." PhD diss., Stanford University.

Quintero, Rummie, founder, Divas de Venezuela. 2003. Interview by the author. Minidisc recording. May 5, Caracas, Venezuela.

Ravelo, Jesús, general coordinator, Unión Afirmativa. 2003. Interview by the author. Minidisc recording. May 8, Caracas, Venezuela.

Robles Gil, Rafael Reygadas. 1998. *Abriendo veredas: Iniciativas públicas y socials de las redes de organizaciones civiles.* México: Convergencia de Organismus Civiles por la Democracia.

Rodriguez, Juana María. 2003. *Queer Latinidad: Identity Practices, Discursive Spaces.* New York: New York University Press.

Roitter, Mario. 2003. "El tercer sector como representación topográfica de la sociedad civil." Paper presented at the *Coloquio Internacional Políticas de Ciudadanía y Sociedad Civil en Tiempos de Globalización. Más Allá de los Debates sobre la Coyuntura en Venezuela.* Caracas, May 23–24, 2004.

Valentine, David. 2007. *Imagining Transgender.* Durham: Duke University Press.

Yuval-Davis, Nira. 1997. "Women, Citizenship, and Difference." *Feminist Review* (57):4–27.

# 35

# *Thinking Figurations Otherwise*
## Reframing Dominant Knowledges of Sex and Gender Variance in Latin America

VEK LEWIS

IN "THINKING FIGURATIONS OTHERWISE," the first chapter of Latin America scholar Vek Lewis's 2010 book *Crossing Sex and Gender in Latin America,* Lewis asks how the critical literature on the representation of *travestismo* in works of culture relates to the actual lives of trans people. Lewis situates his work in opposition to previous work on *travestismo,* which theorizes it as a metaphor for destabilizing the national order; he seeks instead to show how the understanding of gender-variance as destabilizing or excluded from the nation came about in the first place. Thus, Lewis embarks on a genealogy of dominant understandings of *locas, travestis* and *transsexuals.* In both popular imaginaries and critical understandings of Latin American *travestismo,* Lewis claims, the figure of the *travesti* is treated as merely symbolic of a more general crisis in identity-construction. Trans people become convenient tools for thinking *mestizaje*—a term connoting the mixed or hybrid character of Latin American identities—because transness is primarily understood as a hybrid mixture of two sexes, genders, or dispositions. While Lewis critiques Latin American theorists specifically for this error, he also shows how the Anglophone North American theorists of performativity upon whom these writers draw—Marjorie Garber and Judith Butler—make a similar mistake. In advancing this critique, Lewis is attempting to think about gender variance in Latin America in different terms. While gender variant identities and practices in Latin America are indeed shaped by the sociological dimensions of nation, race, and class, seeing gender variance merely as an allegory for personal and political transformations neglects the institutional and material situation of living *travestis, locas* and transsexuals.

## OF REPRESENTATIONS AND EPISTEMES: SOME PRELIMINARIES

In the mural *La katharsis,* which hangs in Mexico City's Palacio de Bellas Artes, the great Mexican postrevolutionary artist José Clemente Orozco depicts a nightmarish panorama of militarism, conflict, and the collapse of a sociopolitical order. The title of the painting suggests a dramatic purgation of demons away from the usual strictures of society; a hell-bent letting loose of destructive energies in a baptism by fire; the perils of war, fascism, technology, and the modern age. In a visual field devoid of any recognizable agents of such forces—the painting is crowded by repeated but anonymous dark shapes flanked suffocatingly by metal coils and armaments—the only complete face and body that appears is that of the woman sprawled naked in the foreground. Her masklike visage stares vacantly and giddily at the viewer. Pearls wrapped around her neck above bare and drooping breasts, legs wide open, she is a prostitute—one of many painted by this artist. What is she doing alongside these indisputable images of the excesses of the bourgeois order: war and imperialism? What is the link? Is the sexual image suggested by this figure symbolic of the orgy of violence indicated in the rest of the painting? Here she is not trampled on or shown as brutalized or subjected to the surrounding terror; rather, she is a surface sign of its deep corruption; the wanton girl-toy of the rich, the Whore of Babylon whose presence is a metonym of the incipient moral decline in Europe—the old dame whose felled head lies next to the prostitute in the painting—and of the excesses of the industrial era.

This study does not concern the pictorial arts, yet Orozco's mural is a useful starting place to explore some of the theoretical and epistemological dimensions to an inquiry into the representation of sexual minorities in literary and filmic production, which is the principal objective of this chapter. Like the prostitute who is invoked as a symbol of the sociopolitical panorama exposed by Orozco—who to be sure, was not alone in his metaphorical use of such figures—*locas, travestis,* and transsexuals in recent decades (1985–2005) have been engaged in many literary and filmic texts from Latin America as symbols of another order—at times represented as purveyors of apocalypse, and at others, of redemptive possibility, among other things.

Orozco's prostitute is lifeless, bereft of individuality and social context: she is a mannequin, a tragicomic exhibit, a condensation of characteristics that embody superficiality, the loss of spirit and meaning, and a hollow decadence. *Locas, travestis,* and transsexuals are at times similarly invoked and manipulated in contemporary cultural production from Latin America, with comparable consequences: the diminution of any sense of inner life, interpersonal history, or subjectivity of the figures so portrayed.

The work of Donna Guy (1991) demonstrates that in the late nineteenth and for much of the twentieth century, the female prostitute was perceived as a threat to family and nation in Argentina. Like prostitutes in Latin American and other cultural contexts, visibly gender nonconforming homosexuals, as well as cross-dressing and cross-living *travestis* and transsexuals, have long been perceived as problematic. As sexual minorities, all these persons have been subject to intensive and objectifying discursive treatments from the late nineteenth century to the end of the millennium—another fin de siècle whose competing anxieties have inspired a resurgence of representations of sex and gender diverse figures seen to transgress the moral order and its sacred divisions.

In the new millennium, recognizing the upsurge in depictions of cross-gender acts, identities, and trans subjects, several critics in Latin American studies are giving more attention to the place of *lo loca* and *lo trans* in representations of nonnormative sexualities and genders. Most of these critics work from the context of Caribbean productions and Chilean representations in art and literature and are Latin American themselves (Arroyo 2003b, the critics from the special issue of *Centro* edited by Sandoval-Sánchez 2003, Richard 1993); others are Latinos writing from the geopolitical space of the United States (Sifuentes-Jáuregui 2001). Many draw on the idea of transvestites as "natural" metaphors for the construal of the national subject. They either understand the place of the *travesti* as embodiment of national colonial identity or resistance to its imposition.[1] Informed by the structuralism of Severo Sarduy, and later, the queer theory work of Marjorie Garber and (early) Judith Butler, all emphasize *travestismo* as a performance, suffused with varying degrees of theatricality, artificiality, and simulation. Literary critics rarely, if ever, draw on Butler's more recent ethically concerned work seen in *Undoing Gender* (2004). Her influential theories of performativity attract attention. Critics do not tie the work of representation to the real-life impacts around gender crossing that Butler has begun to explore, mostly in response to criticism directed at her earlier work. Ben Sifuentes-Jáuregui begins his study by giving a working definition of transvestism: "transvestism is a performance of gender" (2001, 2). Further, for him, transvestism's operational strategy is the "denaturalization of genders," blurring the distinctions between self and other (4). Sifuentes-Jáuregui and his Latin American colleagues are invested in the idea of *travestismo* as symptomatic or instrumental of something; they do not explore the possibilities of the textual inscription of subjectivity.[2] For these critics, the very performativity of *travestismo*—as a ground for configuring through gesture and imitation—establishes it as primordially and preeminently metaphorical in any text in which gender variant figures are present.

This book parts ways with such notions. While sex- and gender-crossing figures have historically been linked to the national sphere, and as a consequence, subject to allegorization, there is nothing "natural" to this representational treatment in culture and discourse. Such a critical determination provides little room to situate representations of *locas, travestis,* and transsexuals that are not preeminently disposed to metaphor and may be informed by emergent, alternative knowledges. In this chapter, and through the analysis of texts undertaken in this book, I lay bare the discursive conditions of possibility that allow *locas, travestis,* and transsexuals to be invoked in the name of the national, and the rhetorical mechanisms that permit them to be appropriated as a sign of change, crisis, or trouble, by engaging in a deconstructive excavation of the genealogy of dominant knowledges about sex and gender variance in the Latin American context. Such dominant knowledges, formed over time, have structured the representation and representability of past and present visions of sex and gender variance. The reigning episteme that encodes effeminacy and *travestismo* in reference to things as diverse as concealment, criminality, subversion, parody, colonial mimesis, and hybridity needs to be situated in terms of its lineage, across the range of sites in which such attributions appear. A fundamental precept of this chapter is that theories that choose sex and gender variance as the object of their inquiry, and that do not lay bare the genealogy of representations in text and culture, can themselves reproduce and prop up dominant visions. As such I include critical approaches to *lo trans* in texts and contexts within the purview of my genealogy, in order to remain alert to this danger but also as a measure that serves to situate my own, very different approach. This approach draws on understandings of the place of subjectivity, which is also addressed in depth in the current chapter. A critical genealogy of dominant frameworks about *locas, travestis,* and transsexuals and their representation in texts has so far not been undertaken by contemporary critics writing on the subject of the cultural representation of sex and gender variance in Latin America, and, as such, is long overdue.

## DISCOURSES OF THE NATIONAL "BODY" AND SOCIAL ORDER: "DEVIANCE," CRISIS, AND METAPHOR

Literary historiography pinpoints the emergence of homosexual types in literary representations in Latin America and how they are forever linked to the social order. David William Foster, in his introduction to *Sexual Textualitier: Essays on Queer/ing Latin American Writing* (1997), for instance, argues that since the appearance of what is recognized as the first modern Latin American "homosexual" novel, Adolfo Camhina's *Bom Crioulo* (Brazil, 1895; *Bom-Crioulo: The Black Man and the Cabin Boy*), there has been a greater emphasis on homoerotic acts rather than questions of individual identity in Latin American literature, especially in modernity. He notes that in this text, and subsequent texts, homosexuality is frequently related to the greater patriarchal order "rather than the emphasis one finds in American writing on questions of personal identity and internal psychological process" (1997, 2). The linking of the libidinal economy of the "passive" homosexual role to the social order lays the conceptual groundwork for the linking of *locas, travestis,* and transsexuals in their gender styles and positionalities to other spheres in contemporary texts.[3]

Outside Latin American literature, in both medico-legal and nationalist discourse, we see precedents of the invocation of sex- and gender-diverse acts and subjects in connection to problems in the national-cultural sphere. The dying years of the nineteenth century and the dawning of the twentieth foresaw the intense scrutiny and taxonomization of subjects in the public gaze who differed from certain standard norms in Argentina, Mexico, Nicaragua, and other Latin American nations (Fernández 2004, 25). Emergent homosexual and *travesti* subcultures were targeted by lawmakers, criminologists, and medical professionals—among other groups such as working-class itinerant laborers, prostitutes, and immigrants as well as indigenous people—as the source of a range of social "vices" that seemingly threatened bourgeois morality, its ideas of property, behavioral and bodily standards, and the safe flow of capital and control of classes.[4] Same-sex erotic practices, cross-dressing and cross-living behaviors became discursively inscribed as a sort of person—the invert—whose nature was aberrant, deviant, and cross-sexed. Further, subjects who displayed such behaviors were associated "scientifically" with crime and grouped alongside prostitutes, professional criminals, swindlers, and violent thieves (25).

The work of Jorge Salessi (2000) is especially illuminating on the discursive forms around gendered others that such codings assumed in Argentina in the period. The "patria"—a masculine, virile entity—was threatened by several perceived enemies. State authorities exhibited a real anxiety over notions of citizen-outsider, private-public, and health-contamination. Several minorities, including homosexuals, *travestis,* and so-called public women, were all visualized as the second term in these categories. A group of *higienistas,* based at the Faculty of Medicine of the University of Buenos Aires, allied with the police and with correctional facilities to criminalize, castigate, and control these "errant" flows. These groups were characterized as *maleantes*—criminals, low-lifes, or bad seeds—who threatened the order and represented forces of anarchy. Their presence and movement through space was conceived of as a form of dangerousness. The most public of these populations—those present in the various *lupanares* (brothels), soliciting while strolling in town plazas or in the port, whether public women or homosexual inverts—were considered agitative and outside "normal" work relations: their traffic and commerce was seen to disturb the healthy flows of the social corpus. Argentina—a healthy masculine body—risked bad circulation and atrophy of its "members." The *higienistas* made recommendations to prevent the spread of a social contamination of the body politic. The *higienistas'* objective was to heal and integrate this nation—in danger of contamination and seduction into deviance (brothels and homosexual cabarets were described as sites of infection). In this way, fin-de-siècle fears around deviance and (sexual) anarchy posited publicly visible same-sex erotic practices and cross-dressing as apocalyptic signs of the end of an order, the end of an era, and the destruction of the "civilized nation."[5] Such sciences of deviance and social control were replicated in Brazil, notes James Green (1999). Salessi's work is the only one to investigate these kinds of discourses in real depth. Similar archives from other countries warrant close attention (Green 1999, 9).

Race and racial mixing also figured strongly in the positivist discourse of the late nineteenth and early twentieth centuries. Of course, the question of racial and cultural heterogeneity—and how to envision a meaningful national community in the postindependence period and modernizing project—has long been one of considerable obsession for Latin American elite thinkers and politicos. The cult of cultural and racial *mestizaje*—so key to colonial consolidation, the efforts of the wars of independence, the formation of the modern nation-state and the mythic forms of *latinidad*—was suddenly radically recontoured by the fin-de-siècle concerns for racial purity that generated considerable fear and obsession and were coded in the language of contagion. In her book *The Rise and Fall of the Cosmic Race: The Cult of Mestizaje in Latin America* (2004), Marilyn Grace Miller argues that *mestizaje* and its relation to national discourse has undergone important transformations and has been used to both racist and antiracist ends. Other writers propose a four-point periodization of different ways of conceptualizing race in relation to nation in the region (Appelbaum, Macpherson, and Rosemblatt 2003). These writers hold that racial difference has been alternately "ignored, expressed, appropriated and transformed" by nationalizing processes and in nation discourse at different times (2). Although engaged in a "positive" sense in the very name of nationalism and nation building in Mexico after the revolution and in Brazil in the 1930s under Getúlio Vargas, *mestizaje* (and, it might be observed, *mulatez)* was often condemned at the turn of the nineteenth century and the first decades of the twentieth; Europeanness and whiteness, linked to progress, were the ideal. In places were *mestizaje* was not reevaluated early in the twentieth century, scientific racism informed the rejection of nonwhite groups or implicitly encoded national citizenship in masculine and white terms in the region at least till the 1940s (Graham 1990, 3). If the specter of plagues induced a sort of hysteria around sexual subjects that demanded the elimination of all "transgressive differences" to constitute and protect the "ideal national community, imagined as a strong and healthy body," *indios, negros, mestizos,* and mulattos became, perhaps more profoundly, targets of blame as imputed historical and enduring sources of sickness, weakness and "retardation" of "la raza nacional" (Nouzeilles 2003, 51–52). Disease became the symptom and metaphor for social disorder. Mechanisms of control and surveillance were recommended by positivist scientists and educators to prevent the spread of an epidemic. In the novel *Salón de belleza,* Mario Bellatin very craftily reroutes the vectors of a metaphorical disease coded in epidemiological terms and attached to his gender-variant characters. Given that the 1980s saw the emergence of the AIDS epidemic, which was fused in the social imaginary in many parts of the world, including Latin America, to homosexuality, it is hardly coincidental that plague metaphors and sexual others still haunt contemporary narratives. Indeed, the convergence of visions of sex and gender otherness with the moral panic around this disease, so prone to rhetorical re-elaboration, is an important dimension for multiple reasons. It is also not an overstatement to signal the importance of the realities of stigma and HIV for *travestis* from that time to the present day. A full elaboration of the discursive connections between marginal others and disease—in all their metaphorically gendered and racialized dimensionalities—is hence crucial.

The discourse of the Argentina's one-time president and Buenos Aires intellectual, Domingo Faustino Sarmiento, is unremitting in its racial profiling of the "barbarism" that threatens future Argentinian society. Sarmiento further plotted the cultured "city dweller" against the rural workers and frontier Pampas gauchos. The characteristic abjection, baseness, primitivism, and, tellingly, passivity and feminization, ascribed to all these racial and ethnic others in his work promulgated the archetypal views on the struggle between the superior "civilized" elements of Latin American culture and the "backward" and debilitating admixture of bad racial "blood" supposedly plaguing the nation.[6]

Jean Franco shows how the endemic "dangerous ill" said to afflict Latin American societies was persistently coded in racial terms (1970, 56–58). Darwinistic theories on the biological predispositions of the allegedly inferior stock of Indians were advanced by the Mexican Francisco Alonso de Bulnes and linked to the perils facing nationhood in *El porvenir de las naciones latinoamericanas* (1899; *The Future of the Latin American Nations).* This work was composed during the era of Porfirio Díaz, a time in which *lo indio* (Indianness) as representative of "la problemática nacional" (the national dilemma) was intensively discussed. In different parts of Latin America, such as Colombia, the Caribbean, and Brazil, blacks were attributed with a "slave mentality" and compliant attitude; Indians were identified for their inherent "resignation" and "passivity" (Franco 1970, 58). These tropes of race and their essentialist frameworks have persisted and interpellated blacks, mulattos, and *indios* as constitutive others to the so-called superior white European citizen of the civilized ideal nation. (Later, in the context of 1930s U.S.-dominated Puerto Rico, we see the repetition of some of these racial tropes and the degradation of the feminine in the nationalist discourse of Antonio S. Pedreira (1992 [1934]).

Further, in the Andean republics and in Mexico, as Jean Franco notes, the Indian was seen as an obstacle to progress and modernity (58). The Bolivian Alcides Arguedas articulated perhaps most vividly the image of the diseased nation in *Pueblo enfermo* (1909), a body stricken by its debilitated constitution and the stupor of the natural environment, both materialized in the Indian. Brazil's complicated history with the problematics of race is underwritten by the facts of slavery there, remembering that the nation was the last to outlaw it in the region. "Branqueamento" as an ideal—whitening and becoming more like the white, via breeding and custom—was prevalent as a philosophy even after the abolition of slavery. Together with Cuba, Brazil has displayed some differences in thinking race in relation to nation that are important—and different moments of mythologization in the name of the national community. In spite of this, racial and cultural difference are still nodes that structure their national elaborations.

Just as the Argentinian *higienistas* sought to heal and integrate the nation—in danger of contamination and seduction into deviance—so, too, did politicians in Argentina and elsewhere in pre-World War II Latin America promote programs to "dilute" the *mestizo* racial stock from its weakening, and feminizing, influences. Writing in the first two decades of the twentieth century, the Argentinian medico-criminologist, sociologist, and psychiatrist José Ingenieros, for instance, favored Germanic European immigration over Italian, Spanish, or French to strengthen the race from its Indio-Hispanic congenital inferiority (Terán 1986). The qualities of barbarity attributed by Sarmiento to *indios* and "mixed-breed" gauchos would be bred out under the civilizing influence of modern European immigrants. Interestingly, Sarmiento himself also warned of the *afeminamiento* (feminization) of Argentinian literature and culture, which for him represented an emasculation of the virility of the society and the nation.

Weak in their dispositions and unnatural in their passions, both racial and sexual subjects, then, were perceived as a threat to the harmony of the imagined social corpus and theorized as a contamination of the national body. Perhaps it is unsurprising to find that the metaphors of abjection and otherness used in reference to the aforementioned racial others are also deployed in reference to *locas, travestis,* and transsexuals. In the heat of anxieties around the possibility of anarchy, sexual minorities were positioned from this time as a source of many ills. Even when *mestizaje* as a sign of mixity was revalorized and appropriated in the name of joining potential contradictions together in state projects of national unity and common imagined histories, both racial and gendered crossings served symbolically to signify the national realm. Hence the connection between racial and gendered others is resignified but does not loosen. In fact, as we will later see in the work of contemporary cultural critics, *travestismo* is so married in Latin American thought to the processes of national identity and *mestizaje* as to create, I will argue, a kind of *travestizaje*, in which the figure of the *travesti* is advanced as a figure par excellence of the process of national identity construction. This is an element of the dominant episteme that is complexly constructed across a range of discursive sites and naturalized by much postmodern (especially queer) theory.

[...]

Apart from the discursive lineage that connects same-sex eroticism and trans practices to problems in the national sphere—as forms of threat to the nation that come from an "afuera" (Salessi 1999)—it is in the fin-de-siècle period that the effeminate or cross-dressed male is first visualized as a shamed and shameful body; as artificial, comic, and grotesque; as excessively "dressed," scandalous, and drawing attention to itself. The new century in Mexico was ushered in with the case of *Los '41*—to which Ben Sifuentes-Jáuregui devotes the first chapter of his book—when police performed a raid on a group of upper class males or *lagartijos* (fops) dancing with cross-dressed partners—and ignited the public imagination around questions of homosexuality, transvestism, and decadence.[8] Many of the attributions inaugurated at this time are still found in media discourse on *travestis* in many locales, which continues to advance the terms of falsity, depravity, criminality, and *malas costumbres* (bad custom). Legal statutes originate from the time in which criminologists determined gender-crossing and effeminate homosexuals as a criminal type; these similarly invoke the terms of *ofensas al pudor público* (offences to public modesty), *las buenas costumbres* (good custom), and the promotion of "escándalo." Inverts then, and *locas* and *travestis* now, represented and represent a rupture in the set terms for the public body in medico-legal discourse. Speaking of the contemporary period, Josefina Fernández notes that these formulations presently circulate so widely that they put limits on seeing *travesti* identity in any other way in dominant culture: they are always located socially "del lado de lo abyecto" (2004,118; "alongside the abject").[9] In political discourse across the region, party politics and the borrowing or stealing of policies of another group are very commonly framed as "travestismo político." Intrigue and corruption at the political level are commonly married to the image of *travestis and travestismo*.[10]

These discursive conditions, then, have made and, to some extent, continue to make it possible to enjoin effeminacy and *travestismo* in the name of imagining crisis and corruption and to conjoin them with the problematics of national identity and its construction. In the next section, I show that, by their over-reliance on the queer theory work on transvestism and transgender, contemporary criticism that treats the representation of *locas, travestis,* and *transexuales* in Latin American cinema and literature fails to question and in fact reenmeshes itself in the dominant views of sex- and gender-variant figures as essentially figurative and symbolic of identity composition or crisis, bypassing a deconstruction of the metaphor and a view of the possibilities of envisioning sex and gender transitivity outside its terms.

## THEORY TROUBLE: ON NOT AVOIDING THE SUBJECT

As alluded to at the beginning of this chapter, theoretical approaches to the representation of sex and gender crossing in Latin American cultural production are inspired by three principal sources: the work of Severo Sarduy (1969; 1982), Marjorie Garber (1992), and Judith Butler (1990; 1993). Some of Sarduy's work anticipates that of the other two thinkers, although it emerged prior to queer theory. In spite of their differences of methodology and approach, in each thinker, the transvestite—as idea, as stage performer, as cultural "role," or as repertoire—is the chosen object for critical view. In virtually all extant work on the literary and cinematic representation of *travestis,* these critics function as the inescapable points of reference. And yet, on a number of counts, such a free application of theory is problematic. First, in relying on work that is largely abstract and devoid of deeper considerations as to the cultural locations of and range of perceptions around *travestis,* at best, critics risk providing generalizing readings; at worst, by uncritically employing the rhetorical turns of structuralist approaches and postmodern queer theory, they verge on celebrating and naturalizing the allegorization of such subjects in literary and cinematic texts, authorizing, via particular academic discourses, the instrumentalist view of the trans figures in texts and culture, wherein sex and gender crossing and change never obtain any status beyond the performative and symbolic. Second, the privileging of the work of, in this instance, Garber and (early) Butler becomes problematic when critics draw on these thinkers to account for representations of *travestis* in Latin American texts but do not account for the important fact that their theories evolved elsewhere and respond to debates and logics that are of U.S. origin. The inclusion of Sarduy's work on transvestites in this contemporary scholarship may, on occasion, function as a de facto attempt to connect Latin American representations to Latin American critical work on the figure of the *travesti* and yet only to the extent that Sarduy's work combines with elements from queer's deconstructive use of "transgender." Those who analyze contemporary cultural representation of *locas, travestis,* and *transexuales* rarely seek out work on sexual and gender subjectivities in a Latin American context; they also do not move outside the terms of *travestismo* as a performative identity vector that inevitably speaks to and embodies other concerns.

Theory's blind spot around its own enmeshment in the dominant ways of thinking about *travestismo* or sex and gender variance is what I address in this section, using the work of several scholars whose objects of analysis, as in the inquiry of Garber and Butler, are also trans people, but who themselves are trans. If queer theory has made "transgender" a key point of its theoretical deliberations, it has also patently brought about an explosion in talk—especially, but not only, in academic sites—around transvestites, transgendered, and transsexual people. And yet much of this talk has been restricted by the privileging of theories about nonnormative gender identities that do little to challenge some of the underpinnings of the trans person as performer or metaphorical figure. I highlight these things in order to situate how and why I opt for a different approach and remains suspicious of the reifying tendencies of queer-inspired contemporary criticism.

The theories of the gay Cuban writer exiled in Paris, Severo Sarduy, elaborated in two of his crucial works, *Escrito sobre un cuerpo* ( 1969; *Written on a Body)* and *La simulación* (1983; *The Simulation),* have been formative in cultural and critical conceptualizations of *travestis* and *transexuales* in Latin America. Writing under the obvious influence of the French poststructuralism of Lacan and Barthes, notions of excess and artificiality are also extended in Sarduy's work on *travestis,* as well as the terms of theatricality, the baroque, and carnivalesque performance. The language of appropriation and incorporation, self and other, so central to Lacan's notions of identity formation, orient Sarduy's visions. Further, in his fictional work that depicts *travestis,* the relation to the national subject is recast; Sarduy draws on the Lacanian analysis of *travestismo* and offers implications for identity formation and its mechanisms, especially in relation to (Cuban) collective and cultural identity.

For Sarduy, *travestismo* is about the appropriation of gesture, clothing, and its extension beyond established limits. It refers to simulation and the covering up of a lack. *Travestismo* is a movement, a chain of infinitely deployed signifiers that have no fixed signified. The *travesti*[11] does not emulate women but, rather, looks at the artifactual construction of Woman and femininity and reproduces it.[12] *Travestismo* concerns a play of surfaces, a successive presentation of masks. The lack or defect to which Sarduy refers concerns castration anxiety and this drives the *travesti* to cross-dress. *Travestismo* becomes for the cross-dresser a way of gesturally identifying with the female, without actually becoming a female "himself." As "he" cross-dresses, he keeps his penis, which reminds him he is still a man. This accentuates the feeling of masculinity and compensates for the sense of psychic loss effected by the fantasy of castration. Sarduy does not hesitate to inscribe this transvestite construction of femininity as thoroughly phallic.[13]

Sarduy never visualizes the possibility of a *travesti* subject—the *travesti* is always essentially male: a male caught in the mirror phase and seduced by symbolic identification with the (m)other. He hence desires to incorporate her, for in Oedipal terms, she has stolen the phallus. *Travestismo* is a way of covering over that loss. Further, *travestismo* is clearly conceived by Sarduy as chiefly a visual effect, a copy of a copy. In these terms it constitutes the reflection in a mirror that dissolves the distinction between self and other, and is the product of a fantasy of identification, incorporation, fusing, and appropriation. This language is often central to the way many critics conceive of the function of *travestis* in literary and visual texts (see especially Richard 2003).

[...]

The deployment of *travestismo* as an organizational grid that is a perfect metaphor from national and regional identity construction in Latin America—in a movement that reconstructs *mestizaje* as *travestizaje*—obtains theoretical authorization when critics cite Garber's and Butler's notions of "transgender" as a matrix of (gender, class, and race) identity construction. The parodic postcard produced by the Chilean-Australian artist, Juan Dávila, *El libertador* (1994; *The Liberator),* is frequently invoked to forward the vision of *travestismo* as conceptually in line with national and cultural identity formation. Dávila's postcard shows a Simón Bolívar atop horse sexually transformed—with both breasts and vagina—cross-dressed and cross-gendered, with putatively Indian features. Richard (1998) reminds us that Dávila's queering of this sacred figure of *latinidad,* so central to nation formation, makes conscious the elements of the subaltern that, while not always celebrated, forge the hybrid synthesis of Latin American culture in the postindependence and modern periods. Arroyo's account of travestismo cultural, meanwhile, also describes cross-gendering as reflective of the combination of subaltern elements—raced and gendered—to produce a whole identity. While Arroyo (2003b) stresses that all subjects do this, she singles out *travestismo* to represent this process of national identification, positing a form of *travestizaje,* literalizing what Dávila's postcard evokes. This is a movement she detects in Cuban and Brazilian discourses of nation; Arroyo does not go far enough, however, to deconstruct the deep logic that fuses *travestismo* with national identity construction or with the image of the mask and play of signifiers. The lacuna in such theorizing is evident in that critics are unable to see past *travestismo* as performative vector or symbol and symptom of national and regional identity; this is not helped by the methodological issue of what forms of knowledge about *travestis they* use. [...]

## AGAINST ALLEGORIES, AGAINST QUEER PARADIGMS

*Crossing sex and gender in Latin America*'s argument distances itself from the theoretical and epistemological assumption that *travestis* or transsexuals are connected to the constitution of national-cultural identity by virtue of inherently common and parallel features in both. It subscribes, instead, to Namaste's view of the metaphorization of transgendered and transsexual people. Applying her theorizations, we can see that two terms are placed together: *locas* and *travestis* or transsexuals in the subsidiary position, and cultural identity and nation in the first. Following Namaste, a metaphor does not contain two subjects that are inherently alike; the two terms are made analogous by their being placed together and their meanings derived from the connotative field, which are often based on other representations and influenced by patriarchal masculinist national discourse, a discourse that has also been pervasive in Latin America as we have seen. The cultural meanings or associated commonplaces, as Max Black calls them, are derived from the kinds of representations that circulate in discourse; they are then extended to order our perception of the principal subject. Common attributions made to *locas, travestis,* and transsexuals include the characteristics of doubleness, charade, bodily and sexual excess or grotesquerie, artificiality, simulation, and appropriation, as discussed in this chapter. Such associative commonplaces, although clearly recurrent in culture, are vigorously contested in this study. Likewise, theory that reproduces them, parsing such attributions with the language and rhetorical turns of Sarduy and queer theory—most dramatically shown in the work of Richard (1993)—is deeply embedded in the logics that this study purposely seeks to disarm. Richard, in advancing her "retoque" (retouching) theory of *travestis* as imitative figures that are symbolic of Latin American identity construction, articulates them into the realm of ritualized falsification, hyperbole, narcissism, illusion, the grotesque, criminality, concealment, and flight. The transformation of *locas, travestis,* and transsexuals into metaphors locks them into a circuit of meaning that hyperbolizes and undermines the possibility of imagining their lives and situatedness at the everyday level in ways that do not draw on the most abject and objectifying forms of knowledge. [...]

## SUBJECTIVITY AND THE POSSIBILITIES OF ITS TEXTUAL INSCRIPTION

How can texts inscribe or make visible gender-variant homosexual and trans subjectivities? How can texts make visible any subjectivity? The two questions are surely linked, and as such, the theoretical arc of this study extends not just to the representation of *locas, travestis,* or transsexuals but also to the representation of any subjectivity in the process of political emergence.

Several contemporary ethnographical studies investigate the self-concepts and identifications of "effeminate" male homosexuals known in different places as *bichas, viados, jotas, cochones* and *colas,* and cross-living *travestis* known also as *vestidas* in other places (Parker 1999; Lancaster 1992; 1998, Prieur 1998; Donoso 1990). These subjects commonly form a subset of the wider homosexual community. Dominant middle-class gays, in contrast, tend to be the more gender normative and structure their relations with one another based more on the so-called egalitarian model. They also do not differentiate these relations in terms of positionality and the related gender role styles to which *travestis* subscribe (Lancaster 1992, 1998; Lumsden 1991; Murray 1995). Much research suggests that in many parts of Latin America, these models of homosexuality exist side by side—the gender differentiated and the non-gender differentiated. The first is more aligned with the popular classes and based on the active-passive distinction (Lumsden 1991; Murray 1995; Carrier 1995).[19] In the active-passive paradigm—called pejoratively by some commentators the "antiquated model" of homoerotic relations—only the passive partner, whose) gender style tends to the feminine, is understood as homosexual. The penetrating, active partner slips by the public radar that assigns gender atypicality thanks to his performance of establishment-aligned masculinity and is hence rarely labeled as homosexual. The *loca* or *travesti* who relates to this paradigm also understands her lover as nonhomosexual (Lumsden 1991; Carrier 1995; Murray 1995; Núñez Noriega 1999).

The psychic dimensions to subjectivity are also interwoven with the social, whose interface is the body. The body becomes a site through which subjectivity is constructed and difference is articulated. Annick Prieur in her study of Mexican *jotas* and *vestidas* argues that her subjects see their corporeality as a personal achievement that imbues them with sensuality and distinctiveness, a vehicle for visibility and definition, and whose gender signs are malleable. Of course, when we speak of the body, we should speak of bodies. Bodies signify, morph, and interact: they are the point of intersubjective relations, the grid work of the experience of being not just a subject among subjects but also the experience of being subjected. Many studies show the great efforts to which *travestis* resort in order to embody their *travestismo*: feminizing body modifications using industrial silicone or oil and incurring some danger in the process, pumping their breasts and hips, and ingesting female hormones scored off the streets. In some places, this feminizing process is understood by subjects as intricately tied up with their sense of sexuality and their desire to signal their availability to men. In other places, it is linked more to their vision of more closely inhabiting the feminine gender with which the subjects have always identified (Kulick 1998, Prieur 1998, Fernández 2004). In Prieur's and Josefina Fernández's studies, respondents claim to have always been *locas* or *travestis* and that only in later years were they able to fully become that vision of themselves. The work of Chilean psychologist, Claudia Espinoza Carraminana (1999), draws a similar trajectory of *travesti* embodiment and calls the process "forjarse mariposa," that is, one's emergence from one form into another, more wondrous creation.

Although studies that center specifically on transsexual lives in Latin America are so scant as to be virtually nonexistent, *Identidad, cultura ysociedad. Un grito desde el silencio (Identity, Culture and Society: A Scream out of Silence)* by Peruvian lawyer and social scientist, Fiorella Cava (2004), provides some insights into Latin American transsexuals. Although *travestis* are different from transsexuals to the extent that many disavow a desire to have sex reassignment surgery (SRS), or even to claim the subjectivity of the "other sex"; both groups, however, experience overlapping forms of oppression. Cava notes the difficulties involved in coming out and then openly transitioning as a transsexual—experiences that cut close to the bone, as the author herself is transsexual. She talks of the trauma that erupts in families, in work, and in social networks, made especially challenging for Latin American transsexuals, in contrast to their Anglo-American counterparts, because of the enduring force of machismo in contemporary Latin culture, according to Cava (67).

Aside from psychic and cultural forces, one's residence in and habitual coursing through certain physical spaces also informs the shaping of subjectivity. All studies on *travestis* in contemporary times point to their commonplace involvement in prostitution, particularly street prostitution. *Travesti* culture is informed to a large degree by the type of work undertaken by its members that is socially stigmatized and open to a variety of risks—running the gamut from abusive clients to corrupt law enforcement officers and their, at times, arbitrary and discriminatory targeting of *travesti* sex workers through fines, incarceration, and sexual abuse. Prostitution, however, also serves as a means of restitution to forge new links, and new families, and to survive where no other work is available. This arises because, due to their visible difference, effeminate homosexuals and *travestis* in many places are expelled from family, school, and neighborhood environments and face grave difficulties in finding conventional forms of employment (Fernández 2004).

Connected to these material realities, the axes of class and ethnicity inform the shape subjectivity takes. Prieur's study shows clear links to her *jotas'* and *vestidas'* gendered stylings of the body and their class (1998, 150). With any subjectivity, attention to what feminists frequently call "intersectionality" is important: How do the various axes of class, race, sexuality, and gender combine and reexpress each other? If one category is simplistically used in a text to symbolize another—by virtue of substitution—what is lost from the picture? These are pivotal to the tension between *lo trans* as explored, complex phenomena and *lo trans* as a rhetorical category or vector that points to other fields in their assumed entirety and hermetic distinction—such as "race," "nation," and "global and postmodern identity."

Subjectivity constantly reconstitutes itself, and this depends to a large extent on another concept, that is, the intersubjective. This concerns the subject's insertion and elaboration alongside and within relation to others in the lifeworld. Subjectivity is facilitated through language via the constant transpositions of the body in the linguistic order. This involves the redrafting and articulating of possible narrative and speaking points by which people make sense of their surroundings and situationality. To realize oneself is to find oneself as part of a community with a common set of experiences and worldviews—or cast out, but that in itself shapes one. *Locas* and *travestis* often also find themselves sidelined in gay culture, as their *actitud escandalosa* (scandalous attitude) is said to be a source of ill repute. Forced out of one community, they form another. This is often the *ambiente,* or the space, of street prostitution: so-called marginal spaces in which one is (out)cast, as we have seen. The distinctive forms of sociolect in subcultures constitute one manifestation of subjectivity. Here one would point to the argot of a group, and specifically with respect to the way its members talk about themselves and are talked about. Such forms of speech are particularly enunciative in the case and cause of a (trans) gendered subjectivity in Spanish, with the use of gendered adjectives and pronouns. The work of Guillermo Núñez Noriega (1997) on homosexual and *travesti* subcultures in Hermosillo, Mexico, and their use of *joteadas,* or camp slang, as well as a study by César O. González Pérez *on jotas and gays travestidos* (2002) in Colima, Mexico, on a similar form of linguistic play called *perreos* provide examples of this. In this way, language might be said to constitute us; however, we also reconstitute language.

Studies by Cuban psychologists Janet Mesa Peña and Diley Hernández Cruz from the *Centra de Investigatión y Desarrollo de la Cultura Cubana* (Center for the Research and Development of Cuban Culture) on *transformistas, travestis,* and *transexuales* in Havana (2004), Sheilla Rodriguez-Madera and José Toro-Alfonso and their pioneering work on transgender people and HIV/AIDS in Puerto Rico (2005), and Mexican Rosio Córdova Plaza on the criminalization of *travesti* sex workers in Xalapa, Veracruz (2007), sketch in considerable detail the social, cultural, and institutional factors that order the lived experiences of real-world *travestis* and transsexuals in their various locales. Such locales are pertinent to this study.

Josefina Fernández, as I have mentioned elsewhere (Lewis 2006), does not only view *lo travesti* as a personal and subjective identity but as a political identity as well, referring to its uneasy articulation in the context of discourses of deviance, control, surveillance, and juridical interpellation. Fernández understands *travestis* in their personal and sociopolitical facets, not simply as an illustration of any single theory. In one part of her study she profiles their struggle to obtain a space in the wider lesbian, gay, bisexual, and transgender (LGBT) movement in Argentina and argues for a recognition of sexual rights by the state. Although Fernández focuses on *travesti* populations in Buenos Aires, her findings extend beyond the borders of Argentina, as gender variant and trans people in Chile, Mexico, and the Caribbean have begun to organize against social and economic exclusion and have thus initiated the politicization of subjectivity. In doing so, they have been importantly involved in the generation of new knowledge frameworks about sex and gender variance and diversity.

Subjectivity does not imply a unified self nor a self that is knowable to itself. Rather, this self is radically decentered, multiple, and dispersed. It emerges through dialogue with others, as well as through participation in visual economies of identification that are embedded in economic relations, such as in music videos, advertising, fashion, style, and other increasingly global semiotic networks that offer promises of newness, becoming, and belonging. Several studies of *travestis* pinpoint the sources of inspiration for their public personae—especially during hours of labor in prostitution—in popular cultural images *of vedettes,* for example (Prieur 1998, Fernández 2004). Subjectivity emerges in varied locations: in the context of the family, labor settings, religious institutions, law courts, recreational and leisure spaces, schools, doctors' offices, and so forth. These are also key domains for *locas, travestis,* and transsexuals as they negotiate the imperiled terrain of public visibility and intersubjective becoming as sexually and gender-diverse peoples.

All of these factors are important in evaluating to what extent a text visualizes the subjectivity of *loca, travesti,* or transsexual characters. If as readers we can state that a text has captured a sense of subjectivity, we need to be able to point to the kind of features of subjectivity mentioned above: its embodied nature, its emergence in and through the sociolinguistic order, and the self's historicity and multiple locations.

## SOME FINAL REMARKS

> No somos viciosas ni enfermas
> No pretendemos engañar a nadie con nuestro aspecto
> No estamos locas por el sexo.

> [We aren't diseased or sick
> We don't mean to trick anyone with our appearance
> We're not just crazy about sex.]

> —Traveschile (a peak Chilean *travesti* group)

In emphasizing the forces that have influenced the formation of the subjectivities and of the real-world subjects known as *locas, travestis,* and *transexuales* in Latin America, this study does not make any facile attempt, of course, to demand that textual representations be seen as mirrors of some outside reality or that literary or cinema critics, indeed, become sociologists. Instead, it serves to remind critical and cultural scholars to extend their views of the possibilities of *loca, travesti,* and transsexual figures in contemporary texts beyond performative or allegorizing paradigms that cannot account for subjectivity and its articulation and that themselves do not break away from the dominant episteme that locates *locas, travestis,* and transsexuals in certain paradigmatic ways. A view that gives countenance to sex- and gender-variant subjects in culture allows the critic to reposition depictions in relation to what is known and knowable among competing knowledges about these subjects in different locations and times, their degrees of social integration, and forms of identification and self-concepts, aspects completely lacking, as we have seen, in queerinspired accounts in much of the work previously discussed. This is particularly fruitful for the reading of texts in which *lorn, travesti,* or transsexual characters move beyond mere stereotype and where a sustained interest in representing these figures as social types is in evidence.[20] Several of the texts that this book examines pursue this line, and thus purely figural understandings of *loca, travesti,* and transsexual lives, embodiments, and emplacements are considered inadequate.

When we speak of "representations," the significance of the term in the study of literature, film, and sexual, ethnic, and other minorities cannot be underestimated. It implies a certain set of priorities, understandings about texts, and readerly orientations: what is it that texts do and make possible for reader interpretation and how might they be seen to speak about people's lives or identities, about stereotypes and cultural context? Committed poststructuralists, following thinkers such as Jacques Derrida and Paul De Man, might assert that no representation can ultimately escape metaphorization, for the very arbitrariness of the processes of signification may lend any representation to allegory. Indeed, the writer Pedro Lemebel, whose work is considered in the closing chapter of this book, reflects on such a problematic. Keeping in mind that representations are never transparent or direct but rather frequently opaque and polysemic, it is taken as axiomatic here that it is better to speak of representational effects accrued in given contexts. Just as in language where a lexical item does not simply have one meaning, and meanings are themselves constructed by the reader, rhetorical operations depend on certain feature s of recognition and connotative association to obtain their effects. This need not set the critic adrift for any lack of a speaking position or valid argument, however. Rather, the predominance of certain constructions of meaning and culturally embedded knowledge formulations in incessant circulation demands an intervention at this level, at the level of the signification, which in turn presents us with a politics of representation. The work of Reinaldo Arenas, as well as the novel by Mario Bellatin, provide good examples of this point. They may not pursue realism in any documentary or faux-objective style, which is the claim of the writer Pedro Juan Gutiérrez in regard to his novel *El Rey de la Habana,* but their depictions of gender-variant and trans acts and people still remit to our knowledge of real-life subjects, situations, and ways of talking about such subjects. They may themselves problematize the connection between literary practices of signification and our knowledge of the real world *or* real subjects—Bellatin's text certainly does this and Arenas's work plays with textual reversals and ironies, that is, the essence of the carnivalesque. Other texts—for example, the film *Las noches de Constantinopla*—work in the comedic vein. In one way or another, however, all these texts still deal with forms of knowledge, worldviews, discourses, and cultural meanings that form their place of production, dissemination, and reception, as well as certain aesthetic traditions in representation.

Literary and filmic texts may not be imitative of some perceived reality, but neither do they exist in isolation. The representation of *lo trans* and gender-variant homosexuality in films and literature cannot be excised from the intertextuality exhibited with other narratives, both literary and nonliterary, visual or verbal, in the culture from which the texts derive—including those outlined in the section on discursive formations about *locus, travestis,* and transsexuals. In their very narrative structure, one may perceive ways of talking that define, construct and produce objects of knowledge (Barker 2000, 390). Representations are thus never free of political import. Not only do they respond to certain knowledges, then, but they also shape them.

Although far from universally true, contemporary Latin American film and literary forms often engage gender-variant or trans acts and subjects figuratively; they may serve a particular structural function in thematic or metaphorical design. However, following Namaste, the mechanisms of the placing together of two terms in metaphor need to be addressed. Added to this, the terms that equate gender atypicality to problems at the level of nation need to be denaturalized and discursively highlighted in terms of their genealogy. The marrying of *travestismo* to *mestizaje—travestizaje—* needs interrogation. This is something that most critics do not undertake currently, as we have also seen. Figurations belong to the realm of rhetoric, which often employs metaphor or tropes; rhetoric as a field relates to the ability of a particular mode of speaking or representation to persuade and influence, but as studies have shown, rhetoric also structures discourse and ultimately the way we think about certain phenomena (Lakoff and Johnson 1980; Morgan 1986; Valverde 1991). Figures of speech, then, become figures of thought.

Critical and cultural codings that posit *locas, travestis,* and transsexuals as enigmatic sphinxes, contradictory ruses, exotic spectacles, deceptive miscreants, that which is beyond what constitutes personhood or livability, and specters of colonial alterity, anarchy, and "end times" need to be exposed as constructions and not naturalized as a priori characteristics of the subjects so described. Clearly, then, for queer theorists, the challenge lies in accounting for trans subjectivities in texts beyond the merely Performative and to locate representations in their social, cultural, and institutional sites of production and reception. For postcolonial critics, the task might be to differentiate between the notion that subjectivities of all kinds are in part molded by overarching (colonial) conditions and the idea that they are simply symbolic of these conditions. The contribution to transgender studies is also valuable, providing a view of trans subjectivities in Latin America that do not always conform to Anglo-American separations between one's sexuality and one's sense of gender, as in the case of *locas* and *travestis.* The readings given here of a selection of literary and filmic texts provide the opportunity for queer, postcolonial, and transgender theorists to reconceptualize some of the common ideas around subjects who live outside normative sex and gender relations and how they are represented in cultural production.

# VIII

## GOING SOMEWHERE

### Transgender Movement(s)

# 36

# *Transgender Without Organs?*
## Mobilizing a Geo-affective Theory of Gender Modification

LUCAS CASSIDY CRAWFORD

IN "TRANSGENDER WITHOUT ORGANS" LUCAS CASSIDY CRAWFORD takes up an increasingly familiar question within transgender theory: why do narratives of gender transition so often rely on a metaphor of geographical migration? He begins by noting how often journey-narratives within transgender cultural texts are stories of migration to big cities from rural or non-metropolitan locations. While acknowledging that such places may lack large trans communities, or have fewer health-care resources for medically-assisted gender transitions, Crawford nevertheless asks, "How might we trouble our certainty that small towns need to be escaped?" He combines this critique of transgender metronormativity with a Deleuzian theorization of deterritorialization, illustrated by anecdotes drawn from his own life growing up in rural and small-town environments. Through its rhetorical structure as well as its content, the essay displaces familiar transgender narratives of moving in a "straight line" away from a "wrong body" trapped in a nonmetropolitan location toward a right (gender-transitioned) body available in the city. Crawford concludes by asking how we might reimagine transgender lives lived in actual small town. He refuses the metronormative logic of "outness" and passing—which dictates that a trans person should both be visible and "out" within a community of identity, but simultaneously be able to escape the weight of one's history always being known by disappearing into the urban crowd—and offers instead the counterexample of "imperceptibility." Imperceptibility, as Crawford reads it via Deleuze and Guattari, indexes a state of being different "like everyone else," and hence unremarkable and unnoticed, that is better suited to small town life—and which may well offer a different mode of living the contradictions of transgender visibility that is equally viable in other locations.

1977, Halifax, Nova Scotia. My parents will work in their hometown, Halifax, until they save enough money to move to the country: not the neopastoral country of idyllic retirement, leisure, or quaintness, but rather a place of quietude, crops, and the moral high ground that (at least reportedly) makes the country such a good place to raise kids. But just now, my mother works in the emergency room of the Halifax Infirmary, has recently married my father, and remembers having had a crush on Billy Conway in high school. Billy comes by Outpatients almost biweekly, and receives a day of psychiatric treatment when he asks the sympathetic but distant doctor for a sex change. One day, Billy arrives with his severed penis wrapped in a Kleenex, is made to dwell slightly longer in the psych ward before once again being released; he then promptly hangs himself in his boarding room in the city's North End. Soon after, when Billy's former doctor plans to marry an ex-nun (dyke?) he knows, a man who claims to be the doctor's lover arrives in the emergency room after his own suicide attempt. The doctor comes out as gay, but dies a year later of a then unfathomable virus. The infirmary closed in 1998 and was demolished in 2005, after Ron Russell, the minister of transportation and public works, condemned the building as "unsafe and unusable."

When the ruggedly boyish character Moira debuted in season three of Showtime's (in)famous program *The L Word,* many of us working-class, rural, or butch dykes finally undid the collective knot in our boxers. Moira's impromptu move from Skokie to Los Angeles coincided with hir transsexual awakening, however, and s/he transitions to become "Max" in subsequent episodes. Relocating from Illinois to California puts Moira not only literally but also figuratively in different states: of mind, of identity, and of desire. The queer pilgrimage to the city is a far from innovative motif, and even in theories that are attuned to the role of place in queer life, the role of the rural is presumed to be inconsequential. For instance, Jay Prosser (1998) claims that narratives of pre- and post-operative transsexuality belie their authors' nostalgia for bodily homes that never existed, a style of feeling that not only shores up the power we attribute to hominess but also traces on our bodies a one-way journey home. As this model configures gender modification as a safe return rather than a risky exploit or experiment in embodied selfhood, Prosser finds relief in the "transgender ambivalence" (177) he finds in the narratives of non-operative gender-variant writers. Their ambivalence towards place, he argues, reflects and generates their nonteleological orientation to practices of gender modification. For both varieties of trans life, styles of affect are constitutive technologies of embodiment; how one is moved emotionally informs and illustrates the mobility of one's gender and one's home.

Even in the transgender texts Prosser analyzes, however, the reader encounters linear and one-way trips from the country to the city—supplemented, at best, with a short trip or two back to the protagonist's hometown. As an (albeit far more interesting) forerunner to *The L Word's* Max, Leslie Feinberg's character Jess in *Stone Butch Blues* moves from "the desert" (15) to Buffalo and eventually to New York City, while the protagonist of her other novel, *Drag King Dreams,* lives out her days in this same urban center. The many representations of Brandon Teena's life (especially in *Boys Don't Cry*) work in tandem with such representations of urban queer freedom, attributing Brandon's murder to regressive, purportedly rural, attitudes that are seldom imagined as characteristics of urban communities.

Philosophical and political accounts of queerness all too often corroborate these valorizations of the urban; Kath Weston describes and decries the "Great Gay Migration" to the city (1995, 253), while Douglas Victor Janoff suggests in *Pink Blood: Homophobic Violence in Canada* that "smaller communities...would benefit from [the] strategy of reaching out to isolated citizens and connecting them with support and services in larger centres" (2005, 243). The link between the city and the queer seems ineluctable in both instances; in the former, smart queers will eventually come to the city, while in the latter, the city eventually comes to all queers. As a small-town trans person whose life is becoming urban and mobile (in various senses), this link certainly feels experientially true for me, as my cities get bigger and my old dot on the map looks smaller.

Given the filmic and literary examples cited above, an attraction to the urban undoubtedly rings true for many other transgender or transsexual people who crave the emotional and medical resources seemingly unavailable in rural spaces. In this ubiquitous city of queer imaginings, such people might join a movement like Queer Nation; change their gender "citizenship," as Susan Stryker recently described transition at a lecture at the University of Alberta; and read Janice G. Raymond's renowned polemic *The Transsexual Empire* or Sandy Stone's famous reply, "The Empire Strikes Back: A Posttranssexual Manifesto." Curiously, the experience of gender modification seemingly demands metaphors of sovereign territoriality as well as literal movement from place to place by those who practice it. This coincidence of various kinds of mobility with various kinds of space motivates some preliminary questions: How do geographical or nationist metaphors of transgender community—empire, citizenship, nation, home—both reflect and reify the apparent need for a transgender person's geographical (urban) relocation? Might something more nuanced than access to medical resources, anonymity, and communities based on identity politics or rooted in urban subcultural practices lie behind the geographical relocation of transgender people? If we can imagine that trans people may remain (or wish to remain) in the country by choice and not by accident or unfortunate circumstances, we could see instead that holding our ground says something about our styles of affect: that each bodily transition (from gender to gender or place to place) may be a matter of spatial ethics as much as sexual ones, of orientation to place as much as to the body, of being moved in certain ways as much as moving.

This essay is animated, then, by the question of how our styles of affect and movement may become "trans" in ways that cast doubt upon our current valorization of cities in representations of queer space. How might we trouble our certainty that small towns need to be escaped, that less populous cities can never quite do the trick or ever offer us enough tricks, that migrating to big cities is an uproblematically happy experience untainted by culture shock, or that one's desire to be there is unsullied by contributory conditions such as class or economic need? My motivation for raising such questions is neither to archive nor to justify existent modes of living gender rurally, but rather to point toward new creative potentials. Drawing on Deleuze and Guattari, my aim is to unsettle—their word, significantly, is "deterritorialize" (1987, 156) – the model of the transgender or transsexual subject, if only because this increasingly coherent model of the subject entails practices that demand medical, subcultural, and financial resources often unavailable to (or undesired by) some rural gender-fuckers—and probably many urban ones as well.¹ Prying open the terms "transgender" and "transsexual" in a way that might allow more people to belong to them or to desire them is an important project; however, the vignettes and theoretical interventions that constitute this essay also revel in the deterritorializing potential of *not* being recognized, not being counted, of being ignored by urban trans theories and cultures, and of finding or crafting ceaseless mobility in seemingly static and conservative locales in ways that may never move trans-urbanites.

## HOW TRANS MOVES US

1996, Kingston, Nova Scotia (population twenty-five hundred). Women in this village wear ties daily-they work at the military base. After I am issued my air cadet uniform, I even wear my tie to school sometimes. I excel at being an air cadet, perhaps because the first year of training could be called "How to Be a (Versatile) Butch Bottom" and summarized thus: 1. No long hair. 2. No insubordination within our playful little roles. 3. No makeup. 4. No fancy jewelry. 5. No problem! Air cadet camp is the sleepaway summer program for twelve-year-old proto-butch kids itching for queer kitsch, for boot-campy kids who wax nostalgic for the drag days of summer drill team when August oranges into rural-school September, and for everyone else who wants to black boots and train their bodies for years to earn the privilege of being called Sir or (like me) Ma'am. In ostensibly impersonal militaristic interactions, more than a few queer kids (who always seem to take the top ranks) thrive on feeling very much in the right body and never quite at home with it in the barracks, parade square, or semiformal dances. We, like the other cadets, cry, but with more grit than melancholy, perhaps because we want a witness to our imperceptible gender-fucking. Perhaps we simply miss our small hometowns. But is "homesickness "just a pessimist's way of describing restlessness, a fever for frequent redeployment? Perhaps we cry because we know the secret of it all. But more often than not, queer cadets can't stop laughing.

In what are probably the three most recognizable transgender narratives in contemporary culture—*Boys Don't Cry, The Crying Game,* and *Stone Butch Blues*—even the titles signal the affect of sadness: characters move from place to place and gender to gender as readers and viewers are moved to tears by these transitions. The concurrence of these different kinds of "being moved" is not simply coincidental; Prosser notes that the "metaphoric territorializing of gender and literal territorializations of physical space have often gone hand in hand" in transgender narrative (1998, 171), an unsurprising collapse, perhaps, given that the singular site of the body is the affective space where both cycles of reification are produced and played out. [...]

While Prosser's work exemplifies the applicability of affect studies to trans life, it also demonstrates the liability of treating affect as an explanation for actions and identities. As he makes clear in *Second Skins: The Body Narratives of Transsexuality* (1998), the feelings associated with inhabiting the "wrong body" are the ones that have, in the manner Cvetkovich describes, formed the most accessible public narrative of transsexuality. Prosser vindicates the transsexual's desire to change sex by way of analyzing and trusting the ways in which the body feels and responds to certain procedures of gender modification, or, conversely, by the lack of such responses. Responding to the widely held assumption that transsexuals are pathological at worst, or falsely conscious Cartesian dupes at best, Prosser states his contention "that transsexuals continue to deploy the image of wrong embodiment because being trapped in the wrong body is simply what transsexuality feels like" (69). In this account, affect is not an expression of transsexuality but is, rather, the definitive condition of it. Prosser arrives at this formulation of affect via his interest in psychoanalyst Dider Anzieu's *The Skin Ego,* which holds that one's ego is a mental projection of what one feels (as the title suggests) through one's skin. Against those who believe that transsexuals are the worst kind of body/mind dualists, Prosser argues that a self who feels accommodated by the wrong body is already corporeal through and through: "Body image... clearly already has a material force for transsexuals" (69), insofar as the ego "is ultimately derived from bodily sensations" (65).

This is a challenging formulation of affect insofar as it implies that feelings are generative rather than reflective, productive rather than derivative, and innovative rather than symptomatic of something less corporeal or more pathological. It is surprising, then, that Prosser thinks that affects "simply" (69) occur or are simply translated into the narratives and conventional procedures of gender modification. Aside from the point that living in the wrong body is certainly not "what transsexuality feels like" (69) *for everyone,* it is worth noting that no bodily sensation carries its own self-evident meaning or orders for action prior to our reformulating these affects into narratives. While the present essay is premised on Prosser's insistence that transsexuality is a matter of affect at least as much as it is a matter of certain procedures of gender transition, Prosser's defense of the wrong-body narrative runs the risk not only of settling on just one definition of the "right" trans affect, but also of figuring affect as an extremely personal phenomenon that has very little to do with others, or with places outside of one's (embodied) home.

The role of Prosser's Freudianism, which trusts that one's psyche will speak through words or through one's signifying body, is obvious in his assumption that a wrong-body narrative is simply a verbal translation of a particular affect. Prosser comes dangerously close to suggesting that wrong-body narratives emanate from our skin without the effects of other people or places, or external ideas about gender. If Freud's taken-for-granted equation of signification and affect allows the latter term to figure unproblematically in our analyses of desire, then it is entirely appropriate to turn to Deleuze and Guattari, whose complex oeuvre aims in part to formulate a specifically anti-Freudian theory of affect, to begin refiguring the relationship between affect and signification. As Freud and Prosser would have it, the formation of the self occurs when one creates a mental projection of the sensations one feels. Affects, for Deleuze and Guattari, operate in precisely the opposite way: they *undo* the subject "like weapons" (1987, 400): they "open a way out" (258) and mount a "counterattack" (400) to even our best attempts to settle on identities and desires. These dangerous bodily occurrences—"arrows," "weapons," and "projectiles" (400), as they are described—are not simply the raw or pre-verbal form of the emotions we know as love, envy, anger, or even the bodily uncanniness that inspires wrong-body narratives. Rather, for Deleuze and Guattari, these narratives of feelings are attempts to harness (and transform) the destructive quality of affect. As they write, "Affect is the active discharge of emotion, the counterattack, whereas feeling is an always displaced, retarded, resisting emotion" (400). As Bonta and Protevi note in *Deleuze and Geophilosophy*, affect is "the capacity to become" (2004, 50), whereas feeling is the reterritorialization of becoming, by means of coding and ultimately controlling it.

Deleuze and Guattari insist vehemently on "an affectability that is no longer that of subjects," but has instead to do with crafting an "assemblage," and with relationships of "symbiosis" (1987, 258). In other words, if affects are generated by proximity, movement, and symbiosis with or between other organisms and environments—a style of relationality that threatens the borders of bodies and identities—why then are they recouped, tamed, and privatized in the name of the subject? This "displaced" and "retarded" (400) harnessing of affect into feelings in fact constitutes "subjectivization," the process through which affect is controlled in order to hold the subject together. For Deleuze and Guattari, affect is the body's capacity to *undermine* our best attempts at deciding on identities and selves. If, in this account, what we call feelings are quite far from bodily sensation, and are actually attempts to maintain the coherence of the subject, then perhaps Prosser is right to say that "being trapped in the wrong body is simply what transsexuality *feels* like" (1998, 69, emphasis mine). When Prosser claims that transsexual transition is a "coming home to the self through body" (83), he describes a spatial trajectory that is the opposite of Bonta and Protevi's gloss on deterritorialization: "the process of leaving home, of altering your habits, of learning new tricks" (2004, 78), a series of exploits that sound much more like camp.

## SMOOTH BODIES

January 2007, Edmonton, Alberta. In a Jasper Avenue bar connected to a Catholic church, I try to convince a pretty (and) brilliant architect that cities built on grids probably help us become straight, insofar as how we move must affect how we are moved, and that the comfortable feeling of knowing where our bodies are at all times might not in fact be a very queer feeling. His soused-up lecture on what was so radical, in the first instance, about the nonmimetic clean straight lines of modern architecture will earn him footnotes later. For now, leaning back on the men's room toilet for a pause, I see his shoes, hear his gentleman's cough at the urinal. I think about him, and his girlfriend, who has reminded me of the excitement of a reciprocated crush.

I will write about this crooked washroom moment and read it at our first drag king show at our one dank and lovely dyke bar—"the last of its kind in Canada," the owner never fails to mention. There have been other shows in years past but nobody seems to know quite when, who, or what they were. "Smooth space does not have a long-term memory with all that that entails, so only microhistories are possible" (Bonta and Protevi 2004, 145).

"You might be able to fill the [thirty] seats," a friend says before the show, but the owner has to lock the door for the first time ever, when this remote back alley bar is almost triple its legal capacity, filled with enthralling people dressed for the occasion of the first drag king show they've ever seen. At intermission I bump into the architect and his girlfriend. "Yep, this is Edmonton, all right," I think: nobody is avoidable and I almost always love this way in which rural accountability permeates our semi-urban space.

A year later, I avoid the temptation to tell the architect that Sarah Ahmed (2006) argues in *Queer Phenomenology* that desire and affect are generated by our various habits of turning and directing the body, writing that "the etymology of 'direct' relates to 'being straight' or getting 'straight to the point.' To go directly is to follow a line without a detour, without mediation. Within the concept of direction is a concept of 'straightness.' To follow a line might be a way of becoming straight, by not deviating at any point" (16). But I don't call the architect, or his girlfriend. Instead, I'll smile obliquely at their summer wedding as they walk down the narrow aisle, looking gorgeously aslant.

Insofar as Deleuze and Guattari consider the affect of a body and its surrounding environment to be mutually constitutive, it is not for rhetorical flourish alone that they continually employ geographical vocabulary and geo-oriented descriptions of the spaces in which affects occur, including their figure of the nomad who "clings to the smooth space left by the receding forest, where the steppe or the desert advances" (1987, 381). It's worth repeating that the word they use to denote the disruptive force of affect is "deterritorialization" (142). In his recent essay, "Space in the Age of Non-Place," Ian Buchanan notes that "deterritorialization names the process whereby the very basis of one's identity, the proverbial ground beneath our feet, is eroded, washed away like the bank of a river swollen by floodwater" (2005, 23). In this decidedly pastoral metaphor, Buchanan reminds us that, just as trans life seems to demand literal and figural movement, so does Deleuze and Guattari's deterritorialization of the subject implicate both body and space. In this sense, the literal shapes we impose upon bodies, buildings, or hillsides are constitutive of how we will be able to move and be moved.

If these nonurban motifs are not accidental, how might a kind of gender nomadism—of refusing home, of refusing the straightest and quickest path between two points—demand a reconfiguration of how we think and feel about space? Deleuze and Guattari's distinction between smooth and striated space suggests that, against any simple rural/urban dichotomy (which is itself instituted only through the boundary-tracing authority of the city), nomadic and radical ways of living with/in (or as) space can happen in any locale, including a rather rural city of a million dispersed people such as Edmonton. To think through the usefulness of this model of striated/smooth for trans relationships to space, I cite at length first Bonta and Protevi, then Deleuze and Guattari:

> Striated space is first griddled and delineated, then occupied, by the drawing of rigid lines that compartmentalize reality into segments, all controlled to a greater or lesser extent through a nested hierarchy of centers .... Thus striated space, because it is composed of centers, is productive of remoteness, of the entire idea that there are places of more and of less importance. [...] The city...is what allows the striation of a larger territory.
>
> (Bonta and Protevi 2004, 154)

> Smooth space [...] is a space of contact, of small tactile or manual actions of contact, rather than a visual space.... Smooth space is a field without conduits or channels. A field, a heterogeneous smooth space, is wedded to a very particular type of multiplicity: nonmetric, acentered, rhizomatic multiplicities that occupy space without "counting" it and can "be explored only by legwork." They do not meet the visual condition of being observable from a point in space external to them.
>
> (Deleuze and Guattari 1987, 371)

With their coded roads, maps, and high straight buildings from which one might see the streets without moving, urban centers seem just what Deleuze and Guattari have in mind when they describe striated space. Perhaps their smooth or nomadic space may not be the random gay bars or drag shows to which one roves in a strange city, but instead, quite literally "a field" (371), the kind where rural queers might have first kisses or redneck trannies might roam, work, or play. In valorizing the work of *Queer Nation,* Lauren Berlant and Elizabeth Freeman suggest that this activist group succeeds in confounding the question of "where" the nation itself might be located; "it names," they say, "multiple locals and national publics; it does not look for a theoretical coherence to regulate in advance all of its tactics: all politics in the *Queer Nation* are imagined on the street" (Berlant and Freeman 1997, 151). This is all too true, insofar as *Queer Nation's* tactics (such as claiming the public space of a shopping mall to hand out pro-queer information) are achieved by using certain versions of publicity, by assuming the possibility of anonymity, and by imagining that "the *street*" somehow belongs and speaks to all queers. Indeed, to the disapproval of Deleuze and Guattari and their privileging of smoothness, this popular model of queer nationhood—and indeed, the very institution of the Pride Parade—assumes the presence of "street" (Berlant and Freeman 1997, 151) and its "direct" centrality to bent queer life.

Interpreting Deleuze and Guattari's distinction of smooth and striated space as merely another way of saying rural and urban would be to oversimplify. To hick trannies for whom public transit is a mere abstraction, a space "explored only by legwork" (Deleuze and Guattari 1987, 371) is concretely familiar. Likewise, while a field appears meticulously organized to a farmer, or a series of landmarks may function as striations for local residents, these people "are not necessarily forces for imparting" the effect of these markings "beyond their own neighbourhood" (Bonta and Protevi 2004, 154), as urban thinkers or planners might be. Insofar as the striation of space is not conducive to becoming, this imperative needs to be actively resisted. That which is striated is, by definition, not remote. Perhaps an overarching revaluing of the very concept of "remoteness" is required to rethink the value of the rural realm and the bodies that (choose to) assemble with/in it. If, for Deleuze and Guattari, "the body or assemblage in question is co-constituted along with the space it occupies" (Bonta and Proveti 2004,146), it is clear that where one lives and moves is more than a blank space into which subjects arrive fully formed; rather, choosing where to live and how to live with/in its spaces are technologies of the (undoing of the) subject, equally as much as those surgical and hormonal technologies we recognize more easily as body/gender modification.

The suggestion that we ought to roam and fuck with the grids and codes of striated spaces deterritorializes the valorization of city dwelling, ownership, and organized urban life that often accompany representations or expectations of trans life. Regarding space and movement as constitutive of one's gender presupposes that, contra Prosser, gender identity is neither simply a matter of the psyche or the skin nor a way in which the subject ought to shore up his or her sense of body homeness. But, if our modes of moving and being moved are indeed so closely intertwined, what ethic of body modification does this reconsideration of remoteness and smooth spaces evoke? Significantly, Bonta and Protevi suggest that "we need to emphasize that striated (and smooth) can be features of non-geographic assemblages [...] and so are not restricted to spaces of interest to geographical pursuits at the scale of the human or the landscape" (2004, 155). In other words, given that processes of gender modification may also be smooth or striated, how do we engage in practices of body morphology that strive toward the smooth, that aim to deterritorialize the subject rather than settle it, to become a nomad rather than come "home to the self through body" (Prosser 1998, 83)? Conceiving of practices of body modification—including gender transition—as a move from one point to another by the straightest line possible seems antithetical to that project. To striate one's body (indeed, even to regard it as so discrete as to call it that) into literal organs and imbue certain of these with a surplus of signifying power also puts one at danger for codifying embodiment in a way that creates remoteness—both of parts of one's "own" body, affect itself, and also those bodies that live elsewhere and morph in different ways. If, instead, one prioritized traits over forms, movement over stasis, and smoothness over striation, gender modification would seem to be at its most deterritorializing when we are emphatically unconcerned with moving from one fixed point to another on the path of least distance and detour. In this sense, an ethics of mobility and spatiality is entailed in and illustrated by any ethics or practice of gender modification. If, by productively unsettling the geo-affective subject, we could create new potentialities for the body, it follows that there is something lacking in our focus on reproducing existent bodies, in the very concept of transition, and in the increasingly coherent practices we pursue in transition's ubiquitously urban home.

Hopefully the applicability of such ideas to rural trans life is becoming clear. Many rural gender-fucking people find—in unconventional ways—unconventional allies, lovers, and mentors in their towns and villages, many of which don't even have geographically accessible hospitals, let alone the legion of certified psychiatrists, surgeons, and endocrinologists who preside over the processes of urban gender transition. What kind of phenomenon is "transgender" if it exists without hormones, surgery, or the extensive medical documentation that accompanies these identifiably trans procedures? Deleuze and Guattari offer resistance to those who might assume such things impossible. In one of their more (in)famous plateaus, "How Do you Make Yourself a Body without Organs?" they speak explicitly about the dangers of reducing a body to a series of cooperative organs. Their phrase "body without organs," (abbreviated BwO in specialist literature) offers resistance to the notion of bodily integrity or unity and calls to mind the dynamic character of transgender bodies—even though its dispensing of a definitive bodily organization clashes with the aspirations of those trans people for whom the acquisition or removal or certain organs constitutes the authenticity of trans subjectivity. While Deleuze and Guattari write of bodies and organs in general, their comments are especially resonant with surgical sex/gender modification. Imbuing certain parts of the body with certain meanings, what they call a focus on "part-objects," is "the approach of a demented experimenter who flays, slices, and anatomizes everything in sight, and then proceeds to sew things randomly back together again" (1987, 171). They contrast the part-object approach and its "fragmented body" (171) with the BwO by arguing that the latter neither presupposes an original unity, nor, more enigmatically, can be contained within one organism or controlled by one singular body. On this last point, they suggest that "it is not 'my' body without organs, instead the 'me' (*moi*) is on it, or what remains of me" (161). The BwO is infinitely unfinished, and it presumes that our environments move us as much as we move through them.

There is nothing necessarily deterritorializing about the gender or body of someone who lives out this kind of transgender without organs.[2] That such a configuration of transgender is possible, however—where passing, nightlife, community, and transition seem or are impossible—reminds us that policing gender identity on the basis of medical procedures also entails a policing of class, race, and a plethora of other cultural and bodily conditions, and also of location. Deterritorializing the system of subjectivity that would have us privilege certain organs and see the body as an integral whole (an idea that undermines trans life in the first instance) does not necessarily entail turning one's body into an assemblage of parts or series of seeming fragments, though this may well be involved. As Deleuze and Guattari note, functioning as a subject is necessary to effect change: "You have to keep small supplies of significance and subjectification, if only to turn them against their own systems when the circumstances demand it" (1987, 160). Transgender and transsexual subjects clearly do and will continue to exist, and for good reason—but hopefully as a way to deterritorialize gender rather than settle it, to take apart their own habits and territories, to help us experiment rather than solve a problem, and to take us wayward rather than directly from one point to the next.

## IMPERCEPTIBLE TRANSGENDERS

October 2007, Los Angeles, California. Like most rural kids I feel frantic here at first, compelled to take advantage of everything offered by a new strange city—lest I not make the most of this opportunity to travel. A few hours after the hotel concierge accepts my credit card, following a ten-minute conversation about how "strange it is you use Laura as a man's name in Canada!," I visit the Los Angeles Holocaust Museum. I shuffle tentatively about the empty rooms until an older woman approaches me, introduces herself as a child survivor, and implores me to sit with her on a bench to hear her story. As she speaks about hiding with her parents in France, and tells me what a fine young man I am for coming to the museum, I think: How will I tell her my name if she asks? Might she consider the incongruence between my acceptance of her appellation, "young man, "and my self-naming as "Laura" to be duplicitous? I ask whether, as a child of nine years old, she had a sense of what was going on around her, as she and her mother hid in a non-Jewish household and snuck food to her father, who lived in a cave nearby. Her response echoes one I have offered to others, when trying to explain the perils and pleasures of my new urban transgender experiences: "Do you have any idea what it's like to never know what people are thinking when they look at you? To be afraid that you'll be found out? "A staff member announcing closing time abbreviates what might have been a considerably difficult and important conversation. Later that day, I stroll a nearly deserted Sunset Boulevard and pass an establishment called Dr. Tea's. An employee on the sidewalk offers me a sample cup and says, "Sir, I'm convinced you need some tea!" I sense he's not alone in that belief. But I don't quite agree. "Could what the drug user or masochist obtains also be obtained in a different fashion... so it would even be possible to use drugs without using drugs, to get soused on pure water?"

(Deleuze and Guattari 1987, 166).

I think of the way in which "passing" is a void notion in a small town where everyone knows you, and I wonder if the way in which rural people are largely ignored by urban queer theory lets us experience something more exhilarating than passing: imperceptibility. Deleuze and Guattari write: "What does becoming-imperceptible signify. ... A first response would be: to be like everyone else.... After a real rupture, one succeeds ... in being just like everyone else. To go unnoticed is by no means easy. ... it is an affair of becoming" (1987, 279).

If rural social lives occur in homes, backyards, and dark fields "rather than [in] a visual space" (371) like a city street, club, organization, or parade, we might ask ourselves a question that any urban postflineur hasn't been able to ask for some time: What *is* it like to remain unseen, both by urban-centered theories of queerness and by our culture at large? While this "indisceribility" (279) may sound like the kind of gender illegibility proffered by some postmodern theories of gender, that sort of unreadability may well be the "too-much-to-be-perceived" (279) of which Deleuze and Guattari write, though visible excess of ambiguous gender undoubtedly has its own value. Instead, the imperceptible lies beneath notice but is still only "like" (280) everybody else. In this account, imperceptibility is something entirely different from being "in the closet," as rural queers are so often read. By seeing imperceptibility as something other than a stopover on the way to a satisfying queer life, this equation of imperceptibility and becoming disrupts the teleology of coming out and transitioning. In so doing, Deleuze and Guattari offer a version of imperceptible trans life (rather than passing) that rural (or otherwise seemingly invisible) trans people might find reassuring or galvanizing: that continually navigating one's imperceptibility, rather than seeking out places where one feels readable or acknowledged as transgender[4] is not necessarily an unmitigated sign of self-loathing or the inability to move to a city; rather, it may be precisely this imperceptibility and lack of recognition that enables rural styles of transgender and the very different affects and lives that could be realized there—ones in which childhood vignettes do not add up to a narrative or to an adult, in which affects don't add up to a fully formed and settled subject, in which body parts and supposed bodily integrity are not cause for premature death, and where bodies that pass or bodies that are imperceptible each assemble in unexpectedly deterritorializing fashion, if only on the way to the next stop, the next desire, the next gender, the next...?

## NOTES

[...]

2. The pun here on genitals as "organs" relies on Deleuze and Guattari's "body without organs" (BwO), mentioned above, by which they hope to inspire an orientation to embodiment and assemblage that is not based on being a complete

organism or focusing on "parts-objects" (1987, 171). [...] The question posed by the pun is, then, In what ways does the concept of transgender-without-organs demand that we rethink the centrality of sexual "organs" to gender? [...]

4. This version of imperceptibility is revisited by Kelly Oliver (2001) in her argument for a postrecognition model of subjectivity in *Witnessing: Beyond Recognition.* In the following, she could remind rural trans people to be wary of political projects that take recognition by urbanites as our main goal. As she writes, "While it seems obvious that oppressed people may engage in struggles for recognition in response to their lack of recognition from the dominant culture, it is less obvious that recognition itself is part of the pathology of oppression and domination" (23).

## WORKS CITED

Ahmed, Sara. 2006. *Queer Phenomenology: Orientations, Objects, Others.* Durham: Duke University Press.

Berlant, Lauren, and Elizabeth Freeman. 1997. "Queer Nationality." In *The Queen of America Goes to Washington City: Essays on Sex and Citizenship.* Durham: Duke University Press.

Bonta, Mark, and John Protevi. 2004. *Deleuze and Geophilosophy: A Guide and Glossary.* Edinburgh: Edinburgh University Press.

Buchanan, Ian. 2005. "Space in the Age of Non-place." In *Deleuze and Space,* ed. 1. Buchanan and G. Lambert. Edinburgh: Edinburgh University Press.

Cvetkovich, Ann. 1992. *Mixed Feelings: Feminism, Mass Culture, and Victorian Sensationalism.* New Brunswick: Rutgers University Press.

Cvetkovich, Ann. 2003. *An Archive of Feelings: Trauma, Sexuality, and Lesbian Public Cultures.* Durham: Duke University Press.

Deleuze, Gilles, and Félix Guattari. 1987. *A Thousand Plateaus: Capitalism and Schizophrenia.* Trans. Brian Massumi. London: Athlone Press.

Janoff, Douglas Victor. 2005. *Pink Blood: Homophobic Violence in Canada.* Toronto: University of Toronto Press.

Oliver, Kelly. 2001. *Witnessing: Beyond Recognition.* Minneapolis: University of Minnesota Press.

Prosser, Jay. 1998. *Second Skins: The Body Narratives of Transsexuality.* New York: Columbia University Press.

Stryker, Susan. 2007. "Transgender Feminism: Queering the Woman Question." Lecture delivered at Edmonton, University of Alberta, March 8.

Weston, Kath. 1995. "Get Thee to a Big City: Sexual Imaginary and the Great Gay Migration." *GLQ* 2(3): 253–78.

# 37

# *Longevity and Limits in Rae Bourbon's Life in Motion*

## DON ROMESBURG

RAE BOURBON, WHO DIED OLD, PENNILESS, AND INCARCERATED in a small Texas town in 1971, lived a long and highly mobile life as an entertainer whose performances, on and off the stage, traversed boundaries of nation, culture, ethnicity, class, sexuality, and gender. In this richly contextualized biographical profile of a remarkable personality, historian Don Romesburg explores the many ways in which Bourbon renounced "borderland belonging"—that is, forms of hybrid identity that constrain movement and possibility—to claim instead a "cosmopolitan transnational citizenship" predicated on the successful transcoding and manipulation of potentially stigmatizing differences in order to promote connectivity, mobility, creativity, wealth, and fame. Rae (or Ray, or possibly Ramon) Bourbon may have been Mexican, Spanish, Tejano, or Anglo; may have been a foster child of aristocratic lineage, may have been illegitimate by birth, or may have been raised by his (or her) birth parents on a south Texas ranch. Bourbon may, or may not, have had genital transformation surgery in Ciudad Juarez in the 1950s: surviving state records and autobiographical representation are wildly contradictory. What is known, however, is that Bourbon appeared in silent movies in both men's and women's roles in the 1910s, was a celebrated "pansy" entertainer in jazz-era Harlem, toured the U.S. with Mae West, performed drag and burlesque routines on the international nightclub circuit, and recorded numerous campy and risqué comedy albums in a career that spanned five decades. Romesburg sees operating behind Bourbon's accomplishments what Chicana Studies scholar Chela Sandoval has termed a "differential consciousness," in which queer-of-color performativity deconstructs and decolonizes the signs of an imposed culture in order to create new possibilities for life.

I said I'd never come back ... but here I am ... here I am
I said I'll keep off your track ... but here I am ... here I am
> —"Here I Am" (1926), performed by Ray Bourbon at the Folies Bergère in 1936

There is no romance or seduction to living on the borders.
> —M. Jacqui Alexander's coda for Gloria Anzaldúa

I have no aversion to the art they term perversion.
I contend that each man's hobby is his own.
You may say that I'm a sissy, in fact an object prissy,
But I've a right to change my mind when I start for home.
(Sometimes I don't get there, but I'll start!)

> —Rae Bourbon, mid-1940s

## INTRODUCTION

What kinds of movement and belonging produce possibilities for a long transgender existence? Comic and female impersonator Rae Bourbon's life, spanning from the end of the nineteenth century into the 1970s, highlights the opportunities and limits of mobility and relationality for material viability and meaningful embodiment on society's margins.

A quick life sketch: Rae had a 60-year career in a profession not known for its longevity. To keep afloat, Bourbon navigated shifting terrains of social attitudes, law enforcement, performance trends, and subcultures. Onstage and off, Rae maneuvered across diverse sexualities, genders, races, and classes. Claiming to be the son of European royalty and born in 1892 in Chihuahua City, Mexico, young Ramon was raised by a wealthy foster family on a large ranch in Hudspeth County, Texas, as a U.S. citizen. After a supposed move to London for schooling, Bourbon went to Hollywood in the late 1910s. There, the performer played male and female stock parts in movies. Ray (sometimes billed "Rae") hit vaudeville as a drag and/or "pansy" performer across the country in the 1920s, then as a bawdy, tuxedoed comic in Hollywood nightclubs and in drag internationally throughout the 1930s. In the mid/late 1940s Bourbon toured in Mae West's shows. A purported 1955 sexual reassignment process in Ciudad Juárez, Mexico, led to a formal change in first name from, as the performer sang in one number, "R-A-Y to R-A-E." Rae's gender ambiguity and contradictory documentation leave unclear the motives for claiming to have undergone such a procedure. From the late 1950s on, Bourbon lived and performed within a blend of self-professed public and private male, female, and trans identities. Rae got banned from the nightclubs of Los Angeles, where s/he had been arrested for impersonating a woman, and, in Miami, cops jailed her/him for impersonating a man. By the 1960s, Bourbon enjoyed few privileges of either of the two "legitimate" sexes. Down but not out, in 1966 Rae mounted *Daddy Was a Lady,* an autobiographical musical, in Colorado. Several years later, a Texas jury found the performer guilty of masterminding a murder in which s/he may or may not have been involved. Bourbon died in a small town under confinement, penniless and alone, in 1971 (Bourbon c. late 1960s–1971; Romesburg 2000).

Showcasing how Bourbon managed for so long to pull off such an eccentric, spectacular, and fierce act affirms the creative dignity of the performer's choices and expressions as tactics of possibility within deeply compromised and changing circumstances. It gives all of us strategies and challenges to connect with the negotiations we make in seeking to fashion our existences. Quality of life for all of us gets constrained, somehow, by our not fitting into the world in which we arrive, and in part gets achieved through demanding, by the practice of our own messy lives, something more. Transgender people, in particular, have had to be especially adept at this to simply continue to live.

Rae's life necessitated multiple forms of mobility and migration. These movements were multidirectional, erratic, and eccentric—across national borders and racial, class, sex/gender and sexual subject positions, through diverse US regions and urban and rural locations, within campy performances with multiple and shifting simultaneous meanings, and via overlapping, transient cultures of kinship and allegiance. Rae's oppositional knowledges, forged through exilic living *and* yearnings for belonging, produced new possibilities, or, as Emma Pérez puts it, "new disidentities," at once deeply relational and fiercely independent (Luibhéid 2008; Pérez 2003: 123–24). The same mobilities which facilitated possibility in particular contexts were turned against the performer in others. Appreciating "how trans moves us" in both spatial and affective ways opens up transgender embodiment as a series of multidirectional, productive, and creative practices (Crawford 2008; Sears 2008; Stryker, Currah, and Moore 2008). Those striving to produce livable lives beyond the confines of heteronormative fusions of sex/gender/sexuality congruence need all the tools they can deploy.

This chapter elaborates on mobilities Bourbon pursued to belong meaningfully in the world. It first considers border excursions and exile in Rae's early years, then explores movement enabled by Bourbon's performances of transgender cosmopolitan citizenship. Next, it examines how queer kinships facilitated Rae's transportation. Finally, it argues that Bourbon's self-narrations suggest transgender talents through which Bourbon grasped toward freedom across decades of shifting fortunes. Rae never was granted the rights required to live this life freely, so instead claimed precarious privilege as a flexible tactic and ethic of entitlement. The magnetic effects of innovative agency and immanent foreclosure tell a story of the possibilities and perils of an oppositional citizen-subject on the go.[1]

## BORDERLAND BELONGING AND EXILIC LIVING

Bourbon's birth has at least three or four versions of the truth. Rae claimed to have been born Ramon Icarez, in either Chihuahua City, Mexico, or "three days out on a ship bound for Vera Cruz," as the illegitimate son of Louisa Bourbon, a Spanish woman, and "Franz Frederick Hapsburg, the grandnephew of the emperor Francis Joseph." Ramon may also have been born on a U.S. ranch near the Mexican border, the child of a mixed Irish- and Mexican-American marriage. Perhaps Rae was born Hal Waddell, son of Frank T. Waddell and "Elizabeth—last name unknown," in Texarkana, Texas. Bourbon's foster parents, also possibly uncle and aunt, also named Waddell, raised Rae as Ramon on a ranch in Hudspeth County below Sierra Blanca, Texas.[2] Bourbon claimed to be unaware until turning twenty-one that the Waddells were foster parents; it was then that Ramon's foster mother supposedly revealed the blue-blooded borderland ancestry. It came as a shock, and yet, as Rae wrote in the memoir, "I had suspected that something was wrong because I didn't seem to belong to the Family that raised Me." Caught up in this whirl of possibilities were serious challenges for Bourbon regarding race, class, legitimacy, documentation, and allegiance during a period of crucial flux for the Texas-Mexico borderlands. As a queer and transgender exilic traveling subject, Rae grappled from birth to death with an ambivalent relationship to the region, its peoples, and the prospects they all held for personal viability. Ultimately, Bourbon chose to identify with a kind of transnational cosmopolitan citizenship over borderland belonging, but never fully left it behind.

In the borderlands of Bourbon's childhood, racial hierarchies, national boundaries, sexual divisions and gender binaries hardened. Anglo Texans increasingly lumped all Mexicans and Tejanos into the same degraded racial category, reconfiguring "Mexicans" as a "culturally and biologically inferior alien race" (Foley 1997: 45). Still, the Eurocentrism of elites during the rule of Porfirio Diaz (1867–1910) in Mexico pushed against flattening racial claims. In border towns such as El Paso, contests continued for decades around whitening performances of class status, Spanish bloodline, and European cultural lineage. Some navigated shifting local conditions in an attempt to retain a *blanqueamiento* citizenship encumbered with a "possessive investment in whiteness" (García 1984; Lipsitz 1998; Montejano 1987). Hardening color lines and sharpened anxieties about mestizo sexuality fused with sexological and state constructions of sexual perversion, modern homosexuality, and gender inversion to make the U.S.–Mexico border a "paradigmatic border" symbolically marking differences of global struggle regarding civilization, modernization, capitalism, and American imperialism (Howe, Zaraysky, and Lorentzen 2008; Luibhéid 2008: 178; Pérez 2003: 126). On Texan soil from the 1890s through the 1900s, Bourbon's body (maybe Mexican, certainly same-sex sexually active and gender transgressive) became socially and scientifically more deviant, primitive, even criminal. Ramon may have recognized how identities and social attitudes were mobile and that moving around might be a way to harness rather than be victim to such flux. Bourbon also learned to appeal to different people by performing diverse racial, gender, sexual, and national identities.

Beyond broader structural and sociocultural contexts, dramatic personal events propelled Ramon outward into exilic living. After an idyllic childhood of private tutoring, servants, and days spent roping, riding, and caring for animals, Bourbon, at 11, grew alienated from the ranch once

Mrs. Waddell took her second husband. The stepfather hated Ramon's affair with George, a ranch foreman. For the next three years, Ramon and George had a relationship that eventually turned sexual. According to the memoir, one day the two went to the Palace Hotel's bar in nearby Sierra Blanca and, without clear reason, a "Mexican" man shot George dead. In true western novel masculine heroics, Rae describes whipping out a gun and killing the assailant before, in true romance novel feminine hysterics, cradling the dying George and collapsing in shock for four days. To protect Ramon from potential retribution, Mrs. Waddell in 1906 supposedly sent Bourbon, age 14, to a private boarding school in London (Bourbon 1970b).

Off the ranch, a wider world opened up, making possible a life filled for performance, flamboyance, and wit. As a gender transgressive, liminally raced queer, Bourbon was far from dominant Texan codes of masculinity. So Bourbon said, as one later routine went, "To Hell with the Range":

> I don't need the hills and plains and the great wide-open spaces
> I can exercise my bronco in some very narrow places. ...
> I thought a ranch might give me a chance for romance and allure
> But one gets so bucolic when they frolic in manure.
>
> (Bourbon 1956a)

Contrasted with Ramon's teenage relationship with the ranch foreman and Rae's later embrace of big cities and their queer cultures, these characterizations highlight Texan backwardness, repression, tedium, and filth. From an early age Rae yearned for a cosmopolitan world.

Exile, for those expressing what Jay Prosser terms "transgender ambivalence" rather than movement toward gender arrival, is a simultaneously coercive and volitional separation from both origin and settled destination. For transpeople as exilic subjects, traveling is "a strategy for living with the exilic condition" (Basu 2004: 131; Prosser 1998: 177). Home, in this context, might be understood as the place of belonging in which an exile can find refuge and recognition. This "home" directs the strategies of movement, circumstances of displacement, and feelings about them for exilic traveling subjects. For Rae, home was not a space or a consciousness but a profoundly interrelational process of associations with others and access to multiple points of contact and departure. This queer translocal mobility, at once nostalgic and disavowing, required shifting affinities, myriad escape hatches, and capacities for flexibly drawing upon multiple cultural and social resources (La Fountain-Stokes 2008).

Rae did not transcend belonging in or exile from the borderlands. Willfully and inadvertently Bourbon returned to Texas and nearby Mexican towns at crucial life junctures. To renegotiate the terms of the journeys, Rae opted for linguistic, social, and material transborder discourses that blurred the increasingly articulated geopolitical and socio-cultural lines between Texas and Mexico. Ramon spoke English and "Mexican Spanish," which, Rae adds in the memoir, was "not unusual because everyone in Texas spoke Mexican Spanish." Healing the wounds of exile involved going back and forth across the border from the 1910s through the 1960s. Rae sometimes referred to Ciudad Juárez as "home" and found it more exciting than other regional towns. Bourbon performed at local clubs such as Hugo's Lobby No. 2, which catered to locals and American tourists with cabaret acts, comics, and striptease. The city also was the site for Rae's purported "sex change operations" and stage performances touting how "She Lost It in Juarez" (Bourbon c. 1969–71, 1970a, 1970b; *El Paso Herald-Post* 1931, 1933; Lomas 2003; Romesburg 2000). Transborder racial and sex/gender performance provided skills of mobility and ambiguity with lifelong utility. Rae appreciated the borderlands' multiple languages, word play, and double entendre, and put these into camp action as a comic and female impersonator. They also allowed Rae to evade Texan systems sex/gender, sexuality, race, and nationalism.

## COSMOPOLITAN CITIZENSHIP AND TRANSNATIONAL TRANSTEXTUALITY

Gender diverse queer migrants must engage in self-authoring to negotiate the multiple relations of power and desire confronting their subjectivities. The challenges and tools at one's disposal differ profoundly for the refugee, transnational laborer, immigrant, tourist, or cosmopolitan citizen (Manalansan 2006). Through literary, interpersonal, and stage performances, Rae reworked the precarious existence of a transnational laborer into a cosmopolitan citizen's grand, gay life.

To distinguish forms of mobility based upon their relationships to capital and labor, Kale Fajardo suggests that we differentiate "travel", which often implies leisure, from "transportation," a disciplined circuit of embodied labor movement between industrialized and consumer spaces. Such circuits, forged in globalization and migration, accommodate alternative queered itineraries and trajectories for those able to navigate its routes (Fajardo 2008). Bourbon found success throughout the first half of the twentieth century along transnational circuits of theater, vaudeville, nightclubs, and movies. Later, circuits became more U.S.-bound, requiring large amounts of transportation to get from one small-town bar to the next big-city female impersonation tourist club. Bourbon navigated shifting laws, policing and immigration bureaucracies regarding cross-dressing, obscenity, and homosexuality, as well as transient profitability. Adept identification of circuits and execution of movement within them made possible the necessary push to get down the road another mile, another year.

Some have articulated the concept of cosmopolitan citizenship in order to underscore statist citizenship's inability to meet the heterogeneous needs of humanity. Others have criticized the elitism bound into cosmopolitanism's claims of virtue. These often support a universalism privileging tourists, intellectuals, tastemakers, industrialists, and artists. Both perspectives emphasize how people's interdependencies exceed the nation-state's capacities to satisfy socio-cultural longings or fulfill economic or political needs (Beck 2004; Linklater 1998). Cosmopolitan citizenship has afforded queer peoples a means to seek affinity beyond state borders and expose the failures of nations to afford viability and respect to sexual and gender-diverse people. Such queer cosmopolitanism has also reproduced power relations bound into empire, globalization, and transnational consumer capitalism (Burns and Davies 2009; Grewal and Kaplan 2001; Rodriguez 2003). Bourbon's movement shows how, for those able to harness them, these two strains need not be contradictory. Claiming such privilege, however, also does not provide real security.

Through self-narration as a transgender cosmopolitan citizen, Rae lived these tensions. The ideal body of cosmopolitan citizenship is one of privilege, capable of accessing many markets, cultures, and locales while appearing to be self-maintaining in core aspects of being. Queer and gender-transgressive bodies (among many others) get positioned as being overwhelmed by desires and the burdens of embodiment and, thus, undeserving of full citizenship (Canaday 2009; Romesburg 2008). Still, Bourbon managed cosmopolitan citizenship as a tactic and ethic. This required awareness of larger forces, flexible accumulation of risk-mitigation strategies, and performance of belonging and entitlement in multiple environments, Rae accessed transportation along circuits of transnational capital in the entertainment industry. As a cultural producer and worker, Bourbon profited from transgressive cultural mobility. Rae's shows were a commodity that brought urbanity to small-town stages, poked fun at rurality and provincial Americanness in big-city nightclubs made lowbrow comedy out of the high art of Western civilization, and lampooned peoples from across the globe. Part of the act, onstage and off, was a claim of transtextual privilege in a global network.

Prosser utilizes transtextuality to underscore multiple, overlapping referents in transpeople's self-narration. These shift depending upon the discourses—legal, medical, social, political—a person must access various moments and locales. To themselves and others, transsexuals (and all people, Prosser suggests) must tell stories about themselves that are not their own in order to more fully realize themselves as viable, recognizable subjects. They also potentially subvert or, at least, make space within these discourses. Film scholar Manthia Diawara refers to transtextuality as "the movement of cultural styles from character to character. ... hybridity, multiple subject positions." This contrasts with immanence, or the "trapping of a cultural role in a character" (Diawara and Kolbowski 1998: 51). Combined, these help explain Bourbon's mobility as one exercise of cosmopolitan citizenship. Through both self-narration and performance, Rae flexibly disidentified with myriad subject positions to subversively embrace the marketplace. Because the navigated forces overwhelmed one person's ability to overcome them, the performer always faced threats of immanence. Being read too literally foreclosed upon possibilities and fixed Rae, perilously, into place. Two illustrations of these tensions are Bourbon's self-positioning around imperial privilege and Rae's racial, sexual, and gender mobilities across space and time.

Bourbon flaunted a royal genealogy and showcased regal associations, bragged about substantial wealth, and claimed a liminal Spanishness. In combination, these supported Bourbon's cosmopolitan citizenship. Both blood parents, Rae told everyone from intimate friends to small-town Texan juries, were from noble European lineage and married outside Paris when the mother was pregnant, then she sailed to America. This lineage even ended up on Bourbon's death certificate (Texas Department of Health—Bureau of Vital Statistics 1971). Rae highlights nobility to showcase sophistication and a capacity to rub shoulders comfortably with the powerful. Bourbon supposedly gave special performances before such luminaries as Shanghai's Chow Ling, "Great Grand-Nephew of the Dowager Empress of China" (1930), England's King Edward (1936), and, most implausibly, with Josephine Baker for Spain's Generalissimo Franco and the Duke and Duchess of Alba (1936). The same was claimed of capitalist royalty, such as Cuban sugar king Jorge Sanchez, Al Capone, and Hollywood celebrities. Rae also performed a privilege-laden trickle-down democratics. In Shanghai, Bourbon refers to a servant as "My Mongol," yet tells him to speak to Rae as he would "anyone else" (Bourbon 1956b, c. 1969–71; Romesburg 2000; State of Texas 1971).[4]

Rae self-presented as rich. In the memoir, Bourbon claims that the birth mother had given a staggering $500,000 to the Waddells to raise Ramon. In a story picked up by the *El Paso Herald-Post* at the height of the Great Depression, Bourbon claimed to receive $1.5 million from the Waddell estate (then plugged a show in Ciudad Juárez). At various times Bourbon claimed to have secret European bank accounts and Texan and Mexican land. Rae kept this up until the end, despite being unable to pay for car repairs, housing, pet boarding, or a defense attorney. In practice, Rae was always scheming to make more and was known for haggling ruthlessly with venue owners. Bourbon had high times, yet filed for bankruptcy in 1944 and struggled with poverty throughout the final two decades (Bourbon c. 1969–71; "Juárez Actor," *El Paso Herald-Post* 1931; Romesburg 2000; Wright and Forrest 1999).

Onstage, Bourbon underscored, as many impersonators did, globe-trotting glamor that appealed to diverse audiences in part because it displayed a democratic-capitalist promise of attainable luxury. Yet Rae also gestured toward the structural challenges for individuals attempting such mobility. Bourbon performed across class identities but always included the lowbrow. Throughout career ups and downs, Rae would don a ratty wig and a dirty, cheap dress to comic effect moments after embodying a high-society maven. Bourbon often sang about performing in drag primarily for the money (Bourbon c. mid-1940s, 1956c). In a comic call to unionize queens entitled "We've Got to Have a Union of Our Own," Bourbon utilizes the symbolics of labor solidarity to urge greater queer and transgender collectivity, making explicit the hard work of entertainment labor and a need to respond to systemic discrimination (Bourbon c. late-1940s a).

In addition to regal relationality and the performance of wealth alongside class mobility, Rae bound racial passing within modes of whiteness into claims of imperial privilege. This allowed for an appeal to a vaguely exotic European ancestry. Emma Pérez suggests that, for subaltern women, assimilation into modes of whiteness can figure as interstitial moves, creating possibilities for personal subject-hood within patriarchal structures that refuse such women comfortable or stable identity (Pérez 1999: 81, 87). For queer and gender diverse people, such tactics brought similar opportunities for subversive navigation. In the memoir, Rae proudly represents a comment by a London theater manager in late 1930s that Bourbon has "no Accent that would associate you with America or with England" to signal cosmopolitanism beyond national or racial origins. Bourbon's light skin would have allowed the performer to claim to be Anglo in many contexts.

Rae also sometimes performed a public and private Castilian identity and found comfort in the use of a loose Spanish. In the memoir, Bourbon, in an aside to the reader, writes, "When I'm out of the United States I unknowingly revert too [sic] Spanish." In jail in 1970, Bourbon frequently closed letters in Spanish (Bourbon c. 1969–71, 1970a, 1970b, 1970c). In songs such as "Spanish," Bourbon claimed Spanishness proudly, even while mocking Latin culture. Without completely disavowing its hybrid relationship to Mexicanness, Bourbon blended Spanishness and borderland belonging, regal relations with lowbrow associations. In the performance for Franco, Rae awed the audience by joining in a robust flamenco complete with castanets, noting, "I hadn't lived along the Rio Grande for nothing." At the subsequent banquet, Bourbon bragged to the Duchess of Alba about learning to dance at the Molino Rojo. "Franco's daughter laughed," Bourbon recalls, "because Molino rojos are all whorehouses. Leave it too Me to make the Faux–pas of My life." (Bourbon c. 1969–71).[5] Time and again, Bourbon blurred lines even when laboring to draw them. Maneuverability let Rae attach to and detach from racial and national allegiances, exercising the flexibility needed for transgender cosmopolitan citizenship.

Bourbon's transgender and racial hybridity, coupled with a keen sense of cultural nuance surrounding socio-economic and social status markers, made movements through carefully calibrated and contextualized performances useful for survival, prosperity, and self-narration. As tactics, however, modes of passing were threatened by potential "discovery" of the "real." In others' eyes, Bourbon sometimes would "go brown," queer, or trans against the performer's intent. Racial/ethnic ambiguity, like sexual and gender ambiguity, was subject not just to Rae's self-presentation but to other people's interpretations of racial, sexual, and gender performance and embodiment. Sometimes that left Bourbon stuck.

In the movies, Bourbon's representational dispersal across time and space allowed movement of queer and transgender possibilities across many eras and locations. Knowing "in the know" showbiz people formed a foundation of contacts through which Rae built a network of possibilities for a lifetime on the go. By the late 1910s, Ramon found transportation routes to Hollywood. Through silent movies and vaudeville circuits, transgender, transracial flexibility was empowering and profitable. Bourbon first got to Hollywood by submitting photos for a competition seeking new screen beauties. As Bob Wright told it, she "[t]urned out to be Ray, this six-foot-one Texan who looked as if he might be a Spanish don with all this luxurious hair." Studio executives said, "We don't want any males who look like you or talk like you." Bourbon replied, "What *do* you want?" They said, "Can you ride a horse?" Rae answered, "I was born on a horse," and got hired as a cross-dressing extra doing actresses' stunts (Wright and Forrest 1999). Bourbon claimed to have been played bit parts in a dozen films from 1919 to 1937, principally with Paramount, where the performer was under contract as a stock player through around 1923.[6] Roles were young and old, male and female, white and nonwhite, spanning across history and around the globe. In *Bella Donna* (1923), Bourbon played a flower vendress and a camel driver. In *Blood and Sand* (1922), Bourbon appears to have played a young bullfighter who dies in Rudolph Valentino's arms and later shows up as a female extra. In *Behind the Rocks* (1922), Rae was an English society woman in the background on a yacht (Bourbon c. 1969–71; Romesburg 2000; Willard 1971: 75).

Bourbon's opportunities to perform racial and gender diversity were furthered by acts that moved transgender queerness globally and transhistorically. Rae later played up this "we are—and I am—

everywhere" sensibility in stage routines from the 1940s through the 1960s. Acts placed same-sex action and gender diversity in medieval Europe, colonial North America, and imperial Asia. Famous historical figures such as Ponce de León, Pocahontas, Cleopatra and George Washington became queens, lesbians, and queers (Bourbon c. late 1940s b, 1956b, 1956d). Later routines played off the performer's longevity. In a 1964 Kansas City performance, Bourbon quipped, "I've been around a long time. When the Man said, 'Let there be light,' I'm the bitch that pulled the switch" (Bourbon 1964; Romesburg 2000). Transgressive camp performance is mobile, refusing fixity. In defiant transtextuality, Bourbon thumbed a nose at immanence. But camp refuses a performer the luxury of autonomy, necessarily soliciting temporary solidarities of double entendre. Such contradictions made Bourbon's self-stylings both nimble and dependent.

Bourbon's movement was driven as much by necessity as yearning for trans-expressivity. Scandal, poverty, and/or illegality dogged Rae whenever success seemed around the corner. In 1923 or 1924, Bourbon's most prolific years of screen work ended after the performer attended a gay party at the house of director Louis Gasiner and Gaston Glass. Police raided the place and Rae hid under dirty laundry to avoid arrest. The next day, Paramount lawyers released all the stock players who had been in attendance from their contracts (Bourbon c. 1969–71; Romesburg 2000; *State of Texas v. Ray Bourbon* 1971: 868).

## TRANSIENCE AND INTIMACIES IN TACIT QUEER RELATIONS

Queer kinships across the globe enabled Bourbon's life as an exilic traveling subject framed though transgender cosmopolitan citizenship. Complicity between associates was necessary for socio-economic mobility, transnational migration, and survival. Tacitness allowed Bourbon to manage those relations to carve out spaces of navigation. These queer tacit associations started at a young age. In the memoir, Bourbon recalls that Maria, the ranch nanny, affirmed specialness worth protecting in Ramon without naming its source, telling others, "I am the only one who understands his Nature; even his Mother does not understand him." Maria, as characterized by Rae, was *entendida,* someone in the know through whom Ramon could find a generous reflection that could, at the same time, remain vague in its specifics. Like the Latina/o concept of being *de ambiente* (in the life), *entendida* assumes something deeply relational and contextual about identity (Decena 2008; Nesvig 2001). As empowering as an *entendida* tacit subjectivity could be, those who could aid and abet could also harm and abandon. As with the Hollywood party raid, betrayals came on the heels of scandalous public disclosures. Associates could and did turn away, transforming what was tacit into plausible deniability to preserve their own security. When they did, Bourbon got stuck in everything from petty jealousies to criminal immanence. Such dependency and vulnerability contradicted Bourbon's desire to embody the privileged ease of cosmopolitan citizenship. To manage this, Rae characterized queer kin as either accompanists or accomplices.

Accompanists were subordinates upon which Bourbon's well-being, status, material prosperity and mobility depended. In addition to houseboys and chauffeur during high times, Bourbon frequently had a traveling companion who played piano for the performer's songs and blue patter. These pianists tended to be young blond, slender, attractive, and male. In the memoir, John "Duke" Kane, who performed with Bourbon on and off from the 1930s through the 1950s, and other accompanists fall in love with Bourbon, a self-testament to Rae's desire to embody importance, maternal and paternal strength, and goodness.

Rae treated employees as if being in the show was a great favor to them. There was some truth to this; Bourbon launched careers for songwriters Bart Howard ("In Other Words (Fly Me to the Moon)") and the team of Robert Wright and Chet Forrest (*Song of Norway*). In 1965, when Bourbon staged *Daddy Was a Lady,* a semi-autobiographical musical, in Cripple Creek, Colorado, the 73-year-old performer made sure that accompanist and lover Pat Lee, an 18-year-old impersonator, had a part

(Bourbon c. 1969–71; FBI 1961–62; Romesburg 2000; Strong 1999; Williamson 2009; Wright and Forrest 1999). These favors, portrayed in the memoir as selfless generosity, were recalled differently by recipients. Through Bourbon, Wright and Forrest secured an MGM contract, then had to pay Rae $10,000 to buy their way out of the favor. Bourbon even threatened their lives (Bourbon c. 1969–71; Wright and Forrest 1999). When Howard left to work at New York's prestigious Rainbow Room, Bourbon sent management a letter calling him an "untrustworthy degenerate" (Gavin 1992: 52–54). Rae's rage suggests how their success disrupted the hierarchy in Bourbon's transgender cosmopolitan citizenship.

Others, accomplices, were fashioned as if they were equals. Some acted as station agents, arranging papers and services necessary for transportation. Examples included chummy bail bondsmen who sprang the performer when tangled up in anti-cross-dressing and indecency charges and friends who helped Rae travel between gigs. Rae enjoyed femme collaboration with well-placed strong women, too. In the early 1930s, Bourbon booked Singapore and Shanghai runs thanks to club owner "Mrs. Merideth." Through the 1940s, Bourbon palled around with the cranky Marge Finocchio, the tough brains behind San Francisco's popular female impersonation tourist bar. During the 1950s and 1960s, Kaye Elledge, a butch lesbian who had performed in Bourbon's band in the 1940s, hosted Rae at Kaye's Happy Landing in Phoenix, Arizona, one of the state's first gay bars. Lifelong friend Mae West gave Rae prominently billed roles in theatrical touring productions of *Catherine Was Great* (1944–46) and *Diamond Lil* (1948–50) (Bourbon c. 1969–71; Romesburg 2000; "Tucson," *Weekly Observer* 1987).

Celebrities were vital to presentation as a transgender cosmopolitan citizen and instrumental to practical issues of reputation, fame, access, and purpose. Onstage Bourbon often called out to famous audience members as if they were old friends. As indicated in the memoir and elsewhere, some were, including West, Lana Turner, Lupe Vélez, Rudolph Valentino, Josephine Baker, Martha Raye, Bob Hope, and Robert Mitchum. Such associations gave Bourbon mainstream publicity few impersonators enjoyed, garnering regular mention in bits by Walter Winchell, Hedda Hopper, and other gossip peddlers nationally syndicated in small-town and big-city newspapers.[7]

Bourbon had special acquaintance with officials who facilitated movement across national borders. One story showcases how this enabled transnational movement against nation-states' attempts to police sexual and gender borders. While performing at the Folies Bergère in 1936, Bourbon arranged handsome, blond cast mate Ferdic Rey's passage to the U.S. through circuitous means. The U.S. Embassy had rejected Rey on moral perversion suspicions. Bourbon arranged for MGM to advance cash to bring Rey to Hollywood for a screen test. Then, at the Mexican Consulate, Carlos, an old flame from "a very Wealthy Mexican Family" with whom Rae had worked in silent movies and shared a romance *de ambiente*, secured Rey's claim of Mexico as the final destination. Next, a young man at the Cuban Consulate approved the visa after telling Bourbon he had seen the performer in Paris and Miami. Bourbon and Duke sailed to New York and took a train to Miami. An immigration officer whom Rae had met on transportation between Miami and Havana gigs, pledged to get Rey into the U.S. on a six-month visa if arriving from Cuba. Bourbon and Duke took a boat to Havana, meeting Rey and his male companion arriving from Europe. Another Vice Consul stamped the visas after Bourbon pledged to send comedy albums. Fast-tracked through customs, the foursome arrived back in Miami. Bourbon bought a Cadillac from a dealership-owning acquaintance and the group headed to Hollywood. Whatever the story's veracity, it highlights the multiple layers of relationship upon which Bourbon relied to conceptualize and manage transnational cosmopolitan citizenship. Fandom, friendship, *entendida* and tacit relationships, and savvy understanding of the mechanics of transport allowed Bourbon to work accomplices to manage international travel. Queer sexuality, racial liminality, and gender diversity required interpersonal work-arounds (Bourbon c. 1969–71; S.S. *Lancastria* 1936).

As useful as accomplices proved to Bourbon's longevity and mobility, they confirmed Bourbon's worst fears of abandonment and immanence in the later years. Those that had enabled Rae's transtextuality and publicity did little when things got dire. While in jail for conspiracy to murder, Bourbon and court-appointed defender William Bell wrote letters to West, California Governor Ronald Reagan, Bob Hope, Gore Vidal, and other Hollywood figures, asking them to testify to Rae's character. None did. Reagan's office sent a terse decline. Hope expressed interest, then never showed. Even West, who called, didn't make the trip. The only person who came from Rae's vast queer kinship network was, ironically, Bob Wright, the partner to 1930s accompanist Chet Forrest that Bourbon had treated with venom long before (Bell 1979, 2000; Romesburg 2000; Wright and Forrest 1999). Bourbon, devastated by these betrayals, on some level understood them. Faced with allegiance to Rae when it meant exposing their own interdependencies with and vulnerabilities to the forces of normativity, nationalism, and the market, most opted for invisibility and passivity. M. Jacqui Alexander suggests that the "meeting place that collapses the enemy, the terrorist, and the sexual pervert is the very one that secures the loyal heterosexual citizen patriot." This place, an orientation within an interchange of interpersonal relationships, cosmopolitan performance, and the state, clarifies borders, boundaries, and belonging. To navigate, Rae reoriented constantly to new contexts upon which the relationships needed for viability and mobility were conditioned (Alexander 2005: 239).

Perhaps the queerest kinship Bourbon sought to establish was with the U.S. government. Where others made patriotic public stances and associations that allowed cover for transgressive personal lives (paging Roy Cohn and Liberace), Rae lived an openly queer transgender life while seeking private alignment with the nation-state. In September 1960, after reading in newspapers about the Soviet defection of U.S. National Security Agency employees William Martin and Bernon Mitchell, Bourbon contacted the FBI, apparently out of patriotism. Rae explained to agents, who viewed the performer as a "notorious female impersonator," that Martin and Mitchell were homosexuals who had attended a Washington, D.C. party thrown by a mutual friend in the honor of Bourbon (Department of the Army 1960; FBI 1961–62).[8]

The agents turned to the matter of Rae's sex. Bourbon claimed having undergone a "Christine Jorgensen operation," and the report notes that "BOURBON laughingly stated his reason ... that he had wanted to save his own life." (Bourbon said it was cancer related.) "Since the operation," it explains, "he has billed himself as RAE BOURBON since actually is now bi-sexual" (male and female). Agents insisted that Bourbon identify "other perverts" in government employ. Rae demurred and refused to meet the agents in person, but continued to phone them for a year. Someone shot the entertainer's windshield, and Bourbon feared an attempted assassination, perhaps by Soviets. The FBI did nothing to aid Bourbon for informing.

Rae had never fit into Americanist gender/sex/sexuality molds either publicly or privately, but by the early 1960s this was truer than ever. Bourbon rejected Cold War cultural logic that presumed a linkage between gender/sex normativity, heterosexuality, and Americanism. Still, Rae believed that communism and the Soviets represented enough of a threat that FBI association was worth risking greater official surveillance by the same legal and administrative system that sought to squash homosexuality and stifle gender diversity in the U.S., at its borders, and beyond.[9] Fear of communist reprisal was the most recent explanation for victimization in a life of being done wrong and let down by intimacies, ranging from the interpersonal to the transnational, that were supposed to provide sustenance and security. By the early 1960s, Rae was turning 70. Bourbon had not regularly made a decent income since touring with Mae West in the 1940s, and had increasingly faced arrest and harassment as a homosexual and/or transsexual performer. Little wonder, then, that Bourbon yearned for freedom, some way to move beyond all of the ugly forces constraining material viability, meaningful embodiment, and intimate belonging on society's margins.

## CONCLUSION: TRANSGENDER TALENTS AND THE LIMITS OF FREEDOM

Rae believed that holding together everything that made up livability through transgender cosmopolitan citizenship, from transborder discourses to transtextuality and queer kinships, relied on talent as the fuel that enabled movement across space and time. In the memoir, Bourbon writes, "Talent is the most requisite of all accoutrements One may possess. Your looks are Nothing. Your background is nothing. Your experience is nothing. If you have TALENT, all else fades into Oblivion.... With me it is not guess work.... I have been in Show-Business over FIFTY-Years" (Bourbon c. 1969–71). Harnessing that talent required a lot of work, discipline, and faith.

Bourbon underscored requisite effort and self-control. While others commented on Rae's heavy drinking and an onstage impulsivity that could work against occupational prosperity and security, Bourbon's self-characterization was sober, contemplative, and striving (Bourbon c. 1969–71; Romesburg 2000; Wright and Forrest 1999). Bourbon did not always actualize this, but it reflected what the performer believed was necessary to stay in the game. "Getting to the top in any Profession is an unceasing Struggle; but in Show Business it is even More so," Rae writes in the memoir. "The Competition is unbelievable, the Envy, Deceit, Treachery, and underhanded tricks innumerable. ... Once you have reached the Top, it is twice as hard to Stay There." Being exceptional was not enough, nor was attainment; one had to ceaselessly reenact greatness, watching one's back and adapting. Bourbon's "rules to live by" set out a host of dictums of withholding as self-preservation, such as "Never let People know what you know; if so, then they know twice as much as You—What they know, plus what you know," and, "Never become overly familiar with people; else they may become so with you." Rae relied more and more on "the babies," dozens of stray dogs and cats hauled around in a trailer from town to town, to supply the unconditional affection otherwise lacking. For all of Rae's interdependencies, intimacy with other people was hard to secure.

All of the struggle and loneliness involved in transforming talent into a trade was worth it, though, because the rewards, beyond transgender livability and longevity, were moments of freedom. Sometimes performance allowed for the sublime. Rae could be carried away, spiritually, to a kind of connectivity beyond material embodiment. At times, this could feel liberating, affirming existence in a way that other maneuvers of transgender cosmopolitan citizenship could not. When others truly saw the performer's talent, Rae felt it supplied a deeper, more freeing recognition, one of the few Bourbon could trust as real.

Bourbon believed talent was god-given. One turned away from it to their own detriment, a manifestation of the "Spiritual Blindness of Man that limits Man." In 1929, destitute and sick with jaundice, Rae had discovered Christian Science through a practitioner's office in the transient vice district of downtown Los Angeles. It was transformative and revelatory. Over the years, Rae corresponded with a handful of women, Christian Science practitioners, who pulled the performer back from "false beliefs" and into a "healing" faith. "We are what we think," Bourbon wrote a friend in one letter from jail. Spirituality gave Rae connectivity for the journey and a way to "deny All that" Rae did not "want expressed in the Body" (Bourbon 1970b).

Revelatory talent could also be unnerving, a reminder of the lack and struggle of life. In a Chicago nightclub in 1931, while singing "You're a Million Miles from Nowhere (When You're One Little Mile from Home)," Bourbon recalls, "I forgot ME, I forgot the Club." Awakened from the state by thunderous applause, Rae was shaken. "There always seems to be one song in every Singers Life, that when they do it they come apart," Bourbon writes. Rae never did the number again (Bourbon c. 1969–71). More than exilic trauma, it was an accidental unveiling of the dependency that said too much.

In the end, Bourbon was caught up in a murder of a Texan pet boarder who, after lack of payment, sold Rae's babies to a laboratory to be used in medical experiments. In the trial, Rae's Texan roots and patriotic anticommunism were downplayed as prosecutors made this queer, racially, and sexually liminal figure into a dangerously mobile drifter and interloping outsider. Tried as a man, Bourbon's gifts for impersonation and transtextuality were recast as capacities for willful deception, pathologies of sexual and gender deviance, and signs of social and economic desperation. Rae's maternal love of pets morphed into a sociopathic, effeminate preference for animals over humans. After a quick deliberation, the jury handed Bourbon a life sentence. Within about a year, on July 20, 1971, Rae died alone under confinement in a small-town Texan hospital.[10] The tools that had sustained a long transgender existence became the means through which to impose brutal immanence.

To what extent should the end of this life come to bear on the rest of it? Literary critic Scott Long suggests that a camp stance exposes "a society that presumes to know what is serious and what is not" as "explicitly inadequate." The loneliness of this position comes from its limits to transform perception more broadly. Camp can only occupy something like a terrorist's status, conducting intermittent raids on the authoritative centers of ignorance" against "a giant backdrop of defeat" (Long 1993: 79, 89–90). Framing Bourbon's life through the final act obscures remarkable resiliency and innovativeness over many decades within structures and systems inadequate to his/her existence. Still, to ignore the end is to elide the real stakes involved. Marcia Ochoa describes how Venezuelan *transformistas,* often street-walking trans sex workers, engage in a self-fashioning through eyebrow plucking, wardrobe, demeanor, and hormonal self-medication that, "without asking permission," allow them to emerge into being through a perversely precarious citizenship. "People who are not subjects of rights are regularly subject to violations of their integrity as human beings and as citizens," she explains, noting that the *transformistas'* innovation and resiliency do not preclude regular disappearing by police and other forms of violence (Ochoa 2008: 149, 155). Bourbon faced similar indignities, often by transforming them into comedy, shaming and maneuvering around officials. The final arrest changed all that. Rae experienced trauma that could not be recontextualized, stripped of the performative privilege on which claims to transgender cosmopolitan citizenship relied. "I didn't know anything like this could happen in the United States," Rae wrote a friend. "I'd read of such things, but NOW, I was going thru it. The tenor, the horror, the face slappings I look. Dear, Dear God. Even to think of it Now the Horror has not lessened one bit" (Bourbon 1970c).

Faced with a precarious existence, Bourbon transformed talent into a long life through transborder discourses, claims of transgender cosmopolitan citizenship, and tenuous but valuable queer kinships. It was a self-fashioning that reiterated a right to personal autonomy and mobility even as it expressed interpersonal, material, performative, and sociopolitical interdependency. But, while performing privilege and entitlement may be like rights, it is not the same as having them. Or freedom. Collaborating with global capital circuits and nation-state paradigms was as obligatory as it was contradictory to Rae's transgression of them. Bourbon never sought to overturn those powerful forces that largely foreclosed upon viability—how, exactly, would that have worked? The spaces Rae was compelled to occupy were not designed to sustain that life.

In closing, a final flight of fancy: Bourbon's maneuvers resonate with Chela Sandoval's methodologies of the oppressed that center on the differential movement of U.S. third world women of color. Rae's uses of transborder, transhistorical camp deconstructed and decolonized signs of culture to create space for multiple possibilities of new consciousness. Claims of imperial privilege and lowbrow democratics appropriated dominant and subcultural forms in potentially transformative ways. Like Sandoval's differential movement, Bourbon's shifting between modes underscore the yearnings for freedom. Rae's persistent mobility calls upon us to recognize one mode of viability for the oppositional citizen-subject. Bourbon's life story gives us, to paraphrase Sandoval, the presence of an obtuse third meaning that shimmers behind all we think we know (Sandoval 2000: 146). The only predictable outcome is transformation itself, and here Bourbon shines. How might Rae's strategies have been different in a world that embraced him/her as a person worthy of support and sustenance? In our neoliberal present, we are encouraged to believe that talent, wealth, celebrity, faith, patriotism, connectivity, and easy transnational movement can protect us from displacements and violence. This old queen might just be a tour guide for us all.

## ACKNOWLEDGEMENTS

I am indebted to Trystan Cotten, Susan Stryker, Julian Carter, Corrie Decker, and Randy Riddle, as well as attendees of presentations in the Sonoma State University Gendered Intersections and University of California, Davis Women and Gender Studies speaker series.

## NOTES

1. On sources and method: Prosser (1998) argues for the primacy of self-authorization in transsexual narratives, but as Halberstam (2005) notes, establishing the archive upon which to base it is challenging for transgender subjects living complex lives that render them unable to provide a coherent narrative. While Bourbon left behind ship manifests, arrest records, court documents, print, sound, and motion picture media, personal letters, performances, and even a half-finished jailhouse memoir, it's not clear how to grant authority. Bourbon used sources to multiple effects: arrest images became publicity stills and the memoir became a front-page story in the *Big Springs Daily Herald* in 1971. Because Bourbon's spotlight-seeking relied on camp's double entendres and unfixed meanings, reading too much earnestness into self-authorized sources would be a disservice. I cross-checked what could be factually ascertained. To get at structures of affect and enabling strategies of self-presentation, I rely on an eccentric subcultural archive of feelings (Cvetkovich 2003), foregrounding Bourbon's performances and personal writings while attentive to more formal historical records and oral histories.
2. For documentation on the various accountings of Bourbon's birth, see Romesburg (2000).
3. [...]
4. Evidence makes some of Bourbon's claims plausible. Ship manifestos prove travel to and from London around the time of the purported performance before the king (*City of Hamburg* 1936; S.S. *Lancastria* 1936).
5. In the 1930s, several lavish whorehouses in Mexican border towns that served mostly U.S. patrons were named "Molino Rojo" (Ruiz 1998: 55).
6. Films in which Bourbon claimed to appear: *Behind the Door* (Famous Players-Lasky/Paramount, 1919); *The Four Horsemen of the Apocalypse* (Metro, 1921); *The Sheik* (Paramount, 1921); *The Young Rajah* (Paramount, 1922); *Blood and Sand* (Paramount, 1922); *Beyond the Rocks* (Paramount, 1922); *Manslaughter* (Paramount, 1922); *Bella Donna* (Famous Players-Lasky/Paramount, 1923); *The Ten Commandments* (Famous Players-Lasky/Paramount, 1923); *Son of Sheik* (United Artists, 1926); *The Volga Boatman* (DeMille Productions/Producers Distributors Corp., 1926); *Gold Diggers of 1937* (Warner Brothers, 1936); *The Hurricane* (United Artists/Samuel Goldwyn, 1937).
7. For sample syndicated column mentions, see Kilgallen (1955); Sullivan (1946); Winchell (1943, 1968).
8. On dubious claims about Martin's and Mitchell's homosexuality see Johnson (2004: 144–46).
9. In the memoir, Rae rants about communism in acting schools and claims having seen it in England, Europe, Africa, Mexico, and the U.S. "COMMUNISM IS A DISEASE," Rae writes (Bourbon c. 1969–71).
10. For trial analyses, see Romesburg (2000, 2007).

# 38

# *The Romance of the Amazing Scalpel*

## "Race," Labor, and Affect in Thai Gender Reassignment Clinics

AREN Z. AIZURA

IN THIS CHAPTER EXCERPTED FROM THE BOOK *QUEER BANKOK*, Aizura, an Australian cultural studies scholar now working in the U.S., offers an ethnographic account of travel to gender reassignment clinics in Thailand. Alongside Iran and Trinidad, Colorado, Thailand is often said to be the global "Mecca" of gender reassignment surgery. Aizura interviews both Thai and non-Thai trans women, surgeons, and clinic staff to reveal the political and racial economies of gender reassignment clinics. Beginning with a paradox of affect—white trans women report feeling very well cared for, while Thai and Vietnamese informants report feeling isolated and neglected—the chapter blends theories of orientalism and self-orientalism, affective labor and biopolitical subjectivity to argue that the uneven distribution of care is a signal of the neoliberal privatization of transnational medical tourism. Within that framework, white trans women are able to access a transformative understanding of their surgery experience. This happens through identification with the perceived "grace" and "beauty" of Thai feminine gender norms, embodied in the affective labor of their Thai female carers. Weaving post-autonomist Marxian theory, trans theory and detailed descriptions of everyday interactions in GRS clinics, Aizura's work calls for more "cross border solidarity" to combat the structural inequalities of health care that nourish such micropolitical and interpersonal power relations.

## WE ALL PAY THE SAME PRICE

The clinic is a pink and white four-story villa on the main highway through Chonburi, a provincial city on the eastern gulf coast of Thailand, one hour's drive from Bangkok.[1] A cosmetic surgery clinic for trans people seeking surgical feminization, it is one of the town's most impressive buildings.[2] The highway is a smog-filled, eight-lane span crossable only by pedestrian overpass. In this chaotic landscape, the clinic radiates an unlikely seeming serenity. Inside, patients relax in the air conditioning and check their email on the wifi network. After undergoing facial feminization surgery, breast augmentation, or, the most complex procedure, genital vaginoplasty, at a private hospital in Chonburi, patients use this clinic not only for consultations with nurses and the surgeon, but also as a lounge or a salon. A number of Thai attendants wait on the patients. Some are nurses, some are administrative assistants, and some are present to fulfill requests for cushions, water, or entertainment, or to provide for less tangible needs such as reassurance or affection.

The non-Thai trans women I spoke with who obtained surgery at this particular clinic described it as a very welcoming place.[3] Although the surgeon's technique is said to be outstanding, patients reported that they do not pay for his surgical skill in creating sensate vaginas and clitorises as much as for the entire "care package". This care package comprises full service from the women one is met at Bangkok airport through lengthy hospital and hotel stays. It ends when a patient gets on a plane to return home, wherever that may be. The service, numerous patients told me, is second to none—even by the high, tourist-targeted medical standards of Thailand. "We provide the Rolls-Royce treatment here," a clinic manager told me.[4] *see Tau + Med.*

This clinic is one of seven or eight gender reassignment clinics in Thailand that service an overwhelmingly foreign clientele. Over the past ten years, gender reassignment surgery or GRS, has become a very profitable procedure for Thai reconstructive surgeons.[5] Thailand is now known by many as one of the premier sites worldwide to obtain vaginoplasty and other cosmetic surgeries; indeed, many surgeons advertise that Bangkok is the "Mecca" of transsexual body modification.[6] While at least one surgeon in Bangkok specializes in masculinizing surgeries for female-to-male transsexuals or trans men, most surgeons performing gender reassignment surgeries in Thailand cater to trans women—that is, persons assigned male gender at birth who now live as women. These clinics see hundreds of patients per year, mainly from overseas.[7] Most clinics, such as the Preecha Aesthetic Institute at Piyawate Hospital in Bangkok, are housed within private hospitals with similarly large proportions of non-Thai patients. These clinics provide one of a range of medical services offered to foreign visitors to Thailand, now an international center for "medical travel", or "medical tourism." They constitute a destination for many people globally who cannot, or who choose not to, access gender reassignment surgeries close to where they reside.

To gain a reputation for managing surgery candidates well involves careful attention to patient care. During major surgery, a process that involves a considerable and prolonged experience of pain, the practice of care demands, above all, attention to a patient's comfort. To offer comfort, of course, is distinct from the state of being "comfortable": One does not guarantee the other. Neither is comfort merely a state that pertains to the corporeal. It registers an affective disposition, and so does its opposite, discomfort. Comfort eases one's passage as one moves through the world. However, if there is difficulty in moving, one may experience discomfort. "If whiteness allows bodies to move with comfort through space," Sara Ahmed writes, "and to inhabit the world as if it were home, then these bodies take up more space. Such physical motility becomes the grounds for social mobility" (2000, 136).

To attend critically to the minute differentiations between comfort and discomfort within the gender clinic I describe above, then, might unfold into more than the mere narration of individual affects. Not all of the trans women I interviewed professed to feel comfortable there. Som, for example, told of difficulty with the aftercare procedures associated with her vaginoplasty, and also of feeling that she could not expect the same service as would be proffered to non-Thai, or white, patients. Som is Thai and grew up in the poor rural north of Thailand. She moved from her village as a teenager, first to Chiang Mai to study and then to Bangkok for work.[8] She met an Australian who became her boyfriend on www.thailadyboy.com, a *kathoey* dating site, and he encouraged her to migrate to Australia to live with him. He also paid for her gender reassignment surgeries at the clinic described above. During our interview, she initially said that her experience of surgery had been excellent. During recovery, she said, she felt like a "princess". Later, we began to discuss the fact that 95 percent of her surgeon's patients are non-Thai, the majority of them affluent American, British, or European trans women. Thailand is famous for its large population of *sao praphet sorng* ("second type of women"), or *kathoey,* male-to-female gender-variant people.[9] It seemed remarkable that non-Thais constituted the overwhelming majority of patients undergoing GRS at the most well-known

498 AREN Z. AIZURA

clinics. As Som commented on this, she revised her previous narrative about the level of care at the clinic she had attended:

A. A.:    When I talked to Dr. ____, he said that most of his patients are farangs [foreigners], some from Japan, some from Europe, America, Australia. But not many Thais.

Som:    Because he is very expensive! He put his prices up!

A. A.:    Many of them put their prices up, I heard. Also Dr. ____?

Som:    Dr. ____, I didn't like. He doesn't even care about the Thais.

A. A.:    What surgeons do Thai kathoey or ladyboys go to?

Som:    Well, they can do [surgery] in a public hospital, which is quite a reasonable price, and the result might not be ... not so good. And sometimes I hear from Thai ladyboys and some people, they said that in photos, it looks weird, it's not the same as ... [Gesturing to herself]

A. A.:    Not the same as your surgery?

Som:    No. It looked terrible. Indeed.

A. A.:    What do you think about this, that the best [clinics] seem to be for farangs [foreigners], and some surgeons don't seem to care about Thais?

Som:    Dr. ____'s staff [at the clinic] too. When I come to meet them, they will be very nice to foreigners. But they forget about Thais. ... Because they think foreigners have lots of money, more than Thai. But we all pay the same price! So, we should deserve to have the same service. But we don't have the right to say that.[10]

Another patient, Emma, is Vietnamese and had been living in Australia for twelve years when she had gender reassignment surgery in Bangkok in 2006. She travelled to Thailand from Australia and stayed in one of Bangkok's premier medical-tourism hospitals, having surgery with the one of most well-known surgeons practicing GRS in Bangkok. Emma was travelling without a support person. By the time I met her, during her recovery from surgery, she had decided that coming to Thailand was a bad idea. She said she would advise trans people in Australia to obtain surgery with Australian surgeons:

Dr. ____ is very busy and it's very difficult to get him to come to see me. I am very annoyed. Also, the nurses do not come to see me. I ring and it takes half an hour for them to come . . . I didn't bring anyone with me to take care of me after the operation. They told me on the phone that the nurses would take care of me, but where are the nurses?[11]

To place these comments in context, the majority of Australian trans women involved in my project were scathing about Australian surgeons' technique. Most agreed that the hospital care available in Thailand far surpassed that available even in Australian private hospitals. Karen, a white trans woman living in Brisbane, Australia, who obtained GRS in an equally well-resourced hospital in Phuket, commented that the hospital felt more like a hotel. "[There were] heaps of nurses, everybody always had lots of time . . . You could ask for something and five minutes later it was in the room."[12] Som's and Emma's stories did not match the overwhelmingly positive narratives I heard from white Americans, Britons, and Australians who attended the same clinics at the same time and underwent the same procedures and who were apparently paying for the same service.

Ahmed appends the lines cited above on comfort and whiteness with a cautionary caveat. "This extension of white motility should not be confused with freedom. To move easily is not [necessarily] to move freely" (2000, 136). It is clear that even white-skinned or affluent gender-variant subjects are not guaranteed freedom. Across the globe, gender reassignment technologies such as hormones and surgery are notoriously difficult for gender-variant people to access. With few exceptions, most governments refuse to cover gender reassignment under public health funding (Lombardi 2007; Namaste 2000). Private health insurance corporations are equally reluctant to cover what is regarded as "elective" treatment (Butler 2006; Gorton 2006). If the provision of gender reassignment surgery began in Thailand as a market serving the large number of local *kathoeys,* over the past ten years it has transformed into a niche medical-tourism market targeted to well-off citizens of affluent nations. Yet the fact that gender reassignment surgery is big business in Thailand does not account for why, in a clinic that is reputed to provide the best care and clearly has the capacity to do so, Som felt that the staff cared more about foreigners than Thais. Neither does it account for why Emma articulated that her needs were not valued. It is dangerous to generalize a distinct frame of experience from two personal accounts, and this is not my intention. Nevertheless, these stories highlight a number of critical questions. Even when gender reassignment technologies are freely available to anyone who can meet the financial cost, which gender-variant bodies carry more value than others? Within the growing globalization of biomedicine along neoliberal lines, which racialized subjects constitute the ideal to whom the labors of care and respect are made available, and which subjects fall outside of that sphere of care and respect?

In the first part of this chapter, I argue that Thai gender reassignment surgery must be theorized as a market, embedded in the historical and economic context of its local development. Next, I investigate how Thai tourist-marketing strategies are always already inflected by a Euro-American, orientalist discourse, wherein Thailand is imagined as the ultimate space of exotic transformation and the fulfillment of desire across multiple sites. In marketing tourism, this becomes a self-orientalizing strategy. Discussing the strategies GRS clinics use to market their services, I suggest that a similar dynamic is at play. I then turn to non-Thai trans women's accounts of GRS in Thailand to highlight the pervasive sense that being present in Thailand somehow facilitates the experience of psychic transformation towards femininity for non-Thai trans women. I ask, what about this sense of transformation specifically comes to bear for *non-Thai* trans women? Finally, I argue that to answer the question of the value of racialized bodies sufficiently, we need to understand the affective labors expended at Thai gender reassignment clinics. The care, the nurturing, and the transmission of affect to non-Thai trans women patients fulfills a medical function *and* facilitates the self-transformation of those patients into more feminine-"feeling" subjects. Affect can be defined as "bodily capacities to affect and be affected or the augmentation or diminution of a body's capacity to act, engage, and to connect" (Clough 2007, 2). Affective labour here registers as both "emotional" work (Hochschild 2003) and as a form of biopolitical production, wherein particular practices reproduce the discursive effects of particular forms of subjectivity.

Before moving on, a few words are in order grounding this chapter geographically and in relationship to queer and gender-variant travel criticism. Thailand is currently undergoing a boom in urban queer sexual cultures in the context of a continuing market in queer tourism. Scholarship on the transnational gendered or sexual dimensions of Thai tourism and migration most often explores tourist involvement in the Thai sex-work economy (McCamish 1999). Aside from some mainstream media coverage, Thailand's gender reassignment tourist market has received little critical attention. Although gender-variant tourism needs to be understood as a distinct (if related) geographical and political circuit, queer tourism offers some useful conceptual tools. Queer tourism, Jasbir Puar notes (2002), is the most visible form of sexual or gendered transnational circulation. However, Puar cautions that queer tourism discourses most often privilege white, middle-class, and affluent queer-tourist practices while relegating the specter of the (non-white) other to the status of the desired object, encouraging and reproducing "colonial constructions of tourism as a travel adventure into uncharted laden with the possibility of taboo sexual encounters, illicit seductions, and dangerous liaisons" (2002, 113). This reminder provokes us to remain alert to the (neo)colonial constructions floating beneath many tourist discourages.

Theorizing trans or gender-variant tourist circuits must take into account the fact that within Euro-American gender-variant discourse, the trope of a "journey" is almost ubiquitous as a metaphor to narrate transsexual transformation from man into woman or vice versa in autobiographies, films (such as *Transamerica*) and novels (Prosser 1999; King 2001). According to Prosser, the "desire to perceive a progressive pattern of becoming underlies the pervasive metaphors of journeying or voyaging in [transsexual] autobiographies" (1999, 91). The trans journey metaphor often encodes within it dominant understandings of East, West home, and elsewhere. In tracing those encodings, we need to draw attention to how flows of global capital intersect with the broad range of gender reassignment technologies (O'Brien 2003). But just as global capital flows in inconsistent transnational trajectories, gender reassignment practices and technologies are equally diverse, inconsistent, and geographically dispersed. Deciphering the complexities of how neoliberal capitalism intersects with gender-variant practices and identities cannot proceed effectively without analysis of the geocultural trajectories of those practices.

These critical frameworks informed my research methods. During clinic observation sessions in Thailand, I would often speak with the patients present, as well as surgeons and staff. This enlarged the fields of GRS candidate interviewee subjects to include people from many different regions globally, I also investigated access to surgical modification for Thais—particularly *kathoeys*, but also *toms,* or trans masculine people.[13] Surgeons performing GRS for a Thai clientele do not tend to advertise as widely on-line or in English, and possibilities for Thais to afford gender reassignment surgery are limited. It is crucial to bring the reader's awareness of these inequities into contact with an analysis of the "Rolls-Royce treatment" in the most luxurious clinics. While Rolls-Royce clinics are a small niche with a much larger local market, their operation nonetheless still warrants analysis.

## GENDER REASSIGNMENT TECHNOLOGIES AND MEDICAL TOURISM IN THAILAND

Within the context of Euro-American theorizations of trans body modification, it is impossible to imagine surgical procedures taking place entirely outside the history of the medicalization of gender variance as gender dysphoria or gender identity disorder. It is equally impossible to imagine surgeries not mediated by psychiatric frameworks governing the categories of gender identity "disorders" (GID), which in turn have determined who is eligible for diagnosis with GID and thus who may access surgeries. Across Europe, North America, Australia, and New Zealand (and increasingly in other regions), most surgeons require surgical candidates to conform to the World Professional Association for Transgender Health (WPATH) Standards of Care. Access to gender reassignment surgeries in Thailand differs from this broadly Euro-American context of medicalization in a number of ways. Despite a history of Thai scholars importing Euro-American psychological arguments against homosexuality and gender variance and deploying them in local research (Jackson 1997a; Jackson and Sullivan 1999, 10–11), gender reassignment is not regarded by most Thai specialists as necessarily requiring psychiatric evaluation. Neither are *kathoey* or *tom* desires for GRS universally understood within a medicalized discourse of transsexuality. *Kathoey* as a category is far more fluid and covers a wider range of cross-gender practices than the English-language category "transsexual". *Kathoey* is sometimes understood as a "third sex" and has been used in the past to refer to effeminate homosexual men as well as those assigned male at birth who feel like, or want to be, women (Jackson 1997b, 170). *Kathoeys,* or *sao praphet sorng,* are not defined within Thai culture by their desires to have gender reassignment surgery, but rather by their feminine behavior. Many begin taking feminizing hormones in adolescence and, by adulthood, may have been living as feminine persons for years. In this cultural context, psychiatric evaluation is regarded as unnecessary. "Patients in Thailand see the plastic surgeon first, not the psychiatrist, because to them, they are normal people," Dr. Preecha Tiewtranon, the surgeon whose clinic is noted above, explained in a 2006 interview. He added, "[They say], 'Psychiatrists are for insane crazy people. I am not insane!'"[15]

The state-subsidized GRS program at Chulalongkorn University Hospital in Bangkok requires Thai GRS candidates to be assessed for gender identity disorder, but this particular program operates on only around thirty patients per year. However, anecdotally it seems that only around 30 percent of *kathoey* desire vaginoplasty.[16] In a study conducted by Nantiya Sukontapatipark on *kathoey/sao praphet sorng* subjectivity only eight of twenty informants had had genital reassignment surgery (Nantiya 2005, 99). In fact, *kathoey* are far more likely to seek "aesthetic" surgical procedures such as rhinoplasty, breast augmentation, eyelid surgery, and silicon injections before full genital reassignment. "Improving" physical appearance through aesthetic surgery is seen as fashionable and desirable for *kathoey* generally.

Non-medicalization, and the greater emphasis placed on *kathoey* beauty, rather than the importance of "female" genitals, have both helped transform gender reassignment surgery services in Thailand into a large, unregulated, and highly commodified industry. This industry operates within an equally sprawling, unregulated, and commodified local cosmetic surgery industry. For this reason, and to contextualize this local industry in relation to the more recent development of a tourist-oriented gender reassignment surgery market, I want briefly to outline the history of gender reassignment surgery in Thailand.

In the late 1970s, Dr. Preecha Tiewtranon, who was then established as a reconstructive surgery specialist in Bangkok, trained himself in vaginoplasty technique. Dr. Preecha trained younger surgeons in this technique, many of whom subsequently established private clinics.[17] As well, what are known as "shophouses" sprang up. Shophouses are cheaper private clinics run by surgeons, who will often rent rooms in private hospitals to perform surgery.

In the mid-1990s, non-Thais began travelling to Thailand in larger numbers to seek GRS. A Thai surgeon quoted by Nantiya attributes this to the large number of *kathoeys* who obtained GRS and then migrated to Europe and North America. Others observe that the explosion of (largely English-language) Internet trans culture in the mid-1990s enabled Thai surgeons to advertise more broadly and led to a sharp increase in the number of non-Thais seeking GRS there. Non-Thai trans women began to travel in Thailand in large numbers to obtain GRS. A small number of surgeons gained reputations outside Thailand and began to attract a large non-Thai customer base. For example, Dr. Suporn Watanyasakul performed twenty to thirty GRS procedures in 1996, mainly on Thai patients. By 2006, he had expanded his operation and was operating on around 220 patients per year.[18] These patients were almost exclusively non-Thai, coming from Europe, North America, and other locales outside Asia. The explosion of popularity of Thai gender reassignment surgeons among non-Thais has pushed up prices for gender reassignment surgery and enabled its rebranding as a luxury service rather than a budget option. One clinic catering mainly to non-Thais raised the price for vaginoplasty from US$2,000 in 2001 to US$15,000 in 2006.[19] Other surgeons followed suit. While even US$2,000 is expensive by Thai standards, the higher prices mean that only very affluent Thais can now afford surgeries with the five or six surgeons with international reputations. Clinic web sites now constitute the main marketing tool to gain non-Thai customers and offer comprehensive information, usually in English, about every aspect of a GRS trip. In seeking recognition as an elite and globally competitive cohort of biomedical specialists, Thai gender reassignment surgeons must also present an image indicating that they comply with internationally recognized standards. Most surgeons who cater to a non-Thai customer base also now require patients to supply evidence of psychiatric assessment and a "Real Life Experience" in line with the WPATH Standards of Care.

## TOURISTIC ORIENTALISM AND FEMININE TRANSFORMATIONS

I turn now to a consideration of specific discourses pervading Thai tourist marketing strategies, and GRS marketing strategies in particular. Although one could argue that gender reassignment surgery candidates visiting Thailand for medical reasons are not tourists, the trans women I interviewed certainly participated in tourist activities. As a popular late twentieth-century tourist destination, Thailand had accrued a particularly dense field of the "conflicted and compulsively repetitious stereotypy" that constitutes Orientalist discourse (Morris 1997, 61). Thailand often figures in this discourse as a space of magic, exotic transformation, and the fulfillment of (Western) desire. Rosalind Morris points to the fantasy of Thailand as a "place of beautiful order and orderly beauty" and simultaneously a place wherein anything goes, whose spaces and people are "responsive to all desires" (1997, 61). This fantasy is always racialized and gendered, often iconized in the image of the responsive Thai woman and, according to Morris, the *kathoey.*[22] Here we witness the production of "ideal" feminine gender through an exoticization of otherness that simultaneously facilitates a moment of self-transformation for the Euro-American subject. Hamilton remarks that this "libidinization" of Thailand is so familiar that it repeats itself in *farang* discourse everywhere (1997, 145).

Thai tourist marketing strategies reflect this libidinization, even in nonsexual arenas, where the promise to the tourist focuses on health. A Tourism Authority of Thailand article promoting health tourism expounds upon Thailand's "traditional" assets thus:

> The Kingdom's legendary tradition of superior service and gracious hospitality is working its magic in a new sector. ... Patients are welcomed as 'guests' and made to feel at home in unfamiliar surroundings. The reception is gracious and courteous. Medical staff consistently provide superior service, often surpassing expectations.
>
> Spa operators likewise report that guests are charmed by the traditional 'wai'—a courteous greeting gesture that conveys profound respect, infinite warmth, hospitality and friendliness. The 'wai' is perceived by visitors to be uniquely and distinctively Thai. The magic is taking hold.[23]

Infinite warmth, magic, grace, and courtesy: all are stereotypically feminine traits. Even if Thai workers meant to embody such attributes are not female and the intended visiting recipients of Thai warmth or grace are not male, this language instantiates a sexualized and racialized economy within the touristic exchange. It comprises part of a strategy I call self-orientalizing, following Aihwa Ong. For Ong, self-orientalization accounts for the fact that "Asian voices are unavoidably inflected by orientalist essentialism that infiltrate all kinds of public exchanges about culture" (1999, 81). Self-orientalization involves the performance of the stereotype of an ethnicity or a nationality to be recognized by the cultural edifice in which the stereotype originates. By framing the Thai medical-tourism experience as particularly beneficial because of Thai rituals and traditions, the marketing language narrates the stereotype of a Thailand freed from the realities of Bangkok smog, traffic, and political instability.[24] Numerous instances of this strategy can be found in generalized tourist marketing, but, as the example above illustrates, it is particularly apparent in health and medical tourism.

Marketing strategies used by Thai gender reassignment clinics follow a similar pattern. When I was interviewing surgeons in Thailand, I found that most were keen to emphasize Thailand's liberal attitudes towards gender variance in comparison with the West. When asked what makes Thailand such a popular place for GRS, for example, Dr. Preecha said, "Thailand is a very open and tolerant society ... There is no Thai law against the operation."[25] Dr. Sanguan Kunaporn, a surgeon who runs Phuket Plastic Surgery and, with Dr. Suporn, is considered by many non-Thai trans women as among the best, explained to me that gender reassignment is a successful industry in Thailand because of surgical technique and the competitive price. He added:

> [Also] the hospitality of the people, not only the staff in the hospital but also the Thai people. Very friendly and welcoming! Compromise, high tolerance. I found that a lot of patients of mine say that

this is the place they would like to live, if they could choose this. Not only in the hospital, but also in the country. They feel safe here when they're walking, or shopping.[26]

We might, however, take these positive interpretations with a grain of salt. Most of the *kathoeys* and *sao prophet sorng* I have spoken with in Thailand describe the difficulties of gender-variant daily life in detail. In fact, many see the "West" as having a far more liberal and "open-minded" culture than Thailand. Homosexual and gender-variant people are not overtly discriminated against in Thai law, and *kathoey* are certainly more visible in Thailand than in North America, Europe, Australia, or New Zealand. Although it may be true that young gender-variant Thais are accepted by family and society without the violence, disavowal, and shame that characterize transphobic Euro-American responses to gender variance, stigma still attaches gender variance in many parts of Thai society. Forms of discrimination against gender-variant people and same-sex relationships do exist (Jackson 1999a, 2003a). In the same manner that ordinary tourists are encouraged to understand Thai culture generally as tunelessly friendly and responsive, Dr. Sanguan's discursive production of Thai culture as universally tolerant of gender-variant subjects seems intended to resonate with potential clients— who are coded implicitly as non-Thai.

A brief survey of graphic representations on GRS clinic web sites offers other examples of self-orientalization in the context of marketing. As noted above, web sites, along with word-of-mouth, constitute the main marketing strategy for Thai GRS surgeons. Here, an explicit connection is made between the "traditional" beauty of feminine Thai bodies and the promises of self-transformation through feminizing surgical procedures. The Phuket Plastic Surgery Clinic web site banner features the face of a smiling, beautiful Thai woman on a background of white orchids, along with a slide show of landscape photographs.[27] The section of Hygeia Beauty's web site concerned with GRS features three glamour shots of equally beautiful women who might be read as *kathoey,* all with long, coiffed hair, evening dresses, and flawless makeup in the style of the "feminine realness" genre of *kathoey* beauty pageants.[28] That the images of bodies represented here are non-trans women or *kathoeys* is not as relevant as how they might be read by prospective customers. The images associate ultra-femininity, the destination (Thailand), and surgical transformation in a promise to the non-Thai browsing trans woman that having GRS in Thailand will not only facilitate her transformation into full womanhood but will also transform her into a *more beautiful* woman.

It is salient to note here that what is now regarded as "traditional" feminine beauty in Thailand emerged relatively recently in historical terms. Recalling Annette Hamilton's remarks on the libidinization of Thailand as it is represented by Thai women characters in English-language expatriate novels, we could read the laughing Thai women on clinic web sites as standing in metonymically for Thailand, as both objects of desire for non-Thai trans women, and the potential vehicle of their own somatic self-transformation. The key difference is between desire and identification. In the novels Hamilton critiques the exchange is a heterosexual relationship. Here, the exchange is about the non-Thai subject's own feminization—both somatically and, perhaps, psychically. This association between travelling to Thailand and self-transformation was reflected back by many non-Thai trans women themselves. Although most were conscious of Thailand's urbanized modernity, many talked about their experiences in Thailand as radically distinct from their daily lives at home. Karen, the Australian trans woman referred to above, described travelling to Thailand as "a magical experience." Other participants commented that, aside from the novel techniques of Thai surgeons, having GRS in Thailand, this "magical" place, was precisely what marked their surgical experiences as a special rite of passage. When I asked her to identify what made getting GRS in Thailand different from having it in Australia, Gemma, a trans woman living in inner-city Sydney, asserted that Thai surgeons were more technically skilled in gender reassignment surgery than Australian surgeons. She added,

It's something kind of tangible and symbolic, to take a journey [to have gender reassignment surgery]. … [To] do things and see people in a situation outside your normal circumstances. … Psychologically it makes quite a difference to go through a process like that and be outside yourself a bit and come home in a different circumstance, having passed a landmark. With a lot of people who have been over [to Thailand] and have had that same experience, you really notice the feeling that they've done a concrete, tangible thing, you know, and been through quite a symbolic journey.[29]

Melanie, a trans woman from the American Midwest, expressed her feelings about how travelling to Thailand had changed her thus:

[Thailand] imprints on you very deeply … It's such a change you know. People come here and it's such a changing experience. And you go outside [the hotel] and it's very urban and you're in a different environment. But still, I don't know, it kinda charms you in a way.[30]

When I asked her to expand on what precisely had charmed her, or imprinted on her so deeply, she said:

It's the people. … There's just a level of kindness and friendliness that I haven't observed really anywhere else. … And [Thai] people, they just, people brighten up, and they wanna help.[31]

It's a convention of the "classical" Western transsexual narrative that genital surgery is the most significant marker of gendered transition: the dramatic final step, what really makes one a woman (or a man, in the case of trans men who obtain genital surgery). The normative psychiatric definition of what a transsexual is depends on the existence of the desire to possess the genitals of the "other" sex. The "traditional" transsexual narrative that emerged in the second half of the twentieth century classically features a case history involving cross-gender behaviors exhibited in early childhood to the desire to live life as a "real" man or woman in adulthood (Spade 2006, Stone 1992). Genital surgical transformation features within that narrative as the desire that confirms one is "truly" transsexual. It is clear that as many ideas about forms of hormonal and surgical transformation exist as there are gender-variant individuals, but the traditional transsexual narrative still dominates many Euro-American gender variant communities and social and scientific theorizations.[32]

As I note above, the geographical "journey" is almost ubiquitous as a metaphor within English-language trans narratives to relate the transsexual transformation from man into woman or vice versa (Prosser 1999, King 2003). The trans women involved in my project seemed to associate the imagined cultural and spatial milieu of Thailand with femininity (implicitly encoding the "West" as the masculine part of a heteronormative East/West dyad). Thus, Thailand is understood as having a transformative power specific to trans (feminine) embodiment. This, in turn, hinges on the perceived transformative power of travelling in general: the alchemical, or magical, properties of journeying to an exotic location. Thus, the imagined geography of Thailand combines a set of orientalizing discourses that permit surgical candidates to imagine themselves as becoming more feminine in that space.

A photomontage produced by one of Dr. Suporn's patients illustrates precisely this metonymic association of popular Thai iconographies, GRS and psychic feminization.[33] Created by a trans woman called Rebecca on an America Online home page, the photomontage accompanies her account of two trips to Thailand for gender reassignment surgery. The page's text reads:

I had SRS with Dr. Suporn Watanyusakul on January 11, 2005. I had the most … wonderful time in Thailand and made friends with some of the most amazing people. If you go to Chonburi leave your inhibitions and worries at the gate. Lose yourself in Thai culture. Enjoy every moment of your experience whether you're heading over for SRS, FFS, AM or just visiting! Thailand is a wonderful place.[34]

The montage presents glamor shots of Rebecca after her GRS and facial feminization surgery, known as FFS, spliced with symbols emblematic of stereotypical "Thai culture." Vividly colored shots of orchids, Thailand's most popular botanical commodity, surround the center of the montage, where Rebecca poses with a fan and a spray of cherry blossom in her hair, in a dress gesturing towards a cheongsam or a kimono. Surprisingly, the outfit looks nothing like Thai "traditional" costume or a tourist interpretation thereof; perhaps this underscores the slippage between the imagined aesthetic of Thailand itself and that of a more generic "Asia". Accompanying an account of Rebecca's experience having surgery in Thailand, the montage associates her journey with her feminization. The incoherently "Asian" iconography is the vehicle through which Rebecca makes explicit the message that she is now a true woman. It also serves to confirm her sense of the power of the exotic to supplement her white-skinned femininity.

To draw attention to the mélange of significations at work in Rebecca's photomontage is not to dismiss her experience of surgery, or of travelling in Thailand, or to dismiss the aesthetic Rebecca deploys to communicate the importance of her trip. Neither do I intend to discount the personal significance of my informants' experiences. Their affective experiences of connection with Thailand are as valid as the felt sense of connection I experience as a traveler to Thailand as a tourist and researcher, and to other locations that are not my "home". Yet to acknowledge the depth, or "truth", of an affective experience is not to naturalize it as an existing outside discourse, quarantined from critical consideration. To return this discussion to questions about the value of particular racialized bodies within the setting of the gender reassignment surgery clinic, I want to suggest that a form of subjectivation in which one can metonymically associate travelling to Thailand for GRS with the power to supplement one's femininity already assumes that subject is non-Thai, non-*kathoey* and non-Asian. To imagine Thailand in such precise ways places one within a specifically Euro-American, Orientalist discourse. A sometime resident of Bangkok such as Som, who booked into a private hospital and an expensive hotel mostly frequented by non-Thais, would almost certainly experience a very different set of expectations, desires, and affective associations about GRS than that reflected in Rebecca, Gemma, and Melanie's accounts. Crucially, Thai culture, landscape, and traditional forms of sociability were not coded as exotic for Som. The marketing discourses that targeted specifically non-Thai, or Euro-American clients, were not developed with her in mind.

## AFFECTIVE LABOR IN THE CLINIC

Thus far, my argument has been limited to the sphere of symbolic representation: website images and photomontages. To relate this to material practices, and to ground my analysis in a critique of economies of feminized and racialized transnational labor, I turn to an analysis of encounters between Thai staff and non-Thai patients in the clinic featured at the beginning of this chapter. As I noted above, many of the clinic's staff are young Thai women (and occasionally *kathoeys*) who fulfill patients' needs. During a visit to this clinic, the British patient-liaison manager and two or three staff members arranged a lunch for me. During lunch I made inquiries about their working conditions, as most of the staff seemed to be on call twenty-four hours a day. The consensus from those assembled was that every clinic employee is expected to be friendly, hospitable, and available whenever a patient expresses a need, no matter how trivial and no matter what the time of day. The Thai financial administrator (who is also the surgeon's wife) described the working atmosphere as "a big family".[35] She also stressed that being employed at the clinic involved hard work and that if an employee did not respect the system, he or she would not last long.

The patient-care manager was a young Thai woman, Mai, who happened to embody precisely the polite, attractive, and courteous standard of so-called traditional Thai femininity. Mai informed me that because the clinic was so busy, she did not take vacations. Sometimes, she said, she was invited to accompany patients on sightseeing trips within Thailand as a guide and assistant, and this gave her a break. Because Mai spoke the most fluent English of all the personal caregivers, patients seemed to approach her most often. Throughout the afternoon, her mobile phone rang constantly with calls from patients. Many of Mai's labors were mediatory. This involved literal Thai–English interpretation between patients and staff members, as well as the task of "translating" Thailand itself for the benefit of the patients as a kind of tour guide: cultural practices, the layout of the town, where to find the best restaurants, and so on.

Since patients at the clinic usually spend at least a month convalescing after surgery, entertainment activities are very popular. These include trips to the local cinema, or to nearby Pattaya to watch *kathoey* cabaret shows and to shop. A Thai massage specialist is employed by the clinic, just as many Thai hotels and guesthouses employ in-house masseurs. Other activities involve learning about feminine skills: the clinic runs small classes on Thai cookery and makeup application. Patients can arrange manicures, pedicures, and hair appointments. To note only these scheduled activities, however, neglects the constant hum of sociality taking place in the clinic, at the hotel, and in the hospital, all of which involved the Thai attendants aiding the mostly non-Thai, Anglo-European trans women patients in whatever they desired to do. This might include playing with each other's hair, or doing each other's nails, or engaging in chitchat. Mai and other employees were not expected merely to behave in a caring way, it seemed that they were also expected (and saw it as their duty) to make friends and to behave as women friends do.

These tasks can be identified as affective labor. As I indicate above, affective labor can be defined as work that blurs the line between a purely commercial transaction and an exchange of feeling. It involves practices of care, the exchange of affect, and work that forms relationships of some kind. Affective labor, or emotional labor, as Arlie Hochschild theorizes it (2003, 138) constitutes part of what has been called the feminization of labor (Cheah 2007, 94); its presence as a micropolitical practice is intimately related to broader shifts within globalization, migration, and the gendered division of labor. Mai and her fellow workers are part of the global population of "third world women workers" (Mohanty 1997), or, within Cheah's theorization of the new international division of reproductive labor, "foreign domestic workers" (2007, 94).

Thailand's service industry, on which tourism so heavily relies, is powered mainly by young women who migrate from rural areas and who perform various forms of service that blur the boundaries between commercial and non-commercial work (Wilson 2004: 84). While these workers are not strictly "foreign domestic workers," since they may not migrate transnationally, rural-to-urban migration may be just as significant as transnational migration in marking these workers as "other" to the metropolitan elites of Bangkok, while also providing the means with which rural migrants can aspire to be modern and socially mobile themselves. For these subjects, domestic work, service industry work in tourism or hospitality, including sexwork, are key industries (along with textiles and other manufacturing activities). As Ara Wilson points out, affective labor is a hallmark of many different service industries in Thailand. She additionally points out that forms of caregiving are naturalized within these economies as traditional Thai behaviors, which conceals their function as commodities:

> [T]he modes of hospitable engagement found in medical tourism—or sex tourism—are often attributed to Thai culture. The labor involved in gracious caretaking is naturalized in this cultural attribution. Without denying the possibility that structures of feeling or the effects of social hierarchies might produce patterned modes of comportment and interaction, it remains worth considering their commodification.
>
> (Wilson 2008)

One of the most important tasks expected of the Suporn Clinic staff was to model femininity itself for the benefit of the patients as a kind of pedagogical practice. The Thai workers were not present just to care for the trans women patients. Through repetition of gendered behaviors, they performed a particular, racialized feminine gender that supplemented the patients' sense of themselves as female. This performative gender modeling may or may not be conscious and certainly is not surprising, given the context. It is also reflective of the generalized orientalization of Thai femininity within tourist cultures. Simultaneously, there is something specific to the production of gender-variant subjectivity happening here. It becomes clearer if we imagine affective labor as biopolitical production: practices that produce and reproduce particular forms of subjectivity. Sandro Mezzadra locates affective labor within theorizations of postfordism undertaken by Paolo Virno (2004), among others:

> Virno stresses the fact that subjectivity itself—with its most intimate qualities: language, affects, desires, and so on—is 'put to value' in contemporary capitalism... [T]his happens not only with particular jobs or in particular 'sectors' (e.g. in the sector of services), being rather a general characteristic of contemporary living labor ... [T]he concept of 'biopolitics' itself should be accordingly reworked.
>
> (Mezzadra 2005, 2)

This reading of Virno by Mezzadra reworks biopolitics in a different direction to Foucault's deployment of the concept to speak about the regulation of populations, as opposed to individuals (Foucault 1995 and 2007). It also steers away from a practical definition of affective labor as work that involves the creation of relationship. Mezzadra also argues that affective labor plays a role in differentiating subjectivities from each other:

> In a situation in which the boundary between friendship and business is itself being blurred ... specific problems arise, which can nurture specific disturbances.
>
> (Mezzadra 2005, 1)

This is what I gesture towards when I ask, "What forms of labor are being performed in a gender clinic in Thailand to produce a particular *non-Thai* trans-feminine subjectivity?" As I have argued throughout this chapter, such a biopolitical production of trans-feminine subjectivity is made possible through the cultural specificities of Thai gender norms. Further, it is an intersubjective process that occurs principally between Thai women, or their images, and non-Thai trans women. Patients attend makeup classes to distract themselves from discomfort and to pass the time, which flows excruciatingly slowly during convalescence. The always already racialized, commodified circulation of feminine-gendered practices unfolds as an unobtrusive excess to the main concern of gender reassignment surgeries. But it is central to the "care package" offered by the clinic.

It is possible to read this scene in a number of ways. We could regard this intersubjective process as a moment of solidarity between equally disenfranchised feminine-identifying subjects under global capitalism. We might also think of it as a moment in which individuals mutually benefit from an economic and social exchange, freely exchanging money for the feeling of being cared for, and wages for acts of caring. Alternatively, we might regard it as a moment in which affective and biopolitical pedagogies producing an idealized, imagined femininity conceal the economic dimensions of the exchange. It is difficult to ignore the fact that the trans women who purchase the surgical product and its attendant services are by and large affluent, by Thai standards, and white. They have privileged access to consumption practices in ways that their Thai caregivers might only aspire to.

I want to steer away, however, from presenting this as a situation in which "first world" trans people exploit "third world" caregivers. Economically, the clinic owners benefit most from this exchange. For their part, the Thai workers at various clinics (and in health tourism more generally) might regard this kind of work as of higher status than other forms of caregiving work, since it is highly paid by Thai standards. Despite the romanticized vision of Thailand evinced by many of the non-Thai trans women I spoke with, they were also grateful to find treatment in a space in which their needs were met and where they were valued as human beings, unlike hospitals in the United States, Europe, and Australia. Additionally, we cannot point to Euro-American gender-variant cultures as commodified without acknowledging that more localized *kathoey* practices of embodied transformation rely just as much on the commodification of gender-variant subjectivity as the gender clinic catering to non-Thai tourists described in the introduction to this chapter. However, recalling Som's and Emma's experiences of not feeling cared for, it seems evident that the intersubjective practices of affective labor supplementing patients' sense of themselves as women within the space of gender reassignment clinics relies on a form of racialization which, no matter how pervasive elsewhere, differentiates between the bodies of more and less valuable, more and less ideal, trans subjects.

## ON GENDER-VARIANT, CROSS-BORDER SOLIDARITY

This chapter began by proposing that gender reassignment clinics in Thailand deploy self-orientalizing images to market surgical services to non-Thai tourists. I then argued that a corollary of this process is that some non-Thai trans women who obtain surgery in Thailand narrate their experiences in terms of a magical, transformative (and finally orientalizing) journey, which has everything to do with their sense of being gendered subjects. Finally, I discussed the affective and micro-political practices within the gender reassignment clinic scene that facilitate the reproduction of that Orientalist narrative. In making this argument, I drew attention to the commodification of gender reassignment surgery as a tourist industry in Thailand, consistent with its commodification elsewhere, but configured in ways specific to the history of Thai gender reassignment surgery and dominant perspectives on gender variance. Most important, I suggested that the biopolitical production of trans subjectivities in this transnational context relies not only on commodification and forms of labor, or on the reproduction of gender norms, or on racialization, but also on simultaneous racialization, gendering and political economy. Each works through, and is inseparable, from the other.

When I asked in my introduction how particular gender-variant bodies circulate within the transnational commodified gender reassignment surgery market, I was thinking already in the context of the low value ascribed to gender-variant bodies within Euro-American surgical cultures. Access to surgical procedures is often dichotomized between what one wishes for and what one bears because it is the only option available. Under these circumstances, it is necessary to place the micro-politics of gender reassignment surgery in Thailand within the context of ongoing political struggles for trans and gender-variant self-determination. It is essential to engage with the power structures that have made gender reassignment surgery into a commodity globally. One of the most important of these is the privatization of health care globally. It is equally as important to target the widely held assumption that gender reassignment surgeries are a "choice" trans people make, and the opposite but equally as pervasive assumption that one cannot be a "real" man or woman, or person, without surgery to make one's genitals congruous with the gender one identifies with. Ideally, gender reassignment technologies would be state-subsidized. But this would not solve the problem that some nations can afford state-funded health care and some cannot. This is the context of global neoliberalism, in which every subjectivity or practice provides another way to extract surplus value. Under these conditions, work within national boundaries is insufficient. More gender-variant, cross-border solidarity work is needed to trace, and cut across, these productive, exploitative flows of transnational capital.

## NOTES

1. This chapter forms part of a book on the valorization of travel metaphors within gender-variant discourses.
2. The expressions trans and gender-variant are used here to describe cross-gender identifications or practices.
3. Interviews were conducted with trans women from the United Kingdom, the Netherlands, the United States, and Australia who obtained surgery at Thai gender reassignment clinics in 2006 and 2007 in Thailand and Australia.
4. The manager asked to remain anonymous. Interview, 15 July 2006.
5. In this chapter I use GRS, gender reassignment surgery, to denote both genital and non-genital procedures. The participants in this project underwent many different surgical procedures, including castration, or orchiectomy; vaginoplasty, the construction of a neo-vagina; breast augmentation, or augmentation mammoplasty (AM), and facial feminization surgery (FFS).
6. See the English-language web site of Dr. Chettawut Tulayaphanich www.chetplasticsurgery.com (accessed 19 May 2007).
7. According to Dr. Preecha's estimates in a 2006 interview, less than one percent of patients at the Preecha Aesthetic Institute were Thai. The Suporn Clinic's manager noted in an interview that the vast majority of Dr. Suporn's patients were non-Thai. The Phuket Plastic Surgery Center had a clientele that was around 95 percent non-Thai in 2006. I follow Thai etiquette in referring to the Thai surgeons by their given names.
8. I use pseudonyms to identify research participants in this chapter to preserve their anonymity.
9. The Thai word *farang* here is generally understood to mean white non-Thais, rather than foreign visitors from other regions in Asia or other non-white, non-Thai people. To avoid any suggestion of Eurocentrism, in this chapter I use Thai-language terms to write about Thai gender-variant identities and practices. *Kathoey* can refer to male-to-female transgender or transsexual categories (Jackson 2003c, paragraph 2), but historically it has had many different connotations, including male homosexuality, a "third sex or gender" *(phet thi-sam)*, and cross-dressers who are assigned male or female at birth (Jackson 1997b, 171). "Ladyboy" is a Thai coinage of English words to mean *kathoey*. *Sao praphet sorng* is a Thai term meaning "second type of woman". It is used by many gender-variant Thais to identify themselves in preference to the term *kathoey*.
10. Interview, Sydney, 18 February 2007.
11. Interview, Bangkok, 18 June 2006.
12. Interview, Brisbane, 30 July 2006.
13. "Trans masculine" here refers to masculine gender-variant identities or practices. Anecdotally, chest reconstruction surgery is popular with *toms* and available in urban and provincial hospitals.
    […]
15. Interview, 18 June 2006.
16. Thirty percent was the figure cited by Sitthiphan Boonyapisomparn, a *sao praphet sorng* activist and health worker who coordinated a Pattaya-based drop-in center for *sao praphet sorng* and *kathoeys*. Interview, Bangkok, 17 January 2008.
17. Interview, 18 June 2006.
18. Interview, Dr. Suporn, 24 June 2006.
19. Personal communication with the clinic manager at the Suporn Clinic, June 2006.
    […]
22. This fantasy is not limited to heterosexuality.
23. Tourism Authority of Thailand, www.tatnews.org/emagazine/1983.asp (accessed 14 June 2007).
24. This is one Thai tourist marketing strategy amongst many. Other narratives stress different aspects of Thailand, such as the "rugged adventure" of visiting hill tribes in the north of the country, or eco-adventures that promise to reveal the "real situation" to the tourist.
25. Interview, 18 June 2006.
26. Interview, 16 July 2006.
27. www.phuket-plasticsurgery.com (accessed 25 May 2008).
28. www.hygeiabeauty.com/sex-change.html (accessed 23 May 2008).
29. Interview, 19 February 2007.
30. Interview, 17 December 2007.
31. Interview, 17 December 2007.
32. The convention that one must obtain genital surgery to be a "real" man or woman has been soundly critiqued within trans theory, beginning with Sandy Stone's "Posttranssexual Manifesto" (1992).
33. See "Rebecca's life on Mars", http://hometown.aol.com/mches48837/ (accessed 12 July 2007).
34. http://hometown.aol.com/mches48837 (accessed 12 July 2007).
35. This situation seems consistent with more generalized labor relations in Thailand, particularly the ideological power of *bun khun* (reciprocal obligation), or family obligations, between employers and employees. Under the terms of *bun khun,* employers occupy a similar symbolic status to parents and employees occupy the position of children who owe their employer-parents loyalty and obedience. See Mills (1999, 122–124).

## WORKS CITED

Anonymous, 2006. "Medical Tourism for Saudi Vacationers in Focus." *Arab News* August 3 2006. <http://www.arabnews.com/?page=1&section=0&article=85985&d=3&m=8&y=2006&pix=kingdom.jpg&category=Kingdom>. Accessed October 1, 2008.

Benjamin, Harry. 1977. *The Transsexual Phenomenon*. New York: Warner.

Brummelheis, Han ten. 1999. "Transformations of Transgender: The Case of the Thai Kathoey." In Peter A. Jackson and Gerard Sullivan (ed), *Lady Boys, Tom Boys, Rent Boys: Male and Female Homosexualities in Contemporary Thailand*. 121-39. London: Routledge, 1999.

Butler, Judith. 2006. "Undiagnosing Gender." In Paisley Currah, Richard M. Juang and Shannon Price (eds) *Transgender Rights*. 274-298. Minneapolis: University of Minnesota Press.

Charoen Kittikanya. 2007. "Foreigners Still Flock to Thai Hospitals, Attracted by Highly Skilled Doctors and Lower Bills." *Bangkok Post Economic Year in Review*. Bangkok Post Website. Accessed June 25, 2008.

Clough, Patricia Ticineto. 2007. "Introduction." In Patricia Ticineto Clough (ed), *The Affective Turn: Theorizing the Social*. 1-33. Durham: Duke University Press.

Foucault, Michel. 1995. *Discipline and Punish: The Birth of the Prison*, trans. Alan Sheridan. London: Vintage.

Foucault, Michel. 2007. *Security, Territory, Population: Lectures at the Collége de France 1977-78*, trans. Graham Burchell. London: Palgrave Macmillan.

Gorton, Nick. 2006. "Health Care and Insurance Issues for Transgender Persons." *American Family Physician* 73: 9, 1591-8.

Hamilton, Annette. 1997. "Primal Dream: Masculinism, Sun, and Salvation in Thailand's Sex Trade." In Lenore Manderson and Margaret Jolly (eds), *Sites of Desire, Economies of Pleasure: Sexualities in Asia and the Pacific*. 145-165. Chicago: University of Chicago Press.

Hochschild, Arlie. 2003. *The Managed Heart: Commercialization of Human Feeling*. Berkeley: University of California Press.

Jackson, Peter A. 1997. "Thai Research on Male Homosexuality and Transgenderism and the Cultural Limits of Foucaultian Analysis." *Journal of the History of Sexuality* 8: 1, 52-85.

Jackson, Peter A. 1997. "Kathoey < > Gay < > Man, The Historical Emergence of Gay Male Identity in Thailand." In Lenore Manderson & Margaret Jolly (eds), *Sites of Desire/Economies of Pleasure: Sexualities in Asia and the Pacific*: 166-190. Chicago: University of Chicago Press.

Jackson, Peter A. 1999. "Tolerant But Unaccepting: The Myth of a Thai 'Gay Paradise.'" In Peter A. Jackson and Nerida Cook (ed). *Genders and Sexualities in Modern Thailand*. 226-242. Chiang Mai: Silkworm Books.

Jackson, Peter A. 2003a. "Space, Theory and Hegemony: The Dual Crises of Asian Area Studies and Cultural Studies." *Sojourn: Social Issues in Southeast Asia* 18(1), 1-41.

Jackson, Peter A. 2003b. "Mapping Poststructuralism's Borders: The Case for Poststructuralist Area Studies." *Sojourn: Social Issues in Southeast Asia.* 18(1), 42-88.

Jackson, Peter A. 2003c. "Performative Genders, Perverse Desires: A Bio-History of Thailand's Same-Sex and Transgender Cultures." *Intersections: Gender, History and Culture in the Asian Context* 9. URL: http://intersections.anu.edu.au/issue9/jackson.html. Accessed June 4 2008.

Jackson, Peter A. 2009. "Capitalism and Global Queering: National Markets, Sex Cultural Parallels, and Multiple Queer Modernities." *GLQ: a Journal of Lesbian and Gay Studies* 15: 3, 357-95.

Jackson, Peter A. and Sullivan, Gerard (eds). 1999. *Lady Boys, Tom Boys, Rent Boys: Male and Female Homosexualities in Contemporary Thailand*. New York: Haworth Press.

King, Dave. 2003. "Gender Migration: A Sociological Analysis (or the Leaving of Liverpool)." *Sexualities*, 6: 2, 173-194.

Lombardi, Emilia. 2007. "Public Health and Trans-People: Barriers to Care and Strategies to Improve Treatment." In Ilan H. Meyer and Mary E. Northridge (eds), *The Health of Sexual Minorities: Public Health Perspectives on Lesbian, Gay, Bisexual and Transgender Populations*. New York: Springer.

McCamish, Malcolm, 1999. "The Friends Thou Hast: Support Systems for Male Commercial Sex Workers in Pattaya, Thailand." In Peter A. Jackson and Gerard Sullivan (ed), *Lady Boys, Tom Boys, Rent Boys: Male and Female Homosexualities in Contemporary Thailand*, 161-91. London: Routledge, 1999.

Mezzadra, Sandro. 2005. "Taking Care: Migration and the Political Economy of Affective Labor." Talk given March 16th 2005 at Goldsmiths University of London, Center for the Study of Invention and Social Process (CSISP). http://www.goldsmiths.ac.uk/csisp/papers/mezzadra_taking_care.pdf. Accessed April 12 2007.

Mills, Mary Beth. 1999. *Thai Women in the Global Labor Force: Consuming Desires, Contested Selves.* New Brunswick: Rutgers University Press.

Mohanty, Chandra Talpade. 1997. "Women Workers and Capitalist Scripts: Ideologies of Common Interests, Domination and the Politics of Solidarity." In M. Jacqui Alexander and Chandra Talpade Mohanty (eds), *Feminist Genealogies, Colonial Legacies, Democratic Futures.* 3-29. New York: Routledge.

Morris, Rosalind. 1997. "Educating Desire: Thailand, Transnationalism, and Transgression." *Social Text* 52/53, 53-79.

Namaste, Viviane. 2000. *Invisible Lives: the Erasure of Transsexual and Transgendered People.* Chicago: University of Chicago Press.

Nantiya Sukontapatipark. 2005. *Relationship Between Modern Medical Technology and Gender Identity in Thailand: Passing From "Male Body" to "Female Body."* Masters Thesis, Mahidol University, Bangkok.

O'Brien, Michelle. 2003. "Tracing this Body: Transsexuality, Pharmaceuticals & Capitalism." At http://www.deadletters.biz/body.pdf. Accessed May 27, 2007.

Ong, Aihwa. 1999. *Flexible Citizenship: The Cultural Logics of Transnationality.* Durham: Duke University Press.

Puar, Jasbir Kaur. 2002. "Circuits of Queer Mobility: Tourism, Travel, and Globalization." *GLQ: A Journal of Lesbian and Gay Studies* 8: 1-2, 101-138.

Prosser, Jay. 1999. "Exception Locations: Transsexual Travelogues." In *Reclaiming Genders: Transsexual Grammars at the Fin de Siecle.* London: Cassell.

Read, Jason. 2003. *The Micropolitics of Capital.* Albany: SUNY Press.

Sanguan Kunaporn. 2001. "Transsexual, Law and Medicine in Thailand." *Journal of Asian Sexology* 2.

Sinnott, Megan. 2004. *Toms and Dees: Transgender Identity and Female Same-Sex Relationships in Thailand.* Honolulu: University of Hawai'i Press.

Spade, Dean. 2006. Mutilating Gender. In Susan Stryker and Stephen Whittle (ed) *The Transgender Studies Reader.* 315-332. New York: Routledge.

Stone, Sandy. 1992. "The Empire Strikes Back: A Posttranssexual Manifesto." *Camera Obscura* 29: 1, 50-176.

Towle, Evan B. and Morgan, Lyyn M. 2002. "Romancing the Transgender Native: Rethinking the Use of the 'Third Gender' Concept." *GLQ: A Journal of Lesbian and Gay Studies* 2002 8: 4, 469-497.

Van Esterik, Penny. 1996. "The Politics of Beauty in Thailand." In Colleeen Ballerino Cohen, Richard Wilk, Beverly Stoeltje (eds), *Beauty Queens on the Global Stage: Gender, Contests and Power.* 203-16. New York: Routledge.

Virno, Paolo. 2004. *A Grammar of the Multitude.* New York: Semiotext(e).

Whittaker, Andrea. 2008. "The Global Quest for a Child: Medical and Reproductive Travel/Tourism in Thailand." Conference paper, International Conference on Thai Studies 10, Bangkok, Thailand.

Wilson, Ara. 2004. *The Intimate Economies of Bangkok: Tomboys, Tycoons, and Avon Ladies in the Global City.* Berkeley: University of California Press.

Wilson, Ara. 2008. "Medical Tourism in Thailand." In Aihwa Ong and Nancy Chen, *Asian Biotech: Ethics and Communities of Fate.* 118-143. Durham: Duke University Press.

World Professional Association for Transgender Health. 2001. *Standards Of Care For Gender Identity Disorders, Sixth Version.* < http://wpath.org/Documents2/socv6.pdf>. Accessed 5 April 2008.

# 39

# *Trans/scriptions*

## Homing Desires, (Trans)sexual Citizenship and Racialized Bodies

NAEL BHANJI

REPRESENTING HIMSELF AS "AN EAST INDIAN/ARAB IMMIGRANT IN CANADA who has spent most of his life in Kenya," Nael Bhanji foregrounds his own embodied knowledges of multi-locationality, movement, race/ethnicity, and gender transition. He interweaves them with what he terms (borrowing a phrase from diaspora studies scholar Avtar Brah) his "homing desires," and a lyrical reading of how notions of home have been deployed in trans theory. To support his argument that home has often functioned within trans theory to reproduce whiteness and Anglophone bias, he offers an extended discussion of a large-scale government-funded study of access to trans-specific healthcare, in which attempts to include diverse multicultural perspectives had the actual effect of producing a nationalist discourse of transsexual citizenship and belonging that perpetuated the marginalization of trans people of color. Bhanji contextualizes this case study within a growing body of critical literature on embodiment, particularly the work of Sara Ahmed, to call for a phenomenology of transsexual consciousness that is more accountable to processes of racialization, and less fixed in ideologies of the nation.

One man's imagined community is another man's political prison.

(Arjun Appadurai)

The idea for this paper was born of a deep frustration with the "imagined community" of transsexual belonging. Consumed by questions of belonging, I began writing in order to understand how our attachments to the perplexing edifice of "home" shape the theoretical routes that we take, the journeys that we embark on and, in the case of transsexuals, the transitions that we make across the borders of gender and/or national identity. I wrote because I was frustrated by transsexual theory's failure to take into account racial difference without resorting to imperializing gestures; because I was tired of reading the kind of theory that Susan Stryker has ingeniously described as limiting itself through an "around the world in eighty genders" approach—a narrative smorgasbord of "gender exotics, culled from native cultures around the world."[1] But, above all, I continue to write because of both my deep respect for trans theory, as well as my skepticism towards it, because it is within these zones of ambivalence and contradiction that we might envision a way forward.

With these paradoxes in mind, my questions are as follows: To what "home"[2] does the trajectory of transition, the act of border-crossing, lead the already in-between diasporic, gender liminal subject?

Who is the correct and proper citizen that gets to speak in the name of a transsexual subjectivity? How can we engage in a more nuanced understanding of the re-circulation, regulation, and re-inscription of the "transsexual empire" in postmodernity? How do we account for the different imaginings of transsexual mobility within a locality? How do we maintain the relationality of trans-identity without slipping into a formless cultural relativism—without rooting ourselves into isolated social and geographical locations? And finally, what are the tacit knowledges that permeate trans scholarship?

The title of this paper, "Trans/scriptions," borrows loosely from Avtar Brah's introductory chapter in her seminal text *Cartographies of Diaspora*. Brah's ruminations on situated identities in unstable cartographies of intersectionality have provided a solid foundation for my own conceptualization of the differential inscriptions of the signifiers of belonging on (trans)sexual and racialized bodies across space and time.[3] Most importantly, her analysis of "homing desires"—which she theorizes as distinct from the desire for a "homeland"—is an invaluable framework through which diaspora and transsexuality may be brought into dialogue with each other.[4] Yet this paper seeks to do more than simply highlight the ways in which racial exclusion within trans theory has resulted in an unspoken white privilege. I prefer, instead, to envision this piece of writing as a theoretical excursion into the turbulent waters of identity politics. Therefore, in the spirit of risky ventures, this journey will be undertaken with neither a map nor a destination; for it is precisely through exploring those stubborn islands of thought—through challenging our own investments in the protective cocoon of homeliness—that we may envision a trans politics that is critical of its (re)turns to "home."

Before moving on, and to make some of my critical allegiances more apparent, this paper intends to problematize *both* "transsexuality" and "transgender" for their lack of engagement with the imaginary and affective conditions of "trans" belonging.[5] Indeed, several contemporary gender theorists have already argued that the catch-all phrase transgender emerges from the Anglo-American gay and lesbian community.[6] But, as this paper will illustrate, the term "transsexual" carries its own imperialist baggage, achieved through the "imposition of a particular world view and conceptual framework."[7] Within both transsexual and transgender scholarship, trans people continue to be "rhetorically inscribed in the articulation of specifically nationalist political programs" that effectively conceal histories of imperialism and social relations of racism.[8] Reduced thus to the purely figural, the deployment of spatial and temporal metaphors can only implicitly and securely locate the (trans)sexual citizen as one marked by the values and norms of the Anglo-American majority.[9]

Ultimately, this paper calls for a much-needed phenomenology of transsexual consciousness that firmly situates narratives of (dis)embodied dissonance within specific historical and political frameworks. Initially conceptualized as a piece of "homework," my preoccupation with the "homing desires" within trans theory stems from my perception of trans politics from the (dis)embodied location of an East Indian/Arab immigrant in Canada who has spent most of his life in Kenya. So if I seem overly occupied with my task of transcribing the multi-placedness of "home" within diasporas onto the lived realities of transsexuality it is because, to borrow from Stuart Hall, "all discourse is 'placed', and the heart has its reasons."[10]

## TRANSIENT TRAJECTORIES

Identities are mapped in real and imaginary, material and metaphorical spaces.

(Richard Phillips, *Mapping Men* 45)

Contemporary American novelist Lars Eighner once wrote, "Home is the natural destination of any homeless person...A homeless life has no storyline."[11] But what do we mean by *home*? Is it, as Chandra Mohanty asks, "the place where I was born? Where I grew up? Where I live and work as an adult?

Where I locate my community- my people? Who are "my people"? Is home a geographical space, a historical space, an emotional sensory space," or a libidinal space?[12] Similarly, when Maya Angelou said, "I long, as does every human being, to be at home wherever I find myself," was she referring to a positioning within the domestic, edifice, or landscape? Must a home be manifested physically or can we also locate it within the self? And when it comes to transsexual theory, do we ask these questions of home because we realize that we have lost home, and if so, does this mean that we were once "at home"? Or is home always something to be traveled towards, an ideal that is constantly re-negotiated and re-imagined? Put simply, what is the work of "home" in transsexual theory?

As a trans-identified person of color living in diaspora, I am deeply aware that the popular saying that "home is where the heart is" has never been as contradictory as it is today. In our increasingly globalized world, a shared experience of profound discontinuity has contributed to the unstable notions of identity and origin. It seems as though "countless people are on the move and even those who have never left their homeland are moved by this restless epoch."[13] So, although many of us are fortunate enough to live in a house, we often find that every house is not a *home*. Forever in transit, we find ourselves living on the borders of homes, "dwelling," as poet Meena Alexander has described, "at the edge of the world," "unhoused," and "unselved."[14] If home is where the heart is, then some of us are actually out of place. And if to "haunt" is to frequent a place habitually, then home, in a sense, is always already haunted.

When I say that the home is "haunted," I am not referring to paranormal activity or supernatural phenomena within the physical realm. Instead, I intend to draw your attention to the *(un)heimlich* specters that continue to haunt the oft-cited metaphorical borderlands of corporeo-psychic uninhabitability in the quest for a livable space of "familiarity, comfort and seamless belonging."[15] Briefly, Sigmund Freud theorizes that the feeling of being "at home," which he calls the *heimlich*, is more a condition of the heart than a physical space. *Heimlich* refers to things that are familiar, intimate, friendly, and "homely."[16] But the word *heimlich* can also be used to refer to things that are hidden, concealed, or shameful: such as the "*heimlich* places (which good manners oblige us to conceal)" or *heimlich* knowledge that should be withheld from others.[17] In other words, the two sets of definitions, whilst not contradictory, suggest that "home" itself is the source of hidden and dangerous knowledge; a knowledge that remains obscure and inaccessible until it coincides with the *unheimlich*. With roots set deep into the ambivalent soil of the *heim*, the uncanny, as Freud explains, "is in reality nothing new or alien, but something which is familiar and old-established in the mind and which has become alienated from it only through the process of repression."[18]

"Home" is a location of dislocation and desire. Often the questions we ask of home lead to other deeper questions, other deeper longings. It is, as Anne-Marie Fortier explains, "a place of disjunction, of unbelonging, of struggles for assimilation/integration, thus a space that *already* harbors desires for hominess."[19] If we consider that the story of home is "a fantasy of incorporation" that is "ambivalent from the very start," homecoming remains impossible because it implies in its subtext a departure and an arrival, a point of coming *from* and arriving *at*.[20] But because the concept of home is fraught with psychical tensions and conflicts, because it is unhomely to begin with, there is almost never a definite arrival "at" home. Instead, the individual is always just "getting there."

With these paradoxes in mind, I have turned to diasporic theories because they offer "critical spaces for thinking about the discordant movements of modernity" without detaching embodied experiences from historical and cultural specificity.[21] [...] By emphasizing multi-locationality within and across national, cultural, and psychic boundaries, a diasporic framework allows us to imagine the ways in which identities are scattered and regrouped into new becomings. And most importantly— at least for the purposes of this paper—the field of diaspora studies makes "the spatialization of identity problematic and interrupts the ontologization of place" thereby bringing the concepts of "home" and "away" into creative tension with each other.[24] [...]

I am aware that my attempts to analyze the transsexual turn to "home" within a diasporic framework runs the risk of homogenizing all difference under the sign of movement itself. Certainly, one of the major pitfalls of diaspora studies is its tendency to flatten experiences of migration, immigration, exile, and estrangement. [...] But perhaps these conversations about homes—discourses that I find myself drawn to again and again—can be rethought through problematizing the neat and tidy borders that they insist upon, borders which often refuse to acknowledge their paradoxical permeability and confinement. Whilst not all trans people of color are diasporic, a diasporic framework, as this paper will illustrate, certainly helps to problematize those unacknowledged "homing desires" within trans theory. In other words, we must pay attention to the different ways in which people (re)imagine and (re)create the edifice of homely belonging; where one's "real" home can only exist as a romanticized cathedral of constancy—like a strongbox of memory kept safe from the siren dance of modernity through spatial and temporal sleight-of-hand that effectively renders it, as Canadian poet Dionne Brand would say, "in another place, not here."[30] Wary of deploying diaspora as a "catch-all phrase to speak of and for all movements, however privileged, and for all dislocations, even symbolic ones," I have chosen instead to interrogate the social and political implications of "homing desires" within narratives of transsexual "homecomings."[31]

In many trans communities, the pressure to pass, to blend into the mainstream, can be intense. The push from pre-op to post-op, from transitioning to transitioned, from transgressive to trans*fixed* results in the transsexual forever rushing onwards to find the space beyond, "the promise of *home* on the other side," and the possibility of *being at home in ones skin*.[32] In Jay Prosser's *Second Skins,* sex-reassignment surgery is described as a transsexual "home-coming"—the return to one's true home in the body—a sort of "somatic repatriation," if you will.[33] Indeed, transsexuality, as Prosser suggests, has always embraced notions of "place, location, and specificity."[34] Contemporary transsexual narratives are often accounts of linear progression: the journey from one location to another—"from fragmentation to integration, from alienation to reconciliation, from loss to restoration"—where one is meant to leave the transgressive space and transition *towards* one's fully embodied identity.[35] The transitional journey itself is merely a link between locations—a sort of gendered non-zone between origin and destination—and not a place to call home. Thus the prefix *trans* signifies multiple crossings, but still within a very confined nexus of homecoming and belonging, of borders and centers.

In transsexual or "*body* narratives," as Prosser has coined, skin seduces as a metaphor for homeliness. Prosser writes of the acute sense of gender dysphoria as akin to the feeling of bodily displacement ... of living without a skin of one's own. Turning to *Stone Butch Blues*, Prosser draws on the experiences of Leslie Feinberg's protagonist, Jess Goldberg, in order to illustrate the extent to which her body—that which should be felt as most familiar—can become radically unhomely. Indeed, Jess's sense of bodily displacement is informed at all points by the longing for "home." Like the female-to-male transsexual, Jess "experiences her female body as that which is most *unheimlich* in herself: as with the transsexual the body that should be home is foreign, the familiar felt as most strange."[36]

Indeed, the analogy between the house and the human body has a long iconographic and metaphorical tradition. As Claudia Benthien explains, the house is the "absolute metaphor" of the body, an orientational guide in the world that provides structure and represents "the totality of reality which can never be experienced and never fully grasped."[37] Furthermore, the absolute metaphor of the body-as-house has always referred to only the skin—that marked epidermal periphery through which we literally feel our way through the world. [...] Ahmed's *Strange Encounters* has summarized the tenuous connections between homeliness, skin and identity as follows:

> We can think of the lived experience of being-at-home in terms of inhabiting a *second skin*, a skin which does not simply contain the homely subject, but which allows the subject to be touched and

> touch the world that is neither simply in the home or away from home.... Movement away is also movement within the constitution of home as such. Movement away is always affective; it affects how homely one might feel and fail to feel.[39]

Certainly, the trope of the "second skin," that "burdensome outer layer," is a recurring leitmotif in narratives of the unhomely transsexual body.[40] For instance, in *Journal of a Transsexual*, Leslie Feinberg writes of hir desire for disembodiment in terms of shedding the unhomely body like a skin: "I think how nice it would be to unzip my body from forehead to navel and go on vacation. But there is no escaping it, I'd have to pack myself along."[41] Encased thus within the baggage of a false, restrictive outer shell, Feinberg's narrative points to the very real work of embodied unhomeliness. But does this mean that a reprieve from this sort of gender dysphoric "home work" is possible only through a disembodied homeliness? In other words, what is the work of "home" within trans theory? How does the trope of homeliness affect different trans bodies? And in an increasingly globalized world, how do these (re)turns to home collude with liberal discourses of social inclusion in order to institute domesticity and normativity as the privileged trajectory of transsexual citizenship? Given the fractured nature of "home," is a transsexual homecoming at all possible?

Ahmed and Stacey write that "skin's memory is burdened with the unconscious."[42] Skin has a phantasmic writerly effect, functioning as "a canvas for what we wish were true- or for what we cannot acknowledge to be true." And transsexual narratives, as Prosser explains in *Skin Memories*, "reveal the skin as a site for unconscious investment, a body memory or fantasy that failed to materialize."[43] A nostalgia for the romanticized ideal of home, the body reconstructed through sex-reassignment surgery—the body that is literally re-membered—is a recovery of the sexed contours that *should* have been:

> What makes the transsexual able and willing to submit to the knife—the splitting, cutting, removal, and reshaping of organs, tissues, and skin that another might conceive as mutilation—is the desire to get the body *back to what it should have been.*[44]

But skin is not simply a "present" surface "in so far as it has multiple histories and unimaginable futures, it is worked upon, and indeed, it is worked towards."[45] In other words, skin can be theorized in spatial and temporal dimensions—remembering, through its imperfect traces, our personal journeys through time and space. As with the act of writing, this testimonial function of skin, "dermographia"—skin writing, from Greek *derma*, skin, and *-graphesis*, writing—"contains the traces of those other contexts in the very living materiality of its forms, even if it cannot be reduced to them."[46] And as with the inevitable erasures in the process of writing, the skin always leaves traces of a not-so-absent past to bear witness on what has yet to be written.

A porous, breathing surface, skin allows us to think about the unstable borders between bodies that are always already criss-crossed by differences that refuse to be contained on the "inside" or the "outside" of the bodies themselves. So rather than fetishize the marked body, through simply reducing it to the least common denominators of difference contained within a singular figure, perhaps we require an approach that is critical of the tacit knowledges which establish the very boundaries that appear to mark out the body. If, as Ahmed and Benthien suggest, skin is always open to being read by others, how can we think about the unstable borders between transsexual bodies that are always already crossed by differences that refuse to be contained on the "inside" or the "outside" of bodies? Reformulating Ahmed's intriguing questions, perhaps we can ask: "How do [trans] bodies re-inhabit space?" and "How do spaces re-inhabit [trans]bodies?"[47]

"Home," as one might imagine in relation to Prosser's model, "is represented as the place in which one finally settles into the comfort of one's true and authentic gender."[48] Thus, to feel "at home in ones skin" is to be taken in the world for who one feels oneself to be. But how are these somatic transitions spurred and enabled by the narrative promise/premise of homeliness? Arguing that a "politics of home" may provide a "powerful organizing trope" for a new transsexual politics of possibility, Prosser writes:

> This "politics of home" would analyze the persistence of sexual difference for organizing identity categories. It would highlight the costs to the subject of not being clearly locatable in relation to sexual difference. Above all, it would not disavow the value of belonging as the basis for a livable identity. The practical applications for such a politics of home are immediate, multiple, and, indeed, transformative.[49]

[...]

What I find most striking about Prosser's work is the way in which the journey towards "home" is conceived of as a form of migration: "an appropriate analogical frame for the transsexual's writing of transition as a journey may be that of *immigration*: the subject conceives of transsexuality as a move to a new life in a new land, allowing the making of home, precisely an act of translation."[52] Akin to the transitory space of an airport terminal, the in-between space of gender transition figures as a site of *future* homely possibility—"the space in which one is almost, but not quite, at home"—where the subject has an itinerary, a destination and a future but has not yet arrived.[53] Thus, in a noteworthy reversal of the diasporic trajectory, the transsexual migrant must leave the space of unhomeliness to arrive at "home."

Like Prosser, I too am interested in the theme of transit, "both as a figure for transsexual transition and as a literal journey undertaken."[54] On the other hand, I am wary of his lack of engagement with the dynamics of race and class. As in "Exceptional Locations", Prosser's *Second Skins* explores the topography of migrational metaphors through a singularly gendered perspective. But he neglects to account for the ways in which power is distributed and wielded across a matrix of over-lapping identities at the same time. The ways in which we theorize transsexuality must necessarily address the question of broader/border traversals. In these contours of citizenship, belonging, and migration, how do the borders themselves deterritorialize and reterritorialize us? Certainly, the borders of gender have a lot in common with those of the home: both police "spaces where those who do not 'belong' are separated from those who do."[55] Bathrooms and border crossings are both equally invested in preserving and maintaining boundaries (between male and female, or citizen and stranger) such that, "at the border it is imperative to produce the right papers and look or act as if we belong—even, paradoxically, when we are sure that we do."[56] In other words, the border marks a sphere of normality, of homeliness, that privileges properly gendered and sexed national bodies.

As Halberstam points out, the "idea of the border sets up some notion of territories to be defended, ground to be held or lost, permeability to be defended against."[57] We turn to these borders in order to separate citizen from stranger, human from alien, insider from outsider, and self from other. Borders allow us to feel safe in the knowledge that whatever is out there, the unsettling potential of Homi Bhabha's *terrere* (terror), will not be able to contaminate the sacred *terre* (earth/land) of the nation-state.[58] The resulting interpenetration of space and the body, and the body and the psyche, means that if geographical borders cannot be separated from the integrity of home, then, equally, the boundaries between differently gendered bodies raise the specter of not being at home in one's body. So, if home is doubly inflected as the task of finding a home in one's body and being able to call the nation home, then concealed under the surface of this "politics of home" is the urge for normality and the desire "to belong without complication to a normative social sphere."[59] Thus, the privileged space of the transsexual homecoming is a fantasy: "a fantasy, moreover, racially and culturally marked as Anglocentric, heteronormative and capitalist."[60]

Aren Z. Aizura is one of the few contemporary trans theorists to recognize that the submerged nationalisms which undergird transsexual theorizing have contributed to a problematic "politics of transsexual citizenship" that is invested in metaphors of homecomings, borders, and boundaries.[61] Furthermore, he argues that narratives of transsexual citizenship have perpetuated this discourse in normality by figuring transition as a necessarily transgressive "but momentary lapse on the way to a proper embodied belonging, a proper home and full social inclusion."[62] This hegemonic construction of linear time and space has obvious implications for the gender liminal body; progress becomes a linear narrative that dictates the body's teleological transition *from* one gender *to* another. So, in a sense, the transitional trope is also the definitive property of a civilizing narrative—an articulation of linear progression towards the ultimate goal of belonging. [...]

If, as Richard Phillips has argued, "men are made, albeit loosely, in the image of their settings," then these adventure stories of transition, too, appear to accommodate and condition those unavowed investments in citizenship discourses that pave the road to transsexual-becoming.[64] In other words, whilst transsexual scholarship appears to romp freely through geographies of liminal adventure, we need to recognize that the fundamental theories undergirding narratives of becoming are rooted in hegemonic notions of embodiment in national, and therefore racialized and gendered, space. [... P]erhaps that "desire to belong" conceals another set of discourses that have as yet gone uninterrogated.

The problem is that metaphorical adoptions of migratory narratives "can have the uncanny effect of using postcolonial rhetorics to redeem colonial contexts" and justify further oppression in the name of the transsexual empire.[67] Such rhetorics assume that the proper solution to painfully wrong embodiment is to migrate to the right body—where, as Halberstam insightfully points out, "rightness may easily depend on whiteness or class privilege as it does on being regendered."[68] So what is needed is a phenomenology of transsexual consciousness that moves away from the notion of "home" as the stasis of being and firmly situates these (dis)embodied dissonances within historical and political frameworks. To quote Ahmed, "the issue of home is not simply about fantasies of belonging but that it is *sentimentalized* as a space of belonging."[69] Wary about the unidirectional impulse towards a transsexual "home," Judith Halberstam has suggested that it might be fruitful to turn to Chicano/a and postcolonial studies where debates about the politics of migration have resulted in "a careful refusal of the dialectic of home and border."[70] Heeding Halberstam's statement that "there is little to be gained theoretically or materially from identifying either home or border as the true place of resistance," I explore next the racial implications of territorial metaphors within the corporeo-theoretical cartography of transsexual writing.[71]

## DIS.ORIENT.ATIONS

Perhaps it is unsurprising that I find myself troubled by the origin stories and narrative marks of arrival in trans theory. Thus far, my intervention is purely theoretical for, try as I might, I have found few resources that do not isolate race from the discourses of transsexual embodiment: and yet "there is a huge difference between becoming a black man or a man of color and becoming a white man, and these differences are bound to create gulfs within transsexual communities."[72] I believe that what we require are interlinking maps of knowledge, theoretical grids that do not shy away from venturing into postcolonial or diasporic theorizing; that any discourse about the "fictional unity" of the transgender collective has to "begin from the premise that genders, sexualities, races, classes, nations, and even continents exist not just as hermetically sealed entities but rather as part of a permeable interwoven relationality."[73]

A little over a year ago, I was hired by a government-funded health collective to assist in a large-scale study of access to trans-specific healthcare. As part of a community engagement team, my role would be to facilitate the creation of a groundbreaking questionnaire that would eventually be circulated to trans-identified individuals across Canada. During the course of my congratulatory phone call, I learned that one of the reasons I was hired was because the collective was striving to be more multicultural in its approach. To this end, the committee had recruited three trans-identified people of color in order to assure diversity within the collective. I never really gave the implications of this multicultural approach any serious thought. At that point in time, I was living in a predominantly white town—a town where a seemingly vague, "you know ... the brown kid with the hair," was usually enough to point someone in my direction—where there were only three other trans-identified people that I knew. So just the prospect of being in a room where there might be dozens of trans-identified men and women excited me; that I might actually *meet* other trans-identified people of color, people who were like me, filled me with the kind of joy that was unfamiliar in its giddy intensity.

On the morning of our first meeting, I walked into the boardroom of a local health center and was quite literally swept off my feet by a stunning South Indian woman, Asha. I had barely recovered from this first onslaught of affection before I felt my hand being grasped, and shaken quite enthusiastically, by Liz, the two-spirited woman who effectively completed our "trio of difference." Over the course of the two-day long meeting, Asha, Liz, and I formed strong bonds with each other. But, this was inevitable. Each meeting found the three of us trying again and again to point out the Eurocentric way in which the health questionnaire had been constructed.

We did not dispute the fact that trans-people had trouble accessing emergency medical care or finding supportive mental healthcare. But what we *did* have a problem with was an unacknowledged elision of the social, political, and cultural nuances that shaped the healthcare system as a whole. For instance, my first appointment with a gender specialist was not as much about my gender identity as it was about whether I, an East-Indian/Arab immigrant from Kenya, was simply having trouble integrating into Canadian society.[74] We were also concerned that the academic jargon used in the questionnaire would alienate both the people who didn't subscribe to those "theoretical pyrotechnics" as well as those for whom English was not a first language.[75] And whilst we were working desperately to get these points across, a hand shot up and a voice, which barely concealed the speaker's exasperation, piped up, "What does race have to do with being trans?!"

In the moments of stunned silence that followed, I remember struggling to contain my emotions. It felt as though I had been betrayed ... both by the collective as well as by my own naïveté. But it was the keen sense of loss that surprised me the most. How do you begin to mourn something that never really existed in the first place? Like three exotic bookmarks marking a chapter in the chronicle of a more diverse and increasingly global trans movement, our presence was meant to signify the dawning of a new era: a proudly Canadian, and therefore multicultural, trans community. Yet, we were, for all intents and purposes, a minority within a minority; held in the discursive grip of a "powerful powerless" we had found ourselves silenced by nationalist discourses of transsexual citizenship.[76]

One might wonder why I was so disenchanted by the siren call of multicultural affiliation. I suppose I should have been grateful, happy even, to have been included in this landmark project. But I felt far removed from the promise of a multicultural trans community. It seemed as though the fragile work of community building elided more elastic, and more complicated, notions of belonging. What it came down to was this: I was unable to pledge allegiance to yet another insulated form of (be)longing whose visions of cultural tolerance inevitably reproduced the very notions of fixed, hegemonic gender identities that the trans movement rebelled against in the first place. By placating us with its call for "respecting difference," not only did this multicultural approach conveniently ignore our autonomy, it also elided the differences *within* our trio of difference. But what, you may wonder, does this story have to do with discourses of nationalism in trans theory?

In her article, "Geography Lessons," Himani Bannerji theorizes that the given-ness of any nation-state is a "construction, a set of representations, embodying certain types of political and cultural communities and their operations."[78] With the ideological category of whiteness set as the core of the Canadian ethos, the ascription of "otherness" not only delimits membership within the cozy centers of the nation-state, but also produces whiteness as its discursive effect such that "European-ness as whiteness thus translates into 'Canada' and provides it with its imagined community."[79] It follows then that narratives of belonging are intimately entwined with indicators of difference. Or, to put it differently, the "affective alliances" which give rise to those feelings of homeliness are rooted within the socially-constructed domain of cultural effects and these affects "define a structure and economy of belonging."[80]

Narratives of belonging are the "effect of inhabitance," as well as the paradoxical affect, and effect, of the unfamiliar and uninhabitable.[81] Haunted by the specter of what is unfamiliar, the domestic landscape of the familiar, and familial, world can only secure itself through a "repetition of gestures" that can never completely eliminate the threat of disappearance and the possibility of psychic displacement.[82] Drawing upon Sara Ahmed, we can understand whiteness as allowing for the linear extension of a properly oriented body through space; and these spaces themselves are the discursive effects of properly orientated bodies. Furthermore, orientation is itself oriented by the repetitions of the things that we "do do" such that what we "do do", and what we "can do," are the effects of difference as well as the mechanisms for the production of difference itself.[83]

Despite the occasional, and sometimes abstract, detour into the quirky world of queer tables, Ahmed's *Queer Phenomenology* highlights how moments of (dis)orientation should be used to think productively about how space is dependent on bodily inhabitance. Ahmed literally queers the "orient" in "orientation" by thinking with, and around, the racialized body in cartographic space. She uses phenomenology to single out the "singling out" of objects, to problematize the orientation of orientation and to destabilize the alignment of alignment. So [...] if orientations are "directional metaphor[s]" turned identification, how can we reconceptualize the body that seemingly repudiates the spatial linearity of socio-historical repetition?

[...]

Ahmed's critique of the socio-scientific construction of racial inheritance illustrates that the perception of race as "property" only serves to reinforce a discursive space in which to further perpetuate racial discourse as "oriented" in particular spatial and temporal frameworks.[89] It follows then that a reproductive discourse that rests on the laurels of socio-scientific inheritance results in space envisioned as the cartographic property of whiteness; and the idea of whiteness as inherited can only continue to allow the white body to affect the spaces of those who must occupy the space of "not-quite-white[ness]."[90] What this indicates is that there is no such thing as "home" itself; that the Oriental, or racialized body, jeopardizes the fictive unity of belonging precisely because of its disorienting presence. So by placing a positive spin on "difference," multiculturalist rhetoric simultaneously "establishes Anglo-Canadian culture as the ethnic core culture while 'tolerating' and hierarchically arranging others around it as 'multiculture.'"[91] Within such a framework, the self-congratulatory slogan "unity in diversity" functions as a mere gesture that implies transcendence as a way to overcome the legitimization crisis of Anglo-Canadian culture.

Drawing upon Bannerji's formulation of the "crisis in [Canadian] citizenship," I would like to suggest that the project of imagining a multicultural transsexual community needs to be further problematized by a sustained critique of both the radical inhabitability of "the idea of belonging" and the exclusionary drive towards a "politics of home" in transsexual theory.[92] The journey home for the transsexual may come at the expense of a recognition that others are permanently dislocated from home—that they occupy the inhospitable territories in between ... the uninhabitable "geographies of ambiguity" at, what bell hooks would call, the very "profound edge[s]" of marginality.[93] Although metaphors of travel and border crossing are inevitable in transsexual discourses, we must recognize that "they are also laden with the histories of other identity negotiations, and they carry the burden of national and colonial discursive histories."[94]

As Halberstam argues, this insistence on linearity within transsexual theory fails to account for bodies that inhabit a "persistent present or a queer temporality that is at once indefinite and virtual but also forceful, resilient, and undeniable."[95] Any trans cartography that prefers to think about transgression using the metaphors of border crossings and homecomings will ultimately fail to take into account the lived realities of those who have no choice but to inhabit the borderlands of non-recognition: "some bodies are never at home, some bodies cannot simply cross from A to B, some bodies recognize and live with the inherent instability of identity."[96] Furthermore, "if the borderlands are uninhabitable for some trans-identified people who imagine that home is just across the border, imagine what a challenge they present to those subjects who do not believe that such a home exists, either metaphorically or literally."[97] Sadly, it seems that the voice that originated from the margins has begun to (re)produce its own marginalized voices.

Of course, these marginal voices can also be produced from the flip side of liberal universalism—cultural relativism—where multicultural cartographies of knowledge tend to be presumed in isolation from the center and from each other. I am all too aware that, in advocating for a race-conscious trans movement, I might end up re-inscribing marginality as the eye of the proverbial storm—a pure state where "they have their culture and we have ours: never the twain shall meet."[98] Indeed, there is plenty of evidence to suggest that this has been the trend within transgender scholarship. Cast as a specific kind of knowledge that can only exist in opposition to "area studies," transgender and transsexual Euro-American academia has often resorted to comparative frameworks that naturalize and reproduce nationalist discourses of sexuality through fetishizing gestures that map racial difference as spectacle. Within this trajectory of knowledge, it is all too apparent that trans-identified people of color have been, to borrow from Appadurai, metonymically frozen in an anthropological taxonomy which, through a spatial and temporal sleight-of-hand, effectively renders them, as Canadian poet Dionne Brand would say, "in another place, not here."[99] Such anthropological[100] narratives, whose DNA contains the genetic blueprint of Judeo-Christian culture, have tended to produce a fetishistic sexuality that can only be understood within the primitive realm: as a "pre-modern, pre-capitalist construction, which in turn enables whiteness to be located within capitalism as well as modernity."[101] In other words, these journeys backwards through time—journeys where "geographical difference across *space* is figured as historical difference across *time*"—produce socio-cultural difference as a space for consumption.[102]

In contemporary trans scholarship these theoretical journeys seem to allow us to consume a veritable buffet of exotic (trans)sexuality—from male transvestite shamans in northwest Venezuela to the shamans in the Vietnamese countryside, from the priestly shamans of West Africa to the transsexual augerers and diviners of Angola, from the "native peoples of the arctic basin" to India's ubiquitous hijras and so forth.[103] [... T]hese accounts of transsexual embodiment engage in a double move of universalizing transsexual difference whilst (re)producing difference as "the body in excess" that can then be consumed.[104] This "additive approach" to trans scholarship is akin to a "family of nations pageant" in which a rotating chain of marginality tends to be pitted against an unstated, white, Western norm, effectively putting relationships amongst others "on hold."[105] In this sense, the radical difference of racial specificity—a specificity that is seemingly unmarked by the shifts and fluxes of relations of social, political, and economic relations over time—inevitably overshadows what could be parallel and productive dialogues of trans embodiment.

As a spatial marker of possibility, the prefix, *trans-* does not just signify movement across or beyond a schism. Instead, it is also evocative of the *transgressions, transmogrifications,* and *transmutations* of established norms. Indeed, one of the functions of *trans-*, as suggested by Song Hwee Lim's article "Is the Trans- in Transnational the Trans- in Transgender," is to destabilize the notion of space as a controlled location. Furthermore, we cannot theorize about the politics of *space* without engaging with the subjective experience of *place*. Each requires the other to fulfill its potential. Borrowing from John Agnew, the simplest explanation of the relationship between space and place can be summarized as follows: "Space refers to location somewhere and place to the occupation of that location. Space is about having an address and place is about living at that address."[106] So if the prefixes *post* (as in postcolonial) and *trans* (as in transsexual) function as temporal and spatial markers, perhaps we should ask what centers and peripheries are necessarily (r)evoked by transsexual theorist Sandy Stone's early formulation of the "posttranssexual empire"?

Written in response to Janice Raymond's anti-transsexual polemic,[107] Stone's "The Empire Strikes Back: A Posttranssexual Manifesto" is still considered to be a monumental call for transsexual self-expression. Drawing upon autobiographical literature, Stone suggests that the transsexual impetus to disappear into "plausible histories"—to become successfully invisible by "passing" as the gender of their choice—forecloses the radical "possibility of a life grounded in the *intertextual* possibilities of the transsexual body."[108] For Stone, the narrative of "passing" is one that denies not just individual history, or political agency, but the destabilizing power of transgression itself. Thus, her "posttranssexual manifesto" calls for a reappropriation of the multiple dissonances of transsexual experience through embracing "physicalities of constantly shifting figure[s] and ground[s] that exceed the frame of any possible representation."[109]

Nevertheless, I find Stone's call of a "posttranssexual" epoch troubling because the "implied openness of the narrative, paradoxically, reveals its own closedness."[110] By positioning the transsexual experience as something outside of both time and space, the "posttranssexual manifesto" has the uncanny effect of erasing the criss-crossing effects of global and local configurations of hegemonic power. In other words, the only way that Stone can address her "brothers" and "sisters" as transsexual kinfolk is by simultaneously denying the plurality, fragmentation, and contingency of identity even as she advocates for it.[111] [...] So perhaps it is only fitting that she re-iterates Raymond's notion of the transsexual "empire"—for Stone's formulation of posttranssexuality assumes a transsexual cosmopolitan elite whose "willful ignorance" is vital to (re)creating trans theory as a "fortress rich world."[113]

The problem with "empires" is that they are dependent on difference and conquest for self-definition. If the "transsexual empire" is evocative of the messy terrain of modern, civilized whiteness that can only be articulated through uncivilized, primitive bodies steeped in exotic culture, then the *post*transsexual empire—which engages in the simultaneous denial of both historic specificity and the complex dynamics of local and global interactions—has produced a muted movement which can only be complicit in re-circulating unequal relations of power. To this end, I agree with Lim's suggestion that "the prefix 'trans'...whether in relation to nation or to gender...while indexing a crossing of boundaries, can in effect fix the boundaries even more firmly and in an essentialist manner."[114]

My concerns about the "posttranssexual" moment are as follows: How can we even begin to acknowledge the multi-layered complexities of this palimpsestic global, transsexual movement if the movement itself has already "moved on" so that it is beyond the reach of both history and the politics of the local/global? Whilst I do not mean to suggest that we re-center notions of a global modernity, I am advocating for an affective approach to transsexual embodiment—one which pays attention to the political ramifications of a movement rooted in the space-beyond, and which interrogates the desires behind the push for transsexual homeliness. The dizzying, free-floating paradigm engendered by Stone's framework effectively ignores the dynamics of power, or the continued hegemony of the center over the margins, by making everyone "equally different, despite specific histories of oppressing or being oppressed."[115] The posttranssexual movement signals a new form of global elite and "evokes the sameness of human differentiation across time by collapsing the processes of time into an unchanging, and highly idealized notion, *the same organized body*."[116] Certainly, it seems as though the transsexual "empire" is drawing its inspiration from Benedict Anderson's formulation of the nation as "an imagined political community—and imagined as both inherently limited and sovereign."[117]

Thus far, I have attempted to illustrate that trans scholarship may be affected by the same discourses of affective mapping that have drawn solid lines between "subject and land ... and between European white subjects and others"; that theory, too, can function as a psychic tool that re-circulates neo-imperialist notions of the externalization and control of bodies and boundaries.[118] In other words, if cartographic tools are "lifelines" that save us from the ravages of the unfamiliar whilst also marking the spaces that are beyond our bodily horizons, and if the act of claiming "empires" is necessarily bound up with the politics of "withness" and "againstness," then transsexual politics, too, are implicated in the game of mastering one's environment without being mastered in return—of ensuring that the "relationship between the knower and the known remains unidirectional."[119] Although these maps allow for spaces of becoming—for a continued investment in the inheritance and reproduction of homely spaces—they simultaneously demand a "turning away" from something else. Trans scholarship is haunted by perpetual discursive acts of psychic violence that can be traced to the ideals of Enlightenment individualism and the European mapping of ownership; that the "antagonism that the imaginary whole of the [trans community] aims to disavow or exclude is thus not just the sign of the failure of any whole to be whole...[rather] it is an ongoing practice of violence."[120] Furthermore, these discursive acts of violence betray the fundamental insecurities in the fictional unity of a transsexual "empire." As such, it is neither home per se that is contested within trans theory, nor the mechanisms that shape home as that contested space. Rather, what are at stake are the things that must necessarily be sacrificed, or disavowed, in order to engage in the very act of imagining home.

## ACKNOWLEDGMENTS

Heartfelt thanks to Aren Z. Aizura, Enakshi Dua, Jane Tolmie, Jin Haritaworn, Heather Sykes, Michelle Murphy, and Trystan T. Cotten whose encouragement and editorial advice have helped shape the best parts of this essay.

## NOTES

1. Susan Stryker, "(De)Subjugated Knowledges: An Introduction to Transgender Studies" in *The Transgender Studies Reader*, eds. Susan Stryker and Stephen Whittle (New York: Routledge, 2006), 14.
2. My interest in the affective conditions of "homework" take into account landscapes that are both metaphorical and literal. The meanings of "home" shift across a number of discourses: from the notion of a stable identity to a fluid concept, from private to public spheres, between the nation as an "imagined community" to a mythic space of belonging, or simply, as a narrative of the self and the "other."
3. Avtar Brah, *Cartographies of Diaspora: Contesting Identities* (New York, NY: Routledge, 1996), 1–10.
4. Avtar Brah, *Cartographies*, 197.
5. Briefly, my use of the word trans as a pseudo-umbrella term—albeit a problematic one—to describe both transsexual and transgender identities follows Jason Cromwell, Aren Z. Aizura, and Bobby Noble's application of trans as an identity category under erasure. Thus, I ask the reader here to read trans not just as a form of categorical indeterminacy, but whilst also keeping in mind the differential modalities of (dis)identification under the sign itself.
6. See Viviane Namaste's *Sex Change, Social Change: Reflections on Identity, Institutions, and Imperialism* (Toronto: Women's Press, 2005), 2. Also Riki Wilchins in Joan Nestle, Claire Howell and Riki Wilchins, *GenderQueer: Voices from Beyond the Sexual Binary* (San Francisco, CA: Alyson Books, 2002), 141–142; Nikki Sullivan, "Transsexual Empires and Transgender Warriors" in *A Critical Introduction to Queer Theory* (New York: NYU Press, 2003).
7. Namaste, *Sex Change, Social Change*, 103.
8. Namaste, *Sex Change, Social Change*, 119.
9. Viviane Namaste, *Invisible Lives: The Erasure of Transsexual and Transgendered People* (Chicago, IL and London: The University of Chicago Press, 2000), 98.
10. Stuart Hall, "Who needs Identity?" in *Questions of Cultural Identity*, eds. Stuart Hall *et al.* (London: Sage Publications, 1996), 234.
11. Lars Eighner, *Travels with Lizbeth: Three Years on the Road and on the Streets* (New York: Ballantine Books, 1993), 97.
12. Chandra Mohanty, "Defining Genealogies: Feminist Reflections on Being South Asian in North America," in *Our Feet Walk the Sky*, eds. Women of South Asian Descent Collective (San Francisco, CA: Aunt Lute Books, 1993), 352.

13. Nikos Papastergiadis, *The Turbulence of Migration: Globalization, Deterritorialization and Hybridity* (Malden, MA: Polity Press, 2000), 2.

14. Meena Alexander, *House of a Thousand Doors* (Washington, DC: Three Continents Press, 1988), 44.

15. Anne-Marie Fortier, "Making Home: Queer Migrations and Motions of Attachment," in *Uprootings/Regroundings: Questions of Home and Migration*, eds. Sara Ahmed et al. (Oxford: Berg, 2003), 130.

16. Sigmund Freud, "The Uncanny," in *Psychological Writings and Letters*, ed. Sander Gilman, trans. Alix Strachey (New York: Continuum, 1995), 125.

17. Freud, "The Uncanny," 125.

18. Freud, "The Uncanny," 142.

19. Anne-Marie Fortier, "Making Home," 127.

20. Stuart Hall, "Cultural Identity and Diaspora," in *Theorizing Diaspora*, eds. Jana Evans Braziel and Anita Mannur (Malden, MA: Blackwell, 2003), 3.

21. Jana Evans Braziel and Anita Mannur, "Nation, Migration, Globalization: Points of Contention in Diaspora Studies," in *Theorizing Diaspora*, eds. Jana Evans Braziel and Anita Mannur (Malden, MA: Blackwell, 2003), 3.

22. Braziel and Mannur, Nation, Migration, Globalization," 1.

23. Braziel and Mannur, Nation, Migration, Globalization," 7.

24. Paul Gilroy, *Between Camps: Nations, Cultures and the Allure of Race* (London: Allen Lane/ Penguin Press, 2000), 122.

    [...]

30. Dionne Brand, *In Another Place, Not Here: A novel.* (New York: Grove, 1997).

31. Braziel and Mannur, "Nation, Migration, Globalization," 3.

32. Jay Prosser, *Second Skins: The Body Narratives of Transsexuality* (Malden, MA: Polity Press, 2000), 489; emphasis mine.

33. Prosser, *Second Skins*, 184.

34. Prosser, *Second Skins*, 488.

35. Prosser, *Second Skins*, 80.

36. Prosser, *Second Skins*, 178.

37. Claudia Benthien, *Skin: On the Cultural Border between Self and the World*, trans. Thomas Dunlap (New York: Columbia University Press, 2002), 25.

    [...]

39. Sara Ahmed, *Strange Encounters: Embodied Others in Post-Coloniality* (New York: Routledge, 2000), 89; emphasis mine.

40. Prosser, *Second Skins*, 68.

41. Leslie Feinberg, *Journal of a Transsexual* (New York: World View, 1980), 20.

42. Ahmed and Stacey, "Introduction," 2.

43. Jay Prosser, "Skin Memories," in *Thinking Through the Skin*, eds. Sara Ahmed and Jackie Stacey (London and New York: Routledge, 2001), 53.

44. Prosser, *Second Skins*, 84; emphasis mine.

45. Ahmed and Stacey, "Introduction," 2.

46. Ahmed and Stacey, "Introduction," 15.

47. Ahmed, *Strange Encounters*, 90.

48. Judith Halberstam, *Female Masculinity* (Durham, NC and London: Duke University Press, 1998), 163.

49. Prosser, *Second Skins*, 204.

    [...]

52. Jay Prosser, "Exceptional Locations: Transsexual Travelogues," in *Reclaiming Genders: Transsexual Grammars at the Fin de Siècle*, eds. Kate More and Stephen Whittle (New York: Continuum International Publishing Group, 1999), 88; emphasis mine.

53. Ahmed, *Strange Encounters*, 78.

54. Prosser, "Exceptional Locations," 88.

55. Aren Z. Aizura, "Of Borders and Homes: The Imaginary Community of (Trans)Sexual Citizenship," *Inter-Asia Cultural Studies* 7.2 (2006): 289.

56. Aizura, "Of Borders and Homes," 29.

57. Halberstam, *Female Masculinity*, 163.

58. Homi K. Bhabha, *The Location of Culture* (London and New York: Routledge, 2007), 142.

59. Aizura, "Of Borders and Homes," 290.

60. Aizura, "Of Borders and Homes," 290.

61. Aizura, "Of Borders and Homes," 290.

62. Aizura, "Of Borders and Homes," 290.

    [...]

64. Richard Phillips, *Mapping Men and Empire: A Geography of Adventure* (London: Routledge, 1997), 66.

    [...]

67. Halberstam, *Female Masculinity*, 172.

68. Halberstam, *Female Masculinity*, 172.

69. Ahmed, *Strange Encounters*, 89.

70. Halberstam, *Female Masculinity*, 170.
71. Halberstam, *Female Masculinity*, 170.
72. Halberstam, *Female Masculinity*, 159.
73. Ella Shohat, "Area Studies, Gender Studies, and the Cartographies of Knowledge," *Social Text* 72 20.3 (2002), 68.
    [...]
75. Gender specialist number two, on the other hand, seemed more willing to talk about the process of transition itself. But, couched in metaphors of migration and assimilation, his navigation of transsexuality still relied upon un/settling narratives of citizenship:

    >He said: "You need to think of transitioning as immigrating to a new country."
    >Silence.
    >I said: "But I've already had to do that once...when I came to Canada."
    >He smiled.
    >He said: "Then it should be easier."

76. Obioma Nnaemeka, "Nego-feminism: Theorizing, Practicing, and Pruning Africa's Way," *Signs* 29.2 (2004), 364.
77. Erella Shadmi, "Between Resistance and Compliance, Feminism and Nationalism: Women in Black in Israel," *Women's Studies International Forum* 23.1 (2000), 30.
78. Himani Bannerji, "Geography Lessons: On Being an Insider/Outsider to the Canadian Nation," in *Dangerous Territories: Struggles for Difference and Equality*, eds. Leslie G. Roman and Linda Eyre (New York: Routledge, 1997), 24.
79. Bannerji, "Geography Lessons," 24.
80. Lawrence Grossberg, *We Gotta Get Out of This Place: Popular Conservatism and Postmodern Culture* (New York: Routledge, 1992), 80.
81. Sara Ahmed, *Queer Phenomenology: Orientations, Objects, Others* (Durham, NC: Duke University, 2006), 7.
82. Ahmed, *Queer Phenomenology*, 57.
83. Ahmed, *Queer Phenomenology*, 59.
    [...]
89. Ahmed, *Queer Phenomenology*, 112.
90. Ahmed, *Queer Phenomenology*, 112.
91. Bannerji, "Geography Lessons," 35.
92. Bannerji, "Geography Lessons," 24; Prosser, *Second Skins*, 204.
93. bell hooks, *Yearning: Race, Gender and Cultural Politics* (Boston, MA: South End Press, 1990), 149.
94. Halberstam, *Female Masculinity*, 165.
95. Judith Halberstam, *In a Queer Time & Place: Transgender Bodies, Subcultural Lives* (New York: New York University Press, 2005), 11.
96. Halberstam, *Female Masculinity*, 165.
97. Halberstam, *Female Masculinity*, 164.
98. M. Jacqui Alexander, *Pedagogies of Crossing: Meditations on Feminism, Sexual Politics, Memory and the Sacred* (Durham, NC: Duke University Press, 2006), 188.
99. Arjun Appadurai, "Putting Hierarchy in its Place," in *Rereading Cultural Anthropology*, ed. George E. Marcus (Durham, NC: Duke University Press, 1992), 34.
100. [...]
101. Mohanram, *Black Body*, 22.
102. James Clifford, *Routes: Travel and Translation in the Late Twentieth Century* (Cambridge MA: Harvard University Press, 1997), 20.
103. Shohat, "Area Studies, Gender Studies," 69; Leslie Feinberg, *Transgender Warriors: Making History from Joan of Arc to Dennis Rodman* (Boston, MA: Beacon Press, 1996), 216.
104. Mohanram, Black Body, 49.
105. Shohat, "Area Studies, Gender Studies," 69.
106. John Agnew, "Space: Place," in *Spaces of Geographical Thought*, eds. Paul Cloke and Ron Johnston (Thousand Oaks, CA: Sage Publications, 2005), 82.
107. First published in 1979, Janice Raymond's *The Transsexual Empire: The Making of the She-Male* is widely criticized for its offensive portrayal of transsexual women as power-hungry rapists who have infiltrated the feminist movement. [...]
108. Sandy Stone, "The Empire Strikes Back: A Posttranssexual Manifesto," in *The Transgender Studies Reader*, eds. Susan Stryker and Stephen Whittle (New York: Routledge, 2006), 231.
109. Stone, "The Empire Strikes Back," 232.
110. Shohat, "Area Studies, Gender Studies," 72.
111. Stone, "The Empire Strikes Back," 232.
    [...]
113. Nandita Sharma, "Canadian Nationalism and the Making of a Global Apartheid," *Women and Environments International Magazine* 68/69 (2005), 10–12.
114. Song Hwee Lim, "Is the Trans- in Transnational the Trans- in Transgender?" *New Cinemas: Journal of Contemporary Film* 5.1 (2007), 47.

115. Smadar Lavie and Ted Swedenburg, "Introduction: Displacement, Diaspora, and Geographies of Identity," in *Displacement, Diaspora, and Geographies of Identity*, eds. Smadar Lavie and Ted Swedenburg (Durham, NC: Duke University Press, 1996), 3.
116. Mohanram, *Black Body*, 31; emphasis mine.
117. Benedict Anderson, "Imagined Communities," in *Nations and Nationalisms: A Reader*, eds. Phillip Spencer and Howard Wollman (Oxford: Rutgers University Press, 2005), 49.
118. Kirby, "Re: Mapping Subjectivity," 49
119. Sara Ahmed, *The Cultural Politics of Emotion* (New York: Routledge, 2004), 17; Kirby, "Re: Mapping Subjectivity," 48.
120. Samira Kawash, "The Homeless Body," *Public Culture* 10.2 (1998), 337.

# 40

# Trans*portation*

## Translating Filipino and Filipino American Tomboy Masculinities through Global Migration and Seafaring

### Kale Bantigue Fajardo

This essay, first published in *GLQ* in 2008 by Asian American Studies scholar Kale Fajardo, draws on extensive ethnographic research with Filipino seamen—on boats, in shipping yards in South East Asia and the U.S., and in several cities across the Pacific Rim. Filipinos constitute 28 percent of the global population of shipping workers. Mostly male, they are the more unfamiliar portion of the population of Overseas Filipino Workers (OFWs)—the better known portion being, of course, Filipina nannies, nurses, house-keepers and other such care-workers across the globe. Fajardo relates how, in her conversations with male shipping workers, some would tell stories about the tomboys in their lives, highlighting how both heterosexual men and transgender tomboys are included in a masculine form of intimacy, pakiisa, that involves trust and interdependence. This, Fajardo argues, illustrates how working-class masculinities are not as "macho" as they are assumed to be. An autoethnographic anecdote about watching cock-fighting videos with workers while at sea shows how, for Fajardo, both heterosexual and transgender OFW masculinities are formed through transportation and movement. Fajardo uses "transportation" as a concept that gestures beyond migration as a journey with a destination, and travel as a leisure activity, to register how structures of transnational capital "move" bodies through trajectories that resemble the repetitions, digressions and loops of shipping routes more than they do a one-way trip. Like overseas workers, Fajardo points out, tomboys are also often in transit—and are constantly negotiating these shifting fields of meaning, as well as the gender essentialisms of states and transnational corporations. Thus, Fajardo rejects both a Euro-American interpretation of tomboys as transgender subjects and a (Philippine) feminist interpretation of tomboys as lesbians. Multiply inscribed through class, Philippine immigrant or OFW status, masculine gender, and affinity with heterosexual non-transgender men, tomboys are "co-produced through routes in and out of Asia."

## A SEA OF (FILIPINO/A) GLOBAL MIGRANTS

Recently, the *New York Times* featured a report on the rising numbers of global migrants who collectively send oceanic-size remittances back home to the global south. The Sunday *Magazine* cover includes a photograph of a Filipina nurse—posed as abandoned, forlorn, and castaway— wearing medical scrubs, white shoes in hand, barefoot on a distant shore (Abu Dhabi?), aquamarine waters in the background; while inside the magazine a lengthy article discusses growing waves of migration from the global south to north, specifically focusing on the near constant outflow of Filipino/a migrants as a case study. The isolated and lonesome Filipina nurse on the magazine cover is revealing. She signifies how global migration and labor in general, and Filipino/a global migration and labor in particular, have been feminized.[1] That is, more women than men from the global south, including the Philippines, migrate to and work in the global north. Beyond suggesting the numerical differences in Filipino/a male and female migration patterns, she evokes a specific genealogy of how the Philippines as a nation and Filipino peoples in general have been feminized through U.S. and Japanese colonial, imperialist, capitalist, and misogynist discourses, which consistently inscribe the Philippines as a feminine and hence "weak nation-state," and the country's citizens and workers as exploited people, largely women.[2] Historically, these discourses have circulated through the figure of the Filipina as "prostitute," "mailorder bride," or "DH" (domestic helper). The wind-tossed and forsaken Filipina nurse brought to a foreign shore by the powerful tides of economic globalization is therefore a new twist on an entrenched discourse of Philippine and Filipino/a feminization, marginalization, and disempowerment.

Within this social context, in the Philippines and the diaspora, sea-based migration and transportation—also known as seafaring—has emerged as an important economic and cultural space through which Filipinos counter these discourses. Because seafaring is a profession where Filipino men are employed in large numbers, seafaring and seamen provide alternative spaces and figures for Filipino state officials, cultural workers, seamen, and even anthropologists to highlight a more masculine occupation and image of the Philippines and its people.[3]

Although a largely invisible migrant group in the United States, Filipino seamen can be found working on ships docked in every major port around the world. They constitute the largest ethnic/racial/national group in the industry's workforce and currently constitute about 28 percent of the labor in global shipping. Setting a national record in 2006, 260,000 Filipino seamen worked on thousands of container ships and oil tankers, which transport 90 percent of the world's goods and commodities, as well as cruise ships, which transport tourists.[4] Locally (in the Philippines), Filipino seamen as "OFWs" (Overseas Filipino Workers) are significant because they contribute huge sums of foreign currency to the national economy. In 2006 Filipino seamen sent home approximately $2 billion.[5] In the same year, OFWs (land- and sea-based) remitted a record high $12.8 billion. This global-local picture suggests why OFWs in general and Filipino seamen in particular are socially significant in Philippine and diasporic contexts.

For ten years I have been researching how working-class Filipino seamen imagine, experience, and create their masculinities through their everyday practices in global shipping, as well as how the Philippine state and other Filipino subjects imagine and produce Filipino masculinities through the sea and seafaring. From 1997 to 2002, I conducted ethnographic fieldwork with Filipino seamen in Manila and Oakland (primarily at maritime ports), and also with state officials, business people, and seafarer advocates in these two port cities. I gained access to Filipino seamen during fieldwork by accompanying (Catholic) seafarer advocates who were visiting ships, and I also visited ships independently. My encounters and conversations with seamen in ports generally ranged in length from a few minutes to an hour, usually during meals or work breaks.[6] In metropolitan Manila and the provinces, I had longer conversations with seamen who were back from sea; those looking to begin or renew contracts with shipping companies; those still attending maritime schools; and retired seamen. In the summer of 2006, as a passenger-ethnographer, I traveled by container ship from the Port of Oakland to the Port of Hong Kong via the northern Pacific Ocean with stops in Tokyo, Osaka (Japan), and Kiaoshung (Taiwan) to complete follow-up research.

Through this fieldwork I observed a recurring narrative about Filipino seamen used by Philippine state officials, cultural workers, and seamen. This narrative suggests that Filipino seamen are largely heterosexual, geographically and sexually mobile, and heroically nationalistic, while simultaneously being family oriented and usually "macho." Although aspects of this narrative accurately describe some Filipino seamen's experiences, my objective has been to intervene in heteropatriarchal understandings by ethnographically addressing the gaps, contradictions, and contingencies in mainstream representations of Filipino (seamen's) masculinities. These fissures become more intelligible when Filipino seamen's masculinities are engaged through their intimate relationalities—that is, through their close social relationships—with Filipino tomboys.[7] Here, the term *tomboy* broadly refers to male- or masculine-identified females or transgendered subjects on the female-to-male (FTM) spectrum of embodiments, practices, and/ or identities in the Philippines or diaspora who often have sexual and emotional relationships with feminine females who identify as "women." As a result of focusing on seamen's relations with tomboys, dominant state narratives of seamen's watertight masculinities begin to leak, revealing instead the connections and fluidities between conventional and transgender masculinities. The Philippines at this intersection is neither a forlorn and castaway nurse nor a macho seaman, but a contact zone between heterogeneously gendered and situated subjects who come together in dialogue on shore and at sea.[8]

As a researcher who enacts and embodies queer and transgender Filipino (American) tomboy masculinity, I learned that upon meeting and getting to know me, Filipino seamen wanted to share commentaries about tomboys in their past and present lives. Conversations with seamen about tomboys enabled me to address ethnographically the relationships between Filipino seamen's heterosexual masculinities and Filipino tomboy masculinities, which in turn provided me with an opportunity to develop a queer, transgender, and transnational narrative intervention and cultural critique—rather than naturalize and reinforce the (Philippine) state's heteronormative constructions of Filipino (seamen's) masculinities. Thus, what at first glance appears to be a heteronormative phenomenon (Filipino seamen in the global shipping industry), actually contains and reveals nonnormative or queer cultural dynamics, including the affinities between working-class Filipino (sea)men and tomboys, as well as a more expansive and inclusive understanding of Filipino masculinities. In this essay, through queer, immigrant, transgender, and transnational Filipino (American) cultural logics, I argue that differently situated Filipino masculinities—heterosexual male and tomboy—must be understood in relation to, *not* apart from, each other.

## TRANSPORTATION

As a (self-identified) queer, immigrant, and transgender Filipino American tomboy situated on both sides of the Pacific (the Philippines and the United States), I emphasize here a queer, transgender Filipino/American translocal, transnational, and transport(ation)-based cultural interpretation of Filipino seafaring and masculinities. Although migration studies often begin with the arrival of the migrant or immigrant in the "receiving country," the transportation framework I suggest includes examining the spaces in between and across countries/localities/spaces (the Philippines, the United States, the Pacific Ocean), and how movement and geographic positioning re/configure Filipino identities and masculinities. In particular, I examine transportation spaces, places, and movements such as ports, seas, ships, seafaring, migration, and travel, and how mobility reinforces, informs, or disrupts cultural meanings.

This understanding of transportation is partially informed by James Clifford's cultural theorizing in *Routes: Travel and Translation in the Late Twentieth Century*, particularly his idea that "travel [movement] is constitutive of culture." Clifford elaborates on the importance of movement by saying that "thinking historically is a process of locating oneself in space and time. And a location, in [this] perspective … is an *itinerary* rather than a bounded site—a series of encounters and translations."[9] Inspired by Clifford's understanding of travel, translations, and itineraries, I foreground cultural encounters and translations in ports and at sea, and suggest how specific embodied practices of mobility and movement—sea-based transportation, migration, and travel—are constitutive of racialized and classed Filipino masculinities. I use the terms *transportation* and *seafaring* to evoke the fact that Filipino seamen are moving through the sea as *sea-based migrant workers*—not as recreational elite travelers, which Clifford acknowledges is what the term *travel* usually connotes. By evoking transportation, I am not suggesting that transportation and seafaring do not involve moments of pleasure or recreation; rather, I do so to acknowledge that the global shipping industry is a (disciplined) site of (largely global south) migrant labor.

In addition to evoking movement across and in between spaces, transportation also calls up gender fluidity and inclusiveness, which the term *transgender* suggests. The "trans" in transgender and transportation evokes movement between and across culturally constructed racialized and classed masculinities and femininities, as well as movement in/through/between spaces. In other words, transportation as a term and framework highlights the intersections of embodied movement and migration (seafaring) *and* the fluidity of (racialized and classed) gender formations. With this transgender-informed understanding of transportation, I suggest that the non-gender-normative and nonheteronormative formations of Filipino tomboy can be interpreted as expressions and embodiments of transgender Filipino masculinities.

Although many middle-class lesbian activists in the Philippines and diaspora regularly use *tomboy* to describe or evoke Filipina working-class butch lesbians, I suggest that Filipino tomboy formations are akin to other transgender female masculinities rooted and routed through Southeast Asia, such as tombois in Indonesia and toms in Thailand. Anthropologist Megan J. Sinnott, for example, writes that toms in and from Thailand can be understood as "female 'men'" or "transgendered females," while anthropologist Evelyn Blackwood writes that "*tomboi* is a term used for females acting in the manner of men (*gaya laki-laki*)."[10] In agreement with these ethnographers, I suggest that the Filipino tomboys can also be understood as a form of female masculinity or an embodiment of female manhood or lalaki (the Tagalog word for male/man/guy). With this understanding of transgender masculinities, in addition to being in conversation with interdisciplinary queer studies scholars in the United States, I also seek to be in dialogue with Filipina feminists in the Philippines and diaspora who regularly advance the idea that Filipino tomboys are always lesbians or women.

Moreover, because tomboy is a term and formation that travels and circulates in and between the Philippines, Southeast Asia, and diasporic locations, I intentionally link queer and transgender with tomboy to indicate my transnationally and diasporically situated subject position and interpretive framework. My intention here is not to transport the terms *queer* or *transgender* to the Philippines in a "Western," U.S. American, or global north colonial or imperialist manner but to emphasize the transnational, trans-Pacific, and transport connections and cultural flows between the Philippines and regional, and diasporic, geographies. That is, Filipino/a peoples and ideas flow back and forth between the Philippines and diasporic locations. While it is important to understand the heterogeneity of Philippine/Asian local understandings and embodiments of tomboyness, it is also important to understand diasporic and immigrant interpretations and practices of tomboy, where tomboy can also signify FTM transgenderism.

Thus I connect Philippine and diasporic cultural logics and critique through the queer diasporic interpretive lens suggested by Gayatri Gopinath.[11] Gopinath forcefully challenges the dominance of Indian nationalist ideologies, which privilege India as a homeland and marginalize South Asian diasporic communities. [...] Building on Gopinath's framework, I intend *not* to privilege the homeland/nation (Philippines) *or* the diaspora (United States) as the original site of cultural purity or queer authenticity. This analytical and political position is based largely on ethnographic fieldwork, but also personal life experiences, which include regular travel between the United States and the Philippines, as well as substantial residency in both locations.[12] As a (self-defined) queer, immigrant, transgender Filipino American tomboy (researcher) who is situated in translocal, transnational, and transport contexts in the Philippines and the United States, I precisely evoke these multiple identity formations (queer, transgender, tomboy, and immigrant), which have different kinds of currency in the Philippines and diaspora (e.g., United States), to emphasize and highlight the complexities of how tomboy as a term, cultural practice, and embodiment circulates, and how tomboy formations are translated and interpreted in different Philippine, diasporic, and immigrant contexts.

The intimate relationalities between Filipino heterosexual (sea)men and Filipino tomboys, as well as the complexities of tomboy formations, became increasingly clear to me through fieldwork in Manila, Oakland, and at sea. As a new ethnographer who lived in the Philippines in the late 1990s, I initially thought that Filipino seamen would speak with me about their lives at sea, the working conditions on ships and in ports, and the politics of Philippine overseas migration policies (since these were my key research areas). Indeed, over the years I have met dozens of Filipino seamen who have shared stories and social commentaries about life at sea and in port(s). However, I also learned that Filipino seamen wanted to converse with me about transgender Filipino masculinities through the figure of the tomboy. These encounters highlighted how my subject position as tomboy enabled—rather than disabled—certain interactions, exchanges, and conversations with Filipino seamen.

During fieldwork, working-class seamen primarily interacted with me as a Filipino masculine and transgendered subject (tomboy), not as a Filipina feminine subject (woman). As I understand these ethnographic moments, they largely occurred because Filipino seamen understood tomboy to be a working-class embodiment of Filipino masculinity that, for them, was not routed or rooted through/in lesbianism or womanhood. With this shared understanding, we co-navigated conversations by discussing tomboys more generally, and more specifically moved toward seamen's stories, memories, and thoughts about tomboy friends, relatives, and acquaintances. Ethnographic encounters also evoked my own memories as a (young) tomboy in the Philippines, especially memories of Filipino men and tomboys closely interacting with one another. [...]

## FILIPINO TOMBOYS: TRANSNATIONAL, TRANS-PACIFIC, TRANSPORT MEANINGS

To understand the full significance of the intimate relation between Filipino heterosexual masculinities and Filipino tomboy masculinities, it is useful to situate and unpack the cultural politics of tomboy cultural meanings in transnational, trans-Pacific, and transport contexts. In Manila and other locations in the Philippines, *tomboy* is a term used to describe a range of gender and sexual practices and identities, including (1) woman-identified lesbianism often transculturated via white U.S.- or European-based notions of gender and sexuality, (2) working-class female-to-male transgender or transsexual embodiments and formations of masculinities where tomboys identify and/or live as lalaki (males/men), and (3) neither "women," "lesbians," or "men" but an entirely different third or fourth gender formation.[15] Cultural interpretations based on the second and third notions do not frequently circulate in scholarly knowledge production, and self-representations by Filipino tomboys are currently limited perhaps because of a lack of economic and educational access (especially in the Philippines). As a result, the first understanding (tomboys as lesbian women) has emerged as a dominant academic and political narrative in the Philippines and in some parts of the diaspora. That is, non-tomboy-authored narratives about tomboys circulate much more widely and have considerable cultural capital.

A significant aspect of how many Filipinos understand tomboy practices and identities in the Philippines and some immigrant communities in North America suggests that being poor or working class is central. This is reflected in popular Philippine discourse where tomboys are often inscribed as poor, working class, unemployed, or working in low-pay service-industry positions as bus conductors, security guards, factory workers, or overseas migrants. While not as visible in popular culture as baklas, poor tomboys can be found in the pages of Manila-based tabloids, as well as in locally made films such as *Tomboy Nora* (1970) and *T- Bird at Ako* (*T-Bird and I*, 1982), both starring the popular Philippine actress Nora Aunor. In an activist example, Information Center Womyn for

Womyn (ICWFW), a lesbian nongovernmental organization in Manila, conducted a study of what they describe as "working-class lesbians." The organization, which codes tomboys as lesbians rather than as transgender, reports that tomboys in their study were employed in positions such as domestic helper, barber, photocopying clerk, street food vendor, train station security guard, tennis court attendant, retail clerk, library assistant, and massage therapist.[16] In a more literary account, Nice Rodriguez (a Filipino tomboy based in Canada) writes in the short story "Every Full Moon" that the tomboy protagonist "Remy" (a.k.a. "Rambo") works as a bus conductor in metropolitan Manila: "A dangerous job meant for men and butches."[17]

Confirming the precarious economic status of tomboys, the video exposé *Behind the Labels: Garment Workers on U.S. Saipan* (dir. Tia Lessin; 2003) features Filipino tomboy antisweatshop activist Chie Abad who worked in a Gap clothing assembly plant for six years in Saipan and who later exposed and organized against the Gap's exploitative employment practices. Abad left the Philippines in the early 1990s to find work in an overseas factory in Saipan. In a personal communication Abad stated, "Many [Filipino] tomboys work abroad as overseas contract workers because they can't find jobs in the Philippines. The Philippines is poor and on top of that tomboys do not want to work in some fields because many companies and government agencies require female employees to wear women's clothing like blouses and skirts."[18] While in Saipan, Abad observed that other tomboys also migrated there for economic reasons. Abad's analysis, which emphasizes a transgender rather than lesbian framework for tomboyness, reveals how the Philippine state's, as well as multinational corporations', heteronormative gender essentialism attempts to police and enforce Filipina femininity and womanhood, severely limiting tomboy masculine gender expressions and both their and our economic opportunities.

Translating and interpreting tomboy in a U.S. context, Gigi Otálvaro-Hormillosa, a queer performance artist of Colombian and Filipino descent writing from the San Francisco Bay Area, asks, "To what extent does the queer Pinay (Filipina) butch enjoy privilege in the U.S. and in the Philippines, since 'butch' or 'tomboy' status deprives her of power in various diasporic settings[?]"[19] Here, Otálvaro-Hormillosa seems to be responding to what she sees as the unequal power relationships between tomboys, whom she equates with butch lesbians or dykes, and Filipino gay men in the diaspora. She responds, more specifically, to what she understands as the "infantilisation of the lesbian" through the term *tomboy* as deployed by anthropologist Martin Manalansan. According to Otálvaro-Hormillosa, Manalansan inadequately addresses queer Pinays, tomboys, and butches, and she critiques him for his "brief derogatory mentions" of Filipina lesbians.[20] Through her critique, Otálvaro-Hormillosa attempts to underscore the power "differences between men and women." That is, she respectively equates baklas and tomboys with manhood and womanhood/lesbianism in an immigrant and diasporic context (the United States). Unlike the previously mentioned accounts, Otálvaro-Hormillosa's analysis does not foreground class as a significant marker of tomboyness. Instead, she emphasizes womanness and diasporic or immigrant queer positionality as the clear central markers of difference in how she deploys and translates tomboy. Although Otálvaro-Hormillosa cites Michael Tan, cautioning, "It is dangerous to transport Western terms onto sexual practices and identities," she does precisely that by unequivocally equating tomboyness with lesbianism and womanhood in her essay. This demonstrates how notions of lesbianism may get universally transposed.

An alternative reading of Otálvaro-Hormillosa may suggest, however, that through transculturation she seeks to highlight a (racialized) queer Pinay/Filipina American framework, suggesting that queer Pinays in the diaspora deploy tomboy to refer to *Filipina* butches, lesbians, dykes, and queers in a U.S. or North American context. In other words, in a diasporic space Otálvaro-Hormillosa seeks to locally rework, translate, and "Filipina-ize" terms, ideologies, and formations that regularly circulate globally (womanness and lesbianism). In this different geopolitical location (in the United States, outside the Philippines), Otálvaro-Hormillosa clearly underscores a queer lesbian Pinay feminist or "peminist" perspective.[21] This is unlike mainstream Filipina feminist notions in the Philippines, which suggest that tomboys are generally *not* feminist or even antifeminist. While articulating a clear feminist perspective that highlights gender and power differences in the diaspora, Otálvaro-Hormillosa sidelines class as an axis of difference that intersects with other axes—race, gender, sexuality, nationality, location—in a coconstitutive nexus.

What Filipina feminist analyses published on both sides of the Pacific have in common is that both often use gender essentialist notions of tomboy. That is, queer Pinay feminists in the United States such as Otálvaro-Hormillosa or Filipina lesbian feminists such as those working for ICWFW in Manila suggest that tomboys are unequivocally women or lesbians. This kind of interpretation is reflected, for example, in Amelia M. de Guzman and Irene R. Chia's report on "working-class lesbians" in the Philippines for the ICWFW. De Guzman and Chia conducted lengthy interviews with nine tomboys (my term, not the ICWFW researchers') in Manila. Based on the interviews, their oral history project documents topics such as when tomboys "discovered they were lesbians," their employment histories, their recreational habits, their butch-femme relationships, and their religious practices. Throughout their analysis, de Guzman and Chia primarily use the term *lesbian* to describe the research participants, although admitting that a "unique element that [they] noticed among the participants is their hesitation to say the word lesbian." At another point in their report, de Guzman and Chia write, "All of them said that they like acting like men. They actually want to become men."[22] In my reading of de Guzman and Chia, they seek to advance a Filipina lesbian feminist perspective by applying the term *lesbian* to poor and working-class tomboys who are clearly uncomfortable with lesbian/woman as an identity and in some cases articulate a desire to become men or live as men.

As a result of how being poor or working class intersects with Filipino tomboy formations in common understandings, my own particular embodiment of tomboy masculinity produced unstable readings in "the field." On any given day in Manila (in different settings), Manileños interpreted my subject position in multifarious ways, for example, as "man," "woman," "bakla," or "tomboy." They also identified how these gender/sexual formations intersect with race, nationality, and class background: namely, "Filipino," "balikbayan," "OFW," "Japanese," "Chinese," or "Korean."[23] But significantly, when I traveled in and through the port area, if I introduced and represented myself as a student researcher (at the time) originally from Malolos, Bulacan, the town and province in the Philippines where I was born, and conversed in Tagalog, Filipino seamen generally interpreted my personhood as tomboy and interacted with me as a masculine/transgender subject.[24] Tomboy here refers to transgender FTM masculinity that is not woman- or lesbian-identified. Their reactions to my "localness" indicate that the Filipino seamen I encountered also understood tomboy formations in classed ways; namely, that tomboys are often locally situated, poor, or working class. Their reading of me as a (transgender) tomboy and their general understanding of tomboy formations were reinforced if I expressed a working-class sensibility or personal genealogy. For example, if I mentioned that I traveled by jeepney (a form of cheap street-level transportation) from Quezon City to the port or Ermita (a neighborhood in Manila where lots of seamen congregate) rather than by taxi, car, or chauffeur, which from the seamen's perspectives are what middle-class, wealthy, or balikbayan Filipinos might use for local transportation, they interacted with me as a (transgender) tomboy. In other cases, if I revealed my family's humble roots in Malolos, or that one of my male cousins was a seaman, or that a female cousin migrated to Kuwait as an OFW, or that an uncle migrated to "Saudi" (Arabia) and lived and worked there for many years, these personal disclosures marked my genealogy, family, and hence myself as more working class, perhaps middle class, but certainly not elite. This reinforced seamen's understandings of tomboy masculinities, which helped them "locate" my positionality and interact with me in terms of these cultural logics. In contrast, if I introduced other aspects of identity formation, for example, that I was from the United States and was a balikbayan and an academic—

three axes of difference that in the Philippines suggest class privilege—working-class seamen were more apt to interact with me as a "woman." If this occurred, I was inspired to contextualize or situate my tomboyness by deepening conversations that highlighted my family's poor and working-class origins. Once I demonstrated an intelligible and locally informed working-class sensibility, my very presence elicited seamen's memories, stories, and thoughts about tomboys.

To illustrate the intimate relationality between working-class Filipino (sea) men and tomboys and our shared spaces of Filipino masculinities, the following paragraphs include four examples of commentaries or conversation excerpts that emerged during fieldwork encounters in Manila and Oakland. The narratives were originally communicated to me in Tagalog but are translated here into English.[25] The seamen's narratives collectively speak to how Filipino heterosexual male masculinities and Filipino transgender tomboy masculinities coexist and are coproduced in Philippine contexts.[26]

> 1. In Manila, a Filipino seaman, "Ernesto" (a crew member on the *Sea Star*), told me about "Percy," a tomboy he knows through his sister who lives and works in Hong Kong: "Percy was a big help to me. I had so many problems in my marriage. I was so depressed one time I was in Hong Kong. Percy took me out and showed me a good time. We went out drinking, went to some bars and I tried to forget my wife and my problems. Percy was the one who reminded me that I should just live my life. My wife wanted a separation. Percy and I were sitting in a bar getting really drunk and Percy said, 'Tapos na, Pare' (It's over, compadre/friend). I was sad, but I knew what Percy said was correct, true."

> 2. In Oakland, a Filipino seaman, "Anthony," remembered his tomboy cousin, nicknamed "Mel": "Mel's mother died when Mel was young, so my mother took care of Mel (plus Mel's two brothers and sister). When the school year started, my mother would buy uniforms and books for my siblings and me. My mother would also buy Mel and my other cousins these things. Mel was close to my age, so we always played together when we were young. Mel is a real guy (tunay na lalaki). Now, Mel has a woman-companion. They've been together a long time. When I have extra money, I send some to Mel. Mel has a small business at the market, but I know that Mel still needs the help."

> 3. In Ermita, a retired Filipino captain, "Jonas," recalled a story about a tomboy he met early on in his career. Now in his late fifties, Jonas remembers: "The captain, who was a Filipino, brought his 'anak,' a tomboy who was around twenty years of age, on board the ship for part of our voyage.[27] The captain thought that maybe his anak would meet a man on board the ship and that this would turn her into a 'real girl.' But none of the men liked the anak. This person was really 'guyish' (or boyish) (lalaking-lalalaki). When the captain was not around, the anak would be included as part of the group. We would talk and tell stories or eat together. But when the captain was around, we acted like this person wasn't part of our group. We didn't want to make the captain mad. The captain eventually sent his anak home because he saw that no one wanted this person."

> 4. And in Oakland, a Filipino seaman, "Ruben," remembered his tomboy cousin "Lou": "We were close in high school. Lou now works at Mega Mall as a security guard. Lou didn't finish college. When I'm on vacation in Manila, I see Lou and we go out drinking with some others from our group. We're still close."

Although these seamen's stories and memories about tomboys were initially unexpected, the regularity of seamen sharing tomboy commentaries begins to reveal how my embodied presence as a Filipino (American) tomboy ethnographer perhaps prompted or encouraged these narratives. That is, it is highly probable that many of the seamen I encountered agreed to talk with me precisely because they had previous experiences with tomboys.[28] The seamen's stories of shared childhood and family experiences and friendships illustrate that in Filipino contexts (particularly among Filipino Christian-based lowlanders) it is culturally sensible and analytically appropriate to analyze Filipino tomboy masculinities in relation to Filipino heterosexual male masculinities, rather than separate them from each other, which frequently happens in feminist accounts.[29] Or, in the case of the (Philippine) state, tomboys are completely ignored or rendered invisible. The seamen's stories and memories speak of overlapping and shared social spaces from and through childhood, youth, kinship/family ties, and friendships where different kinds of Filipino masculinities are cocreated, coproduced, and coexperienced. The seamen's narratives as a whole strongly suggest that Filipino tomboy masculinities can be—indeed, are—a part of Filipino heterosexual male masculinities and vice versa: that is, some heterosexual Filipino men grow up alongside tomboys, and some tomboys develop meaningful friendships and kinship ties with bio-boys and bio-men.

Seamen's commentaries about friendships and family ties with tomboys also collectively reveal an important component of Filipino masculinities: the ability to connect emotionally and create "oneness" with each other, understood in Tagalog as "pakiisa." In a late-1980s Philippines-based ethnographic study, Jane A. Margold notes the inadequacy of conventional understandings of gender for registering the complexities of Filipino masculinities to the extent that they cannot "account for a masculinity that seeks intimacy and reckons a feeling of trust and oneness with another (including other men) as a highly desirable state (*pakikiisa*, in Tagalog)." Critiquing dominant frameworks that define masculinities through "emotional repression and detachment" and which posit the "Filipino man as macho or patriarchal," Margold emphasizes instead *emotional intimacy* between Filipino men and "more fluid, contingent gender identities."[30] The Ilokano overseas migrant men in Margold's study created and enhanced pakiisa through barkadas (friendship groups), which enabled them to endure oppressive social conditions, where employers referred to them as " 'tools,' 'slaves,' and 'dogs,' " and where the threat of (Arab/employer) violence loomed large. Pakiisa as a cultural concept stresses the goal of creating "emotional oneness" through the group, *not* through masculinist individualism, intragroup hierarchies, social competition, and violence that patriarchal European-based notions of dominant masculinities and "male social bonding" have historically reinforced.

In contradistinction, situated in Philippine contexts and cultural logics, pakiisa emphasizes group or collective equality and emotional collaboration, directly suggested in pakiisa's composite parts. As a specialist in Pilipino language studies, Teresita V. Ramos, writes, "The prefix 'paki' is roughly equivalent to the English word 'please.'.. . The topic or focus of the *paki-* verb may be any semantic element *other than the actor*, such as the object or goal [e.g. 'isa'/oneness] … . [In other words], [t]he actor of a *paki-*verb … is always in a *non-focus*."[31] Since *paki-* refers to a polite request to meet a goal— that is, "please collaborate with me to create a sense of emotional oneness"—and *not* a command, pakiisa suggests that group members value equality and interdependence within the group, which is collectively striving to reach the common goal of isa (emotional oneness). Since the object or goal, not individual actors, is the group's primary focus, pakiisa also suggests that the self or personal ego is subordinate and unimportant; in other words, what takes priority is the group or the overall well-being of the larger unit. Although Margold is specifically referring to Ilokanos, her arguments are applicable to other Filipino lowlanders, such as the Tagalogs and Visayans I encountered during fieldwork. This is particularly the case because pakiisa is defined as a Tagalog word, not Ilokano. In seamen's commentaries, they evoke and remember stories of love, loss, brotherhood, and camaraderie with tomboy cousins, friends, and older relatives, demonstrating how working-class Filipino (sea) men and tomboys cocreate masculinities through pakiisa.

Like the working-class Filipino seamen I encountered, I also began to think about moments of pakiisa with other Filipino men and tomboys. Traveling fieldwork encounters with Filipino seamen in Manila, Oakland, and at sea transported me to memories of earlier balikbayan travel where heterogeneous masculinities (straight, tomboy, local, and balikbayan) coexisted. In the following section, I combine ethnographic description, travelogue, and personal reflection to show another example of how heterogeneous Filipino masculinities are cocreated. The vignette further demonstrates how tomboy masculinities are interpretable or translatable as transgender formations, and also highlights how heterogeneous masculinities coexist through transportation, seafaring, and immigrant/balikbayan/ OFW travel.

## SUNDAY COCKFIGHTS (AT SEA AND IN MALOLOS, BULACAN, PHILIPPINES)

It is early evening on a Sunday on the *Penang Prince*, after a mostly blue-sky day at sea. The sun is beginning its descent into the always receding horizon, leaking out electric orange light through a few hazy clouds. The *Prince*, a German-flagged container ship en route from Long Beach, California, to Hamburg, Germany, moves through the steel-blue waters. Winds are steady, but not fierce. The *Prince*'s regular route is to travel back and forth between Western Europe and Southern California, stopping in ports in the Mediterranean, Red Sea, Indian Ocean, Southeast and East Asia, and then crossing the northern Pacific to the U.S. West Coast. I boarded the ship at the Port of Oakland and will disembark at the Port of Hong Kong, our next port of call. I have been a passenger-ethnographer on the *Penang Prince* almost two weeks now. Following the northern Pacific Rim, the *Prince* headed north from the San Francisco Bay Area, up the west coast, and off of the coast of Vancouver, British Columbia, headed west toward Asia, passing through the Gulf of Alaska, the Aleutian Islands, and into the Bering Sea. The *Prince* then traveled toward the south and eventually docked at the Ports of Tokyo, Osaka (Japan), Kiaoshung (Taiwan), and Hong Kong (China). Twenty-one seamen work on board this ship: five Germans (all officers, including the captain), five Filipinos (all officers), and eleven seamen from Kiribati in the South Pacific (all of lower ranks).

The five Filipinos invited me to join them in the officers' recreation room this evening to watch cockfights recorded on a VCD that one of them purchased in Singapore. When I arrive at the gathering, I notice that the second mate has a bottle of Russian vodka and some boxed orange juice, while the chief cook shares small pieces of beef marinated in adobo sauce (soy sauce, garlic, vinegar, and bay leaves) and then baked. My contribution to the group is some Carlsberg beer purchased from the captain's store.

Sunday cockfights remind me of my father's mother, lola (grandmother) Chayong, a small, quiet, and kind woman who in the 1970s ran a food stall at the Malolos Municipal Cockfighting Arena in Bulacan Province. Fortunately for me, my parents'/grandmother's modest home was located directly across from the sabongan (cockfighting arena). As a nine-year-old balikbayan child in 1977, I recall traveling to the Philippines, the cooking frenzy before the cockfights, and then actually watching cockfights with my uncles ("E" and "B") and their tomboy friend ("Jo-Jo"). On Saturday night, my grandmothers, aunts, and older female cousins cooked foods such as bibingka (cassava cake) and ube (sweetened purple yam), and on Sunday morning, they prepped the ingredients for pancit lug-lug, a Central Luzon noodle dish that was my lola's specialty.

All of the action occurred in the kitchen in the morning, but once the cockfights were about to begin, the action moved across the street. On this particular balikbayan trip Titos (uncles) E and B (then in their mid- to late twenties), plus Tito B's tomboy friend, Jo-Jo, who lived in my father's barrio, brought me to watch the cockfights in the upper stands. There, I listened to and observed my uncles and Jo-Jo yelling and placing bets across our section of the arena, the absolute quiet of the place just before the gamecocks clashed, and the crowd's eruption into thunderous cheering and more yelling as one of the gamecocks cut into his opponent's body with a knife attached to an ankle, drawing first blood. Later, some of the losing cocks were butchered near my lola's eatery.

On the ship, the cockfights are much more subdued compared with my childhood immigrant and balikbayan experiences despite the alcohol we have been drinking; there are only six of us, after all.

As the VCD plays on the TV screen, the seamen size up the gamecocks, offering commentary on their overall appearance, noting features like feather color, relative size, personality, and demeanor (e.g., "That one's a beauty, that one's ugly. This cock looks mean, that cock looks cowardly"). On board the *Prince*, no one gambles with real money, only fantasy-greenbacks: the third mate bets one million dollars on the large off-white cock, while the electrician prefers the spotted brown one. The second mate bets five million dollars on the indigo-ink-colored cock with the orange-and-white plume feathers; I agree to root for its opponent. We are captivated with each cockfight, which lasts a few minutes or longer. The fights happen in quick succession because we are watching a cockfighting derby where many elite fighting cocks battled each other at Araneta Coliseum in metro Manila several months ago. We produce a similar stillness that happens in live cockfights and the eruption of noise as the gamecocks clash. The Filipino seamen and I are yelling and swearing as the fights develop: "Ang ganda!" (How beautiful!), "Sige!" (Go on!), "Puta!" (Whore!). And when their chosen cocks are slashed or lose: "Naku, patay na ang manok!" (Wow, the chicken is dead!); "Ang bilis!" (How fast [the gamecock lost]!). Excited, the third mate yells at me: "Mas maganda ito kay sa world cup, di ba?!" (This is more beautiful than the World Cup, right?!). (The 2006 World Cup soccer tournament was concluding during the voyage. While the German seamen tracked the tournament through satellite reports, Filipino seamen had little interest in this event.)

What these Sunday cockfights show is that there are clearly spaces where different kinds of masculine subjects—here, Filipino straight men and tomboys—coexist and cocreate masculinities in and through transportation and travel, that is, immigrant/balikbayan/OFW mobilities in key masculine social spaces (seafaring and cockfights). This is *not* to say that heterogeneous (including queer and transgender) masculinities are created only through practices of mobility and movement, outside the nation-state/"homeland" and in the diaspora. Indeed, my first experiences of cockfights happened precisely in a "local space" (Malolos). In making this clarification, I aim to dialogue with critiques and concerns raised in Asia where gender and sexuality studies scholars and activists suggest that queer (U.S.) diaspora perspectives have become hegemonic (or even colonial), rendering local/regional queer and Asian cultural formations and geographies "less queer," "more normative," and/or "more traditional."[32] These important knowledge/power critiques situated in Asia are critical to keep in mind as queer studies scholars and activists situated in the United States or global north dialogue and debate with counterparts situated in Asia or the global south. Seamen's narratives illustrate that heterogeneous and queer masculinities are produced in various local, regional, transnational, and global nexuses (e.g., Malolos, Manila, Oakland, Philippines/United States/Southeast Asia/Pacific Rim)—not simply in global north, United States, or diasporic contexts. While I am invested in understanding queer/ nonnormative racialized and classed genders and sexualities as they are locally, regionally, transnationally, and globally *rooted in Asia*, I am also committed to showing how heterogeneous masculinities (straight, tomboy, queer, transgender) are also coproduced through transit and transport—*routes in and out of Asia*.

Cross-culturally, cockfights have been largely interpreted as purely "men's spaces" where dominant masculinities are reproduced. This has been especially true in island Southeast Asian studies since Clifford Geertz's watershed essay "Deep Play: Notes on the Balinese Cockfight" has been required anthropological reading in many anthropology departments (and even in gender studies). In and through Geertz's widely acclaimed cultural interpretation, the (Balinese) cockfight has become the signifier par excellence of (Balinese) men and masculinity.[33] [...] Although Geertz writes a complex and informative "thick description" of Balinese cockfighting, he narrativizes the cockfights as an absolute men's space, missing the ways that women participate on the sidelines through the selling of food, drinks, and admission tickets.[35] It is also quite probable that with this kind of understanding of masculinity/gender, he entirely missed the Indonesian tombois (as well as children) who may have been watching the cockfights with male friends or adult relatives.

In light of these gaps, what at first appears to be a highly normative "heterosexual men's space" (Filipino seamen at sea/watching cockfights) can thus also be read and interpreted through a queer and transgender Filipino (American) framework if the presence of alternative masculinity formations (tomboy) are taken into account. Additionally, if the intimate relations among and between working-class Filipino heterosexual masculinities and Filipino queer female masculinities and the concept of pakiisa are treated seriously, we get an entirely different cultural interpretation or ethnographic description of the scene.

Instead of seeing a closed, watertight, and dominant Filipino masculinity, which strongly reinforces a heterosexual reading of seaman, cocks, and cockfighting (i.e., Geertz's cultural interpretation), heterosexual *and transgender tomboys* actually have access to the symbolic meanings of game/cocks and/or the phallus. This illustrates how Filipino masculinities are contingent, fluid, and not naturalized through biology or the body. This dynamic coproduction of masculinities was evident not only through the cockfighting experience but throughout my time on the *Prince*. Filipino seamen during the trans-Pacific voyage engaged a more transgender understanding of Filipino tomboy masculinities. As such, the working-class Filipino seamen on board the *Prince* never used the word *lesbian*, and like many of the seamen who shared tomboy commentaries at the Ports of Manila and Oakland, they used the term *tomboy* to describe masculine Filipino females or FTMs who are more "guy-or-man-like" (lalaking-lalaki) and who have sexual and emotional relationships with "women" (feminine females who identify as such). With this understanding of Filipino gender formations and my own subject positioning and embodiment, the Filipino seamen at sea interacted with me as a Filipino masculine subject (as a tomboy/guy). Subsequently, we shared activities that tomboys and Filipino men share in the Philippines, and which many other seamen recounted during conversations in port: we drank alcohol, ate pulutan (the food that goes with alcohol), talked with each other about sweethearts and lovers (in their case, also wives), discussed relationship and family problems, sang Tagalog songs available on karaoke VCDs, which projected soft porn imagery, cheered Filipino boxing champion Manny Pacquiao as we viewed fights on VCD, and watched sabong (cockfighting) on Sundays.

Moreover, watching the cockfights on the ship with the five Filipino seamen evoked my own memories of spending time with other men and tomboys in the Philippines—specifically with my uncles E and B and their tomboy friend Jo-Jo. My own immigrant and balikbayan experiences as a young tomboy participating in Sunday family rituals and watching sabong reflects many of the seamen's stories from port and sea: men and tomboys—young and old—spending time together as friends, family, companions, and neighbors cocreating heterogeneous masculinities.

## AVAST: TO CEASE HAULING; TO STOP (CONCLUSION)

Seamen's commentaries about tomboy relatives and friends, as well as my (auto) ethnographic travelogue, articulate clear counternarratives to U.S. and Japanese colonial, imperialist, capitalist, and misogynist discourses that seek to construct the Philippines and Filipino/a peoples as disempowered or feminized victims without agency. Seamen, and now tomboys, provide important masculinist alternatives to the figure of the Filipina DH (domestic helper), prostitute, or mail-order bride, through which to imagine the nation and migrant labor. More important, however, by examining and emphasizing how heterogeneous masculinities (straight, transgender, working class, Filipino and Filipino American) are cocreated, coproduced, and clearly contingent, dominant notions of Filipino masculinities are denaturalized and opened up for questioning and challenge. Moreover, the seamen's commentaries, as well as my analysis and autobiographical travelogue of the intimate relations between heterosexual Filipino men and Filipino tomboys, directly contradict Filipina and Filipina American feminist understandings of tomboys as primarily women or lesbians. Interpreting Filipino tomboys as embodiments and formations of transgenderism and FTM manhood, my analytic collage illustrates the importance of addressing the geotemporal place-moments where differently situated Filipino masculinities intersect, contradict, and reinforce each other. [...]

Through situated traveling fieldwork in ports, ships, and seas, as well as immigrant/ balikbayan travel, I have shown that what may appear to be a (hetero)normative cultural moment of gender expression (Filipino men at sea/watching cockfights) reveals other complex cultural dynamics at play: namely, working-class Filipino heterosexual men and tomboys cocreating differently situated masculinities.

Yes, cockfights at sea are more beautiful than the World Cup.

## NOTES

1. See, for example, Nicole Constable, *Maid to Order in Hong Kong: Stories of Filipina Workers* (Ithaca: Cornell University Press, 1997); and Rhacel Salazar Parreñas, *Servants of Globalization: Women, Migration, and Domestic Work* (Stanford: Stanford University Press, 2001).
2. Neferti X. Tadiar, *Fantasy-Production: Sexual Economies and Other Philippine Consequences for the New World Order* (Hong Kong: Hong Kong University Press, 2004).
3. I use the word *seamen* because it is the term commonly used by seamen, their families, and local people in the Philippines. *Seafarer* and *Overseas Filipino Worker* are terms more widely used by the Philippine government and nongovernmental organizations. On state discourse, see Kale Bantigue Fajardo, "Of Galleons and Globalization," *Mains'l Haul: A Journal of Pacific Maritime History* 38, nos. 1–2 (2002): 61–65; for a literary perspective, see Carlos Cortes, *Longitude* (Quezon City: University of the Philippines Press, 1998).
4. Many Filipino seafarers (men and women) work on cruise ships; my research primarily focuses on Filipino seamen on industrial container ships. For information on multinational cruise corporations, see Ross A. Klein, *Cruise Ship Squeeze: The New Pirates of the Seven Seas* (Gabriola Island, BC: New Society, 2005).
5. Maricel Burgonio, "2006 OFW Remittances Hit Record $12.8 B," *Manila Times*, February 16, 2007, www.manilatimes.net/national/2007/feb/16/yehey/top_stories/20070216top4.html.
6. The relatively brief duration of conversations is partially due to the fact that while ships are docked in port, seamen are quite busy. Because of mechanization and increased time pressures, working in port is often more fast paced than working at sea (although this depends on the seaman's position).
7. Scott Morgensen uses the phrase "intimate relationalities" to describe the historically close political and cultural relationships between U.S. sexual minority formations and two-spirit (American Indian) formations. See Morgensen's forthcoming book, *Settler Sexuality and the Politics of Indigeneity*. *Tomboy* is an English word that has been "Tagalog-ized" (i.e., the first *o* is pronounced with an even shorter *o* sound than the English version). Following the historian Noenoe K. Silva's lead, I do not italicize Tagalog words in this essay. Silva states that she does not italicize Hawai'ian words in order "to resist making the native tongue appear foreign" (*Aloha Betrayed: Native Hawaiian Resistance to American Colonialism* [Durham, NC: Duke University Press, 2004], 13).
8. Omise'eke Natasha Tinsley theorizes oceanic spaces (e.g., black Atlantic) as queer racialized spaces. Tinsley's black queer feminist reading of oceans, ships, and shipmates is in dialogue with the analysis here.
9. James Clifford, *Routes: Travel and Translation in the Twentieth Century* (Cambridge, MA: Harvard University Press, 1997), 11, emphasis mine.
10. Megan J. Sinnott, *Toms and Dees: Transgender Identity and Female Same-Sex Relationships in Thailand* (Honolulu: University of Hawai'i Press, 2004); Evelyn Blackwood, "*Tombois* in West Sumatra: Constructing Masculinity and Erotic Desire," in *Female Desires: Same-Sex Relations and Transgender Practices across Cultures*, ed. Evelyn Blackwood and Saskia E. Wieringa (New York: Columbia University Press, 1999).
11. Gayatri Gopinath, *Impossible Desires: Queer Diasporas and South Asian Public Cultures* (Durham, NC: Duke University Press, 2005).
12. I immigrated to the United States in 1973 and have been traveling regularly to the Philippines since then, with trips lasting from ten days to ten months, in the following years: 1977, 1978, 1987, 1988–89, 1992, 1994, 1996, 1997–98, 2000, 2005, and 2006.
13. Anna Tsing, *Friction: An Ethnography of Global Connection* (Princeton: Princeton University Press, 2005), x. [...]
15. The other gender formation often discussed in Filipino/a contexts is bakla (a Filipino/a male femininity or gay men's formation). See, for example, Martin F. Manalansan IV, *Global Divas: Filipino Gay Men in the Diaspora* (Durham, NC: Duke University Press, 2003), and Bobby Benedicto's essay, this issue.
16. Amelia M. de Guzman and Irene R. Chia, "Working Class Lesbians in the Philippines," 2005, www.icwow.org/WCL/WCLenglish.pdf.
17. Nice Rodriguez, *Throw It to the River* (Toronto: Women's Press, 1993), 26.
18. Chie Abad, pers. comm., February 2002.

19. Gigi Otálvaro-Hormillosa, "Performing Citizenship and 'Temporal Hybridity' in a Queer Diaspora," *Antithesis* 11 (2000), www.devilbunny.org/temporal_hybridity.htm.
20. My position is that in *Global Divas* Manalansan does not significantly focus on Filipina tomboys, lesbians, and dykes primarily because it was not within the scope of his study to address these racialized gender/sexuality formations.
21. Melinda L. de Jésus, ed., *Pinay Power: Peminist Critical Theory: Theorizing the Filipina/American Experience* (New York: Routledge, 2005).
22. Guzman and Chia, "Working Class Lesbians in the Philippines," 14, 18.
23. Balikbayan historically refers to Filipinos/as from North America who return to the Philippines. The (Ferdinand) Marcos dictatorship coined this term and promoted tourism with Filipino/a immigrants in Canada and the United States in the 1970s.
24. Various readings emerged quickly upon first meeting with Filipinos/as during fieldwork. [...]
25. Tagalog does not have feminine or masculine pronouns. My translations of the seamen's commentaries reflect the gender-neutral aspects of Tagalog.
26. All names introduced in quotation marks are pseudonyms.
27. Anak is a gender-neutral Tagalog word for child/offspring, and there are no equivalent Tagalog words for "son" or "daughter." A speaker may say, however, "anak na lalaki" (child that is a male) or "anak na babae" (child that is female) to mark a person's gender. Jonas used the word *anak* and did not include "na babae" (that is female). So as to not infantilize the tomboy Jonas was referring to, I do not translate anak here as "child." Anak can also refer to adult children.
28. Situated traveling fieldwork emphasizes short-term ethnographic encounters in contact zones and reflexive/situated cultural analysis in contrast to long-term fieldwork in a bounded field site (e.g., village) with hopes of producing "objective ethnography" (the preferred mode in traditional/colonial anthropology).
29. My discussion is most applicable to the largest Philippine lowlander groups (largely Christian based): Tagalogs, Ilokanos, and Visayans.
30. Jane Margold, "Narratives of Masculinity and Transnational Migration: Filipino Workers in the Middle East," in *Bewitching Women, Pious Men: Gender and Body Politics in South East Asia*, ed. Aihwa Ong and Michael G. Peletz (Berkeley: University of California Press, 1995), 279, 283, 274. Margold's *pakikiisa* is a variant of *pakiisa*.
31. Teresita V. Ramos, *Conversational Tagalog: A Functional-Situational Approach* (Honolulu: University of Hawai'i Press, 1985), 134, emphasis mine. Pilipino—largely Tagalog based—is the national language of the Philippines.
32. I anecdotally heard about these critiques from U.S.-based queer studies scholars who attended the Sexualities, Genders, and Rights in Asia—1st International Conference of Asia Queer Studies, in Bangkok, Thailand, July 7–9, 2005.
33. Clifford Geertz, "Deep Play: Notes on the Balinese Cockfight," in *The Cockfight: A Casebook*, ed. Alan Dundes (Madison: University of Wisconsin Press, 1994), 99.
[...]
35. See Scott Guggenheim, "Cock or Bull: Cockfighting, Social Structure, and Political Commentary in the Philippines," in *The Cockfight: A Casebook*, ed. Alan Dundes (Madison: University of Wisconsin Press, 1994), 149, for a brief discussion of Filipinas who work at cockfighting arenas.

# IX

## *BIOPOLITICS AND THE ADMINISTRATION OF TRANS-EMBODIMENT(S)*

# 41

# *Kaming Mga Talyada (We Who Are Sexy)*

## The Transsexual Whiteness of Christine Jorgensen in the (Post)colonial Philippines

SUSAN STRYKER

SUSAN STRYKER IS CURRENTLY DIRECTOR OF THE INSTITUTE FOR LGBT STUDIES and Associate Professor of Gender and Women's Studies at the University of Arizona. This article, which offers a close reading of the 1962 Filipino feature film *Kaming Mga Talyada* (*We Who Are Sexy*), was originally published in slightly different form in *Social Semiotics*, as part of a special issue on "The Somatechnics of Race and Whiteness." The film is a light comedy that revolves around the appearance of transsexual celebrity Christine Jorgensen at a Manila nightclub; in spite of the film's unassuming tone, Stryker argues, it nevertheless poses substantive questions about the ways in which the medico-juridical discourse of transsexuality has circulated globally with white Eurocentric privilege, and the ways in which it has operated within the densely layered (post) colonial histories of Filipino sex/gender/sexuality/identity—particularly the intertwined categories of *talyada* and *bakla*. Stryker draws on an emerging body of critical literature called *somatechnics*, which elaborates upon the always-already technologized nature of all embodiment and contests the conceptualization of technology as a prosthetic add-on to previously formed "natural bodies." Stryker interprets transsexual embodiment and transgender identity as "somatechnologies" that enmesh individual bodies within the biopolitical project of state-based territorial sovereignty and the governance of national populations. Thus, the micropolitical struggles that the film represents as revolving around the categories of *transsexual* and *talyada* simultaneously enact those same struggles in a different register, on the macro-political scale; here they are an attempt to secure the heteronormative Christian/secular construction of genders that sustain and reproduce Filipino national sovereignty against the twin threats of Islamist and U.S. imperialist challenges to the territorial integrity of the Republic of the Philippines.

*Kaming Mga Talyada* (a.k.a. *We Who Are Sexy*) was produced in 1962 for the Filipino domestic film market by Sampaguita Pictures, one of the major studios in the Philippines (Cayado, 1962). It was an ephemeral piece of popular entertainment that took advantage of the extended appearance of U.S. transsexual celebrity Christine Jorgensen at a Manila nightclub, in order to weave a suprising complex tale of contemporary Filipino gender and sexuality. In spite of the film's light comic tone, *Kaming Mga Talyada* substantively engages with the effects of the newly spectacularized medico-juridical discourse of transsexuality—which circulated globally in the 1950s and 60s via the figure of Christine Jorgensen—on Filipino configurations of sex/gender/sexuality/identity, and thus on the biopolitical equations by means of which sovereign power reproduced and sustained itself.

Veering through several genres (romantic comedy, musical, war story), the film's convoluted storyline narrates the process whereby the production of normative hetero-patriarchal genders secures national territorial sovereignty in the Republic of the Philippines, by simultaneously suppressing a racialized and Orientalized internal Other (the Muslim Moros) while at the same time warding off the destabilizing pull of the U.S. American metropole (figured as white in the person of Christine Jorgensen). In doing so, the film depicts a (post)colonial encounter between two competing "somatechnologies" that allow us to explore the interrelationship between micro-political techniques of subjective individualization (what Michel Foucault called the "anatamo-political") and the macro-scale socio-political organization of state, territory, and population (what Foucault called at the "biopolitical"). It is the "whole intermediary cluster of relations" Foucault describes as linking the anatamo-political to the biopolitical that I seek to identify with the neologism *somatechnics*, which, by supplanting the logic of the *and* in the phrase "embodiment *and* technology," is meant to suggest that material corporeality (*soma*) is inextricably conjoined with the techniques and technologies (*technics*) through which bodies are formed and transformed, and to name the spaces in which, and practices through which, the lives of individual bodies become concretely enmeshed in the lives of nations, states, and capital formations (Foucault 1978, 139).[1]

## THE SPECTACULAR WHITENESS OF AMERICAN TRANSSEXUALITY

Nightclub entertainer Christine Jorgensen spent several months in Manila in 1962, performing at the Safari Club, during an extended tour of the Pacific that also took her to Honolulu, Sydney, and Hong Kong (Jorgensen, 279–282). To the extent that Jorgensen is remembered at all today, it is as an iconic pioneer of the medico-juridical process of somatic transformation that became known in the mid-twentieth-century as "transsexuality." As I and others have recounted elsewhere, Christine Jorgensen made her debut as the first global transsexual celebrity in 1952, at age 26, when news of her genital transformation surgery in Copenhagen made headlines around the world—the first time that surgical and hormonal techniques for "changing sex" had been accorded such attention. (Stryker 1999, 2007; Meyerowitz, 49–98 and *passim.*; Serlin, 159–190, Docter). Jorgensen, a New York native of Danish descent, stayed in the media spotlight for a quarter-century, and it was largely through coverage of her that the phenomenon of transsexuality first became widely known to mass audiences. Shy to the point of reclusiveness before her gender transition, but unable to find routine work due to her notoriety and the stigma attached to transsexuality, Jorgensen developed a lucrative nightclub act that exploited the public's fascination with her, and earned her upwards of $5000 a week throughout the 1950s. She published a best-selling autobiography in 1967 (adapted for the screen in 1970 as the trashy exploitation film *The Christine Jorgensen Story*), and thereafter enjoyed a second career as a sought-after speaker on the college lecture circuit. Even in the 1980s, as Jorgensen's appeal faded, she appeared frequently on television talk shows and at public events, until her death from bladder cancer in 1989 at age 62. Although now little-remembered beyond LGBT people of a certain age, Jorgensen's posthumous reputation has experienced a minor resurgence: in addition to a smattering of academic attention over the past decade or so, the feminist Cleis Press reissued her autobiography in 2000; the A&E Network cable television program *Biography* chronicled her life in 2004; Bradford Louryk's one-person off-Broadway show, *Christine Jorgensen Reveals*, based on an interview Jorgensen recorded with the comedian Nipsey Russell in 1957, received a New York Drama Desk Award in 2006, and psychologist Richard Docter published a short biography of her in 2007.

Although the young Jorgensen undoubtedly cut a charismatic and attractive public figure, and while she certainly exhibited grace under the pressure of unrelenting media attention to intimate details of her life, the scope and intensity of Jorgensen's initial celebrity in the 1950s remains something of a curiosity, given that she was by no means the first person to change legal sex through the use of surgery and hormones. Jorgensen's extremely modest acting, dancing, and vocal talents similarly provide an insufficient explanation of her staying power. The scale and extent of Jorgensen's celebrity in the 1950s thus appear implausible, in retrospect, without taking into consideration the social history that structured the moment of her sudden fame.

As I have noted in previous work on Jorgensen, World War II brought about the largest mobilization of population in United States history—it not only inducted millions of men into military service for deployment around the globe, but also attracted millions more rural residents to coastal cities for wartime work opportunities, and it brought an unprecedented number of women into the paid labor force for the first time. Part of the post-war adjustment was an intense effort to recontain female labor within the domestic sphere, accompanied by much public musing over appropriate gender roles. At the same time, sex-segregated conditions in the military, coupled with new surveillance mechanisms and administrative procedures to root out gay service-members, brought unprecedented attention and visibility to homosexuality as a social issue. Part of what people saw, when they saw Jorgensen, was the spectacle of medical science's supposed ability to engineer both sexuality and gender in ways that produced conventional heterosexuality. These trends cast Jorgensen—and through her the transsexual phenomenon embodied in her person—as a solution to a perceived social problem, and as an emblem of a new era (Berube; Stryker, 1999).

The spectacle of Jorgensen's transsexuality simultaneously evoked the same awe and anxiety associated with the atomic bomb—it offered another instance of scientific prowess seemingly triumphing over matter itself. Just as nuclear technology split the atom to literally destroy matter, transsexual technology destroyed the stable materiality of biological sex, thereby ungrounding gender representation from its presumed physical referent, and demanding new epistemological frameworks for structuring the semiotic production of embodiment's gendered meanings. Jorgensen's spectacularity can thus be read as a map of emergent postmodern and poststructuralist conditions of signification in the mid-twentieth century; the "transsexual phenomenon" she figured can be seen as an ontologizing practice that resignified the relationship between gendered subject and sexed flesh within post-World War II biomedical and technocultural environments (Stryker, 1999).

Building upon this earlier argument, in this article I am interested in using Jorgensen's visit to the former U.S. colony of the Philippines, which had been granted independence only in 1945, to begin remapping the global spectacle of her transsexuality as a white (post)colonial phenomenon. It was not Jorgensen's pale skin or Scandinavian-American cultural heritage that made her white, but rather the processes through which her presence racialized others while obscuring her own racialization, and the means by which her unspoken prerogatives and presumed entitlements over the lives of racialized others circulated invisibly beneath the mask of a falsely universalized mode of being. Jorgensen's light-featured phenotype offered a white screen onto which was projected all that is fantasized of the metropole in relation to the colony: wealth, glamor, mobility, liberation, and self-fashioning, all deployed within a spatialized racial hierarchy that locates darkness in the heart of the colonized territory, and whiteness at the colonizing imperative's point of origin.

Jorgensen's on-screen appearance in *Kaming Mga Talyada* allows us to ask, in the words of Alfred Lopez, "what happens to whiteness after empire," and to assess the ways in which white cultural norms remain embedded in postcolonial societies "as the marker or index of the traces of colonial legacies that yet lie latent (but not dormant) in the postcolonial world's own 'colonial unconscious,' which it owes to itself to uncover and interrogate" (Lopez 4, 6). If we acknowledge that the "white woman's body" has been depicted in U.S. film as the fantasmatic space of the nation's birth since *Birth of a Nation*, perhaps we can begin to trace, through the figure of Christine Jorgensen, the outlines of the new U.S. polity that emerged in the aftermath of World War II—a global (post)colonial neo-empire with its own peculiar administrative logics linking bodies, identities, territories, and populations, that become legible even within seemingly obscure cinematic texts.

## *KAMING MGA TALYADA*: A QUEER KIND OF SEXY

*Kaming Mga Talyada*—filmed principally in Filipino (Tagalog), with some English and Spanish dialog—opens in the lobby of the Philippines National Bank in Manila, where several matronly women are gossiping about their children, when they spy Chelo, a former acquaintance whom they have not seen for ten years. The women somewhat facetiously compliment Chelo, who exudes an over-dressed sense of self-importance, for wearing the most up-to-date fashions, and they tell her that she has become very beautiful, with a figure like Marilyn Monroe (though in truth it is somewhat more ample). When they ask where she has been hiding herself for the past decade, Chelo tells them that she married Captain Antonio Dimagiba, a Filipino man serving in the U.S. military, with whom she has traveled around the world; she has in fact recently returned from "pleasure trips to Hong Kong, Paris, Tokyo and America." Chelo confesses, however, that her husband "loves the army more than her," and has more or less abandoned her to pursue the life of a military man in the United States. To compensate for her partner's preoccupation with his career, Chelo has devoted herself entirely to the pursuit of her own material satisfactions. Thus, before Christine Jorgensen ever appears on screen, the themes of what her transsexuality can be made to represent—a U.S.-centered femininity enmeshed in consumerist hedonism, circulating transnationally with a privilege backed by military power—are prefigured in Chelo's character.

Fortunately, Chelo tells her former acquaintances, she has seven well-behaved, hard-working, unmarried adult daughters who support her financially while her wayward soldier-husband is stationed in the United States. The women become confused, because they remember Chelo as having seven sons. At this point, Chelo produces photographs of her children, and the audience is introduced to the seven Dimagiba siblings—apparently male-bodied individuals, all striking stereotypically fey and feminine poses, several of whom are obviously wearing eye make-up. The film then cuts to a song-and-dance number where Chelo's seven grown children prance about and sing the film's title song:

> We who are talyada, you will always find us in Luneta
> We who are talyada, our beauty is always on display
> In any street, we are always there
> Even Miss Universe will be embarrassed
> By our beautiful talyada bodies and our baby faces
> Oy! Oy! Oy! Oy! Oy! Oy! Oy! Our group is always happy!
> Ay! Ay! Ay! Ay! Ay! Talyada!
> Especially if there are handsome men, our hearts pound and we would
> always look talyada!

In partially rendering the song into English, I have deliberately left the key term *talyada* in the original Filipino, for it is on this term that the film's narrative pivots. The English-language title of *Kaming Mga Talyada* is given in the film's press-packet as *We Who Are Sexy*—this relatively straightforwardly translates *kaming mga* as *we who are*, but the translation of *talyada* into *sexy*, given the context in which it has just been used, is dense with subtextual meanings.

Derived, like many Filipino words, from a Spanish root introduced during the initial European colonization of the Philippine archipelago in the sixteenth century, *talyada* is formed from the verb *tallar*—to sculpt or to measure—and its feminine past-participle, *tallada*. In Tagalog, *talya* literally means a "posture" or "sculpture," whereas *talyada* means something that has been cut or engraved.

(*Tagalog–English Online Dictionary*). The word is commonly used, however, according to Virgilio Almario, a Filipino native-speaker, to mean "a woman's praiseworthy way of carrying herself in public, particularly through the femininity of her clothing and appearance." It thus has a positive connotation when used in reference to female subjects, and conveys much the same sense as the English idiomatic phrase, "she cuts a nice figure." Used in reference to male subjects, however, *talyada* has derogatory implications, and functions as a euphemism for the epithet *bakla*—usually translated, not entirely sastisfactorily, as *faggot*—a term that has been somewhat recuperated within contemporary Filipino usage in much the same manner as the English word *queer* (Benedicto, 2008 (a)).

*Bakla*, in contrast to the currently dominant gender-normative ideology of homosexuality within Eurocentric modernity, refers to a culturally specific combination of biological maleness, same-sex attraction, bodily expression of feminine characteristics or mannerisms, and—often but not always—elements of cross-gender dressing and adornment. According to J. Neil C. Garcia, "*bakla* and homosexual are terms belonging to two different knowledge systems, and therefore [they] can only irrevocably be different from each other" (Garcia, xviii). Martin Manalansan describes the relationship between *gay* and *bakla* as being somewhat more flexible: not "self-contained modes of identity," but rather "two coexisting yet often-times incommensurable cultural ideologies of gender and sexuality" that share a somewhat permeable boundary (Manalansan, 21). Both scholars agree, however, that the fraught transitions between *bakla* and *gay*, where the former symbolizes a Filipino configuration of sex/gender/sexuality/identy and the latter a globally circulating metropolitan homosexuality, represent an epistemological rift within the problematic of (post) colonial representation. (Manalansan, 24; Garcia 39). What I seek to suggest in this article is that the introduction of *transsexual* in the 1950s, and *transgender* in the 1990s, offer different opportunities for articulating *talyada* and *bakla* with Western-dominated processes of sexuality's globalization than are offered by *gay*.

Because it seems important to maintain the linguistic ambiguity through which *talyada* can elide the functions of adjective and noun, throughout this article I'll rely on a somewhat stilted construction that echoes the title of the film: those who are *talyada*. Those who are *talyada* in *We Who Are Sexy* are clearly intended to be read—at a time and in a medium in which a more overt characterization would have been impermissible—as *bakla*. Their exaggerated mannerisms are broad caricatures of male effeminacy; they pin their hair and line their eyes, they mince and sashay in their movements. Luneta (where, according to the lyrics of their song, they can always be found) is Manila's large urban park, where gay men, female prostitutes, and transgender women cruise and stroll for sex. Those who are *talyada* are shown dancing and singing in front of the businesses, adjacent to one another in a low-slung commercial building, through which they support their mother Chelo: a hair salon, a massage parlor, a laundry—all traditional employments of *bakla* individuals who work as *parloristas*. Lynn Pareja, a professor of film and literature at the University of the Philippines, who worked at Sampaguita Pictures when *Kaming Mga Talyada* was made, notes that *talyada* was "slang at the time for gay men." She offers an additional etymology for the term, relating it to *talsik*—a splash or ejaculation—in reference to the way in which effeminate males or sexually unconstrained women are believed incapable of controlling their inner nature, and as a result "splash" portions of their bodies about—head, hips, and especially fingers—and thus appear to "normal" people as "deviants" (David).

And yet, by identifying its protagonists as *talyada* rather than *bakla*, as "sexy" rather than "gay," the film produces intriguing slippages of desire and identification within the Filipino context that elude the conceptual sex/gender/sexuality schemas of Eurocentric modernity. *Talyada* functions not as a mere euphemism: it is a polymorphous category of becoming and possibility that is structured as *sexuality* and *sexiness*, and it structures the entire film. As those who are *talyada* dance and sing in the courtyard of their building, they are secretly observed by seven attractive and conventionally feminine young women, who live in a dormitory next door, where Chelo conveniently happens to be house-mother. The young women are visibly smitten with those who are *talyada*, and the "sexiness" of the meeting-scene can be read in two registers simultaneously: as a heterosexual attraction to the male body that performs the feminine and effiminate gestures, and as a femme–femme attraction that plays out across the division of biological sex difference. One of the young women, who knew the seven Dimagiba siblings in their youth, tells the others that they were not always *talyada,* but had been made so by the unnatural influence of their mother, who wants them to continue supporting her financially rather than marrying and making families of their own. Chelo herself, in her vain preoccupations, can be seen to parody the conventional sense of *talyada* as a complimentary performance of womanhood. The father, Captain Dimagiba, says one of the women, is rumored to be *talyada* himself—why else would he spend so much time away from his wife, in the company of other men? Gayness and heterosexuality, cosmopolitan sexiness and reproductive sexuality, perversity and normativity: each haunts the others whenever one temporarily moves to the foreground as it circulates through the category *talyada*.

The seven young women in the dormitory vow to woo and win as their husbands the seven who are *talyada*, thereby inaugurating the film's overarching plot. Many comic situations based on pronominal confusions, sexual double-codings, and gender transpositions then follow, throughout which those who are *talyada* remain aloof and oblivious to the advances of the women who pursue them. A turning point in the courtship comes, however, when a group date is organized to attend one of Christine Jorgensen's nightclub performances. Considered extra-diagetically, Jorgensen's lengthy performance—consisting of a few songs filled with double-entendres, a quick change number, a Marlene Deitrich impersonation and a rendition of the romantic standard "Dahil Sayo," sung while ethnically cross-dressed in a traditional Filipina costume—leaves much to be desired. Diagetically, however, the scene is meant to represent the height of polysemic metrosexuality, with Jorgensen offering different possibilities for pleasure and identification for all parties involved. In embodying a white American femininity self-evidently achieved though her own practical actions and put on display in Manila, she occupies the spotlight around which the action of the film revolves, betokening a potential for mobility of various sorts, along lines of racial hierarchy that flow toward whiteness across lines that separate colony from metropole, Filipino from American, man from woman, gay from straight, and trans from the stablility of the gender binary.

For all her ambiguities, Jorgensen is unambiguously positioned within the film as part of the "we" who are "sexy" and desirable, and as such her presence adds a further layer of complex connotation to the meaning of *talyada*: she is construed as a formerly male-bodied figure literally cut in an emasculating and feminizing fashion by the surgeon's scalpel and the body-sculpting influence of hormones, who (like a statue or fetish) acquires an artificial form through the exercise of particular craft techniques and who, in enacting a culturally legible womanliness divorced from a biologically female sex, becomes decorative or ornamental, beautiful in an aesthetic sense, but no longer reproductively functional; she exists solely as image and spectacle. Jorgensen thus occupies the traditional space of *talyada*, while pointing beyond it toward a new somatechnic horizon, and demonstrating that the term is capable of inflecting toward the transsexual as easily as toward the homosexual.

## A CHRISTIAN NATIONALIST NORMATIVE SOMATECHNICS

The relationship of the new, globally disseminated transsexual discourse figured in Christine Jorgensen to the pre-existing concepts of *bakla* and *talyada* recapitulates the larger epistemological crisis of (post)colonial representation: it is here, at one point among innumerable others, that a (post)colonial society confronts a colonizing power that organizes embodiment, identity, gender, and sexuality differently than the (post)colonial society does for itself locally. The dramatic turning point of *Kaming Mga Talyada* takes place after the group date to Jorgensen's nightclub performance, when Chelo decides that she will send her children to Europe to become "professionals like Christine"— thus rendering them unsuitable marriage partners for the seven women who love them, and trapping them a non-biologically reproductive feminized form in which they will continue to support their mother. Determined to avoid the calamitous loss of their love objects, the seven young women write to Captain Dimagiba in the United States, urging him to return and to restore (patriarchal) order to his household. He does so, and subsequently drafts his *talyada* children into the Filipino military, in order to subject them to the discipline of a particularly ruthless drill sergeant who represents the last, best hope for restoring their normative masculinity. Another series of comic scenes then ensues, in which those who are *talyada* playfully resist and ultimately thwart the military's efforts to make men of them. In consequence, they wind up in the stockade; their father vows to go to his grave to escape the humiliation and dishonor they bring to the family name, and the seven young women express their deep regret at ever trying to transform those who are *talyada* into marriageable men.

At this point, when the film's narrative movement has ground to an utter halt, an unexpected development takes the plot in an entirely new direction: Muslim insurgents in Mindanao province launch a rebellion against the government of the Philippines that threatens the territorial integrity of the nation, and Captain Dimagiba volunteers himself and his seven children for a suicide mission to nip the uprising in the bud. The film's mood shifts here from comic to dramatic as the Dimagibas' impromptu counterinsurgency squad is whisked away to the southern island of Jolo, in the Sulu archipelago, to seek out and destroy the rebel Datu Roman and his followers. At this point, the film's attention moves from an anatamo-political concern with the production of individual gendered subjectivities, towards the somatechnical linkage between techniques of individualization and the macro-political management of the state.

In relocating its action from Manila to Mindanao, *Kaming Mga Talyada* invokes the history of the multiple colonizations that structure Filipino society. The Sulu archipeligo, stretching from the Zamboanga peninsula of Mindanao south towards Malaysia, had become Islamized as early as the eighth century, through trade contacts with India and the wider Muslim world, and the Sultanate of Jolo was a prosperous regional commercial center. The Muslim population of Mindanao regarded itself as culturally distinct from the pagan animists who populated the northern islands of what, with the advent of Spanish colonization in the sixteenth century, would come to be called the Philippines. The Muslims of Mindanao, whom the Spanish called Moros (derived from *moor*), never recognized Spanish colonial authority, and they resisted, for centuries, Spanish efforts to displace them by resettling Christianized northern islanders in the south. When the Spanish ceded control of the Philippines, including Mindanao, to the United States in the Spanish–American War of 1898, the Moros resisted U.S. colonial authority just as they had resisted the Spanish. And when the United States granted formal independence to the Republic of the Philippines in 1945, the Moros likewise continued to resist Filipino claims to sovereignty over their homeland. Thus, for centuries, the Moro represented the internal Orientalist threat of an ethno-religious Other for a succession of Christian-secular regimes attempting to rule the Philippines (Man, 17–32, 46–62).

In *Kaming Mga Talyada*, the achievement of a normative masculinity for the film's protagonists transpires in the context of war against the Moros. After seeing their father shot and gravely wounded in a jungle ambush, those who are *talyada* become enraged, and they rediscover their manhood in acts of battlefield courage. They defeat the insurgents in bloody hand-to-hand fighting, and return to Manila as military heroes. In keeping with Meyda Yegenoglu's observation in *Colonial Fantasies* that the representational interlocking of cultural and sexual difference is secured by mapping the discourse of Orientalism onto the phallocentric discourse of femininity (Yegenoglu, 73), the femininity of the *talyadas* is symbolically killed off precisely by the act of conquering the Orientalized Muslim men who threaten the territorial integrity of the state. This conceptual operation, rather than the love of good women or the harsh discipline of the military, secures for those who were *talyada* a normative manhood that is simultaneously nationalist and Christian, and that aligns their personal identities with the structures that sustain the project of state territorial sovereignty.

In the film's penultimate scene, the seven young men, now proudly reoriented toward their masculine social identities, visit their wounded father on his birthday as he recuperates in a Manila hospital. As the redomesticated Chelo stands nearby, holding the birthday cake she has baked, they read aloud to him from a special commendation issued by the Secretary of National Defense praising them for their valiant efforts against the Islamic insurgency. The seven women who have pursued the Dimagibas throughout the film show up right on cue, and pair off with their favorites as the beaming parents look on. Christine Jorgensen's nightclub performance seems a far distant event at this apparently happy heteronormative moment, but the film's final scene returns us to the questions Jorgensen's appearance in the film initially raised about the relationship of a normative Filipino Christian nationalist somatechnics to the U.S. imperialist somatechnics that inform the intelligibility of the transsexual discourse. A brief, last-minute detour though another film, uncannily similar in its operative logics to *Kaming Mga Talyada*, paves the way for that discussion.

## TRANSSOMATECHNICS

Allan Punzalan Isaac, in *American Tropics: Articulating Filipino America*, describes the 1939 Gary Cooper vehicle *The Real Glory* as one of several U.S. films about the American Pacific empire that creates "moments of instability in which the management of masculinity becomes the operative trope to resolve internal anxieties of national integrity" (Isaacs, 82). The film opens with the withdrawal of U.S. troops from Mindanao in 1906, which leaves behind only a few civilian administrators and a rag-tag band of Filipino troops to contend with a restive and not-entirely-pacified indigenous Moro population. To stem a deadly outbreak of cholera, American doctor Bill Canavan finds it necessary to boost the masculine self-esteem of the inept Filipino soldiers though the careful application of the latest psychological theories. He thereby transforms them into an effective fighting force capable of repelling the "savage" Moros, and he then leads them on a successful jungle mission to find the dam the Moros have built to block the flow of fresh water into the U.S. fort, which is what has allowed the cholera to breed. Thus, Isaacs concludes, "the movie recounts the birth of Philippine national unity and masculinity against an internal, racialized threat—the Moros—under the auspices of American psychomedical ingenuity" (Isaacs, 85).

Transsexuality is another product of the ""psychomedical ingenuity" that facilitates Eurocentric modernity's biopolitical management of Mindanao and its assimilation into the incipiently nationalist, future (post)colony of the Philippines—it is a deployment and somaticization of categories of being derived from Western sexual science. Considered as a somatechnology, transsexuality functions as an anatomo-political technique for the administration of embodied subjects who contest the double binary of man/woman and homo/hetero that governs identity—and thus the relationship between the individual and state power—within Eurocentric modernity. It is a micro-political practice that recapitulates on the level of individual corporeality the logic of encampment that Giorgio Agamben asserts as the macro-political "space of modernity itself" (Agamben 1997, 113).

In his analysis of concentration camps, Agamben describes what could be called a virtual camp-function, immanent within modern nation-states, that materializes during crises in which a given state's particular nexus of geographical territory (or "determinate localization"), its social apparatuses (or "determinate order"), and the "automatic rules for the inscription of life," or determinate administrative procedures governing birth, education, employment, residence, marriage, health care, death, and the like, begin to break down. (Agamben, 174–75). Encampment is a "state of emergency" organized against a "problem population" that frustrates the routine practices of governmentality through which the subjects best suited for rule by that regime's internal operative logics are produced.

The camp as mechanism for variously segregating, eradicating, or (re)integrating can operate at the level of "problem bodies" as well as problem populations: it is this very operation of sovereign power that transsexual embodiment displays.

Transsexuality is an administrative solution, with biopolitical consequences, particular to certain kinds of problem bodies within Eurocentric modernity—for bodies whose natal sex registration does not match their bodily habituses, whose gendered comportment does not accord with their societal gender status, whose subjective identifications with gender categories are not congruent with those typically associated with their reproductive roles or capacities, and so on. It is the juridico-medical apparatus of an institutional, state-sanctioned power that enmeshes itself with the bare life of individuals whose embodiment problematizes the regulatory function of the gender system. Directed towards a Western state's domestic populations, transsexuality can function, though not without violence, as an internally consistent means to a better life for certain of its subjects; displaced outward, it can become part of the machinery of colonization, performing its operations on different kinds of bodies that may, or may not, be problematic in the contexts in which they are encountered.

In (post)colonial contexts, transsexuality can become—like its counterpart, modern gay identity—one line of flight from colony to metropole for those who are colonized, and who live under the signs of sex/gender/sexuality configurations that hybridize Eurocentric modernity's categorical distinctions. Like modern gay identity, it requires cutting apart things that are elsewhere conjoined as the price of the mobility it promises—but it cuts them differently. To the extent that Filipino nationalism metonymically reproduces against the Moros the same colonizing moves it has experienced through the Spanish and American empires, it must likewise secure the normative somatechnics of gendered embodiment through which it reproduces itself against the pull of an American metropole whose techniques of embodiment simultaneously inform and threaten to undermine the nationalist project: this is the promise and peril embodied by the spectacular transsexual whiteness of Christine Jorgensen in the Philippines.

In the final scene of *Kaming Mga Talyada*, we see the army drill sergeant who earlier had been tasked with masculinizing the Dimagibas through military discipline; he is bawling out a new platoon of raw recruits. As he marches them off toward their barracks, when nobody is watching, the sergeant begins to splash his hips *talyada*-style. Although the closing image is obviously intended to restore the film's initially comic tone, it nonetheless invites new readings that unsettle the apparent correspondences between imperialist and nationalist forms of heteronormative masculine embodiment. The sergeant's swaying hips fleetingly perform and materialize a *talyada* (or *bakla*) sensibility, enacting a repertoire of movements present within a reservoir of Filipino cultural idioms, that, in its incommensurability with modern Eurocentric logics and techniques of administering the embodiment of sex/gender/sexuality, offers a perhaps unexpected resource for (post)colonial resistance.

Although Christine Jorgensen is featured in only one extended scene of *Kaming Mga Talyada*, the spectacle of her transsexuality—spot-lit and center-staged—creates a penumbra within the film where conflicting modes of sex/gender/sexuality collide with one another across the (post)colonial divide. On the one hand, Jorgensen embodies the white, fashionably self-fashioning, glamorous ethos associated with the post-World War II U.S. material culture that the film figures as ultimately desirable, and, on the other hand, she represents a prospect that the film forecloses for its protagonists. The world in which those who are *talyada* can become women physically and irrevocably through transsexual body modification is diametrically opposed to the one in which a performed and fleetingly embodied *talyada* or *bakla* sensibility survives the alignment of normative Filipino masculinity, patriarchal heterosexuality, national territorial sovereignty, and the suppression of a racialized internal Other. Or rather, *talyada* and *bakla* are consonant with these projects in a way that transsexuality is depicted as not being, due to their modes of embodiment and performance. This is not, however, to argue that transsexuality is incompatible with Phillipine nationalism, but rather to suggest that claims of transsexual citizenship and cultural belonging would necessarily need to be advanced along new and different lines.

As the field of transgender studies has taken shape over the past decade or so, it has been criticized for the perceived whiteness and Eurocentrism (or, even more pointedly, the U.S.-centrism) of the term *transgender*: a term that originated among white, middle-class, American male cross-dressers, and which, by some accounts, recapitulates all the colonizing moves by which whiteness functions cross-culturally, between U.S.-Europe and the global South and East, through the capacity attributed to it to name all imaginable non-normative variations of sex/gender/sexuality (Valentine). "Transgender whiteness" has thus become another index of a Northern and Western conceptual imperialism that threatens to overwhelm, subsume, and refigure specific sex/gender/sexuality configurations in colonized locations. But as the close reading of *Kaming Mga Talyada* offered here makes clear, the colonial logics of transgender whiteness have deeper roots.

A strong counter-argument can be advanced, however, that global mappings of disparate and differently subjugated assemblages of sex/gender/sexuality, occupying diverse locations in transnational systems might, by linking with one another through the term *trangender*, offer new possibilities for networks of resistance and transformation. This is why the film's positioning of Christine Jorgensen as *talyada*, along with the queer closing scene of *Kaming Mga Talyada*, are also provocative openings and invitations to reimagine the "scene" of becoming an embodied subject within (post)colonial contexts. In articulating Filipino histories, subjectivities, identities, genders, and sexualities with the category of transsexuality—which originated elsewhere but subsequently has been taken up in unique and specific ways in multiple places—the film offers a sly confirmation that, perhaps all along, "transgender" has been a virtual possibility immanent in many colonized locations. It is not *only* a eurocentric export, and the colonized are not bereft of agency in their uptake of introduced forms.

The Eurocentric whiteness of transgender's theorization within the academy, however, can hardly be denied. In examining Christine Jorgensen's cinematic foray in the Philippines, I hope to model the intellectual and critical contributions that can be made to a transformative or resistive transnational transgender politics by acknowledging and analyzing, rather than by denying, the sometimes oppressive ways in which "transgender whiteness" functions, or how conceptual categories derived from social experience within the United States impinge upon and interact with sex/gender/sexuality/identity configuratations rooted in other socio-cultural formations.

## ACKNOWLEDGEMENTS

Thanks, first, to Joseph Pugliese; many of this article's best insights derive from conversations as we co-edited the special issue of *Social Semiotics* in which a slightly different version of this text originally appeared. Thanks also to Michael David Franklin for locating a copy of *Kaming Mga Talyada*, to Arlene Bag-ao for translating the film's Filipino dialog into English, and to the various artists and scholars of film, gender, race, sexuality and the Philippines who helped me steer my way though a new focus of research for my ongoing interest in transgender phenomena: Bobby Benedicto, Virgilio Almario, Lynn Pareja, Joel David, Helen Leung, Kam Wai Kui, Rani Neutill, Lawrence Cohen, Celine Parreñas-Shimizu, and Warwick Anderson, who suggested in a chance encounter at the 2008 American Anthropological Association annual meeting in San Francisco that I read *American Tropics*. Thanks, too, to audiences at Cornell University, California State University-Northridge, University of California-Berkeley, Netherlands Transgender Film Festival, Gerrit Reitsveld Academy, and the Tate Modern Art Galley in London, where feedback on my screenings and discussions of *Kaming Mga Talyada* has informed my revisions. Meredith Ramirez Talusan offered especially valuable feedback in this regard. Small portions of the descriptive background information on Christine Jorgensen have appeared elsewhere, in somewhat altered form, in works cited below.

## NOTE

1. http://www.somatechnics.mq.edu.au/about/

## WORKS CITED

Agamben, G. 1997. "The Camp as Nomos of the Modern." in *Violence, Identity and Self-Determination* ed. Hent de Vries and Samuel Weber. Stanford: Stanford University Press, 106–118.

Agamben, G. 1998. *Homo Sacer: Sovereign Power and Bare Life*. Stanford, CA: Stanford University Press.

Benedicto, B. 24 August 2008 a. Personal email correspondence to Susan Stryker.

Benedicto, B. 2008b. "The Haunting of Gay Manila: Global Space-Time and Specter of *Kabaklaan*," *GLQ* 14: 2+3, 317–338.

Berube, A. 1991. *Coming Out Under Fire: The History of Gay Men and Women in World War Two*. New York: Free Press.

Cayado, T. 1962. *Kaming Mga Talyada (a.ka. We Who Are Sexy)*. Sampaguita Pictures, Manila, Philippines.

David, J. 5 September 2008. *Personal email correspondence to Susan Stryker.*

Docter, R. 2007. *Becoming a Woman: A Biography of Christine Jorgensen*. New York: Harrington Park Press.

Foucault, M. 1978. *History of Sexuality, Vol. 1,* New York: Vintage.

Garcia, J. 1996. *Philippine Gay Culture: The Last Thirty Years*. Diliman, Quezon City: University of the Philippines Press.

Hill, R. 2007. A Social History of Heterosexual Transvestism in Cold War America. Ph.D. Diss., University of Michigan.

Isaac, A. 2006. *American Tropics: Articulating Filipino America* (University of Minnesota Press.

Jorgensen, C. 2000. *Christine Jorgensen: A Personal Autobiography*. San Francisco: Cleis Press.

Lopez, A. 2005. *Post-Colonial Whiteness: A Critical Reader on Race and Empire*. Albany: State University of New York Press.

Man, W. 1990. *Muslim Separatism: The Moros of Southern Philippines and the Malays of Thailand*. Oxford: Oxford University Press.

Manalansan, M. 2003. *Global Divas: Filipino Gay Men in the Diaspora*. Chapel Hill: Duke University Press.

Meyerowitz, J. 2002. *How Sex Changed: A History of Transsexuality in the United States*. Cambridge: Harvard University Press.

Serlin, D. 2004. *Replaceable You: Engineering the Body in Post-War America*. Chicago: University of Chicago Press.

Stryker, S. 1999. "Christine Jorgensen's Atom Bomb: Mapping Postmodernity though the Emergence of Transsexuality," in E. Ann Kaplan and Susan Squier, eds., *Playing Dolly: Technocultural Formations, Fictions, and Fantasies of Assisted Reproduction*. New Brunswick, NJ: Rutgers University Press, 157–171.

Stryker, S. 2007. "Christine in the Cutting Room: The Cinematic Embodiment of Transsexual Celebrity Christine Jorgensen," *Filmwaves* 33: 20–23.

Valentine, D. 2007. *Imagining Transgender: An Ethnography of a Category*. Chapel Hill: Duke University Press.

Yegenoglu, M. 1998. *Colonial Fantasies: Towards A Feminist Reading of Orientalism*. Cambridge: Cambridge University Press.

*Tagalog–English Online Dictionary*, n.d. http://puwe.de/tag/tagalog.txt

# 42

# *Electric Brilliancy*
## Cross-dressing Law and Freak Show Displays in Nineteenth-century San Francisco

CLARE SEARS

SOCIOLOGIST CLARE SEARS INVESTIGATES THE PRODUCTION of heteronormative public space in 19th-century San Francisco by examining two phenomena that might not seem at first glance to be related: the criminalization of cross-dressing and the spectacularization of gender non-normativity in commercial freak shows. After first calling our attention to the wave of laws against cross-gender dressing that swept the U.S. in the second half of the nineteenth century, Sears argues that these laws were part of a broader class of regulations that targeted queer, foreign, and disabled "problem bodies" that disrupted public norms based on whiteness, able-bodiedness, binary gender, and reproductive heterosexuality. Such problem bodies, she contends, were subjected to operations of exclusion, concentration, segregation, transformation, or extermination that constructed public space as a place in which citizens unmarked by such operations could consider themselves both normal and free. Sears pushes her argument further by showing how some spaces in which problem bodies were operated upon were in fact hyper-visible—Chinatown and sex-worker "tenderloins," for example, both of which were popular destinations for slumming tourists. Freak shows offered another such venue, in which "normal" members of the public could learn to recognize and police the very forms of difference, including gender variance, whose exclusion produced normalcy as its effect.

In 1863, midway through the Civil War, the San Francisco Board of Supervisors passed a local law against cross-dressing that prohibited public appearance "in a dress not belonging to his or her sex" (*Revised Orders* 1863). That city was not alone in this action: between 1848 and 1900, thirty-four cities in twenty-one states passed laws against cross-dressing, as did eleven additional cities before World War I (Eskridge 1999). Far from being a nineteenth-century anachronism, cross-dressing laws had remarkable longevity and became a key tool for policing transgender and queer communities in the 1950s and 1960s. However, although studies have documented the frequent enforcement of these laws in the mid-twentieth century, far less is known about their operations in the nineteenth century, when they were initially passed. In this essay, I examine the legal and cultural history of cross-dressing law in one city—San Francisco—from the 1860s to 1900s. In particular, I explore cross-dressing law's relationship with another nineteenth-century institution that was centrally concerned with cross-gender practices—the dime museum freak show.

Focusing on the complex, contradictory, and sometimes unpredictable relationships between legal regulation, cultural fascination, and gender transgressions, I develop three main arguments. First,

I examine the legal work of cross-dressing law, documenting the range of practices criminalized, people arrested, and punishments faced. Observing that the law exclusively targeted public cross-dressing practices, I argue that it did much more than police the types of clothing that "belonged" to each sex; it also used the visible marker of clothing to police the types of people who "belonged" in public space. Second, I explore the relationship between cross-dressing law and a host of other local laws that targeted human bodies as public nuisances. In doing so, I argue that cross-dressing law was not an isolated act of government, exclusively concerned with gender, but one part of a broader regulatory project that was also concerned with sex, race, citizenship, and city space. Finally, I analyze the case of Milton Matson, a female-bodied man who was recruited from a jail cell to appear in a dime museum freak show in 1890s San Francisco. Based on this analysis, I argue that cross-dressing law and the freak show had similar disciplinary effects, producing and policing the boundaries of normative gender, albeit in incomplete ways.

## A DRESS NOT BELONGING

San Francisco's Board of Supervisors did not initially criminalize cross-dressing as a distinct offense, but as one manifestation of the broader offense of indecency. The full legal text stated:

> If any person shall appear in a public place in a state of nudity, or in a dress not belonging to his or her sex, or in an indecent or lewd dress, or shall make any indecent exposure of his or her person, or be guilty of any lewd or indecent act or behavior, or shall exhibit or perform any indecent, immoral or lewd play, or other representation, he should be guilty of a misdemeanor, and on conviction, shall pay a fine not exceeding five hundred dollars.
>
> (*Revised Orders* 1863)

In turn, this wide-reaching indecency law was not a stand-alone prohibition, but one part of a new chapter of the municipal codebook, titled *Offenses Against Good Morals And Decency*, which also criminalized public intoxication, profane language, and bathing in San Francisco Bay without appropriate clothing. Alongside these newly designated crimes, cross-dressing was one of the very first "offenses against good morals" to be outlawed in the city. In 1866, the original five-hundred-dollar penalty was revised to a five-hundred-dollar fine or six months in jail; in 1875, it increased to a one-thousand-dollar fine, six months in jail, or both (*General Orders* 1866, 1875).

Despite its roots in indecency law, San Francisco's cross-dressing law soon became a flexible tool for policing multiple gender transgressions. Before the end of the nineteenth century, San Francisco police made more than one hundred arrests for the crime of cross-dressing (*Municipal Reports* 1863–64 to 1899–1900).[1] A wide variety of people fell afoul of this law, including feminist dress reformers, female impersonators, "fast" young women who dressed as men for a night on the town, and people whose gender identifications did not match their anatomical sex in legally acceptable ways (people who today would probably—although not definitely—identify as transgender). Those arrested faced police harassment, public exposure, and six months in jail; by the early twentieth century, they also risked psychiatric institutionalization or deportation if they were not U.S. citizens. For example, in 1917, a female-bodied man named Jack Garland was involuntarily institutionalized in a psychiatric ward for refusing to wear women's clothing (Stryker and Van Buskirk 1996), while a male-bodied woman named Geraldine Portica was arrested for violating San Francisco's cross-dressing law and subsequently deported to Mexico (Jesse Brown Cook Scrapbooks n.d.).

San Francisco's cross-dressing law marked the start of a new regulatory approach toward gender transgressions, and it attempted to draw and fix the boundaries of normative gender during a period of rapid social change. However, cross-dressing law signaled not only a new object of regulation, but also a new mechanism of regulation—exclusion from public space. From its inception, cross-dressing law was specifically concerned with public gender displays, and it targeted cross-dressing in public places. Notably, the law made it a crime for someone to "appear *in a public place*...in a dress not belonging to his or her sex," and any clothing practices that occurred in private were beyond its scope (*Revised Orders* 1863; italics mine). As a result, some people confined their cross-dressing practices to private spaces and modified their appearance when in public for fear of arrest.

For example, in the 1890s, a male-bodied San Franciscan who identified as a woman named Jenny reported that although she preferred to wear women's clothing, she only dared do so in private, for fear of arrest on the city streets. In a letter to German sexologist Magnus Hirschfeld, Jenny wrote: "Only because of the arbitrary actions of the police do I wear men's clothing outside of the house. Skirts are a sanctuary to me, and I would rather keep on women's clothing forever if it were allowed on the street" (Hirschfeld 1991, 84). Her fears were not unfounded. In 1895, the police arrested a middle-aged carpenter named Ferdinand Haisch for "masquerading in female attire," after Hayes Valley residents called the cops on the "strange appearing woman" who walked through their neighborhood every evening ("Masqueraded as a Woman," *San Francisco Examiner*, April 16, 1895, 4).[2] The police staked out the neighborhood for several weeks before arresting Haisch, who was wearing the latest women's fashions—a three-quarter-length melton coat, green silk skirt, red stockings, silver-buckled garters, high-heeled shoes, and stylish hat. Following a brief stint in the city prison, Haisch was released by the police court judge on the condition that Haisch ceased wearing these clothes in public. Haisch apparently complied, but her ever-vigilant neighbors were still not satisfied, and they demanded her rearrest for wearing women's clothing at home. However, while predictably sympathetic to the neighbors' complaints, the police admitted that they were powerless to intervene, because the law permitted cross-dressing in private ("Crazy on Female Attire," *The Call*, July 3, 1895, 8).

The exclusion of cross-dressing practices from public space—and their concurrent confinement to private spaces—was a form of legal segregation that had significant political consequences, both for individuals whose public appearance constituted a crime and for the "general" public. First, for people excluded from public space, participation in day-to-day city life was curtailed. Everyday activities, such as going to the shops, enjoying a night on the town, or even walking through one's own neighborhood brought surveillance and arrest. As such, cross-dressing was marked as a deviant and secretive practice, rather than a public activity and identification. Second, by excluding cross-dressing practices from public space, the law also severely restricted people's access to the public sphere, which twentieth-century critical theorist Jürgen Habermas (1991) identified as a fundamental precondition of democracy. [...] By restricting access to these public venues, cross-dressing law effectively excluded multiple people with non-normative gender from civic participation and the democratic life of the city. Finally, cross-dressing law was not only consequential for those excluded from everyday public and political life, but also for the "general" gender-normative public, who faced an artificially narrow range of gender identities in city space. After all, when in public, there were only two ways that people with nonnormative gender presentation could avoid arrest—either changing their clothing to comply with the law or evading police detection by fully "passing." Clearly involving different risks and benefits, these strategies nonetheless had a similar effect on city space, removing different-gender appearances and identities from public view. Indeed, by policing gender hierarchies through public exclusion, cross-dressing law reinforced the very notion of "difference" as anomalous by exaggerating the prevalence of the "norm."

## PROBLEM BODIES, PUBLIC SPACE

Although cross-dressing law marked a particularly literal attempt to produce and police normative gender, it was not an isolated or idiosyncratic act of government. Instead, it was one part of a broader legal matrix that targeted the public visibility of multiple "problem bodies," including those of Chinese immigrants, prostitutes, and individuals deemed maimed or diseased.[3] These local orders constituted a body of law that targeted the atypical human body as a potential public nuisance, and they appeared in the municipal codebook alongside laws that regulated sewage, slaughterhouses, and the keeping of hogs. However, while these nineteenth-century laws differed significantly from each other in their object of concern, their mechanisms of control were very similar, seeking to manage public nuisances—animal, object, or human body—through regulating city space.

Mirroring the regulatory logic of cross-dressing law, some of these laws sought to directly *exclude* problem bodies from public space. For example, in 1867, the Board of Supervisors passed a law that prohibited anyone who was "diseased, maimed, mutilated," or an otherwise "unsightly or disgusting object" from appearing in public (*General Orders* 1869). One part of a broader law, with the name "To Prohibit Street Begging, and to Restrain Certain Persons from Appearing in Streets and Public Places," this law focused on the intersection of disability and poverty, seeking to exclude the potentially sympathetic figure of the disabled beggar from San Francisco streets (Schweik 2007). Two years later, in 1869, the supervisors passed another law that prohibited persons from carrying baskets or bags on poles on the city streets—this way of moving through public space being common among some Chinese immigrant workers (*General Orders* 1872). Similar to cross-dressing law, these laws focused on public appearances and movements and simultaneously policed problem bodies while producing governable city space.

A second set of laws operated through *confinement*, rather than exclusion, seeking to ban problem bodies from particular neighborhoods, rather than from generic public space. A series of laws in the 1880s and 1890s, for example, targeted houses of prostitution on middle-class, residential streets, in an effort to reduce the visibility of commercial sex work for "respectable," middle-class, Anglo-American women and children, through its confinement in carefully designated, racialized vice districts (*General Orders* 1890, 1892, 1898). Subsequent laws and policies went even further in endeavors to confine vice to specific areas. For example, when the owner of a Barbary Coast "den" attempted to buy property in the upscale Pacific Heights neighborhood, following the 1906 earthquake and fire, the police captain promised to block the sale: "This section of the city must be kept free of such places. They have no business outside of the burned district and I propose to drive them back to where they belong" ("Barbary Coast Harpies Seek to Settle Among Homes of Pacific Heights," *The Call*, September 15, 1906, 3). [...]

A third type of legal intervention required the *concealment*, rather than exclusion or confinement, of problem bodies from the "respectable" public's view. Specifically, in 1863, as the Board of Supervisors enacted its wide-ranging indecency law, the local chief of police, Martin Burke, attempted to reduce the visibility of prostitution in Chinatown by requiring the owners of "cribs" (small, street-level rooms from which women solicited sex) to buy and erect large screens at the entrance of the streets that housed them (Burke 1887). This specified not only the geographic spaces of concern (namely, Chinatown), but also the characteristics of "the public" that needed to be shielded from these sights. Burke made this explicit in a subsequent annual report, stating that his purpose was to "hide the degradation and vice…from the view of women and children who ride the streetcar" through the newly developing downtown area (*Municipal Reports* 1865–66).

Finally, there were several legal attempts to bypass intracity boundaries and *remove* problem bodies from the city entirely, aimed exclusively at Chinese immigrants. In 1865, for example, the Board of Supervisors passed an "Order to Remove Chinese Women of Ill-Fame from Certain Limits of the City" (*General Orders* 1866). This was the first local law to explicitly target a single nationality, and under the advice of the city attorney, the supervisors removed the word "Chinese" from the legal text, prior to publication. The intent of the law, however, remained unchanged, and the following year, 137 women—virtually all Chinese—were arrested as "common prostitutes," an enormous increase over the previous year, when there had been one arrest. These women were subsequently removed from the city, and the chief of police boasted that he had used the law to expel three hundred Chinese women, with fewer than two hundred remaining (*Municipal Reports* 1865–66). Additionally, the Board of Supervisors made numerous attempts to harness the power granted by nuisance law to remove all Chinese residents from San Francisco. [...]

Undoubtedly, there were important differences between these laws, as well as between the processes through which cross-dressed, indecent, unsightly, and racialized immigrant bodies were defined as problems and targeted for legal intervention. Nonetheless, I bring these particular laws together here—as they were brought together in nineteenth-century municipal codebooks—for two specific reasons.

First, when these laws are considered together, it becomes clear that cross-dressing law was not alone in its attempt to minimize the public visibility of problem bodies. Instead, it was one part of a broader legal matrix that was concerned not only with gender transgressions, but also with race, citizenship, and disease. Moreover, these were not independent concerns. As numerous scholars have argued, accusations of gender and sexual deviance have frequently been deployed in processes of racialization, while racialized anxieties have informed the policing of gender and sex. In turn, race, gender, and sex have all been linked to disease, and in nineteenth-century San Francisco, the management of public health was key to policing Chinese immigrants and prostitutes. In short, there were numerous intersecting cultural anxieties during this period that become more apparent when cross-dressing law is situated in its broader legal context.

Analyzing cross-dressing law within this context also makes clearer the ways that the law sought to manage not only gender but also city space. As legal historian Lawrence Friedman has stated about nineteenth-century morality laws in general: "What was illegal, then, was not sin itself—and certainly not secret sin—but sin that offended public morality. This was what we might call the Victorian compromise: a certain toleration for vice, or at least a resigned acceptance, so long as it remained in an underground state" (1985, 585). However, before vice in San Francisco could "remain in an underground state," such spaces had to be created. Indecency and nuisance laws were instrumental to this process, creating urban zones where problem bodies could be contained—primarily the racialized vice districts of Chinatown and the Barbary Coast. Consequently, these laws affected not only the public visibility of problem bodies, but also the sociospatial order of the city, drawing a series of territorial boundaries between public and private, visible and concealed, and respectable and vice districts.

## FASCINATION AND FREAKERY

Laws that sought to reduce the visibility of problem bodies—including cross-dressing law—constituted a dense legal matrix that dictated the types of bodies that could move freely through city space and the types of bodies that could not. However, such laws could also incite cultural fascination and the desire to see, which entrepreneurs could exploit. One manifestation of this was the popular commercial "slumming tour," in which tourists were guided through the Barbary Coast and Chinatown, to glimpse the bodies that the law sought to conceal. These tours took in brothels, opium dens, dive bars, and sick rooms housing Chinese patients who were banned from the city's hospital (Evans 1873). Another manifestation was the newspaper scandal, which splashed cross-dressing practices across the front page, as local editors ran sensational stories and interviews with those who broke the law. These scandals publicized normative gender boundaries and ridiculed transgressors, representing gender difference as a titillating private eccentricity or individual moral flaw (Duggan 2000; Sears 2005). However, the starkest manifestation of this cultural fascination was the dime museum freak show, which displayed non-normative bodies and cross-gender performances in seeming conflict with the law.

Dime museum freak shows emerged as a popular form of entertainment in most major U.S. cities after the Civil War, peaking in popularity during the 1880s and 1890s. As one component of the era's new mass entertainment industry, dime museums had their socioeconomic roots in technological, demographic, and economic changes that led to an unprecedented rise in leisure time among working-class and middle-class city residents (Adams 2001).[4] Similar to municipal law, the dime museum freak show was preoccupied with the public appearance of non-normative bodies and offered a variety of attractions for the low price of a dime, including human anatomy exhibits, lectures on morality, sideshow circus artists, and freak show performers. Most studies of dime museums and freak shows have focused on East Coast institutions, with particular emphasis on P. T. Barnum's American Museum in New York (Bogdan 1988; Dennet 1997; McNamara 1974). San Francisco, however, boasted numerous freak shows of its own, ranging from the short-lived Museum of Living Wonders, which operated out of a "leaky tent on Kearny Street" in the early 1870s ("A Shocking Exhibition," *The Call*, December 17, 1873), to the grand exhibitions held at Woodward's Gardens, an expansive family amusement resort that occupied two city blocks in the Mission district from 1866 to 1891 ("Where the 'Old Town' Frolicked," *San Francisco Chronicle*, November 9, 1913, 25). Most of the city's freak shows, however, were clustered on Market Street, operating out of small, seedy, rented storefronts (Asbury 1933; Cowan 1938). Market Street was also home to the Pacific Museum of Anatomy and Science, the city's longest-running dime museum, which claimed to be the "largest anatomical museum in the world" ("Visit Dr. Jordan's Great Museum of Anatomy," *The Call*, September 11, 1902, 2).

In San Francisco, as elsewhere, dime museum entertainment centered upon performances of bodily difference and paid particularly close attention to bodies that challenged gender, racial, and national boundaries or that ostensibly revealed the somatic penalties of immorality through spectacles of disease or deformity. For example, freak shows typically featured a Bearded Lady or Half-Man/Half-Woman character, while anatomy exhibits included hermaphrodite bodies, such as that of the Pacific Museum's display of "a beautiful dissection" of a hermaphrodite cadaver, featuring "the internal arrangements and dissections of this wonderful freak of nature" (Jordan 1868, 19). Another staple attraction was the popular "Missing Link" or "What-Is-It?" exhibit, which usually featured an African American or a white man in blackface who was presented as the "missing link" between man and animal (Cook 1996). Many dime museums also featured pathology rooms that contained displays of diseased sexual organs and other body parts, damaged by syphilis, gonorrhea, and "the filthy habit of self-abuse" (Jordan 1868, 36). Finally, dime museums regularly staged performances of racialized national dominance that corresponded to contemporary wars. One of the first crowd-drawing exhibits at the Pacific Museum of Anatomy and Science, for example, was the preserved head of Joaquin Murietta, the notorious Mexican "bandit" who fought against Anglo dominance and violence in the southern California gold mines, before being killed by state-sponsored rangers in 1853 (Asbury 1933). Murietta was a popular symbol of Mexican resistance, and the display of his severed head graphically dramatized a narrative of Anglo dominance and Mexican defeat, against the backdrop of the Mexican War. Occasionally, dime museum exhibits explicitly linked gender and national boundary transgressions, as when Barnum's American Museum displayed a waxwork figure of Jefferson Davis, the defeated leader of the Southern Confederacy, wearing women's clothing, at the close of the Civil War. This exhibit dramatized rumors that Davis had disguised himself in hoopskirts when trying to escape his northern captors, deploying cultural anxieties about cross-gender practices to emasculate the defeated South, fortify territorial boundaries, and reconsolidate the postwar nation (Silber 1989).[5]

As this brief review suggests, the freak show and the law shared a set of cultural anxieties concerning the shifting boundaries of gender, race, health, and the nation, and the disparate bodies gathered on the freak show stage eerily mirrored the bodies targeted by municipal law—the sexually ambiguous, the indecent, the racialized, and the diseased. However, the relationship between the two institutions was complex, not least because the law prohibited the public visibility of problem bodies while the freak show required their public display. These complexities are illustrated by the case of one man who navigated both legal proscriptions and freak show visibility in 1890s San Francisco—Milton Matson.

In early January 1895, Matson was arrested in San Francisco, in the room of his fiancée, Ellen Fairweather, and charged with obtaining money under false pretenses. Matson was taken to San Jose County Jail and locked up in a cell with several other men, where he remained for two weeks, until the jailer received a bank telegraph, addressed to Miss Luisa Matson, and realized that Matson was female.[6] After complicated legal wrangling, charges against Matson were dropped, and he walked free from the jail in men's clothing, returning to San Francisco the following month.

The exposure of Matson's "true sex" generated a mass of newspaper coverage and the San Francisco dailies ran numerous stories on this "male impersonator" or "pretender," as Matson was described ("Louisa Has Her Say," *The Call*, January 28, 1895, 1; "Will Again Don Woman's Garb," *San Francisco Examiner*, January 30, 1895, 3). In these stories, the press excitedly debated the possibility of Matson's arrest under cross-dressing law and reported that he publicly dared the police to arrest him. Before this could happen, Matson was approached by a local dime museum manager, Frank Clifton, and offered work, sitting upon a museum platform, wearing men's clothing, for the public to view. In need of employment and money, particularly since the press had undermined his ability to live as a man, Matson accepted Clifton's offer. The strangeness of this transition—"from a cell in the San Jose prison to the electric brilliancy of an amusement resort"—was not lost on Matson, who commented: "Funniest thing…I'm getting letters from all sorts of showmen offering good salaries if I will exhibit myself. It amuses me very much….I'm beginning to think it pays to be notorious. It certainly does not seem to be a detriment to people in America" ("Has No Love for Petticoats," *San Francisco Examiner*, February 7, 1895, 16). The appeal of Matson's notoriety proved so popular that several other local freak shows began featuring cross-dressed performers, deceptively advertised as "the only genuine Miss Martson [*sic*] in male attire" ("Louisa Matson's Double Sued," *The Call*, February 15, 1895, 12).

Given the punitive forces impinging on cross-dressing practices in nineteenth-century San Francisco, and the law's insistence on removing them from public view, the concurrent display of cross-dressing performers in city freak shows is initially perplexing. On the one hand, these institutions operated according to very different logics. The law imprisoned, the freak show displayed; the law deprived its subject, the freak show offered a salary; the law disapproved and sought to reduce its subjects' "deviance," the freak show was fascinated and sought to exaggerate and increase it.

On the other hand, the operations of cross-dressing law and the freak show overlapped. After all, Matson was recruited into freak show entertainment directly from a jail cell, following a path that other San Francisco performers had walked before him.[7] Moreover, Matson's participation in a freak show exhibition regulated his offstage behavior in a very direct way; his contract forbade him to wear men's clothing on San Francisco's streets, to preserve the mystique—and profitability—of his show ("She Has Been a Man of the World for Over Twenty-six Years," *San Francisco Examiner*, February 10, 1895, 26). Consequently, although the law and the freak show operated through distinct logics of concealment and display, they could have similar regulatory effects on freak show performers.

The freak show also paralleled cross-dressing law as a normalizing discourse that communicated to audiences, in starkly visual terms, the parameters of acceptable behavior and the penalties for violating these norms. While there are few historical records that speak to the disciplinary impact of cross-dressing performers on freak show audiences, a popular 1890s dime novel is highly suggestive of possible effects. In Archibald Gunter and Fergus Redmond's *A Florida Enchantment*, of 1891, a wealthy white woman, Lillian Travers, purchases a box of African sex change seeds from a dime museum in Florida.[8] Following an argument with her fiancé, she swallows a seed and transitions into a man named Lawrence Talbot. Realizing that a wealthy man needs a male valet, rather than a female housekeeper, Lawrence forces his "mulatto maid," Jane, to also swallow a seed and become a man named Jack. Lawrence later realizes with "fearful horror" that dime museums would love to exhibit him as a freak and he has a nightmare in which the city is covered in gigantic dime museum posters, advertising him as "The Freak of All Ages" and "The Woman Man," appearing alongside "The Living Skeleton" and "The Missing Link." Although doubly fictional (first as appearing in a novel, second as appearing as a dream), this scene illuminates the operations of the freak show in two specific ways.

First, by illustrating Lawrence's horror at the prospect of being displayed as a freak, the nightmare suggests that freak show visibility could have disciplinary effects, operating as a threat against gender transgression and an inducement to conform. Second, the context of Lawrence's nightmare, within the novel, suggests that the disciplinary effects of freak show visibility were informed by racialized anxieties, rather than by a universal fear of being labeled "freak." Specifically, Lawrence's nightmare occurs after he has already entered a dime museum to purchase sex change seeds from Africa and after he has learned that his former maid, now Jack, has begun working at a dime museum as "the greatest freak on earth." Additionally, the poster from his nightmare suggests that part of the horror of being displayed as "The Woman Man" is appearing alongside and in association with the racialized "Missing Link" character and the deformed "Living Skeleton." Indeed, throughout the novel, the dime museum appears as a racialized site that serves as both the source of gender transgression (sex change seeds from Africa) and the space of its containment. This suggests that the potential disciplinary effects of freak show visibility were intricately connected to its association with imperial exoticism and racialized difference.

Finally, freak shows worked in tandem with cross-dressing law by producing not only disciplined audiences schooled in gender normativity, but also vigilant audiences trained in the pleasures of suspicion. The possibility of being duped was central to dime museum entertainment, and show managers encouraged audiences to gain pleasure from suspecting, confronting, and unmasking frauds. Performances of sexual and gender ambiguity were particularly susceptible to this suspicion. For example, the Bearded Lady's combination of feminine dress and masculine facial hair confronted audiences with a fascinating gender dilemma—was this a woman who pushed the female body beyond recognizable femininity or was this a man in drag? Visitors sought to resolve this dilemma by prodding at flesh, tugging at beards, and demanding to know the Bearded Lady's marital and maternal status (Wood 1885). Freak show managers encouraged this questioning and occasionally brought in experts to heighten the drama. At New York's American Museum, for example, P. T. Barnum instigated a confrontation, one that ended in court, in which a freak show visitor accused a Bearded Lady of being male, only to be rebuffed by the latter's husband, father, and numerous doctors who testified that she was, indeed, female. Back in San Francisco, Matson's manager also went to court, to sue rivals of his who allegedly featured "fake" Matsons in their shows. Far from resolving the gender confusion at hand, such events reminded audiences of their susceptibility to being duped. As such, freak shows not only reproduced the boundary between permissible and criminal gender displays that cross-dressing law policed—they also popularized and democratized this boundary, turning audiences into aware and vigilant judges of possible gender "fraud."

Despite their different modes of operation, cross-dressing law and the freak show performed similar cultural work in nineteenth-century San Francisco, as techniques of normalization that strove to produce clear, recognizable boundaries between normative and non-normative gender. Additionally, their mutual preoccupation with cross-dressing bodies did not occur in a vacuum, but was one part of a broader set of cultural concerns about the public visibility of problem bodies, particularly those marked by sexual immorality, race, and disease/deformity.

At the same time, however, freak show displays may have had unintended or ironic effects, particularly when the carefully managed distance between viewer and viewed broke down. As cultural scholar Rachel Adams (2001) has argued, freak shows were not only sites of disidentification and disavowal, where audiences secured a sense of normality through their spatial and existential distance from the freaks on stage, but were also sites of identification, where audiences recognized themselves in the freaks and the freaks in themselves. In part, this occurred because the meaning of the freak show performance (like the meaning of any text) was never completely fixed, but was open to multiple interpretations by different audiences. Moreover, as Adams points out, the interactive format of the freak show amplified the possibility of unintended interpretations, as it facilitated unscripted exchanges between disruptive audience members and the freaks who talked back. Such exchanges encouraged alternative readings of the freak show not only among those who participated in them, but also among the wider audience who collectively observed an unintended show.

Adams makes this argument in the context of discussing African American audiences who identified and unmasked racialized freak show performers as local people of color. Such identification, she claims, undermined the fantasy of complete otherness on which the freak show depended and dissolved the boundary between audience and performer, "relocating [the freak] within the community of onlookers" (2001, 170). However, in the context of gender freaks, particularly Matson, the politics of identification could take a slightly different turn, through identifications and desires that did not relocate the freak within the audience but attracted the onlooker to the cross-gender performer on stage. This attraction could be fueled by a shared sense of female masculinity—after all, Matson was not the only female-bodied person to live as a man in 1890s San Francisco.[9] It could also be fueled by an erotic desire for the cross-gender performer, particularly one such as Matson who had described the pleasures of courting women in the pages of the city press.

There is, unfortunately, scant evidence of such identifications and desires in relation to Matson or other cross-dressed freak show performers, as the voices of those who may have appropriated freak discourse in this manner have not made their way into the archive. However, neglecting this possibility because of insufficient evidence may be more problematic than raising it unsupported by positive proof, as it replicates the structure of the archive, amplifying some voices and silencing others. Within the archive, the voice of the newspaper reporter is prominent; a *San Francisco Examiner* reporter described Matson's dime museum exhibit as follows: "Her part will not be a difficult one. She will be faultlessly attired in patent leathers, a handsome dress suit, embroidered linen and a white tie. She will recline in an easy-chair on a little platform and chat with the socially inclined, but whether she will divulge any of the interesting secrets connected with her numerous love episodes is not definitely known" ("Has No Love for Petticoats," *San Francisco Examiner*, February 7, 1895, 16). Consequently, we can imagine the different ways that different audiences may have interacted with Matson—with fascination and titillation, perhaps; with discomfort and disdain; but also perhaps with identification, attraction, and desire.

## CONCLUSION

Through its focus on cross-dressing law, this essay has demonstrated the centrality of gender regulation to nineteenth-century city life and unearthed the hidden history of a law that has appeared in the footnotes of twentieth-century studies, but has not yet been brought to the fore. The essay has also brought together subjects that rarely share the pages of academic inquiry, despite sharing San Francisco streets: male-bodied women and "unsightly" beggars; female-bodied men and sex workers; freak show managers and city police. In doing so I have argued that the policing of gender transgressions needs to be analyzed in relation to the policing of multiple forms of bodily difference and that legal regulations need to be studied alongside cultural fascination. These analytic insights are crucial not only for a study of nineteenth-century cross-dressing law, but also for future studies of the production and regulation of normative gender.

## NOTES

1. Arrest records were not broken down by gender, but in 1867–68, arrests were reported separately for "wearing female attire" and "wearing male attire." During this year, four people (presumably male bodied) were arrested for "wearing female attire" and two people (presumably female bodied) were arrested for "wearing male attire" (*Municipal Reports* 1867–68).
2. Newspapers did not report on Haisch's own gender identification, but they did describe her going to considerable lengths to publicly present as a woman. Consequently, I use female pronouns when discussing Haisch.
3. I use the term "problem bodies" to collectively refer to the multiple sets of bodies that local government officials defined as social problems and targeted for legal intervention in nineteenth-century San Francisco. In particular, I use "problem bodies" as a term that conceptually precedes the related, but narrower, term "deviant bodies" (Terry and Urla 1995), because I identify the construction of deviance, through processes of normalization, as only one of several different strategies used to manage social, political, and economic conflicts. The concept of problem bodies thus allows a wider range of bodies—and a wider range of conflicts—to be brought into view.
4. Vaudeville theater and minstrel shows were also central components of the new entertainment industry and they shared the freak show's emphasis on cross-gender and cross-racial performances (Lott, 1993; Toll, 1976).
5. Thanks to Susan Stryker for pointing me to the Jefferson Davis reference.
6. Matson was accused of committing this crime in Los Gatos, fifty miles south of San Francisco, and was consequently jailed in San Jose.
7. In 1888, freak show managers recruited another San Francisco performer, "Big Bertha the Queen of Confidence Women," directly from jail, literally paying her bail so as to secure her performance in their Market Street show ("Madame Stanley," *Morning Call*, June 11, 1888, 4).
8. In my discussion of this novel, I draw upon and extend Siobhan Somerville's (2000) earlier analysis.
9. For example, Lou Sullivan (1990) documented the life of Jack Garland (aka Babe Bean), a female-bodied man who lived in or near San Francisco in the late 1890s and 1900s.

## WORKS CITED

Adams, Rachel. 2001. *Sideshow USA: Freaks and the American Cultural Imagination*. Chicago: University of Chicago Press.
Asbury, Herbert. 1933. *The Barbary Coast: An Informal History of the San Francisco Underworld*. New York: A. A. Knopf.
Bogdan, Robert. 1988. *Freak Show: Presenting Human Oddities for Amusement and Profit*. Chicago: University of Chicago Press.
Burke, Martin J. 1887. "The San Francisco Police." Bancroft Library, University of California, Berkeley.
*Chinatown Declared a Nuisance!* 1880. San Francisco: Workingmen's Party of California.
Cook, James W. 1996. "Of Men, Missing Links, and Nondescripts: The Strange Career of P. T. Barnum's 'What Is It?' Exhibition." In *Freakery: Cultural Spectacles of the Extraordinary Body*, ed. R. G. Thomson. New York: New York University Press.
Cowan, Robert Ernest. 1938. *Forgotten Characters of Old San Francisco, 1850–1870*. Los Angeles: Ward Ritchie Press.
Dennett, Andrea Stulman. 1997. *Weird and Wonderful: The Dime Museum in America*. New York: New York University Press.
Duggan, Lisa. 2000. *Sapphic Slashers: Sex, Violence, and American Modernity*. Durham: Duke University Press.
Eskridge, William N. 1999. *Gaylaw: Challenging the Apartheid of the Closet*. Cambridge: Harvard University Press.
Evans, Albert S. 1873. *A la California: Sketch of Life in the Golden State*. San Francisco: A. L. Bancroft.
Friedman, Lawrence Meir. 1985. *A History of American Law*. 2nd ed. New York: Simon and Schuster. ( 1st ed. pub. 1973.)
*General Orders of the Board of Supervisors*. 1866–98. San Francisco: San Francisco Board of Supervisors.
Habermas, Jürgen. 1991. *The Structural Transformation of the Public Sphere: An Inquiry into a Category of Bourgeois Society*. Cambridge: MIT Press (Orig. pub. 1962.)
Hirschfeld, Magnus. 1991. *Transvestites: The Erotic Drive to Cross-Dress*. Buffalo: Prometheus Books (Orig. pub. 1910).

Jesse Brown Cook Scrapbooks Documenting San Francisco History and Law Enforcement. n.d. Vol. 4. The Bancroft Library. University of California, Berkeley. Unit ID: 184.

Jordan, Louis J. 1868. *Handbook of the Pacific Museum of Anatomy and Science.* San Francisco: Francis and Valentine.

Lott, Eric. 1993. *Love and Theft: Blackface Minstrelsy and the American Working Class.* New York: Oxford University Press.

McNamara, Brooks. 1974. "'A Congress of Wonders': The Rise and Fall of the Dime Museum." *ESQ* 20(3):216–31.

*Municipal Reports.* 1863–64 to 1899–1900. San Francisco: San Francisco Board of Supervisors.

Schweik, Susan. 2007. "Begging the Question: Disability, Mendicancy, Speech and the Law." *Narrative* 15(1):58–70.

Sears, Clare. 2005. "A Tremendous Sensation: Cross-Dressing in the Nineteenth Century San Francisco Press." In *News and Sexuality: Media Portraits of Diversity,* ed. L. Casteñada and S. Campbell. Thousand Oaks, CA: Sage Press.

Silber, Nina. 1989. "Intemperate Men, Spiteful Women, and Jefferson Davis: Northern Views of the Defeated South." *American Quarterly* 41(4):614–35.

Somerville, Siobhan. 2000. *Queering the Color Line: Race and the Invention of Homosexuality in American Culture.* Durham: Duke University Press.

Sullivan, Lou. 1990. *From Female to Male: The Life of Jack Bee Garland.* Boston: Alyson.

Stryker, Susan, and Jim Van Buskirk. 1996. *Gay by the Bay: A History of Queer Culture in the San Francisco Bay Area.* San Francisco: Chronicle Books.

*Revised Orders of the City and County of San Francisco.* 1863. San Francisco: San Francisco Board of Supervisors.

Terry, Jennifer, and Jacqueline Urla. 1995. *Deviant Bodies.* Bloomington: Indiana University Press.

Toll, Robert. 1976. *On with the Show! The First Century of Show Business in America.* New York: Oxford University Press.

Wood, J. G. 1885. "Dime Museums." *Atlantic Monthly* 55 (January–June): 759–65.

# 43

# *Shuttling Between Bodies and Borders*

## Iranian Transsexual Refugees and the Politics of Rightful Killing

### Sima Shakhsari

Sima Shakhsari's "Shuttling Between Borders and Bodies" opens with the story of Naz, a transgender Iranian refugee who was featured in two documentaries about transsexuality in Iran, both of which sensationalized that country as a location in which transsexuals were shunned. Unable to find work, and about to be evicted from her apartment, Naz committed suicide a year after being granted asylum in Canada—but this is not the part of her story told by the filmmakers, who frame her narrative as one of successful immigration to a liberal West that is superior to the reactionary Islamic state she left behind. For Shakhsari, an anthropologist based in the U.S.A., this story emblematizes a more extensive representational logic of queer death within the discourse of a "gay internationalism" that allows some deaths to be invested in symbolically, but which renders other deaths literally unthinkable. Shakhsari critically examines the nexus of human rights organizations, media, national governments, gay rights organizations, individuals, and diasporic communities that enables violence towards queer immigrants who do not fit the homonationalist narrative of aspiring to join a modern gay metropolis. At every level, Shakhsari finds, transgender refugees encounter violence and adjudication: from immigration authorities who judge whether they are "real" refugees, to LGBT rights organizations that judge whether their claims for asylum are "convincing" enough to win. This produces a situation in which LGBT organizations actually "coach queer refugees in homonormativity." Shakhsari contrasts such stories with that of Mark Bingham, a gay U.S. citizen who died in the 9/11 attacks, as well as with those of two Iranian teenagers hanged in 2005, which set off a global outcry about the plight of gay Iranians. Many kinds of queers, Shakhsari contends, become cannon fodder and contested subjects in what she calls a "politics of rightful killing," which dictates that those hailed as the future recipients of freedom and democracy, for whom the war on terror is allegedly fought, are precisely those liable to be killed in order to "protect" that vision of putative freedom.

In a documentary film, recorded in Iran and produced in Canada, Naz, a transsexual Iranian woman, tells the interviewer, "*midoonam keh hastam, mikhaam zendegi konam*" ("I know that I am, I want to live").[1] Prodded by different filmmakers to reveal the most intimate matters of her life in front of the camera, Naz has been the subject of several documentary films about transsexuals in Iran. Screened at international film festivals, distributed through YouTube, or broadcast on television outside of

Iran, most of these films juxtapose a repressed life in Iran to a free and violence-free queer life in the West. The films showcase the suffering of working class Iranian transsexual women who are ostracized by their families and subjected to social discrimination, rendering it visible to the often non-Iranian audience. In a peculiar triad of fixation, movement, and affective representation, the viewer is moved, the diasporic filmmaker moves between national borders to document and show, and the "victimized" transgender/transsexual Iranian moves only via her testimonies told in the moving picture. Naz, however, was one of the few subjects of films about transsexual Iranians, who— with the help of a non-profit Canadian organization—traveled to Turkey to apply for refugee status in Canada.

While Naz's life in Iran was represented as an example of the horrific situation of transsexuals in Iran, her story in Canada was never publicized in queer or mainstream media, nor did her story in Canada make it to any documentary films. Almost a year after immigrating to Canada, Naz silently took her life in an apartment she was asked to vacate, as the terms of her subsidized housing had come to an end. [2]

Without undermining the hardship that many queers face in Iran, one is compelled to ask: when and where are queer lives and deaths readily representable, and when and where do they become unrepresentable? When is queer visibility and outness tolerated by the nation? Which queer lives and deaths are representable and which ones are unspeakable? In order to approach these questions, I connect Naz's death to two other stories of queer death. While seemingly separate, all three stories are related if analyzed within the context of the politics of representation during the "war on terror." Through a relational approach (Shohat 2003) and by looking at representations of these deaths by the "gay international"[3] (Massad 2007), I point to the way that representational politics, biopolitics, necropolitics, and geopolitics are connected in the production of universalized sexual identities and the management of life and death of different populations during the war on terror. I argue that representations of queer death are instrumental to how a nexus of state and non-state institutions, individuals, human rights discourses, civilizational discourses, diasporas, and media work together to produce, represent, and manage queer lives and deaths according to national and transnational conventions of citizenship. The Iranian transgender refugee, as a paradigmatic figure of the *homo sacer* (Agamben 1998), is an important site of inquiry in the analysis of the politics of life and death in relation to the gendered norms of citizenship.

## UNSPEAKABLE DEATH: IRANIAN QUEER REFUGEES

Naz was one of around 300 queer refugees who live in transition in remote "satellite towns" in Turkey, waiting for their cases to be handled by the United Nations High Commissioner for Refugees (UNHCR) in Ankara. While most of the Iranian queer asylum seekers in Turkey are gay or lesbian, a small number of transgender people leave Iran in hope of a better life abroad. Even though the numbers are not large, media representations of Iranian transsexual individuals have made them the center of a particular discourse on homosexuality. Within this discourse, Iranian transsexuals are represented as homosexual victims who are *forced* by the Iranian state to go through sex reassignment surgeries (SRSs). Sex change, in this narrative, is seen as a state measure to prevent homosexuality— punishable under the Islamic Republic's sodomy laws. Transsexual Iranians' desires are deemed inauthentic and secondary to an inherent homosexual desire that is persecuted by the state.

It is true that the Islamic state in Iran combines modern medical and religious discourses to produce ideal heteronormative citizen subjects. Post-revolutionary Iran has seen the proliferation of SRSs that can be attributed to Imam Khomeini's fatwa to make these surgeries religiously and legally permissible. Since the early 1980s, numerous SRSs have taken place in Iran, making Iran—by some accounts—the global "SRS capital" after Thailand. While the narrative of "forced surgeries" is an inaccurate account of SRS in Iran, one could argue that the Iranian transsexual is produced as a normalized and "corrected" non-homosexual citizen, governed by modern medical, psychological, legal, and religious discourses and practices (Najmabadi 2008). However, it is undeniable that the Iranian state's religious and biopolitical practices, which enable SRS, have provided relatively amicable opportunities for transgender Iranians, compared to many other states, including those in the so-called free world. The Iranian state offers relatively sizable subsidies and loans for SRSs.[4] In order to protect the privacy of those who undergo surgery, the post-revolutionary Iranian state issues new birth certificates and passports with the post-surgery assigned gender to people diagnosed with Gender Identity Disorder—a pathologizing term that emerged in the 1960s in Iran and was adopted from the American medical and psychological books of the same period in the U.S.A.[5] Despite this official policy, many Iranian transsexuals and transgender people face social harassment, job discrimination, and violence in Iran where—as is the case in many locations such as North America and Europe—modern binaries of sex are naturalized and govern norms of cultural and political citizenship. Along with the much-valorized vision of freedom and democracy in the West, the economic and social hardship endured by many transgendered and transsexual Iranians compels some to seek refugee status in Canada, Australia, and the U.S.A. through the UNHCR offices in neighboring Turkey. While the Iranian transsexual as a "corrected" body is disciplined into norms of heterosexuality in Iran, she is simultaneously produced as a subject of universal rights in need of protection by international human rights regimes. For transsexual Iranians who leave Iran to seek refugee status, the concomitant loss of citizenship rights and the geopolitically driven "protection" of rights entail new forms of regulation according to the norms of the international refugee regimes, as well as those of transitory and destination "host" states.

Ironically, it is under the rhetoric of protection that the refugee has very little or no rights in transition. Turkey extends protection under the 1951 United Nations Convention relating to the Status of Refugees and the amending 1967 Protocol only to persons originating in Europe. However, the Turkish government does permit non-European asylum seekers to remain in Turkey temporarily while their cases are pending with the UNHCR. Iranian refugee applicants are required to register with the Turkish Ministry of the Interior, and with the UNHCR, while waiting to be interviewed several times. If approved as true refugees, they are allowed to apply for resettlement to a third country of asylum. Upon registration with the UNHCR, the applicants are assigned to small "satellite towns," where they are registered by the Turkish Police. There they are required to stay throughout the interview and evaluation process, including medical and sometimes psychological examination by the UNHCR and the embassy of the country of asylum. The entire process—registration with the UNHCR, registration and assignment to small satellite towns in Turkey, interviews with the UNHCR for refugee status determination, and interviews with the third country of asylum—takes years, during which time asylum seekers are required to pay for their own basic expenses.[6] According to a June 2009 report by the Organization for Refuge, Asylum, and Migration (ORAM), queer asylum seekers and refugees in Turkey often have limited or no access to financial support, face consistent harassment from local townspeople, and experience work and housing discrimination. When filing complaints with the Turkish police, they are encouraged to "dress like real men or women" in order to avoid being harassed. According to ORAM, while the UNHCR has improved its guidelines and produced literature to educate its staff, many asylum seekers have reported being asked invasive questions by the Ministry of the Interior in Turkey and the UNHCR about their preferred sexual position, or the number of sexual partners they have had. These questions are meant to verify that the applicants are "true refugees," "true gay and lesbians," or "true transgender" individuals.

A few organizations have advocated for the training of the Turkish government employees and the UNHCR interviewers and criticized the homophobia and transphobia to which refugees are subjected. However, while these organizations' work is important in reducing the violence that queer refugees experience in transitioning between national borders, they keep intact the regulations of border and gender, imposed by the state and the UNHCR. For example, ORAM, an important organization that assists many refugee applicants in Turkey, relies on the UNHCR interpretation of "membership in a particular social group" in its advocacy for queer refugee applicants. Membership in a particular group is interpreted by the UNHCR as either sharing a "characteristic which is immutable or so fundamental to human dignity that [one] should not be compelled to forsake it," or "a characteristic which makes a group cognizable or sets it apart from society at large. The characteristic will often be one which is innate, unchangeable, or which is otherwise fundamental to identity, conscience, or the exercise of one's human rights" (Grungras *et al.*, 44 quoting Neilson 2005). ORAM explains that gay men have the immutable characteristic of being sexually or emotionally attracted to men, and lesbians to women. Transsexuals' gender identity, rather than their sexual orientation, ORAM explains, is viewed as "immutable and fundamental to the person's identity" (Grungras *et al.*, 44 quoting Neilson 2005).

The assumptions of "immutability" embedded in these essentialist juridical discourses produce the refugee as an individual with a fixed, timeless, and universally homogenous identity. It is inevitable that queer refugee applicants repeat essentialist notions of identity in order to fit the "immutability of character," the criterion that qualifies gays, lesbians, and trans people as refugees. Applicants' narratives, their material conditions, and their multiple and complex subjectivities are reduced to rational and linear definitions in order to match the acceptable "immutable" identity, defined and sanctioned by the refugee law, and reified by some diasporic queer organizations that "coach" queer refugees in homonormativity (Duggan 2002). In order to pass the medical and psychological exams successfully, before their interviews with the UNHCR and the embassy of the third country of asylum, Iranian transsexuals—and Iranian queers in general—often rehearse and repeat conventions of "authentic" and believable sexual and gender identities. Thus, through performative acts, universalized and iconic gay, lesbian, transgender, and bisexual (a difficult one to prove for the crisis of mutability it incites) identities are reified and reproduced. However, the regulatory practices of the nation-state and human rights discourses conceal the process of the construction of refugee subjects, by portraying them as already made and prior to discourse. The autonomous subject, as Butler (1992: 12) points out, "can maintain the illusion of its autonomy insofar as it covers over the break out of which it is constituted." In fact, as I have argued elsewhere, the queer refugee is often depicted in dominant representations of the refugee discourse as the subject *in front of law*, as opposed to the subject produced *by law* (Shakhsari 2002).

The Iranian transsexual refugees' performances of immutable gender identity are consistent with modern discourses of sexuality that produce universalized gender and sexual identities. As several scholars have argued (Stone 1991; Spade 2003, 2008; Beauchamp 2009), "transsexual" as a category that signifies "Gender Identity Disorder" was recognized in the U.S.A. through legal and medical discourses. Just as the Harry Benjamin International Gender Dysphoria Association's *Standards of Care for Gender Identity Disorders* was (and is) used to determine the authenticity of a client's claim to "true transsexuality," the Iranian transsexual refugee is tested by the UNHCR for the authenticity of her/his sexual and gender identity, which subsequently qualifies one as a "true refugee."

Normative notions of authentic gender and sexuality are not the only conventions that the queer refugee applicant has to repeat convincingly and without contradictions in multiple interviews. In order to present a successful and legitimate claim to asylum officers, the refugee/asylum seeker often has to repeat a story that inevitably demonizes the "home country" (Luibhéid 1998; Anker 2005; Miller 2005). Given that the credibility of an asylum case is decided according to the 1951 Geneva Convention's notions of what constitutes a human rights violation, human rights groups are heavily involved in gathering and providing information on global human rights abuses. Reports by organizations such as the International Gay and Lesbian Human Rights Commission (IGLHRC), International Gay and Lesbian Association (ILGA), Lesbian and Gay Immigration Rights Task Force, and Amnesty International, together with media reports on the violations of human rights, U.S. State Department country reports, samples of UNHCR assessment of asylum and refugee claims, the applicant's personal testimony, and letters of support from friends and relatives and several other organizations constitute the materials that document "human rights abuses" of queers worldwide. Advocates and UNHCR officers often measure the credibility of an applicant's claim for a "well-founded fear of persecution" against these documents.

Exploring refugee discourse in Canada, Sherene Razack argues that the gendered imperial stories in gender-based asylum cases reconsolidate the "racist notion of the First World helping the Third World out of barbarism and social chaos" (1998: 99). Although Razack's argument pertains to gender-based asylum in Canada, the victim-rescuing narrative remains strong in all Third World/First World refugee narratives. This is not to say that Iranian queer refugee applicants do not have legitimate reasons for seeking asylum. Neither does pointing to the formative and performative processes of asylum suggest that queer refugee applicants and asylum seekers are duped or that they "lie." Clearly, the pressure to tell *the story* is tied in with the refugee's claim to available public spaces and legitimacy of presence (Sanadjian 1995). Even when one is *officially* recognized as a "true refugee" by the international refugee regimes, requests for testimony by the media and random "hosts" (ranging from individuals to universities and LGBT organizations) repeat the interview processes for the refugee. The refusal to answer is exhausted, for it may open the gates to accusations of abusing the asylum privilege, a *right* granted to those who qualify for it by their "lack" in relation to the citizen. As long as the queer refugee defines herself as a refugee (read foreign and victim), she does not trouble the hegemonic binaries of citizen/refugee and First World/Third World. (This autonomy of self-definition also conceals the very constitution of the subject.) If, however, she rejects the subject position of a victim, or resists "speaking up" in testimonies (sometimes through the silence of death), she exhausts her invitation, thus becoming unrepresentable. No more an intelligible subject, the unruly queer refugee becomes disposable through unspeakable death or informal deportation by random citizens ("go back home").[7]

While refugee applicants often have no choice but to repeat the "story" that is expected from them, diasporic Iranian entrepreneurs, including LGBT organizations, may find these stories lucrative in a market where information about human rights abuses in Iran may translate into funding by think tanks, democratizing states, and individual funders.[8] The "war on terror" has provided entrepreneurial opportunities for some opposition groups (queer and otherwise) that compete over envisioning the most democratic future for Iran by providing expertise and "insider" information to the liberating states and think tanks.[9] The exaggerated, and in some cases, fabricated stories of gay persecutions in Iran provide fame and/or fundraising opportunities for some organizations that bank on these stories.[10]

Naz's life and her death exemplify the opportunistic appropriations of queer life and death during the "war on terror." Naz's statement "I know that I am" became the title of an award-winning Canadian documentary film that represents transsexual Iranians as victims of a fundamentalist state, in need of rescue by the "free world." The film repeats a narrative that Anne-Marie Fortier has aptly called "queer homecoming," the familiar story of queer flight from home of oppression to seek refuge in home of freedom in the West. Through testimonial documentary style and juxtaposition of words and images, the film creates a stark opposition between freedom in the West and oppression in Iran. This narrative style is very prominent in the promotional video of the film. While transsexual Iranians are constructed as powerless victims, the white Canadian immigration attorney is depicted as a saint-like figure in a slow-motion caption while her image is juxtaposed with subtitled lyrics that interpellate her as "a savior angel." Not surprisingly, the image of an Iranian clergy is accompanied with lyrics that construct him as an unsympathetic enemy. Ironically, Hojattoleslam Karimnia, the clergy depicted in this promotional video, is a transsexual rights advocate and has played a key role in removing the stigma around sex change by arguing that SRSs are religiously sanctioned.[11]

Representation of lives of queer Iranians as victims may serve purposes other than fundraising and fame and may provide opportunities for immigration for those who produce and reproduce the victim narrative. For example, one of the co-directors of *I Know That I Am* was granted asylum in Canada for making this film. A self-identified straight Iranian non-trans man who assumed the mission of rescuing transsexual Iranians, the co-director told a queer Canadian online journal that he "chose to seek asylum in Canada because of this country's reputation for trans acceptance and human rights protection" (Sheppard 2006). The co-director claimed that he escaped Iran after the government raided his house and confiscated most of his footage. However, several films about transsexual lives have been made and screened in Iran. While the co-director's story may have been true for other reasons, neither being a transsexual individual nor making films about transsexual Iranians constitute a crime or warrant persecution. On July 31, 2008, almost two weeks after Naz's death, the other co-director of the film, Babak Yousefi, wrote in his weblog, "I would like to take this opportunity to share with all my good friends the good news of a first prize Audience Award for the documentary, *I Know That I Am*."[12] Ironically, Yousefi did not acknowledge that the transsexual woman whose life was the subject of the film and whose utterance of "I know that I am" inspired the title of the film, no longer was.

## HEROIC DEATH: AMERICAN QUEER SUBJECTS

> In America, we are free. Free to choose, free to say, free to voice our opinions, free to be ourselves. In many places around the world, I could not be myself. Regardless of others' opinions, I can be who I am, and not have to fear my life. I am proud to be me, proud to be an American, and proud to be gay! Only in America can I be this FREE!!![13]

The production of the queer refugee as one who is in need of rescue and protection by human rights regimes and Western democracies is inevitably connected to the production and representation of queer citizen subjects in First World locations such as the U.S.A., where despite claims of freedom, many queers do not enjoy the same rights as heterosexual citizens. As scholars of citizenship have argued, the universalizing American citizenship is realized through the process of individuation where citizen subjects (as taxpayers and consumers, for example) are constituted and regulated by both the state and social institutions (Ong 1996; Berlant 1997). This process is also entangled with the construction of both dangerous and victimized non-citizens whose elimination or protection through the ethos of American democracy becomes a task which is not limited to the apparatus of the state, but shared by non-state institutions such as human rights organizations (Shakhsari 2002).

As the multicultural U.S.A. hinders the exclusion of racialized and gendered sexualities in its national culture through the myth of equality, it reifies the sovereignty of the figure of the coherent citizen subject vis-à-vis its refugee other. The queer refugee's instability and lack of freedom is juxtaposed to the freedom that First World queer citizens seemingly enjoy. Willing American queer citizen subjects who have historically been excluded from the realms of the "normal" often exercise their belonging to the national culture through attempting to occupy hegemonic positions of citizenship. This often translates into consenting to normative notions of "American-ness" and establishing one's legitimacy as a subject in opposition to the figure of the dangerous terrorist or victimized refugee.[14] September 11, 2001, provided an opportunity for American queer citizens to insert themselves into the imaginations of the nation, in a moment of crisis when particular forms of queerness became tolerable and even encouraged in the American nationalist discourse. As Puar and Rai (2002) have observed, celebrations of outness had an unprecedented prevalence in gay and lesbian cultural circuits in the U.S.A. after September 11. Ellen DeGeneres acting as the emcee for the Emmy Awards as an "out" lesbian, observation of National Coming Out Day on the one-month anniversary of September 11, and window posters and postcards that read, "United We Stand! Gay and Proud," were examples which revealed that being out and patriotic were not contradictory, but necessary for the performance of an American gay identity in times of crisis.[15]

One of the most publicized stories in mainstream media, immediately after the attacks, was that of Mark Bingham. A much praised, openly gay man, Bingham lost his life on September 11, 2001, as he thwarted hijackers' plans to crash United Airlines Flight 93 into the White House. Even though the overarching discourse of male hero and patriotic wife occupied every media representation of Americanness, Mark Bingham was celebrated for his masculinity along with the other three "athletic" men who according to the *Life* magazine "were the hijackers' worst nightmare."[16] The fact that Mark Bingham was a successful white businessman who owned a bicoastal firm made him an ideal type who against all odds (he was gay after all) had reached the American dream.

While the hypervisibility of the post-September 11 American nationalism emphasized the heteronormativity of the nation through images, language, and nationalist practices, queer forms of American nationalism had an overarching presence on gay and lesbian websites.[17] Emulating heteronormative media's praise of Bingham's masculinity, many queer websites focused on how Bingham broke the stereotypes on gay masculinity by showing that gays are "men" too. While attempting to counter homophobic stereotypes, such queer celebrations of Bingham's death constructed his masculinity—which eerily approximated that of the heterosexual citizen soldier—as an ideal to be reached by the patriotic gay American on his path to fulfilling the American dream. While there were instances of dissent, what led the American gay subject to successfully join the imaginations of the nation and citizenship in the mainstream gay and lesbian media was to perform "manhood" and patriotism.[18] For example, in a letter on an online forum dedicated to Mark Bingham, a gay man wrote:

> Thanks be to his Mother who let him become who he was. What a true inspiration he will be to all the scared and intimidated people coming to terms with their sexual identity. For entirely too long we as a society were considered to be less than a man, because of how we felt or what we did in our private life. Mark set the example that so many of us lead day to day. Praise to a Hero, who happened to be gay.[19]

This celebration of a "gay hero" repeats heteronormative conventions of militarized nationalism, where women's role in bearing and rearing of future masculine soldiers is emphasized. While Mark Bingham's mother is praised for rearing a citizen-soldier, Bingham becomes the one who rescues and serves the nation, a task that every queer is expected to perform in order to be intelligible: "I didn't have a gay role model or hero growing up, our future generations now have one. God Bless America!"[20] Like any performance, the drama of patriotism and masculine success require an observer: becoming a citizen subject necessitates visibility and "coming out" into the purview of the nation.

The post-9/11 critical "outing" can be explained through the discourse of protectorship, which has a dual meaning. On one level, the masculine gay man is tolerated as "out" and proud when he performs the hegemonic norms of masculinity and takes on the role of the "protector." On another level, being "out" becomes significant as a patriotic act when it designates a spatial division within a Manichean logic, in which the U.S.A. signifies freedom and democracy and the Muslim world stands for homophobia and gay oppression. In this configuration, queers as markers of freedom are protected (through the violence of war, if need be) by the liberating states against the homophobic enemy. For example, on September 21, 2001, Andrew Sullivan wrote:

> Of all wars, this is surely one in which gay America can take a proud and central part. The men who have launched a war on this country see freedom that gay people have here as one of the central reasons for their hatred… Gay Americans should not merely support this war as a matter of patriotism and pride; they should support it because the enemy sees us as one of their first targets for destruction.[21]

The symbolic space and the opposition between the U.S.A. and the Muslim world are necessary to the construction of the universal gay subject who "needs" protection from the homophobic Muslim. The spatial binary division also involves a mapping of time into space, where the U.S.A. is juxtaposed against a temporally backward Muslim world. For example, Paul Varnell, a gay journalist, associates Islam with backwardness and defines the problem of Islamic fundamentalism as an archaic one that counters the modernity of the "Western culture."[22] These temporal and spatial contrasts, as Weston argues in discussing rural/urban divides, structure the "very subjectivity that allows people to think of themselves or others as gay" (1998: 41). While Islam and Muslims become associated with an archaic past, gayness becomes foundationally American. In this dual field of signification, the American gay citizen subject identifies both as the *protector* and the one who is *protected* from the Muslim enemy. Furthermore, within the discourse of protection, the American gay subject and the victimized Muslim gay are constructed through difference and commonality. As Minoo Moallem (2002: 300) argues, "the barbaric other is there to legitimize and give meaning to the masculine militarism of the 'civilized' and his constant need to 'protect.' Protection enables an alliance between the protector and the protected against a common foe." This common foe to the heterosexually-imagined American nation, the homogenously-imagined visible gay subject, and the victimized queer refugee is the barbaric Muslim other.

The visibility of the queer citizen subject is even more complicated in the paradoxical coupling of visibility and concealment for trans people. As Toby Beauchamp (2009) has convincingly argued, the category of "transsexual" in the U.S.A. is produced through both legal and medical discourses through a double act of concealment and transparency. Those who fit the profile of suffering from "Gender Identity Disorder" are expected to disclose their deviancy to the medico-legal apparatus in order to get approval to medically transition in the form of hormones and/or surgeries. At the same time, trans people are expected to erase any trace of their birth gender in order to fit in, and to re-establish the normalized binaries of gender. "Going stealth," however, as Beauchamp argues, is even more complicated by the post-9/11 "surveillance practices that are intimately tied to state security, nationalism and the 'us/them,' 'either/or' rhetoric that underpins U.S. military and government constructions of safety" (357). While trans people are encouraged by queer advocates to reveal their trans status to circumvent post-9/11 increased security restrictions, not all trans bodies have the same stake in visibility. Beauchamp rightly points out that "[b]odies made visible as abnormal or unruly and in need of constraint or correction may likely experience increased vulnerability and scrutiny" (363). Pointing to the security anxieties provoked by trans concealment, Beauchamp rereads "going stealth" within the context of the "war on terror," as "not simply erasing the signs of one's trans status, but instead, maintaining legibility as a good citizen, a patriotic American—erasing any signs of similarity with the deviant, deceptive terrorist" (364). Once again, successful performances of American citizenship and the visibility and concealment of queer life and death are inevitably tied to the disciplining of queer bodies according to conventions of gendered and raced citizenship in the U.S.A., production of queer difference vis-à-vis the demonized and dangerous Muslim other, and the protection of the victimized Third World queer.

## BARBARIC DEATH: IRANIAN QUEER VICTIMS

An example of the way in which the binary opposition of the backward homophobic Muslim/ civilized queer has been deployed repeatedly during the war on terror is the widely publicized case of the hanging of two young men, Ayaz Marhouni and Mohamad Asgari, in Iran. Marhouni and Asgari were hanged on charges of raping a male minor (*lavat beh onf*) in the city of Mashad, on July 19, 2005. While it is unclear if the two young men were "gay," the international media, international gay and lesbian organizations, and diasporic Iranian opposition groups publicized the case on the internet, alleging that Marhouni and Asgari were hanged because of their sexual orientation.[23] Images of the Mashad hangings spread quickly on news websites, YouTube, and weblogs, while email lists and weblogs were used to mobilize protests internationally in different cities.[24] The overwhelming circulation of the pictures of the hanging on the internet was so extensive that most (and the top) images produced in an image search for the terms "gay" and "Iran" in Google's search engine are still those of Marhouni and Asgari's hanging.

Several groups, including the IGLHRC, Human Rights Watch, and Amnesty International issued statements and disclaimers about the lack of credible information about Marhoni and Asgari's sexuality, or the reasons for their execution. Scott Long, a human rights activist with a long history of working on Iranian cases, argued that the investigations into this case (and similar "gay" cases) are merely based on speculation and are not rooted in any evidence leading to the conclusion that Marhouni and Asgari were gay. The Human Rights Campaign, the Log Cabin Republicans, and Britain's Outrage, however, insisted that Marhoni and Asgari were executed for being gay. Representing Outrage, Peter Tatchell announced that "this is just the latest barbarity by the Islamo-fascists in Iran. ... The entire country is a gigantic prison, with Islamic rule sustained by detention without trial, torture and state-sanctioned murder."[25] Log Cabin Republicans, the conservative American gay group, denounced the execution of Marhouni and Asgari, and reaffirmed their commitment to the global war on terror. Like Sullivan, who used this case to legitimize the war on terror, Patrick Guerrero, the president of the Log Cabin Republicans, stated that "this barbarous slaughter clearly demonstrates the stakes in the global war on terror. Freedom must prevail over radical Islamic extremism."[26] Following suit, several news reports, websites, and activist groups repeated the claim that the young men were hanged for being gay.[27] The case has become the prime example of violence against queers in Iran, inciting the masculine protectorship of the First World and the need to rescue the victimized queer Iranian.[28]

## QUEER MATTER OF LIFE AND DEATH: GEOPOLITICS, BIOPOLITICS, AND NECROPOLITICS

In *Bodies That Matter*, Judith Butler argues that bodies that fail to materialize constitute the "necessary outside" of the heterosexual hegemony (1993: 16). This abjected realm of bodies do not matter, are not worth protecting, saving, or grieving. The three queer death stories I have narrated, however, highlight the fact that while some queer deaths are mourned within nationalist discourses of war on terror, and while some queer deaths become highly representable as evidence of homophobia in the Muslim world, other queer deaths remain ineffable. While Mark Bingham's death on United Flight 93 made him into a masculine American hero (albeit gay), and Mahmood Asgari and Ayaz Marhouni's deaths made them into "gay victims" of the homophobic and savage Iranian state, Naz's death in Canada remains unworthy of news coverage. After all, while some abjected bodies are transformed into intelligible valued ones, not all queer bodies "matter" the same way. Not all queer bodies are the necessary outside of the heterosexual hegemony, but integral to maintaining forms of nationalism that reify hetero and homonormative hegemonies. As such, any analysis of heterosexual hegemony in a transnational context needs to be articulated in relation to other scattered hegemonies (Grewal and Kaplan 1994) such as neoliberal ideals of freedom and liberation and geopolitical deployments of queer life and death. But what does this inconsistency in representations of death tells us about the production and management of democratic life and its entanglement with death in a transnational context?

We may turn to Foucault and Mbembe to understand this aporia where the production of desire for free and democratic life is intertwined with death. Foucault defines populations as "not a collection of juridical subjects in an individual or collective relationship with a sovereign will," but rather as "a set of elements in which we can note constants and regularities even in accidents, in which we can identify the universal of desire regularly producing the benefit of all, and with regard to which we can identify a number of modifiable variables on which it depends" (2007: 74). According to Foucault, desire is the "mainspring of action" of the population, meaning that the regulated play of individual desire will allow the production of collective interests, thus pointing to both the naturalness of population and the artificiality of its management (73). One can expand Foucault's notion of population to the global level and ask what constitutes "all," and how does one define universal desire? Which desires are produced as benefiting the "world population"? How are these desires gendered, sexed, and raced? For whom are those desires considered to be natural and for whom are they seen as ill-fitting? What would happen to the excesses of the art of governmentality; those who are seen as risks to the manufactured desires (for liberal democracy) and thus become the threat and the danger? What happens to those who pose a danger to the population whose desires are produced as the universal yearning for freedom and democracy? Is biopolitics sufficient to analyze the "global" division of populations into those whose lives are produced and managed—sometimes under the rhetoric of "our way of life"—and those whose lives are threatened, not necessarily by the juridical sovereign power of the state, but by international entities and transnational market-driven actors who have close ties to state actors?

Mbembe's notion of necropolitics (2003), which focuses more on the place given to death in relation to human bodies and their inscription in the order of power, is helpful in answering these questions. Using examples of slaves in plantations and the colonized in the colonies, where the absolute lawlessness stems from the denial of humanity to the "native" and where the violence of the state of exception is exercised in the name of civilization, Mbembe argues that the state of exception and the state of siege become the normative basis of the right to kill. Mbembe points out that the modern colonial occupation combines the disciplinary, the biopolitical, and the necropolitical. He argues that the "stage of siege is itself a military institution. It allows a modality of killing that does not distinguish between the external and the internal enemy. Entire populations are the target of the sovereign" (2003: 30).

Mbembe's analysis is an important intervention in the scope and the relevance of the biopolitical in the colonial context. However, neither Foucault's biopolitics nor Mbembe's necropolitics may be sufficient in the analysis of populations that are not reduced to bare life, but whose death is sanctioned in the name of rights. I draw on biopolitics and necropolitics to suggest a form of power over the liminal state between death and a life which is not bare, but is imbued with rights. As a trope, the "people of Iran" constitutes a population which is produced through the discourse of rights and for which death through sanctions and/or bombs is legitimized within the rhetoric of "war on terror." I call this politics of the unstable life, which is at once imbued with—and stripped of— liberal universal rights, *the politics of rightful killing*. Standing between biopolitics and necropolitics, the *politics of rightful killing* explains the contemporary political situation in the "war on terror" where those whose rights and protection are presented as the *raison d'être* of war are sanctioned to death and therefore live a pending death exactly because of those rights. Following Foucault's notion that one's life at the expense of the other's death is compatible with the exercise of biopower (1997: 255), I argue that the management of the life of one population relies on the discipline, control, and ultimately, death and diminishment of the other who stands outside and threatens the interests of the population whose life is worth saving and which may or may not have a territorial boundedness.

*The politics of rightful killing* is not to replace necropolitics or biopolitics, but exists in the same political terrain where bodies are disciplined, normalized, and where bare life is subjected to death. It addresses an impending death, but not the bare life, not the life of the shadow slave, or the life of the absolute enemy (as discussed by Agamben in camps, and by Mbembe in the colonies, plantations, and in Palestine). It is not limited to the state of emergency in the camps or the state of siege—although it is legitimized under those states—but extends itself to the state of normalcy, and is not an exceptional or unique state of lawlessness. In this state of normalcy, while being imbued with rights (rightful), the living dead—the population that lives on the threshold of life and death (Mbembe 2003: 40)—can be killed, *rightfully* in the name of rights and global justice. It can be killed in so far as it contains the danger to the population, "the people" whose life is worth saving, protecting, and managing (even as the living population is eliminating its internal dangers through technologies of government and calculations—Foucault's example of racism). Unlike the *homo sacer*, these living dead cannot be killed by just anyone (certainly not by the illiberal states), but rather only the liberating states who promise them rights, freedom, and democracy.

## CONCLUSION

If the Iranian population at large is subjected to the politics of rightful killing, how does the Iranian transgender refugee figure in the state of normalcy that characterizes the "war on terror"? Here, Agamben's (1998) argument that declarations of rights presuppose man as the natural bearer of rights and a citizen, thus bringing together the biological and the political and making the bare life central to politics in modernity, is instructive. If, as Agamben argues, the camp is the *nomos* of modernity where the state of exception becomes the rule of law, I suggest that the refugee transsexual as a paradigmatic figure of *homo sacer* is an important point of inquiry into the laws of immigration and citizenship, and one who can further complicate the naturalness of rights and the link between the biological and the political. The camp as the state of exception signifies both the body-in-excess and the location one occupies as a refugee, and as such can highlight the limitation of rights associated with the converged notions of the natural and political. Shuttling between life and death, the transsexual refugee is caught between biopolitics (Foucault: 2008) and necropolitics (Mbembe 2003), where her body is produced and managed through religious, medical, psychological, and geopolitical discourses, and her death is sanctioned in the state of exception as a refugee (outside of the nation-state) and transsexual (outside of the naturalized binaries of sex). Just as the simultaneous insistence on revealing the truth and concealing the identity of a trans person's gender/sex is necessary to the maintenance of norms of gender and sexuality,[29] the insistence on visibility and testimonies of oppression of the transgender refugee is necessary to the civilizational narratives of queer oppression in Iran and liberation in North America and Europe. It is in this context and through representational politics that the Iranian transsexual refugee is at once politicized and produced through discourses and practices that authorize war and imperialism in the Middle East, and depoliticized as *homo sacer*—one whose life is disposable once it loses value in neoliberal discourses of tolerance that are tangled with geopolitics. The Iranian transgender refugee, as such, becomes the representable marker of freedom, or lack thereof, in a geopolitical context where the Iranian population becomes subjected to the *politics of rightful killing*. At the same time, the Iranian transgender refugee's visibility exposes her to forms of deadly violence for the crisis it incites in norms of gender and citizenship. In so far as it disrupts the liberatory narratives of transmigration, the economic and physical violence that the transgender refugee faces in the third country of asylum is unrepresentable.

The question of representation is the first step in exploring the management of life and death of Iranian transgender refugees. It does not touch on how Iranian transsexual refugees are nationalized/denationalized, sexed, gendered, raced, and normalized in multiple reterritorializations and through biopolitical and geopolitical practices in Iran, Turkey, and North America. Neither does it explain the way that competing national and international policies and practices of multiple states and human rights regimes, non-governmental organizations, diasporic queer organizations, and standardized medical and psychological discourses articulate and govern normalized national and global bodies who shuttle between rightfulness and rightlessness in transitioning across national boundaries, sexual norms, geopolitical terrains, and neoliberal economies. It does, however, highlight the need for further research in the way that transgender refugees stand at the threshold of life and death as they transition across bodies and borders.

## NOTES

1. *I Know That I Am*. Directors: Peyman Khosravi and Babak Yousefi. 2006. Iran/Canada.
2. It was only in 2010 that ILGA published a sensationalized story by an unknown author about Iranian transgender people. In one short paragraph, the article mentions Naz's death in Canada, focusing the story on abuses she experienced in Iran. The author uses male pronouns, thus undermining Naz's desire to live and die as a trans woman. Ironically, there is very little or no advocacy on behalf of queer refugees after their arrival in a third country of asylum such as the U.S.A. or Canada, where very few job opportunities and services are available to refugees in a market economy where the individual is increasingly responsible for her or his own economic well-being. For ILGA's report see, "Iranian Transgendered People: Harassed, Coerced to Undergo What Turns Out to be Botched Sex Reassignment Procedure." http://ilga.org/ilga/en/article/miNFHPm1NI. Last accessed September 15, 2011.
3. In *Desiring Arabs*, Joseph Massad (2007, 161) defines the gay and lesbian missionary tasks, "the discourses that produce them, and the organizations that represent them" as the Gay International.
4. During Ahmadinejad's first term, the state support for SRSs in the form of grants and loans increased to US$4,500 for operations and hormone therapy and US$5,500 for business startup. The Imam Khomeini Charity Foundation provides loans to help pay for SRS, which is often seen by the religious, legal, medical, and psychological establishments as a "remedy" to prevent homosexual activities among those who are perceived as being ill and in need of correction. Please see: http://www.nytimes.com/2004/08/02/international/middleeast/02iran.html?pagewanted=1&ei=5090&en=97bb9b a99064d599&ex=1249099200&partner=rssuserland; http://www.guardian.co.uk/world/2005/jul/27/gayrights.iran; and http://www.guardian.co.uk/world/2007/sep/25/iran.roberttait All links last accessed September 15, 2011.
5. For the history of emergence of this term in Iran, see Najmabadi's (2008) article, "Transing and Transpassing across Sex-Gender Walls in Iran."
6. While the Turkish government provides limited social and medical services, this requires a fee-based "temporary resident permit" which has to be renewed every six months. The cost in April 2009 was 273 Turkish lira (YTL), which is equal to US$218.
7. A few years ago, I was invited to speak at a college campus about my immigration activism and my asylum in the U.S.A. based on my sexual orientation. After I criticized the anti-immigrant laws such as the Illegal Immigration Reform and Immigrant Responsibility Act of 1996 and the Anti-Terrorist Law, a student asked, "If it is so bad here, why are you here?" This question, which was often asked when I crossed the boundaries between victim/object and activist/subject, seemed to be posed to remind me that I was a refugee who should disclose my story in a testimonial style upon demand.
8. While organizations such as ORAM work to decrease the homophobia and violence that queer applicants are subjected to, a few organizations seem to use queer refugees as opportunities for entrepreneurship. In a gay Iranian man's words, some of these organizations have launched a "queer importing business," without actually supporting those who they claim to protect. There have been accusations of embezzlement by some diasporic queer organizations and individuals who receive awards and funds from fundraising events in the name of assisting queer refugees in Turkey. While these accusations are based on hearsay and dangerously border on gossip, one cannot deny that the "war on terror" has provided an atmosphere where any information that demonizes Iran can be marketable. Women, queers, and journalists seem to be in the center of the sensationalized stories of human rights abuses in Iran.
9. I have discussed neoliberal diasporic entrepreneurship during the "war on terror" elsewhere (Shakhsari 2010).
10. In fact, in my conversation with an ORAM staff member, I learned that in some cases stories of persecution are so outrageous and unbelievable that the UNHCR interviewer rejects the asylum seeker's claim. The role of certain diasporic organizations in convincing asylum seekers to fabricate these stories is more detrimental than helpful.
11. For a promotional video of this film see http://www.youtube.com/watch?v=wF_WOnSndgQ&feature=related.
12. The film won the Melbourne Queer Film Festival Audience Choice Award for Best Documentary. His blog at the address http://www.baabakye.com is no longer active. See the film blog at http://iknowthatiam.blogspot.com/2009_01_01_ archive.html. Last accessed September 15, 2011.
13. A testimony on the Tribute to American Spirit Photo Quilt, an online project sponsored by America OnLine and Kodak. This online photo gallery was established shortly after September 11, 2001 and was available at http://photoquilt.kodak.com.
14. The desire to be included in norms of cultural and political citizenship has seen a shift in the U.S.A. As Escoffier (1998, 226) argues, "queer politics in the late 1980s and early 1990s celebrated the otherness, the differentness, and the marginality of the homosexual, whereas the gay politics of citizenship acknowledges the satisfactions of conforming, passing, belonging, and being accepted."

15. In my research soon after September 11, 2001, a search result for gay, American, and proud produced several images of hypermasculine white gay men covered in an American flag. The images are no longer available with the same search, perhaps due to the disillusionment of American queers with promises of inclusion.

16. This quote from *Life* magazine is a good example of this trend: "Bingham, a six-foot-five surfer and rugby player, had ridden the horns of a bull this summer in Pamplona, Spain and lived to tell about it. The publicly gay San Franciscan had once wrestled a gun from a mugger's hand, then beat up the mugger and his accomplice. He was tough as nails." *Life* 1: 8. November 12, 2001: 89.

17. Some queer sites I explored soon after September 11, 2001, included MetroG, Planetout, The Slant, Gay Today, the Independent Gay Forum, Rainbowquery, Human Rights Campaign (HRC), IGLHRC, National Gay and Lesbian Task Force (NGLTF), Gay and Lesbian Alliance Against Defamation (GLAAD), and Andrew Sullivan's blogs.

18. What is interesting in this playfield of masculinity is that women do not appear in the picture, except as patriotic mothers and wives of heroic men, or as repressed victims of "barbaric" patriarchy. This absence in the political field of citizenship and the nation is also reflected in the gendered imaginations of a gay community that stands proud and united with the rest of America where queer women do not "matter" (Cohler 2006).

19. A letter from the Mark Bingham Forum. http://tenrec.com/forum/index.asp?p=15. Last accessed November 29, 2001.

20. Excerpt from another letter written on the Mark Bingham Forum.

21. Andrew Sullivan, "Our War Too," *PlanetOut*, September 21, 2001.

22. In "The New Culture War," Varnell writes, "Modernity with its individualism, capitalism, rationality, and undermining of religious dominance has more or less invaded an Arabic Muslim culture which is literally in its 1400s, and no doubt feels strange, foreign, threatening, rather as if the same institutions had suddenly appeared in Europe in 1400s." See "The New Culture Wars." *Independent Gay Forum: Forging a Gay Mainstream*. http://www.indegayforum.org/topics/show/27126.html. Last Accessed November 29, 2001. Originally appeared in *Chicago Free Press*, September 19, 2001.

23. For an investigative story on the misrepresentation of this case as "gay hangings," see Richard Kim's "Witness to an Execution" in the August 5, 2005 edition of *The Nation*, http://www.thenation.com/article/witnesses-execution. Last accessed September 15, 2011.

24. For example, see the San Francisco-based gay advocate, Michael Petrelis' blog entry about internet mobilizations to organize offline protests on the anniversary of Marhouni and Asgari's death. http://mpetrelis.blogspot.com/2006/06/iran-stop-killing-gays-apparently.html. Last accessed September 11, 2012.

25. See ILGA's press release, "Iran Executes Gay Teenagers," http://ilga.org/ilga/en/article/675. Last accessed September 11, 2012.

26. See *The Gay Patriot*. http://www.gaypatriot.net/2005/07/26/. Last accessed September 11, 2012.

27. See "Hadd Crimes," http://www.fabmagazine.com/features/309/Hadd_Crimes.html. accessed September, 2012.

28. This case, along with other stories of stoning and execution are often used as evidence to support Iranian queer refugee applicants' cases. The question that needs to be asked here is not whether the representations of these cases are accurate or not (although this question has serious implications in the legitimization of military interventions), but why do norms of citizenship and immigration make it necessary for refugees to repeat these stories in order to support their cases?

29. As Toby Beauchamp has argued, the transgender body's ambiguity translates into deception and concealment of the truth of one's sex and gender.

## BIBLIOGRAPHY

Agamben, Giorgio (1998). *Sovereign Power and Bare Life*. Palo Alto, CA: Stanford University Press.

Anker, Deborah (2005). "Refugee Law, Gender, and the Human Rights Paradigm." In *Passing Lines: Sexuality and Immigration*. Brad Epps, Keja Valens, and Bill Johnson Gonzalez (eds.). Cambridge, Ma: Harvard University Press.

Beauchamp, Toby (2009). "Artful Concealment and Strategic Visibility: Transgender Bodies and U.S. State Surveillance after 9/11." *Surveillance & Society* 6 (4): 356–366.

Berlant, Lauren (1997). *The Queen of America Goes to Washington City: Essays on Sex and Citizenship*. Durham, NC: Duke University Press.

Brown, Wendy (2003). "Neo-liberalism and the End of Liberal Democracy." *Theory and Event* 7 (1): n.p.

Burchell, Graham, Gordon Colin, and Miller Peter (eds.) (1991). *The Foucault Effect: Studies in Governmentality*. Chicago, IL: University of Chicago Press.

Butler, Judith (1992). "Contingent Foundations: Feminism and the Question of Postmodern." In *Feminists Theorize the Political*. Judith Butler and Joan Scott (eds.). London: Routledge.

Butler, Judith (1993). *Bodies That Matter: On the Discursive Limits of Sex*. London: Routledge.

Cohler, Deborah (2006). "Keeping the Home Front Burning: Renegotiating Gender and Sexuality in U.S. Mass Media after September 11." *Feminist Media Studies* 6 (3): 245–261.

Duggan, Lisa (2003). *The Twilight of Equality?: Neoliberalism, Cultural Politics, and the Attack on Democracy.* Boston, MA: Beacon Press.

Escoffier, Jeffrey (1998). *American Homo: Community and Perversity.* Berkeley, CA: University of California Press.

Ferguson, James and Gupta, Akhil (2002). "Spatializing States: Toward an Ethnography of Neo-liberal Governmentality." *American Ethnologist* 29 (4): 981–1002.

Foucault, Michel (1979). "Governmentality." *Ideology and Consciousness,* No. 6, Summer 1986, 5–21.

Foucault, Michel (1997). *Society must be Defended. Lectures at the Collège de France 1975–1976.* Mauro Bertani and Alessandro Fontana (eds.). New York: Picador.

Foucault, Michel (2007). *Security, Territory, Population. Lectures at the Collège de France 1977–1978.* Michel Senellart (ed.). New York: Palgrave Macmillan.

Foucault, Michel (2008). *The Birth of Biopolitics. Lectures at the Collège de France 1978–1979.* Michel Senellart (ed.). New York: Palgrave Macmillan.

Grewal, Inderpal (2005). *Transnational America: Feminisms, Diasporas, Neoliberalisms.* Durham, NC: Duke University Press.

Grewal, Inderpal and Caren Kaplan (1994). "Transnational Feminist Practices and Questions of Postmodernity." In *Scattered Hegemonies.* Inderpal Grewal and Caren Kaplan (eds.). Minneapolis, MN: University of Minnesota Press.

Grungras, Neil, Rachel Levitan and Amy Slotek (2009). "Unsafe Haven: Security Challenges Facing LGBT Asylum Seekers and Refugees in Turkey". *PRAXIS The Fletcher Journal of Human Security* 24.

Grundy-Warr, Carl and Rajaram, Prem Kumar (2004). "The Irregular Migrant as *Homo-Sacer*: Migration and Detention in Australia." *International Migration* 42: 33–64.

Helsinki Citizens' Assembly. Turkey Refugee Advocacy and Support Program, and ORAM. (2009). "Unsafe Haven: The Security Challenges Facing Lesbian, Gay, Bisexual and Transgender Asylum Seekers and Refugees in Turkey." http://www.hyd.org.tr/?sid=23

Kaplan, Caren (1994). "The Politics of Location as Transnational Feminist Critical Practice." In *Scattered Hegemonies.* Inderpal Grewal and Caren Kaplan (eds.). Minneapolis, MN: University of Minnesota Press.

Long, Scott (2009). "Unbearable Witness: How Western Activists (Mis)recognize Sexuality in Iran." *Contemporary Politics* 15 (1): 119–136.

Luibhéid, Eithne (1998). "'Looking Like a Lesbian': The Organization of Sexual Monitoring at the United States-Mexican Border." *Journal of History of Sexuality* 8 (3): 477–506.

Luibhéid, Eithne (2008). "Sexuality, Migration, and Shifting Line between Legal and Illegal Status." *GLQ* 14: 289–315.

Massad, Joseph A. (2007). *Desiring Arabs.* Chicago, IL: University of Chicago Press.

Mbembe, Achille (2003). "Necropolitics." Meintjes, Libby (Trans.). *Public Culture* 15 (1): 11–40.

Miller, Alice M. (2005). "Gay Enough: Some Tensions in Seeking the Grant of Asylum and Protecting Global Sexual Diversity." In *Passing Lines: Sexuality and Immigration.* Brad Epps, Keja Valens, and Bill Johnson Gonzalez (eds.). Cambridge, MA: Harvard University Press.

Moallem, Minoo (2002). "Whose Fundamentalism?" *Meridian* 2 (2): 298–301.

Moallem, Minoo (2005). *Between Warrior Brother and Veiled Sister: Islamic Fundamentalism and the Politics of Patriarchy in Iran.* Berkeley, CA: University of California Press.

Najmabadi, Afsaneh (2008). "Transing and Transpassing across Sex-Gender Walls in Iran." *Women's Studies Quarterly* 36: 3–4.

Neilson, Victoria (2005). "Uncharted Territory: Choosing an Effective Approach in Transgender Based Asylum Claims". *Fordham Urban Law Journal* 32.

Ong, Aihwa (1996). "Cultural Citizenship as Subject-Making." *Current Anthropology* 37 (5): 737–762.

Ong, Aihwa (2006). *Neoliberalism as Exception: Mutations in Citizenship and Sovereignty.* Durham, NC: Duke University Press.

Puar, Jasbir (2007). *Terrorist Assemblages: Homonationalism in Queer Times.* Durham, NC: Duke University Press.

Puar, Jasbir K. and Amit Rai (2002). "Monster, Terrorist, Fag: The War on Terrorism and the Production of Docile Patriots." *Social Text* 20 (3): 117–148.

Razack, Sherene (1998). *Looking White People in the Eye: Gender, Race, and Culture in the Courtrooms and Classrooms*. Toronto: University of Toronto.

Rofel, Lisa (2007). *Desiring China: Experiments in Neoliberalism, Sexuality, and Public Culture*. Durham, NC: Duke University Press.

Rose, Nikolas (2007). *The Politics of Life Itself: Biomedicine, Power, and Subjectivity in the Twenty-First Century*. Princeton, NJ: Princeton University Press.

Sanadjian, Manuchehr (1995). "Temporality of 'home' and Spatiality of Market in Exile: Iranians in Germany." *New German Critique* 64: 3–36.

Sassen, Saskia (2006). *Territory, Authority, Rights: From Medieval to Global Assemblages*. Princeton, NJ: Princeton University Press.

Shakhsari, Sima (2002). *The Discursive Production of Iranian Queer Subjects in Diaspora*. MA Thesis. San Francisco, CA: San Francisco State University.

Shakhsari, Sima (2010). *Blogging, Belonging, and Becoming: Cybergovernmentality and the Production of Gendered and Sexed Diasporic Subjects in Weblogistan*. Ph.D. Dissertation, Stanford, CA: Stanford University.

Sheppard, Denise (2006). "I Know That I Am: A horrifying glimpse into the lives of Iranian transwomen", www.xtra.ca/public/National/I_Know_That_I_Am-1993.aspx, accessed September 12, 2012.

Shohat, Ella (2003). *Multiculturalism, Postcoloniality, and Transnational Media*. New Brunswick, NJ: Rutgers University Press.

Spade, Dean (2003). "Resisting Medicine, Re/modeling Gender." *Berkeley Women's Law Journal* 18: 15–37.

Spade, Dean (2008). "Documenting Gender." *Hastings Law Journal* 59: 731–842.

Stoler, Ann Laura (1995). *Race and the Education of Desire: Foucault's History of Sexuality and the Colonial Order of Things*. Durham, NC: Duke University Press.

Stone, Sandy (1991). "The Empire Strikes Back: A Post-Transsexual Manifesto." *Body Guards: the Cultural Politics of Gender Ambiguity*. Julia Epstein and Kristina Straub (eds.). London: Routledge.

Terry, Jennifer (1995). "Anxious Slippage between 'Us' and 'Them': A Brief History of the Scientific Research for Homosexual Bodies." *Deviant Bodies*. Jennifer Terry and Jacqueline Urla (eds.). Bloomington, IN: Indiana University Press.

Weston, Kath (1998). *Longslowburn: Sexuality and Social Science*. New York: Routledge.

# 44

## *Silhouettes of Defiance*

## Memorializing Historical Sites of Queer and Transgender Resistance in an Age of Neoliberal Inclusivity

CHE GOSSETT

IN THIS ARTICLE, SCHOLAR CHE GOSSETT offers a few observations on mid-twentieth-century U.S. black, queer, and transgender liberation history, and how they reflect on the politics of mourning, resistance, and survival in the historical moment in which he writes. Gossett discusses the famous Stonewall riots in New York in 1969, heralded as the birth of the gay movement, as well as the lesser-known Compton's Cafeteria Riot in San Francisco in 1966, in which trans women and gay hustlers fought back against police oppression. Both radical events, Gossett contends, emerged from the unrealized desires and deferred dreams of marginalized communities of poor urban queer and gender-variant people of color. And yet both events, he continues, through their public memorialization in a time of neoliberal political ascendancy, have been folded narratively into the techniques of governance whereby the state apparatus manages for its own ends the differences of its heterogeneous population—conferring inclusion, belonging, and citizenship to (hetero-, homo-, and trans-) normative subjects while violently disenfranchising others who are noncompliant with racialized gender norms. Gossett draws upon Derrida's *Archive Fever* to suggest that social memory and its enabling condition—the archive—are themselves constituent parts of this epistemic violence; archives select which material traces of which actions by which bodies in which contexts are deemed worthy of saving in the first place, as well as whose stories are worth (re)telling to whom and for what purposes.

The Stonewall rebellion of 1969, in which protesters clashed with the authorities after a violent police raid on a Greenwich Village bar, is a defining moment in the history of the gay rights movement. Now New York City officials hope to capitalize on the 40th anniversary of the uprising, this June, by promoting the city as a gay tourist destination.[1]

In 2009, New York City officials announced the "Rainbow Pilgrimage," a 1.9 million dollar tourist campaign promoting New York as *the* gay tourist destination. Including ads exhorting visitors to "Join the Rainbow Pilgrimage and plan your journey," travel packages, and cross-promotion leading up to the fortieth anniversary of the Stonewall riot, the Rainbow Pilgrimage was designed to capitalize on the estimated ten percent of tourists (who are gay?) who visit New York each year. The designation of

Stonewall as a tourist site would seem to mark the closure of an era characterized by institutionalized police violence against queer and trans people of color—trans women, homeless, poor, and sex workers in particular. Now tourists may view—from a safe distance—the violent past. Yet while such violence may be called forth and then safely archived through memory of the past for some, for others criminalization and police violence are an ever-present reality. Homonormative narratives of queer history that deracialize and deradicalize past insurrections (Stonewall, Compton's, Dewey's) on one hand while presenting "gay rights" as the contemporary "civil rights" struggle on the other, render queer and trans people of color's participation in both movements invisible. Moreover, they construct a limited horizon of queer futurity that is in alignment with the anti-queer, anti-trans, capitalist, and white supremacist state. Yet our histories of resistance refuse to be contained within neoliberal packaging or sanitized by homonormative narratives of progress. Stonewall was one site of resistance to racist, anti-trans, and anti-queer police violence, but there were others that both preceded and followed it.

A close reading of the Rainbow Pilgrimage campaign's description of the "event" of the Stonewall riots raises questions about the politics of memory and memorialization, the archive, and history. In *Archive Fever* Derrida analyzes the violence of the archive, or "archival violence" that imposes a structuring law and order upon memory, domesticating and institutionalizing history, while also homogenizing and flattening its topography of difference and heterogeneity. In order for the archive to be constructed information must be economized. Some information must be preserved while other documents are discarded. This privileging of certain forms of evidence, or documentation, is a form of violence. "An eco-nomic archive in this double sense: it keeps, it puts in reserve, it saves, but in an unnatural fashion, that is to say that in making the law (*nomos*) or in making people respect the law."[2] The archive has its roots in the "archons," or authorities—those who monitored documentation, protected it, and held hermeneutic and interpretative power over it. One of the forms the violence of the archive takes is the violence of this policing: the violence of the archive as police violence. What can this figure of the law, of the policing of the archive, of its securitization, and of its violence tell us about the history of homonormativity and the homonormativization of history?

In her 2008 essay "Transgender History, Homonormativity, and Disciplinarity," scholar, filmmaker, and historian Susan Stryker provides a critical genealogy of "homonormativity" that acknowledges both the socio-political history of the term as well as its multiple trajectories and the history of its terminological use within academic contexts.[3] A central feature of homonormativity that cuts across its varied interpretations and contexts (both before and within our current neoliberal age) is normalization and/or standardization that involves the purging of social undesirables— genderqueer, transgender, transsexual, gender non-conforming, people of color, and those who live and work on the street—as a means of obtaining "rights" and social respectability.

Stryker raises important questions about both the material and epistemic violence, about the politics of knowledge production and power relations embedded in its processes, and she emphasizes the imperative need for radical trans scholarship that works against the grain of disciplining and marginalizing forces of homonormativity. What do the shadows cast by media projections of homonormative history tell us about the ancestral ghosts and haunting presences and pressures past sites of queer and trans resistance impress upon the present political and social imaginaries? How do queer and trans peoples of color posit critical memory in the face of this history of trauma and co-joined violence of historical erasure? If Stonewall was one site, of many, of queer and transgender resistances to police violence, how is it that this violence resurfaces in the construction and preservation of its memory, as "archival violence"? How does this archival violence, this policing of the archive, policing of history, operate in relation to state violence against and invisibilization of queer and transgender bodies, through mass incarceration and the bio- and necropolitics of the prison industrial complex?

The following text is from "NYC gay history essentials" on NYCgo, a website dedicated to tourist marketing for New York City and one of the main platforms used for the Rainbow Pilgrimage campaign. This is how NYCgo tells the story of Stonewall:

> In the predawn hours of June 28, 1969, a handful of City police descended on the Stonewall Inn, a popular neighborhood gay bar. Such raids were commonplace during that era due to strong anti-gay bias, the enforcement of arcane local laws and the connection that some establishments had with organized crime. The bar's patrons, perhaps emboldened by the civil rights movement, refused to disperse peacefully, holding a series of protests during the next few days. In the wake of the Riots, the gay pride movement took hold as groups of New Yorkers formed the Gay Liberation Front, launched the newspaper *Gay* and organized the Gay Activists Alliance. The first Pride March was held to mark the event's one-year anniversary.[4]

What happens when we subject the Rainbow Pilgrimage description of the Stonewall uprising to a historically minded deconstruction? What, in the Derridian sense, is "the event" of the Stonewall uprising? "Let us return to the value of the event," Derrida writes in *Without Alibi*,

> The event affects the "who" and the "what." It affects and changes singularities of all sorts, even as past event, inscribed or archived. The irreducible eventness of the event in question, which, then, must be retained, inscribed, traced, and so forth, can be the thing itself that is thus archived, but it must also be the event of the inscription. Even as it consigns, inscription produces a new event it is supposed to retain, engram, consign, archive.[5]

The event of Stonewall is determined by and recorded through "inscription," while it is also sanitized and naturalized in the process of its archivization. Derrida draws a distinction between the "event one archives" and the "archiving event":

> There is the event one archives, the *archived* event (and there is no archive without a body—I prefer to say "body" rather than "matter," for reasons that that I will try to justify later), and there is the *archiving* event, the archivation. The latter is not the same thing, structurally, as the archived event, even if, in certain cases, it is indissociable from it or even contemporary with it.[6]

Writing further about the body and the archive, Derrida discusses Paul de Man's reading of Rousseau and the "textual event," which changes, through iterations, throughout the body or corpus of de Man's reading. "How does this textual event inscribe itself? What is the operation of its inscription? What is the writing machine, the typewriter that both produces and archives it? What is the body, or even the materiality that confers on this inscription both a support and a resistance?"[7] Here Derrida gestures towards his earlier account of the functioning of the archive in *Archive Fever*, which, "like the media, produces as much as it records the event," and anticipates his later discussions on technologies of writing in *The Paper Machine*.[8] Following Derrida's inquiries, what is the body upon which the archive and the archivization of Stonewall rests and resists? In the construction of the Rainbow Pilgrimage campaign's history of Stonewall, a site of queer and trans resistance to police violence, what bodies are absent, invisible, discarded? What bodies must be sacrificed so that others may live?

The NYCgo article references police violence as a tragedy of the past: "Such raids were commonplace during that era due to strong anti-gay bias, the enforcement of arcane local laws and the connection that some establishments had with organized crime." At the same time, the account rationalizes and excuses the very same violence. It neglects to point out that police raids of gay bars were commonplace not only because of "strong anti-gay bias," but also because of the institutionalized homophobia and transphobia that pervaded juridical, political, and medical discourse and practice. Queerness and gender non-conformity were criminalized and pathologized—as was, and is, blackness. The description of the

Stonewall uprising minimalizes the impact of systematic homophobic, transphobic, and racist police violence.

In Philadelphia, gay cruising areas like Rittenhouse Square were heavily policed in the 1950s and into the 1970s. Frank Rizzo, who conducted raids on gay coffee shops in the 1950s, became police commissioner in 1967.[9] Once he was appointed commissioner, the first of Rizzo's publicized actions responded to high school student protests against segregation and for black studies. Students who gathered in front of the Board of Education were attacked by two busloads of police who had been instructed by Rizzo to "get their black asses."[10] Twenty-two students were critically injured and fifty-seven students were arrested as a result. Philadelphia police used manipulative measures to arrest and criminalize queers, as this report from a 1962 Philadelphia news magazine illustrates:

> The basic method of operation in making homosexual arrests is the same, whether they are being made by members of the Morals Squad or other police units. Generally they work in pairs, one man acting as a decoy, the other as a witness and to aid in apprehension.[11]

In an event that preceded Stonewall, gender non-conforming and queer youth and allies challenged regulations of respectability using direct action and staged a sit-in at Dewey's restaurant in Philadelphia in 1965.[12]

In the sanitization process of archiving and architecting homonormative history, Stonewall is also privileged as the inaugural site of originary (police) violence against which queer and transgender people rebel. "The bar's patrons, perhaps emboldened by the civil rights movement, refused to disperse peacefully, holding a series of protests during the next few days."[13] In a further cleansing of history, queer and transgender people of color are excluded from the archive, just as they are excluded from hormonormative constructions of history. A salutary example is Sylvia Rivera, who was seventeen at the time of the riot and who was quoted as exclaiming, "I'm not missing a minute of this, it's the revolution," and who participated in gay and trans liberation and black and Puerto Rican power movements. Rivera's instrumental involvement in Stonewall only came to broader attention in 1993 with the publication of Martin Duberman's book on the riots. Her involvement in gay liberation movements is still contested by other past gay liberation activists, and she is signally left out of this account. The archivization of Stonewall, the creation of an official narrative, and "the event" privileges certain bodies, while regarding others as socially disposable.

> In the wake of the Riots, the gay pride movement took hold as groups of New Yorkers formed the Gay Liberation Front, launched the newspaper *Gay* and organized the Gay Activists Alliance. The first Pride March was held to mark the event's one-year anniversary.[14]

Based on this description there are no transgender or racialized bodies before or after Stonewall: they are discarded in the process of legitimizing white homonormative history. This description is ahistorical.

Sylvia Rivera and Marsha P. Johnson began informal organizing of Street Transsexual Action Revolutionaries (STAR) shortly after the Stonewall riots; about the same time, Huey P. Newton, pushed by Jean Genet to confront internalized homophobia (organizationally and personally), wrote a letter published in *The Black Panther* newspaper extending a call to gay and women's liberation movements, which resulted in a mass mobilization of Third World Gay revolutionary groups to the Panthers Constitutional Convention at Temple University in Philadelphia in 1970, at which gay liberationist Kiyoshi Kuromiya spoke. In the 1970s local Philadelphia collectives such as the RadicalQueens challenged both gender policing within queer social space as well as anti-trans political violence. The RadicalQueens manifestos perform immanent critique of the politics of history, feminism, and reproductive justice.[15] The manifestos force a reconsideration of feminism: as always already trans and destabilizing of cisgender centrism.

Sites of queer resistance are sanitized and cleansed of undesirables—queers of color, trans and gender-non-conforming people, sex workers—and folded into the state as a means of including particular bodies and politics. This simultaneous inclusion/exclusion operates at the level of the construction of the political "we," which Judith Butler discusses in "Finishing, Starting," and it does so at the level of the archive.[16] As often as sites of queer and transgender resistance are folded into the state through inclusion and tolerance as technologies of governance, the desires of the communities from which those sites emerged are also actively censored, denied, stifled, and extinguished through state and police violence. State recognition in itself, as Jasbir Puar points out in *Terrorist Assemblages*, is not only exclusionary in its privileging of certain queer bodies, it also perpetuates homonationalism:

> The politics of recognition and incorporation entail that certain—but certainly not most—homosexual, gay and queer bodies may be the temporary recipients of the "measures of benevolence" that are afforded by liberal discourses of multicultural tolerance and diversity. This benevolence toward sexual others is contingent upon ever-narrowing parameters of white racial privilege, consumption capabilities, gender and kinship normativity, and bodily integrity.[17]

Tolerance discourse functions as a tool for depoliticization, dominance, and governmentality while distracting from the state violence and exclusion that underpins it.

In *Regulating Aversion*, Wendy Brown figures tolerance as a form of Foucauldian "governmentality." In his thirteen lectures at the College de France, between 1970 and 1984, Foucault responded to criticism of *Discipline and Punish,* in particular his conceptualization of power as capillary and diffuse.[18] Governmentality, seen as a logic and rationality of power and rule, represented a theoretical move away from the "juridical model of sovereignty" and towards an understanding of the ways in which power functions discursively and institutionally. In identifying the state as "the fulcrum of political legitimacy in modern nations," Brown reorients Foucault's "governmentalization of the state" by focusing on the ways the state governs. "A full account of governmentality, then, would attend not only to the production, organization and mobilization of subjects by a variety of powers but also to the problem of legitimizing these operations by the singularly accountable object in the field of political power: the state."[19] Brown argues that tolerance discourse functions to obscure state violence. "Yet at the same time that the state represents itself as securing social equality and rhetorically enjoins the citizenry from prejudice and persecution, the state engages in extralegal and persecutorial actions toward the very group that it calls upon the citizenry to be tolerant toward."[20] Brown perceptively highlights the ruse of universal liberalism that privileges the discourse of rights and individualism while ignoring systematic power relations and social hierarchies. The embrace of liberalism, individualism, and free market rationality (neoliberalism), represents for Brown an insidiously reductive form of depoliticization that crystallizes in tolerance discourse:

> [T]olerance is invoked as a tool for managing what are construed as (non-liberal because "different" and nonpolitical because "essential") culturalized identity claims or identity clashes. As such, tolerance reiterates the depoliticization of those claims and clashes, at the same time depicting itself as a norm-free tool of liberal governance, a mere means for securing freedom of conscience or (perhaps more apt today) freedom of identity.[21]

Nevertheless, the designation of Stonewall as a tourist site on the NYC Rainbow Pilgrimage has been heralded as a form of multicultural inclusion.

In 2006, the Compton's Cafeteria uprising of 1966 was commemorated with a plaque outside the former restaurant. The event was attended by local police and activists and covered by local media.

Media coverage of the event documented the success of trans-inclusion and hailed narratives of progress that treated transphobic police violence as a past issue instead of a current, pressing problem. A *USA Today* article illustrates the pervasiveness of this progress narrative:

> A granite historical marker installed in San Francisco's seedy Tenderloin District this week would be unremarkable if it didn't honor men who dressed in women's clothes and once walked the streets selling sex. The tired transvestites who clashed with police at an all-night greasy spoon here in 1966 never would have expected the city's political elite to show up for a dedication ceremony honoring their struggle as a civil rights milestone. Yet there, at the site of the Compton's Cafeteria riot, among a crowd of unusually tall women and noticeably short men were a pair of city supervisors, the District Attorney, the Police Chief, and a transsexual police sergeant. The California Assembly and the mayor sent proclamations.[22]

In addition to the violent characterization of transgender women as morally repugnant sex workers, "transvestites," and "cross-dressers," the positing of an "unusual," or failed/infantile masculinity ("short men") and failed/unachievable femininity ("tall women"), as well as painting the Tenderloin as a site of corruption, pathos, and hypersexuality, the article boasts an ironic title: "As Gay Pride Hits Stride Transgenders Find More Acceptance." The ostracism of transgender people from the mainstream assimilationist movement for gay rights—i.e. marriage, military, and employment non-discrimination legislation—has functioned as a way for white, homonormative, non-trans gays and lesbians to gain social recognition and state benefits. The formulation of the title should actually be reversed: as gay pride hits stride, transgender people are put on the back of the bus—or the bumper, as Sylvia Rivera said in reference to the Human Rights Campaign in 2001. "One of our [STAR's] main goals now is to destroy the Human Rights Campaign, because I'm tired of sitting on the back of the bumper. It's not even the back of the bus anymore—it's the back of the bumper."[23]

Through its commemoration, the event of the Compton's Cafeteria riot was transformed from an act of queer and transgender resistance to police violence into trans and queer inclusivity and collaboration, both with policing and the state. Central to this was the public recognition awarded to Elliot Blackstone, a police officer who worked with the Mattachine Society and the Daughters of Bilitis in advocating for "trans competency" and police sensitivity during the homophile period and who features as an important character in *Screaming Queens*, the 2005 documentary that first publicized the resistance at Compton's. Blackstone's political commitments were attached to policing and to social and economic justice. He "helped establish an anti-poverty office in the Tenderloin that employed transsexual workers," and when the city refused to pay for hormones for transgender people, he "took up a donation at his church and distributed the drugs for free."[24] The San Francisco Pride Parade saluted his efforts. Such liaisons between representatives of trans community and the police reinforce the idea of benevolent rule that preserves, instead of challenges, structural forces that create systematic oppression in the first place.

Nowadays, it seems, Blackstone's services are no longer necessary. According to a 2006 article in the *San Francisco Chronicle*, the San Francisco Police Department no longer has a GLBT liaison officer. As the article relates, the co-chair of the San Francisco Police Officers' Pride Alliance, Lea Militello, sees this as a natural shift:

> "We don't need one person because we all chip in," she said. The pride alliance has 200 members, some retired, and the department also employs a transgender officer. Police Commissioner Theresa Sparks is a transgender woman. "The department is an easy place to be open about sexual orientation and gender identity."[25]

This quote illustrates Brown's discussion of (trans) inclusivity and of tolerance discourse as a technology of governance and domination. Queerness and transgender bodies are no longer policed, they are doing the policing. Yet although this purportedly represents a movement beyond identity politics, or at the threshold of identity politics, as Brown points out, state violence still continues against these very same communities. Recent research conducted by the National Gay and Lesbian Task Force illustrates the employment hazards that transgender people face.[26] Transgender women of color who do work in the sex economy are often subject to severe transphobic and misogynistic violence. In Memphis, Tennessee, the police violence against and murder of Duanna Johnson in November 2008 was preceded by the murder of Ebony Whitaker in July, Tiffany Berry in 2006, and followed by the hate violence against Leenisha Edwards in December of 2008.[27] The suffering that accompanies incarcerated queer and trans life is ignored. The inclusion of transgender and queer bodies into formations of state militarization like the police and the military represent what Puar identifies as homonationalism (internally) and homo-imperialism (externally). "Victories" like Don't Ask Don't Tell ensure not only imperialism abroad but also that, as Martin Luther King Jr. said of the Vietnam war, "the bombs in Vietnam explode at home," that LGBTQ veterans—disproportionately poor and of color—will continue to suffer from the social misery of homelessness, incarceration, and post-traumatic stress disorder. Such homonationalist endeavors empower gays and lesbians to join the enterprise of occupied zones shadowed by bomb-dropping militarized drones, only to ensure that those who fulfill these roles are treated as disposable by the state upon return.

In *Negotiations* Derrida addresses the history of state violence against the black liberation movement, imprisonment as a tool for de-politicization, and also the death penalty. Rebelling against the tortuous design of the prison, the injustice of American imperialism, and anti-black and anti-poor domestic repression, revolutionary George Jackson authored two highly influential texts, *Soledad Brother* and *Blood in My Eye*, which continue to influence anti-prison, black liberationist political theory and praxis. Derrida's writing on George Jackson raises questions about the violence of the archive, of institutionalized memory, and resistance, and it cautions against treating Jackson's "case" or "affair" as a unique incident, as opposed to part of a systematic, industrialized, capitalist, war machinic targeting of "many Jacksons," who are everywhere under the gaze of the white supremacist state. First published in *Negotiations*, Derrida's "Letter to Jean Genet" deconstructs elements of Jackson's writing in *Soledad Brother* and argues for a shift in envisioning the struggle of Jackson from that of an isolated case to a more systematic understanding of the relationship between anti-black racism and policing as a tool for social control:

> There are more Jacksons than anyone can count. Their prison is also in France you know. And elsewhere. The "testimonials" and "protests" that we might send to the United States must not distract us from this fact. Jackson: "I don't recognize uniqueness, not as it's applied to individualism, because it's too tightly tied into decadent capitalist culture."[28]

Derrida warns against the containment and institutionalization—the archival violence—that accompanies the treatment of Jackson's liberation as an isolated struggle or theatrical spectacle as opposed to a systematic critique of power relations. He also cautions against regarding Jackson as an exceptional talent too great to be imprisoned, which would mean that his exception would then prove the general rule, of the criminalization of blackness—except for its "exemplary figures":

> Finally, if one denounces only a *case* or *affair* (in the sense that, in France, the implications of these *scandals* have always been buried beneath the form of ritualized or fetishistic debates), is there not a risk of closing up the wound of everything that has been broken up by the letters you presented, of reducing these enormous stakes to more or less literary, or even editorial, event, to a French, or

even Parisian, production that an intelligentsia, busying itself with signatures, would have staged for itself?[29]

Derrida ultimately signed a manifesto on behalf of George Jackson, along with Foucault, Roland Barthes, Julia Kristeva, and others, in support of his liberation. In the manifesto, the authors denounce the "ceaseless repression increasingly exerted by the American government against the black movement," demanding the release of political prisoners. The manifesto was sent out in July 1971 and the letter to Genet was authored in August. Derrida would return to the "exemplary figure" of Jackson in 1995, in the essay "For Mumia Abu Jamal." In Derrida's case, on August 20 he had literally only "barely finished writing" his letter to Genet, who was organizing a collection of essays in defense of Jackson. George Jackson was murdered on August 21, and so the letter was never sent.

Derrida's rhetoric of mourning and his eulogic lamentation of the loss of George Jackson brings to the fore his discussion of mourning, loss, and responsibility in *The Work of Mourning*. In this collection of essays Derrida grieves the loss of close friends, mentors, and intellects who inspired and provoked his thought. Derrida grapples with a paradox that accompanies loss and the work of mourning: that every death is at once unique and sequential, that deaths are singular and reiterative. How, Derrida asks, to mourn in the face of this paradox? He argues that mourning entails a responsibility, a refusal of silence and an imperative to speak:

> This being at a loss also has to do with a duty: to let the friend speak, to turn speech over to him, his speech and especially not to take it from him, not to take it in his place—no offense seems worse at the death of a friend (and I feel that I have already fallen prey to it)—allow him to speak, to occupy his silence or to take speech oneself only in order, if this is possible, to give it back to him.[30]

Derrida cautions against certain types of speech—rhetorical strategies that can be self-aggrandizing or eclipsing of the friend—the friend whose loss is always already anticipated, the mourning which is always already pre-figured, the knowledge that one will die before the other.

In "I'm Going to Have to Wander All Alone," written in the wake of Deleuze's death, Derrida raises questions about the singularity of death in relationship to the loss of a generation: "Each death is unique, of course, and therefore unusual." But what can be said about the unusual when, from Barthes to Althusser, from Foucault to Deleuze, it multiples, as in a series, all these uncommon ends in the same "generation"?[31]

Transgender and queer communities of color have endured our generation of suffering and loss through various institutionalized forms of violence: poverty, the criminalization of HIV/AIDS, policing, and racism. When Ronald Reagan created the President's Commission on the Human Immunodeficiency Virus Epidemic, the only states that received federal money for HIV/AIDS care and education were those that implemented "affirmative responsibility" criminal laws around disclosure.[32] The stigmatization of HIV positive incarcerated people, many queers and transgenders, and of color, is not a new feature of the carceral apparatus but rather is a normative occurrence with a long and sordid history connected to the homophobic stigmatization of incarcerated queer people. From 1974–1989 lesbians and gays (and those presumed to be) incarcerated in Florida's Polk County Jail were segregated from the general population and made to wear pink bracelets, the symbolic violence of which links back to the Nazi pink triangle.[33] The racialized, militarized, and anti-poor "war on drugs" and the recently reauthorized needle exchange ban have both drastically heightened the AIDS epidemic.[34]

As a result, incidents or "cases" like that of Gregory Smith—a queer black AIDS activist who, while incarcerated in Camden New Jersey, was additionally charged with attempted murder, making "terroristic threats," and aggravated assault for allegedly biting at two prison guards, sentenced to twenty-five years and died while still in state custody in November 2003—have become common and must not, as Derrida warned, be treated as "exemplary."[35] The more recent "exemplary" legal precedent, the "bio-terrorism" charge waged against Michigan resident Daniel Allen for "use of a harmful biological device"—his HIV status—proves the general, historical rule.[36] While political scientist Cathy Cohen's text *Boundaries of Blackness* is an influential work on the politics of HIV/AIDS in relation to race, there remains a need for further scholarship and activism at the intersections of black radicalism, trans justice and gender self-determination, HIV/AIDS, and prison abolition.

What is the relationship between the memorialization of sites of queer and trans resistance and the politics of loss and mourning? To trauma, violence, and belonging? Through memory work such as the memorialization of these sites of resistance, the trauma and violence that queer and transgender people of color face on a quotidian level is effaced and/or treated as a vestige of an unfortunate past. The memorialization of sites of queer and transgender resistance such as Stonewall and Compton's Cafeteria invisibilize historical and present trauma and cause questions that Derrida raised about the responsibility of mourning to resurface. How are we to mourn for those, such as Marsha P. Johnson, co-founder of STAR, whose body was found floating in the Hudson River in 1992 after the gay pride march?[37] For Sanesha Stewart? "Ex-Con Slays Transsexual Bronx Hooker" was the title provided by the *NY Daily News*, which mirrors the transphobic language of the Compton's Cafeteria article but introduces racist language of black criminality as well: "Ex-Con…"[38] In what ways do media and the state corroborate in their violence and in their perpetuation of transphobic death and death(s)—the symbolism of which we see in the "Death(s) of Ronald Barthes," singular but also plural—how plural must they be, how many more will die? "Impossible mourning" indeed.

Yet, rather than exclusively gravitating towards, we might focus on the reverse and consider survival and resiliency in the face of violence and examine the ways in which those situated at the bio- and necro-political nexus of the prison industrial complex and neoliberal economic policies are also actively combating them:

> Organized, under-organized, and ad hoc movements of imprisoned, homeless, and undocumented people, as well as the activists committed to working beneath and relatively autonomous of the NPIC's political apparatus, may well embody the beginnings of an alternative US-based praxis that displaces the NPIC's apparent domination of political discourse and possibility.[39]

Current movements to change the trans political landscape in Philadelphia, happening outside of the aegis of the non-profit industrial complex—such as Riders Against Gender Exclusion (RAGE), a grassroots, trans and gender-non-conforming movement against gender binary South Eastern Pennsylvania Transit Authority (SEPTA) public transit passes—are indicative of the type of resistance that Dylan Rodriguez references. Moving beyond the constrained political field and vision of the non-profit industrial complex and queer (neo)liberal logic requires disrupting the harmful dynamics that these structures not only maintain but also reproduce.

Queer, gender-non-conforming, and trans people are continuing to center a politics of resistance to policing and prisons, both nationally through conferences such as Transforming Justice and locally in places like Philadelphia, through collectives like Hearts on a Wire. Hearts on a Wire emerged out of a 2007 meeting of activists, providers, trans, and gender-non-conforming people in Philadelphia concerned about the impact of mass incarceration on our communities and committed to creating an advocacy network.[40] Members of Hearts on a Wire conducted a community survey of trans and gender-non-conforming people inside Pennsylvania's prison system. Incarcerated trans and gender-non-conforming people inside—mostly of color—recruited other survey participants in both men's and women's prisons in Pennsylvania. The title of the report, which was actually stamped on a returned piece of mail: "This is a Prison, Glitter is Not Allowed," points to the determined anti-fabulousness and deadly *telos* of the prison regime, its threat to and destructive agenda for queer, trans and gender non-conforming people of color and our communities. Such slogans reflect the transphobic nature of the always already dehumanizing space of the prison—of the cage. These efforts spotlight not only the ways in which the prison industrial complex enacts reproductive and other forms of bio- and also necro-political violence against trans and gender-non-conforming people through the criminalization and penalization of gender expression (infractions like the wearing of make-up mean that you end up in the hole), and the denial of self-determination (placement according to medically assigned sex). They also highlight the ways in which we continue to resist and survive such violence.

## ACKNOWLEDGMENTS

Many thanks to David Kanzanjian, Heather Love, and members of the 2010 Penn Graduate Humanities Forum who generously and critically read this essay in its early iterations and offered valuable insights. Thanks for the encouragement and support of Ben Singer, Eric Stanley, and Jin Haritaworn. Deep appreciation for the many other trans and gender non-conforming activists, organic intellectuals and/or academics who have, in addition to their own work in leftist struggles— be they for a politics of queer and trans prison abolition, or against homonationalism, or for gender self-determining sociopolitical imaginaries and realities—helped to support, influence, inspire, and critique my own projects. Thank you to Peggy Kamuf, with whom I emailed about Derrida's writing on Jackson, Mumia, the death penalty, and the black liberation movement. Thanks also to Aren Aizura for being such a wonderful and committed editor, helping me carry the essay through to publication. Finally, thanks to Susan Stryker for her touchstone contributions to the continually developing field of transgender studies.

## NOTES

1. Sewell Chan, "Stonewall Uprising Given Role in Tourism Campaign," *The New York Times*, April 7, 2009, 1.
2. Jacques Derrida, *Archive Fever* (Chicago, IL: Chicago University Press, 1995), 2–3.
3. Susan Stryker, "Transgender History, Homonormativity, and Disciplinarity," *Radical History Review* 100 (2008), 145–157.
4. David Sokol, *NYC Gay History Essentials*, March 27, 2009, http://www.nycgo.com/articles/nyc-gay-history (accessed January 2, 2010).
5. Jacques Derrida, *Without Alibi* (Palo Alto, CA: Stanford University Press, 2002), 113.
6. Derrida, *Without Alibi*, 113.
7. Derrida, *Without Alibi*, 114.
8. Jacques Derrida, *Archive Fever*, 14.
9. See Marc Stein, *City of Brotherly and Sisterly Loves* (Philadelphia, PA: Temple University Press, 2004), 155–176.
10. Dennis Hevesi, "Frank Rizzo of Philadelphia Dies at 70; A 'Hero' and 'Villain,'" *The New York Times*, July 17, 1991, 1–2.
11. *Greater Philadelphia*, December 1962: 23.
12. Stein, *City of Brotherly and Sisterly Loves*, 245.
13. Sokol, *NYC Gay History Essentials*.
14. Sokol, *NYC Gay History Essentials*.
15. Tommi Avicolli Mecca, *Smash the Church, Smash the State! The Early Years of Gay Liberation* (San Francisco, CA: City Lights Books, 2009).
16. See Judith Butler, "Finishing, Starting" in *Derrida and the Time of the Political*, ed. Pheng Cheah and Suzanne Guerlac (Durham, NC: Duke University Press, 2009), 291–306.
17. Jasbir Puar, *Terrorist Assemblages: Homonationalism in Queer Times* (Durham, NC: Duke University Press, 2007), xii.
18. Graham Burchell, *The Foucault Effect: Studies in Governmentality* (Chicago, IL: University of Chicago Press, 2001).
19. Wendy Brown, *Regulating Aversion* (Princeton, NJ: Princeton University Press, 2008), 83.
20. Brown, *Regulating Aversion*, 84.
21. Brown, *Regulating Aversion*, 24.
22. Lisa Leff, "As Gay Pride Hits Stride, Transgendered Find More Acceptance," *USA Today*, June 24, 2006.
23. Michael Bronski, "On the Back of the Bumper," *Boston Phoenix*, March 21–28, 2002.
24. Wyatt Buchanan, "Pride Parade Salute for an Unlikely Ally," *San Francisco Chronicle,* June 23, 2006.

25. Buchanan, "Pride Parade Salute for an Unlikely Ally."
26. Jeremy W. Peters, "Transgender State Workers Expected to Gain Bias Protection," *The New York Times*, December 29, 2006.
27. Stephen Sprinkle, "Unfinished Lives: Remembering LGBT Hate Crime Victims," *Memphis Nocturne*, January 20, 2009, http://unfinishedlivesblog.com/2009/01/20/memphis-nocturne. Accessed January 2, 2010.
28. Jacques Derrida, *Negotiations* (Palo Alto, CA: Stanford University Press, 2002), 41.
29. Derrida, *Negotiations*, 42.
30. Jacques Derrida, *The Work of Mourning* (Chicago, IL: University of Chicago Press, 2001), 95.
31. Derrida, *The Work of Mourning*, 193.
32. Regan Hoffman, "Sex Crime," *POZ* Magazine, October 2009.
33. Michael F. Welch, *Ironies of Imprisonment* (New York: SAGE Press, 2005), 65.
34. For further information about the global impact of the war on drugs on HIV/AIDS and public health see Kasia Malinowska-Sempruch, *War on Drugs, HIV/AIDS, and Human Rights* (New York: IDEA, 2004).
35. Elihu Rosenblatt, *Criminal Injustice: Confronting the Prison Crisis* (Cambridge: South End Press, 1996), 123.
36. Heywood, Todd, "Accused-HIV-as Terrorism Suspect Rejects Plea Deal," *The Michigan Messenger*, April 9, 2010. http://michiganmessenger.com/36600/accused-hiv-as-terrorism-suspect-rejects-plea-deal.
37. Leslie Feinberg, *Transgender Warriors*, (Boston, MA: Beacon Press, 1996).
38. Hayes, Elizabeth and John Lemire, "Cops: Ex-con Slays Bronx Transsexual 'Hooker,'" *NY Daily News*, February 10, 2008.
39. INCITE! Women of Color Against Violence, *The Revolution Will Not Be Funded* (South End Press, 2005), 31.
40. Pascal Emmer, R. Barrett Marshall, and Adrian Lowe, *This is a Prison, Glitter is Not Allowed: Experiences of Trans and Gender Variant People in Pennsylvania's Prison Systems* (Philadelphia, PA: Hearts on a Wire Collective, 2011).

# 45

## *Neutering the Transgendered*
## Human Rights and Japan's Law No. 111

LAURA H. NORTON

LAURA H. NORTON, A FEDERAL EQUAL EMPLOYMENT PROGRAM MANAGER who holds a Juris Doctorate degree from the University of Washington School of Law, wrote a longer version of this article on the violation of the human rights of transsexual people in Japan as part of a 2006 symposium on queer, transgender, and intersex legal issues at Georgetown University Law Center. Norton first describes the work done in 2003 by Aya Kamikawa, Japan's first openly transgender elected politician, to pass the "Law Concerning Special Cases in Handling Gender for People with Gender Identity Disorder," which was known colloquially as "Law 111." Norton argues that the intent of the law, which was to amend the Family Registry Law in order to allow transgender individuals to petition the courts to change their legal gender designation in Japan's national registry of citizens (the *koseki*), was subverted by the legislative process. As a result of political compromise with conservative legislators, the applicability of Law 111 was narrowed to include only those persons who had never reproduced biologically, or would never do so in the future (as a consequence of the sterilizing effects of their genital transformation surgeries). The argument against passing a broader measure was that, for the sole benefit of a tiny minority, it would require completely overhauling the bureaucratic process through which the entire population was registered and enumerated, and that even if this were done, it would be nonsensical for two individuals designated as female or two individuals designated as male to be entered in the *koseki* as parents of the same offspring. The narrowed scope of the law, however, in spite of the good intentions with which it initially was proposed, actually abrogated fundamental human rights of reproduction and bodily integrity for gender-changing people, as the price for claiming their self-perceived identities. Norton's analysis is consonant with a wider body of work on transgender biopolitics, which locates the micropolitical site of oppression in the very administrative and bureaucratic procedures that regulate all bodies within each particular state or nation. It is because transgender bodies don't readily fit with the ordinary, routine ways of managing most bodies in a given context that their life-chances become diminished.

Aya Kamikawa announced her candidacy in the elections for the Setagaya Ward Assembly in Tokyo, Japan, in March 2003.[1] Kamikawa, a male-to-female transsexual, opted to omit her gender from the requisite application for candidacy. The Public Management Ministry, which oversees elections, instructed ward officials that the Public Offices Elections Law does not require candidates to announce their gender when running for office. Kamikawa, running on a platform that advocated recognition of the civil and human rights of transgendered people, won the election to the Setagaya Ward Assembly as the first openly transgendered politician in Japan's history.[2]

Once in office, Kamikawa focused her clout on lobbying for passage of what would become the Law Concerning Special Cases in Handling Gender for People with Gender Identity Disorder (GID) (Law No. 111 of 2003).[3] The primary effect of Law No. 111 was to redraft the Family Registry Law[4] to permit transgendered people to petition family courts to amend their legal genders to conform to their chosen genders. The Japanese government maintains a national registry of citizens *(koseki)*, the administration of which is subject to the Family Registry Law. *Koseki* records contain a range of personal identifying information, from ancestry to offspring to gender.

Law No. 111 unanimously passed both the Lower and Upper Houses of the Japanese Diet on July 10, 2003, but in a final form much different from the version originally proposed. In order to achieve unanimous passage of the bill, its advocates compromised with the Legislature's conservative majority to narrow the applicability of the law to include only those persons who had never reproduced, and would never do so in the future. It is in its limited applicability that the law impermissibly mandates transgendered persons subject themselves to severe restrictions on their fundamental rights of reproduction and bodily integrity in order to claim their identities.

Because of the discordance between their chosen and legal genders, transgendered persons in Japan are deprived of basic civil entitlements, such as marriage, employment, and health care.[5] Japanese authorities house detainees and prisoners according to legal gender, thereby particularly risking the safety and health of transgendered people in jails and prisons. Japanese judicial and legislative remedies fail to address the underlying challenge to legal classification posed by those persons who will not or cannot conform to a dichotomized schema of gender. Some critics who posit that "transgender individuals are treated very poorly in the [American] legal system,"[6] believe that the international efflorescence of "GID laws" like that promulgated in Japan in 2003 is a positive trend. On the contrary, Japan's statutory response to the transgender challenge benefits very few individuals and violates the human rights of transgendered people.[7] At a more basic level, however, the law reflects a male-female dichotomy that is belied by nature and, as such, fails to accurately reflect social relationships subject to government regulation. Law No. 111 should be amended to remedy those violations and to reflect the complexities of sex and gender.

This Note considers the shortcomings of Law No. 111 through analysis, in Part I, of the *koseki* as a de facto instrument of discrimination. Part II examines organized legal challenges by transgendered activists to the Family Registry Law prior to the passage of Law No. 111. Inquiry into how transgendered persons brought constitutional claims in the Japanese legal system reveals two issues. First, the very saga of Law No. 111's origin is an often-played one of Japanese realpolitik. Like much of Japan's rights-based legislation, Law No. 111 was born of a grassroots activism ignored or rejected by an analytically anemic jurisprudence. Rather, legislative deal-making subdued politically activist goals, thereby facilitating judicial avoidance of implementing Constitutional guarantees of equality. Second, to the extent that case law reflects how gender equality is enshrined in legal systems, much jurisprudence nonetheless seems profoundly unable to resolve the conundrum posed by the ambiguities of gender.

Part III argues, with reference to international human rights law, that Law No. 111 violates the bodily integrity and reproductive freedom of the transgendered through its requirements of childlessness and sexual reassignment surgery (SRS). Part IV examines potential remedies for the law's more egregious features, with reference to international human rights law and to theoretical constructs which challenge binary concepts of sex and gender.

While transgendered individuals comprise a relatively small proportion of the global population, their treatment under the law catalyzes various transnational debates on subjects ranging from gender discrimination to equal marriage rights. As such, the legal resolution of the gender conundrum involves a rethinking of equal protection principles as well as a departure from the perennially contentious battles over the disputed merits of natural law. Nothing could be more natural than sex, and yet the reality of sex is anything but simple despite the law's attempts to make it so.

## I. *KOSEKI* IN CONTEXT: THE FAMILY REGISTRY SYSTEM MAINTAINS SOCIAL HIERARCHY AND FACILITATES DISCRIMINATION

Discrimination in a variety of contexts is facilitated by Japan's family registry system, the *koseki*. The *koseki* is a national system of records maintained by the State and consists of demographic, economic, and genealogical information (including recorded gender at birth) for every citizen in every registered household in Japan.[8] The Family Registry Law provides that "any person" may request registry information.[9] *Koseki* records are regularly accessed by potential employers, insurers, marriage prospects, and spouses in order to determine a subject's ancestral background and family relations; such inquiries would necessarily reveal their subjects' legal genders.[10]

The modem *koseki* is one element of the administrative system instituted by the Supreme Commander of Allied Powers (SCAP) at the end of World War II, but Japan has sporadically maintained the *koseki* in some form since the seventh century. Whether under imperial or democratic auspices, data recorded in the *koseki* serves a variety of state functions, including taxation and identification of individual legal status.

From the time of its reinstatement by the Emperor Meiji in the late nineteenth century, minority groups have criticized the *koseki* as a tool of discrimination contrary to the principles and spirit of a constitutional democracy.[11] As the *koseki* records ancestry, births, and divorces, an individual's ethnic origin, parents' marital status, and other sensitive information may be had through review of the records. Social prejudices are enforced in employment, housing, and health care despite a constitutional guarantee of equal protection.[12] Constitutional challenges to the *koseki* made by the transgendered and other minorities[13] bear many similarities, highlighting the fact that the *koseki* itself is a controversial instrument, no matter the specific shortcomings of Law No. 111. The transgendered are merely among the most recent challengers to a system that reinforces ancient and contemporary hierarchies. Prior to the passage of Law No. 111, transgendered activists began a concerted series of court cases throughout Japan, petitioning in family courts to amend their legal genders as recorded in the *koseki,* relying on various constitutional rights enumerated in Chapter III of the Constitution.[14]

## II. CONSTITUTIONAL DOCTRINES FAIL TO SECURE EQUAL PROTECTION FOR TRANSGENDERED PERSONS IN JAPAN

> To attempt to divide us into rigid categories... is like trying to apply the laws of solids to the state of fluids. ...[15]
>
> —Kate Bornstein, *Gender Outlaw*

The ideological centerpiece of the legal system created by SCAP is the American-authored Constitution, Nihonkoku Kenpō (1946). Japan has developed an indigenous jurisprudence independently from American constitutional doctrines despite the fact that the Kenpō is fairly described as a "thoroughly Anglo-American document."[16] [...] The Japanese judiciary's invariable refusal to engage in the constitutional evaluation of administrative laws compounds the rigidity of the law's treatment of transgendered persons inasmuch as both the law and the courts privilege an exclusivist and majoritarian worldview that punishes the specific and idiosyncratic.

## A. The historical underpinnings of the Japanese legal system enervate judicial review of constitutional questions

The Japanese reception of Western law in the mid-twentieth century laid the framework of the U.S. Constitution over an already extant legal system. The Japanese legal system from 1871 through 1946 was based on a European-style civil code which, in turn, was received in an effort to fend off late-nineteenth-century Western colonialism.[17] SCAP's accommodation of extant imperial power structures, and its failure to hold the Emperor accountable for war crimes,[18] rendered the 1946 Kenpō a document of ambiguous authority. This de facto irrelevance of individual rights allows the conservative executive and judicial branches of the government to consistently and narrowly interpret the Kenpō in a radically different manner from its American cousin. The virtually unbroken control of the political system by conservatives in the postwar era has meant that in spite of substantial similarities in the Japanese and American constitutions, the Japanese judiciary has developed a unique approach to deciding constitutional questions.[19]

The Kenpō is the supreme law of this non-federalist nation and, as such, Japanese judicial review of constitutional questions could be expected to be more robust than that in the United States, because the national government is never required to defer to subordinate political entities like states.[20] Rather, Japanese constitutional review is characterized by an extraordinary degree of judicial restraint and legislative deference.[21] The Japanese Supreme Court has ruled laws unconstitutional only six times, and only once in the first quarter-century following the Occupation.[22] Article 14 of the Kenpō is analogous to the U.S. Constitution's Fourteenth Amendment, Section 1, both of which guarantee legal equality to all people.[23] Ironically, Article 14 is textually more expansive than its American predecessor in its prohibition on both social and economic discrimination for a variety of enumerated protected classes; however, restrictive judicial interpretations of equal protection vitiate Article 14's intent.

Part of the Court's reluctance to wade into murky constitutional waters is historically rooted in the current Constitution's predecessor, the Meiji Kenpō.[24] In an effort to maintain imperial control over the entire legal system, Emperor Meiji forbade the judiciary from adjudicating constitutional questions.[25] As a result, constitutional questions were considered the provenance of the legislature, and remain largely so to this day.

## B. Constitutional rights are defined by social context and legislative prerogative

Constitutional rights in Japan are textually counterbalanced by a standard of conformity with public welfare; that is, rights are not absolute but limited by the social context.[26] The original postwar constitutional jurisprudence references the public welfare standard, but in the last thirty years that standard has been replaced by deference to legislative prerogative.

Nonetheless, judicial sensitivity to the public welfare found full expression in the case law immediately preceding passage of Law No. 111. Shortly after sex reassignment surgery (SRS) was legalized in Japan,[27] postoperative transsexuals petitioned the family courts to amend their *koseki* records to accurately reflect their genders on the basis of Article 14's guarantee of equal protection. Six separate cases were filed at Kanto and Tohoku regional family courts in May 2001.[28] The Tokyo High Court denied the first of the petitions on February 9, 2000, deferring the matter to the Diet.[29]

The Tokyo Family Court took a stronger stand in 2003, noting that the Family Registry Law permits amendment of "contradictions" in the record. The court interpreted contradiction to mean "cases where the records in the register do not match the truth in the beginning."[30] The "truth in the beginning," according to the court, was that the plaintiff was born a "biological female," and plaintiff's self-perception and surgery were therefore irrelevant.

In a case that would eventually find its way to the Supreme Court, a Kanto area family court interpreted "contradiction" differently.[31] The court stated on August 29, 2002, that because the cause of GID was unknown, it could not ascertain whether the plaintiff's gender really did contradict the *koseki* and therefore could not permit amendment. The plaintiff appealed the ruling to the Supreme Court, arguing that being barred from amending the *koseki* prevented him from marrying or obtaining a job and so violated his Constitutional rights to the pursuit of happiness and to equal protection under the law. The plaintiff previously underwent surgery at Saitama Medical Center and had subsequently been denied employment and medical treatment because his apparent gender conflicted with his *koseki* record.[32] The Supreme Court rejected the plaintiff's arguments on June 2, 2003, holding that sexual reassignment surgery did not constitute sufficient ground to justify a change to the *koseki* as the surgery was not indicative of a factual error in the *koseki*.

After three of the six cases failed, culminating in the Supreme Court defeat, activists lobbied the Diet for legislative relief, while simultaneously garnering much media attention.[33] The saga of the court failures was unfortunately unredeemed by passage of Law No. 111, because the legislature, like the courts, ultimately upheld the inviolable nature of the *koseki* over the self-knowledge of transgendered people.

## III. LAW NO. 111 VIOLATES THE REPRODUCTIVE FREEDOM AND BODILY INTEGRITY OF TRANSGENDERED PERSONS

Law No. 111 passed unanimously in a plenary session of the Diet one month after the Supreme Court held that SRS was not sufficient ground to change one's legal gender identity. As currently written, Law No. 111 permits a change of legal gender only when a petitioner is: (1) 20 years of age or older; (2) presently unmarried; (3) childless; (4) without gonads or evincing a persistent lack of gonadal function; and, (5) with genitalia appearing similar to that of the opposite gender.[34] Applicants must also be independently diagnosed by two physicians as having GID.

Under Japan's Eugenics Protection Law, SRS (which removes or incapacitates the reproductive organs) was historically classified as a sterilization procedure, and as such it could not be performed without medical justification. Until 1998, the law did not regard GID as medical justification for the surgery.[35] Transgendered people seeking surgery therefore had to seek medical assistance abroad. In 1997, the Japan Society of Psychiatry and Neurology (JSPN) formulated guidelines for granting SRS, which were instrumental to the amendment of the Eugenics Protection Law legalizing the surgery as medically necessary for people diagnosed with GID. Saitama Medical School performed the first legal SRS in Japan the following year.

### A. Japan legalized sexual reassignment surgery in response to the inclusion of Gender Identity Disorder in the Diagnostic and Statistical Manual of Mental Disorders

The legalization of SRS in Japan was in part a reaction to the American Psychiatric Association's (APA) inclusion of the GID diagnosis in the fourth edition of the Diagnostic and Statistical Manual of Mental Disorders (DSM-IV) [36] and in the International Statistical Classification of Diseases and Related Health Problems (ICD-10).[37] The diagnostic classification of GID as a mental disorder continues to be included in the APA's most recent revision of the manual,[38] although the APA is currently debating its prospective inclusion in the DSM-V. The GID diagnosis has not enjoyed universal acceptance in the psychomedical profession, but it is particularly controversial among transgendered persons, primarily because it pathologizes transgender identities, but also because inclusion in the ICD-10 means that insurance companies will pay for SRS.[39] Despite significant opposition, the diagnosis appears slated for continued acceptance, if only for its pragmatic value in administering various aspects of the lives of transgendered persons.

The DSM-IV-TR diagnostic criteria for GID[40] follow:

- Evidence of a strong and persistent cross-gender identification;
- Evidence of clinically significant distress or impairment in social, occupational, or other important areas of functioning;
- Evidence that cross-gender identification is not merely a desire for the perceived cultural advantages of being the other sex;
- Evidence of persistent discomfort about one's assigned sex or a sense of inappropriateness in the gender role of that sex;
- Absence of a concurrent physical intersex condition.

The mental and emotional functioning of the individual almost entirely defines the GID diagnosis. The exclusion of intersexed persons from the diagnosis belies some preoccupation with the body of the subject, but such preoccupation is far more explicit in the 1997 JSPN Guidelines for SRS. In many regards they are substantially similar to the DSM list, but there is an explicit focus on a requisite rejection of the subject's genitals, in addition to emphases on age and economic status:[41]

- The individual maintains a strong desire to live, act or dress as the opposite sex;
- The individual feels distress from living as his or her birth gender;
- He or she strongly dislikes the physical attributes and functions of the birth gender and desires to have the birth-gender sexual organs removed;
- There has been a continuous desire to change one's sex and he or she has felt 'trapped in the wrong gender' prior to reaching their mid-teens;
- The patient must be at least 20 years of age (changed to 18 in 2002);
- The patient must make follow-up visits with physicians to monitor health (added in 2001).

Saitama Medical School and Okayama University Hospital are the only medical centers in Japan providing sexual reassignment surgery. As of 2002, fourteen people had the surgery.[42] In June 2002, JSPN and the Ethics Committee of the Saitama Medical School jointly demanded that the government ameliorate the ambiguous legal status of transgendered people. In particular, they urged revision of the Family Registry Law to permit postoperative transsexuals to amend their legal gender identities.[43]

### B. Law No. 111 contravenes the spirit of the Japan Society for Psychiatry and Neurology Guidelines through childlessness and non-marital requirements

Contrary to the JSPN guidelines, Law No. 111 dictates that openly transgendered persons cannot have both their legal identities and legal marriages, and further ensures that legally recognized transgendered persons never reproduce.[44] Marital and reproductive restrictions in Law No. 111 originated at the insistence of the majority Liberal Democratic Party in order to secure unanimous passage of the bill.[45] [...]

The Japanese conservative majority insisted that reproduction had to be restricted on the basis that a parent who had changed his or her sex would "shock" a child.[46] Critics of the provision pointed out that a bigger shock might befall children when they discovered their parents' birth genders did not match their perceived genders.[47] Fears of unduly shocking Japan's children, however, are moot because Law No. 111 mandates childlessness for transgendered people if they wish to have their legal genders match their chosen genders. Ironically, the codification of the psychiatric diagnosis of GID exacerbates the violation of the rights of transgendered people because of the law's inclusion of SRS as a criterion for relief.

The Japan Federation of Bar Associations and transgender activists continue to lobby for elimination of the childlessness requirement.[48] It is argued that the stringent requirements of the law render it inapplicable to three-fourths of Japan's transgendered population. Critics also highlight a human rights dilemma posed by the fact that past behavior (i.e., having children) will limit future choices (i.e., changing either one's legal or physical gender). The Japan Federation of Bar Associations has advocated instead a case-by-case assessment of applications that involve children.[49]

Forty percent of individuals diagnosed with GID do not wish to undergo surgery, however, of the sixty percent who indicate they would, many cannot afford the prohibitively expensive surgery, which can cost several million yen.[50] The law therefore poses another equal protection problem in that it discriminates in political and social relations not only on the basis of sex, but also disadvantages the poor in contradiction of Article 14 of the Kenpō, which forbids economic discrimination.

Law No. 111 went into effect on July 16, 2004, and on July 28, 2004, a Naha Family Court granted the first application to amend the *koseki* of a male-to-female transsexual.[51] As justification for its ruling, the court noted the plaintiff's "great psychological pain" and her need for "a stable female identity."[52] While one may be tempted to laud the court's stated compassion for the suffering of the plaintiff, the cold fact remains mat to claim her legal rights she had to place her "great psychological pain" under public scrutiny, not to mention the great physical pain and expense of SRS. Seen from that angle, the compassion of the court's words and the stated purpose of Law No. 111 are belied by the very real human rights dilemma imposed on the transgendered who must be sterilized, thereby undergoing extreme pain, before being allowed to exist according to the dictates of their consciences.

The profound failure of purportedly well-meaning legislatures to provide relief for the transgendered through GID laws like Law No. 111 is precisely attributable to the ambiguity embodied in the transgendered person. Binary legal classifications of gender will never be able to adequately address the diversity extant among the human species, and that is the challenge posed by both transgendered and intersexed persons. Mandatory surgery eases both social and individual anxiety over gender ambiguity through facilitation and perpetuation of the gender binary.[53] Without surgery, a person may impermissibly slip back and forth, not to mention in between, gender categories.

### C. Law No. 111 violates the fundamental human rights of reproductive freedom and bodily integrity

Coincident with Japan's global economic dominance in the 1980s, the State pursued a program of internationalization *(kokusaika),* including the adoption of several international human rights covenants.[54] Between 1979 and 1994, Japan ratified several major international human rights treaties, including: the International Covenant on Economic, Social and Cultural Rights (ICESCR); the International Covenant on Civil and Political Rights (ICCPR); the Convention on the Elimination of All Forms of Discrimination Against Women (CEDAW); and, the Convention on the Rights of the Child. Law No. 111 contradicts several provisions of these four documents, all of which guarantee rights of reproductive self-determination and bodily integrity. Forced sterilization and arbitrary state interference with privacy are internationally condemned practices, and have been since 1948, at the time of the promulgation of the Universal Declaration of Human Rights (UDHR). Of special note in the context of Law No. 111 is the right to health as it is conceived in these international treaties and as subsequently interpreted and elaborated by international bodies.

Article 25.1 of the UDHR is the origin of the right-to-health concept. It provides: "Everyone has the right to a standard of living adequate for the health and well-being of himself [sic] and his [sic] family."[55] The right to health is additionally propounded in the other previously-cited documents to which Japan is a signatory. The ICESCR defines reproductive health in part as "the freedom to decide if and when to reproduce," which freedom is further defined as the "right to control one's health and body, including sexual and reproductive freedom."[56] The ICCPR's reiteration of the UDHR's prohibition of torture, and cruel, inhumane or degrading treatment, and its provision for the special protection of children, include within their scope the abolition of forced sterilization and genital mutilation, consequent to which States Parties have an obligation to recognize equally "various forms of family."[57] CEDAW's reproductive freedom provisions include the ability of persons to "decide freely and responsibly on the number and spacing of children."[58] CEDAW's guarantee of reproductive freedom is internationally regarded as including a ban on genital mutilation.

It may be objected that Law No. 111 does not impose coerced sterilization or genital mutilation on transgendered people, as it is these individuals' choice whether or not to undergo SRS. It must be acknowledged that the situation is much different from that in states which do regularly single out particular racial, ethnic or religious groups for nonconsensual sterilization. As such, transgendered people under Law No. 111's regime are not particularly deprived of access to information about SRS procedures; rather, it is the element of coercion in the law which contravenes the right of reproductive freedom. The paradox of Law No. 111 is that on the one hand it codifies the GID diagnosis, a construct which embodies the idea that transgendered people are compelled to live as a gender different from that assigned to them at birth. On the other hand, to be able to do so fully (i.e., with appropriate legal status), Law No. 111 also compels sterilization and no reproduction prior to sterilization. It is a Hobson's choice and for those who cannot have or do not want SRS, the surgery is a violation of bodily integrity. Either one must undergo sterilization or live with the consequences of a discordant legal identity. Either way, reproductive and privacy rights of the transgendered are violated. In sum, Law No. 111 violates standards of international law which Japan is required to observe.

## IV. BREAKING THE BINARY: NATURAL LAW SHOULD ACCOUNT FOR NATURE, OR WHY WE SHOULD NEUTER THE LAW AND NOT BODIES

> Now when chaos had begun to condense, but force and form were not yet manifest, and there was nought named, nought done, who could know its shape? Nevertheless Heaven and Earth first parted, and the Three Deities performed the commencement of creation; the Passive and Active Essences then developed, and the Two Spirits became the ancestors of all things. Therefore did he enter obscurity and emerge into light, and the Sun and Moon were revealed by the washing of his eyes.
>
> — The *Kojiki* (Records of Ancient Matters) [59]

The most notoriously discriminatory case law involving transgendered persons[60] is saturated with implicit, if not explicit, references to a classical form of natural law that focuses exclusively on invariant laws of nature and disregards the "coincidental aggregates" that emerge from equally natural laws of probability and contingency.[61] If legislatures and courts justify their laws with science, then laws will only be as effective as the underlying empirical data is accurate.

This section sets forth potential remedies for the law's approach to gender in general, and for transgender rights in Japan specifically. Part A addresses [...] the legal conundrum (or resolution) posed by the existence of those who cannot comply with the gender binary. Effective laws are rational laws, but Law No. 111 is neither because it does not reflect the manifold reality of human sexuality.

Part B considers whether legislatures and courts should be in the business of dictating gender. Self-identified transgendered people are subjected to a differential standard of proof in courts and administrative agencies to prove that they are who they say they are, and the State issues the ultimate decision. Such treatment of the transgendered is unjustified and discriminatory, and therefore one solution is to abolish all gender categories in the law. Part C concludes this section with a consideration of how gender classifications perpetuate animus against the gender-variant, and ultimately endanger people's bodies and psyches.

## A. The intersexed body challenges classical natural law on behalf of everybody

The legal system's emphasis on genitals and DNA is a clear indicator of the conflation of genital sex with gender,[62] which in turn reflects the messy state of affairs when attempting to legally classify "sex" and "gender" as distinct concepts, let alone "male" and "female." While Law No. 111 may be perceived as offering greater relief than was previously available from the courts, the law still operates to replicate a falsely dichotomous view of sex, and therefore of gender. [...]

The human reluctance to address gender ambiguity is shot through with the tension between empirical reality and natural law. [...] The empirical evidence is that neither gender nor sex manifest in exclusively binary arrangements. The law engages in self-delusion and undermines its own force when it insists otherwise.

## B. The transgendered carry an extra burden of proof: gender

Traditional jurisprudence, Western or Japanese, does not define male or female, yet laws are replete with the assumption that the distinction is real and natural. A woman bringing a claim of sex discrimination is not required to submit to genetic screening and a physical examination before she is given standing to pursue her claim. Analogously, in the infamous patricide case of *Aizawa v. Japan*,[63] the plaintiff was not genetically screened to determine that she really was her father's daughter before the sentence was imposed on her for his murder. It would seem then that if the fact of a person's transgendered status was never brought to a court's attention, transgendered people would be treated like anyone else similarly situated; that is, their represented gender would not be an occasion for inquiry by the court. The inevitable conclusion is that in cases ranging from sexual discrimination or harassment to domestic relations, the law places a higher burden on the transgendered to prove that they are who they say they are, while anyone else who does not make an issue of their gender, whether or not their perceived gender is accurate, is taken at face-value.

Whether this extra burden upon self-identified transgendered people is justifiable cannot be discerned from the paucity of Japanese case law addressing the necessity of gender categories in the law. Those cases narrowly holding that surgery is not indicative of a contradiction in the registry prove the judiciary's distaste for equal protection analysis.

Indications of possible justifications for gender classifications in the law are provided in English and American case law, however. The English High Court in *Corbett v. Corbett* denied that surgery could alter one's "true sex," but nonetheless opined that "over a very large area the law is indifferent to sex."[64] Where sex did make a difference was in the payment of life insurance or pension premiums, certain employment conditions, and for a few tax purposes.[65] In the United States, statutes criminalizing the statutory rape of minor females but not minor males have been upheld as constitutional despite equal protection challenges.[66] Again, however, any cases brought under such laws do not subject the parties to genetic screening and physical examinations to determine the sex of the parties. As such, imposing an additional burden of proof on self-avowed transgendered people, but not on anyone else (transgendered or not), renders the requirement under-inclusive. Furthermore, these justifications do little to tip the balance in their favor when the grave human rights issues of reproductive freedom and bodily integrity bear so heavily on transgendered people.

## C. Abolition of sex and gender classifications in the law is necessary to achieve gender equality

It may be that the challenge posed by the transgendered person who will not or cannot undergo surgery, nor who wholly identifies as either male or female, is one which can only be answered by abolishing all gender distinctions under the law. International Christian University (ICU) in Tokyo, Japan, responded to transgendered activism in the fall term of 2003 by allowing students to choose their own names and gender identifications, without reference to the *koseki*.[67] The University's Center for Gender Studies has been very vocal in critiquing Law No. 111 for its codification of the GID diagnosis largely because GID pathologizes gender variance.[68] ICU's criticism is not isolated, as many other transgendered activists have decried the medicalization of their sexual identities. If antipathy towards gender variance is really what underlies the law's reluctance to treat transgendered people with justice, then the law implicates many in its disdain who are not transgendered, but merely "different." Ironically, equal protection of the laws for the transgendered is about equal protection for all genders even if gender must be abolished to obtain it.

Law No. 111, for all its shortcomings, does give some definitiveness to the lives of those opting for surgery, and as such is preferable to the situation of outright denial of gender-based rights. To resolve the constitutional and human rights defects in the law, however, the qualifying criteria for amendment of the *koseki* must be liberalized. One step in that direction would be to adopt the Japan Federation of Bar Associations' proposal to do a case-by-case analysis of applications involving children. Ultimately, however, this is a compromise solution that still impermissibly allows for a differential consideration of the reproductive status of transgendered people. Any attempt to constrain the reproduction of transgendered persons should be subjected to rigorous scrutiny given the historical animus against this group.

Significant numbers of gender-variant people do not want surgery,[69] let alone an either/or gender identity. Intersexed people will continue to be born and are increasingly lobbying to prohibit sexual assignment surgeries on infants. The transgendered insist on recognition of their diverse views and their desire to define their gender identities as and when they see fit. [...] One of the primary lessons to be learned from transgendered activists is that the primacy accorded genitals as gender-determinative does not reflect the sexual continuum that exists in nature, and as such the law fails to address accurately the legal relationships it seeks to govern. [...]

Recasting the issue in terms of human rights may mean that transgendered people will be better able to secure their rights in the courts of Japan.[70] In the absence of language to the contrary, Japanese courts tend to view international treaties as self-executing, and have interpreted certain international instruments as creating standing for individual litigants.[71]

Given that Japanese courts treat international instruments on an equal footing with domestic law, a gender-rights-based international covenant would provide a basis for a more effective legal strategy than would a conventional equal protection complaint. The International Bill of Gender Rights (IBGR)[72] has as its central premise the right of all people to self-determination of their gender identities. The IBGR contains provisions addressing reproductive freedom, marriage and employment protections, and access to competent medical and psychiatric care. The IBGR has influenced certain jurisdictions to adopt protections for transgendered people, but as yet the Bill has not received widespread international attention, and the legal identities of the transgendered are therefore more likely to be addressed through local and national nondiscrimination statutes. Nonetheless, Law No. 111 was itself a manifestation of the Japanese government's continued efforts at *kokusaika,* and therefore documents such as the IBGR may yet exert some influence in the future.

On a more immediate and practical level, Japanese residents and citizens would be well-served by increased restrictions on the release of *koseki* records. Virtually open access to these records facilitates a variety of discriminatory practices which could be at least impeded by administrative regulation. Furthermore, regulation of the *koseki* and liberalization of Law No. 111's qualifying criteria would actually accomplish the intent of the law: to prevent discrimination against the transgendered.

## CONCLUSION

Despite the conventional political realities underlying the compromises that trans-formed Law No. 111 from a tool of legal relief to one of discrimination and violation, the fact remains that the rights of transgendered people have received unprecedented attention in Japan over the past few years. Indeed, Japan is not alone among nations in its passage of a GID law, and it remains to be seen whether the interventions of such laws in the lives of transgendered people will prove to be ultimately liberating.

The intensity of the transgender debates belies the relatively small population implicated. This is because much more is at stake than the jobs, families, and marriages of transgendered people. Rather, the means by which laws classify transgendered people are the same means that will classify everyone's gender. The philosophical disaggregation of sex and gender can not resolve the conundrum because neither sex nor gender is purely biological or purely social, and both manifest along continua that defy binary classification. Rather than perpetuate sexual dualism through a sex-gender distinction, emphasis should be placed on individual autonomy and self-determination in accord with human rights-based legal theories. States should be called upon to meet the burden of justifying the necessity of sex and gender classifications, rather man placing the identities of transgendered people under the unpredictable control of courts and legislatures. As long as positive law conflates imperfect social and scientific knowledge with natural law, it invites discrimination from and disrespect for the rule of law.

## NOTES

1. *Man with Gender Identity Disorder to Run as Female,* DAILY YOMIURI, Apr. 16, 2003, at 3 [hereinafter *Man with Gender Identity Disorder*]. [...]
2. *Gender Politics,* S. CHINA MORNING POST, June 21, 2003, at 13, *available at* 2003 WLNR 5933870. [...]
3. Sei doitsusei shogaisha no seibetsu no toriatsukai no tokurei ni kansuru horitsu, Law No. 111 of July 16, 2003 [hereinafter Law No. 111.] For the full text of Law No. 111 as originally passed in Japanese, with an English translation, see Laura Norton, *Neutering the Transgendered: Human Rights and Japan's Law No. 111,* 7 GEO. J. GENDER & LAW 187, Appendices A and B. A summary of the 2003 version of the law's most prominent provisions is available in Yudai Shimizu, *The Law for People with GID to Be Enacted in July* (Apr. 1, 2004), Article ID 0402002, International Christian University Center for Gender Studies, *available at* http://subsite.icu.ac.jp/cgs/article/0402002e.html.
4. Koseki hō [Family Registry Law], Law No. 224 of Dec. 22, 1947 [hereinafter Koseki hō].
5. Full-time employment requires submission to an employer of the *koseki* residency certificate that reflects the applicant's birth gender, but which may not comport with the applicant's perceived gender
6. John M. Ohle, *Constructing the Trannie,* 8 J. GENDER RACE & JUST. 237, 239 (2004).
7. Shimizu, *supra* note 3 (estimating that three-fourths of transgendered people in Japan would not qualify for relief under Law No. 111 because of their marital and reproductive status).
8. Koseki hō, *supra* note 4, arts. 6, 13.
9. Such requests are made in writing to prefectural authorities, and must be accompanied by an explanation of the need for the records. Koseki hō, *supra* note 4, art. 10. While legally considered private, multiple loopholes in the Koseki hō facilitate regular access. Philip Brasor, *Japanese Tradition that Violates Privacy Rights,* JAPAN TIMES, June 9, 2002..
10. A 1976 amendment to the Koseki hō nominally restricted access to records by requiring that all requests for records be accompanied by an explanation, and by vesting city mayors with discretion to deny "unjust" requests. Koseki hō, *supra* note 4, art. 10, nos. 1-3; *see also* Emily A. Su-Lan Reber, *Buraku Mondai in Japan: Historical and Modern Perspectives and Directions for the Future,* 12 HARV. HUM. RTS. J. 297, 358 (1999) (discrimination based on information obtained from the *koseki* remains common).
11. *See* Taimie L. Bryant, *For the Sake of the Country, for the Sake of the Family: The Oppressive Impact of Family Registration on Women and Minorities in Japan,* 39 UCLA L. REV. 109-11 (1991).
12. Article 14, Paragraph 1, of the Japanese Constitution (Nihonkoku Kenpō) (1946) [hereinafter KENPŌ] provides that "all of the people are equal under the law and there shall be no discrimination in political, economic or social relations because of race, creed, sex, social status or family origin." KENPŌ, art. 14, para. 1.
13. The first legal challenges to the *koseki* predate the Occupation (and hence the 1947 Kenpō), and were made by *burakumin,* a Japanese cultural minority. *Burakumin* are a caste with origins in the seventeenth-century Tokugawa Shogunate, who traditionally performed occupations deemed "unclean" under both Buddhist and Shinto philosophies. In 1871, one year prior to reinstituting the *koseki,* the Emperor Meiji issued an Emancipation Edict purportedly "liberating" the *burakumin* from their traditional occupations. Crane Stephen Landis, Comment, *Human Rights Violations in Japan: A Contemporary Survey,* 5 D.C.L. J. INT'L L. & PRAC. 53, 65-66 (1996). Constitutional claims against the family registry system have also been brought by children of unmarried parents, children born of parents of disparate nationalities (if a Japanese father sires a child by a non-citizen, the child is granted merely quasi-citizenship status), and by Japanese

residents of Korean descent (until recently, Koreans were barred from becoming Japanese citizens no matter how many lineal generations had resided in the country, and as such were subject to the dictates of the Alien Registration Law (Gaikokujin tōroku hō, Law No. 125 of 1952)). *Id* at 62-64, 67-68.

14. *Court Vetoes Gender Change on Family Register,* MAINICHI DAILY NEWS, Aug. 29, 2002, at 1 (describing six separate lawsuits filed at family courts throughout the nation requesting permission to amend *koseki* entries).

15. KATE BORNSTEIN, GENDER OUTLAW 69 (1995).

16. H. PAUL VARLEY, JAPANESE CULTURE 269 (3d ed. 1984).

17. Charles Qu, *Parricide, Equality and Proportionality: Japanese Courts' Attitudes Towards the Equality Principle as Reflected in* Aizawa v. Japan, 8 MURDOCH U. ELECTRONIC J.L., para. 57 (2001), http://www.murdoch.edu.au/elaw/issues/v8n2/qu82_text.html.

18. GLEN D. HOOK & GAVAN MCCORMACK, JAPAN'S CONTESTED CONSTITUTION: DOCUMENTS AND ANALYSIS 9-10 (2001) (arguing that SCAP's absolution of Hirohito obfuscated the locus of political power in Japan, thereby corrupting postwar democracy at its very inception).

19. Yasuhiro Okudaira, *The Constitution and Its Various Influences, in* JAPANESE CONSTITUTIONAL LAW 32 (Percy R. Luney & Kazuyuki Takahashi, eds. 1993).

20. *See, e.g.,* U.S. CONST, amend. X (reserving all non-Constitutional powers to the states); CARL GOODMAN, JUSTICE AND CIVIL PROCEDURE IN JAPAN 130 (2004).

21. Okudaira, *supra* note 19, at 16-25.

22. YOSHIYUKI NODA, INTRODUCTION TO JAPANESE LAW 122 (Anthony H. Angelo trans. & ed., 1976) (asserting that only one law voided out of 41,000 cases presenting constitutional questions).

23. " People" is a poor translation of *kokumin,* literally Japanese nationals (i.e., citizens), and therefore excludes resident noncitizens and Japanese nationals of colonial origin, such as those Taiwanese and Koreans forcibly brought to Japan as slave labor. Sylvia Brown Hamano, *Incomplete Revolutions and Not So Alien Transplants: The Japanese Constitution and Human Rights,* 1 U. PA. J. CONST. LAW 415, 436-37 (1999).

24. In this context it is important to note that the 1947 Kenpō is technically an amendment, not a replacement, of the 1889 Dai Nihon Teikoku Kenpō [hereinafter MEIJI KENPŌ]. Hamano, *Id.,* at 421.

25. Percy R. Luney, Jr., *Introduction, in* Luney & Takahashi, *supra* note 19, at i, xi.

26. *See, e.g.,* KENPŌ, art. 12 (the purpose of Constitutional rights is to further the public welfare); art. 13 (guaranteeing the "right to life, liberty, and the pursuit of happiness ... to the extent that it does not interfere with the public welfare"); art. 22 (rights to choose one's residence and occupation are restrained by public interests); art. 29, cl. 2 (property rights are defined "in conformity with the public welfare").

27. The first legal sexual reassignment surgery performed in Japan occurred in 1998. Matsumoto, *supra* note 2; *see also infra* Part IV.

28. *Court Rejects Transsexual's Demand to Alter Gender in Register,* JAPAN ECONOMIC NEWSWIRE, Jan. 12, 2003 [hereinafter *Court Rejects Transsexual's Demand*].

29. Shimizu, *supra* note 3.

30. *Court Rejects Transsexual's Demand, supra* note 28.

31. *Court Vetoes Gender Change on Family Register, supra* note 14.

32. *Family Court Dismisses Suit over Former Female's Registry,* JAPAN TIMES, Aug. 30, 2002. Just two months prior, the Tokyo District Court sanctioned Shobunsha Publications for dismissing an openly transgendered employee, a ruling that temporarily encouraged plaintiffs in the family registry cases. *Japan Activists Hail Ruling on Transgender Sacking,* REUTERS, June 24, 2002, *available at* http://www.vachss.com/help_text/archive/activists_hail.html.

33. Keiji Hirano, *Transsexuals, Supporters Work for Public Understanding,* JAPAN TODAY, Feb. 1, 2003, *available at* http://groups.yahoo.com/group/transgendernews/message/2210.

34. Shimizu, *supra* note 3.

35. Matsumoto, *supra* note 2. In 1969, a Tokyo gynecologist was criminally sentenced for performing three sexual reassignment surgeries in what has become known as the "Blue Boy Scandal." The physician was charged with a violation of Article 28 of the Eugenics Protection Law, which provides that the use of X-rays to incapacitate the reproductive functioning of a patient is prohibited without an "appropriate reason." Article 34 imposes a maximum prison term of one year or a maximum fine of 500,000 [yen] (approx. US $ 4,700) for violations of Article 28. Shimizu, *supra* note 3.

36. AM. PSYCHIATRIC ASS'N, DIAGNOSTIC AND STATISTICAL MANUAL OF MENTAL DISORDERS (1994).

37. WORLD HEALTH ORG., INTERNATIONAL STATISTICAL CLASSIFICATION OF DISEASES AND RELATED HEALTH PROBLEMS, (10th rev., 1992) [hereinafter ICD-10].

38. AM. PSYCHIATRIC ASS'N, DIAGNOSTIC AND STATISTICAL MANUAL OF MENTAL DISORDERS (4th ed., text rev. 2000) [hereinafter DSM-IV-TR].

39. BORNSTEIN, *supra* note 15, at 119 ("Transsexuals ... are heavily invested in maintaining their status as 'diseased' people [because] demedicalization ... would further limit surgery ... and so prohibit insurance companies from footing the bill").

40. DSM-IV-TR, *supra* note 38.

41. Guidelines are as described in Matsumoto, *supra* note 2.

42. Keiji Hirano, *Transsexual to Lecture at Medical School*, KYODO NEWS INT'L, Apr. 15, 2002, *available at* LEXIS, News Library, Japan Science Scan.

43. Matsumoto, *supra* note 2.

44. *New Law Allows Japanese to Officially Change Sex*, MAINICHI DAILY NEWS, July 10, 2003, *available at* 2003 WL 77107530.

45. *Id.*

46. *Id.*

47. *Id.*

48. Shimizu, *supra* note 3.

49. *Id.* Such assessment would include the child(ren)'s age(s), custody arrangements, and family lifestyle.

50. *Id.*

51. *Transsexual's Change Recognized,* AP, July 29, 2004, http://thewe.cc/contents/more/archive2004/july/transsexual_change_recognized.htm. At the time of the ruling, fifteen applications to amend *koseki* records were pending nationwide. *Id.*

52. *Id.*

53. ANNE FAUSTO-STERLING, SEXING THE BODY 34 (2000) ("Historically, hermaphrodites were often regarded as rebellious, disruptive, or even fraudulent").

54. Landis, *supra* note 13, at 75-76.

55. Universal Declaration of Human Rights, G.A. Res. 217A at 71, U.N. GAOR, 3d Sess., 1st plen. mtg., U.N. Doc. A/810 (Dec. 12, 1948) [hereinafter UDHR].

56. Committee on Economic, Social and Cultural Rights, *General Comment 14: The Right to the Highest Attainable Standard of Health (Art. 12),* ¶ 8, U.N. Doc. HRI/GEN/1/Rev. 6 (2003).

57. Human Rights Committee, *General Comment 28: Equality of Rights Between Men and Women,* ¶ 27, U.N. Doc. HRI/GEN/1/Rev. 5 (2001); *see also infra* Part IV(A)(discussing parallels between SRS and genital mutilation). *See also* UDHR, *supra* note 55, arts. 16.1, 16.3 (providing that all persons have the right to "found a family" and that families are entitled to protection).

58. CEDAW, Dec. 18, 1979, 1249 U.N.T.S. 13, art. 16.1(e); *see also Programme of Action of the International Conference on Population and Development,* Cairo, Egypt, Sept. 5-13, 1994, art. 72, U.N. Doc. A/CONF.171/13/Rev. 1 (1995).

59. 1 KOJIKI (RECORDS OF ANCIENT MATTERS), *Preface* (Basil Hall Chamberlain trans., 1882).

60. *See, e.g.,* Corbett v. Corbett, 2 All E.R. 33, 47 (P.1970)(holding birth sex is "true sex"); Littleton v. Prange, 9 S.W.3d 223, 230 (Tex. App. 1999), *cert. denied,* 69 U.S.L.W. 3229 (Oct. 2, 2000)(No. 00-25)(a postoperative male-to-female having "no womb, cervix or ovaries" and retaining "male chromosomes" cannot be a woman under the law).

61. Cynthia W. Crysdale, *Revisioning Natural Law: From the Classicist Paradigm to Emergent Probability*, 56 THEOLOGICAL STUD. 464, 476 (1995).

62. *Cf.* FAUSTO-STERLING, *supra* note 53 at 21 ("Sexuality is a somatic fact *created* by a cultural effect.")(emphasis in original).

63. 27 KEISHU 265 (Sup. Ct., G.B. 1973).

64. Corbett v. Corbett, 2 All E.R. 33, 48 (P. 1970).

65. *Id.* at 33.

66. *See, e.g.,* Michael M. v. Super. Ct. of Sonoma County, 450 U.S. 464, 469-70 (1981).

67. Kazuyoshi Kawasaka, *Living with GID,* Apr. 1, 2004, Art. ID 0312003, International Christian University Center for Gender Studies (on file with author).

68. *Id.*

69. Shimizu, *supra* note 3.

70. Landis, *supra* note 13, at 77-83.

71. Kenneth L. Port, *The Japanese International Law "Revolution": International Human Rights and Its Impact on Japan,* 28 STAN. J. INT'L. L. 139, 154 (1991); Yuji Iwasawa, *Legal Treatment of Koreans in Japan: The Impact of International Human Rights Law on Japanese Law,* 8 HUM. RTS. Q. 131, 135, 142 n.54 (1986).

72. *International Bill of Gender Rights,* in 1996 PROC. FROM THE FIFTH INT'L CONF. ON TRANSGENDER LAW & EMP. POL'Y 7-9.

# X

## *TRANS-ORIENTED PRACTICES, POLICIES, AND SOCIAL CHANGE*

# 46

# "We Won't Know Who You Are"

Contesting Sex Designations in New York City Birth Certificates

PAISLEY CURRAH AND LISA JEAN MOORE

ONE SIMPLE WAY OF READING THIS CHAPTER is as a retrospective narrative account of how New York City has responded to calls to permit trans people to change the gender designation on their birth certificates from 1965 onwards. But Paisley Currah and Lisa Jean Moore have a more complicated political agenda than merely recounting a chronology of historical events; their analytical focus is the legal struggle to redefine sex as a form of self-identification rather than as a genital status. Currah, a transgender legal studies scholar and political scientist, and Moore, a science studies scholar of medicine and biotechnology, were involved in efforts to change the practices of amending birth certificates in New York City in the 2000s. In addition to drawing on the archival record of previous efforts along these lines, the authors also draw on Currah's meeting notes and interviews with other advocates. The resulting dissection of the campaign to change birth certification in NYC shows how gender regulation fits into the biopolitical regulation of the security state. As in countless similar struggles with state administrative bodies, trans advocates in New York clashed with city officials over what constituted "permanence." For officials, genital surgery was a guarantee of the transsexual individual's stability in a chosen gender. Transgender advocates, meanwhile, sought to remove the requirement of reassignment surgery and argued that official sex designation should be changed in line with an individual's self-definition. Ultimately, the effort to change the New York City code failed—and in fact, in the wake of 9/11 state securitization, control over administrative gender markers on documents in many states was made even more restrictive. Currah and Moore show how, as the gendering of bodies reaches a crisis-point, the state seeks to impose stability and stasis in order to maintain legal control.

## DOCUMENTING SEX

How do state agencies link citizens with their birth certificates? If the state is produced through attempting to "render things ... immobile" (Foucault 2007, 256), how is a mutating, trans-sexed body to be fixed, kept in place, and securely moored to the document that purports to describe its subject? What happens when state actors, insisting on the immutability of sexed bodies and their stable alignment to gender identities, are confronted with those whose bodies and gender identities fail to conform to gender expectations? What recurring tropes of sex/gender get invoked to re-anchor these troublesomely sexed subjects? This article examines the regulatory responses of one state actor—the City of New York—to individuals who petition to change the sex classification on their birth certificates.[1]

The identification of citizens or subjects is as vital a function of modern statehood as establishing and policing territorial borders. Indeed, for J. G. Fichte, ensuring "each citizen shall be at all times and places… recognized as this or that particular person" constitutes "the chief principle of a well-regulated police state" (Caplan 2001, 49). The advent of larger, centralized, modern state formations puts greater distances between magistrates and citizens, creating the need for standardized systems for identifying and individuating populations, making citizens legible (Scott 1998). On the birth certificate, sex designation, along with date and location of birth and parentage (when known), functions as an essential classificatory aspect of the "accurate description" meant to establish a permanent correspondence "between a person and a set of signs" (Caplan 2001, 50). This link could be dismissed as a fiction without foundation were it not maintained through the force of law. Although the taxonomies used to classify individuals as of *this* or *that* type (race, sex, national origin, for example) may shift as newer accounts of social difference displace earlier reigning disciplinary knowledges and ontological cartographies, the legitimacy of the traditional "police powers" of the state to establish classifications remains intact.[2]

The ideas associated with what ethnomethodologist Harold Garfinkel labeled the "natural attitude" about sex give sex its cultural credibility as a biometric identifier on identity documents (Garfinkel 2006). For Garfinkel, and for most theorists of gender who have built on his work in the forty years since it first appeared, what we now call gender (but what he referred to as "sex status") is a "managed achievement"—for everyone, not just for transsexuals— produced through social interactions (Garfinkel 2006, 59; West and Zimmerman 1987). […]

The debates that took place between 1965 and 2006 in New York City about the appropriate sex designation on the birth certificates of transsexual people reprise larger assumptions about state administration of the link between genitals and gender identities, and, analogously, between individuals and identity documents. These negotiations over sex definition exemplify the hegemony of the "natural attitude" in the area of sex classification on birth certificates. In the first iteration, in 1965, a transsexual woman attempted to displace the notion that to be classified as female, one must have been born female (and *vice versa*) by arguing that that sexual reassignment surgery should justify a new sex marker. Policymakers were not at all receptive to that position—at the time. Four decades later, transgender rights' advocates attempted again to displace the natural attitude. This time, however, they pushed the argument even further: they suggested that gender identity, rather than (surgically modified) genitals, be the basis for sex re-classification. Unsurprisingly, this argument ultimately failed.

Importantly, in the New York City case, transgender individuals who tried to change the criteria for sex designation on birth certificates were not resisting the imposition of a binary sex/gender frame onto their bodies and identities, which is one aspect of the natural attitude. They were simply attempting to argue that the criteria on which the classification is based should be changed, that they did not reflect current "expert" knowledges, that a misidentification had taken place. The challenge was not articulated as, "By what right does this state agency tell me I am a man or a woman?" Or, "The relationship between what you think is the body's biological sex and gender is not fixed, it's imposed through social norms." Instead, the claim deployed arguments that seem to re-naturalize gender as a legal category—albeit one based on gender identity rather than the body: "I was assigned male at birth but I am now a woman. Get it right." Or, "I was born female but now I am a man. Fix that on my ID, please." The attempt by trans advocates to amend the criteria for legal sex designations resonates with the inescapably liberal quest to be recognized as possessors of the personal attributes we deem central to our selves. For transgender women, recognition means being "Ma'amed" instead of "Sir'ed," having an "F" rather than an "M" on identity papers, and being housed in women's wings in hospitals, residential homes, and prisons.

The pursuit of recognition within a system governed by the logic of the sex binary is disappointing to some in women's, gender, and queer studies (Hausman 1995; Irving 2008). Indeed, as Cressida

Heyes points out, "Whether appropriated to bolster queer theoretical claims, represented as the acid test of constructionism, or attacked for suspect political commitments, transgender has been colonized as a feminist theoretical testing ground" (Heyes 2003, 1098). In the last twenty years, as most of the transgender movement in the United States moved toward a politics of recognition, in the academy much of gender and sexuality studies tacked toward a different horizon, producing trenchant critiques of gender essentialist moves of any sort, mappings of historical formations of disciplinary knowledge regimes across a range of institutions, and close examinations of the processes of normalization and subjectification through which neoliberal institutions create consumers, workers, and citizens (Fraser 1997). [...] A transgender rights framework demanding inclusion and recognition within the institutions, norms, and arrangements structured around gender could be described, if it has not been already, as "trans-normative." Conversely, transgender people fighting "back against the disciplining of their lives" are celebrated as gender revolutionaries who, by implication, might shake and crack the foundations of the disciplinary edifices that structure everyone's legal and normative genders (Irving 2008, 38).

In the introduction to *The Transgender Studies Reader*, Susan Stryker makes a distinction between "the study of transgender phenomena" and the new critical project of "transgender studies." The latter approach ensures that "no voice in the dialog should have the privilege of masking the particularities and specificities of its own speaking position, through which it may claim a false universality or authority" (Stryker 2006, 12). We suggest that evaluating transgender political engagements only *vis-à-vis* feminist or queer commitments can inadvertently normalize existing gender arrangements. One effect of positioning "trans" as the revolutionary subject occupying the liminal spaces at the extremes of gender is the implication that there is a class of non-revolutionary, gender-conforming subjects who *are* correctly interpellated by the gender regime. Hailing *trans*-gender individuals for resisting the classifications of M or F implies that there is no need for non-trans people to oppose the classifications, to protest the imposition of these classifications on their identity documents by burning them. In this process, trans as "revolutionary" slips back into trans as a "special case." Ironically, this trans "exceptionalism" mirrors the approach of state bureaucrats who, when presented with the anomaly of "sex changes," work to come up with a response to a problem they see as limited to a very small class of people. Receding into the background and left largely unexamined, once again, is the attempt to secure the relationship among any bodies, identities, and documents—even those of the unmarked class of the gender normative—through anything but the force of law.

[...] Instead of asking what transgender activism does to/for gender, we invert the usual litmus test and center the effects of the current gender regime on trans people. For trans people, having one's legal sex misclassified carries with it material effects. Birth certificates, for example, are not simply mechanisms for managing populations and the state enforcement of obligations, like taxation or conscription, on individuals; they also create recognition for the distribution of resources from the state to individuals, such as voting, social security, Medicaid, marriage rights, and welfare benefits. [...] Certainly, the birth certificate negotiations showcase fascinating moments of incommensurability among popular, medical, bureaucratic, and advocacy notions about the etiology of sex, its relation to gender identity, the appropriate criteria to use to authenticate gender identity, and so on. But, from the perspective of transgender subjects and others interested in problems of documenting identity, the arguments of officials opposing the notion of gender transitivity are at least of equal importance to the narratives about sex and gender deployed. Paying attention to the governing logics, the changing administrative mandates, the specific configurations of the resistance to changes of sex classification—in this case, the shift from viewing transsexuals as "frauds" in 1965 to basing official recognition of gender transition around the notion of "permanence" in 2005—helps us to understand more about the specific processes of "bioregulation by the state" (Foucault 2003, 250). This sort of research, we hope, can inform researchers and advocates working to find other points of fissure in the micro powers of modern regulatory apparatuses.

In the sections that follow, we examine the negotiations over the legal definition of sex on birth certificates in New York City that took place in 1965–66 and 2002–06. (New York City, for historical reasons, is a "birth registration area" separate from New York State.) During this process, city officials, medical professionals from various fields, and, eventually, transgender advocates produced divergent narratives about the biological basis and measurement of sex, the social and legal consequences of maintaining the status quo, and the perceived risks of changing the sex designation on birth certificates. Our analysis is based on participant observation, ethnography, field notes, in-depth interviews, and content analysis. By triangulating data sources about birth certificates, including scientific texts, health and social policy recommendations, interviews, official meeting minutes, fieldwork, case law, and historical documents, we established various points of analytic comparison to explore multiple concepts about sex classification on birth certificates in different social, medical, and legal contexts (Glaser and Strauss 1967; Strauss and Corbin 1994).

One of the co-authors of this article, Paisley Currah, has been involved in this advocacy since November of 2002, and participated in the most recent round of policy negotiations in the role of an "expert advocate." In co-authoring this article, he is also situated as a researcher of the larger norms at play in the policy reform process. His role as an advocate in the policy reform process enables us to examine these questions not just from the outsider perspective of researchers, but also from the insider perspective of a community member. Our observations are based on Currah's notes from earlier meetings and the official committee meetings, official meeting minutes of the Transgender Advisory Committee (TAC), his retrospective auto-ethnography, interviews with advocates, legal documents, and archival research.[3]

## PROTECTING THE PUBLIC FROM "FRAUD"

In 1965, a transsexual woman asked the City of New York to issue her a new birth certificate identifying her as female. "Anonymous," as she was later described in court documents, had done everything she thought was needed to function socially as a woman: she had had her gender identity affirmed by a medical professional, she had passed the "real-life" test of living as a woman, she had undergone sex reassignment surgery, and she had begun a lifelong course of feminizing hormones (*Anonymous v. Weiner* 1966). But state-issued identity documents still designated Anonymous as male. The "M" gender marker, which revealed her history as a transsexual person to anyone who attempted to authenticate her identity using the description in the document, opened up the possibility that her identity as a woman would be challenged, and thus undermined her ability to function legally and socially as a woman. As historian Joanne Meyerowitz recounts in her comprehensive history of transsexuality in the United States, the Department of Health had previously granted similar requests to three others (Meyerowitz 2002, 243). With Anonymous's request, however, the New York City Commissioner of Health, Dr. George James, decided to look for some guidance. He formally requested the New York Academy of Medicine's Committee on Public Health to "convene a group, including neurologists, gynecologists, endocrinologists, and psychiatrists" to consider the "enormous psychological, legal, and biological implications" of granting these petitions and to advise the DOH on whether or not it should revise its policy (James 1965). After three meetings, some legal research, and the impassioned pleas of transsexual medical advocate Dr. Harry Benjamin, the committee concluded in its 1965 report that "the desire of concealment of a change of sex by the transsexual is outweighed by the public interest for protection against fraud" (New York Academy of Medicine 1966).

The official minutes of the meetings are replete with examples of committee members' concerns about fraud. One doctor paraphrased the New York Penal Code at the time, "nobody is allowed to dress in such a way as to hide his true identity," and noted that a number of "transvestites" had been jailed under that status. Indeed, such statutes were still ubiquitous at the time (Hunter, Joslin, and McGowan 2004; Sears 2008.) In addition, the issue of marriage was often raised during these discussions of fraud. The first draft of the committee's report listed as one public interest "the protection of a prospective spouse against fraud." New birth certificates, the committee was told by a federal official, could be used to get benefits reserved for one gender, or escape obligations for the other (Council 1965).

The committee did consider options to legally recognize the "new sex" of these people—for example, adding a codicil to the birth certificate stating "Now known as female." (There was no discussion of the existence of female-to-male transsexual people.) But, in the end, they concluded that there was no mechanism "not injurious to the public" that would also "make the transsexual happy." The committee members concluded, "for the protection of the general public, [one's status as a transsexual] should be known." As an illustration of this public interest, one doctor cited the case of "a man who marries one of these persons with the expectation of having a family" (New York Academy of Medicine Subcommittee on Birth Certificates 1965).

The fear of fraud makes obvious the entrenched belief on the parts of the medical experts, government officials, and the non-transsexual public that one cannot change one's sex, only its "outward appearance." While the birth sex of infants is almost always assigned based on a visual check of external genitalia, the criterion, according to the committee, should be different for those who have their genitalia surgically altered later in life: they decided that while "ostensibly female," "male-to-female transsexuals are still chromosomally males" (New York Academy of Medicine 1966). Of course, it is precisely because some transsexual women and men can pass in their new gender, can traverse many social, economic, even intimate landscapes as "the other sex," that authorities believe "the public" must be protected from fraud. And the public was safeguarded when the city held that the birth sex of transsexual men and women born in New York City remain on the birth certificate.

The recurring worry in these committee minutes about enabling fraud— producing what one committee member referred to as an "illegal document"— reflects anxiety about aiding transsexuals in concealing their "true identity" from the public. Sociologist Erving Goffman describes the presentation of self to others as having a "promissory character" (Goffman 1959, 2). "The impressions that the others give tend to be treated as claims and promises they have implicitly made, and claims and promises tend to have a moral character" (249). In this sense, birth certificates function as a sort of promissory document not only about an individual's body, but also about the particular history of that body. What is in fact social gender is assumed to guarantee a correspondence between one's present body, its past, and the gender presentation one puts out in the world. The accusation of fraud is made coherent by the "natural attitude" notion, dominant at the time, that framed the body's sexed status as fixed at birth: because the body can't actually ever become the other "sex" physically, any suggestion or performance of the opposite gender is a lie. As Garfinkel pointed out in 1967, "no legitimate path exists between the statuses of male and female" (Garfinkel 2006, 59). Garfinkel's writing suggests that at least since the 1960s, there was already suspicion from the general public ("normals") surrounding changing the birth certificate because of the assumption that sex status is natural, original, and immutable.

While notions of "permanence" rise to the fore in contemporary discussions of sex or gender designation, fraud never entirely disappears from the list of articulated concerns. The 1965 committee report, published in the New York Academy of Medicine's Bulletin in 1966, was cited many times, at least until 2002, by judges in New York State and elsewhere in cases rejecting transgender people's claims for legal sex reclassification. Indeed, as recently as 2000, the highest court in Texas asked, in a sex designation case, "can a physician change the gender of a person with a scalpel, drugs and counseling, or is a person's gender immutably fixed by our Creator at birth?" The court concluded that "there are some things we cannot will into being. They just are" (*Littleton v. Prange* 1999, 222, 224, 231). Similarly, the "transsexual panic" defense invoked in cases where transsexual people are attacked or murdered plays on the same logic of fraud: defense lawyers ask juries to identify with their clients, who were shocked to discover the person they were with was transsexual at the moment of sexual intimacy, or perhaps later (Bettcher, this volume; Craig 2007). For example, in her article about the 2002 murder of Gwen Araujo, Talie Mae Bettcher shows how the logic of "fraud," made coherent by the "natural attitude," is deployed in trans-panic defenses. For "normals," genitalia play the role of "concealed truth" about a person's sex: in contrast to gender presentation, "the sexed body constitutes the hidden, sexual reality" (Bettcher, this volume).

## THE 1971 INTERREGNUM: CERTIFICATES WITHOUT SEX

In 1971, six years after the New York Academy of Medicine presented its report to the Commissioner of Health, the New York City policy was somewhat reformed. Instead of denying the petitions of transsexual men and women and leaving them with a key identity document that listed their birth sex, the city would issue new birth certificates with *no* sex designation: the box for sex was simply eliminated. To be eligible for this "no-sex" certificate, transsexual men and women had to prove they had undergone "convertive" genital surgery, interpreted by the Department of Vital Statistics as phalloplasty or vaginoplasty. Petitioners had to supply a "detailed surgical operative record," a report from a physician detailing a post-operative exam, and a psychiatric exam. The reissued certificates included the following reference: "This certificate is filed pursuant to subsection 5 of subsection (a) of Section 207.05 of the Health Code of the City of New York."

The new certificates thus had two markers revealing the individual's status as transsexual. First, having no box for a sex designation omits a fundamental vital statistic that reviewers of birth certificates—potential employers, the Social Security Administration, drivers' license bureaus, other government agencies and social-service providers—might be looking for, especially when confronted with someone whose appearance or other characteristics might already suggest some kind of gender non-conformity. Second, if one looked up the particular subsection of the Health Code referred to on the amended certificates, one would learn that "The name of the person has been changed pursuant to a court order and proof satisfactory to the Department has been submitted that such person has undergone convertive surgery" (New York City Health Code 1971). While many laypeople might not understand the significance of these markers of a transsexual history, those in the business of document verification, of *re-cognizing* citizens, would. Ironically, deleting this box in some ways makes legal sex more visible through its highly marked absence.

## THE THIRD ITERATION: MANDATING PERMANENCE

The next phase of these negotiations over the legal definition of sex began in 2002 and ended in 2006. This iteration is marked by a significant shift: from the outset, state officials most directly involved in policy-making and all of the medical authorities asked to lend their expertise during negotiations agreed that individuals should be able to change the sex designation on the birth certificate.

Much had changed since the policy iterations of 1965 and 1971. By 2002, a new social movement coalescing under the rubric "transgender" had emerged (Valentine 2007). Annual conferences, newsletters, magazines, advocacy groups, and the Internet had done much to create and solidify trans communities in the United States and beyond (Denny 2006). Most gay, lesbian, and bisexual groups had amended their mission statements to include "transgender" or "gender identity." Media representations of transgender people were beginning to shift from depictions of shock, revulsion, and horror in films such as the *Crying Game* to more sympathetic renderings, such as the films *Normal* and *Boys Don't Cry*. Medical professionals specializing in transgender health had formed an organization to recommend standards of care. Cases involving transgender issues were beginning to have positive outcomes in the courts. A handful of states and dozens of municipalities had banned discrimination against transgender people, including New York City in 2002 (Transgender Law and Policy Institute 2008).

In the area of identity documents, the State Department, the Social Security Administration, and other federal agencies had procedures in place for changing sex designation. By 2002, most states, including New York, had made it possible for transgender people to change their sex on driver's licenses. Although New York City's 1971 policy of issuing new birth certificates with no sex designation had been one of the most liberal in the United States at the time, by 2002 it was very much out of date. With the exception of Idaho, Ohio, and Tennessee, all other jurisdictions in the United States allowed change of sex on the birth certificate. New York City officials, who envisioned the city as a model of progressive social policies in other areas, indicated they were embarrassed that the city was now an outlier on the repressive end of the identity-document spectrum.

In November 2002, a coalition of fourteen organizations "concerned with the civil rights of transgender New Yorkers" sent a letter to the Commissioner of the New York City Department of Health and Mental Hygiene (NYC DHMH). The coalition requested that the no-sex birth-certificate policy be reformed, and that the "voices of those individuals and organizations who are most concerned with this issue" be involved with the policy revision process. Eventually, after two years of preliminary meetings, in December 2004, the NYC DHMH formed the TAC, which met four times between February and May of 2005. Unlike the 1965 subcommittee that was convened by the New York Academy of Medicine, this committee included members of the transgender community. In addition, all of the medical professionals enlisted to serve had experience in treating transgender people, and some were seen as strong allies of the transgender community.

The prevailing view during the 1965 negotiations had been that transsexual people were gender frauds *per se*, that one could never change one's legal sex designation. During the 2002–06 negotiations, the discussions centered on establishing criteria to distinguish those who were temporarily living in the other gender from those whose transition was "permanent and irreversible" (NYC DHMH 2005). The crux of the struggle between transgender advocates and public officials turned on which particular criteria would be appropriate indicia of permanence. Officials initially indicated that the permanence of a transsexual individual's gender identity could be guaranteed only by particular types of genital surgery—vaginoplasty for transgender women, phalloplasty for transgender men. A central component of Garfinkel's "natural attitude" was the belief that individuals "always have been, and always will be" either male or female (Garfinkel 2006, 62). The particular bureaucratic imperative to ensure a permanent change that characterized these negotiations reflects the continued hegemony of this constellation of beliefs—that one "always will be" either male or female. But the notion that one's sex could be re-classified and the permanence of that change assured by genital surgery also shows the evolution and elasticity of the concept: as the "always has been" requisite (pointing to the past) drops out of the bureaucratic mandate for sex classification, but the "always will be" (guaranteeing the future) remains.

For transgender advocates, however, requiring surgery to guarantee permanence belied current models in both transgender health care and in transgender communities' understanding of gender identity. For the officials, sex is determined by the body, and particular surgical body modifications guarantee permanence; for the advocates, in line with transgender communities' views, gender is determined by one's gender identity, and one's legal sex designation should be based on gender identity. As expressed in the International Bill of Gender Rights, one of the foundational documents of transgender activism in the United States, it "is fundamental that individuals have the right to define, and to redefine as their lives unfold, their own gender identities, without regard to chromosomal sex, genitalia, assigned birth sex, or initial gender role" (International Bill of Gender Rights 2006, 328).

Before the first meeting of the committee, the transgender community advocates on the committee, met to strategize ideal and realistic outcomes. Their ideal policy would be to extend the current (1971) policy—no sex marker—to everyone's birth certificates, as an initial step toward getting the state out of the business of defining sex. They decided not to raise this idea since it could have been read by others as naïve, radical, or even unintelligible, and risk leaving the transgender advocates outside the realm of pragmatic policy reform. Two of the advocates were attorneys from a transgender legal service organization, which had many clients who desperately needed birth certificates authenticating their new gender. Moreover, the charge of the committee was to revise the "change-of-sex" policy; the advocates understood that sex would remain in use as a biometric identifier in the near future. In addition, at the time, New York State courts were hearing challenges to the effective ban on same-sex marriage. Officials perhaps understood, though they never stated it outright, that the ban on same-sex marriage depended on the state's power to make sex classifications.[4]

From the advocates' perspective, the next best policy would be to allow individuals to change their birth certificates by affirming their new gender identity in a statement. Officials' preoccupation with permanence, however, made it seem unlikely that individuals could change their legal sex designation without the involvement of specialized experts to "attest" to the permanence of the transition. The most realistic best outcome, advocates decided, would be to eliminate the requirement for "convertive" surgery—to have, in fact, no requirements for body modification of any kind but to have the petition supported by medical experts. Thus, the advocates came to the table with the proposal that "individuals seeking change of sex designation provide a letter from a medical doctor stating that appropriate medical treatment, as medically determined for the individual patient, has been undertaken to ensure that the transition is permanent" (Sylvia Rivera Law Project and Transgender Law and Policy Institute 2003). Advocates understood, but did not emphasize to officials, that many transgender health care specialists would define "*appropriate* medical treatment" to include no hormones or surgery for some individuals.

The idea that the new requirements should ensure that the sex reclassification was permanent dominated preliminary meetings and every meeting of the official TAC. For example, Dr. Schwartz said the Commissioner of Health wanted assurances of permanence and that there would be "no further changes" to the individual. Schwartz stated he was "concerned about people changing their minds about their transitions" and wanted to know "how do we make sure it is really permanent?" The NYC DHMH bureaucrats summed up their concern in the committee's first official meeting by stating, "What is a reasonable minimum standard an individual should have to meet to make a permanent change in one's gender?" A permanent transition, for the officials, initially and ultimately, was one marked by genital surgery. One urologist pointed out, "on the issue of permanence, it can only be met if the source of the opposite hormone were removed, with an orchidectomy or hysterectomy." (Suggesting that these two surgeries could be comparable; however, led to some discomfort in the room on the part of at least one official. The NYC DHMH attorney on the committee stridently pointed out that "having a hysterectomy is not the same thing as having your testicles removed.") Another urologist said that individuals could demonstrate their "commitment to their new gender role" only with an "anatomical change."

The lack of a monolithic approach to the problem on the part of those representing different medical disciplines should not be surprising. As Jacob Hale suggests, expert discourses "do not agree entirely with the 'natural attitude' toward gender, nor with one another" (Hale 1996, 103). Still, he notes, "specialized discourses about gender are by no means immune from the influence of the 'natural attitude' either. Rather, they are shaped by the desire to hold as much, or the most crucial elements, of the 'natural attitude' in place, insofar as this is consistent with their specialized aims; indeed, their specialized aims may, sometimes, take less precedence than upholding some aspect of the 'natural attitude'" (103). While the totality of medical disciplinary knowledges about the sexed and gendered body lacks perfect coherence—the body in some sense becomes a contested terrain of meaning-making between disciplines— traditional beliefs about sexual dimorphism and permanence ultimately continue to hold sway in all these fields.

Establishing a surgical standard would effectively ban the majority of people who wanted to change their legal sex classification from doing so. Most people who transition do not have either of the genital surgeries required by the 1971 policy. One recent study found that 97% of transgender men do not have phalloplasty (Newfield et al. 2006); the number of transgender women who have vaginoplasty is unclear, but reports from social-service providers suggest that the majority of transgender women have not had vaginoplasties. As advocates argued in a memo sent to the NYC DHMH during initial negotiations over the policy, "perhaps the single most erroneous misconception is that sex reassignment consists of a single 'sex-change' operation'" (Sylvia Rivera and Transgender Law and Policy Institute 2003). While transgender people who have phalloplasty or vaginoplasty are also likely to modify their bodies through hormones (testosterone for transgender men, estrogen/progesterone for transgender women), many people transition using only hormones and/or non-genital surgeries (such as double mastectomies for transgender men, breast implants for transgender women). Others transition and live full time in their new genders without any body modification at all. Even for those who would like to have genital surgery, making it a prerequisite for a birth-certificate change imposes an impossible barrier for many.

The surgery requirement would make legal sex—for transgender people, at least—a privileged category legally mediated by one's class status. And for much of the negotiations, the common-sense notion that the body's visual anatomical markers (sexed genitals, in this case) should be the basis for sex definition seemed impenetrable to arguments that a surgical criterion would mean, in effect, that one's legal sex would be dependent on one's location in the social structure. Bluntly put, only by purchasing the anatomical markers ($30,000–$50,000) meant to guarantee permanence could a transgender person meet the metric for legal sex re-classification. The public officials' stated anxiety about gender permanence, then, trumped any concern about the injustice of denying amended birth certificates to the majority of transgender people who could not afford genital surgery. Advocates were well aware of the official resistance to arguments based on class. According to Dean Spade, one of the advocates involved, "Our strategy was to remove the class discussion from the table because the committee would not care about it." To get the policy they wanted, advocates chose to go with a "pro medical authority argument" (interview with Dean Spade, March 23, 2006).

The fundamental strategy of advocates, based on interviews and our analysis of the data, was to "de-medicalize" the policy and, ironically, to rely on the authority of medical experts to do so. They marshaled transgender health-care authorities to acknowledge the myriad procedures and varying rates of success for surgical procedures. At one point, they submitted a memo from a transgender medical doctor listing thirty-one surgical procedures to dispel the "one-surgery" myth. Transgender health-care advocates on the committee argued repeatedly that transgender health care is highly individualized, that there are many routes to transition, and that a requirement for genital surgery was "excessive" since the majority of transgender people do not have it (NYC DHMH 2005). The lone psychiatrist on the committee, for example, argued that the committee would never be able to agree on "what degree of surgery, hormones, and/or anatomical changes would serve as a standard." He stressed that "gender reassignment is not simply based on anatomical changes, but how that person views him/herself and asserts him or herself publicly" (NYC DHMH 2005).

Advocates invoked medical authorities to show that "permanence" could be attained in social relationships without medical intervention. They pointed to recent trends in non-discrimination laws to define gender as much broader than anatomical sex. In Boston, for example, women's facilities, such as bathrooms, showers, and locker rooms, are open to anyone whose "gender identity publicly and exclusively expressed" was female, and *vice versa* for men (Transgender Law and Policy Institute 2008). Schwartz countered that one could not compare standards for access to public restrooms with standards for changes to vital records. "It's a very big deal to change a fact of birth," the NYC DHMH's counsel added (NYC DHMH 2005). Advocates also pointed to the New York State policy on changing sex on driver's licenses, which requires a statement from the physician, psychologist, or psychiatrist certifying that "one gender predominates over the other and the licensee in question is either a male or female." Schwartz countered that "predominates is not enough" (NYC DHMH 2005). What the officials very much wanted was some sort of official "certification" that the change was "permanent and irreversible."

With the exception of the two urologists on the committee, whose medical practices included performing sex reassignment surgeries, all the other medical people pointed out that "permanent" and "irreversible" were concepts that didn't make sense from a medical perspective (NYC DHMH 2005). Most types of body modification can be reversed: individuals can begin a course of feminizing or masculinizing hormones, stop taking them, start taking them again later. In theory, and in very rare cases in actuality, individuals can have a second set of sex reassignment surgeries. Surgery, then, does not guarantee a permanent commitment to a gender identity. But the bureaucratic mandate that particular sex classifications correspond with the corporeal reality of particular genital configurations eventually outweighed the medical arguments.

## "ARE YOU PEOPLE OUT OF YOUR MINDS?": BREEDER DOCUMENTS AND TERRORISTS

Some identity documents have more value in producing identity than others. In the lexicon of vital statistics discourse, the birth certificate is referred to as a "breeder document," a primary identity paper that can be used to authenticate individual identity when applying for other identity documents (NYC DHMH 2005). Its descriptions of the sex and birth history of the infant are understood as fixed pieces of data. Unlike the aspects of identity that are recognizably mutable—name, appearance, ability, for example—the operative principle in vital statistics is that sex, like place of birth and parentage, is a very reliable metric of identification because it is static over one's life course. A birth certificate, then, functions both as a documentary record of a static historical fact and as a primary document authenticating the identity of a person. With those who "change their sex," the dual function of the birth certificate comes into conflict.

The officials' concern with permanence and irreversibility reflected the imperative to render the citizenry, a collection of "identifiable, corporeal bodies," easily legible (Ngai 2004, 36). At the first meeting of the TAC, Schwartz enunciated his concern about linking a transgender "x" to a birth certificate by asserting, "but then we won't know who you are." Changing the definition of sex could loosen too much the link between an individual and the identity document that stands for that individual administratively. This bureaucratic fear of "not knowing" a citizen evokes a central problem of modern statehood, supposedly exacerbated in a post-9/11 era. Indeed, Schwartz proceeded to make a short speech in which he stressed the birth certificate's role as a "breeder document" (NYC DHMH 2005). Pointedly, he cited the 9/11 Commission Report, which recommended new regulations regarding the creation, appearance, and security of birth certificates and other identity documents.

The worry about making identity fraud easier was explicitly connected to security concerns and preventing individuals intent on attacking the United States from obtaining identity documents that mask their true identity. One medical expert on the committee referred to this rationale as the "terrorist straw man" argument—the idea that the policy should not be changed because it might aid terrorists. (Advocates found ludicrous the notion that one might petition the city to change the sex classification on their birth certificate as a way to go underground. A process that mandates one expose one's body and psyche to at least two different medical professionals, who will then write up detailed medical and psychological histories; go to court to change one's name; advertise this name change in a newspaper; and submit all this supporting evidence, including current identity documents, for the review of at least two levels of bureaucracy hardly constitutes a sound plan for avoiding public scrutiny.)

Eventually, the repetition of arguments about the unreliability of genital surgery as a guarantor of permanence convinced the officials on the committee to change the criteria for sex definition. In July of 2005, the committee recommended that the NYC DHMH "recognize… medical and mental health providers most knowledgeable about an individual's transgender health[, who] should determine whether an individual is living fully in the acquired gender." The proposed policy would require affidavits from two medical experts licensed in the United States, one from a board-certified medical doctor and one from a mental-health professional, attesting to the "intended" permanence of the transition. The individual would have to be at least eighteen years of age and indicate that he or she had "lived in the acquired gender for at least two years." Despite the absence of a surgical requirement, in the Western tradition of habeas corpus, the policy required a "detailed diagnosis and case history of the applicant, including results from physical examinations and a description of all medical treatments received by the applicant for the purpose of modifying sexual characteristics" (New York City Department of Health and Mental Hygiene, 2006a). Finally, as in the 1971 policy, the policy mandated an alignment between legal sex and gender norms by requiring the applicant to submit proof that a legal name change had been made.

Overall, however, the policy proposal was viewed largely as a victory by transgender advocates because it marked a shift from the discursive and legal regime of forty years earlier, in which transsexual people were cast inescapably as "frauds," to one in which the new sex of individuals could be listed on their birth certificates, even without surgery. The advocates had begun the process of renegotiating the birth-certificate policy with two goals: first, that re-issued birth certificates list the reassigned sex; second, that the requirement for "convertive surgery" be eliminated. The policy proposal would have accomplished both goals.

When Schwartz presented this policy proposal to the Board of Health—the appointed body that writes the health code for New York City—in September of 2006, there appeared to be general support from the members of the Board of Health present at the meeting. Their questions and comments were innocuous. The new form would read "pursuant to section 207.05" only indicating that the birth certificate had been changed, but not why. A hearing for public comments was scheduled for October 2006, and a vote would be taken at the December meeting of the Board of Health. It was, by all accounts, "expected to pass."

Press coverage following the announcement of the proposed policy, however, generated what could fairly be described as a media firestorm. *The New York Times* published a front-page story titled, "New York Plans to Make Gender a Personal Choice" (Cave 2006, A1). Numerous wire services covered the policy. An editorial from the *Jewish Press* titled "Transgender Folly" railed against dropping the surgery standard (Editorial Board of the Jewish Press 2006). An essay in *Slate*, subtitled "New York City Bungles Transgender Equality," by Kenji Yoshino, an oft-quoted law professor at Yale who writes on gay rights, described the New York City Board of Health as "carried away" by advocates' arguments and invoked national security as one justification for rejecting the proposal (Yoshino 2006).

Although the public testimony submitted about the proposal consisted largely of well-reasoned formal arguments from public interest groups, elected officials, and LGBT institutions in favor of the changes, media coverage elicited less formal email testimony to the Board of Health, almost all in vociferous opposition. The public's expression of the "natural attitude" is illustrated here, though in different forms. "Are you people out of your minds????" asked one member of the public. "How enlightened is a person that refuses to accept that there is a biological difference between a man and a woman? If I wish to call myself a dog, I suppose you people would allow that too?" Another individual opined, "when the terms of male and female are being intentionally blurred, for some rag-tag groups benefit [sic], society loses." A third comment adopts the more elastic version of the "natural attitude," one that allows for re-classification post-genital surgery:

> I am befuddled and wonder if the inmates are now running the asylum ... How might it be possible for someone with male genitals to now be listed as being female? Is everyone expected to be blind? I can understand if one had a sex change but simply dressing [in] the clothing of the opposite sex does not qualify a person of that sex.
>
> (NYC Board of Health 2006)

Just three months after the policy was formally presented, the NYC DHMH summarily withdrew it from consideration. As a justification, they noted "federal identity requirements for vital records post-9/11 and broader societal concerns that were raised during the public comment period." Ultimately, the only change to the 1971 policy that was put in place was to indicate the reassigned sex on re-issued birth certificates. The requirement for convertive surgery remained firmly in place. Significantly, so too did the reference on the amended certificate to the New York City Health Code that refers to the "change-of-sex" provision. Officials cited two main categories of concern: (1) the policy's impact on sex-segregated institutions such as schools, workplaces, hospitals, and prisons; (2) the impact of two pieces of post 9/11 legislation. On the latter, they wrote:

> The United States Congress has recognized the importance of birth certificates in the Intelligence Reform and Terrorism Prevention Act of 2004 ... These acts will, for the first time in the nation's history, impose federal regulations on state and local vital records offices. They will include provisions for birth certificate security, death-birth matching and verification of driver's license applications with birth certificates. We anticipate that automated verification of birth certificate data by federal agencies and state motor vehicle agencies will be a central component of the regulations. Key elements of the birth certificate to be verified are first and last name, date of birth and sex. Given the anticipated federal regulations and the importance of sex as a key element of identity, it is important to wait for their promulgation.
>
> (NYC Department of Health and Mental Hygiene 2006b)

However, in this era of heightened scrutiny of individuals' bodies and histories, transgender people have already found themselves, inadvertently, under increased surveillance. As individuals, similar to undocumented workers and other "suspicious persons," transgender people are constantly forced to account for themselves. When traveling, they are advised to carry not just standard identity documents but legitimating letters from their physicians (National Center for Transgender Equality 2004). In the workplace, employers of transgender people receive "no match" letters from the Social Security Administration (SSA) when the SSA compares the sex on their employee's drivers' licenses to the sex in their SSA records. Because the standards for legal sex definition change across political jurisdictions, and even among different state agencies within the same political jurisdiction (Currah 2009), transgender people are especially vulnerable to any systems of surveillance and "dataveillance" that require data matching (Clarke 1988).

## CONCLUSION

Writ large, these regulatory changes to the classification of sex on the birth certificate illustrate governmental imperatives to secure the relationship between identification and identity, to ensure, in short, that someone is who they say they are. This anxiety about the possible inability of an identity document to secure a constant, socially legible correspondence with an individual is summed up by lead bureaucrat on the issue fretting, "But we won't know who you are." Challenges to the sex designation on the birth certificate center on the tension between sex definition as negotiated by advocates, members of the public, medical experts, and bureaucrats and sex as made real only through the force of law, by legal authority. As the concern about fraud fades from view, permanence emerges as a mechanism for the state to reassert a biological imperative based on the "natural attitude." But what would be the metric that could ensure that this change of sex be one-time, enduring, measurable, and irreversible? In a "natural attitude" lexicon, the solution could only be genital surgery, imagined as final, stable, and non-reversible ("always will be")—very much how the infant body used to function as a guarantee ("once and for all"). Through this process, bureaucrats, with cues from the publics they believe they serve, reworked the "natural attitude" to keep pace with certain biomedical innovations.

Of course, the barrier put in place in New York City to ensure permanence—requiring genital surgery before an M or an F will appear on the reissued document—cannot in fact guarantee the permanence of gender identity or of the genitals. While it is unlikely, it is entirely possible for an individual to have sex reassignment surgery more than once and thus to administratively "switch back" to their original legal sex. This policy does not prevent that from occurring. Nor does it mandate that individuals born in New York City who have undergone genital sex reassignment surgery change their identity documents to match their new body. It does prevent the vast majority of individuals whose gender identity does not match their legal sex from having their gender recognized by the state.

So what version of social order is being maintained by the New York City policy on birth certificates? By mandating that a particular bodily topography— the presence of a penis for men, a vagina for women—establishes the link between the self and the law, the state has hewed close to the traditional biological narrative. The state wants to have irrefutable, stable, and permanent evidence that you are who you say you are. But throughout their lives, people change their bodies, their performances, and their identities. Instead of changing the criteria for markers on identity documents, officials insist that individuals change their bodies to align with the "natural attitude." In so doing, officials can retain the integrity of the ideological and discursive system. The sex/gender binary, which is in perpetual crisis, is actually preserved—not by the physiological requirements guaranteeing permanence and irreversibility, because they can't—but by the legal machinations the state requires of its people.

## ACKNOWLEDGEMENTS

The authors wish to thank Talia Bettcher, Monica Casper, Zillah Eisenstein, Ann Garry, Jamison Green, Judith Lorber, Shoshana Magnet, Lisa Lynn Moore, Ananya Mukherjea, Anna Marie Smith, and Dean Spade for their thoughtful comments on the drafts of this article. We are also indebted to participants at the workshop on "Surveillance and Inequality" held at Arizona State University in March 2007. Paisley Currah's work researching and writing this article was supported by a grant from the PSC-CUNY Research Foundation.

## NOTES

1. Following legal usage, we use "sex" to refer to legal designations as male or female. We also use "sex" when it is the term of art used in the particular discourses we are examining. When not discussing legal classifications or specialized disciplinary deployments of the term, we use "gender." We do not distinguish between "sex" and "gender" to reinforce the notion that there is a dichotomy between sex as biological and gender as social; indeed, we understand legal and medical constructions of "sex" to be an effect of gender and the "natural attitude" we use to frame our argument. "Gender identity" refers to one's sense of oneself as male or female. The gender identity of some people is not traditionally associated with the sex assigned to them at birth. Since the early 1990s, "transgender" has become the term most commonly used to describe people in the United States whose gender identity or gender expression does not conform to social expectations for their birth sex (Currah 2006, 3–4). (In some of the older material we examine, the term "transsexual" is used to describe such individuals, and we use that term when appropriate.) "Transgender men" refers to individuals who were classified as female at birth and whose gender identity is male. "Transgender women" refers to individuals who were classified as male at birth and whose gender identity is female. In our usage, the gender of an individual is determined by his or her gender identity, and pronouns refer to an individual's gender identity.
2. Homer Plessy's lawyer argued against the state's competence in making racial determinations, a rare exception. Ian Haney Lopez shows how individuals from China, India, Japan, and other nations challenged the U.S. racial classification system by arguing, for example, that their particular ancestry should be classified as "white" and hence be eligible for naturalization. In these racial prerequisite cases, the internal logics of the courts' decisions changed when judges stopped invoking scientific accounts of racial difference after early twentieth-century anthropology shifted its emphasis from nature to culture and started deploying dictionary definitions and "common-sense" rationales (Lopez 1996). Over time, challenges to perceived errors in the application of the racial classifications to particular persons in immigration law and other types of law were displaced by challenges to the construction of the categories themselves (Harris 2008). In 1924, U.S. immigration and naturalization classifications shifted to "national origin," which even at the time officials acknowledged was meant to represent and also clarify increasingly murky racial distinctions (Ngai 2004, 31).
3. For this paper, we interviewed several individuals involved as advocates in this issue in New York City and nationally: Dean Spade, at the time an attorney with the Sylvia Rivera Law Project; Chris Daley, at the time the Executive Director of the Transgender Law Center in San Francisco; and Mara Keisling, Executive Director of the National Center for Transgender Equality in Washington, D.C.
4. One participant on the committee remembers at least one official referring to the same-sex marriage issue, but this is not reflected in the official minutes. Interview with Carrie Davis, March 2007.

## REFERENCES

*Anonymous v. Weiner.* 1966. 270 N.Y.S.2d 319.

Bettcher, Talia Mae. 2007. Evil deceivers and make-believers: On transphobic violence and the politics of illusion. *Hypatia* 22 (3): 43–65.

Caplan, Jane. 2001. "This or that particular person": Protocols of identification in nineteenth century Europe. In *Documenting individual identity: The development of state practices in the modern world*, ed. Jane Caplan and John Torpey. Princeton: Princeton University Press.

Cave, Damien. 2006. New York plans to make gender a personal choice. *The New York Times*, November 7.

Clarke, Roger. 1988. Information technology and dataveillance. *Communications of the Association for Computing Machinery* 31 (5): 498–512.

Craig, Elaine. 2007. Trans-phobia and the relational production of gender. *Hastings Women's Law Journal* 18:137–72.

Council, Charles R. 1965. Letter to Carl L. Erhardt, Director of the Bureau of Records and Statistics, The City of New York Health Department, June 11.

Currah, Paisley. 2006. Gender pluralisms under the transgender umbrella. In *Transgender rights*, ed. Paisley Currah, Richard M. Juang, and Shannon Price Minter. Minneapolis: University of Minnesota Press.

Currah, Paisley. 2009. The transgender rights imaginary. In *Feminist and queer legal theory: Intimate encounters, uncomfortable conversations*, ed. Martha Albertson Fineman, Jack E. Jackson, and Adam P. Romero. Burlington, Vt.: Ashgate Press.

Currah, Paisley, and Dean Spade. 2007. The state we're in: Locations of coercion and resistance in trans policy, part I. *Sexuality Research and Social Policy* 4 (4): 1–6.

Denny, Dallas. 2006. Transgender communities of the United States in the late twentieth century. In *Transgender rights*, ed. Paisley Currah, Richard M. Juang, and Shannon Price Minter. Minneapolis: University of Minnesota Press.

Duggan, Lisa. 2003. The *twilight of equality? Neoliberalism, cultural politics, and the attack on democracy*. Boston: Beacon Press.

Editorial Board of the Jewish Press. 2006. Transgender folly. *The Jewish Press*, November 15.

Foucault, Michel. 2003. "*Society must be defended*": Lectures at the Collège de France, 1975–1976, Trans. David Macey. New York: Picador.

Foucault, Michel. 2007. Security, Territory, *Population: Lectures at the Collège de France*, 1977–1978, Trans. David Macey. New York: Palgrave MacMillan.

Fraser, Nancy. 1997. *Justice interruptus*. New York: Routledge.

Garfinkel, Harold. [1967] 2006. Passing and the managed achievement of sex status in an "intersexed" person, part 1. In *Studies in ethnomethodology*. Oxford: Polity Press.

Glaser, Barney, and Anselm Strauss. 1967. *The discovery of grounded theory*. Chicago: Aldine.

Goffman, Erving. 1959. *The presentation of self in everyday life*. New York: Anchor Books.

Hale, Jacob. 1996. Are lesbians women? *Hypatia* 11 (2): 94–121.

Harris, Angela P. 2008. From color line to color chart?: Racism and colorism in the new century. *Berkeley Journal of African-American Law and Policy* 10:52–69.

Hausman, Bernice L. 1995. *Changing sex: Transsexualism, technology, and the idea of gender*. Durham, N.C.: Duke University Press.

Heyes, Cressida J. 2003. Feminist solidarity after queer theory: The case of transgender. *Signs: Journal of Women in Culture and Society* 28 (4): 1093–120.

Hunter, Nan D., Courtney G. Joslin, and Sharon McGowan. 2004. *The rights of lesbians, gay men, bisexuals, and transgender people*. New York: American Civil Liberties Union.

International Bill of Gender Rights. [1990] 2006. In *Transgender rights*, ed. Paisley Currah, Richard M. Juang, and Shannon Price Minter. Minneapolis: University of Minnesota Press.

Irving, Dan. 2008. Normalized transgressions: Legitimating the transsexual body as productive. *Radial History Review* 100:38–59.

James, George. 1965. Letter from George James, Commissioner of Health, to Dr. Henry Kraus, Executive Secretary to the New York Academy of Medicine Committee of Public Health, April 2.

Kessler, Suzanne J., and Wendy McKenna. 1978. Gender: *An ethnomethodological approach*. New York: John Wiley and Sons.

*Littleton v. Prange*. 1999. 9 S.W.3d 231 (Tex. Civ. App. 1999).

Lopez, Ian F. Haney. 1996. *White by law*. New York: New York University Press.

Meyerowitz, Joanne. 2002. *How sex changed: A history of transsexuality in the United States*. Cambridge, Mass.: Harvard University Press.

National Center for Transgender Equality. 2004. Air travel tips for transgender people. Available at http://nctequality.org/Issues/Travel.asp (accessed September 12, 2007).

New York Academy of Medicine Committee on Public Health. 1966. Change of sex on birth certificates for transsexuals. *Bulletin of the New York Academy of Medicine* 42 (8): 721–4.

New York Academy of Medicine Subcommittee on Birth Certificates. 1965. *Birth Certificates, Change of Sex. Committee on Public Health, Public Health Archives*. New York: New York Academy of Medicine.

New York City Board of Health. 2006. Resolution Comments—NYC Birth Certificate for Transgender People.

New York City Department of Health and Mental Hygiene (NYC DHMH). 2005. Minutes of meetings of the Transgender Advisory Committee, February 7–April 18.

New York City Department of Health and Mental Hygiene (NYC DHMH). 2006a. Notice of Intention to Amend Article 207 of the New York City Health Code: Notice of Public Hearing, September 12.

New York City Department of Health and Mental Hygiene (NYC DHMH). 2006b. Response to public comments and additional recommendations regarding Proposal to Amend Section 207.05 of the New York City Health Code, December 5.

New York City Health Code. 1971. Correction of Records; filing of new birth certificates. Section 207.05 (a) (5).

Newfield, Emily, Stacey Hart, Suzanne Dibble, and Lori Kohler. 2006. Female-to-male transgender quality of life. *Quality of Life Research* 15 (9): 1447–57.

Ngai, Mae M. 2004. *Impossible subjects: Illegal aliens and the making of modern America*. Princeton: Princeton University Press.

Scott, James C. 1998. *Seeing like a state*. New Haven: Yale University Press.

Sears, Clare. 2008. Electric brilliancy: Cross-dressing law and freak-show displays in nineteenth-century San Francisco. *Women's Studies Quarterly* 36 (3 and 4): 170–87.

Strauss, Anselm, and Juliet Corbin. 1994. Grounded theory methodology: An overview. In *Handbook in qualitative research*, ed. Norm Denzin and Yvonne Lincoln. London: Sage.

Stryker, Susan. 2006. (De)subjugated knowledges: An introduction to transgender studies. In *The transgender studies reader*, ed. Susan Stryker and Stephen Whittle. New York: Routledge.

Sylvia Rivera Law Project and Transgender Law and Policy Institute. 2003. Birth certificate sex designation: An overview of the issues.

Transgender Law and Policy Institute. 2008. Non-discrimination laws that include gender identity and expression. Available at http://www.transgenderlaw.org/ndlaws/index.htm (accessed March 13, 2008).

Valentine, David. 2007. *Imagining transgender: An ethnography of a category*. Durham, N.C.: Duke University Press.

West, Candace, and Don H. Zimmerman. 1987. Doing gender. *Gender and Society* 1:125–51.

Yoshino, Kenji. 2006. Sex and the city: New York City bungles transgender equality. Available at http://www.slate.com (accessed December 11, 2006).

# 47

# *Reinscribing Normality?*
## The Law and Politics of Transgender Marriage

RUTHANN ROBSON

LESBIAN LEGAL STUDIES SCHOLAR RUTHANN ROBSON offers an astute analysis of the normativizing pressures she sees operating in several landmark early-21st-century legal cases involving transgender marriages in the U.S., notably *Littleton* and *Gardiner*. Robson first discusses the distinction between "formalist" and "functionalist" approaches to interpreting the law. The former relies on formal relations dictated by law, whereas the latter emphasizes actual relations or circumstances pertaining to a given situation. Robson notes that while "functionalism" might appear more humane for queer litigants, it nevertheless tends to promote the most conservative notions of family, kinship, marriage, gender, and sexuality. In her readings of the *Littleton* and *Gardiner* cases, in both of which the marriages of transsexual women to biologically male men were determined to be invalid, Robson notes that not only were trans women definitely the losers, but that the biggest winner was actually a judicial process that reinscribes heterosexuality as the basis of social relationality. The cases were decided against the trans women on the basis of formalist notions of sex-determination, but in examining the functionalist litigation strategies of the defendants, Robson fears that heteronormativity would have been reinforced even had the women won in court. While Robson remains convinced that transgender people can develop a liberatory politics of shared interpersonal life, she considers current strategies and tactics for securing transgender marriage to fall into many of the same normativizing pitfalls that have plagued the gay marriage debate.

Almost thirty years later, I still recall an episode of a television show I saw while I was in law school. I was sitting around with some of my classmates watching a small black-and-white TV, probably drinking and smoking, definitely stalling preparation for another boring class that seemed to have no connection with reality. So, perhaps not surprisingly, the show *Real People* seemed to be a student favorite, this precursor to "reality TV" and a spawn of *Candid Camera*. The show's concept, such as it was, seemed to be that truth is stranger than fiction. It not only provided diversion from unpleasant tasks such as studying fee simple and proximate cause, it invited the viewing audience to laugh at the show's subjects and meanwhile feel reinforced in our own normalcy.

The segment I remember centered on a married couple with children. The twist was that they were transgendered. The man-born one was transitioning to a woman; the woman-born one was transitioning to a man. Importantly, someone said (someone on TV? someone in the room? both?) the couple could still be husband and wife and the children would still have a mother and a father. The audience could laugh—isn't that strange?—but normalcy prevailed. And not merely the normalcy of the viewers, the normalcy of the world. If these two people wanted to "switch," well then, that would be fine. Nothing fundamental would be altered. We could get back to determining the ownership of private property and the liability of tortfeasors.

Recently, long past law school, I experienced déjà vu while reading *Trans-Sister Radio,* by Chris Bohjalian. The novel's plot revolves around the character Dana, transitioning from male to female. For most of the book, Dana is involved with a divorced woman, Allison, whom Dana first meets when he is her male professor. After an intense affair, Allison and the now-female Dana break up what is often described as their lesbian relationship. Dana uneasily dates a few women, but when she falls in love—and lust—it is with Allison's ex-husband. The "switch" from Allison as Dana's partner to her ex-husband as Dana's partner in the last pages of the novel reestablishes heterosexual normalcy.[1] Again, we are reassured that despite a small substitution, nothing fundamental has been altered.

This lack of fundamental alteration is what worries me about the legal discourse surrounding transgendered marriage. Like other movements, including other queer movements, transgendered legal reform has the potential to be merely accommodating, what I have called in other contexts domesticating. The legal discourse surrounding transgendered marriage too often serves to recapitulate and reinscribe the most traditional visions of marriage and heterosexuality. Like the cartoon image of a man and a woman used to represent humanity to alien beings who might discover that NASA launched Pioneer 10 spacecraft, what Michael Warner has termed "heteronormativity" is incessantly being equated with humanness itself.[2]

Perhaps the best known example of such heterosexual insistence occurs in *MT v JT,* decided by a New Jersey court in 1976, in which the court upheld the marriage between M.T., born a male who transitioned to a woman, and J.T., born a male who remained so.[3] The court made explicit that in determining the validity of the marriage, it is "the sexual capacity of the individual which must be scrutinized. Sexual capacity or sexuality in this frame of reference requires the coalescence of both the physical ability and the emotional orientation to engage in sexual intercourse as either a male or a female."[4] On this view, it is heterosexual intercourse, rather than birth certificates, chromosomes, or expert testimony about gender dysphoria, that is the talisman for sex/gender identity.

Traditional heterosexual intercourse is also the shibboleth for marriage itself. While particular distinctions might be made, and the importance of procreation as an outcome of sexual intercourse is often stressed, various doctrines surrounding the marital relation establish that heterosexual intercourse is the underpinning of marriage. For example, generally a marriage can be annulled by one party if the other party does not have the capacity to engage in heterosexual intercourse.[5] Likewise, in states that require grounds for divorce, one party can divorce another on the grounds of "constructive abandonment" for failure to engage in traditional heterosexual intercourse, despite repeated requests to do so.[6] (Interestingly, if the request is for nontraditional heterosexual intercourse, then the refusal will be justified and will not constitute abandonment.)[7]

In one sense, *MT v. JT can* be theorized as upholding a functionalist rather than formalist perspective of marriage and gender identity. The formalist approach relies upon formal relationships dictated by law, while the functionalist approach emphasizes the functions or attributes or "realities" that are deemed to be operative. While this may be described as the difference between law and fact, it is more complex than that, because the argument is really that the law should take into account the "real" facts as opposed to mere formalities. For example, the legal definition of "family" is imbued with a functionalist hue in cases such as *Braschi,* in which New York's highest court interpreted a New York City rent-control regulation disallowing eviction of "either the surviving spouse of the deceased tenant or some other member of the deceased tenant's family."[8] In considering whether Braschi, the surviving partner in a gay relationship, fit into the statutory exemption, the court approvingly referred to factors such as the exclusivity and longevity of the relationship, the level of emotional and financial commitment, the manner in which they conducted their everyday lives and presented themselves, and the reliance they placed upon each other for "family services." The court relied upon underlying facts such as their cohabitation for ten years, their regular visits to each other's relatives, and their joint status as signatories on three safe deposit boxes, bank accounts, and credit cards. Similarly, in the parenting context, the formalist viewpoint rejects any visitation or custody claim of the member of a lesbian couple who has no legal relationship to the child (whether as birth mother or by adoption), since the woman is not a legal parent.[9] The functionalist perspective, on the other hand, is not content with the formal legal definition of "parent" and develops criteria to determine whether a person should be recognized by the law as a parent. These criteria generally include the fostering of the parent-child relationship by the legal parent, the nonlegal parent and child living in the same household, the nonlegal parent's assumption of the obligations of parenthood "by taking responsibility for the child's care, education, and development, including but not limited to financial contribution, and did not expect financial compensation," and the existence of the relationship for a sufficient amount of time to have produced bonding.[10]

A critique of the functionalist approach is that while it may seem more "liberal" than the formalist approach, it actually enshrines the most conservative versions of the categories it determines. It prescribes and enforces its concept of normalcy. For example, if Braschi had been a partner in an "open" relationship that was not sexually exclusive, this fact would have been used to argue that he was not a family member entitled to stay in his home, regardless of any understandings between Braschi and his lover. Likewise, if a lesbian partner agrees to coparent but maintains a separate residence, she will not be deemed a functional parent, again regardless of any understandings between the parents or the quality of relationship with the child.

In the transgender marriage context, the functionalist test employed by the court in *MT v. JT* also requires an application of the most traditional aspects of the functions at issue—here a "wife" or "husband" is judged by the function of heterosexual intercourse. Again, the understandings or sexual satisfactions of the parties are irrelevant.

The law may seem to be considering "reality," but it is imposing a singular and dominant reality. However, in another sense, the functionalist strategy is only necessary because the court is troubled by the formal legal status that would otherwise prevail. In the case of *MT v. JT,* the trial court would never have delved beyond the formal marital status (evidenced by a proper marriage certificate) had not JT argued that the marriage was void, which would release him from his financial obligations of support.

More recently, in *Littleton v. Prange,* the Texas Court of Appeals was also troubled by the formal marital status of Christie Littleton and her deceased husband, Jonathan Littleton.[11] In her medical malpractice suit against the physician who had treated her husband, it became known that Christie had been born male and had undergone sex reassignment surgery before entering into the otherwise valid marriage, again evinced by a proper marriage certificate. Unlike the court in *JT,* however, the Texas courts did not uphold the marriage. Instead, the appellate court resorted to another formalistic document—the birth certificate—to undermine the validity of the formal marriage certificate. According to the court, the original birth certificate, despite the fact that it had been amended to reflect a change of name and gender, was absolutely controlling. In the words of the court, it described things the way "they just are" as opposed to things the way one might "will into being."[12] Born male, Christie remained male, and she could therefore not be the wife of the deceased suing for wrongful death.

The Kansas Supreme Court has likewise refused to recognize a transgendered marriage in *In re Estate of Gardiner,* decided in 2002.[13] As in *MT* and *Littleton,* the court was faced with a challenge to the seemingly lawful marriage of a man to a woman who was MTF. Again, the stakes in *Gardiner* were economic: the challenge came from the estranged son of the man who died intestate, seeking to disinherit his stepmother, J'Noel Gardiner. Ms. Gardiner had been born male, had undergone sex reassignment surgery, had been issued a new birth certificate reflecting a change of name and gender, and several years later had met and married Marshall Gardiner. Invalidating the marriage, the court concluded that J'Noel is not a woman. However, more than the Texas court, the Supreme Court of Kansas recognized that J'Noel's sex/gender had changed. But not to female—to transsexual. This enabled the Kansas Supreme Court to invoke the Kansas so-called little DOMA statute,[14] which defined the marriage contract as a civil contract between "two parties who are of opposite sex" and declared all other marriages contrary to public policy and void. The court interpreted the DOMA statute to exclude transsexuals. "The plain ordinary meaning of 'persons of the opposite sex' contemplates a biological man and a biological woman and not persons who are experiencing gender dysphoria."[15] Such an interpretation presumably precludes transgendered persons from marrying, since they would have no "opposite sex." However, as Julie Greenberg presciently argued, such a position is difficult to defend, given the current constitutional jurisprudence that marriage is a fundamental right and here, as distinct from the same-sex marriage cases, the person is being denied the right to marry "anyone at all."[16]

In both *Littleton* and *Gardiner,* the courts conclude, as a matter of law, that the sex/gender identity of each MTF is not female and thus the marriages to their husbands are invalid. This position is consistent with most of the other cases in the United States that have considered the issue and is now the majority view, although there is more diversity of opinion in other jurisdictions.[17] However, while the result in such cases differs from *MT v. JT,* in all of these cases the courts preserve the heterosexual matrix. In *MT v. JT,* heterosexual intercourse is established, and thus the marriage is valid. In *Littleton* and *Gardiner,* the judicial guardians of heterosexuality have dispatched the pretenders: Christie Littleton remained in reality a man, while J'Noel Gardiner had transitioned from male to transsexual.

It is tempting to argue against the formalistic decisions in *Littleton* and *Gardiner* by favoring the more functionalist approach displayed in *MT v. JT.* Yet such arguments serve to reestablish and reinvigorate the normalcy of heterosexuality. As Andrew Sharpe has demonstrated, judicial approaches to transgender marriage in common law countries have, despite their differences, displayed a concern to "insulate marriage from 'unnatural' homosexual incursion."[18] While Sharpe argues that at times the judicial concern in the non-U.S. context may not be focused on actual sexual functionality but can shift to aesthetic concerns—how the transgendered person appears when unclothed—he nevertheless links the concern with "homophobic anxiety."[19]

The judicial preoccupation with maintaining heterosexuality obviously impacts litigation strategy and also influences and mirrors theoretical and political positions. We may find ourselves objecting to the result in *Littleton* based upon our own preconceptions of the heterosexual arrangement of marriage; a characterization of Ms. Littleton as a "widow" conveys a certain pathos in a heterosexist and sexist society. While perhaps less sympathetic, Ms. Gardiner is also easily stereotyped in sexist and heterosexist terms: she is "hardly the first widow to be accused of marrying a man twice her age for money instead of love with a stepson she first met at her husband's funeral trying to block her inheritance.[20] With relative ease, our understandings of the equity of these cases recapitulate our notions of normalcy and heterosexuality. A slight "switch" is required, but the fundamental social, legal, and political arrangements remain unaltered.

The potentially more subversive situation is the one in which one partner in an extant marriage changes gender. As the transgender theorist and activist Phyllis Randolph Frye has noted, powerful forces militated against such a possibility, given the refusal of the psychiatric and medical community to approve or provide genital surgery to married persons.[21] When such situations do occur the unchanged spouse would most likely be able to procure a divorce, even in states that require grounds.[22] However, dissolving a valid marriage is quite different from declaring a marriage invalid. In the former instance, the legal recognition of the marriage occurs through terminating the legal relation by the divorce. In the latter instance, the marriage is declared void. It is not that the marriage is terminated; it is as if it never existed.

Yet doctrinally, the facts giving rise to the voided marriage occur at the time the marriage is entered into by the parties. Subsequent events may reveal such facts to the parties (e.g., the parties could learn that the husband's previous marriage was not dissolved and thus the current marriage is void for bigamy), but subsequent facts cannot retroactively void the marriage. The application of such well-settled doctrine to the subsequent gender transition of one of the parties to the marriage means, as Frye has argued that "same sex marriages" do exist in the United States.[23] Under the reasoning of *Littleton,* Frye is surely correct. However, given the subsequent judicial pronouncement of *Gardner,* Frye's conclusion has been cast into doubt: the transgendered person is neither female nor male, and just as she or he has no *opposite sex* according to the court, she or he can have no *same* sex. Except, perhaps, another transgendered person, presumably one who has transitioned in the same manner.

As a litigation strategy, Frye is surely astute in recommending that the nontransgendered spouse should initiate or join the litigation, although I am less sanguine that such a person could not "be cast into the role of the degenerate" by a religious or conservative court.[24] Nevertheless, an analogy can be drawn to the U.S. Supreme Court case of *Turner v. Safely,* authored by Justice Sandra Day O'Connor—not known for her liberal views—in which the Court declared unconstitutional a prison regulation limiting marriage for inmates.[25] In a case that could have potentially more resonance than the oft quoted *Loving v. Virginia* in which the Supreme Court finally declared miscegenation laws unconstitutional,[26] the Court in *Turner* de-emphasized heterosexual intercourse as a rationale of marriage. While the Court did include the eventual (heterosexual) consummation of the prison inmate's marriage as significant—implicitly precluding the notion of conjugal visits—the Court first noted the importance of marriage as an expression of "emotional support and public commitment," and next alluded to the religious and spiritual significance of marriage.[27] Additionally, after mentioning the sexual component, the Court recognized the tangible benefits of marriage, such as Social Security benefits and property rights, as well as intangible benefits, such as the legitimation of children.[28]

Yet assimilation to heterosexuality remains strong as a litigation strategy. As Frye notes, the evidence supporting the gender transition document such as the amended birth certificate, which will be used to obtain the marriage certificate, should be sufficient to allow the conclusion that "she has a vagina, or he has a penis, and can be sexually penetrated as a female or can sexually penetrate as a male."[29] While such a view is consistent with *MT v. JT* in which the court upheld the marriage, like *MT,* it makes heterosexual intercourse the sine qua non of marriage. Such a theoretical and social position undermines claims to same-sex marriage.[30]

The larger question is whether marriage—whether heterosexual in fact or heterosexual by law, or even nonheterosexual—is consistent with a liberatory politic. The naturalist arguments for coupling and marriage that proclaim that such arrangements are "just the way things are" echo the *Littleton* court's pronouncement that Christie Littleton's gender just "is" the male gender assigned at birth. Moreover, such a coupling recapitulates and reinforces the dualism displayed by present male/female genders. The traditional model of marriage, as opposed to plural marriage, for example, supports a dyadic and binary mode of social arrangement. The NASA Pioneer spacecraft model of humanity as a "technological but benign Adam and Eve" becomes the theoretical construct and litigation position of this transgender politic.[31]

Moreover, the solution of marriage to the problems faced by M.T., Christie Littleton, and J'Noel Gardiner is, at best, partial. As in same-sex marriage, the specter of benefits to spouses often appears as an advantage—and in these three cases, each putative wife sought an economic gain—yet the political, social, and legal arrangement of marriage can obscure other inequalities. Additionally, it allows the state to impose a bright line rule for the distribution and non distribution of wealth, both private (as in these cases) and public. A regime of marriage allows the state to privatize problems of economic and other inequalities: the solution to a person not having medical care, for example, is not a government policy of universal health care but the individual becoming married to someone whose employer provides good health insurance. In other words, as a matter of reform, it may be expedient to argue for recognizing transgender marriages, but as a matter of critical change, even the success of the argument fails.

I remain convinced that transgendered people can develop a liberatory politic beyond marriage, just as I remain hopeful that lesbians and other queers can develop such a stance, despite what seems to me to be the essential conservatism of present same-sex marriage strategies and theoretical perspectives. In writing on the topic of transgendered marriage, I am cognizant that I am not situated within the transgendered movement, politic, or sensibility, and that my observations and analysis spring from my life as a lesbian and my work on lesbian legal issues, including marriage. Yet when I survey the transgender marriage cases, arguments, scholarship, and theorizing, I confront the same uneasiness I experienced thirty years ago watching shoddy television journalism or more recently reading a popular novel. I am worried that only a few of the characters will be switched. And that nothing fundamental will be altered.

## NOTES

1. The author calls readers' attention to the "switch" character of this plot development by invoking Louisa May Alcott's novel *Little Women* and noting that Laurie, "the lad who lives next door to the March girls," had "spent years wooing the tomboy Jo March, and then, after she finally rebuffed him, he simply moved on to her kid sister Amy and married her. He believed he was destined to become part of the March clan" (Chris Bohjalian, *Trans-Sister Radio* [New York: Crown, 2000], 334–35).
2. See Michael Warner, introduction to *In Fear of a Queer Planet: Queer Politics and Social Theory*, ed. Michael Warner (Minneapolis: University of Minnesota Press, 1993).
3. 355 A.2d 204 (N.J. Superior Ct. Appellate Division 1976).
4. Ibid., 209.
5. For a general discussion of the doctrine, see *Incapacity for Sexual Intercourse as Ground for Annulment*, 52 A.L.R. 589 (1974).
6. For example, section 170 of the New York Domestic Relations Law, which includes as a ground for divorce "the abandonment of the plaintiff by the defendant for a period of one of more years" (NYDRL § 170[2]). [...]
7. Again, as is well settled, the refusal to fulfill the basic marital obligation of sexual relations must be "unjustified, willful, and continue despite repeated requests." See *Silver v. Silver, 757.* [...]
8. *Braschi v. Stahl Associates,* 74 N.Y2d 201, 543 N.E.2d 49, 544 N.YS.2d 784 (1989).
9. This formalist viewpoint is exemplified by *Alison D. v. Virginia M*, 77 NY.2d 651, 569 NY.S.2d 586, 572 N.E.2d 27 (1991), in which the same court that decided *Braschi* rejected the lesbian coparent's claim to visitation based upon her de facto parent status, concluding that she had no "standing" to bring an action for visitation because she was not a parent.
10. See *In re Custody of H.S.H.-K. (Holtzman v. Knott),* 193 Wis. 2d 649, 533 N.W.2d 419 (1995). See also *VC v. MJB,* 163 N.J. 200, 748 A.2d 539 (N.J. 2000).
11. *Littleton v. Prange,* 9 SW.3rd 223 (Tex. Ct. App. 1999), *cert. denied,* 531 U.S. 872 (2000).
12. Ibid., 231.
13. 42 P.3d 120 (Kan. 2002).
14. In response to the Hawai'i Supreme Court's decision allowing room for debate on the subject of same-sex marriage, *Baehr v. Lewin,* 852 P.2d. 44 (Haw. 1993), and the potentiality of other states being compelled to recognize Hawai'i's same-sex marriages under the Constitution's full faith and credit clause, Const. Art. IV §1 ("Full Faith and Credit shall be given in each State to the public Acts, Records, and judicial Proceedings of every other State"), the United States Congress passed the Defense of Marriage Act, DOMA, PL 104–199, 110 Stat. 2419, codified at 28 U.S.C. §1738C (1996), which provides that federal law shall recognize only opposite-sex marriages and that states shall not be required to give effect to same-sex marriages from other states. [...]
15. 42 P.3d at l35.
16. Julie Greenberg, "When Is a Man a Man, and When Is a Woman a Woman?" *Florida Law Review* 52 (2000): 745, 762 (discussion of *Littleton v. Prange*).
17. Other cases in the United States include *In re Ladrach.* 513 N.E.2d 828 (Ohio Probate Ct. 1987) (holding that there is "no authority in Ohio for the issuance of a marriage license to consummate a marriage between a post-operative male to female transsexual person and a male person"); *Frances B. v. Mark B.,* 355 N.Y.S. 2d 712 (1974) (court stating that while the defendant may "function as a male in other situations and relationships," since he does not have male sexual organs or a "normal penis," he is not able to "function as a man"); *Anonymous v. Anonymous,* 325 N.Y.S.2d 499 (1971) (declaring

marriage between a man and a transitioning MTF who had male sex organs at the time of marriage and whom husband believed to be a woman). For discussions of these cases, as well as cases from other nations, see Andrew N. Sharpe, *Transgender Jurisprudence: Dysphoric Bodies of Law* (London: Cavendish, 2002), 89–134 [...]; Mary Coombs, "Sexual Dis-Orientation: Transgendered People and Same-Sex Marriage," *UCLA Women's Law Journal* 8 (1998): 219.

18. Sharpe, *Transgender Jurisprudence*, 115.

19. Ibid., 127–28. [...]

20. Jodi Wilgren, "Suit over Estate Claims a Widow Is Not a Woman," *New York Times,* January 13, 2002.

21. Phyllis Randolph Frye and Alyson Dodi Meiselman, "Same-Sex Marriages Have Existed in the United States for a Long Time *Now*," *Albany Law Review* 64 (2001): 1031, 1039–40 ("Until the 1990s, almost all married transgenders seeking sex reassignment were coerced into divorce by the medical profession").

22. See *Steinke v. Steinke,* 357 A.2d 674 (Super. Ct. Pa. 1975) (holding that wife had grounds for divorce given husband's exploration of the possibility of sex reassignment, including dressing as a woman and taking hormones, although husband did not undergo surgery and eventually "resumed living as a man").

23. Ibid. Frye further argues that same-sex marriage advocates should avail themselves of such transgender same-sex marriage situations as a "wedge issue" to promote same-sex marriage and concludes that their failure to do so is "incomprehensible" (Frye and Meiselman, "Same-Sex Marriages," 1045). Yet given the essential conservatism of the quest for marital recognition, this failure is easily comprehended. It is not only arguments on behalf of transgendered marriage that avail themselves of traditional functionalist strategies; arguments on behalf of same-sex marriage also employ the "we are essentially like you" rhetorical claim.

24. Frye and Meiselman, "Same-Sex Marriages," 1065.

25. *Turner v. Safley,* 482 U.S. 78 (1987).

26. *Loving v. Virginia,* 388 U.S. 1 (1967).The Court's decision in *Pace v. Alabama,* 106 U.S. 583, 585 (1883) was considered the precedent for allowing miscegenation statutes, and previous to *Loving,* the Court three times declined to review constitutional challenges to miscegenation statutes [...]

27. *Turner v. Safley,* 95–96.

28. Ibid., 96.

29. Frye and Meiselman, "Same-Sex Marriages," 1063.

30. Thus, while "the courts in transsexual marriage cases struggle with the same concerns as the opponents to same-sex marriage—the relative significance to marriage of [heterosexual] intercourse and procreation" (Coombs, "Sexual Disorientation," 260), a litigation strategy on behalf of transgendered marriage that argues that the relationship does include heterosexual intercourse is one which accedes to the validity of heterosexual intercourse as definitional of marriage.

31. See Warner, *In Fear of a Queer Planet,* xxiii.

# 48

# *Performance as Intravention*
## Ballroom Culture and the Politics of HIV/AIDS in Detroit

MARLON M. BAILEY

MARLON BAILEY, A SPECIALIST IN AFRICAN DIASPORA STUDIES AND GENDER STUDIES, conducts research on HIV/AIDS prevention practices in queer African-American and Latino/a communities in Detroit, Michigan, using a methodology known as "performance ethnography." Bailey, who trained as an actor before entering academe, works to understand the communities he researches by participating in them, and by performing in the flamboyant, semi-public ritual performances known as "ballroom," in which family-like kinship groups called "houses" compete against one another for fame and money. Ballroom culture has a complex, six-part gender system: butch queens (biological males who have sex with men), femme queens (male-to-female transgender individuals), butch queens up in drags (biological males who have sex with men and sometimes cross-dress but do not live as women), butches (masculinity in a person born female, whether identifying as lesbian or trans man), women (biological females who are feminine women regardless of sexual orientation), and men (heterosexual males who live as men). Participants in the subculture are either children (those who are less established in the scene) or parents (more seasoned members of the scene who act as house mothers or house fathers). In documenting how ballroom culture promotes HIV/AIDS prevention, Bailey demonstrates how communities often deemed to be "at risk" are also "communities of care" whose members look after one another in life-affirming ways. In this article, he argues that ballroom culture accomplishes a public health "intravention" rather than "intervention," enabling better health practices to emerge from within communities in empowering ways, rather than as campaigns imposed on them or imported from the outside.

I see Ballroom as an artistic community that can connect with youth on issues of HIV/AIDS prevention, and the relationship between drugs and unsafe sex.
—Wolfgang Busch, Filmmaker, *How Do I Look*[1]

Despite the feelings of some in black communities that we have been shamed by the immoral behavior of a small subset of community members, those some would label the underclass, scholars must take up the charge to highlight and detail the agency of those on the outside, those who through their acts of nonconformity choose outside status, at least temporarily.
—Cathy J. Cohen, "Deviance as Resistance"[2]

The house structure is geared specifically toward the ball scene (particularly in Detroit). As far as its purpose, houses provide a source of family nurturing that often times a lot of kids don't get at home.
—Prada Escada from the House of Escada in Detroit

"What's going on in the USA? George Bush got us in a disarray. We got soldiers in Baghdad; we should be fighting AIDS instead," chanted Chicago Ballroom commentator Neiman Marcus Escada.[3] Usually spoken in front of a captive crowd of Black queer members of the Ballroom community during a ball, Escada's words serve as both an astute critique of U.S. imperialism in the name of "national security" and its unwillingness to take appropriately aggressive measures to curtail the spread of HIV/AIDS infection among Black gender and sexual marginals locally and abroad. Consisting of Black and Latina/o LGBTQ people, Ballroom culture is a minoritarian social sphere where performance, queer genders and sexualities, and kinship coalesce to create an alternative world. Thus, within and through performance at balls, Neiman Marcus Escada contributes to the creation of a counterdiscourse of HIV/AIDS. This is but one example of the important role that performance plays within Ballroom culture and how it is a part of a critical practice of survival in which many of the members of this community are engaged.

Ballroom culture, sometimes called "house ball culture," is a relatively clandestine community consisting of African American and (in locations such as New York, Miami, and Los Angeles) Latino/a GLBTQ people. Although Jenny Livingston's popular documentary film *Paris Is Burning* (1991) provides only a glimpse into the world of Ballroom culture, it was the first exposé to bring mainstream exposure to Ballroom practices in the late 1980s in New York City. Since its beginnings in Harlem more than fifty years ago, Ballroom culture has expanded rapidly to every major city in the United States, including Chicago, Atlanta, Baltimore, Charlotte, Cleveland, and Philadelphia. Notwithstanding the popular media coverage of Ballroom culture in recent years from its members appearing in Madonna's music video "Vogue" (1990) to the deaths of two of the community's most prominent icons, Pepper LaBejia (2003) and Willie Ninja (2006), to date this unique and generative culture has received scant scholarly attention.

Perhaps more importantly, out of the limited scholarship on Ballroom culture, the disproportionate impact of the HIV/AIDS epidemic on its members has barely been mentioned let alone examined. An increasing number of community-based organizations (CBOs) have received federal and/or state/local funding for prevention programs that target Ballroom communities.[4] Yet the funding support for these prevention programs has yet to garner comprehensive studies that can help determine their overall effectiveness in reducing HIV/AIDS infection among Ballroom communities. As a result, little is known about the sociocultural challenges that members of this community face, and how social practices that are organic to Ballroom culture assist its members in withstanding the scourge of the disease and challenging the stigmatization associated with it.

In this performance ethnography[5] of Ballroom culture and HIV/AIDS in Detroit, Michigan, I delineate three aspects of Ballroom culture that are potential strategies for HIV/AIDS prevention that already exist within the community. First, I highlight three core dimensions of the Ballroom community: the gender and sexual identity system, the kinship structure, and the performances at the ball. Second, I argue that, generally, HIV/AIDS prevention programs that target Black communities have relied on research and intervention models that are based on individual sexual behavior and are devoid of cultural analyses. As a result, the organic practices and strategies of prevention that emerge from within so-called at-risk communities have been woefully neglected. For instance, even though HIV/AIDS infection is disproportionately high among Black men who have sex with men (MSM), a substantial portion of Black MSM remains HIV-negative. More research needs to be conducted to identify and support strategies deployed by Black MSM that protect them from infection. I argue that these strategies are forms of *intravention. Intravention* describes HIV/AIDS *prevention* activities that are conducted and sustained through practices and processes within at-risk communities themselves.[6]

Finally, I delineate three forms of *intravention* that are rooted in Black performance traditions and are integral to Ballroom culture: the creation of a social epistemology, social support, and prevention balls. These three aspects demonstrate that the Black queer members of the Ballroom scene are communities of support rather than simply communities of risk.[7] Looking to performance and other cultural work, in theory and in practice, will not only yield more socioculturally nuanced theories, methods, and models for HIV/AIDS prevention, but it can also help guide CBOs to forge more effective and sustained programs aimed at reducing HIV infection in Black communities in general and Black queer communities in particular.

## BLACK QUEER PERFORMANCE AND HIV/AIDS

I approach this examination of Ballroom culture using the methodology of performance, emphasizing research and community activism in HIV/AIDS prevention. My nine years of performance ethnographic research on Ballroom culture and HIV/AIDS consist of my participation in the very performances and cultural practices that I analyze.[8] Hence, as I describe later in this essay, I competed in balls as a member of both the Detroit and Los Angeles Chapters of the House of Prestige. Accordingly, my performance approach involved me being a member of the Ballroom community and working for two CBOs that collaborated with the Ballroom community.[9] I have also been engaged in extensive HIV/AIDS prevention research and activism among Black gay men and transgender women. Given my particular vantage point, this essay seeks to build a conceptual framework and a language between public health and (Black) cultural studies that can illuminate the central role that performance plays in the lives of Ballroom members as it relates to the epidemic.

By and large, the research on HIV/AIDS and culture has been produced in disparate domains of scholarship. Research on the disproportionate impact of HIV/AIDS on Black communities has been beset by a failure to employ truly interdisciplinary approaches to HIV/AIDS prevention studies to explicate the multifaceted nature of this epidemic, and to identify innovative strategies to combat it. More or less, HIV/AIDS research has been dominated by biomedicine, epidemiology, and social science.[10] Calls for radical interdisciplinarity and cultural criticism have been only marginally addressed at best and outright rejected at worst.[11] As a result, the topic of HIV/AIDS among Black queer communities falls through the cracks, so to speak, of several disparate intellectual conversations that fail to account for the multifarious social context in which Black queer people live. [...]

Theorizing HIV/AIDS through performance, or what Robin D. G. Kelley refers to as cultural labor,[17] necessarily shifts the emphasis in HIV/AIDS research away from individual sexual behavior that supposedly leads to infection to a focus on culture, as an arsenal of resiliency strategies upon which marginalized communities rely to survive the social crisis. For instance, in his analysis of the forms of cultural expression among Black urban youth on the street, Kelley suggests that Black urban youth undertake cultural labor within an increasingly politically powerless and economically deprived urban sphere.[18] Likewise, in my larger project on Ballroom culture, I frame its members' reconstitution of gender and sexual subjectivities, family/kinship, and community as a form of cultural labor as one way to withstand and creatively respond to the sociocultural and economic forms of exclusion that they experience. And, as I will elaborate, in the Ballroom community, these forms of cultural labor are inextricably linked to performance. [...]

Since there is scant research on the Ballroom community and the epidemic, in general, and almost no literature on this topic within public health, this ethnographic study of Ballroom culture in Detroit is an appropriate basis from which to forge cross-disciplinary dialogues and research. For instance, one of the core concepts in HIV/AIDS prevention theory and practice is *intervention*. Within public health, intervention models are designed programmatically to facilitate behavioral change in order to reduce incidence and prevalence of HIV infection among targeted communities that have been identified as "high risk" or as "risk communities." In "AIDS: Keywords," Jan Zita Grover defines "risk groups" as an epidemiological concept that serves to isolate identifiable characteristics among certain communities that are predictive of where infection is most likely to occur so as to contain and prevent it.[20] In other words, within public health, the aim is to identify, isolate, and contain infection within a particular risk community so that the general population remains safe from infection.[21] [...]

Conceptually, I call for a move from *intervention* to *intravention* in HIV/AIDS prevention studies to capture what so-called communities of risk do, based on their own knowledge and ingenuity, to contest, to reduce, and to withstand HIV in their communities. In my critique of the concept of intervention that is so prevalent in public-health and prevention studies, I draw from the work of performance theorist David Román, who suggests that cultural performance is, indeed, an act of intervention into the cultural politics of race, sexuality, and AIDS.[24] Such cultural politics pathologize Black sexuality and represent Black queer men as vectors of HIV infection. Thus, I join performance (as it is an arena in which minoritarian communities engage in social struggle) with Friedman and colleagues' notion of "communities of *intravention*."[25] In their study of HIV/AIDS prevalence among communities of injection drug users (IDU), they further argue, "Cognitive-behavioral theories that focus on the individual may not provide sufficient understanding for such efforts because they lack the concepts and methodologies needed to identify, understand or intervene in structures and processes that are at the cultural system, community network levels."[26]

My analysis here attends to the ways in which such communities of risk deploy strategies to address the correlative social factors that make people more vulnerable to the epidemic such as, but not limited to, social isolation, low self-worth, violence, and poverty. Thus, the concept of *intravention* is a key point of entry for performance into the analysis and development of targeted HIV/AIDS prevention programs within a Black queer cultural context.

In what follows I delineate the aspects of performance that are central to the Ballroom community that intravene in the HIV/AIDS epidemic. Instead of referring to the Ballroom community as a community of risk, I suggest that Ballroom is a community of support. In the Ballroom community, performance is the means through which members create a counterdiscourse (through a social epistemology), provide social support (kin labor) for its members, and produce prevention balls in order to reduce Black queer people's vulnerability to HIV/AIDS infection through competitive performance. Thus, Ballroom cultural practices are a form of intravention, deploying protective and prevention efforts that emerge from within the culture itself, efforts that the larger Black community and society as a whole fail to do. This community constitutes a site of refuge where its members have the opportunity to be nurtured, to experience pleasure, and to access a better quality of life in the face of the AIDS epidemic, particularly for those that are located at the very bottom of society. Clearly, enhancing the quality of life is a precondition to reducing the spread of HIV in the community.

## BALLROOM CULTURE: A COMMUNITY OF SOCIAL SUPPORT

Although Ballroom culture had existed for decades prior to Jennie Livingston's documentary *Paris Is Burning*, the film has become the primary prism through which this rich and longstanding cultural practice is recognized and understood. Even in some of the more recent glances of Ballroom to which the American public has been exposed, very little has been revealed about the day-to-day lives of the people involved and the multiple purposes that the social structures within the community serve.[27]

Two inextricable features sustain the community: flamboyant competitive ball rituals and houses, and the anchoring family-like structures that produce these rituals of performance. Ballroom subjectivities and familial roles are based on an egalitarian gender/sexual identity system that offers

**Table 48.1** Gender/Sexual Identity System

*Ballroom Culture: Three Sexes*

1. Woman (one born with female sex characteristics)
2. Man (one born with male sex characteristics)
3. Intersex (one born with both male and female sex characteristics or with sex characteristics that are indeterminate)

*Six-Part Gender/Sexual Identity System*

1. Butch queens (biologically born male who identify as gay or bisexual and are and can be masculine, hypermasculine, or effeminate)
2. Femme queens (male to female transgender people or at various stages of gender reassignment—that is, hormonal and/or surgical processes)
3. Butch queens up in drags (gay males that perform drag but do not take hormones and who do not live as women)
4. Butches (female to male transgender people or at various stages of gender reassignment or masculine lesbian or a female appearing as male regardless of sexual orientation)
5. Women (biologically born females who are gay or straight identified or queer)
6. Men (biologically born males who live as men and are straight identified)

*House Parents*

1. Mothers: Butch queens, femme queens, and women
2. Fathers: Butch queens, butches, and men

more gender and sexual identities from which to choose than available to members in the "outside" world (see Table 48.1).[28]

Because gender performance is central to self-identification and can imply a whole range of sexual identities in Ballroom culture, the system reflects how the members define themselves largely based on the categories that they walk/perform. All members of the Ballroom community identify as either one of the six categories in the gender/sexual identity system. If/when one "walks a ball," that participant competes in the competitive categories that coincide with their gender/sexual identity within the Ballroom community. For instance, a femme queen can only "walk/perform" in categories that are listed under that heading on the ball flyer. The intensely competitive performances at the ball events create a space of celebration, affirmation, critique, and reconstitution as well as in the everyday lives of its Black queer members.

It is worth noting that there are no balls without houses and there are no houses without balls. And in the kinship system of Ballroom culture, houses are led by "mothers" (butch queens, femme queens, and women) and "fathers" (butch queens and butches), who, regardless of age, sexual orientation, and social status, provide a labor of care and love with/for numerous Black queer people who have been rejected by their blood families, religious institutions, and society at large. Houses, for instance, are one of the core features of the Ballroom community, and houses serve as social, and sometimes literal, homes for its members.[29] Thus the ball, combined with the social relations within the houses outside of it are mutually constitutive and, taken together, make up the world of Ballroom culture.

No doubt, technology has played an integral role in the expansion of Ballroom culture, allowing the members of this national network to stay connected through the Web. For instance, the national Ballroom scene uses various websites, such as www.walk4mewednesdays.com, www.thehouseofballs.com, and www.getyourtens.com, as well as listservs and blogs that are set up and maintained by houses and individual members in order to connect with the community at large and to communicate with their chapters throughout the country. In addition, there are magazines devoted to Ballroom culture, such as *CLIK Magazine*. The National Confederation of Black Gay Prides is an umbrella organization that works with citywide Black gay-pride festivities, bringing together Black and Latino LGBTQ members of the community to participate in national balls. Albeit transient, the Ballroom scene is large and growing, providing a world for Black and Latina/o LGBTQ people to reconstitute, affirm, and celebrate their queer gender and sexual identities. [...]

## BALLROOM CULTURE AND HIV/AIDS

I begin this portion of my examination by situating Ballroom culture and HIV/AIDS within the context of Detroit, Michigan.[31] Given the disproportionate impact of HIV/AIDS on Black communities across the country, and its particular devastation of Black people in Detroit, and given that the Ballroom community is embedded in Black communities in the city, HIV/AIDS and its impact on Ballroom is an instructive case study. Invariably, the interlocking oppressions of race, class, gender, and sexuality shape Black queer people's experiences as they exacerbate the suffering of marginalized groups at the hands of the virus.[32]

In Michigan, although African Americans comprise of only 14 percent of the total population, according to HIV epidemiological data for 2008, new infection rates for African Americans were 59 percent; this was compared to a 35 percent infection rate for whites. By race and gender, HIV infection rates were 41 percent compared to 29 percent for white men. And it is worth noting that African American women make up 73 percent of all HIV cases among women in Michigan.[33] HIV infection rates among MSM were 45 percent compared to 13 percent for heterosexual transmission.[34] Based on this epidemiological data in Michigan, we can infer that Black MSM have increasing disproportionate rates of new HIV infections (that is, there are higher HIV infection rates among Blacks, among Black men, and among Black MSM, and among men, the primary route of HIV transmission is male-to-male sexual intercourse).[35]

Detroit carries the majority of HIV prevalence in Michigan.[36] Known as both the "chocolate city" and the "motor city," Detroit has the most distinct racial and class demographics of any large U.S. city. According to the 2000 U.S. Census, Detroit is the largest city with a Black majority population in the United States. Out of approximately 951,270 residents, 83 percent identified themselves as Black or African American. In socioeconomic terms, Detroit has one of the poorest populations in the country; between 26.8 and 33.4 percent of the city's residents live in poverty.[37] Like many other cities with large Black populations, Detroit is one of the places hardest hit by the disease.[38]

HIV/AIDS workers in Detroit, some of whom are HIV-positive, have a unique vantage point when considering the intersections of gender, sexuality, and HIV/AIDS. The prevention workers that I interviewed suggested that the dominant discourse on HIV/AIDS, one that pathologizes and sutures the disease to homosexuality and that disallows a candid dialogue about sexuality and HIV risk reduction, hampers their ability to reduce infections rates in the city. Compounded by the disturbing socioeconomic conditions, most HIV/AIDS cases among men in Detroit are Black MSM. Black people infected with HIV/AIDS in large cities like Detroit do not have access to AIDS prevention and treatment resources that are equal to their white counterparts.[39] Thus, Black MSM who are infected with or at high risk for HIV/AIDS infection experience a simultaneity of oppression, structured not only by and through race, class, gender, and sexuality, but also through HIV/AIDS.

For example, when I asked Tino Prestige, a butch queen and caseworker at the Horizons Project, an HIV/AIDS prevention and services agency in Detroit, why he thinks the HIV/AIDS epidemic is so severe among African American men in Detroit, he said, "There's a lack of information in the school system, *no* discussion of sexuality, and no discussion of how to be sexually responsible even if you are heterosexual. People have a whole lot of ignorance about LGBTQ issues, and people still think that it's wrong because of their religious views."

Similarly, Noir Prestige, also a butch queen, described how once, while he worked for the Men of Color Motivational Group (MOC), a now-defunct HIV/AIDS prevention agency in Detroit, he delivered a presentation on HIV/AIDS, a school administrator insisted that he not encourage homosexuality, as if HIV/AIDS were "naturally" linked to homosexuality and as if talking about homosexuality would lead to young people adopting it. That is why Noir reiterated the need to "de-gay" or "de-homosexualize" HIV/AIDS so that all people will take the problem seriously. A public discussion of HIV/AIDS, especially among young people, requires this delinking of HIV/AIDS from homosexuality in order to ease homophobic fears held in society. At the same time, prevention workers are faced with a conundrum of sorts because when homosexuality is not discussed Black MSM and/or gay men are rendered invisible, while still viewed as the primary vectors of HIV/AIDS infection.

Both Tino and Noir attest to the fact that explicit and implicit homophobia resulting from familial and cultural expectations to adhere to hegemonic gender and sexual norms directly influence the information that Black queer people receive about HIV/AIDS. As Lester K. Spence argues, in general, the larger Black community's knowledge about HIV/AIDS; Black people's perception of their own risk of contracting the virus; and their preferences concerning HIV/AIDS policy are all intrinsically linked to their views on homosexuality.[40] Ultimately, the treatment and policing of sexuality that Black queer people endure from the outside create deep-seated internal struggles that influence the way they self-identify and interact with others, both gays and heterosexual.

As Spence suggests, Black queer people constitute an "out-group" and are therefore shunned more than any other group in the United States.[41] And in effect, for Black people in Detroit, what should be a consensus issue, HIV/AIDS is instead what Cathy J. Cohen calls a crosscutting issue.[42]

According to Cohen, crosscutting issues disrupt the imagined consensus that disguises hierarchies and inequities as a collective community consciousness. Many of my interlocutors suggested that "the Black community" tends to imagine itself as "straight" and that AIDS has impacted a few sexual deviants within the community who have lost their way. Noir Prestige stated that the family and community that he grew up in believed that, "if you weren't gay, you wouldn't get it [AIDS]." Therefore, crosscutting issues pose challenges for marginal groups disproportionately, and they directly affect a particular segment *within* the marginalized population.[43] It is no surprise, then, that Black communities' response to HIV/AIDS by linking it to homosexuality is an instance of what Cohen terms secondary marginalization, where select, privileged members of Black communities determine the priorities and regulate and police the margins in order to shape a public image that disavows and disciplines the less privileged members or those who do not conform.[44]

Therefore, Ballroom culture is compelled to be proactive and multifaceted in its struggle against the disease and the Othering discourses that accompany it. As David Román aptly points out, AIDS cannot be separated from the discourses that construct and in fact "sustain it."[45] Discourse regarding AIDS informs the specific priorities (defining those whose lives are worth saving) that public-health institutions devise regarding prevention. Recalcitrant racism, sexism, homophobia/heterosexism, poverty, and other forms of disenfranchisement are inextricably linked to scurrilous representations of AIDS as a Black gay disease.

In Michigan, the scant HIV/AIDS reduction strategies consist of the distribution of brochures, condoms, and other safe-sex materials, discussion groups, and safe-sex training,[46] but they ignore the crucial role that cultural values play in shaping the stigmatization associated with race, class, gender, sexuality, and AIDS. Directly related to this issue, few CBOs create programs that move beyond simply reducing individual "risk behaviors," by addressing the social conditions that contribute to them.

For instance, as Noir emphasized firmly, "HIV kills. Why? Stigma. The people living *with it* have to make others comfortable living around it; that's a lot of work. And folks die trying to accomplish that because you end up living in secret. Support is key and very essential in living with the illness or around it." Noir demonstrates how a vicious cycle of stigmatization undermines any prevention program. Unwittingly or not, CBOs extract their prevention techniques from these hegemonic discourses that overdetermine Black MSM as a risk population.

While I was conducting fieldwork, the two organizations that focused on the Black queer community in Detroit enacted prevention programs buttressed by convergent racialized, classed, gendered, and sexualized discourses of risk. But it is the isolating of certain Black groups within the Black community on one level, and the characterization of Black people as a high-risk population on the other, that keeps Ballroom members from utilizing the prevention and treatment resources offered by these organizations. For example, Tino Prestige underscores this when he says, "The Community Health Awareness Group has a mobile testing unit. But when the unit shows up to a ball, people won't be willing to go to it cause people will think something is wrong with them, so they don't want to be seen that way." Simply put, Ballroom members are already stigmatized, the prevention efforts themselves are stigmatized, so our utilization of the services stigmatizes us even more.[47]

## BALLROOM COMMUNITY PRACTICES AS HIV/AIDS INTRAVENTION

What do Black queer members *do* about such conditions? How does the cultural work of creating an alternative minoritarian sphere help to refract feelings of worthlessness caused by stigmatization and oppression? How does Ballroom provide a space to forge alternative realities for its members? Part of what is at stake in the Ballroom community here is a struggle for alternative community representation and community preservation in midst of a health and social crisis.[48] In what follows, I delineate three forms of intravention that are organic aspects of Ballroom culture or what Friedman and colleagues refer to as collective risk-reduction reinforcement.[49] Members of the Ballroom community create a counterdiscourse of HIV/AIDS that recasts its members as people with lives worth saving, not merely risk groups; the structure of the community provides social support; and the community produces prevention balls that are based on Ballroom community values and practices in an attempt to destigmatize HIV/AIDS so that its members can be more receptive to messages of risk reduction.

### Social Epistemology of Ballroom Culture

First, I highlight the ways in which Ballroom members construct a social epistemology as a critical aspect of the overall work of creating an alternative social sphere. This alternative social sphere is a crucial source of value for Ballroom members. I emphasize key characteristics of Ballroom culture/spaces that are strategies for addressing HIV/AIDS that reflect its members' desire for recuperative forms of self and collective representations.[50] I contend that Ballroom practices and their potentialities unveil the difference between *prevention* approaches and the on-the-ground practices of cultural *intravention*.

In his study of the *milieu*, a homosocial underground scene in Abidjan, Ivory Coast, Vinh-Kim Nguyen suggests that social knowledge informs the "social relations and the tactics used to navigate them for individual and collective benefit."[51] This social knowledge is usually contained within dispossessed communities and subaltern spaces and allows its members to comment on their conditions as well as to develop strategies to alter them. For example, social knowledge in the Ballroom community views gender and sexuality as fluid and mutable, kinship/family as not necessarily biological, and performance as integral to community affirmation and preservation. Hence, the creation of a social knowledge is how Ballroom members reconstitute themselves in the midst of the HIV/AIDS crisis in an attempt to change the social consequences of it.

All of my informants agree that doing HIV/AIDS prevention work within the Ballroom scene is difficult; however, some believe that it is a cultural space of hope. One such possibility is the notion of self-renewal, a way of reconstituting the self within Ballroom to contend with the negative representations in the outside world. For instance, Ballroom is what Diva D from the House of Bvlgari calls a "fictitious existence." When I asked him whether "low self-worth" was a motivating factor for Black queer people to join the Ballroom scene, he responded, "Yes, it gives them a brand-new identity; it gives them a brand-new slate. If your family don't care about you because you are gay and what not or if you can't get a job, the Ballroom scene helps you start anew. It creates a brand-new identity that you can feel comfortable with."

The social knowledge of Ballroom links the balls to the community-fashioned kinship system that both sustains the community and facilitates HIV/AIDS prevention. Therefore, Ballroom social knowledge enables effective HIV/AIDS prevention that is based on the values and norms established by its community members as opposed to those imposed on it from the outside.

### Kinship and Social Support

As the house mother of the Detroit chapter of the House of Prestige and former HIV/AIDS prevention worker at the time of the interview, Duchess suggests that Ballroom is built on social relations that redefine prevention work. He stated further, "The structure of the [Ballroom] community already allows for familial prevention work, you know, just in the fact that someone can say to you, 'Now you know you need to wear a condom' and it be from someone that you have built that trust factor with. People in the community do prevention work all of the time."

Within these houses, members consult with their house parents and their siblings on issues that, either by choice or necessity, they do not discuss with their biological kin. House mothers and fathers, in particular, provide daily parental guidance for Ballroom kids on issues such as intimate/romantic relationships, sex, gender and sexual identities, health, hormonal therapy, and body presentation, just to name a few matters.

Siblings in houses provide support for HIV prevention among those not infected, but they also play an integral role by supporting those already infected with HIV as well. For instance, a very thin and increasingly frail-looking Noir Prestige began one of our many interviews by excusing himself to go to the bathroom, apparently to throw up. "Excuse me," said Noir in the living room of his small, tidy apartment that he shares with his boyfriend of eight years. "I just started new meds; this shit is horrible, but I shall survive." Noir went on to describe how his very close relationship with Tino Prestige has helped him cope with his condition.[52]

Noir remarked that he and Tino Prestige have very similar life experiences. They were both infected with the virus in their teens. They are both in long-term relationships (eight years) with partners who are not infected, partners who struggle with the difficulties of loving someone who is HIV-positive and/or living with AIDS. They are both treatment advocates at the Horizons Project. At the balls, they walk in butch realness categories: thug realness and schoolboy realness.[53] Most importantly, they provide treatment for each other. It is worth mentioning here that in Ballroom life, one's age is not based on necessarily one's years on earth; rather, it is based on how long one has been in the Ballroom scene and/or been out in the gay world. Hence, the "big" brother reminded his "little" brother to take his meds, and he often drove him to his appointments with his doctor. They cared for one another especially in moments when each of their partners did not rise to the occasion. In a separate interview I conducted with Tino Prestige, he said, "We are truly brothers." Clearly, these siblings help each other endure the psychic trauma that comes along with HIV/AIDS in ways that their partners could not.

In many cases, house members express love for one another; they serve each other when needed, and undoubtedly they add overall value to each other's lives, especially when facing desperate situations. In general, houses provide what Cornel West describes as nonmarket values: love, care, and service.[54] Not only do these values constitute a labor of care that becomes intensified when the community decides to deal with HIV/AIDS collectively, but they also exist in the quotidian aspect of Ballroom life.

## Black Queer Performance and HIV/AIDS Prevention Balls

Despite the inability of some public-health departments to devise and sustain effective HIV/AIDS prevention strategies for so-called high-risk communities, some Ballroom houses have joined forces with a few CBOs to create "prevention houses" and "prevention balls." As I have noted, Ballroom houses, in general, are spaces of social support that often reinforce messages of HIV/AIDS prevention either directly or indirectly. But, prevention houses usually have formal funding from and/or programmatic ties with CBOs, and they engage in HIV/AIDS prevention activities and coordinate balls based on HIV/AIDS prevention themes.

Again, since there are no houses without balls and there are no balls without houses, part of the important discursive work of prevention houses occurs at prevention balls. On one hand, the importance placed on image and status in Ballroom makes HIV/AIDS prevention work difficult because members distance themselves from the topic of HIV/AIDS for fear that it will tarnish them. But on the other hand, competitive performance, image, and status are used to disseminate and promote messages about HIV risk reduction among Ballroom members. Out of the numerous balls that I attended and/or participated in, most of them were packed with hundreds of Black queer people from all over the country. As Francisco Roque from Gay Men's Health Crisis said, "The Ballroom community is a captive 'at-risk' population, and modeling behavior is built in the community." Albeit imperfect, it is a necessary strategy to use competition and image within a Ballroom cultural context to disseminate information and simultaneously reduce stigma.

As a hallmark of Ballroom culture, competition is another means through which image and status are formed and repaired. Since individual members and houses can gain recognition and status only by "snatching trophies,"[55] competition is an integral aspect of the social world of Ballroom that offers possibilities for effective HIV/AIDS prevention. Former Father of the House of Infiniti and the Executive Director of Empowerment Detroit, an HIV prevention agency targeting Black gay youth, Jonathon Davis confirmed this when he said, "In terms of the Ballroom community in Detroit, if it ain't got nothing to do with a trophy, these girls don't care." And when I asked Pootaman, a twenty-year-old member of the House of Ninja and an HIV/AIDS prevention worker at MOC at the time of the interview, why he became interested in walking balls, he said, "I enjoy the competition, the feeling of sitting someone down to prove a point, that I could take home a trophy." Father Infiniti and Pootaman speak to the centrality of the trophy, the accoutrements that come along with it and how both represent the attainment of value and affirmation that Ballroom members are usually otherwise denied in the outside world.

Last, in order to illustrate more vividly how prevention balls work, I describe my experience as a performance participant and witness. In March 2005, I competed in the annual Love is the Message Ball in Los Angeles.[56] As a member of the Los Angeles chapter of the House of Prestige at the time, I walked, along with Pokka, the father, in the "schoolboy realness versus executive realness" category for the mini grand prize. The description of the category on the flyer read:

> School Boy Realness—Let's see if U were paying attention in Sex Ed. Bring us School Boy realness w/a safe sex production. Props a must and you will be graded on your project and knowledge.
>
> VS.
>
> Executive—U have been promoted to CEO of a condom company of your choice. U must have a prop and be prepared to sell your product to the board.

Pokka planned our performance and was determined to win the trophy and the $100.00 cash prize. Since Pokka and I walk executive realness, I dressed the part and played the role of a CEO, and Pokka was the president of the board of directors of the Lifetime Condoms Corporation. He had spent time and money to prepare everything we needed to mount this miniproduction.

When Kodak Kandinsky, the commentator for the evening, announced our category, members from various houses came out as schoolboy realness wearing clothes with several condoms attached to them. Because I was in the waiting area of the hall, I could not see them perform their miniproduction. When it was our turn, Pokka walked out ahead of me, dressed in an all-black suit and carrying his laptop computer case. As he approached the judges' table, he read a statement about the crisis of HIV/AIDS in the Black community, stressing that condom use is an effective strategy in the fight against the spread of the disease. "Now, I bring to you Professah Prestige, our new CEO, to make a brief statement," said Pokka. I came strutting down the runway in a navy blue suit carrying my laptop computer in a black leather computer bag in one hand and a large black portfolio case full of billboards in the other. When I got to the judges table, I took the microphone and said, "My name is Professah Prestige, the new CEO of Lifetime Condoms. We have new durable condoms that do not reduce sensation. I hope that you all will give them a try. Be safe and use condoms." After my statement, the commentator asked the judges to score me. "Are they real? Do you see it? Judges score him (all of the judges flashed their cards with "10" written on them). Ok, tens across the board. Prestiges step to the side. Next contestants please," said Kodak. "Thank God, I did not get chopped," I thought.

After other competitors were eliminated, "chopped," there were only five competitors left, Pokka and I from the House of Prestige and three members from another house who walked schoolboy realness. Then, someone from the Minority AIDS Project posed the following question to all of us: "What is a dental dam?" Each of us was told to whisper the answer in Kodak's ear. When he came to me, I explained that a dental dam is used for oral sex, and it provides a barrier of protection between the mouth and the anus or the vagina. Then, Kodak announced that only two of us said the correct answer, a schoolboy realness kid from the other house and me. Apparently, Pokka gave him the wrong answer. I felt kind of bad because Pokka had done most of the preparation for our production.

Finally, the judges had to choose who looked more real between the realness kid and me. "Who is realer?" said Kodak. When Kodak got to the final two out of the seven judges, one of them pointed at me and said, "He look like a real executive." At the end, I won the category. I was shocked and thrilled at the same time. They gave me a trophy and the $100.00 prize. I kept the trophy and gave the money to the house mother to put in our house fund. I had won the category for the House of Prestige. Most importantly, within the competitive spirit at the balls, members of the Ballroom community were exposed to knowledge about safe sex without individuals being singled out and stigmatized. Clearly, performance, kinship, and social knowledge function as cultural practices that allow Ballroom community members to intravene radically in the AIDS crisis, since the practices are derived from within the community itself.

## CONCLUSION

Ballroom members perform the labor of caring for and the valuing of lives that are integral to building and sustaining a community in the midst of crisis. Ballroom practices are important alternatives that attend to the multifarious challenges that HIV/AIDS poses, especially the attendant public and scientific discourses that render Black queer people dysfunctional and dangerous, and further stigmatized them as vectors of disease. These values sustain the community and constitute a critical component to any form of intervention not just aimed at reducing the spread of HIV/AIDS, but also attempting to cultivate the necessary systems and structures (within Ballroom) that redress the violence done to Black queers. This is violence not only at the hands of the HIV/AIDS epidemic, but also the Othering discourses that coproduce it.

The focus here is the Ballroom community's creation of "communities" and of new and counter modes of self-representation and self-identification that offer possibilities for members of the minoritarian communities to alter the conditions for themselves. And those of us who are ensconced in notions of "at-risk" communities know that HIV/AIDS—the disease itself—does not discriminate. It has no boundaries. On the contrary, it is the public-health and sociopolitical responses to it, on a local, national, and global scale, that do. This fact marks the difference between *prevention* (from the outside) from *intravention* and the dialectic between the two that are necessary to ameliorate the epidemic.

I do not romanticize performance by suggesting that it can totally overhaul or transform the social and material conditions in which Ballroom members live. Some members fall through the cracks, and many die. But some survive, and they do so with the assistance of fellow Ballroom members. Ballroom culture demonstrates how performance can add value and meaning to the lives of those rendered valueless and meaningless. But, as cultural critic and homo-hip hop artist Tim'm West aptly argues, since there are few safe spaces for Black queers, especially those suffering from HIV, many of us must claim all spaces as salvageable in whichever ways they support our breathing.[57]

## NOTES

1. I interviewed Wolfgang Busch on November 30, 2003 in New York City. His film, *How Do I Look* (2006), is the most recent documentary on Ballroom culture in NYC. During the interview, Wolfgang said that he wants the proceeds from the film to be dedicated to HIV/AIDS prevention. For more information and updates on his work go to http://www. howdoilooknyc.org.
2. Cathy Cohen, "Deviance as Resistance: a New Research Agenda for the Study of Black Politics," *Du Bois Review* 1, no. (2004): 27–45, 27.
3. This chant by Neiman Marcus Escada is taken from a CD of house music mixes called *Bamabounce*.
4. Currently, the Gay Men's Health Crisis (GMHC) has the longest standing HIV/AIDS prevention program that focuses on the Ballroom community. The House of Latex of the GMHC has held its annual Latex Ball (an HIV/AIDS prevention ball) for eighteen years. The Latex Ball is by far the most popular ball in the country, usually drawing between 2,500 and 3,000 audience members/participants. Ironically, the CDC does not recognize this program as an intervention, and it is not federally funded.
5. Performance or performative ethnography is a method of data collection that requires the researcher to actively participate in the very performances and cultural practices that he or she is analyzing. [...]
6. Samuel Friedman, Melissa Bolyard, Carey Maslow, Pedro Mateu-Gelabert, Alan Neaigus, and Milagros Sandoval, "Urging Others to Be Healthy: 'Intravention' by Injection Drug Users as a Community Prevention Goal," *AIDS Education and Prevention* 16, no. 3 (2004): 250–263, at 251.
7. Ibid.
8. E. Patrick Johnson, *Sweet Tea: Black Gay Men of the South* (Chapel Hill: University of North Carolina Press, 2008), 8.
9. In 2003, I worked for Men of Color Motivational Group Inc. (MOC) in Detroit, Michigan. MOC had a CDC-funded program that emphasized HIV/AIDS prevention among the Ballroom community. The program lost its funding, and the organization eventually closed in the midst of controversy. For more information, see Brent Dorian Carpenter, "Sexual Harassment Allegations Rock Men of Color: Funding Could Be at Risk," *Between the Line* (June 2003), 12–18.
10. It is worth noting that most qualitative studies that are conducted on HIV/AIDS within public health are not ethnographic. In my experience working with and among other HIV/AIDS researchers, I am usually the only ethnographer involved in any given research project.
    [...]
17. Robin D. G. Kelley, *Yo' Mama's Disfunktional! Fighting the Culture Wars in Urban America* (Boston: Beacon Press, 1997), 45.
18. Ibid.
    [...]
20. Jan Zita Grover, "AIDS: Keywords," in *AIDS: Cultural Analysis, Cultural Activism,* ed. Douglas Crimp, 17–30 (Cambridge, Mass.: MIT Press, 1998), 27.
21. Cindy Patton, *Fatal Advice: How Safe-Sex Education Went Wrong* (Durham, N.C.: Duke University Press, 1996), 23.
    [...]
24. Román, *Acts of Intervention,* 155.

25. Friedman et al., "Urging Others to Be Healthy," 250.
26. Ibid., 260.
27. Karen McCarthy Brown, "Mimesis in the Face of Fear: Femme Queens, Butch Queens, and Gender Play in the Houses of Greater Newark," in *Passing: Identity and Interpretation in Sexuality, Race, and Religion,* ed. María Carla Sánchez and Linda Schlossberg (New York: New York University Press, 2001), 208–227, at 208.
28. What I call the "gender/sexual identity system" is typically called the "gender system" within Ballroom culture. My outline of the six subjectivities within the system is drawn from ethnographic data that include my attendance/participation in balls, my analysis of numerous ball flyers, and interviews that I conducted with members from all over the country over a nine-year period. Despite a few discrepancies among different sectors of the community, the general components of the system are standard throughout the Ballroom scene. [...]
29. Emily Arnold and Marlon M. Bailey, "Constructing Home and Family: How the Ballroom Community Supports African American GLBTQ Youth in the Face of HIV/AIDS," *Journal of Gay and Lesbian Social Services: Issues in Practice, Policy, & Research* (Summer 2009): 1–34, at 6.
    [...]
31. While I acknowledge the participation of Latina/o queer people in Ballroom culture in some locations, most Ballroom members are Black queer people. Since my primary site of examination is Detroit, where the Ballroom scene is almost exclusively Black, all of my interlocutors and the communities to whom I refer are Black queer people.
32. Brett C. Stockdill, *Activism Against AIDS: At the Intersections of Sexuality, Race, Gender, and Class* (Boulder, Colo.: Lynne Rienner, 2003), 4.
33. All statistics cited here are from the Michigan Department of Community Health (2008), www.michigan.gov/mdch.
34. In a five-city study of HIV infection among Black MSM conducted by the CDC in 2005, it was estimated that 46 percent of Black MSM are infected with HIV/AIDS, and 64 percent of those who tested positive were unaware of their status. "HIV prevalence, unrecognized infection, and HIV testing among men who have sex with men—Five U.S. cities, June 2004—April 2005," *Morbidity and Mortality Weekly Report* 54: 597–601.
35. One of the critical problems with the reporting of HIV epidemiological data by local health departments is that the data is not often disaggregated by race, gender, and "sexual risk categories." As a result, most of the data collected on the local level do not provide specific numbers on Black MSM.
36. Michigan Department of Community Health (2008).
37. U.S. Census (2000), www.census.gov/main/www/cen2000.html.
38. Cathy J. Cohen, "Contested Membership: Black Gay Identities and the Politics of AIDS," in *Queer Theory/Sociology,* ed. Steven Seidman (Cambridge, Mass.: Blackwell, 1996), 372.
39. Roy Cain, "Gay Identity Politics in Community-Based AIDS Organizations," in Ristock and Taylor, *Inside the Academy and Out,* 200. More elaboration on this can be found in Cohen, *The Boundaries of Blackness;* Seidman, *Queer Theory/ Sociology;* and Brett C. Stockdill, *Activism Against AIDS: At the Intersections of Sexuality, Race, Gender, and Class* (Boulder, Colo.: Lynne Rienner, 2003).
40. Lester K. Spence, "Uncovering Black Attitudes About Homosexuality and HIV/AIDS," paper presented at the 2005 National Conference of Black Political Scientists, Alexandria, Va., 1.
41. Ibid., 6.
42. Cohen, *The Boundaries of Blackness,* 70.
43. Ibid.
44. Ibid.
45. Román, *Acts of Intervention,* xxiii.
46. Nancy E. Stoller, *Lessons from the Damned: Queers, Whores, and Junkies Respond to AIDS* (New York: Routledge, 1998), 2.
47. Cain, "Gay Identity Politics," 200.
48. Stuart Hall, "What Is This 'Black' in Black Popular Culture?" in *Black Popular Culture,* ed. Gina Dent, 1–21 (Seattle: Bay Press, 1992), at 24.
49. Friedman et al., "Urging Others to Be Healthy," 251.
50. Kim D. Butler, "Defining Diaspora, Refining a Discourse," *Diaspora* 10, no. 2 (2001): 189–218, at 192.
51. Vinh-Kim Nguyen, "Uses and Pleasures: Sexual Modernity, HIV/AIDS and Confessional Technologies in a West African Metropolis," in *Sex in Development: Science, Sexuality, and Morality in Global Perspective*, ed. Vincanne Adams and Stacy Leigh Pigg, 245–268 (Durham, N.C.: Duke University Press, 2005), 246.
52. Noir Prestige died from complications of HIV/AIDS on May 4, 2005, in Detroit.
53. In Ballroom culture, "realness" refers to a fundamental set of criteria for performance. These criteria have been a part of Ballroom culture throughout its more than five decades of existence. Realness requires strict adherence to certain performances, self-presentations, and embodiments that are believed to capture the authenticity of particular gender and sexual identities. I argue elsewhere that these criteria are established and function based on a schema of race and class that gives realness its discursive power in both the Ballroom scene as well as in society at large. Thus, the performance criteria for schoolboy realness and executive realness include not only "looking like" a schoolboy or an executive, but also performing gender as a man with normative masculinity that signifies "straight" sexuality.

54. Cornel West, "Nihilism in Black America," in Dent, *Black Popular Culture*, 37–47, at 42.

55. In Ballroom lingo, "snatching a trophy" means winning the category and being awarded a trophy and/or a cash prize. This is also called "slay and snatch: slaying the competitors and snatching the trophy."

56. This annual ball is cosponsored by the House of Rodeo and the Minority AIDS Project in Los Angeles.

57. Tim'm West, "Keepin' It Real: Disidentification and Its Discontents," in *Black Cultural Traffic: Crossroads in Global Performance and Popular Culture*, ed. Harry J. Elam Jr. and Kennell Jackson, 162–184 (Ann Arbor: University of Michigan Press, 2005), 163.

# 49

# *Transgender as Mental Illness*

## Nosology, Social Justice, and the Tarnished Golden Mean

## R. Nick Gorton

NICK GORTON, A DOCTOR WHO SPECIALIZES IN TRANSGENDER HEALTH CARE, is a volunteer practitioner at San Francisco's Lyon-Martin Women's Health Services and a consultant on transgender health care. Written in 2007, "Transgender as Mental Illness" engages with ongoing debates about whether transgender should be regarded as a psychiatric disorder or as a medical condition, or neither. Advocates of removing gender identity disorder from the *Diagnostic and Statistical Manual of Mental Disorders (DSM)* argue that transgender and transsexuality are not diseases. Others argue that seeing transness as a "benign variation" would mean procedures used to transform gendered bodies would remove the legitimacy that authorizes trans people's access to social and health services, as well as legal rights. The middle ground, or "golden mean" as Gorton puts it, is to see transness as a medical condition, but not as a stigmatized mental illness. This is the basis for a growing GID reform movement. Gorton takes apart the arguments for GID reform step by step. One important point is that to focus solely on the stigmatization of gender non-conforming people as mentally ill means that other people who are equally stigmatized by being diagnosed with mental disorders keep losing. Moreover, DSM classification confers a legitimacy that justifies the limited health care offered to transgendered prisoners: without that justification, Gorton contends, giving prisoners access to hormones and surgery would be impossible. Although Gorton insists on a physical disease model of transgenderism that is dissonant with the other work collected in this reader, his call for deeper interrogation of the premises on which we base arguments for health care reform remain provocative.

## INTRODUCTION

The question of whether transgenderism is a disease is hotly debated in both the transgender and medical-psychiatric communities. One prevalent view, especially in the transgender community, is that transgenderism is not a disease at all, but a benign normal variant of the human experience akin to left-handedness. Proponents of this view reject the concept of Gender Identity Disorder (GID) as an appropriate descriptor of the transgender experience. Others within the transgender community, and many health care providers, believe that GID (the disease) is an appropriate clinical descriptor for transgenderism. In a prior paper I discussed this question and argued in favor of the classification of transgenderism as a disease.[2] This paper will build on that argument and address the further question of the nosology of transgenderism as a disease.[3] That is, is transgenderism best classified a "medical" or "psychiatric" illness?

Among those within the transgender community who accept that transgenderism is a disease, many reject the idea that GID is a *psychiatric* illness. Instead they advocate a change in both the nomenclature and clinical classification of transgenderism. Instead of designating transgenderism as GID, they favor other disease names such as "gender dysphoria," as well as classification of this entity as a medical rather than a mental illness. Such advocates of transgenderism as a medical diagnosis present their argument as a moderate position between the two poles of "complete depathologization" (that is, transgenderism as a benign variant rather than a disease at all) and "GID as a mental illness." This tantalizing *golden mean* purports to preserve the benefits of the disease model of transgenderism, namely continued access to care within the medical paradigm, legal and social protections, and in some cases the opportunity to have public or private insurance funding for hormonal and surgical treatments. In addition, while preserving these obvious benefits, this school of thought also attempts to eliminate the stigma of "mental illness" to which many transgender people and some health care providers object.

However, while this is a tempting solution to this complex nosological and political problem, the question remains: is this position both logically valid and the most clinically appropriate way of describing transgenderism?

## ARGUMENTS FOR "GID REFORM"

The arguments and motivations for the "GID reform" movement which seeks to reclassify transgenderism as a medical illness are numerous. Several common themes emerge when examining the positions of most advocates of such reform. The three primary types of arguments are: fairness, destigmatization, and scientific justifications. Each of these will be examined below.

### *Fairness*

The appeal to fairness, while common, is perhaps the weakest argument for GID reform. This argument suggests that since homosexuality was declared by mainstream psychiatry as not being a mental illness, that transgenderism similarly deserves depathologization as a fairness issue. A GID reform advocate, Dr. Kelley Winters, has stated:

> Twenty-seven years after the American Psychiatric Association (APA) voted to delete homosexuality as a mental disorder, the diagnostic categories of "gender identity disorder" and "transvestic fetishism" in the *Diagnostic and Statistical Manual of Mental Disorders* continue to raise questions of consistency, validity, and fairness.[4]

Such advocates also often suggest that depathologization would result in the same political and social progress within the transgender community as occurred for gays and lesbians after the removal of homosexuality from the American Psychiatric Association's *Diagnostic and Statistical Manual of Mental Disorders* (DSM). Thus, depathologization becomes a fairness issue not just in the nomenclature of the condition, but also in the benefits supposedly gained from removing the label of mental illness.

However, this argument fails in its weak induction. It is recognized by most transgender rights activists that transgenderism is a unique state that is *not the same as* homosexuality. Both *belong to* the larger LGBTIQ community, but that association does not imply that they should be considered interchangeably.[5] Additionally, while the removal of homosexuality from the DSM in 1973 *preceded* many milestones in the LGB rights movement, attributing these victories to the removal of homosexuality is a *post hoc ergo propter hoc* error. The fallaciousness of this argument is illustrated by the similar ludicrous argument that since the AIDS epidemic began within a decade of homosexuality being removed from the DSM that this removal in some way kindled the epidemic.

### Removal of Stigma

Another common but fairly weak argument to support removal of GID from the DSM is that reform is justified because it will result in the removal of the stigma from transgenderism that is associated with mental illness. This motivation is not a legitimate argument for removal simply because this same argument could be made for all of the diseases that are currently classified as mental illnesses. That is, simply because depression might have less stigma were it considered to be an endocrine disorder, that is not a reasonable argument to remove it from the DSM. However, while removal of stigma is a weak *argument*, it is a major *motivation* for many who wish to reclassify transgenderism as a medical illness, so it is crucial to understand the reasons that underlie the popularity of this argument, as well as its implications.

The question of stigmatization of psychiatric illness exposes deeper moral problems. In one discussion of stigma and GID, Kathy Wilson writes: "Reforming the DSM will not eliminate transgender stigma but will remove its legitimacy."[6] The implication inherent in this simple statement is that those diagnoses which appropriately remain in the DSM are *legitimately stigmatized*. That is, if removal of GID from the DSM will remove the *legitimacy* of its stigmatization, then, as a basic premise of this argument, stigma applied to diagnoses of mental illness should therefore be accepted as legitimate.

A slightly more sophisticated and developed version of this argument attempts to solve this dilemma by stating that while psychiatric illnesses *should not* be stigmatized, in our society they simply *are stigmatized*. Thus, advocates state that no one should be stigmatized because they have a mental illness, however transgender people can reasonably desire to disassociate themselves from that stigma without justifying the pejorative labeling of another group. However, while this argument does not rely on the premise that mental illness *is deserving of* stigma, it makes a more disturbing ethical and political compromise. This argument does not overtly justify the continued marginalization of another disenfranchised group, but it *legitimizes the individual's own role as a passive bystander to that marginalization*. Instead of advocating political and social justice for the larger group, those advocating this position seek to gain acceptance simply by distancing themselves from a larger disenfranchised group. The moral failing of this motivation is illustrated by a quote from Yehuda Bauer, Professor of Holocaust Studies at the Hebrew University of Jerusalem: "I come from a people who gave the Ten Commandments to the world. Time has come to strengthen them by three additional ones, which we ought to adopt and commit ourselves to: thou shall not be a perpetrator; thou shall not be a victim; and thou shall never, but never, be a bystander."

Moreover, in addition to being a morally questionable argument, it also functions to weaken both the transgender community and the larger community of all people with mental illness. Coalition building is one of the pillars of social justice movements. The original union organizing principle remains true: we all do better when we ALL do better. Divisive politics such as distancing and passive acceptance of stigmatization of other groups as the status quo is the antithesis of what builds strong coalitions within larger communities. Lack of such coalitions critically weakens the separate movements. This same sort of divisive politics within the LGB segment of the larger LGBTIQ movement has sometimes resulted in the marginalization of transgender people, but also weakens the power of the larger movement by causing deep rifts. For example, the limited benefit that LGB people might gain by supporting non-trans-inclusive civil rights legislation cannot outweigh the damage produced by disempowering the entire LGBTIQ movement.

So in addition to being a poor *argument* for removal of GID from the DSM, eliminating stigma by distancing oneself from a larger disenfranchised group is morally and politically unjustified as a *motivation for* advocacy for the depathologization of GID.

### Scientific Arguments for Reform

In addition to the above socio-political arguments for reclassification of transgenderism, medical and scientific arguments for reclassification are proposed by reform advocates. These nosological arguments as a whole seek to justify reform by demonstrating that GID is in some way *different from* all of the other illnesses in the DSM, while being more similar to traditional "medical" illnesses.  In general these arguments would seem the most logical and scientific means of arguing for GID reform. That is, if one could show that GID is more like diabetes and hypertension than depression and schizophrenia, it would logically be classified as a disease within the realm of internal medicine rather than psychiatry.

However, while these types of arguments should be the most compelling, the nosological arguments proposed by GID reform advocates universally suffer from either critical inductive or deductive errors. The four primary arguments proposed are:

1. *Etiology is "physical":* There is evidence that GID is caused by genetic and early (pre-natal) environmental aberrations that cause physical changes which result in transgenderism. This basis in "physical" (neurological and endocrine) abnormalities indicates that transgenderism is a medical rather than psychiatric illness.
2. *Treatments are "physical":* Transgender people are treated with physical modalities (drugs and surgery in addition to psychotherapy), which demonstrates the medical rather than mental nature of the illness. This also differentiates transgenderism from other illnesses in the DSM and shows that transgenderism more resembles a medical illness.
3. *Pathology of the body rather than of the mind:* The primary problem with transgender people is not their mind, but their "wrongly gendered" body. Because it is a problem of the body and not of the mind, transgenderism should be seen as a medical illness.
4. *Curability:* Transgenderism can be "cured" (in that no symptoms of dysphoria remain) with "complete" surgical and hormonal reassignment. This differentiates it from psychiatric illness and also possibly indicates that transgender people who are "fully transitioned" no longer have *any* disease at all.

Each of these arguments will be addressed individually, and in doing so demonstrate the errors of the totality of the scientific-nosological argument for reclassification of GID.

## ETIOLOGY IS "PHYSICAL"

Few transgender people or their providers deny that the etiology of transgenderism is biological. It is, like many complex human traits, most likely caused by a poorly understood interaction between an individual's genes and early environmental factors (including prenatal hormonal influences). There is evidence for a significant heritability[7] and many human and animal studies suggest that gender-typical behavior is influenced by the prenatal hormonal milieu.[8] While the evidence is incomplete, the theory that gender identity and behavior are determined largely by genetics and early biological environment best explains the findings from a large number of studies and is for this paper accepted as a true premise.

Given this premise, many advocates of GID reform argue that since the etiology of transgenderism lies in the genes and the physical structure and function of the brain (which developed along cross-gendered pathways), transgenderism is not a psychiatric illness. They compare transgenderism to diseases like hypertension and state that both are biologically and environmentally influenced and ultimately caused by physical differences in the body. In this, advocates argue, transgenderism is differentiated from all other mental illnesses.

However, such arguments ignore the fact that *all* psychiatric illnesses are caused by biological dysfunction. That is, depression, like hypertension, is a flaw in chemistry, not in character. By arguing that transgenderism is different from other mental illnesses due to a "basis in biology," these advocates tacitly accept the common misperception that *other* mental illnesses are not based in biology but are the result of a weak character or personality. The etiology of mental illness in the physical has been accepted for decades by the medical and mental health communities. Older explanations from psychoanalytic theory such as Autism being caused by a "distant mother" have been discredited and no longer are accepted as a valid explanation for mental illness. While environment certainly affects the expression of mental illness, this is also a biological effect in itself (just as environment in the form of diet and sedentary lifestyle produce biological changes which result in diabetes in vulnerable individuals.)

## TREATMENTS ARE "PHYSICAL"

In addition to a physical etiology, many GID reform advocates argue that the treatment of transgenderism with physical modalities (hormones and surgery) indicates that it is a medical rather than psychiatric illness. On the surface, this seems one of the strongest arguments for GID reform. However, a closer evaluation of the premises of this argument reveals several critical problems.

Nosology is the branch of medical science that deals with the classification of diseases. Traditionally, diseases are classified according to: etiology, pathogenesis, symptom, or involved organ system.[9] Moreover, the groupings that emerge in one classification system may not persist when different criteria are applied. For example, if classified by symptoms, both congestive heart failure and asthma would be grouped together as diseases which cause dyspnea.[10] However, if classified by organ system, they would be grouped separately as diseases of the heart and lungs respectively. So the science of nosology seeks to integrate these disparate methods of classification and view the sorting of disease as a multidimensional system in which diseases may occupy multiple groups simultaneously. For example, Down Syndrome can be considered a mental illness (mental retardation) or a chromosomal abnormality (trisomy 21), but can also have a multitude of other problems such as congenital heart disease, sleep apnea, and various orthopedic problems.

However, for the sake of consistency in diagnosis, teaching, research, and medical coding, a unified classification of diseases according to those characteristics is necessary. In such a single system, diseases are grouped according to "best fit" based on their varied characteristics. In this kind of classification system, the multiple different characteristics of a disease are evaluated and it is placed in a "best fit" location determined by the sum of those characteristics.

The particular characteristics that are generally used are etiology, pathogenesis, symptom, or involved organ system. So the argument that GID should be reclassified because its treatments are surgical and medical suffers from two primary difficulties: 1) treatment is not generally accepted as a characteristic on which disease classification should be based, and 2) even if classification by treatment alone did suggest that GID should be reclassified, the fact that other more important aspects of the disease merit classification as a mental illness would still argue for the continued inclusion of GID in the DSM.

In addition, this argument fails to realize that while many mental illnesses are treated with psychotherapy, there are also many that, like transgenderism, are treated with drugs, and even some that are treated with surgery[11] or other physical treatments like electroconvulsive therapy.[12] In addition, one must also consider that in many ways the treatment of mental illness is currently a less

*strang claim
to be made
in this text*

TRANSGENDER AS MENTAL ILLNESS    **649**

overtly scientific practice. The brain is arguably the most complex organ in the human body. Indeed, it is what ultimately makes us human. Our understanding of the inner workings of the brain is barely in its infancy, while the understanding of other branches of medicine is far more developed. So, just as insulin dependent diabetes was no less an illness before the discovery of insulin in the 1920s, mental illnesses will not cease to be mental illnesses if we subsequently develop more physical modalities with which to treat them. The character of an illness does not change even if our understanding of it and ability to treat it evolves.

## PATHOLOGY OF THE BODY RATHER THAN OF THE MIND

This argument claims that the main problem that occurs in transgender people is with their "wrongly-gendered" bodies. Thus, correction of the pathology in the body relieves the illness. Therefore transgenderism should be classified as a physical illness because the etiology is in the body rather than the mind.

This argument is the rhetorical equivalent of the feeling that many transgender people report that they were born in the "wrong body." However, while this is certainly a valid internal experience that many transgender people report, it is neither a valid argument for reclassification of GID, nor consistent with the findings of scientific research.

The research that has been done on the etiology of transgenderism (and gender identity and behavior in general) points to significant differences in the brains of typical males and females. In those instances where there is an alteration from this norm, organisms may have behaviors and feelings that are typical of the opposite gender. For example, sometimes otherwise female animals may demonstrate male typical behaviors due to changes in the brain that occur along typical male-gendered lines.[13] In these types of instances, the cause of the pathology is not that a female body develops where a male body should have, but that a male mind develops incorrectly in an otherwise normal female body. Thus in transgender people who have otherwise normal bodies, normal chromosomal number, and otherwise normal physical development, the pathogenesis of the condition should be seen in the one element that "does not fit," that is, the oppositely gendered-mind.

## CURABILITY

The last common nosological argument supported by advocates of depathologization of GID is that, even if transgender people have a psychopathology before transition, they cease to have that pathology after transition.[14] Thus transgender people who have completed transition no longer have any illness whatsoever.

This argument is slightly different from the global argument that transgenderism is a medical rather than psychological illness. However it is another attempt to achieve a "golden mean" that will still allow transgenderism to be "treated" by medicine, while also purporting to remove the stigma of the mental illness label from transgender patients once transition has been completed.

The primary reason that this argument fails is that despite all currently available medical therapy, it is impossible for any transgender person to have complete assurance that at some time in future will they not be discovered as being transgender. With risk of discovery comes the inevitable risk that transgender people will be treated in a manner inappropriate to their gender identity. For example, if a transgender man was convicted of a crime, he has no assurances that he would not be placed in the women's population in prison. While this is unlikely for most transgender people who have had complete surgical and medical reassignment, and while many times fully transitioned people may be placed in appropriate sex-segregated facilities, there is no guarantee that this will happen. Moreover, while this is an extreme example, there are few transgender people who cannot relate some recent example in their lives of inappropriate gender stereotyping, lack of safe access to

*Fear of Discovery*

the correct sex-segregated facilities, or fear of discovery. Moreover, there are some sex-segregated facilities and accommodations that have been specifically denied to some transgender people based on their transgender status.[15] Thus, for any transgender person, the possibility remains that he will be discovered as transgender and thus not allowed the full rights and responsibilities of his gender. When placed in such a situation, despite completion of hormonal and surgical therapy, a recrudescence of symptoms is reasonably likely due to the same conflict between self-identity and societal treatments and perceptions. Thus, just as the person whose blood pressure remains under 140/90 with the aid of medicines will have a recurrence of hypertension with cessation of medication, the transgender person who loses those rights and privileges gained through surgical and medical reassignment of gender would be expected to also have a recurrence of symptoms. Similarly, as the person with hypertension does not cease to be a hypertensive patient once control of blood pressure is attained, so does the transgender person does not cease to have transgenderism simply because it is controlled with medication and surgery.

## CONCLUSION

While advocates of psychiatric depathologization of transgenderism present numerous arguments justifying their position, all of them suffer from critical inductive or deductive errors. Each argument on the surface appeals to many of the gestalt feelings that transgender people and providers of transgender care may experience. However, when more closely examined, the premises underlying these arguments present far more troublesome intellectual and ethical problems than the problems they purport to solve.

Unfortunately, few if any, people who advocate these positions have deeply examined the underlying assumptions. Worse, such advocates, when challenged about these underlying assumptions, often simply ignore the challenges while advocating the approach that on first blush "feels best" to the majority of people. However such arguments, as always, fail the test of an open and critical evaluation such as presented in this paper.

What may be popular or appealing to the majority of people based on feelings rather than logical analysis is often both without ultimate utility and dangerous in its implications and results. When the arguments are then modified to *approach* the logical truth while still appealing to the feelings of how things "ought to be," this supposed *golden mean* presents an even more insidious argument. This is the danger that the pseudo-philosophy of Intelligent Design presents which Creationism was never able to achieve. The risk lies in such a "tarnished golden mean" mollifying the larger body of detractors who reject the more extreme view after a cursory logical analysis. As Stephen Jay Gould said, "Few arguments are more dangerous than those that 'feel' right but can't be justified."

## FURTHER ANALYSIS

> You can only protect your liberties in this world by protecting the other man's freedom. You can only be free if I am free.
>
> —Clarence Darrow

While the arguments for depathologization have been refuted above, a question remains. While there may be no logical reason or real benefit to depathologization, why resist this movement when it is clearly a passionate issue for many in the transgender community? That is, if no harm comes from certain people having a false belief, why is it necessary to correct this false belief? Why write this article at all?

The primary reason is that while many of the transgender people who argue passionately for depathologization may *feel validated* with the removal of GID from the DSM, there are many more who will suffer greatly. Unfortunately many of these people have little voice in the larger transgender political movement. These are people who inhabit the fringes of society. They are much more dependent on public services and more often have to live and function in sex-segregated facilities like group homes, shelters, and prisons.

These people who are disenfranchised are disproportionately less likely to receive even basic transgender care such as hormones. A classic example is transgender prisoners. While some are able to access hormones, the majority are not. For those who have, it has often required significant lobbying and legal efforts on the part of transgender advocates to allow such prisoners to access care. Fortunately, the current inclusion in the DSM, as well as the treatment recommendations in the American Psychiatric Association's treatment text, *Treatments of Psychiatric Disorders*[16] offer a valid justification for prisoners accessing care. In particular, *Treatments of Psychiatric Disorders*, which is to treatment as the DSM is to diagnosis, is a crucial part of the argument to gain treatment for incarcerated transgender people.

The argument[17] is briefly:

- The 8th Amendment guarantees prisoners the right to medical care.[18]
- Psychiatric care is *specifically* covered under the 8th Amendment protections for prisoners.
- The APA's diagnostic text (DSM-IV-TR) establishes that GID is a psychiatric disease.
- The APA's treatment text (*Treatments of Psychiatric Disorders*) establishes the standards for treating GID. This text includes hormonal treatments as appropriate and medically necessary, recognizes HBIGDA as an important professional authority on transgender care, and in specific states that stopping medical care for prisoners is inappropriate and dangerous.

Loss of the DSM diagnostic category for GID will endanger the access to care, psychological well being, and in some cases, *the very lives* of countless disenfranchised transgender people who are dependent on the medical and psychiatric justification for access to care. Thus the actions of advocates of depathologization not only have their basis in a poor logical argument as described above, but also endanger many transgender people whose voices are rarely, if ever, heard.

## NOTES

1. GID is a disease described in the *Diagnostic and Statistical Manual of Diseases* (DSM-IV-TR) as a mental illness characterized by a persistent cross-gender identification and a persistent discomfort with or sense of inappropriateness of one's sex as assigned at birth.
2. Gorton, R. "Toward a Resolution of GID, the Model of Disease, and the Transgender Community." *Make.* Feb. 2005. (http://www.makezine.org/giddisease.htm)
3. Nosology is the branch of medical science dealing with the classification of disease.
4. From GID Reform Advocates. Accessed 11/02/2005. http://www.transgender.org/gidr/index.html
5. LGBTIQ=Lesbian, Gay, Bisexual, Transgender, Intersex, Queer, and Questioning
6. Wilson, K. "Do Cross-gender Expression and Identity Constitute Mental Illness?" G.I.C. of Colorado, Inc. Accessed on 11/02/2005. http://glbtss.colostate.edu/transgender/Do%20Cross-gender%20Expression%20and%20Identity%20Constitute%20Mental%20Illness.doc
7. Diamond, M. and Hawk, S. "Concordance for Gender Identity among Monozygotic and Dizygotic Twin Pairs." American Psychological Association Annual Meeting. July 28-August 1, 2004, Honolulu, Hawaii.
8. For a review, see Cohen-Bendahan C., et al. "Prenatal Sex Hormone Effects on Child and Adult Sex-typed Behavior: Methods and Findings." *Neurosci Biobehav Rev.* 2005 Apr. 29 (2): 353-84; Hines M., "Abnormal Sexual Development and Psychosexual Issues." *Baillieres Clin Endocrinol Metab.* 1998 Apr 12 (1): 173-89; Hutchison J. "Gender-specific Steroid Metabolism in Neural Differentiation." *Cell Mol Neurobiol.* 1997 17(6): 603-26.
9. Pathogenesis refers to the mechanisms which causes disease, for example: traumatic injury, infectious disease, and genetics.
10. Dyspnea is shortness of breath.
11. Examples of surgery to treat mental illness would include tractotomy and cingulotomy.
12. ECT (electroconvulsive therapy), while having been abused in the past, remains in modern psychiatric treatment a safe, humane, and effective treatment for some forms of major depression that are unresponsive to medication and

psychotherapy. Unlike what was depicted in *One Flew Over the Cuckoo's Nest*, modern ECT is usually done under anesthesia in an operating room.

13. An example of such biological variation is the freemartin. This is an otherwise female cow that exhibits extremely male typical behaviors. These cows are always the product of twin gestations and always have a fraternal male twin. Prenatal androgenizing influences on the freemartin's brain cause this male-typical neural development.

14. Transition usually indicates hormonal and surgical therapy, though to what extent each of these modalities is used varies depending on the individual.

15. An example of such exclusion is the Womyn-Born-Womyn policy of the Michigan Womyn's Music Festival, which states that only cisgender women are allowed into this women's only space.

16. *American Psychiatric Association: Treatments of Psychiatric Disorders*, Third Edition. Washington, DC. American Psychiatric Association, 2001. (First Edition published as: *Treatments of Psychiatric Disorders: A Task Force Report of the American Psychiatric Association*. Washington, DC.)

17. For advocates needing help with providing assistance for disenfranchised transgender people, or needing a more detailed discussion of this topic, please feel free to contact the author.

18. See the ACLU's fact sheet: http://www.aclu.org//prison/medical/14767res20031113.html

# 50

# *Building an Abolitionist Trans and Queer Movement with Everything We've Got*

## Morgan Bassichis, Alexander Lee, and Dean Spade

Trans/genderqueer anti-prison-industrial-complex activists Morgan Bassichis, Alex Lee, and Dean Spade embed a no-holds-barred manifesto for a prison abolition movement that is fully attuned to transgender incarceration issues into a broader call for a transgender movement that embraces prison abolitionism and other fundamental assaults on oppressive aspects of the status quo that might not at first seem to some to be a "transgender" concern. Their manner of framing their work represents a growing tendency in transgender political activism and theorizing. On the one hand, it shifts emphasis away from the mobilization a small minority group of "transgender people" for participation in liberal reform efforts; on the other hand, it links specific kinds of oppression that transgender people face (such as cruel and unusual forms of punishment, including the housing of trans women in male prisons) to larger structural injustices that affect many more sorts of people, whether or not they are trans. The authors argue that hate crime legislation and gay marriage have risen to the top of the political agenda for big LGBT nonprofits that serve the needs of white gays and lesbians better than they serve queer-of-color communities, queer poor people, incarcerated queers, and other multiply marginalized groups. For them, a radical trans social justice movement needs to adopt different tactics, and address different goals. Critical trans resistance to unjust state power must tackle such problems as poverty, racism, and incarceration if it is to do more than consolidate the legitimate citizenship status of the most privileged segments of trans populations.

As we write this, queer and trans people across the United States and in many parts of the world have just celebrated the fortieth anniversary of the Stonewall Rebellion. On that fateful night back in June 1969, sexual and gender outsiders rose up against ongoing brutal police violence in an inspiring act of defiance. These early freedom fighters knew all too well that the NYPD—"New York's finest"—were the frontline threat to queer and trans survival. Stonewall was the culmination of years of domination, resentment, and upheaval in many marginalized communities coming to a new consciousness of the depth of violence committed by the government against poor people, people of color, women, and queer people both within US borders and around the world. The Stonewall Rebellion, the mass demonstrations against the war in Vietnam, and the campaign to free imprisoned Black-liberation activist Assata Shakur were all powerful examples of a groundswell of energy demanding an end to the "business as usual" of US terror during this time.

Could these groundbreaking and often unsung activists have imagined that only forty years later the "official" gay rights agenda would be largely pro-police, pro-prisons, and pro-war—exactly the forces they worked so hard to resist? Just a few decades later, the most visible and well-funded arms of the "LGBT movement" look much more like a corporate strategizing session than a grassroots social justice movement. There are countless examples of this dramatic shift in priorities. What emerged as a fight against racist, anti-poor, and anti-queer police violence now works hand in hand with local and federal law enforcement agencies—district attorneys are asked to speak at trans rallies, cops march in Gay Pride parades. The agendas of prosecutors—those who lock up our family, friends, and lovers—and many queer and trans organizations are becoming increasingly similar, with sentence- and police-enhancing legislation at the top of the priority list. Hate crimes legislation is tacked on to multi-billion dollar "defense" bills to support US military domination in Palestine, Iraq, Afghanistan, and elsewhere. Despite the rhetoric of an "LGBT community," transgender and gender-non-conforming people are repeatedly abandoned and marginalized in the agendas and priorities of our "lead" organizations—most recently in the 2007 gutting of the Employment Non-Discrimination Act of gender identity protections. And as the rate of people (particularly poor queer and trans people of color) without steady jobs, housing, or healthcare continues to rise, and health and social services continue to be cut, those dubbed the leaders of the "LGBT movement" insist that marriage rights are the way to redress the inequalities in our communities.[1]

For more and more queer and trans people, regardless of marital status, there is no inheritance, no health benefits from employers, no legal immigration status, and no state protection of our relationship to our children. Four decades after queer and trans people took to the streets throwing heels, bottles, bricks, and anything else we had to ward off police, the official word is that, except for being able to get married and fight in the military,[2] we are pretty much free, safe, and equal. And those of us who are not must wait our turn until the "priority" battles are won by the largely white, male, upper-class lawyers and lobbyists who know better than us.[3]

Fortunately, radical queer and trans organizing for deep transformation has also grown alongside this "trickle-down"[4] brand of "equality" politics mentioned above. Although there is no neat line between official gay "equality" politics on the one hand, and radical "justice" politics on the other, it is important to draw out some of the key distinctions in how different parts of our movements today are responding to the main problems that queer and trans people face. This is less about creating false dichotomies between "good" and "bad" approaches, and more about clarifying the actual impact that various strategies have, and recognizing that alternative approaches to the "official" solutions are alive, are politically viable, and are being pursued by activists and organizations around the United States and beyond. In the first column, we identify some of these main challenges; in the second, we summarize what solutions are being offered by the well-resourced[5] segments of our movement; and in the third, we outline some approaches being used by more radical and progressive queer and trans organizing to expand possibilities for broad-based, social-justice solutions to these same problems.

## THE CURRENT LANDSCAPE

| Big Problems | "Official" Solutions | Transformative Approaches |
| --- | --- | --- |
| Queer and trans people, poor people, people of color, and immigrants have minimal access to quality healthcare | Legalize same-sex marriage to allow people with health benefits from their jobs to share with same-sex partners | Strengthen Medicaid and Medicare; win universal healthcare; fight for transgender health benefits; end deadly medical neglect of people in state custody |

| Big Problems | "Official" Solutions | Transformative Approaches |
|---|---|---|
| Queer and trans people experience regular and often fatal violence from partners, family members, community members, employers, law enforcement, and institutional officials | Pass hate crimes legislation to increase prison sentences and strengthen local and federal law enforcement; collect statistics on rates of violence; collaborate with local and federal law enforcement to prosecute hate violence and domestic violence | Build community relationships and infrastructure to support the healing and transformation of people who have been impacted by interpersonal and intergenerational violence; join with movements addressing root causes of queer and trans premature death, including police violence, imprisonment, poverty, immigration policies, and lack of healthcare and housing |
| Queer and trans members of the military experience violence and discrimination | Eliminate bans on participation of gays and lesbians in US military | Join with war resisters, radical veterans, and young people to oppose military intervention, occupation, and war abroad and at home, and demand the reduction/elimination of "defense" budgets |
| Queer and trans people are targeted by an unfair and punitive immigration system | Legalize same-sex marriage to allow same-sex international couples to apply for legal residency for the non–US citizen spouse | End the use of immigration policy to criminalize people of color, exploit workers, and maintain the deadly wealth gap between the United States and the Global South; support current detainees and end ICE raids, deportations, and police collaboration |
| Queer and trans families are vulnerable to legal intervention and separation from the state, institutions, and/or non-queer people | Legalize same sex marriage to provide a route to "legalize" families with two parents of the same sex; pass laws banning adoption discrimination on the basis of sexual orientation | Join with struggles of queer/trans and non-queer/trans families of color, imprisoned parents and youth, native families, poor families, military families, and people with disabilities to win community and family self-determination and the right to keep kids, parents, and other family members in their families and communities |
| Institutions fail to recognize family connections outside of heterosexual marriage in contexts like hospital visitation and inheritance | Legalize same-sex marriage to formally recognize same-sex partners in the eyes of the law | Change policies like hospital visitation to recognize a variety of family structures, not just opposite-sex and same-sex couples; abolish inheritance and demand radical redistribution of wealth and an end to poverty |

| Big Problems | "Official" Solutions | Transformative Approaches |
|---|---|---|
| Queer and trans people are disproportionately policed, arrested, and imprisoned, and face high rates of violence in state custody from officials as well as other imprisoned or detained people | Advocate for "cultural competency" training for law enforcement and the construction of queer and trans-specific and "gender-responsive" facilities; create written policies that say that queer and trans people are equal to other people in state custody; stay largely silent on the high rates of imprisonment in queer and trans communities, communities of color, and poor communities | Build ongoing, accountable relationships with and advocate for queer and trans people who are locked up to support their daily well-being, healing, leadership, and survival; build community networks of care to support people coming out of prison and jail; collaborate with other movements to address root causes of queer and trans imprisonment; work to abolish prisons, establish community support for people with disabilities and eliminate medical and psychatric institutionalization, and provide permanent housing rather than shelter beds for all people without homes |

## I. HOW DID WE GET HERE?

The streams of conservative as well as more progressive and radical queer and trans politics developed over time and in the context of a rapidly changing political, economic, and social landscape. [...] *To chart a different course for our movements, we need to understand the road we've traveled.* In particular, we believe that there are two major features of the second half of the twentieth century that shaped the context in which the queer and trans movement developed[6]: (1) the active resistance and challenge by radical movement to state violence, and subsequent systematic backlash,[7] and (2) the massive turmoil and transformation of the global economy.[8] Activists and scholars use a range of terms to describe this era in which power, wealth, and oppression were transformed to respond to these two significant "crises"—including neoliberalism, the "New World Order," empire, globalization, free market democracy, or late capitalism. Each term describes a different aspect or "take" on the current historical moment that we are living in.

It is important to be clear that *none of the strategies of the "New World Order" are new.* They might work faster, use new technologies, and recruit the help of new groups, but they are not new. Oppressive dynamics in the United States are as old as the colonization of this land and the founding of a country based on slavery and genocide. However, they have taken intensified, tricky forms in the past few decades—particularly because our governments keep telling us those institutions and practices have been "abolished." There were no "good old days" in the United States—just times in which our movements and our communities were stronger or weaker, and times when we used different cracks in the system as opportunities for resistance. All in all, we might characterize the past many decades as a time in which policies and ideas were promoted by powerful nations and institutions (such as the World Trade Organization and the International Monetary Fund) to destroy the minimal safety nets set up for vulnerable people, dismantle the gains made by social movements, and redistribute wealth, resources, and life changes upward—away from the poor and toward the elite.[9]

Below are some of the key tactics that the United States and others have used in this most recent chapter of our history:

### Pull Yourself Up by Your Bootstraps, Again

The US government and its ally nations and institutions in the Global North helped pass laws and policies that made it harder for workers to organize into unions; destroyed welfare programs and created the image of people on welfare as immoral and fraudulent; and created international economic policies and trade agreements that reduced safety nets, worker rights, and environmental protections, particularly for nations in the Global South. Together, these efforts have dismantled laws and social programs meant to protect people from poverty, violence, sickness, and other harms of capitalism. [...]

> Example: In 1996, President Clinton signed into law the Personal Responsibility and Work Opportunity Reconciliation Act, which effectively dismantled what existed of a welfare state—creating a range of restrictive and targeting measures that required work, limited aid, and increased penalties for welfare recipients. The federal government abdicated its responsibility to provide minimal safety nets for poor and working-class people, using the rhetoric of "personal responsibility" and "work" to justify the exploitation and pain caused by capitalism and racism. [...] In San Francisco, Mayor Newsom's notorious 2002 "Care Not Cash" program slashed welfare benefits for homeless people, insisting that benefits given to the homeless were being spent on "drugs and alcohol."[12]

### Scapegoating

The decrease in manufacturing jobs and the gutting of social safety nets for the poor and working class created a growing class of people who were marginally employed and housed, and forced into criminalized economies such as sex work and the drug trade. This class of people was blamed for the poverty and inequity they faced—labeled drug dealers, welfare queens, criminals, and hoodlums—and were used to justify harmful policies that expanded violence and harm. At the same time, criminal penalties for behaviors associated with poverty, like drug use, sleeping outside, graffiti, and sex work have increased in many parts the United States, and resources for policing these kinds of "crimes" has also increased. [...]

> Example: Under President Clinton's 1996 welfare reforms, anyone convicted of a drug-related crime is automatically banned for life from receiving cash assistance and food stamps. Some states have since opted out of this ban, but for people living in fifteen states, this draconian measure presents nearly insurmountable barriers to becoming self-sufficient. Unable to receive cash assistance and subject to job discrimination because of their criminal histories, many people with drug-related convictions go back into the drug trade as the only way to earn enough to pay the rent and put food on the table. The lifetime welfare ban has been shown to particularly harm women and their children.[13]

### Fear-Mongering

The government and corporate media used racist, xenophobic, and misogynist fear-mongering to distract us from increasing economic disparity and a growing underclass in the United States and abroad. The War on Drugs in the 1980s and the Bush Administration's War on Terror, both of which are ongoing, created internal and external enemies ("criminals" and "terrorists") to blame for and distract from the ravages of racism, capitalism, patriarchy, and imperialism. In exchange, these enemies (and anyone who looked like them) could be targeted with violence and murder. During this time, the use of prisons, policing, detention, and surveillance skyrocketed as the government declared formal war against all those who it marks as "criminals" or "terrorists." [...]

> Example: Following the September 11, 2001 attacks on the World Trade Center in New York, politicians manipulated the American public's fear and uncertainty to push through a range of new laws and policies justified by a declared "War on Terror." New legislation like the PATRIOT Act, the Immigrant Registration Act, and the Real ID Act, as well as new administrative policies and practices, increased the surveillance state, reduced even the most basic rights and living standards of immigrants, and turned local police, schoolteachers, hospital workers, and others into immigration enforcement officers.

### The Myth That Violence and Discrimination Are Just About "Bad" Individuals

Discrimination laws and hate crimes laws encourage us to understand oppression as something that happens when individuals use bias to deny someone a job because of race or sex or some other characteristic, or beat up or kill someone because of such a characteristic. This way of thinking, sometimes called the "perpetrator perspective,"[14] makes people think about racism, sexism, homophobia, transphobia, and ableism in terms of individual behaviors and bad intentions rather than wide-scale structural oppression that often operates without some obvious individual actor aimed at denying an individual person an opportunity. The violence of imprisoning millions of poor people and people of color, for example, can't be adequately explained by finding one nasty racist individual, but instead requires looking at a whole web of institutions, policies, and practices that make it "normal" and "necessary" to warehouse, displace, discard, and annihilate poor people and people of color. Thinking about violence and oppression as the work of "a few bad apples" undermines our ability to analyze our conditions *systemically* and *intergenerationally,* and to therefore organize for systemic change.

This narrow way of thinking about oppression is repeated in law, policy, the media, and nonprofits. [...]

> Example: As we write this, the Matthew Shepard Local Law Enforcement Enhancement Act has recently passed in the US Senate, and if signed into law would give $10 million to state and local law enforcement agencies, expand federal law enforcement power focused on hate crimes, and add the death penalty as a possible punishment for those convicted. This bill is heralded as a victory for transgender people because it will make gender identity an included category in Federal Hate Crimes law. Like Megan's Law, this law and the advocacy surrounding it (including advocacy by large LGBT nonprofit organizations) focus attention on individuals who kill people because of their identities. These laws frame the problem of violence in our communities as one of individual "hateful" people, when in reality, trans people face short life-spans because of the enormous systemic violence in welfare systems, shelters, prisons, jails, foster care, juvenile punishment systems, and immigration, and the inability to access basic survival resources. These laws do nothing to prevent our deaths, they just use our deaths to expand a system that endangers our lives and places a chokehold on our communities.[16]

### Undermining Transformative Organizing

The second half of the twentieth century saw a major upsurge in radical and revolutionary organizing in oppressed communities in the United States and around the world. This powerful organizing posed a significant threat to the legitimacy of US power and capitalist empire more broadly, and therefore needed to be contained. These movements were undermined by two main strategies: First, the radical movements of the 1960s and '70s were criminalized, with the US government using tactics of imprisonment, torture, sabotage, and assassination to target and destroy groups like the Black Panthers, American Indian Movement, and Young Lords, among others. Second, the growth of the nonprofit sector has seen social movements professionalizing, chasing philanthropic dollars, separating into "issue areas," and moving toward social services and legal reform projects rather than radical projects aimed at the underlying causes of poverty and injustice.[17] These developments left significant sections of the radical left traumatized and decimated, wiping out a generation of revolutionaries and shifting the terms of resistance from revolution and transformation to inclusion and reform, prioritizing state- and foundation-sanctioned legal reforms and social services over mass organizing and direct action. [...]

> Example: In the wake of decades of radical organizing by people in women's prisons and activists on the outside decrying systemic medical neglect, sexual violence, and the destruction of family bonds, California legislators in 2006 proposed a so-called "gender responsive corrections" bill that would allow people in women's prisons to live with their children and receive increased social services. To make this plan work, the bill called for millions of dollars in new prison construction. The message of "improving the lives of women prisoners" and creating more "humane" prisons—rhetoric that is consistently used by those in power to distract us from the fundamentally violent conditions of a capitalist police state—appealed to liberal, well-intentioned feminist researchers, advocates, and legislators. Anti-prison organizations such as Oakland-based Justice Now and others working in solidarity with the resounding sentiment of people in women's prisons, pointed out that this strategy was actually just a back door to creating 4,500 new prison beds for women in California, yet again expanding opportunities to criminalize poor women and transgender people in one of the nation's most imprisoning states.[19]

### The Hero Mindset

The United States loves its heroes and its narratives—Horatio Alger, rags-to-riches, "pull yourself up by your bootstraps," streets "paved with gold," the rugged frontiersman, the benevolent philanthropist, and Obama as savior, among others. These narratives hide the uneven concentration of wealth, resources, and opportunity among different groups of people—the ways in which not *everybody* can just do anything if they put their minds to it and work hard enough. In the second half of the twentieth century, this individualistic and celebrity-obsessed culture had a deep impact on social movements and how we write narratives. Stories of mass struggle became stories of individuals overcoming great odds. The rise of the nonprofit as a key vehicle for social change bolstered this trend, giving incentives to charismatic leaders (often executive directors, often people with privilege) to frame struggles in ways that prioritize symbolic victories (big court cases, sensationalistic media coverage) and ignore the daily work of building a base and a movement for the long haul. This trend also compromises the accountability of leaders and organizations to their constituencies, and devalues activism in the trenches. [...]

> Example: Oprah's well-publicized giveaways—as well as a range of television shows that feature "big wins" such as makeovers, new houses, and new cars—have helped to create the image of social change in our society as individual acts of "charity" rather than concerted efforts by mass groups of people to change relationships of power. These portrayals affirm the false idea that we live in a meritocracy in which any one individual's perseverance and hard work are the only keys needed to wealth and success. Such portrayals hide realities like the racial wealth divide and other conditions that produce and maintain inequality on a group level, ensuring that most people will not rise above or fall below their place in the economy, regardless of their individual actions. In reality, real social change that

alters the relationships of power throughout history have actually come about when large groups of people have worked together toward a common goal.

Together, the tactics that we describe above function as a strategy of *counter-revolution*—an attempt to squash the collective health and political will of oppressed people, and to buy off people with privilege in order to support the status quo. This is a profoundly traumatic process that deepened centuries of pain, loss, and harm experienced by people of color, immigrants, queer and trans people, women, and others marked as "disposable." For many of us, this included losing our lives and our loved ones to the devastating government-sanctioned HIV/AIDS pandemic and ongoing attacks from family, neighbors, and government officials.

Perhaps one of the most painful features of this period has been the separating of oppressed communities and movements from one another. Even though our communities are all overlapping and our struggles for liberation are fundamentally linked, the "divide and conquer" strategy of the "New World Order" has taught us to think of our identities and struggles as separate and competing. In particular, it was useful to maintaining harmful systems and conditions to create a false divide between purportedly separate ("white") gay issues and ("straight") people of color, immigrant, and working-class issues to prevent deep partnerships across multiple lines of difference for social transformation. In this context, the most visible and well-funded arms of LGBT organizing got caught up in fighting for small-scale reforms and battles to be recognized as "equal" and "visible" under the law and in the media without building the sustained power and self-determination of oppressed communities. Instead of trying to change the system, the official LGBT agenda fought to just be welcomed into it, in exchange for helping to keep other oppressed people at the bottom.

But thankfully that's not the end of the story. As we describe below, this period also nurtured powerful strands of radical queer and trans politics organizing at the intersections of oppressions and struggles and in the legacy of the revolutionary freedom fighters of an earlier generation.

## II. RECLAIMING A RADICAL LEGACY

Despite the powerful and destructive impacts that the renewed forces of neoliberal globalization and the "New World Order" have had on our communities and our social movements, there are and always have been radical politics and movements to challenge the exploitation that the United States is founded upon. These politics have been developed in communities of color and in poor and working-class, immigrant, queer, disability, and feminist communities in both "colonized" and "colonizing" nations, from the Black Panther Party in Oakland to the Zapatistas in Chiapas to the Audre Lorde Project in New York. As the story of Stonewall teaches us, our movements didn't start out in the courtroom; they started out in the streets! Informing both the strategies of our movements as well as our everyday decisions about how we live our lives and form our relationships, these radical politics offer queer communities and movements a way out of the murderous politics that are masked as invitations to "inclusion" and "equality" within fundamentally exclusive, unequal systems. Sometimes these spaces for transformation are easier to spot than others—but you can find them everywhere, from church halls to lecture halls, from the lessons of our grandmothers to the lessons we learn surviving in the world, from the post-revolutionary Cuba to post-Katrina New Orleans.

These radical lineages have nurtured and guided transformative branches of queer and trans organizing working at the intersections of identities and struggles for collective liberation. These branches have redefined what count as queer and trans issues, losses, victories, and strategies— putting struggles against policing, imprisonment, borders, globalization, violence, and economic exploitation at the center of struggles for gender and sexual self-determination. Exploding the false division between struggles for (implicitly white and middle-class) sexual and gender justice and (implicitly straight) racial and economic justice, there is a groundswell of radical queer and trans organizing that's changing all the rules—you just have to know where to find it. In the chart below, we draw out a few specific strands of these diverse radical lineages that have paved the way for this work. In the first column, we highlight a value that has emerged from these radical lineages. In the second column, we lift up specific organizations striving to embody these values today.[23]

### Deepening the Path of Those Who Came Before

| Radical Lineage | Contemporary Descendant |
| --- | --- |
| Liberation is a collective process! The conventional nonprofit hierarchical structure is actually a very recent phenomenon, and one that is modeled off corporations. Radical organizations, particularly feminist and women of color-led organizations, have often prioritized working collectively—where group awareness, consensus, and wholeness is valued over majority rule and individual leadership. Collectivism at its best takes up the concerns of the few as the concerns of the whole. For example, when one member of a group or community cannot attend an event or meeting because the building is not wheelchair accessible, it becomes a moment for all to examine and challenge ableism in our culture—instead of just dismissing it as a "problem" that affects only people who use wheelchairs. | The Sylvia Rivera Law Project (SRLP), among many other organizations, has shown just how powerful working collectively can be—with their staff and volunteers, majority people of color, majority trans and gender-non-conforming governing collective, SRLP is showing the world that how we do our work is a vital part of the work, and that doing things collectively helps us to create the world we want to see as we're building it. |
| "Trickle up" change! We know that when those in power say they will "come back" for those at the bottom of the social and economic hierarchy, it will never happen. Marginalization is increased when a part of a marginalized group makes it over the line into the mainstream, leaving others behind and reaffirming the status quo. We've all seen painful examples of this in LGBT politics time after time—from the abandonment of transgender folks in the Employment Non-Discrimination Act (ENDA) to the idea that gay marriage is the first step toward universal healthcare. Instead, we know that freedom and justice for the most oppressed people means freedom and justice for everyone, and that we have to start at the bottom. The changes required to improve the daily material and spiritual lives of low-income queer and transgender people of color would by default include large-scale transformation of our entire economic, education, healthcare, and legal systems. When you put those with the fewest resources and those facing multiple systems of oppression at the center of analysis and organizing, everybody benefits. | Queers for Economic Justice in New York City and the Transgender, Gender Variant, and Intersex Justice Project in San Francisco are two great examples of "trickle up" change—by focusing on queers on welfare, in the shelter system, and in prison systems, these groups demand social and economic justice for those with the fewest resources and the smallest investment in maintaining the system as it is. |

| *Radical Lineage* | *Contemporary Descendant* |
|---|---|
| Be careful of all those welcome mats! Learning from history and other social-justice movements is a key principle. Other movements and other moments have been drained of their original power and purpose and appropriated for purposes opposing their principles, either by governments working to dilute and derail transformation or by corporations looking to turn civil unrest into a fashion statement (or both). Looking back critically at where other movements have done right and gone wrong helps us stay creative and accountable to our communities and our politics. | Critical Resistance is a great example of this commitment. In the group's focus on prison abolition (instead of reform), its members examine their strategies and potential proposals through the question "Will we regret this in ten years?" This question is about taking a long-term view and assessing a potential opportunity (such as any given proposal to "improve" or "reform" prisons or sentencing laws) against their commitment to abolishing—not expanding or even maintaining—the prison industrial complex. The message here is that even though it might feel nice to get an invitation to the party, we would be wise to ask about the occasion. |
| For us, by us! The leadership, wisdom, and labor of those most affected by an issue should be centralized from the start. This allows those with the most to gain from social justice to direct what that justice will look like and gives allies the chance to directly support their leadership. | FIERCE! in New York City is a great example of this principle: By building the power of queer and trans youth of color to run campaigns, organize one another, and challenge gentrification and police violence, FIERCE! has become a powerful force that young people of color see themselves in. At FIERCE!, it is the young people directly facing the intersections of ageism, racism, xenophobia, homophobia, and transphobia who identify what the problems, priorities, and strategies should be rather than people whose expertise on these issues derives from advanced degrees or other criteria. The role of people not directly affected by the issues is to support the youth in manifesting their visions, not to control the political possibilities that they are inventing. |
| Let's practice what we preach! Also known as "praxis," this ideal strives for the alignment of what we do, why we're doing it, and how we do it—not just in our formal work, but also in our daily lives. This goes beyond the campaign goals or strategies of our organizations, and includes how they are organized, how we treat one another, and how we treat ourselves. If we believe that people of color have the most to gain from the end of racism, then we should support and encourage people of color's leadership in fights to end white supremacy, and for a fair economy and an end to the wealth gap. People in our organizations should get paid equally regardless of advanced degrees, and our working conditions and benefits should be generous. If we support a world in which we have time and resources to take care of ourselves, as well as our friends, families, and neighbors, we might not want to work sixty hours a week. | An inspiring example of praxis can be found in the work of Southerners on New Ground (SONG), based in Atlanta, Ga. SONG strives to integrate healing, spirit, and creativity in their work organizing across race, class, gender, and sexuality to embody new (and old!) forms of community, reflective of our commitments to liberation. SONG and other groups show that oppression is traumatic, and trauma needs to be addressed, acknowledged, and held both by individuals and groups of people. If trauma is ignored or swept under the rug, it just comes back as resentment, chaos, and divisiveness. We are all whole, complex human beings that have survived a great deal of violence to get where we are today. Our work must support our full humanity and reflect the world we want to live in. |

| Radical Lineage | Contemporary Descendant |
|---|---|
| Real safety means collective transformation! Oppressed communities have always had ways to deal with violence and harm without relying on police, prisons, immigration, or kicking someone out—knowing that relying on those forces would put them in greater danger. Oppressed people have often known that these forces were the main sources of violence that they faced—the central agent of rape, abuse, murder, and exploitation. The criminal punishment system has tried to convince us that we do not know how to solve our own problems and that locking people up and putting more cops on our streets are the only ways we can stay safe or heal from trauma. Unfortunately we often lack other options. Many organizations and groups of people have been working to interrupt the intergenerational practices of intimate violence, sexual violence, hate violence, and police violence without relying on the institutions that target, warehouse, kill, and shame us. | Groups like Creative Interventions and generationFIVE in Oakland, Calif, Communities Against Rape and Abuse in Seattle, Wash., and the Audre Lorde Project's Safe OUTside the System (SOS) Collective, have been creating exciting ways to support the healing and transformation of people who have survived and caused harm, as well as the conditions that pass violence down from one generation to another. Because violence touches every queer and trans person directly or indirectly, creating ways to respond to violence that are transformative and healing (instead of oppressive, shaming, or traumatizing) is a tremendous opportunity to reclaim our radical legacy. We can no longer allow for our deaths to be the justification for so many other people's deaths through policing, imprisonment, and detention. Locking people up, having more cops in the streets, or throwing more people out will never heal the wounds of abuse or trauma. |

### Resisting the Traps, Ending Trans Imprisonment

Even in the context of growing imprisonment rates and deteriorating safety nets, the past decade has brought with it an upsurge in organizing and activism to challenge the imprisonment and policing of transgender and gender-non-conforming communities.[24] Through high-profile lawsuits, human rights and media documentation, conferences and trainings, grassroots organizing, and coalitional efforts, more individuals and organizations are aware of the dynamics of trans imprisonment than ever. This work has both fallen prey to the tricky traps of the "New World Order" that we described above and also generated courageous new ways of doing the work of transformation and resistance that are in line with the radical values that we also trace. What was once either completely erased or significantly marginalized on the agendas of both the LGBT and anti-prison/prisoner rights movements is now gaining more and more visibility and activity. We think of this as a tremendous opportunity to choose which legacies and practices we want for this work moving forward. This is not about playing the blame game and pointing fingers at which work is radical and which is oppressive, but rather about building on all of our collective successes, losses, and contradictions to do work that will transform society (and all of us) as we know it.

Below are a few helpful lessons that have been guided by the values above and generated at the powerful intersections of prison abolition and gender justice:[25]

### 1. We refuse to create "deserving" vs. "undeserving" victims[26]

Although we understand that transgender and gender-non-conforming people in prisons, jails, and detention centers experience egregious and often specific forms of violence—including sexual assault, rape, medical neglect and discrimination, and humiliation based on transphobic norms— we recognize that all people impacted by the prison industrial complex are facing severe violence. Instead of saying that transgender people are the "most" oppressed in prisons, we can talk about the different forms of violence that people impacted by the prison industrial complex face, and how those forms of violence help maintain the status quo common sense that the "real bad people"—the "rapists," "murderers," "child molesters," in some cases now the "bigots"—deserve to be locked up. Seeking to understand the specific arrangements that cause certain communities to face particular types of violence at the hands of police and in detention can allow us to develop solidarity around shared *and* different experiences with these forces and build effective resistance that gets to the roots of these problems. Building arguments about trans people as "innocent victims" while other prisoners are cast as dangerous and deserving of detention only undermines the power of a shared resistance strategy that sees imprisonment as a violent, dangerous tactic for everybody it touches.

We know that the push for hate crimes laws as the solution to anti-queer and -trans violence will never actually address the fundamental reasons why we are vulnerable to violence in the first place or why homophobia and transphobia are encouraged in our cultures. Individualizing solutions like hate crimes laws create a false binary of "perpetrator" and "victim" or "bad" and "good" people without addressing the underlying systemic problem, and often strengthen that problem. In place of this common sense, we understand that racism, state violence, and capitalism are the root causes of violence in our culture, not individual "bigots" or even prison guards. *We must end the cycle of oppressed people being pitted against one another.*

## 2. We support strategies that weaken oppressive institutions, not strengthen them.

We can respond to the crises that our communities are facing right now while refusing long-term compromises that will strengthen the very institutions that are hurting us. As more and more awareness is being raised about the terrible violence that transgender and gender-non-conforming people face in prisons, jails, and detention centers, some prisoner rights and queer and trans researchers and advocates are suggesting that building trans-specific prisons or jails is the only way that imprisoned transgender and gender-non-conforming people will be safe in the short-term. Particularly in light of the dangerous popularity of "gender responsiveness" among legislators and advocates alike, we reject all notions that we must expand the prison industrial complex to respond to immediate conditions of violence. Funneling more money into prison building of any kind strengthens the prison industrial complex's death hold on our communities. We know that if they build it, they will fill it, and getting trans people out of prison is the only real way to address the safety issues that trans prisoners face. *We want strategies that will reduce and ultimately eliminate the number of people and dollars going into prisons, while attending to the immediate healing and redress of individual imprisoned people.*

## 3. We must transform exploitative dynamics in our work

A lot of oppressed people are hyper-sexualized in dominant culture as a way to create them as a threat, a fetish, or a caricature—transgender women, black men, Asian and Pacific Islander women, to name a few. Despite often good intentions to raise awareness about the treatment of transgender and gender-non-conforming people in prisons, we recognize that much of the "public education" work around these issues often relies on sexualization, voyeurism, sensationalism, and fetishization to get its point across. In general there is a focus on graphic descriptions of people's bodies (specifically their genitals), sexual violence, and the humiliation they have faced. Imprisoned people (who are usually represented as black) and transgender people (who are usually represented as transgender women of color in this context) have long been the target of voyeuristic representation—from porn movies that glorify rape in prison to fetishizing "human rights" research distributed to majority white, middle-class audiences. As transgender people who often have our bodies on display for non-transgender people who feel empowered to question, display, and discuss us, we know that this is a dangerous trend that seriously undercuts the integrity of our work and the types of relationships that can be formed. Unless we address these exploitative power dynamics in our work, even our most "well-intentioned" strategies and movements will reproduce the prison industrial complex's norms of transphobic, misogynist, and racist sexualized violence. *Research, media, cultural work, and activism on this issue needs to be accountable to and directed by low-income transgender people and transgender people of color and our organizations.*

*4. We see ending trans imprisonment as part of the larger struggle for transformation*

The violence that transgender people—significantly low-income transgender people of color—face in prisons, jails, and detention centers and the cycles of poverty and criminalization that leads so many of us to imprisonment is a key place to work for broad-based social and political transformation. There is no way that transgender people can ever be "safe" in prisons as long as prisons exist and, as scholar Fred Moten has written, as long as we live in a society that could even *have* prisons. Building a trans and queer abolitionist movement means building power among people facing multiple systems of oppression in order to imagine a world beyond mass devastation, violence, and inequity that occurs within and between communities. We must resist the trap of being compartmentalized into "issues" and "priorities" and sacrificing a broader political vision and movement to react to the crisis of the here and now. This is the logic that allows many white and middle-class gay and lesbian folks to think that marriage is *the* most important and pressing LGBT issue, without being invested in the real goal of ending racism and capitalism. *Struggling against trans imprisonment is one of many key places to radicalize queer and trans politics, expand anti-prison politics, and join in a larger movement for racial, economic, gender, and social justice to end all forms of militarization, criminalization, and warfare.*

## III. SO YOU THINK WE'RE IMPOSSIBLE?

This stuff is heavy, we realize. Our communities and our movements are up against tremendous odds and have inherited a great deal of trauma that we are still struggling to deal with. A common and reasonable response to these conditions is getting overwhelmed, feeling defeated, losing hope. In this kind of emotional and political climate, when activists call for deep change like prison abolition (or, gasp, an LGBT agenda *centered around* prison abolition), our demands get called "impossible" or "idealistic" or even "divisive." As trans people, we've been hearing this for ages. After all, according to our legal system, the media, science, and many of our families and religions, we shouldn't exist! Our ways of living and expressing ourselves break such fundamental rules that systems crash at our feet, close their doors to us, and attempt to wipe us out. And yet we exist, continuing to build and sustain new ways of looking at gender, bodies, family, desire, resistance, and happiness that nourish us and challenge expectations.

In an age when thousands of people are murdered annually in the name of "democracy," millions of people are locked up to "protect public safety," and LGBT organizations march hand in hand with cops in Pride parades, being impossible may just be the best thing we've got going for ourselves: *Impossibility may very well be our only possibility.*

What would it mean to *embrace*, rather than *shy away from*, the impossibility of our ways of living as well as our political visions? What would it mean to desire a future that we can't even imagine but that we are told couldn't ever exist? We see the abolition of policing, prisons, jails, and detention not strictly as a narrow answer to "imprisonment" and the abuses that occur within prisons, but also as a challenge to the rule of poverty, violence, racism, alienation, and disconnection that we face every day. Abolition is not just about closing the doors to violent institutions, but also about building up and recovering institutions and practices and relationships that nurture wholeness, self-determination, and transformation. Abolition is not some distant future but something we create in every moment when we say no to the traps of empire and yes to the nourishing possibilities dreamed of and practiced by our ancestors and friends. Every time we insist on accessible and affirming healthcare, safe and quality education, meaningful and secure employment, loving and healing relationships, and being our full and whole selves, we are doing abolition. Abolition is about breaking down things that oppress and building up things that nourish. Abolition is the practice of transformation in the here and now and the ever after.

Maybe wrestling with such a significant demand is the wake-up call that an increasingly sleepy LGBT movement needs. The true potential of queer and trans politics cannot be found in attempting to reinforce our tenuous right to exist by undermining someone else's. If it is not clear already, we are all in this together. To claim our legacy of beautiful impossibility is to begin practicing ways of being with one another and making movement that sustain all life on this planet, without exception. It is to begin speaking what we have not yet had the words to wish for.

## NOTES

1. We would like to thank the friends, comrades, and organizations whose work, love, and thinking have paved the path to this paper and our collective movements for liberation, including: Anna Agathangelou, Audre Lorde Project, Community United Against Violence (CUAV), Communities Against Rape and Abuse (CARA), Critical Resistance, Eric Stanley, FIERCE!, INCITE! Women of Color Against Violence, Justice Now, Lala Yantes, Mari Spira, Miss Major, Mordecai Cohen Ettinger, Nat Smith, Southerners on New Ground (SONG), Sylvia Rivera Law Project (SRLP), Transforming Justice Coalition, Transgender, Gender Variant, Intersex Justice Project (TGIJP), and Vanessa Huang.
2. In the wake of the 2011 repeal of Don't Ask Don't Tell, queer and trans people who oppose the horrible violence committed by the US military all over the world have been disappointed not only by pro-military rhetoric of the campaign to allow gays and lesbians to serve, but also by the new debates that have emerged since then about ROTC on college campuses. […]
3. This has been painfully illustrated by a range of LGBT foundation and individual funders who, in the months leading up to the struggle over California's same-sex marriage ban, Proposition 8, declared that marriage equality needed to be the central funding priority and discontinued vital funding for anti-violence, HIV/AIDS, and arts organizations, among others.
4. This is a reference to the "trickle-down" economic policies associated with the Reagan Administration, which promoted tax cuts for the rich under the guise of creating jobs for middle-class and working-class people. The left has rightfully argued that justice, wealth, and safety do not "trickle down," but need to be redistributed first to the people at the bottom of the economic and political ladder. Trickle down policies primarily operate as another opportunity to distribute wealth and security upward.
5. By this we mean the advocacy work and agenda-setting done by wealthy (budgets over $1 million) LGBT-rights organizations such as the Human Rights Campaign and the National Lesbian and Gay Task Force.
6. See the Sylvia Rivera Law Project's *It's War in Here: A Report on the Treatment of Transgender and Gender Non-Conforming People in New York State Prisons* (available online at www.srlp.org) and *Gendered Punishment: Strategies to Protect Transgender, Gender Variant and Intersex People in America's Prisons* (available from TGI Justice Project, info@tgijp.org) for a deeper examination of the cycles of poverty, criminalization, imprisonment, and law-enforcement violence in transgender and gender-non-conforming communities.
7. This was a period of heightened activity by radical and revolutionary national and international movements resisting white supremacy, patriarchy, colonization, and capitalism—embodied by organizations such as the American Indian Movement, the Black Liberation Army, the Young Lords, the Black Panther Party for Self-Defense, the Brown Berets, Earth First!, the Gay Liberation Front, and the Weather Underground in the United States, and anti-colonial organizations in Guinea-Bissau, Jamaica, Vietnam, Puerto Rico, Zimbabwe, and elsewhere. Mass movements throughout the world succeeded in winning major victories against imperialism and white supremacy, and exposing the genocide that lay barely underneath American narratives of democracy, exceptionalism, and liberty.
8. See Ruth Wilson Gilmore, "Globalisation and US Prison Growth: From Military Keynesianism to Post-Keynesian Militarism," *Race and Class,* Vol. 40, No. 2–3, 1998/99.
9. For a compelling analysis of neoliberalism and its impacts on social movements, see Lisa Duggan's *The Twilight of Equality: Neoliberalism, Cultural Politics, and the Attack on Democracy,* published by Beacon Press in 2004. […]
12. Sapphire, "A Homeless Man's Alternative to 'Care Not Cash,'" *Poor Magazine,* July 1, 2003, at http://www.poormagazine.org/index.cfm?L1=news&category= 50&stor=1241.
13. The Sentencing Project, "Life Sentences: Denying Welfare Benefit to Women Convicted of Drug Offenses," at http://www.sentencingprogrject.org/Admin/ Documents/publications/women_smy_lifesentences.pdf.

14. Alan David Freeman, "Legitimizing Racial Discrimination Through Antidiscrimination Law: A Critical Review of Supreme Court Doctrine," 62 MINN. L. REV. 1049, 1052 (1978).
    [...]
16. For a critique of hate crimes legislation, see Carolina Cordero Dyer, "The Passage of Hate Crimes Legislation–No Cause to Celebrate," INCITE! Women of Color Against Violence, March 2001 at http://www.incite-national.org/ news/_march01/editorial.html. Aso see INCITE!-Denver and Denver on Fire's response to the verdict in the 2009 Angie Zapata case at http://www.leftturn. org/?q=node/1310.
17. For an in-depth analysis of the growth and impacts of "nonprofit industrial complex," see INCITE! Women of Color Against Violence's groundbreaking anthology *The Revolution Will Not Be Funded: Beyond the Non-Profit Industrial Complex,* published by South End Press in 2007.
    [...]
19. See Justice Now co-founder Cassandra Shaylor's essay "Neither Kind Nor Gentle: The Perils of 'Gender Responsive Justice'" in *The Violence of Incarceration,* edited by Phil Scraton and Jude McCulloch, published by Routledge in 2008.
    [...]
23. We recognize that we mention only relatively well-funded organizations and mostly organizations in the San Francisco Bay Area and New York City, two strongholds of radical organizing and also places where a significant amount of resources are concentrated. There are hundreds of other organizations around the country and the world that we do not mention and do not know about. *What organizations or spaces do you see embodying radical values?*
24. See the following: The Sylvia Rivera Law Project, http://www.srlp.org; Queers for Economic Justice, http://www.q4ej.org; Transgender, Gender Variant, and Intersex Justice Project, http://www.tgijp.org; Critical Resistance, http://www.criticalresistance.org; FIERCE!, http://www.fiercenyc.org; Southerners on New Ground, http://www.southernersonnewground.org; Creative Interventions, http://www.creative-interventions.org; generationFIVE, http://www.generationfive.org; Communities Against Rape and Abuse, http://www.cara-seattle.org; and Audre Lorde Project's Safe OUTside the System Collective, http://www.alp.org. For examples of LGBTQ-specific organizations creating community-based responses to violence, see the Audre Lorde Project's Safe Outside the System Collective in Brooklyn (www.alp.org), the Northwest Network of BTLG Survivors of Abuse in Seattle, and Community United Against Violence (CUAV) in San Francisco (www.cuav.org). Particularly significant was the Transforming Justice gathering in San Francisco in October 2007, which brought together over two hundred LGBTQ and allied formerly imprisoned people, activists, and attorneys to develop a shared analysis about the cycles of trans poverty, criminalization, and imprisonment and a shared strategy moving forward. Transforming Justice, which has now transitioned to a national coalition, was a culmination of tireless and often invisible work on the part of imprisoned and formerly imprisoned people and their allies over the past many years. For more, see www.transformingjustice.org.
25. See the Transforming Justice Coalition's statement "How We Do Our Work" for a more detailed account of day-to-day organizing ethics, which can be requested from the TGI Justice Project at http://www.tgijp.org.
26. Both of the lessons here were significantly and powerfully articulated and popularized by Critical Resistance and Justice Now, both primarily based in Oakland, CA.

# Permissions

Aizura, Aren Z. "The Romance of the Amazing Scalpel: Race, Affect and Labor in Thai Gender Reassignment Clinics," In Peter A. Jackson (ed), *Queer Bangkok.* (Hong Kong: Hong Kong University Press, 2011), 143–162. Reprinted with permission of the publisher.

Bailey, Marlon. "Performance as Intravention: Ballroom Culture and the Politics of HIV/AIDS in Detroit," *Souls: A Critical Journal of Black Politics, Culture, and Society* 11: 3 (2009), 253–274. Reprinted with permission of the publisher.

Beauchamp, Toby. "Artful Concealment and Strategic Visibility: Transgender Bodies and U.S. State Surveillance After 9/11." *Surveillance and Society* 6: 4 (2009), 356–366. Reprinted with permission from *Surveillance and Society.*

Bettcher, Talia Mae. "Evil Deceivers and Make-Believers: On Transphobic Violence and the Politics of Illusion," *Hypatia* 22: 3 (2007), 43–65. Reprinted with permission of the publisher.

Carlson, Shanna. "Transgender Subjectivity and the Logic of Sexual Difference," in *differences*, 21: 2, 46–72. Copyright, 2010, Brown University and *differences: a Journal of Feminist Cultural Studies.* All rights reserved. Reprinted by permission of the publisher, Duke University Press. www.dukeupress. edu

Cavanagh, Sheila. "Touching Gender: Abjection and the Hygienic Imagination," In *Queering Bathrooms: Gender, Sexuality & The Hygenic Imagination* (Toronto: University of Toronto Press, 2010) (30 pages). Reprinted with permission of the publisher.

Chen, Mel. "Animals Without Genitals: Race and Transsubstantiation," *Women and Performance* 20: 3 (2010), 258-297. Reprinted with permission of the publisher.

Crawford, Lucas. "Transgender Without Organs? Mobilizing a Geo-affective Theory of Gender Modification," *WSQ: Women's Studies Quarterly* 36: 3–4 (Fall/Winter 2008), 127–143. Copyright ©2008 by the Feminist Press at the City University of New York. Used by permission of the publishers, www.feministpressorg. All rights reserved.

Currah, Paisley and Lisa Jean Moore, "'We Won't Know Who You Are': Contesting Sex Designations in New York City Birth Certificates," *Hypatia* 24: 3 (2009), 131–135. Republished with permission of the publisher.

Namaste, Viviane (with Georgia Sitara). "Inclusive Pedagogy in the Women's Studies Classroom: Teaching the Kimberly Nixon Case." *Sex Change, Social Change: Reflections on Identity, Institutions and Imperialism.* (Toronto: Women's Press, 2005), 75–102. Reprinted with permission from publisher.

Noble, Jean Bobby. "Our Bodies Are Not Ourselves: Tranny Guys and the Racialized Class Politics of Incoherence." *Sons of the Movement: FtMs Risking Incoherence on a Post-Queer Cultural Landscape* (Toronto: Women's Press, 2006), 76–100. Reprinted with permission from publisher.

Norton, Laura. "Neutering the Transgendered: Human Rights and Japan's Law No. 111."*Georgetown Journal of Gender and the Law* 7: 2 (2006), 187–216. Republished with permission of author.

Ochoa, Marcia. "Perverse Citizenship: Divas, Marginality, and Participation in 'Loca-Lization.'" *WSQ: Women's Studies Quarterly* 36: 3 & 4 (2008), 146–169. Copyright ©2008 by the Feminist Press at the City University of New York. Used by permission of the publishers, www.feministpressorg. All rights reserved.

Preciado, Beatriz. Originally published as "Pharmaco-pornographic Politics: Toward a New Gender Ecology." *Parallax* 14: 1 (2008), 105–117. Republished with permission of the publisher.

Robson, Ruthann. "Reinscribing Normality: The Law and Politics of Transgender Marriage." In P. Currah, S. Minter, and R. Juang, eds. *Transgender Rights* (Minneapolis, MN: University of Minnesota Press, 2006), 299–309. Republished with permission of the University of Minnesota Press.

Romesberg, Don. "Longevity and Limits in Rae Bourbon's Life in Motion." In Trystan Cotton, ed. *Transgender Migrations* (New York: Routledge, 2011), 119–135.

Roughgarden, Joan. *Evolution's Rainbow: Diversity, Gender, and Sexuality in Nature and People.* © 2004 by the Regents of the University of California. Published by the University of California Press. Reprinted with permission of the publisher.

Salamon, Gayle. "An Ethics of Transsexual Difference: Luce Irigaray and the Place of Sexual Undecideability." *Assuming a Body: Transgender and Rhetorics of Materiality* (New York: Columbia University Press, 2010), 131–145. Reprinted with permission of the publisher.

Sears, Clare. "Electric Brilliancy: Cross-Dressing Law and Freak Show Displays in Nineteenth-Century San Francisco." *WSQ: Women's Studies Quarterly* 36: 3–4 (2008), 170–187. Copyright ©2008 by the Feminist Press at the City University of New York. Used by permission of the publishers, www.feministpressorg. All rights reserved.

Serano, Julia. "Skirt Chasers: Why the Media Depicts the Trans Revolution in Lipstick and High Heels." *Whipping Girl: A Transsexual Woman on Sexism and the Scapegoating of Femininity* (Emeryville, CA: Seal Press, 2007), 35–52. Reprinted with permission of the publisher.

Spade, Dean, Morgan Bassichis, and Alex Lee. "Building an Abolitionist Trans & Queer Movement with Everything We've Got." In Eric Stanley and Nat Smith, eds. *Captive Genders* (Oakland, CA: AK Press, 2011), 15–40. Reprinted with permission of AK Press.

Stryker, Susan. "Kaming Mga Talyada (We Who Are Sexy): The Transsexual Whiteness of Christine Jorgensen in the (Post)Colonial Philippines." *Social Semiotics* 19: 1 (2009), 79–91. Reprinted with permission from the publisher.

Vaccaro, Jeanne. "Felt Matters." *Women and Performance* 20: 3 (2010), 253–266. Reprinted with permission of the publisher.

# Index

9/11 4, 250; homonationalism 571–2; state
    surveillance 46, 49–51, 616, 618

Abad, C. 532
Abidjan 637
abjection 242; anal 388, 436–9; bodily fluids 428–36;
    humanimality 169, 174; hygienic imagination
    426–8; racialization 461–3; sex work 450
ableism 238–40, 243, 261–2
Abraham, N. 185
academia *see* transgender studies
accumulation 17–18, 24–7
*Ace Ventura* 227
acoustics 427, 439
ACT-UP 61
Action T4 268
activism 8; cis- 235–8; harm reduction 61–3;
    internationalization 381; post-Stonewall
    291–2, 295–8; productivism 16–17, 24, 26–7;
    remembrance/necropolitics 30–1, 33–6, 67–74
Adams, R. 562
administrative systems 5, 8, 550–1; Japan 591–3,
    598–600; New York 607–19; post-9/11 48–9,
    657–8
Adorno, T. 440
*Adventures of Sebastian Cole* 228
Advisory 46, 49–54
advocacy groups 36, 40, 53, 61, 612
*Advocate* 296
aestheticism 205, 208
affect 475–8; felt 93, 96–7; haptic cinema 101–2,
    105–11, 115–16; labor/Thai clinics 496–7, 499,
    505–8; mainstream cinema 120, 128
Afghanistan 50, 654
Africa 60, 171
African Americans 263, 559, 562, 630–1, 635
Afro Sisters 80–1
afterlife 66, 68
Agamben, G. 550, 575

Agnew, J. 521
Ahmed, S. 71, 93, 477, 497–8, 515–16, 518, 520
Ahuizotl 329
AIDS *see* HIV/AIDS
*Aizawa v. Japan* 599
Aizura, A.Z. 1–12, 23, 496–511, 517
Al-Qaeda 46, 50
Alabama 292
Albert the Great 339
Albucasis 335, 337–8, 340–1
Alexander, M. Jacqui 492
Alexander, Meena 514
alienation 251, 439–40
Allen, D. 588
Allen, P.G. 350–1
Allen, T. 256
Allison, D. 249
Allred, G. 279
allyship 238–40, 243
Almario, V. 547
Alonso de Bulnes, F. 461
amateurism 91–2
*ambiente* 444–6, 453, 467, 490–1
ambiguity 129, 388–9, 489, 597
America Online 504
America Psychiatric Association (APA) 241, 595, 651
American Indian Movement 659
American Museum 559, 561
American Psychiatric Association 645
American Studies 189
*American Tropics* 550
Amnesty International 569, 573
Amsterdam 254
anal 105, 355, 388, 436–40
anatomy 559; anatamo-politics 544, 549–50;
    anatomists 335–44, 346
*Ancient Bodies, Ancient Lives* 322
ancients 319–31, 388–9 *see also* Greeks
Anderson, B. 522

*Bella Donna* 489
Bellatin, M. 461, 469
belonging 484, 487, 489, 492, 512–13, 517–20
Benjamin, H. 17, 20–5, 267, 568, 610
Benjamin, J. 202
Benjamin, W. 440
Bentham, J. 270
Benthein, C. 515–16
Berlant, L. 478
Berlin 68, 71–4
Bernard of Gordon 345, 347
Berry, T. 586
besides 93
Bettcher, T. 5, 278–90, 612
*Beyond Sexuality* 307
Bhabha, H. 171, 517
Bhanji, N. 12, 512–26
binaries 24; archaeology 320–3; cis/trans 236–44;
    gamete size 150–1; heteronormative 16, 20–2;
    male/female 377, 418, 422–5, 598–9, 619, 627
Bingham, N. 565, 571, 573
bioarchaeology 324
bioeconomy 192, 194
biological body 91, 93
biology: causation of trans 647–8; evolution 147–51,
    156–62; feminisms 233, 235, 242; legal narratives
    619
biomedicine 1, 57–9, 64, 169, 499–501
biopolitics 7, 11, 270; abjection 436; affective
    labor 507–8; necropolitics 66–71; pharmaco-
    pornographic 270–4, 276; (post)colonialism 544,
    550–1; rightful killing 574–5
biotechnology 169, 173–4, 194
birds 148, 151, 159
Birke, L. 163
birth certificates 48, 241, 385, 449, 607–14, 616–19,
    625, 627
birth control 159, 195
bisexuality 302–3, 306
Black Fag 84
Black Panthers 81–2, 295–6, 583, 659–60
Black Power 81–2, 295
*Black Skin, White Masks* 172
blackface 88, 170, 559
blackness 68, 586 *see also* race
Blackstone, E. 585
Blackwood, E. 530
blame-shifting 280–1, 285, 287
blocs 83–4, 89
blood 329, 435–6
*Blood and Sand* 489
Board of Health 617–18
*Bodies That Matter* 306, 308, 573
body 1, 156, 466–8; bodyscape 104–5; deracing 31–
    6; flows/capital 62–3; natural/techno 276; place/
    motion 420–5; politic 460; somatechnics 271,
    544, 551; transitions 91–9, 130–9, 141, 182–6,
    208–11, 253; without organs 168, 173–5, 480

*Body Alchemy* 251
Body Integrity Identity Disorder (BIID) 274–5
Bohjalian, C. 624
Bolívar, S. 447–8, 464
Bolivia 461
Bollas, C. 112
*Bom Crioulo* 459
Bonta, M. 477–8
borders and boundaries 491–2; bodily 182, 184,
    419–25, 477; border-crossing metaphors 515–18,
    520–3; borderlands 483–9, 521; ego 426–8, 431,
    433; gender/nation 559, 561; refugees 568, 576;
    securitization 3–4
Bordwell, D. 102, 104
Bornstein, K. 203–4, 275, 302, 593
Boston 615
*Boundaries of Blackness* 588
Bourbon, R. 11, 483–95
bourgeois 205
Bowers, M. 242
Boylan, J.F. 229
*Boys Don't Cry* 119–20, 123–8, 474–5, 613
Boystown 73
Brah, A. 513
Braham, W. 431
Braidotti, R. 328
brain 647, 649
Brand, D. 255, 515, 521
*Braschi* 624–5
Bravo, A. 454
Brazil 60, 450, 461
breasts 251–3
breeder documents 616–18
Brisbane 498
Bristol Meyers Squibb Company 59–60
Britain 169–71, 267, 426, 430
British Columbia 214–15, 217, 220–1
British Empire 222
*British Nationality Act* 171
Brown, W. 34, 584, 586
Browning, G. 17
Bryld, M. 163
Buchanan, I. 478
Buenos Aires 460–1, 467
Buffalo 474
Buijs, C. 234
Bukowski, C. 271
Bulgaria 72
bureaucracy *see* administrative systems
burial 319–20, 324–6, 329, 358–9
Burke, M. 557
Burroughs, W.S. 271
Burzabadi, A. 384–5
Busch, W. 630
Bush, G.W. 657
butches 424, 428–9, 446; Detroit ballroom 630,
    634–6, 638; look/gaze 121, 128–9; movement(s)
    475, 532; race/class politics 250, 252, 254

phallogocentrism 418
phalloplasty 274, 613, 615
phallus 232, 330, 412, 464, 538; abjection 437–8;
  race 172, 174; subjectivity 304–7, 310, 312
pharmaceuticals 56–65, 266, 268–75
phenomenology 520
Philadelphia 56–8, 61, 63, 583, 588
Philippines 527–38, 543–5, 549–52
Philippines National Bank 546
Phillips, R. 513, 518
Philo, C. 169
Philo, J. de 102, 111, 116
phobias 34
Phoenix 491
Phuket 498, 502–3
*Physics* 418–20
Pill 267, 269, 274–5
Pinays 532–3
Pine, S. 295
*Pink Blood* 474
Piyawate Hospital 497
place 419–24
plague 426, 461
plants 148, 150, 154
plastics 195–6, 269
Plato 34, 305
play 306
*Playboy* 267, 269
Plaza, R.C. 467
pleasure 159, 427; dance 137–8; haptic cinema 106–
  7; medieval anatomies 335–9, 341–6; pharmaco-
  pornographic regime 267, 274
*Plessy v. Ferguson* 50
plutonium 268
poetics 178–9, 350–1
Policansky, D. 159
police 205, 608; biopolitics 555–6, 562, 580–8; Japan
  403–4, 406, 413–14; Latin America 443–4, 447,
  462; New York 292, 294–6; political economy
  35–6, 61, 73; prison-industrial complex 653–4,
  656, 663–5; Rae Bourbon 484, 490, 494
Policía Metropolitana de Caracas (PM) 443–4,
  448–50
political ecology 190, 272–3
political economy 17, 27
politics 452, 463; of home 517, 520; of respectability
  366, 369
Polk County Jail 587
population 5, 574–5
pornography 102, 105–7, 109–10, 266–70, 664
pornosophy 111
Portica, G. 555
positivism 460
postfordism 507
postmodernism 119–20, 129, 462, 481, 545
poststructuralism 1, 464, 469, 545
posttranssexual 3
Potomac River 190, 195–6

poverty 18, 411, 635–6, 655, 657, 659
Povinelli, E. 97
power 297, 436, 446–7, 522, 532; heteronormativity
  16–17; memorialization/necropolitics 31, 39–40,
  574, 584; pharmaceuticals 60, 62–3, 270, 274
praxis 89, 662
Preciado, B. 11, 266–77
Preecha Tiewtranon 497, 500–2
prefix 184, 186
prehistory 319–25, 337
press *see* media
Prestige, House of 635–8
pretense 281–8
Pride 251, 261, 264, 451, 585, 635, 654, 665 *see also*
  Gay Pride
Prieur, A. 466–7
Prince, V. 364–77
Princess of Vix 319–21
Prison Activist Resource Center 62
prisons 6, 294, 651, 653–6, 658–62; abolition 663–6;
  biopolitics 555, 560, 586–9; political economy 24,
  61–2, 68
privacy 51–2, 263–4
privatization 508
privilege 284; cisgender 237–42, 244; counter-
  revolution 659–60; disability 263–4; feminism
  202, 205–6, 208, 231; Rae Bourbon 487–8, 494
problem bodies 554, 556–8, 561
productivity 15, 17, 19–27
profit 60
progesterone 267, 274, 615
progressivism 381
prohibitions 309–10, 427, 430–1
Pronger, B. 437–8
Propecia 59
Proscar 56, 58–9
Prosser, J. 18–19, 69, 93, 201, 252, 473–4, 476–7, 479,
  486–7, 500, 515–17
prosthesis 275
prostitution *see* sex work
protection 214–15, 221–3, 567, 571–3
Protevi, J. 477–8
Proyecto ContraSIDA Por Vida (PCPV) 446
Prozac 268–9, 275
psychiatry 47, 92–3, 132, 265, 275, 500–1, 555;
  Gender Identity Disorder 645–8, 651
*Psychic Life of Power* 314
psychoanalysis 5, 103, 302–4, 306–11, 314
psychotropics 268–9
Puar, J. 53, 93, 499, 570, 584, 586
public health 558, 632–3, 636, 639, 641
public space 554–60
public toilets 426–30, 432–3, 435
Pueblo 359
*Pueblo enfermo* 461
Puerto Rico 291–3, 295–8, 467
punishment 356
punk 79–80, 82–4, 88–9, 269